STAFFORD LIBRARY
COLUMBIA COLLEGE
COLUMBIA, MO 65216

THE
BOOK
OF THE
STATES

1990-91 EDITION

Volume 28

STAFFORD LIBRARY
COLUMBIA COLLEGE
COLUMBIA, MO 65216

The Council of State Governments
Lexington, Kentucky

Copyright 1990
The Council of State Governments
Iron Works Pike
P.O. Box 11910
Lexington, Kentucky 40578-1910

Manufactured in the United States

ISBN 0-87292-955-8
Price $42.50

All rights reserved. Inquiries for use of any material should be directed to:
Executive Editor, The Council of State Governments
Iron Works Pike, P.O. Box 11910, Lexington, Kentucky 40578-1910

CONTENTS

Foreword xi

The State of the States
Deborah Gona 1

Chapter One
STATE CONSTITUTIONS 19
A review of constitutional revision and actions on proposals in the states during 1988-89 and the decade of the 1980s, along with general information on state constitutions, amendment procedures, and constitutional commissions and conventions.

State Constitutions and Constitutional Revision: 1988-89 and the 1980s
Janice May 20

Chapter Two
STATE EXECUTIVE BRANCH 49
An overview of the states' chief executives, other officials, and executive branch activities in 1988-89, as well as current information on the office of the governor — including qualifications for office, compensation, powers, cabinet systems, transition provisions — and the powers, duties, qualifications for office, annual salaries, methods of selection, and length of terms for selected executive branch officials.

The Governors, 1988-89
Thad L. Beyle 50
The Executive Branch: Organization and Issues 1988-89
Thad L. Beyle 75

Chapter Three
STATE LEGISLATIVE BRANCH 107
A review of the evolution of the legislature, with special emphasis on changes in the last two years. Basic information on the state legislatures — including the legal provisions for legislative sessions and a variety of legislative procedures — is presented, along with legislative compensation, statistics on bill introductions and enactments for 1988 and 1989, and membership turnover in the legislatures.

CONTENTS

The State Legislatures
Rich Jones 108

Chapter Four
STATE JUDICIAL BRANCH 193
An exploration of the state of the judiciary, with information on the courts of last resort, intermediate appellate courts, and general trial courts, as well as the compensation and methods of selection and removal of state judges.

State of the Judiciary
Dixie K. Knoebel 194

Chapter Five
STATE ELECTIONS 225
A review of recent state legislation and actions affecting elections and electoral procedures. Information on which state offices will be up for election in 1990-91, primary elections, campaign finance laws and limitations, procedures for passage of initiatives, referendums and recalls, and voter registration information is presented, along with state-by-state voting statistics for recent gubernatorial, non-presidential, and presidential elections.

Election Legislation: 1988-89
Richard G. Smolka 226

Chapter Six
STATE FINANCES 281
An overview of the states' budget procedures, their revenue sources, expenditures, and debts for 1987 and 1988, and tax structures and receipts for 1988.

State Government Finances
Henry S. Wulf 282
Trends in State Taxation: 1988-89
Ronald Alt 310
State Tax Collections in 1988
Gerard T. Keffer 326

Chapter Seven
STATE MANAGEMENT AND ADMINISTRATION 339
An overview of several components of state administration-including personnel management, productivity improvement, facilities and fleet management, purchasing, archives, and information services. Statistics on state government employment and payrolls, as well as public employee retirement systems, are presented for 1987 and 1988.

Developments in State Administration and Management
Wayne W. Hall, Jr. 340
Finances of State-Administered Public Employee Retirement Systems
Henry S. Wulf 366

CONTENTS

Chapter Eight
SELECTED STATE ACTIVITIES, ISSUES, AND SERVICES 379
  An exploration of several areas of concern to the states — including an analysis of who are state innovators, education, health, labor, transportation and highways, criminal justice, and the environment.

Innovators in State Government: Their Organizational and Professional Environment
  Keon S. Chi and Dennis O. Grady 382
Uniform State Laws: 1988-89
  John M. McCabe 405
Labor Legislation: 1988-89
  Richard R. Nelson 446
State Regulation of Occupations and Professions
  Frances Stokes Berry and Pamela L. Brinegar 465
Corrections in the 1990s: States Look to Intermediate Sanctions and Substance Abuse Programming
  Timothy H. Matthews and Kimberly D. Roberts 483
Four State Environmental Protection Initiatives for the 1990s
  R. Steven Brown and John M. Johnson 501
Homelessness in the States
  Lee Walker 511

Chapter Nine
INTERGOVERNMENTAL AFFAIRS 521
  A review of recent developments in the relationship between the federal government and the states and the states and their local governments, and cooperative efforts among the states themselves. Statistics on federal aid and state intergovernmental revenue and expenditures for 1987 and 1988 are included.

Developments in Federal-State Relations
  Norman Beckman 522
Developing State-Local Relationships: 1987-1989
  Joseph F. Zimmerman 533
State Aid to Local Governments
  David Kellerman and Henry S. Wulf 549
Interstate Compacts and Agreements
  Benjamin J. Jones and Deborah Reuter 565
The Council of State Governments 568

Chapter Ten
STATE PAGES 581
  A variety of statistics and information about the states — including capitals, population sizes, land areas, historical data, elected executive branch officials, legislative leaders, and judges of the courts of last resort. State mottos, flowers, songs, birds, and other items unique to the states and other U.S. jurisdictions also are presented.

INDEX 609

TABLES

Chapter One
STATE CONSTITUTIONS
- A State Constitutional Changes by Method of Initiation 1982-83, 1984-85, 1986-87 and 1988-89 21
- B Substantive Changes in State Constitutions: Proposed and Adopted, 1982-83, 1984-85, 1986-87 and 1988-89 22
- 1.1 General Information on State Constitutions 40
- 1.2 Constitutional Amendment Procedure: by Legislature 42
- 1.3 Constitutional Amendment Procedure: by Initiative 44
- 1.4 Procedures for Calling Constitutional Conventions 45
- 1.5 State Constitutional Commissions 47
- 1.6 Constitutional Conventions 1986-87 47

Chapter Two
STATE EXECUTIVE BRANCH
GOVERNORS
- A Costs of Gubernatorial Campaigns, 1988-89 52
- B Total Cost of Gubernatorial Elections: 1977-1989 53
- 2.1 The Governors 1988 62
- 2.2 The Governors: Qualifications for Office . 64
- 2.3 The Governors: Compensation 65
- 2.4 The Governors: Powers 67
- 2.5 Gubernatorial Executive Orders: Authorization, Provisions, Procedures .. 69
- 2.6 State Cabinet Systems 71
- 2.7 The Governors: Provisions and Procedures for Transition 72
- 2.8 Impeachment Provisions in the States 73

EXECUTIVE BRANCH
- 2.9 Constitutional and Statutory Provisions for Length and Number of Terms of Elected State Officials 83
- 2.10 Selected State Administrative Officials: Methods of Selection 85
- 2.11 Selected State Administrative Officials: Annual Salaries 90
- 2.12 Lieutenant Governors: Qualifications and Terms 96
- 2.13 Lieutenant Governors: Powers and Duties 97
- 2.14 Secretaries of State: Qualifications for Office 99
- 2.15 Secretaries of State: Election and Registration Duties 100
- 2.16 Secretaries of State: Custodial, Publication and Legislative Duties 101
- 2.17 Attorneys General: Qualifications for Office 102
- 2.18 Attorneys General: Prosecutorial and Advisory Duties 103
- 2.19 Attorneys General: Consumer Protection Activities, Subpoena Powers, and Antitrust Duties 104
- 2.20 Attorneys General: Duties to Administrative Agencies and Other Responsibilities 105

Chapter Three
STATE LEGISLATIVE BRANCH
- 3.1 Names of State Legislative Bodies and Convening Places 118
- 3.2 Legislative Sessions: Legal Provisions 119
- 3.3 The Legislators: Numbers, Terms, and Party Affiliations 123
- 3.4 Membership Turnover in the Legislatures: 1988 124
- 3.5 The Legislators: Qualifications for Election 125
- 3.6 Senate Leadership Positions: Methods of Selection 127
- 3.7 House Leadership Positions: Methods of Selection 129
- 3.8 Method of Setting Legislative Compensation 131
- 3.9 States in which Legislators' Salaries are Tied or Related to State Employees' Salaries 131
- 3.10 States with Legislative Compensation Commissions 132
- 3.11 Legislative Compensation: Regular and Special Sessions 133
- 3.12 Legislative Compensation: Interim Payments and Other Direct Payments 135
- 3.13 Additional Compensation for Senate Leaders 139
- 3.14 Additional Compensation for House Leaders 141
- 3.15 State Legislative Retirement Benefits 143
- 3.16 Legislators' Use of Surplus Campaign Funds 149
- 3.17 Time Limits on Bill Introductions 151
- 3.18 Bill Prefiling, Reference, and Carryover .. 154
- 3.19 Mechanisms Used to Expedite and Streamline Bill Processing 156

TABLES

3.20 Enacting Legislation: Veto, Veto Override, and Effective Date 157
3.21 Bill and Resolution Introductions and Enactments: 1988 and 1989 Regular Sessions 160
3.22 Bill and Resolution Introductions and Enactments: 1988 and 1989 Special Sessions 163
3.23 Staff for Individual Legislators 165
3.24 Staff for Legislative Standing Committees 166
3.25 Standing Committees: Appointment and Number 167
3.26 Standing Committees: Procedure 126
3.27 Legislative Appropriations Process: Budget Documents and Bills 171
3.28 Fiscal Notes: Content and Distribution .. 173
3.29 Extraordinary Votes Required to take Certain Actions or Pass Specific Types of Legislation-Senate 175
3.30 Extraordinary Votes Required to take Certain Actions or Pass Specific Types of Legislation-House 177
3.31 Legislative Review of Administrative Regulations: Structures and Procedures 179
3.32 Legislative Review of Administrative Regulations: Powers 181
3.33 Summary of Sunset Legislation 183
3.34 Legislative Activities Performed With the Use of Computers 187
3.35 Lobbyists: As Defined in State Statutes .. 189
3.36 Lobbyists: Registration and Reporting ... 191

Chapter Four
STATE JUDICIAL BRANCH

4.1 State Courts of Last Resort 204
4.2 State Intermediate Appellate Courts and General Trial Courts: Number of Judges and Terms 206
4.3 Qualifications of Judges of State Appellate Courts and General Trial Courts 208
4.4 Selection and Retention of State Judges . 210
4.5 Methods for Removal of Judges and Filling of Vacancies 213
4.6 Compensation of Judges of Appellate Courts and General Trial Courts 221
4.7 Selected Data on Court Administrated Offices 223

Chapter Five
STATE ELECTIONS

5.1 State Officials to Be Elected: 1990-91 232
5.2 Methods of Nominating for State Offices 234
5.3 Primary Election Information 236
5.4 Campaign Finance Laws: General Filing Requirements 237
5.5 Campaign Finance Laws: Limitations on Contributions by Organizations 242

5.6 Campaign Finance Laws: Limitations on Contributions by Individuals 247
5.7 Campaign Finance Laws: Limitations on Expenditures 253
5.8 Funding of State Elections: Tax Provisions and Public Financing 259
5.9 Voter Registration Information 261
5.10 Polling Hours: General Elections 262
5.11 Voting Statistics for Gubernatorial Elections 264
5.12 Voter Turnout for Non-Presidential Elections: 1980, 1984, and 1988 265
5.13 Voter Turnout for Presidential Elections: 1980, 1984, and 1988 266
5.14 State Initiatives: Requesting Permission to Circulate a Petition 267
5.15 State Initiatives: Circulating the Petition. 268
5.16 State Initiatives: Preparing the Initiative to be placed on the Ballot 270
5.17 State Initiatives: Voting on the Initiative . 272
5.18 State Referendums: Requesting Permission to Circulate a Petition 273
5.19 State Referendums: Circulating the Petition 274
5.20 State Referendums: Preparing the Referendum to be Placed on the Ballot 275
5.21 State Referendums: Voting on the Referendum 276
5.22 State Recall Provisions: Applicability to State Officials and Petitions 277
5.23 State Recall Provisions: Petition Review, Appeal and Election 279

Chapter Six
STATE FINANCES

FINANCE AND BUDGET
6.1 State Budgetary Calendars 286
6.2 Officials or Agencies Responsible for Budget Preparation, Review, and Controls 287
6.3 State Balanced Budgets and Deficit Limitations: Constitutional and Statutory Provisions 290

REVENUE AND EXPENDITURE
6.4 Summary Financial Aggregates by State: 1987 292
6.5 Summary Financial Aggregates by State: 1988 293
6.6 National Totals of State Government Finances For Selected Years: 1974-1988 . 294
6.7 State General Revenue, By Source and By State: 1987 296
6.8 State General Revenue, By Source and By State: 1988 298
6.9 State Expenditure, By Character and Object and By State: 1987 300
6.10 State Expenditure, By Character and Object and By State: 1988 302
6.11 State General Expenditure, By Function and By State: 1987 304

The Council of State Governments vii

TABLES

6.12 State General Expenditure, By Function and By State: 1988 306
6.13 State Debt Outstanding at End of Fiscal Year, By State: 1987 308
6.14 State Debt Outstanding at End of fiscal Year, By State: 1988 309

TAXES
6.15 Agencies Administering Major State Taxes 313
6.16 State Tax Amnesty Programs 315
6.17 State Excise Rates 316
6.18 Food and Drug Sales Tax Exemptions ... 318
6.19 State Individual Income Taxes 319
6.20 State Personal Income Taxes: Federal Starting Points 320
6.21 Range of State Corporate Income Tax Rates 321
6.22 State Severance Taxes: 1989 323
   A Percent Distribution of State Collections by Major Tax Category 327
   B Selected States' Tax Collections: 1987 ... 327
6.23 National Summary of State Government Tax Revenue, By Type of Tax: 1986-88 . 329
6.24 Summary of State Government Tax Revenue, By State: 1986-1988 330
6.25 State Government Tax Revenue, By Type of Tax: 1988 331
6.26 State Government Sales and Gross Receipts Tax Revenue: 1988 333
6.27 State Government License Tax Revenue: 1988 335
6.28 Fiscal Year, Population and Personal Income, By State 337

Chapter Seven
STATE MANAGEMENT AND ADMINISTRATION

PERSONNEL
7.1 The Office of State Personnel Administrator 345
7.2 State Personnel Administration: Structure and Functions 347
7.3 Classification and Compensation Plans . 349
7.4 Selected Employee Leave Policies 350
7.5 State Employees: Paid Holidays 352

PUBLIC EMPLOYMENT
7.6 Summary of State Government Employment: 1952-1988 355
7.7 Employment and Payrolls of State and Local Governments, By Function: October 1987 356
7.8 Employment and Payrolls of State and Local Governments, By Function: October 1988 357
7.9 State and Local Government Employment, By State: October 1987 .. 358
7.10 State and Local Government Employment, By State: October 1988 359

7.11 State and Local Government Payrolls and Average Earnings of Full-time Employees, By State: October 1987 360
7.12 State and Local Government Payrolls and Average Earnings of Full-time Employees, By State: October 1988 361
7.13 State Government Employment (Full-time Equivalent), For Selected Functions, By State: October 1987 362
7.14 State Government Employment (Full-time Equivalent), For Selected Functions, By State: October 1988 363
7.15 State Government Payrolls For Selected Functions, By State: October 1987 364
7.16 State Government Payrolls For Selected Functions, By State: October 1988 365

RETIREMENT
7.17 Number, Membership and Monthly Benefit Payments of State-Administered Employee Retirement Systems: 1984-85 through 1986-87 371
7.18 National Summary of Finances of State-Administered Employee Retirement Systems, Selected Years, 1976-87 372
7.19 Membership and Benefit Operations of State-Administered Employee Retirement Systems: Last Month of Fiscal Year 1986-87 373
7.20 Finances of State-Administered Employee Retirement Systems, By State: 1986-87 . 375
7.21 Comparative Statistics for State-Administered Public Employee Retirement Systems: 1986-87 377

STATE RECORDS
7.22 Functions and Responsibilities of State Library Agencies 379

Chapter Eight
SELECTED STATE ACTIVITIES, ISSUES, AND SERVICES

INNOVATIONS
A Regional Organization and Distribution of Sample Across Regions 383
B Program Organization and Distribution of Sample Across Policy Areas 384
C Innovation Managers by Region 384
D Program Organization and Distribution of Innovation Managers Across Policy Areas 384
E Educational Background of Innovators .. 385
F Academic Majors of Innovators (Last Degree) 385
G Employment Status of Innovators 386
H Role of Innovators in Developing the Innovation 387
I Ranking of Groups Involved in Innovations' Development (All Innovations) 388

TABLES

J Ranking of Groups Involved in Innovations' Development (Policy Innovations Only) 388
K Rank Ordering of Group Involvement by Policy Areas (Means)................ 389
L Ranking of Groups as Supportive of Innovations (All Innovations) 389
M Ranking of Groups As Supportive of Innovations (Policy Innovation Only) .. 389
N Rank Ordering of Group Support by Policy Areas (Means)................ 390
O Organizational Changes Resulting from Innovations (Percent Responding "Yes") 391
P Innovators' Involvement in Professional Associations 391
Q Innovators' Professionalism by Region .. 392
R Innovators' Professionalism by Policy Area 392
S Innovators' Ranking of Information Sources (Means).................... 392
T Ranking of Information Sources by Policy Area (Means)................ 393
U States With Model Programs........... 393
V Model States by Policy Area (Number of Mentions in Parentheses) 394
W Innovative States by Reputation 394
X Innovative States by Policy Area (Number of Mentions in Parentheses) 395
Y Employment Status of Managers 399
Z Managers' Rating of Group Support for Innovations 399
AA Comparison of Managers' and Innovators' Ratings of Group Support for Innovations Means................... 399
AB Managers Perception of Group Support: Career versus Appointee (Group Means)..................... 400
AC Managers' Rating of Group Support by Policy Areas (Means)................ 400
AD Agency Incentives for Innovative Behavior (Percent Responding Yes) 401
AE Innovation Incentives by Policy Area (Percent Responding Yes) 401
AF Organizational Benefits and Problems Associated with Adopting Innovations . 402

UNIFORM LAWS
8.1 Record of Passage of Uniform Acts..... 409
8.2 Record of Passage of Model Acts....... 416

EDUCATION AND CHILDREN
8.3 Minimum Age for Specified Activities ... 417
8.4 General Revenue of Public School Systems By Source: 1986-87 418
8.5 General Expenditures of Public School Systems: 1986-87 420
8.6 Federal Funds Obligated for Child Nutrition Programs, By State: Fiscal Years 1988 422
8.7 Average Annual Salary of Instructional Staff in Public Elementary and Secondary Schools: 1939-40 to 1988-89 423
8.8 Membership and Attendance in Public Elementary and Secondary Schools, By State: 1987-88 and 1988-89 424
8.9 Enrollment, Average Daily Attendance, and Classroom Teachers in Public Elementary and Secondary Schools, By State 1988-89.................... 425
8.10 State Course Requirements for High School Graduation................... 426
8.11 Number of Institutions of Higher Education and Branches, By Type, Control of Institution, and State: 1987-88 429
8.12 Estimated Undergraduate Tuition and Fees and Room and Board Rates in Institutions of Higher Education, by Control of Institution and By State: 1986-87 430

HIGHWAYS
8.13 Total Road and Street Mileage: 1988 431
8.14 State Receipts for Highways: 1988 432
8.15 State Disbursements for Highways: 1988 . 433
8.16 Apportionment of Federal-Aid Highway Funds: Fiscal 1989 434
8.17 State Motor Vehicle Registrations: 1988 . . 435
8.18 Motor Vehicle Laws 436
8.19 State No-Fault Motor Vehicle Insurance Laws.............................. 438
8.20 Motor Vehicle Operators and Chauffeurs Licenses: 1988 441

COMMISSIONS
8.21 State Public Utility Commissions....... 443
8.22 Selected Regulatory Functions of State Public Utility Commissions 444

LABOR
8.23 Maximum Benefits for Temporary Total Disability Provided by Workers' Compensation Statutes 454
8.24 Estimates for Workers' Compensation Payments, By State and Type of Insurance: 1986-87.................. 456
8.25 Status of Approved State Plans Developed in Accordance with the Federal Occupational Safety and Health Act ... 458
8.26 Selected State Child Labor Standards Affecting Minors Under 18........... 459
8.27 Changes in Basic Minimum Wages in Non-Farm Employment Under State Law: Selected Years 1968 to 1990........... 463

HEALTH
8.28 State Regulation of Selected Occupations and Professions: 1990 471
8.29 State Regulation of Health Occupations and Professions: 1990 472
8.30 Status of Mandatory Continuing Education for Selected Professions: 1989 478

The Council of State Governments   ix

TABLES

8.31 State Health Agencies: Organizational Characteristics and Selected Public Health Responsibilities: Fiscal 1987 ... 479
8.32 Public Health Program Expenditures of State Health Agencies, By Program: Fiscal 1987 480
8.33 Public Health Expenditures of State Health Agencies, By Source of Funds: Fiscal 1987 481

CRIMINAL JUSTICE

A Offenders Under Correctional Supervision - 1988 484
B Percent Positive For Any Drug 487
C Formula Grant Allocations, By State 490
D Allocation of Anti-Drug Abuse Act Funds to the States for Treatment, Education and Law Enforcement 491
E Components of Comprehensive State Departments of Corrections Treatment Strategy for Drug Abuse in Six States .. 492
8.34 Trends in State Prison Population 493
8.35 Adults Admitted to State Prisons, 1980 and 1987 494
8.36 State Prison Capacities, 1988 495
8.37 Adults on Probation, 1988 496
8.38 Adults on Parole, 1988 497
8.39 State Death Penalty (As of December, 1988) 498

ENVIRONMENT

8.40 Interstate Water Agencies 508
8.41 Low-Level Radioactive Waste Compacts . 510

HOUSING

F1 State Legislation Targeted Toward the Homeless 513
F2 Magnitude of the Homelessness Problem (The view from Health, Social Services and Human Resources Agencies) 515
F3 Change in Homelessness (The view from Health, Social Services and Human Resources Agencies) 516

F4 Adequacy of Current Methods to Count the Homelessness (The view from Health, Social Services and Human Resources Agencies) 517

Chapter Nine
INTERGOVERNMENTAL AFFAIRS

9.1 Total Federal Aid to States: Fiscal 1983-1988 532
9.2 Summary of State Intergovernmental Payments: 1942-1988 553
9.3 State Intergovernmental Expenditure, by State: 1980-1988 554
9.4 Per Capita State Intergovernmental Expenditure, by Function and by State: 1987 555
9.5 Per Capita State Intergovernmental Expenditure, by Function and by State: 1988 556
9.6 State Intergovernmental Expenditure, by Function and by State: 1987 557
9.7 State Intergovernmental Expenditure, by Function and by State: 1988 558
9.8 State Intergovernmental Expenditure, by Type of Receiving Government and by State: 1987 559
9.9 State Intergovernmental Expenditure, by Type of Receiving Government and by State: 1988 560
9.10 State Intergovernmental Revenue from Federal and Local Governments: 1987 .. 561
9.11 State Intergovernmental Revenue from Federal and Local Governments: 1988 . 563

Chapter Ten
STATE PAGES

10.1 Official Names of States and Jurisdictions, Capitals, Zip Codes and Central Switchboards 576
10.2 Historical Data on the States 577
10.3 State Statistics 579

FOREWORD

It is with great pride and pleasure that we bring you the new biennial edition of *The Book of the States*, the premier reference work on state government. In recent years we have seen a dramatic shift in responsibility from Washington, DC, to the states, a trend reflected in the essays and data contained in this book. The states are assuming a dominant role in American domestic governance, and it is increasingly important that the institutions and innovations of state governments be widely understood and appreciated. We trust this volume will serve this vital purpose.

May 1990

Dan Sprague
Executive Director
The Council of State Governments

The Book of the States 1990-91 Project Staff

William Carlton Currens, *Project Manager*
Joan Minton, *Assistant Project Manager*
Katherine T. Tyson, *Assistant Project Manager*

Strategic Planning and Innovations

Doris Ball
Martha Hennessey
Juanita Hymer
Nancy L. Olson
Ellen Quinn
E. Norman Sims
Connie C. Whitaker

Communications and Development

Cheri Collis
Doug Dill
Jo Ann Ewalt
Elaine Knapp
Connie LaVake
Janet Murphy
Dag Ryen
Linda Wagar
A. Turner Williams

Acknowledgements

Many thanks to the hundreds of individuals in the states who provided data and information, to the authors who graciously shared their expertise; and to the thousands of state officials who, through their daily work, contributed to the story of state government presented in this volume.

THE STATE OF THE STATES, 1988-89

By Deborah A. Gona

Over the years, The Council of State Governments (CSG), in service to its state constituents, has found value in taking snapshots to record the states in their stages of evolution. Like the photographer taking the group picture, we carefully take a few steps back from our subjects and select the proper lighting and lens settings to show the individual character as well as the collection of "faces."

That is not an unusual activity for an organization charged with strengthening state government, improving state decision-making and preserving the role of the states in the federal system. In fact, this reference work, *The Book of the States*, produced biennially since 1935, is a prime example of one of those records. And this assessment of the "state of the states," originally produced as a message from the states to the 41st president of the United States, is another.[1]

However, that ordinary activity became extraordinary in 1988, because the "state of the states" that year was to form the backdrop for a series of intergovernmental and federal policy-making events set in motion on November 8 — the presidential election, the change in administration, the winding down of the decade of the 80s.

As such, in late 1988, we took those few steps back to snap our photo of the states. We shed the proper illumination on the subjects — highlighting the experiences of the states' leaders — and adjusted the lens to focus on the major issues, problems and opportunities facing the states and their policy-makers.

To understand the issues facing the states adequately, however, we had to begin with a look back over the recent past and the evolving role of state government.

The evolving state of the states during the 1980s

While scholars spent the greater part of the decade assessing the nature and impact of the New Federalism prescribed by Ronald Reagan in 1981, the states were facing the immediate realities of shifting responsibilities and depleted federal funding sources.

The result was not what many had predicted. Instead of less being done by the states, the reverse became true. By emphasizing the tangible — education, housing, pollution control, jobs and economic development — state leaders were able to sell constituents on a governmental role that sometimes included tax increases. The states were propelled into a mode of self-sufficiency, experimentation and innovation.

Analysts on the state and national level found that these "laboratories of democracy" were demonstrating creativity, resilience and a pragmatic approach to governing. In their essay, "Innovators in State Government," (pp. 382-404 of this volume) Keon Chi and Dennis Grady offer a profile of the sorts of individuals who originated or adapted many of the ideas that moved the states to the forefront of innovation.

Soon, however, some of those same analysts discovered that luck may have been playing as much of a role in the states' survival during the years of lean federal support as their pride and natural resilience. Many states and localities found themselves with healthier revenues than they had originally

---

Dr. Deborah A. Gona directs the policy analysis efforts at The Council of State Governments' headquarters office in Lexington, Ky.

anticipated, after the inflation of the 1970s drove up real estate prices and the economic growth of the mid-1980s bolstered tax coffers. According to the National Association of State Budget Officers, between 1982 and 1988 states increased their general fund spending by 51 percent, to $236 billion. During the same period, state aid to local governments increased to $143 billion, up 62 percent from the 1982 level of $88.1 billion.[2]

By the end of the 1980s, though, the fiscal trend appeared to be heading in another direction. While most states reported they were in relatively good financial shape as they closed the books on the 1988-89 fiscal year, several had fallen victim to revenue miscalculations resulting from the federal Tax Reform Act of 1986, the stock market crash of October 1987, sluggish local economies, unexpected expenses and other unforeseen factors.

Most weathered the combined effects of these events, but with the growth of state expenditures and the steadily dropping year-end general fund balances, there was continuing concern among state officials that similar shortfalls were in the offing. In fact, a study by the National Conference of State Legislatures reported that in 1990 over half of the states would be facing serious budget problems, as the slower growth rate for the national economy produced lower-than-expected revenue collections.[3]

Now, analysts argue, the states face a dire predicament. While they have been successful in experimenting with innovative social programs, they are finding it difficult to count on the steady and predictable revenues necessary to sustain them long-term. And the states are bracing for the prospect of less federal money with more federal constraints.

These developments have been coupled with concerns about the implications of recent U.S. Supreme Court decisions that raised the issue of federal taxation of state and local bonds, and even more fundamentally, the protection of the states within the framework of the U.S. Constitution.[4]

What the states had to say

The primary intent of the review of the "state of the states," however, was not to explore the nature of the relationship between the states and the federal government. It was, instead, an attempt to identify, and provide insight into, some of the biggest challenges confronting the states as they headed into the 1990s and the issue areas about which state officials were expressing the greatest concern.

To develop more than a "textbook" perspective on the "state of the states," CSG staff tapped into several information sources: national surveys of the public and state officials; governors' inaugural, budget and state of the state addresses; reviews of priority issues under study by state legislatures; and a variety of studies and analyses on the states.

The overall message was mixed. It was one of innovation, pride and satisfaction. But it was coupled with the understanding that more had to be done to tackle problem areas in the states, and that the "more" had to be weighed against the reality of limited fiscal resources.

Particularly noteworthy was that the public seemed to be relatively pleased with the performance of their states and their state leaders. In the fall of 1988 and 1989, for example, national opinion surveys on the public's perceptions of state government institutions and policy issues revealed a general satisfaction with the way governors and state legislatures were doing their jobs.[5]

In 1988, about 72 percent of those surveyed said their governors were doing a "good" or an "excellent" job, and 64 percent thought the same of their state legislatures. This is compared to the 52 percent who approved of the performance of the members of the U.S. Congress. By 1989, the numbers had dropped slightly for the governors and legislatures, but remained more favorable than the rating given Congress.

Further, most of the respondents felt a little better about their personal finances and the economic conditions of their states than they did about the condition of the national economy. In 1988, about 61 percent of those surveyed described their states' economies as "good" or "excellent," while 45 percent felt the same about national economy. One year later, the public was slightly more pessimistic about future economic conditions, but continued to express more positive feelings about the states' economies than that of the nation.

On the other hand, as the decade ended, the review of state efforts in various policy and program areas was mixed, perhaps more indicative of the public's rising expectations and the changing and expanding role of the states.

While the majority surveyed gave relatively high marks to state efforts in areas such as environmental cleanup, senior citizens' programs and programs to combat illiteracy, they expressed somewhat less approval of efforts in child day care services and child abuse prevention and treatment.

When asked to create hypothetical budgets for their states and chart programs for which they would increase or decrease funding, the respondents were even more revealing. Apart from calling for an increase in education funding, citizens polled did not focus on increases in "traditional" state service areas such as highways and transportation, corrections and prisons or state parks and tourism. Instead, they targeted funding increases for programs related to child day care, drug abuse prevention, illiteracy, senior citizen programs, infant health care, environmental protection and low-income housing.

As the 1980s closed, the public seemed to have developed a positive picture of the states and to be more willing to turn to state government to alleviate problems that the federal government was neglecting. But how did state leaders view the state of the states?

> ... *True to the ideal of federalism, the states in recent years have become genuine centers of creativity, innovation and experimentation in beginning to address the unmet needs of the American people. Assist that creativity by cooperation and shared efforts ....*
> — Respondent to 1988 CSG governing board survey

**The perceptions of state officials —
the major issues, the biggest challenges**

To gain more insight into their views, in the fall of 1988 CSG surveyed a cross-section of senior state officials who are members of its governing board.[6] No one could have predicted the amount of pride in achievement they would express. Although the above quoted response was from a New York state official, it could have come from any state. The survey captured a genuine cross-country, "let-us-show-you-what-we-can-do" spirit.

The officials who responded identified the following as top issues on their states' agendas:

• **Education** — and the elements of reform, restructuring and funding — received the most votes as the priority area of concern across the states.

• **Economic development** — and the concern over long-term growth, employment, infrastructure and rural development.

• **Environment** — including the management of water resources, waste and the protection of natural resources.

• **Human services** — including child day care and welfare reform, and the shortage of affordable housing for low- and middle-income families.

• **Health care** — including AIDS and the costs and availability of quality health care for all segments of the population.

• **Crime and corrections** — from prison overcrowding and construction to drug-related violence and crimes.

While many of the officials expressed genuine satisfaction in seeing their states successfully design, construct and implement programs to address at least some of these concerns, they acknowledged the fiscal challenges that remained. They shared a common concern over state revenues — shortages, instability, new sources, restructuring and tax reform — the impact of the federal deficit, and the prospect of more federal mandates with less money and more strings.

In this essay, we review just some of the problems and challenges the states faced as they approached the end of the decade, as well as some of the actions they had already taken in seven areas: education, employment, environment/natural resources, human services, health care, crime and corrections and infrastructure. Through the essays and tables contained in this book, however, the reader will develop an even better understanding of the states and the nature of state government.

The state of the states — education

An economy threatened by foreign competition and increasingly reliant on complex technologies requires a higher level of education than ever before, and the states have recognized that an educated population is linked to economic success. But they also have recognized that an uneducated population results in higher welfare and social service costs and increases the possibility of criminal behavior.

In 1983, the National Commission on Excellence in Education released *A Nation At Risk*, the catalyst for a nationwide education reform movement. As education reform became a national priority, states heeded the call by providing leadership and commitment. Reams of reports were written, education task forces were formed, and hundreds of programs were enacted across the states, all aimed at fixing up the schools. But the states did more than talk. They also made a financial commitment.

By the end of the decade, however, states began assessing the impact of their reforms. Gains had been made, but the outlook remained bleak, with as many as one million students dropping out of high school every year, and rates in some inner city schools approaching 50 percent. Just as alarming, though, was the evidence that as many as one-quarter of the graduating students were functionally illiterate and ill-equipped for the workforce.

Students at risk

In fact, many school systems had benefited and continue to benefit from the reform movement. But there has been growing concern throughout the states that students at the greatest risk of failure — low-income inner city and minority children — may have been bypassed by the reform movement.

The rapidly-changing demographic composition of public schools is partly to blame. Within the school population, there has been a dramatic increase in the number of children from single-parent, low-income and minority homes. And critics have argued that the first wave of reforms may have placed disadvantaged children at an even greater risk of failure.

While the primary focus of the reform movement was on raising minimum standards of student performance, the states soon learned that measures like more stringent graduation requirements and increased testing could not help students already failing in school.

As a result, many states began to take preventive measures by focusing on early childhood education and pushing to expand efforts at the pre-school level. In Arkansas, the *Home Instruction Program for Preschool Youngsters* (HIPPY) was initiated to serve the dual purpose of involving parents in their children's education and providing assistance to at-risk youth before they reach the first grade. Paraprofessionals work with the mothers of four- and five-year-olds in their homes and teach the moms how to use educational materials. Nearly three-quarters of the states have implemented programs targeted at disadvantaged youth, from infants to third-graders.

But the states continued to provide assistance to disadvantaged students to prevent them from dropping out of school. Everything from remedial programs in basic skills to alternative settings for students who have already dropped out were being developed across the states. In Texas, a program called Y.O.U. was opened to eighth- and ninth-grade students at risk of dropping out of school. Public colleges and universities offer intensive eight-week courses in basic skills which are supplemented by electives and summer jobs.

And the states, in the best position to orchestrate interagency cooperation for providing services to disadvantaged students, began coordinating the services of public and private agencies and forming partnerships with the business community to provide comprehensive assistance to these students.

Management

States also had to begin restructuring the

management and organization of their schools, shifting authority for day-to-day operations away from states and school districts to individual schools. Administrators and teachers increasingly were given the flexibility to make decisions on staffing, curricula, budget priorities and the structure of the school day. Shared-governance was being used to create a more professional environment for teachers and to improve morale.

The state of Washington, for example, initiated a six-year pilot project designed to "remove the shackles of bureaucracy" and promote professionalism. *Schools for the 21st Century* provides funds to schools that have programs designed to enhance the teaching and learning environment, and waives certain laws and regulations in the hope that creativity and innovation will improve overall student performance.

Accountability

In exchange for increased autonomy, however, school districts and individual schools were being asked to accept a greater degree of accountability. And old measures of success in schools — like student/teacher ratios, classroom size and the number of books in the library — were gradually replaced by measures like test scores, student attendance and graduation rates.

But while local school districts and individual schools began to assume greater autonomy, the states still maintained an active role in a variety of ways — by setting clear policy goals and standards for educational achievement, establishing performance criteria coupled with a viable assessment and evaluation program, making provisions for teacher certification and school accreditation, and offering technical assistance to help schools meet goals.

Perhaps most important were the states' efforts to relate sanction and rewards to performance. In the 1988-89 school year, for example, Indiana, with its *A+ Program*, began implementing a performance-based accreditation system, with cash bonuses available to schools that improve test scores and attendance rates.

Parental involvement and choice

According to many educators, one of the most critical factors in determining a child's success in school is parental involvement. However, the changing nature of the American family, including the increase in single-parent and two-career families, prevents many parents from participating. Many states have taken some first steps toward facilitating parental involvement and promoting participation.

In Kentucky, the *Parenthood and Child Education Program* allows parents, who do not have a high school diploma or its equivalent, to get instruction in basic academic skills, while their preschoolers work with child care specialists on developmental skills. And Michigan's *Hispanic Students Dropout Prevention Project* provides weekly parent training sessions to help parents understand the system and to involve them in the schooling process. As a result, parents also are continuing their education. In South Carolina, *School Improvement Councils*, consisting of parents, students, teachers and community representatives, work to improve schools.

Minnesota introduced a plan to give parents a choice about where they will send their children to school. And with surveys indicating that parents who have participated in the *Choose-a-School-Plan* are more satisfied with their children's education, several other states also began considering open enrollment legislation.

As the 1980s came to a close, the states looked back over the education reform movement for signs of success and they found some. But they also recognized that their financial commitment would have to be matched by new and creative efforts to meet their biggest challenge, educating and training a workforce for the changing economy.

The state of the states — employment

Despite the economic recovery of recent years, many national opinion surveys still indicate that employment remains the number one issue with most Americans. The reality of idle factories, dislocated workers and distressed communities are frequent reminders to most Americans of the economic changes taking place across the United States. With the ever-burgeoning federal deficit and the anticipation of another recession by many government officials, Americans understand that prospects for high unemployment, at least in certain areas, remain.

By the end of the 1980s, states were in the vanguard in developing comprehensive economic development strategies to compete in the world economy, strategies that ranged from offering tax and financial incentives to attract and maintain industries to developing research centers to attract high tech industries.

Increasingly, however, the heart of the employment problem for states was not merely business attraction and job expansion. Rather it was to develop a workforce capable of meeting the changing economic reality.

Most new jobs are in the service, information-oriented industries. Technological developments in automation, information and microprocessors require a workforce academically capable of mastering information technology. Further, the movement of women into the workforce has changed the nature and structure of social and family life. And the recent influx of Asian and Latin American immigrants is affecting the economy and the states' provision of services.

Many states recognized these problems early on and began developing innovative ways to combat them. For example, California adopted an *Employment Training Panel* to train and retrain dislocated workers and potential dislocated workers. With programming funded by unemployment insurance taxes and a one percent tax levied on designated employers, the panel contracts with employers and schools to conduct training. A program evaluation reported that trainee wages increased 55 percent after training, and unemployment decreased by 63 percent over a one-year period before and after the training.

As early as 1984, Delaware passed the *Blue Collar Jobs Act* to focus on dislocated workers and youth through school-to-work transition programs. The programs are funded through a one percent tax on the first $8500 of wages per employee, which is paid by the employer. A quarter of the money goes to the state economic development office for industrial recruitment and expansion and the remainder goes to the state's labor department and Private Industry Council to administer the program.

Several states have experimented with entrepreneurial and self-help programs as an employment strategy. Illinois, through its Department of Commerce and Community Affairs, has developed a number of programs to assist small businesses with start-up capital, technical assistance, employee training and government contract procurement. The state also has teamed up with its communities to provide a range of training to potential entrepreneurs. Other states that have experimented with self-help programs include Hawaii, Iowa, Michigan, Minnesota, Mississippi, New Jersey and New York.

The employment outlook

States have been taking the initiative to adjust to technological and demographic changes in the workforce, but employment trends suggest they will have to become even more flexible and adaptable. While the population in Third World countries is increasing, the population in the United States and other industrialized countries is diminishing. Workforces in these underdeveloped countries will be providing an abundance of cheap labor for large, labor-intensive firms, increasing the likelihood of these industries moving out of the U.S.

However, as analysts also have pointed out, the majority of jobs are created by small, existing companies, a factor that is forcing states to rethink their job creation strategies to promote the development of these small businesses. Many states have created business incubator programs as a method of spurring job creation and entrepreneurship. As of May 1987, the number of business incubators was 220; the number at the turn of the 1990s was expected to reach 500.

Pennsylvania's *Small Business Incubator Program*, for example, has been encouraging new business creation and existing business expansion in its communities since 1984. The state provides low-cost rental space, services and technical assistance to new businesses, and once the business becomes operational, it provides technical and financial assistance for business growth.

A neighboring state, Ohio, can lay claim to its *Thomas Edison Program*, which links a venture capital division, six business incubators and eight advanced technology institutes with all of the state's research universities and most of its major industry. The program is designed to allow the state's established firms to gain access to the latest manufacturing, computer and biological technologies, while providing inventors and entrepreneurs with capital and technical assistance.

Another employment trend, however, indicates that minorities, including new immigrants from Asia and Latin America — many of whom have very little education — will make up a large portion of the future workforce. Many young blacks and Hispanics already have drifted into what is being referred to as the "underclass," long-term unemployed individuals who are becoming a sizable population in many urban centers. Many states have found that these individuals not only need to be reeducated to face the realities of the marketplace, but also to find work immediately so they can become productive members of the economy.

Finally, with women entering the workforce at an ever-increasing rate, the nature of economic opportunities available and the types of goods and services state governments will be expected to provide are going to change drastically. States have become involved in family issues, such as parental leave and child day care, to ensure that they will be in step with the changing economic marketplace.

The state of the states — human services

By the late 1980s, a series of family-related issues — child day care, child support, child and spouse abuse, disintegrating families and adoption needs — moved into the national spotlight. Several governors even designated 1988 the "year of the family." But whether it was the result of a growing social consciousness or a practical sense of the economic realities of the changing workforce, that first issue — child care services — succeeded in grabbing the attention of the American public and officials across the states.

The public investment in child day care

The growing number and influence of working mothers heightened social awareness about the availability, affordability and quality of child day care. However, it also gave rise to the powerful family-focused political constituency that pushed the issue of child care support high onto the national and state legislative agendas by 1988.

The facts speak for themselves. Since the 1950s, the number of working women with preschool children has more than quadrupled. Now, approximately 66 percent of mothers aged 18 to 44 work, including an estimated 50 percent of those with children less than one year old. As a result, child care has become much more than a "family issue." It has been transformed into an economic and workforce issue. In his essay, "Labor Legislation: 1988-89," (pp. 446-453 of this volume), Richard Nelson counts child care among the non-traditional labor areas that have received considerable attention in recent years.

For families needing more than one income to maintain a middle-class standard of living, the struggle is to find affordable, quality child day care that will not drain off the benefits of that second paycheck. For low-income families, the availability of affordable child care is often the critical first step toward self-sufficiency. For employers, the new reality is that they will be forced to compete more intensely for a smaller number of new and qualified workers coming into the labor force in the next decade. And demographers have warned that two-thirds of that shrinking number of new job-market entrants will be women, most of them of child-bearing age.

That hard reality has forced policy debates to focus on where family responsibilities end and governmental responsibilities begin. By 1988, the push was on for child care policy at the national level — one that would articulate

STATE OF THE STATES

an overall public commitment to the welfare of children and assist in the states' efforts to respond to the child care service crisis.

At the end of the decade, however, in response to a lack of federal legislation addressing child care issues, 48 states already had enacted nearly 350 laws to try to meet the needs of two-earner and single-parent families. As employers, many states led the way in child care assistance and benefits, providing state employees with more accessible, affordable and quality child care. Connecticut, Washington and Wisconsin put new or additional funds into child care centers for public employees.

Following an example set by Illinois, the states of New Jersey, Oregon and Washington incorporated an income reduction plan for child care expenses as a benefit for state employees. States like California and Wisconsin began requiring that new and remodeled state buildings include child care space.

A number of states also enacted measures to create school-age child care programs, and to support pilot child care projects, start up subsidies for child care facilities, and various incentives for corporate support of day care.

Parental leave

As states began constructing programs to deal with the child care issue, they also had to grapple with a related dilemma — mandating fair leave policies for one or both parents of today's two career families, without interfering with businesses' rights to set company leave policies and ensure efficiency. In the late 1980s, parental leave for the birth, adoption or serious illness of a child continued to be a subject of active interest.

Despite some variance in the duration of leave allowed, states like Connecticut, Minnesota, Oregon, Rhode Island and Tennessee, began requiring employers to grant unpaid leave for a specified period of time and to guarantee returning employees reinstatement to their old job or to a similar one.

Perhaps the most sweeping "leave" legislation, however, was enacted by Wisconsin in 1988. Unlike other previously-adopted provisions, that state's legislation was unique in requiring mandatory time off for both men and women in cases of births, adoptions and family illnesses involving children, spouses or parents.

Welfare reform

That same year, Wisconsin also embarked on a continuing redesign of its welfare system — one with tough, mandatory standards for child support payments and automatic wage withholding, along with work and training programs for welfare recipients and extended medical- and day-care benefits to ease the transition from welfare to work.

Other states, like Arkansas, where "job clubs" offer job hunting skills, and Maryland, where recipients get basic training in literacy and other skills, and California, Massachusetts and Maine, emerged at the forefront of reform efforts. In Georgia, a new state policy encouraging AFDC adult recipients to go to work — one that revised the formula used in calculating the grant amount — took effect at the beginning of 1988. Iowa implemented a comprehensive program — *PROMISE*, Promoting Independence and Self-Sufficiency Through Employment — offering training, job searches, transitional child care and medical benefits, and a cash bonus for certain long-term welfare clients who hold full-time jobs.

The success of those reforms will be measured in years to come. But as the 1980s closed, states had to face and begin resolving another "people" problem.

Homelessness in the states

Homelessness has been recognized as an increasing problem in almost every state, one exacerbated by adverse economic conditions, long-term underemployment and unemployment, critical shortages of low-income and affordable housing, a reduction in federal expenditures for social service programs and the deinstitutionalization and non-institutionalization of the mentally ill. The result is that America's homeless population is increasing annually by an estimated 20 percent, with the fastest growing segment of that population being homeless families with children.

While homeless advocates have pressed for national housing legislation, conservative critics have warned that resurrecting failed "Great Society" programs of the 1960s and 1970s will only worsen the problem. The responsibility for addressing the homeless problem now is resting squarely with state and local governments. In his essay, "Homelessness in the States," (pp. 511-519 of this volume) Lee Walker discusses the states' response to the problem.

By the end of the 1980s, many states had already begun taking legislative action to address the homelessness problem. They started working with non-profit community-based groups, local governments, businesses and the private sector to increase support for emergency shelters, provide support services such as child care and job training, and set up task forces or councils to coordinate assistance to the homeless.

The states also had begun providing health care and other treatment to homeless individuals with special needs; encouraging new financing mechanisms to allow qualified buyers to purchase homes; setting up demonstration programs to encourage the construction, rehabilitation or adaptation of buildings into long-term housing for the homeless; and performing comprehensive studies of homelessness in their state.

However, without additional funds and flexibility from federal programs, additional sources of state and local revenue, and more across-the-board communication and interaction, homelessness is likely to remain a serious fiscal, economic and social liability for the states well into the 1990s.

The state of the states — health care

A spectrum of complicated, sometimes confusing, and more often than not, frustrating health concerns faced the states in the late 1980s: AIDS, long term care for the elderly and disabled, delivery of health care services to the indigent, the impending shortage of nursing services, the growing numbers of uninsured and underinsured and the rising costs of medical care.

Americans were expected to spend more than $450 billion on health care in 1988 alone, about 12 percent of the gross national product. Several factors had combined to influence the increase in health care costs across the states, making the search for adequate solutions even more problematic: the aging population; medical malpractice; the increase in the occurrence of mental health problems, including drug and alcohol abuse; the spiraling cost of medical technology and services; the overbuilding of hospitals; the excess consumption of health services; and changes in utilization patterns. The list continues to grow.

Despite significant initiatives to deal with the range of health-related issues, state officials recognize that much remains to be done. They have become caught in the struggle to provide their citizens with access to adequate and affordable health care services — a struggle complicated by the spread of a disease that, just a few years ago, no one wanted to talk about.

AIDS

As the growing number of cases reflected, Acquired Immunodeficiency Syndrome, better known as AIDS, became the nation's most serious public health concern in the late 1980s. And it is one that is not expected to go away quickly or easily. The U.S. Public Health Service predicts that 80 percent of the AIDS cases diagnosed in the early 1990s would be outside of the current high incidence areas.

Combating its spread, dealing with the costs of health care and treatment, and protecting individual and societal rights are broad concerns associated with the disease. In response, the states have considered hundreds of bills addressing both the social and personal aspects of AIDS and its causative agents. As a result of sharing information across the states, policy-makers have proposed and adopted more comprehensive and innovative ways of dealing with this complex health and social problem.

Through legislation and regulations, the states have addressed antibody testing, blood and blood products, confidentiality, education, employment, housing, informed consent, insurance, marriage, prison populations and the reporting of confirmed cases.

States like Indiana, Georgia, Washington and Wisconsin enacted omnibus AIDS legislation combining many of the above aspects, and most states have dealt with the separate aspects of the problem. But in all states, confirmed cases of AIDS constitute a reportable condition, either by statute or administrative regulation.

By the end of the 1980s, more than half the states had developed measures to instruct and educate the public in the hope of prevention. At least 12 states had enacted legislation mandating AIDS instruction in their public schools. Another 14 had adopted policies through their state boards of education or a combination of board and legislative approval. In Indiana, a statewide public AIDS education and prevention program operated by the state board of health ensures the widespread distribution of timely and useful information, in conjunction with other AIDS-related services and activities.

But the states' programs have not come cheaply. California, which developed some of the most sweeping statutes protecting the confidentiality and civil rights of suspected or actual carriers of the virus, was expected to spend over $63 million on AIDS alone. Even in one of the smaller states, Rhode Island, the governor called for $2.5 million in additional funding for expanded programs in education, treatment and service delivery. But AIDS was just one variable in the health care cost equation states were facing at the end of the 1980s.

Cost containment

States have had to initiate and implement a variety of methods to contain health care costs. Massachusetts, for example, attempted to control hospital costs by setting a revenue ceiling for each hospital. Nevada, on the other hand, required hospitals to itemize and make publicly available charges for services, equipment, supplies and medicines in terms that a patient can understand, and to prepare a summary of charges for services common to patients who are admitted to their facilities.

Other states were trying to put the reins on health care costs through a variety of methods, including:
- Prospective reimbursement, a method establishing the prices hospitals may charge before services are provided, and providing incentives the retrospective fee-for-service system lacks.
- Certificate of need, a method used by many states to control hospital capacity.
- Utilization control, which limits physicians' options by giving financial rewards or by imposing penalties.
- Encouraging competitiveness, by publicizing information on health care providers.
- Self-funding employee health insurance plans, under which employees choosing more costly coverage pay the extra costs.
- Alternative health care, including health maintenance organizations, primary care case management, outpatient care, hospices, homemaker services and adult day care services.

But the success or failure of the states' efforts thus far is not easily measured, as the numbers of consumers of more, longer-term, and consequently, more expensive care continue to increase.

Long-Term Care

America's growing and aging population is requiring more nursing home stays, home health care services and a range of other support activities. In recent years, the elderly population has grown, but the share of total health care dollars spent on the elderly has grown disproportionately. By the end of the 1980s, nearly a third of the annual health care expenditures was going toward treatment of the elderly, who represent about 12 percent of the total population.

But the matter of long-term care extends beyond the age factor. Of those Americans requiring some form of long-term care, about two-thirds are over the age of 65. By the year 2000, however, about 40 percent of those requiring such care are expected to be disabled children and younger adults.

Although they play a joint role in funding and administering federal programs, the states have taken the lead in the search for solutions to the long-term care crisis. Over the past few years, almost 80 percent of the states have instituted state-only, long-term care programs to serve the elderly — programs ranging from adult day care and pharmaceutical assistance to adult foster care, congregate housing and homemaker services.

In 1988 alone, states enacted more than 50 laws dealing with programs and services for the elderly, many addressing the needs of long-term care recipients. Several enacted legislation designed to improve the management of their long-term care service delivery systems, while others established new programs or initiated demonstration projects to test alternative services.

A handful of states began exploring ways to use private insurance to attack a spinoff problem of long-term care — the "spend down" problem that occurs when Medicaid eligibility requires a long-term care patient and his or her spouse to exhaust most of their own resources before they can receive public assistance. For millions across the states, however, any sort of health insurance would be a welcome relief.

Health care for the uninsured and underinsured

According to the U.S. Bureau of the Census, at least 37 million Americans have no health insurance. While the chances of being uninsured are greater for the unemployed, the working poor, minorities and children, more than half of the uninsured are full-time workers. To respond to the health care needs of the uninsured and underinsured, states had to begin searching for more comprehensive solutions through mandates, universal coverage or extension of existing programs.

Many states established task forces and enacted legislation to improve access to care for the medically indigent population. They set up insurance and hospital revenue pools, and began pursuing other initiatives to encourage the development of more affordable health benefit plans for uninsured populations. Several states, for example, considered or had already implemented programs to assist at least some segments of the uninsured/underinsured population, and in some cases, entice employers to provide health insurance for their employees.

By the late 1980s, about half of the states had expanded Medicaid eligibility to include more pregnant women and children. At least 15 had created health insurance pools for high-risk individuals who cannot obtain insurance in the private market. Some states began to provide subsidies and other tax incentives to encourage small businesses to provide health insurance. Others increased taxes and established set-asides and trusts to cover specific groups of the underinsured.

By 1988, however, only two states, Massachusetts and Hawaii, had mandated or guaranteed insurance coverage. Hawaii's program, requiring employers to provide workers with health insurance, has been in effect since the mid-1970s. In 1988, however, the Massachusetts legislature approved a universal health care bill designed to provide basic health insurance for every resident of the state by 1992. By 1989, however, severe budget and financing problems were threatening the Health Care Security Act. For many other states as well, resources simply are not adequate to address the needs of the uninsured population, particularly in poor and economically depressed areas with the most severe health care and service delivery problems.

Shortage of Nursing Services

Discussions of health care service delivery problems typically turn to the shortage of doctors in rural areas or the closing of community hospitals. At the end of the 1980s, however, many states were forced to face and resolve one of the overlooked aspects of service delivery, the impending shortage of nurses.

Like so many other health issues, several factors were at work, making resolution more difficult: internal problems within the nursing profession, early burnout and high turnover rates for practicing nurses and declining enrollment in nursing schools across the states.

Maryland took on one of the most comprehensive responses when its Task Force to Study the Crisis in Nursing released a report early in 1988. The task force advised the state to take immediate steps to avert a potential crisis in health care delivery, and created subcommittees to develop recommendations regarding the state's regulatory environment, nursing education and financing. Other states, including Hawaii, Nebraska, New Jersey, New Mexico, Pennsylvania, South Dakota, Tennessee, Virginia, Washington and Wisconsin, also established study commissions or authorized studies on the magnitude of the problem and its impact on health care.

Several states explored the use of financial incentives to interest individuals in nursing as a profession. Delaware established an incentive program for full-time students in programs leading to licensure as a registered or practical nurse. For each year of continuous employment as a nurse following graduation, one year of the loan's principal and interest amount is forgiven. Indiana expanded its educational assistance program to include students in certificate and associate degree programs. Washington state established a scholarship program for students who agree to spend up to five years practicing in a designated nurse shortage area of the state.

As the range of health problems has expanded, the states' role in developing programs for their treatment and prevention has escalated. The expectations of the American public have done likewise. In the 1988 CSG/UK national opinion survey referred to earlier in this essay, respondents made a strong statement as to where they would slot the money if given the opportunity to construct their state's budget. While 81 percent of the respondents said they would slate increases for improvements in education programs, a little over 72 percent of them said they would increase spending on drug abuse prevention programs.

But substance abuse — apart from its health-related effects — has an unfortunate criminal dimension that states were being forced to deal with as the decade ended.

The state of the states' — crime and corrections

Surveys in recent years have shown that while drug use among high school students and the general population has dropped somewhat, the use of illegal drugs remains one of the biggest problems facing the nation.

It is an issue — one like many others facing the states — that has both personal and social implications. It is the drug link to criminal activity, however, that has created severe enforcement problems for the states, forced them to acknowledge their limited resources, and come up with new approaches to beat the illicit drug industry. With the 1988 reauthorization of the federal grant-in-aid programs provided by the anti-drug abuse act, the states, overall, were expected to receive more funding for drug education, treatment and rehabilitation. But federal grants to the states for drug law enforcement were to be substantially reduced.

In recent years, states like Arizona, Illinois, Kansas, Maine, Minnesota, Nevada and Utah, have enacted legislation requiring dealers of illegal drugs to purchase tax stamps or otherwise pay taxes on their possessions — just one effort to provide a legal weapon against drug dealers.

Other states enacted legislation or considered bills allowing local police and state law enforcement officers to eavesdrop on suspected drug dealers. Still others, like Wisconsin, enacted legislation allowing second degree murder charges to be filed against individuals who supply illegal drugs that result in another person's death.

During 1988, plans also were underway to take the individual states' efforts one step further by establishing regional approaches to combating drug- and crime-related problems. A subcommittee established by the Mid-Atlantic Governors' Drug and Alcohol Abuse Conference was busy drafting a compact calling for, among other things, a declaration of illicit drug use and trafficking as the top law enforcement priority to help ensure sufficient funds, the development of consistent bail and sentencing guidelines to eliminate havens for drug offenders and the creation of model drug education programs.

New Jersey took another tack in fighting drug trafficking, one that quickly captured the attention of other states and localities. In

1987, the state enacted legislation creating drug-free zones around public and private schools across the state, and imposing a minimum of three years in prison for offenders caught in the zones. Since its implementation in June 1987, over 4,000 alleged dealers or users have been arrested on or near school grounds, according to the state attorney general's office.

But while the states and their citizens were ready to take harsh action against the illicit drug industry, by imposing larger fines and prison sentences, they also had to face the reality that those convicted might not have anyplace to be incarcerated.

Prison overcrowding

By the end of the 1980s, the inmate population across the states had rapidly increased, and a majority of the states' correctional facilities had already exceeded their capacity. In more than 30 states, correctional facilities were under court order to alleviate overcrowding. And the costs associated with incarceration forced many states to look at alternatives for their inmate populations.

To deal with the overcrowding problem, the states have had to take on a variety of measures, including new construction, renovation of existing facilities, use of local jails, pretrial diversion, probation, intensive supervision, house arrest, work release and early release. A few states even have used private firms to build, manage and operate state correctional facilities. In their essay, "Corrections in the 90s," (pp. 483-492 of this volume), Timothy Matthews and Kimberly Roberts discuss the variety of policies states have considered or adopted to alleviate the problem.

In 1988, however, building additional prisons remained at the top of the corrections' agenda in several states. Over the preceding five years, California had opened 11 new correctional facilities and added about 17,000 beds to its state correctional system. In lieu of considering other alternatives to incarceration, however, the governor proposed a substantial new bond issue to build more prisons. Similarly, Connecticut planned to add some 2,500 new prison beds to the state's corrections system.

At least 37 states had enacted determinate sentencing and/or mandatory sentencing laws to remove discretionary powers from parole boards and judges. Several states, including Connecticut, Minnesota, and Wisconsin, were using sentencing guidelines with encouraging results. But in 1988, at least one state, Florida, decided to scrap its five-year-old sentencing guidelines and return to a system of case-by-case sentencing with releases determined by a parole and probation commission.

But many states found that in order to make any long-term headway into the prison overcrowding problem, they would have to move away from more traditional measures and turn their attention toward the root causes of criminal behavior. Several states, including Illinois, Maryland, Ohio and Virginia, adopted programs designed to decrease inmate illiteracy, increase skills, and perhaps, decrease recidivism.

The state of the states — environment

Over the years, the states have had to tackle a variety of threats to their environment, from abandoned hazardous waste dumps to toxic air emissions. And, for the most part, the public thought their states were doing a reasonable job in cleaning up the environment, at least in the way of improving air and water quality. About 63 percent of the respondents in the 1988 CSG/UK national opinion survey said their states were doing a "good" or "excellent" job in the area. In their essay, "Four State Environmental Protection Initiatives for the 1990s," (pp. 501-507 of this volume) R. Steven Brown and John Johnson offer examples of states' leadership in environmental management.

In the late 1980s, however, while long-standing environmental protection issues remained, another set of problems moved onto the priority list and captured the attention of the states and their citizens — infectious waste washing up onto beaches, trucks hauling waste that no jurisdiction wanted to claim, drought conditions and gloomy predictions of water shortages in the long-term.

STATE OF THE STATES

Water resources

In what has come to be known as the "drought of 1988," no region was left unaffected. Over 80 percent of the states suffered from abnormal weather conditions and below-normal precipitation levels. Water supplies for irrigated crops were too low, and forest fires raged in several north central and western states, making 1988 the fourth consecutive year of severe forest fire damage.

It was not the first drought period the states had experienced during the 1980s, but it was the drought that heightened awareness and concern for water planning and water resource management. Many states facing the prospect of depleted supplies began turning their attention toward actively developing water resource management plans, programs and legislation.

Some states, like California, Florida, Texas and Arizona, had long been dealing with water resource problems and planning. Other states, including Ohio, Kansas, Oregon and Montana, had to begin formulating long-term water plans.

Unable to control the amount of yearly rainfall, the states have to figure out new and better ways of managing their water resources over the long-run. But they have found themselves in a better position to control other threats to their existing water supplies, their land and their residents — threats in the form of wastes, not only those that can be classified as hazardous, but also infectious and solid.

Infectious waste

With the growing concern over AIDS, and its transmission via blood, blood products or other bodily fluids, infectious waste generated by hospitals and medical laboratories picked up more attention from the media and government authorities in the late 1980s. In the absence of federal statutory guidance, the states had to take the lead in creating or revamping regulatory programs in the area.

According to a CSG survey conducted early in 1988, 11 states already had new or amended infectious wastes statutes or had promulgated regulations since the U.S. Environmental Protection Agency published its 1986 Guidance. In addition to those states, 25 had initiated processes changing their requirements for infectious waste handling, transportation and disposal. States began to zero in on the problem by removing "infectious wastes" from their existing hazardous waste programs and — because of the nature of the problem — creating either a special wastes category or including these wastes under their non-hazardous waste regulations.

Infectious waste — washing up onto coastlines or spilling onto the ground from split bags — succeeded in grabbing the states' attention largely because of its extraordinary and immediate link to the AIDS crisis. But a more ordinary form of waste — solid waste — began to threaten the states simply by its sheer volume.

Solid waste

Landfills all over America are reaching their capacity, and it is estimated that by 1995 about half of them will be closed. Although many of the existing ones are leaking and contaminating groundwater, their long-term alternatives — recycling and waste-to-energy plants — still have not been widely accepted across the states. In some areas of the country, the immediate solution in the late 1980s involved shipping trash to far-off locales.

That "solution," however, appeared to be just as unpopular. In the 1988 CSG/UK national opinion survey, a little over 82 percent of the respondents said their states should prohibit the "importing" of out-of-state wastes. But to protect their own resources, some states like Kentucky had to require existing solid waste landfills, which accept waste from outside the state, to demonstrate that their design protects groundwater.

By the end of the decade, states faced a variety of obstacles in siting new landfills, despite their improved efficiency and design. As a result, they had to begin taking different approaches. For example, Oregon legislation allows the state to preempt local opposition to a landfill site, and Wisconsin negotiates with localities to site new landfills.

However, a few states, including New Jersey, Connecticut, Oregon and Rhode Island, enacted mandatory recycling laws to deal with the disposal problem. In Rhode Island, residents of communities that rely on the state for waste disposal have to separate newspapers and aluminum, glass and metal from their garbage for curbside pickup. New Jersey's Source Separation and Recycling Act — designed with the goal of reducing the amount of waste in the state by 25 percent — requires every state resident to separate materials like newspapers and glass from their household trash.

Waste-to-energy, another alternative that picked up some support from state and local officials, also raised concerns over environmental and health hazards associated with the incinerators' smoke emissions and ash residue. And with limited resources and too many existing facilities that needed "fixing up," some states found that alternative too expensive to warrant serious consideration.

The state of the states — infrastructure

The nation's infrastructure is eroding — a simple statement of a not-so-simple problem that has forced the states to reassess, reprioritize and begin rebuilding America's capital facilities.

One Federal Highway Administration annual bridge report to the U.S. Congress identified 575,607 bridges of which 243,646 or 42 percent were either structurally deficient or functionally obsolete. In 1988, a report by the National Council on Public Improvement warned that most of the nation's mass transit and hazardous waste treatment facilities were dangerously near collapse.

But the concern goes beyond the public's safety and health. Most scholars and practitioners agree that the economic future of the nation is linked to the quality of its capital facilities. The U.S. Department of Commerce has estimated that industrial infrastructure needs will increase by 30 percent in the 1990s. And more and more businesses have begun asking states to make substantial improvements in their infrastructure before they will locate in particular areas. Many economic development analysts suggest that future business recruitment in the states will hinge, at least in part, on their strategies to improve the infrastructure.

But the escalating concern about the impact of the nation's infrastructure crisis on public welfare and economic development has not been matched by government investment in the nation's infrastructure needs. According to Federal Highway Administration projections, $51.4 billion is needed to replace or restore deficient bridges, However, in 1986, for example, only $2.8 billion was spent on bridge repair and federal bridge funding. While state officials pleaded for more funds to repair or replace deficient bridges, bridge funding was reduced by $150 million as a result of the Gramm-Rudman-Hollings Act. State wastewater facilities and sewage disposal programs had similar cuts under the Clean Water Act. With declining federal funding as the decade ended, states had to shoulder more of the responsibility for infrastructure development.

Meeting the challenge

States have tried to meet this challenge in a variety of ways. In many such as Alabama, Colorado, Illinois, Tennessee and Vermont, the governors placed infrastructure development near the top of their agendas.

A number of states addressed the problem by developing comprehensive mechanisms to finance infrastructure development. For example, after experiencing federal reductions in public works moneys in the early 1980s, Washington state took steps toward rebuilding its infrastructure. In 1981, voters approved bond authorities that raised $150 million for the construction of wastewater treatment plants. In 1983, the state legislature raised the state motor fuel tax by two cents per gallon and earmarked the revenue for roads, bridges and highways. At the same time, state officials undertook a study to assess the needs of, and the resources available for public works.

That study led to the establishment in 1985 of the Public Works Trust Fund, which was designed to assist local municipal financing of public works projects. In both 1986 and

1987, a total of $34.6 million in loans made possible $80 million worth of public works construction. In 1988, $36 million in loans was expected to create over $74 million dollars in public works projects.

The Virginia Resource Authority issued $100 million in bonds in 1986 to create a three-year pooled loan program to finance municipally-owned and -operated water and sewage projects. By the late 1980s, 15 projects totaling $60 million had been funded, and applications for the remaining $40 million exceed $90 million.

Illinois made substantial investments in infrastructure under its "Build Illinois" program. Initiated in 1985, this five-year program was aimed at providing new or supplementary funds to improve the state's infrastructure, in the hope of attracting new business or expanding existing business. More than $57 million of the $2.8 billion allocated to the program went into infrastructure improvements, specifically water and sewer programs. Moreover, $372 million was allocated to rebuild the highway system to promote business formation and development. A five-year, $3.6 billion highway construction plan went into effect July 1, 1988.

Many of the eastern states began making substantial improvements in water and sewage facilities. Pennsylvania, for example, approved a $2.5 billion, 25-year grant and loan program to modernize and expand water and sewer facilities. In April 1988, voters approved a $300 million bond issue to supplement the program.

In July 1988, Vermont began a four-year, $52 million project to clean up Lake Champlain. This state-local project was designed to separate sanitary and storm sewers, and upgrade three treatment plants to prevent untreated sewage from going into the lake.

States have been taking the initiative to close the gap between their public infrastructure needs and their ability to pay for those needs. A variety of factors — the changing nature of fiscal federalism; the impact of the new federal tax laws on bond issuance; "pork barrel" politics involved in congressional authorization and distribution of public works projects; and the structural and cyclical changes in the economy — has forced states to strategically plan and prioritize infrastructure developments.

By the end of the 1980s, state policy-makers began to more fully recognize that a high-tech, information-oriented economy calls for different types of infrastructure needs than the manufacturing industry. Similarly, they found that they would need to tailor infrastructure bond financing toward those communities most in need of attracting businesses. The states were becoming responsible not only for setting the fiscal and administrative limits, but also the direction of the effort.

A final look at the state of the states — the challenges and the hopes

In this essay, we reviewed some of the issues and problems facing the states as the 1980s were coming to a close.

But what did state officials think their greatest challenges would be over the next few years? The CSG survey of state leaders identified several, including:

- Building a stronger economic base;
- Financing major reforms;
- Maintaining the quality of life;
- Assuring an adequate supply of clean water;
- Redeveloping rural areas;
- Satisfying a pent-up demand for services;
- Preparing for the 21st century with restricted resources to meet the citizens' needs in education, economic development, health care and environmental protection.

Despite their concerns, however, those state policy-makers expressed pride and optimism in their ability to find creative solutions to often-perplexing problems — as long as they have sufficient resources and latitude to deal with those challenges.

Notes

1. *A Message to the 41st President on the State of the States 1988.* Lexington, Ky: The Council of State Governments, 1988. Released at the CSG Annual Meeting, Kansas

City, Mo., Dec. 3-7, 1988, and presented to President George Bush by Utah Senate President Arnold Christensen, 1989 CSG Chairman, Dec. 19, 1988.

2. *State Aid to Local Governments 1989.* Washington, DC: National Association of State Budget Officers, 1990.

3. Ronald Snell, "The State Fiscal Outlook: 1990 and the Coming Decade," *State Legislative Report* (February 1990), p. 1.

4. *Garcia v. San Antonio Metropolitan Transit Authority* (469 U.S. 528, 83 L.Ed. 2d. 1016, 105 S.Ct. 1005, 1985) and *South Carolina v. Baker* (108 S.Ct. 1355, 99 L.Ed. 2d. 592 12, 1988).

5. National public opinion surveys sponsored by The Council of State Governments and the University of Kentucky's Martin School of Public Administration. In 1988, telephone interviews of 1,000 adults randomly selected from across the U.S. were conducted between Oct. 26 and Nov. 20. In 1989, 1,037 adults were interviewed between Sept. 29 and Oct. 25. Margins of error are +3 percentage points. Throughout this essay, the polls will be referred to as the CSG/UK national survey.

6. This body is composed of the governor and two legislators from each state, as well as other state officials from the legislative, executive and judicial branches who serve on the Council's Executive Committee. The survey was designed to gather information about the ways their states remedied problems, what they thought their states' greatest challenges would be over the next few years and what they wanted to say to the newly-elected president about the "state of the states."

CHAPTER ONE

STATE CONSTITUTIONS

STATE CONSTITUTIONS AND CONSTITUTIONAL REVISION: 1988-89 AND THE 1980s

By Janice C. May

The 1980s may well be remembered as a distinctive decade in the contemporary history of state constitutions. There has been a decline in the overall levels of amendment and revision activity by formal processes. Revision of comprehensive or general scope, including new constitutions, has fallen to the lowest level in 40 and even 50 years.[1] In contrast, the use of the constitutional initiative, which has relatively little effect on overall revision levels, has risen to historic heights during the decade.[2] The increase in the number of constitutional initiatives is part of the recent explosion in the use of the devices of direct democracy, including the statutory initiative, the referendum, and the recall.[3]

Another development has been the revival of state constitutional law.[4] In a significant number of cases, state judges have interpreted their own constitutions independently of the U.S. Constitution regarding civil rights and other controversies. State judicial review is scarcely new, but the emerging body of law is a reminder that state constitutions are changed by judicial interpretation as well as by formal amendment and revision processes. The increasing reliance on state constitutions by judges has been accompanied by an extensive new literature to which the legal profession and many others have contributed. This expanding body of information about state constitutions is a highlight of the decade. It is a reflection of the growing awareness of the importance of state constitutions in the American federal system. This may be the most important development of all, a key to future constitutional change.

General Overview: Use of Authorized Methods

The level of constitutional amendment and revision by formal methods was substantially lower in 1988-89 than at the beginning of the decade. As Table A shows, 267 proposals were referred to the voters in 45 states; 199 were approved, including two adopted in Delaware by legislative action alone. In 1980-81, however, there were 388 proposals and 272 adoptions in 46 states. A comparison of the decade with the 1970s shows an even greater decline. The total number of proposals in the 1980s was 1,513 and the number of adoptions was 1,091. But in the preceding decade, proposals numbered 2,079, or 566 more, and adoptions were 1,305, or 314 more. It is useful to compare propositions and adoptions of statewide applicability only to eliminate the large number of local amendments characteristic of bienniums through 1982-83. (See Table B.) In the 1980s, the statewide proposals and adoptions numbered 1,187 and 811, respectively, compared with 1,520 proposals and 1,011 adoptions in the 1970s. Though less than before, the differences between the decades remain substantial.

The decline in constitutional change by authorized methods was most conspicuous with respect to comprehensive or general revision during the biennium. No new constitution was proposed to the voters or adopted, no constitutional conventions were called by the voters or convened, and only two con-

---

Janice C. May is associate professor of Government at the University of Texas at Austin.

stitutional commissions were active although a third was authorized. The only electoral activity was the defeat by the Illinois voters of a referendum on a convention call, mandated by the Illinois Constitution. For the decade, only one new constitution was adopted, the new Georgia Charter in 1982. In other recent decades more constitutions were approved: six in the 1970s, four in the 1960s, two in the 1950s and three in the 1940s. In the 1980s, five constitutional conventions convened, although the Arkansas convention of 1978 met only briefly in 1980 and the New Hampshire convention of 1974 authorized to serve until 1984 was not active. Other conventions were: New Hampshire (1984), Rhode Island (1986) and the District of Columbia (1982). A comparison by decades shows eight conventions in the 1970s, 14 in the 1960s, nine in the 1950s and six in the 1940s. Nine constitutional commissions were operative in the 1980s, fewer than the other recent decades except for the 1940s. There were 12 in the 1970s, 51 in the 1960s, 14 in the 1950s and six in the 1940s. During the decade, nine convention calls were on ballots but only three were adopted. The numbers called and approved in other recent decades were: 1970s—17-10, 1960s—18-12, 1950s—15-8, and 1940s—7-5. In summary, comprehensive revision as measured by the number of new constitutions, conventions, commissions, and convention calls in the decade of the 1980s was the lowest in 50 years. The numbers of commissions and convention call approvals were the lowest in 40 years.

Use of the constitutional initiative for constitutional change turned out to be an exception to the downward trends. In 1988-89, 21 constitutional amendments were proposed by initiative and 11 were adopted, a record for the decade. In addition, the 55 percent approval rate was a rarity for constitutional initiatives in any biennium in recent years. For the decade, there were 89 proposals and 33 adoptions, the most since the 1930s. The approval rate of 37 percent matched the rate for the last 50 years. Proposals and adoptions by decade were: 1970s—69-21, 1960s—41-17, 1950s—45-16, 1940s—63-28, and 1930s—133-47.

Tables 1.2, 1.3, and 1.4 summarize the procedures associated with each of the three major methods used to initiate state constitutions' amendments and revisions: proposal by the state legislature available in all states; the constitutional initiative provided for in 17 state constitutions; and the constitutional convention accepted as legal in all states although not expressly authorized in nine state constitutions. A fourth method used to initiate and refer proposed constitutional changes to the electorate, the constitutional commission (expressly authorized only in the Florida constitution) was not used in 1988-89 or in any other biennium of the decade.

Legislative proposal, constitutional initiative

Legislative proposal, the most commonly employed method for initiating constitutional amendments, accounted for 246 of the 267 proposals referred to voters during the biennium. Of these, 188 were adopted and 186 (excluding two Delaware propositions) (75.6 percent) were approved by the voters. In the

Table A
State Constitutional Changes by Method of Initiation
1982-83, 1984-85, 1986-87, and 1988-89

Method of Installation	Number of states involved				Total proposals				Total adopted				Percentage adopted			
	1982-83	1984-85	1986-87	1988-89	1982-83	1984-85	1986-87	1988-89	1982-83	1984-85	1986-87	1988-89	1982-83	1984-85	1986-87	1988-89
All methods	45	45	47	45	345	238	275	267	258	158	204	199	73.0	65.5*	74.3*	74.0*
Legislative Proposal	45	45	46	45	330	211	243	246	255	144	191	188	75.5*	67.3*	77.7*	75.6*
Constitutional Initiative	9	10	9	11	16	17	18	21	4	8	5	11†	20.0	47.1	27.7†	55.0†
Constitutional Convention	2	1	1	1	-	10	14	-	-	6	8	-	-	60.0	57.1	-
Constitutional Commission	-	-	-	-	-	-	-	-	-	-	-	-	-	-	-	-

*In calculating these percentages, the amendments adopted in Delaware (where proposals are not submitted to the voters) are excluded.
†Excludes one Nevada constitutional initiative whose final adoption requires a second favorable vote.

CONSTITUTIONS

1980s, 1,392 were proposed and 1043 were adopted, a 74.9 percent approval rate. The legislative proposals constituted 92 percent of proposals by all methods during the biennium and the decade. This is somewhat higher than in other periods because, although there were more constitutional initiatives, only 16 general revision propositions were proposed in 10 years.

The constitutional initiative, which empowers the public by petition to propose amendments directly to the voters, is available in one-third of the states. Appropriate only for making limited constitutional change, the method accounted for a record number of proposals and adoptions during the biennium and decade. The constitutional initiatives, however, amounted to a fairly small percentage of total proposals and adoptions — 8 percent of the proposals for the biennium and 5 percent for the decade and 5 percent of the adoptions for the biennium and 3 percent for the decade. The number of initiative proposals and adoptions by states during the current biennium and the decade are as follows: (Biennium Considered-Passed-Decade Considered-Passed) Arizona (1-1, 4-1), Arkansas (2-1, 9-3), California (4-2, 12-5), Colorado (4-2, 10-4), Florida (2-1, 4-2), Illinois (0-0, 1-1), Massachusetts (0-0,0-0), Michigan (0-0,5-0), Missouri (2-1, 4-3), Montana (0-0, 2-1), Nebraska (1-1, 2-2), Nevada (1--, 7-3), North Dakota (1-0, 4-1), Ohio (0-0, 7-0), Oklahoma (1-1, 3-2), Oregon (0-0, 10-3), South Dakota (2-1, 5-2). California leads the initiative states in numbers of proposals and adoptions by decade and Massachusetts, with no activity, is last.

Constitutional conventions

The constitutional convention is the oldest, best known, and most traditional of the methods for extensively revising an old constitution or writing a new one. As of January 1, 1990, 233 conventions, including the 1982 convention in the District of Columbia, had been held in the United States. During the biennium there were none, and in the decade, five. As Table 1.4 shows, 14 state constitutions require a popular vote periodically on the question of calling a convention. Eight states mandate one every 20 years; one state, every nine years. During the biennium, the only convention referendum question on the ballot was in Illinois, whose constitution is one of the eight to require a vote every 20 years. For Illinois this was the first vote on a call since the new Illinois charter was ratified in 1970. Opposed by the governor and most civic and political leaders, including delegates to

Table B
Substantive Changes in State Constitutions:
Proposed and Adopted, 1982-83, 1984-85, 1986-87, and 1988-89

Subject Matter	Total Proposed				Total Adopted				Percentage Adopted			
	1982 -83	1984 -85	1986 -87	1988 -89	1982 -83	1984 -85	1986 -87	1988 -89	1982 -83	1984 -85	1986 -87	1988 -89
Proposals of state-wide applicability	226	228	251*	228*	149	154	184†	164†	65.9*	67.1*	72.9*	71.6*
Bill of Rights	13	9	12†	21	13	7	10	19	100.0	77.7	81.8*	90.5
Suffrage & elections	5	5	11	12	4	5	10	8	80.0	100.0	90.9	66.7
Legislative branch	32	37	49	44	18	19	35	33	56.3	51.5	71.4	75.0
Executive branch	19	30	23	22	9	20	19	14	47.4	66.7	82.6	63.6
Judicial branch	26	19	18	18	21	16	15	14	80.8	78.9	83.3	77.8
Local government	13	16	17	14	9	13	11	10	69.2	75.0	64.7	71.4
Finance & taxation	48	67	45	54	28	43	29	33‡	58.3	64.2	64.4	62.9‡
State & local debt	26	21	12	6	19	16	8	5	73.1	76.2	66.6	83.3
State functions	31	17	29	22	18	9	22	17	58.1	52.9	75.8	77.3
Amendment & revision	2	2	0	5	1	2	0	2	50.0	100.0	0	40.0
General revision proposals	1	0	14	0	1	0	8	0	100.0	0	57.1	0
Miscellaneous proposals	10	5	22	12	8	4	17	9	80.0	80.0	77.2	75.0
Local amendments	123	10	24	39	107	4	20	35	87.0	40.0	79.1	89.7

*Excludes Delaware where proposals are not submitted to the voters.
†Includes Delaware
‡Excludes one Nevada constitutional initiative whose final adoption requires a second favorable vote.

the 1969-70 Illinois Constitutional Convention, the referendum was defeated in the general election of 1988. The vote was 900,109 in favor and 2,727,144 against; 4,697,192 votes were cast in the election. To pass, the resolution would have had to receive either a majority of the total vote or three-fifths of the vote on the referendum.

Although no constitutional convention convened in 1988 or 1989, a serious effort was mounted in Mississippi by Gov. Ray Mabus to persuade the Mississippi Legislature to place a call on the ballot in 1988. The last volume of *The Book of the States* described the unsuccessful attempt by Gov. William B. Allain, Mabus' predecessor, to win a favorable vote for a referendum on a convention call from the Legislature in 1987. Mabus also failed, but the proposal passed the House for the first time before dying in conference committee. After adjournment, a group of state legislators sought unsuccessfully to revive the Mississippi initiative and referendum as an alternative method of calling a convention. Although adopted by voters in 1914, the initiative and referendum had been invalidated by the Mississippi Supreme Court on procedural grounds in 1922.[5] Encouraged by the reasoning applied in a recent case by the court, *Burrell vs. Mississippi State Tax Commission*, 93 So.2d 848 (Miss. 1988), the legislators hoped that a test case would result in a reversal of the 1922 decision. But the legislators failed in their attempt when they were unable to obtain the required number of signatures for an initiative petition.

Constitutional commissions

Constitutional commissions serve generally two major purposes: to study the constitution and propose changes and to prepare for a constitutional convention. During the biennium, commissions in Oklahoma and Utah were operative, and a third, in Kentucky was authorized to serve to May 1988 although it was not active. During the decade there were nine: Utah, 1977-; Alaska, 1979-80 and 1980-81; Georgia, 1977-1986; New Hampshire, 1983; Rhode Island, 1983; Mississippi, 1985-86; Kentucky, 1987-88; and Oklahoma, 1988-90.

Gov. Henry Bellmon organized the Oklahoma Constitution Study Commission in October 1988 after the Oklahoma Legislature had refused twice to grant his request for funding. The governor named himself, a Republican, and U.S. Senator David Boren, a Democrat, as honorary co-chairs of the 32-member commission. Attorney General Robert Henry was chair. The members included three legislators, other state and local government officers and citizens representing business, law, agriculture, energy, and education interests. Funding was secured from three private foundations. The group organized into eight study committees. In June 1989 a 100-page draft of a revised constitution was reviewed at public hearings in six cities. After further study and revision, the Oklahoma commission gave final approval to three articles, which were submitted to the governor and the Legislature. The final report was expected to be ready in 1990.

The three proposals revised the executive, the ethics, and the corporations articles. The executive article would strengthen the governor's position substantially, which was a key objective of revision leaders. Among the specific changes were: requiring the governor and the lieutenant governor to run as a team, allowing the governor to appoint a majority of boards and commissions soon after inauguration, providing for a cabinet of not more than 15 members, and empowering the first governor elected following the amendment's adoption to reorganize the 347 executive offices and agencies, subject to a legislative veto. Called "anti-business" by the governor, the present corporations article was revised to transfer most of the provisions to the statutes, leaving only those concerning the selection and composition of the Corporation Commission and its general duties. The new ethics article, which made the Ethics Commission a permanent constitutional agency, provided for the method of selection of the five-member body and for its powers and duties. The commission is authorized to promulgate rules of ethical conduct for state officers and employees as well as for campaigns for state office and for initiatives and referenda, including civil penalties for violation of rules.

The rules may be modified or vetoed by legislation, which, in turn, is subject to a gubernatorial veto. Among its other powers, the Ethics Commission is authorized to prosecute violations in state district court.

Backed by the governor, a campaign to place the three constitutional proposals on the ballot in 1990 by the constitutional initiative method was under way by September 1989. Led by a group called Amend Our Constitution Today (ACT), the requisite number of signatures was gathered for each amendment and certified by the secretary of state in time for the next year's elections. At the date of writing, the initiatives were held up by a legal challenge before the Oklahoma Supreme Court. The ballot wording was under legal review for being deceptive, insufficient and not comprehensible on an eighth grade reading level, as required by law. Regardless of the outcome, Oklahoma voters also will have the opportunity to vote on a convention call in 1990, which is mandated by the Oklahoma constitution every 20 years. The governor and other revision leaders are opposed to a convention. Their strategy is to offer to the voters a viable alternative to the convention, the process to begin in 1990.

The Utah Constitutional Revision Commission, a permanent body since 1977, is required by statute to submit recommendations for constitutional revision to the Legislature at least 60 days before each regular session. Major revisions of the articles on local government and debt submitted to the Legislature for action in 1988 were rejected. Also rejected by the Legislature were major revisions of the labor and corporations articles and lesser changes recommended the following year. The most recent recommendations, submitted to the Legislature meeting in 1990, include a major revision of the labor article and two changes to the article on the Legislature. At the 1988 general election, the voters approved two propositions, one on bail and one a "clean-up" measure, both of which had been recommended to the Legislature by the commission. For further information see Table 1.5.

The Kentucky Revision Commission was established in 1987 and served officially until May 1988. In January 1987, the Kentucky Legislative Research Commission (LRC), whose 16 members are legislative leaders, adopted a resolution to create the LRC Special Commission on Constitutional Review. In the resolution, the LRC recognized the need to review the Kentucky constitution but held that a constitutional convention was neither feasible nor warranted. The resolution directed the commission to study all 263 sections of the Kentucky Constitution and to submit an initial report by September 1987.

Most of the 41 members of the commission were appointed by the speaker of the House and the president pro tem of the Senate, the co-chairs of LRC. They appointed 14 citizens; nine representatives of business, labor, and the media (three from each); four legislators (two from each chamber and party); and two mayors and two county executives. The deans of the three state law schools each appointed one of their faculty members and the Chief Justice of the Supreme Court appointed one judge from each of three court levels. Co-chairs of the Elections and Constitutional Amendments Task Force were also members, and the LRC co-chairs served ex officio. The LRC co-chairs named J. William Howerton, Chief Judge of the Court of Appeals, as commission chairman. The director of the LRC supplied staff and support; members were reimbursed for expenses.

The commission organized into six subcommittees, each of which submitted recommendations for inclusion in the full committee report. The full committee did not change the recommendations, but used a mail survey of the members to rank the recommendations on a priority scale of 1 through 5 and to determine how many members supported each proposal. The commission report, which was submitted on Sept. 1, 1987, showed the proposal earning the highest priority called for an Emergency Budget Board to be composed of executive and legislative members and the chief justice or designee to deal with revenue shortfalls between legislative sessions. Among the 77 recommendations were the merit selection of judges, tort caps, electing the governor and lieutenant governor on a joint ticket, allowing the governor to serve while out of the state, a privacy right, and a new equal rights amendment. No recommendations concerning state bonds or a state debt limit were made, and only two recommendations received a unanimous vote.

In 1988, only one of the 77 recommendations was referred by the Legislature to the voters as a constitutional amendment. Backed by the governor, the proposal repealed the constitutional lottery prohibition. The referendum was approved by the voters at the general election.

Substantive Changes

In 1988-89 no general revision proposals were on the ballot. The amendment that came closest to effecting a comprehensive change was the editorial revision of the Maine Constitution in 1988. The editing was limited to removing gender-biased language. A few amendments offered major changes in state and local governmental structure on a piecemeal basis, but most were rejected at the polls. North Dakota voters defeated for the third time during the decade a new executive article, which was the only revision of a major article on the ballot in 1988 or 1989. The West Virginia electorate turned down major reforms of local government, including county home rule, and the executive branch. An amendment establishing a Taxation and Budget Reform Commission in Florida attracted considerable interest. The commission was empowered to propose fiscal amendments directly to the voters as well as to recommend fiscal changes to the Legislature. Constitutional proposals to change governmental policy also were limited in scope, but collectively they served as a guide to state governmental activity. This is particularly true of many fiscal amendments. During the biennium, California Proposition 98 was probably the most important single amendment to be adopted. It required a minimum level of spending for public schools and community colleges and loosened general expenditure limits. Coupled with the defeat of draconian tax reduction measures and the approval of new spending and debt proposals, the trend in 1988-89 was toward a more active state government.

Table B offers an overview of the general subject matter of state constitutional change by two-year periods during the 1980s. Proposals are placed in two major categories: those of general statewide application, which are by far, the most numerous and involved 45 states in 1988-89 and proposed local amendments considered in three states (Alabama, Maryland, and Texas) during the biennium. (Local amendments apply to only one or a few political subdivisions.) Of the 228 statewide propositions, 164 were adopted (including two in Delaware). The voters approved 71.6 percent. Of the 39 local amendments, 35 were approved, or 89.7 percent.

In Table B, statewide amendments are further classified under the principal subject areas of state constitutions, identified for convenience by the titles of articles found in most constitutions.

There is considerable variation among constitutions, however, in the placement of the same or similar subjects by article. The article on finance drew the most propositions (54) and the Legislature was next (44) during the biennium. The highest approval rate was registered by the Bill of Rights (90 percent) and the lowest by amendment and revision (40 percent), which was also the only article to drop below the 50 percent mark. For the decade, the finance and taxation article attracted the most proposals (291), which amounted to 24.5 percent of all statewide propositions. The legislative article was next (196) with 16.5 percent of the total. The highest approval rate for the decade remains with the Bill of Rights (86 percent). The lowest rate was scored by the executive article (62.9 percent). This was somewhat below the rate for finance and taxation (63.5 percent) and the legislative article (64.2 percent).

The Bill of Rights, suffrage and elections

In 1988-89, the number of proposals (21) and adoptions (19) to the state Bills of Rights reached a record-high for the decade. Over half concerned crime, and all of these were approved by the voters. Four added bills of rights for crime victims (Florida, Michigan, Texas, and Washington). They, in effect, constitutionalized statutory rights found in most states, such as the rights to be informed, heard, present, and receive restitution. Four other measures increased the number of exceptions to or otherwise restricted the right to bail (New Mexico, Oklahoma, Rhode Island and Utah). In South Carolina two amendments concerned the establishment of a state grand jury. A Louisiana amendment allows the forfeiture of contraband drugs and property in civil proceedings. In three states, the right to jury trials in civil cases was changed by increasing the value of the matter in dispute (Hawaii and New Hampshire) or allowing smaller juries (Minnesota). The Colorado Bill of Rights was amended to make English the official language; in Arizona and Florida a similar provision was in other articles. The legality of all three provisions has been challenged in federal courts. The U.S. Courts of Appeals of the tenth and eleventh circuits, respectively, failed to find the Colorado and Florida amendments in violation of the Voting Rights Act of 1965 in the cases of *Montero v. Meyer*, 861 F.2d 603 (1988) and *Delgado v. Smith*, 861 F.2d 1489 (1988). The Arizona provision, however, was ruled unconstitutional by a federal district court in *Yniguez v. Mofford*, 730 F. Supp. 309 (1990), decided in February 1990. The judge ruled that the amendment violated rights of expression protected by the First and Fourteenth Amendments of the U.S. Constitution. Arizona officials do not plan to appeal the ruling. Other amendments that passed were: the right to keep and bear arms, including a ban on local government regulation (Nebraska), grant Alaska residents preferred treatment over non-Alaskans to the extent allowable by the U.S. Constitution, a "broad form deed" to restrict strip mining (Kentucky), and permission for classified property taxation (Wyoming). The two amendments that failed were a Florida tort proposal to limit amounts and types of damage awards and a Georgia sovereign immunity measure. Although not placed in state bills of rights, abortion rights measures were on the ballot. A successful Arkansas amendment bans public funding of abortion except to save the mother's life, states a public policy to protect the unborn from conception to birth, and excludes from its provision contraceptives. Colorado voters defeated a proposal to repeal the 1984 amendment banning public funds for abortions.

All but two of the proposed amendments concerning suffrage qualifications were nonsubstantive editorial changes. They included elimination of references to "idiots" and "lunatics" (Washington) and "conforming" provisions to U.S. Constitutional standards (Hawaii—residence, Illinois—residence and age, Colorado—age and gender). Of these, only the Hawaii measure was rejected at the polls. Hawaiians rejected a change to allow a person turning 18 in a given year to vote in all of that year's elections. Nebraskans, however, voters approved an amendment to allow persons who are 18 at the time of the general election to vote in primaries held in the same year. Other proposals concerned elections. The Arizona electorate approved a change to require a run-off election for state executive offices if no candidate received a majority in the general election. This was no doubt a reaction to the plurality election of Gov. Evan Mecham, who was impeached and removed from office. The Delaware Legislature, which does not refer amendments to the voters, gave final approval to an editing change to eliminate gender-bias from the language of election offenses. The remaining election's amendments dealt with the initiative, referendum, or recall. South Dakota voters approved a change from the indirect to the direct statutory initiative. Two changes to restrict the procedures were defeated in North Dakota: removal of the ban on legislative change of provisions adopted by initiative or referendum for seven years and allowing tax measures to remain in effect until election. The remaining measures were adopted: a change from "electors" to "registered voters" to sign petitions (Nebraska), reimbursement of recall expenses limited to state recalls (Colorado); time limit for the initial filing of petitions and use of statistical methods for verification (Nevada); and clarification of timing and publication of texts on statewide questions (New Jersey). During the decade the U.S. Supreme Court required an additional change in provisions on the initiative and referendum. In *Meyer v. Grant*, 108 S. Ct. 1886 (1988), the court held that a Colorado law making it a felony to pay petition circulators was in violation of the right to engage in political speech protected by the First and Fourteenth Amendments.

Three branches of government

Collectively, the proposals to change the legislative, executive, and judicial articles constituted about 36 percent of propositions of statewide applicability during the biennium. The legislative article drew twice as many amendments as the executive and more than twice the number to the judicial article. Three-quarters of the legislative proposals were approved, which marked a decade-high approval rate in this category. The judicial article maintained the decade pattern of high adoptions. But adoptions of executive proposals were only 63 percent, virtually identical to the rate for the decade.

Nineteen of the 44 proposed amendments to the legislative article concerned legislative sessions and organization, procedures, and powers over apportionment and administrative rules. Two of the five amendments on legislative sessions and a part of a third moved away from expansion of the amount of time available for legislative deliberation and action, a goal of older legislative reforms. An Oklahoma constitutional initiative, supported by the group SOS (Shorten Our Sessions) and the governor, and approved by the voters, did not alter the number of days (90) allowed by the constitution for regular sessions. But it reduced the time spent in sessions by specifying dates for the beginning and ending of the sessions. The practice had been to convene for a few days a week for part of the session, thus spreading the 90 days over many weeks. The amendment also added a new deadline for completion of the budget before it was sent to the governor. A Colorado amendment approved by the voters placed a 120-day limit on regular sessions, a change from 140 days in even-numbered years and unlimited sessions in odd-numbered years. A successful Missouri amendment moved the adjournment date of the odd-numbered session to May 30 from June 30 and added a deadline for completion of the budget. A different section of the same amendment was in harmony with the older reforms in that it authorized the Legislature to call special sessions, limited to 30 days, by a vote of three-quarters of the members of each house. A defeated Montana proposal would have substituted annual sessions of 60 and 40 days, respectively, for the current biennial session of 90 days. Part of a successful Louisiana measure concerned organizational sessions. It was added to a provision clarifying the number of days available to the governor for a veto during and after the session.

Two proposals dealt with various rules and procedures governing legislative deliberations. The most novel and intrusive was a successful constitutional initiative called GAVEL (Give a Vote to Every Legislator). It required a committee hearing on all referred bills, an automatic calendar for scheduling bills for floor action, and a prohibition against binding caucus rules in voting decisions. The other measure was a Maryland proposal to save legislative time by allowing bills on first reading to be considered as a group on a consent calendar and to similarly consider vetoes on a veto calendar.

A Georgia amendment to increase the term of office of representatives from two to four years was defeated at the polls. In Hawaii, the voters approved an amendment that sets the beginning of a legislator's term at the time of the general election if the candidate is unopposed after having won the primary. A successful New Jersey measure ensures that the person appointed to fill a vacancy in a legislative seat is of the same political party as the person replaced by allowing the county party to fill the vacancy by a temporary appointment. In Utah, a section of a "clean-up" amendment lowered the maximum size possible of the Senate from 30 members to the current number of 29.

Four propositions would have increased legislative compensation, but only one was approved. A Nebraska measure that raised salaries from $400 to $600 a month won the voters' favor. The Texas electorate turned down two measures in 1989. One would have set the legislative salary as a percentage of the governor's salary — 25 percent for legislators and 50 percent for the speaker and the lieutenant governor, the presiding officer of the Senate. The second proposal would have based per diem compensation on the federal income tax deduction for state legislators' daily expenses. New Mexico legislators, who receive no salary, tried unsuccessfully to obtain voter approval for a legislative annuity, one that had been in effect for some time before an attorney general opinion held it was unconstitutional.

An unsuccessful Hawaii measure on reapportionment would have changed the base from registered voters to population. In Kansas, the voters approved a measure to replace the Kansas census with U.S. Census figures for reapportionment purposes, beginning in 1992. Three other amendments would have allowed the legislature to veto or otherwise regulate administrative rules and regulations; all were defeated by the voters (Nevada, New Hampshire, and Oklahoma).

Among the remaining successful legislative proposals all of which concerned policy matters were: legalizing raffles (Texas), gambling in Deadwood (South Dakota), allowing out-of-state horse races to be shown on closed-circuit television at licensed tracks and parimutuel wagering on these races (Nebraska), allowing the legislature to compensate crime victims (Georgia), and allowing an increase in fines for certain offenses as a source of revenue for jail improvement. Virtually all other changes proposed to the legislative article were fiscal measures.

During the biennium, 22 proposals to amend the executive article were referred to the voters; 14 were approved. The three most comprehensive changes failed at the polls. Some less sweeping reforms were approved.

The governor was the subject of the largest single category of amendments, all of which added to the stature or powers of the office. The only provisions that failed to pass were sections of the new executive article to the North Dakota constitution and an executive reorganization amendment on the ballot the following year. Iowa voters approved the election of the governor and the lieutenant governor on a joint ballot. In Ohio, the governor gained power to fill a vacancy in the office of lieutenant governor, subject to legislative approval. The New Mexico Constitution was changed to clarify and expand the governor's removal powers, which remain subject to legislative exceptions. In Oregon, the chief executive was granted more time to veto bills after adjournment. The amendment also revised the language of the section to make it gender-neutral. In California, the governor may now deny parole to convicted murderers. In Arizona, where Rose Mofford, secretary of state, succeeded Evan Mecham as governor, the state constitution was amended to delete the requirement that state executive officers be male.

Proposals concerning other constitutional executives did not fare as well at the polls. A West Virginia amendment rejected by the voters would have eliminated three constitutional offices (secretary of state, treasurer, and commissioner of agriculture) and left their status and duties to statutes. The measure also would have limited the terms of office of the auditor and attorney general. Three other measures that failed at the polls were: adding the elective superintendent of schools and certain other statewide offices to the state retirement system (Alabama), lifting the two-term limitation on the state treasurer (Arizona), and substituting an appointive for an elective superintendent of schools (Georgia). Adopted were: a companion measure to the Iowa joint-ticket amendment to remove the lieutenant governor as presiding officer of the Senate and to leave powers of the office to the governor or Legislature, and an Oklahoma amendment that restored the appointed commissioner of labor to an elective status.

Only a handful of amendments concerned administrative structure, aside from changes already noted. The most important of these was a rejected 1989 North Dakota proposal that would have authorized a commission to propose a restructuring of the administrative branch into not more than 14 departments. The governor also was allowed to make proposals. Florida voters approved the establishment of two departments (Veterans Affairs and Elderly Affairs). Texans authorized the Legislature to reorganize criminal justice agencies, and South Dakota voters gave statutory replacement of the duties and names of the Board of Charities and Corrections. A proposal to add to the powers of the Louisiana Board of Ethics was defeated.

The 18 proposed amendments to the article on the judiciary dealt with merit selection, districting, terms of office, qualifications, organization and jurisdiction, judicial conduct commissions and jurors.

A New Mexico measure, which was one of two merit selection proposals on the ballot during the biennium, provided for a modified plan under which judges run initially in a partisan election and subsequently in a non-partisan, non-competitive retention election. The voters approved the reform in 1988. The New Mexico Supreme Court upheld the constitutionality of the amendment in *State ex rel. Chavez v. Virgil-Giron*, 766 P.2d 305 (N,M. 1988). In Nevada, the voters rejected merit selection.

Two Louisiana proposals on judicial districting were made in response to federal court decisions that Louisiana judicial districts violated the Voting Rights Act of 1965 by denying minorities a fair opportunity to select judges of their own choosing. One of the amendments divided temporarily the only multi-member supreme court district into two single-member districts. The other amendment authorized the Legislature to divide districts for selection of appellate and district judges; it also authorized a senior judiciary to shelter otherwise displaced judges. The voters rejected both amendments.

In California, a major reform of justice courts (justices of the peace) was approved. The courts became courts of record. The judges, who are required to be attorneys, must meet a variety of requirements, including not practicing private law. A Florida proposal to increase the term of office of county judges from four to six years failed at the polls; in another amendment that passed, the Florida Legislature was authorized to impeach county judges. The electorate approved a Montana amendment that allows the Legislature to set residence requirements for judges other than members of the supreme court, district courts, and justices of the peace.

Four amendments, all of which passed, concerned Judicial Conduct Commissions. Three (Arizona, California, and Washington) were reorganizations or modifications of the commissions, but the fourth established a new commission in Arkansas, styled the Commission for Judicial Discipline, Suspension, Removal, and Disability Retirement. The Arkansas voters also approved an amendment authorizing the Legislature to create juvenile courts. In Indiana, a proposal to limit the number of direct appeals of criminal cases to the supreme court passed. Other voter-approved measures were: authorization for a civil traffic hearing officer (Florida) and allowing judges to to teach part time (California). The Delaware Legislature gave final approval to an amendment changing the status of clerks (prothonotaries) from elective to appointive (by superior courts.).

The remaining two propositions concern jurors; both were adopted. A South Carolina amendment deletes the requirement that jurors must be of good moral character and qualified voters and substituted state residency and other qualifications to be set by the Legislature. An amendment to the executive article of the Texas Constitution permitted a judge to include general information about eligibility for parole and good conduct time in the jury instructions during the punishment phase of the trial.

Local government

Only one of the fourteen proposed constitutional amendments to the local government article provided for a major reform. This was the West Virginia amendment, which was rejected at the polls in 1989. Under the County Organization Reform Amendment the Legislature was required to provide at least three forms of county organization, including the county manager form, from which county voters could choose. The Legislature also could include the power of counties to pass laws and ordinances relating to their local affairs. In addition, the amendment permitted, subject to local voter approval, local government consolidation: of counties, of a division of a county and one or more counties, of a county and a municipality, and of two or more municipalities. Approval of a majority of voters residing in any of the jurisdictions that were merged would be required.

A more limited reform was approved by the New Mexico electorate: counties were permitted to adopt five-member governing boards and to limit the terms of office of county officers. Other successful county measures were: requiring the election of the county assessor (California), making counties liable for acts of sheriffs (New York), and allowing the Legislature to set the qualifications of sheriffs (South Carolina). An Indiana amendment to remove the limit on terms of county offices failed.

Among other successful local government proposals were: allowing the legislature to create hospital districts by special or general law (Texas), permitting hospital district board members to serve four-year terms (Texas), authorizing state assistance to local fire fighters (Texas), liberalizing investment options for municipalities (Texas), and reducing the vote necessary for certain local bond issues if the election is held on general election days (Missouri). Local government proposals concerning bonds, taxes, and certain expenditures will be reviewed under finance and taxation and debt articles.

Finance

State constitutional amendments, proposed and adopted to the finance and taxation article outnumbered those to any other during the biennium and throughout the 1980s with the exception of 1986-87. The most comprehensive of the proposals in 1988-89 was the Louisiana Tax Reform Amendment supported strongly by Gov. Charles E. "Buddy" Roemer as a way to resolve the state's fiscal crisis. Among the provisions were tax changes (sales, income, property, severance), expenditure limit, balanced budget, Revenue Estimating Conference, and several new funds, including a revenue stabilization fund, transportation trust fund, and a wetlands fund. The voters rejected the amendment in a special election on April 29, 1989. Several of the provisions were submitted separately on October 7; three were adopted.

Taxes were the target of most amendments to the finance and taxation article. In a continuation of the trend that began in the 1980-81 biennium, the voters rejected two proposals modeled after Proposition 13, the tax reduction initiative adopted in California in 1978. The most expansive and restrictive of the two was a Colorado constitutional initiative called the "Taxpayers Bill of Rights" by its sponsors and a "Terroristic Amendment" by Gov. Roy Romer who actively opposed it. The major provisions were: limit residential property taxes to 1 percent of assessed market value and limit further increases, reduce the income tax and use only a single rate, repeal 1988 tax increases and require voter approval for future changes, require notice of election to raise taxes to be mailed to every voter residence, limit average annual percent increase in state spending, and extend the initiative and referendum to all local governments. The measure was defeated by a vote of 567,884 for and 778,075 against at the general election in 1988. The other proposal, also a constitutional initiative, was on the general election ballot in South Dakota. "Dakota Proposition II" was, as its title suggests, the second such proposal in the state, the first having failed in 1980. The measure would have lowered property taxes to a maximum limit of 2½ percent of true value on non-agricultural land and 1 percent on agricultural land, restricted future increases, and required a two-thirds vote of local and state governments to impose special taxes or increase tax collections, respectively. The only other significant tax reduction measure during the biennium was a Nevada constitutional initiative that prohibited the personal income tax. The tax is not presently levied in the state. The voters gave the first of two approvals required by the Nevada constitution in the 1988 general election. The next election will be in 1990.

In contrast to these tax reduction efforts, several amendments required tax increases. The most publicized was probably Proposition 99, the California cigarette and tobacco amendment approved in the 1988 general election. The measure raised the cigarette tax by a substantial 25 cents (from 10 cents to 35 cents a pack) and imposed a new excise tax on other types of tobacco products. The new revenue, expected to be in the $600 million range the first year, was to be deposited in the Cigarette and Tobacco Tax Benefit Fund, the proceeds to be spent on health and medical programs and services with a small amount dedicated to wildlife and parks and recreation. Among other amendments to raise or increase taxes passed by the voters were: severance tax on minerals (Nevada), tax on all government property to the extent permitted by the U.S. Constitution (Oklahoma), continue a sales tax of .1 percent for conservation and parks (Missouri), and increase the gasoline tax (Louisiana). The Louisiana proposal was one of two affecting automobiles. One replaced the $3 license fee that had been set during the days of Huey Long with a larger one (from $10 to $50) based on the value of the motor vehicle. The other ended the general sales tax on gasoline and motor fuels but added 44 cents to the 16-cent gasoline tax already levied.

A substantial number of amendments to increase, add, or mix taxes failed to pass during the biennium. One was the Louisiana Tax Reform Amendment, the tax provisions of which might have yielded $116 million in new revenue in 1989-90.[6] Four measures to reform or change school financing methods were among the rejected amendments. Michigan voters were offered two options: Proposal A would have increased the sales tax by ½ of 1 percent and Proposal B, by 2½ percent. Proposal B, a far more complex alternative, included among its provisions statewide property tax relief. The other two school propositions were on the ballot in Oregon (new tax base limits) and West Virginia (uniform property tax levy). In Pennsylvania, an amendment requiring local governments to reduce residential real estate tax rates to the extent of additional personal income tax revenues also died. And a Wisconsin measure to allow property or sales tax refunds and credits on the income tax failed. Although not proposing a specific tax increase, an Arkansas constitutional initiative would likely have had that effect. The voters rejected the amendment sponsored by Gov. Bill Clinton to reduce the legislative voting majority required to pass tax measures from 75 percent to 60 percent.

A large number of amendments not yet reviewed concerned the property tax. Seven of these, all of which passed, gave tax reductions or exemptions to veterans, the elderly, widowers or family heads in California, Colorado, Florida, New Jersey, New Mexico, Texas, and Washington. Property tax exemptions also were approved in Colorado (certain mining claims) and in Texas (the "freeport" exemption subject to local option). Several amendments were specifically designed to promote economic development. An Oklahoma amendment to liberalize tax exemptions for new business was adopted, but two in Louisiana were rejected (property tax freeze for improvements in economic districts and review board authority to exempt certain new or expanding business from property taxes on inventory). (A third Louisiana proposal that relied on the sales tax to promote economic industrial growth also was defeated.) Among successful property tax measures were special tax valuations for historic places (Georgia) and on land producing high water recharge to aquifers (Florida).

Significant fiscal developments occurred during the biennium with respect to appropriation limits and other spending proposals. Voter response to general expenditure limits may signal a turning point in their popularity. Of five such proposals on the ballot in 1988-89, the most important was Proposition 98, a constitutional initiative to change the California Constitution. This amendment, which the voters adopted, breached the Gann expenditure limits adopted in 1979 (named after Paul Gann, the sponsor). The new amendment requires a minimum level of spending on public schools and community colleges (K-14). The larger of two methods for calculating the minimum level must be selected (either a percentage of the state general fund revenue allocated to K-14 schools or the same total amount of funds from the general fund in 1988-87). In addition surplus revenue in excess of the expenditure limits must be spent on public schools (up to 4 percent of the minimum school funding level) instead of returning the entire surplus to the taxpayers. The new money made available for the schools must be used for "instructional improvement and accountability" and cannot be used to displace existing funds. An annual "report card" on school accountability is required from school districts. The amendment provides for a temporary suspension of the distribution of new funds and for their termination. The program will cease when the California averages on school expenditures per student and class size match the averages of the 10 states having the highest expenditure averages and smallest class sizes.

Two other amendments on general expenditure limits were defeated by the California voters in the 1988 primaries. One would have allowed more spending and the second, which was supported by Gann, would have increased spending for transportation by diverting money from the general revenue fund and also would have added tax and spending restrictions. Expenditure limits incorporated in the Colorado tax reduction and the Louisiana omnibus tax reform amendments died with the defeat of the propositions.

Another way to regulate spending is by "rainy day" and other types of reserve funds. During the biennium, a Texas amendment setting up an economic stabilization fund was adopted, whereas a provision for a similar fund in the Louisiana Tax Reform Amendment failed. Reserve funds were required by most of the tax reduction and expenditure limits proposals, including Proposition 98.

A host of other spending proposals were on the ballot in 1988-89, and most were accepted by the electorate. Many increased spending by dedicating a tax or by diversion of other revenues to a special fund to be used to support government programs such as transportation, health, welfare, environmental protection, energy conservation, culture and history and economic development. Only one of these proposals was designed to cut back expenditures. This was an amendment, approved by the Montana voters, to allow the Legislature to reduce welfare spending by eliminating a constitutional mandate to provide economic and certain other assistance to all those in need. By way of contact, the Georgia voters approved an expansion of Medicaid under the Indigent Care Trust Fund and help to the homeless by the Housing Trust Fund. Even more expansive was the proposed Missouri Health Care Trust Fund. It would have provided health care coverage for catastrophic illnesses and to certain uninsured persons and would have assisted with Medicaid payments. The program would have been financed by an earnings tax and federal funds. A constitutional initiative, it was one of the few spending propositions to be defeated. Among the funds to promote economic development were: the Georgia Seed Capital Fund, a source of funding for innovative firms, the Texas Growth Fund to be used to help start new businesses and expand existing businesses, and the Georgia Export Finance Fund. Only the latter failed at the polls. In addition, the Oklahoma Constitution was amended to authorize the Oklahoma Center for the Advancement of Science and Technology to promote economic development through grants, loans, or other means, such as purchase of stock.

Seven amendments on the ballot in six states changed some aspect of fund administration; all but two passed. Amendments to the California, Montana and Texas constitutions loosened restrictions on management of public funds; only the Montana provision failed. Among the others was a California proposal that allowed the deposit of state money in federally insured loan companies and a Texas amendment that removed long-standing restrictions on the investment of the Permanent University Fund by the University of Texas Board of Regents.

Twenty-three proposals during the biennium

directly concerned debt or state credit; 18 were adopted. One of the rejected proposals, an amendment to allow the Alabama Music Hall of Fame to issue general obligation bonds, was adopted in a second election. The four other defeated measures concerned local debt. A Nevada proposition to increase the bonding capacity of the state from 1 to 2 percent of the assessed value of taxable property was passed, but measures in Virginia and Georgia to increase local debt capacity failed. The other amendments specified the purpose for the bonds or use of state credit. Most were proposed to promote economic development or improve infrastructure. Measures on the ballot in Arizona, Florida, New York, and Oklahoma concerned transportation. All passed except the Arizona proposition, which increased allowable municipal borrowing authority for municipal streets and bridges. A trio of amendments authorizing bonds for water development or clean water in Missouri, Oregon, and Texas were approved. Another three allowing bonds for economic development were adopted in Oklahoma, South Carolina and Texas. Education was the subject of two amendments in Texas (long-term construction bonds for school facilities and college bonds). Two concerned bonds for the Alabama Music Hall of Fame, as mentioned, the second of which passed. The other amendments were: general obligation bonds for construction of prison and mental health facilities (approved in Texas), borrowing for county library books (approved in New Mexico), and a Georgia amendment to issue temporary loans on behalf of special service districts, which failed. The two remaining amendments, which were adopted, were changes to the Washington Constitution to allow the use of public credit to encourage energy conservation by private households and businesses.

Functions, amendments and revisions, and miscellaneous

Most contemporary state constitutions contain separate articles on major policy or functional areas, primarily education, corporations, health and welfare, and conservation.

Policy provisions also are incorporated in the legislative, finance and several other articles. This means that amendments to change policy articles are not indicative of all policy changes in any given biennium.

The total number of proposed changes to articles on government functions dropped to 22 in 1988-89, the second lowest of the decade, but the percentage approved (77.2 percent) was the highest. The most proposals are typically on education. This was true of the biennium; half (eleven) of the propositions were education amendments of which nine were adopted. Most of the education amendments during the biennium related to government structure and the management of school funds and lands. The most significant of these was the Educational Reorganization Amendment on the West Virginia ballot. It would have removed the state Board of Education and the appointed superintendent of schools from the constitution, leaving the executive structure for the "supervision of free schools" to the Legislature's discretion. The voters turned down the proposal. A successful Hawaii amendment was the first during the decade to provide for a high school student to serve as a non-voting member of the state Board of Education. The student would be selected by the Hawaii State Student Council. A North Dakota proposition to allow changes in the composition of the State Board of Higher Education failed. Seven other proposed changes concerned school funds and lands; all passed (one each in Nevada and Oklahoma, two in Texas, and three in Oregon). One of the Oregon measures removes the constitutional requirement that proceeds from property forfeited to the state be placed in the Common School Fund. The change will allow the proceeds to be used for drug law enforcement. The second allows Common School Fund investment in corporate stocks and investment income to be applied to management expenses. The third is a "Buy Oregon" type of measure. It restricts the sale or export of timber from the Common School Lands unless it is processed in Oregon.

Next to education, the largest number of proposals pertain to the corporation article.

Five of these were on the ballot in 1988-89; three passed. The general purpose of amendments to the Alabama, Mississippi, and Missouri constitutions was to loosen or end restrictions on corporations. For example, the Mississippi proposal repealed the ban on building, leasing, or operating railroads by foreign corporations. The Alabama and Mississippi measures were approved, but the Missouri measure failed. A second proposal that gave certain powers to shareholders was adopted in Missouri. The last proposal, which was defeated, would have repealed the constitutional requirement that the Arizona Corporation Commission must use the "fair value" method to determine the value of public utility property.

Two of the remaining amendments pertained to resources; both passed. The Hawaii provision asserted the right of the state to regulate resources in an exclusive economic zone; the Oregon water development fund loans were expanded. Other amendments have been reviewed under different constitutional articles.

Five changes to the amendment and revision article were considered by the voters in 1988-89; two were adopted. These numbers, though low, were the second highest of the decade. Although all proposals are significant, the Florida proposition that established a second commission empowered to propose amendments directly to the voters is unique. Approved at the 1988 general election, the new Taxation and Budget Reform Commission is authorized to propose amendments on "matters relating directly to taxation and the state budgetary process." The Florida Constitution Revision Commission, created 20 years ago by the Florida Constitution, will no longer have power to propose amendments on the fiscal subjects to the voters. The Taxation and Budget Reform Commission is to be established every 10 years, beginning in 1990. Eleven of the 29 commission members will be appointed by the governor and seven each by the speaker of the House and the president pro tem of the Senate. In addition, four legislators (a minority and a majority representative and their senate counterparts) appointed by their presiding officers will serve ex officio without voting privileges. The commission's chair will be appointed by the other commissioners. The amendment lists a formidable array of topics for the new commission to review. Commission members can then make recommendations for statutory change to the Legislature or propose constitutional amendments to the voters. Any proposed amendment must, however, run a procedural gauntlet: a two-thirds favorable vote by the whole commission and a majority of each of three groups identified by their appointing authority (governor, speaker, president pro tem). The amendment also must be timely filed before the general election of the second year following the commission's establishment.

The only other change to the amendment and revision article to be approved was the South Carolina measure. Applying only to the 1990 election, it authorized article-by-article revision notwithstanding a permanent provision that requires separate submission of multiple amendments. Although described as temporary on the ballot, it has applied to every general election since 1970. The three propositions that failed were: editing of the Georgia Constitution after every general election by a commission composed of the governor, speaker, president of the Senate, and legislative counsel; removing the attorney general from the Georgia commission that prepares official summaries of amendments; and liberalizing the procedures of the Mississippi Constitution to permit limited or unlimited amendment and revision.

Most state charters contain a Miscellaneous or General Provisions Article for placement of provisions that do not fit elsewhere or apply to more than one article, such as an oath of office. In 1988-89 nine such propositions were proposed and six were adopted, far fewer than two years ago but typical of the decade as a whole. Adding two amendments from the legislative article to four in miscellaneous, six proposals concerned lotteries, the same member as in the preceding biennium. Lotteries were newly legalized in Idaho, Indiana, Kentucky, and Minnesota, but rejected in North Dakota for the second time in four years.

The Missouri amendment modified the state lottery to increase prize money and end advertising restrictions. No two of the other miscellaneous amendments were on the same subject. Two not already reviewed were a Texas amendment, which passed, to change the oath of office required of elective and appointive officers and a Maine proposition, which failed at the polls, to increase affordable housing. With the backing of the full faith and credit of the state, mortgages for low and moderate income people would have been insured by the Maine State Housing Authority.

For convenience, three amendments limited to editing but changing different sections and articles were counted under the miscellaneous column because they are not general revisions. All were adopted. The most significant was the editorial revision of the Maine document to provide gender-neutral language. A Utah amendment, described in the caption as "Providing Miscellaneous Technical and 'Cleanup' Changes", revised nine sections in three articles. The third proposition, also labeled a "cleanup" amendment, changed six sections in four articles of the Colorado Constitution. One of the amended sections allowed the Legislature to make exceptions to the mandatory eight-hour work day for miners, an historic provision originally adopted in 1902.

Sources and resources

The remarkable upsurge in the number of publications and conferences on state constitutions reported in recent volumes of *The Book of the States* showed no sign of abating in 1988-89, but on the contrary seemed to reach even higher levels. Although most of the new materials are state constitutional law publications, other perspectives on state constitutions are becoming more common in the literature. The bicentennial commemoration of the U.S. Constitution has been a contributing factor.

Highly significant contributions to state constitutional resources were made in 1988-89 by the National Association of Attorneys General (NAAG). Financed by grants from the State Judicial Institute, the NAAG's State Constitutional Law Clearinghouse Project was established. Two new publications were launched: the *State Constitutional Law Bulletin*, published monthly from October-July (first issue, December 1987), and *Emerging Issue in State Constitutional Law*, an annual law review (first issue, 1988). In addition, annual constitutional law seminars have been held (the first in 1988). The NAAG also sponsors the annual Graduate and Law School Writing Competition.

The U.S. Advisory Commission on Intergovernmental Relations (ACIR) has continued to support research on state constitutions. The agency published the first case book on state constitutional law in 1988: *State Constitutional Law: Cases and Materials* by Robert F. Williams. In another publication, *State Constitutions in the Federal System: Selected Issues and Opportunities for State Initiatives* (July 1989), the commission issued a major policy statement based on research findings of scholars in the field. Briefly stated, the ACIR affirmed the essential role of state constitutions and state constitutional law in the federal system. It stressed the need for more public understanding of state charters and recommended more instruction about state constitutions in law schools and other education levels.

The Edward McNall Burns Center for State Constitutional Studies was newly established during the biennium at Rutgers University in New Brunswick, New Jersey. Edited by Stanley H. Friedelbaum, the director of the Center, a quarterly review, *State Constitutional Commentaries and Notes*, made its debut in the fall of 1989.

Several new historical studies of state constitutions and state constitutional law have been published or are scheduled for publication in 1990. Edited by Paul Finkelman and Stephen Gottlieb, *Toward a Usable Past* will be published by the University of Georgia Press. It is an outgrowth of a two-day conference sponsored by the New York Bicentennial Commission and held at the Albany Law School in October 1988. The Conference of

Chief Justices has commissioned a special study of state constitutional traditions to be edited by A.E. Dick Howard and published by the National Center for State Courts. Among recent books on individual state constitutions are *The Constitution of South Carolina, Vol. II: The Journey Toward Local Self Government* by James Lowell Underwood (South Carolina University Press, 1989) and *Rocky Mountain Constitution Making, 1850-1912* by Gordon Morris Bakken (Greenwood Press, 1987).

The first three volumes of the projected 52-volume series on state constitutions in the United States, to be edited by G. Alan Tarr and published by Greenwood Press, were scheduled for publication in 1990: New Jersey by Robert F. Williams, New York by Peter J. Galie, and Michigan by Susan P. Fino. Two books on individual rights protected by state constitutions are: *Human Rights in the States, New Directions in Constitutional Policymaking*, edited by Stanley H. Friedelbaum (Greenwood Press, 1988), and *The Texas Bill of Rights: A Commentary and Litigation Manual* by James C. Harrington (Butterworth, 1987).

An extensive bibliographical collection of documents was made available in 1989 by the Congressional Information Service (CIS). *State Constitutional Conventions, Commissions, and Amendments, 1979-1988* is part 5 of a compilation of materials on microform that spans the 200-year period from 1776 to the present. All parts are accompanied by an annotated bibliography that serves as a locater of documents and an independent reference source.

Another benchmark of the biennium and the decade was the inauguration of a new series of annual reviews of state constitutional law by the *Rutgers Law Journal* (Rutgers University School of Law at Camden). The first review, published in the summer of 1989 (vol. 20), included a selected bibliography for 1980-89. The editors drew a parallel between the new series and annual surveys of state constitutional developments published for 20 years until discontinued in 1949 in the *American Political Science Review*.

Three state constitutions, Arizona, Oregon, and Texas, were highlighted by law schools and reviews during the biennium. The Arizona Constitution was the subject of articles in the spring 1988 issue (vol. 20) of the *Arizona State Law Journal* (Arizona State University College of Law at Tempe). In 1988 the *Oregon Law Review* (vol. 67) reproduced remarks on the work of the Commission for Constitutional Review of 1961 at a 1987 symposium at the law school. The final report of the Oregon commission was reprinted. The University of Texas School of Law and the *Texas Law Review* co-sponsored a one-and-a-half day meeting on the Texas Constitution in October 1989. The papers will appear in a future issue of the law review.

In addition, symposiums focused on the Montana and Maryland constitutions in 1989 in advance of the 1990 mandated referenda on a convention call in both states. The University of Montana School of Law and Salisbury University were the respective hosts. Brochures and citizen guides were planned for the elections. Following the report of the Kentucky Constitutional Revision Commission, a series of forums sponsored by the Kentucky Chamber of Commerce and the Kentucky Bar Association were held. In 1987, the Kentucky Legislative Research Commission published a revised edition of *A Citizens Guide to the Kentucky Constitution*. In New Mexico the "Fourth New Mexico Town Hall" convening in Las Cruces in 1989 issued a policy report that made the calling of a constitutional convention to revise the New Mexico constitution its first priority. The town halls are a creation of New Mexico First, a private, nonpartisan organization founded in 1986 by the state's two U.S. Senators, Pete V. Domenici and Jeff Bingaman.

Literature and conferences on specialized state constitutional topics are too numerous to review, but among the meetings was the "Pacific Rim State Constitutional Law Conference" organized by the Oregon Criminal Defense Lawyers Association and held in Kono, Hawaii in November 1989.

The selected list of references at the end of this summary analysis includes several works of particular significance: *Sources and Documents of United States Constitution* (edited and annotated by William F. Swindler with Donald Musch) designed to integrate national and state constitutional documents into a reference collection on American constitutional developments; *Model State Constitution*, first published by the National Municipal League in 1923 and since revised six times; and the *Index Digest of State Constitutions* prepared by the Legislative Drafting Research Fund of Columbia University. The selected list necessarily excludes many specific items developed for constitutional reform of particular state constitutions, including official documents, special studies, and a vast quantity of ephemeral material stored in state libraries and archives. Of particular value are the complete, annotated, and comparative analyses of the Illinois and Texas constitutions, prepared for delegates to the constitutional conventions of those states. Also excluded from the list are numerous materials prepared by groups long identified with state constitutions, the League of Women Voters, the National Civic League, and The Council of State Governments. Excepting the holdings of the Library of Congress, probably the most extensive collection of fugitive and published materials are those of the National Civic League and The Council of State Governments.

Sources of periodic reviews and updates of state constitutional developments include the biennial summary of official activities in *The Book of the States*. The 1982-83 volume featured a 50-year review of state constitutional history and bibliography. From 1982-1986 Ronald K. L. Collins authored articles on state constitutional law that appeared periodically in *The National Law Journal*. From 1970 through 1985, Albert L. Sturm contributed an annual survey of state constitutional developments to the *National Civic Review*.

Footnotes

1. Janice C. May, "Constitutional Revision in 1988," *Emerging Issues in State Constitutional Law 2* (1989): 61-62. The data on comprehensive revision cited in the following pages of this review are from this source.

2. Janice C. May, "The Constitutional Initiative: A Threat to Rights?" *Human Rights in the States, New Directions in Constitutional Policymaking*, ed. Stanley H. Friedelbaum (Westport, Conn.: Greenwood Press, 1988), pp. 165-166. The data on constitutional initiatives cited in the following pages of this review are from this source and the current biennial survey of state election officials.

3. For recent studies of this development see David B. Magleby, *Direct Legislation: Voting on Ballot Propositions in the United States* (Baltimore and London: Johns Hopkins University Press, 1984) and Thomas E. Cronin, *Direct Democracy, The Politics of Initiative, Referendum, and Recall* (Cambridge, Mass. and London: Harvard University Press, 1989.)

4. Robert F. Williams and Earl M. Maltz, "Introduction — Annual Issue on State Constitutional Law," *Rutgers Law Journal* 20 (Summer 1989): 877. The two law professors contend that "the 1980's might well be designated as the decade of revival of state constitutional law."

5. The case was *Power v. Robertson*, 93 So. 769 (1922). For a discussion see May, "Constitutional Revision in 1988," at 64-69.

6. Thomas H. Ferrell, "Louisiana Voters Reject Tax Reform Amendment," *State Constitutional Commentaries and Notes* 1 (Fall 1989): 17.

Selected References

"Annual Issue on State Constitutional Law." *Rutgers Law Journal* 20, 4 (Summer 1989): 877-1113. Includes Bibliography, 1980-89.

Bamberger, Phylis Skloot, ed. *Recent Developments in State Constitutional Law*, New York, N.Y.: Practising Law Institutite, 1985.

Brammer, Dana B. and John Winkle III, eds. *A Contemporary Analysis of Mississippi's Constitutional Government: Proceedings of a Forum May 2-3, 1986*. Oxford, Miss.: The Public Policy Research Center, University of Mississippi, October 1986.

Brown, Cynthia E., comp. *State Constitutional Conventions: From Independence to the Completion of the Present Union, A Bibliography.* Westport, Conn.: Greenwood Press, 1973.

Clem, Alan L., ed. *Contemporary Approaches to State Constitutional Revision.* Vermillion, S.D.: Governmental Research Bureau, University of South Dakota, 1970.

Collins, Ronald K.L., comp. and ed. "Bills and Declarations of Rights Digest." *The American Bench, Judges of the Nation.* 3rd ed. Minneapolis, Minn.: Reginald Bishop Forster and Associates, Inc., 1985, 2483-2655.

Constitutions of the United States: National and State, 2nd ed. 2 vols. Dobbs Ferry, N.Y. Oceana Publications, 1974. Loose leaf. Updated periodically.

Cornwell, Elmer E., Jr. et al. *Constitutional Conventions: The Politics of Revision.* New York, N.Y.: National Municipal league, 1974. (In second series of the National Municipal League's State Constitution Studies.)

Dishman, Robert B., *State Constitutions: The Shape of the Document.* Rev. ed. New York, N.Y.: National Municipal League, 2968 (In first series of the National Municipal League's State Constitution Studies.)

Edwards, William A., ed. *Index Digest of State Constitutions* 2nd ed. Dobbs Ferry, N.Y.: Oceana Publications, 1959. Prepared by the Legislative Drafting Research Fund, Columbia University.

Elazar, Daniel J., ed. Series of articles on American state constitutions and the constitutions of selected foreign states. *Publius: The Journal of Federalism* 12, 2 (Winter 1982): entire issue.

Emerging Issues in State Constitutional Law. Annual Law Review. Washington, D.C.: National Association of Attorneys General 1988-.

Friedelbaum, Stanley H. ed. *Human Rights in the States, New Directions in Constitutional Policymaking.* Westport, Conn.: Greenwood Press, 1988.

Grad, Frank P., *The State Constitution: Its Function and Form for Our Time.* New York, N.Y.: National Municipal League, 1968. Reprinted from *Virginia Law Review* 54,5 (June 1968). (In first series of the National Municipal League's State Constitution Studies.)

Graves, W. Brooke. "State Constitutional Law: A Twenty-five Year Summary." *William and Mary Law Review* 8,1 (Fall 1966): 1-48.

_____, ed. *Major Problems in State Constitutional Revision.* Chicago: Public Administration Service, 1960.

Harrington, James C. *The Texas Bill of Rights: A Commentary and Litigation Manual.* Austin, Texas: Butterworth, 1987.

Kincaid, John, special ed. "State Constitutions in a Federal System." *The Annals of the American Academy of Political and Social Sciences* 496 (March 1988): entire issue.

Leach, Richard H., ed. *Compacts of Antiquity: State Constitutions.* Atlanta, Ga.: Southern Newspaper Publishers Association Foundation, 1969.

Leshy, John D. "The Making of the Arizona Constitution." *Arizona State Law Journal* 20, 1 (Spring 1988): 1-113.

May, Janice C. "Constitutional Amendment and Revision Revisited." *Publius: The Journal of Federalism* 17, 1 (Winter 1987): 153-179.

_____. "The Constitutional Initiative: A Threat to Rights?" In *Human Rights in the States, New Directions in Constitutional Policymaking*, Stanley H. Freidelbaum, ed.: 163-184.

_____. "Texas Constitutional Revision: Lessons and Laments." *National Civic Review* 66, 2 (February 1977): 64-69.

_____, *The Texas Constitutional Revision Experience in the Seventies.* Austin, Tex.: Sterling Swift Publishing Company, 1975.

McGraw, Bradley D., ed. *Developments in State Constitutional Law*, The Williamsburg Conference, St. Paul, Minn.: West Publishing Co., 1985.

Model State Constitution. 6th ed. New York, N.Y.: National Municipal League, 1963. Revised 1968.

Pisciotte, Joseph P., ed. *Studies in Illinois Constitution Making.* 10 vols. Urbana, Ill.:

CONSTITUTIONS

University of Illinois Press, 1972-1980.

Report of the Special Commission on Constitutional Revision. Research Report No. 226. Frankfort, Kentucky: Legislative Research Commission, September 1987.

Sachs, Barbara Faith, ed. *Index to Constitutions of the United States: National and State.* London, Rome and New York: Oceana Publications. 1980. Prepared by the Legislative Drafting Research Fund. Columbia University. The first two in the series are: *Fundamental Liberties and Rights: A Fifty-State Index* (1980), and *Laws, Legislatures and Legislative Procedures: A Fifty-State Index* (1982).

Schrag, Philip G. *Behind the Scenes: The Politics of a Constitutional Convention.* Washington, D.C.: Georgetown University Press, 1985.

Southwick, Leslie H. "State Constitutional Revision: Mississippi and the South." *The Mississippi Lawyer* 32, 3 (November-December 1985): 21-25.

_____ and C. Victor Welsh, III. "Method of Constitutional Revision: Which Way Mississippi?" *Mississippi Law Journal* 56, 1 (April 1986): 17-71.

State Constitutional Commentaries and Notes, A Quarterly Review. New Brunswick, N.J.: Edward McNall Burns Center for State Constitutional Studies, Fall 1989-.

State Constitutional Conventions, Commissions, and Amendments, 1979-1988. Annotated Bibliography and Microfiche Collection, Part 5. Bethesda, Maryland: Congressional Information Service, 1989. Parts 1-4 (1776-1978) published irregularly. For annotated bibliography published separately for Part 1 (1776-1959) see Cynthia Brown entry.

State Constitutional Convention Studies. 11 vols. New York, N.Y.: National Muncipal League, 1969-1978.

State Constitution Studies. 10 vols. in two series. New York, N.Y.: National Municipal League, 1960-1965.

State Constitutional Law Bulletin. Monthly from July-August. Washington, D.C.: National Association of Attorneys General, Dec. 1987.

Sturm, Albert L., *A Bibliography on State Constitutions and Constitutional Revision,* 1945-1975. Englewood, Colo.: The Citizens Conference on State Legislatures, August 1975.

_____. Annual summary analyses of state constitutional developments. Published in the January or February issues of the *National Civic Review* 1970-1985.

_____. "The Development of American State Constitutions." *Publius: The Journal of Federalism* 12.2 (Winter 1982): 57-98.

_____. *Thirty Years of State Constitution Making,* 1938-1968. New York, N.Y.: National Municipal League, 1970.

Swindler, William F., ed. *Sources of Documents of United States Constitutions.* 10 vols. Dobbs Ferry, N.Y.: Oceana Publications, Inc. 1973-1979.

_____ ed. (vol.1), with Donald Musch (vols. 2-4). *Sources and Documents of U.S. Constitutions, Second Series 1492-1800.* 4 vols. Dobbs Ferry, N.Y.: Oceana Publications, Inc. 1982-1986.

"A Symposium on State Constitutional Revision." *Oregon Law Review* 67, 1 (1988): 1-238.

"Symposium on the Arizona Constitution." *Arizona State Law Journal* 20, 1 (Spring 1988): 1-368.

"Symposium on Constitutional Revision in Mississippi," *Mississippi Law Journal,* 56, 1 (April 1986): 1-163.

"Symposium: The Emergence of State Constitutional Law." *Texas Law Review* 63, 6 and 7 (March/April 1985): 959-1375.

Tarr, G. Alan and Mary Cornelia Porter, eds. "New Developments in State Constitutional Law." *Publius: The Journal of Federalism* 17,1 (Winter 1987): entire issue.

Wheeler, John P., Jr. *The Constitutional Convention: A Manual on Its Planning, Organization and Operation.* New York, N.Y.: National Municipal League, 1961.

_____. ed. *Salient Issues of Constitutional Revision.* New York, N.Y.: National Municipal League, 1961.

Williams, Robert F. *State Constitutional Law: Cases and Materials.* Publication M-159. Washington, D.C.: Advisory Commission on Intergovernmental Relations, 1988.

CONSTITUTIONS

Table 1.1
GENERAL INFORMATION ON STATE CONSTITUTIONS
(As of January 1, 1990)

State or other jurisdiction	Number of constitutions*	Dates of adoption	Effective date of present constitution	Estimated length (number of words)	Number of amendments Submitted to voters	Number of amendments Adopted
Alabama	6	1819, 1861, 1865, 1868, 1875, 1901	Nov. 28, 1901	174,000	726	513
Alaska	1	1956	Jan. 3, 1959	13,000	31	22
Arizona	1	1911	Feb. 14, 1912	28,876 (a)	198	109
Arkansas	5	1836, 1861, 1864, 1868, 1874	Oct. 30, 1874	40,720 (a)	164	76 (b)
California	2	1849, 1879	July 4, 1879	33,350	781	471
Colorado	1	1876	Aug. 1, 1876	45,679	239	115
Connecticut	4	1818 (c), 1965	Dec. 30, 1965	9,564	26	25
Delaware	4	1776, 1792, 1831, 1897	June 10, 1897	19,000	(d)	119
Florida	6	1839, 1861, 1865, 1868, 1886, 1968	Jan. 7, 1969	25,100	79	53
Georgia	10	1777, 1789, 1798, 1861, 1865, 1868, 1877, 1945, 1976, 1982	July 1, 1983	25,000	35 (e)	24
Hawaii	1 (f)	1950	Aug. 21, 1959	17,453 (a)	93	82
Idaho	1	1889	July 3, 1890	21,500	187	107
Illinois	4	1818, 1848, 1870, 1970	July 1, 1971	13,200	11	6
Indiana	2	1816, 1851	Nov. 1, 1851	9,377 (a)	70	38
Iowa	2	1846, 1857	Sept. 3, 1857	12,500	51	48 (g)
Kansas	1	1859	Jan. 29, 1861	11,865	115	87
Kentucky	4	1792, 1799, 1850, 1891	Sept. 28, 1891	23,500	58	29
Louisiana	11	1812, 1845, 1852, 1861, 1864, 1868, 1879, 1898, 1913, 1921, 1974	Jan. 1, 1975	51,448 (a)	51	27
Maine	1	1819	March 15, 1820	13,500	186	157 (h)
Maryland	4	1776, 1851, 1864, 1867	Oct. 5, 1867	41,349 (a)	233	200
Massachusetts	1	1780	Oct. 25, 1780	36,690 (a,i)	143	116
Michigan	4	1835, 1850, 1908, 1963	Jan. 1, 1964	20,000	47	16
Minnesota	1	1857	May 11, 1858	9,500	206	112
Mississippi	4	1817, 1832, 1869, 1890	Nov. 1, 1890	24,000	133	102
Missouri	4	1820, 1865, 1875, 1945	March 30, 1945	42,000	115	74
Montana	2	1889, 1972	July 1, 1973	11,866 (a)	25	15
Nebraska	2	1866, 1875	Oct. 12, 1875	20,048 (a)	283	189
Nevada	1	1864	Oct. 31, 1864	20,770	175	108 (g)
New Hampshire	2	1776, 1784	June 2, 1784	9,200	274 (j)	142 (j)
New Jersey	3	1776, 1844, 1947	Jan. 1, 1948	17,086	52	39
New Mexico	1	1911	Jan. 6, 1912	27,200	231	120
New York	4	1777, 1822, 1846, 1894	Jan. 1, 1895	80,000	274	207
North Carolina	3	1776, 1868, 1970	July 1, 1971	11,000	34	27
North Dakota	1	1889	Nov. 2, 1889	20,564	222 (k)	125 (k)
Ohio	2	1802, 1851	Sept. 1, 1851	36,900	245	145
Oklahoma	1	1907	Nov. 16, 1907	68,800	274 (l)	133 (l)
Oregon	1	1857	Feb. 14, 1859	26,090	367	188
Pennsylvania	5	1776, 1790, 1838, 1873, 1968 (m)	1968 (m)	21,675	25 (m)	19 (m)
Rhode Island	2	1842 (c)	May 2, 1843	19,026 (a,i)	99	53
South Carolina	7	1776, 1778, 1790, 1861, 1865, 1868, 1895	Jan. 1, 1896	22,500 (n)	647 (o)	463
South Dakota	1	1889	Nov. 2, 1889	23,300	185	97
Tennessee	3	1796, 1835, 1870	Feb. 23, 1870	15,300	55	32
Texas	5	1845, 1861, 1866, 1869, 1876	Feb. 15, 1876	62,000	483	326
Utah	1	1895	Jan. 4, 1896	11,000	126	77
Vermont	3	1777, 1786, 1793	July 9, 1793	6,600	208	50
Virginia	6	1776, 1830, 1851, 1869, 1902, 1970	July 1, 1971	18,500	23	20
Washington	1	1889	Nov. 11, 1889	29,400	153	86
West Virginia	2	1863, 1872	April 9, 1872	25,600	107	62
Wisconsin	1	1848	May 29, 1848	13,500	168	124 (g)
Wyoming	1	1889	July 10, 1890	31,800	97	57
American Samoa	2	1960, 1967	July 1, 1967	6,000	13	7
No. Mariana Islands	1	1977	Jan. 9, 1978	11,000	47 (p)	45 (p,q)
Puerto Rico	1	1952	July 25, 1952	9,281 (a)	6	6

CONSTITUTIONS

GENERAL INFORMATION ON STATE CONSTITUTIONS—Continued

* The constitutions referred to in this table include those Civil War documents customarily listed by the individual states.
(a) Actual word count.
(b) Eight of the approved amendments have been superseded and are not printed in the current edition of the constitution. The total adopted does not include five amendments that were invalidated.
(c) Colonial charters with some alterations served as the first constitutions in Connecticut (1638, 1662) and in Rhode Island (1663).
(d) Proposed amendments are not submitted to the voters in Delaware.
(e) The new Georgia constitution eliminates the need for local amendments, which have been a long-term problem for state constitution makers.
(f) As a kingdom and a republic, Hawaii had five constitutions.
(g) The figure given includes amendments approved by the voters and later nullified by the state supreme court in Iowa (three), Kansas (one), Nevada (six) and Wisconsin (two).
(h) The figure does not include one amendment approved by the voters in 1967 that is inoperative until implemented by legislation.
(i) The printed constitution includes many provisions that have been annulled. The length of effective provisions is an estimated 24,122 words (12,400 annulled) in Massachusetts and, in Rhode Island before the "rewrite" of the constitution in 1986, it was 11,399 words (7,627 annulled).
(j) The constitution of 1784 was extensively revised in 1792. Figures show proposals and adoptions since the constitution was adopted in 1784.
(k) The figures do not include submission and approval of the constitution of 1889 itself and of Article XX; these are constitutional questions included in some counts of constitutional amendments and would add two to the figure in each column.
(l) The figures include five amendments submitted to, and approved by the voters which were, by decisions of the Oklahoma or U.S. Supreme Courts, rendered inoperative or ruled invalid, unconstitutional, or illegally submitted.
(m) Certain sections of the constitution were revised by the limited constitutional convention of 1967-68. Amendments proposed and adopted are since 1968.
(n) Of the estimated length, approximately two-thirds is of general statewide effect; the remainder is local amendments.
(o) As of 1981, of the 626 proposed amendments submitted to the voters, 130 were of general statewide effect and 496 were local; the voters rejected 83 (12 statewide, 71 local). Of the remaining 543, the General Assembly refused to approve 100 (22 statewide, 78 local), and 443 (96 statewide, 347 local) were finally added to the constitution.
(p) The number of amendments is from 1984-1989.
(q) The total excludes one amendment ruled void by a federal district court.

CONSTITUTIONS

Table 1.2
CONSTITUTIONAL AMENDMENT PROCEDURE: BY THE LEGISLATURE
Constitutional Provisions

State or other jurisdiction	Legislative vote required for proposal (a)	Consideration by two sessions required	Vote required for ratification	Limitation on the number of amendments submitted at one election
Alabama	3/5	No	Majority vote on amendment	None
Alaska	2/3	No	Majority vote on amendment	None
Arizona	Majority	No	Majority vote on amendment	None
Arkansas	Majority	No	Majority vote on amendment	3
California	2/3	No	Majority vote on amendment	None
Colorado	2/3	No	Majority vote on amendment	None (b)
Connecticut	(c)	(c)	Majority vote on amendment	None
Delaware	2/3	Yes	Not required	No referendum
Florida	3/5	No	Majority vote on amendment	None
Georgia	2/3	No	Majority vote on amendment	None
Hawaii	(d)	(d)	Majority vote on amendment (e)	None
Idaho	2/3	No	Majority vote on amendment	None
Illinois	3/5	No	(f)	3 articles
Indiana	Majority	Yes	Majority vote on amendment	None
Iowa	Majority	Yes	Majority vote on amendment	None
Kansas	2/3	No	Majority vote on amendment	5
Kentucky	3/5	No	Majority vote on amendment	4
Louisiana	2/3	No	Majority vote on amendment (g)	None
Maine	2/3 (h)	No	Majority vote on amendment	None
Maryland	3/5	No	Majority vote on amendment	None
Massachusetts	Majority (i)	Yes	Majority vote on amendment	None
Michigan	2/3	No	Majority vote on amendment	None
Minnesota	Majority	No	Majority vote in election	None
Mississippi	2/3 (j)	No	Majority vote on amendment	None
Missouri	Majority	No	Majority vote on amendment	None
Montana	2/3 (h)	No	Majority vote on amendment	None
Nebraska	3/5	No	Majority vote on amendment (e)	None
Nevada	Majority	Yes	Majority vote on amendment	None
New Hampshire	3/5	No	2/3 vote on amendment	None
New Jersey	(k)	(k)	Majority vote on amendment	None (l)
New Mexico	Majority (m)	No	Majority vote on amendment (m)	None
New York	Majority	Yes	Majority vote on amendment	None
North Carolina	3/5	No	Majority vote on amendment	None
North Dakota	Majority	No	Majority vote on amendment	None
Ohio	3/5	No	Majority vote on amendment	None
Oklahoma	Majority	No	Majority vote on amendment	None
Oregon	(n)	No	Majority vote on amendment	None
Pennsylvania	Majority (o)	Yes (o)	Majority vote on amendment	None
Rhode Island	Majority	No	Majority vote on amendment	None
South Carolina	2/3 (p)	Yes (p)	Majority vote on amendment	None
South Dakota	Majority	No	Majority vote on amendment	None
Tennessee	(q)	Yes (q)	Majority vote in election (r)	None
Texas	2/3	No	Majority vote on amendment	None
Utah	2/3	No	Majority vote on amendment	None
Vermont	(s)	Yes	Majority vote on amendment	None
Virginia	Majority	Yes	Majority vote on amendment	None
Washington	2/3	No	Majority vote on amendment	None
West Virginia	2/3	No	Majority vote on amendment	None
Wisconsin	Majority	Yes	Majority vote on amendment	None
Wyoming	2/3	No	Majority vote in election	None
American Samoa	3/5	No	Majority vote on amendment (t)	None
No. Mariana Islands	3/4	No	Majority vote on amendment	None
Puerto Rico	2/3 (u)	No	Majority vote on amendment	3

CONSTITUTIONS

CONSTITUTIONAL AMENDMENT PROCEDURE: BY THE LEGISLATURE—
Continued

(a) In all states not otherwise noted, the figure shown in the column refers to the proportion of elected members in each house required for approval of proposed constitutional amendments.

(b) Legislature may not propose amendments to more than six articles of the constitution in the same legislative session.

(c) Three-fourths vote in each house at one session, or majority vote in each house in two sessions between which an election has intervened.

(d) Two-thirds vote in each house at one session, or majority vote in each house in two sessions.

(e) Majority vote on amendment must be at least 50 percent of the total votes cast at the election; or, at a special election, a majority of the votes tallied which must be at least 30 percent of the total number of registered voters.

(f) Majority voting in election or three-fifths voting on amendment.

(g) If five or fewer political subdivisions of the state are affected, majority in state as a whole and also in affected subdivision(s) is required.

(h) Two-thirds of both houses.

(i) Majority of members elected sitting in joint session.

(j) The two-thirds must include not less than a majority elected to each house.

(k) Three-fifths of all members of each house at one session, or majority of all members of each house for two successive sessions.

(l) If a proposed amendment is not approved at the election when submitted, neither the same amendment nor one which would make substantially the same change for the constitution may be again submitted to the people before the third general election thereafter.

(m) Amendments concerning certain elective franchise and education matters require three-fourths vote of members elected and approval by three-fourths of electors voting in state and two-thirds of those voting in each county.

(n) Majority vote to amend constitution, two-thirds to revise ("revise" includes all or a part of the constitution).

(o) Emergency amendments may be passed by two-thirds vote of each house, followed by ratification by majority vote of electors in election held at least one month after legislative approval.

(p) Two-thirds of members of each house, first passage; majority of members of each house after popular ratification.

(q) Majority of members elected to both houses, first passage; two-thirds of members elected to both houses, second passage.

(r) Majority of all citizens voting for governor.

(s) Two-thirds vote senate, majority vote house, first passage; majority both houses, second passage. As of 1974, amendments may be submitted only every four years.

(t) Within 30 days after voter approval, governor must submit amendment(s) to U.S. Secretary of the Interior for approval.

(u) If approved by two-thirds of members of each house, amendment(s) submitted to voters at special referendum; if approved by not less than three-fourths of total members of each house, referendum may be held at next general election.

CONSTITUTIONS

Table 1.3
CONSTITUTIONAL AMENDMENT PROCEDURE: BY INITIATIVE
Constitutional Provisions

State or other jurisdiction	Number of signatures required on initiative petition	Distribution of signatures	Referendum vote
Arizona	15% of total votes cast for all candidates for governor at last election.	None specified.	Majority vote on amendment.
Arkansas	10% of voters for governor at last election.	Must include 5% of voters for governor in each of 15 counties.	Majority vote on amendment.
California	8% of total voters for all candidates for governor at last election.	None specified.	Majority vote on amendment.
Colorado	5% of total legal votes for all candidates for secretary of state at last general election.	None specified.	Majority vote on amendment.
Florida	8% of total votes cast in the state in the last election for presidential electors.	8% of total votes cast in each of 1/2 of the congressional districts.	Majority vote on amendment.
Illinois (a)	8% of total votes cast for candidates for governor at last election.	None specified.	Majority voting in election or 3/5 voting on amendment.
Massachusetts (b)	3% of total votes cast for governor at preceding biennial state election (not less than 25,000 qualified voters).	No more than 1/4 from any one county.	Majority vote on amendment which must be 30% of total ballots cast at election.
Michigan	10% of total voters for all candidates at last gubernatorial election.	None specified.	Majority vote on amendment.
Missouri	8% of legal voters for all candidates for governor at last election.	The 8% must be in each of 2/3 of the congressional districts in the state.	Majority vote on amendment.
Montana	10% of qualified electors, the number of qualified electors to be determined by number of votes cast for governor in preceding general election.	The 10% to include at least 10% of qualified electors in each of 2/5 of the legislative districts.	Majority vote on amendment.
Nebraska	10% of total votes for governor at last election.	The 10% must include 5% in each of 2/5 of the counties.	Majority vote on amendment which must be at least 35% of total vote at the election.
Nevada	10% of voters who voted in entire state in last general election.	10% of total voters who voted in each of 75% of the counties.	Majority vote on amendment, in two consecutive general elections.
North Dakota	4% of population of the state.	None specified.	Majority vote on amendment.
Ohio	10% of total number of electors who voted for governor in last election.	At least 5% of qualified electors in each of 1/2 of counties in the state.	Majority vote on amendment.
Oklahoma	15% of legal voters for state office receiving highest number of voters at last general state election.	None specified.	Majority vote on amendment.
Oregon	8% of total votes for all candidates for governor at last election at which governor was elected for four-year term.	None specified.	Majority vote on amendment.
South Dakota	10% of total votes for governor in last election.	None specified.	Majority vote on amendment.
No. Mariana Islands	50% of qualified voters of commonwealth	In addition, 25% of qualified voters in each senatorial district	Majority vote on amendment if legislature approved it by majority vote; if not, at least 2/3 vote in each of two senatorial districts in addition to a majority vote.

(a) Only Article IV, the Legislature, may be amended by initiative petition.
(b) Before being submitted to the electorate for ratification, initiative measures must be approved at two sessions of a successively elected legislature by not less than one-fourth of all members elected, sitting in joint session.

CONSTITUTIONS

Table 1.4
PROCEDURES FOR CALLING CONSTITUTIONAL CONVENTIONS
Constitutional Provisions

State or other jurisdiction	Provision for convention	Legislative vote for submission of convention question (a)	Popular vote to authorize convention	Periodic submission of convention question required (b)	Popular vote required for ratification of convention proposals
Alabama	Yes	Majority	ME	No	Not specified
Alaska	Yes	No provision (c,d)	(c)	10 years (c)	Not specified (c)
Arizona	Yes	Majority	(e)	No	MP
Arkansas	No		No		
California	Yes	2/3	MP	No	MP
Colorado	Yes	2/3	MP	No	ME
Connecticut	Yes	2/3	MP	20 years (f)	MP
Delaware	Yes	2/3	MP	No	No provision
Florida	Yes	(g)	MP	No	Not specified
Georgia	Yes	(d)	No	No	MP
Hawaii	Yes	Not specified	MP	9 years	MP (h)
Idaho	Yes	2/3	MP	No	Not specified
Illinois	Yes	3/5	(i)	20 years; 1988	MP
Indiana	No		No		
Iowa	Yes	Majority	MP	10 years; 1970	MP
Kansas	Yes	2/3	MP	No	MP
Kentucky	Yes	Majority (j)	MP (k)	No	No provision
Louisiana	Yes	(d)	No	No	MP
Maine	Yes	(d)	No	No	No provision
Maryland	Yes	Majority	ME	20 years; 1970	MP
Massachusetts	No			No	Not specified
Michigan	Yes	Majority	MP	16 years; 1978	MP
Minnesota	Yes	2/3	ME	No	3/5 voting on proposal
Mississippi	No		No		
Missouri	Yes	Majority	MP	20 years; 1962	Not specified (l)
Montana	Yes (m)	2/3 (n)	MP	20 years	MP
Nebraska	Yes	3/5	MP (o)	No	MP
Nevada	Yes	2/3	ME	No	No provision
New Hampshire	Yes	Majority	MP	10 years	2/3 voting on proposal
New Jersey	No		No		
New Mexico	Yes	2/3	MP	No	Not specified
New York	Yes	Majority	MP	20 years; 1957	MP
North Carolina	Yes	2/3	MP	No	MP
North Dakota	No		No		
Ohio	Yes	2/3	MP	20 years; 1932	MP
Oklahoma	Yes	Majority	(e)	20 years	MP
Oregon	Yes	Majority	(e)	No	No provision
Pennsylvania	No		No		
Rhode Island	Yes	Majority	MP	10 years	MP
South Carolina	Yes	(d)	ME	No	No provision
South Dakota	Yes	(d)	(d)	No	(p)
Tennessee	Yes (q)	Majority	MP	No	MP
Texas	No		No		
Utah	Yes	2/3	ME	No	MP
Vermont	No		No		
Virginia	Yes	(d)	No	No	MP
Washington	Yes	2/3	ME	No	Not specified
West Virginia	Yes	Majority	MP	No	Not specified
Wisconsin	Yes	Majority	MP	No	No provision
Wyoming	Yes	2/3	ME	No	Not specified
American Samoa	Yes	(r)	No	No	ME (s)
No. Mariana Islands	Yes	Majority (t)	2/3	No (u)	MP and at least 2/3 in each of 2 senatorial districts
Puerto Rico	Yes	2/3	MP	No	MP

CONSTITUTIONS

PROCEDURES FOR CALLING CONSTITUTIONAL CONVENTIONS—Continued

Key:
MP — Majority voting on the proposal.
ME — Majority voting in the election.

(a) In all states not otherwise noted, the entries in this column refer to the proportion of members elected to each house required to submit to the electorate the question of calling a constitutional convention.

(b) The number listed is the interval between required submissions on the question of calling a constitutional convention; where given, the date is that of the first required submission of the convention question.

(c) Unless provided otherwise by law, convention calls are to conform as nearly as possible to the act calling the 1955 convention, which provided for a legislative vote of a majority of members elected to each house and ratification by a majority vote on the proposals. The legislature may call a constitutional convention at any time.

(d) In these states, the legislature may call a convention without submitting the question to the people. The legislative vote required is two-thirds of the members elected to each house in Georgia, Louisiana, South Carolina and Virginia; two-thirds concurrent vote of both branches in Maine; three-fourths of all members of each house in South Dakota; and not specified in Alaska, but bills require majority vote of membership of each house. In South Dakota, the question of calling a convention may be initiated by the people in the same manner as an amendment to the constitution (see Table 1.3) and requires a majority vote on the question for approval.

(e) The law calling a convention must be approved by the people.

(f) The legislature shall submit the question 20 years after the last convention, or 20 years after the last vote on the question of calling a convention, whichever date is last.

(g) The power to call a convention is reserved to the people by petition.

(h) The majority must be 50 percent of the total votes cast at a general election or at a special election, a majority of the votes tallied which must be at least 30 percent of the total number of registered voters.

(i) Majority voting in the election, or three-fifths voting on the question.

(j) Must be approved during two legislative sessions.

(k) Majority must equal one-fourth of qualified voters at last general election.

(l) Majority of those voting on the proposal is assumed.

(m) The question of calling a constitutional convention may be submitted either by the legislature or by initiative petition to the secretary of state in the same manner as provided for initiated amendments (see Table 1.3).

(n) Two-thirds of all members of the legislature.

(o) Majority must be 35 percent of total votes cast at the election.

(p) Convention proposals are submitted to the electorate at a special election in a manner to be determined by the convention. Ratification by a majority of votes cast.

(q) Conventions may not be held more often than once in six years.

(r) Five years after effective date of constitutions, governor shall call a constitutional convention to consider changes proposed by a constitutional committee appointed by the governor. Delegates to the convention are to be elected by their county councils. A convention was held in 1972.

(s) If proposed amendments are approved by the voters, they must be submitted to the U.S. Secretary of the Interior for approval.

(t) The initiative may also be used to place a referendum convention call on the ballot. The petition must be signed by 25% of the qualified voters or at least 75% in a senatorial district.

(u) The legislature was required to submit the referendum no later than seven years after the effective date of the constitution. The convention was held in 1985; 45 amendments were submitted to the voters.

CONSTITUTIONS

Table 1.5
STATE CONSTITUTIONAL COMMISSIONS
(Operative during January 1, 1987 to January 1, 1990)

State	Name of commission	Method and date of creation and period of operation	Membership: number and type	Funding	Purpose of commission	Proposals and action
Kentucky	LRC Special Commission on Constitutional Review.	Legislative: Resolution of Legislative Research Commission (LRC). January 1987-May 1988. Initial report September 1, 1987.	41 members. LRC co-chairs (Speaker and president pro tem ex officio, co-chairs of legislative task force. LRC co-chairs appointed 14 citizens, 3 media, 3 business, 3 labor, 2 mayors, 2 county executives, 2 representatives and 2 senators (bi-partisan), Deans of 3 law schools appoint 1 faculty member from each school, Chief Justice appoints 3 judges, 1 from each level.	LRC budget-staff and support, member expenses.	To study each of 263 sections of constitution and submit recommendations to LRC.	September 1, 1987 initial report: 77 recommendations from 6 subcommittees ranked in order of priority (1-5) and percent of commission favoring each recommendation using a mail survey. To be included, over 50 percent support required. One recommendation (lottery) referred to voters and approved in 1988.
Oklahoma	Oklahoma Constitution Study Commission.	Executive; appointed by invitation. October 1988-1990, (indefinite termination date).	Governor and U.S. senator honorary chairs, attorney general chair. 32 members: 3 legislators and other state and local officials, representatives of business, law, agriculture, energy, education.	No appropriation; private funding from 3 foundations, $65,000; members not reimbursed for expenses.	To study entire constitution; submit revised constitution by June 1989.	Preliminary 100-page draft ready for citizen comment in June 1989; final approval given.
Utah	Utah Constitutional Revision Commission.	Statutory; Ch. 89, *Laws of Utah*, 1969; amended by Ch. 107, *Laws*, 1975; amended by Ch. 159, *Laws*, 1977, which made the commission permanent as of July 1, 1977. (Codified at Ch. 54, Title 63, *Utah Code Annotated*, 1953).	16; 1 ex officio, 9 appointed: by the speaker of the House (3), president of the Senate (3) and governor (3) — no more than 2 of each group to be from the same party; and 6 additional members appointed by the 9 previously appointed members.	Appropriations through 1989 totalled $693,000 (The 1989 appropriation was $50,000, the same as for 1988).	Study constitution and recommend desirable changes, including proposed drafts.	Mandated to report recommendations at least 60 days before legislature convenes. Voter action on the commission's recommendations through 1987 included: approval of revised articles on the executive branch, revenue and taxation, the judicial branch, the legislative branch and education. Proposed revisions of articles on local government and public debt to legislature for 1988 session rejected; major revisions of labor and corporations articles submitted for 1989 session rejected; major revision of labor article and two changes to legislative article submitted in 1989 for 1990 session.

Table 1.6
STATE CONSTITUTIONAL CONVENTIONS
1988-89

State	Convention dates	Type of convention	Referendum on convention questions	Preparatory bodies	Appropriations	Convention delegates	Convention proposals	Referendum on convention proposals
				----- None -----				

CHAPTER TWO

STATE EXECUTIVE BRANCH

THE GOVERNORS, 1988-89

By Thad L. Beyle

The two-year period was marked by relative calm for the governors after a few years of turmoil on several levels. First, there was less political activity with only 12 races in 1988 and two in 1989. However, in 1988, the unsuccessful Democratic candidate for president was a governor, and in 1989 much attention focused on the election of a black governor in Virginia. Second, the series of investigations into gubernatorial actions and character which had generated so much negative publicity in the mid-1980s had passed, and no new major problems surfaced. The action was more policy related as governors grappled with increasing demands for state services and funds while state revenues weakened.

Gubernatorial Elections

Fourteen governorships were decided by elections in 1988-89. In nine of these contests the incumbent stood for an additional term, with eight winning re-election. The winning incumbents were Michael Castle (R-Delaware), John Ashcroft (R-Missouri), James Martin (R-North Carolina), George Sinner (D-North Dakota), Edward DiPrete (R-Rhode Island), Norman Bangerter (R-Utah), Madeleine Kunin (D-Vermont) and Booth Gardner (D-Washington). The one incumbent who was defeated in the general election was Arch Moore (R-West Virginia). He had served as Governor of West Virginia for 12 years, from 1969-1977 and from 1985-1989.

Looking at the 163 gubernatorial elections in the 13-year period, 1977-1989, incumbents were eligible to seek another term in 74 percent of the contests. Eligible incumbents did seek re-election 78 percent of the time and had a 74 percent success rate. However, breaking these elections down into the three most recent blocks of four elections each, beginning with the 1978 elections, we see there was some variation in these percentages. For example, in the first election block of 1978-1981, 76 percent of the 54 incumbents were eligible to seek another term, 83 percent of them did, and 68 percent were successful. In the second grouping, 1982-1985, 80 percent of the 54 incumbents were eligible to seek another term, 74 percent did, and 75 percent won. In the most recent elections of 1986-1989, 66 percent of the 53 incumbents were eligible to seek re-election, 77 percent did, and over 81 percent were successful.

Thus, while the number of incumbent governors eligible to seek re-election varied between 80 and 66 percent over the period, and their rate of seeking re-election also varied between 74 and 83 percent, their success rate steadily climbed from 68 to 75 to 81 percent. Incumbency is obviously growing as a major factor in electoral success for governors, much as it is for other elected officials in the federal system.[1] For example, over the four congressional elections in the 1980s, incumbent return rates rose from slightly over 90 percent to over 98 percent.[2]

The six newly elected governors display some of the diversity that exists in the routes taken to the governor's chair. Two moved directly up from other statewide elected positions to become governor, Evan Bayh (D-Indiana) from secretary of state and Douglas Wilder (D-Virginia) from lieutenant governor. Two moved directly from congressional seats, Judd Gregg (R-New Hampshire) and James

---

Thad L. Beyle is Professor of Political Science at the University of North Carolina at Chapel Hill.

Florio (D-New Jersey). The two others, Stan Stephens (R-Montana) and Gasper Caperton (D-West Virginia), moved from the private sector, although Stephens had served sixteen years in the state legislature, many of these as a legislative leader. Lieutenant Governor Robert J. Miller (D-Nevada) succeeded to the governor's chair in January 1989 when incumbent Governor Richard Bryan, who won the U.S. Senate race in 1988, was sworn into office.

Among those who sought the governorship unsuccessfully were two lieutenant governors, John Mutz (R-Indiana) and Robert Jordan (D-North Carolina), two congressmen, Jim Courter (R-New Jersey) and Stan Parris (R-Virginia), a U.S. senator, Paul Trible (R-Virginia), a former governor, Thomas Judge (D-Montana) and a former governor's wife and state legislator, Betty Hearnes (D-Missouri). Many other legislators and legislative leaders, mayors and former mayors unsuccessfully sought governorships.

The partisan affiliation of the winners in 1988-89 was evenly split as Democrats and Republicans each won seven races. However, since there were more open seats previously held by Democrats, the Republicans were able to close the gap in the statehouses to 29 Democrats and 21 Republicans. However, governors in 30 of the states will face legislatures with one or both houses controlled by the opposite party. Split ticket voting is alive and well in the states.

Cost of Gubernatorial Elections

The costs of gubernatorial elections continue to escalate with the most expensive elections generally associated with highly contested primaries, especially when there is an open seat, or with efforts to unseat an incumbent, and when someone with considerable money of their own wants to become governor. Table A indicates the cost of the most recent gubernatorial campaigns for each of the states in actual dollars for the year involved.

Table B presents the total cost of gubernatorial elections by year, normalized to 1987 dollars. In nine of the 12 years for which there is earlier comparable data, these elections have cost more, ranging from only three percent between 1984-1988 to 134 percent between 1985-1989. The latter figure demonstrates how expensive contests for open seats can be, as both the New Jersey and Virginia incumbent governors were constitutionally prohibited from seeking another term in 1989. These were the most expensive races ever recorded in either state.

Over the 1977-1989 period, during which campaign expenditure data is available in most states, the ten most expensive governors' chairs (in 1987 dollars) have been: Texas (an average of $26.8 million), Louisiana ($21.7 million), New York ($20.7 million), California ($20.5 million), Kentucky ($18.4 million), Florida ($14 million), New Jersey ($13.8 million), Tennessee ($11.7 million), Virginia ($10.6 million) and Pennsylvania ($10 million). All are either among the nine largest states in population or are southern states. Three states still have gubernatorial campaigns which have averaged less than one million dollars in total expenditures over the period: Vermont ($0.8 million), Delaware ($0.7 million), and North Dakota ($0.6 million).

The most expensive individual gubernatorial campaigns in the two-year period were in Virginia, with losing candidate Marshall Coleman (R) spending $9.4 million and winner Wilder (D) spending $6.9 million, in New Jersey, with winner Florio (D) and loser Courter (R) each spending over $7.7 million and in North Carolina, with incumbent winner Martin (R) spending over $6.3 million. In each of these cases, they were the most expensive individual gubernatorial campaigns ever recorded for the state.

There was a very high correlation between spending the most money and winning the election in these 14 races. In 12 of the races, the winner spent the most money, and eight of them were the incumbent governors. Incumbency still breeds funds for a re-election campaign. In the Virginia race, the winner, Wilder (D), did outspend his rival, Coleman (R), in the general election, but Coleman had to fund an expensive three-way Republican nomination fight.[1] In Indiana, the losing candidate, Mutz (R), outspent winner Bayh

GOVERNORS

Table A
COSTS OF GUBERNATORIAL CAMPAIGNS, MOST RECENT ELECTION

State	Year	W	Total campaign expenditures (1) All candidates	Winner spent	Winner's percentage of all expenditures	Winner's vote percent	Cost (2) per total vote
Alabama	1986	R*	$9,990,777	$960,866	10	56	$8.10
Alaska	1986	D**	6,311,219	1,380,146	22	47	114.26
Arizona	1986	R#	6,922,216	1,168,193	17	40	7.98
Arkansas	1986	D*	2,252,907	1,597,163	71	64	3.27
California	1986	R*	22,464,928	13,714,233	61	61	3.18
Colorado	1986	D#	6,204,938	1,797,709	29	58	5.91
Connecticut	1986	D*	3,878,640	2,550,437	66	58	3.94
Delaware	1988	R*	885,731	838,523	95	71	3.69
Florida	1986	R#	23,990,965	4,279,212	18	55	7.09
Georgia	1986	D*	807,906	702,314	87	71	.69
Hawaii	1986	D#	6,711,865	1,830,720	27	52	20.09
Idaho	1986	D#	1,834,373	994,207	54	50	4.78
Illinois	1986	R*	8,916,247	6,634,929	74	53	2.82
Indiana	1988	D#	8,239,770	3,820,016	40	53	3.85
Iowa	1986	R*	2,990,628	1,792,324	60	52	3.29
Kansas	1986	R#	6,390,771	1,575,269	25	52	7.60
Kentucky	1987	D#	18,366,985	9,961,460	54	65	12.81
Louisiana	1987	D**	13,142,072	2,640,637	20	33	8.43
Maine	1986	R#	5,362,179	1,302,763	24	40	12.56
Maryland	1986	D#	4,949,183	3,689,563	75	82	4.49
Massachusetts	1986	D*	4,054,859	3,503,635	86	69	2.41
Michigan	1986	D*	9,362,420	2,988,839	32	68	3.98
Minnesota	1986	D*	4,744,363	2,032,523	43	56	3.41
Mississippi	1987	D#	8,702,740	2,952,105	34	61	12.06
Missouri	1988	R*	4,292,387	3,510,484	82	64	2.08
Montana	1988	R#	3,225,864	1,128,901	35	53	8.96
Nebraska	1986	R#	3,992,790	1,486,116	37	53	7.09
Nevada	1986	D*	1,833,735	1,478,553	81	72	7.06
New Hampshire	1988	R#	1,520,087	788,552	52	61	3.46
New Jersey	1989	D#	26,172,262	7,736,580	30	61	11.66
New Mexico	1986	R#	2,572,787	1,630,000	63	53	6.52
New York	1986	D*	6,998,540	5,458,457	78	65	1.64
North Carolina	1988	R*	11,275,235	6,338,185	56	56	5.17
North Dakota	1988	D*	673,000	435,000	65	60	2.25
Ohio	1986	D*	7,917,191	4,797,278	61	61	7.58
Oklahoma	1986	R#	3,856,218	1,234,944	32	47	5.12
Oregon	1986	D#	5,049,211	2,880,230	57	52	5.54
Pennsylvania	1986	D#	16,168,820	7,291,155	45	51	4.85
Rhode Island	1988	R*	5,037,168	2,590,397	51	51	12.58
South Carolina	1986	R#	6,865,817	3,018,144	44	51	9.20
South Dakota	1986	R#	2,482,094	1,172,662	47	52	8.43
Tennessee	1986	D#	14,635,833	4,113,698	28	54	12.10
Texas	1986	R***	35,313,071	12,160,386	34	53	10.39 (3)
Utah	1988	R*	3,513,295	1,321,432	38	40	4.53
Vermont	1988	D*	1,139,676	698,203	61	55	4.76
Virginia	1989	D#	21,730,000	6,860,000	32	50	12.14
Washington	1988	D*	2,586,735	1,581,194	61	62	1.38
West Virginia	1988	D***	8,533,441	4,589,009	54	59	13.14
Wisconsin	1986	R***	2,900,140	1,188,406	41	53	1.93
Wyoming	1986	D#	2,428,892	312,877	13	54	14.75
1986 election totals		19D/17R	255,933,237(3)	104,974,359(3)	41	(36 states)	
1987 election totals		3D/0R	40,211,797(3)	15,554,202(3)	39	(3 states)	
1988 election totals		5D/7R	50,922,389	27,639,896	54	(12 states)	
1989 election totals		2D/0R	47,902,262	14,596,580	30	(2 states)	
Total (53 states) 29D, 24R Winners							

Sources: State campaign finance filing offices; The Council of State Governments; and Scott Mouw of the Department of Political Science, University of North Carolina at Chapel Hill.

Key:
(1) Includes primaries and general elections; all figures are actual dollars for the year involved.
(2) Determined by dividing total campaign expenditures by total general elections votes for the office.
(3) Change from earlier reported numbers due to additional reports received.

D Democrat
R Republican
* Incumbent ran and won.
** Incumbent ran and lost in party primary.
*** Incumbent ran and lost in general electin.
# Open seat.

GOVERNORS

Table B
TOTAL COST OF GUBERNATORIAL ELECTIONS: 1977-1989
(In thousands of dollars)

Year	Number of Races	Total Campaign Costs		Average Cost per state 1987 $	Percent Change in Similar Elections (1)
		Actual $	1987 $		
1977	2	9,118	16,948	8,474	—
1978	36	99,733	169,903	4,720	—
1979	3	32,744	49,239	16,413	—
1980	13	35,551	47,528	3,656	—
1981	2	19,996	24,535	12,267	+45%
1982	36	181,743	214,826	5,967	+26%
1983	3	39,954	45,506	15,169	−8%
1984	13	46,830	51,349	3,950	+8%
1985	2	18,142	19,157	9,579	−22%
1986	36	255,933	259,830	7,218	+21%
1987	3	40,212	40,212	13,404	−12%
1988	12	50,922	48,869	4,072	+3%
1989	2	47,902	44,894	22,427	+134%
Totals	163	878,780	1,032,796	6,336	

(1) This represents the percent increase or decrease over the last bank of similar elections, i.e., 1977 vs. 1981, 1978 vs. 1982, 1979 vs. 1983, etc.

by $4.4 million to $3.8 million, even though Bayh had a nominal contest for the Democratic nomination. The one incumbent governor losing his seat, Moore (R) of West Virginia, was outspent by winner Caperton $4.6 million to $2.4 million.

There were at least 78 separate candidates in these 14 governors races in 1988-89 as measured by those who filed campaign expenditure reports. Many of these candidates spent little or no money campaigning. New Jersey with eleven and West Virginia with nine topped the states with crowded fields of candidates. In New Jersey the fight was in the Republican primary with eight candidates vying for the nomination. In West Virginia the fight was in the Democratic primary with seven candidates.

Gubernatorial Powers

In a 1987 study, the National Governors' Association (NGA) analyzed "The Institutionalized Powers of the Governorship, 1965-1985."[1] Based on previous studies by political scientists,[2] the NGA study used a numerical scoring system to measure the governors' tenure potential, appointive powers, budget-making powers and veto powers, plus the legislature's budget changing authority and amount of party control the governor has in the legislature. The results indicate that over a 20-year period, the governor's power over the executive branch has increased while power vis-a-vis the legislative branch has declined.[3]

An updated study, using the same NGA measures but extending the comparisons through 1990, corroborated and reinforced these trends. The governors gaining the most power were in those states classified as Republican in terms of level of party competition, states in the mid-west and in the less populous states suggesting that the more populous states had already provided their governors with greater powers.[4]

Another recent study of the institutional powers of the governors in 1990 added the governors' removal powers to this equation leading to a comparison of the relative powers of the 50 state governors.[5] In this presentation, the editors made three significant shifts in how the rankings were calculated. First, they averaged the scores instead of using actual scores. Then they broadened the range for moderate powers. Finally the states were given an absolute ranking rather than just placed in a broad category.

In general, the governorships group together as moderately powerful in the amount and type of institutional powers they hold. There are no states in the very weak category, and only one, Maryland, in the very strong category. Four states, Massachusetts, New York, South Dakota and West Virginia are rated strong, while seven states fall into the weak category.

In that study, seven states weak on gubernatorial powers and their weaknesses are: North Carolina (lack of veto, restricted removal power); New Hampshire (short term, restricted veto power); Nevada (restricted removal and veto powers); Rhode Island (short term, restricted veto power and split partisan control); South Carolina (restricted appointment power, split partisan control); Texas (restricted appointment power, weak budget power and split partisan control); and Vermont (short term, restricted veto power).[6]

Gubernatorial Veto. The governor's power to veto legislation, either in toto, by item, or in part, continues to be controversial in the states. In Florida, controversy erupted when Governor Martinez vetoed only a portion of line-item projects, which legislators felt overstepped his veto power. The legislators argued that it was the principal and not the amount of money involved. For example, the governor eliminated an $80,000 position at one university, but not the entire budget line. So a law suit will have to determine what constitutes a line-item veto.[1]

In Wisconsin, gubernatorial-legislative warfare continues over Governor Tommy Thompson's use of the item veto to alter language in legislation by saving letters from some words and then using the letters to make new words. In a June 1988 four-to-three split decision, the state's Supreme Court sided with the governor arguing that the "partial" veto provision in the Wisconsin constitution confers broader authority to the governor than do item veto provisions found in other state constitutions.[2]

The Wisconsin court established only two tests to determine whether the governor's action is legitimate: Is the result a "complete, entire, and workable law," and are the revisions "germane" to the original? In addition, the court "overtly invoked political considerations, including advice to a co-equal branch of government (the legislature) on how to restructure its internal practices" to avoid perceived abuse of gubernatorial power. The court's suggestions were to keep the legislature's "internally generated initiatives out of budget bills, or (amend) . . . the state constitution."[3] The Wisconsin legislature placed a constitutional amendment before the voters prohibiting the practice of "pick-a-letter" vetoes,[4] and Democratic Speaker of the Assembly Tom Loftus is challenging Republican Governor Thompson for the governorship in the 1990 election. Wisconsin voters approved the prohibition of "pick-a-letter" vetoes by 62 percent vote in April 1990. Still pending in a court suit is the question of a govenor vetoing selected numbers.[5]

In Oregon, the state's Supreme Court took a considerably more restrictive view of the use of the gubernatorial veto.[6] Here, the case concerned whether the veto power could be extended to "any" provision in a bill bearing an emergency clause. The court, in declining to grant greater veto power to the governor by limiting it to the emergency clause alone, argued that the "governor's veto power is not the kind of provision that must find new applications in changing technical, economic, or social conditions."[7]

Despite these conflicts and court decisions, a recent study of the item veto experience in the states concludes there is no one clear trend toward either gubernatorial or legislative dominance.[8] There is continuing punching and counter-punching with mixed signals from the referees. And as for an item veto for the president, one careful observer notes "[S]tate experience indicates the item veto is not a magic wand capable of making the deficit disappear. The old-fashioned medicine of political leadership remains the only viable cure."[9]

At the ballot box in 1988, Oregon voters amended their constitution to extend the deadlines for vetoes and now require the governor to give more notice of planned vetoes.[10] North Carolina's Governor Martin continues to push for a constitutional amendment providing him or his successors with the veto power. Calling 1989 the "Year of the Veto," he called on the legislature to act; there was action but nothing like getting an amendment onto the ballot. It was clear that to get to that voter hurdle, major compromises between the governor and the legislature would be needed in developing a "balance of powers" package that gives something to the legislature (longer terms, off-presidential year elections) as well as the governor.[11]

Gubernatorial Appointment Power. Governors have greatly increased the number of women they appoint to state-level cabinet positions. Between 1981 and 1989 the number of women in these positions increased by 114 percent. However, the increase was only 15 percent between 1987 and 1989. Those with the largest percentages were Governors Baliles (VA) with 42 percent, Schaefer (MD) with 39 percent, Clinton (AR) with 36 percent, the two Thompsons (IL and WI) with 32 percent, Bellmon (OK) and Roemer (LA) with 30 percent. Governor Ashcroft (MO) was the only governor who had not appointed a woman at the cabinet level. These figures do not include appointments to governors' own personal staffs.[1]

A recent survey of fifteen states on the legislature's role in the governor's appointment power found that informal relations between the governor's office and legislative staff seem to facilitate confirmation of the governor's appointments, at least in these specific administrations. However, legislative refusal is seen as an ever-present danger.[2]

Governors have also become more interested in the ways they can evaluate and monitor the performance of those they appoint to executive branch positions. A recent report suggests the bottom line is the governor's individual style, and how he or she defines performance expectations.[3] The Oklahoma governor's office has developed an elaborate computer-based appointment management system to monitor the appointment process.[4]

Governors' Offices

A recent 50-state study of the governors' offices found the governors faced with an interesting challenge. They must "run a well-organized and clearly structured executive team . . . (while maintaining) a high degree of flexibility to deal with complex variables" which are constantly changing. Relying on a small staff and using the chief-of-staff model seem to be the ways governors approach this challenge. In addition, the study found no "single best way" to structure the governor's office, and that the governors themselves may "be the best source of information about the ways organization and management are achieved" in the office.[1]

There have been changes in who the governors have hired to serve on their staff. Comparing surveys of gubernatorial staffs in the late 1960s with those serving between 1982-1986 found: more women (31 percent, up from 7 percent in the earlier period); more non-whites (7 percent, up from 3 percent); more with an urban upbringing (54 percent, up from 39 percent); and more with an occupation in public administration or management (20 percent, up from 10 percent). There were also fewer journalists (14 percent, down from 20 percent); slightly fewer native born residents of the state (55 percent, down from 62 percent). There was little change in age (mid 30s), whether they had a college degree (84 percent did) and whether they were attorneys (slightly less than 50 percent were).[2]

The areas of expertise of the staff members also had changed between the two time periods. In the late 1960s, the top five areas of expertise were: budgeting, state government generalists, education, legislative relations and intergovernmental relations. In the mid 1980s, the top five areas were media/public relations, budgeting, legislative relations, legal issues and education.[3]

Changes in the 'Rules of the Game'

There have been several changes made in the "rules of the game" for elections in the states over the past two years. As an aftermath to the election and impeachment of Arizona Governor Evan Mecham (R), who served in 1987-88, that state adopted a run-off provision for general elections. Unless a candidate receives a majority of the vote in the general election, there will be a run-off.[1] Mecham won with only 40 percent of the vote in the three-candidate 1986 governor's race.

Mecham is also challenging the so-called "Dracula" clause in the state constitution by seeking the governorship again. The clause, which bars impeached officials from seeking and holding office, has prompted several interpretations. The first is that Mecham is clearly barred from office by the successful impeachment action. The second is that the senate vote on the issue, taken immediately after it had convicted him of the impeachment charges by a two-thirds vote, failed to gain the necessary two-thirds vote, so he is not subject to the "Dracula" clause. A third interpretation is that only the conviction needed a two-thirds vote, not the "Dracula" clause which only needed a majority vote.[2] The attorney general sided with the second interpretation and Mecham is in the 1990 race.

Also in the 1988 elections, Arizona voters removed an outdated provision that constitutional officers be male; Iowa voters decided to have the governor and lieutenant governor run and be elected as a team beginning with the 1990 election.[3] Beginning with the 1990 primaries, candidates for office in North Carolina will need only 40 percent, rather than 50 percent, of the party primary vote to become the party nominee. This change was made in an attempt to give minority candidates a better chance to become the party nominee, and to reduce the number of second primaries.

Indiana is gradually changing how it allows state government to assist state parties in raising money. In 1986, Republican Governor Robert D. Orr ended the practice of allowing motor vehicle branches to use "profits" for partisan purposes. Up until then, the county party chair of the governor's party controlled the branches and the "profits" often found their way into the state party coffers. In 1989, Democratic Governor Bayh ended the practice of deducting party dues from governmental employee's pay checks.[4]

Separately Elected Officials

The concept of separately electing executive branch officials continues to be alive and well in the states. In 1988, Georgia voters soundly rejected a constitutional amendment which would have made the currently elected state school superintendent an appointed position,[1] while Oklahoma voters supported a switch back to an elected commissioner of labor.[2]

In 1989, West Virginia voters soundly rejected a gubernatorially supported amendment to the state's constitution which would have eliminated the separately elected offices of secretary of state, treasurer and agriculture commissioner. At the same time they rejected another amendment which would have eliminated the state board of education and the state superintendent as constitutional offices in favor of gubernatorial appointments.[3]

Lieutenant Governors. This office continues to be the focus of controversy. As noted earlier, it can serve as a launching pad for a run for the governorship, and it can be a powerful legislative position. For example, in 1989, lieutenant governors presided over the state senate in 28 states, can vote in case of a tie in 25 states, can assign bills to committees in fifteen states and appoint committees and committee chairs in seven states.[1]

Lieutenant governors can also be a power in the executive branch not only as the successor to the governor — the "heartbeat" power (42 states) — but also by serving as acting governor when the governor is disabled (40 states) or out of state (27 states), as executive branch board members (31 states), or as a member of the governor's cabinet or advisory body (20 states). Moreover, they can perform other duties assigned by the governor (33 states) and can make appointments to executive branch boards and commissions (6 states).[2] Under Governor Robert Orr (R-Indiana), Lt. Governor Mutz served as the executive director of the state commerce department and secretary of agriculture.[3]

Some of the 42 states with the office have considered abolishing it as did a legislative study committee in Kansas. Some of the eight states without the office have considered adding it. In other states, there are moves to expand the scope of the office's responsibility such as in Kentucky where the lieutenant governor wants to merge the office with that of the treasurer and the secretary of state.[4]

There are continuing political problems surrounding the office of lieutenant governor. After 1988 elections in North Carolina, the state senate reduced the powers of the lieutenant governor as presiding officer. Why? For the first time in this century, a Republican was elected to preside over the Democratic body.[5] Mississippians recently found out that their lieutenant governor since 1980, Brad Dye, has made more than $23,000 "moonlighting" as governor whenever the governor leaves the state. He is paid at a rate of $172.60 per day, more than the $25 daily rate a lieutenant governor can make in Wisconsin, but less than the $239 in Texas. Eight states have such a provision.[6]

On the personal side, the dean of lieutenant governors, John A. Cherberg (D-Washington) retired in 1989 after serving in the office for 32 years, the longest tenure as lieutenant governor of any state in history. He was preceded in that office by Vic Meyers, who had served from 1933 to 1953. Washington had just two lieutenant governors over the 62-year span.[7]

Attorneys General. Recent actions by attorneys general in several states has led some to pin a rising activist bent on this office. Most of these initiatives focused on trying to regulate certain business activities. For example, eight state attorneys general joined in a suit against major insurers over what they alleged was collusion in liability insurance coverage restrictions.[1] They lost their first round in this case, but found that multi-state efforts reduce the cost of litigation, while enhancing the impact of undertaking a case.[2]

Some attorneys general have also initiated action against airlines and car rental firms for misleading advertisements, and have taken steps to control or forestall mergers and takeovers.[3] Three attorneys general were reported to be investigating anti-trust activities in a proposed takeover in the textile industry.[4] Most recently, twenty-nine state attorneys general joined in a suit against the asbestos industry in an attempt to have the industry foot the bill for removing cancer-causing asbestos from public buildings, including schools.[5]

These actions obviously were controversial, even among the attorneys general. While many argued that inaction by the federal government on some of these issues led to this activism, the attorney general of New Mexico argued this was only interfering in federal regulation of interstate business by placing the National Association of Attorneys General (NAAG) into the role of "a shadow Congress . . . using the cover of 'consumer protection' to impose their own anti-business, pro-government-regulation views on the entire nation."[6] One observer suggested that NAAG should be renamed the "National Association of Aspiring Governors".[7]

In Georgia, a controversy between the attorney general and the state bar association over the power of the bar to discipline the attorney general for breaching normal client-lawyer relations was resolved in favor of the officeholder. The case involved a suit brought by the attorney general against the state personnel board for violating the open meetings law, and the bar argued that since the attorney general was the attorney for the board, this violated rules which forbid lawyers from suing their clients. The bar appealed but lost in a lower court decision.[8]

In another area of conflict involving the attorney general, there is growing realization of the tension in roles they must perform as the lawyer for the state, state agencies and state officials, and their role as the people's counsel. This often places the attorney general in the position of suing a state agency or seeking prosecution of a state official while representing them officially.[9]

In Virginia, the attorney general and prospective 1993 gubernatorial candidate Mary Sue Terry is involved in a conflict over whether the all-male Virginia Military Institute should admit women. On one side of the argument is tradition, alumni and some important political interests; on the other is the women's movement. Adding to the general controversy is the question of whether the attorney general is taking a political step in contesting the case, or is doing so as the commonwealth's lawyer?

The attorney general of Illinois was criticized for settling an abortion suit out of court rather than pursuing it all the way to a U.S. Supreme Court decision.[10]

Secretaries of State. A recent study indicated that this office could entail as many as 26 separate duties falling into five general categories: electoral, registration, custodial, publication and legislative.[1] Individual state offices ranged from a high of 23 duties in Missouri to a low of six in Virginia; the average across the 50 states was 15.6.[2]

The office also has a strong political character. Over the 20th century, 20 of the 1,087 serving governors (1.8 percent) had previously served as secretary of state. There have been two basic patterns of moving from the office to the governorship. The first is by being in the direct line of succession should anything happen to the governor. Something did happen to a number of chief executives and thirteen secretaries of state became governor in this manner, all in the western states of Wyoming (7), Arizona (3), Oregon (2), and Alaska (1). Ten of these successions occurred before 1950.[3]

The second pattern involves using the position as a stepping stone to run for governor (5 cases) or for an intermediate office such as lieutenant governor or attorney general en route to the governorship (2). Because of the individual-political nature of this route, no state had more than one such individual.[4] This pattern is of more recent vintage — no secretary of state was elected to the governorship prior to 1966 — and interestingly all in this pattern were Democrats. Currently, three former secretaries of state are serving as governor, Evan Bayh of Indiana, Mario Cuomo of New York, and Rose Mofford of Arizona.[5]

The dean of secretaries of state, Thad Eure (D-NC), the self-proclaimed "oldest rat in the Democratic barn," retired in 1989 after 52 years of service in the position. Beginning with his election in 1936, he served with twelve separate governors over the period.[6]

Treasurers. The Council of State Governments recently issued a report on the activities and functions of state treasurers.[1] While most of these officials are elected, eight are appointed by the governor, and four are selected by the legislature. In addition to their specified duties related to cash management in the state treasury, most also serve on a range of boards and commissions, primarily those having to do with the raising or investment of local and state funds.[2]

In California, the state's Supreme Court had to decide whether Governor Deukmejian's appointment of U.S. Representative Dan Lungren as state treasurer had been adequately confirmed by the state legislature as required under a new amendment to the state constitution. The appointment, made to fill out the remaining portion of the late Treasurer Jesse Unruh's term, was approved by the state house but was rejected by one vote in the state senate. In 1988, the court decided unanimously that the appointment required confirmation by both houses before Lungren could take office. Five of the seven judges on the Court were Deukmejian appointees.[3]

In 1988, Arizona voters repealed the limitation of their treasurer's tenure by removing a two consecutive elected term ban.[4]

National Governors' Association

During the 1989-1990 fiscal year, NGA and the new national administration attempted to join cause on several common interests. The most visible of these interests was education, as highlighted by the September summit in Charlottesville, Virginia between the governors and President George Bush. From this summit flowed an NGA Task Force on Education which is working with President Bush on educational reform. The results of this cooperative effort were seen in the president's 1990 State of the Union Address where he outlined the national education goals that he and the governors had agreed upon.[1] Subsequently the president attended the winter meeting of NGA to continue the discussion on educational reforms, and to endorse the six goals and 21 objectives developed by the NGA Task Force.[2]

Footnotes

Gubernatorial Elections

1. See Gerald Benjamin, "The Power of Incumbency," *Empire State Report* (April 1987), 33-37.

2. David Shribman, "Drive to Restrict Tenure in Congress to 12 Years Is Pressed in Capital and One-Third of the States," *Wall Street Journal* (March 12, 1990), A12.

Costs of Gubernatorial Campaigns

1. Larry Sabato, "The 1989 Gubernatorial Election in Virginia," (Charlottesville, VA: Department of Government and Foreign Affairs, 1990), and letter to the author, February 14, 1990.

Gubernatorial Power

1. Office of State Services, *State Management Notes*, "The Institutionalized Powers of the Governorship, *State Management Notes* 1965-1985," (Washington, DC: National Governors' Association, 1987).
2. Joseph A. Schlesinger, "The Politics of the Executive," in Herbert Jacob and Kenneth N. Vines, eds., *Politics in the American States: A Comparative Analysis* 1st. ed. (Glenview, IL: Little, Brown, 1965), 207-237, and 2nd. ed. (1971), 220-234; and Thad L. Beyle, "Governors," in Virginia Gray, Herbert Jacob and Robert Albritton, eds., *Politics in the American States* 5th. ed. (Glenview, IL: Scott Foresman, 1990), 201-251.
3. Thad L. Beyle, "The Institutionalized Powers of the Governorship, 1965-1985," *Comparative State Politics Newsletter* 9:1 (February 1988), 26-27.
4. Author's and NGA calculations.
5. Thad L. Beyle, "The Chief Executive: The Powers of the Governor of North Carolina," *North Carolina Insight* 12:2 (March 1990), 27-45.
6. Ibid., 41-43.

Gubernatorial Veto

1. "Gubernatorial power," *State Government News* 31:9 (September 1988), 26.
2. *State ex rel State Senate v. Thompson*, 144, Wis 2d 429, 424 NW2d 385, 386, n. 3 (1988).
3. David Frohnmayer, "The Courts as Referee," in Lawrence Baum and Frohnmayer, eds., *The Courts: Sharing and Separating Powers*, Eagleton's 1988 Symposium on the State of the States, (New Brunswick, NJ: Eagleton Institute of Politics, 1988), 62.
4. "Gubernatorial power," 26. For more on this fight see also: "Wisc. Court Asked to Veto Vetoes," *Governing* 1:4 (January 1988), 58; "Wisconsin Veto Flap, Chapter 2," *Governing* 1:5 (March 1988), 68; and, Tony Hutchison, "Legislating Via Veto," *State Legislatures* 18:1 (January 1989), 20-22.
5. "Veto Powers," *State Policy Reports* 8:8 (April 1990), 24.
6. Cf. *Lipscomb, et al v. Oregon St. Bd. of Higher Educ.*, 305 Or 472, 478, 753 P2d 939, 942 (1988).
7. Frohnmayer, 62.
8. J. Pottorff, "Political Stew: Item Veto Issues Bubbling to the Top in State Court Jurisdictions," *Emerging Issues in State Constitutional Law* (National Association of Attorneys General, Inaugural Issue, 1988), 1. See also Office of State Services, "Gubernatorial Item Veto Authority," *Management Briefs*, (Washington, D.C.: National Governors' Association, 1988).
9. Calvin Bellamy, "Item Veto: Dangerous Constitutional Tinkering," *Public Administration Review* 49:1 (January/February 1989), 51.
10. Elaine S. Knapp, "Voters like lotteries, reject tax cuts," *State Government News* 31:12 (December 1988), 27.
11. Phung Nguyen and Alva W. Stewart, "North Carolina Governors and the Veto Power," *Comparative State Politics Newsletter* 10:4, (August, 1989) 26-32. See also the symposium on the veto in North Carolina in *North Carolina Insight* 12:2 (March 1990), 2-26.

Gubernatorial Appointment Power

1. "Women in politics," *State Government News* 32:4 April 1989), 28.
2. Office of State Services, "Legislative Confirmation of Gubernatorial Appointees," *Management Briefs* (Washington, DC: National Governors' Association, January 10, 1990).
3. Office of State Services, "Managing the Performance of Gubernatorial Appointees," *Management Notes* (Washington, DC: National Governors' Association, February 1988), 18.

4. Office of State Services, "Appointments, Management and Tracking Systems," *Management Briefs* (Washington, D.C.: National Governors' Association 1989).

The Governors' Offices

1. Office of State Services, "Organization and Staffing Patterns In the Governor's Office," *Management Notes (Washington, DC: National Governors' Association, November, 1988),* 16.
2. Donald P. Sprengel, "Trends in Staffing the Governors' Office," *Comparative State Politics Newsletter* 9:3 (June 1988), 11.
3. Sprengel, 14.

Changes in the 'Rules of the Game'

1. Knapp, 27.
2. Kathleen Sylvester, "Mecham Wants to Know If Dracula Law Has Teeth," *Governing* 2:11 (August 1989), 71-72.
3. Knapp, 27.
4. Rob Gurwitt, "Indiana Curbs Party Payroll Deductions," *Governing* 2:11 (August 1989), 16.

Separately Elected Officials

1. George H. Cox, Jr., "1988 Referendum Results From Georgia," *Comparative State Politics Newsletter* 10:1 (February 1989), 18-19.
2. Knapp, 27.
3. "West Virginia Setbacks," *State Policy Reports* 7:18 (September 1989), 23.

Lieutenant Governors

1. Ran Coble, "Comparison of Powers of the Lieutenant Governors Among the 50 States," *North Carolina Insight* 11: 2-3 (April 1989), 164. See also Kathleen Sylvester, "Lieutenant Governors: Giving Up Real Power For Real Opportunity," *Governing* 2:5 (February 1989), 46-50.
2. Ibid.
3. Sylvester, "Lieutenant Governors."
4. "Lieutenant Governors," *State Policy Reports* 7:16 (August 1989), 31.
5. Coble, 162-163.
6. Jonathan Walters, "Lieutenant Governor Reaps a Stand-In's Bonanza," *Governing* 2:8 (May 1989), 78.
7. Hugh A. Bone, "Record Setting Incumbent Retires in Washington State," *Comparative State Politics Newsletter* 9:6 (December 1988), 2-3.

Attorneys General

1. "Activist Attorneys General," *State Policy Reports* 6:7 (April 1988), 18-19.
2. Elder Witt, "AGs Fire on Asbestos Industry," *Governing* 3:7 (April 1990), 12.
3. "Why the States Are Ganging Up on Some Giant Companies," *Business Week* (April 11, 1988). See also Randall Bloomquist, "Can the States Regulate National Ads?," *Governing* 2:10 (July 1989), 64-65.
4. The states were New York, North Carolina and South Carolina. "Activist Attorneys General," *State Policy Reports* 6:8 (April 1988), 21.
5. Witt, 12.
6. "Insurance, Attorneys General, and State Insurance Regulators," *State Policy Reports* 6:12 (June 1988), 12.
7. "Activist Attorneys General," *State Policy Reports* 6:8 (April 1988), 21.
8. "Power of Attorneys General to Sue State Officials," *State Policy Reports* 6:8 (April 1988), 27.
9. Dave Frohnmayer, "Representing the Public: Public Interest Comes First," *Journal of State Government* 61:3 (April/May 1988), 92.
10. "Attorney General Roles," *State Policy Reports* 8:5 (March 1990), 16-17.

Secretaries of State

1. Joy Hart Seibert, *The Secretary of State: The Office and Duties,* (Lexington, KY: Council of State Governments, 1987).
2. Jack Betts, "The Department of the Secretary of State: Which Way Now?," *North Carolina Insight* 11:4 (August 1989), 7, 10.
3. Those secretaries of state who initially succeeded to the office of governor were: Fenimore C. Chatterton (R-WY, 1903); Frank Benson (R-OR, 1909); Frank Houx (D-WY, 1917); Ben Olcott (R-OR, 1919); Frank Lucas (R-WY, 1924); Alonzo Clark (R-WY, 1931); Dan Garvey (D-AZ, 1948); Arthur Crane (R-WY, 1949); Clifford Rogers (R-WY, 1953);

Jack Gage (D-WY, 1961); Keith Miller (R-AK, 1969); Wesley Bolin (D-AZ, 1977); and Rose Mofford (D-AZ, 1988).

4. Those secretaries of state elected to the office of governor were: Kenneth Curtis (D-ME, 1966); Tom McCall (D-OR, 1966); Edmund G "Gerry" Brown (D-CA, 1974); Jay Rockefeller (D-WV, 1976); Mario Cuomo (D-NY, 1982); Mark White (D-TX, 1982); and, Birch Bayh, Jr., (D-IN, 1988).

5. Thad L. Beyle, "Secretaries of State Who Became Governor in the 1970s and 1980s," *North Carolina Insight* 11:4 (August 1989), 16.

6. Betts, 5.

Treasurers

1. *State Treasury Activities and Functions* (Lexington, KY: Council of State Governments, 1988).

2. "The Role of State Treasurers," *State Policy Reports* 6:16 (August 1988), 30-31.

3. "Court to Deukmejian: Forget Lungren," *Governing* 1:11 (August 1988), 15.

4. "Election '88: State-by-State, Arizona," *USA/TODAY* (November 10, 1989), 8A.

National Governors' Association

1. "Education: Consensus on Goals Reached by Bush, NGA Task Force," *Governors' Weekly Bulletin* 24:5 (February 2, 1990), 1-2.

2. "Bush Endorses National Education Goals Adopted by the Governors This Week," *Governors' Weekly Bulletin* 24:8 (March 2, 1990).

Table 2.1
THE GOVERNORS
1990

State or other jurisdiction	Name and Party	Length of regular term in years	Date of first service	Present term ends	Number of previous terms	Maximum consecutive terms allowed by constitution	Joint election of governor and lieutenant governor (a)	Official who succeeds governor	Birthdate	Birthplace
Alabama	Harold Guy Hunt (R)	4	01/87	01/91		2	No	LG	06/17/33	Ala.
Alaska	Steve Cowper (D)	4	12/86	12/90		2	Yes	LG	08/21/38	Va.
Arizona	Rose Mofford (D)	4	04/88	01/91 (s)			(b)	SS	06/10/22	Ariz.
Arkansas	Bill Clinton (D)	4	01/79	01/91	3 (c)	2 (c)	No	LG	08/19/46	Ark.
California	George Deukmejian (R)	4	01/83	01/91	1		No	LG	06/06/28	N.Y.
Colorado	Roy Romer (D)	4	01/87	01/91			Yes	LG	10/28/28	Colo.
Connecticut	William A. O'Neill (D)	4	12/80	01/91	1 (d)		Yes	LG	08/11/30	Conn.
Delaware	Michael N. Castle (R)	4	01/87	01/93		2 (e)	No	LG	07/02/29	Del.
Florida	Bob Martinez (D)	4	01/87	01/91		2	Yes	LG	12/25/34	Fla.
Georgia	Joe Frank Harris (D)	4	01/83	01/91	1		No	LG	02/26/36	Ga.
Hawaii	John D. Waihee III (D)	4	01/86	12/90		2	Yes	LG	05/19/46	Hawaii
Idaho	Cecil D. Andrus (D)	4	01/71	01/91	2 (f)		No	LG	08/25/31	Ore.
Illinois	James R. Thompson (R)	4	01/77	01/91	3 (g)		Yes	LG	05/08/36	Ill.
Indiana	Evan Bayh (D)	4	01/89	01/93		2	Yes	LG	12/26/55	Ind.
Iowa	Terry Branstad (R)	4	01/83	01/91	1	2	No	LG	11/17/46	Iowa
Kansas	Mike Hayden (R)	4	01/87	01/91		2	Yes	LG	03/16/44	Kan.
Kentucky	Wallace G. Wilkinson (D)	4	12/87	12/91		(h)	No	LG	12/12/41	Ky.
Louisiana	Buddy Roemer (D)	4	03/88	03/92		2	(b)	PS	10/04/43	La.
Maine	John R. McKernan Jr. (R)	4	01/87	01/91		2	Yes	PS	05/20/48	Maine
Maryland	William Donald Schaefer (D)	4	01/87	01/91		2	Yes	LG	11/02/21	Md.
Massachusetts	Michael S. Dukakis (D)	4	01/75	01/91	2 (i)		Yes	LG	11/03/33	Mass.
Michigan	James J. Blanchard (D)	4	01/83	01/91	1		Yes	LG	08/08/42	Mich.
Minnesota	Rudy Perpich (DFL)	4	12/76	01/91	1 (j)		Yes	LG	06/27/28	Minn.
Mississippi	Ray Mabus (D)	4	01/88	01/92		1	No	LG	10/11/48	Miss.
Missouri	John Ashcroft (R)	4	01/85	01/93	1	2 (e)	No	LG	05/09/42	Mo.
Montana	Stan Stephens (R)	4	01/89	01/93		2	Yes	LG	09/16/29	Canada
Nebraska	Kay A. Orr (R)	4	01/87	01/91		2	Yes	LG	01/02/39	Iowa
Nevada	Bob Miller (D)	4	11/88	01/91 (t)			No	LG	03/30/45	Ill.
New Hampshire	Judd Gregg (R)	2	01/89	01/91			(b)	PS	02/14/47	N.H.
New Jersey	James S. Florio (D)	4	01/90	01/94		2	(b)	PS	08/29/37	N.Y.
New Mexico	Garry E. Carruthers (R)	4	01/87	01/91		(h,k)	Yes	LG	8/29/39	Colo.
New York	Mario M. Cuomo (D)	4	01/83	01/91	1		Yes	LG	06/15/32	N.Y.
North Carolina	James G. Martin (R)	4	01/85	01/93	1	2 (e)	No	LG	12/11/36	Ga.
North Dakota	George A. Sinner (D)	4	01/85	01/93	1		Yes	LG	05/29/28	N.D.
Ohio	Richard F. Celeste (D)	4	01/83	01/91	1	2	Yes	LG	11/11/37	Ohio
Oklahoma	Henry Bellmon (R)	4	01/63	01/91	1 (l)	2 (m)	No	LG	09/03/21	Okla.
Oregon	Neil Goldschmidt (D)	4	01/87	01/91		2	(b)	SS	06/16/40	Ore.
Pennsylvania	Robert P. Casey (D)	4	01/87	01/91			Yes	LG	01/09/32	N.Y.
Rhode Island	Edward D. DiPrete (R)	2	01/85	01/91	1		No	LG	07/08/34	R.I.
South Carolina	Carroll A. Campbell Jr. (R)	4	01/87	01/91		2	No	LG	07/24/40	S.C.
South Dakota	George S. Mickelson (R)	4	01/87	01/91		2	Yes	LG	01/31/41	S.D.
Tennessee	Ned Ray McWherter (D)	4	01/87	01/91		2	No	SpS (o)	10/15/30	Tenn.
Texas	William P. Clements Jr. (R)	4	01/79	01/91	1 (m)		No	LG	04/13/17	Texas
Utah	Norman H. Bangerter (R)	4	01/85	01/93	1		Yes	LG	01/04/33	Utah
Vermont	Madeleine Kunin (D)	2	01/85	01/91	2		No	LG	09/28/33	Switzerland

THE GOVERNORS—Continued

State or other jurisdiction	Name and Party	Length of regular term in years	Date of first service	Present term ends	Number of previous terms	Maximum consecutive terms allowed by constitution	Joint election of governor and lieutenant governor (a)	Official who succeeds governor	Birthdate	Birthplace
Virginia	L. Douglas Wilder (D)	4	01/90	01/94		(h)	No	LG	01/17/31	Va.
Washington	Booth Gardner (D)	4	01/85	01/93	1		No	LG	08/21/36	Wash.
West Virginia	Gaston Caperton (D)	4	01/89	01/93			(b)	PS	02/21/40	W.V.
Wisconsin	Tommy Thompson (R)	4	01/87	01/91		2 (p)	Yes	LG	11/19/41	Wis.
Wyoming	Michael (Mike) J. Sullivan (D)	4	01/87	01/91			(b)	SS	09/22/39	Neb.
American Samoa	Peter T. Coleman (R)	4	01/56	01/93	3 (u)	2 (q)	Yes	LG	12/08/19	A.S.
Guam	Joseph Ada (R)	4	01/87	01/91		2	Yes	LG	12/03/43	Guam
No. Mariana Islands	Lorenzo I. DeLeon Guerrero (R)	4	01/90	01/94		3 (r)	Yes	LG	01/25/35	Saipan
Puerto Rico	Rafael Hernandez-Colon (PDP)	4	01/73	01/93	2 (v)		(b)	SS	10/24/36	P.R.
U.S. Virgin Islands	Alexander A. Farrelly (D)	4	01/87	01/91		2	Yes	LG	12/29/33	V.I.

Key:
D — Democrat
PDP — Popular Democratic Party
R — Republican
LG — Lieutenant governor
SS — Secretary of state
PS — President of the senate
SpS — Speaker of the senate

(a) The following also choose candidates for governor and lieutenant governor through a joint nomination process: Florida, Kansas, Maryland, Minnesota, Montana, North Dakota, Ohio, Utah, American Samoa, and Guam.
(b) No lieutenant governor.
(c) Served 1979-81, 1983-85, and 1985-87. In 1984, a constitutional amendment passed which changes to four years the length of the governor's term, with a maximum of two terms (effective with the 1986 election).
(d) Succeeded to governor's office December 1980. Elected to first full term November 1982.
(e) Absolute two-term limit, but not necessarily consecutive.
(f) Resigned in 1977 to accept appointment as U.S. Secretary of the Interior.
(g) First term was for two years, four years thereafter.
(h) Successive terms forbidden.
(i) Served 1975-79 and 1983-87.
(j) Succeeded to governor's office December 1976 to serve remainder of unexpired term. Elected to first full term November 1982.
(k) Beginning in 1991, governor limited to 2 consecutive 4-year terms.
(l) Served 1963-67.
(m) Prohibited from serving more than eight years out of a twelve year period.
(n) Served 1979-83.
(o) Official bears the additional statutory title of "lieutenant governor."
(p) Prohibited from serving in the term immediately following two consecutive terms regardless of whether the terms were filled in whole or in part.
(q) Limit is statutory.
(r) Absolute three-term limitation, but not necessarily consecutive.
(s) Succeeded to governor's office April 1988 as a result of her predecessor's impeachment.
(t) Succeeded to governor's office November 1988 to serve remainder of unexpired term.
(u) Presidentially appointed Governor 1956-61. Elected to three-year term in 1978; four-year terms in 1981 and 1989.
(v) Served 1973-1977 and 1985-1989.

Table 2.2
THE GOVERNORS: QUALIFICATIONS FOR OFFICE

State or other jurisdiction	Minimum age	State citizen (years)	U.S. citizen (years)	State resident (years)	Qualified voter (years)
Alabama	30	7	10	7	. . .
Alaska	30	. . .	7	7	★
Arizona	25	5	10	. . .	. . .
Arkansas	30	. . .	★	7	★
California	18	. . .	5	5	★
Colorado	30	. . .	★	2	. . .
Connecticut	30	. . .	. . .	. . .	★
Delaware	30	. . .	12	6	. . .
Florida	30	. . .	. . .	7	★
Georgia	30	6	15	6	. . .
Hawaii	30	. . .	★	5	★
Idaho	30	. . .	★	2	. . .
Illinois	25	. . .	★	3	. . .
Indiana	30	. . .	5	5	. . .
Iowa	30	. . .	★	2	. . .
Kansas	. . .	. . .	. . .	. . .	. . .
Kentucky	30	6	★	6	. . .
Louisiana	25	5	5	. . .	★
Maine	30	. . .	15	5	. . .
Maryland	30	. . .	(a)	5	5
Massachusetts	. . .	. . .	. . .	7	. . .
Michigan (b)	30	. . .	. . .	. . .	4
Minnesota	25	. . .	★	1	. . .
Mississippi	30	. . .	20	5	. . .
Missouri	30	. . .	15	10	. . .
Montana (c)	25	★	★	2	. . .
Nebraska	30	5	5	5	. . .
Nevada	25	2	. . .	2	★
New Hampshire	30	. . .	. . .	7	. . .
New Jersey	30	. . .	20	7	. . .
New Mexico	30	. . .	★	5	★
New York	30	. . .	★	5	. . .
North Carolina	30	. . .	5	2	. . .
North Dakota	30	. . .	★	5	★
Ohio (d)	. . .	. . .	★	. . .	★
Oklahoma	31	. . .	★	. . .	10
Oregon	30	. . .	★	3	. . .
Pennsylvania	30	. . .	★	7	. . .
Rhode Island (e)	. . .	. . .	. . .	. . .	★
South Carolina	30	5	★	5	. . .
South Dakota	. . .	. . .	2	2	. . .
Tennessee	30	7	★	. . .	. . .
Texas	30	. . .	★	5	. . .
Utah	30	5	. . .	5	★
Vermont	. . .	. . .	. . .	4	. . .
Virginia	30	. . .	★	5	5
Washington	18	. . .	★	. . .	★
West Virginia	30	5	★	★	★
Wisconsin	. . .	. . .	★	. . .	★
Wyoming	30	. . .	★	5	★
American Samoa	35	. . .	★ (f)	5	. . .
Guam	30	. . .	5	5	★
No. Mariana Islands	35	. . .	. . .	10	★
Puerto Rico	35	5	5	5	. . .
U.S. Virgin Islands	30	. . .	5	5	★

Note: This table includes constitutional and statutory qualifications.
Key:
★ — Formal provision; number of years not specified.
. . . — No formal provision.
(a) *Crosse* v. *Board of Supervisors of Elections* 243 Md. 555, 221A.2d431 (1966) — opinion rendered indicated that U.S. citizenship was, by necessity, a requirement for office.
(b) A person convicted of felony or breach of public trust is not eligible to the office for a period of 20 years after conviction.
(c) A person convicted of a felony is not eligible to hold office until his final discharge from state supervision.
(d) A person convicted of embezzlement of public funds is not eligible to hold office.
(e) A person convicted of bribery is not eligible to hold office.
(f) U.S. citizen or U.S. national.

GOVERNORS

Table 2.3
THE GOVERNORS: COMPENSATION

State or other jurisdiction	Salary	Governor's office staff (a)	Access to state transportation			Travel allowance	Official residence
			Automobile	Airplane	Helicopter		
Alabama............	$ 70,223	22	★	★	★	(b)	★
Alaska..............	81,648	67	★	★	★	(b)	★
Arizona.............	75,000	50	★	★	★	(b)	...
Arkansas...........	35,000	48	★	...	...	(c)	★
California..........	85,000	86	★	...	...	(c)	(d)
Colorado	70,000	41.5	★	★	...	(e)	★
Connecticut	78,000	38	★	...	(f)	(e)	★
Delaware	80,000	22	★	...	★	$ 21,900 (c)	★
Florida.............	100,883	129 (g)	★	★	...	(b)	★
Georgia	88,872	55	★	★	★	(e)	★
Hawaii	94,780	28 (g)	★	...	...	(e)	★
Idaho	55,000	16 (h)	★	★	...	(e)	...
Illinois.............	93,266	173	★	★	★	(b)	★
Indiana.............	77,194	34	★	★	★	0	★
Iowa	72,500	10	★	★	...	(b)	★
Kansas	73,137	22	★	★	...	(e)	★
Kentucky	69,731	78	★	★	★	(b)	★
Louisiana	66,096	46	★	...	★	(p)	★
Maine	70,000	21	★	★	...	(e)	★
Maryland	85,000	104 (j)	★	★	★	(e)	★
Massachusetts	75,000	81	★	★	★	(e)	...
Michigan	106,690	45	★	★	★	(e)	★
Minnesota	103,860	30	★	★	★	(e)	★
Mississippi	75,600	39 (k)	★	★	★	24,017 (c,e)	★
Missouri	88,541	34	★	★	...	(c)	★
Montana............	51,713	24	★	★	★	(b)	★
Nebraska	58,000	16	★	★	★	(b)	★
Nevada	70,857 (l)	17	★	...	...	(c)	★
New Hampshire ...	75,753	27	★	★	...	(e)	★ (i)
New Jersey.........	85,000	60	★	...	★	(m)	★ (i)
New Mexico........	90,000	38	★	★	★	(c)	★
New York	130,000 (m)	216	★	★	★	(b)	★
North Carolina	123,000	86	★	★	★	11,500	★
North Dakota	65,196	18.25	★	★	...	(e)	★
Ohio	65,000	60	★	★	★	(e)	★
Oklahoma	70,000	34	★	★	...	(e)	★
Oregon	77,500	44	★	...	...	0	★
Pennsylvania	85,000	60	★	★	...	(b)	★
Rhode Island	69,000	47	★	★	★	(e)	...
South Carolina	84,897	30	★	★	★	(e)	★
South Dakota	60,819	26	★	★	...	(e)	★
Tennessee	85,000	40	★	★	★	(e)	★
Texas...............	93,432	178	...	★	★	(b)	★
Utah	69,992	18	★	★	...	26,000	★
Vermont............	75,800	21	★	...	...	(e)	...
Virginia.............	85,000	36	★	★	★	(b)	★
Washington	96,700	37	★	★	...	N.A.	★
West Virginia	72,000	30	★	★	★	(n)	★
Wisconsin	86,149	38	★	★	...	(e)	★
Wyoming	70,000	8 (o)	★	★	...	(c)	★
American Samoa ...	50,000	25	★	...	...	(c)	★
Guam	75,000	N.A.	...	...	...	N.A.	★
No. Mariana Islands ...	50,000	N.A.	N.A.	N.A.	N.A.	N.A.	N.A.
Puerto Rico	45,000	N.A.	★	★	★	(e)	★
U.S. Virgin Islands	64,400	N.A.	★	...	...	N.A.	★

THE GOVERNORS: COMPENSATION—Continued

Key:
★ — Yes
... — No
N.A. — Not available

(a) Definitions of "governor's office staff" vary across the states—from general office support to staffing for various operations within the executive office.

(b) Reimbursed for travel expenses. Alabama—reimbursed up to $40/d in state; actual expenses out of state. Alaska—governor is reimbursed $80/d or if exceed for actual amount. Arizona—reimbursed for actual expenses to a maximum of $52.50/d in state and $55/d out of state. Florida—reimbursed at same rate as other state officials: in state, choice between $50 per diem or actual expenses; out of state, actual expenses. Idaho—standard per diem, $15/d in state; $20/d out of state. Illinois—No set allowance. Iowa—Limit set in annual office budget. Kentucky—mileage at same rate as other state employees. Montana—reimbursed for actual and necessary expenses in state up to $55/d, and actual lodging plus meal allowance up to $30/d out of state (no annual limit). Nebraska—reasonable and necessary expenses. New York—reimbursed for actual and necessary expenses. Pennsylvania—reimbursed for reasonable expenses. Texas—reimbursed for actual expenses.

(c) Amount includes travel allowance for entire staff. Arkansas, Michigan, Missouri—amount not available. California—$130,000 in state; $27,000 out of state. Nevada—$19,411 in state, $9,389 out of state. New Mexico—$67,400 in state, $48,400 out of state. Wyoming—$45,536 in state; $46,158 out of state. American Samoa—$142,000.

(d) In California—provided by Governor's Residence Foundation, a non-profit organization which provides a residence for the governor of California. No rent is charged; maintenance and operational costs are provided by California Department of General Services.

(e) Travel allowance included in office budget.

(f) Emergency authorization for use of National Guard's.

(g) In Florida, does not include Office of Planning and Budgeting and a number of state commissions located within executive office of governor for budget purposes. In Hawaii, does not include offices and commissions attached to governor's office.

(h) Number on staff varies from 12 to 20 during the year.

(i) Governor does not occupy residence.

(j) Includes positions added when Criminal Justice Coordinating Council moved into governor's office.

(k) Currently 18; budget request is for 39.

(l) On employee/employer paid retirement system.

(m) Accepts $100,000.

(n) Included in general expense account.

(o) Also has state planning coordinator.

(p) Provided as needed within budgetary constraints.

Table 2.4
THE GOVERNORS: POWERS

State or other jurisdiction	Budget-making power – Full responsibility	Budget-making power – Shares responsibility	No item veto	Item veto—2/3 legislators present to override	Item veto—majority legislators elected to override	Item veto—3/5 legislators elected to override	Item veto—at least 2/3 legislators elected to override	Authorization for reorganization through executive order (b)	Other statewide elected officials (c) – Number of officials	Number of agencies
Alabama	★				★				17	8 (d)
Alaska	★								1	0
Arizona	★						★	C	8	6
Arkansas	★				★				6	6
California	★						★	S	7	7
Colorado		★					★		4	16
Connecticut	★						★	C	6	5
Delaware	★			★		★			5	5
Florida	★							S	6	6
Georgia	★					★			13	9
Hawaii	★						★	(e)	22	2
Idaho	★							C	6	7
Illinois	★					★		C	15	0
Indiana	★		★						6	7
Iowa	★						★		6	6
Kansas	★			★	★			C	15	6
Kentucky		★★						S	7	7
Louisiana							★		21	10
Maine			★						0	0
Maryland	★					★		C	3	3
Massachusetts	★ (f)			★				C	5	6
Michigan	★ (f)						★	C	35	7
Minnesota		★					★	S	5	5
Mississippi	★						★	S	13	9
Missouri	★							C	5	15
Montana	★			★				S	11	15
Nebraska	★					★			26	8
Nevada	★		★★						23	7
New Hampshire	★		★★				★		5	1
New Jersey	★			★					0	0
New Mexico	★						(k)		19	8
New York		★	(g)				★	C	3	3
North Carolina		★		★			★		9	9
North Dakota	★								13	11
Ohio	★								6	29
Oklahoma	★ (f)			★			★	S	9	7
Oregon	★ (f)								5	5
Pennsylvania	★ (f)		★				★		4	4
Rhode Island	★	★							4	4
South Carolina		★		★					8	10 (h)
South Dakota	★							C	9	7
Tennessee	★				★			S	3	1
Texas		★					★		9	7
Utah	★			★★					4	30
Vermont	★		★	★				S	5	5

THE GOVERNORS: POWERS—Continued

State or other jurisdiction	Budget-making power		No item veto	Veto power (a)				Authorization for reorganization through executive order (b)	Other statewide elected officials (c)	
	Full responsibility	Shares responsibility		Item veto—2/3 legislators present to override	Item veto—majority legislators elected to override	Item veto—3/5 legislators elected to override	Item veto—at least 2/3 legislators elected to override		Number of officials	Number of agencies
Virginia	★	...	...	★	...	...	...	S (i)	2	2
Washington	★	...	...	★	...	...	...	...	8	8
West Virginia	...	★	...	★	...	...	...	S	4	7
Wisconsin	★	...	...	★ (j)	...	...	...	...	5	5
Wyoming	★	...	...	...	...	...	★	...	4	4
American Samoa	...	★	...	...	...	...	★	S	1	1
Guam	★	...	...	...	...	...	★	...	36	3
No. Mariana Islands	★	...	...	...	...	...	★	C	1	1
Puerto Rico	★	...	...	...	...	...	...	...	0	0
U.S. Virgin Islands	★	...	...	...	...	...	...	...	1	1

Sources: The National Governors' Association 1985 survey of governors' offices; The Council of State Governments; and state constitutions and statutes.

Key:
C — Constitutional
S — Statutory

(a) In all states, except North Carolina, governor has the power to veto bills passed by the state legislature. The information presented here refers to the governor's power to *item* veto—veto items within a bill—and the votes needed in the state legislature to override the item veto. For additional information on vetoes and veto overrides, as well as the number of days the governor is allowed to consider bills, see Table 3.14, "Enacting Legislation: Veto, Veto Overrides and Effective Date."
(b) For additional information on executive orders, see Table 2.5, "Gubernatorial Executive Orders: Authorization, Provisions, Procedures."
(c) Includes only executive branch officials who are popularly elected either on a constitutional or statutory basis (elected members of state boards of education, public utilities commissions, university regents, or other state boards or commissions are also included); the number of agencies involving these officials is also listed.
(d) Lieutenant governor's office is part of governor's office.
(e) Implied through a broad interpretation of gubernatorial authority; no formal provision.
(f) Full to propose; legislature adopts or revises; and governor signs or vetoes.
(g) Governor has no veto power.
(h) Divisions within governor's office.
(i) For shifting agencies between secretarial offices; all other reorganizations require legislative approval.
(j) In Wisconsin, governor has "partial" veto over appropriation bills. The partial veto is broader than item veto.
(k) In New York, governor has item veto over appropriations.

Table 2.5
GUBERNATORIAL EXECUTIVE ORDERS: AUTHORIZATION, PROVISIONS, PROCEDURES

State or other jurisdiction	Authorization for executive orders	Provisions: Civil defense disasters, public emergencies	Energy emergencies and conservation	Other emergencies	Executive branch reorganization plans and agency creation	Create advisory, coordinating, study or investigative committees/commissions	Respond to federal programs and requirements	State personnel administration	Other administration	Procedures: Filing and publication procedures	Subject to administrative procedure act	Subject to legislative review
Alabama	S,I (a)	★	.	★ (b)	.	.	.	.	.	★ (c,d)	.	★
Alaska	C	★★	★ (a)	★★ (a)	★	★★	.	.	.	★★★	.	.
Arizona	I	.	.	.	.	.	.	.	.	.	.	.
Arkansas	S,I (e)	★★	★★	★★★	★★	★★	★★	★★	★★	★★★	.	.
California	S	★	★	.	.	.	.	.	.	★	.	.
Colorado	S	★	.	★ (f)	.	.	.	.	.	.	.	.
Connecticut	S	★★	.	.	.	.	.	.	.	.	.	.
Delaware	C	★★	.	★★ (qq)	★★	★★★★	★★★	★★★	★★ (g,h)	★★ (c)	.	★ (k)
Florida	C,S	★★	★★	★★★	★★	★★★★	★★★	★★★	★★ (g,h)	★★★	.	.
Georgia	S,I (e)	★★	★★	.	★	.	.	.	.	.	.	.
Hawaii	.	.	.	.	.	.	.	.	.	.	.	.
Idaho	S	★★	.	.	.	.	.	.	.	.	.	.
Illinois	C	★★	.	.	.	I	I	I	.	★★ (c)	.	.
Indiana	I	.	.	.	★	.	.	.	.	★★ (c)	.	.
Iowa	S	.	.	.	.	.	.	.	.	.	.	.
Kansas	S	★★	.	★ (n)	★★	★★	★	★	★★ (l)	★★ (c,d,m)	.	.
Kentucky	S	.	.	.	★★★	.	.	.	★ (k,o,p,q)	★★ (c)	.	.
Louisiana	S (r)	★★	★ (rr)	★★ (u,v)	★★	★★	★	.	★ (j,s,t)	★★ (m)	★	★★ (s,t)
Maine	S	★	.	.	.	.	.	.	.	★ (d)	.	★ (x)
Maryland	C,S	★★	★	★ (f,u)	★★	★★★	★★	★	★ (w)	★★ (m)	.	.
Massachusetts	C,I	★★	★★	★ (f,u)	★★	★★	★	.	★ (q)	★★★ (c)	.	★★ (y)
Michigan	C,S	★★	★★	.	★★	★★	★★	.	★ (z)	★★ (c,m)	.	★★ (x)
Minnesota	S	★	★	.	★★	★	★★	.	★ (aa,bb)	★★ (c)	★	★★ (x,cc)
Mississippi	S	★★	.	.	★	.	.	.	.	★	.	.
Missouri	C	.	.	.	★	.	.	.	★ (q)	★ (c)	.	.
Montana	S,I	★★	★★ (a)	★★ (dd)	.	.	.	.	★ (q)	.	.	.
Nebraska	S	★★	.	.	★	.	.	.	★ (bb)	.	.	.
Nevada	I	★★	.	.	★	.	.	.	.	.	.	.
New Hampshire	S	.	.	.	S,C	.	.	.	.	★	.	★ (x)
New Jersey	S	★★	.	★★	★	★	★	★	.	★	★	★
New Mexico	S	.	.	.	.	.	.	.	.	.	.	.
New York	I	.	.	.	★	.	.	S	★ (bb)	S	.	.
North Carolina	S,I	.	.	.	.	I	I	I	.	.	.	.
North Dakota	S,I	★★	★	.	.	.	.	.	.	★★ (c)	.	.
Ohio	C,S	★★	.	.	.	★	.	.	.	★ (c)	.	.
Oklahoma	S,I	★★	★	★ (u)	★	★	.	.	★ (ee)	★ (c)	.	.
Oregon	S	★★	.	★★ (i,n,u,w)	.	.	.	.	★ (ff)	★ (c,m)	.	.
Pennsylvania	S (a)	★★	.	★ (h,j)	.	.	.	.	★ (l)	★ (l)	.	★ (x)
Rhode Island	I (e)	★ (bb)	.	.	★	★	★	.	.	★ (c,d,gg)	.	.
South Carolina												

GUBERNATORIAL EXECUTIVE ORDERS—Continued

State or other jurisdiction	Authorization for executive orders	Civil defense disasters, public emergencies	Energy emergencies and conservation	Other emergencies	Executive branch reorganization plans and agency creation	Create advisory, coordinating, study or investigative committees/commissions	Respond to federal programs and requirements	State personnel administration	Other administration	Filing and publication procedures	Subject to administrative procedure act	Subject to legislative review
South Dakota	C	...	★	...	...	...	...	...	...	...	...	...
Tennessee	S,I	★	★	★	★	...	...	★	★	★ (c)	...	★
Texas	S	★	★	★	...	★	★	★	★	★	★	★
Utah	S	★	★	...	(hh)	★	★	★	...	...	...	...
Vermont	S,I	★	★	...	...	...	...	...	...	★ (ii)	...	★ (jj)
Virginia	S,I	★	★	★ (r)	...	...	...	...	★ (h,ff,ll,mm)	★ (c)	...	...
Washington	S	...	★	...	...	...	...	...	...	...	...	...
West Virginia	S,I (e)	★	★	★	(kk)	★	...	★	★ (nn)	★ (c,m)	...	...
Wisconsin	S	★	★	★	★	★	...	★	★ (bb,oo,p)	★	...	...
Wyoming	I	...	...	...	...	...	...	...	...	...	...	...
American Samoa	C,S	...	★	...	★	★	...	★	★	★ (pp)	★ (pp)	...
No. Mariana Islands	C	...	...	...	...	...	...	...	...	...	...	...
Puerto Rico	I	...	...	...	...	...	...	...	...	...	...	...

Sources: Massachusetts, Legislative Research Council, "Report Relative to Gubernatorial Executive Orders," House Document No. 6557, April 3, 1981, pp. 89-94; E. Lee Burnick, Department of Political Science, University of North Carolina at Greensboro; The Governors Center at Duke University (Survey, March 1984); The National Governors' Association 1985 survey; updated by The Council of State Governments' survey (1989).

Key:
C — Constitutional
S — Statutory
I — Implied
★ — Formal provision
... — No formal provision
(a) Broad interpretation of gubernatorial authority.
(b) To activate or veto environmental improvement authorities.
(c) Executive orders must be filed with secretary of state or other designated officer. In Idaho, must also be published in state general circulation newspaper.
(d) Governor required to keep record in office. In Maine, also sends copy to Legislative Counsel, State Law Library, and all county law libraries in state.
(e) Some or all provisions implied from constitution.
(f) To regulate distribution of necessities during shortages.
(g) To reassign state attorneys and public defenders.
(h) To suspend certain officials and/or other civil actions.
(i) To declare water, crop and refugee emergencies.
(j) To designate game and wildlife areas or other public areas.
(k) Only if involves a change in statute.
(l) To transfer allocated funds.
(m) Included in state register or code.
(n) To give immediate effect to state regulations in emergencies.
(o) To control administration of state contracts and procedures.
(p) To impound or freeze certain state matching funds.
(q) To reduce state expenditures in revenue shortfall.
(r) Broad grant of authority.
(s) Appointive powers.
(t) To suspend rules and regulations of the bureaucracy.
(u) For fire emergencies.
(v) For financial institution emergencies.
(w) To control procedures for dealing with public.
(x) Reorganization plans and agency creation.
(y) Legislative appropriations committees must approve orders issued to handle a revenue shortfall.
(z) To assign duties to lieutenant governor, issue writ of special election.
(aa) To control prison and pardon administration.
(bb) To administer and govern the armed forces of the state.
(cc) For meeting federal program requirements.
(dd) To declare air pollution emergencies.
(ee) Relating to local governments.
(ff) To transfer funds in an emergency.
(gg) Must be published in register if they have general applicability and legal effect.
(hh) Can reorganize, but not create.
(ii) Filed with legislature.
(jj) Only executive branch reorganization.
(kk) To shift agencies between secretarial offices; all other reorganizations require legislative approval.
(ll) To control state-owned motor vehicles.
(mm) Delegate powers to secretaries and other executive branch officials.
(nn) Regarding annual reports of state agencies.
(oo) To transfer functions between agencies.
(pp) If executive order fits definition of rule.
(qq) Local financial emergency, shore erosion, polluted discharge and energy shortage.
(rr) If an energy emergency is declared by the state's Executive Council or Legislature.

GOVERNORS

Table 2.6
STATE CABINET SYSTEMS

State or jurisdiction	Authorization for cabinet system					Criteria for membership			Number of members in cabinet (including governor)	Frequency of cabinet meetings	Open cabinet meetings
	Statute	Constitution	Governor	Tradition		Appointed to specified office	Elected to specified office	Gubernatorial appointment regardless of office			
Alabama	...	...	...	★		...	...	★	28	Twice monthly (a)	★
Alaska	...	...	★	...		★	...	...	17	Regularly	★ (b)
Arizona	...	...	★	...		★	...	...	19	Weekly	...
Arkansas	★	...	...	...		★	...	...	17	Regularly	...
California	...	...	★	...		★	...	★	11	Every two weeks	...
Colorado	...	★	...	...		★	...	...	21	Twice monthly	★
Connecticut	★	...	...	...		★	...	...	24	Gov.'s discretion	...
Delaware	★	...	...	...		...	...	★ (c)	19	Gov.'s discretion	★
Florida	...	★	...	...		...	★	...	7	Every two weeks	★
Georgia	----	----	----	----		---- (d) ----	----	----	----	----	----
Hawaii	...	...	...	★		★	...	★	24	Gov.'s discretion	...
Idaho	----	----	----	----		---- (d) ----	----	----	----	----	----
Illinois	★	...	...	...		★ (c)	...	...	42 (e)	Gov.'s discretion (f)	★
Indiana	----	----	----	----		---- (d) ----	----	----	----	----	----
Iowa	★	...	...	...		...	★	...	5	Weekly	★
Kansas	...	...	★	...		...	...	★	14	Monthly (a)	...
Kentucky	★	...	...	...		★	...	...	13	Weekly	...
Louisiana	★	★	...	...		★	★	...	21	Monthly	...
Maine	...	...	...	★		...	...	★ (c)	20	Gov.'s discretion	...
Maryland	★	...	...	...		★ (c)	...	...	20	Weekly	...
Massachusetts	★	...	...	...		★	...	...	11	Twice monthly	...
Michigan	...	...	★	...		★	★	★	30	Gov.'s discretion	...
Minnesota	...	...	★	...		★	...	...	26 (h)	Regularly	...
Mississippi	----	----	----	----		---- (d) ----	----	----	----	----	----
Missouri	...	★	...	★		★	...	...	16	Gov.'s discretion	...
Montana	...	...	★	...		★	...	...	24	Monthly	★
Nebraska	...	...	★	...		★	...	...	27	Monthly	...
Nevada	----	----	----	----		---- (d) ----	----	----	----	----	----
New Hampshire	----	----	----	----		---- (d) ----	----	----	----	----	----
New Jersey	★	★	...	...		★	...	...	21	Once or twice monthly	...
New Mexico	★	...	...	...		★	...	...	15	Weekly	...
New York	...	...	...	★		★	...	...	16	Gov.'s discretion	...
North Carolina (i)	...	...	...	...		...	...	★	10	Monthly	...
North Dakota	----	----	----	----		---- (d) ----	----	----	----	----	----
Ohio	★	...	...	...		★	...	★	27	Gov.'s discretion	(g)
Oklahoma	★	...	...	...		...	...	★	11 (j)	Gov.'s discretion	...
Oregon	...	...	★	...		...	...	★	21	As needed	...
Pennsylvania	★	...	...	...		★	...	...	20	Gov.'s discretion	★
Rhode Island	----	----	----	----		---- (d) ----	----	----	----	----	----
South Carolina	----	----	----	----		---- (d) ----	----	----	----	----	----
South Dakota	...	...	★	...		★	...	★	22	Gov.'s discretion	...
Tennessee	★	...	...	★		★	...	...	29	Gov.'s discretion	★
Texas	----	----	----	----		---- (d) ----	----	----	----	----	----
Utah	...	...	★	(k)		★	...	...	31	Monthly	★
Vermont	★	...	...	...		★	...	...	6	Gov.'s discretion	...
Virginia	★	...	...	...		★	...	...	9	Gov.'s discretion	...
Washington	...	...	★	...		★	...	...	26	Twice monthly	...
West Virginia	★	...	...	...		...	...	★	8	Weekly	...
Wisconsin	★	...	...	...		★	...	...	9	Monthly	★
Wyoming (l)	★	...	...	...		★	...	...	4	Gov.'s discretion	★
Puerto Rico	★	★	...	...		★	...	...	17	Weekly	...

Key:
★ — Yes
... — No

(a) More often during legislative sessions. Kansas—bi-weekly.
(b) Except when in executive session.
(c) With the consent of the Senate.
(d) No formal cabinet system. In Idaho, however, sub-cabinets have been formed, by executive order; the chairmen report to the governor when requested.
(e) Includes directors of three independent bonding agencies.
(f) Sub-cabinets meet monthly.
(g) In practice, the media and others do not attend, but cabinet meetings have not been formally designated closed.
(h) Five sub-cabinets have been formed.
(i) Constitution provides for a Council of State made up of elective state administrative officials, which makes policy decisions for the state while the cabinet acts more in an advisory capacity.
(j) Each cabinet member is chair of a sub-cabinet (each state agency). These sub-cabinets meet quarterly.
(k) State Planning Advisory Committee, composed of all department heads serves as an informal cabinet. Committee meets at discretion of state planning coordinator.
(l) A 4-year, phased-in executive reorganization currently being implemented. The first three cabinet-level agencies go on-line in July 1990.

GOVERNORS

Table 2.7
THE GOVERNORS: PROVISIONS AND PROCEDURES FOR TRANSITION

State or other jurisdiction	Legislation pertaining to gubernatorial transition	Appropriations available to gov-elect	Gov-elect's participation in state budget for coming fiscal year	Gov-elect to hire staff to assist during transition	State personnel to be made available to assist gov-elect	Office space in buildings to be made available to gov-elect	Acquainting gov-elect staff with office procedures and routine office functions	Transfer of information (files, records, etc.)
Alabama	...	...	•	(a)	•	•	•	...
Alaska	...	★	...	...	★	•	★	•
Arizona	...	...	★	...	•	•	•	•
Arkansas	★	60,000 (b)	★	★	•	•	...	...
California	★	450,000	★	★	★	★	•	•
Colorado	★	10,000	...	★	★	★	★	★
Connecticut	★	25,000	•	★	•	★	...	★
Delaware	★	(j)	...	...	•	•	•	•
Florida	•	300,000 (d)	★	•	•	•	•	•
Georgia	★	★	...	★	★	★	•	★
Hawaii	★	100,000	★	★	★	★	★	★
Idaho	★	15,000	★	★	★	★	★	★
Illinois	★	...	★	★ (e)	★	★	★	★
Indiana	★	45,000	★	★	★	★	★	★
Iowa	★ (f)	10,000	★	★	• (g)	•	•	★ (h)
Kansas	★	100,000	★	★	★	★	★	★
Kentucky	★	Unspecified	★	★	★	★	★	★
Louisiana	★	10,000	★	★	...	★	★	★
Maine	★	5,000	★	★	★ (i)	•	★	•
Maryland	★	50,000	★	★	★	★	★	★
Massachusetts	...	★	•	★	★	★	•	•
Michigan	★	1,000,000 (c)	•	★	★	★	★	...
Minnesota	★	29,600	★	★	★	★	★	•
Mississippi	★	30,000	★	★	★	★	★	★
Missouri	★	100,000	★	★	★	★	•	• (r)
Montana	★	5,000	★	★	★	★	★	★
Nebraska	...	44,000 (j)	★	•	•	★	•	•
Nevada	...	5,000 (k)	★	...	•	•	•	★
New Hampshire	★	5,000	★	★	★	★	★	...
New Jersey	★	295,000	★	★	★	★	•	★
New Mexico	★	(l)	★	★	•	★	•	•
New York	...	...	•	•	•	•	•	•
North Carolina	★	50,000 (d)	• (m)	★	★	★	•	•
North Dakota	...	... (n)	...	...	•	...	•	★
Ohio	★	(l)	...	★	★	•	...	...
Oklahoma	★	40,000	★	★	...	•	...	...
Oregon	★	20,000	★	★	★	★	★	★
Pennsylvania	★	100,000	...	★	•	★	★	...
Rhode Island	...	...	★	...	...	...	...	...
South Carolina	★	50,000	...	★	•	★	★	★
South Dakota	★	10,000 (o)	•	★	•	★	•	★
Tennessee	★	★	...	...	...	...	•	•
Texas	...	...	★	★	•	•	...	...
Utah	...	Unspecified	...	...	...	...	...	(q)
Vermont	...	40,000	★ (p)	•	•	•	...	(q)
Virginia	...	(j)	...	★ (r)	★ (r)	★ (r)	★ (r)	★ (r)
Washington	★	80,000	•	•	•	•	•	•
West Virginia	...	...	...	...	...	...	...	...
Wisconsin	★	Unspecified	★	★	★	★	★	★
Wyoming	...	(l)	★	★	•	•	•	•
American Samoa	...	Unspecified	★ (s)	•	•	•	•	•
Guam	...	...	...	...	...	...	...	...
No. Mariana Islands	...	...	...	...	...	...	...	...
Puerto Rico	...	250,000 (d)	...	•	•	•	•	...
U.S. Virgin Islands	...	...	...	...	...	...	...	...

Sources: The National Governors' Association 1985 survey, and The Council of State Governments.

Key:
... — No provisions or procedures
★ — Formal provisions or procedures
• — No formal provisions, occurs informally
(a) Governor usually hires several incoming key staff during transition.
(b) Made available in 1983.
(c) Made available in 1982.
(d) Inaugural expenses are paid from this amount.
(e) On a contractual basis.
(f) Pertains only to funds.
(g) Provided on irregular basis.
(h) Arrangement for transfer of criminal files.
(i) Budget personnel.
(j) Determined prior to each election by legislature.
(k) Is not adequate and is augmented by legislature.
(l) Legislature required to make appropriation; no dollar amount stated in legislation. In New Mexico, $50,000 was made available in 1986. In Wyoming, $10,000 for governor elected in 1990 pending legislative approval.
(m) New governor can submit supplemental budget.
(n) If necessary, submit request to State Emergency Commission.
(o) Made available for 1987.
(p) Responsible for the preparation of the budget; staff made available.
(q) Not transferred but use may be authorized.
(r) Activity is traditional and routine, although there is no specific statutory provision.
(s) Can submit reprogramming or supplemental appropriation measure for current fiscal year.

Table 2.8
IMPEACHMENT PROVISIONS IN THE STATES

State or other jurisdiction	Governor and other state executive and judicial officers subject to impeachment	Legislative body which holds power of impeachment	Vote required for impeachment	Legislative body which conducts impeachment trial	Chief justice presides at impeachment trial (a)	Vote required for conviction	Official who serves as acting governor	Legislature may call special session for impeachment
Alabama	★ (b)	H	2/3 mbrs.	S	★	2/3 mbrs.	LG	★
Alaska	★	S	maj. mbrs.	H		2/3 mbrs.	SS	★
Arizona	★ (d)	H		S	★	2/3 mbrs.		
Arkansas	★	H		S	★	2/3 mbrs.	LG	
California	★	H		S		2/3 mbrs.		
Colorado	★ (d)	H	maj. mbrs.	S	★	2/3 mbrs.	LG	★
Connecticut	★	H		S	★	2/3 mbrs. present		
Delaware	★	H	2/3 mbrs.	S	★	2/3 mbrs.	LG	
Florida	★	H	2/3 mbrs.	S	★	2/3 mbrs. present	LG	
Georgia	★ (e)	H		S	★	2/3 mbrs. present		★
Hawaii	★ (f)	H		S	★	2/3 mbrs.	LG	★
Idaho	★	H		S	★	2/3 mbrs.	LG	★
Illinois	★	H	maj. mbrs.	S		2/3 mbrs.		
Indiana	★	H	2/3 mbrs.	S		2/3 mbrs.		
Iowa	★	H		S		2/3 mbrs. present	LG	
Kansas	★	H		S		2/3 mbrs.	LG	
Kentucky	★	H		S		2/3 mbrs. present	LG	★
Louisiana	★	H		S		2/3 mbrs.	LG	★
Maine	★	H		S		2/3 mbrs. present		
Maryland	★	H	maj. mbrs.	S		2/3 mbrs.	PS	
Massachusetts	★	H		S (g)		2/3 mbrs.	LG	★
Michigan	★	H	maj. mbrs.	S	★	2/3 mbrs.		
Minnesota	★	H	maj. mbrs.	S		2/3 mbrs.	LG	
Mississippi	★	H	2/3 mbrs. present	S	★	2/3 mbrs.	LG	
Missouri	★	H		(h)	(h)	(h)		
Montana	★	H	2/3 mbrs.	S		2/3 mbrs.	LG	★
Nebraska	★ (d)	S (i)	maj. mbrs.	(j)	(j)	(i)		
Nevada	★	H	maj. mbrs.	S	★	2/3 mbrs.	LG	
New Hampshire	★	H		S	★			★
New Jersey	★ (k)	H	maj. mbrs.	S		2/3 mbrs.	PS	
New Mexico	★	H	maj. mbrs.	S	★	2/3 mbrs.	LG	★
New York	★	H	maj. mbrs.	(l)		2/3 mbrs. present	LG	★
North Carolina	★ (d)	H		S	★	2/3 mbrs. present	LG	★
North Dakota	★	H	maj. mbrs.	S		2/3 mbrs.	LG	
Ohio	★	H	maj. mbrs.	S		2/3 mbrs.		★
Oklahoma	★ (b)	H		S	★ (m)	2/3 mbrs. present	LG	★
Oregon	★	H		S	★	2/3 mbrs.	LG	
Pennsylvania	★	H	(n)	S	★	2/3 mbrs.	LG	
Rhode Island	★	H	2/3 mbrs.	S		2/3 mbrs.	LG	
South Carolina	★	H		S				
South Dakota	★ (d)	H	maj. mbrs.	S	★	2/3 mbrs.	LG	★
Tennessee	★	H		S	★	2/3 mbrs. (o)	LG	
Texas	★	H	2/3 mbrs.	S	★	2/3 mbrs. present	LG	
Utah	★ (d)	H	2/3 mbrs.	S		2/3 mbrs.	LG	
Vermont	★	H		S		2/3 mbrs. present		

IMPEACHMENT PROVISIONS IN THE STATES—Continued

State or other jurisdiction	Governor and other state executive and judicial officers subject to impeachment	Legislative body which holds power of impeachment	Vote required for impeachment	Legislative body which conducts impeachment trial	Chief justice presides at impeachment trial (a)	Vote required for conviction	Official who serves as acting governor	Legislature may call special session for impeachment
Virginia	★	H	maj. mbrs.	S	...	2/3 mbrs. present	...	★
Washington	★ (d)	H	...	S	★	2/3 mbrs.	...	★
West Virginia	★	H	maj. mbrs.	S	★	2/3 mbrs.	LG	★
Wisconsin	★	H	maj. mbrs.	S	...	2/3 mbrs. present	SS	...
Wyoming	★ (d)	H		S	★	2/3 mbrs.		
Dist. of Columbia				(p)				
American Samoa	(q)	H	2/3 mbrs.	S	★	2/3 mbrs.	...	...
Guam				(p)				
No. Mariana Islands	★	H	2/3 mbrs.	S	★	2/3 mbrs.	...	★
Puerto Rico	(r)	H	2/3 mbrs.	S	★	3/4 mbrs.	...	...
U.S. Virgin Islands				(p)				

Sources: Legislative Drafting Research Fund, Columbia University, *Constitutions of the United States: National and State* (Dobbs Ferry, N.Y.: Oceana Press, 1982, 1983); *The Book of the States, 1986-87*; and state statutes. Information compiled by Joe Farrell, Public Administration Program, University of North Carolina at Chapel Hill; and The Council of State Governments.

Note: The information in this table is based on a literal reading of the state constitutions and statutes. For information on other methods for removing state officials, see Table 4.5, "Methods for Removal of Judges and Filling of Vacancies," and Table 5.16, "Provisions for Recall of State Officials."

Key:
★ — Yes; provision for
... — Not specified, or no provision for
H — House or Assembly (lower chamber)
S — Senate
LG — Lieutenant governor
PS — President of the Senate
SS — Secretary of state
(a) Presiding justice of state court of last resort. In many states, provision indicates that chief justice presides only on occasion of impeachment of governor. Other judicial officers not subject to impeachment.
(b) Includes justices of Supreme Court.
(c) A Supreme Court justice designated by the court.
(d) With exception of certain judicial officers. In Arizona, Washington, and Wyoming—justices of courts not of record. In Colorado—county judges and justices of the peace. In Nevada and Utah—justices of the peace. In North Dakota and South Dakota—county judges, justices of the peace, and police magistrates.
(e) All persons who have been or may be in office.
(f) Governor, lieutenant governor, and any appointive officer for whose removal the consent of the Senate is required.
(g) House elects three members to prosecute impeachment.
(h) All impeachments are tried before the state Supreme Court, except that the governor or a member of the Supreme Court is tried by a special commission of seven eminent jurists to be elected by the Senate. A vote of 5/7 of the court of special commission is necessary to convict.
(i) Unicameral legislature; members use the title "senator."
(j) Court of impeachment is composed of chief justice and all district court judges in the state. A vote of 2/3 of the court is necessary to convict.
(k) All state officers while in office and for two years thereafter.
(l) Court for trial of impeachment composed of president of the Senate, senators (or major part of them), and judges of Court of Appeals (or major part of them).
(m) No provision for impeachment. Public officers may be tried for incompetency, corruption, malfeasance, or delinquency in office in same manner as criminal offenses.
(n) Vote of 2/3 members required for an impeachment of the governor.
(o) Vote of 2/3 of members sworn to try the officer impeached.
(p) Removal of elected officials by recall procedure only.
(q) Governor, lieutenant governor.
(r) Governor and Supreme Court justices.

THE EXECUTIVE BRANCH: ORGANIZATION AND ISSUES, 1988-89

By Thad L. Beyle

Executive Branch Reorganization

Reorganization of state executive branches has occurred in four distinct waves over the 20th Century usually following similar efforts at the national level. The most recent wave began in the mid 1960s and included 22 different states through 1987.[1]

A study by James K. Conant of the most recent efforts in these 22 states examines each reorganization, its genesis, process, outcomes and effects.[2] Several of the author's findings are of interest. The average germination period (the years between the last and the most recent reorganization) was 45 years, with a range from no previous effort in Iowa, to 84 years in Florida, to 5 years in California. The governor was the initiator or key figure in 18 of the 22 reorganizations, the governor and the legislature jointly initiated the effort in three other states (Florida, Missouri, Louisiana), while the legislature initiated the action in Colorado.

The goals articulated by those seeking reform were "modernization and streamlining of the executive branch machinery, efficiency, effectiveness, economy, responsiveness and gubernatorial control."[3] The authorizing mechanism of choice was a constitutional amendment. In half of the states a numerical limit was set on the number of departments allowed. In Louisiana reform was accomplished via a new constitution. The process was elaborated by either statutes or executive orders. In 10 states the authorizing mechanism was statutory, and in Kentucky it was an executive order.[4]

Gubernatorial-legislative conflict over reorganization varied across the 22 states, with over half going through the process with relatively little conflict between the two branches.[5] There was considerable conflict over reorganization in 5 states (Arkansas, Florida, Massachusetts, Michigan and Wisconsin) and a moderate level of conflict in 4 states (Connecticut, Delaware, Georgia and Iowa).

There was good reason for gubernatorial-legislative conflict in terms of what resulted from these reorganizations. For example, in several states there was a significant increase in potential gubernatorial power as the number of independent boards, commissions and agencies decreased from a range of 300 (Georgia and Louisiana) to 85 (Wisconsin) pre-reorganization, to a range of 30 (Wisconsin) to 7 (Virginia) post-reorganization.[6]

The governors' appointment powers also increased considerably depending on the model used for the reorganized state executive branch. There are three generic models: the traditional model with many agencies (over 17) and a low degree of functional consolidation; the cabinet model with nine to 16 agencies with moderate functional consolidation into single-function agencies (over 50 percent into single function agencies); and the secretary/coordinator model with one to eight agencies with high consolidation into broad single-function or large multiple-function agencies.[7]

For the four states opting to use the secretary/coordinator model, governors were able to appoint 80 percent or more of the department heads;[8] and for those nine states moving to the cabinet model, the governors were

---

Thad L. Beyle is Professor of Political Science at the University of North Carolina at Chapel Hill.

able to appoint 60 percent or more.[9] For those ten states selecting the traditional model, the increases in appointment power were much less significant, ranging from a high of 58 percent in North Carolina to a low of 17 percent in Wisconsin.[10]

However, despite the avowed goal of achieving efficiency, effectiveness and economy, actual savings occurred in only six of the 22 states, and in three of these the savings were modest. In fact, only Georgia and Iowa even made attempts to document "the bottom line results of the reorganization." This led Conant to argue that reorganization proponents "should be more cautious about the bottom line results they expect from reorganization, but they need not abandon the pursuit of a modernized, streamlined executive branch or strong executive leadership."[11]

A recent NGA study of governors' cabinets found that "effective cabinets do not just happen. They require careful preparation and regular attention" from the governor and his or her senior staff.[12] Further, the cabinet's role "is a function of the governor's style and priorities, the governor's relations with his or her appointees, and his or her view of the governor's role in the day-to-day administration of state government."[13]

The Minnesota governor has the authority to transfer powers and duties among executive branch agencies by executive reorganization orders. These transfers can be made to "improve efficiency and avoid duplication," must be made in the form of a reorganization order effective upon being filed with the secretary of state, and may only be made to agencies in existence for over a year prior to the order. There are some limitations on this power: a governor cannot transfer "all or substantially all the powers or duties or personnel of a department, the Housing Finance Agency, or the Pollution Control Agency" without legislative ratification, and each January the commissioner of administration must submit, in bill form, all the statutory changes necessitated by the governor's reorganization orders. If no action is taken by the legislature, the order stands.[14]

Between 1970 and 1988, five Minnesota governors issued 155 reorganization orders, most of which were merely administrative in nature and were often issued to carry out the intent of new legislation. Several recent orders have involved more significant transfers.[15]

Over the past two years there has not been a high level of action on state government reorganization. In 1988, Mississippi Governor Ray Mabus induced the legislature to create a 25-member commission to study his reorganization proposal which would reduce the number of state agencies from 160 to as few as 15.[16] In 1989, West Virginia Governor Gaston Caperton was able to gain legislative approval for consolidating 150 executive boards and agencies into seven new departments;[17] but as noted earlier, he was unable to get voter approval of a constitutional amendment to abolish three constitutionally elected offices.

Partial Reorganizations

Economic development

There has been considerable ferment in this area of state concern in recent years. Part of the drive for this has been the changing view of what economic development means in the states today. This changing view has been the basis of much gubernatorial action that looks at the question of economic development from the perspective of America's and each state's changing role in a global economy and not necessarily from the perspective of new programs or more spending.[1]

In a recent study of what he calls the "decade of enormous innovation at the state level," David Osborne classified the various gubernatorial efforts of the 1980s into 10 categories: improving the intellectual infrastructure; improving the skills and education levels of the work force; improving the quality of life; improving the entrepreneurial climate; improving access to risk capital; improving the market for new products and processes; assisting industrial modernization; changing the culture of industry; improving social organization; and, bringing the poor into the growth process.[2]

Osborne clearly sets out two agendas that some governors have followed. The first is to create economic growth as a staple of gubernatorial goals and actions. The second agenda, however, is to bring the poor — individuals and communities — into the the growth process. From Osborne's observations of gubernatorial and state actions, the most successful address both agendas.[3]

Some examples of this approach follow: In 1988, Colorado formed an Office Economic Development to consolidate international trade, minority, women's and small business agencies in the governor's office in order to provide a more cohesive mission and to strengthen the governor's control.[4] Florida created the Office of Space Programs to help the state stay in the forefront of space technology, attract corporations with an interest in building in space and in becoming the home for the first commercial spaceport.[5] Pennsylvania created a Governor's Response Team to work on limiting the bureaucratic red tape businesses must wade through when locating in the state.[6]

Also in 1988, Mississippi reorganized its Department of Economic Development by abolishing the board which had directed the agency and replacing it with a director appointed by the governor and confirmed by the state senate. The agency also received some of the functions previously performed by the abolished Research and Development Center.

States continued to establish funding mechanisms to assist citizens and businesses in furthering economic development. Kentucky established a Rural Economic Development Authority in 1988 which will issue revenue bonds to finance manufacturing projects in high unemployment counties. Louisiana combined all the Department of Economic Development's financial assistance and investment programs in an Economic Development Corporation in order to provide one-stop shopping for those businesses and communities interested in financial aid.[7] Vermont created the Vermont Captive Insurance program to enable businesses to become self-insured, and thereby reduce premiums.[8]

North Carolina created the N.C. Enterprise Corporation, a public/private organization to assist development in rural areas by providing loans and capital for business expansion in 1988.[9] At the same time, Maryland created the Economic Development Opportunities Program Fund to assist in attracting or retaining commercial, industrial, educational or research entities.[10]

Corrections

Privatizing state correctional systems continues to be an option despite unresolved arguments over many of the issues involved. There are several trends now seen in the states: some states are expanding the authority of the corrections department (state and local) to make greater use of privatization; there is a growing private sector capacity to provide an array of correctional services; and contracts are being let by state and local governments for larger and more secure corrections facilities.[1]

The activities undertaken in a private/public relationship in corrections fall into five models: services, construction, management, ownership and operation, and take-over. The private services model is the oldest and best known and is used to provide selected services in a more efficient manner. In the private construction model, private firms usually handle all aspects of prison construction free of governmental control. Proponents argue this saves money, time and avoids delays. The private management model is as named: a private firm is contracted to run prisons and jails. The private ownership and operation model takes this last relationship one step further by allowing the private business to own the prison. The take-over model, in which the the entire system is placed in the private sector has been suggested but not adopted in any state.[2]

Some specific actions in the corrections area are as follows: In 1988, Mississippi replaced the independent Board of Corrections, and reorganized the corrections department, putting it under the control of a director appointed by the governor with senate approval.[3] In 1988, California voters gave the governor the power to review decisions of the Parole Board through a constitutional amendment.[4]

Environment

In 1989, the Michigan legislature decided not to fund the Toxic Control Commission which had been established in 1979 as a watchdog of the agriculture, natural resources and public health departments. This came in response to the accidental mixing of a chemical flame retardant with livestock feed, which was not detected for a year. In 1990, the governor transferred the toxic emergency response powers from the defunct commission to the Department of Public Health.[1]

Higher Education

Maryland took major steps to reorganize its system of higher education in 1988. An 11-campus system was established to be run by a single Board of Regents, and the campus at College Park was designated as the flagship of the system. The Maryland Higher Education Commission was also established to coordinate all public and private institutions in the state.[1]

In July 1989, a three judge federal panel ruled that Louisiana's governing structure for higher education must be revamped. The court mandated abolishing the current system with four separate boards as they "perpetuated illegal segregation", and called for a single 17-member board appointed by the governor and confirmed by the senate. This decision paralleled an earlier proposal made by the governor but rejected by the legislature.[2]

Management Techniques

The current trend in analyzing the role of governors is to view them as managers and to look at what managers in other organizations and situations, especially in the private sector, do. The "Governor as Manager" model has prompted several articles and publications suggesting, examining, and assessing this potential role for governors and the styles that several governors have used.[1] However, one observer has cautioned that while the techniques currently associated with helping a governor fulfill this role may be helpful to the governor and could lead to better state government, they should not replace the hard work and thinking needed "to set state goals or make decisions."[2]

Sunset

Another method of achieving change within the executive branch is sunset laws and procedures to terminate agencies, boards, commissions, or committees unless the legislature specifically reauthorizes them. Started by Colorado in 1976, the concept spread rapidly so that every state and even Congress has considered it. By 1981, at its highwater mark, 36 states had adopted some form of sunset legislation. A recent survey found that by 1989 six states had repealed their laws,[1] and six others had allowed theirs to lapse into inactivity.[2] One of these states, Connecticut, has rescheduled the sunset review cycle to 1995 after postponing it twice. All but one of the states (Illinois) dropping their sunset law had part-time legislatures with below average spending on the legislative institution suggesting "that weak legislative bodies are not well suited to implement sunset review."[3]

There has been variable success with sunset laws in the states. Termination of agencies continues but not at the same rate as in initial reviews. Few of the agencies terminated were of "major" status; most were of a peripheral nature and had lost their usefulness or relevance. There have also been some changes made in agency status and activities flowing from the sunset review process, mostly "aimed at improving the efficiency of agency and board operations," i.e., "92 percent have added public members to to licensing boards or agencies."[4] But in Oklahoma, the governor was able to combine his veto power and sunset legislation to make serious inroads on minor regulatory agency's independence.[5]

Productivity

When reorganization fails to create more cost-effective government, states often turn to other types of programs to reduce costs.

Several states have implemented programs to reward state employees for money saving ideas or innovations. In 1988, Governor John Waihee of Hawaii started "A Committee for Excellence" (ACE) to seek innovative ways state government could serve the public. Other states with employee incentive or recognition programs include Delaware, Indiana, Missouri, Oklahoma, Oregon and Tennessee.[1]

Planning

Policy and program analysis still are elusive parts of decision-making agendas in state and local governments. A recent reissue of a study and guide to this process suggests that successful analyses tend to be well timed in terms of making the findings available to the policy makers when they need them, include explicit political and administrative considerations that could affect implementation, and focus on clearly-defined problems rather than on broad issues.[1]

One of the joint approaches that governors and other state policy makers are using to enhance their planning capabilites is the development of the State Scanning Network coordinated by the Council of State Planning Agencies and NGA. This process of "scanning" various sources for clues as to trends and new issues by many separate observers, with their observations then screened for broad trends by a review panel, has helped states identify new issues of importance to state policy makers.[2] This process has also been used on the regional level by such organizations as the Southern Growth Policies Board.

State Agency Heads

Since 1964, Deil Wright has conducted periodic surveys of state agency heads. Comparing the results of the 1964 and 1988 surveys, he finds that the typical administrator is now slightly less male (83 percent vs. 98 percent in 1964), slightly less white (91 percent vs. 98 percent), younger (median age of 46 vs. 52), and more educated (only 1 percent have high school or less vs. 18 percent in 1964). The number of agency heads with a graduate or professional degree has risen to 55 percent from 40 percent. These administrators arrived at their position mainly by promotion up through the agency (37 percent) or from another agency in the same state (19 percent). A small number (5 percent) were hired from another state.[1]

Ethics

Ethics in government continues to be an issue across the states. The New York State Commission on Government Integrity in its report, "Restoring the Public Trust: A Blueprint for Government Integrity," called on the state legislature to consider tougher laws in several areas, including campaign finance, ballot access, judicial selection, pension forfeiture, and the closing of loopholes in the 1976 Open Meetings Law and the 1987 Ethics in Government Act.[1]

Authors of a major study of state ethics codes wonder if the recent introduction across the states of reforms which "opened the electoral process, fostered accountability measures and increased clarification of conflict of interest", and setting standards of quality, "have not been at least as significant as the other reforms" the states have undertaken over the past two decades.[2]

In 1988, voters in Arkansas approved a gubernatorially sponsored ethics measure which will set standards of conduct for lobbyists and state officials. Voters in Mississippi also supported their governor's push for reformed county governments by adopting centralized county road administrations to replace the current corrupt systems.[3] The Oklahoma Ethics Commission was renamed the Oklahoma Council on Campaign Compliance and Ethical Standards, its funding doubled, and several gray areas in the law clarified.[4]

There were some very serious situations in the states in which ethical questions graded over into charges of corruption. West Virginia's popular state treasurer, A. James Manchin, who had run unopposed in November 1988, was caught in a scandal when outside auditors found record losses in the state's Consolidated Investment Fund of nearly $300 million in December 1988.[5] Although he initially refused to resign, Manchin did so in July after being impeached by the House of Delegates, just before his trial in the Senate began. While criminal corruption was not shown, someone on Manchin's staff had mismanaged agency funds in a pooled investment with the result that they lost half their value.[6]

The state seemed snakebit as Attorney General Charlie Brown resigned one month later after being accused of perjury and facing a grand jury investigation into the financing of his 1984 and 1988 campaigns.[7] Then, three state senators resigned over money corruption issues.[8] It was a hard year for the state; even the governor got involved in a messy divorce. Finally, in April 1990 former Governor Arch Moore (R, 1969-77, 1985-89) agreed to plead guilty to extortion, mail fraud, tax fraud and obstruction of justice. These were tied to his successful 1984 campaign, unsuccessful 1988 campaign, and his third term as govenor.[9] It is reported that 50 other officials may be facing criminal charges in the state.[10]

Tennessee is undergoing an FBI investigation into allegations of corruption in the state-run bingo operation. Top officials are charged with setting up phony charities so bingo games could be run. Governor McWherter has issued tighter ethics rules for any gubernatorial appointees in the wake of the scandal.[11]

Recently, several states have established inspector general offices, which are to probe into allegations of wrong doing in state government. Beginning with Massachusetts in 1981, four other states set up such an office in the last five years: Louisiana, New York, Ohio and Pennsylvania. While often limited in their authority over the legislative and judicial branches, and other separately elected officials, they all can investigate allegations in agencies under the governor. In Massachusetts, the authority also extends to local governments. But not all the office's activities are in response to allegations, as they can "identify programs or departments that might be vulnerable to corruption." Some other states argue that the attorney general's office or the auditor have these responsibilities.[12]

Footnotes

Executive Branch Reorganization

1. The 22 states in chronological order are: Michigan, Wisconsin, California, Colorado, Florida, Massachusetts, Delaware, Maryland, Montana, Maine, North Carolina, Arkansas, Virginia, Georgia, South Dakota, Kentucky, Missouri, Idaho, Louisiana, New Mexico, Connecticut and Iowa.
2. James K. Conant, "In the Shadow of Wilson and Brownlow: Executive Branch Reorganization in the States, 1965 to 1987," *Public Administration Review* 48:5 (September/October 1988), 892-902.
3. Ibid., 895.
4. Ibid.
5. Those states with low conflict over reorganiztion were: California, Colorado, Maryland, Montana, North Carolina, Virginia, Maine, South Dakota, Kentucky, Idaho, Louisiana and New Mexico.
6. Conant, 895.
7. ACIR, *The Question of State Government Capability* (Washington, DC: ACIR, 1985), 149.
8. Those state adopting the secretary/coordinator model were California, Massachusetts, Virginia and Kentucky.
9. Those states adopting the cabinet model were Delaware, Maryland, Maine, Arkansas, South Dakota, Missouri, Louisiana (mix with traditional), New Mexico and Iowa.
10. Those states adopting the traditional model were Michigan, Wisconsin, Colorado, Florida, Montana, North Carolina, Georgia, Idaho, Louisiana (mix with cabinet) and Connecticut.
11. Conant, 892.
12. Barry Van Lare, Office of State Services, "The Role of Cabinets in State Government," *Management Notes* (Washington, DC: National Governors' Association, November 1988), 11.
13. Ibid.
14. Mark Shepard, "Governors' Reorganization Powers," House Research Information Brief, (St. Paul: Research Department, Minnesota House of Representatives, 1988), 2.
15. Ibid., 3.

16. Joseph Parker, "Mississippi Governor Goes Two for Four in First Legislative Session," *Comparative State Politics Newsletter* 9:3 (June 1988), 20-21.

17. Elder Witt, "A Governor Seeks Less Government," *Governing* 2:9 (June 1989), 66.

Economic Development

1. David Osborne, "States lead economic rebirth," *State Government News* 31:11 (November 1988), 12-14.

2. Osborne, 13-14.

3. "The States as Laboratories," *State Policy Reports* 6:11 (June 1988), 20-21.

4. Linda Wagar, "Economic development: States hone strategies," *State Government News* 31:11 (November 1988), 8

5. Wagar, 10.

6. Wagar, 11.

7. Wagar, 10.

8. Wagar, 11.

9. Joel Thompson, "North Carolina's 1988 Short Session: Missed Opportunities," *Comparative State Politics Newsletter* 9:4 (August 1988), 26.

10. Andree E. Reeves, "Controversies & Accomplishments of the 1988 Maryland General Assembly," *Comparative State Politics Newsletter* 9:4 (August 1988), 30.

Corrections

1. Keon S. Chi, "Prison Overcrowding and Privatization: Models and Opportunities," *The Journal of State Government* 62:2 (March/April 1989), 70.

2. Chi, 70-72.

3. Thomas H. Handy, "Mississippi Focuses on Education & Economic Development," *Comparative State Politics Newsletter* 9:4 (August 1988), 23.

4. "Election '88: State-by-State: California," *USA/TODAY* (November 10, 1988), 8A.

Environment

1. Brenda L. Wilson, "Toothless Watchdog Commission Quits," *Governing* 3:7 (April 1990), 13-14.

Higher Education.

1. Reeves, 29-30.

2. Thomas H. Ferrell, "Federal Court Orders Restructuring of Higher Education in Louisiana," *Comparative State Politics Newsletter* 10:4 (August 1989), 8-9. See also "Higher Education Segregation," *State Policy Report* 6:17 (September 1988), 23-24.

Managerial Techniques

1. See especially the July/August, 1989 issue of *The Journal of State Government* for different perspectives on this subject.

2. Joseph Fisher, "Formal Mechanisms: Helping the Governor to Manage," ibid., 131.

Sunset

1. Arkansas, Mississippi, Nebraska, New Hampshire, North Carolina, Wyoming.

2. Connecticut, Illinois, Montana, Nevada, Rhode Island, South Dakota.

3. Richard C. Kearney, "Sunset: A Survey and Analysis of the State Experience," *Public Administration Review* 50:1 (January/February 1990), 55.

4. Kearney, 52-53.

5. "Sunset Legislation in Oklahoma," *State Policy Reports* 6:10 (May 1988), 24.

Productivity

1. Fara Croson, "State Awards Programs Recognize Innovative Ideas from Employees," *Governors' Weekly Bulletin* 23:17 (April 28, 1989), 3-4; and "Productivity," *Governors' Weekly Bulletin* 23:18 (May 5, 1989), 4.

Planning

1. Harry Hatry, *Program Analysis for State and Local Governments* (Washington, DC: Urban Institute, 1988), reviewed in *State Policy Reports* 6:16 (August 1988), 29-30.

2. "Scanning Network", *Governors' Weekly Bulletin* 22:10 (March 4, 1988), 4.

State Agency Heads

1. Data provided by Deil S. Wright. For the comparison between the 1964 and 1984 re-

sults, see Peter J. Haas and Deil S. Wright, "Research Update: The Changing Profile of State Administrators," *The Journal of State Government* 60:6 (November/December 1987), 270-278.

Ethics

1. Joseph F. Zimmerman, "Commission Calls for Tougher Ethics Reform laws for New York," *Comparative State Politics Newsletter* 10:1 (February 1989), 24-25. See also Zimmerman, "Government Integrity in New York," *Comparative State Politics Newsletter* 9:1 (February 1988), 14-16.

2. Fran Burke and George Benson, "Written Rules: State Ethics Codes, Commissions and Conflicts," *The Journal of State Government* 62:5 (September/October 1989), 198.

3. Elaine S. Knapp, "Voters like lotteries, reject tax cuts," *State Government News* 31:12 (December 1988), 27. See also, Jonathan Walters, "In Arkansas, A New Twist On Use of Initiatives," *Governing* 2:2 (November 1988), 72.

4. Casey Hamilton and K.C. Moon, "Oklahoma 1988 Session Highlights," *Comparative State Politics Newsletter* 10:1 (February 1989), 7.

5. "In Briefs: West Virginia," *Comparative State Politics Newsletter* 10:2 (April 1989), 47.

6. "West Virginia Woes," *State Policy Reports* 7:17 (September 1989), 30.

7. LaDonna Sloan, "In Briefs: West Virginia," *Comparative State Politics Newsletter* 10:6 (December 1989), 37.

8. "West Virginia Setbacks," *State Policy Reports* 7:18 (September 1989) 23-24.

9. AP wire story, "Former governor of West Virginia to plead guilty," (Raleigh) *News and Observer* (April 13, 1990), 8A.

10. "West Virginia Problems," *State Policy Reports* 8:8 (April 1990), 24

11. Janice L. Davis, "In Briefs: Tennessee," *Comparative State Politics Newsletter* 11:1 (February 1990), 34.

12. Cheri Collis, "State inspectors general: The watchdog over state agencies," *State Government News* 33:4 (April 1990), 13.

EXECUTIVE BRANCH

Table 2.9
CONSTITUTIONAL AND STATUTORY PROVISIONS FOR LENGTH AND NUMBER OF TERMS OF ELECTED STATE OFFICIALS

State or other jurisdiction	Governor	Lt. governor	Secretary of state	Attorney general	Treasurer	Auditor	Comptroller	Education	Agriculture	Labor	Insurance	Other
Alabama	4/2	4/2	4/2	4/2	4/2	4/2	...	...	4/2 (a)	...	...	Bd. of Education—4/-; Public Service Comm.—4/-
Alaska	4/2 (b)	4/2	(c)	...	...	...	...	...	...	...	...	
Arizona	4/-	(d)	4/-	4/-	4/2	...	...	4/-	...	...	...	Corporation Comm.—6/-; Mine inspector—2/-
Arkansas	4/-	4/-	4/-	4/-	4/-	4/-	(e)	...	...	...	...	Land Cmsr.—4/-
California	4/-	4/-	4/-	4/-	4/-	...	4/-	4/-	...	...	...	Bd. of Equalization—4/-
Colorado	4/-	4/-	4/-	4/-	4/-	...	...	...	...	...	...	Regents of Univ. of Colo.—6/-; Bd. of Education—6/-
Connecticut	4/-	4/-	4/-	4/-	4/-	...	4/-	...	...	...	...	
Delaware	4/2 (f)	4/-	...	4/-	4/-	4/-	...	...	...	...	4/-	
Florida	4/2	4/-	4/-	4/-	4/-	...	4/-	4/-	4/-	...	(g)	
Georgia	4/2	4/-	4/-	4/-	...	...	4/-	4/-	4/-	4/-	(h)	Public Service Comm.—6/-
Hawaii	4/2	4/2	(c)	...	...	...	...	...	...	...	...	Bd. of Education—4/U
Idaho	4/-	4/-	4/-	4/-	4/-	4/-	(i)	4/-	...	...	...	
Illinois	4/-	4/-	4/-	4/-	4/-	...	4/-	...	...	...	...	Bd. of Trustees, Univ. of Ill.—6/-
Indiana	4/2 (j)	4/-	4/2 (j)	4/-	4/2 (j)	4/2 (j)	(i)	4/-	(c)	...	...	
Iowa	4/U	4/U	4/U	4/U	4/U	4/U	...	...	4/U	...	...	
Kansas	4/2	4/2	4/-	4/-	4/-	4/-	...	...	...	...	4/-	Bd. of Education—4/-
Kentucky	4/0	4/0	4/0	4/0	4/0	4/0	(e)	4/0	4/0	...	...	Railroad Comm.—4/-
Louisiana	4/2	4/-	4/-	4/-	4/-	4/-	...	(k)	...	4/-	...	Bd. of Education—4/-; Public Service Comm.—6/-; Elections Cmsr.—4/-
Maine	4/2	(l)	...	...	...	...	...	...	...	...	...	
Maryland	4/2 (b)	4/-	...	4/U	...	...	4/-	...	...	...	...	
Massachusetts	4/-	4/-	4/-	4/-	4/-	4/-	...	...	...	...	...	Exec. Council—2/-
Michigan	4/-	4/-	4/-	4/-	...	...	(m)	...	...	...	...	Univ. Regents—8/-; Bd. of Education—8/-
Minnesota	4/-	4/-	4/-	4/-	4/-	4/-	...	...	...	...	...	
Mississippi	4/1	4/-	4/-	4/1	4/-	4/-	(i)	...	4/-	...	4/-	Public Service Comm.—4/-; Highway Comm.—4/-
Missouri	4/2 (f)	4/-	4/-	4/-	4/-	4/2 (f)	4/U	...	...	...	...	
Montana	4/-	4/-	4/-	4/-	...	4/-	...	4/-	...	...	(i)	Public Service Comm.—4/-
Nebraska	4/2 (b)	4/-	4/-	4/-	4/2 (n)	4/-	...	...	...	...	...	Regents of Univ. of Neb.—6/-; Bd. of Education—4/-; Public Service Comm.—6/-
Nevada	4/2	4/-	4/-	4/-	4/-	...	4/-	...	...	...	...	Bd. of Regents—6/-; Bd. of Education—4/3
New Hampshire	2/-	(l)	...	...	...	...	...	...	...	...	...	Exec. Council—2/-
New Jersey	4/2	(l)	...	...	...	...	...	...	...	...	...	
New Mexico	4/1 (o)	4/1 (o)	4/1 (o)	4/1 (o)	4/1 (o)	4/1 (o)	...	...	...	...	...	Cmsr. of Public Lands—4/1(o); Bd. of Education—6/-; Corporation Comm.—6/-
New York	4/-	4/-	...	4/-	...	(p)	4/-	...	...	...	...	
North Carolina	4/2 (f)	4/2 (f)	4/-	4/-	4/-	4/-	(q)	4/-	4/-	4/-	4/-	
North Dakota	4/-	4/-	4/-	4/-	4/2	4/-	...	4/-	4/- (r)	4/- (r)	4/-	Public Service Comm.—6/-; Tax Cmsr.—4/-
Ohio	4/2	4/-	4/-	4/-	4/-	4/-	(m)	...	...	...	...	Bd. of Education—6/-
Oklahoma	4/2	4/U	...	4/U	4/U	4/U	...	4/U	...	...	4/-	Corporation Comm.—6/-
Oregon	4/2 (j)	(d)	4/2 (j)	4/-	4/2 (j)	(s)	...	4/-	...	4/-	...	
Pennsylvania	4/2	4/2	(d)	4/2	4/2 (t)	4/2	...	...	...	...	...	
Rhode Island	2/-	2/-	2/-	2/-	2/-	...	...	...	...	...	...	
South Carolina	4/2	4/-	4/-	4/-	4/-	...	4/-	4/-	4/-	...	...	Adjutant General—4/-

EXECUTIVE BRANCH

LENGTH AND NUMBER OF TERMS—Continued

State or other jurisdiction	Governor	Lt. governor	Secretary of state	Attorney general	Treasurer	Auditor	Comptroller	Education	Agriculture	Labor	Insurance	Other
South Dakota	4/2	4/2	4/-	4/-	4/-	4/-	(i)	...	...	...	...	Cmsr. of School & Public Lands—4/-; Public Utilities Comm.—6/-
Tennessee	4/2	(l)	...	...	...	(p)	...	...	...	...	...	Public Service Comm.—6/-
Texas	4/-	4/-	...	4/-	4/-	...	4/-	...	4/-	...	...	Cmsr. of General Land Off.—6/-; Railroad Comm.—6/-
Utah	4/-	4/-	(c)	4/-	4/-	4/-	...	...	...	...	...	Bd. of Education—4/-
Vermont	2/-	2/-	2/-	2/-	2/-	2/-	...	...	...	...	...	
Virginia	4/0	4/U	...	4/U	...	...	...	...	...	...	...	
Washington	4/-	4/-	4/-	4/-	4/-	4/-	(m)	4/-	...	...	4/-	Cmsr. of Public Lands—4/-
West Virginia	4/2	(l)	4/-	4/-	4/-	4/-	(i)	...	4/-	...	...	
Wisconsin	4/-	4/-	4/-	4/-	4/-	...	(e)	4/-	...	...	...	
Wyoming	4/-	(d)	4/-	...	4/-	4/-	...	4/-	...	...	...	
Dist. of Columbia	4/U (u)	...	...	...	...	...	...	...	...	...	...	Chmn. of Council of Dist. of Col.—4/U
American Samoa	4/2	4/2	(c)	...	...	(m)	...	...	...	...	...	
Guam	4/2(b)	4/-	(c)	...	...	...	...	...	...	...	(v)	Bd. of Education—4/-; Village Cmsr.—4/U
No. Mariana Islands	4/3	4/-	...	...	...	...	(e)	...	(w)	...	...	
Puerto Rico	4/-	(d)	...	...	...	...	...	...	...	...	...	
U.S. Virgin Islands	4/2 (b)	4/-	(c)	...	(e)	...	...	...	...	...	(c)	

Note: First entry in a column refers to number of years per term. Entry following the slash refers to the maximum number of consecutive terms allowed. This table reflects a literal reading of the state constitutions and statutes. Blank cells indicate no specific administrative official performs function.

Key:
- — No provision specifying number of terms allowed
0 — Provision specifying officeholder may not succeed self
U — Provision specifying individual may hold office for an unlimited number of terms
... — Position is appointed or elected by governmental entity (not chosen by electorate)
(a) Commissioner of agriculture and industries.
(b) After two consecutive terms, must wait four years before being eligible again.
(c) Lieutenant governor performs function.
(d) Secretary of state is next in line of succession to the governorship.
(e) Finance administrator performs function.
(f) Absolute two-term limitation, but not necessarily consecutive.
(g) State treasurer also serves as insurance commissioner.
(h) Comptroller general is ex-officio insurance commissioner.
(i) State auditor performs function.
(j) Eligible for eight out of 12 years.
(k) Head of administration performs function.
(l) President of the senate is next in line of succession to the governorship. In Tennessee, speaker of the senate has the statutory title "lieutenant governor."
(m) State treasurer performs function.
(n) After two consecutive terms, must wait two years before being eligible again.
(o) Limited to two consecutive 4-year terms.
(p) Comptroller performs function.
(q) Budget administrator performs function.
(r) Constitution provides for a secretary of agriculture and labor. However, the legislature was given constitutional authority to provide for (and has provided for) a department of labor distinct from agriculture, and a commissioner of labor distinct from the commissioner of agriculture.
(s) Secretary of state's office performs function.
(t) Treasurer must wait four years before being eligible to the office of auditor general.
(u) Mayor.
(v) Taxation administrator performs function.
(w) Natural resources administrator performs function.

EXECUTIVE BRANCH

Table 2.10
SELECTED STATE ADMINISTRATIVE OFFICIALS: METHODS OF SELECTION

State	Governor	Lieutenant governor	Secretary of state	Attorney general	Treasurer	Adjutant general	Administration	Agriculture	Banking	Budget
Alabama	CE	CE	CE	CE	CE	G	...	CE	GS	N.A.
Alaska	CE	CE	...	GB	A	GB	GB	A	A	A
Arizona	CE	...	CE	CE	CE	G	GS	GS	GS	A
Arkansas	CE	CE	CE	CE	CE	G	G	G	G	AG
California	CE	CE	CE	CE	CE	GS	...	GS	GS	(a-9)
Colorado	CE	CE	CE	CE	CE	GS	GS	GD	CS	GS
Connecticut	CE	CE	CE	CE	CE	GE	GE	GE	GE	CS
Delaware	CE	CE	GS	CE	CE	GS	GS	GS	G	GS
Florida	CE	CE	CE	CE	CE	GS	GS	CE	(a-13)	GS
Georgia	CE	CE	CE	CE	A	G	GS	CE	GS	G
Hawaii	CE	CE	CE	GS	GS	GS	G	G	AG	GS
Idaho	CE	CE	CE	CE	CE	GS	GS	GS	GS	AG
Illinois	CE	CE	CE	CE	CE	GS	GS	GS	GS	GS
Indiana	CE	CE	CE	CE	CE	G	G	A	G	G
Iowa	CE	CE	CE	CE	CE	GS	GS	CE	GS	GS
Kansas	CE	CE	CE	CE	SE	GS	GS	BS	GS	G
Kentucky	CE	CE	CE	CE	CE	G	G	CE	G	G
Louisiana	CE	CE	CE	CE	CE	GS	GS	CE	GS	CS
Maine (b)	CE	...	CL	CL	CL	G	G	GLS	GLS	AG
Maryland	CE	CE	GS	CE	CL	G	GS	GS	AG	GS
Massachusetts	CE	CE	CE	CE	CE	G	G	G	G	G
Michigan	CE	CE	CE	CE	GS	GS	GS	B	GS	GS
Minnesota	CE	CE	CE	CE	CE	G	GS	GS	A	GS
Mississippi	CE	CE	CE	CE	CE	GS	N.A.	CE	GS	GS
Missouri	CE	CE	CE	CE	CE	GS	GS	GS	AS	A
Montana	CE	CE	CE	CE	A	GS	GS	GS	A	G
Nebraska	CE	CE	CE	CE	CE	GE	GE	GE	GE	GE
Nevada	CE	CE	CE	CE	CE	G	G	BG	AG	(a-6)
New Hampshire	CE	...	CL	GC	CL	GC	GC	GC	GC	AGC
New Jersey	CE	...	GS	GS	GS	GS	AGC	BG	GS	GS
New Mexico	SE	SE	SE	SE	SE	SE	GS	GS	A	A
New York	CE	CE	GS	CE	(m)	G	GS	GS	GS	G
North Carolina	CE	CE	SE	SE	SE	G	G	SE	G	G
North Dakota	CE	CE	CE	CE	CE	G	(a-33)	CE	GS	(ii)
Ohio	CE	CE	CE	CE	CE	G	GS	GS	A	G
Oklahoma	CE	CE	GS	CE	CE	GS	GS	B	GD/GS	GS
Oregon	CE	...	CE	SE	CE	G	GS	GS	A	AG
Pennsylvania	CE	CE	GS	CE	CE	GS	GS	GS	GS	G
Rhode Island	CE	CE	CE	CE	CE	G	GS	CS	CS	CS
South Carolina	CE	CE	CE	CE	CE	CE	B	CE	(a-4)	B
South Dakota	CE	CE	CE	CE	CE	GS	GS	GS	A	A
Tennessee	CE	(w)	CL	CT	CL	G	G	G	G	A
Texas	CE	CL	GS	CE	CE	GS	B	SE	BS	G
Utah	SE	SE	SE	SE	SE	GS	GS	GS	GS	G
Vermont	CE	CE	CE	CE	CE	SL	GS	GS	GS	AGS
Virginia	CE	CE	GB	CE	GB	GB	GB	GB	B	GB
Washington	CE	CE	CE	CE	CE	G	G	G	CS	G
West Virginia	CE	...	CE	CE	CE	GS	GS	CE	GS	CS
Wisconsin	CE	CE	CE	CE	CE	GS	GS	B	GS	A
Wyoming	SE	...	SE	G	SE	G	G	B	GS	AG

Note: The chief administrative officials responsible for each function were determined from information given by the states for the same function as listed in *State Administrative Officials Classified by Function 1989-90*, published by The Council of State Governments.

Key:
N.A. — Not available
... — No specific chief administrative official or agency in charge of function
CE — Constitutional, elected by public
CL — Constitutional, elected by legislature
SE — Statutory, elected by public
SL — Statutory, elected by legislature
L — Selected by legislature or one of its organs
CT — Constitutional, elected by state Supreme Court

Appointed by:
G — Governor
GS — Governor
GG — Governor
GB — Governor
GE — Governor
GC — Governor
GD — Governor
GLS — Governor

Approved by:
Senate
General Assembly
Both houses
Either house
Council
Departmental board
Appropriate legislative committe & Senate

GOC — Governor & Council or cabinet
LG — Lieutenant governor
AT — Attorny general
SS — Secretary of state

Appointed by:
A — Agency head
AB — Agency head
AG — Agency head
AGC — Agency head
AS — Agency head
AGS — Agency head
ASH — Agency head
B — Board or commission
BG — Board
BGC — Board
BGS — Board
BS — Board or commission
BA — Board or commission
CS — Civil Service
ACB — Nominated by audit committee

Approved by:
Board
Governor
Governor & Council
Senate
Governor & Senate
Senate president & House speaker
Governor
Governor & Council
Governor & Senate
Senate
Agency head
Both houses

EXECUTIVE BRANCH

SELECTED OFFICIALS: METHODS OF SELECTION—Continued

State	Civil rights	Commerce	Community affairs	Comptroller	Computer services	Consumer affairs	Corrections	Economic development	Education	Election administration
Alabama	...	G	G	N.A.	N.A.	N.A.	B	(a-12)	B	N.A.
Alaska	A	GB	GB	A	A	A	GB	GB	GB	A
Arizona	A	GS	...	...	A	A	GS	GS	CE	(a-2)
Arkansas	N.A.	...	G	G	G	(a-3)	G	G	G	CE
California	GS	GS	G	CE	G	GS	GS	(a-11)	CE	A
Colorado	CS	GE	CS	CS	CS	AS	GS	G	GS	A
Connecticut	B	GE	A	CE	A	GE	GE	GE	B	CS
Delaware	G	(a-2)	GS	AG	A	AG	GS	GS	B	GS
Florida	A	GS	GS	CE	G	A	GS	A	CE	A
Georgia	G	B	B	CE	A	G	B	B	CE	A
Hawaii	...	GS	...	GS	CS	G	GS	GS	B	CE
Idaho	B	GS	A	CE	(a-6)	(a-3)	GS	(a-11)	CE	A
Illinois	GS	GS	(a-11)	CE	(a-6)	(a-3)	GS	(a-11)	GS	GS
Indiana	G	CE	A	CE	G	A	G	A	CE	A
Iowa	GS	GS	A	GS	CS	A	GS	GS	GS	(a-2)
Kansas	BG	GS	A	A	A	AT	GS	(a-11)	B	SS
Kentucky	G	G	G	G	(a-13)	(a-3)	G	(a-11)	CE	B
Louisiana	(a-3)	(a-16)	CS	(a-6)	CS	...	GS	GS	B	CE
Maine (b)	B	GS	BG	BG	BG	GLS	AG	(a-11)	GLS	(a-2)
Maryland	(f)	AG	A	CE	A	A	AGS	(a-11)	B	G
Massachusetts	G	(a-16)	G	G	G	G	G	G	G	SS
Michigan	B	GS	CS	CS	CS	CS	B	CS	B	(a-2)
Minnesota	GS	GS	A	(a-9)	A	AT	GS	A	GS	S
Mississippi	N.A.	(a-16)	A	(a-9)	B	AT	GS	GS	BS	SS
Missouri	B	(a-16)	(a-16)	A	A	N.A.	GS	GS	B	SS
Montana	B	GS	A	(a-6)	A	A	GS	A	CE	A
Nebraska	BS	(a-16)	A	A	A	A	GE	GE	(k)	(a-2)
Nevada	G	G	G	CE	G	AG	G	G	B	(a-2)
New Hampshire	CS	AGC	(a-34)	AGC	AGC	(a-3)	GC	AGC	BGC	(a-2)
New Jersey	GOC	GS	GS	(a-9)	A	GS	GS	A	GS	(ee)
New Mexico	G	(a-16)	GS	(a-4)	A	AT	GS	GS	B	SS
New York	G	GS	(a-2)	(a-4)	(a-6)	GS	GS	(a-11)	B	B
North Carolina	AG	G	AG	GG	AG	A	G	AG	SE	G
North Dakota	(a-29)	(a-16)	A	(ii)	A	AT	GS	G	CE	(a-2)
Ohio	GS	(n)	A	(a-4)	A	B	B	A	B	SS
Oklahoma	B	GS	(a-11)	A	A	B	B	(a-11)	CE	G
Oregon	A	(a-28)	G	CE	AG	...	GS	A	CE	A
Pennsylvania	G	GS	GS	A	G	A	GS	(a-11)	G	A
Rhode Island	BG	(a-16)	...	CS	CS	GB	GS	GS	BGC	GS
South Carolina	B	(a-16)	G	CE	B	B	B	B	CE	BG
South Dakota	A	GS	(a-16)	CE	G	A	AG	GS	(oo)	(a-2)
Tennessee	B	G	(a-11)	CL	A	A	G	(a-11)	G	SS
Texas	B	B	GS	CE	B	AT	B	(a-11)	B	SS
Utah	B	GS	(q)	AG	AG	AG	GS	AG	B	SE
Vermont	AT	AG	AG	(a-9)	CS	AT	AG	AG	BG	(qq)
Virginia	...	GB	A	GB	GB	A	GB	GB	GB	GB
Washington	B	G	G	(a-4)	A	A	G	(a-11)	CE	CS
West Virginia	GS	(x)	G	CE	CS	AT	GS	G	B	(a-2)
Wisconsin	A	GS	A	CS	CS	(t)	GS	CS	CE	B
Wyoming	AG	G	(a-16)	SE	AG	AT	B	GS	SE	(vv)

(a) Chief administrative official or agency in charge of function:
(a-1) Lieutenant governor
(a-2) Secretary of state
(a-3) Attorney general
(a-4) Treasurer
(a-5) Adjutant general
(a-6) Administration
(a-7) Agriculture
(a-8) Banking
(a-9) Budget
(a-10) Civil rights
(a-11) Commerce
(a-12) Community affairs
(a-13) Comptroller
(a-14) Computer services
(a-15) Consumer affairs
(a-16) Economic development
(a-17) Education (chief state school officer)
(a-18) Emergency management
(a-19) Employment services
(a-20) Energy resources
(a-21) Environmental protection
(a-22) Finance
(a-23) Fish and wildlife
(a-24) General services
(a-25) Health
(a-26) Highways
(a-27) Historic preservation
(a-28) Insurance
(a-29) Labor
(a-30) Mental health and retardation
(a-31) Natural resources
(a-32) Parks and recreation
(a-33) Personnel
(a-34) Planning
(a-35) Post audit
(a-36) Public utility regulation
(a-37) Public welfare
(a-38) Purchasing
(a-39) Revenue
(a-40) Social services
(a-41) Solid waste management
(a-42) Transportation
(b) Information based on Council of State Governments survey (1988).
(c) Responsibilities shared between Assistant Secretary, Office of Mental Retardation, Health & Human Resources Department and Assistant Secretary, Department of Health & Hospitals.
(d) Responsibilities shared between Commissioner, Division of Administration and Legislative Auditor, Office of Legislative Auditor.

EXECUTIVE BRANCH

SELECTED OFFICIALS: METHODS OF SELECTION—Continued

State	Emergency management	Employment services	Energy resources	Environmental protection	Finance	Fish & wildlife	General services	Health	Higher education	Highways
Alabama	G	AG	AG	B	G	(a-31)	N.A.	B	B	G
Alaska	A	A	...	GB	A	GB	A	GB	GB	(a-42)
Arizona	A	A	A	GS	A	B	A	GS	...	A
Arkansas	G	G	A	G	G	BG	G	G	G	B
California	GS	GS	GS	GS	GS	GS	GS	GS	B	GS
Colorado	CS	GS	CS	CS	(a-13)	CS	GS	GS	GS	GS
Connecticut	A	A	A	GE	GE	GS	(a-6)	GE	B	A
Delaware	AG	(a-29)	A	GS	GS	AG	(a-6)	AG	B	AG
Florida	A	A	G	GS	A	B	GOC	A	B	(a-42)
Georgia	G	A	G	BG	A	A	(a-6)	A	B	(a-42)
Hawaii	GS	CS	CS	GS	(a-9)	CS	(a-13)	GS	B	CS
Idaho	A	GS	A	A	(a-9)	GS	A	GS	B	(a-42)
Illinois	GS	GS	(a-31)	GS	(a-39)	GS	(a-6)	GS	GS	(a-42)
Indiana	G	G	A	G	(a-9)	A	(a-6)	G	N.A.	G
Iowa	GS	GS	CS	CS	(a-13)	CS	(a-6)	GS	B	A
Kansas	A	(a-29)	GS	A	(a-9)	(a-32)	(a-6)	GS	B	(a-42)
Kentucky	AG	AG	(a-31)	(a-31)	(a-13)	AG	(a-13)	AG	G	AG
Louisiana	GS	GS	GS	GS	(a-6)	GS	(a-6)	A	B	GS
Maine (b)	AG	GLS	G	GLS	GLS	GLS	(a-22)	A	GLS	GLS
Maryland	AG	AG	A	GS	(a-13)	A	GS	GS	G	A
Massachusetts	G	G	G	G	(a-6)	G	G	G	G	G
Michigan	CS	CS	N.A.	CS	(a-9)	(a-31)	CS	GS	CS	(a-42)
Minnesota	CS	A	A	A	(i)	CS	(a-6)	GS	B	A
Mississippi	GS	GD	(a-42)	A	N.A.	A	(a-9)	B	B	B
Missouri	A	A	A	A	(j)	B	A	GS	B	(a-42)
Montana	A	A	A	A	(a-9)	A	N.A.	A	B	GS
Nebraska	(a-5)	A	GE	GE	(l)	(a-32)	(a-6)	GE	BS	(a-42)
Nevada	G	G	G	A	(a-13)	G	GS	G	B	(a-42)
New Hampshire	G	GC	G	GC	(a-6)	BGC	AGC	AGC	BGC	(a-42)
New Jersey	A	AGC	GS	GS	(a-4)	BG	(a-6)	GS	BG	(a-42)
New Mexico	GS	GS	GS	A	GS	B	GS	A	GS	GS
New York	GS	GS	GS	GS	(a-4)	(a-21)	(a-6)	(a-18)	(a-17)	GS
North Carolina	AG	G	AG	(a-31)	(a-9)	BG	AG	AG	B	AG
North Dakota	A	G	A	A	(a-9)	G	(a-9)	G	B	G
Ohio	AG	GS	GS	GS	(a-9)	A	(a-6)	GS	BG	(a-42)
Oklahoma	(a-5)	(a-33)	A	B	(a-9)	B	(a-6)	B	B	(a-42)
Oregon	AG	AG	GS	B	(a-9)	B	GS	AG	B	A
Pennsylvania	G	A	LG	GS	(a-39)	(mm)	GS	GS	B	A
Rhode Island	(a-5)	GS	(a-36)	GS	(a-9)	CS	CS	GS	BGC	(a-42)
South Carolina	A	B	G	A	(a-6)	B	B	B	B	(a-42)
South Dakota	A	A	A	A	(a-9)	G	(a-6)	GS	B	A
Tennessee	A	G	G	A	(a-6)	B	G	G	B	(a-42)
Texas	G	B	B	A	(a-13)	B	(a-6)	B	B	B
Utah	AG	B	AG	AG	(a-13)	AG	(a-6)	GS	B	(a-42)
Vermont	A	GS	GS	AG	(a-9)	AG	AGS	AG	CS	GS
Virginia	GB	GB	A	GB	GB	B	GB	GB	GB	GB
Washington	A	A	G	G	(a-9)	(rr)	(a-6)	G	B	(a-42)
West Virginia	G	GS	(y)	(z)	(a-6)	CS	CS	(uu)	GS	GS
Wisconsin	GS	A	A	A	A	CS	A	A	B	A
Wyoming	AG	A	A	G	(a-13)	B	(a-6)	G	GS	(a-42)

(e) Responsibilities shared between Commissioner, Division of Administration and State Director of Purchasing, same office.
(f) Appointed by Governor from list of five names submitted by the commissioners. Position is subject to removal by the Governor upon the recommendation of 2/3 of the commissioners.
(g) Responsibilities shared between Director, Developmental Disabilities Administration, Department of Health & Mental Hygiene and Assistant Secretary, Mental Health-Addictions, Developmental Disabilities.
(h) Responsibilities shared between Commissioner of Revenue, Bureau of Revenue, Department of Treasury and Director, Local Finance Programs, same department.
(i) Responsibilities shared between Commissioner, Pollution Control Agency and Executive Director, Environmental Quality Board.
(j) Functions are covered by several different departments including Department of Revenue, Office of Administration and State Treasurer.
(k) Responsibilities shared between Commissioner, Department of Education and President, State Board of Education.
(l) Responsibilities shared between Budget Administrator, Budget Division Administrative Services Department, Auditor of Public Accounts and State Tax Commissioner, Department of Revenue.
(m) Responsibilities shared between Comptroller, Office of State Comptroller and Commissioner, Department of Taxation and Finance.
(n) Responsibilities shared between Director, Department of Development and Director, Department of Commerce.
(o) Responsibilities shared between Director, Department of Mental Health and Director, Developmental Disabilities Services, Department of Human Services.
(p) Responsibilities shared between Assistant Administrator, Programs for Developmental Disabilities, Department of Human Resources and Administrator, Mental Health Division, same department.
(q) Responsibilities shared between Deputy Director, Division of Community Development, Community & Economic Development Department and Deputy Director, Division of Business & Economic Development, same department.
(r) Responsibilities shared between Commissioner, Department of Mental Retardation and Commissioner, Department of Mental Health.
(s) Responsibilities shared between Administrator, Developmental Disabilities, Department of Social Services and Secretary, Department of Human Services.
(t) Responsibilities shared between Administrator, Trade & Consumer Protection Division, Agriculture, Trade and Consumer Protection and Director, Office of Consumer Protection, Department of Justice.
(u) Responsibilities shared between Director, Division of Mental Health & Hospitals, Department of Human Services and Director, Division of Developmental Disabilities, same department.
(v) Responsibilities shared between Director, Commission on Tourism and Chairman, Gaming Control Board.
(w) Speaker of the Senate has statutory title of Lieutenant Governor, and is elected by the Senate from among its membership.

The Council of State Governments

EXECUTIVE BRANCH

SELECTED OFFICIALS: METHODS OF SELECTION—Continued

State	Historic preservation	Insurance	Labor	Licensing	Mental health & retardation	Natural resources	Parks & recreation	Personnel	Plannning	Post audit
Alabama	B	G	G	...	B	G	N.A.	B	...	L
Alaska	G	A	GB	A	A	GB	A	A	...	L
Arizona	G	GS	B	...	...	GS	B	A	GS	L
Arkansas	A	G	G	...	BG	G	G	AG	...	L
California	G	(ww)	GS	GS	GS	GS	GS	GS	G	ACB
Colorado	...	CS	CS	GS	CS	GS	CS	GS	(a-9)	L
Connecticut	BG	GE	GE	A	(r)	(a-21)	CS	A	A	L
Delaware	AG	CE	GS	AG	AG	GS	AG	GS	G	CE
Florida	A	CE	G	A	A	GOC	A	GS	(a-9)	L
Georgia	A	CE	SE	A	A	BG	A	GS	G	SL
Hawaii	G	AG	GS	GS	CS	G	CS	GS	G	CS
Idaho	B	GS	GS	A	A	...	B	B	(a-11)	L
Illinois	GS	GS	GS	GS	GS	GS	GS	A	AG	SL
Indiana	N.A.	G	G	G	G	G	A	G	A	G
Iowa	GS	GS	GS	GS	A	G	CS	GS	(a-16)	CE
Kansas	B	SE	GS	N.A.	A	(a-21)	GS	A	(a-9)	L
Kentucky	B	G	G	AG	AG	G	G	G	(a-9)	CE
Louisiana	CS	CE	GS	CS	(c)	GS	LGS	CS	CS	(d)
Maine (b)	B	A	A	BG	BG	(a-21)	B	BG	G	SL
Maryland	A	AGS	AG	GS	(g)	GS	A	GS	G	ASH
Massachusetts	SS	G	G	G	(xx)	G	A	A	(a-16)	CE
Michigan	CS	GS	GS	GS	GS	B	CS	B	N.A.	CL
Minnesota	B	GS	GS	CS	A	GS	CS	GS	GS	CE
Mississippi	B	CE	N.A.	N.A.	B	BG	A	B	A	CE
Missouri	A	AS	GS	A	B	GS	A	G	(a-6)	CE
Montana	A	A	GS	A	(yy)	GS	A	A	(a-9)	L
Nebraska	BS	GE	GE	A	(dd)	GE	BS	GE	GE	CE
Nevada	A	AG	G	N.A.	G	G	A	G	A	AB
New Hampshire	BGC	GC	GC	(a-2)	AGC	GC	AGC	AGC	G	L
New Jersey	A	GS	GS	(a-15)	(u)	A	A	GS	G	L
New Mexico	A	B	A	(ff)	(gg)	GS	A	BS	...	SE
New York	GS	GS	(a-19)	(a-2)	(hh)	(a-21)	(a-27)	GS	GS	(a-4)
North Carolina	AG	SE	SE	...	AG	G	AG	G	AG	SE
North Dakota	B	CE	SE	(a-2)	A	...	G	AB	(a-20)	(jj)
Ohio	...	GS	GS	...	(kk)	G	A	GS	(a-9)	CE
Oklahoma	B	CE	GS	...	(o)	B	(a-31)	GS	...	CE
Oregon	(ll)	GS	SE	(a-28)	(p)	G	B	AG	B	A
Pennsylvania	A	GS	GS	GS	A	(a-21)	A	A	G	CE
Rhode Island	BG	GS	GS	CS	GS	(a-21)	CS	CS	CS	(nn)
South Carolina	A	B	GS	...	(r)	G	B	B	(a-33)	B
South Dakota	GS	(a-11)	GS	A	(s)	GS	GS	GS	...	L
Tennessee	AG	G	G	A	G	G	A	G	G	(a-13)
Texas	B	BS	...	B	B	B	(a-23)	...	(a-9)	L
Utah	AG	GS	GS	AG	(zz)	GS	AG	GS	(a-9)	(pp)
Vermont	CS	GS	GS	CS	AG	GS	CS	AGS	G	CE
Virginia	GG	(a-8)	GB	GB	GB	GB	(a-27)	GB	(a-9)	GB
Washington	A	CE	G	(a-6)	A	CE	B	G	(a-9)	CE
West Virginia	(aa)	GS	GS	...	AG	(a-21)	AG	GS	(a-6)	SL
Wisconsin	CS	GS	GS	GS	CS	B	CS	GS	(a-9)	L
Wyoming	B	G	GS	A	G	AG	A	AG	G	(a-13)

(x) Responsibilities shared between Director, Division of Commerce and Secretary, Department of Commerce, Labor and Environmental Resources.
(y) Responsibilities shared between Commissioner, Oil and Gas Conservation Commission and Commissioner, Division of Energy.
(z) Responsibilities shared between Director, Environmental Health Service, Director, Division of Natural Resources, and Director, Air Pollution Control Commission.
(aa) Responsibilities shared between Administrator, Historic Preservation Unit, Division of Culture and History and Commissioner, Division of Culture and History.
(bb) Responsibilities shared between Secretary, Department of Tax and Revenue and Commissioner, State Tax Division.
(cc) Responsibilities shared between Secretary, Department of Public Safety and Superintendent, Division of Public Safety.
(dd) Responsibilities shared between Director, Medical Serivces Division, Department of Public Institutions and Director, Office of Mental Retardation, Department of Public Institutions.
(ee) Responsibilities shared between Director, Election Division and Executive Director, Election Law Enforcement Commission, Department of Law and Public Safety.
(ff) Responsibilities shared between Board Administrator, Boards and Commission, Department of Regulation and Licensing, and Superintendent, Department of Regulation and Licensing.
(gg) Responsibilities shared between Chief, Developmental Disabilities Bureau, Department of Health and Environment and Bureau Chief, Mental Health Bureau, Department of Health and Environment.
(hh) Responsibilities shared between Cmmissioner, Office of Mental Health, and Commissioner, Mental Retardation and Development Disabilities.
(ii) Responsibilities shared between Director, Office of Management and Budget and Executive Budget Analyst, Office of Management and Budget.
(jj) Responsibilities shared between State Auditor, and Legislative Budget Analyst, Fiscal Division, Legislative Council.
(kk) Responsibilities shared between Director, Department of Mental Retardation and Director, Department of Mental Health.
(ll) Responsibilities shared by Executive Director, Historical Society and Preservation Officer, Parks and Recreation Division, Department of Transportation.
(mm) Responsibilities shared between Executive Director, Game Commission and Executive Director, Fish Commission.
(nn) Responsibilities shared between Auditor General, Office of Auditor General and Director, Bureau of Audits.
(oo) Responsibilities shared between Secretary, Department of Education and State Superintendent of Education, Cultural Affairs Department, Department of Education.
(pp) Responsibilities shared between State Auditor, Office of State Auditor and Audit Manager, Office of State Auditor.
(qq) Responsibilities shared between Secretary of State and Director, Office of Secretary of State.

EXECUTIVE BRANCH

SELECTED OFFICIALS: METHODS OF SELECTION—Continued

State	Pre-audit	Public library	Public utility regulation	Public welfare	Purchasing	Revenue	Social services	Solid waste management	State police	Tourism	Transportation
Alabama	(a-13)	B	CE	B	N.A.	G	(a-37)	N.A.	A	G	N.A.
Alaska	A	A	G	A	(a-24)	A	GB	A	A	A	GB
Arizona	...	A	B	...	A	GS	A	A	GS	GS	GS
Arkansas	A	G	G	...	AG	G	A	G	G	A	B
California	CE	A	GS	GS	A	B	GS	GS	GS	G	GS
Colorado	(a-13)	GS	GS	(a-40)	CS	GS	GS	CS	CS	CS	...
Connecticut	(a-13)	B	GE	GE	A	GE	GE	CS	GE	CS	GE
Delaware	CE	AG	AG	AG	AG	AG	GS	...	AG	A	GS
Florida	A	A	L	A	A	GOC	A	A	A	A	GS
Georgia	SL	B	SE	(a-40)	A	GS	A	A	BG	A	B
Hawaii	CS	B	G	CS	CS	GS	GS	AG	...	GS	GS
Idaho	(a-13)	A	GS	A	A	GS	A	A	GS	(a-11)	GS
Illinois	(a-13)	SS	GS	GS	(a-6)	GS	GS	(a-31)	GS	(a-11)	GS
Indiana	(a-13)	G	G	G	(a-6)	G	(a-37)	A	G	A	G
Iowa	(a-39)	A	GS	CS	CS	GS	A	CS	A	A	GS
Kansas	(a-13)	GS	GS	A	A	GS	GS	(a-21)	GS	A	GS
Kentucky	(a-11)	G	G	AG	AG	G	AG	AG	G	G	G
Louisiana	(a-6)	LGS	B	GS	(e)	GS	GS	GS	AS	LGS	GS
Maine (b)	(a-13)	BG	G	A	BG	BG	(a-37)	(a-21)	AG	N.A.	(a-26)
Maryland	CS	A	GS	A	A	(a-13)	A	A	GS	A	GS
Massachusetts	(a-13)	G	G	G	G	G	G	A	G	A	G
Michigan	(a-35)	CL	GS	GS	CS	(h)	GS	CS	GS	GS	B
Minnesota	A	CS	A	CS	CS	GS	A	CS	A	CS	GS
Mississippi	(a-9)	B	B	BG	A	GS	N.A.	A	GS	A	A
Missouri	(a-13)	B	GS	A	A	GS	GS	A	GS	B	A
Montana	N.A.	B	SE	GS	A	GS	GS	A	AT	A	A
Nebraska	(a-13)	BS	B	(a-40)	A	GE	GE	(a-21)	GE	A	GE
Nevada	(a-6)	G	G	G	AG	G	G	A	AG	(v)	B
New Hampshire	AGC	AGC	GC	AGC	(a-24)	GC	GC	AGC	AGC	CS	GC
New Jersey	(a-9)	A	GS	AB	AGC	GS	GS	A	(a-18)	A	GS
New Mexico	A	A	GS	A	A	GS	A	A	GS	A	G
New York	(a-4)	(a-17)	GS	GS	(a-6)	GS	(a-37)	(a-21)	GS	GS	(a-26)
North Carolina	...	AG	AG	G	AG	G	AG	AG	G	AG	G
North Dakota	(a-9)	A	CE	G	A	CE	G	A	G	A	...
Ohio	(a-35)	B	GS	GS	A	G	(a-37)	GS	AG	G	GS
Oklahoma	(a-9)	B	B	B	A	GS	B	A	B	(a-31)	B
Oregon	...	B	GS	AG	A	GS	GS	(a-21)	GS	A	BS
Pennsylvania	(a-4)	...	CB	GS	A	(a-39)	A	A	GS	(a-11)	GS
Rhode Island	CS	GS	GS	CS	CS	CS	GS	B	G	A	GS
South Carolina	(a-13)	B	GS	(a-40)	B	GS	B	A	A	A	B
South Dakota	...	B	SE	AG	A	GS	GS	(a-21)	AG	A	GS
Tennessee	A	SS	CE	G	A	G	A	A	G	G	G
Texas	(a-13)	B	(a-20)	B	(a-6)	(a-13)	(a-37)	A	B	A	(a-26)
Utah	(a-13)	AG	AG	AG	AG	GS	GS	AG	AG	AG	GS
Vermont	(a-9)	GD	GS	AG	CS	AGS	CS	CS	A	CS	GS
Virginia	(a-13)	GB	(a-8)	GB	A	G	GB	A	GB	A	GB
Washington	...	(ss)	G	(tt)	A	G	(a-37)	CS	G	G	G
West Virginia	(a-6)	B	G	GS	CS	(bb)	CS	CS	(cc)	AG	GS
Wisconsin	CS	CS	GS	A	CS	GS	GS	CS	A	A	GS
Wyoming	(a-13)	B	GS	G	AG	GS	G	A	B	B	B

(rr) Responsibilities shared between Director, Department of Fisheries and Director, Department of Wildlife.
(ss) Responsibilities shared between State Librarian, State Library and Serials Manager, State Library.
(tt) Responsibilities shared between Secretary, Department of Social and Health Services, and Director, Income Assistance Services, Department of Social and Health Services
(uu) Responsibilities shared between Secretary, Health and Human Resources and Director, Division of Health
(vv) Responsibilities shared between Secretary of State and Elections Assistant, Office of Secretary of State.
(ww) Effective November 1990 will be SE.
(xx) Responsibilities shared between Commission, Department of Mental Health and Commissioner, Department of Mental Retardation.
(yy) Responsibilities shared between Administrator, Mental Health Division, Department of Institutions and Administrator, Developmental Disabilities Division, Social and Rehabilitation Services Department.
(zz) Responsibilities shared between Director, Division of Mental Health, Department of Social Services and Director, Services to the Handicapped Division, Department of Social Services.

EXECUTIVE BRANCH

Table 2.11
SELECTED STATE ADMINISTRATIVE OFFICIALS: ANNUAL SALARIES

State	Governor	Lieutenant governor	Secretary of state	Attorney general	Treasurer	Adjutant general	Administration	Agriculture	Banking	Budget
Alabama	70,223	43,860	36,234	77,420	49,500	56,812	...	49,156	56,812	88,504
Alaska	81,648	66,816 (d)	66,816 (d)	66,816 (d)	66,816 (d)	66,816 (d)	66,816 (d)	65,508 (d)	62,508 (d)	62,508 (d)
Arizona	75,000	...	50,000	70,000	50,000	46,606 (d)	61,362 (d)	46,606 (d)	46,606 (d)	46,606 (d)
Arkansas	35,000	14,000	22,500	46,785	22,500	50,864	71,905	48,405	64,061	49,199
California	85,000	72,500	72,500	77,500	72,500	79,399 (d)	...	101,343	95,052	(a-22)
Colorado	70,000	48,500	48,500	60,000	48,500	75,583	72,624	58,464	58,464	77,813
Connecticut	78,000	55,000	50,000	60,000	50,000	59,789 (d)	78,732 (d)	59,789 (d)	67,639 (d)	72,819 (d)
Delaware	80,000	35,100	69,900	81,400	63,000	60,400	65,600	60,400	68,300	76,100
Florida	100,883	91,301	52,762	91,301	91,301	78,192	84,925	91,301	(a-13)	73,547
Georgia	88,872	57,702	71,184	72,824	67,164	75,474	69,001	71,186	69,003	78,984
Hawaii	94,780	90,041	90,041	85,302	85,302	88,107	90,041	85,302	67,716	85,302
Idaho	55,000	15,000	45,000	48,000	45,000	65,000	58,947	58,947	58,947	58,947
Illinois	93,266	65,835	82,294	82,294	71,321	40,598	68,578	65,835	68,250	81,500
Indiana	77,194	63,986	45,994	59,202	45,994	57,018	67,990	41,834	61,204	65,000
Iowa	72,500	25,100	55,700	69,600	55,700	59,800	52,700 (d)	55,700	42,600 (d)	56,400 (d)
Kansas	73,137	20,688	56,400	65,345	56,816	58,850	73,323	60,000	49,307	66,908
Kentucky	69,731	59,263	59,263	59,263	59,263	64,260	69,594	59,263	52,500	64,260
Louisiana	66,096	63,367	60,169	66,566	60,169	78,749	66,492	60,164	73,000	48,732
Maine (c)	70,000	...	47,154	56,366	44,926	39,613	51,739	49,404	48,761	50,346
Maryland	85,000	72,500	45,000	72,500	72,500	70,092 (d)	81,756 (d)	81,756 (d)	60,093 (d)	95,360 (d)
Massachusetts	75,000	60,000	60,000	65,000	60,000	78,200	80,000	58,000	63,000	77,500
Michigan	106,690	80,300	89,000	89,000	80,300	72,500	80,300	80,300	65,000	80,300
Minnesota	103,860	57,125	57,125	81,138	54,042	66,607	67,500	67,500	64,039	78,500
Mississippi	75,600	40,800	54,000	61,200	54,000	50,400	...	54,000	49,200	56,791 (d)
Missouri	88,541	53,277	70,909	76,786	70,909	59,016	76,786	67,970	57,945	64,299
Montana	51,713	37,098	35,031	47,166	30,561	51,763	48,500	51,763	39,541	51,763
Nebraska	58,000	40,000	40,000	57,500	35,000	46,519	50,500	59,613	66,351	54,612
Nevada	70,857	12,500	50,500	62,500	49,000	54,794	62,009	48,584	48,310	(a-6)
New Hampshire	75,753	...	60,410	67,625	60,410	64,029	67,625	50,499	64,029	60,410
New Jersey	85,000	46,667	95,000	95,000	95,000	95,000	60,000 (d)	95,000	95,000	79,697 (d)
New Mexico	90,000	40,425	40,425	46,200	40,425	54,558	62,067	62,067	53,123	53,123
New York	130,000	110,000	87,338	110,000	(n)	87,338	91,957	87,338	87,338	96,662
North Carolina	123,000	70,992	70,992	70,992	70,992	64,548	70,992	70,992	68,304	38,549 (d)
North Dakota	65,196	53,496	49,300	55,704	49,300	76,920	(a-33)	49,296	49,800	(jj)
Ohio	65,000	46,883	66,997	66,997	66,997	65,416	58,843 (d)	53,331 (d)	53,331 (d)	53,331 (d)
Oklahoma	70,000	40,000	37,500	55,000	50,000	63,450	60,019	51,115	64,045	62,245
Oregon	77,500	(a-2)	59,500	64,000	59,500	69,180	84,072	69,180	56,904	76,224
Pennsylvania	85,000	67,500	58,000	84,000	84,000	58,000	65,000	58,000	58,000	65,000
Rhode Island	69,000	52,000	52,000	55,000	52,000	50,671 (d)	72,785 (d)	33,068 (d)	45,754 (d)	65,412 (d)
South Carolina	84,897	37,142	72,161	72,161	72,161	72,161	93,619 (d)	72,161	(a-4)	69,246 (d)
South Dakota	60,819	52,915	41,309	51,626	41,309	57,242	53,622	51,480	59,738	63,773
Tennessee	85,000	49,500	65,000	65,650	65,000	57,500	65,000	55,500	58,000	64,000
Texas	93,432	7,200	72,549	74,698	74,698	59,790	69,300	74,698	84,941	63,000
Utah	69,992	52,499	52,499	56,014	52,998	60,008	68,078	55,536	53,498	65,770
Vermont	75,800	31,600	47,700	57,300	47,700	49,254	65,229	55,744	54,205	57,013
Virginia	85,000	28,000	59,247	75,000	84,248	69,119	92,913	76,830	83,713	90,058
Washington	96,700	51,100	52,600	75,700	65,000	78,191	79,620	79,620	60,688	82,000
West Virginia	72,000	...	43,200	50,400	50,400	35,700	70,000	46,800	38,300	25,152 (d)
Wisconsin	86,149	46,360	42,098	73,903	42,098	50,461 (d)	62,964 (d)	54,323 (d)	46,871 (d)	50,461 (d)
Wyoming	70,000	52,500	52,500	63,147	52,500	58,525	66,329	63,013	55,008	60,000

Note: The chief administrative officials responsible for each function were determined from information given by the states for the same function as listed in *State Administrative Officials Classified by Function 1989-90*, published by The Council of State Governments.

Key:
N.A. — Not available
... — No specific chief administrative official or agency in charge of function
(a) Chief administrative official or agency in charge of function:
(a-1) Lieutenant governor
(a-2) Secretary of state
(a-3) Attorney general
(a-4) Treasurer
(a-5) Adjutant general
(a-6) Administration
(a-7) Agriculture
(a-8) Banking
(a-9) Budget
(a-10) Civil rights
(a-11) Commerce
(a-12) Community affairs
(a-13) Comptroller
(a-14) Computer services
(a-15) Consumer affairs
(a-16) Economic development
(a-17) Education (chief state school officer)
(a-18) Emergency management
(a-19) Employment services
(a-20) Energy resources
(a-21) Environmental protection
(a-22) Finance
(a-23) Fish and wildlife
(a-24) General services
(a-25) Health
(a-26) Highways
(a-27) Historic preservation
(a-28) Insurance
(a-29) Labor
(a-30) Mental health and retardation
(a-31) Natural resources
(a-32) Parks and recreation
(a-33) Personnel
(a-34) Planning
(a-35) Post audit
(a-36) Public utility regulation
(a-37) Public welfare
(a-38) Purchasing
(a-39) Revenue
(a-40) Social services
(a-41) Solid waste management
(a-42) Transportation

EXECUTIVE BRANCH

SELECTED OFFICIALS: ANNUAL SALARIES—Continued

State	Civil rights	Commerce	Community affairs	Comptroller	Computer services	Consumer affairs	Corrections	Economic development	Education	Election administration
Alabama	...	86,764	56,812	61,022	56,654	34,554	68,576	(a-12)	103,856	29,796
Alaska	62,508 (d)	66,816 (d)	66,816 (d)	56,244 (d)	62,508 (d)	56,244 (d)	66,816 (d)	66,816 (d)	66,816 (d)	62,508 (d)
Arizona	51,074 (d)	51,074 (d)	...	...	46,606 (d)	55,989 (d)	67,225 (d)	51,074 (d)	50,000	(a-2)
Arkansas	N.A.	...	71,905	71,905	65,047	(a-3)	65,000	60,839	70,879	22,500
California	95,052	95,052	67,824	72,500	86,544	95,052	95,052	(a-11)	72,500	5,364 (d)
Colorado	...	...	58,464	58,464	58,464	59,056	70,000	77,813	79,742	41,556
Connecticut	63,246 (d)	67,639 (d)	50,009 (d)	50,000	63,246 (d)	67,639 (d)	72,681 (d)	77,681 (d)	78,732 (d)	55,415 (d)
Delaware	42,806	(a-2)	65,600	61,178	74,769	42,961	76,100	76,100	93,300	39,625
Florida	36,798	61,200 (d)	84,926	91,301	63,018	36,720 (d)	84,925	58,656	91,301	54,499
Georgia	55,194	77,850	77,838	71,172	67,200	61,098	69,000	77,850	72,824	61,500
Hawaii	...	85,302	...	85,302	63,348	65,000	85,302	85,302	90,041	90,041
Idaho	36,171	48,485	34,445	45,000	(a-6)	(a-3)	60,424	(a-11)	45,000	46,488
Illinois	57,057	65,835	(a-11)	71,321	(a-6)	(a-3)	65,835	(a-11)	108,696	63,000
Indiana	43,498	63,986	31,356	45,994	56,108	58,188	68,302	55,484	63,102	37,024
Iowa	38,500 (d)	52,700 (d)	49,046 (d)	56,400 (d)	49,064 (d)	47,257 (d)	56,400 (d)	63,000 (d)	63,000 (d)	(a-2)
Kansas	40,500	71,550	51,263	63,655	61,107	42,708	72,267	(a-11)	86,000	36,000
Kentucky	60,000	64,260	56,111	64,260	(a-13)	(a-3)	64,260	(a-11)	59,263	42,682
Louisiana	(a-3)	(a-16)	34,128	(a-6)	55,260	...	58,000	58,000	95,000	60,169
Maine (c)	39,527	59,821	39,056	48,033	67,464	40,248	47,026	(a-11)	59,816	(a-2)
Maryland	64,900 (d)	60,093 (d)	60,093 (d)	72,500	60,093 (d)	60,093 (d)	70,092 (d)	(a-11)	88,296 (d)	60,093 (d)
Massachusetts	58,100	(a-16)	67,000	75,000	63,200	64,500	77,500	70,700	77,500	49,300
Michigan	80,300	80,300	46,980 (d)	29,838 (d)	29,838 (d)	61,825 (d)	83,100	29,838 (d)	80,516	(a-2)
Minnesota	60,000	67,500	64,206	(a-9)	64,122	66,691	67,500	36,644	78,500	34,034
Mississippi	...	(a-16)	37,172 (d)	(a-9)	52,450 (d)	37,548 (d)	48,000	59,400 (d)	55,685 (d)	45,604 (d)
Missouri	50,340	(a-16)	(a-16)	57,973	57,973	...	67,970	67,970	75,252	29,532
Montana	32,868	51,763	41,425	(a-6)	47,393	33,731	51,763	37,195	40,643	23,061
Nebraska	66,036	(a-16)	37,800	53,568	57,324	26,928	66,612	68,783	(l)	(a-2)
Nevada	48,800	57,443	46,600	49,000	53,516	33,607	65,322	55,525	61,004	(a-2)
New Hampshire	37,947	50,499	(a-34)	53,209	60,410	(a-3)	60,410	50,499	67,625	(a-2)
New Jersey	59,471 (d)	95,000	95,000	(a-9)	85,000	62,445 (d)	95,000	73,150	95,000	(ff)
New Mexico	50,294	(a-16)	62,067	(a-4)	50,315	48,693	62,067	62,067	63,877	51,314
New York	79,437	87,338	(a-2)	(a-4)	(a-6)	73,482	98,399	(a-11)	131,250	79,437
North Carolina	38,549 (d)	70,992	40,377 (d)	110,772	61,474 (d)	46,411 (d)	70,992	42,229 (d)	70,992	46,411 (d)
North Dakota	(a-29)	(a-16)	41,736	(jj)	57,276	30,384	51,948	47,724	50,304	(a-2)
Ohio	43,867 (d)	(o)	39,832 (d)	(a-4)	39,832 (d)	43,867 (d)	58,843 (d)	39,832 (d)	97,677	40,394 (d)
Oklahoma	39,985	68,650	(a-11)	58,145	45,774	42,768	65,400	(a-11)	55,000	61,400
Oregon	56,904	(a-28)	62,700	59,500	62,700	...	76,224	56,904	59,500	51,576
Pennsylvania	64,998	61,500	58,000	54,000	64,626	60,401	61,500	(a-11)	65,000	41,500
Rhode Island	33,068 (d)	(a-16)	...	50,671 (d)	42,548 (d)	30,616 (d)	72,785 (d)	67,868 (d)	91,000	34,684
South Carolina	56,989 (d)	(a-16)	32,988	72,161	71,113 (d)	66,722 (d)	93,619 (d)	80,225 (d)	72,161	49,212 (d)
South Dakota	22,922	53,498	(a-16)	41,309	54,309	37,336	52,998	80,000	(pp)	(a-2)
Tennessee	52,000	64,500	(a-11)	65,000	63,000	38,000	62,000	(a-11)	90,000	41,500
Texas	52,133	74,970	58,800	74,698	75,600	75,283	84,000	(a-11)	114,474	52,730
Utah	45,157	62,150	(r)	65,936	56,389	37,294	62,150	50,814	69,742	52,499
Vermont	53,186	48,526	52,333	(a-9)	51,293	53,186	53,768	48,526	61,651	(rr)
Virginia	...	92,913	71,512	87,054	83,640	39,935	92,111	93,883	96,529	61,617
Washington	59,713	79,620	79,620	(a-4)	57,760	73,185	79,620	(a-11)	69,800	40,873
West Virginia	40,000	(y)	63,600	46,800	42,204 (d)	39,900 (d)	45,000	63,600	70,600	(a-2)
Wisconsin	40,442 (d)	54,324 (d)	43,389 (d)	43,389 (d)	40,442 (d)	(u)	54,324 (d)	37,567 (d)	72,337	40,442 (d)
Wyoming	54,149	62,500	(a-16)	52,500	57,486	35,486	62,121	58,658	52,500	(ww)

(b) Salary listed may be of military grade.
(c) Council of State Governments' survey (1988).
(d) Minimum figure in range; top of range follows:
Alaska: Lieutenant governor, $92,676; Attorney General, $92,676; Treasurer, $92,676; Adjutant general, $92,676; Administration, $92,676; Agriculture, $86,292; Banking, $86,292; Budget, $86,292; Civil rights, $86,292; Commerce, $92,676; Community affairs, $92,676; Comptroller, $77,424; Computer services, $86,292; Consumer affairs, $77,424; Corrections, $92,676; Economic development, $92,676; Education, $92,676; Elections administration, $86,292; Emergency management, $86,292; Employment services, $72,420; Environmental protection, $92,676; Finance, $77,424; Fish and wildlife, $92,676; General services, $86,292; Health, $92,676; Higher education, $89,580; Historic preservation, $63,084; Insurance, $86,292; Labor, $92,676; Licensing, $86,292; Mental health & retardation, $86,292; Natural resources, $92,676; Parks & recreation, $86,292; Personnel, $86,292; Post audit, $86,292; Pre-audit $86,292; Public library, $86,292; Public utility regulation, $86,292; Public welfare, $86,292; Revenue, $86,292; Social Services, $92,676; Solid waste management, $67,548; State police, $86,292; Tourism, $86,292; Transportation, $92,676
Arizona: Adjutant general, $70,532; Administration, $92,863; Agriculture, $70,532; Banking, $70,532; Budget, $70,532; Civil rights, $77,294; Commerce, $77,294; Computer services, $70,532; Consumer affairs, $84,734; Corrections, $101,738; Economic development, $77,294; Education, $50,000; Elections administration, $50,000; Emergency management, $53,553; Employment services, $53,553; Energy resources, $53,553; Environmental protection, $84,734; Finance, $77,294; Fish and wildlife, $70,532; General services, $58,699; Health, $101,738; Highways, $84,734; Historic preservation, $44,716; Insurance, $70,532; Labor, $77,294; Natural resources, $84,734; Parks & recreation, $64,320; Personnel, $77,294; Planning, $77,294; Post audit, $82,262; Public library, $40,215; Public utility regulation, $70,532; Purchasing, $64,320; Revenue, $92,863; Social Services, $77,294; Solid waste management, $64,320; State police, $85,000; Tourism, $70,532; Transportation, $101,738
California: Adjutant general, $92,111; Elections administration, $5,913; Public library, $5,005; Purchasing, $6,503
Connecticut: Adjutant general, $72,538; Administration, $99,913; Agriculture, $72,538; Banking, $81,686; Budget, $93,541; Civil rights, $76,424; Commerce, $81,686; Community affairs, $63,028; Computer services, $76,424; Consumer affairs, $81,686; Corrections, $88,024;; Economic development, $88,024; Education, $95,155; Elections administration, $71,083; Emergency management, $54,819; Employment services, $76,424; Energy resources, $72,538; Environmental protection, $88,024;; Finance, $99,913; Fish and wildlife, $76,882; Health, $88,024;; Highways, $76,424; Historic preservation, $49,933; Insurance, $81,686; Labor, $81,686; Licensing, $73,923; Parks & recreation, $76,802; Personnel, $76,424; Planning, $72,538; Post audit, $79,961; Public library, $72,538; Public utility regulation, $89,948; Public welfare, $88,024;; Purchasing, $76,424; Revenue, $81,686; Social Services, $81,686; Solid waste management, $76,882; State police, $88,024;; Tourism, $56,173; Transportation, $99,913; Delaware: Tourism, $60,040

The Council of State Governments 91

EXECUTIVE BRANCH

SELECTED OFFICIALS: ANNUAL SALARIES—Continued

State	Emergency management	Employment services	Energy resources	Environmental protection	Finance	Fish & wildlife	General services	Health	Higher education	Highways
Alabama	56,812	62,556	51,600	52,598	56,812	(a-31)	52,598	113,977	97,940	56,812
Alaska	62,508 (d)	52,548 (d)	...	66,816 (d)	56,244 (d)	66,816	62,508 (d)	66,816 (d)	64,620 (d)	(a-42)
Arizona	35,386 (d)	35,386 (d)	35,386 (d)	55,989 (d)	51,074 (d)	46,606	38,788 (d)	67,225 (d)	...	55,989 (d)
Arkansas	39,133	67,896	54,900	55,000	71,905	58,088	71,905	72,907	72,867	76,708
California	83,869	95,052	90,860	101,343	101,343	95,052	95,052	95,052	100,834	95,052
Colorado	48,108	72,624	43,992	55,680	(a-13)	58,464	72,624	83,830	88,000	80,925
Connecticut	45,311 (d)	63,246 (d)	59,789 (d)	72,681 (d)	82,669 (d)	59,935 (d)	(a-6)	78,732 (d)	101,800	63,246 (d)
Delaware	44,473	(a-29)	46,666	70,900	81,400	49,024	(a-6)	97,509	49,900	73,541
Florida	66,288	60,756	51,000	84,925	58,472	84,926	84,926	61,200 (d)	137,945	(a-42)
Georgia	75,474	59,688	61,098	78,349	67,164	67,234	(a-6)	95,962	133,300	(a-42)
Hawaii	88,107	(a-29)	60,912	74,880	(a-9)	33,000	(a-13)	85,302	90,041	68,784
Idaho	47,341	58,947	(a-31)	53,456	(a-9)	66,622	41,870	68,245	74,506	(a-42)
Illinois	40,598	71,321	(a-31)	65,835	(a-39)	65,835	(a-6)	71,321	124,200	(a-42)
Indiana	34,944	62,010	39,858	67,522	(a-9)	44,538	(a-6)	87,230	N.A.	69,992
Iowa	25,600 (d)	52,700 (d)	49,046 (d)	49,064 (d)	(a-13)	49,064 (d)	(a-6)	52,700 (d)	63,000 (d)	51,397 (d)
Kansas	41,107	(a-29)	38,880	60,878	(a-9)	(a-32)	(a-6)	100,225	91,500	(a-42)
Kentucky	43,291	51,511	(a-31)	(a-31)	(a-13)	58,000	(a-13)	94,570	82,344	56,700
Louisiana	32,360	45,228	53,164	58,000	(a-6)	58,000	(a-6)	110,000	78,479	58,455
Maine (c)	38,627	40,834	50,346	49,404	59,816	42,723	(a-22)	54,353	(x)	(a-26)
Maryland	51,520 (d)	64,900 (d)	39,383 (d)	81,756 (d)	(a-13)	42,534 (d)	81,756 (d)	95,360 (d)	88,296 (d)	89,903
Massachusetts	54,100	72,100	62,000	70,700	(a-6)	63,300	73,100	77,600	100,000	77,500
Michigan	44,370 (d)	29,838 (d)	...	29,838 (d)	(a-9)	(a-31)	29,838 (d)	80,300	50,863 (d)	(a-42)
Minnesota	51,553	64,248	54,643	(j)	(a-9)	57,190	(a-6)	67,500	83,875	73,351
Mississippi	33,600	51,606	(a-42)	42,119 (d)	...	38,696 (d)	(a-9)	67,290 (d)	98,000	54,000
Missouri	52,203	64,191	54,390	57,945	(k)	69,972	54,423	87,456	75,000	(a-42)
Montana	30,891	44,292	38,954	47,393	(a-9)	34,815	35,695	46,436	79,200	51,763
Nebraska	(a-5)	44,904	47,914	47,444	(m)	65,000	(a-6)	69,187	39,192	(a-42)
Nevada	38,447	53,516	46,600	51,689	(a-13)	48,676	52,968	50,320	107,100	(a-42)
New Hampshire	52,000	60,410	34,000	65,831	(a-6)	50,499	53,209	65,831	43,283	(a-42)
New Jersey	85,273 (d)	60,000 (d)	95,000	95,000	(a-4)	56,640 (d)	(a-6)	95,000	95,000	(a-42)
New Mexico	62,067	62,067	62,067	57,408	62,067	56,222	62,067	62,067	65,000	62,067
New York	98,399	91,957	87,338	91,957	(a-4)	(a-21)	(a-6)	(a-18)	(a-17)	98,399
North Carolina	36,823 (d)	68,304	38,549 (d)	(a-31)	(a-9)	58,884	35,143 (d)	78,057 (d)	134,450	56,000 (d)
North Dakota	39,744	55,596	41,736	60,144	(a-9)	48,180	(a-9)	78,012	93,528	58,100
Ohio	32,698 (d)	58,843 (d)	40,394 (d)	58,843 (d)	(a-9)	40,394 (d)	(a-6)	58,843 (d)	115,003	(a-42)
Oklahoma	(a-5)	(a-33)	51,115	39,985	(a-9)	60,949	(a-6)	87,288	120,000	(a-42)
Oregon	56,904	69,180	62,700	69,180	(a-9)	69,180	76,224	69,180	120,000	76,224
Pennsylvania	60,910	62,250	64,997	65,000	(a-39)	(nn)	61,500	65,000	64,500	64,500
Rhode Island	(a-5)	67,868 (d)	(a-36)	67,868 (d)	(a-9)	37,034 (d)	60,497 (d)	100,696	87,120	(a-42)
South Carolina	39,047	86,268	55,161	66,930 (d)	(a-6)	65,349 (d)	71,113 (d)	93,619 (d)	77,700 (d)	(a-42)
South Dakota	40,123	29,307	43,514	46,405	(a-9)	53,165	(a-6)	52,208	86,000	52,666
Tennessee	52,000	57,500	64,500	62,000	(a-6)	57,500	55,500	61,000	98,500	(a-42)
Texas	52,500	77,700	61,425	67,515	(a-13)	75,600	(a-6)	84,000	117,923	84,000
Utah	44,346	69,342	N.A.	58,760	(a-13)	48,422	(a-6)	80,517	N.A.	(a-42)
Vermont	39,042	53,061	58,157	49,005	(a-9)	47,008	50,003	63,003	39,624	61,714
Virginia	63,357	75,996	43,654	63,713	92,913	60,567	84,826	93,018	94,636	96,528
Washington	52,337	54,969	59,713	79,620	(a-9)	(ss)	(a-6)	79,620	85,000	(a-42)
West Virginia	32,000	45,000	(z)	(aa)	(a-6)	31,812 (d)	25,152 (d)	(vv)	70,000	60,000
Wisconsin	37,567 (d)	46,871 (d)	43,539 (d)	50,461 (d)	46,871 (d)	40,442 (d)	46,871 (d)	54,324	72,971 (d)	50,461 (d)
Wyoming	37,992	55,509	32,094	57,000	(a-13)	61,800	(a-6)	78,418	60,000	(a-42)

Florida: Commerce, $106,733; Consumer affairs, $63,371; Health, $106,733

Iowa: Administration, $64,700; Banking, $57,000; Budget, $75,100; Civil rights, $51,600; Commerce, $64,700; Community affairs, $61,984; Comptroller, $75,100; Computer services, $61,984; Consumer affairs, $64,958; Corrections, $75,100; Economic development, $89,300; Education, $89,300; Emergency management, $42,600; Employment services, $64,700; Energy resources, $61,984; Environmental protection, $61,984; Finance, $75,100; Fish and wildlife, $61,984; General services, $64,700; Health, $64,700; Higher education, $89,300; Highways, $64,958; Historic preservation, $64,700; Insurance, $64,100; Labor, $64,100; Licensing, $42,600; Mental health & retardation, $68,078; Natural resources, $75,100; Parks & recreation, $53,851; Personnel, $64,700; Planning, $89,300; Pre-audit $75,100; Public library, $49,700; Public utility regulation, $64,100; Public welfare, $53,851; Purchasing, $53,851; Revenue, $75,100; Social Services, $68,078; Solid waste management, $53,851; State police, $64,958; Tourism, $53,851; Transportation, $89,300

Maryland: Adjutant general, $86,205; Administration, $100,550; Agriculture, $100,550; Banking, $73,907; Budget, $117,281; Civil rights, $79,819; Commerce, $73,907; Community affairs, $73,907; Computer services, $73,907; Consumer affairs, $73,907; Corrections, $86,205; Economic development, 73,907; Education, $108,593; Elections administration, $73,907; Emergency management, $63,364; Employment services, $79,819; Energy resources, $51,730; Environmental protection, $100,550; Fish and wildlife, $55,869; General services, $100,550; Health, $117,281; Higher education, $108,593; Historic preservation, $73,907; Insurance, $73,907; Labor, $73,907; Licensing, $100,550; Mental health & retardation, $86,205; Natural resources, $108,593; Parks & recreation, $79,819; Personnel, $100,550; Planning, $79,819; Post audit, $93,102; Pre-audit $35,287; Public library, $73,907; Public utility regulation, $86,205; Public welfare, $79,819; Purchasing, $51,730; Social Services, $79,819; Solid waste management, $68,433; State police, $86,205; Tourism, $79,819; Transportation, $117,281

Michigan: Community affairs, $62,911; Comptroller, $77,987; Computer services, $77,987; Consumer affairs, $83,394; Economic development, $77,987; Emergency management, $59,299; Employment services, $77,987; Environmental protection, $83,478; General services, $72,140; Higher education, $68,027; Historic preservation, $77,987; Parks & recreation, $68,027; Purchasing, $77,987; Revenue, $72,140; Solid waste management, $83,478

Mississippi: Budget, $72,152; Commerce, $75,471; Community affairs, $47,232; Comptroller, $72,153; Computer services, $66,622; Consumer affairs, $56,228; Economic development, 75,471; Education, $70,733; Elections administration, $53,765; Environmental protection, $63,073; Fish and wildlife, $57,939; General services, $72,152; Health, $86,366; Natural resources, $67,623; Parks & recreation, $50,911; Personnel, $65,641; Planning, $47,232; Pre-audit $72,153; Public welfare, $75,471; Purchasing, $52,972; Solid waste management, $57,083; Tourism, $43,600

92 The Book of the States 1990-91

EXECUTIVE BRANCH

SELECTED OFFICIALS: ANNUAL SALARIES—Continued

State	Historic preservation	Insurance	Labor	Licensing	Mental health & retardation	Natural resources	Parks & recreation	Personnel	Plannning	Post audit
Alabama	55,900	56,812	56,811	...	82,160	56,812	46,488	79,407	...	84,240
Alaska	45,972 (d)	62,508 (d)	66,816 (d)	62,508 (d)	62,508 (d)	66,816 (d)	62,508 (d)	62,508 (d)	...	62,508 (d)
Arizona	29,549 (d)	46,606 (d)	51,074 (d)	...	...	55,989 (d)	42,500 (d)	51,074	51,074 (d)	82,262 (d)
Arkansas	43,773	55,493	59,182	...	54,112	43,773	54,841	49,199	...	71,133
California	64,668	95,052	101,343	95,052	95,052	83,869	95,052	95,052	86,820	101,134
Colorado	...	52,932	58,464	72,624	58,464	75,219	58,464	63,246 (d)	(a-9)	72,908
Connecticut	38,929 (d)	67,639 (d)	67,639 (d)	57,632 (d)	(s)	(a-21)	59,935 (d)	63,246 (d)	59,789 (d)	62,336 (d)
Delaware	53,724	60,400	65,600	45,920	83,546	70,900	58,091	70,900	55,650	60,400
Florida	57,904	91,301	65,894	53,489	68,244	84,925	68,752	84,925	(a-9)	87,144
Georgia	51,492	71,172	71,184	61,218	95,962	78,349	61,676	77,862	78,984	70,640
Hawaii	85,302	67,716	85,302	85,302	42,132	85,302	48,504	85,302	85,302	64,356
Idaho	46,176	57,533	52,187	43,971	56,139	...	58,947	56,139	(a-11)	52,187
Illinois	67,792	60,349	61,488	61,488	71,321	57,057	65,835	57,504	56,710	68,250
Indiana	N.A.	50,024	50,024	39,260	63,024	65,702	54,938	66,820	47,684	57,980
Iowa	52,700 (d)	49,700 (d)	49,700 (d)	25,600 (d)	53,851 (d)	56,400 (d)	42,598 (d)	52,700 (d)	(a-16)	55,700
Kansas	39,708	56,816	58,575	N.A.	63,000	(a-21)	72,267	65,368	(a-9)	69,036
Kentucky	52,103	53,550	66,283	40,057	66,434	64,260	52,500	64,504	(a-9)	59,263
Louisiana	33,288	60,169	56,016	38,148	(g)	58,000	43,841	59,532	39,792	(f)
Maine (c)	35,114	48,825	49,404	32,656	54,272	(a-21)	42,794	45,781	52,874	37,085
Maryland	60,093 (d)	60,093 (d)	60,093 (d)	81,756 (d)	(h)	88,296 (d)	64,900 (d)	81,756 (d)	64,900 (d)	75,700 (d)
Massachusetts	44,100	63,300	52,100	52,100	(xx)	69,100	52,100	73,200	(a-16)	70,000
Michigan	29,838 (d)	72,015	65,020	80,300	80,300	83,100	50,863 (d)	80,300	...	69,500
Minnesota	N.A.	67,500	67,500	35,747	61,283	67,500	50,905	67,500	67,500	62,320
Mississippi	44,400	54,000	...	...	64,800	53,243 (d)	20,642 (d)	51,657 (d)	37,172 (d)	54,000
Missouri	30,072	57,945	67,970	54,396	75,930	67,970	57,945	54,423	(a-6)	70,909
Montana	28,819	36,048	51,763	44,292	(yy)	51,763	38,164	42,517	(a-9)	59,446
Nebraska	54,996	57,040	45,862	46,320	(ee)	51,492	65,000	51,500	47,914	35,000
Nevada	37,319	52,900	43,300	...	69,000	55,982	45,900	49,498	36,757	59,147
New Hampshire	39,684	67,625	50,499	(a-2)	65,831	67,625	50,499	55,001	52,000	61,000
New Jersey	38,336 (d)	95,000	95,000	(a-15)	(v)	78,500	59,471 (d)	95,000	95,000	80,000
New Mexico	45,573	50,232	46,592	(gg)	(hh)	62,067	53,872	53,123	...	40,425
New York	87,338	87,338	(a-19)	(a-2)	(ii)	(a-21)	(a-27)	87,338	87,338	(a-4)
North Carolina	32,023 (d)	70,992	70,992	...	53,383 (d)	70,992	38,549 (d)	70,992	38,549 (d)	70,992
North Dakota	28,620	49,300	45,996	(a-2)	50,652	...	44,532	49,116	(a-20)	(kk)
Ohio	...	48,360 (d)	48,360 (d)	...	(ll)	58,843 (d)	40,394 (d)	36,088 (d)	(a-9)	66,997
Oklahoma	48,400	75,400	42,140	...	(p)	55,000	(a-31)	55,400	...	50,000
Oregon	(mm)	76,224	59,500	(a-28)	(q)	59,700	62,500	69,180	62,700	59,700
Pennsylvania	51,462	58,000	65,000	50,600	57,487	(a-21)	60,988	64,000	51,000	84,000
Rhode Island	N.A.	67,868 (d)	60,497 (d)	37,034 (d)	75,240 (d)	(a-21)	38,388 (d)	53,128 (d)	53,218 (d)	(oo)
South Carolina	32,093	66,722 (d)	60,244 (d)	...	(s)	55,161	61,891 (d)	69,246 (d)	(a-33)	69,246 (d)
South Dakota	37,502	(a-11)	52,208	21,008	(t)	65,000	42,328	50,794	...	51,355
Tennessee	36,500	57,500	55,500	40,000	61,000	57,500	52,000	57,500	58,000	(a-13)
Texas	50,299	69,300	...	58,907	88,480	70,711	(a-23)	...	(a-9)	81,230
Utah	48,277	55,515	60,819	44,075	(zz)	65,770	50,315	62,150	(a-9)	(qq)
Vermont	37,045	54,205	51,646	26,416	63,107	62,026	50,835	52,562	45,989	47,700
Virginia	65,590	(a-8)	66,324	57,795	92,706	92,913	(a-27)	81,880	(a-9)	87,992
Washington	44,764	63,900	79,620	(a-6)	70,368	69,800	73,932	79,620	(a-9)	67,100
West Virginia	(bb)	36,700	35,700	...	47,250	(a-21)	49,980	38,300	(a)	N.A.
Wisconsin	37,567 (d)	50,461 (d)	54,324 (d)	46,871 (d)	34,809 (d)	58,483 (d)	(a-9)	54,324 (d)	32,253	37,567 (d)
Wyoming	51,425	44,160 (d)	45,556	31,563	44,437	41,272	30,566	54,149	48,880	(a-13)

New Jersey: Administration, $80,000; Budget, $111,519; Civil rights, $83,261; Comptroller, $111,519; Consumer affairs, $87,418; Elections administration, $59,178; Emergency management, $111,414; Employment services, $80,000; Fish and wildlife, $79,293; General services, $80,000; Historic preservation, $53,670; Licensing, $87,418; Mental health & retardation, $87,418; Parks & recreation, $83,261; Purchasing, $80,000; Revenue, $101,203; Solid waste management, $68,491; State police, $111,414

North Carolina: Budget, $63,072; Civil rights, $63,072; Community affairs, $66,096; Computer services, $101,688; Consumer affairs, $76,332; Economic development, 69,336; Elections administration, $76,332; Emergency management, $60,204; Energy resources, $63,072; Finance, $63,072; General services, $57,432; Health, $129,492; Highways, $92,400; Historic preservation, $52,284; Mental health & retardation, $88,104; Parks & recreation, $63,072; Planning, $63,072; Public library, $69,336; Purchasing, $72,768; Social Services, $80,052; Solid waste management, $66,096; State police, $76,332; Tourism, $66,096

Ohio: Administration, $82,680; Agriculture, $76,586; Banking, $76,586; Budget, $76,586; Civil rights, $64,251; Commerce, $76,586; Community affairs, $58,843; Computer services, $58,843; Consumer affairs, $64,251; Corrections, $82,680; Economic development, $58,843; Elections administration, $52,936; Emergency management, $49,317; Employment services, $82,680; Energy resources, $52,936; Environmental protection, $82,680;

Finance, $76,586; Fish and wildlife, $52,936; General services, $82,680; Health, $82,680; Highways, $82,680; Insurance, $70,138; Labor, $70,138; Mental health & retardation, $82,680; Natural resources, $82,680; Parks & recreation, $53,936; Personnel, $53,851; Planning, $76,586; Public library, $64,251; Public utility regulation, $82,680; Public welfare, $76,586; Purchasing, $53,851; Revenue, $76,586; Social Services, $76,586; Solid waste management, $52,936; State police, $64,251; Tourism, $64,251; Transportation, $82,680

Rhode Island: Adjutant general, $58,040; Administration, $80,156; Agriculture, $37,432; Banking, $53,128; Budget, $72,785; Civil rights, $37,432; Commerce, $75,240; Comptroller, $58,040; Computer services, $48,215; Consumer affairs, $34,624; Corrections, $80,156; Economic development, $75,240; Emergency management, $58,040; Employment services, $75,240; Energy resources, $70,326; Environmental protection, $75,240; Finance, $67,868; Fish and wildlife, $41,943; General services, $67,868; Highways, $80,156; Insurance, $75,240; Labor, $67,868; Licensing, $41,943; Mental health & retardation, $82,611; Natural resources, $75,240; Parks & recreation, $43,503; Personnel, $60,497; Planning, $60,497; Pre-audit $29,513; Public library, $62,956; Public utility regulation, $70,326; Public welfare, $58,040; Purchasing, $62,956; Revenue, $65,412; Social Services, $80,156; Transportation, $80,156

EXECUTIVE BRANCH

SELECTED OFFICIALS: ANNUAL SALARIES—Continued

State	Pre-audit	Public library	Public utility regulation	Public welfare	Purchasing	Revenue	Social services	Solid waste management	State police	Tourism	Transportation
Alabama	(a-13)	55,000	47,891	56,812	61,022	56,812	(a-37)	47,658	50,102	56,812	33,134
Alaska	62,508 (d)	62,508 (d)	62,508 (d)	62,508 (d)	(a-24)	62,508 (d)	66,816 (d)	49,140 (d)	62,508 (d)	62,508 (d)	66,816 (d)
Arizona	...	40,215	46,606 (d)	...	42,500 (d)	61,362 (d)	51,074 (d)	42,500 (d)	85,000	46,606 (d)	67,225 (d)
Arkansas	31,136	50,136	58,183	...	49,199	53,210	58,022	55,000	49,174	38,327	76,708
California	72,500	4,540	90,860	95,052	5,898 (d)	95,052	95,052	79,676	101,343	67,824	95,052
Colorado	(a-13)	56,210	48,400	(a-40)	55,680	83,000	75,000	58,464	58,464	58,464	...
Connecticut	(a-13)	59,789 (d)	70,117 (d)	72,681 (d)	63,246 (d)	67,639 (d)	67,639 (d)	59,935 (d)	72,681 (d)	43,790 (d)	82,669 (d)
Delaware	60,400	42,012	46,301	66,641	48,589	70,469	81,400	...	67,841	36,054 (d)	76,100
Florida	74,460	62,194	84,925	67,989	61,556	85,292	70,686	65,468	70,386	58,624	86,700
Georgia	70,640	73,614	68,490	(a-40)	65,412	69,804	75,903	66,396	75,854	73,776	93,530
Hawaii	60,912	85,302	74,880	61,488	51,420	85,302	85,302	74,880	...	85,302	85,302
Idaho	(a-13)	34,445	50,003	60,424	40,872	39,749	54,787	46,176	48,485	(a-11)	73,445
Illinois	(a-13)	61,692	70,455	71,321	(a-6)	71,321	65,835	(a-31)	65,835	(a-11)	71,321
Indiana	(a-13)	57,096	53,014	65,000	(a-6)	65,000	(a-37)	38,844	59,956	45,916	55,016
Iowa	(a-39)	35,200 (d)	49,700 (d)	42,598 (d)	42,598 (d)	56,400 (d)	53,851 (d)	42,598 (d)	51,397 (d)	42,598 (d)	63,000 (d)
Kansas	(a-13)	53,295	74,347	53,500	56,286	72,267	72,795	(a-21)	55,710	49,400	72,267
Kentucky	(a-11)	53,028	60,900	65,098	44,404	64,260	59,322	50,431	64,260	64,260	64,260
Louisiana	(a-6)	48,713	61,536	53,500	(g)	58,000	58,000	51,000	52,000	43,842	58,455
Maine (c)	(a-13)	38,885	59,109	40,019	38,858	46,490	(a-37)	(a-21)	49,339	32,947 (c)	(a-26)
Maryland	26,867 (d)	60,093 (d)	70,092 (d)	64,900 (d)	39,383 (d)	(a-13)	64,900 (d)	55,642 (d)	70,092 (d)	64,900 (d)	95,360 (d)
Massachusetts	(a-13)	48,800	63,300	77,600	69,000	77,500	80,000	44,000	69,000	46,200	70,600
Michigan	(a-35)	...	65,000	80,300	29,838 (d)	(i)	80,300	29,838 (d)	80,300	72,119	80,300
Minnesota	68,361	59,299	45,790	51,052	63,141	78,500	55,228	62,181	58,005	63,600	78,500
Mississippi	(a-9)	44,400	33,600	59,713 (d)	35,356 (d)	60,000	N.A.	38,111 (d)	48,000	29,116 (d)	48,000
Missouri	(a-13)	60,462	67,970	61,521	54,423	76,787	70,909	41,508	63,700	54,396	79,788
Montana	...	42,517	38,295	51,763	39,763	51,763	51,763	39,763	44,579	39,541	33,731
Nebraska	(a-13)	48,144	37,992	(a-40)	44,736	66,612	63,370	(a-21)	51,565	38,388	65,522
Nevada	(a-6)	44,626	64,100	56,530	46,715	60,700	64,749	51,689	50,033	(w)	64,475
New Hampshire	53,209	50,499	67,625	53,209	(a-24)	67,625	67,625	39,685 (d)	60,410	33,248 (d)	67,625
New Jersey	(a-9)	76,990	95,000	76,000	60,000 (d)	72,286 (d)	95,000	48,929 (d)	(a-18)	75,625	95,000
New Mexico	46,592	40,789	56,077	41,621	49,317	62,067	53,123	54,558	58,760	52,884	62,067
New York	(a-4)	(a-17)	91,957	91,957	(a-6)	91,957	(a-37)	(a-21)	91,957	87,338	(a-26)
North Carolina	...	42,229 (d)	70,992	70,992	44,286 (d)	70,992	48,629 (d)	40,377 (d)	46,411 (d)	40,377 (d)	70,992
North Dakota	(a-9)	42,168	49,300	71,556	50,220	49,296	66,192	47,448	46,175	36,216	...
Ohio	(a-35)	43,867 (d)	58,843 (d)	53,331 (d)	36,088 (d)	53,331 (d)	(a-37)	40,394 (d)	43,867 (d)	43,867 (d)	58,843 (d)
Oklahoma	(a-9)	47,906	51,115	87,287	59,573	62,922	87,287	31,272	59,400	(a-31)	67,400
Oregon	...	62,700	69,180	76,224	51,576	76,224	84,072	(a-21)	76,224	56,904	76,224
Pennsylvania	(a-4)	...	57,519	65,000	49,135	(a-39)	57,750	53,790	61,500	(a-11)	65,000
Rhode Island	25,369 (d)	55,584 (d)	62,956 (d)	50,671 (d)	55,584 (d)	58,040 (d)	72,785 (d)	...	81,111	38,937	72,785 (d)
South Carolina	(a-13)	50,87 (d)	57,673	(a-40)	43,825 (d)	63,448	82,091 (d)	40,609 (d)	58,250 (d)	42,237 (d)	97,351 (d)
South Dakota	...	38,750	30,992	66,040	35,006	52,208	66,040	(a-21)	47,341	49,317	59,073
Tennessee	54,000	64,500	65,000	61,000	40,000	61,000	45,500	52,000	55,500	57,500	61,000
Texas	(a-13)	54,600	(a-20)	84,000	(a-8)	(a-13)	(a-37)	58,244	79,800	64,260	(a-26)
Utah	(a-13)	51,334	51,542	55,515	47,008	65,166	68,078	51,834	54,142	49,816	68,058
Vermont	(a-9)	48,714	64,646	57,220	37,128	54,038	46,446	47,944	55,155	50,544	61,714
Virginia	(a-13)	76,830	(a-8)	84,131	74,499	90,055	84,131	60,407	81,880	68,157	96,528
Washington	...	(tt)	73,932	(uu)	53,629	79,620	(a-37)	42,226	79,620	56,346	98,459
West Virginia	(a-6)	47,500	50,000	47,800	27,636 (d)	(cc)	26,364 (d)	31,812	(dd)	47,250	70,000
Wisconsin	32,253 (d)	37,567 (d)	50,462 (d)	54,324 (d)	40,442 (d)	58,483 (d)	67,783 (d)	40,442 (d)	46,871 (d)	43,739 (d)	58,483 (d)
Wyoming	(a-13)	35,316 (d)	55,509	51,540	43,363	62,809	51,540	45,556	50,291	56,445	69,320

South Carolina: Administration, $126,661; Budget, $93,686; Civil rights, $77,103; Commerce, $108,539; Computer services, $96,211; Consumer affairs, $90,270; Corrections, $126,661; Economic development, $108,539; Elections administration, $66,580; Environmental protection, $100,394; Finance, $126,661; Fish and wildlife, $88,413; General services, $96,211; Health, $126,661; Higher education, $105,124; Highways, $131,711; Insurance, $90,270; Labor, $81,506; Mental health & retardation, $111,065; Parks & recreation, $83,735; Personnel, $93,686; Planning, $93,686; Post audit, $93,686; Public library, $66,819; Public welfare, $111,065; Purchasing, $65,737; Social Services, $111,065; Solid waste management, $60,913; State police, $87,376; Tourism, $63,355; Transportation, $131,711

West Virginia: Budget, $46,044; Computer services, $61,068; Consumer affairs, $47,250; Fish and wildlife, $58,248; General services, $46,044; Historic preservation, $38,220; Planning, $46,044; Purchasing, $50,568; Social Services, $48,264; Solid waste management, $58,248

Wisconsin: Adjutant general, $76,615; Administration, $86,149; Agriculture, $83,117; Banking, $70,629; Budget, $76,615; Civil rights, $60,047; Commerce, $83,117; Community affairs, $65,121; Comptroller, $65,121; Computer services, $60,047; Consumer affairs, $65,121; Corrections, $83,117; Economic development, $55,376; Elections administration, $60,047; Emergency management, $55,376; Employment services, $70,629; Energy resources, $65,121; Environmental protection, $76,615; Finance, $70,629; Fish and wildlife, $60,047; General services, $70,629; Health, $83,117; Higher education, $111,650; Highways, $76,615; Historic preser-

vation, $55,376; Insurance, $76,615; Labor, $83,117; Licensing, $70,629; Mental health & retardation, $50,591; Natural resources, $86,149; Parks & recreation, $60,047; Personnel, $86,149; Planning, $76,615; Post audit, $83,117; Pre-audit $46,882; Public library, $55,376; Public utility regulation, $76,615; Public welfare, $83,117; Purchasing, $60,047; Revenue, $86,149; Social Services, $86,149; Solid waste management, $60,047; State police, $70,629; Tourism, $65,121; Transportation, $86,149

Wyoming: Insurance, $69,900; Public library, $55,104.

(e) Responsibilities shared between Assistant Secretary, Office of Mental Retardation, Health & Human Resources Department, $63,327 and Assistant Secretary, Department of Health & Hospitals.

(f) Responsibilities shared between Commissioner, Division of Administration, $66,492 and Legislative Auditor, Office of Legislative Auditor.

(g) Responsibilities shared between Commissioner Division of Administration, $46,848 and State Director of Purchasing, same office.

(h) Responsibilities shared between Director, Developmental Disabilities Administration, Department of Health & Mental Hygiene, $70,092-$86,205 and Assistant Secretary, Mental Health-Addictions, Developmental Disabilities.

(i) Responsibilities shared between Commissioner of Revenue, Bureau of Revenue, Department of Treasury, $72,140 and Director, Local Finance Programs, same department $29,838-$72,140.

(j) Responsibilities shared between Commissioner, Pollution Control Agency, $67,500 and Executive Director, Environmental Quality Board.

EXECUTIVE BRANCH

SELECTED OFFICIALS: ANNUAL SALARIES—Continued

(k) Functions are covered by several different departments including Department of Revenue, Office of Administration, $76,786 and State Treasurer, $70,909.

(l) Responsibilities shared between Commissioner, Department of Education, $82,656 and President, State Board of Education.

(m) Responsibilities shared between Budget Administrator, Budget Division Administrative Services Department, $54,612 and Auditor of Public Accounts, $35,000 and State Tax Commissioner, Department of Revenue, $66,612.

(n) Responsibilities shared between Comptroller, Office of State Comptroller, $110,000 and Commissioner, Department of Taxation and Finance, $110,000.

(o) Responsibilities shared between Director, Department of Development and Director, Department of Commerce, $48,360.

(p) Responsibilities shared between Director, Department of Mental Health, $87,288 and Director, Developmental Disabilities Services, Department of Human Services.

(q) Responsibilities shared between Assistant Administrator, Programs for Developmental Disabilities Department of Human Resources and Administrator, Mental Health Division, same department, $76,224.

(r) Responsibilities shared between Deputy Director, Division of Community Development, Community & Economic Development Department, $55,515 and Deputy Director, Division of Business & Economic Development, same department.

(s) Responsibilities shared between Commissioner, Department of Mental Retardation, $82,091-$111,065 and Commissioner, Department of Mental Health.

(t) Responsibilities shared between Administrator, Developmental Disabilities, Department of Social Services, $42,952 and Secretary, Department of Human Services.

(u) Responsibilities shared between Administrator, Trade & Consumer Protection Division, Agriculture, Trade and Consumer Protection, $43,539-$65,121 and Director, Office of Consumer Protection, Department of Justice.

(v) Responsibilities shared between Director, Division of Mental Health & Hospitals Department of Human Services, $22,500 and Director, Division of Developmental Disabilities, same department.

(w) Responsibilities shared between Director, Commission on Tourism, $60,800 and Chairman, Gaming Control Board.

(x) Receives $55 per diem plus expenses.

(y) Responsibilities shared between Director, Division of Commerce, Labor and Environmental Resources, $65,000 and Commissioner, Department of Commerce, Labor and Environmental Resources $70,000.

(z) Responsibilities shared between Commissioner, Oil and Gas Conservation Commission, $40,000 and Commissioner, Division of Energy, $65,000.

(aa) Responsibilities shared between Director, Environmental Health Services, $46,606, Director, Division of Natural Resources, $47,800, and Director, Air Pollution Control Commission, $44,800.

(bb) Responsibilities shared between Administrator, Historic Preservation Unit, Division of Culture and History, $20,916 - $38,220, and Commissioner, Division of Culture and History, $38,300.

(cc) Responsibilities shared between Secretary, Department of Tax and Revenue $70,000 and Commissioner, State Tax Division, $26,364 - $48,264.

(dd) Responsibilities shared between Secretary, Department of Public Safety, $70,000 and Superintendent, Division of Public Safety, $40,000.

(ee) Responsibilities shared between Director, Medical Serivces Division, Department of Public Institutions, $49,824 and Director, Office of Mental Retardation, Department of Public Institutions.

(ff) Responsibilities shared between Director, Election Division, $59,178 and Executive Director, Election Law Enforcement Commission, Department of Law and Public Safety.

(gg) Responsibilities shared between Board Administrator, Boards and Commission, Department of Regulation and Licensing, $32,136 and Superintendent, Department of Regulation and Licensing.

(hh) Responsibilities shared between Chief, Developmental Disabilities Bureau, Department of Health and Environment, $36,421 and Bureau Chief, Mental Health Bureau, Department of Health and Environment.

(ii) Responsibilities shared between Cmmissioner, Office of Mental Health, $98,399 and Commissioner, Mental Retardation and Development Disabilities, $98,399.

(jj) Responsibilities shared between Director, Office of Management and Budget, $82,998 and Executive Budget Analyst, Office of Management and Budget.

(kk) Responsibilities shared between State Auditor, $49,300 and Legislative Budget Analyst, Fiscal Division, Legislative Council.

(ll) Responsibilities shared between Director, Department of Mental Retardation, $58,843 and Director, Department of Mental Health, $82.680.

(mm) Responsibilities shared by Executive Director, Historical Society, $65,000 and Preservation Officer, Parks and Recreation Division, Department of Transportation.

(nn) Responsibilities shared between Executive Director, Game Commission, $63,414 and Executive Director, Fish Commission, $63,414.

(oo) Responsibilities shared between Auditor General, Office of Auditor General, $75,190 and Director, Bureau of Audits.

(pp) Responsibilities shared between Secretary, Department of Education, $53,498 and State Superintendent of Education, Cultural Affairs Department, Department of Education.

(qq) Responsibilities shared between State Auditor, Office of State Auditor, $52,998 and Audit Manager, Office of State Auditor.

(rr) Responsibilities shared between Secretary of State, $47,700 and Director, Office of Secretary of State.

(ss) Responsibilities shared between Director, Department of Fisheries, $479,620 and Director, Department of Wildlife.

(tt) Responsibilities shared between State Librarian, State Library, $73,932 and Serials Manager, State Library.

(uu) Responsibilities shared between Secretary, Department of Social and Health Services, $98,459 and Director, Income Assistance Services, Department of Social and Health Services

(vv) Responsibilities shared between Secretary, Health and Human Resources, $70,000 and Director, Division of Health, $57,200.

(ww) Responsibilities shared between Secretary of State, $52,500 and Elections Assistant, Office of Secretary of State.

(xx) Responsibilities shared between Commission, Department of Mental Health, $77,500 and Commissioner, Department of Mental Retardation, $77,500.

(yy) Responsibilities shared between Administrator, Mental Health Division, Department of Institutions, $34,967 and Administrator, Developmental Disabilities Division, Social and Rehabilitiation Services Department.

(zz) Responsibilities shared between Director, Division of Mental Health, Department of Social Services, $60,819 and Director, Services to Handicapped Division, Department of Social Services.

EXECUTIVE BRANCH

Table 2.12
LIEUTENANT GOVERNORS: QUALIFICATIONS AND TERMS

State or other jurisdiction	Minimum age	State citizen (years) (a)	U.S. citizen (years)	State resident (years)	Qualified voter (years)	Length of term (years)	Maximum consecutive terms allowed
Alabama	30	7	10	7	...	4	2
Alaska	30	7	7	7	★	4	...
Arizona	--- (a) ---
Arkansas	30	...	★	7	★	2	...
California	18	...	5	5	★	4	...
Colorado	30	...	★	2	...	4	...
Connecticut	30	...	...	...	★	4	...
Delaware	30	...	12	6	...	4	...
Florida	30	...	...	7	★	4	...
Georgia	30	6	15	6	...	4	...
Hawaii	30	...	★	5	★	4	2
Idaho	30	...	★	2	...	4	...
Illinois	25	...	★	3	...	4	...
Indiana	30	...	5	5	...	4	...
Iowa	30	...	★	2	...	4	...
Kansas	...	...	...	...	...	4	2
Kentucky	30	6	★	6	...	4	(c)
Louisiana	25	5	5	...	★	4	...
Maine	--- (b) ---
Maryland	30	...	(d)	5	5	4	...
Massachusetts	...	...	...	7	...	4	...
Michigan (e)	30	...	...	...	4	4	...
Minnesota	25	...	★	1	...	4	...
Mississippi	30	...	20	5	...	4	...
Missouri	30	...	15	10	...	4	...
Montana	25	...	★	2	...	4	...
Nebraska	30	5	5	5	...	4	...
Nevada	25	2	...	2	★	4	...
New Hampshire	--- (b) ---
New Jersey	--- (b) ---
New Mexico	30	...	★	5	★	4	1 (f)
New York	30	5	★	5	...	4	...
North Carolina	30	...	5	2	...	4	2
North Dakota	30	...	★	5	★	4	...
Ohio	...	...	★	...	★	4	2
Oklahoma	31	...	★	...	10	4	...
Oregon	--- (b) ---
Pennsylvania	30	...	★	7	...	4	2
Rhode Island	...	...	...	...	★	2	...
South Carolina	30	5	★	5	...	4	...
South Dakota	...	...	2	2	...	4	2
Tennessee	--- (b) ---
Texas	30	...	★	5	...	4	...
Utah	30	5	...	5	★	4	...
Vermont	...	...	...	4	...	2	...
Virginia	30	...	★	5	5	4	...
Washington	...	...	★	...	★	4	...
West Virginia	--- (b) ---
Wisconsin	18	...	★	...	★	4	...
Wyoming	--- (b) ---
American Samoa	35	...	★	5	...	4	2
Guam	30	5	5	★	★	4	...
No. Mariana Islands	35	...	...	...	★	4	...
Puerto Rico	--- (b) ---
U.S. Virgin Islands	30	...	5	5	★	4	2

Note: This table includes constitutional and statutory qualifications.

Key:
★ — Formal provision; number of years not specified.
... — No formal provision.
(a) Some state constitutions have requirements for "state citizenship." This may be different than state residency.
(b) No lieutenant governor. In Maine, Tables 3.3 and 3.5 contain information on qualifications and terms of the President of the Senate. In Tennessee, the speaker of the senate, elected from senate membership, has statutory title of "lieutenant governor."
(c) Successive terms forbidden.
(d) *Crosse* v. *Board of Supervisors of Elections* 243 Md. 555, 221 A.2d 431 (1966)—opinion rendered indicated that U.S. citizenship was, by necessity, a requirement for office.
(e) A person who has been convicted of felony or breach of public trust is not eligible to the office for a period of 20 years after conviction.
(f) Limited to 2 consecutive 4-year terms.

EXECUTIVE BRANCH

Table 2.13
LIEUTENANT GOVERNORS: POWERS AND DUTIES

State or other jurisdiction	Presides over Senate	Appoints committees	Breaks roll-call ties	Assigns bills	Authority for governor to assign duties	Member of governor's cabinet or advisory body	Serves as acting governor when governor out of state
Alabama	★	★ (a)	★	★	...	...	★ (b)
Alaska	...	...	...	...	★	★	★ (c)
Arizona	————	————	————	(d)	————	————	————
Arkansas	★	...	★	...	...	...	★
California	★	...	★	...	★	...	★
Colorado	...	...	...	...	★	★	★
Connecticut	★	...	★	★	★	★	★
Delaware	★	...	★	★	★	★	...
Florida	...	...	...	...	★	...	...
Georgia	★	★ (a)	...	★	★	...	...
Hawaii	...	...	...	...	★	★	★
Idaho	★	...	★	...	★	...	★
Illinois	...	...	...	...	★	★	...
Indiana	★	...	★	...	★	★	...
Iowa	★ (h)	...	(e)	★	... (h)	...	...
Kansas	...	...	...	...	★	(g)	(f)
Kentucky	★	...	★	...	★	★	★
Louisiana	...	...	...	...	★	...	★
Maine	————	————	————	(d)	————	————	————
Maryland	...	...	...	...	★	★	★
Massachusetts	...	...	...	...	★	★	★
Michigan	★	...	★	...	★	★	★
Minnesota	...	...	...	...	★	...	...
Mississippi	★	★ (a)	★	★	...	...	★
Missouri	★	...	★	...	★	...	★
Montana	...	...	...	...	★	★	★ (b)
Nebraska	★ (i)	...	★ (j)	...	★	★	★
Nevada	★	...	★	...	...	...	★
New Hampshire	————	————	————	(d)	————	————	————
New Jersey	————	————	————	(d)	————	————	————
New Mexico	★	(k)	★	...	★	★	★
New York	★	...	★	...	★	...	★
North Carolina	★	...	★	...	★	★ (r)	★
North Dakota	★	...	★	★	★	...	★
Ohio	...	...	...	...	(l)	★	(m)
Oklahoma	★	...	★	...	★	★	★
Oregon	————	————	————	(d)	————	————	————
Pennsylvania	★	...	★ (j)	★	★	★	...
Rhode Island	★	...	★	★	★	...	★
South Carolina	★	...	★	...	...	...	(f)
South Dakota	★	(n)	★	★	★	★	(o)
Tennessee	————	————	————	(d)	————	————	————
Texas	★	★ (a)	★	★	...	...	★
Utah	...	...	...	...	★	...	...
Vermont	★	★ (a)	★	★	...	...	★
Virginia	★	...	★	...	★	★	...
Washington	★	(p)	★ (j)	...	★	...	★
West Virginia	————	————	————	(d)	————	————	————
Wisconsin	...	...	...	...	★	★	(q)
Wyoming	————	————	————	(d)	————	————	————
American Samoa	...	...	...	...	★	★	★
Guam	...	...	...	...	★	★	★
No. Mariana Islands	...	★	...	...	★	★	★
Puerto Rico	————	————	————	(d)	————	————	————
U.S. Virgin Islands	...	...	...	...	★ (l)	★	★

EXECUTIVE BRANCH

LIEUTENANT GOVERNORS: POWERS AND DUTIES—Continued

Source: The Council of State Governments, Spring 1990.
Key:
★ — Provision for responsibility.
. . . — No provision for responsibility.

(a) Appoints all standing committees. Alabama—appoints some special committees; Georgia—appoints all Senate members of conference committees and all senators who serve on interim study committees; Mississippi—appoints members of conference, joint and special committees; Texas—appoints subcommittees and temporary committees; Vermont— appoints all committees as a member of the Committee on Committees.

(b) After 20 days absence. In Montana, after 45 days.

(c) Alaska constitution identifies two types of absence from state: (1) temporary absence during which the lieutenant serves as acting governor; and (2) continuous absence for a period of six months, after which the governor's office is declared vacant and lieutenant governor succeeds to the office.

(d) No lieutenant governor; secretary of state is next in line of succession to governorship. In New Jersey, Senate President is next in line of succession to governorship. In Tennessee, speaker of the Senate bears the additional statutory title of "lieutenant governor."

(e) Only when final passage is not an issue.

(f) Only in emergency situations.

(g) Governor's cabinet is made up of heads of the state departments; since the state's statutes provide that the lieutenant governor may be assigned to serve as head of a department, the officeholder could become part of the official cabinet at some point during the tenure.

(h) Commencing January 1, 1991, the lieutenant governor shall have duties provided by law and assigned by the governor.

(i) Unicameral legislative body.

(j) Except on final enactments.

(k) Special committees only for joint sessions to inform the House and the governor.

(l) Presides over cabinet meetings in absence of governor.

(m) Only if governor asks the lieutenant to serve in that capacity, in the former's absence.

(n) Conference committees.

(o) Only in event of governor's continuous absence from state.

(p) In theory, lieutenant governor is responsible; in practice, appointments are made by majority caucus.

(q) Only in situations of an absence which prevents governor from discharging duties which need to be undertaken prior to his return.

(r) Member of *Council of State* per state constitution. Also sits on Governor's Cabinet, by invitation.

EXECUTIVE BRANCH

Table 2.14
SECRETARIES OF STATE: QUALIFICATIONS FOR OFFICE

State or other jurisdiction	Minimum age	U.S. citizen (years)	State resident (years)	Qualified voter (years)	Method of selection to office
Alabama	25	7	5	★	E
Alaska	----------	----------	(a) ----------	----------	----------
Arizona	25	10	5	★	E
Arkansas	18	★	★	★	E
California	18	★	★	★	E
Colorado	25	★	★	. . .	E
Connecticut	18	★	★	★	E
Delaware	. . .	. . .	. . .	. . .	A
Florida	30	. . .	7	★	E
Georgia	25	10	4	. . .	E
Hawaii	----------	----------	(a) ----------	----------	----------
Idaho	25	★	2	. . .	E
Illinois	25	★	3	. . .	E
Indiana	. . .	. . .	. . .	. . .	E
Iowa	. . .	. . .	★	. . .	E
Kansas	. . .	. . .	. . .	. . .	E
Kentucky	30	2	2 (b)	. . .	E
Louisiana	25	5	(b)	★	E
Maine	. . .	. . .	. . .	. . .	(c)
Maryland	. . .	. . .	. . .	★	A
Massachusetts	. . .	. . .	5	. . .	E
Michigan(d)	. . .	. . .	. . .	★	E
Minnesota	21	★	★	★	E
Mississippi	25	★	5 (b)	★	E
Missouri	18	★	★	★	E
Montana (e)	25	★	2	. . .	E
Nebraska (f)	18	★	. . .	. . .	E
Nevada	25	★	2	★	E
New Hampshire	18	★	★	★	(c)
New Jersey	. . .	. . .	. . .	. . .	A
New Mexico	30	★	★	★	E
New York	18	★	★	. . .	A
North Carolina	21	. . .	. . .	★	E
North Dakota	25	★	. . .	★	E
Ohio	18	★	★	★	E
Oklahoma	31	★	10	10	A
Oregon	18	★	. . .	★	E
Pennsylvania	. . .	. . .	. . .	. . .	A
Rhode Island	18	★	★	★	E
South Carolina	21	. . .	★	★	E
South Dakota	18	★	★	. . .	E
Tennessee	21	★	★	★	(c)
Texas	. . .	. . .	. . .	. . .	A
Utah	----------	----------	(a) ----------	----------	----------
Vermont	. . .	. . .	. . .	. . .	E
Virginia	. . .	. . .	. . .	. . .	A
Washington	18	★	30 da.	★	E
West Virginia	18	★	★	. . .	E
Wisconsin	18	. . .	10 da.	. . .	E
Wyoming	25	★	★	. . .	E
American Samoa	----------	----------	(a) ----------	----------	----------
Guam	----------	----------	(a) ----------	----------	----------
No. Mariana Islands	----------	----------	(a) ----------	----------	----------
Puerto Rico	35	★	★	★	A
U.S. Virgin Islands	----------	----------	(a) ----------	----------	----------

Source: The Book of the States 1988-89.
Note: This table contains constitutional and statutory provisions. "Qualified voter" provision may infer additional residency and citizenship requirements.
Key:
★ — Formal provision; number of years not specified
. . . — No formal provision
A — Appointed by governor
E — Elected by voters
(a) No secretary of state.
(b) Additional state citizenship requirement. Kentucky-two years. Louisiana, Mississippi-five years.
(c) Chosen by joint ballot of state senators and representatives. In Maine and New Hampshire, every two years. In Tennessee, every four years.
(d) A person convicted of a felony or breach of public trust is not eligible to the office for a period of 20 years after conviction.
(e) No person convicted of a felony is eligible to hold public office until final discharge from state supervision.
(f) No person in default as a collector and custodian of public money or property shall be eligible to public office; no person convicted of a felony shall be eligible unless restored to civil rights.

EXECUTIVE BRANCH

Table 2.15
SECRETARIES OF STATE: ELECTION AND REGISTRATION DUTIES

State or other jurisdiction	Chief election officer	Determines ballot eligibility of political parties	Receives initiative and/or referendum petition	Files certificate of nomination or election	Supplies election ballots or materials to local officials	Files candidates' expense papers	Files other campaign reports	Conducts voter education programs	Prepares extradition papers or warrants of arrest	Registers corporations (a)	Processes and/or commissions notaries public	Registers securities	Registers trade names/marks
Alabama	★	★	...	★	★	★	★	★	★	★	...	...	★
Alaska (b)	★	★	★	★	★	...	...	★	...	★	★	...	...
Arizona	★	★	★	★	★	★	★	★	...	...	★	...	★
Arkansas	★	★	★	★	★	★	★	★	...	★	★	...	★
California	★	★	...	★	★	★	★	★	...	...	★	...	...
Colorado	★	★	★	★	★	★	★	★	...	★ (c)	★	...	★
Connecticut	★	★	...	★	★	★	★	★	...	★	★	...	★
Delaware	...	...	...	...	...	...	★	...	...	★	★	...	★
Florida	★	★	...	★	★	★	★	★	...	★	★	...	★
Georgia	★	★	...	★	★	★	★	★	...	★	★	★	★
Hawaii (b)	★	★	...	★	★	...	★	★	...	★	★	...	★
Idaho	★	★	★	...	★	★	★	★	...	★	★	...	★
Illinois	...	...	...	★	...	...	...	...	★	★	★	★	★
Indiana	...	...	...	★	...	...	★	...	★	★	★	★	★
Iowa	★	★	...	★	★	...	★	★	...	★	★	...	★
Kansas	★	★	...	★	★	★	★	★	...	★	★	...	★
Kentucky	★	★	...	★	★	...	...	★	...	★	★	...	★
Louisiana	★	★	...	★	★	★ (d)	★	★	...	★	★	...	★
Maine	★	★	★	★	...	...	★	★	...	★	★	...	★
Maryland	...	...	★	...	...	...	...	...	★	...	★	...	★
Massachusetts	★	★	★	★	★	★	★	★	...	★	★	★	★
Michigan	★	...	★	★	★	★	★	★	...	★	★	...	...
Minnesota	★	★	...	★	★	...	★	★	...	★	★	...	★
Mississippi	(e)	★	...	★	★	★	★	★	...	★	★	★	★
Missouri	★	★	★	★	★	★	★	★	★	★	★	★	★
Montana	★	★	★	★	...	...	...	...	★	★	★	...	★
Nebraska	★	★	★	...	...	...	...	...	...	★	★	...	...
Nevada	★	★	★	★	★	★	★	★	...	★	★	★	★
New Hampshire	★	★	★	★	★	★	★	...	...	★	★	...	★
New Jersey	★	★	...	★	★	★	★	★	...	...	★	...	...
New Mexico	★	★	★	★	...	★	★	★	...	...	★	...	★
New York	...	...	...	...	...	...	...	...	...	★	★	★	★
North Carolina	...	...	...	★	...	...	★	...	...	★	★	...	★
North Dakota	★	★	★	★	★	★	★	★	...	★	★	...	★
Ohio	★	★	★	★	★	★	★	★	...	★	★	...	★
Oklahoma	...	...	★	...	...	...	...	...	...	★	★	...	★
Oregon	★	★	★	★	★	★	★	★	...	★	★	...	★
Pennsylvania	★	★	...	★	★	★	★	★	★	★	★	...	★
Rhode Island	★	...	...	★	★	...	★	★	...	★	★	...	★
South Carolina	...	...	...	...	...	★	...	...	...	★	★	★	★
South Dakota	★	★	★	★	★	★	★	★	★	★	★	...	★
Tennessee	(f)	★	...	★	★	...	...	...	...	★	★	...	★
Texas	★	★	...	★	★	★	★	★	...	★	★	...	★
Utah (b)	★	★	★	★	★	★	★	★	...	...	...	...	...
Vermont	★	★	...	★	★	★	★	★	...	★	★	...	★
Virginia	...	...	...	...	...	...	...	...	★	...	★	...	...
Washington	★	★	★	★	★	...	...	★	...	★	★	...	★
West Virginia	★	★	...	★	★	★	★	★	★	★	★	...	★
Wisconsin	...	...	...	...	...	...	...	...	...	★	★	...	★
Wyoming	★	★	★	★	★	★	★	★	...	★	★	★	★
American Samoa (b)	...	...	...	...	...	...	...	...	N/A	N/A	N/A	N/A	N/A
Puerto Rico	...	...	...	...	...	...	...	...	...	★	★	...	★
U.S. Virgin Islands (b)	...	...	...	...	...	...	...	...	...	★ (g)	...	★	★

Source: National Association of Secretaries' of State survey (1990). Preliminary data.

Key:
★ — Responsible for activity
... — Not responsible for activity
N/A — Does not apply
(a) Unless otherwise indicated, office registers domestic, foreign and non-profit corporations.
(b) No secretary of state. Duties indicated are performed by lieutenant governor.
(c) Receives registration applications for foreign profit/non-profit corporations.
(d) Receives these from federal candidates only.
(e) State Election Commission composed of governor, secretary of state and attorney general.
(f) Secretary appoints state coordinator of elections.
(g) Both domestic and foreign profit; but only domestic non-profit.

EXECUTIVE BRANCH

Table 2.16
SECRETARIES OF STATE: CUSTODIAL, PUBLICATION AND LEGISLATIVE DUTIES

State or other jurisdiction	Custodial: Archives state records and documents	Files state agency rules and regulations	Administers uniform commercial code provisions	Files other corporate documents	Publication: State manual or directory	Session laws	State constitution	Statutes	Administrative rules and regulations	Legislative: Opens legislative sessions (a)	Enrolls or engrosses bills	Retains copies of bills	Registers lobbyists
Alabama	...	★	★	★	...	★	...	★	...	...	★	★	...
Alaska (b)	...	★	...	...	...	...	★	...	★	★	...	★	...
Arizona	...	★	★	★	★	...	★	★	★	...	...	★	★
Arkansas	...	★	★	★	★	★	★	★	...	...	...	★	★
California	★	★	★	★	★	...	...	...	...	...	...	★	★
Colorado	...	★	★	★	★	...	★	...	...	...	...	★	★
Connecticut	★	★	★	★	★	...	★	...	...	S	...	★	...
Delaware	★	★	★	★	...	...	...	...	...	N/A	N/A	N/A	...
Florida	★	★	★	★	...	...	★	★	★	...	...	...	...
Georgia	★	★	...	★	★	★	★	★	★	...	...	★	★
Hawaii (b)	(c)	★	...	...	★	...	...	(d)	...	...	...	★	...
Idaho	...	...	★	★	★	...	★	...	...	...	...	★	★
Illinois	★	★	★	★	★	★	★	...	★	H	...	...	★
Indiana	★	★	★	★	★	...	...	...	...	H	...	...	★
Iowa	...	...	★	★	★	...	★	...	...	...	...	★	...
Kansas	...	★	★	★	★	★	★	...	★	★	★	★	★
Kentucky	★	...	★	★	...	...	...	...	...	...	...	...	...
Louisiana	★	...	...	★	★	...	★	...	...	...	...	★	★
Maine	...	★	★	★	...	...	...	...	...	...	...	★	★
Maryland	... (e)	★	...	...	...	...	...	...	★	...	...	★	...
Massachusetts	★	★	★	★	★	★	★	★	★	...	...	★	★
Michigan	★	★	★	...	★	...	...	...	...	...	★	★	★
Minnesota	...	★	★	★	★	...	...	...	...	H	...	★	...
Mississippi	★	★	★	★	★	★	★	★	★	...	★	★	★
Missouri	★	★	★	★	★	★	★	★	★	★	...	★	...
Montana	★ (e)	★	★	★	★	...	★	...	★	H	...	★	...
Nebraska	★	★	★	★	★	★	★	...	★	(f)	★	★	...
Nevada	...	★	★	★	★	...	★	...	...	H	...	★	★
New Hampshire	★	...	★	★	★	...	...	...	...	...	★	★	★
New Jersey	★	...	★	★	...	...	★	...	...	...	...	★	...
New Mexico	★	...	★	...	★	★	★	★	...	H	...	★	★
New York	...	★	★	★	★	...	★	...	★	...	...	...	...
North Carolina	...	...	★	★	★	★	★	...	...	...	...	★	★
North Dakota	...	★	★	★	...	★	...	...	...	...	...	...	★
Ohio	...	★	★	★	★	★	★	...	...	...	...	★	...
Oklahoma	...	★	★	★	...	★	...	...	...	...	...	★	...
Oregon	★	★	★	★	...	...	...	...	★	...	...	★	★
Pennsylvania	...	★	★	★	...	...	...	...	...	...	★	★	...
Rhode Island	★	★	★	★	...	★	...	...	★	...	...	★	★
South Carolina	...	...	★	★	...	...	...	...	...	...	...	...	★
South Dakota	...	★	★	★	★	...	★	...	...	★	...	★	★
Tennessee	★	★	★	★	...	★	★	★	★	...	...	★	...
Texas	★	★	★	...	...	...	...	★	★	...	...	★	★
Utah (b)	...	...	...	★	...	...	...	...	...	★	...	★	★
Vermont	★	★	★	★	★	★	★	...	...	H (g)	...	★	★
Virginia	...	...	...	★	★	...	...	...	...	...	...	...	★
Washington	★	...	...	★	...	...	...	...	...	...	...	★	...
West Virginia	...	★	★	★	...	...	...	...	★	...	...	★	...
Wisconsin	★	★	★	★	...	...	...	...	...	...	...	...	★
Wyoming	...	★	★	★	★	...	★	...	...	H	...	★	...
Puerto Rico	...	★	...	★	...	★	★	★	...	...	...	...	...
U.S. Virgin Islands (b)	...	★	★	★	...	...	...	...	...	...	★	★	...

Source: National Association of Secretaries' of State survey (1990). Preliminary data.

Key:
★ — Responsible for activity
... — Not responsible for activity
N/A — Does not apply
U/A — Information not available
(a) In this column only: ★ — Both houses; H — House; S — Senate.
(b) No secretary of state. Duties indicated are performed by lieutenant governor.
(c) Limited responsibility.
(d) Distributes and sells session laws, statutes and administrative rules and regulations.
(e) As specified by law. In Maryland, Hall of Records is the archivist.
(f) Certifies and seats members of unicameral legislature.
(g) Until speaker is elected.

EXECUTIVE BRANCH

Table 2.17
ATTORNEYS GENERAL: QUALIFICATIONS FOR OFFICE

State or other jurisdiction	Minimum age	U.S. citizen (years)	State resident (years)	Qualified voter (years)	Licensed attorney (years)	Membership in the state bar (years)	Method of selection to office
Alabama	25	7	5	...	...	...	E
Alaska	...	★	...	...	...	...	A
Arizona	25	10	5	...	...	...	E
Arkansas	18	★	★	★	...	...	E
California	18	...	...	...	(a)	(a)	E
Colorado	25	★	2	...	★	...	E
Connecticut	18	★	★	★	10	10	E
Delaware	...	...	...	...	...	...	E
Florida	30	...	7	★	5	5	E
Georgia	25	10	4	...	7	7	E
Hawaii	...	★	1	...	...	...	A
Idaho	30	★	2	...	★	★	E
Illinois	25	★	3	...	...	...	E
Indiana	...	...	(b)	...	★	...	E
Iowa	...	...	...	...	...	...	E
Kansas	...	...	...	...	...	...	E
Kentucky	30	2	2 (b)	...	8	2	E
Louisiana	25	5	(b)	★	5	5	E
Maine	...	...	...	...	...	...	(c)
Maryland	...	★ (d)	10 (b)	★	10	10 (e)	E
Massachusetts	...	...	5	...	...	★	E
Michigan (f)	...	...	...	★	...	...	E
Minnesota	21	...	30 da.	★	...	...	E
Mississippi	26	...	5 (b)	...	5	5	E
Missouri	...	★	1	...	...	...	E
Montana (g)	25	★	2	...	5	★	E
Nebraska (h)	21 (e)	...	(e)	...	(e)	...	E
Nevada	25	★	2 (b)	★	...	...	E
New Hampshire	...	...	...	...	★	★	A
New Jersey	18 (e)	...	★	...	★	★	A
New Mexico	30	★	5	...	★	★	E
New York	30	★	5	...	(e)	...	E
North Carolina	21	...	...	★	★	(e)	E
North Dakota	25	★	★	★	...	...	E
Ohio	18	★	★	★	...	...	E
Oklahoma	31	★	10	10	...	...	E
Oregon	18	★	6 mos.	★	...	...	E
Pennsylvania	30	★	7	...	★	★	E
Rhode Island	18	★	★	★	...	...	E
South Carolina	...	...	★	★	...	...	E
South Dakota	...	★	★	...	★	★	E
Tennessee	...	...	...	...	...	...	(i)
Texas	...	...	...	...	★	★	E
Utah	25	...	5 (b)	★	★	★	E
Vermont	...	...	...	...	...	...	E
Virginia	30	★	5 (j)	...	...	5 (j)	E
Washington	...	★	...	★	★	★	E
West Virginia	25	★	(b)	...	...	...	E
Wisconsin	...	★	★	...	...	...	E
Wyoming	...	...	★	★	4	4	A
American Samoa	...	★	...	...	...	...	A
Guam	...	...	...	...	...	...	A
No. Mariana Islands	...	...	3	...	5	...	A
Puerto Rico	21 (e)	★	...	...	(e)	(e)	A
U.S. Virgin Islands	...	★	...	...	(k)	...	A

Note: This table contains constitutional and statutory provisions. "Qualified voter" provision may infer additional residency and citizenship requirements.

Key:
★ — Formal provision; number of years not specified.
... — No formal provision.
A — Appointed by governor.
E — Elected by voters.
(a) No statute specifically requires this, but the State Bar act can be interpreted as making this a qualification.
(b) Additional state citizenship requirement. Kentucky, Nevada—two years. Louisiana, Mississippi, Utah, West Virginia—five years.
(c) Chosen biennially by joint ballot of state senators and representatives.
(d) *Crosse* v. *Board of Supervisors of Elections* 243 Md. 555, 2221A. 2d431 (1966)—opinion rendered indicated that U.S. citizenship was, by necessity, a requirement for office.
(e) Implied.
(f) A person convicted of a felony or breach of public trust is not eligible to the office for a period of 20 years after conviction.
(g) No person convicted of felony is eligible to hold public office until final discharge from state supervision.
(h) No person in default as a collector and custodian of public money or property shall be eligible to public office; no person convicted of a felony shall be eligible unless restored to civil rights.
(i) Appointed by judges of state Supreme Court.
(j) Same as qualifications of a judge of a court of record.
(k) Must be admitted to practice before highest court.

EXECUTIVE BRANCH

Table 2.18
ATTORNEYS GENERAL: PROSECUTORIAL AND ADVISORY DUTIES

State or other jurisdiction	Authority in local prosecutions: Authority to initiate local prosecutions	Authority in local prosecutions: May intervene in local prosecutions	Authority in local prosecutions: May assist local prosecutor	Authority in local prosecutions: May supersede local prosecutor	Issues advisory opinions: To state executive officials	Issues advisory opinions: To legislators	Issues advisory opinions: To local prosecutors	Issues advisory opinions: On the interpretation of statutes	Issues advisory opinions: On the constitutionality of bills or ordinances	Reviews legislation: Prior to passage	Reviews legislation: Before signing
Alabama	A	A,D	A,D	A	★	★	★	★	★	★	...
Alaska	(a)	(a)	(a)	(a)	★	★	...	★	★	★	★
Arizona	A,B,C,D,F	B,D	B,D	B	★	★	★	★	★	★	...
Arkansas	...	D	D	...	★	★	★	★	★	...	...
California	A,B,D,E,F	A,B,D,E	A,B,D,E	A,B,D,E	★	★	★	★	★	★	★
Colorado	B,F	B	D,F (b)	B	★	★	★	★	★	★	★
Connecticut	...	...	...	...	★	★ (d)	...	★	★	★	★
Delaware	(a)	(a)	(a)	(a)	★	★	(a)	★	★	★	★
Florida	F	D	D	...	★	★	★	★	...	★	★
Georgia	A,B,F	A,B,D,G	A,B,D,F	B	★	★	★	★	...	★	★
Hawaii	E	A,D,G	A,D	A,G	★	★	★	★	★	★	★
Idaho	A,D,F	A	A,D	A	★	★	★	★	...	★	★
Illinois	D,F	D,F	D,F	F	★	★ (m)	★	★	★	(c)	(c)
Indiana	F (b)	...	A,D,E,F	G	★	★	...	★	★	...	★
Iowa	D,F	D	D	...	★	★	★	★	★	★	★
Kansas	B,C,D,F	D	D	A,F	★	★	★	★	★	(c)	(c)
Kentucky	A,B	B,D	B,D,F	G	★	★	★	★	★	★	...
Louisiana	G	G	D	G	★	★	★	★	★	★	★
Maine	A	A	A	A	★	★	...	★	★	★	★
Maryland	B,C,F	B,C,D	B,C,D	B,C	★	★	★	★	★	★	★
Massachusetts	A	A	A,D	A	★	★ (g)	★	★	★	(c)	(c)
Michigan	A	A	D	A	★	★	★	★	★	★	★
Minnesota	B	B,D,G	A,B,D	B	★	(g)	★	★	...	...	(c)
Mississippi	B,D,E,F	D	B,D,F	E	★	★	★	★	★	(c)	(c)
Missouri	F	...	B	...	★	★	★	★	...	★	★
Montana	C,F	A,B,C,D	A,B,C,D,F	A,C	★	★ (d)	★	★	(k)	★	★
Nebraska	A	A	A,D	A	★	★	★	★	★	★	★
Nevada	D,F,G (e)	D (e)	(e,f)	G,F	★	...	★	★	(l)	...	...
New Hampshire	A	A	A	A	★	...	...	★	★	★	★
New Jersey	A	A,B,D,G	A,D	A,B,D,G	★	★	★	★	★	★	★
New Mexico	A	A	D	B	★	★	★	★	★	★	★
New York	B,F	B	D	B	★	★	...	★	★	...	★
North Carolina	...	D	D	...	★	★	★	★	★	★	...
North Dakota	A,G	A,D	A,D	A	★	★	★	★	...	...	(c)
Ohio	B,C,F	B,F	F	B,C	★	★ (g)	★	★	...	...	...
Oklahoma	B,C,F	B,C	B,C	...	★	★	★	★	★	★	★
Oregon	B,F	B,D	B,D	B	★	★	★	★	★	(c)	(c)
Pennsylvania	A,D,F,G	D,G	D	G	★	★	★	★	★	★	★
Rhode Island	...	A	A	...	★	★	★	★	★	...	...
South Carolina	A,D (b)	A,D	A,D	...	★	★	★	★	★	★	★
South Dakota	A (h)	A	A	A	★	...	★	★	★	★	★
Tennessee	D,F,G (b)	D,G (b)	D	F	★	★	★	★	★	(c)	(c)
Texas	F	...	D	...	★	★	★	★	★	★	★
Utah	A,B,D,E,F,G	E,G	D,E	E	★	★ (n)	★	★	★	(c)	(c)
Vermont	A	A	A	...	★	★	★	★	★	★	★
Virginia	B,F	A,B,D,F	B,D,F	B	★	★	★	★	★	★	★
Washington	B,D,G	B,D,G	D	B	★	★	★	★	★	★	★
West Virginia	...	...	D	...	★	★ (d)	★	★	★	(i)	(i)
Wisconsin	B,C,F	B,C,D	D	B	★	★	★	★	★ (k)	(i)	(i)
Wyoming	B,D (e),F	B,D	B,D	...	★	★	★	★	...	★	★
American Samoa	A,E	A,E	A,E	A,E	★	★	...	★	★	★	★
No. Mariana Islands	A	...	...	...	★	★	...	★	★	★	★
Puerto Rico	A,B,E	A,B,E	A,E	A,B,E	★	★	...	★	★	★	★
U.S. Virgin Islands	A	...	...	...	★	★	...	★	★	★	★

Source: The Council of State Governments, *The Book of the States* 1988-89.

Key:
A — On own initiative.
B — On request of governor.
C — On request of legislature.
D — On request of local prosecutor.
E — When in state's interest.
F — Under certain statutes for specific crimes.
G — On authorization of court or other body.
★ — Has authority in area.
... — Does not have authority in area.
(a) Local prosecutors serve at pleasure of attorney general.
(b) Certain statutes provide for concurrent jurisdiction with local prosecutors.
(c) Only when requested by governor or legislature.
(d) To legislative leadership.
(e) In connection with grand jury cases.
(f) Will prosecute as a matter of practice when requested.
(g) To legislature as a whole not individual legislators.
(h) Has concurrent jurisdiction with states' attorneys.
(i) No legal authority, but sometimes informally reviews laws at request of legislature.
(j) If the governor removes the district attorney for cause.
(k) Bills, not ordinances.
(l) On the constitutionality of legislation.
(m) Opinion may be issued to officers of either branch of General Assembly or to Chairman or Minority Spokesman of committees or commissions thereof.
(n) Only when requested by legislature.

EXECUTIVE BRANCH

Table 2.19
ATTORNEYS GENERAL: CONSUMER PROTECTION ACTIVITIES, SUBPOENA POWERS AND ANTITRUST DUTIES

State or other jurisdiction	May commence civil proceedings	May commence criminal proceedings	Represents the state before regulatory agencies (a)	Administers consumer protection programs	Handles consumer complaints	Subpoena powers (b)	Antitrust duties
Alabama	★	★	...	★	★	•	A,B
Alaska	★	★	★	★	★	★	B,C
Arizona	★	...	...	★	★	★	A,B,D
Arkansas	★	...	★	★	★	★	B,C
California	★	★	★	★	★	★	A,B,C,D (c)
Colorado	★	★	★	★	★	•	B,C,D (k)
Connecticut	★	(e)	★	★	...	•	A,B,D
Delaware	★	★	★	★	...	★	A,B,C
Florida	★	...	...	...	★	★	A,B,C,D (j)
Georgia	★	★	★	...	...	•	B,C
Hawaii	★	★	★	★ (e,f)	...	•	A,B,C,D
Idaho	★	...	★	★	★	•	D
Illinois	★	★	★	★	★	•	A,B,C,D
Indiana	★	...	...	★	★	...	B,C,D
Iowa	★	★	★	★	★	•	A,B,C,D
Kansas	★	★	★	★	★	★	B,C,D
Kentucky	★	★	★	★	★	(c)	A,B,D
Louisiana	★	★	★	★	★	★	A,B,C,D
Maine	★	★	★	★	★	★	A,B,C
Maryland	★	★	★	★	★	★	B,C,D
Massachusetts	★	★	★	★	★	•	A,B,C,D
Michigan	★	★	★	★	★	•	A,B,C,D
Minnesota	★	...	★	★	★	•	B,C,D
Mississippi	★	★	...	★	★	•	A,B,C,D
Missouri	★	...	...	...	★	•	A,B,C,D
Montana	★	★	★	...	...	★	B,C,D
Nebraska	★	...	★	★	★	•	A,B,C (d),D
Nevada	★	★	...	...	★	★	A,B,C,D
New Hampshire	★	★	★	...	★	•	B,C,D
New Jersey	★	★	★	★	★	★	A,B,C,D
New Mexico	★	★	★	★	★	•	A,C
New York	★	★	...	...	★	★	A,B,C,D
North Carolina	★	...	★	★	★	•	A,B,C,D
North Dakota	★	...	★	★	★	★	A,B,D
Ohio	★	★	★	★	★	•	B,C,D
Oklahoma	★	...	(e)	★	★	•	B,D
Oregon	★	★	(c)	★	★	•	A,B,C,D
Pennsylvania	★	★	★	★	★	•	A,B,C,D
Rhode Island	★	★	★	★	★	•	A,B,C,D
South Carolina	★	★	★	...	★	•	A,B,C,D
South Dakota	★	★	★	★	★	•	A,B,C,D
Tennessee	★	★	★ (c)	★	★	•	A,B,C,D
Texas	★	...	★	★	★	•	B,D
Utah	★ (d)	...	★ (d,f)	...	★ (f)	★	A (g),B,C,D (g)
Vermont	★	★	★	★	★	•	A,B,C,D
Virginia	★	(e)	★	★ (f)	★ (f)	•	A,B,C,D
Washington	★	...	★	★	★	•	A,B,D
West Virginia	★	...	★	★	★	•	A,B,D
Wisconsin	★	...	★	★	★	•	B,C
Wyoming	★	...	...	★	★	...	...
American Samoa	★	★	★	...	...	★	...
No. Mariana Islands	★	★	★	...	...	★	B,C,D
Puerto Rico	★	★	★	★ (e)	★ (e)	★	A,B,C
U.S. Virgin Islands	★	★ (h)	★	...	...	★	A,B (i),C,D

Source: The Council of State Governments' survey, Spring 1990.
Key:
A — Has *parens patriae* authority to commence suits on behalf of consumers in state antitrust damage actions in state courts.
B — May initiate damage actions on behalf of state in state courts.
C — May commence criminal proceedings.
D — May represent cities, counties and other governmental entities in recovering civil damages under federal or state law.
★ — Has authority in area.
. . . — Does not have authority in area.
(a) May represent state on behalf of: the "people" of the state; an agency of the state; or the state before a federal regulatory agency.
(b) In this column only: ★ broad powers and • limited powers.
(c) When permitted to intervene.
(d) Attorney general has exclusive authority.
(e) To a limited extent.
(f) Attorney general handles legal matters only with no administrative handling of complaints.
(g) Opinion only, since there are no controlling precedents.
(h) May prosecute in inferior courts. May prosecute in district court only by request or consent of U.S. Attorney General.
(i) May initiate damage actions on behalf of jurisdiction in district court.
(j) May commence criminal proceedings with local state attorney.
(k) Only under Rule 23 of the Rules of Civil Procedure.

EXECUTIVE BRANCH

Table 2.20
ATTORNEYS GENERAL: DUTIES TO ADMINISTRATIVE AGENCIES AND OTHER RESPONSIBILITIES

State or other jurisdiction	Serves as counsel for state	Appears for state in criminal appeals	Issues official advice	Interprets statutes or regulations	In behalf of agency	Against agency	Prepares or reviews legal documents	Represents the public before the agency	Involved in rule-making	Reviews rules for legality
Alabama	A,B,C	★ (a)	★	★	★	★	★	(b)	...	★
Alaska	A,B,C	★	★	★	★	★	★	...	★	★
Arizona	A,B,C	(c,d)	★	★	★	★	★	...	★	★
Arkansas	A,B,C	★ (a)	★	★	★	...	★	★	★	★
California	A,B,C	★ (a)	★	★	★	★	★	...	...	...
Colorado	A,B,C	★ (a)	★	★	★	★	★	...	★	★
Connecticut	A,B,C	(b)	★	★	★	(b)	★	(b)	★	★
Delaware	A,B,C	★ (a)	★	★	★	★	★	★	★	★
Florida	A,B,C	★ (a)	★	★	★	...	★	★	★	...
Georgia	A,B,C	(b,c)	★	★	★	★	★	...	★	★
Hawaii	A,B	(b,c)	★	★	★	★	★	★	★	★
Idaho	A,B,C	★ (a)	★	★	★	★	★	...	★	★
Illinois	A,B,C	(b,c,e)	★	★	★	★	★	★	...	...
Indiana	A,B,C	★ (a)	★	★	★	...	★	...	★	★
Iowa	A,B,C	★ (a)	★	★	★	★	★	...	...	★
Kansas	A,B,C	★ (a)	★	★	★	★	★	...	...	★
Kentucky	A,B*,C	★	★	★	★	★	★	...	★	★
Louisiana	A,B,C	(c)	★	★	★	★	★	...	★	★
Maine	A,B,C	(b,d)	★	★	★	(b)	★	(b)	★	★
Maryland	A,B,C	★	★	★	★	(b)	★	★	★	★
Massachusetts	A,B,C	(b,c,d)	★	★	★	★	★	★	★	★
Michigan	A,B,C	(b,c,d)	★	★	★	...	★	★	★	★
Minnesota	A,B,C	(c,d)	★	★	(a)	★	★	★	★	★
Mississippi	A,B,C	★	★	★	★	★	★	★	★	★
Missouri	A,B,C	★	★	★	★	★	★	...	★	★
Montana	A,B,C	★	★	★	★	...	★	...	★	★
Nebraska	A,B,C	★	★	★	★	★	★	...	...	★
Nevada	A,B,C	★ (d)	★	★	★	...	★	★	★	★
New Hampshire	A,B,C	★ (a)	★	★	★	★	★	★	★	★
New Jersey	A,B,C	★ (d)	★	★	★	★	★	...	★	★
New Mexico	A,B,C	★ (a)	★	★	★	★	★	...	★	★
New York	A,B,C	(b)	★	★	★	★	★	★	★	...
North Carolina	A,B,C	★	★	★	★	★	★	(b)	★	★
North Dakota	A,B,C	(b)	★	★	★	...	★	★	★	★
Ohio	A,B,C	...	★	★	★	★	★	★	★	...
Oklahoma	A,B,C	(b)	★	★	★	★	★	★	★	★
Oregon	A,B,C	★	★	★	★	...	★	...	★	★
Pennsylvania	A,B,C	★	★	★	★	★	★	...	★	★
Rhode Island	A,B,C	★ (a)	★	★	★	★	★	★	★	★
South Carolina	A,B,C	★ (d)	★	★	★	...	★	...	★	★
South Dakota	A,B,C	★ (a)	★	★	★	...	★	...	★	...
Tennessee	A,B,C	★ (a)	★	★	★	...	★	(b)	★	★
Texas	A,B,C	(c)	★	★	★	★	★	...	★	★
Utah	A,B,C	★ (a)	★	★	★	★	★	★	★	★
Vermont	A,B,C	★	★	★	★	...	★	★	★	★
Virginia	A,B,C	★ (a)	★	★	★	★	★	★	★	★
Washington	A,B,C	(c,f)	★	★	★	★	★	★	★	★
West Virginia	A,B,C	★ (a)	★	★	★	(f)	★	★	★	...
Wisconsin	A,B,C	(b)	★	★	★	(b)	(b)	(b)	(b)	...
Wyoming	A,B,C	★ (a)	★	★	★	...	★	...	★	★
American Samoa	A,B,C	★ (a)	★	★	★	...	★	...	★	★
No. Mariana Islands	A,B,C	★	★	★	★	...	★	...	★	★
Puerto Rico	A,B,C	★	★	★	★	...	★	...	★	★
U.S. Virgin Islands	A,B,C (g)	★	★	★	★	★	★	...	★	★

Source: The Council of State Governments' survey, Spring 1990.
Key:
A — Defend state law when challenged on federal constitutional grounds.
B — Conduct litigation on behalf of state in federal and other states' courts.
C — Prosecute actions against another state in U.S. Supreme Court.
* — Only in federal courts.
★ — Has authority in area.
... — Does not have authority in area.

(a) Attorney general has exclusive jurisdiction.
(b) In certain cases only.
(c) When assisting local prosecutor in the appeal.
(d) Can appear on own discretion.
(e) In certain courts only.
(f) If authorized by the governor.
(g) Except in cases in which the U.S. Attorney is representing the Government of the U.S. Virgin Islands.

CHAPTER THREE

STATE LEGISLATIVE BRANCH

THE STATE LEGISLATURES

By Rich Jones

State legislatures are dramatically different institutions than they were 25 years ago. In 1965, as the effort to modernize and improve state legislatures began in earnest, legislatures were generally considered 18th century relics, incapable of meeting the challenges set before them. One prominent author described them as a drag on the states' ability to function effectively in the federal system. His assessment was not that they had done anything terribly wrong but that they had not done much of anything. They were malapportioned and generally dominated by rural interests. There was little or no staff, and legislators were heavily dependent on executive agencies and lobbyists for information. They met infrequently and had limited ability to adjust the length and frequency of their sessions. Members in most states did not have office space and committee rooms were often too small to accommodate citizens wanting to participate in the legislative process. Their procedures and committee systems were antiquated.[1] A new member of the Illinois House of Representatives was quoted in 1965 as stating he was, "appalled by the conditions under which we have to work."[2] Because of these weaknesses state legislatures were characterized as a "series of sometime governments: their presence is rarely felt or rarely missed."[3]

Several factors propelled the revitalization and modernization of state legislatures. One was the series of state and federal court decisions following the U.S. Supreme Court rulings on legislative districting in *Baker vs. Carr* (1963) and *Reynolds vs. Simms* (1965). These decisions required districts in both houses of state legislatures be apportioned based on equal population ("One man, one vote"). As a result, many legislatures became more representative of the population and power shifted from rural to urban and suburban interests. The composition of the membership changed as the number of farmers declined and the number of educators, professionals, women and racial minorities grew. Another factor was the series of studies of the legislative process conducted by national organizations, citizen groups in the states and the legislatures themselves. These studies examined the problems confronting legislatures and provided recommendations for improvement. The recommendations advocated most frequently included:

- eliminating and relaxing constitutional limits on legislative sessions and salaries;
- developing and expanding legislative staff;
- expanding and improving legislative facilities;
- reforming legislative rules and procedures to open the process up to greater public participation and scrutiny;
- expanding the legislatures' capacity to review and oversee state budgets; and
- developing statutes to govern legislative ethics, campaign finance, disclosure and conflict of interest.

State legislatures enter the 1990s having incorporated most of the reformers' recommendations. Some legislatures have eliminated constitutional limits on sessions while others have expanded the time available for legislative sessions. Currently, 43 states meet in annual sessions as compared to 20 in 1966. Legislative compensation has increased significantly. Only six states have constitutional

---

Rich Jones is the director of Legislative Programs at the National Conference of State Legislatures.

limits on legislative salaries. Staffing is probably the area that has changed the most. In 1988, there were more than 33,000 staff working in state legislatures, 41 percent of whom were full-time professional staff. Legislatures have added office space, expanded committee rooms and renovated their capitols. Many legislatures now provide district offices for the members in addition to space in the capitol. Legislatures have streamlined their procedures and adopted open meeting and open records laws that have made the process more accessible to the public. Legislatures currently play an active role in reviewing and monitoring state budgets as well as overseeing the operation of state agencies. The majority of legislatures have enacted statutes that govern legislative ethics, campaign finance and conflict of interest. As a result of these changes, legislatures have become co-equal partners in state government and in the process have transformed into a leading source of policy innovation in the nation.

Legislative Operations, Organization and Procedures

As legislatures have assumed a more active policy-making role, the number and complexity of the issues they address and the public attention they receive have expanded. Consequently, legislative workloads have grown. To meet these increased demands and to more effectively complete their business within prescribed time limits, legislatures have devoted considerable attention to streamlining and improving their operations. Providing increased public access to the legislative process and improving the legislature's use of its time in session and during the interim have been the primary objectives of these efforts.

Since 1987, studies of legislative procedures and operations have been conducted in Alaska, Florida, Kansas, Minnesota, Missouri, Nevada, New York and Washington. Studies are underway in Delaware and Maine. The legislatures used different approaches in conducting these studies, but they all had the common objective of identifying methods to streamline legislative procedures, become more efficient and more effectively handle the increased workload.

Length of Legislative Sessions

During the last two decades limitations on the length of sessions and restrictions on the legislature's ability to call itself into special session were relaxed. Currently, 12 states place no limit on session length, 32 states have constitutional limits and six states have statutory or indirect limitations based on cutoffs in legislators' salaries or per diem expense payments. All but seven states (Arkansas, Kentucky, Montana, Nevada, North Dakota, Oregon and Texas) meet in annual sessions. Following World War II, only four states held annual sessions. By 1966 this number increased to 20 states, and by 1974, 42 states met annually.

More recently, however, there has been increased interest, particularly on the part of the public, in limiting legislative sessions. In 1988, Colorado voters approved a constitutional amendment that limited legislative sessions to 120 calendar days. Previously, the first year of the session was unlimited with a 140-day limit placed on the second year. A constitutional amendment adopted by the voters in Oklahoma in 1989 specified that the Legislature could meet only from February through May. This was a change from the prior language which limited the Legislature to 90 legislative days. Meeting four days per week, the Legislature was in session most years from early January through June. Because the legislature has kept to its four-day a week meeting schedule, this change has had the effect of limiting the time spent in session. Alaska adopted a 120-day session limit in 1984. There have been several attempts to limit sessions in Michigan, and New Hampshire has considered returning to biennial sessions. Arizona and Nevada limit their sessions by legislative rules that reduce the salary or per diem expenses for the members if they stay in session beyond the prescribed limit. The effectiveness of these measures is questionable. Throughout the 1980s, the Nevada Legislature has repeatedly exceeded its limit; the 1987 and 1989 sessions have been the longest to date. Arizona has exceeded its session cut-off by about one month in each year since 1985. Although more restrictive limits are placed on sessions, the legislatures' workload continues to grow. Colorado and Oklahoma, after moving toward more limited sessions, met in special session during 1989 to complete action on issues left unresolved during their regular sessions. Nationwide, 37 special sessions were convened in 28 states during 1989.[1]

Full-Time Legislatures and Legislators

Debates over the amount of time legislatures spend in session often center around the desire to preserve the citizen legislature versus the need to develop professional or full-time legislatures similar to the U.S. Congress. The amount of time a legislature spends in session and the level of compensation paid to its members have a direct effect on the type of member found in legislative bodies. Those states with longer sessions and higher salaries have, for the most part, a larger number of members that consider the legislature their career. Traditionally, it has been argued that legislatures benefit by having members who represent a variety of vocations, who come to the legislature for a short period of time and then return to their other occupations. In recent years, many have argued that the complexities of the issues and the demands placed on legislatures have increased the need for full-time legislators.

Several factors such as the amount of time spent in session, level of compensation, amount of staff and turnover in membership can be used to measure whether a legislature is considered full-time. In addition, full-time legislatures tend to provide district offices for the members, place a high priority on constituent service and have a large number of members who consider themselves full-time legislators.

A 1988 National Conference of State Legislatures (NCSL) study grouped the legislatures into three categories depending on the extent to which they exhibit the characteristics of a full-time legislature. California, Illinois, Massachusetts, Michigan, New York, Ohio, Pennsylvania and Wisconsin are considered to be full-time legislatures. They meet in session longer than the other legislatures, have relatively high salaries, large staffs and stable memberships. At the other end of the spectrum are the 17 states with clearly part-time legislatures. They meet in short sessions, have low salaries and small staffs and exhibit high turnover among the members. In between are the 25 states whose legislatures may have some of the characteristics of the full-time legislatures but not all. Florida, for example, has a large legislative staff but meets in a short session and ranks in the midrange on legislative pay. New Jersey meets most of the full-time characteristics except for a relatively high turnover rate among its membership. Given the increased demands placed on legislatures, it is likely that states such as Florida, Missouri and New Jersey will move into the full-time category during the coming decade. Others, such as Maine and North Carolina are likely to evolve from being part-time bodies and begin to take on more characteristics of full-time legislatures.[1]

The number of members who consider themselves to be full-time legislators is increasing. In a 1986 study conducted by NCSL, 11 percent of all legislators designate the legislature as their sole profession. It can be argued that the actual percentage of full-time legislators is even higher. If the occupational categories of retired, student and homemaker are included, full-time legislators would exceed 20 percent of all legislators. More than 60 percent of the members in the Pennsylvania and New York legislatures consider themselves full-time lawmakers and more than half the legislators in the middle Atlantic states serve full time. About 19 percent of all women legislators consider themselves to be full-time legislators with an additional 13 percent indicating that they are homemakers.[2]

This study also found that the number of attorneys serving in state legislatures declined significantly, dropping from 22 percent of the total in 1976 to 16 percent in 1986. Stringent disclosure laws and the ability to advertise their services may account for some of this decline. Also, many of the former attorneys may now consider themselves to be full-time legislators. The largest percentage of lawyer legislators is in the South, with Virginia having the highest percentage of any legislature (45 percent). In rank order, the largest self designated occupational categories are: attorney (16 percent), business owner (14 percent), full-time legislator (11 percent), agricultural occupations (10 percent) and educator (8 percent).

The makeup of state legislatures is changing in other ways. The number of women and minorities serving in state legislatures continues to grow. In 1989, 1,261 legislators or almost 17 percent were women. This is a 400 percent increase since 1969, when 301 or 4 percent of all legislators were women, and a 163 percent increase since 1979, when 770 or 10 percent of all legislators were women.[3] One result of the increase in the number of women legislators is the increase in the number of women that hold leadership positions. In 1989, 15 women held positions as presiding officer, majority or minority leader. This compares to four women holding similar positions in 1979.[4] In 1989, there were 407 Black state legislators and 128 Hispanic state legislators.[5]

Legislative Scheduling

Making the best use of time during a session is a major concern in state legislatures. A majority of legislatures have experimented with floor and committee scheduling systems and the use of deadlines. Deadline systems, which establish specific dates for committee consideration and cut off dates for floor consideration, are used in at least 10 states.[1] These systems provide a more even work flow throughout the legislative session and can reduce the end-of-session logjams.[2] Another effect of these systems is to kill bills at various stages of the legislative process — often providing a convenient excuse for inaction — rather than having all of the bills that have been introduced remain alive throughout the session.

Bill Introductions

Limiting the number of bills introduced and establishing deadlines for introducing bills are two tools that legislatures use to help manage their workload. Although controversial, the Colorado, Indiana (short session only), Montana, Nebraska and North Dakota legislatures and the Tennessee Senate limit the number of bills that members can introduce. Colorado limits each member to six bills in the first year of a session and four bills in the second.

More than 35 legislatures have established deadlines for the introduction of bills and at least 38 have provisions allowing bills to be prefiled. These procedures are designed to encourage the introduction of bills earlier in the session so that committees can begin work immediately upon convening. In addition, 13 legislative chambers use proposed short form or skeleton bills. If, after consideration, there is interest in pursuing the policies embodied in the skeleton bills a complete bill will be drafted. By using skeleton bills the legislature reduces the number of full bills introduced, eases the burden on bill drafters and gives committees the opportunity to combine duplicate proposals into a single bill.[1]

On average, legislatures consider more than 200,000 bills each biennium. The number introduced in each state during a biennium varies from a low of about 1,000 in Alaska, Colorado, North Dakota, Vermont and Wyoming to highs of more than 30,000 in New York and 18,000 in Massachusetts. Legislatures pass approximately 21 percent of the bills introduced or about 42,000 bills in an average biennium. The passage rate for state legislation has remained fairly constant since the late 1970s.[2]

Legislative Compensation

Adequate pay for state legislators was a key recommendation of the legislative reform movement. Proponents argued that increased salaries, additional staff resources and extended time in session would help attract and retain higher quality members. In the mid 1960s, lawmakers salaries were set in the constitutions of 26 states. Those states with constitutionally established salaries paid legislators less than those that set salaries by statute. Increasing constitutionally set salaries was politically and administratively difficult to do.[1] Over the past 25 years, all but six states have removed legislators' salaries from their constitutions. Those states that still retain the constitutional limits pay relatively low salaries such, as Alabama's $10 per day for 30 session days, New Hampshire's $100 per year and Rhode Island's $5 per day for 60 session days.[2]

Deciding appropriate salaries for state legislators is a difficult task that involves balancing the philosophical idea of a citizen legislature with the practical considerations of the time and cost of serving in the legislature. Legislatures in 28 states are responsible for setting their own salaries. Compensation commissions are used in 20 states. In most of these states, the legislature must approve the commission's recommendations before they can take effect. However, in five states (Delaware, Hawaii, Idaho, Michigan and Washington), the commission's recommendations go into effect automatically unless rejected by the legislature. In Oklahoma, the Compensation Review Board sets legislators' salaries without approval or rejection by the legislature. Seven states (Florida, Georgia, Kansas, Missouri, Montana, North Carolina, and Oregon) tie legislators' salaries to those paid to state employees.

In 1990, salaries range from a low of $100 per year in New Hampshire to a high of $57,500 per year in New York. Ten states will pay legislators $30,000 a year or more in 1990. All but five states pay legislators a per diem to cover living expenses. In 43 states, presiding officers and majority or minority leaders receive additional compensation. In 16 states, additional pay is given to other leaders such as deputy majority leaders, whips, caucus chairs and policy chairs. Committee chairs get extra pay in 15 states.

In addition to salaries, legislators are eligible for retirement benefits in 42 states. In 46 states they receive various insurance benefits such as health and hospitalization, dental, life, disability and optical. In most of these states, legislators receive the same insurance benefits as state employees. All but three states (Hawaii, Massachusetts and New Jersey) reimburse legislators for the use of their cars. California and Pennsylvania provide monthly allowances to lease automobiles, and certain legislative leaders are provided with a state car in Arkansas, Missouri, New Jersey and Washington.

A relatively new and growing aspect of legislative compensation is the allowances paid to members in 33 states for district or capitol office expenses. These range from relatively small postage budgets in Minnesota and Nevada to staffing allowances in excess of $100,000 paid to members in California, Michigan, New York and Texas.

Legislative Staffing

The cornerstone of the modern state legislature is the legislative staff. The growth and development of legislative staff has significantly affected the operations of state legislatures. Through its ability to gather, evaluate, process and synthesize information, staff provide legislatures with greater independence. No longer must legislators rely exclusively on the information provided by lobbyists and executive agencies.

Modern legislative staffing can be traced to 1901 when the Wisconsin Legislative Reference Bureau, the nation's first permanent legislative staff, was created. Up to that point, staff was generally limited to the clerk and secretary, two positions derived from English parliamentary tradition. In 1933, Kansas created the nation's first legislative council staff, and throughout the 1940s and 1950s a majority of the states created similar operations. Council staff were organized on a nonpartisan basis to provide research and policy analysis to members of both chambers. In the early 1960s, 44 legislatures had legislative councils.

Legislatures began to add specialized staff beginning in the 1950s with the appearance of fiscal and budget staff. All 50 states had staff to provide independent budget analysis and information by 1975. Post audit and program evaluation staff were added to legislatures in the early 1970s, with most states adopting this capability by the mid-1980s. Computer staff, science and technical staff and a wide range of specialists on policy issues were added to legislatures throughout the 1970s and 1980s.

Legislative staffing underwent several significant changes in the 1980s. First, the number of staff working in state legislatures grew by approximately 24 percent, from almost 27,000 total staff in 1979 to over 33,000 total staff in 1988. Most of the increase came in the area of full-time professional staff, which grew by 5,400 or almost 65 percent. This growth represents nearly 85 percent of the total staff change since 1979. The number of session-only staff declined by 12 percent from 1979 to 1988.[1]

The growth rate in legislative staff has not been uniform across all states. The states with the largest number of staff in 1979 accounted for more than 65 percent of the total growth during the 1980s. States with the largest legislative staffs in 1988 are in rank order New York, California, Pennsylvania, Texas, Florida, Illinois and Michigan.

The decentralization of legislative staff that has occurred since the mid-1960s is continuing, but in a different way. There have been almost no recent examples of decentralization occurring through the breakup and reassignment of central legislative staff agencies. Rather, decentralization is occurring through growth in staff outside of these legislative staff agencies. Staff added during the 1980s tended to be personal staff to individual members, staff assigned to the party caucuses and policy staff assigned to work directly with legislative committees. Since 1979, at least 17 states report they have increased the number of personal staff available to members. The growth in this type of staff has decentralized staff resources and consequently, power within state legislatures.

Recent changes to central legislative staff agencies have tended toward consolidation. In 1989, Alaska combined House and Senate research agencies into a single research unit for the entire Legislature. Prior to the 1989 session, Oregon abolished a central research office, eliminated session staff assigned to committees and created full-time committee staff in the House and Senate. Recent reorganizations in Maine and Arkansas have consolidated the operations of their central staff agencies.

One result of the growth and professionalization of legislative staff is the need for improved personnel management systems. Several legislatures, including Connecticut and Maine, have undertaken comprehensive reviews of their position classification systems and pay plans. Formal evaluation systems have been established in a majority of legislatures, and programs that offer professional development for staff are being implemented in a number of legislatures, including Florida and Texas.

Legislative Facilities

Legislatures have come a long way from the time when the only space the members had was a desk on the chamber floor. Modern telecommunications and computer technology, longer sessions, increased public desire for access to the legislature and the expanding number of staff are some of the factors driving the legislatures' need for additional and more sophisticated space. The Connecticut Legislature recently completed a legislative office building, Pennsylvania added a wing to its main capitol, Alabama renovated a highway department building and converted it for the Legislature's use, and Wisconsin moved legislative staff into leased space outside of the capitol. Plans are underway for constructing legislative office buildings in Arizona, Michigan and Texas.

Concurrent with this drive for additional space, legislatures have embarked on an effort to restore and preserve the historic quality of their capitols. During the 1980s, major renovation projects were undertaken in California, Connecticut, Indiana, Michigan, Minnesota, Mississippi, New York, Pennsylvania, Tennessee and Wisconsin. New Jersey almost has finished restoring its capitol and New Mexico is about to begin a restoration project.[1]

Information Systems

The evolution of computer technology — particularly the development of powerful, relatively inexpensive personal computers — has changed significantly the operations of state legislatures. Computers have enhanced the legislatures' policy-making capacity, increased the efficiency of legislative functions such as bill drafting and journal production and expanded legislators' ability to provide constituent services. Through the use of networking capabilities, legislative computer systems can be connected with executive agency systems and the legislature's computers can be linked together. The North Carolina Legislature receives expenditure information from the executive agencies as it is entered into the agencies' systems, allowing lawmakers to monitor agency budgets continuously. California and New Jersey link computers in the district offices to the legislatures' main information system at their capitols. California, Florida and Washington are among the states that use computer technology to produce legislative journals. By using computer software to do the layout and by electronically transmitting the information to the printer, the journal can be produced more quickly and at lower costs. In almost every state, legislators have access to word processing systems that increases their ability to communicate with constituents.

Computers will have an enormous impact on the 1990 reapportionment process. The increased access to powerful computers coupled with the availability of digital data from the U.S. Census Bureau will mean legislative districts can be drawn with greater precision. More people, inside and outside the legislature, will have access to the technology and information to develop redistricting plans. The results are likely to be more alternative plans being considered, a weakening of the leaders' control over the process and more court challenges based on the ability to draw alternative plans that meet legal requirements.

As more members familiar with computers are elected to the legislature, the demand for additional technology will increase. In 1990, the Michigan Senate installed computers on the floor for every senator who wanted one. Senators can vote through the computer, review the bill being considered, as well as proposed amendments, receive and send messages through an electronic mail system, and access the computer system in their offices to draft correspondence and communicate with staff. The trend toward greater use of computers to provide constituent services is likely to continue unabated throughout the 1990s, giving rise to questions about the line separating campaign activities from legislative business. Legislatures also are becoming more involved in setting policies for state-wide computer information systems. They are establishing standards and creating agencies to coordinate the development of executive branch computer systems so that duplication and incompatibility can be avoided.

Party Control

Democrats continued to dominate state legislatures throughout the 1980s and during the 1989-90 biennium. As of November 1989, there were 4,449 Democratic legislators, 2,940 Republican legislators, 49 nonpartisan members of the Nebraska unicameral, six independents and 17 vacancies. Democrats control 29 legislatures, Republicans control eight, and 12 legislatures where each party controls one chamber. (The Nebraska unicameral is elected on a nonpartisan basis.)[1] The Indiana House of Representatives was equally divided between Republicans and Democrats (50-50) following the 1988 election. The House adopted an elaborate organization plan that established co-speakers (one from each party) who presided every other day, co-chairs of all committees and an equal number of members from each party on all committees. In the closing days of the 1990 session, a Democratic member switched parties, giving the Republicans a 51 to 49 advantage. However, the organization agreement requires a two-thirds majority to amend it.[2]

During 1989, cross-party coalitions were formed in several states, resulting in the removal of long-tenured legislative leaders. A coalition of conservative Democrats and Republicans controls the Florida Senate and a similar coalition tried unsuccessfully to organize the Florida House. The Tennessee Senate is also controlled by a coalition. Dissident Democrats and Republicans joined together in North Carolina to control the House and replace the long-time speaker. Republicans joined with disaffected Democrats to limit the powers of the majority leader in the Rhode Island Senate, and Connecticut saw a group of Democrats and Republicans unseat the speaker of the House.[3] In a move unrelated to coalition politics, the Oklahoma Legislature replaced its house speaker in the closing days of the 1989 session.[4] The use of coalitions to organize state legislatures has been prevalent in recent years, having been used in Alaska, California and New Mexico during the 1980s. Political scientists argue that independence among the members, the quest for power, and a decline in party discipline have given rise to the increased use of coalitions. Malcolm Jewell of the University of Kentucky believes there may be regional patterns that affect the creation of coalitions. He argues that the possibility for bipartisan coalitions exists strongly in the south because liberal-conservative lines may mean more than Democratic or Republican alliances.[5]

The Evolving Legislature

The legislative modernization movement was successful in strengthening state legislatures, turning them into independent institutions capable of devising innovative solutions to complex public policy issues. This enhanced capacity along with New Federalism policies of the 1980s and growing federal budget deficits propel legislatures into the forefront of the policy debate on a wide range of issues, including education, economic development, health care, delivery of social services and environmental protection.

These reforms also had several consequences for the legislative institution. Increased staff, better office space, including district offices, access to computers, and the ability to raise campaign funds directly from political action committees, have made the individual legislator more independent. Consequently, the power of legislative leaders and their ability to forge consensus on divisive issues has declined.

Higher salaries, better working conditions and greater visibility have attracted people to the legislature who consider politics their career. Occupational data indicates that the number of full-time legislators is growing. Increasingly, people are coming to the legislature with little work experience or from other careers in government and politics. In several states there is a growing number of legislators who are former legislative staff. In California, for example, approximately 20 percent of the members are former staffers, and in Wisconsin one out of six members either worked for the Congress or the Legislature. These members want to stay in public office for the long term, rarely leave the legislature voluntarily and increasingly have ambitions for higher office. They devote considerable attention to their re-election efforts and to constituent services.[1]

The public's awareness and approval of state legislatures are increasing. Nationwide surveys on legislative performance conducted by the National Conference of State Legislatures in 1979 and The Council of State Governments in 1987-1989, show an increase in positive evaluations of job performance. Legislatures received high marks on job performance from 61 percent of the respondents in 1989 compared to 31 percent in 1979.[2]

There are three broad trends likely to affect state legislatures throughout the 1990's. The first trend is that of the growing demands placed on legislative time. The increased number of complex issues, greater recognition of state legislatures by the general public, more intense media scrutiny and the continued flow of responsibilities from the federal government will combine to crowd already filled agendas. The ideal of the citizen legislature will run headlong into the practical necessity of spending more time on legislative business. Legislatures will likely react to these demands by re-examining their procedures in a quest to gain greater efficiencies by streamlining their operations.

The growth in legislative staff also is likely to continue but at a slower rate. The growth in staff in the 1990s will again be concentrated in aides to individual members, caucus staff and issue specialists. As a result, power within legislatures will be further diffused.

Increased partisan competition is the third major trend that will affect state legislatures in the 1990s. The increased number of partisan staff and the pivitol role legislatures will play in the reapportionment process will add to already rising levels of partisanship. The new-found strength of the Republican party in the South, particularly in states such as Florida, North Carolina and Texas, will bring partisan competition to states that until recently have been dominated by the Democratic party. Increasing partisan competition will lead to higher campaign costs, the use of more sophisticated campaign techniques and more negative campaigns. It is likely that the fallout from these hard fought and more bitter campaigns will carry over into the legislative sessions.

References

Introduction

1. John Burns, The Sometime Governments (New York: Bantam Books, 1971), pp. 27-34.
2. The Council of State Governments, The Book of the States, 1966-67 ed. (Lexington, KY: The Council of State Governments, 1966) p. 38.
3. Burns, The Sometime Governments, p. 32.

Length of Legislative Sessions

1. National Conference of State Legislatures, "1989 Regular and Special Session Dates," 31 December 1989.

Full-Time Legislatures and Legislators

1. Karl T. Kurtz, "Changing State Legislatures," Presentation at the National Conference of State Legislatures Legislative Organization and Management Committee meeting, 20 October 1989.
2. Beth Bazar, State Legislators' Occupations: A Decade of Change, (Denver, Colorado: National Conference of State Legislatures, [1987], pp. 1-6.
3. Center for the American Woman and Politics, "Women in State Legislatures 1989," Fact Sheet, Eagleton Institute of Politics, Rutgers University, 1 May 1989.
4. National Conference of State Legislatures, A Compilation of Women Legislative Leaders, January 1989.
5. National Conference of State Legislatures, A Compilation of Black and Hispanic Legislators, November 1989.

Legislative Scheduling

1. American Society of Legislative Clerks and Secretaries and National Conference of State Legislatures, Inside the Legislative Process, 1988 ed., (Denver, Colorado: National Conference of State Legislatures, 1988), p.82.
2. Harvey J. Tucker, Legislative Logjams: A Comparative State Analysis, (College Station, Texas: Public Policy Resources Laboratory, Texas A&M University, 1984), p. 14.

Legislative Compensation

1. Council of State Governments, The Book of the States 1966 Ed., pp. 42-43.
2. The data on legislators' compensation is taken from the National Conference of State Legislatures 1990 Compensation Survey and reflects salaries, per diems and benefits paid to legislators as of January 31, 1990.

Legislative Staffing

1. Brian Weberg, "Changes in Legislative Staff," Journal of State Government 61 (November/December 1988): pp. 191-197.

Legislative Facilities

1. Sharon Randall, "Saving History and Making Room: States Do Both," State Legislatures, February 1988, pp. 15-18.

Party Control

1. National Conference of State Legislatures, A Compilation of State Election Results, 16 November 1989.
2. Patrick J. Traub, "Speakers Du Jour in Indiana," State Legislatures, July 1989, p. 17.
3. Karen Hansen, "Are Coalitions Really on the Rise?," State Legislatures, April 1989, p. 11.
4. "Oklahoma Ousts Speaker," State Legislatures, July 1989, p. 9.

5. Karen Hansen, "Are Coalitions Really on the Rise?", p. 12.

The Evolving Legislature

1. Alan Rosenthal, "The Legislative Institution — Transformation and/or Decline," A paper prepared for State of the States Symposium, Eagleton Institute of Politics, Rutgers University, December 1987, pp. 11-13.

2. Karl T. Kurtz, "The Public Standing of the Legislature," A paper prepared for the Symposium on the Legislature in the Twenty-first Century, National Conference of State Legislatures, March 1990, p. 4.

LEGISLATURES

Table 3.1
NAMES OF STATE LEGISLATIVE BODIES AND CONVENING PLACES

State or other jurisdiction	Both bodies	Upper house	Lower house	Convening place
Alabama	Legislature	Senate	House of Representatives	State Capitol
Alaska	Legislature	Senate	House of Representatives	State Capitol
Arizona	Legislature	Senate	House of Representatives	State Capitol
Arkansas	General Assembly	Senate	House of Representatives	State Capitol
California	Legislature	Senate	Assembly	State Capitol
Colorado	General Assembly	Senate	House of Representatives	State Capitol
Connecticut	General Assembly	Senate	House of Representatives	State Capitol
Delaware	General Assembly	Senate	House of Representatives	Legislative Hall
Florida	Legislature	Senate	House of Representatives	The Capitol
Georgia	General Assembly	Senate	House of Representatives	State Capitol
Hawaii	Legislature	Senate	House of Representatives	State Capitol
Idaho	Legislature	Senate	House of Representatives	State Capitol
Illinois	General Assembly	Senate	House of Representatives	State House
Indiana	General Assembly	Senate	House of Representatives	State House
Iowa	General Assembly	Senate	House of Representatives	State Capitol
Kansas	Legislature	Senate	House of Representatives	State House
Kentucky	General Assembly	Senate	House of Representatives	State Capitol
Louisiana	Legislature	Senate	House of Representatives	State Capitol
Maine	Legislature	Senate	House of Representatives	State House
Maryland	General Assembly	Senate	House of Delegates	State House
Massachusetts	General Court	Senate	House of Representatives	State House
Michigan	Legislature	Senate	House of Representatives	State Capitol
Minnesota	Legislature	Senate	House of Representatives	State Capitol
Mississippi	Legislature	Senate	House of Representatives	New Capitol
Missouri	General Assembly	Senate	House of Representatives	State Capitol
Montana	Legislature	Senate	House of Representatives	State Capitol
Nebraska	Legislature	(a)		State Capitol
Nevada	Legislature	Senate	Assembly	Legislative Building
New Hampshire	General Court	Senate	House of Representatives	State House
New Jersey	Legislature	Senate	General Assembly	State House
New Mexico	Legislature	Senate	House of Representatives	State Capitol
New York	Legislature	Senate	Assembly	State Capitol
North Carolina	General Assembly	Senate	House of Representatives	State Legislative Building
North Dakota	Legislative Assembly	Senate	House of Representatives	State Capitol
Ohio	General Assembly	Senate	House of Representatives	State House
Oklahoma	Legislature	Senate	House of Representatives	State Capitol
Oregon	Legislative Assembly	Senate	House of Representatives	State Capitol
Pennsylvania	General Assembly	Senate	House of Representatives	Main Capitol Building
Rhode Island	General Assembly	Senate	House of Representatives	State House
South Carolina	General Assembly	Senate	House of Representatives	State House
South Dakota	Legislature	Senate	House of Representatives	State Capitol
Tennessee	General Assembly	Senate	House of Representatives	State Capitol
Texas	Legislature	Senate	House of Representatives	State Capitol
Utah	Legislature	Senate	House of Representatives	State Capitol
Vermont	General Assembly	Senate	House of Representatives	State House
Virginia	General Assembly	Senate	House of Delegates	State Capitol
Washington	Legislature	Senate	House of Representatives	Legislative Building
West Virginia	Legislature	Senate	House of Delegates	State Capitol
Wisconsin	Legislature	Senate	Assembly (b)	State Capitol
Wyoming	Legislature	Senate	House of Representatives	State Capitol
Dist. of Columbia	Council of the District of Columbia	(a)		District Building
American Samoa	Legislature	Senate	House of Representatives	Maota Fono
Guam	Legislature	(a)		Congress Building
No. Mariana Islands	Legislature	Senate	House of Representatives	Civic Center
Puerto Rico	Legislative Assembly	Senate	House of Representatives	The Capitol
Federated States of Micronesia	Congress	(a)		Congress Office Building
U.S. Virgin Islands	Legislature	(a)		Capitol Building

(a) Unicameral legislature. Except in Dist. of Columbia, members go by the title Senator.
(b) Members of the lower house go by the title Representative.

Table 3.2
LEGISLATIVE SESSIONS: LEGAL PROVISIONS

State or other jurisdiction	Regular sessions				Special sessions		
	Legislature convenes			Limitation on length of session (a)	Legislature may call	Legislature may determine subject	Limitation on length of session
	Year	Month	Day				
Alabama	Annual	Jan. Apr. Feb.	2nd Tues. (b) 3rd Tues. (c,d) 1st Tues. (e)	30 L in 105 C	No	Yes (f)	12 L in 30 C
Alaska	Annual	Jan. Jan.	3rd Mon. (c) 2nd Mon. (e)	120 C (g)	By 2/3 vote of members	Yes (h)	30 C
Arizona	Annual	Jan.	2nd Mon.	(i)	By petition, 2/3 members, each house	Yes (h)	None
Arkansas	Biennial-odd year	Jan.	2nd Mon.	60 C (g)	No	Yes (f,j)	(j)
California	(k)	Jan.	1st Mon. (d)	None	No	No	None
Colorado	Annual	Jan.	Wed. after 1st Tues.	(l)	By request, 2/3 members, each house	Yes (h)	None
Connecticut	Annual (m)	Jan. Feb.	Wed. after 1st Mon. (n) Wed. after 1st Mon. (o)	(p)	Yes (q)	(q)	None (r)
Delaware	Annual	Jan.	2nd Tues.	June 30	Joint call, presiding officers, both houses	Yes	None
Florida	Annual	Apr.	Tues. after 1st Mon. (d)	60 C (g)	Joint call, presiding officers, both houses	Yes	20 C (g)
Georgia	Annual	Jan.	2nd Mon. (d)	40 L	By petition, 3/5 members, each house	Yes (h)	(s)
Hawaii	Annual	Jan.	3rd Wed.	60 L (g)	By petition, 2/3 members, each house	Yes	30 L (g)
Idaho	Annual	Jan.	Mon. on or nearest 9th day	None	No	No	20 C
Illinois	Annual	Jan.	2nd Wed.	None	Joint call, presiding officers, both houses	Yes	None
Indiana	Annual	Jan.	2nd Mon. (d,t)	odd-61 L or Apr. 30; even-30 L or Mar. 15	No	Yes	30 L in 40 C
Iowa	Annual	Jan.	2nd Mon.	(u)	By petition, 2/3 members, both houses	Yes	None
Kansas	Annual	Jan.	2nd Mon.	odd-None; even-90 C (g)	Petition to governor of 2/3 members, each house	Yes	None
Kentucky	Biennial-even yr.	Jan.	Tues. after 1st Mon. (d)	60 L (v)	No	No	None
Louisiana	Annual	Apr.	3rd Mon.	60 L in 85 C	By petition, majority, each house	Yes (h)	30 C
Maine	(k,m)	Dec. Jan.	1st Wed.(b) Wed. after 1st Tues. (o)	100 L (g) 50 L (g)	Joint call, presiding officers, with consent of majority of members of each political party, each house	Yes (h)	None
Maryland	Annual	Jan.	2nd Wed.	90 C (g)	By petition, majority, each house	Yes	30 C
Massachusetts	Annual	Jan.	1st Wed.	None	By petition (w)	Yes	None
Michigan	Annual	Jan.	2nd Wed. (d)	None	No	No	None

LEGISLATIVE SESSIONS: LEGAL PROVISIONS—Continued

State or other jurisdiction	Regular sessions				Special sessions		
	Legislature convenes			Limitation on length of session (a)	Legislature may call	Legislature may determine subject	Limitation on length of session
	Year	Month	Day				
Minnesota	(x)	Jan.	Tues. after 1st Mon. (n)	120 L or 1st Mon. after 3rd Sat. in May (x)	No	Yes	None
Mississippi	Annual	Jan.	Tues. after 1st Mon.	125 C (g,y); 90 C (g,y)	No	No	None
Missouri	Annual	Jan.	Wed. after 1st Mon.	odd-June 30; even-May 15	No	No	60 C
Montana	Biennial-odd yr.	Jan.	1st Mon.	90 L (g)	By petition, majority, both houses	Yes	None
Nebraska	Annual	Jan.	Wed. after 1st Mon.	odd-90 L (g); even-60 L (g)	By petition, 2/3 members, each house	Yes	None
Nevada	Biennial-odd yr.	Jan.	3rd Mon.	60 C (u)	No	No	20 C(u)
New Hampshire	Annual	Jan.	Wed. after 1st Tues. (d)	45 L	By 2/3 vote of members	Yes	(u)
New Jersey	Annual	Jan.	2nd Tues.	None	By petition, majority, each house	Yes	None
New Mexico	Annual (m)	Jan.	3rd Tues.	odd-60 C; even-30 C	By petition, 3/5 members, each house	Yes (h)	30 C
New York	Annual	Jan.	Wed. after 1st Mon.	None	By petition, 2/3 members, each house	Yes (h)	None
North Carolina	(x)	Jan.	Wed. after 2nd Mon. (n)	None (x)	By petition, 3/5 members, each house	Yes	None
North Dakota	Biennial-odd yr.	Jan.	Tues. after Jan. 3, but not later than Jan. 11 (d)	80 L (z)	No	Yes	None
Ohio	Annual	Jan.	1st Mon.	None	Joint call, presiding officers, both houses	Yes	None
Oklahoma	Annual	Feb.	(ff)	90 L	By 2/3 vote of members	Yes	None
Oregon	Biennial-odd yr.	Jan.	2nd Mon.	None	By petition, majority, each house	Yes	None
Pennsylvania	Annual	Jan.	1st Tues.	None	By petition, majority, each house	No	None
Rhode Island	Annual	Jan.	1st Tues.	60 L (u)	No	Yes	None
South Carolina	Annual	Jan.	2nd Tues. (d)	1st Thurs. in June (g)	No	No	None
South Dakota	Annual	Jan.	Tues. after 1st Mon.	odd-40 L; even-35 L	No	No	None
Tennessee	(x)	Jan.	(aa)	90 L (u)	By petition, 2/3 members, each house	Yes	30 L (u)
Texas	Biennial-odd yr.	Jan.	2nd Tues.	140 C	No	No	30 C
Utah	Annual	Jan.	2nd Mon.	60 C	No	No	30 C
Vermont	(x)	Jan.	Wed. after 1st Mon. (n)	(u)	No	Yes	None
Virginia	Annual	Jan.	2nd Wed.	odd-30 C (g); even-60 C (g)	By petition, 2/3 members, each house	Yes	30 C
Washington	Annual	Jan.	2nd Mon.	odd-105 C; even-60 C	By petition, 2/3 members, each house	Yes	30 C

LEGISLATIVE SESSIONS: LEGAL PROVISIONS—Continued

State or other jurisdiction	Regular sessions					Special sessions		
	Legislature convenes				Limitation on length of session (a)	Legislature may call	Legislature may determine subject	Limitation on length of session
	Year	Month	Day					
West Virginia	Annual	Feb. Jan.	2nd Wed. (c,d) 2nd Wed. (e)		60 C (g)	By petition, 3/5 members, each house	Yes (bb)	None
Wisconsin	Annual (cc)	Jan.	1st Tues. after Jan. 8 (d,n)		None	No	No	None
Wyoming	Annual (m)	Jan. Feb.	2nd Tues. (n) 2nd Tues. (o)		odd-40 L; even-20 L	No	Yes	None
Dist. of Columbia	(dd)	Jan.	2nd day		None			
American Samoa	Annual	Jan. July	2nd Mon. 2nd Mon.		45 L 45 L	No	No	None
Guam	Annual	Jan.	1st Mon. (ee)		None	No	No	None
Puerto Rico	Annual	Jan.	2nd Mon.		Apr. 30 (g)	No	No	20 C
U.S. Virgin Islands	Annual	Jan.	2nd Mon.		75 L	No	No	15 C

LEGISLATIVE SESSIONS: LEGAL PROVISIONS—Continued

Note: Some legislatures will also reconvene after normal session to consider bills vetoed by governor.

Connecticut—if governor vetoes any bill, secretary of state must reconvene General Assembly on second Monday after the last day on which governor is either authorized to transmit or has transmitted every bill with his objections, whichever occurs first; General Assembly must adjourn *sine die* not later than three days after its reconvening. Hawaii—legislature may reconvene on 45th day after adjournment *sine die*, in special session, without call. Louisiana—legislature meets in a maximum five-day veto session on the 40th day after final adjournment. Missouri—if governor returns any bill on or after the fifth day before the last day on which legislature may consider bills (in even-numbered years), legislature automatically reconvenes on first Monday in September for a maximum 10 C session. New Jersey—legislature meets in special session (without call or petition) to act on bills returned by governor on 45th day after *sine die* adjournment of the first year of a two-year legislature; a special session may not be convened if the 45th day falls on or after the last day of the legislative year in which the second session occurs. Virginia—legislature reconvenes on sixth Wednesday after adjournment for a maximum three-day session (may be extended to seven days upon vote of majority of members elected to each house). Utah—if 2/3 of the members of each house favor reconvening to consider vetoed bills, a maximum five-day session is set by the presiding officers. Washington—upon petition of 2/3 of the members of each house, legislature meets 45 days after adjournment for a maximum five-day session.

Key:
C — Calendar day
L — Legislative day (in some states, called a session day or workday; definition may vary slightly, however, generally refers to any day on which either house of the legislature is in session)

(a) Applies to each year unless otherwise indicated.
(b) General election year (quadrennial election).
(c) Year after quadrennial election.
(d) Legal provision for organizational session prior to stated convening date. Alabama—in the year after quadrennial election, on the second Tuesday in January for 10 C. California—in the even-numbered, general election year, on first Monday in December for an organizational session, recess until the first Monday in January of the odd-numbered year. Florida—in general election year, 14th day after election. Georgia—in odd-numbered year. Indiana—third Tuesday after first Monday in November. Kentucky—in odd-numbered year, Tuesday after first Monday in January for 10 L. Michigan—held in odd-numbered year. New Hampshire—in even-numbered year, first Wednesday in December. North Dakota—in even-numbered year, Tuesday after first Monday in December of three-day session. South Carolina—in even-numbered year, Tuesday after certification of election of its members for a maximum three-day session. West Virginia—in year after general election, on second Wednesday in January.
(e) Other years.
(f) By 2/3 vote each house.
(g) Session may be extended by vote of members in both houses. Alaska: 2/3 vote for 10-day extension. Arkansas: 2/3 vote. Florida: 3/5 vote. Hawaii: petition of 2/3 membership for maximum 15-day extension. Kansas: 2/3 vote. Maryland: 3/5 vote for maximum 30 C. Mississippi: 2/3 vote for 30-day extension, no limit on number of extensions. Nebraska: 4/5 vote. South Carolina: 2/3 vote. Virginia: 2/3 vote for 30-day extension. West Virginia: 2/3 vote (or if budget bill has not been acted upon three days before session ends, governor issues proclamation extending session). Puerto Rico: joint resolution.
(h) Only if legislature convenes itself. Special sessions called by the legislature are unlimited in scope in Arizona, Georgia, Maine, and New Mexico.
(i) No constitutional or statutory provision; however, legislative rules require that regular sessions adjourn no later than Saturday of the week during which the 100th day of the session falls.
(j) After governor's business has been disposed of, members may remain in session up to 15 C by a 2/3 vote of both houses.
(k) Regular sessions begin in December after general election, in December of even-numbered year. In California, legislature meets in December for an organizational session, recesses until the first Monday in January of the odd-numbered year and continues in session until Nov. 30 of next even-numbered year. In Maine, session which begins in December of general election year runs into the following year (odd-numbered); second session begins in next even-numbered year.
(l) A 1989 constitutional amendment imposed a time limit of 120 C on regular sessions
(m) Second session limited to consideration of specific types of legislation. Connecticut—individual legislators may only introduce bills of a fiscal nature. Maine—budgetary matters; legislation in the governor's call; emergency legislation; legislation referred to committees for study. New Mexico—budgets, appropriations and revenue bills; bills drawn pursuant to governor's message; vetoed bills. Wyoming—budget bills.
(n) Odd-numbered years.
(o) Even-numbered years.
(p) Odd-numbered years—not later than Wednesday after first Monday in June; even-numbered years—not later than Wednesday after first Monday in May.
(q) Constitution provides for regular session convening dates and allows that sessions may also be held "...at such other times as the General Assembly shall judge necessary." Call by majority of legislators is implied.
(r) Upon completion of business.
(s) Limited to 40 days if called by governor and 30 days if called by petition of the legislature, except in cases of impeachment proceedings.
(t) Legislators may reconvene at any time after organizational meeting; however, second Monday in January is the final date by which regular session must be in process.
(u) Indirect limitation; usually restrictions on legislator's pay, per diem, or daily allowance.
(v) May not extend beyond April 15.
(w) Joint rules provide for the submission of a written statement requesting special session by a specified number of members of each chamber.
(x) Legal provision for session in odd-numbered year; however, legislature may divide, and in practice has divided, to meet in even-numbered years as well.
(y) A 1968 constitutional amendment calls for 90 C sessions every year, except the first year of a gubernatorial administration during which the legislative session runs for 125 C.
(z) No legislative day is shorter than a natural day.
(aa) Commencement of regular session depends on concluding date of organizational session. Legislature meets, then returns on the Tuesday following the conclusion of the organizational session.
(bb) According to a 1955 attorney general's opinion, when the legislature has petitioned to the governor not to be called into session, it may then act on any matter.
(cc) The legislature, by joint resolution, establishes the session schedule of activity for the remainder of the biennium at the beginning of the odd-numbered year.
(dd) Each Council period begins on January 2 of each odd-numbered year and ends on January 1 of the following odd-numbered year.
(ee) Legislature meets on the first Monday of each month following its initial session in January.
(ff) Odd number years will include the 1st Tues. after the 1st Mon. in January. On this day, limited constitutional duties can be performed.

LEGISLATURES

Table 3.3
THE LEGISLATORS
Numbers, Terms, and Party Affiliations

State or other jurisdiction	Senate						House						Senate and House totals
	Democrats	Republicans	Other	Vacancies	Total	Term	Democrats	Republicans	Other	Vacancies	House total	Term	
All states	1,192	751	1	2	1,995		3,277	2,176	4	9	5,466		7,461
Alabama	28	6	...	1	35	4	85	17	...	3	105	4	140
Alaska	8	12	...	...	20	4	23	17	...	...	40	2	60
Arizona	13	17	...	...	30	2	26	34	...	...	60	2	90
Arkansas	31	4	...	...	35	4	88	11	1 (a)	...	100	2	135
California	24	15	1 (a)	...	40	4	46	33	...	1	80	2	120
Colorado	11	24	...	...	35	4	26	39	...	...	65	2	100
Connecticut	23	13	...	...	36	2	88	63	...	...	151	2	187
Delaware	13	8	...	...	21	4	18	23	...	...	41	2	62
Florida	23	17	...	...	40	4	73	47	...	...	120	2	160
Georgia	45	11	...	...	56	2	144	36	...	...	180	2	236
Hawaii	22	3	...	...	25	4	45	6	...	...	51	2	76
Idaho	19	23	...	...	42	2	20	64	...	...	84	2	126
Illinois	31	28	...	...	59	4 (b)	67	51	...	...	118	2	177
Indiana	24	26	...	...	50	4	50	50	...	...	100	2	150
Iowa	30	20	...	...	50	4	61	39	...	...	100	2	150
Kansas	18	22	...	...	40	4	58	67	...	...	125	2	165
Kentucky	30	8	...	...	38	4	72	28	...	...	100	2	138
Louisiana	34	5	...	...	39	4	86	17	...	2	105	4	144
Maine	20	15	...	...	35	2	97	54	...	...	151	2	186
Maryland	40	7	...	...	47	4	125	16	...	...	141	4	188
Massachusetts	32	8	...	...	40	2	128	32	...	...	160	2	200
Michigan	18	20	...	...	38	4	61	49	...	...	110	2	148
Minnesota	44 (c)	23 (d)	...	...	67	4	80 (c)	53 (d)	...	1	134	2	201
Mississippi	44	8	...	...	52	4	112	9	1 (e)	...	122	4	174
Missouri	22	12	...	...	34	4	104	58	...	1	163	2	197
Montana	23	27	...	...	50	4 (f)	52	48	...	...	100	2	150
Nebraska	---------- Nonpartisan election ----------				49	4	---------------------- Unicameral ----------------------						49
Nevada	8	13	...	...	21	4	30	12	...	...	42	2	63
New Hampshire	8	16	...	...	24	2	119	281	...	...	400	2	424
New Jersey	22	17	...	1	40	4 (g)	44	36	...	...	80	2	120
New Mexico	26	16	...	...	42	4	45	25	...	...	70	2	112
New York	27	34	...	...	61	2	92	58	...	...	150	2	211
North Carolina	37	13	...	...	50	2	74	46	...	...	120	2	170
North Dakota	32	21	...	...	53	4	45	61	...	...	106	2	159
Ohio	14	19	...	...	33	4	59	40	...	...	99	2	132
Oklahoma	33	15	...	...	48	4	68	32	...	1	101	2	149
Oregon	19	11	...	...	30	4	32	28	...	...	60	2	90
Pennsylvania	23	27	...	...	50	4	104	99	...	...	203	2	253
Rhode Island	41	9	...	...	50	2	83	17	...	...	100	2	150
South Carolina	35	11	...	...	46	4	87	37	...	...	124	2	170
South Dakota	15	20	...	...	35	2	24	46	...	...	70	2	105
Tennessee	22	11	...	...	33	4	59	40	...	...	99	2	132
Texas	23	8	...	...	31	4	93	57	...	...	150	2	181
Utah	7	22	...	...	29	4	28	47	...	...	75	2	104
Vermont	16	14	...	...	30	2	74	76	...	...	150	2	180
Virginia	30	10	...	...	40	4	59	39	2 (a)	...	100	2	140
Washington	24	25	...	...	49	4	63	35	...	...	98	2	147
West Virginia	29	5	...	...	34	4	81	19	...	...	100	2	134
Wisconsin	20	13	...	...	33	4	56	43	...	...	99	2	132
Wyoming	11	19	...	...	30	4	23	41	...	...	64	2	94
Dist. of Columbia	12	0	1 (a)	...	13	4	---------------------- Unicameral ----------------------						13
American Samoa	---- Nonpartisan selection ----			4	18	4	----- Nonpartisan election -----		1		21	2	39
Guam	13	8	...	...	21	2	---------------------- Unicameral ----------------------						21
No. Mariana Islands	2	7	...	...	9	4	8	7	...	...	15	2	24
Puerto Rico	18 (i)	8 (j)	1 (k)	...	27	4	36 (j)	14 (j)	1 (k)	...	51	4	78
U.S. Virgin Islands	1 5 9	3	3 (l)	...	15	2	---------------------- Unicameral ----------------------						

Note: This table reflects the legislatures as of January 1989, except for New Jersey, Virginia and the No. Mariana Islands; information for those jurisdictions is for 1990.
(a) Independent.
(b) The entire Senate is up for election every ten years, beginning in 1972. Senate districts are divided into three groups. One group elects senators for terms of 4-years, 4-years and 2-years, the second group for terms of 4-years, 2-years and 4-years, the third group for terms of 2-years, 4 years and 4-years.
(c) Democrat-Farmer-Labor.
(d) Independent-Republican.
(e) Independent-Democrat.
(f) After each decennial reapportionment, lots are drawn for half of the senators to serve an initial 2-year term. Subsequent elections are for 4-year terms.
(g) Senate terms beginning in January of second year following the U.S. decennial census are for 2 years only.
(h) Council of the District of Columbia.
(i) Popular Democratic Party.
(j) New Progressive Party.
(k) Puerto Rican Independent Party (also known as the Independent Puerto Rico Party).
(l) Independent (2); Independent Citizens Movement (1).

LEGISLATURES

Table 3.4
MEMBERSHIP TURNOVER IN THE LEGISLATURES: 1988

	Senate			House		
State	Total number of members	Number of membership changes	Percentage change of total	Total number of members	Number of membership changes	Percentage change of total
Alabama	35 (a)	...	...	105 (a)	...	...
Alaska	20 (b)	4	20	40	7	18
Arizona	30	7	23	60	18	30
Arkansas	35 (b)	1	3	100	10	10
California	40 (b)	3	8	80	8	10
Colorado	35 (b)	9	26	65	15	23
Connecticut	36	4	11	151	28	19
Delaware	21 (b)	3	14	41	3	7
Florida	40 (b)	7	18	120	22	18
Georgia	56	9	16	180	27	15
Hawaii	25 (b)	4	16	51	10	20
Idaho	42	7	17	84	17	20
Illinois	59 (b)	1	2	118	10	8
Indiana	50 (b)	10	20	100	9	9
Iowa	50 (b)	7	14	100	12	12
Kansas	40	10	25	125	24	19
Kentucky	38 (b)	5	13	100	13	13
Louisiana	39 (a)	9	23	105 (c)	33	31
Maine	35	7	20	151	36	24
Maryland	47 (a)	...	...	141 (a)	...	...
Massachusetts	40	6	15	160	18	11
Michigan	38 (a)	...	...	110	10	9
Minnesota	67 (a)	...	...	134	17	13
Mississippi	52 (a)	...	...	122 (a)	...	...
Missouri	34 (b)	2	6	163	28	17
Montana	50	7	14	100	31	31
Nebraska	49 (b)	9	18	---Unicameral---		
Nevada	21 (b)	3	14	42	7	17
New Hampshire	24	4	17	400	145	36
New Jersey	40 (c)	3	8	80 (c)	20	25
New Mexico	42	13	31	70	9	13
New York	61	5	8	150	17	11
North Carolina	50	10	20	120	24	20
North Dakota	53 (b)	6	11	106	23	22
Ohio	33 (b)	2	6	99	7	7
Oklahoma	48 (b)	14	29	101	31	31
Oregon	30 (b)	8	27	60	19	32
Pennsylvania	50 (b)	7	14	203	27	13
Rhode Island	50	8	16	100	17	17
South Carolina	46	10	22	124	26	21
South Dakota	35	10	29	70	18	26
Tennessee	33 (b)	3	9	99	16	16
Texas	31 (b)	5	16	150	26	17
Utah	29 (b)	6	21	75	21	28
Vermont	30	14	47	150	33	22
Virginia	40 (d)	...	...	100 (c)	14	14
Washington	49 (b)	9	18	98	20	20
West Virginia	34 (b)	10	29	100	45	45
Wisconsin	33 (b)	5	15	99	19	19
Wyoming	30 (b)	7	23	64	13	20

Source: Survey conducted by The Council of State Governments, Lexington, Kentucky, 1989.
Note: *Turnover calculated after 1988 legislative elections. Data was obtained by comparing the 1987-88 and 1989-90 editions of *State Elective Officials and the Legislatures*, published by The Council of State Governments.

(a) No election held in 1988.
(b) Entire Senate membership not up for reelection in 1988.
(c) Election held in 1989.
(d) Entire Senate to be elected in 1991.

Table 3.5
THE LEGISLATORS: QUALIFICATIONS FOR ELECTION

State or other jurisdiction	House					Senate				
	Minimum age	U.S. citizen (years)	State resident (years)	District resident (years)	Qualified voter (years)	Minimum age	U.S. citizen (years)	State resident (years)	District resident (years)	Qualified voter (years)
Alabama	21	...	3 (a)	1	...	25	...	3 (a)	1	...
Alaska	21	...	3	1	★	25	...	3	1	★
Arizona	25	★	3	1	...	25	★	3	1	...
Arkansas	21	★	2	1	★	25	★	2	1	★
California	18	3	3	...	★	18	3	3	...	★
Colorado	25	★	...	1	...	25	★	...	1	...
Connecticut	18	...	...	★	★	18	...	...	★	★
Delaware	24	...	3 (a)	1	...	27	...	3 (a)	1	...
Florida	21	...	2	★	★	21	...	2	★	★
Georgia	21	★	(a)	1	...	25	★	(a)	1	★
Hawaii	18	...	3	(b)	★	18	...	3	(b)	★
Idaho	18	★	...	1	★	18	★	...	1	★
Illinois	21	★	...	2 (c)	...	21	★	...	2 (c)	...
Indiana	21	★	2	1	★	25	★	2	1	★
Iowa	21	★	1	60 da.	...	25	★	1	60 da.	...
Kansas	18	...	2 (a)	★	★	18	...	6 (a)	★	★
Kentucky	24	...	2	1	...	30	...	2	1	...
Louisiana	18	...	2	1	★	18	...	2	1	★
Maine	21	5	1	(r)	...	25	5	1	(r)	...
Maryland	21	...	1 (a)	6 mo. (d)	★	25	...	1 (a)	6 mo. (d)	★
Massachusetts	18	...	...	1	...	18	...	5	...	...
Michigan (e)	21	★	...	(b)	★	21	★	...	(b)	★
Minnesota	21	...	1	6 mo.	★	21	...	1	6 mo.	★
Mississippi	21	...	4 (a)	...	★	25	...	4	...	4
Missouri	24	...	...	1 (f)	2	30	...	...	1 (f)	3
Montana (g)	18	...	1 (a)	6 mo. (h)	★	18	...	1 (a)	6 mo. (h)	★
Nebraska	U	U	U	U	U	21	...	1 (a)	1	...
Nevada	21	...	1 (a)	(b)	★	21	...	1 (a)	(b)	★
New Hampshire	18	...	2 (a)	★	...	30	...	7 (a)	★	...
New Jersey	21	...	2 (a)	1	...	30	...	4 (a)	1	...
New Mexico	21	...	...	...	...	25	...	5	...	...
New York	18	★	5	1 (i)	★	18	★	5	1 (i)	★
North Carolina	(j)	★	1	...	★	25	★	2 (a)	...	★
North Dakota	18	...	1	(b)	★	18	...	1	(b)	★
Ohio(k)	18	...	...	...	★	18	...	...	...	★
Oklahoma	21	...	...	(b)	★	25	...	...	(b)	★
Oregon	21	★	...	1	...	21	★	...	1	...
Pennsylvania	21	...	4 (a)	★	...	25	...	4 (a)	★	...
Rhode Island(l)	18	...	...	(b)	★	18	...	...	(b)	★
South Carolina	21	...	...	...	★	25	...	...	...	★
South Dakota(k,l)	25	★	2	(b)	★	25	★	2	(b)	★
Tennessee	21	★	(a)	1 (b)	★	30	★	3	1 (b)	★
Texas	21	★	2	1	★	26	★	5	1	★
Utah	25	...	3	...	★	25	...	3	...	★
Vermont	18	...	2	6 mo. (b)	...	18	...	2	6 mo. (b)	...

THE LEGISLATORS: QUALIFICATIONS FOR ELECTION—Continued

State or other jurisdiction	House					Senate				
	Minimum age	U.S. citizen (years)	State resident (years)	District resident (years)	Qualified voter (years)	Minimum age	U.S. citizen (years)	State resident (years)	District resident (years)	Qualified voter (years)
Virginia	21	...	...	★	★	21	...	...	★	★
Washington	18	★	...	(b)	★	18	★	...	(b)	★
West Virginia(l)	18	...	(a)	1	★	25	...	(a)	1	★
Wisconsin	18	...	1	(b)	★	18	...	1	(b)	★
Wyoming	21	★	(a)	...	...	25	★	(a)	...	...
Dist. of Columbia	U	U	U	U	U	18	...	1	★	★
American Samoa (l)	25	★ (m)	5	1	...	30 (n)	★ (m)	5	1	...
Guam (o)	U	U	U	U	★	25	★	5	...	★
No. Mariana Islands	21	...	3	...	...	25	...	5	...	...
Puerto Rico(p)	25	★	2 (a)	i (q)	...	30	★	2 (a)	i (q)	...
U.S. Virgin Islands (o)	U	U	U	U	U	21	★	3	...	★

Note: This table includes constitutional and statutory provisions.

Key:
U — Unicameral legislature; members are called senators, except in District of Columbia.
★ — Formal provision; number of years not specified.
... — No formal provision.

(a) Additional state citizenship requirement. Alabama, Delaware—three years. Georgia, New Jersey, House, two years; Senate, four years. Mississippi—four years. New Hampshire—seven years. North Carolina—two years. Pennsylvania—four years. West Virginia—five years.
(b) Must be a qualified voter of the district; number of years not specified.
(c) Following redistricting, a candidate may be elected from any district that contains a part of the district in which he resided at the time of redistricting, and reelected if a resident of the new district he represents for 18 months prior to reelection.
(d) If the district was established for less than six months, residency is length of establishment of district.
(e) No person convicted of a felony or breach of public trust within preceding 20 years or convicted of subversion shall be eligible.
(f) Only if the district has been in existence for one year; if not, then legislator must have been a one year resident of the district(s) from which the new district was created.
(g) No person convicted of a felony is eligible to hold office until final discharge from state supervision.
(h) Shall be a resident of the county if it contains one or more districts or of the district if it contains all or parts of more than one county.
(i) After redistricting, must have been a resident of the county in which the district is contained for one year immediately preceding election.
(j) A conflict exists between two articles of the constitution, one specifying age for House members (i.e., "qualified voter of the state") and the other related to general eligibility for elective office (i.e., "every qualified voter . . . who is 21 years of age . . . shall be eligible for election").
(k) No person convicted of embezzlement of public funds shall hold any office.
(l) Disqualification for bribery. In South Dakota and West Virginia, disqualification also for perjury or other infamous crimes. In American Samoa, also for felony.
(m) Or U.S. national.
(n) Must be registered matai.
(o) Disqualification for felony or crime involving moral turpitude unless person received pardon restoring civil rights.
(p) Read and write the Spanish or English language.
(q) When there is more than one representative district in a municipality, residence in the municipality shall satisfy this requirement.
(r) Must be district resident at time of nomination.

Table 3.6
SENATE LEADERSHIP POSITIONS—METHODS OF SELECTION*

State or other jurisdiction	President	President pro tem	Majority leader	Assistant majority leader	Majority floor leader	Assistant majority floor leader	Majority whip	Majority caucus chairman	Minority leader	Assistant minority leader	Minority floor leader	Assistant minority floor leader	Minority whip	Minority caucus chairman
Alabama	(a)	ES	EC	...	...	...	...	...	EC	...	...	...	...	...
Alaska	ES	(b)	EC	EC	...	...	...	...	EC	EC	...	...	EC	...
Arizona	ES	ES	...	...	...	...	EC	EC	...	...	EC	...	EC	EC
Arkansas	ES	ES	...	...	...	...	...	...	...	...	...	...	...	...
California	(a)	ES	...	EC	EC	...	EC	EC	EC	EC	EC	...	...	EC
Colorado	EC	EC	EC	EC	EC	EC	...	EC	EC	EC AL/6 (c)	EC	...	...	EC
Connecticut	(a)	ES	EC	AT/8 (c)	...	...	...	EC	EC	...	...	...	EC	...
Delaware	(a)	ES	EC	EC (d)	...	...	EC	...	EC	EC (d)	EC	...	EC AL AL	EC AL EC
Florida	ES	ES	EC	...	...	...	EC	EC	EC	...	...	...	AL	...
Georgia	(a)	ES	EC	...	...	...	EC	EC	EC	...	...	...	EC	EC
Hawaii	ES	ES (e)	EC	EC	EC	EC	(f)	EC	EC	EC	EC	...	(f)	...
Idaho	(a)	ES	EC	EC	EC	EC	...	EC AP	...	EC AL/5	...	...	...	EC AL
Illinois	ES (g)	ES	(g)	AP/6	AT	...	AT	EC	EC	EC/3	EC	AL	AL	EC
Indiana	ES	ES	EC	EC/3	...	...	EC	...	EC	...	...	...	...	...
Iowa	ES	ES	EC	...	...	...	...	EC	EC	EC	EC	...	EC	EC
Kansas	ES	ES (e)	EC	EC	EC	EC	EC	EC	EC	EC	EC	...	EC	EC
Kentucky	(a)	ES	EC	EC	EC	...	...	EC	EC	EC	EC	...	EC	...
Louisiana	(a)	ES	...	...	...	...	...	...	...	...	...	...	...	...
Maine	(a)	ES	EC	EC	EC	...	EC	EC	EC	EC	EC	...	EC	EC
Maryland	(a)	ES	AP	AP (h)	AP (h)	AP (h)	AP (h)	EC	EC	...	EC	...	EC	...
Massachusetts	ES (i)	EC	EC	EC	AP	AP	EC	(i)	AP	EC	AL/3	EC	EC (i)
Michigan	(a)	EL (j)	EC	EC	EC	EC	EC/4	EC	EC	EC	EC	EC/4	EC	EC
Minnesota	ES	ES	...	...	...	...	...	...	...	...	...	...	...	...
Mississippi	(a)	AP (e)	AP	AP	...	...	...	...	...	...	...	...	...	...
Missouri	ES	ES	EC	EC/4	EC	EC	EC	EC	EC	EC	EC	EC	EC	EC
Montana	ES	ES	EC	...	EC	...	EC	EC	AP EC	...	EC	...	EC	EC
Nebraska (U)	(a)	ES	(k)	...	...	...	...	...	...	...	...	...	...	...
Nevada	ES	ES (k)	EC	AT	...	...	EC AT	EC AT	EC EC EC EC	AL EC/2	EC EC	AL/3 EC EC/4	EC AL/2 EC	EC AL EC
New Hampshire	ES	ES	EC	EC	EC	...	EC	(i)	EC	AL	EC	EC/4	EC	(i)
New Jersey	ES	ES	EC	EC	EC	...	EC	EC	EC	...	EC	EC	EC	EC
New Mexico	(a)	ES	EC	...	EC	EC	EC	EC	EC	AL	EC	...	EC	EC
New York	(a)	ES	EC	AT	...	...	AT	AT	EC	...	EC	...	AL/2	AL
North Carolina	(a)	ES	EC	EC	EC	EC	EC	(i)	EC	ES	EC	...	EC	EC
North Dakota	(a)	ES	EC	EC	...	...	ES	ES	ES (i)	...	...	...	ES	(i)
Ohio	ES (i)	ES	...	...	...	...	...	...	...	...	...	...	...	...
Oklahoma	(a)	ES	EC	EC/3	EC	EC	EC	EC	EC	EC/2	EC	EC	EC	EC
Oregon	ES	ES	EC	EC/3	...	...	EC	EC	EC	EC/2	...	...	EC	EC
Pennsylvania	(a)	ES	EC	...	...	...	EC	EC	EC	...	...	...	EC	AL
Rhode Island	(a)	ES	EC	...	...	...	EC	EC	EC	...	...	...	EC	(i)
South Carolina	(a)	ES	EC	EC/7	...	...	EC	EC	EC	...	...	...	EC	EC

SENATE LEADERSHIP POSITIONS—METHODS OF SELECTION—Continued

State or other jurisdiction	President	President pro tem	Majority leader	Assistant majority leader	Majority floor leader	Assistant majority floor leader	Majority whip	Majority caucus chairman	Minority leader	Assistant minority leader	Minority floor leader	Assistant minority floor leader	Minority whip	Minority caucus chairman
South Dakota	(a)	ES	EC	EC	...	...	...	EC	EC	EC	...	...	...	EC
Tennessee	ES (j)	ES	...	...	EC	...	EC/4	...	...	...	EC	...	...	...
Texas	(a)	ES	...	...	...	...	...	...	...	...	...	...	EC	...
Utah	(a)	ES	EC	EC	...	...	EC	EC	EC	EC	...	...	...	EC
Vermont	(a)	ES	EC	EC	...	...	EC	EC	EC	EC	...	...	...	EC
Virginia	(a)	EC	EC	...	...	...	EC	EC	EC	...	...	...	...	...
Washington	(a)	ES	EC	EC	...	...	AP	EC	EC	EC	...	...	EC	EC
West Virginia	ES	AP	AP	EC	...	...	...	EC	EC	EC	...	...	...	EC
Wisconsin	ES	...	EC	EC	...	...	...	...	EC	...	...	...	...	EC
Wyoming	ES	ES (e)	...	...	EC	...	...	...	...	...	EC	...	...	...
Dist. of Columbia (U)	(l)	(m)	...	...	...	...	...	...	...	...	...	...	...	...
American Samoa	ES	ES	...	...	...	...	...	...	EC (i)	EC	EC	...	...	(i)
Guam (U)	ES (j)	ES (e)	EC	EC	...	...	EC	(i)	EC (i)	...	EC	...	...	...
Puerto Rico	ES (i)	EC (e)	EC	EC	EC	...	...	EC	(o)	...	EC	...	EC	EC
U.S. Virgin Islands (U)	ES	ES (e)	ES (n)	...	...	...	...	...	...	...	...	...	...	...

Note: In some states, the leadership positions in the Senate are not empowered by the law or by the rules of the chamber, but rather by the party members themselves. Entry following slash indicates number of individuals holding specified position.

Key:
ES — Elected or confirmed by all members of the Senate.
EC — Elected by party caucus.
AP — Appointed by president.
AT — Appointed by president pro tempore.
AL — Appointed by party leader.
(U) — Unicameral legislative body.
... — Position does not exist or is not selected on a regular basis.

(a) Lieutenant governor is president of the Senate by virtue of the office.
(b) President *may* name any member as president pro tempore to serve during the former's absence. The appointment may extend throughout the session unless terminated by the Senate.
(c) Assistant majority leader: two deputy majority leaders and six assistant majority leaders. Assistant minority leader: deputy minority leader and four assistant minority leaders.
(d) Official titles are majority leader pro tempore and minority leader pro tempore.
(e) Official title is vice president. In Guam, vice speaker. In New Hampshire there is one president pro tem and one vice president.
(f) Majority policy leader; minority policy leader.
(g) President is also majority leader.
(h) Joint appointment by president and the majority leader.
(i) President and minority floor leader are also caucus chairmen. In Ohio and Puerto Rico, president and minority leader.
(j) Official title is speaker of the legislature in Nebraska. Officer has the statutory title of "lieutenant governor" in Tennessee; official title is speaker of the Senate.
(k) President pro tempore is also majority leader.
(l) Chairman of the Council, which is an elected position.
(m) Appointed by the chairman; official title is chairman pro tem.
(n) Officer designated by a majority of the members.
(o) Any three or more senators may meet in order to select the minority leader.

Table 3.7
HOUSE LEADERSHIP POSITIONS—METHODS OF SELECTION

LEGISLATURES

State or other jurisdiction	Speaker	Speaker pro tem	Majority leader	Assistant majority leader	Majority floor leader	Assistant majority floor leader	Majority whip	Majority caucus chairman	Minority leader	Assistant minority leader	Minority floor leader	Assistant minority floor leader	Minority whip	Minority caucus chairman
Alabama	EH	EH	EC	...	...	...	EC	...	EC	...	...	...	EC	...
Alaska	EH	AS	EC	...	...	...	EC	...	EC	EC	...	...	EC	...
Arizona	EH	AS	(a)	...	...	...	EC	...	EC	EC	...	...	EC	EC
Arkansas	EH	EH	...	...	AS (b)	...	...	...	...	...	...	...	EC/2	...
Colorado	EH	AS/2 (c)	EC	EC	...	...	EC	EC	EC	...	EC	...	AL/2	EC
Connecticut	EH	EH	EC	AL/15 (d)	...	...	EC	EC	EC	AL (d)	EC	EC/2	EC	AL
Delaware	EH	EH	AS	...	...	...	AS/4	EC	EC	EC (e)	EC	...	AL/4	EC
Florida	EH	EH	EC	...	...	...	EC	EC	EC	...	EC	...	EC	...
Georgia	EH	EH	...	...	...	...	...	...	...	...	...	...	...	...
Hawaii	EH	EH (f)	EC	EC	EC	EC/6	EC	EC	EC	EC	EC	EC/2	AS	EC
Idaho	EH	EH	EC	AS/6	EC	...	...	AS	EC	AL/5	EC	AS	EC	EC
Illinois	EH	AS	AS	EC/4	EC	AS	AS	EC	EC	EC/4	EC	...	EC	EC
Indiana	EH	EH	EC	...	...	...	...	...	EC	EC	EC	...	EC	EC
Iowa	EH	EH	...	...	...	...	...	...	...	...	...	...	...	...
Kansas	EH	EH	EC	EC	EC	...	EC	EC	EC	EC	EC	EC	EC	EC
Kentucky	EH	EH	EC	...	EC	...	...	...	EC	...	EC	...	EC	EC
Louisiana	EH	EH	...	...	...	...	...	...	...	...	...	...	...	...
Maine	EH	EH	EC	EC	EC	EC	EC	AS	EC	EC	EC	EC	EC	...
Maryland	EH	EH	AS	AS	...	...	AS	EC	EC	...	...	...	EC	...
Massachusetts	EH (g)	...	AS	AS/2	EC	...	EC	(g)	EC (g)	AL/2	EC	...	EC	(g)
Michigan	EH (g)	EH	EC	EC/4	EC	...	EC	EC	EC (g)	EC	EC	...	EC	EC
Minnesota	EH	...	...	...	AS/8	...	AS	EC	EC	EC/4	EC	...	EC	...
Mississippi	EH	...	...	...	...	...	...	...	...	...	...	...	...	...
Missouri	EH	EH	EC	...	EC	...	EC	...	EC	EC	EC	EC	EC	...
Montana	EH	EH	AS	...	EC	EC	EC	...	EC	EC	EC	EC	AL	...
Nebraska (h)	...	...	...	...	...	...	AS	...	...	AL/5	...	...	EC	(g)
Nevada	EH	EH	EC	AS/2	EC	...	AS	...	AS	EC/3	EC	...	AL	EC
New Hampshire	EH	EH	AS	EC	AS/8	...	EC/4	...	EC	...	EC	EC	EC	...
New Jersey	EH	EH	EC	...	...	AS/6 (i)	...	...	...	...	...	...	...	...
New Mexico	EH	AS	AS	...	EC	...	EC	EC	AS	AL/5	EC	...	EC	EC
New York	EH	EH	EC	...	...	...	AS	EC	EC	EC	EC	...	AL	EC
North Carolina	EH	EH	EC	...	...	...	EC	EC	EC	EC	EC	...	AL	EC
North Dakota	EH	AS	...	...	...	...	...	...	...	...	...	...	...	...
Ohio	EH	EH	EC	EC	EH	EH	EH	EH	EH	EH	EH	...	EH	...
Oklahoma	EH	EH	EC	EC	AS	...	EC	EC	EC	EC	EC	...	EC	EC
Oregon	EH	EC	EC	...	...	...	AS	EC	EC	EC	EC	EC/3	EC	EC
Pennsylvania	EH	AS	EC	...	...	...	EC	...	EC	EC	EC	...	AL	EC
Rhode Island	EH	EH	EC	EC/10	...	...	EC	EC	EC	...	EC	...	EC	EC
South Carolina	EH	EH	EC	...	...	...	EC	...	EC	EC/5	EC	...	EC	...

The Council of State Governments

HOUSE LEADERSHIP POSITIONS—METHODS OF SELECTION—Continued

State or other jurisdiction	Speaker	Speaker pro tem	Majority leader	Assistant majority leader	Majority floor leader	Assistant majority floor leader	Majority whip	Majority caucus chairman	Minority leader	Assistant minority leader	Minority floor leader	Assistant minority floor leader	Minority whip	Minority caucus chairman
South Dakota	EH	EH	EC	EC	EC	...	EC	EC	EC	EC	EC	...	EC/2	EC
Tennessee	EH	EH	EC	...	EC	...	EC	EC	EC	...	EC	...	EC	EC
Texas	EH	AS	...	...	...	...	...	...	...	...	...	...	...	...
Utah	EH	...	EC	...	...	...	EC	EC	EC	...	EC	...	EC	EC
Vermont	EH	...	EC	...	EC	...	EC	EC	EC	...	EC	...	EC	EC
Virginia	EH	...	EC	...	...	...	...	EC	EC	...	EC	...	EC	EC
Washington	EH	AS	EC	AS/2 (i)	...	...	(j)	EC (i)	EC	...	EC	...	AL	EC
West Virginia	EH	EH	AS	EC	...	...	...	(j)	EC	...	EC	...	EC	EC
Wisconsin	EH	EH	EC	...	EC	...	EC	EC	EC	EC	EC	...	EC	EC
Wyoming	EH	...	...	...	...	...	...	...	...	...	...	...	...	...
Dist. of Columbia (h)	EH	EH (f)	...	...	...	...	...	...	...	...	...	...	...	...
American Samoa	...	...	...	...	...	...	...	...	...	...	...	...	...	...
Guam (h)	EH	EC (f)	EC	...	EC	...	...	(k)	EC (k)	...	EC	...	...	(k)
Puerto Rico	EH	...	...	...	...	...	...	...	...	...	...	...	...	...
U.S. Virgin Islands (h)	EH (k)	...	...	...	...	...	...	...	...	...	...	...	...	...

Note: In some states, the leadership positions in the House are not empowered by the law or by the rules of the chamber, but rather by the party members themselves. Entry following slash indicates number of individuals holding specified position.

Key:
EH — Elected or confirmed by all members of the House.
EC — Elected by party caucus.
AS — Appointed by speaker.
AL — Appointed by party leader.
... — Position does not exist or is not selected on a regular basis.

(a) Outgoing speaker, by agreement of the House.
(b) Appointed by speaker, after consultation with members of supporting majority.
(c) Official title is deputy speaker.
(d) Assistant majority leader: two deputy majority leaders (appointed by majority leader), and 13 assistant majority floor leaders. Assistant minority leader: two deputy minority leaders (appointed by minority leader) and eight assistant minority leaders.
(e) Minority leader pro tempore.
(f) Official title is vice speaker.
(g) Speaker and minority leader are also caucus chairmen.
(h) Unicameral legislature; see entries in table on Senate leadership positions.
(i) Assistant majority floor leader: first assistant floor leader, three assistant floor leaders.
(j) One also serves as majority whip; the other also serves as majority caucus chairman.
(k) Also serves as caucus chairman.

LEGISLATURES

Table 3.8
METHOD OF SETTING LEGISLATIVE COMPENSATION
(As of January 31, 1990)

State or jurisdiction	Constitution	Legislature	Legislature and compensation commission	State or jurisdiction	Constitution	Legislature	Legislature and compensation commission
Alabama	★	...	...	New Mexico	...	★	...
Alaska	...	★ (a)	...	New York	...	★	...
Arizona (b)	...	...	...	North Carolina	...	★	...
Arkansas	★	...	...	North Dakota	...	...	★
California	...	★ (c)	...	Ohio	...	★	...
Colorado	...	★	...	Oklahoma (d)	...	...	...
Connecticut	...	...	★	Oregon	...	★	...
Delaware	...	...	★	Pennsylvania	...	★	...
Florida	...	★	...	Rhode Island	★	...	...
Georgia	...	★	...	South Carolina	...	★	...
Hawaii	...	...	★	South Dakota	...	★	...
Idaho	...	...	★	Tennessee	...	★	...
Illinois	...	...	★	Texas	★	...	...
Indiana	...	★	...	Utah	...	...	★
Iowa	...	...	★	Vermont	...	★	...
Kansas	...	★	...	Virginia	...	★	...
Kentucky	...	★	...	Washington	...	...	★
Louisiana	...	★	...	West Virginia	...	...	★
Maine	...	...	★	Wisconsin	...	★	...
Maryland	...	...	★	Wyoming	...	★	...
Massachusetts	...	★	...	Dist. of Columbia	...	★	...
Michigan	...	...	★				
Minnesota	...	...	★				
Mississippi	...	★	...				
Missouri	...	★	...				
Montana	...	★	...				
Nebraska	★	...	...				
Nevada	...	★	...				
New Hampshire	★	...	...				
New Jersey	...	★	...				

Source: National Conference of State Legislatures.
(a) Salary commission in non-binding.
(b) Arizona Compensation Commission submits recommendation to vote of people.
(c) California constitution allows statutory increases not to exceed 5% per year.
(d) Oklahoma Compensation Board sets salary without legislative action.

Table 3.9
STATES IN WHICH LEGISLATORS' SALARIES ARE TIED OR RELATED TO STATE EMPLOYEES' SALARIES
(As of January 31, 1990)

State	Description
Florida	Tied to average percentage increase for state career service employees for the fiscal year just concluded. [Florida Statutes, Sec. 11.13(1)(b)].
Georgia	Legislators receive a cost of living adjustment equal to one-half the percentage increase given to executive, legislative and judicial employees.
Kansas	Legislators receive same margin of increase given to civil service employees.
Missouri	Legislators receive all cost of living raises that state employees receive.
Montana	Tied to statutory value of a Grade 8 Step 2 classified state employee. For a given biennium, value remains as it was set on the first day of the session.
North Carolina	Increases are made in amounts equal to the average increases for state employees [N.C.G.S. 120-3(b)].
Oregon	Increases are tied to State Management Service Schedule for state employees.
Wisconsin	Legislators' salary level is recommended by Director of Dept. of Employment Relations to Joint Committee on Employment Relations, which sets salary and per diem.

Source: National Conference of State Legislatures.

LEGISLATURES

Table 3.10
STATES WITH LEGISLATIVE COMPENSATION COMMISSIONS
(As of January 31, 1990)

State	Description
Alabama	...
Alaska	Commission makes report, but doesn't have constitutional power to change salary, which is set by statute.
Arizona	Commission meets every two years; recommendation submitted to voters.
Arkansas	...
California	...
Colorado	...
Connecticut	Legislature enacts salary and can make adjustments to commission's recommendation.
Delaware	Commission meets every four years. Recommendation goes into effect automatically if legislature doesn't reject it.
Florida	Commission serves as an advisory body to study trends and developments in compensating public officers. It reports its findings and recommendations to the legislature not later than March 1 of every odd-numbered year.
Georgia	...
Hawaii	Legislature must disapprove by a certain date or recommendation goes into effect automatically.
Idaho	Salary recommendation goes into effect unless rejected by the 25th legislative day by concurrent resolution of the legislature.
Illinois	Compensation Review Board makes recommendation and legislature sets salary (can reject or reduce recommendation).
Indiana	...
Iowa	Salary set by statute; commission meets every two years to make recommendation.
Kansas	(a)
Kentucky	(b)
Louisiana	...
Maine	State Compensation Commission recommends in the form of a bill that legislature can enact or not.
Maryland	The recommendation of the General Assembly Compensation Commission is presented to the legislature in January of the final year of a four-year term. The legislative body can accept or reduce, but not increase, commission's proposal.
Massachusetts	Compensation commission reports findings in each odd-numbered year. Findings have no effect without legislative action.
Michigan	Two-thirds vote of each house can reject but not modify recommendation.
Minnesota	Compensation Council recommends percentage, which can be modified or ratified by legislature.
Mississippi	...
Missouri	...
Montana	...
Nebraska	...
Nevada	New compensation commission will make recommendations each biennium for consideration by legislature, which will have the option of rejecting the recommendation.
New Hampshire	...
New Jersey	...
New Mexico	...
New York	...
North Carolina	...
North Dakota	Legislature can statutorily approve, reject or modify the recommendation of the Legislative Compensation Commission.
Ohio	...
Oklahoma	Constitutional provision gives salary commission authority to set salary. (Commission's biennial recommendation goes into effect without legislative action.)
Oregon	...
Pennsylvania	...
Rhode Island	...
South Carolina	...
South Dakota	...
Tennessee	...
Texas	...
Utah	Legislature can approve, reject or lower, but not raise, recommended salary.
Vermont	...
Virginia	...
Washington	Salary commission sets salary and effective date.
West Virginia	Constitutional provision sets up Citizens' Legislative Compensation Commission, which meets every four years to recommend salary. Legislature sets salary statutorily.
Wisconsin	(a,c)
Wyoming	...

Source: National Conference of State Legislatures.
Key:
... — Not applicable
(a) Kansas and Wisconsin do not have a "compensation commission" as such.
(b) Kentucky statute (KRS 6.191) provides for a Legislative Compensation Commission, but the commission is not active.
(c) In Wisconsin, salary is recommended by director of Department of Employment Relations to Joint Committee on Employment Relations, which sets salary and per diem with governor's approval.

LEGISLATURES

Table 3.11
LEGISLATIVE COMPENSATION: REGULAR AND SPECIAL SESSIONS
(As of January 31, 1990)

State or jurisdiction	Regular sessions		Salaries	Special session		Travel allowance		
	Per diem salary	Limit on days	Annual salaries	Per diem salary	Limit on days	Cents per mile	Round trips home to capitol during session	Per diem living expenses
Alabama	$10	30L		$10	36C	10	One	$40 (U) (a)
Alaska	...	...	$22,140	...	30C	(b)	...	$80 ($60 for Juneau Legislators) (U)
Arizona	...	...	$15,000	...	...	25.5	Weekly (c)	$60 ($35 for those living within 50 miles of capitol (V) (d)
Arkansas	...	...	$7,500	...	...	23	Weekly	$74 (U)
California	...	...	$40,816	...	...	15	...	$88 (V)
Colorado	...	...	$17,500	...	...	20 (24 for 4-wheel drive	Weekly (e)	$99 (V) ($45 for Denver area legislators)
Connecticut	...	...	$16,760	...	...	21	One	Senators - $4,500/y; Representatives - $3,500/y (U)
Delaware	...	...	$23,282	...	...	20	Unlimited	$5,500/y (U)
Florida	...	...	$21,684	...	20C	20	Weekly (f)	$50 (U)
Georgia	...	...	$10,376	...	...	21	Weekly (f)	$59 (U) (g)
Hawaii	...	...	$27,000	...	...	0	...	(h)
Idaho	$30 (i)	...	...	$30	30C	(j)	(j)	$60 (U) ($35 for legislators who do not establish a second residence); plus $200/y allowance to cover office expense) (U)
Illinois	...	...	$35,661	...	...	24	Weekly (f)	$74 (V)
Indiana	...	...	$11,600	...	...	25	Weekly	$88 (U)
Iowa	...	...	$16,600	$40	...	21	Weekly	$40 ($25 for Polk County legislators) (U)
Kansas	$59	90C	...	$59	None	22.5	Weekly	$69 subsistence (U)
Kentucky*	$100	60L	...	$100	...	22.5	Weekly	$75 (U)
Louisiana	...	...	$16,800	$75	30C	21	Weekly	$75 (V)
Maine	...	...	(k)	$55	None	22	Weekly (l)	$60 (V)
Maryland	...	...	$25,000	...	30C	23	Weekly (m)	$84 (V)
Massachusetts	...	...	$30,000	...	...	0	...	$5 to $50 depending on distance from capitol (U) plus $2,400/y (U)
Michigan	...	...	$45,450	...	...	(n)	Weekly	$8,500/y (U)
Minnesota	...	...	$26,395	...	...	27	(o)	$48 (U) plus $400/m housing for senators, $200-$450/m for representatives (V)
Mississippi	...	...	$10,000	$50	30C	20	Weekly	$76 (U) (None for Jackson legislators)
Missouri	...	...	$22,414.20	...	...	20.5	Weekly	$35 (U)
Montana*	$52.13	90L	...	$52.13	None	25.5	four	$50 (U)
Nebraska	...	...	$12,000	...	...	21	(p)	$67 (V) ($26 for legislators residing within 50 miles of capitol)
Nevada*	$130	60C	...	$130	20C	25.5	One	$66 (V) plus actual expenses for relocating to capitol once per session)
New Hampshire	...	...	$100	$3	15L	38 for first 45 miles; 19 thereafter	Unlimited	None
New Jersey	...	...	$35,000	...	...	0	...	None
New Mexico*	$75	60C (odd y) 30C (even y)	...	$75	30C	25	One	None
New York	...	...	$57,500	...	...	23	Weekly	$75 (V)
North Carolina	...	...	$11,124	...	...	25	Weekly	$81 (U) plus $465/m (U) expenses allowance
North Dakota	$90 (q)	80C	...	$90	None	20	Weekly	$35, not to exceed $600/m (V)
Ohio	...	...	(r)	...	...	20.5	Weekly	None

LEGISLATIVE COMPENSATION: REGULAR AND SPECIAL SESSIONS—Continued

State or jurisdiction	Salaries			Special session		Travel allowance			
	Regular sessions		Annual salaries	Per diem salary	Limit on days	Cents per mile	Round trips home to capitol during session	Per diem living expenses	
	Per diem salary	Limit on days							
Oklahoma	...	...	$32,000	...	...	(y)	(y)	$35 (V)	
Oregon	...	...	$11,868 (s)	...	...	22	One	$66 (U)	
Pennsylvania	...	...	$47,000	...	...	20	Weekly	$88 (V) plus $10,000/y (V) expenses	
Rhode Island	$5	60L	...	...	...	8	One	None	
South Carolina	...	...	$10,000	$250	...	21	Weekly	$74 subsistence for actual attendance on session days	
South Dakota	...	...	$4,267 (odd y) $3,733 (even y)	106.72	...	22	Weekly (z)	$75 (U)	
Tennessee	...	...	$16,500	...	...	21	Weekly (t)	$78 (Y)	
Texas	$65	...	$7,200	$65	30C	24 (u)	Weekly	$30 (U)	
Utah	...	60C	...	...	30C	24	Weekly (v)	$25 (U), $50 lodging allowance for legislators residing outside Davis County	
Vermont	...	...	$6,750 (w)	$90	...	24	Weekly (x)	$87 (U) ($32/d plus mileage for legislators who commute)	
Virginia	...	...	$18,000	...	...	24	Weekly	$82 (U)	
Washington	...	...	$17,900	...	30C	10	One	$66 (U)	
West Virginia	...	...	$6,500	$50	None	20	Weekly	$70 (V); $50 for special session and interim legislative business (U)	
Wisconsin	...	...	$32,239	...	...	24	Weekly	$64 maximum (U)	
Wyoming*	$75	60L	...	$75	None	35 (aa)	One	$60 (V)	
Dist. of Columbia	...	...	$71,885	...	...	21	...	$118 plus transportation for out-of-town travel during session (V)	

Source: National Conference of State Legislatures.

Note: In many states, legislators who receive an annual salary or per diem salary also receive an additional per diem amount for living expenses. Consult appropriate columns for a more complete picture of legislative compensation during sessions. For information on interim compensation and other direct payments and services to legislators, see Table 3.9, "Legislative Compensation: Interim Compensation and Other Direct Payments."

Key:
C — Calendar
L — Legislative day
(U) — Unvouchered
(V) — Vouchered
d — day
w — week
m — month
y — year
* — biennium
... — Not applicable

(a) $40 one additional day per week for committee meeting attendance.
(b) 25 cents per mile for travel other than to and from capitol.
(c) For members residing outside capitol county (daily for in-county members). Can get airfare in lieu of mileage.
(d) After 120L, $20 ($10 for those living within 50 miles of capitol).
(e) For members outside the Denver Metro area; one roundtrip a day for Denver Metro area members.
(f) In Florida and Georgia, members have option of airfare. Illinois includes air or train travel.
(g) Legislators also receive $4,800/y expense allowance (V) which includes office space.

(h) $65 per diem (V) travel to a neighbor island on legislative business, excluding legislative session attendance; plus $5,000/y expense allowance.
(i) $15/d outside of session (session equals about 70¢; interim days average 5 to 8).
(j) $25 maximum, one roundtrip daily for legislators living in Ada County; for members outside Ada County, maximum of seven round trips.
(k) 1990 - $6,600/y; 1991 - $10,500/y.
(l) Or 22 cents a mile in lieu of lodging, up to $34/d.
(m) If claiming lodging; one roundtrip daily if not claiming lodging.
(n) House - 25.5 cents a mile; Senate - 28.5 cents a mile.
(o) Representatives receive one roundtrip weekly, either mileage or airfare. Senators are not limited to the number of trips.
(p) One roundtrip a week for legislators residing 50 miles or more from capitol; one roundtrip a day for those inside 50-mile radius.
(q) Plus $180 each month legislator is in office.
(r) New members receive $38,482.45. Other members at $36,649.95 or $34,904.71 (rate to increase 5 percent a year through 1992).
(s) Will increase four percent in February 1991.
(t) Members living more than 100 miles from Nashville can get one coach airfare a week plus cab fare.
(u) For travel by aircraft legislators are reimbursed 35 cents per mile in a single-engine aircraft.
(v) Daily if in Salt Lake City or Davis County.
(w) 1991 - $480/w; 1992 - $510/w for an average of 15 weeks.
(x) For commuters, one roundtrip a day.
(y) If not claiming lodging, mileage is part of per diem.
(z) One roundtrip is reimbursed at 5 cents per mile (airfare if less than mileage).
(aa) May elect to receive only 24 cents per mile.

Table 3.12
LEGISLATIVE COMPENSATION: INTERIM PAYMENTS AND OTHER DIRECT PAYMENTS
(As of January 31, 1990)

State or jurisdiction	Compensation for committee or official business during interim			Other direct payments or services to legislators
	Per diem compensation for committee or official business	Travel allowance (cents per mile)	Per diem living expenses	
Alabama	$40	10 (a)	...	$1,900/m for district expenses (U)
Alaska	$50-55	25	$80-90 ($60 for Juneau legislators (V)	$4,000/y for district or capitol office. Office space and telephone also provided (U). Primary staffing is provided by the legislature
Arizona	...	25.5 or airfare	$60 ($35 for those living within 50 mile radius), one day a week except leaders, who are allowed two days a week (V)	...
Arkansas	$78	23	...	$485/m, $545/m or $600/m for office expenses, travel, meals, lodging and clerical staff salaries. Committee chairmen are eligible for an additional $150/m
California	...	15 (b)	$88; up to $147 for travel outside the capitol (V)	$279,380/y in assembly for both capitol and district office expenses. In senate, allowance varies based on staffing level and geographic location of district office
Colorado	$99	20 (24 for 4-wheel drive)	Actual and necessary (V)	...
Connecticut	...	21	(c)	(d)
Delaware	...	20	(c)	...
Florida	...	20 or airfare	$50 or actual amount for single occupancy room and meals (V)	$1,500/m for district office and staffing (e)
Georgia	...	21	$59(V) (c)	$4,800/y (includes office expenses) (V)
Hawaii	...	...	$10 on island residence; $65 other than island of residence; $120 out of state (c)	...
Idaho	$30 (f)	20.5	Actual expenses (V)	(c)
Illinois	...	24	Actual expenses up to $69 (V)	Senators receive $57,000/y (maximum); representatives receive $42,000/y (maximum) for office expenses and staffing of district offices
Indiana	...	25	$88 (V)	$25 a day, seven days a week for district office, when not in session (U)
Iowa	$40	21	Actual and reasonable lodging expenses; $30 meals (V)	$75/m for travel and other district office costs
Kansas	$59	22.5	$69 (V)	$600/m during nine month interim for office expenses and in-district travel, etc. (U)
Kentucky	$100	22.5	Actual expenses (V)	$950/m (U) in interim for secretarial assistance and other expenses; $50/session stationery allowance
Louisiana	$75	21	Out of state, actual (V)	$325/m (V) to cover rent, and other expenses for a district office. $1,047/m for legislative assistant. An increase of 5 percent a year up to $1,652/m is provided (g)
Maine	$55	22	$26 for meals plus actual expenses for lodging (V)	$500/y "Constituent Service Allowance" (U). Members do not have district offices

LEGISLATIVE COMPENSATION: INTERIM PAYMENTS AND OTHER DIRECT PAYMENTS—Continued

State or jurisdiction	Compensation for committee or official business during interim			
	Per diem compensation for committee or official business	Travel allowance (cents per mile)	Per diem living expenses	Other direct payments or services to legislators
Maryland	...	23	Up to $84, of which $33 allowed for meals (V)	(h)
Massachusetts	Included in expense allowance (c)	Included in expense allowance (c)	Ranges from $5 to $50 (V) depending on distance legislator's district is from the capitol	...
Michigan	...	28.5 Senate 25.5 House	(c)	Senators receive $47,000/y for office expenses, in-district travel and temporary staff. Members do not have district offices. Representatives do not have an office budget. Majority senators receive $168,727/y for staffing plus 5 benefit packages. Minority senators receive $102,883/y plus 3 benefit packages. Representatives do not receive a staffing allowance
Minnesota	$50 Senate $48 House	26	$55 (V) for lodging (House)	Legislators receive a postage allowance
Mississippi	$40	20	$76 (U)	$800/m during interim
Missouri	...	20.5	Lodging and meals (V)	Legislators receive $600/m for office expenses, in-district travel and district office staffing
Montana	$52.13	25.5	In state: $14.50 for meals and $24.96 for lodging (V); Out of state: $22.50 meals, actual lodging and mileage (V)	...
Nebraska	...	21	...	...
Nevada	$130	25.5 or airfare	In state: up to $58; Out of state, up to $24 plus reasonable single-room rate (V)	$2,800 biennium telephone allowance; $60 biennium postage allowance; plus $2,800 biennium communication allowance for phone, etc. (Leaders and committee chairs receive additional $900)
New Hampshire	...	38 for first 45 miles, 19 thereafter	...	...
New Jersey	...	...	...	District office rent up to $12,000. Up to $1,500/y for supplies and furniture. $60,000/y for staffing
New Mexico	$75	25	...	...
New York	$75 (i)	23	(i)	$1,600/y for incidental expenses. Major office expenses are covered by the legislature. Approximately $130,000 to $250,000 for district and capitol staff, depending on position of legislator
North Carolina	...	25	$81 for actual attendance (U)	$1,500/biennium for postage and telephone expenses
North Dakota	$62.50	20 (j)	In state: $35 for lodging, $17 for meals; Out of state: actual lodging, $30 meals (V)	...
Ohio	...	20.5 (a)	...	...
Oklahoma	...	20.5	$25, up to 20 days (V)	$350 for office supplies, $750 postage and $600 phone allowance
Oregon	...	22	$66 (V)	$400-550/m depending on district size; $1,491/m for personal secretary and $1,781/m for legislative assistant (in session)
Pennsylvania	...	24 Senate 22.5 House	$88 (V) or actual expenses for lodging and meals plus partial per diem	Senators receive $20,000/y office expenses. Representatives receive $10,000/y. Representatives also receive $2,000/y postage allowance

LEGISLATIVE COMPENSATION: INTERIM PAYMENTS AND OTHER DIRECT PAYMENTS—Continued

State or jurisdiction	Per diem compensation for committee or official business	Travel allowance (cents per mile)	Per diem living expenses	Other direct payments or services to legislators
Rhode Island	...	...	...	...
South Carolina	$35	21	$74 (V)	$300/m in-district expenses; $400 during session for postage
South Dakota	$75	22	$23 (plus tax) for lodging. $6 for meals (U)	...
Tennessee	...	21 or airfare	$78 (IRS rate) (V)	$525/m for office expenses. Senate and house speakers receive an additional $5,700/y in office expenses
Texas	...	24 (k)	Senate: actual expenses (V) House: $81 (V)	Senators are reimbursed for district office expenses (no set limit); Representatives receive $7,000/m in session and $6,000/m in interim for district office, capitol office, staffing and travel
Utah	$65	24	$25 (V) plus $50 lodging for legislators residing outside Salt Lake City or Davis County (U)	...
Vermont	$90	24	Actual expenses (V)	...
Virginia	$100	24	$35 for meals plus actual expenses for lodging and miscellaneous (V)	$6,000/y for office expenses and supplied (U). Senate president pro tem, senate majority and minority floor leaders and house majority and minority floor leaders receive $7,200/y office expense and $22,500/y for staffing. House speaker gets $70,000/y for staffing. Other legislators receive $15,000/y for secretary or administrative assistant
Washington	...	24	$66 plus actual expenses for travel to high-cost cities (V)	$300/m year-round for office expenses and travel
West Virginia	$50	20	$30 for meals, $40 for lodging (V)	...
Wisconsin	...	24	$64 (U). Out-of-session allowance of $75/m for senators, $25/m house (U)	Senators receive $25,825 for two-year session for office expenses and travel. Senators receive the cost of one district-wide mailing a year (approx. $9,924). Representatives do not have district offices but receive $10,852/biennium for office supplies, printing, mailing. Senators receive $109,646 for two-year session for administrative staff. (Salary and benefits for two people plus others without benefits subject to approval.) Representatives' staff are paid out of the general budget
Wyoming	$75	35	$60 (V)	...
Dist. of Columbia	...	(l)	Up to $118 plus transportation for out-of-town travel (V)	Council members receive staff allowances (m)

LEGISLATIVE COMPENSATION: INTERIM PAYMENTS AND OTHER DIRECT PAYMENTS—Continued

Source: National Conference of State Legislatures.
Note: For more information on legislative compensation, see Table 3.8, "Legislative Compensation."
Regular and Special Sessions."

Key:
... — Not applicable
(U) — Unvouchered
(V) — Vouchered
d — day
m — month
y — year

(a) For maximum one round trip per week in interim.
(b) Mileage rates applies when own car is used. State or rental cars are also available.
(c) For additional allowance see Table 3.8 on "Legislative Compensation: Regular and Special Sessions."
(d) Senate Democratic caucus receives approximately $20,000/y for each senator's constituent caseworker; the senate Republican caucus receives approximately $20,000 for every three senators for caseworkers. House caucuses receive approximately $20,000 for every four rank and file members for caseworkers.
(e) The speaker, senate president and senators who have three district employees for 16 or more calendar days in each month receive $1,750. Senators also receive $6,000/y for in-state travel and office expenses (V). Representatives receive $7,100/y for mailing newsletters.

(f) For official business; additional $15 for each calendar day not in session.
(g) Newly elected members receive $1,000 one time for equipment and furniture; returning members $250 per term for equipment and furniture.
(h) For office expenses, members receive the following: senate presiding officer, majority leader, minority leader and standing committee chairs - $18,796/y; other senators - $17,395/y; house speaker, speaker pro tem, majority leader, minority leader and standing committee chairs - $17,818/y; house delegation chairs - $17,002/y; and other representatives - $16,197/y.
(i) Members receive $100 on official business in counties with populations of one million or more or out of state; $75 in Albany and other counties; and $45 for partial days (V).
(j) For travel 150 miles beyond border, 18 cents a mile; private aircraft reimbursed at 35 cents a mile.
(k) For travel by aircraft legislators are reimbursed: 35 cents per mile for a single-engine aircraft, 65 cents per mile in a single-engine aircraft, 55 cents per mile in a twin-engine aircraft, $1.00 per mile in a turbine-powered aircraft.
(l) Optional local travel allowance of $50/m.
(m) Staffing allowances are as follows: Chair (six personal staff positions) - $229,724; Chair (10 committee staff positions) - $360,140; Chair Pro tem (5 personal staff positions) - $176,210; Chair Pro Tem (5 committee staff positions) - $164,074; Eight councilmembers, who each have an average of 5 personal staff - $131,999 (approximately); two councilmembers, each with 5 personal staff positions - $157,733; one council member (5 personal staff positions) - $153,224.

LEGISLATURES

Table 3.13
ADDITIONAL COMPENSATION FOR SENATE LEADERS
(As of January 31, 1990)

State	President	President pro tem	Majority leader	Minority leader	Other
Alabama	$2/LD (a)	0	...	...	
Alaska	$500/y	...	0	0	
Arizona	0	...	0	0	
Arkansas	$2,500/y (a)	(b)	...	...	
California	(a)	0	0	0	
Colorado	$99/d leg. business (during interim)	$99/d leg. business (during interim)	$99/d leg. business (during interim)	$99/d leg. business (during interim)	
Connecticut	(a)	$6,400/y	$5,290/y	$5,290/y	Dep. Maj. Ldr., Dep. Min. Ldr: $3,860/y; Asst. Maj. Ldr., Asst. Min. Ldr., Joint Standing Cmte Chair: $2,540/y; Ranking Min. Mbrs of all standing cmtes.: $1,440/y
Delaware	(a)	$9,000/y	$7,000/y	$7,000/y	Maj. Whip, Min. Whip: $4,500/y; Jt. Finance Cmte. Mbrs.: $5,500/y; Jt. Finance Cmte. Chair and V-Chair: $6,500/y
Florida	$8,436/y	0	0	0	
Georgia	(a)	$47,326/y	$2,400/y	$2,400/y	Maj. & Min. Admn. Fl. Ldrs.: $2,400/y; Asst. Maj. & Min. Admn. Fl. Ldrs.: $1,200/y
Hawaii	$5,000/y	0 (c)	0	0	
Idaho	(a)	0	0	0	
Illinois (d)	$10,972/y (e)	...	(e)	$10,972/y	Asst. Maj. Ldr., Asst. Min. Ldr., Maj. Caucus Chair., Min. Caucus Chair., $6,584/y
Indiana	(a)	$6,500/y	$4,500/y	$5,500/y	Maj. Caucus Chair., Min. Caucus Chair., Asst. Maj. Flr. Ldr., Asst. Min. Flr. Ldr.: $4,500; Finance Cmte. Chair: $5,000/y; Asst. Pres. Pro Tem: $4,000; Finance Cmte. ranking minority mbr., $3,500; budget subcommittee chair, $3,000/yr; Maj. Whip, Min. Whip: $1,500
Iowa	$7,300/y (a,f)	0	$7,300/y	$6,300/y	
Kansas	$9,415/y	$4,805/y (c)	$8,493/y	$8,493/y	Asst. Maj. Ldr., Asst. Min. Ldr.: $4,805; Ways & Means Chair: $7,571/y
Kentucky	$25/LD (a)	$25/LD	$20/LD	$20/LD	Asst. Pres. Pro Tem, Maj. Whip, Min. Whip, Maj. Caucus Chair, Min. Caucus Chair: $15/LD. All cmte. chairs $10/LD for cmte. meetings
Louisiana	$15,200/y (g)	0	...	...	
Maine	$3,300/y (1990) $5,250/y (1991)	... ...	$1,650/y (1990) $2,625/y (1991)	$1,650/y (1990) $2,625/y (1991)	1990 - Asst. Maj. Ldr., Asst. Min. Ldr.: $825/y 1991 - Asst. Maj. Ldr., Asst. Min Ldr.: $1,312/y
Maryland	$7,500/y (h)	0	0	0	(i)
Massachusetts	$35,000/y	...	$22,500/y	$22,500/y	Asst. Maj. Flr. Ldr., Asst. Min. Flr. Ldr., 2nd Asst. Maj. Flr. Ldr., 2nd and 3rd Asst. Min. Flr. Ldrs., Post Audit & Oversight, Taxation Cmte. Chairs, Ways & Means Cmte. V-Chair.: $15,000/y; Ways & Means Cmte. Chair: $25,000/y; Other Cmte. Chair, Ways & Means Asst. V. Chair: $7,500/y
Michigan	(a)	0	$21,000/y	$17,000/y	Maj. Flr. Ldr.: $10,000/y; Min. Flr. Ldr.: $8,000/y; Appropriations & Judiciary Cmte. Chairs: $5,000/y Finance and Taxes Chair: $5,279/y
Minnesota	0	...	$10,558/y	$10,558/y	
Mississippi	$40,800/y (a)	0	...	...	
Missouri	(a)	$2,500/y	$1,500/y	$1,500/y	
Montana	$5/LD ($450/y)	0	0	0	
Nebraska	(a)	0	...	...	
Nevada	$2/LD (a)	0	0	0	(j)
New Hampshire	$25/y	0	0	0	Finance cmte. Chair: $160/d (k)
New Jersey	$11,667/y	0	0	0	
New Mexico	(a)	0	0	0	
New York	(a)	$30,000/y (e)	(e)	$25,000/y	Other leadership positions: between $6,500/y and $25,000/y; Cmte. Chair: between $9,000/y and $24,500/y
North Carolina	(a)	$19,104/y (l)	$2,564/y (l)	$2,564/y (l)	Dep. Pres. Pro Tem: $16,080/y (l)
North Dakota	(a)	0	$10CD	$10CD	Standing and Interim Cmte. Chair: $5 CD
Ohio	$21,503/y	$16,248/y	...	$16,248/y	Asst. Pres. Pro Tem: $13,072/y; Asst. Min. Ldr.: $11,487/y; Maj. Whip: $9,899/y; Min. Whip: $6,726/y; Min. Flr. Ldr.: $1,777/y; All cmte. chairs: $5,000/y; Cmte. V-Chairs and ranking minority members, $3,609/y

LEGISLATURES

ADDITIONAL COMPENSATION FOR SENATE LEADERS—Continued

State	President	President pro tem	Majority leader	Minority leader	Other
Oklahoma	(a)	$14,944/y	$10,304/y	$10,304/y	
Oregon	$11,868/y	0	0	0	
Pennsylvania	(a)	$26,370/y	$21,097/y	$21,097/y	Maj. Whip, Min. Whip, Appropriations Chair, Min. Chair: $16,011/y; Maj. Caucus Chair., Min. Caucus Chair: $9,983/y; Maj. Caucus Secy., Min. Caucus Secy., Maj. Policy Chair., Maj. Caucus Admin., Min. Caucus Admin.: $6,593/y
Rhode Island	(a)	0	0	0	
South Carolina	$1,575/y (a,m)	$7,500/y	...	...	Standing Cmte. Chair: $400/y
South Dakota	(a)	0	0	0	
Tennessee	$33,000/y (a,n)	0	0	0	
Texas	(a)	0	...	...	
Utah	$1,000/y	...	$500/y	$500/y	
Vermont	(a)	$7,700/y	0	0	
Virginia	(a)	0	0	0	
Washington	(a)	0	$900/y	$900/y	
West Virginia	$50/LD (o)	0	$25/LD	$25/LD	
Wisconsin	0	...	0	0	
Wyoming	$3/LD	0 (c)	0	0	

Source: National Conference of State Legislatures.
Key:
LD — Legislative day
CD — Calendar day in session
m — month
y — year
... — Position does not exist or is not selected on a regular basis
(a) Lieutenant governor is president of the Senate. Additional compensation noted is that which the lieutenant governor receives for services as president of the Senate. In Mississippi, constitution states that the salary of the lieutenant governor must be the same as that of the speaker of the House ($40,800), and that the lieutenant governor also receive the same per diem and expenses as members while in session. In Tennessee, lieutenant governor is a statutory title.
(b) Receives a special public relations expense allowance of $10,000/y plus free housing in a state-owned building and a travel allowance of $450/m.
(c) Official title is vice-president.
(d) Pay levels for legislative leaders have been enacted into law but are presently under litigation on the grounds that members cannot vote themselves a mid-term salary change. Thus, legislative leaders are still receiving the same levels of additional pay as last year.
(e) President also serves as majority leader. In New York, president pro tempore serves as majority leader.
(f) Lieutenant governor receives additional $20/day per diem.
(g) Senate presiding officer receives $10,000 expense allowance in addition to per diem.
(h) Leaders also receive additional amounts for district office expenses.
(i) Committee chairs except Executive Nominations and Rules Committee Chair receives $1,401/y for office expenses and staffing.
(j) All Standing Committee Chairs receive an additional unvouchered communications aliowance of $900/biennium.
(k) For no more than 10 days/biennium to attend Governor's budget hearings.
(l) President Pro Tem receives $833/m expenses; Deputy President Pro Tem, $554/m; Majority and Minority Leaders, $554/m.
(m) Lieutenant Governor receives $1,300/y travel allowance.
(n) Official title is Speaker of the Senate. Speaker receives $750 ex officio services in session, in addition to $5,700/y for district office expenses.
(o) President also receives $100/day for up to 80 days per year in interim.

LEGISLATURES

Table 3.14
ADDITIONAL COMPENSATION FOR HOUSE LEADERS
(As of January 31, 1990)

State	Speaker	Speaker pro tem	Majority leader	Minority leader	Other
Alabama	$2/LD	0	...	...	
Alaska	$500/y	...	0	0	
Arizona	0	0	0	0	
Arkansas	$2,500/y (a)	0	0	0	
California	0	0	0	0	
Colorado	$99/d legis. business (during interim)	...	$99/d legis. business (during interim)	$99/d legis. business (during interim)	
Connecticut	$6,400/y	$3,860/y	$5,290/y	$5,290/y	Dep. Maj. Ldr., Dep. Min. Ldr.: $3,860/y; Asst. Maj. Ldr., Asst. Min. Ldr., Standing Cmte. Chairs: $2,540/y; Ranking Min. Mbrs. of all Standing Cmtes.: $1,440/y
Delaware	$9,000/y	...	$7,000/y	$7,000/y	Maj. Whip, Min. Whip: $4,500/y; Jt. Finance Cmte. Mbrs.: $5,500/y; Jt. Finance Cmte. Chair & V-Chair: $6,500
Florida	$8,436/y	0	0	0	
Georgia	$47,326/y	0	$2,400/y	$2,400/y	Maj. & Min. Admn. Flr. Ldrs.: $2,400/y; Maj. & Min. Asst. Flr. Ldrs.: $1,200/y
Hawaii	$5,000/y	0 (c)	0	0	
Idaho	0	...	0	0	
Illinois (d)	$10,972/y	...	$8,229/y	$10,972/y	Asst. Maj. Ldrs., Asst. Min. Ldrs., Maj. Caucus Chair., Min. Caucus Chair: $6,584
Indiana (e)	$6,500/y	$5,000/y	$5,000/y	$5,000/y	Caucus Chair, Ways & Means Chair,: $5,000/y; Maj. Asst. Flr. Ldr., Min. Asst. Flr. Ldr.; Maj. Whip, Min. Whip: $3,500/y; Ways & Means Cmte. ranking members, $3,000/y
Iowa	$7,300/y (f)	0	$6,300/y	$6,300/y	
Kansas	$9,415/y	$4,805/y	$8,493/y	$8,493/y	Asst. Maj. Ldr., Asst. Min. Ldr.: $4,805/y; Appropriations Cmte. Chair: $7,571/y
Kentucky	$25/LD	$15/LD	$20/LD	$20/LD	Maj. Whip, Min. Whip, Maj. Caucus Chair, Min. Caucus Chair: $15/LD; All committee chairs: $10/d (for committee meetings)
Louisiana	$15,200 (g)	0	...	...	
Maine	$3,300/y (1990) $5,250/y (1991)	...	$1,650/y (1990) $2,625/y (1991)	$1,650/y (1990) $2,625/y (1991)	1990—Asst. Maj. Ldr., Asst. Min. Ldr.: $825/y 1991—Asst. Maj. Ldr., Asst. Min. Ldr.: $1,312/y
Maryland	$7,500/y	0	0	0	(h)
Massachusetts	$35,000/y	...	$22,500/y	$22,500/y	Asst. Maj. Flr. Ldr., Asst. Min. Flr. Ldr., 2nd Asst. Maj. Ldr., 2nd Asst. Min. Flr. Ldr., 3rd Asst. Min. Flr. Ldr., Post Audit, Taxation Cmte. Chairs, Ways & Means Cmte. V-Chair: $15,000/y; Ways & Means Cmte. Chair: $25,000/y; All other Cmte. Chairs, Ways & Means Cmte. Asst. V-Chair, Post Audit V-Chair: $7,500/y
Michigan	$23,000/y	0	$10,000/y	$17,000/y	Min. Flr. Ldr.: $8,000/y; Appropriations Cmte. Chair, Judiciary Cmte. Chair: $5,000/y
Minnesota	$10,588/y	...	$10,558/y	$10,558/y	
Mississippi	$40,800/y	...	...	...	
Missouri	$2,500/y	$1,500/y	$1,500/y	$1,500/y	
Montana	$5/LD ($450/y)	0	0	0	
Nebraska	---------- Unicameral Legislature ----------				
Nevada	$2/LD	0	0	0	(i)
New Hampshire	$25/y	...	0	0	Appropriations Cmte. Chair: $160/LD (j)
New Jersey	$11,667/y	0	0	0	
New Mexico	0	...	0	0	
New York	$30,000/y	$18,000/y	$25,000/y	$25,000/y	Other leadership positions: between $6,500/y and $25,000/y; All Cmte. Chairs: between $9,000/y and $24,500/y
North Carolina	$20,100/y	$6,468/y (k,l)	(k,l)	$2,564/y (l)	
North Dakota	$10/CD	...	$10/CD	$10/CD	Standing and Interim Cmte. Chairs: $5/CD
Ohio	$21,503/y	$16,248/y	$13,072/y	$16,248/y	Asst. Min. Ldr., $11,487/y; Asst. Maj. Flr. Ldr., $9,899/y; Maj. Whip, Min. Whip, $6,726/y; Asst. Maj. Whip: $3,552/y; Asst. Min. Whip: $1,777/y; All Cmte. Chairs: $5,000/y; All cmte V-Chairs and ranking minority mbrs.: $3,609
Oklahoma	$14,944/y	0	$10,304/y	$10,304/y	
Oregon	$11,868/y	0	0	0	
Pennsylvania	$26,370/y	...	$21,097/y	$21,097/y	Maj. Whip, Min. Whip, Appropriations Chair and Min. Chair: $16,011/y; Maj. Caucus Chair, Min. Caucus Chair: $9,983/y; Maj. Caucus Secy., Min. Caucus Secy., Maj. Policy Chair, Min. Policy Chair, Maj. Cacus Administr., Min. Caucus Administr.: $6,593/y
Rhode Island	$5/d ($300/y)	0	0	0	
South Carolina	$11,000/y (m)	$3,600/y (k)	0 (k)	0	Standing Cmte. Chairs: $400/y

LEGISLATURES

ADDITIONAL COMPENSATION FOR HOUSE LEADERS—Continued

State	Speaker	Speaker pro tem	Majority leader	Minority leader	Other
South Dakota	0	0	0	0	
Tennessee	$33,000/y (n)	0	0	0	
Texas	0	0	...	...	
Utah	$1,000/y	...	$500/y	$500/y	
Vermont	$7,700/y	...	0	0	
Virginia	$10,000/y	...	0	0	
Washington	$1,800/y	0	0	0	$900/y
West Virginia	$50 LD (o)	0	$25/LD	$25/LD	
Wisconsin	$25/m	0	0	0	
Wyoming	$3/LD	0	0	0	
Dist. of Columbia	$10,000/y (p)	...	...	...	

Source: National Conference of State Legislatures.
Note: This table reflects the amount paid the leadership in addition to their regular legislative compensation.
Key:
LD — Legislative day
CD — Calendar day in session
d — day
m — month
y — year
... — Position does not exist or is not selected on a regular basis
(a) Receives a special public relations expenses allowance of $10,000/y plus free housing in a state-owned building.
(b) Official title is deputy speaker.
(c) Official title is vice speaker.
(d) Pay levels for legislative leaders have been enacted into law but are presently under litigation on the grounds that members cannot vote themselves a mid-term salary change. Thus, legislative leaders are still receiving the same levels of additional pay as last year.

(e) The Indiana House is tied as of the 1988 election. Officers of both parties receive equal amounts of additional pay.
(f) Speaker receives additional $20/d per diem.
(g) Speaker receives $10,000 expenses allowance in addition to per diem.
(h) Committee chairs except the Rules Committee Chair receive an additional office/staffing allowance of $1,621/y.
(i) All Standing Committee Chairs receive an additional unvouchered communications allowance of $900 per biennium.
(j) For no more than $10/d biennium to attend Governor's budget hearings.
(k) Speaker Pro Tem is also majority leader.
(l) Speaker receives $1,175/m expenses; Speaker Pro Tem receives $694/m; Minority Leader receives $554/m.
(m) Speaker receives $1,300/y travel allowance.
(n) Speaker receives $750 for ex officio services in session, in addition to $5,700/y for district office expenses.
(o) Speaker receives $100/d for up to 80 days per year in interim.
(p) Council Chair.

TABLE 3.15
STATE LEGISLATIVE RETIREMENT BENEFITS
(As of January 1990)

State or jurisdiction	Participation	Requirements for regular retirement	Contribution rate	1990 salary*	Monthly benefit estimates					Benefit formula	Same as state employees
					4 yrs	8 yrs	12 yrs	16 yrs	20 yrs		
Alaska	Optional	Age 60, 5 yrs service; Age 55, 5 yrs service if vested before 7/1/86	6.75%	$22,140	Not eligible	$668	$988	$1,337	$1,696	2% x avg monthly salary x length of service before 7/1/86 to 10 yrs of service; 2.25% x avg monthly salary x length of service as of 7/1/86 and from 10-20 yrs of service	Yes
Arizona	Mandatory	Age 65, 5 yrs service; Age 62, 10 yrs service; Age 60, 25 yrs service	1.27%	$15,000	Not eligible	$400	$600	$800	$1,000	4% x yrs of service x final salary rate (maximum = 80% of salary)	No
Arkansas	Mandatory	Non-contributory plan: Age 65, 10 yrs service; Age 55, 17 1/2 yrs	0% after 1/1/78 non-contrib. members	$7,500	Not eligible	Not eligible (Non-contributory plan—after 1978)	$270	$360	$450	Non-contributory: 1.8% x 5 yr avg salary x 2 x yrs of service	No
	Optional	Contributory plan: Age 60, 10 yrs service; Age 55, 14 yrs service; Age 50, 18 yrs service	6% before 1/1/78 contrib. members		Not eligible	Not eligible (Contributory plan—before 1978)	$314	$314	$314	Contributory	
California	Optional	Age 60, 4 yrs service; Any age, 20 yrs service	8%	$40,816	$448	$996	$1,344	$1,782	$2,190	5% yr of service x $500 up to 15 yrs service; + 3% per yr x $500 for service in excess of 15 yrs	No
Colorado	Optional	Age 65 and over, 5 yrs service; Age 60-65, 20 yrs service; Age 55-59, 30 yrs service; Any age, 35 yrs service	8%	$17,500	Not eligible	$292	$438	$583	$729	2.5 x highest 3 yr avg salary x yrs of service for first 20 yrs; additional 1% per yr above 20 yrs	Yes
Connecticut	Mandatory	Age 65, 10 yrs service	0%	$16,760	Not eligible	Not eligible	$223	$297	$372	(.0133 x avg annual salary) + [.005 x avg annual salary in excess of "breakpoint" (specific dollar amount for each year)] x yrs credited service	Yes
Delaware	Mandatory	Age 60, 5 yrs service; Age 55, 10 yrs service	6%	$23,282	Not eligible	$238	$358	$477	$596	$29.80/month per yr of service	No
Florida	Optional	Age 62, 8 yrs service; Any age, 30 yrs service	0%	$21,684	Not eligible	$415	$622	$830	$1,037	3% x yrs of service x highest 5 yr avg salary	Yes
Georgia	Optional	Age 65, 8 yrs creditable service (incl. military); Age 62, 8 yrs membership service	3.75% plus $7/month	$10,376	$80	$160	$240	$320	$400	$20/month x yrs of service	Yes

STATE LEGISLATIVE RETIREMENT BENEFITS, JANUARY 1990—Continued

State	Participation	Requirements for regular retirement	Contribution rate	1990 salary*	4 yrs	8 yrs	12 yrs	16 yrs	20 yrs	Benefit formula	Same as state employees
						Monthly benefit estimates					
Hawaii	Mandatory	Age 55, 5 yrs service; Any age, 10 yrs service	7.8%	$27,000	Not eligible	$630	$945	$1,260	$1,575	(3.5% x final avg salary x yrs of service) + monthly annuity based on age and member's contribution (maximum 75% of final avg compensation)	Yes (a)
Idaho	Mandatory	Age 65, 5 yrs service	5.3%	$6,525*	Not eligible	$70	$104	$139	$174	$8.70/month x yrs of service	Yes
Illinois	Optional	Age 62, 4 yrs service; Age 55, 8 yrs service	11.5% (b)	$35,661	$357	$802	$1,337	$1,931	$2,525	3% x final salary x first 4 yrs service; 3.5% next 2 yrs service; 4% next 2 yrs service; 4.5% next 4 yrs service; 5% for each yr in excess of 12 yrs service (limit 85% of final salary)	Yes (c)
Indiana	Mandatory	Age 65, 10 yrs service	5%	$11,600	Not eligible	Not eligible	(d)	(d)	(d)	Lump sum is returned to member at time of retirement; at present salary, benefit would equal $2,900 plus interest per yr of service	No
Iowa	Optional	Age 62, 30 yrs service; Or, total of age and yrs of service = 92	3.7%	$16,600	$92	$184	$277	$369	$461	50% x highest 3 yr avg salary based on 30 yrs service. Benefit prorated for less than 30 yrs service	Yes
Kansas	Optional	Age 65, 8 yrs service	Plan 1: 4% / Plan 2: 5%	$21,948 (e) (e)	Plan 1: Not eligible / Plan 2: Not eligible	$205	$307	$410	$512	Plan 1: 1.4% x highest 4 yr avg salary x yrs of service / Plan 2: 2% x highest 3 yr avg salary x yrs of service	Yes
Kentucky	Optional	Age 65, 5 yrs service	5%	$27,500	Not eligible	$293	$439	$585	$732	2.75% x yrs of service x final salary	No
Louisiana	Optional	Age 60, 10 yrs service; Age 55, 12 yrs service; Any age, 16 yrs service	11.5%	$16,800	Not eligible	$504	$756	$1,008	$1,260	Highest 3 yr avg salary x [(2.5% x yrs of service as state employee) + (1% x yrs in legislature)]	No

STATE LEGISLATIVE RETIREMENT BENEFITS, JANUARY 1990—Continued

State	Participation	Requirements for regular retirement	Contribution rate	1990 salary*	Monthly benefit estimates					Benefit formula	Same as state employees
					4 yrs	8 yrs	12 yrs	16 yrs	20 yrs		
Maine	Mandatory	Age 60, 1 yr service; Any age, 25 yrs service	4%	$6,600 (f)	$59	$118	$176	$235	$294	2% x highest 3 yr avg salary x yrs service	Yes (but employee contribution = 6.5%)
Maryland	Optional	Age 60, 8 yrs service	5%	$25,000	Not eligible	$417	$625	$833	$1,042	2.5% x highest yr salary x yrs of service (maximum 24 yrs or 60%)	No
Massachusetts	Optional	Age 65, 6 yrs service	Before 1975: 5%; 1975-83: 7%; 1983-1/88: 8%; after 1/88: 8% of first $30,000 salary and 10% of additional salary	$30,000	Not eligible	$500	$750	$1,000	$1,250	2.5% x 3 yr avg salary x yrs of service	Yes (g)
Michigan	Optional	Age 55, 5 yrs service Or age + yrs service = 70	9%	$45,450	Not eligible	$1,212	$1,818	$2,424	$2,576	20% x final salary x yrs of service after 5 yrs service; 4% of highest salary per yr for yrs 6-15; 1% per yr for yrs 16-20 (maximum 64%)	No
Minnesota	Mandatory	Age 62, 6 yrs service	9%	$26,395	Not eligible	$524	$786	$1,048	$1,310	2.5% x yrs of service x high 5 yr avg salary including regular and special session per diem (maximum 20 yrs service credit)	Yes
Mississippi	Optional	Age 60, 4 yrs service Age 55, 25 yrs service Any age, 30 yrs service	6.5% (h)	$10,000	$200	$375	$575	$750	$938	(1.875% x high 4 yr avg salary x yrs service) + 50% of PERS benefit for legislative time	No (h)
Missouri	Mandatory	Age 60, 6 yrs service	0%	$22,414	Not eligible	$320	$630	$840	$1,300	$80/month x number of terms served (for first 3-4 terms); $105/month x number of terms from 5-9; $130/month x number of terms for 10 or more terms	No
Montana	Optional	Age 65 Age 60, 5 yrs service Any age, 30 yrs service	6%	$13,554*	$75 (if age 65)	$151	$226	$301	$377	1.67% x yrs of service x highest 3 yr avg salary	Yes
Nevada	Mandatory	Age 60, 10 yrs service	15%	$3,900	Not eligible	Not eligible	$300	$400	$500	$25/month per yr of service up to 30 yrs	No

STATE LEGISLATIVE RETIREMENT BENEFITS, JANUARY 1990—Continued

State	Participation	Requirements for regular retirement	Contribution rate	1990 salary*	Monthly benefit estimates					Benefit formula	Same as state employees
					4 yrs	8 yrs	12 yrs	16 yrs	20 yrs		
New Jersey	Mandatory	Age 60	5%	$35,000	$350	$700	$1,050	$1,400	$1,750	3% x highest 3 yr avg salary x yrs of service	Yes
New York (i)	Mandatory	Age 62, 10 yrs service	3%	$57,500	Not eligible	Not eligible	$955	$1,273	$1,591	1.66% x final avg salary x yrs service	Yes
North Carolina	Mandatory	Age 65, 5 yrs service	7%	$11,124	Not eligible	$297	$445	$594	$695	4% x final salary x yrs of service (maximum = 75% of salary)	No
Ohio	Optional	Age 60, 5 yrs service; Age 55, 25 yrs service; Any age, 30 yrs service	8.5%	$38,482	Not eligible	$539	$808	$1,077	$1,347	2.1% x 3 yr avg salary x yrs of service (maximum 90% of salary) up to 30 yrs service; 2.5% for each additional yr service after 30 yrs	Yes, but mandatory for state employees
Oklahoma	Optional	Age 60, 6 yrs service	4.5% to 10% (member chooses contrib. rate) 10% from $25,000 to $40,000	$32,000	Not eligible	$316–$666 (j)	$480–$1,000 (j)	$633–$1,333 (j)	$792–$1,667 (j)	Final salary x yrs of service x compensation factor based on contrib. rate selected (.019 for 4.5% CR)	No
Oregon	Optional	Age 58; Age 55, 30 yrs service	0%	$11,868	$79	$158	$237	$316	$396	2% x final avg salary x yrs service	Yes (k)
Pennsylvania	Optional	Age 50, 3 yrs service; Any age, 35 years service; If in system before 3/1/74, age 50, 21 yrs service	Tier 1: before 3/1/74: 18.75% Tier 2: 3/1/74–7/22/83: 5% Tier 3: after 7/22/83: 6.25%	$47,000	Tier 1: $1,175 Tiers 2 and 3: $313	$2,350	$3,525	$4,700	$5,875	Tier 1: 2% x highest 3 yrs avg salary x yrs of service x 3.75 Tiers 2 and 3: 2% x highest 3 yrs avg salary x yrs service	Yes (l)
Rhode Island	Optional	Age 55, 8 yrs service	30% or $90/yr	$300	Not eligible	$627	$940	$1,253	$1,567	$600/yr of service (maximum $12,000/yr at 20 yrs of service)	No (m)
South Carolina	Mandatory	Age 60; Any age, 30 yrs service	10%	$13,600 (n)	$213	$437	$656	$874	$1,093	4.82% x yrs of service x "normal compensation" (1990 normal comp. = $10,000 salary + $3,600)	No
Tennessee	Optional	Age 55, 4 yrs service	0%	$16,500	$280	$560	$840	$1,120	$1,400	$70/month x yrs service	No

LEGISLATURES

STATE LEGISLATIVE RETIREMENT BENEFITS, JANUARY 1990—Continued

State	Participation	Requirements for regular retirement	Contribution rate	1990 salary*	Monthly benefit estimates					Benefit formula	Same as state employees
					4 yrs	8 yrs	12 yrs	16 yrs	20 yrs		
Texas	Optional	Before 8/31/83: Age 60, 8 yrs service Age 55, 12 yrs service After 8/31/83: Age 60, 10 yrs service Age 55, 30 yrs service	8%	$7,200	Not eligible	$1,017	$1,526	$2,035	$2,544	2% x yrs of service x state district judge's salary (currently $76,308)	Yes
Utah	Optional	Age 65, 4 yrs service	0%	$65/day	$40	$80	$120	$160	$200	$10/month x yrs service	No
Virginia	Mandatory	Age 65, 5 yrs service Age 55, 30 yrs service	0%	$18,000	Not eligible	$185	$277	$370	$462	If avg salary is less than $13,200: .015 x highest 3 yr avg x yrs of service. If avg salary is greater than $13,200 .0165 x (highest 3 yr avg salary minus $1,200) x yrs of service	Yes
Washington	Optional	Plan 1: Age 60, 5 yrs service Age 55, 25 yrs service Any age, 30 yrs service Plan 2: Age 65, 5 yrs service	Plan 1: Before 10/1/77: 6% Plan 2: After 10/1/77: 4.9%	$16,500	Plan 1: Not eligible Not eligible	$330 $220	$495 $330	$660 $440	$825 $550	Plan 1: 3% x highest 2 yr avg salary x yrs of service Plan 2: 2% x highest 5 yr avg salary x yrs of service	Yes
West Virginia	Optional	Age 60, 5 yrs service	4.5%	$6,500	Not eligible	$87	$130	$173	$217	2% x yrs of service x highest 3 consecutive yr avg salary	Yes
Wisconsin	Mandatory	Age 62	.5%	$32,239	$226	$451	$677	$903	$1,128	2.1% x statutory salary when leaving office x yrs of service	Yes (o)
Dist. of Columbia	Mandatory	Age 62, 5 yrs service Age 60, 20 yrs service Age 55, 30 yrs service	7%	$71,885	Not eligible	$764	$1,213	$1,692	$2,172	1.5% x highest 3 yr avg salary x first 5 yrs service; 1.75% x highest 3 yr avg salary x yrs 6-10; 2% x highest 3 yr avg salary x all service over 10 yrs	Yes

STATE LEGISLATIVE RETIREMENT BENEFITS, JANUARY 1990—Continued

Source: National Conference of State Legislatures.

Note: The following states do not have legislative retirement benefits: Alabama, Nebraska, New Hampshire, New Mexico, North Dakota, South Dakota, Vermont and Wyoming.

* An estimated, annualized salary is used for purposes of computing retirement benefits.

(a) Plans for legislators are the same as for state employees except that state employees have a different benefit formula (2 percent rather than 3.5 percent).

(b) Member contribution is 8.5 percent plus 1 percent for an automatic annual increase in annuity plus 2 percent for a survivor annuity that is refunded if the member is unmarried at time of retirement.

(c) Plans are the same except that legislators' plan has higher contribution rate and higher payout (maximum achieved sooner).

(d) New retirement plan allows members to withdraw entire lump sum upon retirement and purchase their own annuities. State's contribution is 20 percent of salary. Some members elected to stay in the state's prior legislative retirement plan, but as of April 30, 1989, all new members will enter the new plan.

(e) Members may figure their contribution rate based on base pay alone ($21,948/yr); base pay plus interim expense allowance ($27,348/yr); or base pay, interim expense allowance and session expenses ($53,016).

(f) Since even-year salaries are lower for Maine legislators, the highest three year average salary would be computed based on the 1989 salary of $9,900, the 1987 salary of $9,000 and the 1985 salary of $7,550; thus, the average for purposes of these benefit computations is $8,817.

(g) Plans are the same except that state employees are vested for 10 years.

(h) Legislators are eligible for both regular retirement at 6.5 percent employee contribution rate and legislative supplement retirement system at 3 percent contribution rate.

(i) Represents only Tier 4 of a four tier system.

(j) Benefit estimates based on the salary cap of $25,000 and contribution range of 4.5 percent to 10 percent.

(k) Plans are the same except that state employees' benefits are figured using a factor of 1.67 percent (rather than 2 percent).

(l) Plans for legislators are the same as for state employees except that normal retirement for state employees is at age 60, and legislators in the system prior to 1974 receive higher benefits than newer legislators and other state employees.

(m) State employees contribute 7.5 percent of their annual salaries.

(n) Annual salary plus in-district expenses.

(o) Plan for legislators is the same as for state employees except that retirement age for employees is 65.

LEGISLATURES

Table 3.16
LEGISLATORS' USE OF SURPLUS CAMPAIGN FUNDS
(As of January 31, 1990)

State or jurisdiction	Description
Alabama	Qualified yes. According to Fair Campaign Practices Act of Sept. 28, 1988, surplus funds may be used to defray any ordinary and necessary expenses occurring pursuant to the holding of office; contributed to a charitable organization; transferred to another political committee; or "used for any other lawful purpose."
Alaska	Yes. (2 AAC 50.400.)
Arizona	Yes. (But legislators must report such use, and funds become taxable income.)
Arkansas	Yes. (No limitation set by law.)
California	Qualified yes. Funds can be used for expenses associated with election to the office or holding the office, but cannot be contributed to another candidate or used for personal purposes.
Colorado	No. Funds can be used for campaigning only. Can contribute to other campaigns on file with Secretary of State or leave in own fund for next campaign.
Connecticut	No. Funds must be distributed to one or more of the following: 1. Party committee (state central or local); 2. Political committee for ongoing political activity; 3. Tax-exempt organization under IRS Code 501 (c) (3); or 4. Contributors (funds prorated). Funds cannot be given to a committee to finance a future campaign by the legislator. A successful candidate may use surplus funds to pay costs incurred in preparing to take office.
Delaware	No. Can contribute to other candidates or repay a *loan* made to campaign. Must itemize expenditures in report to election commission.
Florida	Qualified yes. If candidate wins election, he/she can keep some funds for an office account as follows: statewide office—$10,000; state legislator—$5,000; supreme court justice—$6,000. Additional funds and those of unsuccessful candidates must be: 1. Pro-rated to each contributor; 2. Donated to a charity under IRS code 501 (c) (3); 3. Donated to a political party of which the candidate is a member; or 4. Given to the General Revenue Fund (if candidate ran for state office) or the county or city general fund if the candidate ran for local office.
Georgia	Yes. (No limitations.)
Hawaii	No. Legislator can reimburse self for campaign *loan*.
Idaho	Yes. (No limitations.)
Illinois	No. All funds must be refunded to contributors or transferred to other charitable or political organizations; legislator may repay own *loan* to campaign.
Indiana	No. Must be used for campaign or political purposes or given to other party organizations, the state election board, or non-profit organizations.
Iowa	No. Funds must be used for campaign expenses, but legislator may repay his or her own *loan* to the campaign.
Kansas	Yes. (No provision.)
Kentucky	No. [KRS 121.180(10).]
Louisiana	No. As of January 1, 1991, funds received on or after July 15, 1988, cannot be used for purposes unrelated to the campaign or office. Such funds may be returned pro rata to contributors, given to charity, used to support another candidate, or kept in escrow for future campaigns. Prior to July 15, 1988, funds received can be converted to personal use any time in future. Funds received from July 15, 1988, to January 1, 1991, can be converted to personal use at any time between those dates.
Maine	No. Funds can be used to repay candidate's own *loan* to campaign; pro-rated to contributors; given to a qualified political party within the state; given as an unrestricted gift to the state; carried forward to the candidate's own subsequent campaign committee: or transferred to one or more other candidates (within contribution limitations).
Maryland	No. Funds must be: 1. Returned pro rata to contributors; 2. Paid to state central committee of candidate's party; 3. Paid to a local central committee of candidate's party; 4. Paid to a local board of education or a recognized non-profit organization for the benefit of pupils or teachers; or 5. Paid to a recognized charitable organization. (Candidates have the option of having a continuing committee, from election to election.)
Massachusetts	No. Any surplus funds be used for another campaign or given to a local aid fund.
Michigan	Yes, with some limitations. Legislator can repay a *loan* to campaign or transfer funds to an "office-holder expense fund" for payment of expenses incidental to the office. Funds may also be given to charity, returned to contributors, or given to the party committee.
Minnesota	Yes, but expenditures must be reported to the Ethical Practices Board.
Mississippi	Yes. (No limitations.)
Missouri	Yes.
Montana	Yes. No limitations, but expenditures must be reported.
Nevada	Yes.
Nebraska	Yes. Can repay own expenses or use for in-district travel or staff travel.
New Hampshire	Yes. No limitations, but expenditures must be reported.
New Jersey	No. Must be transmitted to another candidate or political committee; returned on a pro rata basis to contributors of $100 or more; used to repay the candidate's *loans* to the campaign; donated to an organization under Internal Revenue Code 170(c); or retained for a future campaign.
New Mexico	Yes, but must disclose expenditures and report any personal use as income.
New York	No. Sec. 14-130 of election law prohibits personal use "unrelated to a political campaign or the holding of a public office or party position."
North Carolina	Yes, but any funds returned to the legislator become taxable income and must be reported.
North Dakota	Yes. No limitations, but expenditures must be reported.
Ohio	Yes, with limitations. Can contribute to another campaign committee or use to pay conference fees or expenses related to the office.
Oklahoma	Yes.
Oregon	Yes. No limitations, but expenditures must be reported.
Pennsylvania	No.
Rhode Island	Yes.
South Carolina	Yes, but must disclose all expenditures.
South Dakota	Yes.
Tennessee	Yes, but must be reported as income.
Texas	No. May be used for any "legitimate political purpose, banning personal use, as long as there is no perceived violation of the public trust."
Utah	Yes. Can be used as income, used to defray legislative expenses, or returned to contributors.
Vermont	No.

LEGISLATORS' USE OF SURPLUS CAMPAIGN FUNDS—Continued

State or jurisdiction	Description
Virginia	Yes, but must disclose expenditures.
Washington	Yes, but use is limited. Legislator may: 1. Return funds to contributors; 2. Reimburse self for lost earnings (must prove); 3. Transfer funds to another candidate or party; 4. Donate to a charitable organization; 5. Transfer to the state treasury for the general fund; or 6. Hold for future election.
West Virginia	No. Can use for political purposes in a subsequent campaign by the candidate or another candidate.
Wisconsin	No. Funds are for political purposes only. Can give to another candidate or to the school fund.
Wyoming	Yes. No applicable statutes.
Dist. of Columbia	No.

Source: National Conference of State Legislatures.

LEGISLATURES

Table 3.17
TIME LIMITS ON BILL INTRODUCTION

State or other jurisdiction	Time limit on introduction of bills	Procedure for granting exception to time limits
Alabama	24th L day of regular session (a).	House: 4/5 vote of quorum present and voting. Senate: majority vote after consideration by Rules Committee.
Alaska	35th C day of 2nd regular session (b).	2/3 vote of membership (concurrent resolution).
Arizona	By 29th day of regular session; By 10th day of special session.	Permission of Rules Committee.
Arkansas	55th day of regular session (50th day for appropriations bills).	2/3 vote of membership of each house.
California	March 6 of odd-year session; Feb. 19 of even-year session.	(c)
Colorado	House: 22nd L day of regular session. Senate: 17th L day of regular session (d).	House, Senate Committees on Delayed Bills may extend deadline.
Connecticut	Depends on schedule set out by joint rules adopted for biennium (e).	2/3 vote of members present.
Delaware	House: no introductions during last 30 C days of 2nd session. Senate: no limit.	
Florida	House: noon 2nd day of regular session (b); Senate: noon 4th L day of regular session (d,f).	Senate: majority of those present; Committee on Rules and Calendar determine whether existence of emergency compels bill's consideration. House: 2/3 vote of members present.
Georgia	House: 30th L day of regular session because of Senate ruling; Senate: 33rd L day of regular session.	House: unanimous vote. Senate: 2/3 vote of membership.
Hawaii	Actual dates established during session.	Unanimous vote of membership.
Idaho	House: 20th day of session (b); 45th day of session (g). Senate: 12th day of session (b); 35th day of session (g).	
Illinois	April 7 of odd year of session (h).	House: rules governing limitations may not be suspended. Senate: rules may be suspended by affirmative vote of majority of members; suspensions approved by Rules Committee, adopted by majority of members present.
Indiana	House: 16th day of 1st regular session; 4th day of 2nd regular session. Senate: 10th day of 1st regular session; 4th day of 2nd regular session	House: 2/3 vote of membership; Senate: consent of Rules and Legislative Procedures Committee.
Iowa	House: Friday of 7th week of 1st regular session; Friday of 2nd week of 2nd regular session (i,j). Senate: Friday of 7th week of 1st regular session (i,j); Friday of 2nd week of 2nd regular session (b,i).	Constitutional majority.
Kansas	15th C day in 1989 regular session and 1990 sessions (k); 45th day of regular sessions for committees (l).	Resolution adopted by majority of members of either house may make specific exceptions to deadlines.
Kentucky	House: 38th L day of regular session; Senate: no introductions during last 20 L days of session.	Majority vote of membership each house.
Louisiana	15th C day of regular session (m).	2/3 vote of elected members of each house.
Maine	Last Friday in December of 1st regular session; deadlines for 2nd regular session established by Legislative Council (b,n).	Approval of majority of members of Legislative Council.
Maryland	No introductions during last 35 C days of regular session.	2/3 vote of elected members of each house.
Massachusetts	1st Wednesday in December even numbered years, preceeding regular session (o). 1st Wednesday in November odd numbered years, preceeding regular session (o).	Favorable vote of Rules Committee followed by 4/5 vote of members of each house.
Michigan	No limit.	
Minnesota	No limit.	
Mississippi	14th C day of 90-day session; 51st C day of 125-day session (d,p).	2/3 vote of members present and voting.
Missouri	60th L day of regular session (d).	Majority vote of elected members each house; governor's request for consideration of bill by special message.
Montana	Individual introductions: 14th L day; revenue bills: 21st L day; committee bills and resolutions: 40th L day; committee bills: 78th L day; committee revenue bills: 66th L day (q).	2/3 vote of members.

LEGISLATURES

TIME LIMITS ON BILL INTRODUCTION—Continued

State or other jurisdiction	Time limit on introduction of bills	Procedure for granting exception to time limits
Nebraska	10th L day of any session (d,r).	3/5 vote of elected membership (s).
Nevada	10th C day of regular session(t).	2/3 vote of members present; also standing committee of a house if request is approved by 2/3 members of committee. Consent to suspend rule may be given only by affirmative vote of majority members elected.
New Hampshire	Actual dates established during session: 1989, must file by title on or after May 11 and fully prepared by November 20.	2/3 vote of both bodies voting separately or approval of 3/5 of Rules Committee.
New Jersey	No limit.	
New Mexico	30th L day of regular session (d,u); appropriations bills: 50th L day of regular session.	2/3 vote of members present.
New York	Assembly: for unlimited introduction of bills, 1st Tuesday in March; for introduction of 10 or fewer bills, last Tuesday in March (v). Senate: not prior to the 1st Tuesday of March (w).	Unanimous vote (x).
North Carolina	Last Thursday in February of 1st biennial session (y).	House: 2/3 of members present and voting; Senate: 2/3 vote of membership, except in case of deadline for local bills which may be suspended by 4/5 of senators present and voting.
North Dakota	15th L day (z); resolutions: 18th L day (aa); bills requested by executive agency or Supreme Court: Dec. 15 prior to regular session.	2/3 vote or approval of majority of Committee on Delayed Bills.
Ohio	After March 15 of 2nd regular session, either house by majority vote of its members may end bill introductions.	House majority vote on recommendation of bill by Reference Committee. Senate: 3/5 vote of elected members.
Oklahoma	27th L day for house of origin in 1st session (bb); 19th L day of 2nd session (cc).	2/3 vote of membership.
Oregon	House: 36th C day of session(dd); Senate: 36th C day following election of Senate president (ee).	
Pennsylvania	No limit (ff).	
Rhode Island	Actual dates established during session: 1989, February 16 (gg).	House: 2/3 vote of members present. Senate: majority present and voting.
South Carolina	House: April 15 of regular session; May 1 for bills first introduced in Senate (d,hh). Senate: May 1 of regular session for bills originating in House.	House: 2/3 vote of members present and voting; Senate: 2/3 vote of membership.
South Dakota	40-day session: 15th L day; committee bills and joint resolutions, 16th L day. 35-day session: 10th L day; committee bills and joint resolutions, 11th L day; bills introduced at request of department, board, commission or state agency: 2nd L day (ii).	2/3 of membership.
Tennessee	House: general bills, 10th L day of regular session (jj).	House: 2/3 vote of all members; Senate: 2/3 vote of members
	Senate: general bills, 10th L day of regular session; resolutions, 40th L day.	or unanimous consent of Committee on Delayed Bills.
Texas	60th C day of regular session (kk).	4/5 vote of members present and voting.
Utah	42nd C day of session. (d)	House: 2/3 vote of all members present; Senate: majority of membership.
Vermont	House, Individual introductions: 1st session, March 1; 2nd session, Feb. 1. Committees: 10 days after 1st Tuesday in March(ll). Senate: Individual and committee: 1st session, 53rd C day; 2nd session, sponsor requests bill drafting 25th C day before session (mm).	Approval by Rules Committee.
Virginia	Deadlines may be set during session.	
Washington	(Constitutional limit) No introductions during final 10 days of regular session (d,nn).	2/3 vote of elected members of each house.
West Virginia	House: 50th day of regular session (b,d); Senate: 41st day of regular session (d).	2/3 vote of members present.
Wisconsin	No limit.	
Wyoming	15th L day of session (d).	2/3 of elected members of either house.
American Samoa	15th L day.	2/3 of elected members.
Guam	No limit.	

LEGISLATURES

TIME LIMITS ON BILL INTRODUCTION—Continued

State or other jurisdiction	Time limit on introduction of bills	Procedure for granting exception to time limits
Puerto Rico	60th day.	Majority vote of membership.
U.S. Virgin Islands	No limit.	

Key:
C — Calendar
L — Legislative

(a) Not applicable to local bills that have been advertised or general bills of local application.
(b) Not applicable to bills sponsored by any joint committees. In Florida, also does not apply to short-form bills.
(c) Not applicable to constitutional amendments, committee bills introduced pursuant to Assembly Rule 47 or Senate Rule 23, bills introduced in Assembly with permission of speaker or bills introduced in Senate with permission of Senate Rules Committee. Subject to these deadlines, bills may be introduced at any time, except when the houses are in joint summer, interim, or final recess.
(d) Not applicable to appropriations bills. In West Virginia, supplementary appropriations bills.
(e) Not applicable to (1) bills providing for current government expenditures; (2) bills the presiding officers certify are of an emergency nature; (3) bills the governor requests because of emergency or necessity; and (4) the legislative commissioners' revisor's bills and omnibus validating act.
(f) Not applicable to local bills and joint resolutions.
(g) Not applicable to House State Affairs, Appropriations, Revenue and Taxation, or Ways and Means committees, nor to Senate State Affairs, Finance, or Judiciary and Rules committees.
(h) Final day for introduction of bills: House and Senate—April 7 (except in the House if bill has been requested from Legislative Reference Bureau by March 15); final day for standing committee to report bills: House—April 14/Senate—May 30. Appropriation bills in even numbered years referred to Rules Committee. Non-applicable for emergency bills of the Rules Committee.
(i) Unless written request for drafting bill had been filed before deadline.
(j) Not applicable to bills co-sponsored by majority and minority floor leaders.
(k) Deadline for introduction by individual members may be changed to an earlier date in either house by resolution adopted by majority of members.
(l) Not applicable to Ways and Means and Federal and State Affairs committees, the select committees of either house or the House Committee on Calendar and Printing.
(m) Not applicable to concurrent resolutions proposing suspension of law and bills reported by substitute.
(n) Not applicable to bills intended to facilitate legislative business.
(o) Not applicable to messages from governor, reports required or authorized to be made to legislature, petitions filed or approved by voters of cities or towns (or by mayors and city councils) for enactment of special legislation and which do not affect the powers and duties of state departments, boards, or commissions.
(p) Not applicable to revenue, local and private bills.
(q) Not applicable to interim study resolutions or joint resolutions concerning administration.
(r) Not applicable to "A" bills and those introduced at the request of the governor.
(s) For standing or special committee to introduce bill after 10th L day.
(t) Requests submitted to legislative counsel for bill drafting. Does not apply to standing committees or to member who had requested bill drafting before 11th C day of session.
(u) Not applicable to bills to provide for current government expenses; bills referred to legislature by governor by special message setting forth emergency necessitating legislation.
(v) Does not apply to bills introduced by Rules Committee, by message from the Senate, with consent of the speaker or by members elected at special election who take office on or after the first Tuesday of March.
(w) Bills recommended by state department or agency must be submitted to office of temporary president not later than March 1. Bills proposed by governor, attorney general, comptroller, department of education or office of court administration must be submitted to office of temporary president no later than first Tuesday in April.
(x) In no case may a bill be introduced on Fridays, unless submitted by governor or introduced by Rules Committee or by message from Senate.
(y) Not applicable to those honoring memory of the deceased.
(z) No member may introduce more than three bills as prime sponsor after 9th L day.
(aa) Not applicable to resolutions proposing amendments to U.S. Constitution or directing Legislative Council to carry out a study (deadline, 34th L day).
(bb) Final date for consideration on floor in house of origin during first session. Bills introduced after date are not placed on calendar for consideration until second session.
(cc) Not applicable to reapportionment bills.
(dd) Not applicable to measures approved by Committee on Legislative Rules, Operations and Reform or by speaker; appropriation or fiscal measures sponsored by Joint Committee on Ways and Means; true substitute measures sponsored by standing, special or joint committees, or measures drafted by legislative counsel.
(ee) Not applicable to measures approved by Rules Committee, appropriation or fiscal measures sponsored by Joint Committee on Ways and Means; measures requested for drafting by legislative counsel.
(ff) Resolutions fixing the last day for introduction of bills in the House are referred to the Rules Committee before consideration by the full House.
(gg) Not applicable to resolutions of condolence or congratulations, corporate charter renewals, claims bills or city and town bills.
(hh) Not applicable to joint resolutions approving or disapproving agency regulations.
(ii) Not applicable to governor's bills.
(jj) Not applicable to certain local bills or a bill correcting a typographical error or an earlier enactment of the Committee on Delayed Bills.
(kk) Not applicable to local bills, resolutions, emergency appropriations, all emergency matters submitted by governor in special messages to the legislature.
(ll) Not applicable to Appropriations or Ways and Means committees.
(mm) Not applicable to Appropriations or Finance committees.
(nn) Not applicable to substitute bills reported by standing committees for bills pending before such committees.

Table 3.18
BILL PRE-FILING, REFERENCE, AND CARRYOVER

State or other jurisdiction	Pre-filing of bills allowed (a)	Bills referred to committee by: Senate	Bills referred to committee by: House	Bill referral restricted by rule Senate	Bill referral restricted by rule House	Bill carryover allowed (b)
Alabama	★ (c)	President (d)	Speaker			...
Alaska	★ (e)	President	Speaker	★	★	★
Arizona	★	President	Speaker			...
Arkansas	★	President	Speaker	★	★	
California	(f)	Rules Cmte.	Rules Cmte.	★		★ (g)
Colorado	★	President	Speaker			...
Connecticut	★	President (d)	Speaker	★	★	...
Delaware	★	President (d)	Speaker		★	★
Florida	★	President	Speaker	★	★	...
Georgia	...	President (d)	Speaker			★
Hawaii	(h)	President	Speaker	★	★	★
Idaho	...	President (d)	Speaker			...
Illinois	★	Cmte. on Assignment	Cmte. on Assignment			★
Indiana	★	Pres. Pro Tempore	Speaker			...
Iowa	★	President (d)	Speaker	★		★
Kansas	★	President	Speaker	★	★	★
Kentucky	★	Cmte. on Cmtes. (i)	Cmte. on Cmtes.	★	★	
Louisiana	★	President (j)	Speaker (j)	★	★	...
Maine	★ (k)	-------- Secy. of Senate and Clerk of House (l) --------				...
Maryland	★	President	Speaker	(m)	(m)	...
Massachusetts	★	Clerk (j)	Clerk (j)	★	★	
Michigan	...	Majority Ldr.	Speaker			★
Minnesota	★ (n)	President	Speaker	(m)	(m)	★
Mississippi	★	President (d)	Speaker			...
Missouri	★	Pres. Pro Tempore	Speaker	★	★	★
Montana	★	President	Speaker			
Nebraska (U)	★	Reference Cmte.		★		★
Nevada	★	Majority Ldr.	Speaker	★		
New Hampshire	★	President	Speaker		★	
New Jersey	★ (k)	President	Speaker			★
New Mexico	...	Pres. Pro Tempore	Speaker	(m)	(m)	...
New York	★	Pres. Pro Tempore (o)	Speaker			★
North Carolina	...	President (d)	Speaker	(m)	(m)	★
North Dakota	★	President (d)	Speaker	★	★	
Ohio	★	Reference Cmte.	Reference Cmte.			★
Oklahoma	★	Pres. Pro Tempore	Speaker			★
Oregon	★	President	Speaker	★	★	
Pennsylvania	★	President (d)	Speaker			★
Rhode Island	★	President (d)	Speaker			★
South Carolina	★	Pres. Pro Tempore	Speaker			★
South Dakota	★	President (d)	Speaker			...
Tennessee	★	Speaker	Speaker	★	★	★
Texas	★	President (d)	Speaker		★	
Utah	★	President	Speaker			...
Vermont	★	President (d)	Speaker	★	★	★
Virginia	★	Clerk	Speaker	★	★	★
Washington	★	President	Speaker			★
West Virginia	★	President	Speaker			...
Wisconsin	★	Presiding Officer	Presiding Officer			★ (p)
Wyoming	★ (k)	President	Speaker			...
American Samoa	★	President	Speaker	★	★	★
Guam (U)	★	Rules Cmte.		★		★
Puerto Rico	★	President	President	★	★	★
U.S. Virgin Islands (U)	★	President				★

LEGISLATURES

BILL PRE-FILING, REFERENCE, AND CARRYOVER—Continued

Key:
★ — Procedure allowed
. . . — Procedure not allowed
(U) — Unicameral legislature

(a) Unless otherwise indicated by footnote, bills may be introduced prior to convening each session of the legislature. In this column only: ★—pre-filing is allowed in both chambers (or in the case of Nebraska, Guam, and the Virgin Islands, in the unicameral legislature); . . .—pre-filing is not allowed in either chamber.

(b) Bills carry over from the first year of a legislature to the second (does not apply to legislatures meeting in session once every two years). Bills generally do not carry over after an intervening legislative election.

(c) Except between the end of the last regular session of the legislature in any quadrennium and the organizational session following the general election.

(d) Lieutenant governor is the president of the Senate.

(e) Maximum 10 bills per member.

(f) California has a continuous legislature. Members may introduce bills at any time during the biennium.

(g) Bills introduced in the first year of the regular session and passed by the house of origin on or before January 30 of the second year are "carryover bills."

(h) House only in even-numbered years.

(i) Lieutenant governor as president of the Senate is a member of committee.

(j) Subject to approval or disapproval. Louisiana—majority of members present. Massachusetts—by presiding officer and Committe on Steering and Policy.

(k) Prior to convening of first regular session only.

(l) For the joint standing committee system. Secretary of Senate and clerk of House, after conferring, suggest an appropriate committee reference for every bill, resolve and petition offered in either house. If they are unable to agree, the question of reference is referred to a conference of the president of the Senate and speaker of the House. If the presiding officers cannot agree, the question is resolved by the Legislative Council.

(m) Not restricted, except: Maryland—in House, local bills; in Senate, local bills and bills creating judgeships. Minnesota—bills on government structure and bills appropriating funds which are referred to Finance Committee. New Mexico—in House, bills referred to Appropriations and Finance Committee; in Senate, bills referred to Finance Committee. North Carolina—bills referred to Appropriations, Finance, and Ways and Means committees.

(n) Prior to convening of second regular session only.

(o) Also serves as majority leader.

(p) Any bill, joint resolution on which final action has not been taken at the conclusion of the last general-business floor period in the odd-numbered year shall be carried forward to the even-numbered year.

LEGISLATURES

Table 3.19
MECHANISMS USED TO EXPEDITE AND STREAMLINE BILL PROCESSING

State or other jurisdiction	Prefiling of bills	Carryover of bills from 1st session	Companion bills	Deadlines for the introduction of bills	Deadlines for committee action	Deadlines for 1st and 2nd House action	Committee bills
Alabama	B	...	S	S	S	S	...
Alaska	B	B	B	B (a)	...	...	...
Arizona	B	...	...	B	B	H	...
Arkansas	B	...	H	B	...	...	B
California	...	S	...	B	B	B	H
Colorado	B	...	...	B	B	B	S
Connecticut	B	...	...	B	B	...	B
Delaware	B	B	...	H	H	...	...
Florida	B	...	B	B	H	...	B
Georgia	...	B	...	B	...	S	...
Hawaii	B	B	H	B	B	B	...
Idaho	...	...	...	B	S	S	H
Illinois	B	B	S	B	B	B	B
Indiana	B	...	...	B	B	B	...
Iowa	B	B	B	S	B	B	B
Kansas	B	B	...	B	...	S	H
Kentucky	B	...	B	B	...	...	S
Louisiana	B	...	...	B	...	...	...
Maine	B	B	...	B	B	...	...
Maryland	B	...	B	B	S	...	...
Massachusetts	B	...	...	B	B	...	B
Michigan	S	...	S	...	H	...	...
Minnesota	S	B	B	...	B	B	B
Mississippi	B	...	...	B	B	B	...
Missouri	B	S	...	B	...	...	...
Montana	B	...	...	B	...	S	B
Nebraska	S	S	...	S	...	...	S
Nevada	...	...	...	...	...	...	S
New Hampshire	B	S	...	B	H	B	...
New Jersey	B	S	B	...	...	...	...
New Mexico	...	...	H	B	...	...	...
New York	B	B	B	B	S	...	...
North Carolina	B	H	B	B	H	B	...
North Dakota	B	...	...	B	B	B	B
Ohio	S	B	...	H	...	...	...
Oklahoma	B	B	H	B	B	S	...
Oregon	B	...	...	B	H	H	H
Pennsylvania	B	B	...	...	...	...	...
Rhode Island	...	...	...	...	...	...	...
South Carolina	B	B	H	B	...	...	H
South Dakota	B	...	...	B	S	B	S
Tennessee	B	B	B	B	...	...	S
Texas	B	...	H	B	...	...	...
Utah	B	...	H	B	H	...	H
Vermont	H	H	...	H	H	H	H
Virginia	H	H	H	H	H	...	...
Washington	B	B	S	S	B	B	B
West Virginia	B	H	B	B	H	H	H
Wisconsin	S	B	B	...	...	...	S
Wyoming	B	...	...	B	H	H	B
American Samoa	...	H	...	H	H	...	...
Puerto Rico	...	S	...	...	...	...	...

Source: National Conference of State Legislatures.
(a) Personal bill deadline—35th day of the second session.

Key:
S — Senate
H — House
B — Both
... — Not applicable

Table 3.20
ENACTING LEGISLATION: VETO, VETO OVERRIDE AND EFFECTIVE DATE

State or other jurisdiction	Governor may item veto appropriation bills — Amount	Governor may item veto appropriation bills — Other (b)	Days allowed governor to consider bill (a) — During session — Bill becomes law unless vetoed	Days allowed governor to consider bill (a) — After session — Bill becomes law unless vetoed	Days allowed governor to consider bill (a) — After session — Bill dies unless signed	Votes required in each house to pass bills or items over veto (c)	Effective date of enacted legislation (d)
Alabama	★	★	6	20P		Majority elected	Immediately (e)
Alaska	★ (f)	...	15	10A		2/3 elected (g)	90 days after enactment
Arizona	★	...	5	10A		2/3 elected	90 days after adjournment
Arkansas	★	...	5	20A (h)		Majority elected	90 days after adjournment
California	★ (f)	...	12 (h,i)	(i)		2/3 elected	(j)
Colorado	★	★	10 (h)	30A (h)		2/3 elected	Immediately (k)
Connecticut	★	...	5	15P (h)		2/3 elected	Oct. 1
Delaware	★	★	10		30A (h)	3/5 elected	Immediately
Florida	★	★	7 (h)	15P (h)		2/3 elected	60 days after adjournment
Georgia (i)	★	...	6	40A (m)		2/3 elected	July 1 (n)
Hawaii (l)	★ (f)	...	10 (o,p)	45A (o,p)	(p)	2/3 elected	Immediately
Idaho	★	...	5	10A		2/3 elected	60 days after adjournment
Illinois	★ (f)	...	60 (h)	60P (h)		3/5 elected (g)	Jan. 1 (n)
Indiana	...	...	7	7A		Majority elected	(q)
Iowa	★	★	3	(r)	(r)	2/3 elected	July 1 (n)
Kansas	★	...	10 (h)	10P		2/3 elected	Upon publication
Kentucky	★	★	10 (h)	10A		Majority elected	90 days after adjournment
Louisiana (l)	★	★	10 (h)	20P (h)		2/3 elected	60 days after adjournment
Maine (l)	★	★	10	(m)		2/3 present	90 days after adjournment
Maryland (l)	...	★	6	30P (m)		3/5 elected	June 1 (s)
Massachusetts	★ (f)	★	10		10P	2/3 present	90 days after enactment
Michigan	★	★	14 (h)	10A	14P (h)	2/3 elected and serving	90 days after adjournment
Minnesota	★	★	3	20P (h)	14P	2/3 elected	Aug. 1 (t)
Mississippi	...	...	5	15P (m)		2/3 elected	60 days after enactment
Missouri	★	...	15 (r)	45P (m,r)		2/3 elected	90 days after adjournment (t,u)
Montana	★ (f)	★	5 (h)	25A (h)		2/3 present	Oct. 1 (u)
Nebraska	★ (v)	...	5	5A		3/5 elected	3 months after adjournment
Nevada	...	...	5	10A		2/3 elected	July 1
New Hampshire	...	...	5		5P	2/3 elected	60 days after enactment
New Jersey	★ (f)	...	(w)	(w)	(w)	2/3 elected	July 4
New Mexico	★	...	3		20A	2/3 present	90 days after adjournment (t)
New York	★	...	10		30A	2/3 elected	20 days after enactment
North Carolina	...	...		(x)			30 days after enactment
North Dakota	★ (f)	★	3	15A		2/3 elected	90 days after enactment
Ohio	★	★	10	10A		3/5 elected	90 days after filed with secretary of state
Oklahoma	★	...	5		15A	2/3 elected (g)	90 days after adjournment
Oregon	★	★	5	20A		2/3 present	90 days after adjournment
Pennsylvania	★ (f)	...	10 (h)	30A (h)		2/3 elected	60 days after enactment
Rhode Island	★	...	6	10A (h)		3/5 present	10 days after enactment
South Carolina	★	★	5	(m)		2/3 present	20 days after enactment
South Dakota	★	★	5	15A		2/3 elected	90 days after enactment
Tennessee	★ (f)	...	10	10A		Majority elected	40 days after enactment
Texas	★	...	10	20A		2/3 present	90 days after adjournment
Utah	★	...	10 (h)	20A (h)		2/3 elected	60 days after adjournment
Vermont	...	...	5		3A	2/3 present	July 1

VETO, VETO OVERRIDE AND EFFECTIVE DATE—Continued

State or other jurisdiction	Governor may item veto appropriation bills		Days allowed governor to consider bill (a)			Votes required in each house to pass bills or items over veto (c)	Effective date of enacted legislation (d)
	Amount	Other (b)	During session Bill becomes law unless vetoed	After session Bill becomes law unless vetoed	After session Bill dies unless signed		
Virginia	★		7 (h)		30A (h)	2/3 present (y)	July 1 (v,z)
Washington	★	★	5	20A		2/3 present	90 days after adjournment
West Virginia	★	★	5	15A (aa)		Majority elected (g)	90 days after enactment
Wisconsin	★	★	6		6P	2/3 present	Day after publication
Wyoming	★	...	3	15A (h)		2/3 elected	Immediately
American Samoa	★		10		30P	2/3 elected	60 days after adjournment (bb)
Guam	★	(f)	10		30P	2/3 elected	Immediately (cc)
No. Mariana Islands	★		40 (dd)			2/3 elected	Immediately
Puerto Rico	★	(f)	10		30P (h)	2/3 elected	Specified in act
U.S. Virgin Islands	★		10		30P (h)	2/3 elected	Immediately

Note: Some legislatures reconvene after normal session to consider bills vetoed by governor. Connecticut—if governor vetoes any bill, secretary of state must reconvene General Assembly on second Monday after the last day on which governor is either authorized to transmit or has transmitted every bill with his objections, whichever occurs first; General Assembly must adjourn *sine die* not later than three days after its reconvening. Hawaii—legislature may reconvene on 45th day after adjournment *sine die*, in special session, without call. Louisiana—legislature meets in a maximum five-day veto session on the 40th day after final adjournment. Missouri—if governor returns any bill on or after the fifth day before the last day on which legislature may consider bills (in even-numbered years), legislature automatically reconvenes on first Monday in September for a maximum 10C session. New Jersey—legislature meets in special session (without call or petition) to act on bills returned by governor on 45th day after *sine die* adjournment of the first year of a two-year legislature; a special session may not be convened if the 45th day falls on or after the last day of the legislative year in which the second session occurs. Virginia—legislature reconvenes on sixth Wednesday after adjournment for a maximum three-day session (may be extended to seven days upon vote of majority of members elected to each house). Utah—if 2/3 of the members of each house favor reconvening to consider vetoed bills, a maximum five-day session is set by the presiding officers. Washington—upon petition of 2/3 of the members elected to each house, legislature meets 45 days after adjournment for a maximum five-day session.

Key:
★ — Yes
... — No
A — days after adjournment of legislature
P — days after presentation to governor

(a) Sundays excluded, unless otherwise indicated.
(b) Includes language in appropriations bill.
(c) Bill returned to house of origin with governor's objections.
(d) Effective date may be established by the law itself or may be otherwise changed by vote of the legislature. Special or emergency acts are usually effective immediately.
(e) Penal acts, 60 days.
(f) Governor can also reduce amounts in appropriations bills. In Hawaii, governor can reduce items in executive appropriations measures, but cannot reduce nor item veto amounts appropriated for the judicial or legislative branches.
(g) Different number of votes required for revenue and appropriations bills. Alaska—3/4 elected, Illinois—appropriations reductions, majority elected. Oklahoma—emergency bills, 3/4 vote. West Virginia—budget and supplemental appropriations, 2/3 elected.
(h) Sundays included.
(i) A bill presented to the governor that is not returned within 12 days becomes a law; provided that any bill passed before Sept. 1 of the second calendar year of the biennium of the legislative session and in the possession of the governor on or after Sept. 1 that is not returned by the governor on or before Sept. 30 of that year becomes law. The legislature may not present to the governor any bill after Nov. 15 of the second calendar year of the biennium of the session. If the legislature, by adjournment of a special session prevents the return of a bill with the veto message, the bill becomes law unless the governor vetoes within 12 days by depositing it and the veto message in the office of the secretary of state.
(j) For legislation enacted in regular sessions: Jan. 1 next following 90-day period from date of enactment. For legislation enacted in special sessions: 91 days after adjournment. Does not apply to statutes calling elections, statutes providing for tax levies or appropriations for the usual current state expenses or urgency statutes, all of which take effect immediately.
(k) An act takes effect on the date stated in the act, or if no date is stated in the act, then on its passage.
(l) Constitution withholds right to veto constitutional amendments.
(m) Bills vetoed after adjournment are returned to the legislature for reconsideration. Georgia: bills vetoed during last three days of session and not considered for overriding, and all bills vetoed after *sine die* adjournment may be considered at next session. Maine: returned within three days after the next meeting of the same legislature which enacted the bill or resolution. Maryland: reconsidered at the next meeting of the General Assembly. Mississippi: returned within three days after the beginning of the next session. Missouri: bills returned within four days of adjournment or later in first session are considered at beginning of second session; bills returned in second session are considered in automatic veto session. South Carolina: within two days after the next meeting.
(n) Effective date for bills which become law on or after July 1. Georgia—Jan. 1, unless a specific date has been provided for in legislation. Illinois—a bill passed after June 30 does not become effective prior to July 1 of the next calendar year unless legislature, by a 3/5 vote provided for an earlier effective date. Iowa—if governor signs bill after July 1, bill becomes law on Aug. 15; for special sessions, 90 days after adjournment. South Dakota—91 days after adjournment.
(o) Except Sundays and legal holidays. In Hawaii, except Saturdays, Sundays, holidays and any days in which the legislature is in recess prior to its adjournment.
(p) The governor must notify the legislature 10 days before the 45th day of his intent to veto a measure on that day. The legislature may convene on the 45th day after adjournment to consider the vetoed measures. If the legislature fails to reconvene, the bill does not become law. If the legislature reconvenes, it may pass the measure over the governor's veto or it may amend the law to meet the governor's objections. If the law is amended, the governor must sign the bill within 10 days after it is presented to him in order for it to become law.
(q) No act takes effect until it has been published and circulated in the counties, by authority, except in cases of emergency.
(r) Governor must sign or veto all bills presented to him. Iowa—any bill submitted to the governor for his approval during the last three days of a session must be deposited by him in the secretary of state's office within 30 days after adjournment with his approval or objections. Missouri—otherwise, legislature, by joint resolution, reciting fact of such failure, may direct the secretary of state to enroll the bill as an authentic act and it becomes law.
(s) Bills passed over governor's veto are effective in 30 days or on date specified in bill, whichever is later.
(t) Different date for fiscal legislation. Minnesota, Montana—July 1. Missouri, New Mexico—immediately.
(u) In event of a recess of 30 days or more, legislature may prescribe, by joint resolution, that laws previously passed and not effective shall take effect 90 days from beginning of recess.
(v) No appropriation can be made in excess of the recommendations contained in the governor's budget except by a 2/3 vote. The excess is not subject to veto by the governor.
(y) If a bill is not returned by the governor within 10 days after it is presented to him (excluding Sundays), it becomes law, unless the house of origin is in temporary adjournment. In that case, the legislature comes law on the day the house of origin reconvenes. If on the 10th day, the legislature is in adjournment

VETO, VETO OVERRIDE AND EFFECTIVE DATE—Continued

sine die, the bill becomes law if the governor signs it within 45 days (excluding Sundays) after the adjournment. On the 45th day, the bill becomes law unless he returns it with his objections (1) on the 45th day if the house of origin has convened in regular or special session of the same two-year legislature; (2) on the day upon which the house reconvenes, if it is in temporary adjournment on the 45th day; or (3) on the 45th day (if the house is in adjournment *sine die*) at the special session which convenes on that day (without petition or call) for the sole purpose of acting on returned bills.

(x) Governor has no approval or veto power.
(y) Must include majority of elected members.
(z) Special sessions—first day of fourth month after adjournment.
(aa) Five days for appropriations bills.
(bb) Laws required to be approved only by the governor. An act required to be approved by the U.S. Secretary of the Interior only after it is vetoed by the governor and so approved takes effect 40 days after it is returned to the governor by the secretary.
(cc) U.S. Congress may annul.
(dd) Twenty days for appropriations bills.

LEGISLATURES

Table 3.21
BILL AND RESOLUTION INTRODUCTIONS AND ENACTMENTS: 1988 AND 1989 REGULAR SESSIONS

State or jurisdiction	Duration of session*	Introductions Bills	Introductions Resolutions	Enactments Bills	Enactments Resolutions	Measures vetoed by governor	Length of session
Alabama	Feb. 2-May 5, 1988	1,751	756	396	704	13 (a)	30L
	Feb. 2-May 11, 1989	1,803	936	590	886	3	(b)
Alaska	Jan. 11-May 10, 1988	446	141	176	77	3	120C
	Jan.9-May 9, 1989	691	205	119	73	2	121C
Arizona	Jan. 11-July 1, 1988	928	50	351	23	9	172C
	Jan. 9-May 9, 1989	1,134	59	313	14	9	158C
California	Jan. 4-Aug. 31, 1988	3,207	181	1,647	164	385	122L
	Dec. 5, 1988-Sept. 15, 1989	4,260	280	1,467	187	275	133L
Colorado	Jan. 6-May 24, 1988	564	114	314	84	5	140C
	Jan. 11-May 10, 1989	626	84	378	63	7	120C
Connecticut	Feb 3-May 4, 1988	1,682	151	444	N.A.	2	71L
	Jan.4-June 7, 1989	3,686	169	173	N.A.	3	117L
Delaware	Jan.13-June 30, 1988	1,198	841	426	841	24	55C
	Jan. 10-June 30, 1989	767	431	136	395	10	51C
Florida	April 5-June 7, 1988	2,969 (c)	171 (d)	556 (c)	148 (d)	20	64C
	April 4-June 3, 1989	3,232 (c)	176 (d)	532 (c)	151 (d)	21	61C
Georgia	Jan. 12-March 7, 1988	1,781	921	684	720	9	40L
	Jan. 9-March 15, 1989	1,542	834	704	698	10	40L
Hawaii	Jan. 20-April 27, 1988	3,085	1,382	404	532	28	62L
	Jan. 18-April 26, 1989	3,970	1,355	397	547	35	62L
Idaho	Jan.11-March 31, 1988	734	77	385	37	9	81L
	Jan. 9-March 29, 1989	752	104	434	63	8	80L
Illinois	Jan. 13, 1988-Jan. 10, 1989	2,094	1,993	442	1,972	22 (e)	(b)
	Jan. 10-Nov. 3, 1989	4,366	2,074	1,027	1,941	120	(b)
Indiana	Nov. 17, 1987-Feb. 29, 1988	980	6	212	0	2	30L
	Nov. 22, 1988-April 29, 1989	1,630	18	338	3	12	61L
Iowa	Jan. 11-April 19, 1988	1,368	105	208	19	18	98C
	Jan. 19-May 7, 1989	1,347	115	324	34	24	119C
Kansas	Jan. 11-June 3, 1988	842 (f)	46 (g)	399	22	2	71L
	Jan. 9-June 26, 1989	991	57 (g)	313	22	2	(b)
Kentucky	Jan. 5-April 15, 1988	1,429	440	399	38	11	59L
	No regular session in 1989						
Louisiana	April 18-July 11, 1988	2,957	556	1,009	338	30	(b)
	April 17-July 5, 1989	2,669	405	848	272	20	(b)
Maine	Jan. 6-May 5, 1988	725	45 (h)	396	43 (h)	8	72L
	Dec. 7, 1988-July 1, 1989	1,781	53	734	53	0	92L
Maryland	Jan. 13-April 11, 1988	2,373	96	792	15	80 (a)	90C
	Jan. 11-April 10, 1989	2,537	63	929	22	98	90C
Massachusetts	Jan. 6-Nov. 23, 1988	8,304	5	335	5	0	322C
	Jan. 4, 1989-Jan. 2, 1989	8,733	4	731	4	0	364C
Michigan	Jan.13-Dec. 29, 1988	1,148	10	521	1	10	352C
	Jan. 11-Dec. 28, 1989	2,114	29	307	1	1	352C
Minnesota	Feb. 9-May 25, 1988	2,168 (t)	26	593	21	3	76C
	Jan. 3-May 22, 1989	3,466 (t)	53	709	31	7	139C
Mississippi	Jan. 5-May 8, 1988	2,603	349	646	202	6	125C
	Jan. 3-April 10, 1989	2,597	411	603	191	7	98C
Missouri	Jan. 6-May 13, 1988	1,347	65	178	33	8	(b)
	Jan. 4-May 30, 1989	1,404	48	81	1	7	77L
Montana	No regular session in 1988						
	Jan 2-April 21, 1989	1,268	90	796	72	14	90L
Nebraska	Jan. 6-April 8, 1988	451	213	259	N.A.	33 (a)	60L
	Jan. 4-May 24, 1989	817	243	308	N.A.	38 (a)	90L
Nevada	No regular session in 1988						
	Jan. 16-July 1, 1989	1,518	271	891	201	2 (a)	123L
New Hampshire	Jan. 6-May 3, 1988	597 (i)	61	294 (j)	44	8	23L
	Dec. 7, 1988-June 28, 1989	965	65	421	44	5	30L

LEGISLATURES

BILL AND RESOLUTION INTRODUCTIONS AND ENACTMENTS—Continued

State or jurisdiction	Duration of session*	Introductions		Enactments		Measures vetoed by governor	Length of session
		Bills	Resolutions	Bills	Resolutions		
New Jersey	Jan. 12, 1988-Jan. 10, 1989	7,804	640	186	20	41	56L
	Jan. 10, 1989-Jan 8, 1990	2,114	235	351	9	81	45L
New Mexico	Jan. 19-Feb. 18, 1988	900	30	165	7	25	30C
	Jan. 17-March 18, 1989	1,733	38	468	13	76	60C
New York	Jan. 6, 1988-(k)	18,077	N.A.	794	N.A.	61	151L
	Jan. 4, 1989-(k)	14,902	N.A.	779	N.A.	N.A.	142L
North Carolina	June 2-July 12, 1988	805	21	233	12	N.A.	28L
	Jan. 11-Aug. 12, 1989	3,375	100	802	34	N.A.	(b)
North Dakota	No regular session in 1988						
	Jan. 4-April 20, 1989	1,216	168	783	135 (l)	9	75L
Ohio	Jan. 5-Dec. 31, 1988	411	50 (m)	210	18	3	(b)
	Jan. 3-Dec. 31, 1989	1010	78 (m)	117	43	1	(b)
Oklahoma	Jan. 5-July 12, 1988	791	253	330	136	37 (a)	90L
	Jan. 3-May 26, 1989	1,084	402	248	139	30 (a)	83L
Oregon	No regular session in 1988						
	Jan. 9-July 4, 1989	2,856	125	1,083	48	15	177C
Pennsylvania	Jan. 5-Nov. 30, 1988 (m)	1,127	261	262	164	11 (a)	(b)
	Jan. 3, 1989-Jan. 2, 1990	3,572	433	163	206	1	(b)
Rhode Island	Jan. 5-June 4, 1988	4,570	547	1,331	547	84 (a)	69L
	Jan.3-July 6, 1989	4,445	563	1,211	563	56	86L
South Carolina	Jan. 12-June 21, 1988	1,793 (n)	(n)	518 (n)	(n)	18 (a)	96L
	Jan. 10-June 22, 1989	2,041 (n)	(n)	310 (n)	(n)	76 (a)	(b)
South Dakota	Feb. 12-March 14, 1988	697	6	424	4	14 (a)	35L
	Jan. 10-March 20, 1989	761	7	452	3	2	40L
Tennessee	Jan. 12-April 29, 1988 (o)	2,114	919	692	784	0	45L
	Jan. 10-May 25, 1989 (p)	N.A.	N.A.	N.A.	N.A.	N.A.	53L
Texas	No regular session in 1988						
	Jan.10-May 29, 1989	5,069	2,723	1,318	2,309	56	140C
Utah	Jan. 11-Feb. 24 1988 (o)	619	131	260	83	7	45C
	Jan. 9-Feb. 22, 1989 (p)	678	105	283	56	4	45C
Vermont	Jan. 5-May 20, 1988	554	106	174	81	2	85L
	Jan. 4-May 7, 1989	793	114	136	80	1	74L
Virginia	Jan. 13-March 12, 1988	1,561	436	907	354	8	58C
	Jan. 11-Feb. 25, 1989	1,516 (q)	479	745	418	7	47C
Washington	Jan. 11-March 10, 1988	1,459	289	108	22	3	60C
	Jan. 9-April 23, 1989	2,388	129	446	28	18	105C
West Virginia	Jan. 13-March 12, 1988 (r)	1,993	206	153	62	13	62C
	Feb. 8-April 8, 1989 (r)	1,496	198	221	75	4	65C
Wisconsin	Jan. 5, 1987-Jan. 3, 1989	1,631	217	413	123	53	133L
	Jan. 3, 1989-Jan. 7, 1991	1,369 (s)	243 (s)	116 (s)	101 (s)	17 (s)	115l (s)
Wyoming	Feb. 15-March 12, 1988	330	24	102	4	4	21L
	Jan. 10-March 1, 1989	752	37	293	5	6	38L
Puerto Rico	Jan. 11-June 10, 1988	574	1,154	298	322	37	152C
	Jan. 9-July 3, 1989 and	1,608	2,414	204	233	28	176C
	Sept. 11-October 31, 1989						59C

LEGISLATURES

BILL AND RESOLUTION INTRODUCTIONS AND ENACTMENTS—Continued

* Actual adjournment dates are listed regardless of constitutional or statutory limitations. For more information on provisions, see Table 3.2, "Legislative Sessions: Legal Provisions."

Key:
C — Calendar day
L — Legislative day (in some states, called a session or workday; definition may vary slightly, however, generally refers to any day on which either chamber of the legislature is in session).
N.A. — Not available

(a) Number of vetoes overriden: Alabama: 1988 - 1; Colorado: 1988 - 1; Illinois: 1988 - 2, 1989 - 9; Indiana: 1989 - 2; Maryland: 1988 - 1; Nebraska: 1988 - 17, 1989 - 4; Nevada: 1989 - 1; Oklahoma: 1988 - 6, 1989 - 7; Pennsylvania: 1988 - 1; Rhode Island: 1988 - 7; South Carolina: 1988 - 10, 1989 - 13; South Dakota: 1988 - 3. Plus line item vetoes: Alaska: 1988 - 1; North Dakota: 1988 - 1; Oklahoma: 1988 - 10, 1989 - 8.

(b) Alabama: 1989—Senate 28L, House 29L; Illinois: 1988—Senate 56L, House 55L; 1989—Senate 69L, House 76L; Kansas: 1989—Senate 72L, House 73L; Louisiana: 1988—Senate 48L, House 57L; 1989—Senate 42L, House 53L; Missouri: 1988—Senate 67L, House 68L; North Carolina: 1989—Senate 128L, House 137L; Ohio: 1988—Senate 116L, House 101L; 1989—Senate 121L, House 120L; Pennsylvania: 1988—Senate 67L, House 68L; 1989—Senate 73L, House 77L; South Carolina: 1989—Senate 100L, House 90L.

(c) Includes general, local, joint resolutions, and memorials.
(d) Includes concurrent resolutions and one-chamber resolutions.
(e) Amendatory vetoes 40; amendatory vetoes accepted, 16; amendatory vetoes overriden, 4.
(f) Plus 582 bills carried over from 1987.
(g) Plus 36 concurrent resolutions carried over from 1987. In 1988 240 simple resolutions (house only or senate only) were introduced, 236 were adopted. In 1989, 211 simple resolutions were introduced, 187 were adopted.
(h) Of the total, 42 joint resolutions were introduced and enacted.
(i) Does not include 155 pieces of legislation re-referred from 1987 session.
(j) Includes re-referred legislation that was enacted.
(k) Adjourned *sine die*.
(l) In addition, a total of 1,705 simple resolutions were introduced in 1988; 1,310 in 1989.
(m) Expired constitutionally.
(n) Includes resolutions.
(o) Second year of two year session.
(p) First year of two year session.
(q) Includes 268 carryovers.
(r) Extended by proclamation by governor for consideration of budget in 1988 to March 14; in 1989 to April 12.
(s) All data as of February 24, 1990.
(t) Includes simultaneous introductions.

LEGISLATURES

Table 3.22
BILL AND RESOLUTION INTRODUCTIONS AND ENACTMENTS: 1988 AND 1989 SPECIAL SESSIONS

State or jurisdiction	Duration of session*	Introductions Bills	Introductions Resolutions	Enactments Bills	Enactments Resolutions	Measures vetoed by governor	Length of session
Alabama	Aug. 30-Sept. 22, 1988	594	405	223	172	18 (a)	12L
	Sept. 26-Sept. 30, 1988	114	86	26	73	3	5L
	Dec. 4-Dec. 21, 1989	89	114	19	70	1	6L
Alaska	No special sessions in 1988/1989						
Arizona	No special sessions in 1988						
	Sept. 20-Sept. 22, 1989	15	5	5	0	1	3C
	Nov. 21-Nov. 22, 1989	6	1	3	0	0	2C
Arkansas	Jan. 26-Feb. 5, 1988	54	25	35	22	5	8C
	July 11-July 14, 1988	37	42	26	40	4	4C
	June 20-June 23, 1989	294	6	286	5	1	4C
	July 25-July 27, 1989	10	8	3	6	2	3C
	Oct. 23-Nov. 3, 1989	195	45	100	36	18	12C
California	Nov. 9-Nov. 10, 1988	9	0	3	0	0	2L
	Nov. 2-April 19, 1990 (k)	104	5	24	1	0	(k)
Colorado	Aug. 3-Aug. 5, 1988	9	12	7	12	0	3C
	June 21-July 1, 1989	26	11	5	5	0	10C
Connecticut	June 20-June 20, 1988	0	8	0	0	0	1L
	July 17-July 17, 1989	0	10	0	0	0	1L
Delaware	No special sessions in 1988						
	Dec. 18-Dec. 20, 1989	7	0	0	0	0	1C
Florida	Feb. 2-Feb. 4, 1988	25 (c)	0	7 (c)	0	1	3C
	June 8-June 8, 1988	3 (c)	0	3 (c)	0	0	1C
	June 3-June 3, 1989	7 (c)	0	3 (c)	0	0	1C
	June 19-June 20, 1989	35 (c)	1 (d)	14 (c)	1 (d)	0	2C
	Oct. 10-Oct. 11, 1989	32 (c)	0	0	0	0	2C
	Nov. 15-Nov. 18, 1989	66 (c)	5 (d)	14 (c)	5 (d)	0	4C
Georgia	No special sessions in 1988						
	Sept. 9-Sept. 15, 1989	18	18	11	18	0	5L
Hawaii	May 20-May 23, 1988	2	0	2	0	0	2L
	No special sessions in 1989						
Idaho	No special sessions in 1988/1989						
Illinois	No special sessions in 1988/1989						
Indiana	No special sessions in 1988						
	May 2-May 4, 1989	28	0	28	0	2	3L
Iowa	No special sessions in 1988/1989						
Kansas	No special sessions in 1988						
	Dec. 8-Dec. 9, 1989	15	5 (e)	2	2 (e)	0	2L
Kentucky	Nov. 28-Dec. 14, 1988	7	77	3	3	0	17C
	Jan. 6-Jan. 6, 1989	0	12	0	1	0	1C
Louisiana	March 21-March 26, 1988	17	46	16	32	0	6L
	Oct. 2-Oct. 25, 1988	50	52	22	41	2	(b)
	Feb. 22-March 7, 1989	34	54	16	50	0	(b)
	July 5-July 10, 1989	141	32	30	29	1	6L
Maine	Sept. 15-Sept. 15, 1988	43	34	1	1	0	1L
	Nov. 28-Nov. 28, 1988	11	0	8	0	0	1L
	Aug. 21-Aug. 22, 1989	34	0	26	0	0	2L
Maryland	No special sessions in 1988/1989						
Massachusetts	No special sessions in 1988/1989						
Michigan	No special sessions in 1988/1989						
Minnesota	No special sessions in 1988						
	Sept. 27-Sept. 29, 1989	8 (f)	0	4 (f)	0	0	3L
Mississippi	Aug. 10-Aug. 16, 1988	42	22	21	16	0	7C
	April 17-April 19, 1989	5	32	3	23	0	3C
Missouri	No special sessions in 1988						
	July 5-July 12, 1989	11	0	1	0	0	8L

LEGISLATURES

BILL AND RESOLUTION INTRODUCTIONS AND ENACTMENTS—Continued

State or jurisdiction	Duration of session*	Introductions Bills	Introductions Resolutions	Enactments Bills	Enactments Resolutions	Measures vetoed by governor	Length of session
Montana	No special sessions in 1988 June 19-July 14, 1989	94	3	15	1	2	21L
Nebraska	Jan. 11-Jan. 18, 1988 Nov. 8-Nov. 17, 1989	3 9	5 11	3 4	4 9	0 0	7L 7L
Nevada	No special sessions in 1988 Nov. 21-Nov. 21, 1989	2	4	2	4	0	1L
New Hampshire	No special sessions in 1988 Dec. 14-Dec. 14, 1989	3	2	1	2	0	1L
New Jersey	No special sessions in 1988/1989						
New Mexico	Feb. 18-Feb. 19, 1988 No special sessions in 1989	3	0	3	0	0	1C
New York	No special sessions in 1988/1989						
North Carolina	No special sessions in 1988 Dec. 7-Dec. 7, 1989	6	0	1	0	0	1L
North Dakota	No special sessions in 1988/1989						
Ohio	No special sessions in 1988/1989						
Oklahoma	Aug. 29-Sept. 2, 1988 Aug. 14, 1989-March 5, 1990 (g)	6 34	14 39	4 0	13 30	1 (a) 0	5L (g)
Oregon	No special sessions in 1988/1989						
Pennsylvania	Nov. 9-Nov. 30, 1988 (h) No special sessions in 1989	7	0	2	1	0	56L
Rhode Island	No special sessions in 1988/1989						
South Carolina	No special sessions in 1988/1989						
South Dakota	No special sessions in 1988/1989						
Tennessee	No special sessions in 1988/1989						
Texas	No special sessions in 1988 June 20-July 19, 1989 Nov. 14-Dec. 12, 1989	253 178	453 448	45 1	419 394	0 0	30C 29C
Utah	July 5-July 6, 1988 April 7-April 7, 1989	17 2	2 0	16 2	2 0	0 0	2C 1C
Vermont	No special sessions in 1988/1989						
Virginia	No special sessions in 1988 April 5-April 5, 1989 April 24-April 27, 1989	0 23	6 25	0 12	6 23	0 0	1C 4C
Washington	March 11-March 12, 1988 April 24-May 10, 1989 May 17-May 20, 1989	19 21 17	11 21 10	3 29 (i) 4	7 8 8	0 0 0	2C 17C 4C
West Virginia	March 22-March 22, 1988 June 1-June 10, 1988 June 14-June 28, 1988 Jan. 25-Feb. 1, 1989	8 19 49 4	10 15 10 1	4 4 10 4	8 12 8 1	0 0 0 0	1C 10C 15C 8C
Wisconsin	September 1987 November 1987 June 1988 Oct. 10, 1989-Feb. 24, 1990 (j)	2 19 4 46	1 3 4 5	2 5 2 6	1 3 4 4	0 3 0 2	4L 20L 2L (j)
Wyoming	No special sessions in 1988/1989						
Puerto Rico	No special sessions in 1988 Nov. 29-Dec. 18, 1989	34	56	12	3	0	19C

* Actual adjournment dates are listed regardless of constitutional or statutory limitations. For more information on provisions, see Table 3.2, "Legislative Sessions: Legal Provisions."

Key:
C — Calendar day
L — Legislative day
(a) Number of vetoes overriden: Alabama: 1988—1; plus line item vetoes: Oklahoma: 1988—1.
(b) Louisiana: 1988 Senate—16L, House—19L; 1989 Senate—11L, House—12L.
(c) Includes general, local, joint resolutions and memorials.
(d) Includes concurrent resolutions and one chamber resolutions.
(e) Concurrent resolutions.
(f) Includes simultaneous introductions.
(g) Through March 5, 1990; still in session as of April 20, 1990.
(h) Expired constitutionally.
(i) Includes regular session bills.
(j) Active session: all data as of Feb. 24, 1990.
(k) Still in session as of April 19, 1990.

LEGISLATURES

Table 3.23
STAFF FOR INDIVIDUAL LEGISLATORS

State or other jurisdiction	Senate Capitol Personal	Senate Capitol Shared	Senate District	House Capitol Personal	House Capitol Shared	House District
Alabama	SO	...	YR	...	YR/5	YR
Alaska	YR (a)	...	...	YR (a)	...	...
Arizona	YR	YR/1.3	...	YR	YR/3.6	...
Arkansas	...	YR	...	...	YR	...
California	YR	YR (l)	YR	YR	YR (l)	YR
Colorado	...	YR/3	...	...	YR/5	...
Connecticut	YR	YR/0.5	...	...	YR/1	...
Delaware	SO	YR/2	...	SO	YR/3	...
Florida	...	...	YR	...	...	YR
Georgia	YR (b)	YR/2	...	YR (b)	YR/6	...
Hawaii	YR	YR (c)	...	YR	YR (c)	...
Idaho	...	YR/25	...	...	SO/25	...
Illinois	YR	(c)	(d)	...	YR (e)	(d)
Indiana	...	YR/3	...	...	YR/2	...
Iowa	SO	...	...	SO	...	...
Kansas	SO	...	...	...	SO/3	...
Kentucky	...	YR/1.7	...	...	YR/1.7	...
Louisiana	...	...	YR	...	...	YR
Maine	(f)	SO/10	...	...	SO/30	...
Maryland	YR	...	YR	SO	...	YR
Massachusetts	YR	...	...	YR	...	...
Michigan	YR	...	...	YR	...	...
Minnesota	YR	...	...	YR	YR/3	...
Mississippi	...	YR	...	...	YR	...
Missouri	YR	...	YR	SO	IO	YR
Montana	...	SO/5	...	...	SO/10	...
Nebraska	YR	...	...	Unicameral		
Nevada	...	YR	...	...	YR	...
New Hampshire	...	SO/3	...	...	YR/20	...
New Jersey	YR (g)	...	YR (g)	YR (g)	...	YR (g)
New Mexico	SO	SO/3.5	...	SO	SO/7.5	...
New York	YR (d)	...	YR	YR	...	YR
North Carolina	SO	...	...	SO	...	...
North Dakota	...	SO/13	...	...	SO/15	...
Ohio	YR	YR (h)	(i)	YR	YR	... (i)
Oklahoma	(b)	IO/5	...	SO	YR/2	...
Oregon	YR	...	...	YR	...	...
Pennsylvania	YR	...	YR	YR	...	YR
Rhode Island	...	YR/8	...	...	YR/7	...
South Carolina	YR	YR	...	SO	YR	...
South Dakota	...	SO	...	...	SO	...
Tennessee	YR	...	...	YR	...	...
Texas	YR	...	YR	YR	...	YR
Utah	...	SO/2	...	...	SO/5	...
Vermont	...	YR (j)	...	...	YR (j)	...
Virginia	YR	SO/2	YR	YR	SO/2	YR
Washington	YR	YR/1	YR	YR	YR/1	YR
West Virginia	SO	...	...	...	SO/20	...
Wisconsin	YR	...	(e)	YR	...	...
Wyoming	...	YR (k)	...	...	YR (k)	...
American Samoa	...	...	...	...	...	...
Puerto Rico	YR	...	...	YR	...	YR
U.S. Virgin Islands	YR	YR	YR	Unicameral		

Note: For entries under column heading "Shared," figures after slash indicates approximate number of legislators per staff person, where available.

Key:
... — Staff not provided for individual legislators.
YR — Year-round
SO — Session only
IO — Interim only

(a) Personal staff work in Juneau during session and in the district during the interim.
(b) Personal staff provided for Chairmen of Committees. In Oklahoma, staff is also provided for leadership; all others are during session only.
(c) Majority and minority offices provide staff year-round.
(d) District office expenses allocated per year from which one or two legislative assistants may be employed.
(e) House leadership offices provide staff year-round.
(f) Personal staff provided to leadership only.
(g) Personal and district staff are the same. In Wisconsin, the total of all employees' salaries for each senator must be within the limits established by the Senate.
(h) There are three types of staff positions that provide staff to senators in a shared arrangement; 33 senators to 2 steno pool staff and 25 caucus assistants to 33 senators; and 1 constituent aide for every 4 senators.
(i) Some legislators have established district offices at their own expense.
(j) Shared pool covers staff.
(k) During sessions, legislators are served by temporary sessional staff; during interim period, by Legislative Service office.
(l) Secretarial staff.

LEGISLATURES

Table 3.24
STAFF FOR LEGISLATIVE STANDING COMMITTEES

State or other jurisdiction	Committee staff assistance				Source of staff services*								
	Senate		House		Joint central agency (a)		Chamber agency (b)		Caucus or leadership		Committee or committee chairman	
	Prof.	Cler.	Prof.	Cler.	Prof.	Cler.	Prof.	Cler.	Prof.	Cler.	Prof.	Cler.
Alabama	(c)	★	(c)	★	B						B	B
Alaska	★	★	★	★	B			B	B	B	B	B
Arizona	★	★	★	★	(d)		B	B	B	B	B	
Arkansas	★	★	★	★	B	B		B				
California	★		★				B	B				
Colorado	★	...	★	...	B							
Connecticut	★ (e)	★ (e)	★ (e)	★ (e)	(e)	(e)						
Delaware	(c)	★ (f)	(c)	★ (f)	B	B		B	B			
Florida	★	★	★	★							B	B
Georgia	★	★ (f)	★	★ (f)	B		S			B	H	
Hawaii	(g)	★	(g)	★	B	B	B	B	B	B	B	B
Idaho	(c)	★	(c)	★	B							B
Illinois	★	★	★	★					B	B		
Indiana	★	★	★	...	B						S	
Iowa	★	★	★	★	B			B (h)	B			B (h)
Kansas	★	★	★	★	B	B		B		B		B
Kentucky	★	★	★	★	B	B						
Louisiana	★	★	★	★				B			B	B
Maine	★ (e)	★ (e)	★ (e)	★ (e)	(e)							(e)
Maryland	★	★	★	★	B							B
Massachusetts	★	★	★	★	B		B		B	B	B	
Michigan	★	★	★	★				H	B		B	B
Minnesota	★	★	★	★							B	B
Mississippi	•	★	★	★	B	B						
Missouri	(c,f)	★	(c,f)	★					B	B	B	B
Montana	★	★	★	★	B	B						B
Nebraska	★	★					U	U			U	U
Nevada	(c)	★	(c)	★	B			B				
New Hampshire	•	★ (f)	•	★ (f)	B	B			H			
New Jersey	★	★	★	★	B	B						
New Mexico	•	★	•	★	B			B				
New York	★	★	★	★	B	B	B	B	B	B	B	B
North Carolina	•	★	•	★	B		B	B				
North Dakota	(c)	★	(c)	★	B							
Ohio	★	★	★	★	B				B	B		
Oklahoma	•	★	•	★			B	B				
Oregon	★	★	★	★							B	B
Pennsylvania	★	★	★	★			B	B				
Rhode Island	★	★	★	★							B	B
South Carolina	•	★	•	★	B	B	B	B		B	B	B
South Dakota	★	★	★	★	B					B		
Tennessee	★	★	★	★	B				B	B	S	B
Texas	★	★	★	★	B	B	B (f)			B	B	B
Utah	★	★	★	★	B							
Vermont	★	★	★	★	B	B						
Virginia	★	★	★	★	B			B				B (h)
Washington	★	★	★	★			B	B	B		B	
West Virginia	★	★	★	★	B	B	B	B			B	B
Wisconsin	★	★	★	★	B		B		B			
Wyoming	★ (f)	★	★ (f)	★	B							
American Samoa	★ (f)	...	★ (f)	...	B							
Guam	★	★			U	U			U	U	U	U
Puerto Rico	★	★	★	★	B						B	B
Virgin Islands	★	★			U	U						U

Source: The Council of State Governments' Legislative Survey (1988).
* Multiple entries reflect a combination of organizational location of services.
Key:
★ — All committees
• — Some committees
... — No committees
B — Both chambers
H — House
S — Senate
U — Unicameral
(a) Includes legislative council or service agency or central management agency.
(b) Includes chamber management agency, office of clerk or secretary and House or Senate research office.
(c) Money committees only.
(d) Joint Legislative Budget Committee provides staff assistance to the fiscal committees of both houses.
(e) Standing committees are joint House and Senate committees.
(f) Provided on a pool basis.
(g) All professional committee staff (except Finance committees) during session only. During interim, assistance provided by year-round majority and minority research offices.
(h) The Senate secretary and House clerk maintain supervision of committee clerks. Iowa: during the session each committee selects its own clerk.

LEGISLATURES

Table 3.25
STANDING COMMITTEES: APPOINTMENT AND NUMBER

State or other jurisdiction	Committee members appointed by:		Committee chairpersons appointed by:		Number of standing committees during regular 1989 session (a)	
	Senate	House	Senate	House	Senate	House
Alabama	P (b)	S	P (b)	S	18	24
Alaska	CC (c)	CC (c)	CC (c)	CC (c)	9 (d)	9 (d)
Arizona	P	S	P	S	10 (d)	16 (d)
Arkansas	CC	S	CC	(e)	10 (d)	10 (d)
California	CR	S	CR	S (f)	22 (d)	26 (d)
Colorado	MjL,MnL	S,MnL	MjL	S	10	10
Connecticut	PT	S	PT	S	(g)	(g)
Delaware	PT	S (h)	PT	S	22 (d)	19 (d)
Florida	P	S	P	S	22 (d)	29 (d)
Georgia	P (b)	S	P (b)	S	25	28
Hawaii	P (i)	(j)	P (i)	(j)	18	18
Idaho	PT (k)	S	PT (l)	S	11	14
Illinois	CC	S,MnL	P	S	19	25
Indiana	PT	S	PT	S	17	29
Iowa	MjL, MnL (m)	S	MjL,MnL (m)	S	15 (d)	16 (d)
Kansas	(n)	S	(n)	S	18 (d)	21 (d)
Kentucky	CC	CC	CC	CC	15	15
Louisiana	P	S	P	S	15	15
Maine	P	S	P	S	4 (g)	6 (g)
Maryland	P	S	P	S	6 (d)	7 (d)
Massachusetts	P	S	P	S	6	6
Michigan	MjL	S	MjL	S	15	30
Minnesota	(o)	S	(o)	S	18	20
Mississippi	P (b)	S	P (b)	S	29 (d)	30 (d)
Missouri	PT (p)	S	PT	S	25 (d)	49 (d)
Montana	CC	S	CC	S	16	15
Nebraska (U)	CC		(q)		13	
Nevada	(r)	S	MjL	S	9	13
New Hampshire	P (s)	S (t)	P (s)	S	15 (d)	23 (d)
New Jersey	P	S	P	S	17 (d)	24 (d)
New Mexico	CC	S	CC	S	7	15
New York	PT (u)	S	PT (u)	S	32 (d)	37 (d)
North Carolina	PT,MnL	S	PT,MnL	S	34	53
North Dakota	CC	S	MjL	S	11 (d)	15 (d)
Ohio	(v)	S	CC	S	17	26
Oklahoma	PT (t)	S	PT	S	18 (d)	28 (d)
Oregon	P	S	P	S	16 (d)	17 (d)
Pennsylvania	PT	S	PT	S	21	21
Rhode Island	MjL	S	MjL	S	6	6
South Carolina	E (w)	S	E	E	15	11
South Dakota	(x)	S	(x)	S	13 (d)	13 (d)
Tennessee	S	S	S	S	9 (d)	11 (d)
Texas	P (b)	S (y)	P (b)	S	12	36
Utah	P	S	P	S	10 (d)	12 (d)
Vermont	P (b)	S	P (b)	S	12 (d)	15 (d)
Virginia	E	S (z)	(aa)	S	10	17
Washington	P (b,bb)	S (cc)	(dd)	S (dd)	14	21
West Virginia	P	S	P	S	15 (d)	13 (d)
Wisconsin	(ee)	S	(ee)	S	15 (d)	26 (d)
Wyoming	P (ff)	S (ff)	P (ff)	S (ff)	12 (d)	12 (d)
Dist. of Columbia (U)	(gg)		(gg)		10	
American Samoa	P,E	S,E	P	S	18	13
Guam (U)	(hh)		E		13	
Puerto Rico	P	S	P	S	19 (d)	25 (d)
U.S. Virgin Islands	P		P		10	

LEGISLATURES

STANDING COMMITTEES: APPOINTMENT AND NUMBER—Continued

Note: Standing committees are those which regularly consider legislation during the legislative session.

Key:
CC — Committee on Committees
CR — Committee on Rules
E — Election
MjL — Majority Leader
MnL — Minority Leader
P — President
PT — President pro tempore
S — Speaker
(U) — Unicameral Legislature

(a) Taken from state legislative rulebooks, 1990, 1989, 1988 and 1987.
(b) Lieutenant governor is president of the Senate.
(c) Report of Committee on Committees is subject to approval by majority vote of chamber's membership.
(d) Also, joint standing committees. Alaska, 2; Arizona, 4; Arkansas, 5; California, 16; Delaware, 2; Florida, 5; Iowa, 1; Kansas, 6; Maryland, 2 (and 9 joint statutory); Mississippi, 6; Missouri, 6; New Hampshire, 3; New Jersey, 4; New York, 15; North Dakota, 1; Oklahoma, 3; Oregon, 2; South Dakota, 1; Tennessee, 1; Utah, 10; Vermont, 4; West Virginia, 2; Wisconsin, 7; Wyoming, 1; and Puerto Rico, 2.
(e) Chair of the standing committee is the ranking member of the committee on senority basis.
(f) Chair and vice-chair of the standing and special committees are to be members of different parties.
(g) Substantive standing committees are joint committees. Connecticut, 20; Maine, 20; Massachusetts, 21.
(h) Shall include members of two political parties.
(i) President appoints committee members and chairs; minority members on committees are nominated by minority party caucus.
(j) By resolution, with members of majority party designating the chair, vice-chairs and majority party members of committees, and members of minority party designating minority party members.
(k) Committee members appointed by the Senate leadership under the direction of the president pro tempore, by and with the Senate's advice.
(l) Chair is appointed from the membership of the political party having a majority of the Senate.
(m) Appointments made after consultation with the president.
(n) Committee on Organization, Calendar and Rules.
(o) Subcommittee on Committees of the Committee on Rules and Administration.
(p) Minority leader appoints committee members from minority party.
(q) Secret ballot by legislature as a whole.
(r) Committee composition and leadership usually determined by party caucus.
(s) Appointments made after consultation with the minority leader.
(t) Minority floor leader apopints minority members of committees (subject to Senate approval).
(u) President pro tempore is also majority leader.
(v) Appointed by Senate.
(w) Seniority system is retained in process.
(x) Presiding officer announces committee membership after selection by president pro tempore, majority and minority leaders.
(y) A maximum of one-half of the membership on each standing committee, exclusive of the chair and vice chair, is determined by seniority; the remaining membership is appointed by the speaker.
(z) Unless specially directed by the House, in which case they shall be appointed by ballot and a plurality of votes shall prevail.
(aa) Senior member of the majority part on the committee is the chair.
(bb) Confirmed by the Senate.
(cc) By each party caucus.
(dd) By majority caucus.
(ee) Committee on Senate Organization.
(ff) With the advice and consent of the Rules and Procedures Committee.
(gg) Chair of the Council.
(hh) Chair of each committee.

LEGISLATURES

Table 3.26
STANDING COMMITTEES: PROCEDURE

State or other jurisdiction	Uniform rules of committee procedure			Public access to committee meetings				Recorded roll call on vote to report bill to floor	
				Open to public		Advance notice required (number of days)			
	Senate	House	Joint	Senate	House	Senate	House	Senate	House
Alabama	...	★		★	★	...	...	Al	Nv
Alaska	...	...		★	★	...	...	Sm	Sm
Arizona	...	★		★	★	5	(a)	Nv	Al
Arkansas	★	★	★	★	★	2	1	Sm	Sm
California	★	★	★	★	★	(a)	(a)	Al	Al
Colorado	★	★		★	★	...	...	Al	Al
Connecticut			★	★ (b)	★ (b)	1	1	Al	Al
Delaware	★	★		★	★	(a)	(a)	Al	Al
Florida	★	★		★	★	1 (c)	2 (d)	Al	Al
Georgia	...	...		★	★	...	...	Sm	Nv
Hawaii	★	★		★ (b)	★	2	2	Al	Al
Idaho	★	★		★	★	...	...	Us	Us
Illinois	★	★	...	★	★	6	6.5	Al	Al
Indiana	...	...		★	★	2	(a)	Al	Al
Iowa	★	★		★	★	...	...	Al	Al
Kansas	★	★		★	★	...	(a)	Sm	Al
Kentucky	...	...		★	★	...	3	Al	Al
Louisiana	★	★		★	★	(a)	(a)	Sm	Al
Maine			★	★	★	(a)	(a)	Sm	Sm
Maryland	★	★		★	★	(a)	(a)	Al	Al
Massachusetts	...	...	...	★	★	...	...	Nv	Sm
Michigan	★	★		★	★	(e)	(e)	Al	Al
Minnesota	★	★	★	★	★	3	3	Sm	Sm
Mississippi	...	...	...	★	★	...	...	Sm	Sm
Missouri	★	★	★	★	★	(a)	1	Al	Al
Montana	...	...		★	★	(f)	(f)	Al	Al
Nebraska (U)	★			★		7		Al	
Nevada	★	★		★	★	(a)	5 (g)	Al	Al
New Hampshire	...	★		★	★	3	3	Al	Al
New Jersey	★	★		★	★	10	5	Al	Al
New Mexico	★	★		★	★	...	...	Sm	Sm
New York	★	★		★	★	7	5	Nv	Nv
North Carolina	...	...	...	★ (b)	★ (b)	(a)	(a)	Sm	Sm
North Dakota	...	...		★	★	(h)	(h)	Al	Al
Ohio	★	★		★	★	2	(a)	Al	Al
Oklahoma	★	★		★	★	(a)	(a)	Sm	Sm
Oregon	★	★		★	★	1 (i)	1 (j)	Al	Al
Pennsylvania	...	...		★	★	3	3	Al	Al
Rhode Island	★	★	★	★	★	...	...	Sm	Al
South Carolina	★	★	★	★	★	1	1	Sm	Sm
South Dakota	★	★		★	★	2	2	Us	Us
Tennessee	★	★		★	★	(k)	(k)	Al	Al
Texas	...	★		★	★	1	5	Sm	Al
Utah	★	★	★	★	★	1	1	Al	Al
Vermont	★	★	★	★	★	...	...	Sm	Sm
Virginia	★	★		★	★ (l)	(a)	(a)	Al	Al
Washington	★	★		★	★	5	5	Al	Al
West Virginia	...	...		★	★ (b)	...	...	Sm	Sm
Wisconsin	★	★	★	★	★	7	7	Al	Al
Wyoming	...	...	...	★ (b)	★	...	...	Al	Al
American Samoa	...	...	...	★	★	(d)	1.5	Nv	Nv
Guam (U)	★			★ (b)		7		Al	
Puerto Rico	★	★		★	★	...	...	Nv	Nv
U.S. Virgin Islands (U)	★			★		7 (m)		Us	

The Council of State Governments 169

LEGISLATURES

STANDING COMMITTEES: PROCEDURE—Continued

Key:
★ — Yes
... — No
Al — Always
Us — Usually
Sm — Sometimes
Nv — Never
(U) — Unicameral legislature

(a) No specified time. Kansas—"due notice" required by House rules. Maine—usually seven days notice given. Maryland—"from time to time," usually seven days. Nevada—"adequate notice." North Carolina—notice must be given in the House or Senate; two methods to waive notice in the Senate. Ohio—"due notice," usually seven days. Virginia—notice published in the daily calendar.

(b) Certain matters specified by statute can be discussed in executive session. Connecticut—upon a 2/3 vote of committee members present and voting and stating the reason for such executive session. North Carolina—appropriations committees are required to sit jointly in open session. Guam—hearings are open to the public, but meetings may be closed.

(c) During session—one day notice for first 50 days, two hours thereafter.

(d) During session—two days notice for first 45 days, two hours thereafter.

(e) Committees meet on regular schedule during sessions. For rescheduled or special meetings 18 hours notice, unless legislature is adjourned or recessed for less than 18 hours.

(f) There is an informal agreement to give three days notice.

(g) Public hearings on bills or resolutions of "high public importance" must receive five calendar days notice. All other committee meetings must have 24 hours notice.

(h) Rules require posting of bills and resolutions to be considered at each meeting and provide deadlines for such posting depending upon the schedules for particular committees.

(i) Except in case of meeting to resolve conflicts or inconsistencies among two or more measures, in which case posting and notice to the public shall be given immediately upon call of the meeting, and notice of the meeting shall be announced on the floor if the Senate is in session.

(j) In case of actual emergency, a meeting may be held upon such notice as is appropriate to the circumstances.

(k) Committees meet on a fixed schedule during sessions. Senate: five days notice required during interim, three days otherwise. House: 72 hours notice required during interim.

(l) Committee meetings are required to be open for final vote on bill.

(m) Advance notice may be waived if the committee determines there is cause to conduct a meeting sooner. In that case, notice must be given at least 48 hours in advance. Items on the agenda may be considered by unanimous consent.

LEGISLATURES

Table 3.27
LEGISLATIVE APPROPRIATIONS PROCESS: BUDGET DOCUMENTS AND BILLS

State or other jurisdiction	Legal source of deadline		Budget document submission — Submission date relative to convening					Budget bill introduction		
	Constitutional	Statutory	Prior to session	Within one week	Within two weeks	Within one month	Over one month	Same time as budget document	Another time	Not until committee review of budget document
Alabama............	...	★	...	2nd day	...	...	...	★	...	...
Alaska.............	...	★	...	★	...	...	...	★	...	...
Arizona............	...	★	...	★	...	...	...	...	...	★
Arkansas	...	...	(a)	...	...	...	...	...	...	★
California..........	★	...	...	...	...	...	★	★	...	...
Colorado	...	★	★ (b)	...	...	...	...	...	...	★
Connecticut	...	★	...	...	...	★ (c)	...	★	...	...
Delaware	...	★	...	...	...	by Feb. 1	...	★ (d)	...	...
Florida	...	★	45 days	...	...	...	...	...	...	★ (d)
Georgia............	★	...	...	★	...	...	...	★	...	...
Hawaii	...	★	30 days	...	...	...	...	...	★	...
Idaho	...	★	...	★	...	...	...	...	...	★
Illinois.............	...	★	...	...	...	...	★	...	★	...
Indiana............	...	★	7 days (e)	...	...	...	...	★	...	...
Iowa	...	★	...	...	...	★ (a)	...	...	...	★ (d)
Kansas	...	★	...	...	★ (g)	...	...	...	★	...
Kentucky	...	...	...	...	...	...	(f)	★	...	...
Louisiana	...	★	...	1st day	...	★ (a)	...	...	(h)	...
Maine	...	★	...	★ (g)	...	...	...	★	...	...
Maryland	★	...	...	★ (g)	...	...	...	★ (i)	...	...
Massachusetts	★	...	...	...	...	★ (g)	...	★ (j)	...	...
Michigan	...	★	...	...	...	★	...	★	...	...
Minnesota	...	★	...	...	...	★ (a)	...	...	...	★
Mississippi	...	★	...	1st day	...	...	...	...	...	★
Missouri...........	★	...	...	...	...	★ (g)	...	★	...	...
Montana...........	...	★	...	1st day	...	...	...	...	★	...
Nebraska	...	★	...	...	...	★ (a,g)	...	★ (d)	...	...
Nevada	...	★	...	...	★	...	...	...	...	★
New Hampshire	...	★	...	...	...	...	★	★	...	...
New Jersey.........	...	★	...	...	...	★ (g)	...	★	...	...
New Mexico........	...	★	...	...	...	(k)	...	★	...	...
New York	★	...	...	...	★ (g)	...	...	★ (l)	...	...
North Carolina	...	...	...	(m)	...	...	...	★	...	...
North Dakota	...	★	(n)	...	...	...	...	...	★	★
Ohio	...	★	...	...	...	★ (g)	...	★	...	...
Oklahoma	...	★	...	★	...	...	...	★	...	...
Oregon	...	★	Dec. 1 (g)	...	...	...	...	...	★ (a)	...
Pennsylvania	...	★	...	...	...	...	★ (g,o)	...	...	★
Rhode Island	...	★	...	...	...	...	★	★	...	...
South Carolina	...	★	(a,b)	...	...	...	...	...	...	★
South Dakota	...	★	★	...	...	...	...	...	...	★
Tennessee..........	...	★	...	...	★ (a,g)	...	...	★	...	...
Texas..............	...	★	...	★	...	...	...	★	...	...
Utah	...	★	(p)	...	★ (c)	...	...	...	...	★
Vermont	...	★	...	...	...	★	...	...	...	★
Virginia............	...	★	...	1st day	...	...	...	★	...	...
Washington	...	★	Dec.20(c)	...	...	...	...	...	★	...
West Virginia	★	...	...	1st day(g)	...	...	...	★	...	...
Wisconsin..........	...	★	...	...	...	★ (q)	...	★	...	...
Wyoming	...	★	Dec. 1	...	...	...	...	...	...	★
American Samoa ...	...	...	(m)	...	...	...	...	...	★	...
Guam	...	★	...	...	...	★	...	★	...	...
Puerto Rico	★	...	...	...	...	★	...	...	...	★
U.S. Virgin Islands ...	...	★	...	...	...	★ (r)	...	★	...	...

LEGISLATURES

LEGISLATIVE APPROPRIATIONS PROCESS—Copntinued

KEY:
★ — Yes
... — No

(a) Specific time limitations: Arkansas—60 days; Connecticut—odd numbered years, no later than the first session day following the third session day in Feb.; Iowa—No later than Feb. 1; Louisiana—within 15 days; Minnesota—fourth Monday in January during biennial session; Nebraska—by Jan 15; New Hampshire—by Feb. 15; Oregon—Dec. 15; South Carolina—first Tuesday in January; South Dakota—first Tuesday after the first Monday in Dec.;Tennessee—on or before Feb. 1; Vermont—within three weeks.

(b) Copies of agency budgets to be presented to the legislature by November 1. Governor's budget usually is presented in January.

(c) Even numbered years.

(d) Executive budget bill is introduced and used as a working tool for committee. Delaware: after hearings on executive bill, a new bill is then introduced. The committee bill is considered by the legislature.

(e) Budget document submitted prior to session does not necessarily reflect budget message which is given sometime during the first three weeks of session.

(f) No set time.

(g) Later for first session of a new governor. Kansas—21 days; Maine—By Feb. 1; Maryland—by third Wed. in Jan.; Massachusetts—three weeks; Missouri—30 days; Nebraska—Feb 1; New Jersey—Feb. 15; New York—Feb. 1; Ohio—March 16; Oregon—Feb. 1; Pennsylvania—first full week in March; Tennessee—March 1; West Virginia—10 days.

(h) Subject to 15 day limit.

(i) Appropriations bills other than the budget bill (supplementary) may be introduced at any time. They must provide their own tax source and may not be enacted until the budget bill is enacted.

(j) General appropriations bills only.

(k) Statutes provide for submission by the 25th legislative day; however, the executive budget is usually presented by the first day of the session.

(l) Governor has 30 days to amend or supplement the budget; he may submit any amendments to any bills, or submit supplemental bills.

(m) By custom only. No statutory or constitutional provisions.

(n) For whole legislature. The Legislative Council only received budget on December 1.

(o) Submitted by governor as sson as possible after General Assembly organizes, but not later than the first full week in February.

(p) Must submit to fiscal analyst 30 days prior to session.

(q) Last Tuesday in January. A later submission date may be requested by the governor.

(r) Organic Act specifies at opening of each regular session; statute specifies on or before May 30.

LEGISLATURES

Table 3.28
FISCAL NOTES: CONTENT AND DISTRIBUTION

	Content						Distribution					
								Legislators				
										Appropriations committee		
State or other jurisdiction	Intent or purpose of bill	Cost involved	Projected future cost	Proposed source of revenue	Fiscal impact on local government	Other	All	Available on request	Bill sponsor	Members	Chairman only	Fiscal staff	Executive budget staff
Alabama	...	★	...	★	★		★(a)	...	...	...	...	...	...
Alaska	...	★	★	★(b)	...		★(c)	...	...	...	...	...	...
Arizona	...	★	★	★	★		★	...	...	...	...	★	★
Arkansas	...	★	★	...	★		...	...	...	...	...	★	...
California	★	★	★	★	★		★	...	...	...	...	★	★
Colorado	★	★	★	★	★		★	...	...	...	...	★	...
Connecticut	...	★	★	...	★		...	...	...	...	...	★	...
Delaware	...	★	★	...	...	★(d)	...	★	...	★	...	★	★
Florida	...	★	★	★	★	★(e)	★	...	...	...	...	★	★
Georgia	...	★	★	★	★		...	★	...	...	...	...	...
Hawaii													
Idaho	★	★	★	★(f)	★		★	...	...	...	...	...	...
Illinois	...	★	★	★	★	(g)	...	★(h)	★(h)	...	...	★	★
Indiana	★	★	★	★	★		★	...	...	...	...	...	...
Iowa	...	★	★	★	★		★	...	...	...	...	...	...
Kansas	★	★	★	★	★		...	★	...	...	★(i)	★	★
Kentucky	★	★	★	★	...		...	★	★	★	...	★	...
Louisiana	...	★	★	...	★		...	★	★	...	...	★(j)	...
Maine	...	★	★	...	...		★	...	...	...	...	★	...
Maryland	★	★	★	★	★		...	★	★	★(i)	...	★	★
Massachusetts	...	★(k)	...	...	...		★	★	...	...	...	★	...
Michigan	★	★	★	★	★	★(l)	★(m)	★	...	...	...	★	...
Minnesota	★	★	★	★	...		...	★	★	★	...	...	...
Mississippi	★	★	★	...	★		...	★	...	...	★	...	...
Missouri	...	★	★	★	★		★	...	...	...	...	...	...
Montana	...	★	★	★	★	★(e)	★	...	...	...	...	★	★
Nebraska	...	★	★	★	★		★	...	...	...	...	★	★
Nevada	★	★	★	★	★		★	...	...	...	...	...	...
New Hampshire	★	★	★	★	★		★	...	...	...	...	★	★
New Jersey	★	★	★	...	★	★	★(n)	...	...	...	...	★	★
New Mexico	★	★	★	...	(f)	★(o)	...	(p)	...	...	★(p)	...	...
New York	★	★(q)	...	...	★		...	★	★	★	...	★	...
North Carolina	...	★	★	...	★	★(r)	...	★	...	...	...	★	...
North Dakota	★	★	★(s)	★	★		...	★	★	★	...	★	...
Ohio	★	★	★	★	★		★(t)	★	★	★	...	★	...
Oklahoma	...	...	...	...	...		...	...	...	...	...	...	...
Oregon	...	★	★	★	★		★	...	...	...	...	...	...
Pennsylvania	...	★	★	★	★	★(g)	★	...	...	...	...	★	★
Rhode Island	...	★	★	...	★	★(u)	...	★	★	...	★	★	★
South Carolina	...	★	★	...	...		...	...	...	...	...	...	...
South Dakota	...	★	★	★	★		...	★	...	...	...	★	★
Tennessee	★	★	★	★	★	★(v)	★	★	★	★(i)	...	...	★
Texas	...	★	★	★	★		...	★	★	★(i)	...	...	...
Utah	...	★	★	★	★		★	...	...	...	★	...	...
Vermont	★	★	★	★	...		...	★	...	...	...	...	...
Virginia	★	★	★	★(w)	...	★	...	★	★	★	...	...	...
Washington	★	★	★	★	★		...	★	★	★	...	★	★
West Virginia	★	★	★	★	★(x)		★	...	...	...	...	...	...
Wisconsin	...	★	★	★	★		★	...	...	...	...	...	...
Wyoming	...	★	★	★	★		★	...	...	...	...	...	...
American Samoa													
Guam	★	★	★	★	★		★	...	...	...	...	★	★
Puerto Rico	...	★	...	...	★		★	...	...	...	...	...	...
U.S. Virgin Islands	★	★	...	★	...		★	...	...	...	...	...	...

LEGISLATURES

FISCAL NOTES: CONTENT AND DISTRIBUTION—Continued

Key:
★ — Yes
... — No

(a) Fiscal notes are included in bills for final passage calendar.
(b) Contained in the bill, not in the fiscal note.
(c) Fiscal notes are attached to the bill before it is reported to the Rules Committee. Governor's bills must have fiscal note before introduction.
(d) Relevant data and prior fiscal year cost information.
(e) Mechanical defects in bill and effective date.
(f) Occasionally.
(g) Bill proposing changes in retirement system of state or local government must have an actuarial note.
(h) A summary of the fiscal note is attached to the summary of the relevant bill in the Legislative Synopsis and Digest. Fiscal notes are prepared for the sponsor of the bill and are attached to the bill on file in either the office of the clerk of the House or the secretary of the Senate.
(i) Or to committee to which referred.
(j) Prepared by Legislative Fiscal Office; copies sent to House and Senate staff offices respectively.
(k) Fiscal notes are prepared only if cost exceeds $100,000 or matter has not been acted upon by the Joint Committee on Ways and Means.
(l) Other revelant data.

(m) Analyses prepared by Senate Fiscal Agency, distributed to Senate members only; analyses prepared by House Fiscal Agency, distributed to House members only.
(n) Sponsor may disapprove fiscal note; if disapproved, fiscal note is not printed or distributed.
(o) Impact of revenue bills reviewed by Legislative Council Service and executive agencies.
(p) Legislative Finance Committee staff prepared fiscal notes for Appropriations Committee chairman; other fiscal impact statements prepared by Legislative Council Service and executive agencies are available to anyone upon request.
(q) Rules of the Assembly require sponsors' memoranda to include estimate of cost to state and/or local government. Fiscal note required by law to be included on all pension bills.
(r) Fiscal note required in Senate. In House, staff prepares a summary.
(s) A two-year projection.
(t) If a bill comes up for floor consideration.
(u) Technical or mechanical defects may be noted.
(v) Effects of revenue bills.
(w) The Department of Taxation prepares revenue impact notes including the intent and revenue impact.
(x) House of Delegates only.

LEGISLATURES

Table 3.29
EXTRAORDINARY VOTES REQUIRED TO TAKE CERTAIN ACTIONS OR PASS SPECIFIC TYPES OF LEGISLATION — SENATE

State or other jurisdiction	Tax bills	Constitutional amendments	State Borrowing	Removal of judge	Expulsion of member	Emergency enactment of legislation	Overriding gubernatorial veto	Suspend constitutional requirements	Other (c)
Alabama	...	★	...	...	...	...	...	...	...
Alaska	...	★	...	...	★	...	★	...	(c)
Arizona	...	...	...	...	...	★	★	...	...
Arkansas	★ (a)	...	...	...	...	★	...	...	...
California	★	★	...	...	★	★	★	★	...
Colorado	...	★	...	★	...	...	★	...	...
Connecticut	...	★	...	★	★	...	★	...	...
Delaware	★	★	★	...	★	...	★	...	(d)
Florida	...	★	...	★ (b)	★	...	★	...	(e)
Georgia	...	★	...	★	...	...	...	...	...
Hawaii	...	★	...	...	...	...	★	...	(f)
Idaho	...	★	...	...	...	...	★	★	...
Illinois	...	★	★	...	★	★	★	...	...
Indiana	...	...	...	...	...	...	★	★	...
Iowa	...	★	...	...	★	...	★	...	(g)
Kansas	...	★	...	...	★	★	★	...	...
Kentucky	...	★	...	...	★	...	...	...	...
Louisiana	★	★	★	★	★	...	★	...	(h)
Maine	...	★	...	...	★	★	★	...	(i)
Maryland	...	...	...	★	★	...	...	...	(j)
Massachusetts	...	...	★	...	★	★	★	...	...
Michigan	...	★	★	★	★	...	★	...	(k)
Minnesota	...	...	★	...	...	★	★	★	...
Mississippi	...	★	...	...	★	★	★	★	...
Missouri	...	...	...	...	...	★	★	...	...
Montana	...	★	...	...	★	...	...	★	...
Nebraska	...	...	...	...	★	★	...	...	(l)
Nevada	...	...	...	★	★	★	★	★	(m)
New Hampshire	...	...	...	...	...	...	★	...	...
New Jersey	...	★	...	...	★	★	★	...	...
New Mexico	...	...	...	...	★	★	★	...	...
New York	...	★	...	...	...	...	★	...	...
North Carolina	...	★	...	★	...	...	...	...	(n)
North Dakota	...	...	...	...	...	★	★	...	(o)
Ohio	...	...	...	...	★	★	★	★	(p)
Oklahoma	...	...	...	...	...	★	★	★	(q)
Oregon	...	...	...	...	★	...	★	...	(r)
Pennsylvania	...	...	...	★	★	...	...	...	(s)
Rhode Island	...	...	...	...	...	...	★	...	...
South Carolina	...	★	...	...	★	...	★	...	(t)
South Dakota	★	★	★	★	★	★	★	★	...
Tennessee	...	★	...	...	...	...	...	...	...
Texas	...	★	...	...	★	★	★	★	(u)
Utah	...	★	...	...	...	★	★	...	(v)
Vermont	...	...	...	...	...	...	...	...	...
Virginia	...	...	...	...	...	...	...	...	...
Washington	...	★	...	...	...	...	...	...	...
West Virginia	...	★	...	...	★	...	★	★	...
Wisconsin	...	...	...	★	★	...	★	...	(w)
Wyoming	...	★	...	...	★	...	★	...	(x)
Puerto Rico	...	★	...	...	★	...	★	...	(y)

LEGISLATURES

EXTRAORDINARY VOTES REQUIRED — SENATE—Continued

Source: National Conference of State Legislatures.
Key:
. . . — No provision
(a) Most taxes, sales tax only takes 51 percent.
(b) Impeachment of judge.
(c) Change daily order of business; take up reconsideration of vote on the same day as original measure; amend uniform rules; title change other body's bill; court rule change; adopt effective date other than 90 days; advance bill from 2nd to 3rd reading the same day.
(d) Spend "rainy day fund"; exceed 98 percent spending limit.
(e) Issuance of bonds over $50 million; increase or decrease number of judgeships recommended by Supreme Court; extension of session; authorize interest above 5 percent on certain bonds.
(f) Exceed debt limit; authorize issuance of special purpose revenue bonds.
(g) Confirm gubernatorial appointees; ex post facto compensation bills; convene special sessions; impeachment.
(h) Create judgeship; change a parish; create a parish.
(i) Overturn committee recommendation of confirmation; bond authorization acts; recalling bills from legislative files; items calling for U.S. constitutional conventions; introduction in the 2nd regular session of measures rejected in the 1st regular session.
(j) To force a bill or joint resolution from the Committee on Rules; to repeal or amend any rules; to limit debate; to introduce a Senate resolution or Senate joint resolution during the last 35 calendar days of a regular session; to give a bill two readings on the same day; to introduce a bill during the last 35 days of a regular session; to adjourn the Senate to any other place than that in which it may be sitting.
(k) Appropriations for private or local purposes; immediate effect.
(l) Constitutional amendment proposed on the primary election ballot.
(m) Impeachment proceedings of Governor, Lt. Governor, state or judicial officers.
(n) Determine mental incapacity of Governor by joint resolution; convention of people (concurrence to proposition for voter approval); ruling of chair appealed; remove from table (unfavorable report); recall from committee; 3rd reading on same day as 2nd (non roll-call measure); remove from table (defeated measure embodied in another measure); remove from table (postponed indefinitely); remove from table (placed by motion); send to House same day as passed by Senate; convene extra session (both bodies of General Assembly); incorporate city/town (limits: 1 mile--5,000; 3 miles--10,000; 4 miles--25,000; 5 miles--50,000); acceptance and use of properties--State Nature & Historic Preserve.
(o) Amend or repeal initiated or referred measure within seven years after enactment or approval.
(p) To close any proceeding; to allow outside group to use chamber.
(q) To call a special session for an amendment to the constitution.
(r) Revision of constitution.
(s) Some confirmations of Governor's nominations.
(t) Enact property tax exemption.
(u) Immediate effect on any bill; impeachment of any officer; confirm nominees of Governor.
(v) Change rules governing the limitation of debate; change rules governing the lifting of a tabled bill from committee; change rules governing consideration of bills during the last three days of a session; change rules governing voting.
(w) Trial of impeachment; rescind motion to message Assembly.
(x) To introduce nonbudget bills in the budget session.
(y) Removal of judge of the Supreme Court, the Comptroller and the Ombudsman.

LEGISLATURES

Table 3.30
EXTRAORDINARY VOTES REQUIRED TO TAKE CERTAIN ACTIONS OR PASS SPECIFIC TYPES OF LEGISLATION — HOUSE

State or other jurisdiction	Tax bills	Constitutional amendments	State Borrowing	Removal of judge	Expulsion of member	Emergency enactment of legislation	Overriding gubernatorial veto	Suspend constitutional requirements	Other (c)
Alabama	...	★	...	...	...	...	...	...	(a)
Alaska	...	★	...	...	★	★	...	...	(b)
Arizona	...	...	...	...	★	★	★	...	...
Arkansas	★	...	...	...	...	★	...	★	...
California	★ (c)	★	★	★	★	★	★	★	...
Colorado	...	★	...	...	...	...	★	...	(d)
Connecticut	...	...	...	★	★	...	★	...	...
Delaware	★	★	★	...	★	...	★	...	(e)
Florida	...	★	...	★	★	★	★	★	(f)
Georgia	...	★	...	...	...	...	★	...	(g)
Hawaii	...	★	...	...	★	...	★	...	(h)
Idaho	...	★	...	...	...	...	★	★	...
Illinois	...	★	★ (i)	...	★	...	★	...	(j)
Indiana	...	...	...	...	★	...	...	★	(k)
Iowa	...	★	...	...	...	...	★	...	(l)
Kansas	...	★	...	...	★	★	★	...	...
Kentucky	...	★	...	...	...	...	...	...	...
Louisiana	★	★	★	...	...	...	★	...	...
Maine	...	★	★	...	...	★	★	...	...
Maryland	...	...	...	★	...	...	...	...	(m)
Massachusetts	...	...	★	...	...	★	★	...	(n)
Michigan	...	★	★	★	★ (o)	...	...	...	...
Minnesota	...	...	★	...	★	★	★	★	...
Mississippi	...	★	...	...	★	...	★	...	(p)
Missouri	...	...	...	...	★	★	★	...	...
Montana	...	★	...	...	...	...	★	...	(q)
Nebraska	...	...	...	Unicameral	...	...	...	...	...
Nevada	...	...	...	★	★	★	★	★	...
New Hampshire	...	★	...	...	...	★	★	...	...
New Jersey	...	...	...	...	...	★	...	...	...
New Mexico	...	★	...	★	★	★	★	...	...
New York	...	...	...	...	...	...	★	...	(r)
North Carolina	★	★	★	...	...	...	...	★	(s)
North Dakota	...	...	...	...	...	★	★	...	(t)
Ohio	...	...	...	...	...	★	...	...	...
Oklahoma	...	...	...	...	...	★	★	★	...
Oregon	...	...	...	...	★	...	★	★	...
Pennsylvania	...	...	...	...	...	...	★	...	(u)
Rhode Island	...	...	...	...	...	...	...	...	...
South Carolina	...	★	...	...	...	...	...	...	...
South Dakota	★	...	...	...	...	★	★	...	(v)
Tennessee	...	★	...	...	...	...	...	...	...
Texas	...	★	...	★	...	★	★	★	...
Utah	...	★	...	...	...	★	★	...	...
Vermont	...	★	...	...	...	...	★	...	...
Virginia	...	...	★ (w)	...	...	★	★	★	(x)
Washington	...	★	★	...	...	...	★	...	...
West Virginia	...	★	...	...	★	...	★ (y)	...	...
Wisconsin	...	...	...	★	★	...	★	...	...
Wyoming	...	★	...	...	...	...	★	...	(z)
American Samoa	...	...	...	...	★	...	★	...	(aa)
Puerto Rico	...	...	...	...	...	...	...	...	...

EXTRAORDINARY VOTES REQUIRED — HOUSE—Continued

Source: National Conference of State Legislatures.

(a) Bills appropriating state funds to private schools and nonstate agencies.
(b) Change daily order of business; take up reconsideration of a vote on the same day as original passage; amend uniform rules; adopt an effective date other than 90 days; court rule change; advance bill from 2nd to 3rd reading the same day.
(c) If increasing taxes.
(d) Change in number of district judges.
(e) To appropriate public money to any county, municipality or corporation; to issue or loan bonds of the state to any county, municipality or corporation; to pledge the credit of the state by guaranteeing or endorsing the bonds or other undertakings of any county, municipality or corporation; to lay out, open, alter or maintain roads and highways which form continuous roads or highways through at least a portion of the three counties; to create courts other than constitutional courts; to grant jurisdiction over additional misdemeanors to inferior courts; to initiate impeachment proceedings; to enact or amend the general corporation law; to enact any special act of incorporation; to appropriate for any fiscal year funds in excess of 98% of the estimated state general fund revenue for that fiscal year; to impose or levy any new license fees.
(f) Impeach an officer (governor, lt. governor, cabinet, supreme court).
(g) Local acts affecting revenue or expenditures.
(h) Convene a special session; extension of session.
(i) To incur state debt without a referendum.
(j) Close session or committee meeting to the public; deny or limit home rule power or limit home rule debt.
(k) Amend on 3rd reading.
(l) Private act.
(m) Extension of session; introduce a bill during last 35 days; give a bill two readings on the same day; force a bill from the Rules Committee.
(n) Legislation recommended by the governor which applies to a single city or town.
(o) If breach of public trust, only takes a majority of those elected and serving.
(p) Restore suffrage; granting gratuity or donation.
(q) Remove a call of the House.
(r) Adoption of emergency funds affecting certain local governments; bills appropriating state funds to particular local governments.
(s) Rules of chair appealed; consideration of defeated bill; two readings on same day; recall from committee.
(t) Amend or repeal initiated or referred measure within seven years after enactment or approval.
(u) Non-preferred appropriation bills.
(v) Special appropriation of money expenditure.
(w) For certain types of bonds.
(x) Property tax exemption.
(y) Appropriation bills.
(z) To introduce nonbudget bills in the budget session.
(aa) Lands and titles.

LEGISLATURES

Table 3.31
LEGISLATIVE REVIEW OF ADMINISTRATIVE REGULATIONS: STRUCTURES AND PROCEDURES

State	Type of reviewing committee	All rules reviewed	Time limits for submission of rules for review
Alabama	Mbrs. Legislative Council	P	60 days.
Alaska	Joint bipartisan	P,E	...
Arizona	(a)		
Arkansas	Joint bipartisan	P,E	...
California	(a)		
Colorado	Joint bipartisan	E	...
Connecticut	Joint bipartisan	P	65 days.
Delaware	(a)		
Florida	Joint bipartisan	P,E	...
Georgia	Standing committee	P	30 days.
Hawaii	(a)		
Idaho	Germane joint subcommittees	P	...
Illinois	Joint bipartisan	P,E	90 days
Indiana	Joint bipartisan	E	Legislature has authority to intervene only after rules have been adopted.
Iowa	Joint bipartisan	P,E	Not stated in Iowa Code
Kansas	Joint bipartisan	E	45 days following publication in the *Kansas Register*.
Kentucky	Joint bipartisan subcommittee	P	Not stated in statute.
Louisiana	Standing committee	P	All proposed rules and fees are submitted to designated standing committees of the legislature. If unacceptable, the committee sends a written report to the governor. The Governor has ten days to disapprove the committee report. If both senate and house committees fail to find the rule unacceptable, or if the governor disapproves the action of a committee within 10 days, the agency may adopt the rule change.
Maine	Jt. standing cmtes & Executive Dir of the Legislative Council	E	Any group of 100 or more registered voters, or any person directly, substantially, and adversely affected by a rule may file an application for review with the executive director of the legislative council. One-third or more of the appropriate standing committee must request a review within 15 days of receipt of the application.
Maryland	Joint bipartisan	P,E	The committee has no power to suspend or veto proposed regulations.
Massachusetts	Jt. standing cmte. & Commisioner of Administration and Finance	P	If the rule is not approved by the general court and the governor within 90 days of filing, it is deemed to have been disapproved.
Michigan	Joint bipartisan	P	Joint committee on Administrative Rules has 2 months (3 months by vote of committee) to approve/disapprove proposed rule. If committee disapproves rule or certifies an impasse, the rule cannot be promulgated by the agency unless legislature overrules The JCAR action by passing a concurrent resolution within 60 days.
Minnesota	Joint Legislative Commission	E	The commission may not take action until the standing committees of both houses report to the commission or after 60 days have lapsed.
Mississippi	(a)		
Missouri	Joint bipartisan	P,E	...
Montana	Joint bipartisan	P,E	...
Nebraska	(a)		
Nevada	Joint bipartisan	P	If an agency refuses to revise a regulation, the commission may postpone the filing of the regulation until the 30th day of the next regular session. Before the 30th day of the next regular session the legislature may, by concurrent resolution, declare that the regulation may not become effective.
New Hampshire	Joint bipartisan	P	Within 45 days of the filing the committee may approve or object.
New Jersey	(a)		
New Mexico	(a)		
New York	Joint bipartisan commission	P,E	The commission is advisory only, it cannot veto, suspend, amend or otherwise prevent a rule from becoming effective.
North Carolina	Public membership appointed by legislature	P	Must be reviewed within 30 days.
North Dakota	Interim committee with possible public membership	P,E	Within 14 days the agency must respond in writing to the committee's objection. Objections are published in the supplement to the *North Dakota Code*.
Ohio	Joint bipartisan	P,E	60 days before adoption.
Oklahoma	Standing cmte. or cmte. appointed by leadership of both houses	E	Failure of legislature to disapprove a rule within 30 L days results in automatic approval. Upon approval by legislature and the governor or a direct approval by joint resolution of the legislture, a rule is considered finally adopted and is effective 10 days after being published in the *Oklahoma Register*.
Oregon	Joint bipartisan	P,E	...
Pennsylvania	Standing committee	P	Standing committee has 20 days to review the final form regulation. If no action is taken, it is approved. If the committee disapproves a regulation, the committee has 14 days to introduce a concurrent resolution and within 10L days or 30C days both chambers must vote to disapprove the regulation.
Rhode Island	(a)		
South Carolina	Standing committee	P	If no action is taken within 1st 60C days, the regulations are placed on the agenda of the full committee. If no action is taken by either house or senate to introduce a resolution to disapprove the regulation or not approved by legislature within 120 days after submission to the general assembly, the regulations are effective upon publication in the *Senate Review*.

LEGISLATURES

LEGISLATIVE REVIEW OF ADMINISTRATIVE REGULATIONS—Continued

State	Type of reviewing committee	All rules reviewed	Time limits for submission of rules for review
South Dakota	Joint bipartisan	P	A proposed or provisional rule can be suspended until July 1 following the next legislative session, if five of the committee's six members agree.
Tennessee	Joint standing committee	P	. . .
Texas	Appropriate standing committees	P	. . .
Utah	Joint bipartisan	P	. . .
Vermont	Joint bipartisan	P,E	All final proposed rules must be submitted to the committee, which has 30 days to review them. Within 14 days of receiving an objection the agency must respond in writing. If the committee still objects it may file its objection with the secretary of state.
Virginia	Standing committee	P,E	Legislative review is optional. Within 21 days after the receipt of an objection, the agency shall file a response with the registrar, the objecting legislative committee and the governor. After an objection is filed, the regulation unless withdrwn by the agency shall become effective on a date specified by the agency which shall be after the 21-day extension period.
Washington	Joint bipartisan	P,E	If the committee determines that a proposed rule does not comply with legislative intent, a written notice is sent to the agency. The notice must be sent seven days before any hearing. Within 30 days after notification, the agency must schedule a public hearing on the rule. Within seven days after a hearing the agency notifies the committee of its action. If the agency fails to hold the hearing or does not amend, modify, withdraw or repeal the rule to conform to legislative intent, the committee may, within 30 days, file a notice of objection and a statement of its reasons with the Code Reviser.
West Virginia	Joint bipartisan	P	No later than 40 days before the sixtieth day of each regular session, the committee submits to the legislature all proposed rules. If legislature fails during regular session to enact a statute authorizing the agency to promulgate a legislative rule, the agency may not issue the rule or take action unless authorized to do so.
Wisconsin	Joint bipartisan	P	The standing committee has 30 days to conduct their review. Within 30 days of suspending a rule, JCRAR must introduce a bill and secure legislative enactment to repeal the suspended rule. If legislature does not pass the bill, the rule stands and JCRAR may not suspend it again.
Wyoming	Joint bipartisan	P,E	Legislative action must take place before the end of the next succeeding legislative session in order to nullify a rule.

Source: National Conference of State Legislatures and state statutes.

(a) No formal mechanism for legislative review of administrative rules.

Key:
P — Proposed rules
E — Existing rules
. . . — Not available

Table 3.32
LEGISLATIVE REVIEW OF ADMINISTRATIVE REGULATIONS: POWERS

State	Reviewing committee's powers:				Legislative powers:		
	Review of proposed rules	Review of existing rules	No objection constitutes approval of proposed rule	Committee may suspend rule	Legislature must sustain committee action	Time limit for legislative action	Legislature can amend or modify rule
Alabama	★	...	★	★	★	End of regular session	...
Alaska	★	★	...	★	★	30 days after convening of regular session	...
Arizona	----------	----------	----------	(a)	----------	----------	----------
Arkansas	★	★	...	...	...		...
California	----------	----------	----------	(a)	----------	----------	----------
Colorado	...	★	★	...	★	Next regular session	★ (c)
Connecticut	★	...	★	★	(b)	(b)	
Delaware	----------	----------	----------	(a)	----------	----------	----------
Florida	★	★	...	...	...		...
Georgia	★	...	★	...	...	30 days after convening of regular session	...
Hawaii	(d)	★	N.A.	...	...		...
Idaho	★	...	★	...	★	End of regular session	...
Illinois	★	★	...	★	★	150 days	★
Indiana	(e)	★	...	...	...		...
Iowa	★	★	★	★	★	End of regular session	...
Kansas	...	★	★	...	★	End of regular session	...
Kentucky	★	...	★	...	(f)		...
Louisiana	★	...	★	★ (g)	...		★
Maine	...	★	N.A.	...	...		...
Maryland	★	★	★	★ (h)	...		...
Massachusetts	★ (i)	...	★ (j)	...	★	Practices vary	...
Michigan	★	...	(k)	(l)	(m)	(n)	...
Minnesota	(o)	★	...	★	(p)	End of next regular session	...
Mississippi	----------	----------	----------	(a)	----------	----------	----------
Missouri	★	★	★	★	...		...
Montana	★	★	...	...	...	None	★
Nebraska	...	★	...	...	★	Next regular session	...
Nevada	★	...	★	(q)	★	30 session days	...
New Hampshire	★	...	★	(r)	...		...
New Jersey	----------	----------	----------	(a)	----------	----------	----------
New Mexico	----------	----------	----------	(a)	----------	----------	----------
New York	★	★	★	...	...		...
North Carolina	----------	----------	----------	(a,s,t)	----------	----------	----------
North Dakota	★	★	★	...	...		...
Ohio	★	★	...	★	★	60 days	...
Oklahoma	...	★	★	(u)	...	30 legislative days	...
Oregon	★	★	N.A.	...	...		...
Pennsylvania	★	★ (v)	★	...	★	20 days for proposed regulations from date published in *Pennsylvania Bulletin*	...
Rhode Island	----------	----------	----------	(a,x)	----------	----------	----------
South Carolina	★	...	★	...	★	Next regular session	...
South Dakota	★	...	★	★	★	End of next regular session	★
Tennessee	★	...	N.A.	★	...		...
Texas	----------	----------	----------	(u)	----------	----------	----------
Utah	★	...	N.A.	...	...		...
Vermont	★	★	★	...	...		...
Virginia (w)	★	★	N.A.	...	...	End of regular session	...
Washington	★	★	N.A.	(y)	...		...
West Virginia	★	...	...	...	★	End of session	★
Wisconsin	★	★	★	★	★	End of next regular session	★ (z)
Wyoming	★	★	N.A.	...	★	End of next regular session	...

LEGISLATURES

LEGISLATIVE REVIEW OF ADMINISTRATIVE REGULATIONS—Continued

Source: National Conference of State Legislatures and State Statutes.
Note: See note Table 3.23.
Key:
★ — Yes
... — No
N.A. — Not available

(a) No formal mechanism for legislative review of administrative rules.
(b) It is not mandatory for legislature to approve or disapprove committee action. However, disapproval of a rule implementing a federally subsidized program must be sustained by legislature before end of the regular session or committee's action is reversed.
(c) Committee may disapprove a part of a rule.
(d) Reviews rules when adopted, amended, or repealed.
(e) Committee shall receive and may review complaints regarding an agency rule or practice. Committee may also review an agency rule or practice on its own motion, and may recommend that a rule be modified, repealed, or adopted.
(f) Legislation passed in 1986 states that all regulations shall expire 90 days after the adjournment of the next General Assembly. Those regulations that an administrative body wishes to remain in effect must be enacted into the statutes.
(g) If committee determines that rule is unacceptable, it submits a report to the governor. The governor has ten days to accept or reject the report.
(h) May suspend for 30 days.
(i) Provided in statute for certain rules but not others.
(j) If rule is not approved within 90 days by general court and Governor; it is considered disapproved.
(k) Committee must approve rules before they take effect.
(l) Committee may suspend rules during interim only, if granted authorization to do so by legislature.
(m) Legislature may overrule committee disapproval of rules by passing a Joint Resolution adopting the rules.
(n) Legislature has 60 days to pass a Joint Resolution approving rules which the commitee has disapproved.
(o) Some rules may be submitted for "review and comment."
(p) Yes, if the commission action is to suspend a rule; otherwise its recommendations are self-executing.
(q) Constitutional amendment pending 3-88 authorizing legislation review of regulations.
(r) Committee may object to rule. Rule may be adopted over committee objection, but committee can shift burden of proof to agency.
(s) Committee abolished.
(t) The Rules Commission is an executive branch agency, however the members are appointed by the General Assembly, and reports on actions are made to the General Assembly when there is an objection to a rule.
(u) No formal committee; committees may be established for advisory purposes only.
(v) Then recommendation goes to existing agency.
(w) Legislative review of rules is optional.
(x) Auditor is empowered by legislature to review rules.
(y) By a two-third's vote, the committee may request the governor to approve suspension of a rule upon which the committee has made an adverse finding. If suspended, the rule must be stayed until 90 days following the next legislative session.
(z) For a proposed rule, the Legislature can amend or modify with the agreement of the promulgating agency. However, it cannot do so for an existing rule.

Table 3.33
SUMMARY OF SUNSET LEGISLATION

State	Scope	Preliminary evaluation conducted by	Other legislative review	Other oversight mechanisms in bill	Phase-out period	Life of each agency (in years)	Other provisions
Alabama	C	Select Jt. Cmte.	Dept. of Examiners of Public Accounts	Zero-base budgeting	180/d	4	1-hour time limit on floor debate on each bill.
Alaska	R	Standing cmtes.	...	Perf. audit	1/y	Varies (usually 4)	Specific programs authorized for termination by Legis. Budget & Audit Cmte.
Arizona	C	Off. of the Auditor General	Committees of reference appointed at beginning of legislative term	Perf. audit	(a)	10	1984 legislation allows Jt. Legis. Oversight Cmte. to establish priorities for and reschedule sunset audits. Cmte. may also request special performance audits not required by sunset schedule.
Arkansas	(b)	...	...	...	...	...	...
California	(c)	...	...	...	...	...	...
Colorado	C	Dept. of Regulatory Agencies reports to Joint Legis. Sunrise & Sunset Cmte. by July 1, preceding year of termination	Standing cmtes.	Perf. audit	1/y	10	There also is legislation requiring a study of 20 principal depts. of state government on a schedule concluding in 1994.
Connecticut	(d)	...	...	...	...	...	...
Delaware	C	Agencies under review submit reports to Del. Sunset Comm. based on criteria for review and set forth in statute. Comm. staff conducts separate review	...	Perf. audit	Dec. 31 of next succeeding calendar year	4	Yearly Sunset Review schedules must include at least 9 agencies. If the number automatically scheduled for review or added by the General Assembly is less than a full schedule, additional agencies shall be added in order of their appearance in the Del. Code to complete the review schedule.
Florida	R	Appropriate substantive cmte. shall begin review 15 months prior to repeal date	...	...	1/y	10	Provides for periodic review of limitations on the initial entry into a profession, occupation, business industry, or other endeavor.
Georgia	R	Dept. of Audits	Standing Cmtes.	Perf. audit	1/y	1-6	A performance audit of each regulatory agency must be conducted at least once every 6 years.
Hawaii	R	Legis. Auditor	Consumer Protection Cmte. of each house	...	None	6	Proposed new regulatory measures must be referred to the Auditor for sunrise analysis.
Idaho				No program			
Illinois	(e)	...	Off. of Auditor General; standing cmtes. of each house	...	...	...	...

Key:
C — Comprehensive
R — Regulatory
S — Selective
D — Discretionary
d — day
m — month
y — year

LEGISLATURES

SUNSET LEGISLATION—Continued

State	Scope	Preliminary evaluation conducted by	Other legislative review	Other oversight mechanisms in bill	Phase-out period	Life of each agency (in years)	Other provisions
Indiana	C	Off. of Fiscal and Management Analysis	Interim and Standing Legislative Cmtes.	...	None (f)	...	Each newly-established agency subject to termination with certain life span. Agencies established by exec. order, terminate when a Governor leaves office. Agencies established by concurrent resolution by General Assembly terminate after adjournment of the 2nd session.
Iowa	(c)	...	...	...	...	...	...
Kansas	R (g)	Standing cmtes. of each house	Legis. Post Audit, if directed by legislative cmte., or Legis. Post Audit Cmte.	Perf. audit	1/y	Subject to legislative discretion	Act terminates in July 1992 unless reenacted.
Kentucky				No program			
Louisiana	C	Standing cmtes. of the two houses which have usual jurisdiction over the affairs of the entity. Process begins 2 years prior to the termination date	Bill authorizing recreation referred to cmte. performing initial review	Zero budget review (h)	1/y	9	Standing cmtes. may conduct a more extensive evaluation of selected statutory entities under their jurisdiction or of particular programs of such entities.
Maine	C	Off. of Fiscal & Prog. Review	...	Perf. eval.	1/y	10	Performance reviews also scheduled for executive departments (no terminations).
Maryland	R	Dept. of Fiscal Services	Standing cmtes.	...	1/y	10	Sunset cycle was completed in 1983, resumed in 1987.
Massachusetts				No program			
Michigan	(c)	...	...	...	...	...	...
Minnesota	(c)	...	...	...	...	...	...
Mississippi	(i)	...	...	...	...	...	...
Missouri				No program			
Montana	(j)	...	...	...	...	...	...
Nebraska	(k)	...	...	...	...	...	...
Nevada	(l)	...	...	...	...	...	...
New Hampshire	(m)	...	...	...	...	...	...
New Jersey	(c)	...	...	...	...	...	...
New Mexico	R	Legis. Finance Cmte.	...	...	(a)	6	Legis. Finance Cmte. is responsible for introducing legislation to continue any agency reviewed.

Key:
C — Comprehensive
R — Regulatory
S — Selective
D — Discretionary
d — day
m — month
y — year

SUNSET LEGISLATION—Continued

LEGISLATURES

State	Scope	Preliminary evaluation conducted by	Other legislative review	Other oversight mechanisms in bill	Phase-out period	Life of each agency (in years)	Other provisions
New York				——No program——			
North Carolina	(n)	...	...	...	...	...	...
North Dakota				——No program——			
Ohio	(c)	...	...	...	...	...	...
Oklahoma	R	Jt. Cmte. on Sunset Review	Standing cmtes.	...	1/y	6	Rules & regulations of terminated agencies continue in effect unless terminated by law; includes agencies established by exec. order.
Oregon	R	Interim cmte.	Standing cmtes.	...	None	8	...
Pennsylvania	S	Legis. Budget and Finance Cmte.	Standing cmtes.	Perf. eval.	6/m	10	...
Rhode Island	(j)	...	Reorganization Comm.; standing cmtes.	Perf. audit	1/y	6	...
South Carolina	R	Legis. Audit Council					
South Dakota	(o)	...	...	...	...	...	...
Tennessee	C	Special evaluation cmte. in each house	State Auditor	Perf. audit	1/y	8	Establishment of new agencies subject to review by Govt. Operations cmtes. of each house.
Texas	C	Sunset Advisory Comm.	...	Perf. eval.	1/y	12	Initial review conducted by agencies themselves.
Utah	R	Interim study cmte.	Off. of Legis. Research & General Counsel	Interim cmte's discretion	1/y	Varies (usually not more than 10)	Legis. Audit Cmte. may at its discretion coordinate the audit of state agencies with the interim cmte's sunset review.
Vermont	R	Legis. Council staff	Standing cmtes.	...	None	...	...
Virginia	(p)	...	...	...	...	...	...
Washington	C	Legis. Budget Cmte.	Standing cmtes.	Prog. review	1/y	(q)	Select jt. cmte. prepares termination legislation.
West Virginia	S	Jt. Cmte. on Govt. Operations	Legis. Post Audit Div.	Perf. audit	1/y	6	Jt. Cmte. on Govt. Operations composed of 5 House members, 5 Senate members & 5 citizens appointed by Governor. Agencies may be reviewed more frequently.
Wisconsin	(c)	...	...	...	...	...	...
Wyoming	(r)	...	...	...	...	...	...

Key:
C — Comprehensive
R — Regulatory
S — Selective
D — Discretionary
d — day
m — month
y — year

SUNSET LEGISLATION—Continued

(a) Agency termination is scheduled on July 1 of the year prior to the scheduled termination of statutory authority for that agency.
(b) Arkansas' legislature voted for repeal in 1983, but a clerical error halted the repeal process, which has for all practical purposes been abandoned.
(c) While they have not enacted sunset legislation in the same sense as the other states with detailed information in this table, the legislatures in California, Iowa, Michigan, Minnesota, New Jersey, Ohio, and Wisconsin have included sunset clauses in selected programs.
(d) Sunset suspended in 1983. Next review cycle is scheduled for 1995.
(e) Illinois sunset law remains on the books but without any staff support since summer 1985.
(f) Through an executive order, the governor may provide a terminated agency with one year to wind up its affairs.
(g) Primarily.
(h) Louisiana no longer uses zero based budgeting, but the sunset law has not been revised.
(i) Sunset Act terminated December 31, 1984.
(j) Sunset suspended in 1983.
(k) Nebraska's Sunset Act terminated in 1985.
(l) Nevada law provided for a one-cycle pilot program under which three agencies were reviewed in 1980. No further expansion of the law has been enacted.
(m) New Hampshire's Sunset Committee was repealed July 1, 1986.
(n) North Carolina's sunset law terminated on July 30, 1981. Successor vehicle, The Legislative Cmte. on Agency Review, operated until June 30, 1983.
(o) South Dakota suspended Sunset in 1979.
(p) By joint resolution, Senate and House of Delegates establish a schedule for review of "functional areas" of state government. Program evaluation is carried out by Joint Legislative Audit and Review Commission. Agencies are not scheduled for automatic termination. Commission reports are made to standing committees which conduct public hearings.
(q) Subject to legislative discretion.
(r) Wyoming repealed Sunset in 1988.

Table 3.34
LEGISLATIVE ACTIVITIES PERFORMED WITH THE USE OF COMPUTERS

State or other jurisdiction	Statutory, bill systems, legal applications							Fiscal, budget, economic applications										Legislative management			
	Statutory retrieval	Bill drafting	Bill status report	Statutory revision	Case law retrieval	Redistricting	Other	Revenue forecasting	Revenue analysis	Budget comparison	Budget effects of legislation	Fiscal notes	Local fiscal notes	Economic impact notes	Impact of salary and fringe changes	State aid formulas	Tracking federal dollars	Other	Computer printing	Legislative accounting	Mailing lists	Other
Alabama	★	★	★	...	...	★	...	★	★	★	★	★	★	...	★	★	★	(a)	★	...	...	
Alaska	★	★	★	★	...	...	(b)	★	★	★	★	★	★	...	★	★	★		★	★	★	
Arizona	★	★	★	★	...	...		★	★	★	★	★	★	★	★	★	★		★	★	★	
Arkansas	★	★	★	★	★	★	(ii)	★	★	★	★	★	★	★	★	★	...		★	★	★	(ii)
California	★	★	...	★	★	★		★	★	★	★	★	★	★	★	★	★		★	★	★	
Colorado	★	★	★	★	...	★	(e)	★	★	★	★	★	★	★	★	★	★		★	★	★	(d)
Connecticut	★	★	★	★	★	...		★	★	...	★	★	★	★	★	★	★		★	★	★	
Delaware	★	★	★	★	★	...	(b)	★	★	★	★	★	★	★	★	...	...	(b)	★	★	★	
Florida	★	★	★	★	★	★	(b)	★	★	★	★	★	★	★	★	★	★	(f)	★	★	★	
Georgia	★	★	★	★	★	...		★	★	...	★	★	★	★	★	★	★		★	★	★	
Hawaii	★	★	★	★	...	...		★	★	★	★	...	...	★	★	★	★		★	★	★	
Idaho	★	★	★	★	...	...		★	★	★	★	★	★	★	★	★	...		★	...	★	(e)
Illinois	★	★	★	★	...	★		★	★	★	★	★	★	★	★	★	★		★	★	★	
Indiana	★	★	★	★	★	...		★	★	...	★	★	★	★	★	★	★		★	...	★	
Iowa	★	★	★	★	★	...		★	★	★	★	★	★	★	★	★	★		★	★	★	
Kansas	★	★	★	★	...	★	(g)	★	★	★	★	★	★	★	★	★	★	(h)	★	★	★	(i),(b,j)
Kentucky	★	★	★	★	★	★		★	★	★	★	★	★	★	★	★	★		★	★	★	
Louisiana	★	★	★	★	★	★		★	★	★	★	★	★	★	★	★	★		★	★	★	
Maine	★	★	★	★	★	...		★	★	★	★	★	★	★	★	★	★		★	★	★	
Maryland	★	★	★	★	★	...		★	★	★	★	★	★	(k)	★	★	★		★	★	★	
Massachusetts	★	★	★	★	...	★		★	★	★	★	★	★	★	★	★	★		★	★	★	(j)
Michigan	★	★	★	★	S	★		S	S	...	★	S	S	★	★	★	★ H	(l)	★	★	★	
Minnesota	★	★	★	S	★	★		S	S	★	★	S	★	★	★	★	★		★	★	★	
Mississippi	★	★	★	★	...	★		★	★	★	★	★	★	★	★	★	★		★	★	★	
Missouri	★	★	★	★	★	★		★	★	★	★	★	★	★	★	★	★		★	★	★	
Montana	★	★	★	★	★	★	(m,n,o)	★	★	★	★	★	★	★	★	★	★	(p)	★	★	★	(q)
Nebraska	★	★	★	★	★	★		★	★	★	★	★	★	★	★	★	...		★	★	★	
Nevada	★	★	★	★	★	★		★	★	★	★	★	★	★	★	★	...		★	★	★	(r,s,t)
New Hampshire	★	★	★	...	★	★		★	★	★	...	...	...	...	...	★	...		...	★	★	
New Jersey	★	★	★	★	★	...		...	...	★	★	★	★	★	★	★	...		★	★	★	
New Mexico	...	★	★	★	★	★	(v)	★	★	★	★	★	★	★	★	★	★	(u)	★	★	★	(t),(q,t,u)
New York	★	★	★	★	★	★		★	★	★	★	★	★	...	★	★	★	(j,t)	★	★	★	
North Carolina	★	★	★	★	★	...		★	★	★	★	★	★	★	★	★	★		★	★	★	
North Dakota	★	★	★	★	★	...	(n)	★	★	...	★	...	...	★	★	★	...	(x)	★	★	★	
Ohio	★	★	★	★	★	...		★	★	★	★	★	★	★	★	...	★		★	★	★	(c,s,y,e)

LEGISLATIVE ACTIVITIES PERFORMED WITH THE USE OF COMPUTERS—Continued

LEGISLATURES

State or other jurisdiction	Statutory, bill systems, legal applications							Fiscal, budget, economic applications											Legislative management				
	Statutory retrieval	Bill drafting	Bill status report	Statutory revision	Case law retrieval	Redistricting	Other	Revenue forecasting	Revenue analysis	Budget comparison	Budget effects of legislation	Fiscal notes	Local fiscal notes	Economic impact notes	Impact of salary and fringe changes	State aid formulas	Tracking federal dollars	Other	Computer printing	Legislative accounting	Mailing lists	Other
Oklahoma	★	★	★	★	S	★		H	★	★	★	S	S		★	★	H			★	★	(n,e,z)
Oregon	★	★	★	★		★	(aa)	★	★	★	★	★	★		★	★		(bb)	★	★	★	(cc)
Pennsylvania	★	★	★	★	★	★	(n,e,o)	★	★	★	★	★	★		★	★	★			★		
Rhode Island	★	★	★	★		★	(dd)	★	★	★	★	★	★		★	★	★		★	★	★	
South Carolina	★	★	★	★	★	★		★	★	★	★	★	★	★	★	★	★		★	★	★	
South Dakota	★	★	★	★		★			★	★	★	★	★	★	★	★	★		★	★	★	
Tennessee	★	★	★	★	(b)	★		★	★	★	★	★	★	★	★	★	★		★	★		
Texas	★	★	★	★	★	★	(n)	★	★	★	★	★	★		★	★	★	(a)	★	★	★	(j,ee)
Utah	★	★	★	★	★	★		★	★	★	★	★	★	S	★	★	★		★	★	★	(q)
Vermont	★	★	★	★						★										★		
Virginia	★	★	★	★	(b)	★			★	★	S	★		S	★	S	★		★	★	★	
Washington	★	★	★	★	S	S		S	★	★	★	★	★		★	S			★	★	★	
West Virginia	★	★	★	★	★	★			★	★	★		★		★	★				★	★	
Wisconsin	★	★		★	★	★		★	★	★	★	★		S	★	★	★	(gg)	★	★	★	(n,ff)
Wyoming	★	★	★	★	★	★		★	★	★	★	★	★		★	★	★		★	★	★	(hh)
American Samoa	★		★																	★	★	
Puerto Rico	★	★	★	★	★				★	★	★								★	★	★	
U.S. Virgin Islands	★																	★			?	

Key:
★ — Existing application
⋯ — Not an existing application
S — Performed in Senate only
H — Performed in House only
(a) Preparation of appropriation bill.
(b) Legal, legislative tracking or other databases searches.
(c) Scheduling.
(d) Legislative budget analysis.
(e) Roll calls and/or voting.
(f) Producing fiscal analysis reports.
(g) Bill citator, session statistics. In House, subject bill index and subject act index.
(h) Budget preparation, program evaluation.
(i) Workload tracking, personnel records.
(j) Personnel and/or payroll.
(k) Economic impact analysis (do not do economic impact notes).
(l) Property tax modeling, income tax modeling, school aids modeling.
(m) Voting system, public subscriber on-line access.
(n) Preparation/printing of journals, calendars, public laws and/or supplements/annotations.
(o) Photocomposition.
(p) Local government financial reporting.
(q) General word processing/document management.
(r) Workload analysis, work flow tracking, lists of publications.
(s) Electronic mail.
(u) Electronic publishing (desk top publishing, business graphics, etc.).
(v) Research INCLGIS.
(w) Bill request tracking, workload management for attorneys.
(w) Project management.
(x) Access to state personnel system.
(y) Legislative analysis in Legislative Budget Office.
(z) Floor management.
(aa) Indexes.
(bb) State mandates.
(cc) Registered lobbyists, executive nominations, leave accounting, inventory, state-wide election results, payroll and benefits.
(dd) Citations/omnibus bill.
(ee) Travel per diem, legislative budget.
(ff) Committee meetings.
(gg) Tax modeling.
(hh) Questionnaire processing.
(ii) Bill history, vote retrieval, staff bill analysis.
(jj) Constituent case work management, payroll, inventory control.

LEGISLATURES

Table 3.35
LOBBYISTS: AS DEFINED IN STATE STATUTES

State or jurisdiction	Legislative/Parliamentary lobbying	Administrative agency lobbying	Elective officials as lobbyists	Public employees as lobbyists	Compensation standard	Expenditure standard	Time standard	Making campaign contributions at any time	Making campaign contributions during legislative sessions	Making expenditures in excess of $ per official per year	Solicitation by officials or employees for contributions or gifts	Other
Alabama	★	★	...	...	...	...	...	...	...	...	★	...
Alaska	★	★	...	...	...	...	★	...	...	...	...	...
Arizona	★	★	...	...	...	...	...	...	...	...	...	...
Arkansas	★	★	...	...	...	...	...	...	...	...	...	...
California	...	...	...	...	...	...	...	...	...	...	...	(b)
Colorado	★	...	★	...	★	★	...	...	...	...	...	...
Connecticut	★	★	...	★	...	★	★	...	...	$ 50	★ (b)	(c,d,e)
Delaware	★	...	...	...	...	★	...	...	...	...	...	...
Florida	★	...	★	...	...	...	...	...	...	...	★	(f,g,h)
Georgia	★	...	...	...	...	...	...	...	...	...	...	(c,f)
Hawaii	★	★	...	...	★	★	★	...	...	...	...	(c)
Idaho	★	...	...	...	★	...	...	...	...	...	...	...
Illinois	...	...	...	...	...	...	...	...	...	...	...	(c)
Indiana	★	...	...	...	★	★	★	...	...	...	★	...
Iowa	★	...	★	★	★	★	...	...	...	...	...	...
Kansas	★	★	...	...	...	★	...	...	...	$100	...	(i)
Kentucky	★	...	...	...	...	...	...	...	...	...	...	(j)
Louisiana	★	...	...	...	★	...	...	...	...	...	...	(k)
Maine	★	...	...	...	...	...	★	...	...	...	...	...
Maryland	★	★	...	...	★	★	★	...	...	...	★	(c)
Massachusetts	★	★	...	...	...	...	...	...	...	$100	...	...
Michigan	★	★	...	...	★	★	★	...	...	(b)	...	...
Minnesota	★	★	...	...	...	★	★	...	...	...	...	(l)
Mississippi	★	...	...	★	...	...	...	...	...	...	...	(c)
Missouri	★	...	...	...	...	...	...	...	...	...	...	...
Montana	★	...	...	★	...	...	...	...	...	...	...	...
Nebraska	★	★	...	...	...	...	...	...	...	$ 25	...	...
Nevada	★	...	...	...	...	...	...	...	...	$100	★	(c,e,e,m,)
New Hampshire	★	...	...	...	...	...	...	...	...	...	...	...
New Jersey	★	...	...	...	★	★	★	...	...	...	...	...
New Mexico	★	...	...	...	...	...	...	...	...	...	...	...
New York	★	★	...	...	...	...	...	...	...	...	...	(c)
North Carolina	★	...	...	...	...	...	...	...	...	...	...	(c)
North Dakota	★	★	★	...	...	...	...	...	...	...	...	...
Ohio	★	...	...	...	...	...	...	...	...	...	...	...
Oklahoma	★	...	...	...	★	★	...	...	...	...	...	(c,h,m)
Oregon	★	...	★	★	...	★	★	★	...	...	★	(c,h,)
Pennsylvania	★	★	...	...	★	...	...	...	...	...	...	...
Rhode Island	★	...	...	...	...	...	...	...	...	...	...	...
South Carolina	★	...	...	...	...	...	...	...	...	...	...	(c)
South Dakota	★	...	...	...	...	...	...	...	...	...	...	...
Tennessee	★	★	★	★	...	...	...	...	...	...	...	...
Texas	★	★	...	...	★	★	★	★	...	...	...	(c,n)
Utah	★	★	...	...	★	★	★	...	...	...	...	...
Vermont	★	...	...	...	★	...	...	...	...	...	...	...
Virginia	★	...	...	...	...	★	★	...	...	...	...	...
Washington	★	★	★	★	★	★	★	...	...	...	...	...
West Virginia	★	...	...	...	...	...	...	...	...	...	...	...
Wisconsin	★	★	...	★	★	★	★	...	...	$ 0	★	(c,e)
Wyoming	★	...	...	...	★	...	...	...	...	...	...	...
Dist. of Columbia	★	★	...	...	★	★	★	...	...	$100	...	...

LOBBYISTS: AS DEFINED IN STATE STATUTES—Continued

Source: Campaign Finance, Ethics and Lobby Law, 1988. The Council of State Governments, Council on Governmental Ethics.

Key:
. . . — Not applicable
★ — Application exists
(a) Number of contacts.
(b) Lobbyists making gifts in excess of the following thresholds to state officials: California, $10 per month per official; Connecticut, $50 per gift; Michigan, $31 per gift; Nebraska, $25 per month per official.
(c) Contingency basis lobbying.
(d) Placing public officials under personal obligation.
(e) Instigating legislative and or administrative action for the purpose of obtaining employment in support or defeat thereof.
(f) Offering or proposing anything which may be reasonbly construed to improperly influence a legislator's official acts, decisions or votes.
(g) Attempting to influence the selection of officers and employees of the House.
(h) Making false statements or misrepresentation to legislators.
(i) Paying or agreeing to pay any state officer or employee or candidate for state office compensation for property or services substantially in excess of that charged in the ordinary course of business.
(j) $3,000 limitation per campaign.
(k) Purchase anything other than food and drink for state officials.
(l) Political contributions not to be included in Lobbyist Disbursement Reports.
(m) Using information from lobbyists reports in soliciting contributions.
(n) Restricted from the floor of either house while in session.

LEGISLATURES

Table 3.36
LOBBYISTS: REGISTRATION AND REPORTING

State or jurisdiction	Agency which administers registration and reporting requirements for lobbyists	Frequency	Legislation/Administrative Action Seeking to Influence	Expenditures Benefiting Public Officials or Employees	Compensation Received [Broken Down by Employer(s)]	Total Compensation Received	Categories of Expenditures	Total Expenditures	Other
Alabama	Ethics Comm.	Monthly (a)	★	★	...	...	★	...	...
Alaska	Alaska Public Offices Comm.	Monthly (b)	★	★	★	★	★	★	...
Arizona	Secretary of State	Annually (c)	...	(d)	...	...	...	...	...
Arkansas			...	...	...	...	...	...	...
California	Secretary of State Off.	Quarterly	★	★	★	★	★	★	...
Colorado	Secretary of State	Monthly	★	★	★	...	★	...	...
Connecticut	State Ethics Comm.	Monthly (e)	...	(f)	★	★	★	★	...
Delaware	Legislative Council	Quarterly	...	...	...	...	...	★	...
Florida	House Clerks Off.	Semi-annually	...	...	...	...	★	...	(g)
Georgia	Off. of Secretary of State	...	...	...	...	...	...	...	...
Hawaii	State Ethics Comm.	Semi-annually	★	★	★	★	...	★	(h)
Idaho	Sec. of State Off.	Monthly (a) and annually	★	★	...	...	★	★	(i)
Illinois	Secretary of State	Apr., July and year end	...	...	...	...	...	...	(j)
Indiana	Secretary of State	Semi-annually	...	★	★	★	★	★	...
Iowa	Secretary of Senate	Monthly	★	★	...	...	...	★	...
Kansas	Secretary of State	Monthly (k)	...	★	...	...	★	...	...
Kentucky	Attorney General	After session	★	...	...	...	...	★	...
Louisiana	Secretary of Senate	...	...	...	...	...	...	...	...
Maine	Dept. of State	Monthly (a) and annually	...	★	★	★	...	★	...
Maryland	Ethics Comm.	Semi-annually	★	★	★	★	★	★	(m)
Massachusetts	Secretary of State	Semi-annually	...	★	★	★	★	★	(n)
Michigan	Secretary of State	Semi-annually	...	★	...	...	★	★	...
Minnesota	Ethical Practices Bd.	Quarterly and annually	★	★	...	...	★	★	(o)
Mississippi	Secretary of State	Annually	...	...	...	...	...	★	...
Missouri	Clerk of House, Sec. of Senate	3 times during session	★	★	...	...	★	...	...
Montana	Commr. of Political Practices	...	...	★	★	★	★	★	...
Nebraska	Accountability & Disclosure Comm.	Monthly (p)	★	...	★	...	★	★	(q)
Nevada	Dir. Leg. Counsel Bureau	Monthly	★	...	...	...	★	★	...
New Hampshire	Secretary of State	Apr. 15, Aug. 15, Dec. 1	...	...	★	...	★	★	...
New Jersey	Attorney General	Annually	★	★	★	★	★	★	★
New Mexico	Secretary of State	After session	...	★	...	...	★	★	...
New York	State Comm. on Lobbying	Quarterly	★	★	★	★	...	★	...
North Carolina	Secretary of State	Annually	...	...	...	...	★	...	...
North Dakota	Secretary of State	Annually	...	(r)	...	...	...	...	...
Ohio	Jt. Cmte. on Agency Rule Review	Semi-annually	...	★	...	...	...	...	...
Oklahoma	Jt. Legislative Ethics. cmte.	Semi-annually	...	★	...	...	...	...	...
Oregon	Govt. Ethics Comm.	Quarterly	...	★	...	...	★	★	...
Pennsylvania	Clerk of House, Sec. of Senate	Semi-annually	...	★	...	...	★	★	...
Rhode Island	Secretary of State	(s)	★	...	★	★	★	★	...
South Carolina	Secretary of State	After session	...	★	...	...	...	...	...
South Dakota	Secretary of State	Annually	...	...	...	...	...	...	(j)
Tennessee	State Librarian & Archives	Semi-annually	...	...	...	...	...	...	...
Texas	Secretary of State	Monthly (a); quarterly	★	...	...	...	★	★	...
Utah	Lieutenant Governor	...	...	...	...	...	...	...	...
Vermont	Secretary of State	Semi-annually (t)	...	...	...	...	...	...	...
Virginia	Sec. of Commonwealth	After session and annually	★	★	★	★	★	★	...
Washington	Public Disclosure Comm.	Monthly	★	★	★	★	★	★	...
West Virginia	Secretary of State	After session and annually	...	...	...	...	...	★	...
Wisconsin	Secretary of State	Semi-annually (v)	★	★	★	...	★	★	(w)
Wyoming	Dir., Legislative Service Office	...	...	...	...	...	...	...	...
Dist. of Columbia	Bd. of Elections & Ethics	Biennially	★	★	★	★	★	★	...

LEGISLATURES

LOBBYISTS: REGISTRATION AND REPORTING—Continued

Source: Campaign Finance, Ethics and Lobby Law, 1988. The Council of State Governments, Council on Governmental Ethics Laws.

Key:
. . . — Not applicable
★ — Application exists
(a) During legislative session.
(b) During legislative session, quarterly thereafter.
(c) Also monthly during those months in which any single expenditure exceeds $25.
(d) Entertainment expenses.
(e) During legislative session, a year end report is required of those terminating registration during the year.
(f) Expenditures of over $15 per occassion.
(g) Amount, source, purpose of money spent on legislators (exlusive of personal expenses for travel, meals, lodging).
(h) Contributions of $25 or more received by lobbyist or lobbyist employer.
(i) Advertising, telephone, travel and office expenses which are not reimbursed.
(j) Generally, expenditure made for the purpose or promoting or opposing the passage of legislation.
(k) When $100 or more is spent.
(l) The lobbyist and lobbyist employer file a joint annual report.
(m) Special events, office expenses, witness fees, publication, research.
(n) Itemization of expenses over $35/day for lobbyists and $50/day for employers.
(o) Original sources of funds in excess of $500 in a calender year for lobbying purposes; lobbyist's receipts of over $500 for lobbyist's salary, fees, expenses for lobbying purposes.
(p) Monthly during legislative sessions, at end of legislative session during the interim.
(q) Lobbyist fees.
(r) If over $25.
(s) At specified times during legislative session and at end of legislative session.
(t) January 20 for preceding year; March 10 for January and February.
(u) Copies of registration and report sent to clerk of House.
(v) The lobbyist's report goes to his employer and is attached to the employer's report.
(w) Nature and interest of employer.

CHAPTER FOUR

STATE JUDICIAL BRANCH

THE STATE OF THE JUDICIARY

By Dixie K. Knoebel

Introduction

What is the status of the state judicial systems as we begin the final decade of the 20th century? The 50 state court systems and the District of Columbia are remarkably diverse. Court structures, operations, and procedures can vary greatly from one state to another, as well as between jurisdictions within each state. This diversity may be found in the method of selection for judges and other court officials, the configuration and jurisdiction of courts, the way in which caseloads and juries are managed, the areas and degree of automation, the source and level of funding for the courts, court personnel and function, and judicial compensation and fringe benefits.

Court systems are by nature reactive. Their response must be limited to the issues brought before them. Issues are brought to the courts by the public in the form of cases, and by the legislators in the form of laws and directives that affect how cases are to be handled. The ability of the courts to deal with what is brought before them is largely dependent upon the resources, particularly financial, that are available.

This chapter on the state judicial systems focuses on some progressive and innovative solutions explored by many court systems to respond to current demands. These solutions involve technology, case management, court access and awareness, fairness, and judicial selection and compensation.

Technology and the Courts

All levels of state courts have been effected to some extent by technology: appellate, civil, criminal, domestic relations, small claims, juvenile, and traffic. Technological systems have been developed to automate support payments, fine/bail accounts, jury selection and management, payroll and personnel, accounting, and case management. Significant attention has focused in recent years on automation to collect child support payments and to track cases.

Automation may be seen as one way to help court systems become more efficient. One of the more popular technologies and the one most helpful to judges is a computerized legal data base such as LEXIS and WESTLAW. Many state appellate and some trial court personnel have access to these data bases. Their use, however, is largely dependent upon the availability of funding for this service.

Technology beyond LEXIS and WESTLAW has not been as widespread. The complex organizational structure of the courts and limited financial resources are two reasons cited for the slowness with which the courts have caught on to automation. Judge Donald P. Smith, Jr., of the Colorado Court of Appeals explains, "The very nature of the law's reliance on precedence leaves judges and court systems behind the times not only in the use of computerized legal research but also with many of the other basic technological tools ... such as word processing, electronic transcriptions of court reporters' keystrokes, and case management systems."[1]

Many court systems have been reluctant to incorporate automation and computer technology into their operations. There are jurisdictions, however, taking the lead in automation, sometimes participating in pilot court projects.

Dixie K. Knoebel is director of Information Service for the National Center for State Courts.

Montgomery County, Penn., has been recognized as a pioneer in computer use. Remote computer access to this court's record database has been available to attorneys for years. Constructed to provide for inquiry only, the access service is free and available on a dial-up basis 24 hours every day. Harris County, Texas (Houston), and Rockville and Baltimore, Md., have instituted programs to allow public access to court records via remote computers. Recently the office of the administrator of the courts of Washington developed a pilot project for dial-up access to the comprehensive state Superior Court judicial information system.[2]

Collection of delinquent fines and fees can be made much easier through automation. Computerized record keeping allows automatic notification of delinquent accounts so that the parties can be notified by the court. Evidence suggests that one of the simplest methods of encouraging payment of fines is to remind the offender. Computers make it easier to record the offender's payment schedule and other data to enable automatic preparation of reminder notices as a payment date nears or a warning when such a date has passed without payment. Computers also make installment plans much easier to institute. In Maine, court procedure includes setting an amount for periodic payments, establishing a schedule for the payments, and a fixed date on which the final payment is due. At the Phoenix Municipal Court a payment schedule is entered into a computer; missed payments automatically result in a computer-generated warning letter.[3] Similarly, the Pittsburgh Court of Common Pleas child support division has instituted a computer network that allows for the tracking of incoming checks, disbursements, deliquencies, and notification to the judge as necessary.

Use of Facsimile Machines to Transmit Court Documents

There has been a proliferation in the use of fax machines in courts. Many judges are showing a surprising readiness to accept the use of facsimiles, adjusting rules and procedures to accommodate their use. Minnesota appears to be in the forefront, permitting attorneys to file documents by fax. Effective Jan. 1, 1989, the Minnesota Supreme Court authorized the installation of fax machines in all the state's courthouses, authorizing the filing of any paper with the court by fax. The rule also requires the subsequent filing, within five days, of the original document, with a $5 transmission fee and any applicable filing fees. Fax machines are also used in Cook County, Ill., (notice of compliance in garnishments), New York Civil Court, Oregon (service of papers statewide) and Michigan (two counties using fax machines to issue search warrants authorizing blood alcohol tests).

Other courts are considering similar experiments. Potential problems associated with the advent of fax machines, however, will need to be addressed: the ability of one fax machine to monopolize another machine by sending junk fax, the use of thermal paper by most machines, which turns black under sunlight or intense heat, and collection of filing fees applicable to pleadings that are filed by fax.[4]

Videotape as the Court Record

In 1982 Judge James S. Chenault of the Madison County (Richmond, Ky.) Circuit Court instituted video recording to serve as the court record. This videotape record was not transcribed; the tape itself served as the official record. At this early point, an operator was required to control the cameras. In 1984, however, operatorless video recording was introduced in a Louisville, Ky., court. Since then, video recording as the official court record has expanded to various jurisdictions in Arizona, Arkansas, California, Florida, Hawaii, Michigan, North Carolina, Oregon, Virginia, and Washington. The impact of videotape on other methods of conventional court recording, particularly court reporting where reporters enter and then transcribe the record, is still unclear.[5]

"Courts of the Future"

In pilot "courts of the future" in Chicago, Phoenix, and Detroit, computers have been installed so that court reporters take testimony, which is translated within seconds to words on computer terminals. These terminals enable judges and lawyers to read the testimony almost simultaneously on their computer screens.[6] These computers also may be used by court participants who are hearing-impaired.

In Fairfax County (Virginia) Circuit Court, terminals at the judge's bench are linked to the clerk's office, allowing for the cataloging of cases, compilation of dockets, and assignment of cases. In Brevard County, Fla., a two-way audio-visual microwave network has been hooked up, linking jails and courthouses, allowing for "long distance" initial proceedings, second appearances, bond hearings, enforcement hearings, motions, pleas, and sentencing. This system is expected to save $100,000 a year in transportation and vehicle maintenance costs. It allows court proceedings to be conducted with inmates under the watchful eye of sheriff's deputies while all other court personnel remain in the courthouse. Not only does this offer a high degree of security, but it also is intended to speed up the caseflow process.[7]

Two other innovations may be on the horizon for court systems. "Bar code readers" recently have become a part of the automated data collection system (known as STAT-SCAN) of the California Administrative Office of the Courts. These devices, used extensively in many industrial and commercial environments to collect information on inventory control and document tracking, may be transferable to the court environment, enabling collection of data, reporting, and compilation of cases. When a case is filed, a bar code label with the court's case number is placed on the case file. Appropriate entries are made to record transactions that occur during the life of that case.[8]

Another first for courts has been the development of an interactive video terminal in the courthouse in Golden, Colo., designed to assist persons representing themselves in small claims and child support matters. A touch sensitive screen allows the user to direct the computer to information by touching a picture or portion of the screen that represents the choice. Users may read or listen to a voice in either Spanish or English. The computer automatically performs calculations for the child support worksheet and completes small claims forms that can be submitted to the clerk's office to initiate the case.[9]

State Court Case Management

Delay in case processing is a problem for many court systems. The reasons for this problem include the complexity of litigation, an inundation of drug cases, overcrowded jails, increased workload, and debate over who controls the movement of cases.

The National Center for State Courts, in a recent study on the pace of litigation in 26 urban trial courts[10], found that early and continuous court control was the most important factor regarding the pace of litigation. It was more important than court resources in obtaining faster disposition times in civil and felony cases. Effective caseflow and resource management were found to be clearly related to a faster pace of litigation. Control meant establishing firm policies against postponement of trial dates in felonies and early court control over the scheduling of case events in civil cases.

Another attempt to gain control over case processing has been the adoption by 23 states of time standards, requiring that cases be heard within a certain period of time.[11] The Conference of State Court Administrators in 1983 and the American Bar Association's National Conference of State Trial Judges in 1984 developed and adopted time standards for the processing of civil and criminal cases. These time standards allow the monitoring of efforts to reduce the number of case delays. Nine counties in California are participating in a three-year pilot program designed to move cases through the courts, as mandated by the 1986 Trial Court Delay Reduction Act. This program is a precursor to possible statewide time standards for case dispositions by 1991. The standards require general civil cases to be resolved within one year of filing and 90 percent of felony cases to be resolved within four months of arrest, 100 percent within one year.[12]

Specialized Drug Courts

An increase in drug-related cases has been cited as the most serious factor effecting felony court delay.[13] In response to this serious problem, jurisdictions in some areas of the country are creating drug courts or courts with special drug sessions to process drug cases. Drug courts have been established in New York City and Jersey City. In Cook County, Ill., officials plan to open five evening narcotics courts in the criminal court.[14] Proponents of drug courts maintain that this attention enhances the prosecution of drug cases, uses court personnel more efficiently, and insures the consistency of sentencing.[15] Another response to drug-related cases is the Comprehensive Adjudication of Drug Arrestees (CADA) Program, funded by the Bureau of Justice Assistance (BJA) in Rhode Island, Flint, Mich., New Orleans and Santa Clara County, Calif. The goal of these programs is to reduce delays in the courts and to more efficiently process drug cases.[16]

Another case disposition method recently gaining popularity is differentiated case management (DCM). DCM relates the speed and method of case disposition to the cases' actual resource and management requirements (including both court and attorney), not dependent on the order in which they are filed. DCM is used as a response to the surge of drug cases, as an alternative to creation of drug courts, and for dealing with case delay in general.

Civil DCM programs are in place in a number of jurisdictions in Alaska, California, Connecticut, Kentucky, Massachusetts, Michigan, New Jersey, and Washington, DC.[17] In Bergen County, N.J., the civil division assigns cases to one of three tracks — expedited, standard, or complex — and cases are handled according to procedures tailored to that particular track. Similar to medical triage, by evaluating the likely complexity of each case, events and processing time can be tailored to procedural requirements.[18] Experimental criminal case DCM programs are used by courts in New Jersey, Michigan, and Washington.[19] Early evaluation signs point to positive experiences with this new process.

Alternative Dispute Resolution

Alternative dispute resolution (ADR) is another program designed to overcome deficiencies in the traditional (and overburdened) justice system and to provide a more timely and accessible process. A survey of the Conference of State Court Administrators (COSCA) in 1986 revealed that the types of cases handled by the various ADR programs include minor criminal, some felony, and many types of civil disputes, particularly those in the domestic relations area. At last count, 24 states and D.C. were operating a court-annexed arbitration program(s). In addition to court-annexed arbitration, other ADR methods have been implemented, such as mediation, pretrial settlement, summary jury trials, and medical malpractice screening.[20] Alternative dispute resolution is also available in many states through private organizations such as Endispute and Judicate.

The ABA Committee on Standards of Judicial Administration included provisions for alternative dispute resolution for the first time in the recent draft revisions to the ABA Standards Relating to Court Organization. In the Discussion Draft from June 1, 1989, and included in the standards adopted in February 1990, the committee created a standard that acknowledged alternative dispute resolution as a viable alternative to formal court adjudication (Standard 1.12.5). The standards address ADR administration, education and experience of ADR professionals, and referral procedures to ADR programs. The standards acknowledge court-annexed arbitration programs and court-referred ADR programs.[21]

Some litigants have turned away from the traditional court adjudication route and hired private judges to hear their disputes. These private decision makers are paid by the parties, both of whom must consent to the process. Although the speed of such a process may be attractive, a serious concern is that such a system is available only to those who can afford private judges, while leaving the traditional court route to the poor and those accused of crimes. Those opposed to private judging are fearful that it may erode the quantity and quality of services provided by court systems by attracting the best judges to a private business where there is high pay, modern facilities, and fewer and more interesting cases.[22] California's 117-year old private judging law is being studied to investigate the effect of that statute and report to the California Judicial Council.[23] Because California state court dockets have lengthened in the past decade, this once little-used statute has gained considerable popularity for those parties who seek speed, privacy, a customized procedure or a specialized decision-maker, and can afford the process. New York and Washington have similar laws (as do approximately seven other states). In some states the verdicts can be reviewed by appeals courts.[24]

Public Perception of and Access to the Courts

The judiciary is gradually becoming aware that the public is woefully misinformed about the state court systems and the way in which they operate. Many judges and court personnel acknowledge the judiciary would be viewed in a better light if the public were accurately and more fully informed about the general operations of the third branch.

To this end, judges and court administrators across the country are working with schools, churches, and business groups to promote law-related education programs and to develop formal judicial speakers bureaus. For example, in Colorado the Committee on Public Education, a standing committee of the Supreme Court, has been created to develop programs to give the public a better understanding of the judiciary and ultimately foster greater confidence in the courts. The focus has been on schools, the community, and the media.[25] In many states, judges and local school representatives work together to coordinate and conduct mock trial tournaments for students. State court systems also are working closely with schools to educate students on the basics of the local and state judiciary by developing brochures that describe the individual state court systems and inviting classes to observe court proceedings.

Both the bar (state and local) and the media can be of assistance in promoting a more accurate and positive image of the courts. In many states, committees of bench/bar and bench/bar/media representatives have been created to improve the judicial system and to develop programs that will have a positive affect on the image of the judiciary. Although the relationship between the media and the court has generally been an uncomfortable one at best, these committees are based on the premise that cooperation and communication will result in a better informed public without compromising the basic tenets of the Code of Judicial Conduct.

Another way to help educate the public about the judicial branch has been through television coverage of courtroom proceedings. Today only six states and the District of Columbia do not allow television coverage at any level of court.[26] Colorado was the first state to permit courtroom television coverage in 1956; most states began to allow cameras to televise courtroom proceedings in the late 1970's through the 1980's. In all instances where cameras are allowed, there are specific guidelines governing coverage.[27] Judges and court administrators generally have recognized that cameras in the courtroom promotes a positive judicial image and helps foster a better public understanding of the court system.

One effort to make courts more accessible to the public has been by extending court hours and conducting court proceedings in the evenings and weekends. Night court, as it is often called, is defined as "any hours after normal closing hours during which a court remains open for court appearances or the payment of fines."[28] Establishing night courts appear to be more popular in larger cities, because the operating costs of extended hours can be financially prohibitive in less populated areas. Examples of extended hours include Phoenix, where the clerk's office has opened a window between the hours of 6 p.m. and midnight, permitting payments and case filings. Most recently, Los Angeles has remained open into the evening hours to hear trials.[29]

Increased public accessibility to the courts also means an increased responsibility in terms of safety. Although no statistics exist on courtroom violence at the state court level, according to the U.S. Marshals Service, threats are increasing against judges, prosecutors, jurors and witnesses in federal courts. It is apparent, particularly in courts that hear domestic relations cases, that violence is on the rise. Court officials have begun to address the need for security by increasing prevention and detection methods, such as metal detectors at the doors to the courthouses and restricted access to judicial chambers.[30]

Fairness in the Courts

The judiciary is in contact with many diverse groups, including women, minorities, the mentally and physically handicapped and people stricken with AIDS. The judicial decisionmaker may no longer be a white anglo-saxon male; there has been an increase in the number of women and minorities attaining the bench. This diversity, both on and off the bench, has served as a vehicle for the judiciary to examine its interactions with attorneys, litigants, judges, witnesses, jurors, and court employees.

In October 1982 the first state supreme court task force on gender bias in the courts was established in New Jersey. By 1989, that number had increased to 27 task forces all across the country. Results from these task forces have included documentation of incidences of gender bias in the courts and strategies for addressing the problems, including such recommendations as legislative reforms, changes in court procedures, judicial education, and changes in law school curricula.

The ABA standing committee on Ethics and Professional Responsibility on May 1, 1989 circulated a discussion draft of revisions to the ABA Code of Judicial Conduct. Specifically, all language in the proposed revised code would be gender neutral, and commentaries to the proposed revised Canons 2 and 3 would be expanded to give illustrative guidance to determine what appears to be and is improper judicial conduct as it relates to gender bias.[31]

Task forces on race and ethnic bias also have been established by courts in California, Michigan, New Jersey, New York, Washington, and Florida to examine discrimination in such areas as bail determinations, jury selection, sentencing, and disparity in jury awards. The New York task force found that courts are staffed so overwhelmingly by whites that minorities do not trust the court system. The Washington task force also found that minorities believe they won't receive equal treatment in the court system.[32]

Fair and equal treatment is also an issue for those litigants and others appearing in court who are hearing-impaired or do not speak English. Because of the recent influx of non-English speaking immigrants, many state courts have had to find court interpreters. Standards for and certification of court interpreters is being or has been developed in Arizona, California, Massachusetts, New Jersey, and New Mexico. Not only must the interpreter be intimately familiar with the second language, but also must have knowledge of courtroom procedure and legal vocabulary.[33]

For the hearing-impaired, all states but Alaska have statutes providing for interpretation for hearing-impaired persons. Proficiency in sign language is required for interpreters for deaf persons.[34] In Los Angeles Superior Court, the court has begun to provide sign language interpreters for hearing-impaired citizens selected for jury service.[35]

Acquired Immune Deficiency Syndrome and the Courts. As the number of people infected with the AIDS virus continues to increase, so does the number of AIDS-infected individuals appearing in the state courts. The state courts of Alaska, Arizona, Colorado, Connecticut, Illinois, Massachusetts, Minnesota, New York, Oregon, Vermont, and Virginia, as well as the U.S. Fourth Circuit Court of Appeals, have developed guidelines or rules to assist court personnel in conducting court proceedings where one or more of the participants has AIDS, as well as for resolving workplace issues such as HIV (human immunodeficiency virus)-infected employees.

In 1989, the American Bar Association (ABA) adopted a policy on AIDS for the criminal justice system that states that attorneys should not refuse to represent or modify representation because of a person's known or perceived HIV status. Court proceedings involving the HIV-infected should proceed as in any other case unless the court participant exhibits violent behavior or attempts to escape. When a person's HIV status is an issue in a case, the ABA policy states that the court must be provided with the most current, accurate and objective medical information about the person's condition.[36]

The Judge:
Selection, Retention and Compensation

As of December 1988 there were 354 justices/judges serving the court of last resort, 804 judges on intermediate appellate courts (in the 37 states where that level of court exists), 8,937 judges serving general jurisdiction courts, and 18,563 judges serving limited jurisdiction courts.[37] Many methods are used to select these judges: partisan and non-partisan election, gubernatorial appointment, recommendations from judicial nominating commissions, legislative selection, and court selection. Methods not only vary from one state to another but several methods may be used for different judicial levels within one state as well. Thirty-four states and the District of Columbia use judicial nominating commissions (bodies that present candidates for judicial office to the governor for appointment), in at least at one level of their state court system.[38]

Most recently the citizens of New Mexico (November 1988) voted to institute a hybrid system of judicial selection. There, a judge is nominated by a judicial nominating commission and appointed by the governor. At the next general election, that judge must then run in a partisan election. If that judge wins, at the next general election the judge faces a retention election, where the voters only need to vote yes or no to retain that judge in office.

Other states continue to wrestle with what the best method is to select judges. In Alabama, Florida, Louisiana, New York, Texas and Washington, where judges are elected, and in South Carolina and Virginia, where judges are selected by the legislature, alternative judicial selection procedures are being examined, such as gubernatorial appointment following recommendations from a judicial nominating commission.[39]

The configuration of voting boundaries to select judges within states also has been an issue. Several states have been challenged under the Voting Rights Act of 1985. Plaintiffs argue that judges should fall under this act because of possible discrimination regarding minority access not only to the bench but also in voting area configurations that determine who should sit on the bench. Minority plaintiffs have brought suit against Alabama, Florida, Georgia, Louisiana, Mississippi, Ohio and Texas, contending their voting strength has been diluted because of the way in which judges are elected. There has been no definitive answer regarding judicial selection and the Voting Rights Act, and the Supreme Court has refused to consider a writ of certiorari. Remedies to address lawsuit concerns, however, are presently being fashioned in Illinois, Louisiana and Ohio.[40]

Another issue effecting many judges is that of mandatory retirement. Many states authorize mandatory retirement for judges, usually at age 70. The Age Discrimination in Employment Act, or ADEA (1986), promotes employment of older persons and prohibits age discrimination in employment. Elected and appointed judges are bringing lawsuits under the ADEA and the Equal Employment Opportunity Act (EEOA), challenging their states' mandatory retirement laws. Rulings have generally abided with state mandatory retirement requirements, superceding the ADEA amendments and EEO Commission concerns. This is an issue, however, that has not been resolved.[41]

Concern also has been expressed that judges are not receiving adequate judicial compensation, in the area of salaries and fringe benefits. As of Jan. 1, 1990, the average salaries of justices/judges of courts of last resort was $81,337; judges of intermediate appellate courts $80,044; and judges of general jurisdiction trial courts $73,208.[42]

Edward B. McConnell, president of the National Center for State Courts, recently stated, "... to have good judges, a state must be able to get good lawyers to leave the practice of law and go on the bench, and must keep good judges from leaving the bench to return to the practice of law ... it is axiomatic in business that you get what you pay for. Because of this correlation between quality and compensation, a state cannot expect to attract and retain good judges and thereby maintain a top-quality court system at compensation levels that are comparable to those of the less experienced or less competent lawyers." It is clear that inadequate judicial pay scales, found to be the case in most states, are deterring the best qualified and experienced lawyers. The quality of justice is diminished when less than the best qualified candidates are serving on the bench.[43]

In 1988, the ABA published A Survey of Judicial Fringe Benefits.[44] The ABA recommended that judges who are at least age 65 with at least 15 years of service should be eligible to receive a pension equal to 75 percent of the currently effective salary of the office from which he or she retired, that the state judicial retirement fund be underwritten by the state, and that authorization of adequate leave be given, including periodic paid sabbaticals. The ABA House of Delegates at their 1988 annual meeting approved a resolution endorsing judicial sabbaticals, providing six month (at full pay) or one year (at half pay) sabbaticals after six continuous years of full-time service. Presently only three states (Alaska, Oregon and Minnesota) and Puerto Rico have provisions for extended judicial leave, but without pay.[45]

Conclusion

In addition to technological advances affecting the judiciary, many court systems are concerned with efficiency and adequate financial allocation. Several states have determined that a more forward-looking stance would help them respond to these challenges, and are creating future's commissions. Their goal is to examine what may lie ahead for the judiciary and how the courts can most effectively and efficiently respond to changes. Recommendations from two of these commissions have stressed structural and procedural changes to help the court systems operate more efficiently.

In 1987, the Commission on the Future of Virginia's Judicial System was created to develop a vision for an effectively functioning justice system for the 21st century. Recommendations included the establishment of county public defender offices, time standards and improved calendar management practices, use of videotape recordings of the courtroom proceedings as the official trial record, abolishment of the jury sentencing system, development of alternative dispute resolution programs, establishment of a single-tiered trial court with divisions, a state-funded court system with the exception of court facilities, the establishment of a trial court administrator's office, the abolishment of the office of the elected clerk of court, and the use of judicial nominating commissions to select judges.[46]

In 1988, Arizona established the Commission on the Courts. The charge was to develop a long-range plan for the Arizona courts through 2000, prepare recommendations for improving the court system, devise a plan for providing change and promote a receptive environment for change outside the judiciary. Recommendations from the report, similar to those outlined by Virginia, include a three-tiered court system, merit selection system for all judges, responsibilities of the clerk of court carried out under the direction of a court executive, the position of clerk of court to be appointive rather than elective, and state funding of the maintenance and operations of the entire court system.[47]

Other states also have begun to establish similar bodies. Massachusetts recently established the Chief Justice Commission on the Future of the Courts. Iowa appointed a Year 2000 Committee to review the existing structure and internal operating procedures of Iowa's appellate courts. The New Hampshire Supreme Court established a Long-Range Planning Task Force, to enable the Supreme

Court to establish a clear focus and to better allocate resources in meeting the mission of the judicial branch into the 21st century. Alabama has appointed a Commission on the Future of the Alabama Juvenile Justice System, to look at the areas of administration, delinquent children, and neglected or abused children.[48]

Footnotes

1. Court Technology Conference, April 1988, as reported in the National Law Journal, "Computer Age Eludes the Courts", May 30, 1988.
2. Information Service memorandum IS 89.2524 on Remote Computer Access to Automated Court Records and to Other Public Records, January 11, 1990.
3. Information Service memorandum IS 89.1859 on Collection and Enforcement on Fines and Fees, December 20, 1989.
4. Information Service memorandum IS 89.2292 on Fax Machines in Courts, December 29, 1989.
5. Videotaped Trial Records: Evaluation and Guide, National Center for State Courts, January 15, 1990.
6. "Court of Future is Here", ABA Journal, February 1989.
7. "Microwave Network Improves Court Security and Reduces Manpower", Court Review, (Florida), Summer 1988.
8. The Magic Wand: Bar Code Technology in the California Courts, Western Regional Office, National Center for State Courts, January 1989 and "STATSCAN: California's Automated Data Collection and Tracking System", State Court Journal, Spring 1987.
9. "Nation's First Computerized Information Center in Golden", Colorado Courts, October 1988.
10. Examining Court Delay, National Center for State Courts, 1989.
11. Most of the focus has been on delay in the trial courts, although delay is beginning to be addressed at the appellate level as evidenced by development of appellate case processing time standards in several states. In 1986, Idaho became the first state to adopt comprehensive time standards for appellate cases. California is joining the intermediate appellate courts in Connecticut, Louisiana, Virginia and Wisconsin to design and implement delay reduction programs based upon the ABA's Standards Relating to Appellate Delay Reduction. (Case Processing Goals, Howard Schwartz, July 20, 1988).
12. "Pilot Program Seeks to Reduce Civil Delay in California", Judicature, February-March 1988.
13. Examining Court Delay, National Center for State Courts, 1989.
14. "Court Overwhelmed by Drug Cases", Justice Policies, October 2, 1989.
15. "Drug Court", Detroit Free Press, March 27, 1989, and "Numerous Drug Arrests Bringing Cases to New York City Courts", Criminal Justice Newsletter, May 1, 1989.
16. 1988 Report on Drug Control, Bureau of Justice Assistance, Office of Justice Programs, U.S. Department of Justice, 1989.
17. "Case Differentiation: An Approach to Individualized Case Management", Judicature, June-July 1989.
18. "Differentiated Case Management Project: Assessments of the Bergen Experience", New Jersey Law Journal, June 9, 1988.
19. "Case Differentiation: An Approach to Individualized Case Management", Judicature, June-July 1989.
20. "State Adoption of Alternative Dispute Resolution", State Court Journal, Spring 1988.
21. Draft Revisions to ABA Standards Relating to Court Organization, Discussion Draft, American Bar Association, June 1, 1989.
22. "Private Judging: A Challenge to Public Justice", ABA Journal, September 1, 1988.
23. "'Rent a Judge' Law Reviewed", Alternatives to the High Cost of Litigation, December 1989.
24. "Judges for Hire", Virginia Lawyers Weekly, October 1989.
25. "Colorado Judicial Department Public Education Program", Colorado Lawyer, June 1988.
26. These states are Indiana, Missouri, Mis-

sissippi, South Carolina, South Dakota, and Texas.

27. Summary of TV Cameras in the State Courts, Information Service, November 22, 1989.

28. Other reasons expressed for establishing night court programs include reducing delay between arrest and release on bail, reducing jail overcrowding, convenience for participants including the police, maximizing the use of existing courtroom space, and spreading the court's workload over more hours.

29. Information Service memorandum IS 86.055 on Use of Night Courts.

30. Report on Trends in the State Courts, Information Service, June 1989.

31. Draft Revisions to ABA Code of Judicial Conduct, Discussion Draft, American Bar Association, May 1, 1989.

32. Report on Trends in the State Courts, Information Service, June 1989.

33. Information Service memorandum IS 89.1323 on Developing Standards for Court Interpreters.

34. Report on Trends in the State Courts, Information Service, June 1989.

35. Press release, Jury Commissioner, LA Superior Court, April 25, 1989.

36. Report on Trends in the State Courts, Information Service, June 1989.

37. Court Caseload Statistics: Annual Report 1988, National Center for State Courts, 1990.

38. State Court Organization 1987, National Center for State Courts, 1988.

39. Report in Trends in the State Courts, Information Service, June 1989.

40. "The Voting Rights Act: Are Its Provisions Applicable to the Judiciary?", State Court Journal, Summer 1989.

41. Report on Trends in the State Courts, Information Service, 1989.

42. Survey of Judicial Salaries, National Center for State Courts, November 1989.

43. "State Judicial Salaries: A National Perspective", The Journal of State Government, September/October 1988.

44. ABA/JAD Committee on State Judicial Salaries and Compensation, American Bar Association, March 1988.

45. ABA National Conference of Special Court Judges Report to the House of Delegates, Recommendations, American Bar Association, draft dated December 1, 1988.

46. Courts in Transition: The Report of the Commission on the Future of Virginia's Judicial System, May 1, 1989.

47. The Future of Arizona Courts, Report of the Commission on the Courts, 1989.

48. Report on Trends in the State Courts, Information Service, 1989.

Table 4.1
STATE COURTS OF LAST RESORT

State or other jurisdiction	Name of court	Justices chosen (a) At large	Justices chosen (a) By district	No. of judges (b)	Term (in years) (c)	Chief justice Method of selection	Chief justice Term of service as chief justice
Alabama	S.C.	★		9	6	Popular election	6 years
Alaska	S.C.	★		5	10	By court	3 years (d)
Arizona	S.C.	★		5	6	By court	5 years
Arkansas	S.C.	★		7	8	Popular election	8 years
California	S.C.	★		7	12	Appointed by governor (e)	12 years
Colorado	S.C.	★		7	10	By court	At pleasure of court
Connecticut	S.C.	★		7	8	Nominated by governor, appointed by General Assembly	8 years
Delaware	S.C.	★		5	12	Appointed by governor with consent of Senate	12 years
Florida	S.C.	★		7	6	By court	2 years
Georgia	S.C.	★		7	6	By court	4 years
Hawaii	S.C.	★		5	10	Appointed by governor, with consent of Senate	10 years
Idaho	S.C.	★		5	6	By court	4 years
Illinois	S.C.		★	7	10	By court	3 years
Indiana	S.C.	★		5	10 (f)	Selected by judicial nominating commission from S.C. members	5 years
Iowa	S.C.	★		9	8	By court	Remainder of term
Kansas	S.C.	★		7	6	By seniority of service (g)	Remainder of term
Kentucky	S.C.		★	7	8	By court	4 years
Louisiana	S.C.		★	7	10	By seniority of service	Remainder pf term
Maine	S.J.C.	★		7	7	Appointed by governor, with consent of Senate	7 years
Maryland	C.A.	★		7	10	Designated by governor	Remainder of term
Massachusetts	S.J.C.	★		7	To age 70	Appointed by governor	To age 70
Michigan	S.C.	★		7	8	By court	2 years
Minnesota	S.C.	★		7	6	Popular election	6 years
Mississippi	S.C.		★	9	8	By seniority of service	Remainder of term
Missouri	S.C.	★		7	12	By court	2 years
Montana	S.C.	★		7	8	Popular election	8 years
Nebraska	S.C.		★ (h)	7	6	Appointed by governor	Life
Nevada	S.C.	★		5	6	By seniority of service (i)	1-2 years
New Hampshire	S.C.	★		5	To age 70	Appointed by governor and Council	To age 70
New Jersey	S.C.	★		7	7 (j)	Appointed by governor, with consent of Senate	7 years (j)
New Mexico	S.C.	★		5	8	By court	2 years
New York	C.A.	★		7	14 (j)	Appointed by governor, with consent of Senate	14 years (j)
North Carolina	S.C.	★		7	8	Popular election	8 years
North Dakota	S.C.	★		5	10	By Supremem and district court judges	5 years (k)
Ohio	S.C.	★		7	6	Popular election	6 years
Oklahoma	S.C.		★	9	6	By court	2 years
Oregon	C.C.A.		★	3	6	By court	2 years
Pennsylvania	S.C.	★		7	6	By court	6 years
Rhode Island	S.C.	★		7	10	By seniority of service	Remainder of term
South Carolina	S.C.	★		5	Life	By legislature	Life
South Dakota	S.C.		★ (l)	5	10	Joint public vote of General Assembly	10 years
Tennessee	S.C.	★		5	8	By court	4 years
Texas	S.C.	★		9	8	By court	18 months
Texas	C.C.A.	★		9	6	Popular election	6 years
Utah	S.C.	★		5	10 (n)	Popular election (m)	6 years (m)
Vermont	S.C.	★		5	6	Appointed by governor, with consent of Senate	6 years

STATE COURTS OF LAST RESORT—Continued

State or other jurisdiction	Name of court	Justices chosen (a)		No. of judges (b)	Term (in years) (c)	Chief justice	
		At large	By district			Method of selection	Term of service as chief justice
Virginia	S.C.			7	12	By seniority of service	Remainder of term
Washington	S.C.	★		9	6	By seniority of service	2 years
West Virginia	S.C.	★		5	12	By seniority of service	1 year
Wisconsin	S.C.	★		7	10	By seniority of service (o)	Remainder of term
Wyoming	S.C.	★		5	8	By court	2 years
Dist. of Columbia	C.A.	★		9	15	Designated by President (p)	4 years
American Samoa	H.C.			8 years (q)	(r)	Appointed by Secretary of the Interior	(r)
Puerto Rico	S.C.	★		8	To age 70	Appointed by President with consent of Senate	To age 70

Sources: National Center for State Courts, *State Court Organization 1987*; state constitutions and statutes.

Key:
S.C. — Supreme Court
S.C.A. — Supreme Court of Appeals
S.J.C. — Supreme Judicial Court
C.A. — Court of Appeals
C.C.A. — Court of Criminal Appeals
H.C. — High Court

(a) See Table 4.4, "Selection and Retention of Judges," for details.
(b) Number includes chief justice.
(c) The initial term may be shorter. See Table 4.4, "Selection and Retention of Judges," for details.
(d) A justice may serve more than one term as chief justice, but may not serve consecutive terms in that position.

(e) Subsequently, must run on record for retention.
(f) Initial two years; retention 10 years.
(g) If two or more qualify, then senior in age.
(h) Chief justice chosen statewide; associate judges chosen by district.
(i) If two or more qualify, then determined by lot.
(j) May be reappointed to age 70.
(k) Or expiration of term, whichever is first.
(l) Initially chosen by district; retention determined statewide.
(m) Presiding judge of Court of Criminal Appeals.
(n) Initial three years; retention 10 years.
(o) If two or more qualify, then justice with least number of years remaining in term.
(p) From list of nominees submitted by Judicial Nominating Commission.
(q) Chief judges and associate judges sit on appellate and trial divisions.
(r) For good behavior.

Table 4.2
STATE INTERMEDIATE APPELLATE COURTS AND GENERAL TRIAL COURTS: NUMBER OF JUDGES AND TERMS

State or other jurisdiction	Intermediate appellate court				General trial court		
	Name of court	No. of judges	Term (years)		Name of court	No. of judges	Term (years)
Alabama	Court of Criminal Appeals	5	6		Circuit courts	124	6
	Court of Civil Appeals	3	6				
Alaska	Court of Appeals	3	8		Superior courts	30	6
Arizona	Court of Appeals	18	6		Superior courts	101	4
Arkansas	Court of Appeals	6	8		Chancery courts	34	4
					Circuit courts	33	6
California	Courts of Appeal	88	12		Superior courts	725	6
Colorado	Court of Appeals	13	8		District Court	110	6
Connecticut	Appellate Court	9	8		Superior courts	139	8
Delaware					Superior courts	15 (a)	12
Florida	District Court of Appeals	46	6		Circuit courts	372	6
Georgia	Court of Appeals	9	6		Superior courts	137	4 (b)
Hawaii	Intermediate Court of Appeals	3	10		Circuit courts	24	10
Idaho	Court of Appeals	3	6		District courts	33	4
Illinois	Appellate Court	34	10		Circuit courts	760 (c)	6
Indiana	Court of Appeals	12	10 (d)		Superior Court	129	6
					Circuit courts	90	6
Iowa	Court of Appeals	6	6		District courts	100 (e)	6
Kansas	Court of Appeals	10	4		District courts	146 (f)	4
Kentucky	Court of Appeals	14	8		Circuit courts	91	8
Louisiana	Court of Appeals	52	10		District courts	192	6
Maine					Superior Court	16	7
Maryland	Court of Special Appeals	13	10		Circuit courts	109 (g)	15
Massachusetts	Appeals Court	14	(i)		Trial Court	320	(i)
Michigan	Court of Appeals	18	6		Circuit courts	167	6
Minnesota	Court of Appeals	13	6		District courts	230	6
Mississippi					Chancery courts	39	4
					Circuit courts	40	4
Missouri	Court of Appeals	32	12		Circuit courts	133 (h)	6
Montana					District courts	36	6
Nebraska					District courts	48	6
Nevada					District courts	39	6
New Hampshire					Superior Court	25	(i)
New Jersey	Appellate Division of Superior Court	28	7		Superior Court	349	7
New Mexico	Court of Appeals	7	8		District courts	59	6
New York	Appellate Division of Supreme Court	47	5 (i)		Supreme Court	484	14 (i)
	Appellate Terms of Supreme Court	15	5 (i)				
North Carolina	Court of Appeals	12	8		Superior Court	74	8
North Dakota	Court of Appeals (temporary)	3			District courts	27	6
Ohio	Court of Appeals	59	6		Courts of common pleas	344	6
Oklahoma	Court of Appeals	12	6		District Court	71 (j)	4
Oregon	Court of Appeals	10	6		Circuit courts	87	6
	Tax Court	1	6				
Pennsylvania	Superior Court	15	10		Courts of common pleas	341	10
	Commonwealth Court	9	10				
Rhode Island					Superior Court	20	Life
South Carolina	Court of Appeals	6	6		Circuit Court	31	6

STATE INTERMEDIATE APPELLATE COURTS AND GENERAL TRIAL COURTS—Continued

State or other jurisdiction	Intermediate appellate court			General trial court		
	Name of court	No. of judges	Term (years)	Name of court	No. of judges	Term (years)
South Dakota	...	...	...	Circuit courts	35	8
Tennessee	Court of Appeals	12	8	Chancery courts	35	8
	Court of Criminal Appeals	9	8	Circuit courts	97 (k)	8
Texas	Courts of Appeals	80	6	District courts	385	4
Utah	Court of Appeals	7	10 (l)	District courts	29	6
				Superior courts	10	6
Vermont	...	...	...	District courts	15	6
Virginia	Court of Appeals	10	8	Circuit courts	122	8
Washington	Court of Appeals	16	6	Superior courts	136	4
West Virginia	...	...	...	Circuit courts	60	8
Wisconsin	Court of Appeals	13	6	Circuit courts	208	6
Wyoming	...	...	...	District courts	17	6
Dist. of Columbia	...	...	...	Superior Court	51	15
American Samoa	...	...	...	High Court: trial level	8 (m)	(n)
Guam	...	...	...	Superior Court	6	7
Puerto Rico	...	...	...	Superior Court	95	12

Sources: National Center for State Courts, *State Court Caseload Statistics: 1988 Annual Report;* state statutes and court administration offices.

Key:
... — Court does not exist in jurisdiction
(a) President judge, three resident judges and 11 associate judges.
(b) For judges of the Superior Court of the Atlanta Judicial Court, term of office is eight years.
(c) 389 authorized circuit, 371 associate circuit, plus 50 permissive associate judges.
(d) Two years initial; 10 years retention.
(e) Plus 42 district associate judges and 19 senior judges.
(f) Plus 69 district associate judges and 70 district magistrates.
(g) Includes judges of Circuit Court for Baltimore City.
(h) Plus 170 associate circuit judges.
(i) To age 70.
(j) Plus 77 associate judges and 60 special judges.
(k) With civil jurisdiction, 69 judges; with criminal jurisdiction, 28.
(l) Three years initial; 10 years retention.
(m) Chief justice and associate judges sit on appellate and trial divisions.
(n) For good behavior.

JUDICIARY

Table 4.3
QUALIFICATIONS OF JUDGES OF STATE APPELLATE COURTS AND GENERAL TRIAL COURTS

State or other jurisdiction	U.S. citizenship (years)		Years of minimum residence				Minimum age		Member of state bar (years)		Other	
			In state		In district							
	A	T	A	T	A	T	A	T	A	T	A	T
Alabama	5	5	(a)	(a)	...	1	25	25	★	★	...	...
Alaska	★	★	5 (a)	5 (a)	...	...	...	...	★ (b)	★ (b)	...	...
Arizona	...	...	10 (c)	5	3 (d,e)	...	30 (d)	30	10 (c)	5	(f,g)	(f,g)
Arkansas	★	★	2	2	...	...	30	28	(h,i)	(h,i)	(f)	(f)
California	...	...	...	...	...	...	...	...	10 (i)	10 (i)	...	...
Colorado	...	...	(e)	...	...	(e)	...	...	5	5	(g)	(g)
Connecticut	...	...	...	...	...	...	18	...	★	★	...	...
Delaware	...	...	(a)	(a)	...	...	...	...	(h)	(h)	...	...
Florida	...	...	(e)	(e)	★	★	...	...	10	5	(g)	(g)
Georgia	3	3	(a)	(a)	...	...	30	30	7	7	...	...
Hawaii	★	★	★ (a)	★ (a)	...	...	...	...	10	10	...	...
Idaho	★	★	2	2	...	(e)	30	30	★	(h)	...	...
Illinois	★	★	...	...	★	★	...	...	★	★	...	...
Indiana	★	★	...	...	★	★	...	...	10 (i)	★	...	...
Iowa	...	...	...	...	...	...	...	...	★	★	...	...
Kansas	...	...	...	...	...	★	30	30	★ (i)	★ (i)	...	...
Kentucky	★	★	2	2	2	2	...	...	8	8	...	...
Louisiana	...	...	5	...	2	2	25	...	5	5	(f)	(f)
Maine	...	...	...	...	...	...	...	...	(h)	(h)	(f)	(f)
Maryland	...	...	5 (a,e)	5 (a,e)	6 mo.	6 mo.	30	30	★	★	(f)	(f)
Massachusetts	...	...	...	...	...	...	...	...	...	...	...	...
Michigan	...	...	(e)	...	(e)	(e)	...	...	★	★	(g,j)	(g,j)
Minnesota	...	...	...	...	...	...	...	...	(h)	(h)	...	...
Mississippi	...	...	(a)	(a)	...	...	30	26	5	5	...	...
Missouri	15	10	(e)	(e)	★	1	30	30	★	★	...	...
Montana	★	★	2	2	...	...	...	...	5	5	...	...
Nebraska	★	★	3	...	★ (e)	★	30	30	5 (i)	5 (i)	...	...
Nevada	...	...	2 (e)	2 (e)	...	...	25	25	★	★	(k)	(k)
New Hampshire	...	...	...	...	...	...	...	...	...	...	(l)	(l)
New Jersey	...	...	...	...	...	...	...	...	10	10	...	...
New Mexico	...	...	3	3	...	★	30	30	3 (h,i)	3 (h,i)	...	...
New York	...	...	...	...	...	...	...	...	10	10	...	...
North Carolina	...	...	1	...	...	...	21	...	★	★	...	...
North Dakota	★	★	★	★	...	...	...	...	★ (h)	★ (h)	...	...
Ohio	...	...	...	...	...	★	...	...	6 (i)	6 (i)	(g)	(g)
Oklahoma	...	...	(e)	...	(e)	(e)	30	...	5 (i)	4 (i)	...	...
Oregon	★	★	3	★	(e)	★	...	...	★	★	...	...
Pennsylvania	★	★	1 (a)	(a)	...	1	...	...	★	★	...	...
Rhode Island	...	...	...	...	...	...	...	...	...	...	...	...
South Carolina	★	★	5 (a)	5 (a)	...	★ (e)	26	26	5	5	...	...
South Dakota	★	★	★	★	★ (e)	★ (e)	...	...	★	★	...	...
Tennessee	...	...	5 (a)	5	...	1	35 (m)	30	★	★	...	...
Texas	★	★	(a)	(a)	(d)	2	35	25	★ (i)	★ (i)	...	...
Utah	...	...	5	3	...	★	30	25	★	★	...	...
Vermont	...	...	★	★	...	...	...	...	★ (i)	★ (i)	...	...
Virginia	...	...	★	★	...	...	...	...	5	5	...	...
Washington	...	...	1	...	1	1	...	...	★ (n)	★	...	...
West Virginia	...	...	5	5	...	...	30	30	★ (i)	★ (i)	...	...
Wisconsin	...	...	(e)	...	...	(e)	...	...	5	5	...	...
Wyoming	★	★	3	2	...	...	30	28	1 (h,i)	1 (h)	...	...
Dist. of Columbia	★	★	...	...	90 days	...	...	...	5 (i)	5 (i)	...	...
American Samoa	★	★	...	...	...	...	...	...	★	★	...	...
Guam	...	★	...	...	...	...	...	...	...	(h)	...	...
No. Mariana Islands	...	★	...	...	...	...	...	30	...	(h)	...	...
Puerto Rico	★	★	...	...	...	...	...	25	★ (i)	★ (i)	...	...

JUDICIARY

QUALIFICATIONS OF JUDGES—Continued

Sources: National Center for State Courts, *State Court Organization 1987;* state constitutions and statutes.

Note: The information in this table is based on a literal reading of the state constitutions and statutes. Requirements that an individual be a member of the state bar or a qualified elector may imply additional requirements.

Key:
A — Judges of courts of last resort and intermediate appellate courts.
T — Judges of general trial courts.
★ — Provision; length of time not specified.
. . . — No specific provision.

(a) Citizen of the state. In Alabama, Mississippi and Tennessee (court of criminal appeals), five years; in Georgia, three years.

(b) Must have been engaged in active practice of law for specific number of years. Alaska: appellate — eight years; trial—five years.

(c) For court of appeals, five years.

(d) For court of appeals judges only.

(e) Qualified elector. For Arizona court of appeals, must be elector of county of residence. For Michigan Supreme Court, elector in state; court of appeals, elector of appellate circuit. For Missouri Supreme and appellate courts, electors for nine years; for circuit courts, electors for three years. For Oklahoma Supreme Court and Court of Criminal Appeals, elector for one year; court of appeals and district courts, elector for six months. For Oregon court of appeals, qualified elector in county.

(f) Specific personal characteristics. Arizona, Arkansas—good moral character. Maine—sobriety of manners. Maryland—integrity, wisdom and sound legal knowledge.

(g) Nominee must be under certain age to be eligible. Arizona—under 65. Colorado—under 72, except when name is submitted for vacancy. Florida—under 70, except upon temporary assignment or to complete a term. Michigan, Ohio—under 70.

(h) Learned in law.

(i) Years as a practicing lawyer and/or service on bench of court of record in state may satisfy requirement. Arkansas—appellate: eight years; trial: six years. Indiana—10 years admitted to practice or must have served as a circuit, superior or criminal court judge in the state for at least five years. Kansas—appellate: 10 years; trial: five years (must have served as an associate district judge in state for two years). Texas—appellate: 10 years; trial: four years. Vermont—five of 10 years preceding appointment. West Virginia—appellate: 10 years; trial: five years. Puerto Rico—appellate: 10 years; trial: five years.

(j) A person convicted of a felony or breach of public trust is not eligible to the office for a period of 20 years after conviction.

(k) May not have been previously removed from judicial office.

(l) Except that record of birth is required.

(m) Thirty years for judges of court of appeals and court of criminal appeals.

(n) For court of appeals, admitted to practice for five years.

JUDICIARY

Table 4.4
SELECTION AND RETENTION OF JUDGES

State or other jurisdiction	How selected and retained
Alabama	Appellate, circuit, district and probate judges elected on partisan ballots. Municipal court judges appointed by the governing body of the municipality (majority vote of its members).
Alaska	Supreme Court, court of appeals, superior court and district court judges appointed by governor from nominations submitted by Judicial Council. Supreme Court, court of appeals and superior court judges approved or rejected at first general election held more than three years after appointment. Reconfirmation every 10 and six years, respectively. District court judges approved or rejected at first general election held more than one year after appointment. Reconfirmation every four years. District court magistrates appointed by and serve at pleasure of presiding judge of superior court in each judicial district.
Arizona	Supreme Court justices and court of appeals judges appointed by governor from a list of not less than three nominees submitted by a nine-member Commission on Appellate Court Appointments. Superior court judges (in counties with population of at least 150,000) appointed by governor from a list of not less than three nominees submitted by a nine-member commission on trial court appointments. Judges initially hold office for term ending 60 days following next regular general election after expiration of two-year term. Judges who file declaration of intention to be retained in office run at next regular general election on non-partisan ballot. Superior court judges in counties having population less than 150,000 elected on non-partisan ballot; justices of the peace elected on partisan ballot; police judges and magistrates selected as provided by charter or ordinance; Tucson city magistrates appointed by mayor and council from nominees submitted by non-partisan Merit Selection Commission on magistrate appointments.
Arkansas	All elected on partisan ballot.
California	Supreme Court and courts of appeal judges appointed by governor, confirmed by Commission on Judicial Appointments. Judges run unopposed on non-partisan retention ballot at next general election after appointment. Superior court judges elected on non-partisan ballot or selected by method described above; judges elected to full term at next general election on non-partisan ballot. Municipal court and justice court judges initially appointed by governor and county board of supervisors, respectively, retain office by election on non-partisan ballot.
Colorado	Supreme Court and court of appeals judges appointed by governor from nominees submitted by Supreme Court Nominating Commission. Other judges appointed by governor from nominees submitted by Judicial District Nominating Commission. After initial appointive term of two years, judges run on record for retention. Municipal judges appointed by municipal governing body. Denver County judges appointed by mayor from list submitted by nominating commission; judges run on record for retention.
Connecticut	All nonelected judges appointed by legislature from nominations submitted by governor exclusively from candidates submitted by the Judicial Selection Commission. Judicial Review Council makes recommendations on nominations for reappointment. Probate judges elected on partisan ballots.
Delaware	All appointed by governor from list submitted by a judicial nominating commission (which is established by executive order) with consent of majority of senate.
Florida	Supreme Court and district court of appeals judges appointed by governor from nominees submitted by appropriate judicial nominating commission. Judges run for retention at next general election preceding expiration of term. Circuit and county court judges elected on non-partisan ballots.
Georgia	Supreme Court, court of appeals and superior court judges elected on non-partisan ballots. Probate judges and justices of peace elected on partisan ballots. Other county and city court judges appointed.
Hawaii	Supreme Court and intermediate court of appeals justices and circuit court judges nominated by Judicial Selection Commission (on list of at least six names) and appointed by governor with consent of senate. Judges reappointed to subsequent terms by the Judicial Selection Commission. District court judges nominated by Commission (on list of at least six names) and appointed by chief justice.
Idaho	Supreme Court and court of appeals justices and district court judges elected on non-partisan ballot. Magistrates appointed on merit basis by District Magistrates Commission and run for retention in first general election next succeeding the 18-month period following initial appointment; thereafter, run every four years.
Illinois	Supreme Court, appellate court and circuit court judges nominated at primary elections or by petition and elected at general or judicial elections on partisan ballot. Judges run in uncontested retention elections for subsequent terms. Circuit court associate judges appointed by circuit judges for four-year terms.
Indiana	Supreme Court justices and court of appeals judges appointed by governor from list of three nominees submitted by seven-member Judicial Nominating Commission. Judges serve until next general election after two years from appointment date; thereafter, run for retention on record. Circuit, superior and county judges in most counties run on partisan ballot. Marion County municipal judges appointed by governor from nominees submitted by county nominating commission.
Iowa	Supreme Court, court of appeals and district court judges appointed by governor from lists submitted by nominating commissions. Judges serve initial one-year term and until January 1 following next general election, run on records for retention. Full-time judicial magistrates appointed by district judges in judicial election district from nominations submitted by county judicial magistrate appointing commission. Part-time magistrates appointed by county judicial magistrate appointing commission.
Kansas	Supreme Court and court of appeals judges appointed by governor from nominations submitted by Supreme Court Nominating Commission. Judges serve until second Monday in January following first general election after one year in office; thereafter run on record for retention every six (Supreme Court) and four (court of appeals) years. District judges in most judicial districts selected by non-partisan commission plan.
Kentucky	All judges elected on non-partisan ballot.
Louisiana	All justices and judges (except Orleans Parish District and Family Court judges) elected on non-partisan ballot.
Maine	All appointed by governor with confirmation of the senate, except probate judges who are elected on partisan ballot.
Maryland	Court of Appeals and special appeals judges nominated by Judicial Nominating Commission, and appointed by governor with advice and consent of senate. Judges run on record for retention after one year of service. Judges of circuit courts and Supreme Bench of Baltimore City nominated by Commission and appointed by governor. Judges run in first general election after year of service (may be challenged by other candidates). District court judges nominated by Commission and appointed by governor, subject to senate confirmation.

JUDICIARY

SELECTION AND RETENTION OF JUDGES—Continued

State or other jurisdiction	How selected and retained
Massachusetts	All nominated and appointed by governor with advice and consent of Governor's Council. Judicial Nominating Commission, established by executive order, submits names on non-partisan basis to governor.
Michigan	All elected on non-partisan ballot, except remaining municipal judges who are selected in accordance with local procedures for selecting public officials.
Minnesota	All elected on non-partisan ballot.
Mississippi	All elected on partisan ballot, except municipal court judges who are appointed by governing authority of each municipality.
Missouri	Judges of Supreme Court, court of appeals and several circuit courts appointed initially by governor from nominations submitted by judicial selection commissions. Judges run for retention after one year in office. All other judges elected on partisan ballot.
Montana	All elected on non-partisan ballot. Judges unopposed in reelection effort, run for retention.
Nebraska	All judges appointed initially by governor from nominees submitted by judicial nominating commissions. Judges run for retention on non-partisan ballot in general election following initial three-year term; subsequent terms are six years.
Nevada	All elected on non-partisan ballot.
New Hampshire	All appointed by governor and confirmed by majority vote of five-member Executive Council.
New Jersey	All appointed by governor with advice and consent of senate, except judges of municipal courts serving a single municipality who are appointed by the governing body. Judges are reappointed by the governor (to age 70) with the advice and consent of senate.
New Mexico	Supreme Court, Court of Appeals, district and municipal judges appointed by governor from list submitted by a judicial nominating commission. At next general election, after appointment, judges run for full terms in partisan, contested election. If appointed judge wins the contested election, the judge runs for subsequent terms in uncontested retention elections.
New York	All elected on partisan ballot, except judges of Court of Appeals who are appointed by governor with advice and consent of senate. Governor also appoints judges of court of claims and designates members of appellate division of supreme court. Mayor of New York City appoints judges of criminal and family courts in the city from list submitted by a judicial nominating commission, established by mayor's executive order.
North Carolina	All elected on partisan ballot, except special judges of superior court who are appointed by governor.
North Dakota	All elected on non-partisan ballot.
Ohio	All elected on non-partisan ballot, except court of claims judges who may be appointed by chief justice of Supreme Court from ranks of Supreme Court, court of appeals, court of common pleas or retired judges.
Oklahoma	Supreme Court justices and Court of Criminal Appeals judges appointed by governor from lists of three submitted by Judicial Nominating Commission. Judges run for retention on non-partisan ballot at first general election following completion of one year's service. Judges of court of appeals, and district and associate district judges elected on non-partisan ballot. Special judges appointed by district judges within judicial administrative districts. Municipal judges appointed by governing body of municipality.
Oregon	All judges elected on non-partisan ballot for six-year terms, except municipal judges who are generally appointed and serve as prescribed by city council.
Pennsylvania	All initially elected on partisan ballot and thereafter on non-partisan retention ballot, except judges of traffic court and magistrates (Pittsburgh) who are appointed by mayor.
Rhode Island	Supreme Court justices elected by legislature. Superior, district and family court judges appointed by governor with advice and consent of senate. By executive order, governor selects appointees from names submitted by a judicial nominating commission. Probate and municipal court judges appointed by city or town councils.
South Carolina	Supreme Court, court of appeals, circuit court and family court judges elected by legislature from names submitted on a non-partisan basis by judiciary committee of legislature. Probate judges elected on partisan ballot. Magistrates appointed by governor with advice and consent of senate. Municipal judges appointed by mayor and alderman of city.
South Dakota	Supreme Court justices appointed by governor from nominees submitted by Judicial Qualifications Commission. Justices run for retention at first general election after three years in office. Circuit court judges elected on non-partisan ballot. Magistrates appointed by presiding judge of judicial court.
Tennessee	Judges of intermediate appellate courts appointed initially by governor from list of three nominees submitted by Appellate Court Nominating Commission. Judges run for election to full term at biennial general election held more than 30 days after occurrence of vacancy. Supreme Court judges and all other judges elected on partisan ballot, except some municipal judges who are appointed by governing body of city.
Texas	All elected on partisan ballot (method of selection for municipal judges determined by city charter or local ordinance).
Utah	Supreme Court, district court, circuit court and juvenile court judges appointed by governor from list of at least three nominees submitted by Judicial Nominating Commission. Judges run unopposed for retention in general election following initial three-year term; thereafter run on record for retention every 10 (Supreme Court) and six (other courts of record) years.
Vermont	Supreme Court justices, superior court and district court judges nominated by Judicial Nominating Board and appointed by governor with advice and consent of senate. Judges retained in office unless legislature votes for removal.
Virginia	All full-time judges elected by majority vote of legislature.
Washington	All elected on non-partisan ballot (method of selection for some municipal judges locally determined).
West Virginia	Supreme Court of Appeals judges, circuit court judges and magistrates elected on partisan ballot.
Wisconsin	Supreme Court, court of appeals and circuit court judges elected on non-partisan ballot. Method of selection for municipal judges determined locally.

JUDICIARY

SELECTION AND RETENTION OF JUDGES—Continued

State or other jurisdiction	How selected and retained
Wyoming	Supreme Court justices, district and county court judges appointed by governor from list of three nominees submitted by judicial nominating commission. Judges run for retention on non-partisan ballot at first general election occurring more than one year after appointment. Justices of the peace elected on non-partisan ballot. Municipal (police) judges appointed by mayor with consent of council.
Dist. of Columbia	Court of appeals and superior court judges nominated by president of the United States from a list of persons recommended by District of Columbia Judicial Nominating Commission; appointed upon advice and consent of U.S. Senate.
American Samoa	Chief justice and associate justice(s) appointed by the U.S. Secretary of the Interior pursuant to presidential delegation of authority. Associate judges appointed by governor of American Samoa on recommendation of the chief justice, and subsequently confirmed by the senate of American Samoa.
Guam	All appointed by governor with consent of legislature from list of nominees submitted by Judicial Council; thereafter, run on record for retention every seven years.
No. Mariana Islands	All appointed by governor with advice and consent of senate.
Puerto Rico	All appointed by governor with advice and consent of senate.
U.S. Virgin Islands	All appointed by governor with advice and consent of legislature.

Sources: Larry Berkson, Scott Beller and Michele Grimaldi, *Judicial Selection in the United States: A Compendium of Provisions* (Chicago: American Judicature Society) and update; Donna Vandenberg, "Judicial Merit Selection: Current Status," American Judicature Society; American Judicature Society and state constitutions and statutes.

JUDICIARY

Table 4.5
METHODS FOR REMOVAL OF JUDGES AND FILLING OF VACANCIES

State or other jurisdiction	How removed	Vacancies: how filled
Alabama	Judicial Inquiry Commission investigates, receives or initiates complaints concerning any judge. Complaints are filed with the Court of the Judiciary which is empowered to remove, suspend, censure or otherwise discipline judges in the state.	By gubernatorial appointment. At next general election held after appointee has been in office one year, office is filled for a full term. In some counties, vacancies in circuit and district courts are filled by gubernatorial appointment on nominations made by judicial commission.
Alaska	Justices and judges subject to impeachment for malfeasance or misfeasance in performance of official duties. On recommendation of Judicial Qualifications Commission or on its own motion, Supreme Court may suspend judge without salary when judge pleads guilty or no contest or is found guilty of a crime punishable as felony under state or federal law or of any other crime involving moral turpitude under that law. If conviction is reversed, suspension terminates and judge is paid salary for period of suspension. If conviction becomes final, judge is removed from office by Supreme Court. On recommendation of Judicial Qualifications Commission, Supreme Court may censure or remove a judge for action (occurring not more than six years before commencement of current term) which constitutes willful misconduct in office, willful and persistent failure to perform duties, habitual intemperance or conduct prejudicial to the administration of justice that brings the judicial office into disrepute. The Court may also retire a judge for a disability that seriously interferes with the performance of duties and is (or is likely to become) permanent.	By gubernatorial appointment, from nominations submitted by Judicial Council.
Arizona	Judges subject to recall election. Electors, equal in number to 25% of votes cast in last election for judge, may petition for judge's recall. All Supreme Court, court of appeals and superior court judges (judges of courts of record) are subject to impeachment. On recommendation of Commission on Judicial Qualifications or on its own motion, Supreme Court may suspend without salary, a judge who pleads guilty or no contest or is found guilty of a crime punishable as felony or involving moral turpitude under state or federal law. If conviction is reversed, suspension terminates and judge is paid salary for period of suspension. If conviction becomes final, judge is removed from office by Supreme Court. Upon recommendation of Commission on Judicial Qualifications, Supreme Court may remove a judge for willful misconduct in office, willful and persistent failure to perform duties, habitual intemperance or conduct prejudicial to the administration of justice that brings the office into disrepute. The Court may also retire a judge for a disability that seriously interferes with performance of duties and is (or is likely to become) permanent.	Vacancies on Supreme Court, court of appeals and superior courts (in counties with population over 150,000) are filled as in initial selection. Vacancies on superior courts in counties of less than 150,000 may be filled by gubernatorial appointment until next general election when judge is elected to fill remainder of unexpired term. Vacancies on justice courts are filled by appointment by county board of supervisors.
Arkansas	Supreme, appellate, circuit and chancery court judges are subject to removal by impeachment or by the governor upon the joint address of 2/3 of the members elected to each house of General Assembly.	By gubernatorial appointment. Appointee serves remainder of unexpired term if it expires at next general election.
California	All judges subject to impeachment for misconduct. All judges subject to recall election. On recommendation of the Commission on Judicial Performance or on its own motion, the Supreme Court may suspend a judge without salary when the judge pleads guilty or no contest or is found guilty of a crime punishable as a felony or any other crime that involves moral turpitude under that law. If conviction is reversed, suspension terminates and judge is paid salary for period of suspension. If conviction becomes final, judge is removed from office by Supreme Court. Upon recommendation of Commission on Judicial Performance, Supreme Court may remove judge for willful misconduct in office, persistent failure or inability to perform duties, habitual intemperance or conduct prejudicial to the administration of justice that brings the office into disrepute. The Court may also retire a judge for disability that seriously interferes with performance of duties and is (or is likely to become) permanent.	Vacancies on appellate courts are filled by gubernatorial appointment with approval of Commission on Judicial Appointments until next general election at which appointee has the right to become a candidate. Vacancies on superior courts are filled by gubernatorial appointment until next election. Vacancies on municipal courts are filled by gubernatorial appointment for remainder of unexpired term; on justice courts by appointment of county board of supervisors or by nonpartisan special election.
Colorado	Supreme, appeals and district court judges are subject to impeachment for high crimes and misdemeanors or malfeasance in office by 2/3 vote of senate. Supreme Court, on its own motion or upon petition, may remove a judge from office upon final conviction for a crime punishable as felony under state or federal law or of any other crime involving moral turpitude under that law. Upon recommendation of Commission on Judicial Discipline, Supreme Court may remove or discipline a judge for willful misconduct in office, willful or persistent failure to perform the duties of office, intemperance or violation of judicial conduct, or for disability that seriously interferes with performance and is (or is likely to become) permanent. Denver county judges are removed in accordance with charter and ordinance provisions.	By gubernatorial appointment (or mayoral appointment in case of Denver county court from names submitted by appropriate judicial nominating commission.

The Council of State Governments 213

JUDICIARY

METHODS FOR REMOVAL OF JUDGES—Continued

State or other jurisdiction	How removed	Vacancies: how filled
Connecticut	Supreme and superior court judges are subject to removal by impeachment or by the governor on the address of 2/3 of each house of the General Assembly. On recommendation of Judicial Review Council or on its own motion, the Supreme Court may remove or suspend a judge of the Supreme or superior court after an investigation and hearing. If the investigation involves a Supreme Court justice, such judge is disqualified from participating in the proceedings. If a judge becomes permanently incapacitated and cannot adequately fulfill the duties of office, the judge may be retired for disability by the Judicial Review Council on its own motion or on application of the judge.	If General Assembly is in session, vacancies are filled by gubernatorial nomination and legislative appointment. Otherwise vacancies are filled temporarily by gubernatorial appointment.
Delaware	Judges are subject to impeachment for treason, bribery or any high crime or misdemeanor. The Court on the Judiciary may (after investigation and hearing) censure or remove a judge for willful misconduct in office, willful and persistent failure to perform the duties of office or an offense involving moral turpitude or other persistent misconduct in violation of judicial ethics. The Court may also retire a judge for permanent mental or physical disability interfering with the performance of duties.	Vacancies are filled as in initial selection.
Florida	Supreme Court, district courts of appeal and circuit court judges are subject to impeachment for misdemeanors in office. On recommendation of Judicial Qualifications Commission, Supreme Court may discipline or remove a judge for willful or persistent failure to perform duties or for conduct unbecoming to a member of the judiciary, or retire a judge for a disability that seriously interferes with the performance of duties and is (or is likely to become) permanent.	By gubernatorial appointment, from nominees recommended by appropriate judicial nominating commission.
Georgia	Judges are subject to impeachment for cause. Upon recommendation of the Judicial Qualifications Commission (after investigation of alleged misconduct), the Supreme Court may retire, remove or censure any judge.	By gubernatorial appointment (by executive order) on nonpartisan basis from names submitted by Judicial Nominating Commission.
Hawaii	Upon recommendation of the Commission on Judicial Discipline (after investigation and hearings), the Supreme Court may reprimand, discipline, suspend (with or without salary), retire or remove any judge as a result of misconduct or disability.	Vacancies on Supreme, intermediate court of appeals and circuit courts are filled by gubernatorial appointment (subject to consent of senate) from names submitted by Judicial Selection Committee. Vacancies on district courts are filled by appointment by chief justice from names submitted by Committee.
Idaho	Judges are subject to impeachment for cause. Upon recommendation by Judicial Council, Supreme Court (after investigation) may remove judges of Supreme Court, court of appeals and district court judges. District court judges (or judicial district sitting en banc), by majority vote in accordance with Supreme Court rules, may remove magistrates for cause. District Magistrate's Commission may remove magistrates without cause during first 18 months of service.	Vacancies on Supreme Court, court of appeals and district courts are filled by gubernatorial appointment from names submitted by Judicial Council for unexpired term. Vacancies in magistrates' division of district court are filled by District Magistrate's Commission for remainder of unexpired term.
Illinois	Judges are subject to impeachment for cause. The Judicial Inquiry Board receives (or initiates) and investigates complaints, and files complaints with the Courts Commission which may remove, suspend without pay, censure or reprimand a judge for willful misconduct in office, persistent failure to perform duties or other conduct prejudicial to the administration of justice or that brings the judicial office into disrepute. The Commission may also suspend (with or without pay) or retire a judge for mental or physical disability.	Vacancies on Supreme, appellate and circuit courts are filled by appointment by Supreme Court until general election. Associate judge vacancies on circuit courts are filled as as in initial selection.
Indiana	Upon the recommendation of the Judicial Qualifications Commission or on its own motion, the Supreme Court may suspend or remove an appellate judge for pleading guilty or no contest to a felony or crime involving moral turpitude. The Supreme Court may also retire, censure or remove a judge for other matters. The Supreme Court may also discipline or suspend without pay a non-appellate judge.	Appellate vacancies are filled as in initial selection. Vacancies on circuit courts are filled by gubernatorial appointment until general election. Vacancies on most superior courts are filled by gubernatorial appointment.

214 The Book of the States 1990-91

JUDICIARY

METHODS FOR REMOVAL OF JUDGES—Continued

State or other jurisdiction	How removed	Vacancies: how filled
Iowa	Supreme and district court judges are subject to impeachment for misdemeanor or malfeasance in office. Upon recommendation of Commission on Judicial Qualifications, the Supreme Court may retire a Supreme, district or associate district judge for permanent disability, or remove such judge for failure to perform duties, habitual intemperance, willful misconduct, conduct which brings the office into disrepute or substantial violations of the canons of judicial ethics. Judicial magistrates may be removed by a tribunal in the judicial election district of the magistrate's residence.	Vacancies are filled as in initial selection.
Kansas	All judges are subject to impeachment for treason, bribery or other high crimes and misdemeanors. Supreme Court justices are subject to retirement upon certification to the governor (after a hearing by the Supreme Court nominating commission) that such justice is so incapacitated as to be unable to perform adequately the duties of office. Upon recommendation of the Judicial Qualifications Commission, the Supreme Court may retire for incapacity, discipline, suspend or remove for cause any judge below the Supreme Court level.	Vacancies on Supreme Court and court of appeals are filled as in initial selection. Vacancies on district courts (in areas where commission plan has not been adopted) are filled by gubernatorial appointment until next general election, when vacancy is filled for remainder of unexpired term; in areas where commission plan has been adopted, vacancies are filled by gubernatorial appointment from names submitted by judicial nominating commission.
Kentucky	Judges are subject to impeachment for misdemeanors in office. Retirement and Removal Commission, subject to rules of procedure established by Supreme Court, may retire for disability, suspend without pay or remove for good cause any judge. The Commission's actions are subject to review by Supreme Court.	By gubernatorial appointment (from names submitted by appropriate judicial nominating commission) or by chief justice if governor fails to act within 60 days. Appointees serve until next general election after their appointment at which time vacancy is filled.
Louisiana	Judges are subject to impeachment for commission or conviction of felony or malfeasance or gross misconduct. Upon investigation and recommendation by Judiciary Commission, Supreme Court may censure, suspend (with or without salary), remove from office or retire involuntarily a judge for misconduct relating to official duties, willful and persistent failure to perform duties, persistent and public conduct prejudicial to the administration of justice that brings the office into disrepute, or conduct while in office which would constitute a felony or conviction of felony. The Court may also retire a judge for disability which is (or is likely to become) permanent.	Vacancies are filled by Supreme Court appointment if remainder of unexpired term is six months or less; if longer than six months, vacancies are filled in special election.
Maine	Judges are subject to removal by impeachment or by governor upon the joint address of the legislature. Upon recommendation of the Committee on Judicial Responsibility and Disability, the Supreme Judicial Court may remove, retire or discipline any judge.	Vacancies are filled as in initial selection.
Maryland	Judges are subject to impeachment. Judges of Court of Appeals, court of special appeals, trial courts of general jurisdiction and district courts are subject to removal by governor on judge's conviction in court of law, impeachment, or physical or mental disability. Judges are also subject to removal upon joint address of the legislature. Upon recommendation of the Commission on Judicial Disabilities (after hearing), the Court of Appeals may remove or retire a judge for misconduct in office, persistent failure to perform duties, conduct prejudicial to the proper administration of justice, or disability that seriously interferes with the performance of duties and is (or is likely to become) permanent. Elected judges convicted of felony or misdemeanor relating to public duties and involving moral turpitude may be removed from office by operation of law when conviction becomes final.	Vacancies are filled as in initial selection.
Massachusetts	Judges are subject to impeachment. The governor, with the consent of the Executive Council, may remove judges upon joint address of the legislature, and may also (after a hearing and with consent of the Council) retire a judge because of advanced age or mental or physical disability. The Commission on Judicial Conduct, using rules of procedure approved by the Supreme Judicial Court, may investigate the action of any judge that may, by consequence of willful misconduct in office, willful or persistent failure to perform his duties, habitual intemperance or other conduct prejudicial to the administration of justice, bring the office into disrepute.	Vacancies are filled as in initial selection.

JUDICIARY

METHODS FOR REMOVAL OF JUDGES—Continued

State or other jurisdiction	How removed	Vacancies: how filled
Michigan	Judges are subject to impeachment. With the concurrence of 2/3 of the members of the legislature, the governor may remove a judge for reasonable cause insufficient for impeachment. Upon recommendation of Judicial Tenure Commission, Supreme Court may censure, suspend (with or without salary), retire or remove a judge for conviction of a felony, a physical or mental disability, or a persistent failure to perform duties, misconduct in office, habitual intemperance or conduct clearly prejudicial to the administration of justice.	Vacancies in all courts of record are filled by gubernatorial appointment from nominees recommended by a bar committee. Appointee serves until next general election at which successor is selected for remainder of unexpired term. Vacancies on municipal courts are filled by appointment by city councils.
Minnesota	Supreme and district court judges are subject to impeachment. Upon recommendation of Board of Judicial Standards, Supreme Court may censure, suspend (with or without salary), retire or remove a judge for conviction of a felony, physical or mental disability, or persistent failure to perform duties, misconduct in office, habitual intemperance or conduct prejudicial to the administration of justice.	As a result of executive order, by gubernatorial appointment from names submitted by appropriate committee on judicial nominations. Appointee serves until general election occurring more than one year after appointment at which time a successor is elected to serve a full term.
Mississippi	Judges are subject to impeachment. For reasonable cause which is not sufficient for impeachment, the governor may, on joint address of legislature, remove judges of Supreme and inferior courts. Upon recommendation of Commission on Judicial Performance, Supreme Court may remove, suspend, fine, publicly censure or reprimand a judge for conviction of a felony (in a court outside the state), willful misconduct, willful and persistent failure to perform duties, habitual intemperance or conduct prejudicial to the administration of justice which brings the office into disrepute. The Commission may also retire any judge for physical or mental disabilitythat seriously interferes with performance of duties and is (or is likely to become) permanent.	By gubernatorial appointment, from names submitted by a nominating commission. The office is filled for remainder of unexpired term at next state or congressional election held more than seven months after vacancy.
Missouri	Upon recommendation of Commission on Retirement, Removal and Discipline, Supreme Court may retire, remove or discipline any judge.	Vacancies on Supreme Court, court of appeals and circuit courts which have adopted commission plan are filled as in initial selection. Vacancies on other circuit courts and municipal courts are filled, respectively, by special election and mayoral appointment.
Montana	All judges are subject to impeachment. Upon recommendation of Judicial Standards Commission, Supreme Court may suspend a judge and remove same upon conviction of a felony or other crime involving moral turpitude. The Supreme Court may retire any judge for a disability that seriously interferes with the performance of duties, and that is (or may become) permanent. The Court may also censure, suspend, or remove any judge for willful misconduct in office, willful and persistent failure to perform duties, violation of canons of judicial ethics adopted by the Supreme Court, or habitual intemperance.	Vacancies on Supreme and district courts are filled by gubernatorial appointment (with confirmation by senate) from names submitted by judicial nominating commission. Vacancies on municipal and city courts are filled by appointment by city councils for remainder of unexpired term.
Nebraska	Judges are subject to impeachment. In case of impeachment of Supreme Court justice, judges of district court sit as court of impeachment with 2/3 concurrence required for conviction. In case of other judicial impeachments, Supreme Court sits as court of impeachment. Upon recommendation of the Commission on Judicial Qualifications, the Supreme Court may reprimand, discipline, censure, suspend or remove a judge for willful misconduct in office, willful failure to perform duties, habitual intemperance, conviction of crime involving moral turpitude, disbarment or conduct prejudicial to the administration of justice that brings the office into disrepute. The Supreme Court also may retire a judge for physical or mental disability that seriously interferes with performance of duties and is (or is likely to become) permanent.	Vacancies are filled as in initial selection.
Nevada	All judges, except justices of peace, are subject to impeachment. Judges are also subject to removal by legislative resolution and by recall election. The Commission on Judicial Discipline may censure, retire or remove a Supreme Court justice or district judge for willful misconduct, willful or persistent failure to perform duties or habitual intemperance, or retire a judge for advanced age which interferes with performance of duties or for mental or physical disability that is (or is likely to become) permanent.	Vacancies on Supreme or district courts are filled by gubernatorial appointment from among three nominees submitted by Commission on Judicial Selection. Vacancies on justice courts are filled by appointment by board of county commissioners or by special election.

JUDICIARY

METHODS FOR REMOVAL OF JUDGES—Continued

State or other jurisdiction	How removed	Vacancies: how filled
New Hampshire	Judges are subject to impeachment. Governor, with consent of Executive Council, may remove judges upon address of both houses of legislature.	Vacancies are filled as in initial selection.
New Jersey	Supreme and superior court judges are subject to impeachment by the legislature. Except for Supreme Court justices, judges are subject to a statutory removal proceeding that is initiated by the filing of a complaint by the Supreme Court on its own motion or the governoror either house of the legislature acting by a majority of its total membership. Prior to institution of the formal proceedings, complaints are usually referred to the Supreme Court's ASdvisory Committee on Judicial Conduct, which conducts a preliminary investigation, makes findings of fact and either dismisses the charges or recommends that formal proceedings be instituted. The Supreme Court's determination is based on a plenary hearing procedure, although the Court is supplied with a record created by the Committee. The formal statutory removal hearing may be either before the Supreme Court sitting en banc or before three justices or judges (or combination thereof) specifically designated by chief justice. If Supreme Court certifies to governor that it appears a Supreme Court or superior court judge is so incapacitated as to substantially prevent the judge from performing the duties of office, the governor appoints a commission of three persons to inquire into the circumstances. On their recommendation, the governor may retire the justice or judge from office, on pension, as may be provided by law.	Vacancies on Supreme, superior, appellate division of superior, county, district, tax and municipal courts are filled as in initial selection.
New Mexico	Judges are subject to impeachment. The Judicial Standards Commission may discipline or remove a judge for willful misconduct in office, willful and persistent failure to perform duties or habitual intemperance, or retire a judge for disability that seriously interferes with performance of duties and is (or is likely to become) permanent.	Vacancies on Supreme and district courts are filled by gubernatorial appointment from names submitted by judicial nominating commission.
New York	All judges are subject to impeachment. Court of Appeals and supreme court judges may be removed by 2/3 concurrence of both houses of legislature. Court of claims, county court, surrogate's court, family court, civil and criminal court (NYC) and district court judges may be removed by 2/3 vote of the senate on recommendation of governor. Commission on Judicial Conduct may determine that a judge be admonished, censured or removed from office for cause, or retired for disability, subject to appeal to the Court of Appeals.	Vacancies on Court of Appeals and appellate division of supreme court are filled as in initial selection. Vacancies in elective judgeships (outside NYC) are filled at the next general election for full term; until election, governor makes appointment (with consent of senate if in session).
North Carolina	Upon recommendation of Judicial Standards Commission, Supreme Court may censure or remove a court of appeals or trial court judge for willful misconduct in office, willful and persistent failure to perform duties, habitual intemperance, conviction of a crime involving moral turpitude, conduct prejudicial to the administration of justice that brings the office into disrepute, or mental or physical incapacity that interferes with the performance of duties and is (or is likely to become) permanent. Upon recommendation of Judicial Standards Commission, a seven-member panel of the court of appeals may censure or remove (for the above reasons) any Supreme Court judge.	Vacancies on Supreme, appeals and superior courts are filled by gubernatorial appointment until next general election.
North Dakota	Supreme and district court judges are subject to impeachment for habitual intemperance, crimes, corrupt conduct, malfeasance or misdemeanor in office. Governor may remove county judges after hearing. All judges are subject to recall election. On recommendation of Commission on Judicial Qualifications or on its own motion, Supreme Court may suspend a judge without salary when judge pleads guilty or no contest or is found guilty of a crime punishable as a felony under state or federal law or any other crime involving moral turpitude under that law. If conviction is reversed, suspension terminates and judge is paid salary for period of suspension. If conviction becomes final, judge is removed by Supreme Court. Upon recommendation of Commission on Judicial Qualifications, Supreme Court may censure or remove a judge for willful misconduct, willful failure to perform duties, willful violation of the code of judicial conduct or habitual intemperance. The Court may also retire a judge for disability that seriously interferes with the performance of duties and is (or is likely to become) permanent.	Vacancies on Supreme and district courts are filled by gubernatorial appointment from nominees submitted by Judicial Nominating Committee until next general election, unless governor calls for a special election to fill vacancy for remainder of term. Vacancies on county courts are filled by appointment by board of county commissioners from names submitted by nominating commission.
Ohio	Judges are subject to impeachment. Judges may be removed by concurrent resolution of 2/3 members of both houses of legislature or removed for cause upon filing of a petition signed by 15% of electors in preceding gubernatorial election. The Board of Commissioners on Grievances and Discipline of the Judiciary may disqualify a judge from office when judge has been indicted for a crime punishable as felony under state or federal law. Board may also remove or suspend a judge for willful and persistent failure to perform duties, habitual intemperance, conduct prejudicial to the administration of justice or which would bring the office into disrepute, or suspension from practice of law, or retire a judge for physical or mental disability that prevents discharge of duties. Judge may appeal action to Supreme Court.	Vacancies are filled by gubernatorial appointment until next general election when successor is elected to fill unexpired term. If unexpired term ends within one year following such election, appointment is made for unexpired term.

JUDICIARY

METHODS FOR REMOVAL OF JUDGES—Continued

State or other jurisdiction	How removed	Vacancies: how filled
Oklahoma	Judges are subject to impeachment for willful neglect of duty, corruption in office, habitual intemperance, incompetency or any offense involving moral turpitude. Upon recommendation of Council on Judicial Complaints, chief justice of Supreme Court may bring charges against any judge in the Court on the Judiciary. Court on the Judiciary may order removal of judge for gross neglect of duty, corruption in office, habitual intemperance, an offense involving moral turpitude, gross partiality in office, oppression in office, or any other ground specified by law. Judge may also be retired (with or without salary) for mental or physical disability that prevents performance of duties, or for incompetence to perform duties.	Vacancies on Supreme Court and Court of Criminal Appeals are filled as in initial selection. Vacancies on court of appeals and district courts are filled by gubernatorial appointment from nominees submitted by Judicial Nominating Commission. For court of appeals vacancies, judge is elected to fill unexpired term at next general election.
Oregon	On recommendation of Commission on Judicial Fitness, Supreme Court may remove a judge for conviction of a felony or crime involving moral turpitude, willful misconduct in office, willful or persistent failure to perform judicial duties, habitual intemperance, illegal use of narcotic drugs, willful violation of rules of conduct prescribed by Supreme Court or general incompetence. A judge may also be retired for mental or physical disability after certification by Commission. Judge may appeal action to Supreme Court.	Vacancies on Supreme Court, court of appeals and circuit courts are filled by gubernatorial appointment, until next general election when judge is selected to fill unexpired term.
Pennsylvania	All judges are subject to impeachment for misdemeanor in office. Upon recommendation of Judicial Inquiry and Review Board, a judge may be suspended, removed or otherwise disciplined by Supreme Court for specific forms of misconduct, neglect of duty or disability.	By gubernatorial appointment (with advice and consent of senate), from names submitted by appropriate nominating commission. Appointee serves until next election if the election is more than 10 months after vacancy occurred.
Rhode Island	All judges are subject to impeachment. The Supreme Court on its own motion may suspend a judge who pleaded guilty or no contest or was found guilty of a crime punishable as felony under state or federal law or any other crime involving moral turpitude. Upon recommendation of the Commission on Judicial Tenure and Discipline, the Supreme Court may censure, suspend, reprimand or remove from office a judge guilty of a serious violation of the canons of judicial ethics or for willful or persistent failure to perform duties, a disabling addiction to alcohol, drugs or narcotics, or conduct that brings the office into disrepute. The Supreme Court may also retire a judge for physical or mental disability that seriously interferes with performance of duties and is (or is likely to become) permanent. Whenever the Commission recommends removal of a Supreme Court justice, the Supreme Court transmits the findings to the speaker of the house of representatives, recommending the initiation of proceedings for the removal of the justice by resolution of the legislature.	Vacancies on Supreme Court are filled by the two houses of the legislature in grand committee until the next election. In case of a judge's temporary inability, governor may appoint a person to fill vacancy. Vacancies on superior, family and district courts are filled by gubernatorial appointment (with advice and consent of senate).
South Carolina	Judges are subject to removal by impeachment or by governor on address of 2/3 of each house of legislature. Supreme Court may retire judges for mental and/or physical disability. Judicial Standards Commission enforces code of judicial conduct.	Vacancies are filled as in initial selection for remainder of unexpired term; if remainder is less than one year, vacancy is filled by gubernatorial appointment. Vacancies on probate courts are filled by gubernatorial appointment until next general election.
South Dakota	Supreme Court justices and circuit court judges are subject to removal by impeachment. Upon recommendation of Judicial Qualifications Commission, Supreme Court may remove a judge from office.	Vacancies on Supreme and circuit courts are filled by gubernatorial appointment from names submitted by Judicial Qualifications Commission for balance of unexpired term.
Tennessee	Judges are subject to impeachment for misfeasance or malfeasance in office. Upon recommendation of the Court on the Judiciary, the legislature (by concurrent resolution) may remove a judge for willful misconduct in office or physical or mental disability.	Vacancies on Supreme, circuit, criminal and chancery courts are filled by gubernatorial appointment until next biennial election held more than 30 days after vacancy occurred. At election, successor is chosen as in initial selection. Vacancies on court of appeals and court of criminal appeals are filled as in initial selection.

JUDICIARY

METHODS FOR REMOVAL OF JUDGES—Continued

State or other jurisdiction	How removed	Vacancies: how filled
Texas	Supreme Court, court of appeals and district court judges are subject to removal by impeachment or by joint address of both houses. Supreme Court may remove district judges from office. District judges may remove county judges and justices of the peace. Upon charges filed by the State Commission on Judicial Conduct, the Supreme Court may remove a judge for willful or persistent violation of the code of judicial conduct, and willful or persistent conduct that is clearly inconsistent with the proper performance of duties, or casts public discredit upon the judiciary or administration of justice. The Court may also retire a judge for disability.	Vacancies on appellate and district courts are filled by gubernatorial appointment until next general election, at which time a successor is chosen. Vacancies on county courts are filled by appointment by county commissioner's court until next election when successor is chosen. Vacancies on municipal courts are filled by governing body of municipality for remainder of unexpired term.
Utah	All judges, except justices of the peace, are subject to impeachment. Following investigations and hearings, the Judicial Conduct Commission may order the reprimand, censure, suspension, removal, or involuntary retirement of any judge for willful misconduct, final conviction of a crime punishable as a felony under state or federal law, willful or persistent failure to perform judicial duties, disability that seriously interferes with performance, or conduct prejudicial to the administration of justice that bring the judicial office into disrepute. Prior to implementation, the Supreme Court reviews the order. Lay justices of the peace may be removed for willful failure to participate in judicial education program.	Vacancies on Supreme, district and circuit courts are filled by gubernatorial appointment from candidates submitted by appropriate nominating commission.
Vermont	All judges are subject to impeachment. Supreme Court may discipline, impose sanctions on, or suspend from duties any judge in the state.	Vacancies on Supreme, superior and district courts are filled as in initial selection if senate is in session. Otherwise, by gubernatorial appointment from nominees submitted by judicial nominating board.
Virginia	All judges are subject to impeachment. Upon certification of charges against judge by Judicial Inquiry and Review Commission, Supreme Court may remove a judge.	Vacancies are filled as in initial selection if General Assembly is in session. Otherwise, by gubernatorial appointment, with appointee serving until 30 days after commencement of next legislative session.
Washington	A judge of any court of record is subject to impeachment. After notice, hearing and recommendation of Judicial Qualifications Commission, Supreme Court may censure, suspend or remove a judge for violating a rule of judicial conduct. The Supreme Court may also retire a judge for disability that seriously interferes with the performance of duties and is (or is likely to become) permanent.	Vacancies on appellate and general trial courts are filled by gubernatorial appointment until next general election when successor is elected to fill remainder of term.
West Virginia	Judges are subject to impeachment for maladministration, corruption, incompetency, gross immorality, neglect of duty or any crime or misdemeanor. The Supreme Court of Appeals may censure or suspend a judge for any violation of the judicial code of ethics or retire a judge who is incapable of performing duties because of advancing age, disease or physical or mental infirmity.	Vacancies on appellate and general trial courts are filled by gubernatorial appointment. If unexpired term is less than two years (or such additional period not exceeding three years), appointee serves for remainder of term. If unexpired term is more than three years, appointee serves until next general election, at which time successor is chosen to fill remainder of term.
Wisconsin	All judges are subject to impeachment. Supreme Court, court of appeals and circuit court judges are subject to removal by address of both houses of legislature with 2/3 of members concurring, and by recall election. As judges of courts of record must be licensed to practice law in state, removal of judge may also be by disbarment. Upon petition of Judicial Commission or on its own motion, Supreme Court may declare a judgeship vacant for judge's misconduct or disability. In case of disability, judge receives salary and benefits for balance of term or until temporary vacancy terminates, whichever comes first.	Vacancies on Supreme Court, court of appeals and circuit courts are filled by gubernatorial appointment from nominees submitted by nominating commission.
Wyoming	All judges, except justices of peace, are subject to impeachment. Upon recommendation of Judicial Supervisory Commission, the Supreme Court may retire or remove a judge. After a hearing before a panel of three district judges, the Supreme Court may remove justices of the peace.	Vacancies are filled as in initial selection. Vacancies on justice of the peace courts are filled by appointment by county commissioners until next general election.

JUDICIARY

METHODS FOR REMOVAL OF JUDGES—Continued

State or other jurisdiction	How removed	Vacancies: how filled
Dist. of Columbia	Commission on Judicial Disabilities and Tenure may remove a judge upon conviction of a felony (including a federal crime), for willful misconduct in office, willful and persistent failure to perform judicial duties or for other conduct prejudicial to the administration of justice which brings the office into disrepute.	Vacancies are filled as in initial selection, unless president of the United States fails to nominate candidate within 60 days of receipt of list of nominees from D.C. Judicial Nominating Commission; then Commission nominates and appoints, wth advice and consent of U.S. Senate.
American Samoa	U.S. Secretary of the Interior may remove chief and associate justices for cause. Upon recommendation of governor, chief justice may remove associate judges for cause.	Vacancies are filled as in initial selection.
Guam	On recommendation of Judicial Qualifications Commission, a special court of three judges may remove a judge for misconduct or incapacity.	By gubernatorial appointment.
No. Mariana Islands	Judges are subject to impeachment for treason, commission of a felony, corruption or neglect of duty. Upon recommendation of an advisory commission on the judiciary, the governor may remove, suspend or otherwise sanction a judge for illegal or improper conduct.	By gubernatorial appointment.
Puerto Rico	Supreme Court justices are subject to impeachment for treason, bribery, other felonies and misdemeanors involving moral turpitude. Supreme Court may remove other judges for cause (as provided by judiciary act) after a hearing on charges brought by order of chief justice, who disqualifies self from final proceedings.	Vacancies are filled as in initial selection.

Source: American Judicature Society (Spring, 1988), (used with permission).

JUDICIARY

Table 4.6
COMPENSATION OF JUDGES OF APPELLATE COURTS AND GENERAL TRIAL COURTS

State or other jurisdiction	Appellate courts				General trial courts	Salary
	Court of last resort	Salary	Intermediate appellate court	Salary		
Alabama	Supreme Court	$ 82,880 (a)	Court of Criminal Appeals	$ 81,880 (b)	Circuit courts	$56,760 (c)
			Court of Civil Appeals	81,880 (b)		
Alaska	Supreme Court	85,728 (d)	Court of Appeals	79,992	Superior courts	77,304 (d)
Arizona	Supreme Court	84,000 (a)	Court of Appeals	82,000	Superior courts	80,000
Arkansas	Supreme Court	72,716 (a,q)	Court of Appeals	70,240 (b,q)	Chancery courts	67,761 (q)
					Circuit courts	67,761 (q)
California	Supreme Court	115,161 (a)	Courts of Appeal	(e)	Superior courts	94,344
Colorado	Supreme Court	72,000 (a)	Court of Appeals	67,500 (b)	District Court	63,000
Connecticut	Supreme Court	92,045 (a,i,q)	Appellate Court	85,587 (b,i,q)	Superior courts	81,760 (i,q)
Delaware	Supreme Court	95,200 (a)	. . .	. . .	Superior courts	90,500 (b)
Florida	Supreme Court	97,518	District Court of Appeals	91,782	Circuit courts	86,046
Georgia	Supreme Court	90,514	Court of Appeals	89,931	Superior courts	68,838 (c)
Hawaii	Supreme Court	78,500 (a)	Intermediate Court	73,500 (b)	Circuit courts	69,500
Idaho	Supreme Court	65,874 (a)	Court of Appeals	64,874	District courts	61,740
Illinois	Supreme Court	93,266	Appellate Court	87,780	Circuit courts	75,113 (b)
Indiana	Supreme Court	69,300 (a,f)	Court of Appeals	64,050 (b,f)	Circuit courts	58,800 (c)
					Superior courts	58,800 (c)
Iowa	Supreme Court	78,900 (a)	Court of Appeals	75,800 (b)	District courts	72,000 (b)
Kansas	Supreme Court	75,052 (a)	Court of Appeals	72,373 (b)	District courts	(g)
Kentucky	Supreme Court	70,293 (a)	Court of Appeals	67,424 (b)	Circuit courts	64,555
Louisiana	Supreme Court	76,166	Court of Appeals	72,967	District courts	69,769
Maine	Supreme Judicial Court	80,392 (a)	. . .	. . .	Superior Court	76,024 (b)
Maryland	Court of Appeals	90,400 (a)	Court of Special Appeals	87,200 (b)	Circuit courts	85,500
Massachusetts	Supreme Judicial Court	90,450 (a)	Appeals Court	83,708 (b)	Trial Court (h)	80,360 (b)
Michigan	Supreme Court	106,610	Court of Appeals	102,346	Circuit courts	58,633 (c)
					Recorder's Court (Detroit)	98,081
Minnesota	Supreme Court	84,011 (a)	Court of Appeals	77,502 (b)	District courts	74,309
Mississippi	Supreme Court	75,800 (a)	. . .	. . .	Chancery courts	66,200
					Circuit courts	66,200
Missouri	Supreme Court	85,602 (a)	Court of Appeals	79,725	Circuit courts	65,031 (b,l)
					Municipal division of circuit courts	up to $69,000
Montana	Supreme Court	56,452 (a,q)	. . .	. . .	District courts	55,178 (q)
Nebraska	Supreme Court	70,023 (q)	. . .	. . .	District courts	64,772 (q)
Nevada	Supreme Court	73,500	. . .	. . .	District courts	67,000
New Hampshire	Supreme Court	84,000 (a)	. . .	. . .	Superior Court	78,750 (b)
New Jersey	Supreme Court	93,000 (a)	Appellate division of Superior Court	90,000	Superior Court	85,000 (m)
New Mexico	Supreme Court	68,595 (a,q)	Court of Appeals	65,150 (b,q)	District courts	61,740 (q)
New York	Court of Appeals	115,000 (a)	Appellate divisions of Supreme Court	102,500 (n)	Supreme Court	95,000
North Carolina	Supreme Court	84,456 (a,j)	Court of Appeals	79,968 (b,j)	Superior Court	70,992 (b,j)
North Dakota	Supreme Court	68,342 (a)	. . .	. . .	District courts	62,969 (b)
Ohio	Supreme Court	91,750 (a)	Court of Appeals	85,450	Courts of common pleas	65,900 (c)
Oklahoma	Supreme Court	71,806 (a)	Court of Appeals	67,344	District Court	(o)
Oregon	Supreme Court	76,400 (a,q)	Court of Appeals	74,600 (b,q)	Circuit courts	69,600 (q)
			Tax Court	71,800 (q)	District Court	69,600 (q)
Pennsylvania	Supreme Court	91,500 (a)	Superior Court	89,500 (b)	Courts of common pleas	80,000 (b)
			Commonwealth Court	89,500 (b)		
Rhode Island	Supreme Court	90,618 (a,k)	. . .	. . .	Superior Court	81,587 (b,k)
South Carolina	Supreme Court	87,238 (a)	Court of Appeals	82,877 (b)	Circuit Court	82,877
South Dakota	Supreme Court	61,618 (a)	. . .	. . .	Circuit courts	57,546 (b)
Tennessee	Supreme Court	85,500 (r)	Court of Appeals	81,500 (r)	Chancery courts	78,000 (r)
			Court of Criminal Appeals	81,500 (r)	Circuit courts	78,000 (r)
					Criminal courts	78,000 (r)
Texas	Supreme Court	89,250 (a)	Court of Appeals	80,325 (b,c)	District courts	76,309 (c)
Utah	Supreme Court	75,000 (a)	Court of Appeals	71,250 (b)	District courts	67,500
Vermont	Supreme Court	68,055 (a)	. . .	. . .	Superior courts	64,645 (b)
					District courts	64,645 (b)
Virginia	Supreme Court	94,907 (a)	Court of Appeals	90,162 (b)	Circuit courts	88,106
Washington	Supreme Court	89,300 (s)	Court of Appeals	84,900 (s)	Superior courts	80,500 (s)
					District Court	76,600 (s)
West Virginia	Supreme Court of Appeals	72,000	. . .	. . .	Circuit courts	65,000
Wisconsin	Supreme Court	82,623 (a)	Court of Appeals	77,871	Circuit courts	73,003
Wyoming	Supreme Court	66,500	. . .	. . .	Distict courts	63,500
Dist. of Columbia	Court of Appeals	102,500 (a)	. . .	. . .	Superior Court	96,600
American Samoa	High Court	74,303	. . .	. . .	(p)	(p)
Guam	. . .	. . .	. . .	. . .	Superior Court	60,000 (b)
Puerto Rico	Supreme Court	60,000 (a)	. . .	. . .	Superior Court	48,000
					District Court	42,000
U.S. Virgin Islands	. . .	. . .	. . .	. . .	Territorial Court	62,000 (b)

JUDICIARY

COMPENSATION OF JUDGES—Continued

Source: National Center for State Courts, Survey of Judicial Salaries.
Note: Compensation is shown according to most recent legislation, even though laws may not yet have taken effect.

(a) These jurisdictions pay the following additional amounts to the chief justice or presiding judge of court of last resort:
Alabama, Utah—$1,000.
Arizona, Indiana, New Jersey, South Dakota—$2,000.
Arkansas—$6,454.
California—$5,603.
Colorado, Missouri, Oklahoma, Pennsylvania—$2,500.
Connecticut—$8,576.
Delaware—$3,500.
Hawaii, Idaho—$1,500.
Iowa—$3,000.
Kansas—$2,080.
Kentucky—$1,435.
Maine—$4,020.
Maryland—$1,550.
Massachusetts—$3,258.
Minnesota—$6,509.
Mississippi—chief justice, $1,200; presiding judge, $600.
Montana—$1,270.
New Hampshire—$2,625.
New Mexico—$1,065.
New York—$5,000.
North Carolina—$1,776.
North Dakota—$1,901.
Ohio—$5,850.
Oregon—$1,800.
Rhode Island—$7,964.
South Carolina—$4,591.
Texas—$2,625.
Vermont—$2,900.
Virginia—$6,275 (plus $6,500 in lieu of travel expenses).
Wisconsin—$9,113.
District of Columbia—$500.
American Samoa—plus nonforeign post differentials where applicable.
Puerto Rico—$2,600.

(b) Additional amounts paid to various judges:
Alabama—presiding judge, $500.
Arkansas—chief judge, $1,238.
Colorado—chief judge, $2,500.
Connecticut—state court administrator who is also a judge of superior court, $4,859; chief judge, $5,283.
Delaware—presiding judge, $3,500.
Hawaii, Kansas—chief judge, $2,000.
Illinois—chief judge, $5,486.
Indiana—chief judge, $2,675.
Iowa—chief judge of court of appeals, $3,000; chief judge of district court, $3,000.
Kentucky—chief judge, $717.
Maine—chief justice, $3,801.
Maryland—chief judge of court of special appeals, $1,600.
Massachusetts—chief justice of appeals court, $3,259; superior court chief justice, $3,348.
Minnesota—chief judge, $3,315.
Missouri—chief judge, $8,816.
New Hampshire—chief judge of superior court, $5,250.
New Mexico—chief judge, $1,090.
New York—presiding judge of appellate division of supreme court, $5,000.
North Carolina—chief judge of court of appeals, $1,788; senior judge of superior court, $2,340.
North Dakota—presiding judge, $1,493.
Oregon—chief judge, $1,800.
Pennsylvania—presiding judges of superior court and commonwealth court, $1,500; president judges of courts of common pleas, additional amounts to $2,500, depending on number of judges and population.
Rhode Island—presiding judge of superior court, $7,564.
South Carolina—chief judge, $3,488.
South Dakota—presiding circuit judge, $2,000.
Texas—chief judge, $525.
Utah, Virginia—chief judge, $1,000.
Vermont—administrative judges of superior and district courts, $3,410.
District of Columbia—chief judge of superior court, $500.
Guam—presiding judge, $2,500.
U.S. Virgin Islands—presiding judge of territorial court, $4,000.

(c) Plus local supplements, if any. In Texas, for court of appeals, supplements to salary $1,000 less than salary for supreme court justice; for district court, supplements to salary $2,000 less than salary of supreme court justice.

(d) Salaries range from $85,728 to $97,728 for supreme court justices and $77,304 to $90,828 for superior court judges, depending on location and cost-of-living differentials.

(e) Level III, $107,964; Level II, $113,612

(f) Plus $3,000 subsistence allowance.

(g) Salary varies according to designation: district judge designated as administrative judge, $65,990; district judge, $65,246; district magistrate judge, $30,806.

(h) Superior court department of the trial court.

(i) Plus 3 percent for 25 or more years, 3/4 of 3 percent for 20-25 years, 1/2 of 3 percent for 15-20 years, and 1/4 of 3 percent for 10-15 years

(j) Plus 4.8 percent after 5 years, 9.6 percent after 10 years, 14.4 percent after 15 years, and 19.2 percent after 20 years

(k) Plus 5 percent after 7 years, 10 percent after 11 years, 15 percent after 15 years, 17.5 percent after 20 years, and 20 percent after 25 years.

(l) State may pay if municipality elects to transfer jurisdiction of municipal ordinance violations to Circuit Court.

(m) Assignment judges recieve $88,000.

(n) Appellate Division of the Supreme Court in the 1st, 2nd, 3rd, and 4th departments, the presiding justice, $107,500 and the associate justice, $102,500. Appellate terms of the Supreme Court, 1st, 2nd, 9th, 10th, 11th, and 12th districts, the presiding justice, $100,000, and the associate justice, $97,500.

(o) District judges, $59,906. Associate district judges paid on basis of population ranges: over 30,000—$56,506; 10,000 to 30,000—$50,272; under 10,000—$47,154.

(p) General trial court responsibilities handled by the chief justice or associate judges of the High Court.

(q) Effective July 1, 1990.
(r) Effective September 1, 1990.
(s) Effective September 3, 1990.

JUDICIARY

Table 4.7
SELECTED DATA ON COURT ADMINISTRATIVE OFFICES

State or other jurisdiction	Title	Established	Appointed by (a)	Salary
Alabama	Administrative Director of Courts (b)	1971	CJ	$ 80,184
Alaska	Administrative Director	1959	CJ (b)	83,728
Arizona	Administrative Director of Courts	1960	SC	80,000
Arkansas	Director, Administrative Office of the Courts	1965	CJ (c)	54,316
California	Administrative Director of the Courts	1960	JC	107,964
Colorado	State Court Administrator	1959	SC	67,500
Connecticut	Chief Court Administrator (d)	1965	CJ	96,136 (h)
Delaware	Director, Administrative Office of the Courts	1971	CJ	64,900
Florida	State Courts Administrator	1972	SC	72,800
Georgia	Director, Administrative Office of the Courts	1973	JC	67,138
Hawaii	Administrative Director of the Courts	1959	CJ (b)	68,400
Idaho	Administrative Director of the Courts	1967	SC	66,854
Illinois	Administrative Director of the Courts	1959	SC	87,780
Indiana	Executive Director, Division of State Court Administration	1975	SC	61,800
Iowa	Court Administrator	1971	SC	52,200 to 75,700
Kansas	Judicial Administrator	1965	CJ	63,746
Kentucky	Administrative Director of the Courts	1976	CJ	64,560
Louisiana	Judicial Administrator	1954	SC	69,769
Maine	Court Administrator	1975	CJ	65,291
Maryland	State Court Administrator (b)	1955	CJ	78,000
Massachusetts	Administrator, Supreme Judicial Court (b)	1978	SC	86,967
Michigan	State Court Administrator	1952	SC	93,605
Minnesota	State Court Administrator	1963	SC	not to exceed 74,309
Mississippi	Court Administrator	1974	SC	61,200
Missouri	State Courts Administrator	1970	SC	65,738
Montana	State Court Administrator	1975	SC	38,216
Nebraska	State Court Administrator	1972	CJ	56,714
Nevada	Director, Office of Court Administration	1971	SC	57,800
New Hampshire	Director of Administrative Services	1980	SC	67,765
New Jersey	Administrative Director of the Courts	1948	CJ	90,000
New Mexico	Director, Administrative Office of the Courts	1959	SC	58,456
New York	Chief Administrator of the Courts (e)	1978	CJ (f)	107,500
North Carolina	Director, Administrative Office of the Courts	1965	CJ	73,332 (h)
North Dakota	Court Administrator (g)	1971	CJ	57,371
Ohio	Administrative Director of the Courts	1955	SC	73,736
Oklahoma	Administrative Director of the Courts	1967	SC	67,344
Oregon	Court Administrator	1971	CJ	67,600
Pennsylvania	Court Administrator	1968	SC	79,000
Rhode Island	State Court Administrator	1969	CJ	72,785 (h)
South Carolina	Director of Court Administration	1973	CJ	68,372
South Dakota	State Court Administrator	1974	SC	38,729 to 58,115
Tennessee	Executive Secretary of the Supreme Court	1963	SC	63,125
Texas	Administrative Director of the Courts (i)	1977	SC	77,490
Utah	Court Administrator	1973	SC	67,500
Vermont	Court Administrator (j)	1967	SC	64,645
Virginia	Executive Secretary to the Supreme Court	1952	SC	88,106
Washington	Administrator for the Courts	1957	SC (k)	78,200
West Virginia	Administrative Director of the Supreme Court of Appeals	1975	SC	51,000
Wisconsin	Director of State Courts	1978	SC	77,871
Wyoming	Court Coordinator	1974	SC	42,241
Dist. of Columbia	Executive Officer, Courts of D.C.	1971	(l)	89,500
American Samoa	Court Administrator	1977	CJ (m)	27,092
Guam	Administrative Director of Superior Court	N.A.	CJ (m,n)	43,000
Puerto Rico	Administrative Director of the Court	1952	CJ (m)	50,000
U.S. Virgin Islands	Court/Administraive Clerk	N.A.	(m)	46,600

Source: Salary information was taken from *Survey of Judicial Salaries,* published by National Center for State Courts.
  Key:
  SC—State court of last resort.
  CJ—Chief justice or chief judge of court of last resort.
  JC—Judicial council.
  (a) Term of office for all court administrators is at pleasure of appointing authority.
  (b) With approval of Supreme Court.
  (c) With approval of Judicial Council.
  (d) Administrator is an associate judge of the Supreme Court.
  (e) If incumbent is a judge, the title is Chief Administrative Judge of the Courts.
  (f) With advice and consent of Administrative Board of the Courts.
  (g) Serves as executive secretary to Judicial Council.
  (h) Base pay supplemented by increments for length of service.
  (i) Serves as executive director of Judicial council.
  (j) Also clerk of the Supreme Court.
  (k) Appointed from list of five submitted by governor.
  (l) Joint Committee on Judicial Administration.
  (m) From 1988-89 edition of *The Book of the States.*
  (n) Presiding judge of Superior Court (general trial court).

CHAPTER FIVE

STATE ELECTIONS

ELECTION LEGISLATION

by Richard G. Smolka

Much of the legislation passed in the last two years has been intended to reverse the long term trend of declining voter participation in national elections and in most state elections. During this time states continued a quarter-century trend to make it easier to register and to vote and to have the vote counted. Their efforts included procedures to aid not only able-bodied citizens but also the elderly and those with physical handicaps.

Laws were passed increasing the ways in which citizens could register to vote, and to make it possible for administrators to make voting more convenient. Some laws made it easier to obtain an absentee ballot and to return the ballot in time to be counted, especially for overseas citizens and military personnel.

Although few changes in election technology occurred during the past two years, lawmakers were more concerned than in the past about the impact of technology on the voter and on the counting of the ballots. Legislative committees looked into the impact of ballot format and design, and the security and accuracy of computer vote-counting methods.

In addition, some laws have attempted to address growing public dissatisfaction with the electoral system. Legislators have responded to those who believe campaigns are too expensive or who think candidates may become indebted to large contributors. In the past two years, campaign finance laws in general and increased campaign spending in particular have occupied lawmakers attention.

Voter Registration

The liberalization of laws relating to voter registration continued unabated during the past two years. Although no dramatic changes were made, several states adopted laws making marginal changes and many used administrative rules and regulations to ease voter registration.

Most interest was shown in the "motor-voter" concept of voter registration. With "motor-voter," any person applying for a driver's license, or seeking to renew a driver's license, is automatically offered a chance to register to vote.

The "motor-voter" registration idea, first used in Michigan in 1976, was based on the fact that far more people are licensed to drive than are registered to vote. By combining the procedures, states attempted to increase voter registration to include all eligible voters who also had driver's licenses.

By early 1990, six states, Arizona, Colorado, Michigan, Minnesota, Nevada, and Washington, as well as the District of Columbia offered an opportunity to register to vote with the driver's license application or renewal. The registration opportunity was either through a combined form used for both purposes or by a procedural requirement to ask all driver's license applicants whether they wished to register to vote.

Several other states, including Iowa, North Carolina, Ohio and Vermont, also offered the opportunity to vote through motor vehicle agencies but the procedure was passive. The voter registration form was available but the driver had to pick up the form or request it from a motor vehicle agency employee. The motor vehicle agency would accept the completed forms for forwarding to the appropri-

---

Richard G. Smolka is Professor of Government at The American University in Washington, D.C. and Editor of Election Administration Reports.

ate election official but was not required to offer the applicant assistance in completing the form.

In both forms, the "motor-voter" concept has been accepted in the states in which it is used. No state that introduced the "motor-voter" form of voter registration has considered repealing it. "Motor-voter" became the centerpiece of federal voter registration legislation considered by the 101st Congress.

In many states, opportunities to register were increased through voter outreach programs designed to register those who for lack of information or opportunity had failed to register. These methods included public service advertising, deputy registrars in busy locations — especially in areas where registration had been traditionally lower than average — and even the use of a drive-in window in Sonoma County, Calif. to pick-up and return voter registration forms.

Minnesota included preprinted postcard voter registration forms in the income tax booklet and forms mailed to each state taxpayer. The state reported more than 100,000 registration forms were received from the tax year 1988 booklets.

Handicapped Access to the Polls

The states continued to enact legislation and administrative regulations to comply with the federal Voting Accessibility for the Elderly and Handicapped Act. The law, in effect for the first time during the 1986 election, requires states to make all polling places in federal elections accessible to the handicapped unless the chief election officer of a state determines that no alternative is available. The law also requires the Federal Election Commission (FEC) to report to Congress on state compliance with the law after each federal election.

The 1989 FEC report to Congress noted substantial improvement in the states between the 1986 and 1988 elections. Of polling places evaluated, 79 percent were considered accessible, an increase of six percentage points over 1986. Progress was deemed greater because most states imposed more stringent accessibility standards than were imposed in the initial year of the law.

Election Technology

States continued to draft laws to meet requirements of new technology in elections including those related to voter registration and vote counting methods. Some new laws or interpretations of existing election statutes have permitted the use of electronic signatures that previously required an original signature.

The most common changes are occurring as a result of signature digitization. New laws allow the original signature of the voter to be optically scanned and stored electronically. The signature image is then used to verify petition signatures, and in some instances, to verify identification of voters. Only in cases of doubt is the original signature needed. New York is currently drafting regulations prescribing procedures to verify voter signatures at the polls from electronically reproduced original signatures, thereby eliminating the need for the heavy binders containing original voter registration cards at the polls.

The states most concerned with accuracy and integrity in vote counting have also passed legislation in anticipation of and to comply with the Federal Election Commission's Voluntary Voting Systems Standards. The standards, adopted in February 1990, were developed over five-years in consultation with state and local election officials, vendors, legislators, and computer experts interested in the election process. The goal was to establish performance and procedural standards for punchcard, marksense, and direct electronic recording voting systems.

The standards, which include hardware and software requirements, will be supplemented by management guidelines to offer alternative approaches for their implementation and enforcement.

The FEC standards were adopted in part, even before they were finalized, by seven states, California, Florida, Georgia, Minnesota, New Mexico, New York and Washington. Other states are expected to adopt these or other voting system standards in the near future.

Florida law was changed to give the state greater authority over voting format and equipment used after some politically inexplicable results in the 1988 election for the U.S. Senate. The ratio of votes cast for president compared to the total votes cast for U.S. Senator in various counties created a bizarre pattern. In 34 of Florida's 67 counties, more votes were cast for presidential candidates than for Senate candidates, but the dropoff in eight of these counties exceeded 10 percent and ranged up to 24.5 percent in Hillsborough County. At the same time, in the other 33 counties, the number of votes cast for the same U.S. Senate candidates was as much as 17 percent more than the number of votes cast for the presidential candidates. In nine counties, more than eight percent more votes were cast in the U.S. Senate race than for presidential candidates. The pattern appears to be unprecedented in these counties, in Florida voting history and perhaps in the nation.

Geography, media market, voting behavior, or candidate or party political bases appeared to have no relationship to the county turnout variations. The only significant differences appeared to be the type of ballot formats and the voting systems used. The state wants to increase uniformity in the ballot system to avoid similar results in the future. Although the final margin was only 33,000 votes (less than .8%) out of a total of more than 4.1 million voters who went to the polls, no recount was requested.

Oklahoma passed a law requiring a centralized computerized and automated election management system. The state is purchasing computer hardware and software to implement a complete and uniform statewide voter registration and election system that will be operational by 1992. Alabama mandated a state voter file maintenance system and uniform procedures for maintaining the registry.

In unusual but authorized activities, the town of Calais, Vermont in November 1989, transmitted two absentee ballots via facsimile to California because there would have been insufficient time to mail ballots and have them returned by the deadline. Detroit accepted a copy of a candidate's signature on a required identification affidavit that was transmitted by facsimile from California. Burton, Michigan used a portable computer to record voter activity at the polls in a school district election. The voting activity record was later loaded into the city's mainframe computer, thus updating all records for voting history.

Absentee Voting

Experiences with absentee voting laws have produced different types of legislation in the states. Those states with more restrictive laws are passing legislation to liberalize the absentee voting procedure and to extend the deadlines for receipt of ballots not mailed to the voters in time to be returned. Others, where very liberal absentee voter laws exist, have considered more restrictive procedures to guard against vote fraud.

Absentee ballots have become a political weapon in states where any voter, regardless of whether they will be absent from the community on election day, may request an absentee ballot. Candidates and political parties have organized to make full use of these laws to encourage their supporters to vote by absentee ballot as soon as legally possible. Practice in California has created situations in local elections where up to 50 percent of all votes have been cast by absentee ballot.

A similar situation appears to be developing in Texas, which has similar laws. In the 1990 primary election, more than 15 percent of all votes cast in both political party primary elections were by absentee ballot. Most of these were cast in-person in advance of the election rather than by mail. Some counties made in-person absentee voting exceptionally easy to do. For example, Bexar County, (San Antonio) Texas established 27 voting substations throughout the county where any registered voter in the county could vote in person. Voters could obtain the absentee ballot appropriate to their residence address at any one of the substations. The Bexar County in-person advance absentee vote in both political parties totalled 41,290 — 29 percent of all votes cast in the county. By contrast, absentee ballots returned through the mail accounted for only one percent of the total vote.

Clearly, absentee voting has a new meaning here, referring to the procedures used, not the physical location of the voter.

Campaign Finance Regulation

In recent years, criticism over the costs of political campaigns and the relationships between contributors and candidates have grown increasingly strident. Some public figures have announced their unwillingness to be a candidate because of fundraising pressures. During 1988-89, most state legislatures actively considered and many passed campaign finance reform bills limiting campaign spending, increasing disclosure requirements, initiating or increasing the amount of public funding of elections, or other options. Since 1973, 26 states have offered some type of public funding of elections, and 23 states retain active programs.

The least controversial legislation usually pertains to campaign disclosure requirements. The trend has been consistently to require more reports at more frequent intervals from more candidates or contributors. At least 12 states enacted enhanced campaign disclosure laws during 1988-89.

The number and type of organizations prohibited from making political contributions to certain offices was increased in several states. In Georgia, candidates for insurance commissioner are prohibited from receiving contributions from insurance companies and related industries and PACs. In Indiana, those who have made contributions to statewide candidates within a three-year period may not become vendors for the state lottery commission.

State agencies administering campaign finance laws were given increased authority to levy fines and penalties against those who failed to comply.

New Hampshire attempted to put a cap on campaign spending by providing easy ballot access to candidates who voluntarily agree to comply with prescribed limits for various federal, state and local offices. Those who do not must pay greatly increased filing fees and meet substantial petition requirements as well. The Federal Election Commission issued an advisory opinion[1] that the law cannot be applied to candidates for the U.S. Senate and House of Representatives. New Hampshire, however, announced its intention to enforce the law in 1990 and to defend it as necessary in the courts.

The states that provide public funding for campaigns in exchange for limits on campaign spending determine the amount available in one of two ways. Public funding may be provided by general appropriations, or the amount may be determined by provisions that require taxpayers to designate on their income tax forms, a small amount — one or two dollars — for this purpose. In some states, the system is simply a check-off, a designation at no cost to the taxpayer. In other states, the taxpayer who makes such a designation adds to his tax liability.

In 1988, North Carolina adopted a tax add-on to help fund campaigns for governor and other state offices. The same year, Arizona passed a law providing for funding for political parties through an optional tax add-on.

New York City paid a total of $4,498,348 in matching funds to candidates in the 1989 elections. Under New York City's new campaign finance law, candidates for mayor, city council president, comptroller, borough president, and city council become eligible to receive matching funds when they agree to accept contribution and spending limits for their campaigns. Forty-eight candidates received at least some matching funds. Mayoral candidate David Dinkins who won the election received matching funds of $461,739 for the primary election and $524,410 for the general election. His major opponent, Rudolph W. Giuliani, received $756,188 during the primary and $464,766 during the general election.

Two states with public financing of state elections made significant changes in the law in 1989.[2] New Jersey, which introduced the first public financing of elections law in the states in 1974, effective for the 1977 gubernatorial election, increased the amount candidates are required to raise from private sources to qualify for public funding from $50,000 to $150,000.

Once the threshold is met, the candidates receive two-for-one matching funds from the state for all funds except the first $50,000 privately raised. The state will contribute a maximum of $1,350,000 to each candidate's primary election campaign. For general elections, the threshold is again $150,000. Candidates meeting the threshold qualify for two-to-one matching funds up to a total of $3.3 million in public funds.

New Jersey raised candidate expenditure limits from $1.1 million to $2.2 million for the primary election and to $5 million for the general election. The law also raised contribution limits from $800 to $1,500 for both the primary and general elections.

Five candidates for governor qualified for the maximum public funding in the primary election. Three others received some public funding for their campaigns.

Michigan also amended its campaign finance law to raise the expenditure limit from $1 million to $1.5 million each for the primary and general election. For primary elections, candidates will receive up to 66 percent of the limit, and general election candidates will receive 75 percent of the limit.

Michigan gubernatorial candidates are required to raise $75,000 (five percent) of the limit, in private contributions of $100 or less to become eligible for public funding.

The new Michigan law also includes a provision to reduce the influence of a candidate's personal wealth in a campaign. If a candidate who is not receiving public funds spends more than $340,000 of family money, an opponent who does qualify for public funds would be permitted to exceed the $1.5 million spending limit by raising additional unmatched funds from private sources.

The Michigan law also allows minor parties and independent candidates to receive public funds on a one-to-one matching basis. Matching funds may not exceed 50 percent of the expenditure limit.

The Future

Whether any or all of these laws will have an effect on voter turnout and voter attitudes toward the electoral system remains uncertain. A recent Library of Congress study[3] found it impossible to come to any conclusion about whether "motor-voter" or mail registration increased voter registration or voter turnout. The author considered the evidence difficult to evaluate because of variations in state voter registration, purge procedures, and reporting practices, as well as how the law was administered in the states. The basic data, he concluded, was of such mixed and unknown quality that no valid conclusions could be drawn.

The Congress is once again considering a major voter registration bill that will mandate the states to register voters by mail, by "motor-voter," through various state and local government agencies dealing with the public, and to report on registration practices and results to Congress. If Congress plays an active role in this area, heretofore the exclusive province of the states, new laws, periodic amendments to federal election laws, and federal regulations can be expected. States would be required to ignore their own constitutional provisions, state laws, and administrative practices if they conflicted with federal election law or regulation of federal elections.

Concern for this possibility has led some state party officials and political leaders to consider a separation of federal and state elections. If the states scheduled all state and local elections completely independent of federal elections, and prohibited any combination of federal and state or local elections, election laws passed by Congress would be restricted in their impact to federal elections only. State and local elections, perhaps conducted in odd-numbered years, would be insulated from unforseen and unintended consequences of future federal legislation or regulation designed primarily for federal elections.

Notes

1. Federal Election Commission, A.O. 1989-25, November 30, 1989.

2. Herbert E. Alexander. "Public Financing of State Elections," a paper presented to the State of the States Symposium, Eagleton Institute of Politics, Rutgers University, December 14-15, 1989.

3. Royce Crocker. "Voter Registration and Turnout in States with Mail and Motor Voter Registration Systems." Congressional Research Service, Library of Congress, February 23, 1990.

Selected References

Alexander, Herbert E., "Public Financing of State Elections," a paper presented to the State of the States Symposium, Eagleton Institute of Politics, Rutgers University, December 14-15, 1989. Available through Citizens' Research Foundation, University of Southern California.

_____. ed. *Comparative Political Finance in the 1980s.* Cambridge: Cambridge University Press, 1989.

_____. *Financing the 1988 Election*, Los Angeles: Citizens' Research Foundation, (forthcoming).

Committee for the Study of the American Electorate, "Creating the Opportunity, How Changes in Registration and Voting Law Can Enhance Voter Participation" Washington, D.C., 1987.

Crocker, Royce. "Voter Registration and Turnout in States with Mail and Motor Voter Registration Systems," Congressional Research Service, Library of Congress, February 23, 1990.

Darcy, R. and Ian McAllister, Ballot Position Effects, *Electoral Studies*, Volume 9, No. 1, March, 1990

Donsanto, Craig C. *Federal Prosecution of Election Offenses*, 5th ed. Washington, D.C. U. S. Department of Justice, May, 1988.

Eshleman, Kenneth L. *Where Should Students Vote?*, Lanham, Md.: University Press of America, 1989.

Federal Election Commission, *Performance and Test Standards for Punchcard, Marksense, and Direct Electronic Voting Systems*, Washington, D.C., 1990.

Federal Election Commission, *Polling Place Accessibility in the 1988 General Election*, Washington, D.C., 1989.

_____. *The FEC Journal of Election Administration*, Volume 15, Autumn, 1988.

Federal Voting Assistance Program, Department of Defense. *'88-89 Voting Assistance Guide*, Washington, D.C. 1989.

Gans, Curtis B. "Declining Voter Participation," John F. Kennedy School of Government, Harvard University, Institute of Politics *Quarterly Report*, Vol II, No. 1, Fall, 1988.

Landers, Robert K., "Why America Doesn't Vote," *Congressional Quarterly Editorial Research Reports*, Vol 1, No. 7, February 19, 1988.

Michaelson, Ronald D. *1989 Campaign Finance Update: Legislation and Litigation* Los Angeles: Citizens' Research Foundation, 1990.

Orren, Gary R. "Declining Voter Participation, Who Cares?" John F. Kennedy School of Government, Harvard University, Institute of Politics *Quarterly Report*, Vol. II, No. 1, Fall, 1988.

Palmer, James A. and Edward D. Feigenbaum, eds. *Campaign Finance Law '88*, Washington, D.C.: Government Printing Office, 1988. (Document No. 052-006-00041-4.)

Smolka, Richard G. *Election Administration Reports*, a biweekly newsletter for election officials, Washington, D.C.

Table 5.1
STATE OFFICIALS TO BE ELECTED: 1990 AND 1991

State or other jurisdiction	Date of general elections in 1990 (a)	Governor	Lieutenant governor	Secretary of state	Attorney general	Treasurer	Auditor	Judges of court of last resort (b)	Judges of intermediate appellate court (b)	Board of education members	Public utilities commissioners	Superintendent of public instruction	Other	State legislatures: members to be elected — Senate	House
Alabama	Nov. 6	★	★	★	★	★	★	1	5 (c)	★	2	...	Commr. of agriculture & industry	All	All
Alaska	Nov. 6	★	★	...	...	...	...	1	...	...	...	...	...	1/2 (d)	All
Arizona	Nov. 6	★	...	★	★	★	★	3	7	...	...	★	State mine inspector; corporation commr.	All	All
Arkansas	Nov. 6	★	★	★	★	★	★	3	...	...	...	...	Land commr.	1/2 (d)	All
California	Nov. 6	★	★	★	★	★	...	...	...	...	...	★	Insurance commr., board of equalization (4)	1/2	All
Colorado	Nov. 6	★	...	★	★	★	...	1	8	2	...	...	...	1/2 (d)	All
Connecticut	Nov. 6	★	★	★	★	★	...	...	...	...	...	...	Insurance commr.	All	All
Delaware	Nov. 6	...	...	...	...	★	★	...	...	...	...	...	Commr. agriculture	1/2 (d)	All
Florida	Nov. 6	★	★	★	★	★	★	★	3	★	2	★	Commr. agriculture, commr. labor	1/2	All
Georgia	Nov. 6	★	★	★	★	...	...	1	...	...	...	★	...	All	All
Hawaii	Nov. 6	★	★	...	...	...	...	2	1	6	...	...	Office of Hawaiin Affairs (5)	1/2 (d)	All
Idaho	Nov. 6	★	★	★	★	★	★	3	9	...	...	★	...	All	All
Illinois	Nov. 6	★	★	★	★	★	★	...	...	...	...	...	University of Illinois trustees (3)	1/3 (d)	All
Indiana	Nov. 6	...	...	★	...	★	★	...	...	...	...	★	...	1/2	All
Iowa	Nov. 6	★	★	★	★	★	★	3	4	...	...	...	Secretary of agriculture	1/2	All
Kansas	Nov. 6	★	★	★	★	★	...	4	7	5	...	...	Insurance commr.	All	All
Kentucky (1991)	Nov. 6	...	...	...	...	...	...	4	13	★	...	...	Commr. of agriculture	1/2	All
Louisiana (1991)	(e)	★	...	★	...	★	★	1	...	...	...	...	Public service commr.	...	...
Maine	Nov. 6	...	...	...	...	...	★	...	...	...	...	...	...	All	All
Maryland	Nov. 6	★	★	...	★	...	...	3	5	...	...	...	...	All	All
Massachusetts	Nov. 6	★	★	★	★	★	★	...	...	...	...	...	Governors counselor, registrar of probate	All	All
Michigan	Nov. 6	★	★	★	★	...	...	2	9	2	...	...	Board of trustees, Univ. of Michigan (2); board of regents, Michigan State Univ. (2); Wayne State Univ., board of governors (2)	1/2	All
Minnesota	Nov. 6	★	★	★	★	★	★	5	7	...	...	...	...	All	All
Mississippi (1991)	Nov. 6	...	...	...	...	...	...	3	4	...	2	...	...	...	...
Missouri	Nov. 6	...	...	★	★	★	★	3	...	...	...	...	...	1/2	All
Montana	Nov. 6	...	...	...	...	N.A.	★	2	...	...	...	1	...	1/2 (d)	All
Nebraska	Nov. 6	★	★	★	★	★	★	2	...	...	...	...	...	1/2 (d)	U
Nevada	Nov. 6	★	★	★	★	★	★	2	...	5	...	...	3 university regents	All	All
New Hampshire	Nov. 6	★	...	...	...	...	...	...	...	...	...	...	5 executive councillors	2	All
New Jersey (1991)	Nov. 5	...	...	...	...	...	...	...	...	...	...	...	...	All	...
New Mexico	Nov. 6	★	★	★	★	★	2	1	6	...	...	...	Corporation commr., commr. of public lands	All	All
New York	Nov. 6	★	★	...	★	...	★	...	6	...	...	...	...	All	All
North Carolina	Nov. 6	...	...	...	...	...	...	3	6	...	...	...	Commr. of agriculture, commr. of insurance, commr. of labor	All	All
North Dakota	Nov. 6	...	...	★	★	★	★	1	...	...	...	...	...	1/2	All
Ohio	Nov. 6	★	★	★	★	★	★	2	All	1/3	...	...	Commr. of labor, public service commr.	1/2	All

232   The Book of the States 1990-91

ELECTIONS

STATE OFFICIALS TO BE ELECTED: 1990 AND 1991—Continued

State or other jurisdiction	Date of general elections in 1990 (a)	Governor	Lieutenant governor	Secretary of state	Attorney general	Treasurer	Auditor	Judges of court of last resort (b)	Judges of intermediate appellate court (b)	Board of education members	Public utilities commissioners	Superintendent of public instruction	Other	State legislatures: members to be elected Senate	State legislatures: members to be elected House
Oklahoma	Nov. 6	★	★	...	★	★	★	3	4	...	...	★	Corporation commr., commr. of labor, state insurance commr.	1/2	All
Oregon	Nov. 6	★	...	...	★	★	...	2	3	...	...	...	Commr. of the bureau of labor and industry	1/2 (d)	All
Pennsylvania	Nov. 6	★	★	...	...	★	★	...	...	...	...	...	...	1/2	All
Rhode Island	Nov. 6	★	★	★	★	★	...	...	...	...	...	...	...	All	All
South Carolina	Nov. 6	★	★	★	★	★	★	...	...	...	...	★	Commr. of agriculture, adjutant general	1	All
South Dakota	Nov. 6	★	★	★	★	★	★	3	...	...	1	...	Commr. of school and public lands	All	All
Tennessee	Nov. 6	★	...	...	...	...	...	5	35	...	...	...	Public service commr.	1/2 (d)	All
Texas	Nov. 6	★	★	...	★	★	...	3	All	...	...	...	Railroad commr. (1), commr. of general land office, commr. of agriculture	1/2	All
Utah	Nov. 6	...	...	...	...	...	★	...	4	...	...	...	...	1/2 (d)	All
Vermont	Nov. 6	★	★	★	★	★	★	...	...	5	...	...	...	All	All
Virginia	Nov. 6	...	...	...	...	...	...	...	...	...	...	...	...	All	All
Washington	Nov. 6	...	...	...	...	★	...	3	4	...	...	★	Insurance commr., commr. of public lands	1/2 (d)	All
West Virginia	Nov. 6	...	...	...	...	★	★	1	...	...	...	...	...	1/2	All
Wisconsin	April 3	...	...	...	...	...	...	...	4	...	...	...	...	1/2 (d)	All
Wyoming	Sept. 13	★	...	★	★	★	★	2	...	...	...	★	...	1/2	All
Dist. of Columbia	Nov. 6	...	...	...	...	...	...	...	...	6	...	...	Mayor, 7 council seats	(f)	...
American Samoa	Nov. 6	...	...	...	...	...	...	...	...	...	...	...	...	All	U
Guam	Nov. 6	★	...	...	...	...	...	2	...	...	...	...	Village commrs.	3	All
No. Mariana Islands	Nov. 4	...	...	...	...	...	...	...	...	...	...	...	...	...	...
Puerto Rico	Nov. 6	...	...	...	...	...	...	...	...	...	...	...	...	...	...
U.S. Virgin Islands	Nov. 6	...	...	...	...	...	...	...	...	...	...	...	...	1/2	All, U

Source: State election administration offices.

Note: In several states, elections for some state offices do not occur in 1990 or 1991. When a number appears in a column instead of a star, the figure indicates the number of individuals on the state court or other government body up for election in 1990 or 1991. The information in this table is current as of March 1989.

Key:
★ — Office up for election
... — Office not up for election
U — Unicameral legislative body
N.A. — Not applicable
(a) Elections for 1991 are indicated by (1991) before date for general election.
(b) For some states, information on number of judges facing election in 1990 or 1991 is tentative given the nature of the selection and retention processes.
(c) Court of Civil Appeals-1; Criminal Court of Appeals-4.
(d) Actual number of seats up for election: Alaska (10); Arkansas (22); Colorado (17); Delaware (10); Hawaii (12); Illinois (20); Nebraska (24); Nevada (11); Oregon (15); Tennessee (17); Utah (15); and Wisconsin (17).
(e) Under Louisiana's election law, candidates of all parties run together on a single ballot in Spetember; if no candidate for an office wins a majority of the vote, the top two finishers oppose each other in a November runoff. In 1990 the elections will be held on October 6, 1990 and November 6, 1990. In 1991, the elections will be held on October 19, 1991 and November 16, 1991.
(f) Seven members of the Council of the District of Columbia; includes Chairman of the Council.

ELECTIONS

Table 5.2
METHODS OF NOMINATING CANDIDATES FOR STATE OFFICES

State or jurisdiction	Method(s) of nominating candidates
Alabama	Primary election; however, the state executive committee or other governing body of any political party may choose instead to hold a state convention for the purpose of nominating candidates (meetings must be held at least 60 days prior to the date on which primaries are conducted).
Alaska	Primary election.
Arizona	Primary election.
Arkansas	Primary election.
California	Primary election.
Colorado	Convention/primary; however, a political party may hold a pre-primary convention (at least 65 days before the primary) for the designation of candidates. Each candidate who receives at least 30 percent of the delegates vote of those present in voting is listed on the primary ballot, with the candidate receiving the most votes listed first. If no candidate recieves at least 30 percent of the vote, a second ballot shall be taken on all candidates, and the two candidates with the highest number of votes will be the candidate placed on the primary ballot. If any candidate receives less than ten percent of the votes, they are precluded from petitioning further.
Connecticut	Convention/primary election. Political parties hold state conventions (convening not earlier than the 68th day and closing not later than the 50th day before the date of the primary) for the purpose of endorsing candidates. If no one challenges the endorsed candidate, no primary election is held. However, if anyone (who received at least 20 percent of the delegate vote on the roll call at the convention) challenges the endorsed candidate, a primary election is held to determine the party nominee for the general election.
Delaware	Primary election.
Florida	Primary election.
Georgia	Primary election.
Hawaii	Primary election.
Idaho	Primary election.
Illinois	Primary election; however, state conventions are held for the nomination of candidates for trustees of the University of Illinois.
Indiana	Primary election held for the nomination of candidates for governor and U.S. senator; state party conventions held for the nomination of candidates for other state offices.
Iowa	Primary election; however, if there are more than two candidates for any nomination and none receives at least 35 percent of the primary vote, the primary is deemed inconclusive and the nomination is made by party convention.
Kansas	Primary election; however, candidates of any political party whose secretary of state did not poll at least 5 percent of the total vote cast for all candidates for that office in the preceding general election are restricted to nomination by delegate or mass convention.
Kentucky	Primary election.
Louisiana	Primary election. Open primary system requires all candidates, regardless of party affiliation, to appear on a single ballot. Candidate who receives over 50 percent of the vote in the primary is elected to office; if no candidate receives a majority vote, a runoff election is held between the two candidates who received the most votes.
Maine	Primary election.
Maryland	Primary election.
Massachusetts	Primary election.
Michigan	Primary election held for the nomination of candidates for governor, U.S. congressional seats and state senators and representatives; state conventions held for the nomination of candidates for lieutenant governor, secretary of state and attorney general.
Minnesota	Primary election.
Mississippi	Primary election.
Missouri	Primary election.
Montana	Primary election.
Nebraska	Primary election.
Nevada	Primary election.
New Hampshire	Primary election.
New Jersey	Primary election.
New Mexico	Primary election.
New York	Committee meeting/primary election. The person who receives the majority vote at the state party committee meeting becomes the designated candidate for nomination; however, all other persons who received at least 25 percent of the convention vote may demand that their names appear on the primary ballot as candidates for nomination.

ELECTIONS

METHODS OF NOMINATING CANDIDATES FOR STATE OFFICES —Continued

State or jurisdiction	Method(s) of nominating candidates
North Carolina	Primary election.
North Dakota	Primary election.
Ohio	Primary election.
Oklahoma	Primary election.
Oregon	Primary election.
Pennsylvania	Primary election.
Rhode Island	Primary election.
South Carolina	Primary election for republicans and democrats; party conventions held for four minor parties. All must file with proper election commission by varying dates depending on office.
South Dakota	Primary election. Any candidate who receives a plurality of the primary vote becomes the nominee; however, if no individual receives at least 35 percent of the vote for the candidacy for the offices of governor, U.S. Senator, or U.S. congressman, a runoff election is held 2 weeks later.
Tennessee	Primary election.
Texas	Primary election.
Utah	Convention/primary election. Delegates from the county primary conventions are elected to the state primary convention for the purpose of selecting the political party nominees to run at the regular primary election.
Vermont	Primary election.
Virginia	Primary election; however, the state executive committee or other governing body of any political party may choose instead to hold a state convention for the purpose of nominating candidates (party opting for convention can only do so within 32 days prior to date on which primary elections are normally held).
Washington	Primary election.
West Virginia	Primary election.
Wisconsin	Primary election.
Wyoming	Primary election.
Dist. of Columbia	Primary election.

Note: The nominating methods described here are for state offices; procedures may vary for local candidates. Also, independent candidates may have to petition for nomination. For more information on primaries, see Table 5.3, "Primary Election Information."

ELECTIONS

Table 5.3
PRIMARY ELECTION INFORMATION

State or other jurisdiction	Dates of 1990 primaries for state officials		Party affiliation for primary voting		Voters receive ballot of:	
	Primary	Runoff (a)	Voters must declare/change affiliation prior to election day	Voters select party on election day	One party (b)	All parties participating (c)
Alabama	June 5	June 26	...	★	★	...
Alaska	Aug. 28	...	...	(d)	...	★ (d)
Arizona	Sept. 11	...	At least 50 days before	...	★	...
Arkansas	May 29	June 12	...	★	★	...
California	June 5	...	At least 29 days before	...	★	...
Colorado	Aug. 14	...	At least 25 days before	(c)	★	...
Connecticut	Sept. 11	...	At least 6 months before (e)	(c)	★	...
Delaware	Sept. 8	...	By March 1 of election year	...	★	...
Florida	Sept. 4	Oct. 2	At least 30 days before	...	★	...
Georgia	July 17	Aug. 7	...	★	★	...
Hawaii	Sept. 22	...	...	★	...	★
Idaho	May 22	...	...	★	...	★
Illinois	March 20	...	...	★	★	...
Indiana	May 8	...	...	★	★	...
Iowa	June 5	...	...	★	★	...
Kansas	Aug. 7	...	At least 20 days before (e)	(e)	★	...
Kentucky	May 29	...	At least 30 days before	...	★	...
Louisiana	Sept. 29	Nov. 6 (f)	At least 24 days before (f)	...	...	(f)
Maine	June 12	...	At least 90 days before (e)	(e)	★	...
Maryland	Sept. 11	...	At least 84 days before (e)	...	★	...
Massachusetts	Sept. 18	...	At least 28 days before (e)	(e)	★	...
Michigan	Aug. 7	...	...	★	...	★
Minnesota	Sept. 11	...	...	★	...	★
Mississippi	June 5	June 26	...	★	★	...
Missouri	Aug. 7	...	...	★	...	★
Montana	June 5	...	...	★	...	★
Nebraska	May 15	...	By 2nd Friday before election	...	★	...
Nevada	Sept. 4	...	At least 30 days before	...	★	...
New Hampshire	Sept. 11	...	At least 10 days before	...	★	...
New Jersey	June 5	...	At least 50 days before (e)	...	★	...
New Mexico	June 5	...	By Jan. 25 of election year (g)	...	★	...
New York	Sept. 11	...	At least 1 year before (e)	...	★	...
North Carolina	May 8	June 5	At least 21 days before (h)	(c)	★	...
North Dakota	June 12	...	...	★	★	...
Ohio	May 8	...	...	★	★	...
Oklahoma	Aug. 28	Sept. 18	At least 10 days before (i)	(i)	★	...
Oregon	May 15	...	At least 20 days before (e)	...	★	...
Pennsylvania	May 15	...	At least 30 days before	...	★	...
Rhode Island	Sept. 11	...	At least 90 days before (e)	(e)	★	...
South Carolina	June 12	June 26	...	★	...	★
South Dakota	June 5	...	At least 15 days before	...	★	...
Tennessee	Aug. 2	...	...	★	...	★
Texas	March 13	April 10	...	★	★	...
Utah	Aug. 21	...	...	★	...	★
Vermont	Sept. 11	...	...	★	...	★
Virginia	June 12	...	...	★	...	★
Washington	Sept. 18	...	...	(d)	...	★ (d)
West Virginia	May 8	...	At least 30 days before	...	★	...
Wisconsin	Sept. 11	...	...	★	...	★
Wyoming	Aug. 21	...	...	★	★	...
Dist. of Columbia	Aug. 11	...	At least 30 days before	...	★	...
Guam	Sept. 1	...	...	★	...	★
U.S. Virgin Islands	Sept. 11	...	At least 30 days before	...	★	...

Sources: Federal Election Commission; League of Women Voters, *Vote! The First Steps*; state election administration offices.

Key:
... — No provision

(a) A runoff election between the top two candidates is held if the leading candidate does not get a majority of the votes cast in the first primary.

(b) The type of primary in which voters receive only the ballot of their party choice in a primary (voters must declare their affiliation on, or prior to, election day) is generally referred to as a *closed* primary.

(c) The type of primary in which voters receive a ballot for all parties and select the party of their choice in the privacy of the voting booth is generally referred to as an *open* primary.

(d) Voters are not restricted to one party. In Alaska and Washington, voters participate in a *blanket* primary. As in regular open primaries, voters receive a ballot that contains the primary ballot for all parties. However, a voter in the blanket primary may pick and choose among the parties in moving through the lists of candidates for various offices. The only restriction is that the voter can indicate only one preference for each office.

(e) Applies to previously affiliated registered voters. In Connecticut, unaffiliated voters may now vote in some Republican primaries but not in Democratic primaries. In Colorado, Connecticut, Kansas, Louisiana, Maine, Massachusetts, New Hampshire, New Jersey (new voters) and Rhode Island, unaffiliated voters may declare party at the polls. North Carolina may choose Republican at the polls. In Maryland and Oregon, new registrants declare at time of registration. In New York, new voters declare affiliation at least 30 days before, while previously eligible voters declare at least 60 days before.

(f) Louisiana has an open primary which requires all candidates, regardless of party affiliation, to appear on a single ballot. If a candidate receives over 50 percent of the vote in the primary, he is elected to the office. If no candidate receives a majority vote, then a single election is held between the two candidates receiving the most votes.

(g) Previously affiliated voters may not change party affiliation after proclamation of primary.

(h) Business days.

(i) New registrants declare at time of registration; however, no changes in party affiliation are allowed between July 1 and Sept. 30 in an even-numbered year.

ELECTIONS

Table 5.4
CAMPAIGN FINANCE LAWS: GENERAL FILING REQUIREMENTS
(As of January 1988)

State or jurisdiction	Statements required from	Statements filed with	Time for filing
Alabama	Political committees.	Secy. of state for statewide and judicial offices. Secy. of state and probate judge in county of residence for legislative office.	15 days after primary or runoff and 30 days after any other election.
Alaska	Candidates; groups and individuals who contribute $250 or more per year to any group or candidate; a business entity, labor organization or municipality making a contribution or expenditure; suppliers receiving more than $250 from a candidate or group.	Alaska Public Offices Commission, central office.	30 days and 1 week before and 10 days after election; annually on Dec. 31 for contributions and expenditures received but not reported that year. (a)
Arizona	Candidates, committees and continuing political organizations.	Secy. of state.	10-15 days before and 20 days after primary; 10-15 days before and 20 days after general or special election; supplemental reports annually by Apr. 1 for contributions and expenditures subsequent to post-election report.
Arkansas	Candidates and persons acting on their behalf receiving contributions in excess of $250/election from any person.	Secy. of state and county clerk in county of residence.	Contributions: 25 and 7 days before and 30 days after election. Expenditures: 30 days after election. Supplemental reports for expenditures subsequent to post-election report.
California	Candidates and certain committees and elected officers whose salary is $100 or more per month.	Secy. of state, registrar of Los Angeles and San Francisco and clerk of county of residence; legislative candidates, board of equalization, court of appeals and superior court judges also file with clerk of county with largest number of registered voters in district.	Semiannual: July and Jan. 31; periodic: March 22, May 26, Oct. 5 and 27. 40 and 12 days before election. (b)
Colorado	Candidates; certain political committees; persons making independent expenditures of more than $100.	Secy. of state.	11 days before and 30 days after election. Supplemental reports annually on the anniversary of the election until no unexpended balance or deficit. (c)
Connecticut	Candidates, political committees, and party committees receiving or spending over $500 in a single election.	Secy. of state.	2nd Thurs. of Jan., Apr., July, Oct.; 7 days before and 30 days after primary (45 days after general election). Supplemental reports for deficits: 90 days after election and within 30 days after any change and within 7 days after distribution of surplus funds.
Delaware	Candidates, committees.	State election commissioner.	20 days before election, Dec. 31 of election year, Dec. 31 of post-election year and annually by Dec. 31 until fund closes.
Florida	Candidates; political committees; committees of continuous existence; party executive committees; persons making independent expenditures of $100 or more.	Qualifying officer and supervisor of elections in county of residence for candidates. Division of elections in county where election is held for statewide committees.	Pre-election: 10th day of each calendar quarter from time treasurer is appointed through last day of qualifying for office; office; the 4th, 18th and 32nd days preceding the first and second primaries, and the 4th and 18th days preceding the general election for unopposed candidates. Post-election report 10 days after each quarter until no unexpended balance.
Georgia	Candidates, committees, and certain other individuals or organizations.	Secy. of state and copy to probate judge or superintendent of elections in candidate's county of residence.	45 and 15 days before and 10 days after primary and 15 days before general or special election; 6 days before genral and non-partisan runoff elections; Dec. 31 of election year; and annually on Dec. 31 for winning candidates.
Hawaii	Candidates, parties, committees.	Campaign Spending Commission.	10 working days before each election; 20 days after primary and 30 days after general or special election. Supplemental reports in event of surplus or deficit over $250 on 5th day after the last day of election year, and every 6 months thereafter.

ELECTIONS

GENERAL FILING REQUIREMENTS—Continued

State or jurisdiction	Statements required from	Statements filed with	Time for filing
Idaho	Candidates; political committees; organizations which contribute more than $500 to a political committee; persons making independent expenditures of more than $50.	Secy. of state.	By 7 days before election and 30 days after. (d) Supplemental reports on Jan. 31 annually in the event of an unexpended balance or expenditure deficit.
Illinois	Political committees and treasurers of state.	State Board of Elections.	Contributions: 15 days before election and 90 days after each general election. Annual reports of contributions and expenditures: July 31.
Indiana	Political candidates, regular party and political action committees.	State Election Board; legislative candidate committees file duplicate with elections board of candidate's county of residence.	14 days (if postmarked) or 11 days (if hand-delivered) before election or convention; 20 days after convention, if no pre-convention report is filed; annually by Jan. 15; (political party committee March 1).
Iowa	Candidates and committees receiving contributions of or spending more than $250.	Campaign Finance Disclosure Commission.	20th day of Jan., May, July and Oct. annually. In years in which the candidate does not stand for election, the May and July reports are not required of a candidate committee.
Kansas	Candidates; political committees; party committees; persons making independent expenditures of more than $100.	Secy. of state.	6 days before election and Dec. 10 of election years.
Kentucky	Candidates, campaign committees, political party executive committees, permanent committees.	Kentucky Registry of Election Finance with duplicates to clerk of county where candidate resides. Campaign committees file with appropriate central campaign committees.	Candidates and campaign committees: 32 and 12 days before and 30 days after election. Political party executive committees: 30 days after election. Permanent committees: last day of each calendar quarter. Semiannual supplemental reports June 30 and Dec. 31 until fund shows a zero balance.
Louisiana	Candidates; political committees; any person (not a candidate) making independent expenditures or accepting contributions (other than to or from a candidate) of more than $500.	Supervisory Committee.	Candidates and committees: 180, 90, 30 and 10 days before primary; 10 days before and 40 days after general election; Feb. 15 annually until a deficit has been paid, or Jan. 15 if the candidate or committee has received contributions or made expenditures during the year. (e)
Maine	Candidates; political committees; state party committees; political action committees; any person (not a candidate) making expenditures of more than $50.	Commission on Governmental Ethics and Election Practices.	7 days before and 42 days after election; gubernatorial candidates also file Jan. 15 after non-election years if they received or spent more than $1,000 in that year, and 42 days before election. All; disposition of surplus or deficit in excess of $50 on 1st day of each quarter of fiscal year. (f)
Maryland	Candidates receiving contributions of or spending $300 or more; political committtees; party central committees; states.	Board at which candidate filed certificate of candidacy. Central committees and political committees file with State Administrative Board of Election Laws.	4th Tues. before primary; 2nd Fri. before any election; 3rd Tues. after general election or before taking office, whichever is earlier. Disposition of surplus or deficit 6 months after general election and annually on anniversary of election until eliminated. Central and continuing committees also file annually on the date of the last general election.
Massachusetts	Candidates and political committees.	Director of campaign and political finance.	8 days before election and Jan. 10 of year after general election for General Assembly candidates; 3rd business day after designating depository and Jan. 10 of year after general election for others.
Michigan	Candidates; political committees; party committees; persons making independent expenditures of $100 or more in calendar year.	Secy. of state.	Committees supporting or opposing candidates; 11 days before and 30 days after election; committees other than independent committees by Jan. 31 of each year. (g)

ELECTIONS

GENERAL FILING REQUIREMENTS—Continued

State or jurisdiction	Statements required from	Statements filed with	Time for filing
Minnesota	Candidates; political committees; party committees; and individuals making independent expenditures over $100.	Ethical Practices Board. Legislative candidates file copies with auditor of each county in district.	10 days before election and Jan. 31 annually (h)
Mississippi	Candidates and political committees.	Secy. of state.	For 1991 and every 4th year thereafter, detailed reporting dates are specified; other years: 7 days before election, complete through 10 days before election; Jan. 31 to cover entire prior calendar year.
Missouri	Candidates who spend or receive more than $1,000 or who receive a single contribution in excess of $250; committees; and persons making independent expenditures of $500 or more.	Secy. of state for statewide candidates and committees, and candidates for Supreme Court or appellate court; candidates for legislature file with secy. of state and election authority of candidate's place of residence.	40 and 7 days before and 30 days after election. Supplemental reports each Jan. 15 if contributions or expenditures of $500 or more were made or received since last report. Quarterly reports if post-election report shows outstanding debts of more than $500, until deficit is below $500. (i)
Montana	Candidates and political committees.	Commissioner of Political Practices and county clerk or recorder where candidate resides or political committee has headquarters.	Statewide office: March 10 and Sept. 10 in election years. 15 and 25 days before and 20 days after election; supplemental reports March 10 and Sept. 10 annually until closing statement is filed. Legislative office: 10 days before and 20 days after election. (j)
Nebraska	Candidate committees, political party committees, and certain other committees.	Nebraska Accountability and Disclosure Commission and election commissioner or clerk of candidate's county of residence.	30 and 10 days before and 40 days after election. Jan. 31 annually if statements not required during previous year or did not expend more than $2,000 during previous year. (k)
Nevada	Candidates, party committees, and other committees spending over $500.	Officer with whom candidate filed declaration of candidacy.	15 days before primary and 15 days before and 30 days after general election.
New Hampshire	Candidates, and political committees spending over $500.	Secy. of state.	Wed. 3 weeks before and Wed. immediately before election; 2nd Fri. after election and every 6 months thereafter until outstanding debt or obligation is satisfied or surplus depleted. (l)
New Jersey	Candidates and political committees. Reports not required if total expenditures do not exceed $2,000; single expenditures over $100 must be reported. Exemptions may be provided for political committees and continuing political committees.	Election Law Enforcement Commission.	29 and 11 days before and 20 days after election; every 60 days after election (starting with the 19th day after election) until no balance remains. (m)
New Mexico	Candidates who anticipate receiving or spending more than $500; political committees.	Secy. of state.	10 days before and 30 days after election; 6 months after if any contributions are unspent or debt remains unpaid, and 12 months after an election (and annually thereafter) if debt remains unpaid.
New York	Candidates and political committees spending or receiving more than $1,000 in a filing period or $50 in calendar year.	State Board of Elections.	Primary election reports filed on the 32nd and 11th day before, and 10th day after contested primary; general election reports filed 32nd and 11th day before, and 27th day after. Additional statements on Jan. 15 and July 15 until satisfaction of all liabilities and disposition of all assets. (n)
North Carolina	Candidates, political committees, and individuals making independent expenditures over $100.	State Board of Elections for statewide and multicounty district offices. County board of elections for others.	10 days before and after election (losing candidates in primary file 10 days after election). Supplemental reports due Jan. 7 after general election and annually following years in which contributions are received or expenditures made. Independent expenditure reports are filed within 10 days after expenditure is made.

ELECTIONS

GENERAL FILING REQUIREMENTS—Continued

State or jurisdiction	Statements required from	Statements filed with	Time for filing
North Dakota	Candidates receiving more than $100 in contributions; political parties receiving contributions of more than $100 or contributing more than $100 to a candidate; political committees.	Secy. of state. Legislative candidates file with county auditor of candidate's county of residence.	Candidates: 10 days before election and 30 days after close of calendar year. Political committees: by Oct. 15, with supplemental report by Jan. 30. Political parties: by Jan. 30. (o)
Ohio	Candidate campaign committees, political committees, political parties.	Secy. of state. Legislative candidates file with Board of Elections for county with largest population.	12 days before and 38 days after election and last business day of Jan. annually, except in year post-general-election statement is filed.
Oklahoma	Candidates, political parties, and organizations.	Oklahoma Ethics Commission.	10 days before election and 40 days after general election. Supplemental reports within 6 months and 10 days after general election if any contributions are received or expenditures made within 6 months after general election.
Oregon	Candidates, political committees.	Secy. of state.	29-39 and 5-7 days before and 30 days after election. If post-election statement shows an unexpended balance of contributions or a deficit, supplemental reports are required until there is no balance or deficit. (p)
Pennsylvania	Candidates and political committees receiving or spending over $250.	Secy. of the commonwealth or appropriate county board of elections.	6th Tues. and 2nd Fri. before and 30 days after election. Annual reports required on Jan. 31 until there is no balance or debt in the report.
Rhode Island	Candidates, political action committees and political party committees spending more than $5,000 or receiving any contribution in excess of $200 from one source.	State Board of Elections.	28 and 7 days before and 28 days after election. Party committees also file by March 1 annually. Supplemental reports are required at 90-day intervals commencing 120 days after election until dissolution.
South Carolina	Candidates and committees.	State Ethics Commission; Senate or House Ethics Committee for legislative office.	30 days after election and 10 days after end of each calendar quarter in which funds are received or spent.
South Dakota	Candidates and certain committees.	Secy. of state.	Last Tues. before election and Feb. 1 of each year (for statewide offices); July 1 and Dec. 31 of each year (for legislative office). (q)
Tennessee	Candidates and political campaign committees.	Secy. of state; copy filed with county election commission of residence for legislative office.	7 days before any election and 48 days after election. Supplemental report one year after election (or sooner if no surplus or deficit). Multi-candidate political campaign committees: 10 days after each quarter.
Texas	Candidates, political committees, officeholders and individuals making unreimbursed expenditures more than $100.	Secy. of state.	Pre-election reports: 30 and 8 days before and 30 days after election. Opposed candidates must file semi-annually by the 15th of July and Jan. (r)
Utah	Personal campaign committees for governor, lt. governor, state auditor, treasurer, atty. gen.; state senate or house of representatives candidates; political party committees.	Lt. governor.	10th day of July, Oct. and Dec. of election year and 5th day before election for state office candidates and for political parties 30 days after election for legislative candidates.
Vermont	Candidates spending or receiving more than $500; political parties and political committees that have accepted contributions or made expenditures of more than $500 in a calendar year.	Secy. of state for state office, political parties and political committees. Legislative office, officer with whom candidate files.	State office, political parties and political committees: 40 and 10 days before any election and 10 days after general election. Supplemental reports annually on July 15 until all expenditures are accounted for and all deficits are eliminated. Legislative office: within 10 days before any election and within 30 days after general election.
Virginia	Candidates and political party committees meeting certain thresholds.	State Board of Elections and election board where candidate resides.	May general election—by May 1 of election year, 8th day before primary, 15th of July and Aug., 8th day before general election, Dec. 1st, 15th of Jan. and July next year and Jan. 15th of subsequent years. Also, pre-election-year annual report by Jan. 15th. State executive offices by Oct. 1st of election year. (s)

ELECTIONS

GENERAL FILING REQUIREMENTS—Continued

State or jurisdiction	Statements required from	Statements filed with	Time for filing
Washington	Candidates and political committees. Exemptions exist at certain thresholds.	Public Disclosure Commission and county auditor or elections officer in county of candidate's residence. Continuing political political committees: Public Disclosure Commission, elections officer and auditor in county where committee maintains its office.	Initial report at time of appointment of treasurer; 21 and 7 days before election and 21 days after any election; 10th day of each month in which no other report is filed if total contributions or expenditures since last report exceed $200. (t)
West Virginia	Candidates and their financial agents; party committees, persons and treasurers supporting or opposing any candidate.	Secy. of state for state and multicounty offices. Clerk of county commission for single-county office.	Last Sat. in March or 15 days after that day before a primary; 7-10 days before and 25-30 days after any election. (u)
Wisconsin	Candidates; political party committees, political committees, and others receiving or spending over $25.	State Elections Board. Legislative candidates also file duplicate with county clerk of most populous jurisdiction.	8-14 days before election; continuing reports by committees and individuals, Jan. 1-31 and July 1-10 semi-annually. (v)
Wyoming	Candidates, political party committees, and political action committees.	Secy. of state. Legislative candidates also file with county clerk.	10 days after election. Non-party committees: 14 days after election; party committees: 7 days after election. Committees formed after election report July 1 and Dec. 31 of odd-numbered years until all debts are paid.
Dist. of Columbia	Candidates spending more than $250; political committees; and individuals making independent expenditures of $50 or more.	Director of Campaign Finance.	Each year: Jan. 31. Election years: 10th day of March, June, Aug., Oct., and Dec. and 8 days before election. Non-election years: July 31. (w)

Source: James A. Palmer and Edward D. Feigenbaum, *Campaign Finance Law 1988* (Washington, D.C.: National Clearinghouse on Election Administration, Federal Election Commission, 1988).

Note: This table deals with filing requirements for statewide and legislative offices in general terms. For detailed legal requirements or requirements for county and local offices, state statutes should be consulted.

(a) Contributions exceeding $250 made within one week before the election must be reported within 24 hours.
(b) Contributions or independent expenditures of $1,000 or more received after the final pre-election report must be reported within 48 hours.
(c) Contributions exceeding $500 received within 16 days before the election must be reported within 48 hours.
(d) Winning candidates in a primary do not file a post-primary report.
(e) Special report is required within 48 hours after receipt of a contribution equal to the reporting amount, or a candidate's expenditure of more than $200 to any candidate, committee, or other person required to file disclosure reports who makes endorsements during the period from 20 days before any election through election day.
(f) Contributions to or expenditures by candidates of $1,000 or more made after the 11th day and more than 48 hours before any election must be reported.
(g) Contributions of $200 or more received after the closing date of a pre-election statement, but before the second day prior to the election, must be reported within 48 hours after receipt.
(h) Contributions of $2,000 or more ($400 or more for a legislative candidate) received between the closing date of the last pre-election report and the election must be reported within 48 hours after receipt.
(i) Contributions of more than $1,000 ($500 for any other committee) received after the closing date of the last pre-election report but before election day must be reported within 48 hours after receipt.
(j) Contributions of $500 or more received by a statewide candidate between the 20th day before the election and election day must be reported within 24 hours. Contributions of $100 or more received by a legislative candidate between the 15th day before the election and election day must be reported within 24 hours.

(k) Contributions of $500 or more received after last pre-election statement must be reported within five days after receipt.
(l) Contributions exceeding $500 received after Wednesday before any election must be reported within 24 hours.
(m) Contributions of $250 or more received by a candidate or political committee between the 13th day before and the election day must be reported within 48 hours.
(n) Contributions of more than $1,000 received after the final pre-election statement must be reported within 24 hours after receipt.
(o) Contributions of $500 or more received by a candidate in the 15-day period before any election must be reported within 48 hours of receipt.
(p) Contributions of $500 or more received after the eighth day and before the day preceding the election must be reported on the day before the election.
(q) Contributions of $500 or more received within the nine days immediately prior to the election must be reported within 48 hours after receipt.
(r) Opposed candidates may opt for semi-annual reports if contributions are less than $500. Certain large aggregate pre-election contributions must be reported within 48 hours of acceptance.
(s) Contributions of $1,000 or more received between the 11th day before any nomination or election and the day of nomination or election must be reported within 72 hours, but no later than the day prior to the day of nomination or election.
(t) Contributions of $500 or more made or received after the last pre-election report or within 21 days of general election must be reported within 24 hours after the contribution is made or 48 hours after contribution is received. Candidates and committees may also qualify for abbreviated reporting.
(u) Also annually on last Saturday in March within 15 days if contributions or expenditures exceed $500 or any loan is outstanding.
(v) Contributions of more than $500 received within 15 days of election must be reported within 48 hours after receipt.
(w) Contributions of $200 or more received after last pre-election report must be reported within 24 hours.

ELECTIONS

Table 5.5
CAMPAIGN FINANCE LAWS: LIMITATIONS ON CONTRIBUTIONS BY ORGANIZATIONS
(As of January 1988)

State or jurisdiction	Corporate	Labor union	Separate segregated fund—political action committee (PAC)	Regulated industry	Political party
Alabama	Limited to $500 to any one candidate, political committee, or political party per election.	Unlimited.	Unlimited.	Public utility regulated by public service commission may only contribute through a PAC.	Unlimited.
Alaska (a)	Limited to $1,000 per year for each elective office.	Same as corporate.	Same as corporate.	...	Unlimited.
Arizona	Prohibited.	Prohibited.	Limited to $2,500 for statewide candidate, $1,000 for other candidates.	Prohibited.	Unlimited.
Arkansas(a)	Limited to $1,500 per candidate, per election.	Same as corporate.	Same as corporate.	...	Limited to $2,500 per candidate, per election.
California(a)	Unlimited.	Unlimited.	Unlimited.	...	Unlimited.
Colorado(a)	Unlimited.	Unlimited.	Unlimited.	...	Unlimited.
Connecticut(a)	Prohibited.	Prohibited.	Labor organization PAC limited to an aggregate of $50,000 per election, and same limits per candidate as individuals. Corporate PAC limited to an aggregate of $100,000 per election, and twice the limits per candidate as individuals.	Prohibited.	Unlimited.
Delaware(a)	Limited to $1,000 per statewide candidate per election, $500 per non-statewide candidate, per election.	Same as corporate.	Same as corporate.	...	...
Florida(a)	Limited to $3,000 for statewide office candidate per election; $2,000 for candidate for retention as district court of appeal judge; $1,000 for any other candidate or committee, per election.	Same as corporate.	Same as corporate.	...	Unlimited, except that party may not contribute to a candidate for judicial office.
Georgia	Unlimited.	Unlimited.	Unlimited.	Public utility corporation regulated by public service commission may not contribute, directly or indirectly.	Unlimited.
Hawaii(a)	Limited to $2,000 in any election period.	Same as corporate.	Same as corporate.	...	Sliding scale percentage limit based upon candidate expenditure limits.
Idaho	Unlimited.	Unlimited.	Unlimited.	...	Unlimited.
Illinois	Unlimited.	Unlimited.	Unlimited.	Prohibited for insurance companies doing business in Illinois or for anyone holding 5% or more stock in a horse racing organization.	Unlimited.

ELECTIONS

LIMITATIONS ON CONTRIBUTIONS BY ORGANIZATIONS—Continued

State or jurisdiction	Corporate	Labor union	Separate segregated fund— political action committee (PAC)	Regulated industry	Political party
Indiana	Limited to an aggregate of $5,000 for statewide candidates; an aggregate of $5,000 for state party central committees; an aggregate of $2,000 for other offices; and an aggregate of $2,000 for other party committees.	Same as corporate.	Unlimited.	...	Unlimited.
Iowa	Prohibited.	Unlimited.	Unlimited.	Prohibited for insurance companies.	Unlimited.
Kansas	Limited to $3,000 per statewide candidate per election, and $750 per candidate, per election for house and senate seats.	Same as corporate.	Same as corporate.	Same as corporate.	Unlimited.
Kentucky (a)	Prohibited.	Unlimited.	Limited to $4,000 per candidate per election.	Prohibited.	Unlimited.
Louisiana (a)	Unlimited.	Unlimited.	Unlimited.	...	Unlimited.
Maine	Limited to $5,000 per candidate per election.	Same as corporate.	Same as corporate.	Same as corporate.	Same as corporate.
Maryland (a)	Limited to an aggregate of $2,500 per election and $1,000 per candidate, per election.	Same as corporate.	Unlimited (if registered under Maryland law).	...	Unlimited.
Massachusetts (a)	Prohibited.	Unlimited.	Unlimited.	Prohibited.	Unlimited.
Michigan (a)	Prohibited for candidate elections.	Limited to $1,700 for a statewide office, $450 for state senator, $250 for state representative candidates per election.	Same as labor union. A separate segregated fund which qualifies as an independent committee may contribute 10 times these amounts.	Prohibited, except through a separate segregated fund.	State central committee is limited to $34,000 for a statewide office, $4,500 for state senator, $2,500 for state representative candidates, per election. Local party is limited to $17,000 for a statewide office, $4,500 for a state senator, $2,500 for state representative candidates, per election.
Minnesota	Prohibited.	Limited to $60,000 per election year for governor/lt. governor ($12,000 in non-election years); $10,000 per election year for attorney general ($2,000 in non-election years); $5,000 per election year for other statewide offices ($1,000 in non-election years); $1,500 per election year for state senator ($300 in non-election years); $750 per election year for state representative ($150 in non-election years).	Same as labor union.	Prohibited for insurance companies.	Limited to $300,000 per election year for governor/lt. governor ($60,000 in non-election years); $50,000 per election year for attorney general ($10,000 in non-election years); $25,000 per election year for other statewide offices ($5,000 in non-election years); $7,500 per election year for state senator ($1,500 in non-election years); $3,750 per election year for state representative ($750 in non-election years).

LIMITATIONS ON CONTRIBUTIONS BY ORGANIZATIONS—Continued

State or jurisdiction	Corporate	Labor union	Separate segregated fund—political action committee (PAC)	Regulated industry	Political party
Mississippi	Limited to $1,000 per candidate per year.	Unlimited.	Unlimited.	Generally prohibited.	Unlimited.
Missouri (a)	Unlimited.	Unlimited.	Unlimited.	...	Unlimited.
Montana	Prohibited.	Limited for all elections in a campaign to $1,500 for governor/lt. governor; $750 for other statewide candidates; $400 for public service commissioner, district court judge or state senator; $250 for other candidates.	Limited for all elections in a campaign to $8,000 for governor/lt. governor; $2,000 for other statewide candidates; $1,000 for public service commissioner; $600 for state senator ($1,000 total from all non-party political committees); $300 for other candidates ($600 total for house candidates from all non-party political committees).	Prohibited.	Contributions to judicial candidates are prohibited; otherwise, same as PAC.
Nebraska (a)	Unlimited, but may not receive contributions unless separate segregated fund is established.	Same as corporate.	Unlimited.	Same as corporate.	Unlimited.
Nevada	Unlimited.	Unlimited.	Unlimited.	Unlimited.	Unlimited.
New Hampshire	Prohibited.	Prohibited.	Limited to $5,000.	Prohibited.	Unlimited.
New Jersey (a)	Unlimited, except in contributions to governor in any primary or general election ($800 limit).	Same as corporate.	Same as corporate.	Prohibited for insurance corporations or associations and certain other corporations.	Unlimited, except state committee contribution to governor in general election ($800 limit).
New Mexico	Unlimited.	Unlimited.	Unlimited.	...	Prohibited in primary elections, otherwise unlimited.
New York (a)	Limited to an aggregate of $5,000 per calendar year.	Unlimited.	Unlimited.	Unlimited if not corporation. If corporation, limited to $5,000 per calendar year. Public utilities may not contribute from public service revenues unless cost is charged to shareholders.	Unlimited.
North Carolina (a)	Prohibited.	Prohibited.	Limited to $4,000 per committee or candidate, per election.	Prohibited.	Unlimited.
North Dakota	Prohibited.	Prohibited.	Unlimited.	Prohibited.	Unlimited.
Ohio (a)	Prohibited.	Unlimited.	Unlimited.	Prohibited.	Unlimited.
Oklahoma	Prohibited.	Limited to $5,000 to a political party or organization or a state office, and $1,000 for a local office candidate.	Same as labor union.	Prohibited.	Same as labor union.
Oregon	Unlimited.	Unlimited.	Unlimited.	Unlimited.	Unlimited.
Pennsylvania (a)	Prohibited.	Prohibited.	Unlimited.	Prohibited.	Unlimited.
Rhode Island	Unlimited.	Unlimited.	Unlimited.	...	Unlimited.

ELECTIONS

LIMITATIONS ON CONTRIBUTIONS BY ORGANIZATIONS—Continued

State or jurisdiction	Corporate	Labor union	Separate segregated fund—political action committee (PAC)	Regulated industry	Political party
South Carolina	Unlimited.	Unlimited.	Unlimited.	...	Unlimited.
South Dakota	Prohibited.	Prohibited if union is a corporation. Permitted if an association, but not out of dues or treasury fund.	Unlimited.	Prohibited.	Unlimited.
Tennessee	Prohibited.	Unlimited.	Unlimited.	Prohibited.	Unlimited.
Texas (a)	Prohibited.	Prohibited.	Unlimited, but may not be made mandatory assessments from corporation employees or labor organization members. Contributions from out-of-state political committees are subject to special notification and reporting requirements.	Prohibited.	Unlimited.
Utah	Unlimited.	Unlimited.	Unlimited.	Unlimited.	Unlimited.
Vermont (a)	Limited to $1,000 per candidate or committee, per election.	Same as corporate.	Limited to $5,000 per candidate or committee per election.	Same as corporate.	Unlimited.
Virginia	Unlimited.	Unlimited.	Unlimited.	...	Unlimited.
Washington (a)	Unlimited, except aggregate contributions of more than $5,000 may not be made to a candidate or political committee within 21 days of a general election.	Same as corporate.	Same as corporate.	Same as corporate.	Unlimited.
West Virginia (a)	Prohibited.	Limited to $1,000 per candidate, per election.	Same as labor union.	Prohibited.	Same as labor union.
Wisconsin (a)	Prohibited, except concerning referendum.	Prohibited if it is a Chapter 185 association, except concerning a referendum.	Limited according to formula for statewide candidates; and $1,000 for state senator; $500 for state representative; and $6,000 for political parties in calendar year.	Public utilities may not offer special privileges to candidates, political committees and individuals making independent dispersements.	Certain specified percentage limits per candidate.
Wyoming	Prohibited.	Prohibited.	Unlimited.	Prohibited.	Prohibited in primary elections, otherwise unlimited.
Dist. of Columbia (a)	Limited to an aggregate of $4,000 per election and $2,000 for mayor, $1,500 for council chairman, $1,000 for council member at-large, $400 for council member from a district and board of education member at-large, $200 for board of education member from a district or a party official, $25 for neighborhood advisory commission member.	Same as corporate.	Same as corporate.	...	...

LIMITATIONS ON CONTRIBUTIONS BY ORGANIZATIONS—Continued

Source: James A. Palmer and Edward D. Feigenbaum. *Campaign Finance Law 1988*. (Washington, D.C.: National Clearinghouse on Election Administration, Federal Election Commission, 1988).
Note: Consult state statutes for more details.
Key:
. . . — No reference to contribution in the law.
(a) Restriction on cash contributions. In Alaska, Arkansas, California, Colorado, Florida, Kentucky, Maryland, Missouri, New York, North Carolina, Ohio and Texas (no limit for general purpose committee): must be $100 or less. In Connecticut, Delaware, Massachusetts, Nebraska, Vermont, Washington (if no receipt), West Virginia and Wisconsin: must be $50 or less. In Hawaii: cash contribution of more than $100 requires a receipt to the donor and a record of the transaction. In Louisiana: cash contributions of more than $300 must be by written instrument; all cash contributions by corporations, labor organizations and associations must be by check. In New Jersey: cash contributions are prohibited unless in response to public solicitation, or a written contributor statement is filed (cumulative maximum of $100). In Pennsylvania: must be $100 or less per candidate. In Vermont, contributions over $50 must be itemized by contributor and single contributions over $50 must be made by check. In Michigan, contributions must be less than $20. In Wisconsin, contributions over $50 to be made by negotiable instrument or credit card.

ELECTIONS

Table 5.6
CAMPAIGN FINANCE LAWS: LIMITATIONS ON CONTRIBUTIONS BY INDIVIDUALS
(As of January 1988)

State or jurisdiction	Individual	Candidate	Candidate's family member	Government employees	Anonymous or in name of another
Alabama	Unlimited.	Unlimited.	Unlimited.	No solicitation of state employees for state political activities. City employees may contribute to county/state political activities; county employees may contribute to city/state political activities.	...
Alaska (a)	Limited to $1,000 per year for each elective office.	Unlimited.	Same as individual.	Contribution may not be required of state employees.	Prohibited.
Arizona	Limited to $500 per candidate and $2,000 per calendar year.	Unlimited.	Same as individual.	...	...
Arkansas (a)	Limited to $1,500 per candidate, per election.	Unlimited.	Same as individual.	Contribution may not be required of state employees. State division of social services/county board of public welfare employees may not solicit, nor may certain judges solicit for campaigns other than their own.	Anonymous contribution must be less than $50 per year. Contribution in the name of another prohibited.
California (a)	Unlimited.	Unlimited.	Unlimited.	Must be less than $100. Local agency employees may not solicit employees of their agency except incidentally through a large solicitation.	Anonymous contribution prohibited. Contributions in the name of another is unlimited.
Colorado (a)	Unlimited.	Unlimited.	Unlimited.	...	Contribution in the name of another prohibited.
Connecticut (a)	Limited to an aggregate of $15,000 per election and $2,500 for governor; $1,500 for other statewide office; $1,000 for sheriff; $500 for state senator or probate judge; $250 for state representative, town, city or borough office; $5,000 per year to state party.	Unlimited.	Unlimited.	May not be required. State department heads and deputy department heads may not solicit.	Anonymous contribution must be less than $15. Contribution in the name of another prohibited.
Delaware (a)	Limited to $1,000 per statewide candidate, per election; $500 per non-statewide candidate per election.	Limited to $5,000 per election.	Same as candidate.	...	Prohibited.
Florida (a)	Limited to $3,000 for statewide office candidate per election; $2,000 for candidate for retention as district court of appeal judge; $1,000 for any other candidate or committee per election.	Unlimited.	Same as individual.	Judges not elected in public elections between competing candidates may not make contributions. Solicitation generally prohibited for state employees. Judges may not solicit contributions.	Contribution in the name of another prohibited.

ELECTIONS

LIMITATIONS ON CONTRIBUTIONS BY INDIVIDUALS—Continued

State or jurisdiction	Individual	Candidate	Candidate's family member	Government employees	Anonymous or in name of another
Georgia	Unlimited.	Unlimited.	Unlimited.	State employee may not coerce another state employee into contributing.	Anonymous contribution prohibited.
Hawaii (a)	Limited to $2,000 in any election period.	Limited to an aggregate of $50,000 in any election year.	Same as candidate.	Solicitation of contributions prohibited. Contribution to other employees is prohibited.	Prohibited.
Idaho	Unlimited.	Unlimited.	Unlimited.	Contributions permitted. State employee may not coerce another state employee into contributing.	Anonymous contribution must be $50 or less. Contribution in the name of another prohibited.
Illinois	Unlimited.	Unlimited.	Unlimited.	Generally prohibited.	Prohibited.
Indiana	Unlimited.	Unlimited.	Unlimited.	Contribution may not be required. Employees may not solicit or receive contributions.	Contribution in the name of another prohibited.
Iowa	Unlimited.	Unlimited.	Unlimited.	State employees may not coerce another state employee into contributing.	Prohibited.
Kansas	Limited to $3,000 per statewide candidate, per election; and $750 per candidate per election for house and senate seats.	Unlimited.	Spouse is unlimited.	Contribution may not be required.	Anonymous contribution must be $10 or less. Contribution in the name of another prohibited.
Kentucky (a)	Limited to $4,000 per candidate per election, or $2,000 to a PAC.	Unlimited (loans are limited).	Limited to $4,000 per candidate per election except for minors having a lower threshold.	Contribution may not be required. Contribution may be prohibited, depending on who is recipient.	Anonymous contribution must be $100 or less. Contribution in the name of another prohibited.
Louisiana (a)	Unlimited.	Unlimited.	Unlimited.	Contribution may not be solicited.	Anonymous contribution generally prohibited if more than $25. Contribution in the name of another prohibited.
Maine	Limited to an aggregate of $25,000 in a calendar year and $1,000 per candidate, per election.	Unlimited.	Spouse is unlimited.	State employee may not coerce another state employee into contributing.	Contribution in the name of another prohibited.
Maryland (a)	Limited to an aggregate of $2,500 per election and $1,000 per candidate per election.	Unlimited.	Spouse is unlimited.	Contribution may not be required.	Prohibited.
Massachusetts (a)	Limited to $1,000 per candidate, per year. Minors limited to $25 per year.	Unlimited.	Same as individual.	Contribution may not be required. Solicitation generally prohibited.	Contribution in the name of another prohibited.
Michigan (a)	Limited to $1,700 for statewide office, $450 for state senator, $250 for state representative candidates per election.	Unlimited, except for $25,000 per gubernatorial campaign.	Same as candidate.	Contribution may not be required.	Prohibited.

248 The Book of the States 1990-91

ELECTIONS

LIMITATIONS ON CONTRIBUTIONS BY INDIVIDUALS—Continued

State or jurisdiction	Individual	Candidate	Candidate's family member	Government employees	Anonymous or in name of another
Minnesota	Limited to $60,000 per election year for governor/lt. governor ($12,000 in non-election years); $10,000 per election year for attorney general ($2,000 in non-election years); $5,000 per election year for other state-wide offices ($1,000 in non-election years); $1,500 per election year for state senate ($300 in non-election years); $750 per election year for state representative ($150 in non-election years).	Unlimited.	Same as individual.	Contribution may not be required. Solicitation prohibited during hours of employment.	Anonymous contribution must be less than $20. Contribution in the name of another prohibited.
Mississippi	Unlimited.	Unlimited	Unlimited.	Contribution may not be required. Employees of certain specified agencies may not contribute. Solicitation prohibited from employees of certain specified agencies.	...
Missouri (a)	Unlimited.	Unlimited.	Unlimited.	...	Anonymous contribution must be $10 or less. Contribution in the name of another prohibited.
Montana	Limited for all elections in a campaign to $1,500 for governor/lt. governor; $750 for other statewide candidates; $500 for public service commissioner, district court judge, or state senator; $250 for other candidates.	Unlimited.	Same as individual.	Contributions by municipal employees in city with municipal commission form of government prohibited. Solicitation by municipal government employees prohibited.	Prohibited.
Nebraska (a)	Unlimited.	Unlimited.	Unlimited.	...	Prohibited.
Nevada	Unlimited.	Unlimited.	Unlimited.	...	...
New Hampshire	Limited to $5,000.	Unlimited.	Same as individual.	...	Prohibited.
New Jersey	Unlimited, except in contribution to governor in any primary or general election ($800 limit). Contributor's spouse may contribute up to $800 for governor in general election.	Unlimited, but if receiving public funds for governor, limited to $25,000 per election from own funds.	Unlimited, except in contribution to governor in any primary or general election ($800 limit).	Prohibited to demand from other public employees.	Prohibited.
New Mexico	Unlimited.	Unlimited.	Unlimited.	Solicitation prohibited while on duty. Judges may not solicit from litigants in pending cases or attorneys or for non-judicial candidates.	Anonymous contribution in excess of $50 subject to special report.

ELECTIONS

LIMITATIONS ON CONTRIBUTIONS BY INDIVIDUALS—Continued

State or jurisdiction	Individual	Candidate	Candidate's family member	Government employees	Anonymous or in name of another
New York (a)	Limited to an aggregate of $150,000 in a calendar year and a maximum aggregate per office. Statewide: $0.025 x voters (voters in party in state). Senate or assembly: $0.05 x voters in district (voters in party in district) with $2,500 min./ $50,000 max. for assembly member, and $4,000 min./ $50,000 max. for senator.	Unlimited.	Spouse is unlimited. Other family member contributions are aggregated and subject to a maximum aggregate per office. Statewide: $0.025 x voters (voters in party in state). Senate or assembly: $0.25 x voters in district (voters in party in district) with $20,000 min./ $100,000 max. for senator; $12,500 min./$100,000 max. for assembly member.	Contributions permitted, but may not be required. Judicial candidates may not solicit government employees or receive contributions from them. Police force members may not solicit for contributions from government employees.	Prohibited.
North Carolina (a)	Limited to $4,000 per committee or candidate, per election.	Unlimited.	Unlimited.	Contributions permitted expressly for a judge or judicial candidate to contribute to a judicial candidate. Judge or judicial candidate may not solicit contributions.	Prohibited.
North Dakota	Unlimited.	Unlimited.	Unlimited.	...	Prohibited.
Ohio (a)	Unlimited.	Unlimited.	Unlimited.	Classified service employees may not solicit or be solicited. Judge should not contribute to a political party in the year of candidacy. Court employees may not be solicited for a judicial candidate.	Prohibited.
Oklahoma	Limited to $5,000 to a political party or organization or a state office, and $1,000 for a local office candidate, per person or family.	Unlimited.	Same as individual.	Judges and state highway patrolmen may not solicit. State employees and judges may not receive contributions.	Prohibited.
Oregon	Unlimited.	Unlimited.	Unlimited.	Contribution may not be demanded to pay any political assessment. Solicitation prohibited during hours of employment.	Prohibited.
Pennsylvania (a)	Unlimited.	Unlimited.	Unlimited.	State employees may not be solicited.	Prohibited.
Rhode Island	Unlimited.	Unlimited.	Unlimited.	State classified employees may not be solicited, and may not solicit other state employees.	Prohibited.
South Carolina	Unlimited.	Unlimited.	Unlimited.	Judges may contribute only to a political party or organization to extent permitted by law. Judges may not solicit.	...
South Dakota	Limited to $1,000 for any statewide candidate; $250 for any other candidate; or $3,000 to a political party in any calendar year.	Unlimited.	Unlimited.	...	...

ELECTIONS

LIMITATIONS ON CONTRIBUTIONS BY INDIVIDUALS—Continued

State or jurisdiction	Individual	Candidate	Candidate's family member	Government employees	Anonymous or in name of another
Tennessee	Unlimited.	Unlimited.	Unlimited.	Superiors may not solicit their employees. Certain government contractors may not be solicited. Judges may not solicit. Judges expressly permitted to contribute only to political party or candidate.	...
Texas	Unlimited.	Unlimited.	Unlimited.	...	Contribution in the name of another prohibited unless there is disclosure.
Utah	Unlimited.	Unlimited.	Unlimited.	Solicitation prohibited during hours of employment. Judges are not permitted to make contributions to a political party or organization.	...
Vermont (a)	Limited to $1,000 per candidate or committee, per election.	Unlimited.	Unlimited.	Solicitation by employees prohibited.	...
Virginia	Unlimited.	Unlimited.	Unlimited.	...	...
Washington	Unlimited, except aggregate contributions of more than $5,000 may not be made to a candidate or political committee within 21 days of a general election.	Same as individual.	Same as individual.	...	Prohibited.
West Virginia (a)	Limited to $1,000 per candidate, per election.	Same as individual.	Same as individual.	Contribution may not be solicited.	Anonymous contribution prohibited. Contributor disclosure required for contribution in the name of another.
Wisconsin	Limited to $10,000 for statewide candidates; $1,000 for state senator; $500 for state representative in calendar year; other offices by formula.	Unlimited, unless candidate receives a grant from the election campaign fund, then limited to 200% of individual limit.	Limited to same amounts as individual, however, unlimited as to funds or property owned jointly or as marital property by candidate and spouse.	Contribution and solicitation prohibited during hours of employment, or while engaged in official duties. Judges may not contribute or solicit for a political party.	Anonymous contribution must be less than $10. Contribution in the name of another prohibited.
Wyoming	Limited to an aggregate of $25,000 and $1,000 per candidate in any general election year and the year preceding.	Unlimited.	Unlimited.	Judges may not solicit.	...
Dist. of Columbia (a)	Limited to an aggregate of $4,000 per election and $2,000 for mayor, $1,500 for council chairman, $1,000 for council member at-large, $400 for council member from a district or board of education member at-large, $200 for board of education member from a district or a party official, $25 for neighborhood advisory commission member.	Same as individual.	Same as individual.	Contributions permitted, but district employees may not solicit or collect political contributions.	Anonymous contributions prohibited.

LIMITATIONS ON CONTRIBUTIONS BY INDIVIDUALS—Continued

Source: James A. Palmer and Edward D. Feigenbaum. *Campaign Finance Law 1988.* (Washington, D.C.: National Clearinghouse on Election Administration, Federal Election Commission, 1988).

Note: Consult state statutes for more details.

Key:

. . . — No reference to contribution in the law.

(a) Restriction on cash contributions. In Alaska, Arkansas, Florida, Kentucky, Maryland, New York, North Carolina, and Ohio: must be $100 or less. In California and Colorado: must be less than $100. In Connecticut, Delaware, Massachusetts, Nebraska, Vermont, West Virginia: must be $50 or less. In Hawaii and Missouri: cash contribution of more than $100 requires a receipt to the donor and a record of the transaction. In Louisiana: cash contributions of more than $300 must be by written instrument. In Michigan: must be $20 or less. In Pennsylvania: must be $100 or less per candidate. In District of Columbia: must be less than $50.

ELECTIONS

Table 5.7
CAMPAIGN FINANCE LAWS: LIMITATIONS ON EXPENDITURES
(As of January 1988)

State or jurisdiction	Who may make expenditures	Total expenditures allowed	Expenditures prior to first filing	For certain purposes	Use of surplus funds (a)
Alabama	Committee named and designated by candidate.	...	...	Candidate's travel, filing fees, stenographic work, clerks for mailings, communications and stationery, voter lists, office rent, broadcast, advertising, campaign literature, compensation to those distributing literature, rent for rally halls, bands.	...
Alaska (b)	Candidate, treasurer, deputy treasurer.	...	None permitted, except for personal travel expenses and public opinion surveys/polls.	...	May be given to charity, used to repay contributors, spent on a future campaign, used to repay candidate or used as income, contributed to another committee, or transferred to office allowance fund.
Arizona	...	...	None permitted until registration form is properly filed.	...	...
Arkansas (b)	...	...	...	...	...
California (b)	Must have authorization of treasurer or treasurer's designated agents.	...	...	...	...
Colorado b)	...	...	...	Must be reasonably related to election, voter registration, or political education.	May be contributed to a non-profit or charitable organization or to the state or political subdivision, but not to candidate or party.
Connecticut (b)	Treasurer or those authorized by the treasurer	...	None permitted until treasurer and campaign depository have been properly designated.	Polls, meeting halls and rally expenses, printing and advertising, professional services fee, travel, staff salaries, rent, supplies, voter transportation, communications, expenses incurred in circulating nominating petitions, and other necessary expenses permitted by the commission.	May be donated to another committee (c) or distributed on a pro rata basis to contributors or used for transition expenses. Ballot question committees may distribute surplus to government agencies or tax exempt organizations.
Delaware	Those with candidate's written approval.	Primary: statewide candidates: $.25 x qualified voters; senate: greater of $.25 x qualified voters or $4,000; house: greater of $.25 x qualified voters or $2,000. General election: all figures doubled.	None permitted until registration form is properly filed.	Staff salaries, travel expenses, filing fees, communications and printing, food, office supplies, voter lists and canvasses, poll watchers, rent, advertising, rallies, state licensed counsel.	May be contributed to tax-exempt charitable or political organization with candidate's authorization.

The Council of State Governments 253

LIMITATIONS ON EXPENDITURES—Continued

State or jurisdiction	Who may make expenditures	Total expenditures allowed	Expenditures prior to first filing	For certain purposes	Use of surplus funds (a)
Florida (b)	...	...	...	Expenditures only to influence results of election.	May be used to reimburse a candidate for his contributions; transferred to a public office account in amount up to $10,000 for statewide candidate, $5,000 for multi-county candidate, and $2,500 x number of years in term of office for which legislative candidate is elected; returned pro rata to contributors; donated to a non-profit or charitable organization; or given to state or political subdivision.
Georgia	...	...	...	...	...
Hawaii	Campaign treasurer and deputy treasurer.	Voluntary election year limits: gov.: $1.25 x qualified voters; lt. gov.: $.70 x qualified voters; mayor: $1 x qualified voters; house/senate/council/prosecutor: $.70 x qualified voters; others: $.10 x qualified voters.	...	Donations to community, youth, social, or recreational organizations; reports, surveys, or polls.	May be used for fundraising; candidate-sponsored politically-related activity; ordinary and necessary officeholder expenses; or donated to any community service, scientific, educational, youth, recreational, charitable, or literary organization.
Idaho (b)	...	...	...	...	...
Illinois	...	...	...	...	...
Indiana	Treasurer.	...	...	...	May be transferred to one or more political party committees or to the state election board.
Iowa	...	...	...	Only for legitimate campaign purposes in general elections, including salaries, rent, advertising, supplies, travel, campaign paraphernalia, contributions to other candidates, and the like.	(d)
Kansas	...	...	None permitted until registration form is properly filed.	...	...
Kentucky	Treasurer must make or authorize all expenditures on behalf of candidate.	...	None permitted until primary campaign depository is designated.	Political parties receiving tax money may only use these funds to support this party's candidates in a general election and for administrative costs of maintaining a party headquarters.	May be returned pro rata to all contributors, transferred to candidate's party committee, or retained for election to the same office or escheat to state's treasury.
Louisiana (b)	...	...	None aggregating in excess of $500 until statement of organization is properly filed.	...	...
Maine	Candidate, treasurer.	Political action committee limited to $5,000 per candidate or political committee in any election.	...	...	...

LIMITATIONS ON EXPENDITURES—Continued

ELECTIONS

State or jurisdiction	Who may make expenditures	Total expenditures allowed	Expenditures prior to first filing	For certain purposes	Use of surplus funds (a)
Maryland (b)	Public funds may only be spent upon authority of candidate or treasurer; other expenditures must be made by or through treasurer.	Publicly-financed candidates for the governor and lieutenant governor unit limited to $0.20 x qualified voters.	None permitted until registration form is properly filed.	Public contributions may only be used to further candidate's nomination or election, for legal purposes, and for expenses not incurred later than 30 days after election.	Surplus public contributions must be paid not later than 60 days after the election for which the funds were granted. Other funds must be returned on a pro rata basis to contributors, paid to a party central committee, or donated to a local board of education, recognized non-profit educational organization, or charitable organization.
Massachusetts (b)	...	...	...	Candidates: limited to reasonable and necessary expenses directly related to candidate's campaign. Other committees: for enhancement of political future of candidate or principle.	Pro rata portion of public funds revert to state. Other funds must be donated to local aid fund.
Michigan (b)	Expenditure may only be made with authorization of treasurer or treasurer's designee.	Gubernatorial candidates limited to $1 million per election. (f)	...	Public funds may be spent only on services, facilities, materials, or other things of value to further candidate's election during election year.	Surplus public funds must be promptly repaid and may not be used in subsequent election. Other funds may be transferred to another committee, party, tax-exempt charitable institution or returned to contributors.
Minnesota	Authorized by treasurer or deputy treasurer of committee or fund.	Publicly-financed candidates limited in election year to following amounts. Gov./lt. gov.: $600,000; atty. gen.: $100,000; secy. of state, treas., aud.: $50,000; senate: $15,000; house: $7,500. In non-election year, 20% of applicable limit.	...	Salaries, wages, fees, communications, mailing, transportation and travel, advertising and printing, office space and furnishings, supplies, and other expenses reasonably related to election.	...
Mississippi	...	...	...	...	...
Missouri (b)	Expenditures must be made by or through treasurer; when treasurer's office is vacant candidate serves as treasurer.	...	...	...	...
Montana	Campaign treasurers, authorized deputy campaign treasurers of candidates and political committees.	...	None may be made by committee until it files statement of organization and has treasurer.	...	...
Nebraska (b)	Treasurers or treasurer's designees; however candidates and agents also permitted to make expenditures.	...	...	Committee (other than political party committee) may use funds for goods, materials, services, or facilities to assist or oppose candidate or ballot question. (g)	...

LIMITATIONS ON EXPENDITURES—Continued

State or jurisdiction	Who may make expenditures	Total expenditures allowed	Expenditures prior to first filing	For certain purposes	Use of surplus funds (a)
Nevada	...	...	...	...	...
New Hampshire	Candidate or fiscal agent, treasurer of political committee.	...	None may be made by non-party political committee until registration statement is filed and (if organized to support a candidate) written consent of candidate or financial agent has been secured and filed.	...	...
New Jersey	Treasurer or deputy treasurer of candidate, political party committee, political committee, and continuing political committees.	Max. amount for gov. in primary: $.35 x number of voters in preceding presidential election; in general election: $.70 x number of voters in preceding presidential election.	...	...	...
New Mexico	Treasurer of candidate or political committee.	...	None permitted until treasurer appointed.	...	...
New York (b)	Treasurer of candidate or political committee.	...	None may be made by a political committee until designation of treasurer and depository have been filed.	Any lawful purpose.	Surplus campaign funds may be used for any lawful purpose, including transfer to political party committee, return to donor, or held for use in subsequent campaign.
North Carolina (b)	Treasurer or asst. treasurer of candidate or political committee. (h)	...	None permitted until treasurer appointed and certified. (h)	...	...
North Dakota	... (h)	...	...	...	...
Ohio	Campaign treasurer, authorized deputy campaign treasurers for a campaign committee.	...	None may be made by candidate's campaign committee until candidate designates treasurer.	...	...
Oklahoma	Agents and sub-agents in the case of candidates and political parties.	...	...	Only to defray campaign expenditures or ordinary and necessary expenses incurred in connection with duties of public officeholder.	...
Oregon (b)	...	...	...	...	...
Pennsylvania	...	...	...	No expenditures except as provided by law.	...
Rhode Island	Campaign treasurers, deputy campaign treasurers.	...	None may be made until the appointment of a treasurer and the filing of such designation.	...	...
South Carolina	...	...	...	...	...
South Dakota	...	...	...	Necessary expenditure of money for ordinary or usual expense of conducting political campaign unless expressly forbidden.	...

LIMITATIONS ON EXPENDITURES—Continued

State or jurisdiction	Who may make expenditures	Total expenditures allowed	Expenditures prior to first filing	For certain purposes	Use of surplus funds (a)
Tennessee	Political treasurer of candidate and political campaign committee.	...	None permitted until candidate and political committee certify name and address of treasurer.	Clerical/office force, dissemination of literature, public speakers, newspaper announcement of candidacy and transportation of voters unable to go to polls.	...
Texas	Candidate for candidates own election, political committee, campaign treasurer or asst. campaign treasurer acting in official capacity and an individual who makes independent, unreimbursed expenditures.	...	None permitted until name of campaign treasurer has been filed.	Use of public funds for advertising is prohibited.	...
Utah	Candidate and secretary and members of personal campaign committee in case of candidate.	...	None permitted until state office candidate files statement of appointment of personal campaign committee.	Any expenditures may be made, except those prohibited by law.	...
Vermont (b)	Designated treasurer.	...	...	...	May be used by candidate to reduce personal campaign debts.
Virginia (b)	...	...	(i)	...	After filing of final report, surplus funds may be used for next election.
Washington (b)	Campaign treasurer or candidate or person on authority of campaign treasurer or candidate.	...	...	...	...
West Virginia	Candidates, financial agents, political party committee treasurers.	...	None may be made by political party committee until treasurer appointed.	...	...
Wisconsin (b)	Treasurer of candidate, political committee, political group, or individual.	State office candidates who receive election campaign fund grant may not spend more for campaign than amount specified in authorized disbursement schedule. (j)	None permitted until registration statement is filed and campaign depository account is established.	For any lawful purpose.	...
Wyoming	...	...	...	...	...
Dist. of Columbia (b)	Chairman, treasurer, or designated agents.	...	...	...	May be contributed to a political party for political purposes; returned to donors; transferred to a scientific, technical, or literacy or educational organization; or used for constituent services with certain limitations.

LIMITATIONS ON EXPENDITURES—Continued

Source: James A. Palmer and Edward D. Feigenbaum, *Campaign Finance Law 1986*. (Washington, D.C.: National Clearinghouse on Election Administration, Federal Election Commission, 1986).

Note: Consult state statutes for more details.

Key:
. . . — No reference in the law.
(a) Post election.
(b) Restrictions on cash expenditures. In Alaska, California, Colorado, Florida, Maryland, Missouri, New York and North Carolina: may not exceed $100. In Arkansas, Connecticut, Idaho, Massachusetts, Nebraska, Vermont, Wisconsin and District of Columbia: may not exceed $50. In Michigan: may not exceed $20. In Virginia: petty cash expenditures of less than $25 are permitted; otherwise, only by check. In Washington: receipt is needed for cash contributions over $50.
(c) Except one established to further the candidate's future campaigns.
(d) Unless otherwise provided by the committee in its statement of organization.
(e) Public funds may not be used to lease or purchase any item whose benefits extend beyond the time within which the funds must be spent.
(f) Except up to $200,000 more can be spent to solicit contributions, and additional expenditures are authorized in response to editorials, endorsements, and the like.
(g) After an election, a committee may expend or transfer funds for: continued operation of campaign offices; social events for workers and volunteers; obtaining public input and opinion; repayment of campaign loans; newsletters and other political communications; gifts of acknowledgement; and candidate-related meals, lodging, and travel by officeholder and family.
(h) Except for independent expenditures.
(i) Candidate must appoint one campaign treasurer no later than upon acceptance of a contribution, expenditure of funds, or qualification as a candidate, whichever occurs first.
(j) Unless opponents not accepting a grant do not agree to comply with the limit voluntarily.

Table 5.8
FUNDING OF STATE ELECTIONS: TAX PROVISIONS AND PUBLIC FINANCING
(As of January 1988)

State or jurisdiction	Tax provisions relating to individuals				Public financing	
	Credit	Deduction	Checkoff	Surcharge	Source of funds	Distribution of funds
Alabama	...	...	...	$1 (a)	Surcharge	To political party designated by taxpayer
Alaska	$50	...	...	...	...	...
Arizona	...	$100 (a)	...	...	...	...
Arkansas	...	...	...	...	...	...
California	...	$100	...	$1, $5, $10, or $25 (b)	Surcharge and an equal amount matched by state	To political parties for party activities and distribution to statewide general election candidates
Hawaii	...	$100 for contribution to central or county party committees or $500 for contributions to candidates who abide by expenditure limits, with max. of $100 of a total contribution to a single candidate deductible	$2 (a)	...	Checkoff, appropriated funds, other moneys	To candidates for all non-federal elective offices
Idaho	...	...	$1	...	Checkoff	To political party designated by taxpayer
Indiana	...	...	...	...	Revenue from personalized motor vehicle license plates	Percentage divided equally between the qualified political parties
Iowa	...	...	$1.50 (a)	...	Checkoff	To political party designated by taxpayer; if not specified, amount divided among qualifying parties for party activities and distribution to general election candidates
Kentucky	...	...	$2 (a)	...	Checkoff	To political party designated by taxpayer for party activities and distribution to general election candidates
Maine	...	...	...	Any amount	Surcharge	To political party designated by taxpayer
Maryland	...	...	...	...	Direct appropriations	To candidates for governor and lieutenant governor in 1990 only
Massachusetts	...	...	...	$1 (a)	Surcharge	To candidates in statewide primary and general elections
Michigan	...	...	$2 (a)	...	Checkoff and an equal amount matched by state	To candidates in gubernatorial primaries and candidates for governor and lt. governor in general election
Minnesota	...	...	$5 (a)	...	Checkoff and excess anonymous contributions	To qualifying candidates for governor, lt. governor, attorney general, secretary of state, state auditor, state treasurer, state senator and representative in primary and general elections
Montana	...	$100 (a)	...	$1 (a)	Surcharge	To candidates opposed in elections for governor, lt. governor, Supreme Court chief justice and justices
New Jersey	...	...	$1 (a)	...	Direct appropriations and checkoff	To gubernatorial candidates

FUNDING OF STATE ELECTIONS—Continued

State or jurisdiction	Tax provisions relating to individuals				Public financing	
	Credit	Deduction	Checkoff	Surcharge	Source of funds	Distribution of funds
North Carolina	...	$25 for political contribution or newsletter fund contribution	$1 (a)	...	Checkoff	Divided among political parties according to registration. In non-general election year not more than 50% in election campaign fund to state party and 50% to presidential election year candidates fund. In general election year 100% in election campaign fund to state party (with 50% to special party committee). If presidential election year, 100% in presidential election year candidates fund to state party (with 50% to special party committee
Ohio	...	...	$1 (a)	...	Checkoff	Divided equally among major political parties each calendar quarter. Party allocation divided: 1/2 to state executive committee of party and 1/2 to county executive committees of party according to proportion of income from tax return checkoffs in each county to total checkoff income
Oklahoma	...	$100	...	...	...	...
Oregon	Lesser of 50% of contribution to max. $50 (a) or the taxpayer's tax liability	...	...	Amount designated by taxpayer from income tax refund	Surcharge	To political party designated by taxpayer. State central committees allocate funds. Major political party; not less than 50% to county central committees and not less than 50% of remainder to party candidates; not less than 50% of funds to each county committee is to go to party candidates. Minor political party: not less than 50% to party candidates
Rhode Island	(e)	...	$2 (a)	...	Credit/("credit")	To eligible political party designated by taxpayer. If a party is not designated, 5% of the amount is allocated to each party for each state officer elected and the remainder to each party in proportion to the votes received in previous statewide election
Utah	...	...	$1	...	Checkoff (although funds are actually from revenue from sales and use taxes)	To political party designated by taxpayer: 50% to state central committee and 50% to county central committees in proportion to the number of taxpayers designating the party in each county to the total number of taxpayers in the state who designate the party
Virginia	...	...	...	$2 (a)	Surcharge	To political party designated by taxpayer
Wisconsin	...	...	$1 (a)	...	Checkoff	According to formula, to general election candidates for state executive office, Supreme Court, and legislative offices (f)
Dist. of Columbia	50% of contribution to max. $50 (a)	...	...	...	...	...

Source: James A. Palmer and Edward D. Feigenbaum, *Campaign Finance Law 1988*, (Washington, D.C.: National Clearinghouse on Election Administration, Federal Election Commission, 1988).
Note: This table shows only those states that have a tax provision relating to individuals or a provision for public financing of state elections. Credits and deductions may be allowed only for certain types of candidates and/or political parties. Consult state laws for further details.
Key:
— No provision.
... — For joint returns, amount indicated above may be doubled.
(a) For joint returns, amount indicated above may be doubled.
(b) And a separate designation of $1, $5, $10, or $25.
(c) 10 percent to each party and remainder divided according to registration figures.
(d) 20 percent for governor, 15 percent for lieutenant governor, 15 percent for attorney general and 10 percent each for state treasurer, state auditor and inspector, commissioner of insurance, superintendent of public instruction, and corporation commissioner.
(e) See checkoff; designated to specified party or to non-partisan general account.
(f) Candidates must meet certain qualifications.

ELECTIONS

Table 5.9
VOTER REGISTRATION INFORMATION

State or other jurisdiction	Mail registration allowed for all voters	Closing date for registration before general election (days)	Persons eligible for absentee registration (a)	Automatic cancellation of registration for failure to vote for ____ years
Alabama		10	M/O	—
Alaska	★	30	(b)	2
Arizona		50	D,O	1 general election
Arkansas		20	B,D,S,T	4
California	★	29	(b)	—
Colorado		25	D	2 general elections
Connecticut	★	21 (e)	(b)	—
Delaware	★	3rd Sat. in Oct. (c)	(b)	2 general elections
Florida		30	B,D,E,R,S,T	2
Georgia		30	P	3
Hawaii	★	30	(d)	2
Idaho		17/10 (e)	T	4
Illinois		28	M/O	4
Indiana		29	B,D,S,T	2
Iowa	★	10	(b)	4
Kansas	★	20	(b)	2 general elections
Kentucky	★	30	(b)	4
Louisiana		24	D	4
Maine	★	Election day	(b)	—
Maryland	★	29	(b)	5
Massachusetts		28	D	1
Michigan		30	D,T	10
Minnesota	★	Election day (g)	(b)	4
Mississippi		30	M/O	4
Missouri		28	B,D,E,R,S,T	—
Montana	★	30	(b)	1 presidential election
Nebraska	★	(j)	(b)	—
Nevada		30	M/O	1 general election
New Hampshire		10	B,D,E,R,S,T	10
New Jersey	★	29	(b)	4
New Mexico		28	T	1 general election
New York	★	30 (c)	(b)	4
North Carolina		21 (h)	M/O	2 presidential elections
North Dakota (i)				—
Ohio	★	30	(b)	4
Oklahoma		10	M/O	8
Oregon	★	21	(b)	2
Pennsylvania	★	30	(b)	2
Rhode Island		30	D	5
South Carolina	★	30	(b)	2 general elections
South Dakota	★	15	(b)	4
Tennessee	★	29	(b)	4
Texas	★	30	(b)	—
Utah	★	5 (k)	(b)	4
Vermont		17	(d)	4
Virginia		31	(t)	4
Washington		30	M/O	2 (l)
West Virginia	★	30	(b)	2 general elections
Wisconsin	★	Election day (k)	(b)	2 general elections
Wyoming		(g)	B,D,E,R,S,T	1 general election
Dist. of Columbia	★	30	(b)	4
American Samoa		30	M/O	2 general elections
Guam	★	10	(b)	1 general election
Puerto Rico		50	(b)	1 general election
U.S. Virgin Islands		30	(g)	2 general elections

Source: Adapted from *Vote! The First Steps*. League of Women Voters Education Fund, 1730 M St., N.W., Washington, D.C. (Copyright 1988), and state election administration officials.

Key:
— — No automatic cancellation
(a) In this column: B-Absent on business; C-Senior citizen; D-Disabled persons; E-Not absent, but prevented by employment from registering; M/O-No absentee registration except military and oversees citizens as required by federal law; O-Out of state; P-Out of precinct; R-Absent for religious reasons; S-Students; T-Temporarily out of jurisdiction.
(b) All voters. See column on mail registration.
(c) Closing date differs for primary election. In Connecticut, 1 day; Delaware, 21 days; New York, 60 days.
(d) Anyone unable to register in person.
(e) With precinct registrar, 17 days before; with county clerk, 10 days.
(f) No one is eligible to register absentee.
(g) Minnesota-20 days or election day; Wyoming-30 days or primary election day.
(h) Business days.
(i) No voter registration.
(j) 2nd Friday before election day.
(k) By mail: Utah, 20 days; Wisconsin, 13 days.
(l) 4 years if person voted in presidential election.

ELECTIONS

Table 5.10
POLLING HOURS: GENERAL ELECTIONS

State or other jurisdiction	Polls open	Polls close	Notes on hours (a)
Alabama	No later than 8 a.m.	Between 6 and 8 p.m.	Polls must be open at least 10 consecutive hours; hours set by county commissioner.
Alaska	7 a.m.	8 p.m.	
Arizona	6 a.m.	7 p.m.	
Arkansas	Between 7 and 8 a.m.	7:30 p.m.	
California	7 a.m.	8 p.m.	Polls must be open at least 8 consecutive hours; hours set by municipal governing body.
Colorado	7 a.m.	7 p.m.	
Connecticut	6 a.m.	8 p.m.	
Delaware	7 a.m.	8 p.m.	
Florida	7 a.m.	7 p.m.	
Georgia	7 a.m.	7 p.m.	
Hawaii	7 a.m.	6 p.m.	
Idaho	8 a.m.	8 p.m.	Polls may open earlier at option of county clerk, but not earlier than 7 a.m. Polls may close earlier if all registered electors in a precinct have voted.
Illinois	6 a.m.	7 p.m.	
Indiana	6 a.m.	6 p.m. local time	
Iowa	7 a.m.	9 p.m.	
Kansas	Between 6 and 7 a.m.	Between 7 and 8 p.m.	Hours may be changed by county election officer, but polls must be open at least 12 consecutive hours between 6 a.m. and 8 p.m.
Kentucky	6 a.m.	6 p.m.	Persons in line may vote only until 7 p.m.
Louisiana	6 a.m.	8 p.m.	
Maine	Between 6 and 9 a.m.	8 p.m.	Towns with population less than 100 may close after all registered voters have voted.
Maryland	7 a.m.	8 p.m.	
Massachusetts	7 a.m.	8 p.m.	
Michigan	7 a.m.	8 p.m.	
Minnesota	7 a.m.	8 p.m.	Municipalities of less than 500 may establish hours of no later than 10 a.m. to 8 p.m.
Mississippi	7 a.m.	7 p.m.	
Missouri	6 a.m.	7 p.m.	
Montana	7 a.m. noon	8 p.m. 8 p.m.	In precincts of over 200 registered voters. In precincts of less than 200 registered voters, polls may close when all registered electors have voted.
Nebraska	7 a.m. 8 a.m.	7 p.m. 8 p.m.	Mountain Time Zone. Central Time Zone.
Nevada	7 a.m.	7 p.m.	
New Hampshire	Varies 11 a.m.	Varies cities 7 p.m. towns	Cities: Polls open not less than 8 hours and may be opened not earlier than 6 a.m. nor later than 8 p.m. Small towns: In towns of less than 700 population the polls must be open at least five consecutive hours. In towns of less than 100 population, the polls close if all registered voters have appeared.
New Jersey	7 a.m.	8 p.m.	
New Mexico	7 a.m.	7 p.m.	
New York	6 a.m.	9 p.m.	
North Carolina	6:30 a.m.	7:30 p.m.	In precincts where voting machines are used, county board of elections may permit closing at 8:30 p.m., permitting that all precincts remain open until 8:30 p.m.
North Dakota	Between 7 and 9 a.m.	Between 7 and 9 p.m.	In precincts where less than 75 votes were cast in previous election, polls may open at noon.
Ohio	6:30 a.m.	7:30 p.m.	

POLLING HOURS: GENERAL ELECTIONS—Continued

State or other jurisdiction	Polls open	Polls close	Notes on hours (a)
Oklahoma	7 a.m.	7 p.m.	
Oregon	7 a.m.	8 p.m.	
Pennsylvania	7 a.m.	8 p.m.	
Rhode Island	Between 6 a.m. and noon	9 p.m.	Opening hours vary across cities and towns.
South Carolina	7 a.m.	7 p.m.	
South Dakota	7 a.m. 8 a.m.	7 p.m. 8 p.m.	Mountain Time Zone. Central Time Zone.
Tennessee	7 a.m. (CST) 8 a.m. (EST)	7 p.m. (CST) 8 p.m. (EST)	Counties with population over 120,000 may not open later than 8 a.m. Must be open at least 10 hours and no more than 13 hours.
Texas	7 a.m.	7 p.m.	
Utah	7 a.m.	8 p.m.	
Vermont	Between 6 and 10 a.m.	7 p.m.	
Virginia	6 a.m.	7 p.m.	
Washington	7 a.m.	8 p.m.	
West Virginia	7:30 a.m.	7:30 p.m.	
Wisconsin	7 a.m. Between 7 and 9 a.m.	8 p.m. 8 p.m.	1st, 2nd, 3rd class cities. 4th class cities, towns and villages.
Wyoming	7 a.m.	7 p.m.	
Dist. of Columbia	7 a.m.	8 p.m.	
American Samoa	8 a.m.	6 p.m.	
Guam	8 a.m.	8 p.m.	
Northern Mariana Is.	6:30 a.m.	6:30 p.m.	
Puerto Rico	8 a.m.	2 p.m.	
Virgin Islands	8 a.m.	6 p.m.	

Sources: State statutes and state election administration offices.
Note: Hours for primary, municipal and special elections may differ from those noted.

(a) In all states, voters standing in line when the polls close are allowed to vote; however, provisions for handling those voters vary across jurisdictions.

ELECTIONS

Table 5.11
VOTING STATISTICS FOR GUBERNATORIAL ELECTIONS*

State	Primary election			General election						Total votes
	Republican	Democrat	Total votes	Republican	Percent	Democrat	Percent	Other	Percent	
Alabama..........	29,194	940,088 (a)	969,282	696,203	56.3	537,163	43.5	2,864	0.2	1,236,230
Alaska...........	84,004	63,486	147,490	76,515	42.6	84,943	47.3	18,097	10.1	179,555
Arizona..........	226,296	210,688	436,984	343,913	39.7	298,986	34.5	224,085	25.8	866,984
Arkansas	22,346	520,628	542,974	248,427	36.1	439,882	63.9	242	0.0	688,551
California.......	2,059,413	2,168,625	4,228,038	4,506,601	60.5	2,781,714	37.4	155,236	2.1	7,443,551
Colorado	187,820	unopposed	187,820	434,420	41.0	616,325	58.2	8,183	0.8	1,058,928
Connecticut	94,536	(b)	94,536	408,489	41.1	575,638	57.9	9,565	1.0	993,692
Delaware ‡.......	unopposed	unopposed	0	169,733	70.7	70,236	29.3	0	0.0	239,969
Florida	554,663 (a)	1,006,662 (a)	1,561,325	1,847,525	54.6	1,538,620	45.4	26	0.0	3,386,171
Georgia..........	unopposed	611,463	611,463	346,512	29.5	828,465	70.5	137	0.0	1,175,114
Hawaii	41,001	231,560	272,561	160,460	48.0	173,655	52.0	0	0.0	334,115
Idaho	unopposed	unopposed	0	189,794	49.0	193,429	49.9	4,203	1.1	387,426
Illinois.........	497,982	791,180	1,289,162	1,655,849	52.7	208,830 (c)	6.6	1,279,299	40.7	3,143,978
Indiana ‡	unopposed	903,040	903,040	1,002,207	46.8	1,138,574	53.2	0	0.0	2,140,781
Iowa	unopposed	134,191	134,191	472,712	51.9	436,987	48.0	924	0.1	910,623
Kansas	276,126	unopposed	276,126	436,267	51.9	404,338	48.1	0	0.0	840,605
Kentucky †......	90,370	633,718	724,088	273,141	35.1	504,674	64.9	0	0.0	777,815
Louisiana †	(d)	(d)	(d)	(d)	(d)	(d)	(d)	(d)	(d)	(d)
Maine	116,129	118,436	234,565	170,312	39.9	128,744	30.2	127,805	29.9	426,861
Maryland	unopposed	639,964	639,964	194,185	17.6	907,291	82.4	0	0.0	1,101,476
Massachusetts ...	64,373	unopposed	64,373	525,364	31.2	1,157,786	68.7	929	0.1	1,684,079
Michigan	582,337	457,087	1,039,424	753,647	31.4	1,632,138	68.1	10,779	0.4	2,396,564
Minnesota	192,153	510,495	702,648	606,755	42.9	790,138	55.8	19,096	1.3	1,415,989
Mississippi †	18,855	807,990 (a)	826,845	336,006	46.6	385,689	53.4	0	0.0	721,695
Missouri ‡	unopposed	460,973	460,973	1,339,531	64.2	724,919	34.8	21,478	0.1	2,085,928
Montana ‡.......	87,921	118,058	205,979	190,604	51.9	169,313	46.1	7,104	0.2	367,021
Nebraska	192,851	145,057	337,908	298,325	52.9	265,156	47.0	941	0.2	564,422
Nevada	68,236	89,960	158,196	65,081	25.0	187,268	71.9	8,026	3.1	260,375
New Hampshire ...	83,271	unopposed	83,271	267,064	60.4	172,543	39.0	2,316	0.6	441,923
New Jersey §	395,059	381,015	776,074	838,553	36.7	1,379,937	60.0	35,274	3.3	2,286,693
New Mexico......	89,107	unopposed	89,107	209,455	53.0	185,378	47.0	0	0.0	394,833
New York	unopposed	unopposed	0	1,363,810	31.8	2,775,229	64.6	155,085	3.6	4,294,124
North Carolina ‡ ..	unopposed	506,073	506,073	1,222,338	56.1	957,687	43.9	0	0.0	2,180,025
North Dakota ‡ ...	unopposed	unopposed	0	119,986	40.1	179,094	59.9	0	0.0	299,080
Ohio	730,946	unopposed	730,946	1,207,264	39.4	1,858,372	60.6	975	0.0	3,066,611
Oklahoma	158,899	517,310 (a)	676,209	431,762	47.5	405,295	44.5	72,868	8.0	909,925
Oregon	284,937	317,517	602,454	506,986	47.8	549,456	51.9	3,188	0.3	1,059,630
Pennsylvania	unopposed	973,210	973,210	1,638,268	48.4	1,717,484	50.7	32,523	1.0	3,388,275
Rhode Island	unopposed	75,393	75,393	203,550	50.8	196,936	49.2	30	0.0	400,516
South Carolina ..	unopposed	329,496	329,496	384,565	51.0	361,325	47.9	7,861	1.0	753,751
South Dakota	116,098	71,944	188,042	152,543	51.8	141,898	48.2	0	0.0	294,441
Tennessee	236,141	740,469	976,610	553,449	45.7	656,602	54.2	288	0.0	1,210,339
Texas	544,719	1,096,552	1,641,271	1,813,779	52.7	1,584,515	46.0	43,166	1.3	3,441,460
Utah ‡	(b)	(b)	(b)	260,462	40.1	249,321	38.4	139,331	2.5	649,114
Vermont	unopposed	unopposed	0	105,191	43.3	134,438	55.4	3,250	1.3	242,879
Virginia §	401,887	(b)	401,887	89,195	9.0	896,936	90.8	1,947	0.2	988,078
Washington ‡	334,441	595,244	929,685	708,481	37.8	1,166,448	62.2	0	0.0	1,874,929
West Virginia ‡ ..	147,468	348,886	496,354	267,172	41.1	382,421	58.9	0	0.0	649,593
Wisconsin	301,118	268,169	569,287	805,090	52.7	705,578	46.2	16,292	1.1	1,526,960
Wyoming	94,068	41,265	135,333	75,841	46.0	88,879	54.0	0	0.0	164,720

Source: *America Votes*. New Jersey and Virginia by state elections offices.
* Figures are for 1986, except where indicated: † 1987; ‡ 1988; § 1989.
(a) Total shown is for first primary. Total votes for runoff election: Alabama, 931,345; Florida, Republican-390,985, Democrat-848,041; Mississippi, 666,922; Oklahoma, 446,763.
(b) Candidates nominated by convention.
(c) No Democratic candidate for Governor on ballot; Fairchild "paired" Democrat for Lieutenant Governor; Democratic vote cast for "no name" and Fairchild.
(d) Louisiana has an open primary which requires all candidates, regardless of party affiliation, to appear on a single ballot. If a candidate receives over 50 percent of the vote in the primary, he is elected to the office. If no candidate receives a majority vote, then a single election is held between the two candidates receiving the most votes.

ELECTIONS

Table 5.12
VOTER TURNOUT IN NON-PRESIDENTIAL ELECTION YEARS: 1978, 1982 AND 1986
(In thousands)

State or jurisdiction	1986 Voting age population (a)	1986 Number registered	1986 Number voting (b)	1982 Voting age population (a)	1982 Number registered	1982 Number voting (b)	1978 Voting age population (a)	1978 Number registered	1978 Number voting (b)
United States....	182,628	121,089	64,803	169,339	110,477	67,592	158,373	104,829	61,038
Alabama..........	3,010	2,362	1,236	2,812	2,136	1,128 (c)	2,669	1,938	730 (d)
Alaska...........	385	292	181	287	266	195 (c)	269	238	130
Arizona..........	2,605	1,598	867	2,061	1,141	726 (c)	1,766	969	551
Arkansas.........	1,761	1,189	695	1,650	1,116	789 (c)	1,575	1,047	524 (c)
California........	20,8785	12,834	7,444	18,277	11,559	7,876 (c)	16,546	10,130	7,132
Colorado	2,489	1,822	1,061	2,225	1,456	956 (c)	1,974	1,345	848
Connecticut	2,492	1,673	994	2,378	1,647	1,084 (c)	2,254	1,626	1,061
Delaware	490	296	161	443	286	191 (d)	426	278	166
Florida	9,614	5,631	3,430	8,169	4,866	2,689 (c)	6,862	4,217	2,530
Georgia..........	4,665	2,576	1,225	4,040	2,316	1,169 (c)	3,667	2,183	663 (c)
Hawaii	824	420	334	716	405	312 (c)	657	395	293
Idaho	701	550	387	661	541	327 (c)	612	526	297
Illinois...........	8,550	6,004	3,144	8,346	5,965	3,691 (f)	8,132	5,809	3,343
Indiana	4,068	2,878	1,556	3,904	2,937	1,817 (d)	3,812	2,851	1,405
Iowa	2,068	1,622	911	2,094	1,586	1,038 (c)	2,075	1,588	843 (c)
Kansas	1,829	1,173	841	1,759	1,186	763 (c)	1,681	1,182	749 (d)
Kentucky	2,746	1,999	677	2,620	1,827	700 (e)	2,528	1,666	477 (d)
Louisiana	3,175	2,179	1,370	3,055	1,965	(g)	2,760	1,821	840
Maine	893	790	427	831	766	460 (c)	791	692	375 (d)
Maryland	3,491	2,140	1,113	3,190	1,968	1,139 (c)	3,014	1,888	1,012 (c)
Massachusetts	4,535	3,006	1,684	4,394	3,027	2,051 (d)	4,213	2,920	2,044
Michigan	6,791	5,791	2,397	6,554	5,625	3,040 (c)	6,406	5,230	2,985
Minnesota	3,161	2,615	1,416	2,988	2,668	1,805 (d)	2,823	2,511	1,625
Mississippi	1,867	1,652	524	1,745	1,508	645 (d)	1,672	1,150 (h)	584 (d)
Missouri	3,821	2,769	1,477	3,640	2,749	1,544 (d)	3,499	2,579	1,546 (i)
Montana.........	586	444	318	569	446	321 (d)	548	410	297
Nebraska	1,167	850	564	1,144	832	548 (c)	1,108	833	511
Nevada	780	368	262	661	322	240 (d)	520	268	195
New Hampshire ...	823	551	251	697	462	285 (c)	638	489	279
New Jersey.......	5,943	3,777	1,554	5,544	3,681	2,194 (d)	5,326	3,602	2,060
New Mexico......	1,101	633	395	936	583	407 (c)	841	598	357
New York	13,480	8,071	4,294	13,153	7,635	5,222 (c)	12,912	7,801	4,929
North Carolina ...	4,913	3,081	1,591	4,417	2,675	1,321 (e)	4,088	2,430	1,136 (d)
North Dakota	483	(j)	289	473	(j)	262 (d)	455	(j)	235
Ohio	7,970	5,987	3,121	7,793	5,674	3,395 (d)	7,638	5,222	3,018
Oklahoma	2,404	2,018	910	2,299	1,614	883 (c)	2,081	1,366	801
Oregon	2,051	1,502	1,060	1,954	1,517	1,042 (c)	1,808	1,473	911 (c)
Pennsylvania	9,060	5,847	3,388	8,883	5,703	3,684 (c)	8,673	5,590	3,742 (c)
Rhode Island	764	525	323	726	534	343 (d)	707	534	332
South Carolina ...	2,534	1,299	754	2,291	1,229	672 (c)	2,104	1,098	633 (d)
South Dakota	509	428	296	482	426	279 (c)	480	421	260 (c)
Tennessee	3,661	2,446	1,210	3,375	2,273	1,260 (d)	3,179	2,138	1,190 (c)
Texas............	12,270	7,287	3,441	10,793	6,415	3,191 (c)	9,350	5,682	2,370 (c)
Utah	1,078	763	435	986	749	531 (d)	858	667	385
Vermont	412	328	197	379	316	169 (c)	353	286	125
Virginia..........	4,544	2,610	1,043	4,078	2,234	1,415 (d)	3,794	2,027	1,251
Washington	3,417	2,230	1,337	3,154	2,106	1,368 (d)	2,792	1,961	1,029
West Virginia	1,398	946	396	1,408	948	565 (d)	1,363	1,021	493
Wisconsin........	3,563	(j)	1,527	3,464	(j)	1,580 (c)	3,263	1,682	1,501 (c)
Wyoming	351	235	165	354	230	169 (c)	296	201	142
Dist. of Columbia...	489	282	132	487	361	111 (e)	515	250	103

Sources: U.S. Department of Commerce, Bureau of the Census, *Statistical Abstract of the United States* and unpublished data from the Republican National Committee.
(a) Estimated as of November 1 of the year indicated. Includes armed forces stationed in each state, aliens and institutional population.
(b) Number represents total voting in general election for all races for the year indicated, except where noted. Total persons voting restricted to number of ballots recorded by secretaries of state as having been cast. 1986-Highest number if votes cast for the Senatorial election, the gubernatorial election or all races for the U.S. House of Representatives.
(c) Total vote for largest race—governor.
(d) Total vote for largest race—senator.
(e) Total vote for largest race—congressional.
(f) Total vote for largest race—secretary of state.
(g) Under Louisiana's election law, candidates of all parties run together on a single non-partisan ballot in September. If no candidate wins a majority of the vote, the top two finishers, regardless of party, oppose each other in a November runoff. In 1982, the congressional incumbents were reelected in the September race.
(h) Estimated.
(i) Total vote for largest race—state auditor.
(j) No required statewide registration.
(k) Total vote for largest race—mayor.

ELECTIONS

Table 5.13
VOTER TURNOUT FOR PRESIDENTIAL ELECTIONS: 1980, 1984 AND 1988
(In thousands)

State or jurisdiction	1988 Voting age population (a)	1988 Number registered	1988 Number voting (b)	1984 Voting age population (a)	1984 Number registered	1984 Number voting (b)	1980 Voting age population (a)	1980 Number registered	1980 Number voting (b)
Alabama	3,010	2,380	1,378	2,892	2,343	1,442	2,757	2,132	1,342
Alaska	385	294	200	351	305	208	277	259	158
Arizona	2,605	1,798	1,172	2,268	1,463	1,026	1,970	1,121	874
Arkansas	1,761	1,203	828	1,607	1,268	884	1,628	1,186	838
California	20,875	14,004	9,887	19,181	13,074	9,505	17,548	1,1361	8,587
Colorado	2,489	2,030	1,372	2,353	1,621	1,295	2,123	1,434	1,184
Connecticut	2,492	1,784	1,443	2,401	1,806	1,467	2,304	1,706	1,406
Delaware	490	318	250	459	314	255	432	301	236
Florida	9,614	6,047	4,302	8,665	5,547	4,180	7,578	4,810	3,687
Georgia	4,665	2,941	1,810	4,231	2,372	1,776	3,870	2,377	1,597
Hawaii	824	444	354	758	419	336	697	403	303
Idaho	701	572	409	686	582	411	646	581	437
Illinois	8,550	6,357	4,559	8,438	6,470	4,819	8,235	6,230	4,740
Indiana	4,068	2,866	2,169	3,993	3,054	2,233	3,892	2,944	2,242
Iowa	2,068	1,690	1,226	2,120	1,729	1,320	2,099	1,717	1,318
Kansas	1,829	1,266	993	1,798	1,291	1,022	1,730	1,291	980
Kentucky	2,746	2,026	1,323	2,697	2,023	1,369	2,596	1,759	1,295
Louisiana	3,175	2,228	1,628	3,129	2,262	1,707	2,919	2,015	1,549
Maine	893	855	555	854	811	553	811	760	523
Maryland	3,491	2,310	1,714	3,260	2,253	1,676	3,080	2,065	1,540
Massachusetts	4,535	3,275	2,633	4,443	3,254	2,559	4,278	3,153	2,524
Michigan	6,791	5,953	3,669	6,566	5,889	3,802	6,520	5,726	3,910
Minnesota	3,161	2,917	2,097	3,058	2,893	2,084	2,933	2,353	2,052
Mississippi	1,867	1,596	932	1,802	1,670	941	1,723	1,482	893
Missouri	3,821	2,942	2,094	3,708	2,969	2,123	3,578	2,841	2,100
Montana	586	506	366	591	527	384	560	496	364
Nebraska	1,167	899	661	1,172	903	652	1,133	856	641
Nevada	780	445	350	691	356	287	602	297	248
New Hampshire	823	650	451	734	544	389	672	523	384
New Jersey	5,943	4,011	3,100	5,687	4,073	3,218	5,422	3,766	2,976
New Mexico	1,101	675	521	1,002	651	514	900	653	457
New York	13,480	8,612	6,486	13,301	9,044	6,807	12,933	7,898	6,202
North Carolina	4,913	3,432	2,134	4,593	3,271	2,715	4,274	2,775	1,856
North Dakota	483	(c)	297	493	(c)	309	467	(c)	302
Ohio	7,970	6,323	4,394	7,841	6,358	4,548	7,744	5,887	4,284
Oklahoma	2,404	2,199	1,171	2,408	1,950	1,256	2,207	1,458	1,150
Oregon	2,051	1,524	1,202	1,984	1,609	1,227	1,929	1,569	1,182
Pennsylvania	9,060	5,876	4,536	8,975	6,194	4,845	8,787	5,754	4,562
Rhode Island	764	549	405	735	542	410	710	531	416
South Carolina	2,534	1,438	986	2,382	1,396	969	2,215	1,236	894
South Dakota	509	440	313	508	443	318	488	448	328
Tennessee	3,661	2,417	1,636	3,490	2,580	1,712	3,323	2,149	1,618
Texas	12,270	8,202	5,427	11,436	7,900	5,398	10,130	6,640	4,542
Utah	1,078	807	647	1,023	840	630	935	782	604
Vermont	412	348	243	392	322	235	370	312	213
Virginia	4,544	2,877	2,192	4,235	2,552	2,147	3,930	2,302	1,866
Washington	3,417	2,499	1,865	3,228	2,458	1,884	3,040	2,182	1,742
West Virginia	1,398	969	653	1,422	1,025	736	1,400	1,035	738
Wisconsin	3,536	(c)	2,192	3,485	(c)	2,112	3,375	(c)	2,273
Wyoming	351	226	177	354	240	189	332	219	177
Dist. of Columbia	489	300	193	489	275	211	495	289	175

Source: U.S. Department of Commerce, Bureau of the Census, *Statistical Abstract of the United States, 1989-90.*
(a) Estimated population, 18 years old and over. Includes armed forces in each state, aliens, and institutional population.
(b) "Number voting" is number of ballots cast in presidential race.
(c) No statewide registration required. Excluded from totals for persons registered.

ELECTIONS

Table 5.14
STATE INITIATIVES: REQUESTING PERMISSION TO CIRCULATE A PETITION

State	Applied to (a) Amendment	Applied to (a) Statute	Signatures required to request a petition (b) Amendment	Signatures required to request a petition (b) Statute	Request submitted to	Request form furnished by (c)	Restricted subject matter (d)	Individual responsible for petition Title	Individual responsible for petition Summary	Financial contributions reported (e)	Deposit required (f)
Alabama	...	...	...	...	...	...	...	...	...	...	...
Alaska	...	D	...	100	LG	SP	Y	LG	LG	Y	$100.00
Arizona	D	D	15% EV	10% EV	SS	ST	N	...	...	Y	...
Arkansas	D	D	...	...	AG	SP	N	AG	AG	N	...
California	D	D	...	...	AG	SP	N	AG	AG	Y	$200.00
Colorado	D	D	...	...	...	...	N	(g)	(g)	Y	...
Connecticut	...	...	...	...	...	...	...	...	...	...	...
Delaware	...	...	...	...	...	...	...	...	...	...	...
Florida	D	...	...	...	SS	SP	N	P	P	Y	...
Georgia	...	...	...	...	...	...	...	...	...	...	...
Hawaii	...	...	...	...	...	...	...	...	...	...	...
Idaho	...	D	...	20	SS	SP	N	AG	AG	Y	...
Illinois	D	...	...	...	...	...	...	...	...	...	...
Indiana	...	...	...	...	...	...	...	...	...	...	...
Iowa	...	...	...	...	...	...	...	...	...	...	...
Kansas	...	...	...	...	...	...	...	...	...	...	...
Kentucky	...	...	...	...	...	...	...	...	...	...	...
Louisiana	...	...	...	...	...	...	...	...	...	...	...
Maine	...	I	...	...	...	SP	Y	P	P	Y	...
Maryland	...	...	...	...	...	...	...	...	...	...	...
Massachusetts	I	I	10	10	AG	ST	Y	AG	AG	Y	...
Michigan	D	I	...	...	...	...	Y	...	...	Y	...
Minnesota	...	...	...	...	...	...	...	...	...	...	...
Mississippi	...	...	...	...	...	...	...	...	...	...	...
Missouri	D	D	...	...	SS	SP	Y	SS,AG	...	Y	...
Montana	D	D	...	...	SS	SP	Y	AG	AG	Y (h)	...
Nebraska	D	D	...	...	SS	SP	Y	AG	AG	Y	N
Nevada	D	I	...	...	SS	SP	Y	P	P	Y (i)	...
New Hampshire	...	...	...	...	...	...	...	...	...	...	...
New Jersey	...	...	...	...	...	...	...	...	...	...	...
New Mexico	...	...	...	...	...	...	...	...	...	...	...
New York	...	...	...	...	...	...	...	...	...	...	...
North Carolina	...	...	...	...	...	...	...	...	...	...	...
North Dakota	D	D	25	25	SS	SP	Y	SS,AG	SS,AG	Y (e)	...
Ohio	D	I	...	...	SS	SP	Y	...	AG	Y	...
Oklahoma	D	D	...	...	SS	SP	N	AG	AG	Y	...
Oregon	D	D	25	25	SS	SP	N	AG	AG	Y	...
Pennsylvania	...	...	...	...	...	...	...	...	...	...	...
Rhode Island	...	...	...	...	...	...	...	...	...	...	...
South Carolina	...	...	...	...	...	...	...	...	...	...	...
South Dakota	D	D	...	...	SS	SP	N	P	...	Y	...
Tennessee	...	...	...	...	...	...	...	...	...	...	...
Texas	...	...	...	...	...	...	...	...	...	...	...
Utah	...	I,D	...	5	LG	SP	N	LG	LG	N	...
Vermont	...	...	...	...	...	...	...	...	...	...	...
Virginia	...	...	...	...	...	...	...	...	...	...	...
Washington	...	I,D	...	1	SS	SP	N	AG	AG	Y	N
West Virginia	...	...	...	...	...	...	...	...	...	...	...
Wisconsin	...	...	...	...	...	...	...	...	...	...	...
Wyoming	...	D	...	100	SS	SP	Y	AG,SS	AG,SS	Y	$100.00

Source: State election administration offices.

Key:
... — Not applicable
D — Direct
I — Indirect
EV — Eligible voters
LG — Lieutenant Governor
SS — Secretary of State
AG — Attorney General
P — Proponent
ST — State
SP — Sponsor
Y — Yes
N — No

(a) An initiative may provide a Constitutional Amendment or develop a new statute, and may be formed either directly or indirectly. The direct initiative allows a proposed measure to be placed on the ballot after a specific number of signatures have been secured on a petition. The indirect initiative must first be submitted to the legislature for decision after the required number of signatures have been secured on a petition, prior to placing the proposed measure on the ballot.

(b) Prior to circulating a statewide petition, a request for permission to do so must first be submitted to a specified state officer.
(c) The form on which the request for petition is submitted may be the responsibility of the sponsor or may be furnished by the state.
(d) Restrictions may exist regarding the subject matter to which an initiative may be applied. The majority of these restrictions pertain to the dedication of state revenues and appropriations, and laws that maintain the preservation of public peace, safety, and health.
(e) In some states, a list of financial contributors and the amount of their contributions must be submitted to the specified state officer with whom the petition is filed. In North Dakota, if over $100 in aggregate for calendar year.
(f) A deposit may be required after permission to circulate a petition has been granted. This amount is refunded when the completed petition has been filed correctly.
(g) Title Setting Board—SS, AG, Director of Legislative Legal Services.
(h) Contributions reported to Commissioner of Political Practices; petitions filed with SS.
(i) Expenditures made in excess of $500.00 for the purpose of advocating the passage or defeat of the measure must be reported.

Table 5.15
STATE INITIATIVES: CIRCULATING THE PETITION

State or other jurisdiction	Basis for signatures (see key below) Amendment	Basis for signatures Statute	Maximum time period allowed for petition circulation (a)	Can signatures be removed from petition (b)	Completed petition filed with	Days prior to election Amendment	Days prior to election Statute
Alabama	...	...	...	...	...	...	...
Alaska	15% VG	10% TV from 2/3 ED	1 year	Y	LG	...	...
Arizona	10% VG, 5% each from 15 co.	10% VG	2 years	Y	SS	4 months	4 months
Arkansas	8% VG	8% VEG, 5% each from 15 co.	...	...	SS	...	...
California	...	5% VG	150 days	Y	SS	131 days	131 days
Colorado	5% VSS	5% VSS	6 months	...	SS	3 months	...
Connecticut	...	...	...	...	...	...	...
Delaware	...	...	...	...	...	...	...
Florida	8% VEP, 8% from 1/2 CD	...	...	...	SS	91 days	...
Georgia	...	...	...	...	...	...	...
Hawaii	...	...	...	...	...	...	...
Idaho	8% VG	10% VG	...	...	SS	6 months	4 months
Illinois	...	...	2 years	Y	SS	...	...
Indiana	...	...	...	...	...	...	...
Iowa	...	...	...	...	...	...	...
Kansas	...	...	...	...	...	...	...
Kentucky	...	...	...	...	...	...	...
Louisiana	...	10% VG	1 year	...	...	...	...
Maine	...	...	...	...	...	...	...
Maryland	...	...	...	...	...	...	...
Massachusetts	3% VG, no more than 25% from 1 co.	3% VG, no more than 25% from 1 co. (c)	...	Y	SS	...	...
Michigan	10% VG	8% VG	(d)	...	SS	(e)	(e)
Minnesota	...	...	...	...	...	...	...
Mississippi	...	...	...	Y	SS	...	...
Missouri	8% VG, 8% each from 2/3 CG	5% VG, 5% each from 2/3 CD	12 months	...	...	4 months	...
Montana	10% VG, 10% each from 2/5 SLD	5% VG, 5% each from 1/3 SLD	1 year	Y	SS	(f)	(f)
Nebraska	10% EV, 5% each from 2/5 co.	7% EV, 5% each from 2/5 co.	...	Y	SS	4 months	4 months
Nevada	10% TV, 10% each from 3/4 co.	10% TV, 10% each from 3/4 co.	(g)	...	SS	30 days prior to LS	30 days
New Hampshire	...	...	...	...	...	...	...
New Jersey	...	...	...	...	...	...	...
New Mexico	...	...	...	...	...	...	...
New York	...	...	...	...	...	...	...
North Carolina	4% resident population	2% resident population	...	...	...	...	...
North Dakota	10% VG, 1.5% each from 1/2 co.	3% VG, 1.5% each from 1/2 co. (h)	...	...	SS	90 days	90 days
Ohio	...	...	...	Y	SS	90 days	90 days
Oklahoma	15% VH	8% VH	90 days	N	SS	...	...
Oregon	8% VG	6% VG	...	...	SS	4 months	4 months
Pennsylvania	...	...	...	...	...	...	...
Rhode Island	...	...	...	...	...	...	...
South Carolina	...	...	...	...	...	...	...
South Dakota	10% VG	5% VG	1 year	...	SS	one year	189 days
Tennessee	...	...	...	...	...	...	...
Texas	...	...	...	...	...	...	...
Utah	...	10% VG, 10% each from 1/2 co.	2 years	Y	LG	...	150 days
Vermont	...	...	...	...	...	...	...

STATE INITIATIVES: CIRCULATING THE PETITION—Continued

State or other jurisdiction	Basis for signatures		Maximum time period allowed for petition circulation (a)	Can signatures be removed from petition (b)	Completed petition filed with	Days prior to election	
	Amendment	Statute (see key below)				Amendment	Statute
Virginia	...	...	...	...	...	...	...
Washington	...	8% VG	(h)	Y	SS	...	(i)
West Virginia	...	...	...	...	...	...	...
Wisconsin	...	...	...	...	...	...	...
Wyoming	...	15% TV	18 months	Y	SS	...	60 days

Source: State election administrative offices.

Key:
... — Not applicable
VG — Total votes cast for the position of governor last election
EV — Eligible voters
VH — Total votes cast for the office receiving the highest number of votes cast last general election
TV — Total voters in last general election
ED — Election district
co. — county
SS — Secretary of State
LS — Legislative Session

(a) The petition circulation period begins when petition forms have been approved and provided to sponsors. Sponsors are those individuals granted permission to circulate a petition, and are therefore responsible for the validity of each signature on a given petition.
(b) Should an individual wish to remove his/her name from a petition, a request to do so must be submitted in writing to the state officer with whom the petition is filed.
(c) First Wednesday in December.
(d) In Michigan, signatures dated more than 180 days prior to the filing date are ruled invalid.
(e) Constitutional Amendment—not less than 120 days prior to the next general election; statute—approximately 160 days prior to the next general election.
(f) Second Friday of the fourth month prior to election (3 1/2 months).
(g) Constitutional Amendment—276 days; Amend or create a statute—291 days.
(h) Direct—6 months; Indirect—10 months.
(i) Direct—4 months; Indirect—10 months prior to legislative session.

ELECTIONS

Table 5.16
STATE INITIATIVES: PREPARING THE INITIATIVE TO BE PLACED ON THE BALLOT

State	Signatures verified by who (a)	Within how many days after filing	Number of days to complete a petition that is: Incomplete (b)	Number of days to complete a petition that is: Not accepted (c)	Penalty for falsifying petition (denotes fine, jail term)	Petition certified (d) by who
Alabama	Director of Elections	60 days	...	...	Class B misdemeanor	LG
Alaska	SS, county recorder	10 days (g)	30 days	...	Class 1 misdemeanor	SS
Arizona	Clerk or registrar of voters	15 days	10 days	15 days	$50-$100.00, 1-5 yrs	SS
Arkansas		25-105 days	30 days	...		
California						
Colorado	SS	21 days	...	...	...	SS
Connecticut	...	...	...	...	...	...
Delaware	Supervisor of elections	...	...	...	...	SS
Florida		...	...	...	...	...
Georgia						
Hawaii	County clerk	...	...	...	...	SS
Idaho	SBE and Election Auth.	14 days	...	10 days	$5,000.00, 2 yrs	SBE
Illinois	...	...	...	...	...	...
Indiana	...	...	...	...	...	...
Iowa	...	25 days	...	...	...	SS
Kansas						
Kentucky						
Louisiana						
Maine						
Maryland						
Massachusetts	Local board of registrar	2 weeks	4 weeks (e)	...	...	...
Michigan	City and township clerks	...	...	...	...	...
Minnesota	...	...	...	...	...	...
Mississippi	...	...	...	...	...	...
Missouri	SS, local election auth.	...	Prior to filing deadline	...	Class A misdemeanor	SS
Montana	County registrar	4 weeks	...	...	$500.00, 6 months	SS
Nebraska	County clerk or election commr.	40 days	...	10 days	Class IV felony	SS
Nevada	County clerk or registrar	20-50 days	...	...	$10,000.00, 1-10 yrs	SS
New Hampshire	...	...	...	...	...	...
New Jersey	...	...	...	...	...	...
New Mexico	...	...	...	...	...	...
New York	...	...	...	...	...	...
North Carolina	SS	35 days	20 days	...	...	SS
North Dakota	...	...	10 days	...	...	SS
Ohio	County board of elections	...	...	...	$1,000.00, 6 months	SS
Oklahoma	SS, county elections official	15 days	...	...	...	SS
Oregon	...	...	...	...	...	...
Pennsylvania	...	...	...	...	...	...
Rhode Island	...	...	...	...	...	...
South Carolina	SS	...	...	...	...	SS
South Dakota	...	...	...	...	...	...
Tennessee	...	...	...	...	...	...
Texas	...	...	...	...	...	...
Utah	County clerks	...	...	...	$500.00, 2 yrs	LG
Vermont	...	...	...	...	...	...

STATE INITIATIVES: PREPARING THE INITIATIVE TO BE PLACED ON THE BALLOT—Continued

State	Signatures verified by who (a)	Within how many days after filing	Number of days to complete a petition that is:		Penalty for falsifying petition (denotes fine, jail term)	Petition certified (d) by who
			Incomplete (b)	Not accepted (c)		
Virginia	...	...	...	...	...	...
Washington	SS	(f)	...	10 days (h)	...	SS
West Virginia	...	...	...	...	...	...
Wisconsin	...	...	...	...	...	...
Wyoming	SS	60 days	60 days	60 days	$1,000.00, 1 yr	...

Source: State election administration offices.

Key:
... — Not applicable
SS — Secretary of State
LG — Lieutenant Governor
BSC — Board of State Canvassers
SBE — State Board of Elections
LS — Legislative session

(a) The validity of the signatures, as well as the correct number of required signatures must be verified before the initiative is allowed on the ballot.
(b) If an insufficient number of signatures are submitted, sponsors may amend the original petition by filing additional signatures within a given number of days after filing. If the necessary number of signatures have not been submitted by this date, the petition is declared void.
(c) In some cases, the state officer will not accept a valid petition. In such a case, sponsors may appeal this decision to the Supreme Court, where the sufficiency of the petition will be determined. If the petition is determined to be sufficient, the initiative is required to be placed on the ballot.
(d) A petition is certified for the ballot when the required number of signatures have been submitted by the filing deadline, and are determined to be valid.
(e) Applies to statuatory initiatives.
(f) Direct—no specific limit; Indirect—45 days.
(g) In Arizona, the secretary of state has 48 hours to count signatures and 15 days to complete random sample; the county recorder then has 10 days to verify signatures.
(h) In Washington, a petition that is not accepted may be *appealed* in 10 days.

ELECTIONS

Table 5.17
STATE INITIATIVES: VOTING ON THE INITIATIVE

State	Ballot (a) Title by	Ballot (a) Summary by	Election where initiative voted on	Effective date of approved initiative (b) Amendment	Effective date of approved initiative (b) Statute	Days to contest election results (c)	Can an approved initiative be: Amended	Can an approved initiative be: Vetoed	Can an approved initiative be: Repealed	Can a defeated initiative be refiled
Alabama	...	...	...	...	...	...	...	...	...	...
Alaska	LG	...	(d)	...	...	90 days	Y	N	after 2 yrs	Y
Arizona	...	...	GE	IM	IM	5 days	Y	N	Y	...
Arkansas	AG	AG	...	30 days	30 days	60 days	...	N	N	...
California	AG	AG	GE	IM (b)	IM (b)	5 days	Y	...	Y	Y
Colorado	SS,AG,LS	SS,AG,LS	next biennial election	30 days	30 days	...	...	N	...	Y
Connecticut	...	...	...	...	...	...	...	...	...	...
Delaware	...	...	...	...	...	...	...	...	...	...
Florida	P,AG	P,AG	GE	(f)	...	10 days	Y	N	N	Y
Georgia	...	...	...	...	...	...	...	...	...	...
Hawaii	...	...	...	...	...	...	...	...	...	...
Idaho	AG	AG	GE	...	30 days	20 days	...	...	...	...
Illinois	SBE	SBE	GE	20 days	...	15 days	...	...	...	...
Indiana	...	...	...	...	...	...	...	...	...	...
Iowa	...	...	...	...	...	...	...	...	...	...
Kansas	...	...	...	...	...	...	...	...	...	...
Kentucky	...	...	...	...	...	...	...	...	...	...
Louisiana	...	...	...	...	...	...	...	...	...	...
Maine	...	...	REG or SP	30 days after 2nd vote	...	...	N	N	N	...
Maryland	...	...	...	...	...	...	...	...	...	...
Massachusetts	AG	AG	GE	30 days	30 days	10 days	Y	Y	Y	6 years
Michigan	BSC	BSC	GE	45 days (b)	10 days (b)	2 days	Y	N	Y	...
Minnesota	...	...	...	...	...	...	...	...	...	...
Mississippi	...	...	...	...	...	...	...	...	...	...
Missouri	...	LC	GE or SP	30 days	IM	30 days	...	N	...	Y
Montana	...	AG	GE	July 1	Oct. 1	...	...	N	...	Y
Nebraska	AG	AG	GE 4 mo. after filing	10 days (b)	10 days (b)	40 days	...	N	...	after 3 yrs
Nevada	SS,AG	SS,AG	GE	10 days (e)	10 days (e)	10 days	N	N	N	Y
New Hampshire	...	...	...	...	...	...	...	...	...	...
New Jersey	...	...	...	...	...	...	...	...	...	...
New Mexico	...	...	...	...	...	...	...	...	...	...
New York	...	...	...	...	...	...	...	...	...	...
North Carolina	...	...	...	...	...	...	...	...	...	...
North Dakota	...	...	PR,SP, or GE	30 days	30 days	...	w/i 7 Yrs	N	w/i 7 yrs	Y
Ohio	SS	Ohio Ballot Board	(g)	...	...	15 days	...	N	...	Y
Oklahoma	AG	AG	...	IM	IM	...	...	N	Y	after 3 yrs
Oregon	AG	...	GE even years	30 days	30 days	40 days	N	N	Y	Y
Pennsylvania	...	...	...	...	...	...	...	...	...	...
Rhode Island	...	...	...	...	...	...	...	...	...	...
South Carolina	...	...	...	...	...	...	...	...	...	...
South Dakota	...	AG	GE	1 day	1 day	10 days	...	N	Y	Y
Tennessee	...	...	...	...	...	...	...	...	...	...
Texas	...	...	...	...	...	...	...	...	...	...
Utah	LC	LC	GE	...	5 day	5 days	Y	N	...	Y
Vermont	...	...	...	...	...	...	...	...	...	...
Virginia	...	...	...	...	...	...	...	...	...	...
Washington	AG	AG	GE	...	IM	3	after 2 yrs	...	after 2 yrs	Y
West Virginia	...	...	...	...	...	...	...	...	...	...
Wisconsin	...	...	...	...	...	...	...	...	...	...
Wyoming	SS	SS,AG	GE 120 days after LS	...	90 days	...	Y	N	after 2 yrs	after 5 yrs

Source: State election administrative offices.

Key:
- ... — Not applicable
- LG — Lieutenant Governor
- SS — Secretary of State
- AG — Attorney General
- P — Proponent
- LC — Legislative Council
- BSC — Board of State Canvassers
- SBE — State Board of Elections
- GE — General election
- REG — Regular election
- SP — Special election
- IM — Immediately
- LS — Legislative legal services
- Y — Yes
- N — No

(a) In some states, the ballot title and summary will differ from that on the petition.

(b) A majority of the popular vote is required to enact a measure. In Massachusetts and Nebraska, apart from satisfying the requisite majority vote, the measure must receive, respectively, 30% and 35% of the total votes cast in favor. An initiative approved by the voters may be put into effect immediately after the approving votes have been canvassed—California and Nebraska; or after a certain number of days have passed following the election in which the initiative was voted on; Michigan—Constitutional Amendment or after certification - statutory initiative.

(c) Individuals may contest the results of a vote on an initiative within a certain number of days after the election including the measure proposed.

(d) First statewide election at least 120 days after the legislative session.

(e) Fourth Wednesday in November.

(f) First Tuesday after the first Monday in January following the general election.

(g) General election at least 90 days after filing.

ELECTIONS

Table 5.18
STATE REFERENDUMS: REQUESTING PERMISSION TO CIRCULATE A PETITION

State	Citizen petition	Types of referendum (a) Legislative	Constitutional convention	Signatures required to request a petition (b)	Request submitted to	Request forms furnished by (c)	Restricted subject matter (d)	State officer responsible for petition Title	Summary	Financial contributions reported (e)	Deposit required (f)
Alabama	...	...	...	...	...	...	...	...	...	...	...
Alaska	Y	N	...	100	LG	SP	Y	LG	LG	Y	$100.00
Arizona	Y	Y	...	5% EV	SS	ST	N	...	...	Y	...
Arkansas	Y	...	...	...	AG	SP	N	AG	AG	N	...
California	Y	...	Y	...	AG	SP	N	AG	AG	Y	N
Colorado	Y	Y	...	...	...	...	N	(h)	(h)	Y	...
Connecticut	...	Y	...	...	...	...	...	...	...	...	...
Delaware	...	...	...	...	...	...	...	...	...	...	...
Florida	...	...	...	...	...	...	...	...	...	...	...
Georgia	...	...	...	...	...	...	...	...	...	...	...
Hawaii	...	...	...	...	...	...	...	...	...	...	...
Idaho	Y	...	...	20	SS	SP	N	AG	AG	Y	...
Illinois	Y	Y	...	...	...	...	...	...	...	...	...
Indiana	...	...	...	...	...	...	...	...	...	...	...
Iowa	...	...	Y	...	...	...	...	...	...	...	...
Kansas	...	...	Y	...	...	...	...	...	...	...	...
Kentucky	Y	Y	Y	...	SS	...	...	...	...	...	...
Louisiana	...	...	...	...	...	...	...	...	...	...	...
Maine	Y	Y	Y	...	SS	SP	Y	SS	SS	Y	...
Maryland	Y	...	...	...	SS	...	...	...	...	...	...
Massachusetts	Y	...	...	10	SS	ST	...	AG	AG	Y	...
Michigan	Y	Y	Y	...	...	...	Y	...	...	Y	...
Minnesota	...	...	...	...	...	...	...	...	...	...	...
Mississippi	...	...	...	...	...	...	...	...	...	...	...
Missouri	Y	Y	...	...	SS	SP	N	SS,AG	...	Y	...
Montana	Y	Y	...	...	SS	SP	N	AG	AG	Y	N
Nebraska	Y	...	...	5% EV	SS	SP	Y	AG	AG	Y	N
Nevada	Y	...	...	...	SS	SP	N	...	...	(g)	N
New Hampshire	...	...	...	...	...	...	...	...	...	...	...
New Jersey	...	Y	Y	...	...	...	...	...	...	...	...
New Mexico	Y	...	Y	...	SS	...	...	SS	SS	...	...
New York	...	...	Y	...	SS	...	...	...	...	...	...
North Carolina	...	...	Y	...	SS	...	...	...	...	...	...
North Dakota	Y	...	...	...	SS	SP	Y	SS	SS	Y (e)	...
Ohio	Y	Y	Y	...	SS	SP	Y	...	AG	Y	N
Oklahoma	Y	Y	Y	...	SS	SP	N	SS	SS	Y	...
Oregon	Y	...	...	...	SS	SP	N	SS	SS	Y	...
Pennsylvania	...	...	Y	...	...	...	...	...	...	...	...
Rhode Island	...	...	Y	...	...	...	...	...	...	...	...
South Carolina	...	...	...	...	...	...	...	...	...	...	...
South Dakota	Y	...	...	...	SS	SP	Y	P	...	Y	N
Tennessee	...	...	...	...	...	...	...	...	...	...	...
Texas	...	...	...	...	...	...	...	...	...	...	...
Utah	Y	...	...	5	LG	SP	N	LG	LG	N	...
Vermont	...	...	...	...	...	...	...	...	...	...	...
Virginia	...	...	...	...	...	...	...	...	...	...	...
Washington	Y	Y	...	1	SS	SP	Y	AG	AG	Y	N
West Virginia	...	...	...	...	...	...	...	...	...	...	...
Wisconsin	...	Y	Y	...	...	...	...	...	...	...	...
Wyoming	Y	...	...	100	SS	SP	Y	SS	SS	Y	$100.00

Source: State election administration offices.

Key:
... — Not applicable
EV — Eligible voters
LG — Lieutenant Governor
SS — Secretary of State
AG — Attorney General
P — Proponent
ST — State
SP — Sponsor
Y — Yes
N — No

(a) Three forms of referendum exist: Citizen petition, Submission by the legislature and Constitutional requirement. The table outlines the steps necessary to enact a citizens petition.
(b) Prior to circulating a statewide petition, a request for permission to do so must first be submitted to a specified state officer. Some states require such signatures to be those only of eligible voters.
(c) The form on which the request for petition is submitted may be the responsibility of the sponsor (SP) or may be furnished by the state (ST).
(d) Restrictions may exist regarding the subject matter to which a referendum may be applied. The majority of these restrictions pertain to the dedication of state revenues and appropriations, and laws that maintain the preservation of public peace, safety and health.
(e) In some states, a list of individuals who contribute financially to the referendum campaign must be submitted to the specified state officer with whom the petition is filed. In North Dakota, if over $100 in aggregate for calendar year.
(f) A deposit may be required after permission to circulate a petition has been granted. This amount is refunded when the completed petition has been filed correctly.
(g) Expenditures advocating defeat or passage of the question in excess of $500.00 must be reported.
(h) Title Setting Board—SS, AG, Legislative legal services.

ELECTIONS

Table 5.19
STATE REFERENDUMS: CIRCULATING THE PETITION

State	Basis for signatures (see key below)	Maximum time period allowed for petition circulation (a)	Can signatures be removed from petition (b)	Completed Petition filed: With who	Number of days after legislative session
Alabama	...	...	...	...	...
Alaska	10% TVE, from 2/3 ED	w/i 90 days of LS	Y	LG	90 days
Arizona	5% VG	w/i 90 days after LS	Y	SS	90 days
Arkansas	...	...	...	SS	...
California	5% VG	90 days	Y	SS	90 days
Colorado	5% VSS	6 months	...	SS	90 days
Connecticut	...	...	...	...	...
Delaware	...	...	...	...	...
Florida	...	...	...	...	...
Georgia	...	...	...	...	...
Hawaii	...	...	...	...	...
Idaho	10% VG	...	...	SS	60 days
Illinois	10% VG	2 years	Y	SS	6 months prior to GE
Indiana	...	...	...	...	...
Iowa	...	...	...	...	...
Kansas	...	...	...	...	...
Kentucky	5% VG	...	...	SS	4 months
Louisiana	...	...	...	...	...
Maine	10% VG	1 year	...	SS	90 days
Maryland	3% VG	...	...	...	...
Massachusetts	3% VG	90 days	...	...	90 days
Michigan	5% VG	...	...	SS	90 days
Minnesota	...	...	...	...	...
Mississippi	...	...	...	...	...
Missouri	5% VG from 2/3 ED	...	Y	SS	90 days
Montana	5% VG, from 1/3 ED	1 year	Y	SS	6 months
Nebraska	5% VG, from 2/5 co.	...	...	SS	90 days
Nevada	10% EV last GE	276 days	...	SS	120 prior to next GE
New Hampshire	...	...	...	...	...
New Jersey	...	...	...	...	...
New Mexico	10% EV last GE, from 3/4 co.	...	...	...	4 months prior to next GE
New York	...	...	...	...	...
North Carolina	...	...	...	...	...
North Dakota	2% total population	...	...	SS	90 days after receiving
Ohio	6% EV, 3% each from 1/2 co.	...	...	SS	90 days
Oklahoma	5% HV	...	N	SS	90 days
Oregon	4% VG	...	N	SS	90 days
Pennsylvania	...	...	...	...	...
Rhode Island	...	...	...	...	...
South Carolina	...	...	...	...	...
South Dakota	5% VG	90 days	N	SS	90 days
Tennessee	...	...	...	...	...
Texas	...	...	...	...	...
Utah	10% VG	...	...	LG	60 days
Vermont	...	...	...	...	...
Virginia	...	...	...	...	...
Washington	4% VG	w/i 90 days after LS	Y	SS	90 days
West Virginia	...	...	...	...	...
Wisconsin	...	...	...	...	...
Wyoming	15% TVE	18 months	Y	SS	90 days

Source: State election administration offices.
Key:
... — Not applicable
VG — Total votes cast for the position of governor last election
EV — Eligible voters
TVE — Total votes cast in the last general election
ED — Election district
co. — county
SS — Secretary of State
LG — Lieutenant Governor
Y — Yes
N — No

(a) The petition circulation period begins when petition forms have been approved and provided to or by the sponsors. Sponsors are those individuals granted permission to circulate a petition, and are therefore responsible for the validity of each signature on a given petition.
(b) Should an individual wish to remove his/her name from a petition, a request to do so must first be submitted in writing to the state officer with whom the petition is filed.

ELECTIONS

Table 5.20
STATE REFERENDUMS: PREPARING THE REFERENDUM TO BE PLACED ON THE BALLOT

State	Signatures verified by (a)	Within how many days after filing	# days to amend/appeal petition that is Incomplete (b)	# days to amend/appeal petition that is Not accepted (c)	Penalty for falsifying petition (denotes fine, jail term)	Petition certified (d) by
Alabama	...	...	...	...	...	...
Alaska	Director of elections	60 days	10 days (e)	...	Class B misdemeanor	LG
Arizona	SS, county recorder	10 days (f)	...	10 days	Class 1 misdemeanor	SS
Arkansas	SS	...	30 days	15 days	$50-$100.00, 1-5 yrs	...
California	County clerk or registrar of voters	...	...	...	...	SS
Colorado	...	...	...	...	...	...
Connecticut	...	...	...	...	...	...
Delaware	...	...	...	...	...	...
Florida	SS, Election superintendent	...	...	...	...	...
Georgia	...	...	...	...	...	...
Hawaii	...	...	...	...	...	...
Idaho	SS, county clerk	...	...	...	$5,000.00, 2 yrs	...
Illinois	SBE and election auth.	14 days	...	...	...	SBE
Indiana	...	...	...	...	...	...
Iowa	...	...	...	...	...	...
Kansas	...	...	...	...	...	...
Kentucky	...	...	...	...	...	...
Louisiana	...	...	...	...	...	...
Maine	SS	...	...	...	...	...
Maryland	...	...	...	...	...	...
Massachusetts	...	...	...	...	...	...
Michigan	City and township clerks	...	...	...	...	BSC
Minnesota	...	...	...	...	...	...
Mississippi	...	...	...	...	...	...
Missouri	SS, local election authorities	...	...	...	Class A misdemeanor	SS
Montana	County registrar	28 days	...	...	$500.00, 6 mo. jail	SS
Nebraska	SS, county clerk, election commr.	40 days	...	...	Class IV felony	SS
Nevada	County clerk, registrar	20-50 days	...	...	$10,000.00, 1-10 yrs	SS
New Hampshire	...	...	...	...	...	...
New Jersey	...	...	...	...	...	...
New Mexico	...	...	30 days	15 days	...	...
New York	...	...	...	...	...	...
North Carolina	...	...	...	...	...	...
North Dakota	SS	...	20 days	...	...	...
Ohio	County board of elections	...	10 days	...	$1000.00, 6 months	SS
Oklahoma	...	...	...	...	$500.00, 2 yrs	...
Oregon	SS, county elections officials	15 days	...	...	...	SS
Pennsylvania	...	...	...	...	...	...
Rhode Island	...	...	...	...	...	...
South Carolina	...	...	...	...	...	...
South Dakota	SS	...	...	...	...	SS
Tennessee	...	...	...	...	...	...
Texas	...	...	...	...	...	...
Utah	County clerks	...	...	...	$1500.00, 2 yrs	LG
Vermont	...	...	...	...	...	...
Virginia	...	...	...	...	...	...
Washington	SS	(h)	...	10 days (g)	...	SS
West Virginia	...	...	...	...	...	...
Wisconsin	...	...	...	...	...	...
Wyoming	SS	60 days	60 days	60 days	$1,000.00, 1 yr	...

Source: State election administration offices.
Key:
... — Not applicable
SS — Secretary of State
LG — Lieutenant Governor
BSC — Board of State Canvassers
SBE — State Board of Elections
(a) The validity of the signatures, as well as the correct number of required signatures must be verified before the referendum is allowed on the ballot.
(b) If an insufficient number of signatures are submitted, sponsors may amend the original petition by filing additional signatures within a given number of days after filing. If the necessary number of signatures have not been submitted by this date, the petition is declared void.
(c) In some cases, the state officer will not accept a valid petition. In such cases, sponsors may appeal this decision to the Supreme Court, where the sufficiency of the petition will be determined. If the petition is determined to be sufficient, the referendum is required to be placed on the ballot.
(d) A petition is certified for the ballot when the required number of signatures have been submitted by the filing deadline, and are determined to be valid.
(e) If within 90 days of the legislative session.
(f) In Arizona, the secretary of state has 48 hours to count signatures and 15 days to complete random sample; the county recorder then has 10 days to verify signatures.
(g) In Washington, a petition that is not accepted may be appealed in 10 days.
(h) No specified time.

ELECTIONS

Table 5.21
STATE REFERENDUMS: VOTING ON THE REFERENDUM

State	Ballot (a) Title by	Ballot (a) Summary by	Election where referendum voted on	Effective date of approved referendum (b)	Days to contest election results (c)
Alabama	...	...	...	...	...
Alaska	LG,AG	LG,AG	1st statewide election 180 days after LS	30 days	5 days
Arizona	...	...	GE	IM	5 days
Arkansas	AG	AG	...	30 days	60 days
California	AG	AG	GE or SP 31 days after LS	IM	...
Colorado	SS,AG,LS	SS,AG,LS	GE	30 days	...
Connecticut	...	...	...	...	...
Delaware	...	...	...	...	...
Florida	...	...	...	...	...
Georgia	...	...	...	...	...
Hawaii	...	...	...	...	...
Idaho	AG	AG	Biennial or REG	30 days	...
Illinois	SBE	SBE	GE	20 days	30 days
Indiana	...	...	...	...	...
Iowa	...	...	...	...	...
Kansas	...	...	...	...	...
Kentucky	...	...	GE or SP	IM	...
Louisiana	...	...	...	...	...
Maine	...	...	GE or SP more than 60 days but less than 6 mo after LS	30 days	...
Maryland	...	...	...	30 days	...
Massachusetts	...	...	GE more than 60 days after filing	30 days	...
Michigan	BSC	BSC	GE	10 days	2 days
Minnesota	...	...	...	...	...
Mississippi	...	...	...	...	...
Missouri	SS	LC	GE	IM	30 days
Montana	AG	AG	GE	Oct. 1 (d)	...
Nebraska	AG	AG	GE not less than 30 days after filing	10 days	40 days
Nevada	SS,AG	SS,AG	GE	IM	10 days
New Hampshire	...	...	...	...	...
New Jersey	...	...	...	...	...
New Mexico	SS	...	GE	IM	...
New York	...	...	...	...	...
North Carolina	...	...	...	...	...
North Dakota	SS	...	PR or SP	30 days	...
Ohio	...	Ohio Ballot Board	GE more than 60 days after filing	30 days	15 days
Oklahoma	SS	...	GE or SP	IM	...
Oregon	AG	...	GE or SP	30 days	40 days
Pennsylvania	...	...	...	...	...
Rhode Island	...	...	...	...	...
South Carolina	...	...	...	...	...
South Dakota	...	AG	GE	1 day	10 days
Tennessee	...	...	...	...	...
Texas	...	...	...	...	...
Utah	LC	LC	GE	5 days (d)	5 days
Vermont	...	...	...	...	...
Virginia	...	...	...	...	...
Washington	AG	AG	GE	IM	3 days
West Virginia	...	...	...	...	...
Wisconsin	...	...	...	...	...
Wyoming	SS	SS,AG	GE more than 180 days after LS	30 days	30 days

Source: State election administration offices.

Key:
... — Not applicable
LG — Lieutenant Governor
AG — Attorney General
SS — Secretary of State
BSC — Board of State Canvassers
SBE — State Board of Elections
LC — Legislative Council
GE — General Election
PR — Primary
REG — Regular Election
SP — Special election
IM — Immediately
LS — Legislative Legal Services
Y — Yes
N — No

(a) In some states, the ballot title and summary will differ from that on the petition.
(b) A majority of the popular vote is required to enact a measure in every state. In Nebraska, a referendum approved by the voters may be put into effect immediately after the approving votes have been canvassed by the governor or after a certain number of days have passed following the vote for a successful referendum. In Massachusetts the measure must also receive at least 30 percent of the total ballots cast in the last election.
(c) Individuals may contest the results of a vote on a referendum within a certain number of days after the election including this matter. In Alaska, five days to request recount with appeal to the court within five days after recount.
(d) Unless otherwise specified.

ELECTIONS

Table 5.22
STATE RECALL PROVISIONS: APPLICABILITY TO STATE OFFICIALS AND PETITIONS

State	Officers to whom recall is applicable (a)	# times recall can be attempted	Recall may be initiated after official has been in office	Recall may not be initiated with days remaining in term	Basis for signatures (b) (see key below) Statewide officers	Others	Maximum time period allowed for petition circulation (c)
Alabama							
Alaska	All but judicial officers		120 days	180 days	25% VO	25% VO	
Arizona	All	(d)	6 mo./5 days legislators		25% VO	25% VO	120 days
Arkansas							
California	All	(e)	No limit		12% VO, 1% from 5 co.	20% VO	160 days
Colorado	All	(f)	6 mo./5 days general assembly		25% VO	25% VO	
Connecticut							
Delaware							
Florida							
Georgia	All		180 days	180 days	15% VO, 1/15 from each cong. district	30% VO	90 days
Hawaii							
Idaho	All but judicial officers	(d)	90 days		20% EVg	20% EV	60 days
Illinois							
Indiana							
Iowa							
Kansas	All but judicial officers	1 time	120 days	200 days	40% VO	40% VO	90 days
Kentucky							
Louisiana	All but jud. officers of records	(g)			33 1/3% EV (h)	33 1/3% EV (h)	180 days
Maine							
Maryland							
Massachusetts							
Michigan	All but jud. officers of records		6 months		25% EVg	25% EVg	(i)
Minnesota							
Mississippi							
Missouri							
Montana	All public officers elected or appt.	(d)	2 months		15% EV	(j)	3 months
Nebraska	All public officers	(k)	6 months (l)		25% EV in given jurisdiction	25% EV in given jurisdiction	60 days
Nevada							
New Hampshire							
New Jersey							
New Mexico							
New York							
North Carolina							
North Dakota	All	1 time			25% EVg	25% EVg	
Ohio							
Oklahoma							
Oregon	All	(d)	6 mo./5 days general assembly		15% voters for state supreme justice	15% voters for state supreme justice	90 days
Pennsylvania							
Rhode Island							
South Carolina							

STATE RECALL PROVISIONS—Continued

State	Officers to whom recall is applicable (a)	# times recall can be attempted	Recall may be initiated after official has been in office	Recall may not be initiated with days remaining in term	Basis for signatures (b) (see key below) Statewide officers	Basis for signatures (b) (see key below) Others	Maximum time period allowed for petition circulation (c)
South Dakota	...	...	...	...	...	...	...
Tennessee	...	...	...	...	...	...	...
Texas	...	...	...	...	...	...	...
Vermont	...	...	...	...	...	...	...
Virginia	...	...	...	180 days	...	...	...
Washington	All but judges of courts of records	...	IM	...	25% VO	35% VO	(m)
West Virginia	...	...	...	...	...	...	...
Wisconsin	All	1 time	1 year	...	25% VG	25% VG	60 days
Wyoming	...	...	...	...	...	...	...

Source: State election administration offices.

Key:
... — Not applicable
All — All elective officials
Vo — Number of votes cast in the last election for the office or official being recalled
EVg — Number of eligible voters in the last general election for governor
EV — eligible voters
IM — Immediately

(a) An *elective* official may be recalled by qualified voters entitled to vote for the recalled official's successor. An *appointed* official may be recalled by qualified voters entitled to vote for the successor(s) of the elective officer(s) authorized to appoint an individual to the position.
(b) Signature requirements for recall of those other than state elective officials are based on votes in the jurisdiction to which the said official has been elected.
(c) The petition circulation period begins when petition forms have been approved and provided to sponsors. Sponsors are those individuals granted permission to circulate a petition, and are therefore responsible for the validity of each signature on a given petition.
(d) If the treasury is reimbursed the cost of the first recall attempt.
(e) Must wait until 6 months after the first recall attempt.
(f) If signatures are obtained at least equal in number to 50% of those voting in the last general election.
(g) Must wait at least until 18 months after the first recall attempt.
(h) Basis for signatures — 33 1/3% if over 1,000 EV; 40% if under 1,000 EV.
(i) In Michigan, signatures dated more than 90 days prior to the filing deadline are ruled invalid.
(j) 15% EV for district or county officials, 10% EV for municipal or school officials.
(k) If the treasury is reimbursed the cost of subsequent recall efforts.
(l) Six months or 10 days after legislative session begins for legislators.
(m) Statewide officials—270 days; others—180 days.

ELECTIONS

Table 5.23
STATE RECALL PROVISIONS: PETITION REVIEW, APPEAL AND ELECTION

State	Signatures verified by (a)	Days to amend/appeal a petition that is: Incomplete (a)	Days to amend/appeal a petition that is: Not accepted (c)	Penalty for falsifying petition (denotes fines, jail time)	Time allowed for petition to be certified (d)	Days to step down after certification (e)	Voting on the recall (f) Election held	Voting on the recall (f) Election type	Days contest election results (g)
Alabama	...	...	...	...	...	...	...	...	...
Alaska	Director of Elections	20 days	20 days	Class B misdemeanor	30 days	...	60-90 days after cert.	SP,GE or PR	5 days
Arizona	SS, county recorder	...	10 days	Class 1 misdemeanor	75 days	5	100-120 days after cert.	SP	5 days
Arkansas	...	...	...	$50-$100.00, 1-5 yrs	...	...	...	...	...
California	County clerk/registrar of voters	...	...	...	...	...	60-80 days after cert.	SP	...
Colorado	...	...	...	...	30-60 days	...	60-90 days after cert.	SP or GE	...
Connecticut	...	...	...	...	...	...	...	...	...
Delaware	...	...	...	...	...	...	...	...	...
Florida	Election supervisor	Not allowed	10 days	$1,000.00, 12 months	30-45 days	...	30-45 days after cert.	SP or GE	5 days
Georgia	...	...	...	...	...	...	...	...	...
Hawaii	...	...	...	...	...	...	...	...	...
Idaho	SS, county clerk	30 days	10 days	$5,000.00, 2 yrs	10 days	5	45-60 days after cert.	SP or GE	...
Illinois	...	...	...	...	...	...	...	...	...
Indiana	...	...	...	...	...	...	...	...	...
Iowa	...	...	...	...	...	...	...	...	...
Kansas	County election officer	...	...	...	30 days	...	60-90 days after cert.	SP or GE	30 days
Kentucky	...	...	...	...	...	...	...	...	...
Louisiana	Registrar of voters	...	...	$100-1,000,30-90 days	10 days	...	at least 60 days after cert.	SP	30 days
Maine	...	...	...	...	...	...	...	...	...
Maryland	...	...	...	...	...	...	...	...	...
Massachusetts	...	...	...	...	...	...	...	...	...
Michigan	SS	...	...	...	...	IM	w/i 60 days after cert.	SP	2 days
Minnesota	...	...	...	...	...	...	...	...	...
Mississippi	...	...	...	...	...	...	...	...	...
Missouri	...	...	...	...	...	...	...	...	...
Montana	County clerk	20 days	...	$500.00, 6 mo.	30 days	5	3 months after cert.	SP or GE	...
Nebraska	...	...	...	...	...	...	...	...	...
Nevada	County clerk, registrar	...	...	$10,000.00,1-10 yrs	20-50 days	5	(h)	SP	10 days
New Hampshire	...	...	...	...	...	...	...	...	...
New Jersey	...	...	...	...	...	...	...	...	...
New Mexico	...	...	...	...	...	...	...	...	...
New York	...	...	...	...	...	...	...	...	...
North Carolina	...	...	...	...	...	...	...	...	...
North Dakota	SS	20 days	...	...	35 days	10	30-90 days after cert.	SP or GE	...
Ohio	...	...	...	...	...	...	...	...	...
Oklahoma	...	...	...	...	...	...	...	...	...
Oregon	SS or county clerk	...	...	...	10 days	5	35 days after cert.	SP	40 days
Pennsylvania	...	...	...	...	...	...	...	...	...
Rhode Island	...	...	...	...	...	...	...	...	...
South Carolina	...	...	...	...	...	...	...	...	...
South Dakota	...	...	...	...	...	...	...	...	...
Tennessee	...	...	...	...	...	...	...	...	...
Texas	...	...	...	...	...	...	...	...	...
Utah	...	...	...	...	...	...	...	...	...
Vermont	...	...	...	...	...	...	...	...	...

STATE RECALL PROVISIONS—Continued

State	Signatures verified by (a)	Days to amend/appeal a petition that is:		Penalty for falsifying petition (denotes fines, jail time)	Time allowed for petition to be certified (d)	Days to step down after certification (e)	Voting on the recall (f)		Days contest election results (g)
		Incomplete (a)	Not accepted (c)				Election held	Election type	
Virginia	...	...	...	...	...	...	...	...	...
Washington	SS, county auditor	...	10 days (i)	felony	w/i 10 days	IM	45-60 days after cert.	SP	10 days
West Virginia	...	...	...	...	...	...	...	...	...
Wisconsin	...	5 days	...	...	45 days	10	6 weeks after filed	SP or GE	...
Wyoming	...	...	...	...	...	...	...	...	...

Source: State election administration offices.

Key:
... — Not applicable
SS — Secretary of State
SP — Special election
GE — General election
PR — Primary election
IM — Immediate and automatic removal from office

(a) The validity of the signatures, as well as the correct number of required signatures must be verified before the recall is allowed on the ballot.
(b) If an insufficient number of signatures are submitted, sponsors may amend the original petition by filing additional signatures within a given number of days. If the necessary number of signatures have not been submitted by this date, the petition is declared void.
(c) In some cases, the state officer will not accept a valid petition. In such a case, sponsors may appeal this decision to the supreme court, where the sufficiency of the petition will be determined. When this is declared, the initiative is required to be placed on the ballot.
(d) A petition is certified for the ballot when the required number of signatures have been submitted by the filing deadline, and are determined to be valid.
(e) The official to whom a recall is proposed has a certain number of days to step down from his position before a recall election is initiated, if he desires to do so.
(f) A majority of the popular vote is required to recall an official in each state.
(g) Individuals may contest the results of a vote on a recall within a certain number of days after the results are certified. In Alaska, five days to request recount with appeal to court within five days of recount.
(h) A recall election is held 10-20 days after the court determines a recall election is to be held.
(i) In Washington, a petition that is not accepted may be appealed in 10 days.

CHAPTER SIX

STATE FINANCES

STATE GOVERNMENT FINANCES

By Henry S. Wulf

Introduction and Summary

State governments are important economic entities. A recent compilation combined information from Fortune magazine's ranking of the 500 largest industrial corporations with Bureau of the Census data on state government finances. The state with the least amount of fiscal activity, South Dakota, ranked 355th on this list, ahead of "such well known American corporations as: Macmillan, Fruit of the Loom, Bausch and Lomb, Champion Spark Plug . . . Fairchild Industries and Dr. Pepper/Seven Up." California ranked 5th between IBM and General Electric and New York 8th between Mobil and Chrysler.

The sheer magnitude of their economic activity aside, the real importance of state governments lies in the vital role they play in delivering or financing public services. In the past year this role has become increasingly more difficult as changes continue in the restructuring of American fiscal federalism.

Total state government revenues amounted to $541.8 billion in fiscal year 1988, an increase of 4.9 percent over 1987. This is the smallest single-year increase since 1955 and considerably below the 7.3 percent rise from 1986 to 1987. The major revenue sources and their share of total revenues were: taxes (49 percent), funds from the federal government (19 percent) insurance trust revenue (17 percent) and current charges (6 percent).

Expenditures in 1988 totaled $485 billion. This rise of 6.4 percent over the previous year was smaller than the 7.4 percent increase between 1986 and 1987. In accord with their role as financier of government services, states gave more than 3 out of every 10 dollars to local governments. Education and public welfare outlays together comprised more than one-half of all state expenditures, accounting for 32.9 and 17.4 percent, respectively.

The state government indebtedness total of $276.8 billion at the end of fiscal year 1988 had increased only 4.2 percent over the previous year. State government indebtedness, however, isn't as significant as that of local governments, which carry an additional $200 billion in debt. Compared with the federal government, state governments had only one-tenth as much indebtedness.

Cash and investment holdings were $783.4 billion in 1988. Only $112 billion, however, were in funds not committed to specific purposes such as insurance trust or bond redemption. The single largest amount of assets, $435 billion, was in state employee retirement systems.

The following discussion compares changes in state finances between 1987 and 1988 with changes that occurred in previous periods. The benchmarks used most often are the five-year period from 1983 to 1988 and the ten-year period from 1978 to 1988. The measure used to represent changes over time is a calculation of the average annual percentage change.

State Government Revenue

The overall revenue increase of 4.9 percent contained some diversity as shown in Table A. The two largest revenue sources, taxes and federal intergovernmental revenue, has higher growth than the average for all revenues, although the difference appears to be signifi-

---

Henry S. Wulf is Chief, Finance Branch, Governments Division, U.S. Bureau of the Census.

FINANCE AND BUDGET

cant only for taxes. The major revenue source that kept the overall rate so low was the decrease in insurance trust revenues. Two factors contributed to this. First, the earnings of employee retirement systems decreased nearly $2 billion, a result of difficulties in the financial markets after October 1987. Second, in their unemployment trust funds, eight states had repayments of prior year federal advances that resulted in a decrease of $1.7 billion of revenue in those trust funds.

Table A
Sources of state revenue and change from 1987 to 1988

	1988 % change 1987 to 1988	% of total revenue
Current charges	7.9	6.4
Taxes	7.1	48.7
Revenue from the Federal government	5.2	18.5
TOTAL REVENUE	4.9	100.0
Miscellaneous general revenue	3.9	7.3
Utility revenue	2.2	.6
Insurance trust revenue	-1.3	16.7
Liquor stores	-1.6	.5
Revenue from local governments	-2.2	1.2

The two largest sources of tax revenue, general sales and individual income taxes, contributed $87.0 and $80.1 billion respectively to the tax total of $264 billion. The 1988 general sales tax amount was up 9.8 percent over 1987 while the individual income tax increased 5.1 percent. Over the past 5 years general sales taxes have been growing at a rate of 10.2 percent annually and individual income taxes 10.0 percent annually. That the individual income tax rise was considerably lower (5.1 percent) than in recent experience (10.0 percent) was due, in part, to changes in federal income taxes that affected state individual income tax collections. Though many states enacted legislation in the wake of federal changes, collections in a number of cases were considerably less than had been expected.

There are two other aspects of state revenue that deserve comment, current charges and revenues from the federal government. All levels of government have shown increased interest in determining whether charges for specific services are commensurate with the cost. In state governments nearly four out of every five dollars in current charges derive from education (primarily tuition from public colleges and universities) and state hospitals. Without examining specific *quid pro quo* arguments concerning fees and services, one way to look at how the general attitude toward charges has affected collections is to see how quickly they're rising compared with other state revenues.

Over the past five years, all current charges have been rising at an average annual rate (8.2 percent) slightly lower than all revenue (8.7 percent). The average annual increases for both education (8.0 percent) and hospital services (7.0 percent) were considerably below those for all other charges such as highways, parks and natural resources, which grew at a combined annual rate of 10.0 percent. The general conclusion seems to be that, compared with other state revenues, current charges have been at least keeping pace over the past five years.

It is useful to compare growth rates in revenues the states received from the federal government in 1988 with those it received five years ago and 10 years ago. The year 1978 marked the height of federal revenues as a percent of all state and local government revenues. At that time the state governments themselves were direct recipients of money from the federal General Revenue Sharing (GRS) program. By 1983, only local governments were receiving GRS funds and a new philosophy was beginning to reshape the federal fiscal structure.

As the data in Table B show, there was significant disparity in the growth rates between funds the states were generating themselves and the money they were receiving from the federal government in the five years from 1978 to 1983. However, in the following five years, although the rise in federal revenue was lower, it was reasonably close to the growth of the states' own source revenues. Whatever separate forces might be driving either of these growth patterns, federal revenues in recent years are maintaining a similar pattern to the states themselves.

State Government Expenditure

Compared with recent history, the changes from 1987 to 1988 showed restrained growth

FINANCE AND BUDGET

Table B
Average annual percentage changes in selected state revenues

	Average Annual Percentage Change		
	1978 to 1983	1983 to 1988	1978 to 1988
From Own Sources	10.6	8.8	9.7
From the Federal Government	6.6	7.8	7.2

in nearly every outlay category. The data in Table C illustrate this clearly.

The only type of expenditure showing a marked difference from the experience of the past five years was interest on debt. Unlike the other categories which were slightly below the five-year average, interest on debt was substantially lower. This sizable change, however, is related to the considerable slowdown in the bond market, especially compared with the period 1983-1986.

Also related in part to changes in the bond market are the data on capital expenditures as seen in Table C. Though still among the most rapidly rising portions of state expenditures, capital outlay growth has slowed. From 1983 to 1986 it rose at an average annual rate of 14.4 percent, but dropped to 7.7 percent from 1986 to 1987 and 9.3 percent from 1987 to 1988. Part of the reason for the increasing emphasis in the states on capital outlays is the growing awareness of the need to provide adequate public infrastructure.

From the perspective of functional expenditures, education and public welfare were dominant, comprising slightly more than one-half of the total. These two, combined with the other major activities of insurance trust expenditures, highways, hospitals and interest on debt, account for three out of every four state dollars.

Among basic functions there was no pattern in the changes from 1987 to 1988 with one exception. Three criminal justice activities — correction, judicial and legal and police protection — rose from the previous year, respectively, 13.7, 12.9 and 11.4 percent. Each of these rose about twice as fast as the overall increase in expenditures. In total these three activities amounted to about 4.7 percent of all state expenditures. This bears watching to see if the level of increase will be sustained.

In addition to their roles as direct providers of government services, state governments also play a major part in the financing of local government services. In 1988, for example, more than 30 percent of all expenditures were intergovernmental payments to local governments. More than three-fifths of these payments were in support of education, but there were also significant amounts passed on for public welfare, unrestricted local government support and highways.

Table C
State expenditures by character and object

	Annual percent change		1988 % of total expenditure
	1987 to 1988	Average, 1983 to 1988	
Capital outlay	9.3	12.0	8.4
Intergovernmental expenditure	7.2	8.4	31.3
Salaries and wages	7.0	7.6	17.9
Current operations other than salaries and wages	6.7	8.6	26.0
TOTAL EXPENDITURE	6.4	7.7	100.0
Interest on debt	.4	11.5	4.2
Insurance benefits and repayments	2.1	.9	9.1
Assistance and subsidies	2.0	5.5	3.1

The continuing series of court cases concerning the equity of education financing might be the stimuli for very large and rapid increases in intergovernmental aid to education. Some observers think, however, that if the states suffer serious financial difficulties, they will, in turn, shift more of the financial burden of education to local governments.

State Government Indebtedness

State government indebtedness at the end of fiscal year 1988 was $276.8 billion. The percentage increase of only 4.2 percent over the previous year was the lowest in 35 years. This follows a period from 1983 to 1986 when the average annual percentage increase in debt was 14.0 percent.

The reasons for the sudden shift in debt financing are complex. They involve changes in federal law, general economic conditions, the fiscal condition of the states and priorities.

What future direction this segment of state finances will take is unclear. A number of states, with bond ratings lower than they've had in the recent past, will probably continue to borrow only minimal amounts. Capital spending by the states, on the other hand, continues to rise and the traditional source for this money has been debt obligations. Furthermore, there is increasing discussion about the need to replace deteriorating infrastructure. The major indicators and reports from the bond market appear to show a continuation of borrowing by the states similar to the slow growth of 1987 and 1988.

State Government Cash and Investments

Most of the state government cash and investment holdings total of $783 billion is dedicated for specific purposes and, therefore, is unavailable for financing general government activities. More than three-fifths of the total, for example, is for insurance trust activities such as state-administered retirement, unemployment compensation and workers' compensation. An additional one-fourth is held either as offsets for retiring long-term debt or in bond funds prior to the disbursement of bond issues. Thus, only 14 percent of the total, or $111.8 billion, is actually available to states in general accounts and specialized accounting reserves such as so-called rainy day funds.

A large portion of what is theoretically available, however, is encumbered by state constitutions or laws that severely restrict access to the funds. Two examples that are also among the largest of these specially restricted funds are the Texas Permanent School Fund and the Alaska Permanent Fund.

The overall growth in state cash and security holdings from 1987 to 1988 was 12.7 percent. In general, the prevailing financial conditions govern increases in these assets since state government contributions are normally fairly consistent.

Issues in State Finances

There are two important financial concerns for the states with both short-term and long-term implications. They are: Will there be significant changes in the general economy that will require serious financial adjustments? And, where are changes in fiscal relationships with the federal and local governments headed?

The National Conference of State Legislatures, in a recent survey of state finances, found that more than one-half of the states anticipate revenue shortfalls due primarily to slower economic growth. Eight states in the Northeast, according to the report, face deficits in the near future. The survey concludes that, "the substantial economic growth and low inflation of the 1980s enabled states to manage some difficult, long-term fiscal problems rather than solve them," but that these problems will be "less manageable" if the projected economic growth slows, as they predict. The executive director of the National Association of State Budget Officers has estimated that state revenues will decrease $4 billion for every 1 point increase in the unemployment rate.

Bureau of Economic Analysis data seem to buttress this argument of increasing financial difficulties for the states. The reported balance in state government "other funds" (excluding all trust funds) has become increasingly negative over the past four years: 1985, plus $0.8 billion; 1986, minus $0.6 billion; 1987, minus $9.7 billion; and 1988, minus $16.5 billion.

If these forecasts are correct, what does this portend for the states' ability to cope financially in what has been dubbed as the era of "competitive federalism?" The states have been filling gaps in recent years, according to some observers, left by the federal government's disinclination to maintain or increase certain services. The latest poll by the Advisory Commission on Intergovernmental Relations on public attitudes on government, however, showed that on the question of which level of government gave them the most for their money, the respondents picked the federal government first (33 percent), local governments next (29 percent) and state governments last (22 percent). A real question for the states is whether they can assume new responsibilities for services at the same time that there is apparently some reluctance among the public to give them the means to do this.

FINANCE AND BUDGET

6.1 STATE BUDGETARY CALENDARS

State	Budget guidelines to agencies	Agency requests submitted to Governor	Agency hearings held	Governor's Budget sent to legislature	Legislature adopts budget	Fiscal year begins	Frequency of legislative/ budget cycles
Alabama	July	Oct/Nov	December	February	Feb/May	October	Annual/Annual
Alaska	August	October	November	December	May	July	Annual/Annual
Arizona	June	September	October	January	April	July	Annual/Annual
Arkansas	March	July	August	Sept/Dec	Jan/April	July	Biennial/Biennial
California	July/Nov	Aug/Sept	Aug/Oct	January	June	July	Annual/Annual
Colorado	June	August	September	November(a)	April	July	Annual/Annual
Connecticut	July	September	February	February	May/June(b)	July	Annual/Annual
Delaware	August	Oct/Nov	Oct/Nov	January	June	July	Annual/Annual
Florida	July/August	Oct/Nov	November	February	June	July	Annual/Biennial(c)
Georgia	May	September	Nov/Dec	January	March	July	Annual/Annual
Hawaii	June/July	Aug/Sept	November	January(d)	April	July	Annual/Biennial
Idaho	May	September	November	January	March	July	Annual/Annual
Illinois	August	Nov/Dec	Nov/Dec	March	June	July	Annual/Annual
Indiana	June	September	Oct/Nov	January	April/May	July	Annual/Annual
Iowa	June	September	Nov/Dec	January	April/May	July	Annual/Annual
Kansas	June	September	Oct/Nov	January	April/May	July	Annual/Annual
Kentucky	July	October	Oct/Dec	January	March/April	July	Biennial/Biennial
Louisiana	September	December	January	April	July	July	Annual/Annual
Maine	July	September	Oct/Dec	January	June	July	Biennial/Biennial
Maryland	July	Aug/Sept	Oct/Nov	January	April	July	Annual/Annual
Massachusetts	August	October	October	Juanary	June	July	Annual/Annual
Michigan	June	Sept/Nov	Oct/Dec	February	June	October	Annual/Annual
Minnesota	May	October	November	January	May	July	Annual/Biennial
Mississippi	June	August	September	December	March/April	July	Annual/Annual
Missouri	July	October	. . .	January	April/May	July	Annual/Annual
Montana	June	Aug/Sept	. . .	December	April	July	Biennial/Biennial
Nebraska	July	September	January	January	April	July	Annual/Biennial
Nevada	June	September	Sept/Dec	January	June	July	Biennial/Annual
New Hampshire	June	October	November	February	June	July	Annual/Biennial
New Jersey	May	October	. . .	January	June	July	Annual/Annual
New Mexico	July	September	Oct/Dec	January	Feb/March	July	Annual/Annual
New York	July	September	Oct/Nov	January	March	April	Annual/Annual
North Carolina	March	July	November	February	July	July	Biennial/Biennial(e)
North Dakota	March	June/July	July/Oct	December	Jan/April	July	Biennial/Biennial
Ohio	July	Sept/Oct	Sept/Nov	Jan/March(f)	June	July	Biennial/Biennial(h)
Oklahoma	July	September	Sept/Nov	February	May	July	Annual/Annual
Oregon	March	Aug/Sept	Oct/Nov	December	June/July	July	Biennial/Biennial
Pennsylvania	August	October	Dec/Jan	February(g)	June	July	Annual/Annual
Rhode Island	June/July	October	November	February	May/June	July	Annual/Annual
South Carolina	May	August	September	January	June	July	Annual/Annual
South Dakota	June/July	September	September	December	March	July	Annual/Annual
Tennessee	August	October	November	January	April/May	July	Annula/Annual
Texas	March	June	July/Sept	January	May	September	Biennial/Biennial
Utah	July/August	Sept/Oct	November	December	February	July	Annual/Annual
Vermont	August	October	Sept/Oct	January	May	July	Annual/Annual
Virginia	May(h)	August(h)	Sept/Nov	January	March	July	Annual/Biennial(i)
Washington	April	September	October	December	May	July	Annual/Biennial(j)
West Virginia	July/August	September	Oct/Dec	January	March	July	Annual/Annual
Wisconsin	May	October	March	January	June	July	Annual/Annual
Wyoming	July/August	Oct/Nov	November	December	March	July	Annual/Biennial

Source: National Association of State Budget Officers, *Budgetary Process in the States* (July 1989).
 (a) Governor submits approved department budgets to legislature November 1. Final statewide budget is submitted in January.
 (b) Legislature adopts budget during June of odd years, May of even years.
 (c) Biennial budget submission but annual appropriation.
 (d) Budget document due to legislature at end of December. Appropriations bill due in January.
 (e) With annual updates.
 (f) Budget is submitted in January except during inauguration, then sumittted in in March. Appropriations are annual.
 (g) Budget is submitted in March when governor has been elected for first full term.
 (h) These dates are for the operating expense budget. For the capital budget, guidelines are sent to agencies in December, with requests due by March 1.
 (i) Virginia adopts a biennial budget in the even-numbered year. It is amended by the General Assembly in the odd-numbered year.
 (j) There are annual updates of the budget.

FINANCE AND BUDGET

Table 6.2
OFFICIALS OR AGENCIES RESPONSIBLE FOR BUDGET PREPARATION, REVIEW AND CONTROLS

State or other jurisdiction	Official/agency responsible for preparing budget document	Special budget review agency in legislative branch	Agency(ies) responsible for budgetary and related accounting controls
Alabama	State Budget Off., Dept. of Finance	Legislative Fiscal Off.	Dept. of Finance
Alaska	Director, Off. of Mgt. & Budget, Off. of the Governor	Div. of Legislative Audit; Div. of Legislative Finance; Administrative Services Div., Legislative Affairs Agcy.	Off. of Commissioner, Dept. of Revenue
Arizona	Director, Executive Budget Off., Dept. of Admn.	Jt. Legislative Budget Cmte.	Div. of Finance, Dept. of Admn.
Arkansas	Director, Off. of Budget, Dept. of Finance & Admn.	Fiscal & Tax Research Services, Bur. of Legislative Research	Dept. of Finance & Admn.
California	Director, Dept. of Finance	Jt. Legislative Budget Cmte.; Cmte. on Ways & Means	Dept. of Finance
Colorado	Director, Off. of State Planning & Budgeting	Jt. Budget Cmte.; Legislative Council	Div. of Accounts & Control, Dept. of Admn.
Connecticut	Executive Budget Officer, Budget & Finance Div., Off. of Policy & Mgt.	Off. of Fiscal Analysis	Off. of Policy & Mgt.
Delaware	Director, Off. of the Budget	Off. of Controller General, Legislative Council	Dept. of Finance
Florida	Director, Off. of Planning & Budgeting, Off. of the Governor	Senate, House Appropriations Cmtes.	Finance Div., Dept. of Banking & Finance
Georgia	Director, Off. of Planning & Budget	Legislative Budget Analyst, Legislative Budget Off.	Fiscal Div., Dept. of Administrative Services
Hawaii	Director, Dept. of Budget & Finance	Senate Ways & Means Cmte.; House Finance Cmte.	Dept. of Budget & Finance
Idaho	Administrator, Div. of Financial Mgt., Off. of the Governor	Legislative Budget Off.	Div. of Financial Mgt., Off. of the Governor
Illinois	Director, Bur. of the Budget, Off. of the Governor	Economic & Fiscal Comm.; Senate House Appropriations Cmtes.	Dept. of Revenue; Bur. of the Budget, Off. of the Governor
Indiana	Director, Budget Agcy.	Off. of Fiscal & Mgt. Analysis, Legislative Services Agcy.	Budget Agcy.
Iowa	Director, Dept. of Mgt.	Legislatiove Fiscal Bur.	Dept. of Mgt.
Kansas	Director, Div. of the Budget., Dept. of Admn.	Fiscal Analyst, Legislative Research Dept.	Div. of the Budget, Dept. of Admn.
Kentucky	State Budget Director, Governor's Off. for Policy & Mgt.	Budget Review Off., Legislative Research Comm.; Program Review & Investigation Cmte.; Interim Jt. Cmte. on Appropriations & Revenue	Finance & Admn. Cabinet
Louisiana	Budget Director, Div. of Admn., Office of the Governor	Legislative Fiscal Off.; Fiscal Services, Senate Research Services	Div. of Admn.
Maine	State Budget Officer, Bur. of the Budget, Dept. of Finance & Admn.	Off. of Fiscal & Program Review, Legislative Council	Dept. of Finance
Maryland	Secretary, Dept. of Budget & Fiscal Planning	Div. of Budget Review; Div. of Fiscal Research, Dept. of Fiscal Services	Comptroller of the Treasury
Massachusetts	Budget Director, Executive Off. for Admn. & Finance	Senate, House Ways & Means Cmtes.	Executive Off. for Admn. & Finance
Michigan	Director, Dept. of Mgt. & Budget	Senate, House Fiscal Agencies	Dept. of Mgt. & Budget
Minnesota	Commissioner, Dept. of Finance	Senate Finance Cmte.; House Ways & Means Cmte.	Dept. of Finance
Mississippi	Executive Director, Dept. of Finance & Admn.	Jt. Legislative Budget Off.	Dept. of Finance & Mgt.; Jt. Legislative Budget Off.
Missouri	Commissioner, Off. of Admn.	Oversight Div.	Office of Admn.
Montana	Director, Budget & Program Planning, Off. of the Governor	Off. of Legislative Fiscal Analyst	Budget & Program Planning, Off. of the Governor

FINANCE AND BUDGET

BUDGET OFFICIALS OR AGENCIES—Continued

State or other jurisdiction	Official/agency responsible for preparing budget document	Special budget review agency in legislative branch	Agency(ies) responsible for budgetary and related accounting controls
Nebraska	Budget Administrator, Budget Div., Administrative Services Dept.	Legislative Fiscal Analyst, Legislative Council	Budget Div., Administrative Services Dept.; Auditor of Public Accounts; Dept. of Revenue
Nevada	Director, Budget Div., Dept. of Admn.	Fiscal Analyst Div., Legislative Counsel Bur.	Controller
New Hampshire	Commissioner, Administrative Services Dept.; Budget Officer	Legislative Budget Assistant's Off.	Administrative Services Dept.
New Jersey	Director, Off. of Mgt. & Budget	Legislative Budget & Finance Off.; Central Mgt. Unit., Off. of Legislative Services	Treasury Dept.
New Mexico	Director, Budget Div., Dept. of Finance & Admn.	Legislative Finance Cmte.	Dept. of Finance & Admn.
New York	Director, Div. of Budget, Executive Dept.	Senate Finance Cmte.; Assembly Ways & Means Cmte.	Off. of the State Comptroller
North Carolina	Executive Assistant, Off. of State Budget	Fiscal Research Div., Legislative Services Off.	Off. of State Budget
North Dakota	Executive Budget Analyst; Director, Off. of Mgt. & Budget	Legislative Budget Analyst & Auditor, Legislative Council	Off. of Mgt. & Budget
Ohio	Off. of Budget & Mgt.	Legislative Budget Off., Legislative Services Comm.	Off. of Budget & Mgt.
Oklahoma	Director, Off. of State Finance	House of Rep., Fiscal Div.; Appropriations Coordinator, Senate Fiscal Staff	Off. of State Finance
Oregon	Administrator, Budget & Mgt. Div., Executive Dept.	Legislative Fiscal Off.	Budget & Mgt. Div., Executive Dept.
Pennsylvania	Secretary, Off. of Budget, Off. of the Governor	Senate, House Appropriations Cmtes. Legislative Budget & Finance Cmte.; Jt. Staff Government Comm.	Dept. of Revenue
Rhode Island	Deputy Director, Dept. of Admn.	Senate, House Fiscal Advisory Staffs	Dept. of Admn.
South Carolina	Director, Budget Div., Budget & Control Bd.	State Auditor	Budget & Control Bd.
South Dakota	Commissioner, Bur. of Finance & Mgt.	Legislative Research Council	Bur. of Finance & Mgt.
Tennessee	Commissioner, Budget Div., Dept. of Finance & Admn.	Fiscal Review Cmte.	Dept. of Finance & Admn.
Texas	Director, Governor's Off. of Budget & Planning	Legislative Budget Bd.	Public Accounts
Utah	Director, Off. of Planning & Budget	Off. of Legislative Fiscal Analyst	Div. of Finance, Administrative Services Dept.
Vermont	Commissioner, Dept. of Finance & Mgt.	Jt. Fiscal Cmte.	Dept. of Finance & Mgt., Agency of Admn.
Virginia	Director, Dept. of Planning & Budget	Senate Finance Cmte.; House Appropriations Cmte.	Off. of Finance
Washington	Director, Off. of Financial Mgt.	Ways & Means Cmte.	Off. of Financial Mgt.
West Virginia	Director, Budget Div., Dept. of Finance & Admn.	Budget Div., Legislative Auditor	Dept. of Finance & Admn.
Wisconsin	Administrator, State Executive Budget & Planning, Dept. of Admn.	Legislative Fiscal Bur.	Finance & Program Mgt., Dept. of Admn.
Wyoming	Administrator, Budget Div., Admn. & Fiscal Control Dept.	Audit & Fiscal Div., Legislative Services Off.	Off. of State Auditor
Dist. of Columbia	Director, Off. of the Budget	Cmte. of the Whole	Financial Mgt.
American Samoa	Director, Program Planning & Budget Development	Legislative Fiscal Off.	Dept. of Treasury
Guam	Director, Bur. of Budget & Mgt. Research	Ways & Means Cmte.	Dept. of Admn.

FINANCE AND BUDGET

BUDGET OFFICIALS OR AGENCIES—Continued

State or other jurisdiction	Official/agency responsible for preparing budget document	Special budget review agency in legislative branch	Agency(ies) responsible for budgetary and related accounting controls
No. Mariana Islands	Planning & Budget, Off. of the Governor	Senate Fiscal Affairs Cmte.; House Ways & Means Cmte.	Finance & Accounting Dept.
Puerto Rico	Director, Off. of Budget & Mgt.	Off. of Legislative Services; Senate Budget Off.; House Budget & Finance Off.	Off. of Budget & Mgt.
U.S. Virgin Islands	Director, Off. of Mgt. & Budget	Post Audit Div.	Dept. of Finance

Sources: The Council of State Governments, *State Legislative Leadership, Committees and Staff: 1989-90* and *State Administrative Officials Classified by Function: 1989-90.*

Table 6.3
STATE BALANCED BUDGETS: CONSTITUTIONAL AND STATUTORY PROVISIONS GUBERNATORIAL AND LEGISLATIVE AUTHORITY

State	Constitutional and Statutory Provisions				Gubernatorial Authority				Legislative Authority	
	Governor must submit a balanced budget	Legislature must pass a balanced budget	Governor must sign a balanced budget	May carry over deficit	Governor has line item veto	Can reduce budget without legislative approval	Restrictions on budget reductions	Votes required to override gubernatorial veto	Votes required to pass revenue increase	Votes required to pass budget
Alabama	C,S	C,S	C,S	...	*	*	ATB	Majority elected	Majority	Majority
Alaska	C	S	...	*	*	*	...	3/4 elected (a)	Majority elected	Majority elected
Arizona	C	C	C	...	*	*	(c)	2/3 elected	1/2 elected	1/2 elected
Arkansas	S	S	S	* (b)	*	*	ATB,MR	Majority elected	3/4 elected	3/4 elected
California	C	...	...	*	*	...	*	2/3 elected	2/3 elected	2/3 elected
Colorado	...	C	C	...	*	*	MR	2/3 elected	Majority present	Majority present
Connecticut	S	S	S	...	...	(e)	*	3/5 elected	Majority present (d)	Majority present (d)
Delaware	C	C	S	...	*	(f)	...	3/5 elected	3/5 elected	Majority elected
Florida	S	C	C	...	*	*	...	2/3 elected	Majority	Majority
Georgia	C	C	C	...	...	*	ATB	2/3 elected	Majority	Majority
Hawaii	C,S	...	C,S	...	*	*	...	2/3 elected	Majority elected	Majority elected (g)
Idaho	C	C	C	...	*	*	...	2/3 elected	Majority elected	Majority
Illinois	C	C	C	...	*	*	...	3/5 elected	Majority elected	Majority elected (h)
Indiana	C	C	C	*	...	*	...	Majority	Majority	Majority
Iowa	C	C	C	...	*	...	ATB	2/3 elected	Majority	Majority
Kansas	C	C	C	...	*	*	MR (i)	2/3 elected	Majority elected	Majority
Kentucky	C,S	S	C	...	*	*	*	2/3 elected	Majority elected	Majority present
Louisiana	C,S	C	C,S	*	*	*	MR	2/3 present	2/3 elected	1/2 elected
Maine	S	C	S	...	...	*	ATB (j)	2/3 present	Majority elected	(k)
Maryland	C	C	C	...	*	*	...	(l)	Majority	Majority
Massachusetts	C	C	C	...	*	*	...	2/3 present	Majority	Majority (m)
Michigan	C	C	C	...	*	*	*	2/3 elected	Majority	Majority elected
Minnesota	S	S	S	...	*	*	MR	2/3 elected	2/3 elected	Majority elected
Mississippi	S	S	S	...	*	*	MR	3/5 elected	Majority	Majority
Missouri	C	C	C	...	*	*	...	2/3 elected	Majority elected	Majority elected
Montana	C	C	C	...	*	*	MR	2/3 elected	Majority	Majority
Nebraska	C	C	C	...	*	*	...	3/5 elected	Majority	3/5 elected
Nevada	S	C	S	...	...	*	...	2/3 elected	Majority	Majority
New Hampshire	C	C	C	*	...	* (n)	...	2/3 elected	Majority	Majority present
New Jersey	C	C	C	...	*	*	...	2/3 elected	Majority	Majority
New Mexico	C	C	...	...	*	* (o)	...	2/3 present	Majority	Majority
New York	C	C	C	...	*	* (q)	(q)	2/3 elected	Majority	Majority
North Carolina	C	S	...	...	...	*	ATB	...	Majority	Majority
North Dakota	S	S	S	...	*	*	...	2/3 elected	Majority (r)	Majority (r)
Ohio	...	...	...	...	*	*	...	3/5 elected	Majority elected	Majority elected
Oklahoma	C,S	C	C	...	*	*	ATB	2/3 elected (t)	Majority	Majority (t)
Oregon	C	C	C	...	...	*	... (u)	2/3 elected	Majority elected	Majority
Pennsylvania	C,S	S	S	...	*	*	...	2/3 elected	Majority	Majority elected
Rhode Island	C	C	C	* (v)	...	*	ATB	3/5 elected	Majority	Majority elected
South Carolina	...	C	C	...	*	*	ATB	2/3 present	Majority	Majority
South Dakota	C	C	C	...	*	*	...	2/3 elected	2/3 elected	Majority elected
Tennessee	C	C	...	...	*	...	...	Majority elected	Majority elected	Majority elected
Texas	...	...	...	...	*	...	...	2/3 elected	Majority	Majority
Utah	S	S	S	...	...	*	ATB	2/3 elected	Majority	Majority
Vermont	... (w)	...	...	*	...	*	... (x)	2/3 present	Majority	Majority

STATE BALANCED BUDGETS—Continued

	Constitutional and Statutory Provisions			Gubernatorial Authority			Legislative Authority	
State	Governor must submit a balanced budget	Legislature must pass a balanced budget	Governor must sign a balanced budget	May carry over deficit	Governor has line item veto	Can reduce budget without legislative approval	Restrictions on budget reductions	Votes required to override gubernatorial veto	Votes required to pass revenue increase	Votes required to pass budget
Virginia	S	...	...	...	*	*	MR (z)	2/3 present	Majority elected	Majority elected
Washington	S	...	...	... (y)	*	*	ATB	2/3 elected	51%	51%
West Virginia	...	C	C	...	*	* (aa)	ATB (aa)	2/3 elected	Majority	Majority
Wisconsin	C	C	C	...	*	...	...	2/3 present	Majority present	Majority present
Wyoming	C	C	C	...	*	...	...	2/3 elected	Majority	Majority

Source: National Association of State Budget Officers, *Budgetary Processes in the States*, 1989.

Key: C - Constitutional
S - Statutory
ATB - Across the board
MR - Maximum reduction dictated
* - Yes
... - No

(a) Joint session.
(b) May carry over "casual deficits," i.e., not anticipated.
(c) Governor may reduce budgets of administration-appointed agencies only.
(d) Must have quorum.
(e) Budget reductions are limited to executive branch only.
(f) The Governor and elected cabinet may reduce the budget. The reductions must be reported to the legislature and advice as to proposed reductions may be offered.
(g) If general fund expenditure ceiling is exceeded, 2/3 vote required; otherwise majority of elected members.
(h) After June 30, 1990, need 3/5 to become effective immediately.
(i) Reductions allowed only to get back to a balanced budget.
(j) Governor may expend funds up to one year. Certain restrictions apply to ATB reductions.
(k) For emergency enactment, 2/3 votes required.
(l) Governor has no veto power over the budget bill, but vote of 3/5 elected required to override veto on other bills.
(m) For capital budget, 2/3 votes required.
(n) May not reduce debt service.
(o) May reduce budget of agencies under Governor's control only.
(p) Technically, the Governor is not required to sign a balanced budget, however, in order to consummate the spring borrowing the Governor must certify that the budget is in balance.
(q) May reduce budget without approval only for state operations; only restriction on reductions is that reductions in aid to localities cannot be made without legislative approval.
(r) Emergency measures and measures that amend a statute that has been referred or enacted through an initiated measure within the last seven years must pass both houses by a 2/3 majority.
(s) There is no constitutional or statutory requirement that the Governor submit or the legislature enact a balanced budget. There is a constitutional requirement that the legislature provide sufficient revenues to meet state expenses. The Governor is required by statute to examine monthly the relationship between appropriations and estimated revenues and to reduce expenditures to prevent imbalance.
(t) Emergency measures require a 3/4 majority for override. Budget bills usually require Emergency Clauses and therefore require 2/3 vote for passage.
(u) Governor recommends a biennial budget that is subject to legislative approval.
(v) May carry over deficit into subsequent year only.
(w) Formal budget submitted by Budget and Control Board, not Governor.
(x) May not change legislative intent when reducing budget.
(y) The Constitution specifies that expenditures shall not exceed revenues at the end of the biennial period.
(z) The Governor has power to withhold allotments of appropriations, but cannot reduce legislative appropriations.
(aa) May reduce spending authority.

REVENUE AND EXPENDITURE

Table 6.4
SUMMARY FINANCIAL AGGREGATES, BY STATE: 1987
(In millions of dollars)

State	Revenue				Expenditure				Debt outstanding at end of fiscal year	Cash and security holdings at end of fiscal year
	Total	General	Utilities and liquor store	Insurance trust	Total	General	Utilities and liquor store	Insurance trust		
United States	$517,019	$419,487	$5,776	$91,756	$455,752	$403,937	$8,442	$43,373	$265,677	$695,821
Alabama	7,077	5,954	140	983	6,333	5,769	130	434	3,729	9,447
Alaska	4,892	4,245	2	645	4,416	4,037	98	282	6,189	18,410
Arizona	6,673	5,213	8	1,452	5,904	5,402	10	492	1,937	8,907
Arkansas	3,888	3,253	0	635	3,473	3,220	0	254	1,441	4,929
California	70,336	55,884	88	14,363	62,481	55,440	6	7,035	22,405	91,409
Colorado	6,723	4,926	0	1,798	5,456	4,714	0	743	2,320	9,387
Connecticut	7,595	6,888	18	689	6,666	6,062	75	529	8,014	9,273
Delaware	1,980	1,701	4	276	1,553	1,449	11	93	2,787	2,546
Florida	17,394	14,436	5	2,953	15,426	14,570	23	833	7,806	23,604
Georgia	10,241	8,631	0	1,609	9,061	8,423	0	638	2,601	11,807
Hawaii	3,164	2,638	0	526	2,614	2,392	0	222	2,868	4,536
Idaho	1,868	1,439	36	392	1,605	1,399	29	177	614	2,341
Illinois	20,632	17,276	0	3,356	18,821	17,085	0	1,735	12,665	22,720
Indiana	9,037	8,202	0	835	8,342	7,874	0	468	2,731	8,308
Iowa	5,481	4,665	104	712	5,075	4,694	79	302	1,776	5,435
Kansas	4,112	3,431	0	681	3,629	3,302	0	327	370	3,832
Kentucky	6,926	5,860	0	1,066	6,334	5,844	0	489	4,669	8,755
Louisiana	9,257	7,719	0	1,539	8,460	7,205	0	1,255	11,075	12,464
Maine	2,651	2,278	50	323	2,287	2,043	49	195	1,621	3,007
Maryland	9,700	8,430	58	1,212	8,714	7,731	177	806	5,336	10,923
Massachusetts	14,001	13,022	33	947	14,015	13,000	37	978	12,800	14,378
Michigan	21,493	17,474	426	3,593	18,791	16,504	414	1,873	7,700	24,637
Minnesota	10,643	8,834	0	1,809	9,205	8,425	0	780	3,587	13,463
Mississippi	4,413	3,618	112	684	3,956	3,555	90	310	1,322	5,447
Missouri	7,761	6,486	0	1,275	7,095	6,629	0	466	4,307	11,829
Montana	1,816	1,433	36	347	1,697	1,430	32	236	1,146	3,086
Nebraska	2,475	2,285	0	190	2,282	2,210	0	73	1,478	2,646
Nevada	2,475	1,662	42	771	2,010	1,630	45	334	1,226	4,136
New Hampshire	1,759	1,382	168	208	1,484	1,295	133	56	2,362	2,111
New Jersey	19,542	15,936	315	3,291	17,175	14,586	878	1,712	17,489	29,239
New Mexico	3,842	3,268	0	574	3,306	3,074	0	233	1,780	9,010
New York	55,572	44,600	1,735	9,236	47,505	40,053	3,855	3,597	40,631	78,644
North Carolina	11,874	9,765	0	2,110	10,133	9,380	0	754	2,726	15,788
North Dakota	1,545	1,352	0	193	1,584	1,452	0	132	792	2,011
Ohio	25,067	16,698	337	8,032	20,753	16,817	285	3,651	9,440	40,221
Oklahoma	5,781	4,785	170	826	5,510	4,619	266	625	4,105	8,135
Oregon	6,146	4,627	138	1,381	5,140	4,441	89	610	7,143	14,828
Pennsylvania	23,803	18,886	613	4,304	20,571	17,603	592	2,376	8,820	25,384
Rhode Island	2,575	2,151	7	417	2,259	2,011	22	226	2,785	3,406
South Carolina	6,766	5,271	480	1,015	5,959	5,107	471	380	3,722	10,111
South Dakota	1,241	1,044	0	197	1,281	1,236	0	46	1,544	2,687
Tennessee	7,383	6,308	0	1,074	6,641	6,162	0	480	2,261	8,774
Texas	24,038	19,608	0	4,430	21,717	19,275	0	2,443	5,329	36,457
Utah	3,400	2,809	69	523	3,262	2,932	51	279	1,418	4,279
Vermont	1,294	1,151	29	114	1,153	1,076	28	49	955	1,446
Virginia	11,174	9,224	253	1,697	9,693	9,040	211	442	4,199	12,829
Washington	11,575	8,772	216	2,587	9,982	8,382	184	1,416	3,841	14,808
West Virginia	3,965	3,240	57	669	3,884	3,239	51	595	2,241	4,249
Wisconsin	12,167	9,183	0	2,984	9,427	8,669	0	758	4,795	15,181
Wyoming	1,802	1,544	28	229	1,630	1,450	24	155	780	4,564

Source: U.S. Bureau of the Census, *State Government Finances in 1987*.
Note: Detail may not add to totals due to rounding. Data presented are statistical in nature and do not represent an accounting statement. Therefore, a difference between an individual government's total revenues and expenditures does not necessarily indicate a budget surplus or deficit.

REVENUE AND EXPENDITURE

Table 6.5
SUMMARY FINANCIAL AGGREGATES, BY STATE: 1988
(In millions of dollars)

	Revenue				Expenditure				Debt outstanding at end of fiscal year	Cash and security holdings at end of fiscal year
State	Total	General	Utilities and liquor store	Insurance trust	Total	General	Utilities and liquor store	Insurance trust		
United States	$541,786	$445,498	$5,796	$90,491	$484,984	$432,157	$8,610	$44,217	$276,786	$783,357
Alabama	8,022	6,504	141	1,377	6,877	6,290	123	464	3,180	11,063
Alaska	5,592	5,040	2	550	4,198	3,870	57	271	6,097	19,211
Arizona	6,883	5,588	16	1,279	6,319	5,719	15	585	1,992	10,916
Arkansas	3,958	3,447	0	511	3,570	3,298	0	273	1,639	5,625
California	73,229	56,684	128	16,417	66,903	59,680	5	7,218	24,116	91,277
Colorado	6,527	5,027	0	1,501	5,620	4,890	2	728	2,289	10,662
Connecticut	8,113	7,022	18	1,073	7,518	6,892	65	560	8,266	12,567
Delaware	2,036	1,844	4	188	1,741	1,643	11	87	2,756	4,347
Florida	19,362	16,863	5	2,493	17,833	16,933	25	875	8,296	25,423
Georgia	10,892	9,278	0	1,614	9,763	9,109	0	654	3,138	14,100
Hawaii	3,619	3,127	0	492	2,808	2,571	0	237	2,928	5,745
Idaho	1,913	1,550	34	328	1,692	1,496	27	168	677	2,572
Illinois	20,549	17,850	0	2,699	19,212	17,451	0	1,761	13,149	26,709
Indiana	9,744	8,942	0	802	8,848	8,400	0	448	3,085	8,709
Iowa	5,814	4,933	78	803	5,316	4,976	57	284	1,365	5,987
Kansas	4,390	3,877	0	514	3,814	3,486	0	328	368	3,983
Kentucky	7,352	6,316	0	1,036	6,858	6,352	5	501	5,040	9,983
Louisiana	7,845	7,606	0	239	8,252	7,295	0	957	11,257	14,711
Maine	2,909	2,582	72	254	2,500	2,240	52	208	1,724	3,437
Maryland	11,942	9,356	64	2,521	9,442	8,390	163	889	5,616	13,592
Massachusetts	14,721	13,636	36	1,050	15,367	14,258	48	1,060	13,831	15,424
Michigan	21,549	18,479	413	2,657	20,380	18,069	354	1,956	8,464	28,223
Minnesota	11,453	9,727	0	1,726	9,648	8,835	0	813	3,607	14,733
Mississippi	4,610	3,915	111	585	4,145	3,765	89	292	1,470	5,999
Missouri	8,150	7,016	0	1,134	7,498	6,909	0	589	4,569	13,296
Montana	2,026	1,593	34	399	1,695	1,423	30	242	1,237	3,396
Nebraska	2,624	2,456	0	168	2,347	2,274	0	73	1,359	2,743
Nevada	2,487	1,741	48	697	2,293	1,873	54	365	1,362	4,574
New Hampshire	1,771	1,388	172	211	1,610	1,420	137	53	2,705	4,281
New Jersey	20,957	16,647	317	3,993	18,952	16,274	809	1,870	17,410	36,957
New Mexico	4,136	3,564	0	573	3,504	3,247	0	257	1,741	9,408
New York	57,278	46,262	1,724	9,292	50,429	42,592	4,142	3,695	41,882	90,320
North Carolina	12,806	10,626	0	2,180	11,022	10,277	0	745	2,728	18,210
North Dakota	1,615	1,440	0	175	1,597	1,472	0	125	797	2,038
Ohio	25,642	17,358	326	7,958	21,395	17,306	295	3,794	9,800	45,150
Oklahoma	6,425	5,398	168	858	5,781	4,917	259	605	3,753	8,477
Oregon	6,266	4,761	139	1,366	5,255	4,572	89	594	6,810	16,566
Pennsylvania	23,824	19,435	605	3,783	21,397	18,635	586	2,177	9,303	29,594
Rhode Island	2,719	2,241	7	470	2,480	2,189	46	244	2,871	4,687
South Carolina	7,344	5,794	492	1,058	6,383	5,464	523	396	3,645	11,179
South Dakota	1,393	1,169	0	223	1,133	1,081	0	52	1,554	2,951
Tennessee	7,798	6,853	0	945	7,082	6,625	0	457	2,254	9,729
Texas	26,659	22,495	0	4,164	22,790	20,661	0	2,129	7,120	40,086
Utah	3,691	2,995	65	631	3,224	2,909	50	265	1,515	4,976
Vermont	1,401	1,248	29	124	1,268	1,189	27	52	925	1,591
Virginia	11,833	10,190	248	1,394	10,683	10,004	209	469	4,513	14,732
Washington	12,465	9,220	217	3,027	11,404	9,322	185	1,897	4,272	16,618
West Virginia	3,701	3,247	54	400	3,809	3,178	46	585	2,464	4,760
Wisconsin	12,061	9,716	0	2,345	9,822	9,074	0	748	5,012	17,562
Wyoming	1,691	1,453	27	211	1,509	1,360	25	125	838	4,476

Source: U.S. Bureau of the Census, *State Government Finances in 1988.*
Note: Detail may not add to totals due to rounding. Data presented are statistical in nature and do not represent an accounting statement. Therefore, a difference between an individual government's total revenues and expenditures does not necessarily indicate a budget surplus or deficit.

REVENUE AND EXPENDITURE

Table 6.6
NATIONAL TOTALS OF STATE GOVERNMENT FINANCES FOR SELECTED YEARS: 1974-88

Item	1988	1987	1986	1985	1984	1982	1980	1978	1976	1974	Percentage change 1987 to 1988	Percentage change 1986 to 1987	Per capita 1988	Per capita 1987
Revenue total	$541,786	$516,509	$481,174	$439,416	$397,087	$330,898	$276,962	$225,011	$183,821	$140,816	4.8	7.4	$2,209.66	$2,129.60
General revenue	445,498	419,054	393,476	365,835(r)	330,740	275,111	233,592	189,099	152,118	122,327	6.2	6.6	1,816.95	1,727.86
Taxes total	264,080	246,501	228,054	215,893(r)	196,795	162,607	137,075	113,261	89,256	74,207	6.9	8.3	1,077.04	1,017.11
Intergovernmental revenue	107,225	102,381	98,574	89,887	81,450	69,166	64,326	53,461	44,717	33,170	4.7	3.9	437.31	421.71
From federal government	100,461	95,463	92,666	84,434	76,140	66,026	61,892	50,200	42,013	31,632	5.2	3.0	409.73	393.21
Public welfare	47,908	44,969	41802	38,664	35,423	31,510	24,680	20,007	16,867	13,320	6.5	7.6	195.39	185.23
Education	17,970	16,883	16,523	15,307	13,975	13,149	12,765	9,819	8,661	6,720	6.4	2.2	73.29	68.54
Highways	13,467	12,963	13,855	12,702	10,380	8,304	8,860	6,301	6,262	4,503	3.9	-6.4	54.93	53.39
General revenue sharing	(b)	(b)	(b)	(b)	(b)	(b)	2,278	2,255	2,102	2,045	0.0	0.0	(b)	(b)
Employment security administration	2,896	2,794	2,790	2,594	2,606	2,352	2,050	1,887	1,658	1,295	3.7	.1	11.81	11.51
Other	18,220	17,852	17,696	15,167	13,756	10,711	11,258	9,931	6,463	3,749	2.1	.9	74.32	73.52
From local governments	6,763	6,918	5,908	5,453	5,310	3,139	2,434	3,261	6,704	1,538	-2.2	17.1	27.58	28.50
Charges and miscellaneous revenue	74,193	70,173	66,848	60,055(r)	52,495	43,338	32,190	22,377	18,145	14,950	5.7	5.0	302.59	289.04
Utility revenue (a)	3,030	2,964	2,907	2,921(r)	2,638	2,085	1,304	962	0	0	2.2	2.0	12.36	12.21
Liquor stores revenue	2,767	2,812	2,807	2,753	2,759	2,854	2,765	2,388	2,196	2,049	-1.6	.2	11.28	11.58
Insurance trust revenue	90,491	91,678	81,984	67,907	60,950	50,848	39,301	32,562	29,508	16,439	-1.3	11.7	369.07	377.94
Unemployment compensation	17,187	18,839	18,173	17,596	16,671	16,854	13,468	13,083	15,068	5,711	-8.8	3.7	70.10	77.60
Employee retirement	63,556	64,405	56,820	43,993	38,564	29,035	21,146	16,026	12,171	8,919	-1.3	13.3	259.21	265.59
Other	9,749	8,434	6,991	6,319	5,715	4,959	4,686	3,452	2,269	1,809	15.6	20.6	39.76	34.75
Debt outstanding at end of fiscal year, total	276,786	265,506	247,715	211,917(r)	186,377	147,470	121,958	102,569	84,825	65,296	4.3	7.3	1,128.86	1,094.32
Long-term	275,448	263,898	246,109	209,125(r)	183,208	143,702	119,821	99,671	78,814	61,697	4.3	7.3	1,123.41	187.71
Non-guaranteed	207,312	197,554	181,469	148,693	125,859	92,195	70,457	53,356	39,972	30,842	5.1	8.7	845.52	812.73
Full-faith and credit	68,136	66,344	64,640	60,432	57,349	51,507	49,364	46,316	38,842	30,855	2.1	3.3	277.89	274.98
Short-term	1,338	1,606	1,606	2,792	3,168	3,768	2,137	2,897	6,011	3,599	-16.7	0.0	5.46	6.62
Net long-term	108,829	141,815	129,119	110,361	101,681	87,047	79,810	72,089	62,488	53,847	-23.3	9.8	443.86	584.13
Full-faith and credit only	54,154	51,168	50,212	47,894	46,976	39,766	39,357	39,147	33,708	26,967	5.8	1.9	220.87	210.76
Expenditure and debt redemption	505,824	476,047	439,793	402,450	361,810	317,482	263,494	208,533	184,511	134,948	6.3	8.2	2,062.98	1,961.07
Debt redemption	20,840	20,351	15,577	11,708	10,364	7,190	5,682	4,701	3,585	2,814	2.4	30.6	84.99	83.83
Expenditure, total	484,984	455,696	424,216	390,742(r)	351,446	310,292	257,812	203,832	180,926	132,134	6.4	7.4	1,977.99	1,877.24
General expenditure	432,157	403,939	380,346	349,685	309,684	269,490	228,223	179,802	153,690	119,891	7.0	7.0	1,762.54	1,663.81
Education	159,500	149,901	140,189	128,604	116,058	102,984	87,939	69,702	59,630	46,860	6.4	6.9	650.52	617.44
Intergovernmental expenditure	95,391	88,253	81,929	74,937	67,485	60,684	52,688	40,125	34,084	27,107	8.1	7.7	389.05	363.51
State institutions of higher education	52,410	50,710	47,928	44,264	40,016	34,296	27,927	23,259	29,700	15,395	3.4	5.8	213.75	208.87
Other	11,700	10,937	10,332	9,403	8,557	8,005	7,324	6,318	5,839	4,358	7.0	6.0	47.71	45.05
Public welfare	84,235	78,454	72,554	67,263(r)	62,749	55,257	44,219	35,776	29,633	22,538	7.4	8.3	343.55	323.15
Intergovernmental expenditure	17,665	17,331	16,298	14,629	13,628	13,744	10,977	10,047	9,476	7,369	1.9	6.3	72.04	71.39
Cash assistance, categorical programs	9,803	9,590	9,277	8,388	8,297	7,337	6,831	5,712	5,203	4,984	2.2	3.4	39.98	39.50
Cash assistance, other	1,153	1,140	1,161	1,148	1,154	875	687	623	212		1.1	-1.8	4.70	4.70
Other public welfare	55,614	50,393	45,817	43,099	39,670	33,301	25,725	19,393	14,601	9,974	10.0	10.0	226.82	207.57
Highways	40,681	38,273	36,661	33,154(r)	28,937	25,131	25,044	18,479	18,100	15,847	6.3	4.4	165.92	157.65
Regular state highway facilities	31,509	29,713	28,598	25,791	21,971	19,078	19,652	13,970	14,223	11,887	6.0	3.9	128.51	122.39
State toll highway facilities	2,222	1,776	1,593	1,343	1,154	1,025	1,009	687	636	749	25.1	11.5	9.06	7.32
Intergovernmental expenditure	6,949	6,785	6,470	6,019	5,688	5,028	4,383	3,821	3,241	3,211	2.4	4.9	28.34	27.95
Health and hospitals	34,872	32,131	30,131	27,595	24,982	22,284	17,855	13,883	11,110	8,443	8.5	6.6	142.22	132.35
State hospitals and institutions for handicapped	19,489	17,862	16,962	15,802	15,068	13,681	11,015	8,979	7,572	5,957	9.1	5.1	79.49	73.57
Other	18,383	14,269	13,169	11,793	9,914	8,603	6,840	4,905	3,538	2,486	29.0	8.0	74.97	75.71
Natural resources	8,300	7,816	7,312	6,758	5,945	5,485	4,346	3,411	2,480	3,053	6.2	6.9	33.85	32.19
Corrections	13,303	11,704	10,771	9,171	7,732	5,889	4,449	3,275	1,812	1,594	13.7	8.7	54.26	48.21
Financial administration	6,969	6,459	5,855	5,019(r)	4,517	3,735	3,031	2,482	1,955	1,688	7.9	10.3	28.42	26.60
General control	6,922	6,191	5,767	5,231	4,654	3,909	3,232	2,331	1,688	1,273	12.0	7.0	28.23	25.50
Employment security administration	2,842	2,741	2,697	2,582(r)	2,546	2,278	2,001	1,757	1,570	1,304	3.7	1.6	11.59	11.29
Police	4,508	4,048	3,714	3,518	3,140	2,730	2,263	1,826	1,569	1,262	11.4	9.0	18.39	16.67

294 The Book of the States 1990-91

REVENUE AND EXPENDITURE

NATIONAL TOTALS OF STATE GOVERNMENT FINANCES—Continued

Item	Amount (in millions)									Percentage change 1987 to 1988	Percentage change 1986 to 1987	Per capita 1988	Per capita 1987
	1988	1987	1986	1985	1984	1982	1980	1978	1976	1974				
Interest	19,367	18,583	16,876	14,982	13,137	9,015	6,763	5,268	4,140	2,863	4.2	10.1	78.99	76.54
Veteran's services	134	129	122	113	99	64	61	54	64	156	3.9	5.7	.55	.53
Utility expenditure (a)	6,232	5,971	5,530	5,364	4,817	3,730	2,401	1,544			4.4	8.0	25.42	24.59
Liquor expenditure	2,378	2,470	2,418	2,391	2,313	2,408	2,206	1,991	1,781	1,653	-3.7	2.2	9.70	10.17
Insurance trust expenditure	44,217	43,316	39,749	37,940	34,632	34,664	24,981	20,495	25,455	10,590	2.1	8.8	180.34	178.65
Unemployment compensation	13,024	15,174	14,821	14,928	13,987	18,027	12,006	10,672	17,780	4,673	-14.2	2.4	53.12	62.74
Employee retirement	24,196	22,189	19,878	18,230	16,467	13,133	10,257	7,811	6,045	4,591	9.0	11.6	98.68	91.40
Other	6,997	5,952	5,051	4,782	4,178	3,503	2,718	2,011	1,629	1,326	17.6	17.8	28.54	24.51
Total expenditure by character and object	484,984	455,696	424,216	390,742(r)	351,446	310,292	257,812	203,832	180,926	132,134	6.4	7.4	1,977.99	1,877.24
Direct expenditure	333,322	314,270	292,249	269,171(r)	243,073	211,549	173,307	136,545	123,069	86,193	6.1	7.5	1,359.44	1,294.71
Current operation	213,231	199,659	186,188	172,124(r)	156,734	133,152	108,131	86,153	68,175	50,803	6.8	7.3	869.66	822.39
Capital outlay	40,666	37,209	34,550	30,657	25,583	23,466	23,325	16,064	18,009	15,417	9.3	7.6	165.86	153.26
Construction	31,421	28,174	26,557	23,877(r)	19,671	19,560	19,736	13,260	15,285	12,655	11.5	6.1	128.15	116.05
Purchase of land and existing structures	3,081	2,594	2,177	1,833	1,816	1,316	1,345	1,171	1,274	1,540	18.8	17.6	12.57	10.71
Equipment	6,164	6,440	5,816	4,947	4,096	2,590	2,243	1,633	1,450	1,222	-4.3	10.7	25.14	26.50
Assistance and subsidies	15,000	14,705	14,162	12,842	12,386	10,867	9,818	8,341	7,290	6,521	2.0	3.8	61.18	60.57
Interest on debt	20,208	19,382	17,601	15,608	13,738	9,400	7,052	5,493	4,140	2,863	4.3	10.1	82.42	79.83
Insurance benefits and repayments	44,217	43,316	39,749	37,940	34,632	34,664	24,981	20,495	25,455	10,590	2.1	8.8	180.34	178.65
Intergovernmental expenditure	151,662	141,426	131,966	121,571	108,373	98,743	84,504	67,287	57,858	45,941	7.2	7.2	618.55	582.53
Cash and security holdings at end of fiscal year	783,357	694,943	610,975	519,014(r)	443,366	338,274	273,047	207,107	157,210	134,493	12.6	13.9	3,194.90	2,866.08
Unemployment fund balance in U.S. Treasury	27,398	22,431	18,019	8,629	5,707	6,789	11,945	7,450	4,425	10,773	22.1	24.5	111.74	92.39
Cash and deposits	N.A.	N.A.	47,164	44,569	45,232	35,400	30,782	25,345	18,477	18,387	N.A.	N.A.	N.A.	N.A.
Securities	N.A.	607,658	534,481	453,128(r)	392,427	296,084	230,320	179,312	134,308	105,332	N.A.	13.7	N.A.	2,502.94
Total by purpose:														
Insurance trust	483,149	443,168	377,152	318,204	274,378	211,493	166,656	124,371	94,679	80,840	9.0	17.5	1,970.51	1,825.39
Debt offsets	166,619	122,256	116,990	98,764	81,527	56,655	40,011	27,582	15,880	7,849	36.3	4.5	679.55	503.57
Other	133,589	130,400	116,833	102,046	87,461	70,126	66,381	60,154	46,651	45,804	2.4	11.6	544.84	537.12

Sources: U.S. Bureau of the Census, annual reports on *State Government Finances* and *Historical Statistics on Governmental Finances and Employment* (vol. 6, no. 4, of the 1977 *Census of Governments*).
Key:
N.A. — Not available
(a) Reported separately only since 1977, previously included with general revenue or general expenditure.
(b) State participation ended September 1980.
(r) Revised.

Table 6.7
STATE GENERAL REVENUE, BY SOURCE AND BY STATE: 1987
(In thousands of dollars)

State	Total general revenue (a)	Total (b)	Sales and gross receipts Total (b)	Sales and gross receipts General	Taxes Motor fuels	Licenses Total (b)	Licenses Motor vehicle	Individual income	Corporation net income	Intergovernmental revenue	Charges and miscellaneous general revenue
United States	$419,486,709	$246,933,216	$119,837,528	$79,637,645	$15,705,469	$15,999,845	$8,308,708	$75,964,843	$20,724,145	$102,380,659	$70,172,834
Alabama	5,953,977	3,222,201	1,740,745	883,762	262,744	279,291	104,077	887,427	161,832	1,514,717	1,217,059
Alaska	4,245,157	1,062,391	81,725	0	32,117	68,737	17,688	427	141,068	488,932	2,693,834
Arizona	5,213,456	3,469,477	2,124,694	1,547,425	309,534	243,162	179,582	762,128	198,948	1,000,081	743,898
Arkansas	3,252,525	1,889,066	1,081,990	715,636	206,457	124,624	69,443	535,317	115,620	912,977	450,482
California	55,884,203	35,790,750	13,758,531	10,934,653	1,248,218	1,426,331	946,287	13,874,104	4,758,950	12,693,621	7,399,832
Colorado	4,925,579	2,561,477	1,216,438	718,646	291,575	141,839	77,538	1,034,676	124,085	1,245,627	1,118,475
Connecticut	6,888,306	4,359,175	2,696,144	1,823,025	254,123	246,200	174,696	465,968	680,242	1,229,293	1,299,838
Delaware	1,700,779	941,932	138,037	0	77,664	295,294	42,551	358,612	105,097	280,538	478,309
Florida	14,435,691	9,846,189	7,588,430	5,478,278	716,019	662,708	363,139	0	596,434	2,902,105	1,687,397
Georgia	8,631,416	5,323,689	2,487,090	1,739,304	385,698	169,623	73,123	2,149,111	449,176	2,342,370	965,357
Hawaii	2,638,319	1,697,424	1,040,995	817,525	48,089	27,802	17,604	543,093	76,793	429,661	511,234
Idaho	1,439,422	829,698	438,696	297,896	82,227	76,272	32,821	265,336	47,308	391,961	217,763
Illinois	17,276,208	10,429,524	5,388,013	3,405,309	740,786	767,214	579,787	3,095,177	862,435	4,109,404	2,737,280
Indiana	8,202,302	4,774,190	2,856,221	2,252,060	397,254	132,918	89,468	1,454,886	235,709	1,921,558	1,506,554
Iowa	4,664,918	2,662,110	1,245,335	826,107	252,041	255,572	176,462	955,232	149,602	1,121,355	881,453
Kansas	3,431,057	2,085,490	1,062,093	726,833	156,753	126,185	73,915	634,479	137,061	816,083	529,484
Kentucky	5,859,962	3,520,409	1,563,175	892,042	294,472	254,499	140,422	920,968	267,378	1,424,620	914,933
Louisiana	7,718,612	3,448,641	1,954,964	1,189,690	357,400	369,550	71,286	438,643	191,189	2,476,047	1,793,924
Maine	2,278,088	1,288,480	668,494	439,399	97,278	87,018	46,657	423,209	68,336	611,499	378,109
Maryland	8,429,916	5,204,499	2,305,755	1,302,463	328,335	168,568	85,544	2,181,080	270,489	1,767,093	1,458,324
Massachusetts	13,021,606	8,463,874	2,757,566	1,866,748	310,397	251,056	131,605	3,979,026	1,203,940	2,517,022	2,040,710
Michigan	17,474,164	9,857,122	4,092,375	2,828,516	717,796	563,591	339,746	3,208,459	1,644,692	4,518,404	3,098,638
Minnesota	8,833,624	5,546,422	2,407,445	1,468,608	356,870	367,875	265,234	2,312,044	422,999	1,993,472	1,293,730
Mississippi	3,617,723	1,943,388	1,301,047	1,015,402	128,125	164,131	57,714	315,449	102,865	1,165,851	508,484
Missouri	6,485,756	3,942,295	2,093,344	1,624,025	215,212	322,716	185,017	1,247,536	235,352	1,571,389	972,072
Montana	1,432,705	591,001	148,705	0	85,490	61,010	30,464	194,675	34,568	499,359	342,345
Nebraska	2,285,158	1,203,344	663,649	390,546	161,842	99,599	50,586	359,803	67,423	585,625	496,189
Nevada	1,662,157	1,131,312	956,296	552,995	97,900	123,485	49,919	0	0	308,570	222,275
New Hampshire	1,382,347	562,712	243,189	0	83,615	84,326	43,051	8,678	151,793	360,518	459,117
New Jersey	15,935,856	9,491,417	4,911,270	2,911,780	343,542	576,744	324,080	2,603,334	1,088,311	3,004,775	3,439,664
New Mexico	3,267,965	1,574,692	924,356	699,564	107,684	66,894	36,631	242,622	99,139	601,433	1,091,840
New York	44,600,158	24,676,346	7,876,098	5,097,847	495,922	733,000	410,000	12,476,941	2,143,390	14,669,952	5,253,860
North Carolina	9,764,630	6,235,163	2,530,090	1,456,024	554,254	415,486	204,414	2,565,878	566,480	2,194,137	1,335,330
North Dakota	1,352,003	573,465	299,667	193,779	55,441	60,241	31,093	80,150	33,442	381,967	396,571
Ohio	16,697,667	9,717,146	5,131,010	3,382,985	641,771	822,529	339,154	3,217,989	474,588	3,882,584	3,097,937
Oklahoma	4,784,641	2,669,188	1,169,464	613,769	204,931	305,972	218,025	678,828	83,703	1,134,466	980,987
Oregon	4,626,603	2,235,073	302,113	0	150,345	266,236	170,821	1,461,609	136,376	1,208,602	1,182,928
Pennsylvania	18,885,770	11,378,764	5,733,514	3,568,903	651,124	1,168,468	404,895	2,749,784	1,015,814	4,724,798	2,782,208
Rhode Island	2,151,032	1,050,144	531,499	350,811	52,666	40,527	27,463	359,005	87,675	519,509	581,379
South Carolina	5,271,248	3,158,453	1,739,972	1,175,411	262,054	167,592	73,300	1,008,938	190,474	1,232,507	880,288

STATE GENERAL REVENUE, BY SOURCE AND BY STATE: 1987—Continued

State	Total general revenue (a)	Taxes Total (b)	Sales and gross receipts Total (b)	Sales and gross receipts General	Sales and gross receipts Motor fuels	Licenses Total (b)	Licenses Motor vehicle	Individual income	Corporation net income	Intergovernmental revenue	Charges and miscellaneous general revenue
South Dakota	1,044,450	416,386	326,504	205,480	56,751	50,097	33,837	0	24,212	349,374	278,690
Tennessee	6,308,275	3,603,331	2,785,525	1,994,313	489,224	351,296	130,347	68,123	298,644	1,883,423	821,521
Texas	19,608,051	11,227,796	8,116,106	4,601,385	1,273,136	1,816,263	697,428	0	0	4,525,129	3,855,126
Utah	2,808,851	1,438,325	752,813	559,208	127,378	68,792	39,860	531,674	60,891	804,265	566,261
Vermont	1,151,197	537,905	277,525	109,450	40,208	46,552	32,429	161,971	38,445	338,247	275,045
Virginia	9,224,246	5,526,557	2,259,632	1,102,670	438,691	329,803	227,709	2,445,816	320,598	2,085,530	1,612,159
Washington	8,771,819	5,639,369	4,244,763	3,284,378	448,682	295,315	137,838	0	0	2,089,117	1,043,333
West Virginia	3,239,733	1,830,168	1,134,027	790,406	161,649	111,390	68,401	482,205	89,890	927,727	481,838
Wisconsin	9,182,988	5,673,577	2,479,614	1,651,907	418,527	287,348	149,107	2,224,053	470,689	2,176,634	1,332,777
Wyoming	1,544,393	631,669	210,785	150,682	35,458	58,104	36,450	0	0	446,731	465,993

Source: U.S. Bureau of the Census, *State Government Finances in 1987.*
Note: Detail may not add to totals due to rounding.
(a) Total general revenue equals total taxes plus intergovernmental revenue plus charges and miscellaneous revenue.
(b) Total includes other taxes not shown separately in this table.

REVENUE AND EXPENDITURE

Table 6.8
STATE GENERAL REVENUE, BY SOURCE AND BY STATE: 1988
(In thousands of dollars)

State	Total general revenue (a)	Taxes Total (b)	Sales and gross receipts Total (b)	Sales and gross receipts General	Sales and gross receipts Motor fuels	Licenses Total (b)	Licenses Motor vehicle	Individual income	Corporation net income	Intergovernmental revenue	Charges and miscellaneous general revenue
United States	$445,498,310	$264,080,470	$130,135,502	$87,009,688	$17,196,209	$17,043,316	$8,879,338	$80,133,133	$21,684,670	$107,224,621	$74,193,219
Alabama	6,503,697	3,374,056	1,825,240	927,750	275,750	280,666	107,933	929,459	177,657	1,745,442	1,384,199
Alaska	5,039,744	1,251,021	81,710	0	33,676	72,234	18,358	449	181,387	746,769	3,041,954
Arizona	5,588,006	3,722,112	2,290,007	1,706,342	314,928	257,043	190,519	857,710	148,134	1,021,965	843,929
Arkansas	3,447,111	2,020,721	1,147,721	777,073	216,965	125,078	68,718	596,899	116,202	946,061	480,329
California	56,683,778	36,075,033	14,543,985	11,515,266	1,292,300	1,670,571	1,062,730	12,864,291	4,781,873	13,036,411	7,572,334
Colorado	5,026,892	2,725,767	1,214,576	724,300	300,032	159,078	82,358	1,159,923	146,776	1,190,227	1,110,898
Connecticut	7,021,731	4,376,395	2,908,988	1,983,977	292,515	260,592	185,170	352,031	601,212	1,342,864	1,302,472
Delaware	1,843,817	1,018,367	144,793		81,402	327,530	44,892	377,782	119,323	292,391	533,059
Florida	16,863,265	11,460,299	9,122,497	6,862,627	764,040	685,279	377,858	0	624,032	3,235,790	2,167,176
Georgia	9,277,960	5,782,247	2,628,575	1,856,625	411,706	179,259	75,107	2,391,771	478,969	2,488,806	1,006,907
Hawaii	3,127,352	2,039,375	1,294,497	919,796	49,806	29,709	18,411	625,594	78,053	497,462	590,515
Idaho	1,549,846	893,658	478,290	328,453	95,204	70,344	31,659	280,991	61,352	435,392	220,796
Illinois	17,850,468	11,018,693	5,802,525	3,677,354	701,971	814,621	619,767	3,161,110	973,704	4,011,942	2,759,833
Indiana	8,941,796	5,311,824	3,018,823	2,361,910	401,452	178,452	129,288	1,764,498	261,125	1,991,780	1,638,192
Iowa	4,932,768	2,841,657	1,302,013	859,033	266,094	254,887	184,489	1,064,816	158,040	1,136,948	954,163
Kansas	3,876,719	2,445,284	1,131,923	775,633	170,035	135,926	78,339	826,318	195,520	852,546	578,889
Kentucky	6,315,593	3,663,591	1,684,790	951,756	322,736	183,927	76,672	1,006,992	255,760	1,638,016	1,013,986
Louisiana	7,605,985	3,776,254	2,068,833	1,300,885	366,798	368,558	76,445	575,693	219,894	1,920,062	1,909,669
Maine	2,582,470	1,505,523	737,112	491,936	105,779	96,188	55,052	555,212	84,704	634,050	442,897
Maryland	9,356,478	5,830,888	2,552,272	1,423,585	441,618	228,658	133,141	2,432,698	313,070	1,950,585	1,575,005
Massachusetts	13,635,732	8,521,404	2,913,743	2,021,093	305,517	248,379	145,000	3,984,746	1,068,341	2,912,621	2,201,707
Michigan	18,478,996	10,515,368	4,064,211	2,919,055	687,308	579,931	413,715	3,587,860	1,856,105	4,653,115	3,310,513
Minnesota	9,727,066	6,143,956	2,702,528	1,676,632	391,657	375,120	272,876	2,625,405	411,960	2,201,768	1,381,342
Mississippi	3,914,652	2,126,254	1,402,715	1,007,276	229,060	185,431	74,507	353,227	96,170	1,255,910	532,488
Missouri	7,015,941	4,405,501	2,286,839	1,683,481	339,738	337,566	195,344	1,515,970	224,228	1,577,569	1,032,871
Montana	1,592,985	715,083	182,094	0	102,404	74,058	29,796	243,768	46,200	528,283	349,619
Nebraska	2,455,997	1,342,868	726,593	447,790	165,798	98,465	50,464	432,035	73,783	595,477	517,652
Nevada	1,741,495	1,186,445	982,050	546,409	99,238	149,346	57,233	0	0	309,520	245,530
New Hampshire	1,388,324	583,168	256,878		83,016	82,680	45,857	29,844	145,680	370,130	435,026
New Jersey	16,646,749	9,762,360	5,152,735	3,136,801	330,866	593,844	322,421	2,557,694	1,181,849	3,586,372	3,298,017
New Mexico	3,563,510	1,793,387	1,013,390	739,904	138,703	127,565	98,473	303,733	49,576	646,969	1,123,154
New York	46,261,827	26,171,362	8,379,003	5,510,790	500,180	778,359	417,660	13,569,288	2,172,245	14,583,898	5,506,567
North Carolina	10,626,327	6,922,990	2,821,701	1,627,672	596,573	456,240	215,513	2,784,385	712,975	2,319,443	1,383,894
North Dakota	1,439,803	633,339	326,187	204,793	63,668	59,495	33,118	114,020	39,094	413,730	392,734
Ohio	17,357,889	9,990,514	5,169,277	3,218,959	811,365	806,389	350,133	3,364,689	582,026	4,213,160	3,154,215
Oklahoma	5,398,374	3,150,072	1,457,067	756,916	311,367	336,752	244,761	832,779	83,725	1,188,269	1,060,033
Oregon	4,760,881	2,110,963	314,949		166,072	298,191	191,569	1,283,647	167,047	1,350,992	1,298,896
Pennsylvania	19,435,494	11,825,044	6,015,886	3,846,585	672,262	1,201,892	419,812	2,805,432	1,046,443	4,742,001	2,868,449
Rhode Island	2,241,276	1,120,534	574,630	383,209	54,763	42,919	31,457	388,461	79,194	593,364	527,378
South Carolina	5,793,863	3,438,186	1,865,982	1,249,430	305,989	171,023	68,256	1,141,076	203,959	1,384,779	970,898

STATE GENERAL REVENUE, BY SOURCE AND BY STATE: 1988—Continued

State	Total general revenue (a)	Taxes Total (b)	Sales and gross receipts Total (b)	Sales and gross receipts General	Sales and gross receipts Motor fuels	Licenses Total (b)	Licenses Motor vehicle	Individual income	Corporation net income	Intergovernmental revenue	Charges and miscellaneous general revenue
South Dakota	1,169,400	475,701	392,944	262,348	61,844	37,589	20,869	0	26,357	392,114	301,585
Tennessee	6,853,089	3,855,027	2,946,730	2,142,276	503,496	381,598	144,464	79,650	352,120	2,092,266	905,796
Texas	22,495,090	13,425,516	10,276,793	6,271,018	1,473,821	1,981,504	693,988	0	0	5,136,774	3,932,800
Utah	2,994,743	1,602,093	786,820	589,480	129,370	73,204	40,349	637,511	71,663	790,014	602,636
Vermont	1,247,556	616,553	303,322	123,490	42,435	48,338	33,094	201,660	44,688	334,345	296,658
Virginia	10,189,775	6,136,607	2,527,280	1,188,856	593,677	342,380	232,882	2,757,868	334,382	2,151,078	1,902,090
Washington	9,220,287	5,994,964	4,511,633	3,553,516	435,456	329,349	155,977	0	0	2,141,081	1,084,242
West Virginia	3,246,819	1,743,871	924,408	537,499	167,658	108,372	67,868	394,181	176,704	982,398	520,550
Wisconsin	9,716,268	6,005,545	2,674,857	1,769,062	491,323	297,811	154,275	2,319,967	461,369	2,225,054	1,485,669
Wyoming	1,452,656	573,030	203,087	151,047	36,778	60,926	40,701	0	0	436,618	443,008

Source: U.S. Bureau of the Census, *State Government Finances in 1988*.
Note: Detail may not add to totals due to rounding.
(a) Total general revenue equals total taxes plus intergovernmental revenue plus charges and miscellaneous revenue.
(b) Total includes other taxes not shown separately in this table.

Table 6.9
STATE EXPENDITURE, BY CHARACTER AND OBJECT AND BY STATE: 1987
(In thousands of dollars)

State	Intergovernmental expenditure	Total	Current operation	Direct expenditure — Capital outlay — Total	Construction	Land and existing structures	Equipment	Assistance and subsidies	Interest on debt	Insurance benefits and repayments	Exhibit: Total salaries and wages
United States	$141,425,744	$314,326,007	$199,659,219	$37,207,018	$28,174,048	$2,600,008	$6,432,962	$14,705,345	$19,381,604	$43,372,821	$81,261,431
Alabama	1,628,921	4,704,074	3,373,465	480,543	339,949	44,646	95,948	160,783	255,699	433,584	1,454,168
Alaska	937,086	3,479,111	2,025,355	416,958	353,295	10,206	53,457	83,090	671,891	281,817	754,970
Arizona	1,981,109	3,923,312	2,387,335	838,526	588,048	166,279	84,199	140,856	64,550	492,045	922,302
Arkansas	990,802	2,482,416	1,725,021	312,904	250,780	14,476	47,648	92,190	98,630	253,671	783,428
California	27,625,639	34,854,914	23,095,895	2,608,735	1,849,946	258,657	500,132	422,634	1,692,684	7,034,966	8,355,540
Colorado	1,527,581	3,928,867	2,529,234	415,829	315,408	27,872	72,549	34,901	206,122	742,781	1,195,798
Connecticut	1,299,536	5,366,045	3,319,459	644,163	544,838	44,153	55,172	276,943	596,949	528,531	1,472,823
Delaware	281,350	1,272,104	817,785	152,866	106,790	9,340	36,736	37,865	170,454	93,134	405,031
Florida	5,890,208	9,536,069	6,219,566	1,445,912	1,001,728	270,798	173,386	469,151	568,347	833,093	3,411,839
Georgia	2,791,541	6,269,163	4,150,082	1,043,617	795,089	104,817	143,711	274,787	163,149	637,528	1,814,983
Hawaii	43,842	2,570,352	1,664,844	382,758	317,433	8,316	57,009	93,251	207,368	222,131	921,105
Idaho	433,384	1,171,776	707,269	207,914	162,637	11,851	33,426	30,506	48,863	177,224	290,329
Illinois	5,151,843	13,668,957	7,856,412	1,563,272	1,217,279	72,115	273,878	1,569,194	944,621	1,735,458	2,800,214
Indiana	2,779,292	5,562,587	4,098,585	691,553	502,520	38,898	150,135	99,839	204,904	467,706	1,612,760
Iowa	1,557,314	3,517,505	2,364,936	505,962	380,489	28,089	97,384	223,901	120,247	302,459	1,039,505
Kansas	981,336	2,647,517	1,791,157	400,972	318,682	4,909	77,381	113,075	15,578	326,735	924,442
Kentucky	1,565,480	4,768,352	3,099,303	715,173	550,586	57,886	106,701	183,008	281,489	489,379	1,346,729
Louisiana	1,811,000	6,648,791	3,766,192	817,871	674,597	77,620	65,654	203,188	606,585	1,254,955	1,551,401
Maine	464,779	1,822,516	1,229,376	145,921	47,449	66,094	32,378	122,761	129,855	194,603	401,430
Maryland	2,048,764	6,665,521	4,118,530	999,718	758,620	111,767	129,331	367,009	373,825	806,439	1,694,063
Massachusetts	3,891,302	10,123,945	6,647,354	889,633	775,790	26,381	87,462	751,948	856,525	978,485	2,538,030
Michigan	5,143,979	13,646,819	8,736,992	919,792	692,509	41,556	185,727	1,541,920	574,954	1,873,161	3,732,689
Minnesota	3,438,831	5,766,125	3,965,856	644,131	495,002	56,560	92,569	110,558	265,219	780,361	1,921,036
Mississippi	1,346,201	2,609,808	1,785,575	294,171	250,277	8,719	35,175	113,075	106,868	310,119	665,871
Missouri	2,091,007	5,003,773	3,196,691	770,064	623,462	54,248	92,354	246,676	324,770	465,572	1,532,282
Montana	318,184	1,379,274	762,827	237,718	204,450	12,546	20,722	50,742	92,128	235,859	336,408
Nebraska	547,691	1,734,740	1,208,812	250,720	186,336	20,449	43,935	79,294	123,038	72,876	609,675
Nevada	650,462	1,359,124	731,331	165,331	146,809	3,053	15,469	24,582	103,536	334,344	361,884
New Hampshire	182,019	1,301,581	900,772	142,728	109,206	11,043	22,479	35,555	166,497	56,029	397,548
New Jersey	4,959,157	12,215,738	7,459,453	1,654,577	1,311,378	192,759	150,440	154,417	1,235,781	1,711,510	2,623,950
New Mexico	1,166,268	2,140,198	1,379,225	336,301	286,121	23,579	26,601	68,652	123,388	232,632	624,385
New York	16,248,656	31,255,944	19,936,525	3,966,770	2,382,638	59,295	1,524,837	734,981	3,020,493	3,597,175	7,625,857
North Carolina	3,651,320	6,481,976	4,434,196	831,447	593,095	16,954	221,398	286,558	176,028	753,747	2,182,448
North Dakota	361,184	1,223,148	879,124	132,090	112,263	7	19,820	22,959	56,829	132,146	339,763
Ohio	6,027,790	14,724,768	7,914,255	1,554,525	1,247,758	95,298	211,469	887,606	717,846	3,650,536	3,155,243
Oklahoma	1,360,835	4,149,031	2,624,760	415,563	345,971	14,793	54,799	181,486	302,523	624,699	1,194,834
Oregon	1,190,596	3,949,286	2,244,967	431,212	328,644	22,465	80,103	155,048	508,367	609,692	1,007,856
Pennsylvania	5,720,515	14,850,868	9,051,193	1,363,382	1,128,970	56,048	178,364	1,481,961	578,008	2,376,324	2,705,404
Rhode Island	367,086	1,891,614	1,193,507	157,054	121,867	17,047	18,140	94,877	220,551	225,625	455,228
South Carolina	1,465,863	4,492,659	3,105,973	567,899	399,579	34,908	133,412	137,893	300,448	380,446	1,464,912

REVENUE AND EXPENDITURE

STATE EXPENDITURE, BY CHARACTER AND OBJECT AND BY STATE: 1987—Continued

State	Intergovernmental expenditure	Total	Current operation	Direct expenditure							Exhibit: Total salaries and wages
				Capital outlay				Assistance and subsidies	Interest on debt	Insurance benefits and repayments	
				Total	Construction	Land and existing structures	Equipment				
South Dakota	204,596	1,076,770	580,792	312,204	289,215	1,311	21,678	26,293	111,858	45,623	248,395
Tennessee	1,585,739	5,055,502	3,549,651	689,774	508,772	81,237	99,765	176,736	159,812	479,529	1,446,047
Texas	6,225,435	15,491,828	9,546,985	2,361,815	1,865,325	181,125	315,365	673,061	467,321	2,442,646	3,410,270
Utah	787,955	2,474,511	1,654,000	347,042	266,990	15,855	64,197	81,004	112,969	279,496	657,949
Vermont	179,476	973,973	691,058	88,970	67,117	2,513	19,340	64,035	80,705	49,205	258,513
Virginia	2,761,290	6,931,597	4,879,669	1,016,129	805,502	71,322	139,305	272,329	321,227	442,243	2,288,627
Washington	2,908,212	7,073,378	4,034,230	867,611	690,380	21,716	155,515	477,109	278,081	1,416,347	1,861,116
West Virginia	894,505	2,989,787	1,800,070	335,018	300,083	2,091	32,844	120,973	139,060	594,666	649,023
Wisconsin	3,409,036	6,018,379	3,813,888	453,499	363,469	24,820	65,210	624,652	367,936	758,404	1,548,989
Wyoming	549,747	1,079,914	609,687	218,681	198,907	1,521	18,253	29,433	67,028	155,085	264,339

Source: U.S. Bureau of the Census, *State Government Finances in 1987.*
Note: Detail may not add to totals due to rounding.

Table 6.10
STATE EXPENDITURE, BY CHARACTER AND OBJECT AND BY STATE: 1988
(In thousands of dollars)

State	Intergovernmental expenditure	Total	Direct expenditure								
			Current operation	Capital outlay			Assistance and subsidies	Interest on debt	Insurance benefits and repayments	Exhibit: Total salaries and wages
				Total	Construction	Land and existing structures	Equipment				
United States	$151,661,866	$333,322,103	$213,230,967	$40,666,340	$31,421,064	$3,081,389	$6,163,887	$14,999,984	$20,207,528	$44,217,284	$86,931,345
Alabama	1,772,140	5,104,944	3,625,843	649,150	494,489	26,973	127,688	162,390	203,117	464,444	1,543,738
Alaska	794,294	3,403,608	2,176,998	259,813	226,136	1,947	31,730	93,969	602,032	270,796	749,500
Arizona	2,014,460	4,304,944	2,558,325	841,409	554,680	206,406	80,323	167,873	152,100	585,237	979,232
Arkansas	1,053,029	2,517,230	1,763,100	288,319	227,156	13,121	48,042	96,369	96,922	272,520	789,520
California	29,754,786	37,148,167	25,321,688	2,525,442	1,828,490	248,853	448,099	348,052	1,734,972	7,218,013	8,873,965
Colorado	1,601,393	4,018,253	2,496,382	577,711	469,112	36,297	72,302	33,782	182,485	727,893	1,400,797
Connecticut	1,477,198	6,040,614	3,877,483	719,004	566,868	36,997	115,139	294,979	589,002	560,146	1,652,982
Delaware	317,800	1,422,947	886,665	201,098	154,786	21,882	24,430	38,847	209,475	86,862	446,211
Florida	6,500,752	11,332,345	7,469,221	1,823,380	1,218,759	425,263	179,358	527,779	636,637	875,328	3,776,035
Georgia	2,928,597	6,834,053	4,506,694	1,182,626	934,722	108,390	139,514	321,470	169,234	654,029	1,891,433
Hawaii	49,776	2,758,280	1,829,482	397,800	316,365	14,262	67,173	99,191	194,684	237,123	989,841
Idaho	489,765	1,201,834	746,416	209,620	166,793	14,721	28,106	29,139	48,210	168,449	313,827
Illinois	5,274,272	13,937,860	8,040,948	1,771,469	1,420,413	58,708	292,348	1,418,736	945,989	1,760,718	2,927,080
Indiana	2,995,457	5,852,303	4,313,395	779,804	569,327	28,393	182,084	112,536	198,984	447,584	1,767,697
Iowa	1,802,094	3,514,351	2,354,268	546,105	451,323	17,252	77,530	222,609	107,811	283,558	1,163,131
Kansas	1,073,214	2,740,780	1,836,484	393,879	330,613	3,960	59,306	150,776	31,580	328,061	913,234
Kentucky	1,741,531	5,116,459	3,329,587	797,585	635,419	49,850	112,316	189,494	299,030	500,763	1,271,501
Louisiana	1,865,441	6,386,686	3,765,091	701,564	562,356	88,226	50,982	218,128	744,758	957,145	1,634,867
Maine	544,712	1,955,376	1,342,974	156,349	36,130	89,697	30,522	115,294	132,774	207,985	427,005
Maryland	2,233,494	7,208,010	4,392,041	1,144,452	919,108	89,410	135,934	414,594	368,382	888,541	1,881,744
Massachusetts	4,127,655	11,238,938	7,431,384	975,587	809,712	48,186	117,689	835,492	936,317	1,060,158	2,802,057
Michigan	5,813,874	14,565,704	9,000,322	1,425,070	681,033	469,505	274,532	1,602,570	581,385	1,956,357	3,672,972
Minnesota	3,621,482	6,026,197	4,178,532	664,155	522,943	90,418	50,794	115,569	255,382	812,559	2,029,699
Mississippi	1,391,664	2,753,546	1,892,849	335,659	277,763	7,508	50,388	131,368	102,081	291,589	715,186
Missouri	2,303,781	5,193,795	3,252,877	766,953	587,843	74,816	104,294	259,212	326,225	588,528	1,529,778
Montana	308,044	1,386,785	802,237	203,162	176,920	5,525	20,717	48,405	91,336	241,645	334,520
Nebraska	552,488	1,794,641	1,238,026	292,892	228,607	11,753	52,532	75,258	115,557	72,908	670,968
Nevada	725,283	1,567,230	794,247	262,855	232,434	2,990	27,431	31,047	113,735	365,346	388,922
New Hampshire	204,898	1,404,980	967,361	169,183	145,663	11,129	12,391	39,311	175,862	53,263	369,802
New Jersey	5,462,250	13,489,533	8,107,065	1,956,371	1,603,625	95,973	256,773	179,511	1,377,038	1,869,548	3,068,921
New Mexico	1,244,887	2,258,998	1,462,131	338,049	288,339	10,810	38,900	81,344	120,896	256,578	659,579
New York	16,767,678	33,661,576	22,026,644	4,112,098	3,153,745	99,846	858,507	641,548	3,185,797	3,695,489	8,267,105
North Carolina	4,066,203	6,955,823	4,699,397	1,010,010	763,998	10,216	235,796	316,505	184,541	745,370	2,313,394
North Dakota	365,329	1,231,505	865,114	157,324	130,217	1,953	25,154	24,456	59,769	124,842	332,764
Ohio	6,315,346	15,079,748	8,085,861	1,599,554	1,319,235	65,655	214,664	884,141	716,436	3,793,756	3,422,726
Oklahoma	1,447,844	4,333,376	2,782,062	472,341	387,801	16,428	68,112	192,715	281,293	604,965	1,235,463
Oregon	1,201,765	4,052,940	2,458,277	343,448	271,859	3,789	67,800	157,393	500,119	593,703	1,109,408
Pennsylvania	6,119,723	15,277,467	9,484,926	1,491,416	1,266,237	42,708	182,471	1,489,458	635,095	2,176,572	2,854,947
Rhode Island	374,269	2,105,784	1,302,328	255,665	189,411	21,524	44,730	98,062	205,388	244,341	519,662
South Carolina	1,574,229	4,808,486	3,278,998	707,018	539,312	49,428	118,278	137,255	289,271	395,944	1,588,542

STATE EXPENDITURE, BY CHARACTER AND OBJECT AND BY STATE: 1988

State	Intergovernmental expenditure	Total	Current operation	Direct expenditure				Assistance and subsidies	Interest on debt	Insurance benefits and repayments	Exhibit: Total salaries and wages
					Capital outlay						
				Total	Construction	Land and existing structures	Equipment				
South Dakota	221,219	911,773	573,223	136,461	110,852	1,623	23,986	29,387	121,040	51,662	243,050
Tennessee	1,685,450	5,396,687	3,864,718	709,122	591,983	49,271	67,868	193,241	172,727	456,879	1,491,929
Texas	6,625,955	16,163,884	9,987,931	2,679,085	2,194,108	133,802	351,175	764,917	603,127	2,128,824	3,861,240
Utah	842,039	2,382,115	1,623,897	301,658	218,991	23,424	59,243	80,618	110,829	265,113	683,265
Vermont	213,223	1,055,159	741,882	118,797	88,456	3,584	26,757	63,948	78,639	51,893	269,827
Virginia	3,038,790	7,643,711	5,278,709	1,268,854	982,578	104,285	181,991	283,457	343,411	469,280	2,503,157
Washington	3,485,095	7,919,332	4,329,859	957,860	776,113	20,030	161,717	457,429	276,793	1,897,391	2,029,480
West Virginia	870,197	2,939,257	1,720,820	369,598	321,724	3,246	44,628	120,391	143,565	584,883	652,479
Wisconsin	3,855,521	5,966,796	3,851,134	400,088	274,742	18,687	106,659	576,687	390,740	748,147	1,655,586
Wyoming	551,480	957,293	515,071	219,428	201,775	2,669	14,984	33,282	64,956	124,556	261,577

Source: U.S. Bureau of the Census, *State Government Finances in 1988*.
Note: Detail may not add to totals due to rounding.

Table 6.11
STATE GENERAL EXPENDITURE, BY FUNCTION AND BY STATE: 1987
(In thousands of dollars)

State	Total general expenditure (a)	Education	Public welfare	Highways	Hospitals	Natural resources	Health	Corrections	Financial administration	Employment security administration	Police
United States	$403,937,262	$149,900,675	$78,453,819	$38,272,844	$18,048,409	$7,815,820	$14,082,525	$11,703,622	$6,458,626	$2,741,100	$4,047,906
Alabama	5,769,291	2,746,552	635,826	555,098	418,124	120,652	205,600	129,414	108,549	33,288	48,283
Alaska	4,036,769	971,097	280,361	501,546	27,326	142,178	61,780	92,915	92,987	18,569	34,195
Arizona	5,402,250	2,169,109	586,556	1,049,956	64,054	86,903	153,335	249,689	130,600	16,147	82,455
Arkansas	3,219,547	1,346,723	540,055	468,403	133,184	98,985	96,959	58,923	61,729	32,832	26,819
California	55,439,787	22,225,667	12,444,027	2,653,050	1,604,310	1,273,976	2,147,399	1,855,856	1,105,131	256,631	610,466
Colorado	4,713,667	1,970,132	850,555	585,358	234,588	113,941	128,379	126,655	91,480	19,266	50,588
Connecticut	6,062,397	1,539,082	1,094,514	618,025	466,596	59,079	164,642	159,273	111,798	53,243	72,008
Delaware	1,449,315	561,423	139,549	147,978	36,472	26,954	58,116	48,543	37,910	5,425	25,461
Florida	14,570,274	5,744,313	1,905,156	1,466,365	392,391	516,356	981,880	508,194	185,681	31,585	206,985
Georgia	8,423,176	3,645,183	1,430,849	926,762	409,031	232,182	305,685	311,462	111,897	63,307	88,860
Hawaii	2,392,063	820,672	307,478	93,694	110,894	53,052	84,482	85,059	35,971	15,439	2,949
Idaho	1,399,119	618,443	153,786	208,654	24,341	65,811	46,690	23,771	20,189	9,749	14,637
Illinois	17,085,342	6,027,593	3,724,321	1,830,595	506,302	216,415	548,048	443,402	281,420	150,946	173,639
Indiana	7,874,173	3,529,948	1,240,920	868,977	325,287	124,706	223,919	173,204	107,891	55,884	67,045
Iowa	4,693,559	2,012,464	769,293	666,561	308,477	114,410	67,750	97,547	49,607	36,074	38,191
Kansas	3,302,118	1,457,514	515,563	476,162	215,842	84,997	48,349	86,214	71,759	15,195	19,317
Kentucky	5,844,453	2,318,365	985,769	850,602	155,962	174,827	152,760	130,109	115,317	39,233	76,109
Louisiana	7,204,836	2,590,472	1,046,149	711,646	554,712	262,039	170,310	204,032	58,419	50,612	100,531
Maine	2,043,449	673,814	510,523	196,404	53,375	54,269	59,350	36,930	26,682	16,798	21,635
Maryland	7,731,282	2,302,336	1,385,486	1,077,588	271,994	170,559	355,713	362,057	135,474	31,156	180,061
Massachusetts	13,000,043	3,130,280	3,063,088	668,726	586,988	165,538	613,584	279,832	201,178	87,410	103,968
Michigan	16,503,577	5,286,713	4,173,573	1,212,929	730,263	238,656	1,118,450	562,471	149,687	129,990	153,691
Minnesota	8,424,595	3,185,409	1,625,654	844,607	427,073	218,352	153,651	106,516	96,995	77,863	57,611
Mississippi	3,555,483	1,497,570	544,760	386,804	175,201	102,142	103,754	68,562	27,881	38,548	30,798
Missouri	6,629,208	2,841,716	1,075,517	708,250	371,568	150,556	214,221	172,845	107,295	54,238	72,649
Montana	1,429,702	466,276	234,592	245,374	33,950	77,611	49,399	24,865	42,131	8,537	18,205
Nebraska	2,209,555	755,164	396,144	342,168	136,661	68,041	69,423	44,161	23,429	20,932	21,658
Nevada	1,629,929	614,687	143,235	202,990	29,999	29,797	33,566	58,032	47,601	18,629	12,320
New Hampshire	1,294,628	292,402	243,727	182,777	42,751	24,133	81,639	24,234	22,875	12,424	16,710
New Jersey	14,585,706	4,358,460	2,546,571	1,255,895	599,460	159,258	393,105	401,453	216,662	54,992	195,175
New Mexico	3,073,834	1,298,021	316,770	381,861	138,131	57,806	96,696	78,859	48,261	25,381	27,915
New York	40,052,756	11,376,780	11,548,157	1,922,111	2,620,176	222,824	1,235,399	1,298,857	682,097	327,267	330,968
North Carolina	9,379,549	4,473,137	1,205,315	1,923,098	502,143	197,319	316,248	375,387	99,931	42,123	105,487
North Dakota	1,452,186	542,805	225,908	170,096	70,436	51,280	37,206	11,222	17,019	13,027	5,558
Ohio	16,816,792	6,422,446	3,833,853	1,497,052	878,455	165,277	425,982	545,289	276,056	124,548	107,978
Oklahoma	4,619,327	1,971,246	853,355	543,803	234,610	89,635	129,311	132,772	93,661	36,319	37,340
Oregon	4,441,369	1,399,419	562,371	588,069	206,599	139,323	117,721	93,325	133,166	29,186	52,645
Pennsylvania	17,603,464	5,571,418	4,487,492	2,186,058	826,894	275,621	485,486	301,821	235,002	124,675	204,703
Rhode Island	2,011,449	556,666	496,730	123,735	107,379	13,023	85,143	43,908	57,544	16,126	17,804
South Carolina	5,107,330	2,355,267	610,690	395,287	329,814	120,180	258,342	200,550	81,580	46,230	57,049
South Dakota	1,235,743	318,256	143,706	148,560	29,641	40,957	37,553	19,985	14,629	11,682	10,505
Tennessee	6,161,712	2,353,584	1,185,317	806,296	296,652	96,516	251,682	221,333	72,016	46,950	46,943
Texas	19,274,617	9,787,767	2,580,561	2,543,513	918,840	289,083	488,362	523,457	215,309	192,139	145,062
Utah	2,931,896	1,382,521	390,686	279,117	149,397	125,498	107,575	87,703	47,937	36,739	26,322
Vermont	1,076,230	355,315	196,790	144,554	21,933	28,592	29,680	18,686	21,687	14,910	15,014

304   The Book of the States 1990-91

STATE GENERAL EXPENDITURE, BY FUNCTION AND BY STATE: 1987—Continued

State	Total general expenditure (a)	Education	Public welfare	Highways	Hospitals	Natural resources	Health	Corrections	Financial administration	Employment security administration	Police
Virginia	9,039,910	3,677,587	1,059,112	1,316,372	672,300	142,242	313,481	449,610	173,362	57,025	91,413
Washington	8,381,588	3,811,326	1,511,806	888,188	274,640	200,435	255,381	187,451	124,927	51,741	65,567
West Virginia	3,238,828	1,286,900	510,870	462,632	58,888	86,420	102,646	26,247	61,423	23,399	26,183
Wisconsin	8,669,011	2,766,708	2,029,429	670,278	237,003	168,183	349,112	141,518	101,880	56,128	37,135
Wyoming	1,450,378	493,927	111,304	278,220	27,302	79,231	67,581	19,422	24,914	10,563	13,296

Source: U.S. Bureau of the Census, *State Government Finances in 1987*.
Note: Totals may not add due to rounding.

(a) Does not represent sum of state figures because total includes miscellaneous expenditure not shown seperately.

REVENUE AND EXPENDITURE

Table 6.12
STATE GENERAL EXPENDITURE, BY FUNCTION AND BY STATE: 1988
(In thousands of dollars)

State	Total general expenditure (a)	Education	Public welfare	Highways	Hospitals	Natural resources	Health	Corrections	Financial administration	Employment security administration	Police
United States	$432,156,750	$159,500,270	$84,234,602	$40,680,854	$19,670,009	$8,300,307	$15,202,071	$13,302,910	$6,968,745	$2,841,813	$4,508,218
Alabama	6,289,741	3,020,224	685,796	680,800	450,519	137,144	222,007	147,481	110,487	32,389	49,404
Alaska	3,869,779	948,388	306,957	438,086	26,106	150,535	68,111	94,372	77,535	15,663	33,915
Arizona	5,718,965	2,199,436	672,960	1,050,739	71,314	88,090	154,214	255,424	126,322	17,661	92,077
Arkansas	3,297,739	1,442,204	557,378	433,747	137,275	96,145	104,869	61,797	57,242	31,855	25,706
California	59,680,059	23,820,249	13,539,353	2,747,468	1,755,498	1,451,509	2,305,337	2,246,806	1,072,892	256,570	653,244
Colorado	4,890,051	2,079,734	801,144	582,482	248,736	120,572	140,933	141,112	106,843	50,492	34,946
Connecticut	6,892,359	1,818,145	1,227,248	735,443	545,236	60,478	195,771	199,165	134,637	48,582	78,768
Delaware	1,643,380	598,073	132,972	171,658	46,884	26,179	67,518	54,569	50,654	5,394	27,368
Florida	16,932,849	6,860,852	2,266,353	1,894,012	429,199	522,911	1,000,740	654,237	322,654	29,574	216,598
Georgia	9,108,621	3,953,720	1,622,302	968,474	457,759	238,898	330,625	341,791	120,497	69,733	103,245
Hawaii	2,570,933	882,730	319,299	115,384	114,465	54,206	103,597	71,887	40,066	17,883	3,622
Idaho	1,495,766	619,137	182,968	219,780	28,791	75,603	47,407	37,264	24,509	15,645	16,420
Illinois	17,451,414	5,961,915	3,811,865	1,941,147	525,994	224,711	552,241	475,151	275,999	160,053	179,396
Indiana	8,400,176	3,660,862	1,446,670	903,246	362,234	117,162	241,871	186,750	111,274	61,590	74,427
Iowa	4,976,336	2,222,235	825,809	702,979	271,818	99,742	78,062	105,060	54,171	37,132	32,752
Kansas	3,485,933	1,496,027	543,439	494,025	232,230	87,956	73,403	98,919	93,683	14,512	20,379
Kentucky	6,352,212	2,591,254	1,105,215	805,361	212,435	168,702	163,706	150,391	104,962	35,771	74,868
Louisiana	7,294,982	2,689,648	1,090,821	643,633	560,032	220,131	169,825	227,664	58,184	51,795	99,481
Maine	2,239,977	756,390	544,984	205,855	51,948	68,427	71,140	43,604	32,416	16,161	22,447
Maryland	8,390,006	2,423,343	1,527,633	1,244,987	292,537	176,201	388,490	367,837	153,302	35,888	184,397
Massachusetts	14,258,453	3,297,673	3,367,701	672,983	706,521	203,693	642,388	342,597	309,174	89,790	135,483
Michigan	18,068,827	6,115,660	4,310,227	1,236,521	914,897	258,283	1,275,272	614,643	160,121	139,380	166,281
Minnesota	8,835,120	3,285,624	1,679,152	886,353	445,382	233,785	187,659	121,227	104,464	81,665	75,894
Mississippi	3,764,766	1,587,370	618,255	394,070	188,130	120,287	114,758	57,472	39,537	38,051	33,879
Missouri	6,909,048	2,942,922	1,126,974	764,568	377,004	155,036	226,447	183,301	103,784	56,114	81,094
Montana	1,423,402	476,558	235,632	222,352	33,454	87,098	55,544	23,557	43,218	8,258	15,600
Nebraska	2,274,221	747,904	417,132	358,987	150,134	75,727	76,924	48,644	27,926	21,251	25,910
Nevada	1,872,922	688,811	154,245	210,026	36,151	40,547	39,140	103,791	56,260	20,456	16,539
New Hampshire	1,420,036	333,319	252,868	202,149	53,205	30,187	86,956	29,856	27,388	12,011	19,929
New Jersey	16,273,660	4,758,960	2,821,538	1,582,294	684,323	178,523	454,049	455,524	240,154	56,723	265,446
New Mexico	3,247,307	1,387,656	351,381	365,030	154,417	61,823	105,468	86,649	48,344	34,534	31,379
New York	42,591,841	12,182,347	12,231,589	1,828,424	2,871,771	255,936	1,411,894	1,511,929	670,578	328,295	349,858
North Carolina	10,276,656	4,860,172	1,341,942	1,096,632	502,302	230,309	359,298	421,935	106,499	39,728	110,733
North Dakota	1,471,992	546,502	234,361	188,099	58,463	53,895	16,933	14,363	22,805	5,883	6,833
Ohio	17,305,856	6,316,369	4,073,471	1,614,023	877,764	150,903	483,964	556,554	272,073	128,875	107,916
Oklahoma	4,916,974	2,073,553	937,192	618,192	253,658	81,833	131,956	142,404	105,724	36,964	40,761
Oregon	4,572,260	1,464,966	628,952	520,483	258,103	168,583	136,348	100,405	143,998	29,793	55,861
Pennsylvania	18,634,704	5,862,209	4,628,863	2,213,716	851,755	309,650	555,554	336,105	255,013	124,830	219,810
Rhode Island	2,189,261	622,428	500,913	158,394	118,582	16,825	103,312	52,359	49,828	18,266	18,605
South Carolina	5,464,019	2,389,564	636,972	503,748	352,897	145,075	288,572	231,780	87,652	49,909	62,952
South Dakota	1,081,330	305,446	153,434	158,832	26,273	43,877	45,278	19,625	16,035	13,079	10,785
Tennessee	6,625,258	2,409,840	1,433,799	855,152	316,393	100,947	215,687	266,407	80,427	50,498	48,857
Texas	20,661,015	10,088,270	2,924,134	2,862,835	990,587	311,871	489,405	652,870	253,245	213,138	171,419
Utah	2,909,179	1,439,253	370,747	291,738	170,643	67,894	84,040	75,945	47,534	31,594	24,109
Vermont	1,189,219	419,749	204,623	135,433	22,666	33,336	33,699	21,599	23,449	7,142	19,026

STATE GENERAL EXPENDITURE, BY FUNCTION AND BY STATE: 1988—Continued

State	Total general expenditure (a)	Education	Public welfare	Highways	Hospitals	Natural resources	Health	Corrections	Financial administration	Employment security administration	Police
Virginia	10,003,909	3,958,768	1,174,758	1,551,109	780,441	140,838	331,246	435,565	195,258	59,032	219,565
Washington	9,322,149	4,265,457	1,645,147	847,725	289,046	221,903	254,074	206,530	132,644	49,569	78,257
West Virginia	3,178,316	1,273,214	489,604	489,141	65,280	73,006	93,493	29,144	67,737	23,319	24,613
Wisconsin	9,074,170	3,163,623	1,986,248	646,368	272,112	159,310	338,791	180,083	117,378	59,154	33,400
Wyoming	1,359,602	485,517	91,583	226,171	26,645	104,025	84,055	18,766	32,169	10,169	13,964

Source: U.S. Bureau of the Census, *State Government Finances in 1988.*
Note: Totals may not add due to rounding.
(a) Includes miscellaneous expenditures not shown separately in this table.

REVENUE AND EXPENDITURE

Table 6.13
STATE DEBT OUTSTANDING AT END OF FISCAL YEAR, BY STATE: 1987
(In thousands of dollars, except per capita amounts)

State	Total	Per capita	Long-term Total	Long-term Full faith and credit	Long-term Nonguaranteed	Short-term	Net long-term (a) Total	Net long-term (a) Full faith and credit
United States	$265,676,763	$ 1,094.23	$264,071,179	$66,757,606	$197,313,573	$1,605,584	$141,815,056	$51,168,384
Alabama	3,728,623	912.98	3,728,623	1,868,203	1,860,420	0	1,797,878	1,311,593
Alaska	6,188,794	11,810.68	6,182,368	1,448,476	4,733,892	6,426	1,967,000	560,375
Arizona	1,936,738	569.63	1,936,738	0	1,936,738	0	1,159,520	0
Arkansas	1,440,955	603.41	1,440,955	0	1,440,955	0	431,652	0
California	22,405,137	810.22	22,405,137	5,109,944	17,295,193	0	12,919,187	2,175,558
Colorado	2,319,634	704.41	2,308,404	0	2,308,404	11,230	630,266	0
Connecticut	8,013,818	2,494.96	8,003,518	2,252,815	5,750,703	10,300	4,730,620	1,976,069
Delaware	2,786,999	4,300.92	2,778,161	524,139	2,254,022	8,838	2,355,933	518,536
Florida	7,805,781	649.29	7,805,781	1,780,376	6,025,405	0	3,282,199	1,069,434
Georgia	2,600,784	417.66	2,600,784	1,608,266	992,518	0	2,025,982	1,608,250
Hawaii	2,867,947	2,650.60	2,796,476	1,823,677	972,799	71,471	2,270,632	1,813,253
Idaho	613,692	613.69	613,692	0	613,692	0	144,422	0
Illinois	12,665,135	1,093.33	12,655,460	3,806,220	8,849,240	9,675	6,863,558	3,680,793
Indiana	2,731,350	493.92	2,691,507	0	2,691,507	39,843	1,004,090	0
Iowa	1,775,728	629.02	1,290,192	0	1,290,192	485,536	578,972	−711,220
Kansas	369,936	149.47	369,936	0	369,936	0	339,593	0
Kentucky	4,668,955	1,254.08	4,668,955	142,480	4,526,475	0	2,942,878	69,264
Louisiana	11,075,130	2,489.91	11,074,988	3,463,219	7,611,769	142	7,303,250	3,390,095
Maine	1,621,025	1,366.80	1,621,025	296,575	1,324,450	0	309,434	296,575
Maryland	5,336,095	1,176.39	5,330,370	2,040,910	3,289,460	5,725	2,658,728	2,012,859
Massachusetts	12,800,267	2,185.84	12,606,698	4,406,692	8,200,006	193,569	5,774,033	4,383,862
Michigan	7,700,322	836.54	7,669,138	561,300	7,107,838	31,184	3,097,769	534,300
Minnesota	3,586,866	845.16	3,586,866	1,142,372	2,444,494	0	1,438,744	965,939
Mississippi	1,322,458	503.99	1,322,458	420,986	901,472	0	558,616	394,902
Missouri	4,306,689	843.29	4,306,687	686,525	3,620,162	2	1,809,542	613,856
Montana	1,146,145	1,416.74	1,118,555	99,402	1,019,153	27,590	360,781	90,868
Nebraska	1,478,397	927.48	1,463,632	0	1,463,632	14,765	572,708	0
Nevada	1,226,184	1,218.87	1,226,184	367,175	859,009	0	577,105	348,256
New Hampshire	2,362,126	2,236.86	2,362,126	454,505	1,907,621	0	1,526,465	379,155
New Jersey	17,488,666	2,278.95	17,480,566	2,774,440	14,706,126	8,100	11,829,360	2,765,389
New Mexico	1,780,016	1,189.85	1,777,316	115,291	1,662,025	2,700	390,199	−10,936
New York	40,630,801	2,278.15	40,403,499	4,717,852	35,685,647	227,302	22,286,095	2,804,926
North Carolina	2,725,698	425.29	2,713,291	780,664	1,932,627	12,407	1,707,874	721,891
North Dakota	791,706	1,179.89	791,706	0	791,706	0	41,395	0
Ohio	9,439,644	872.75	9,329,644	2,731,455	6,598,189	110,000	7,070,960	2,727,044
Oklahoma	4,105,135	1,259.63	4,105,135	88,641	4,016,494	0	2,150,253	88,641
Oregon	7,143,426	2,623.37	6,958,426	6,231,380	727,046	185,000	1,743,818	1,501,862
Pennsylvania	8,819,566	738.53	8,816,954	4,371,872	4,445,082	2,612	6,878,053	4,315,540
Rhode Island	2,785,175	2,824.72	2,732,375	301,470	2,430,905	52,800	1,286,429	301,470
South Carolina	3,722,490	1,086.54	3,722,280	693,458	3,028,822	210	2,386,397	471,782
South Dakota	1,544,118	2,177.88	1,544,118	0	1,544,118	0	227,605	0
Tennessee	2,260,765	465.66	2,183,726	802,143	1,381,583	77,039	996,847	729,073
Texas	5,328,886	317.55	5,325,921	2,080,588	3,245,333	2,965	2,740,110	648,703
Utah	1,417,516	843.76	1,412,106	255,155	1,156,951	5,410	334,439	239,025
Vermont	955,067	1,746.01	952,324	266,702	685,622	2,743	336,038	266,702
Virginia	4,198,991	710.01	4,198,991	389,747	3,809,244	0	670,435	389,747
Washington	3,841,031	845.67	3,841,031	3,073,190	767,841	0	3,209,991	3,036,956
West Virginia	2,240,820	1,180.62	2,240,820	619,916	1,620,904	0	1,303,922	565,280
Wisconsin	4,795,159	997.54	4,795,159	2,159,385	2,635,774	0	2,761,712	2,122,717
Wyoming	780,377	1,592.61	780,377	0	780,377	0	31,567	0

Source: U.S. Bureau of the Census, *State Government Finances in 1987.*
Note: Debt figures include revenue bonds and other special obligations of state agencies as well as state general obligations.

(a) Long-term debt outstanding minus long-term debt offsets.

REVENUE AND EXPENDITURE

Table 6.14
STATE DEBT OUTSTANDING AT END OF FISCAL YEAR, BY STATE: 1988
(In thousands of dollars, except per capita amounts)

State	Total	Per capita	Long-term Total	Long-term Full-faith and credit	Long-term Nonguaranteed	Short-term	Net long-term (a) Total	Net long-term (a) Full-faith and credit
United States	$276,786,404	$1,128.86	$275,448,173	$68,135,781	$207,312,392	$1,338,231	$108,829,189	$54,154,353
Alabama	3,180,220	775.29	3,180,220	1,322,165	1,858,055	0	1,734,238	1,286,079
Alaska	6,096,612	11,634.76	6,096,612	1,447,538	4,649,074	0	2,058,460	657,969
Arizona	1,992,337	571.03	1,992,337	0	1,992,337	0	1,111,685	0
Arkansas	1,639,409	684.51	1,636,573	14,245	1,622,328	2,836	387,809	14,245
California	24,116,216	851.74	24,116,216	4,896,553	19,219,663	0	6,823,148	2,594,740
Colorado	2,288,683	693.33	2,288,348	75,665	2,212,683	335	233,151	75,665
Connecticut	8,265,744	2,556.68	8,251,344	2,591,763	5,659,581	14,400	2,669,970	2,196,116
Delaware	2,755,743	4,175.37	2,746,366	513,169	2,233,197	9,377	708,776	502,570
Florida	8,296,461	672.60	8,287,455	1,850,585	6,436,870	9,006	3,513,549	817,937
Georgia	3,138,090	494.81	3,138,090	2,187,210	950,880	0	2,149,449	2,118,607
Hawaii	2,927,718	2,666.41	2,854,912	1,847,983	1,006,929	72,806	2,387,529	1,835,665
Idaho	677,446	675.42	677,446	0	677,446	0	189,942	0
Illinois	13,148,589	1,132.13	13,147,701	3,917,373	9,230,328	888	4,887,853	3,791,393
Indiana	3,085,427	555.33	3,069,147	0	3,069,147	16,280	1,075,681	0
Iowa	1,364,581	481.50	1,364,581	0	1,364,581	0	399,493	0
Kansas	367,527	147.31	366,909	0	366,909	618	284,369	0
Kentucky	5,040,295	1,352.37	5,040,295	119,460	4,920,835	0	2,617,784	84,025
Louisiana	11,256,703	2,553.70	11,066,290	3,266,631	7,799,659	190,413	4,758,832	3,196,413
Maine	1,723,686	1,430.44	1,722,785	308,275	1,414,510	901	324,378	308,275
Maryland	5,615,514	1,214.95	5,615,514	2,100,991	3,514,523	0	2,900,383	2,070,984
Massachusetts	13,830,594	2,348.55	13,600,794	4,877,757	8,723,037	229,800	5,467,793	4,856,672
Michigan	8,463,922	916.01	8,463,108	527,300	7,935,808	814	1,819,023	527,300
Minnesota	3,606,620	837.39	3,606,620	1,274,123	2,332,497	0	1,545,450	1,274,123
Mississippi	1,470,266	561.17	1,466,719	499,873	966,846	3,547	680,714	473,661
Missouri	4,568,735	888.69	4,568,317	804,330	3,763,987	418	982,469	709,301
Montana	1,236,851	1,536.46	1,207,634	91,542	1,116,092	29,217	341,033	91,542
Nebraska	1,359,420	848.58	1,345,273	0	1,345,273	14,147	478,465	0
Nevada	1,361,667	1,291.90	1,361,667	532,615	829,052	0	755,500	523,940
New Hampshire	2,704,756	2,492.86	2,704,756	445,655	2,259,101	0	407,486	317,359
New Jersey	17,409,738	2,254.86	17,347,468	2,607,825	14,739,643	62,270	6,984,492	2,600,501
New Mexico	1,741,314	1,155.48	1,737,662	104,990	1,632,672	3,652	407,477	104,990
New York	41,882,229	2,338.61	41,530,953	4,760,555	36,770,398	351,276	17,821,407	2,914,187
North Carolina	2,728,302	420.45	2,728,224	712,640	2,015,584	78	863,278	668,970
North Dakota	796,908	1,194.76	796,908	0	796,908	0	45,799	0
Ohio	9,800,359	902.84	9,630,359	2,807,945	6,822,414	170,000	4,598,700	2,807,945
Oklahoma	3,753,349	1,157.73	3,753,349	80,376	3,672,973	0	1,826,897	70,026
Oregon	6,809,976	2,461.14	6,809,976	6,054,546	755,430	0	1,730,360	1,455,392
Pennsylvania	9,302,790	775.17	9,297,291	4,441,502	4,855,789	5,499	5,816,099	4,437,684
Rhode Island	2,870,529	2,890.76	2,870,229	390,090	2,480,139	300	682,146	390,090
South Carolina	3,644,778	1,050.37	3,641,775	681,613	2,960,162	3,003	2,304,435	391,989
South Dakota	1,553,692	2,179.09	1,553,692	0	1,553,692	0	228,382	0
Tennessee	2,254,391	460.55	2,185,559	733,737	1,451,822	68,832	917,427	667,384
Texas	7,119,634	422.76	7,119,544	2,602,190	4,517,354	90	2,901,868	747,649
Utah	1,515,384	896.68	1,511,634	291,005	1,220,629	3,750	358,443	274,351
Vermont	924,747	1,660.23	924,709	19,197	905,512	38	283,057	19,197
Virginia	4,512,950	750.28	4,512,950	346,200	4,166,750	0	768,036	346,200
Washington	4,271,565	919.01	4,271,280	3,360,400	910,880	285	3,469,244	3,315,079
West Virginia	2,464,001	1,313.43	2,464,001	569,544	1,894,457	0	1,001,316	559,513
Wisconsin	5,012,233	1,032.39	4,938,878	2,057,895	2,880,983	73,355	2,090,312	2,057,895
Wyoming	837,703	1,748.86	837,703	0	836,973	0	35,602	730

Source: U.S. Bureau of the Census, *State Government Finances in 1988.*
Note: Debt figures include revenue bonds and other special obligations of state agencies as well as state general obligations.
(a) Long-term debt outstanding minus long-term debt offsets.

TRENDS IN STATE TAXATION: 1988-89

By Ronald Alt

During 1988 and 1989, increases in state tax rates have exhibited a trend away from broad-based taxes toward selective excise taxes. More states raised motor fuel excise tax rates than any other tax (29 states). Next in frequency was the tobacco excise tax, which was raised in 16 states, and alcohol beverage taxes, increased in 8 states. Meanwhile, the general sales tax rate was raised in 8 states, while income tax rates (personal and corporate) were increased in 10 states.

However, most state income tax systems are tied to federal gross income. The federal tax reform act of 1986 broadened the income tax base, leading to an increase in revenue in many states. As a result, many states decreased income tax rates, increased the standard deductions or exemptions, changed tax brackets, or enacted some combination of the three. In fact, three states followed the lead of the federal government by simplifying the number of brackets and tax rates in 1988 and 1989. Several other states had done so in 1987.

On March 28, 1989, the U.S. Supreme Court invalidated Michigan's policy of taxing federal civil service pensions while exempting state and local retirement benefits (*Davis v. Michigan Department of the Treasury*). In response to this decision, 18 states have made changes equalizing the tax treatment of all public employee pensions. Litigation seeking refunds is currently under way in 24 states.

Personal Income Tax

Eight states made changes to their personal income tax systems during 1988. Three of these states, Oklahoma (for taxpayers deducting federal taxes), Utah and Vermont, lowered their tax rates. Utah also changed its provisions to allow taxpayers to deduct one-third of their federal taxes. Hawaii increased while Idaho lowered the personal exemption. And, Nebraska lowered its standard deduction to the federal amount.

Two of the states making changes completely reformed their income tax systems. Kansas reduced the number of tax brackets from 8 to 2, increased the personal exemption and repealed the deduction for federal income taxes. Maine reduced the number of brackets from 8 to 4, and revised the personal exemption and standard deductions.

In 1989, 16 states made changes affecting personal income taxes. Six of these raised personal income tax rates. They are: Connecticut (interest and dividends), Illinois, Massachusetts, Montana (added a five percent surcharge), North Dakota and Vermont. Five states, Hawaii, Kansas, Nebraska, South Carolina and Utah, directly reduced their tax rates. Five states, Hawaii, Maine, New York, South Carolina and Virginia, revised their tax brackets reducing the effective tax rates. Maine changed its personal exemptions and standard deductions to conform to the federal tax system. Hawaii raised its standard deduction, while Kansas, Maryland and Nebraska raised their exemptions. Two states changed the deductibility of federal income taxes. Kansas set up a different set of rates for individuals deducting federal income tax payments, while Utah increased the deductibility from one-third to one-half.

In 1989, North Carolina simplified its personal income tax structure by reducing the number of brackets from 5 to 2 and adopting federal taxable income as the starting point.

Ronald Alt is a senior research associate with the Federation of Tax Administrators.

The state, however, will not include federal indexing.

In response to the Davis case (overturning the way Michigan taxed federal and state pensions), 18 states changed the allowable exemptions on public employee pensions. The new caps on public pension exemptions are: Arizona, $2,500; Arkansas, $6,000; Colorado, $20,000; Georgia, $10,000; Iowa, $0 ($5,000 in 1989); Louisiana, (All); Michigan, (All); Missouri, $6,000 ($3,000 in 1989); New York, (All); North Carolina, $4,000; North Dakota, 5,000; Oklahoma, $5,500; Oregon, $5,000; South Carolina, $3,000; Utah, $0; Virginia, $16,000; West Virginia, $2,000; and Wisconsin, (All for certain systems entered before 1964).

Corporate Income Tax

Only two states made changes to their corporate income taxes in 1988. Arizona repealed the special rate applicable to capital gains and South Carolina lowered the tax rate to 5.5 percent.

Ten states changed their corporate income tax rates during 1989. Eight states increased the tax rate: Connecticut (20 percent surcharge), Illinois (20 percent surcharge), Missouri (added two brackets for higher income business), Montana (5 percent surcharge), New Jersey (0.375 percent surtax), North Dakota (alternate minimum tax increased 1 percent), Rhode Island (1 percent increase) and the District of Columbia (5 percent surcharge). Two states, South Carolina and West Virginia, lowered the tax rates to 5.0 percent and 9.45 percent, respectively.

Sales Taxes

During 1988, only three states made changes to their sales tax rates. Two states, Florida and West Virginia, raised the rate by one percentage point. Meanwhile, South Dakota lowered the sales tax rate one percent to 4 percent.

In 1989 seven states changed their general sales tax rates. States raising their tax rates were: California (a temporary 0.25 percent increase for earthquake relief), Connecticut (0.5 percent), Georgia (1 percent), Kansas (0.25 percent) and Missouri (0.2 percent). North Dakota raised its rate 0.5 percent in May and lowered it 1 percent (to 5 percent) after a voter referendum in December. Utah lowered the general sales tax rate by 3/32 to 5 percent.

Beginning on January 1, 1990, Illinois' municipalities lost the right to impose a local option sales tax. In lieu of a local tax, the state raised its general sales tax rate by 1.25 percent and will distribute the proceeds to local governments.

Motor Fuel Tax Rates

In 1988, 16 states raised their excise tax rate on gasoline. These states are Arizona, a 1 cent increase; Connecticut, 1 cent; Idaho, 3.5 cents; Indiana, 1 cent; Iowa, 2 cents; Maine, 2 cents; Minnesota, 3 cents; Mississippi, 1 cent; Nevada, 2 cents; New Mexico, 0.2 cent; New Jersey, 2.5 cents; Ohio, 0.1 cent; Oregon, 2 cents; South Carolina, 1 cent; South Dakota, 5 cents; and Wisconsin, 0.9 cent.

The excise tax rate on gasoline was increased in 17 states during 1989, and in three more states effective January, 1990. This raised the median state tax rate to 16.25 cents. The changes were: Colorado, a 2 cents increase; District of Columbia, 2.5 cents; Illinois, 3 cents; Kansas, 4 cents; Maine, 1 cent; Nebraska, 3.8 cents; New Mexico, 2 cents; Ohio, 3.2 cents; Oklahoma, 1 cent; Oregon, 2 cents; Rhode Island, raised the minimum rate by 5 cents; Tennessee, 4 cents; Vermont, 3 cents; Virginia, 0.2 cent; West Virginia, 5 cents; and Wyoming, 1 cent. North Carolina raised its tax rate an equivalent of 5.2 cents when the fixed rate was increased from 14 cents to 17 cents and the variable component raised from 3 percent to 7 percent of the wholesale price. In North Dakota, a voter referendum reversed a 3 cent fuel tax increase. On January 1, 1990, the tax rate on gasoline increased in three states: Illinois by another 3 cents, Louisiana by 4 cents, and Oregon by 2 cents.

All but five of these states raised the diesel rate by the same amount as gasoline. As a result, the median state diesel fuel tax rate increased to 17.0 cents. New Mexico raised the diesel fuel rate in 1988 but not in 1989. Maine increased the tax rate by 5 cents in 1988, while adding a penny in 1989. Colorado, on the other hand, lowered its tax rate by 2 cents for 1990. Meanwhile, Tennessee raised the diesel fuel rate by only 1 cent. On January 1, 1990, Nevada raised the diesel fuel rate by an additional 2 cents.

Tobacco Tax Rates

During 1988, only three states raised their tax rates applicable to cigarettes. Iowa raised its rate by 8 cents, Michigan by 4 cents, and Rhode Island by 2 cents. Iowa also raised the tax rate applicable to other tobacco products to 19 percent of the wholesale price. Alaska imposed a 25 percent tax on the wholesale price of other tobacco products.

Fourteen states increased their tobacco excise tax rates in 1989, raising the median state rate to 21 cents per pack. The tax rate increases are: Alaska, 13 cents; California, 25 cents; Connecticut, 14 cents; Illinois, 10 cents; Maine, 3 cents; Montana, 2 cents; Nevada, 15 cents; New Hampshire, 4 cents; New York, 12 cents; North Dakota, 3 cents; Oregon, 1 cent; Rhode Island, 10 cents; Washington, 3 cents and Wyoming, 4 cents. In Iowa, legislation approved in the previous year reduced the tax rate on cigarettes by 3 cents in 1989.

Two states enacted a tax on tobacco products other than cigarettes (OTP). New York imposed a tax rate of 15 percent on wholesale sales, while Connecticut imposed a tax rate of 20 percent. North Dakota and Maine raised their OTP tax rates to 30 percent and 50 percent, respectively.

Alcohol Beverage Tax Rates

Only two states raised alcohol beverage excise tax rates during 1988. Alabama raised its percentage based tax by 8 percent, while the indexation provision in Hawaii's law raised its liquor and beer rates. The gallonage rate on liquor increased 22 cents and beer increased a penny.

In 1989, seven states raised their excise tax rates on alcohol beverages. However, these increases raised the median state gallonage tax rates for distilled spirits (counting only those states with licensed distributors) to $2.80; for table wine, $0.55; and for beer, $0.14. The indexation provision in Hawaii raised liquor and beer rates by 33 cents and 4 cents, respectively. Rhode Island raised all alcohol beverage tax rates by 50 percent, while Connecticut raised the rate on liquor by 50 percent and beer and wine by 100 percent. Meanwhile, New York raised the spirits tax rate by 30 percent, table wine by 56 percent, and doubled the beer tax rate. The District of Columbia set its tax rates for beer and wine equal to neighboring Maryland's. Washington added a temporary tax to all three beverages, and Ohio raised the beer excise tax rate by 40 percent.

Amnesty Programs

During the last two years, three states conducted tax amnesty programs. This makes a total of 30 states and the District of Columbia that have conducted amnesty programs since 1982. The Florida program, begun in 1988, covered all taxes except intangibles (covered under another program) and generated net revenues of $8.4 million. The Kentucky program, also begun in 1988, generated $60.1 million and covered all taxes. And finally, the North Carolina program covered all taxes and generated $37.6 million in 1989. Virginia will become the latest state to initiate a tax amnesty when its program begins in 1990.

TAXES

Table 6.15
AGENCIES ADMINISTERING MAJOR STATE TAXES
(As of January 1, 1990)

State or jurisdiction	Income	Sales	Gasoline	Motor vehicle
Alabama	Dept. of Revenue	Dept. of Revenue	Dept. of Revenue	Dept. of Revenue
Alaska	Dept. of Revenue	...	Dept. of Revenue	Dept. of Public Safety
Arizona	Dept. of Revenue	Dept. of Revenue	Dept. of Transportation	Dept. of Transportation
Arkansas	Dept. of Fin. & Admin.	Dept. of Fin. & Admin.	Dept. of Fin. & Admin.	Dept. of Fin. & Admin.
California	Franchise Tax Bd.	Bd. of Equalization	Bd. of Equalization	Dept. of Motor Vehicles
Colorado	Dept. of Revenue	Dept. of Revenue	Dept. of Revenue	Dept. of Revenue
Connecticut	Dept. of Revenue Serv.	Dept. of Revenue Serv.	Dept. of Revenue Serv.	Dept. of Motor Vehicles
Delaware	Div. of Revenue	...	Dept. of Public Safety	Dept. of Public Safety
Florida	Dept. of Revenue	Dept. of Revenue	Dept. of Revenue	Div. of Motor Vehicles
Georgia	Dept. of Revenue	Dept. of Revenue	Dept. of Revenue	Dept. of Revenue
Hawaii	Dept. of Taxation	Dept. of Taxation	Dept. of Taxation	County Treasurer
Idaho	Dept. of Revenue & Tax.	Dept. of Revenue & Tax.	Dept. of Revenue & Tax.	Transportation Dept.
Illinois	Dept. of Revenue	Dept. of Revenue	Dept. of Revenue	Secretary of State
Indiana	Dept. of Revenue	Dept. of Revenue	Dept. of Revenue	Bur. of Motor Vehicles
Iowa	Dept. of Revenue & Finance	Dept. of Revenue & Finance	Dept. of Revenue & Finance	Dept. of Transportation
Kansas	Dept. of Revenue	Dept. of Revenue	Dept. of Revenue	Local
Kentucky	Revenue Cabinet	Revenue Cabinet	Revenue Cabinet	Transportation Cabinet
Louisiana	Dept. of Revenue & Tax.	Dept. of Revenue & Tax.	Dept. of Revenue & Tax.	Dept. of Public Safety
Maine	Bur. of Taxation	Bur. of Taxation	Bur. of Taxation	Secretary of State
Maryland	Comptroller	Comptroller	Comptroller	Dept. of Transportation
Massachusetts	Dept. of Revenue	Dept. of Revenue	Dept. of Revenue	Reg. of Motor Vehicles
Michigan	Dept. of Treasury	Dept. of Treasury	Dept. of Treasury	Secretary of State
Minnesota	Dept. of Revenue	Dept. of Revenue	Dept. of Revenue	Dept. of Public Safety
Mississippi	Tax Comm.	Tax Comm.	Tax Comm.	Tax Comm.
Missouri	Dept. of Revenue	Dept. of Revenue	Dept. of Revenue	Dept. of Revenue
Montana	Dept. of Revenue	...	Dept. of Revenue	Local
Nebraska	Dept. of Revenue	Dept. of Revenue	Dept. of Revenue	Dept. of Motor Vehicles
Nevada	...	Dept. of Taxation	Dept. of Taxation	Dept. of Motor Vehicles
New Hampshire	Dept. of Revenue Admin.	...	Dept. of Safety	Dept. of Safety
New Jersey	Dept. of Treasury	Dept. of Treasury	Dept. of Treasury	Dept. of Law & Public Safety
New Mexico	Tax & Revenue Dept.	Tax & Revenue Dept.	Tax & Revenue Dept.	Tax & Revenue Dept.
New York	Dept. of Tax. & Finance	Dept. of Tax. & Finance	Dept. of Tax. & Finance	Dept. of Motor Vehicles
North Carolina	Dept. of Revenue	Dept. of Revenue	Dept. of Revenue	Dept. of Transportation
North Dakota	Tax Cmsr.	Tax Cmsr.	Tax Cmsr.	Dept. of Motor Vehicles
Ohio	Dept. of Taxation	Dept. of Taxation	Dept. of Taxation	Bur. of Motor Vehicles
Oklahoma	Tax Comm.	Tax Comm.	Tax Comm.	Tax Comm.
Oregon	Dept. of Revenue	...	Dept. of Transportation	Dept. of Transportation
Pennsylvania	Dept. of Revenue	Dept. of Revenue	Dept. of Revenue	Dept. of Transportation
Rhode Island	Dept. of Administration	Dept. of Administration	Dept. of Administration	Dept. of Transportation
South Carolina	Tax Comm.	Tax Comm.	Tax Comm.	Dept. of Hwys. & Pub. Transportation
South Dakota	...	Dept. of Revenue	Dept. of Revenue	Dept. of Motor Vehicles
Tennessee	Dept. of Revenue	Dept. of Revenue	Dept. of Revenue	Dept. of Revenue
Texas	...	Comptroller	Comptroller	Dept. of Hwys. & Pub. Transportation
Utah	Tax Comm.	Tax Comm.	Tax Comm.	Tax Comm.
Vermont	Cmsr. of Taxes	Cmsr. of Taxes	Cmsr. of Motor Vehicles	Cmsr. of Motor Vehicles
Virginia	Dept. of Taxation	Dept. of Taxation	Dept. of Motor Vehicles	Dept. of Motor Vehicles
Washington	...	Dept. of Revenue	Dept. of Licensing	Dept. of Licensing
West Virginia	Tax Dept.	Tax Dept.	Tax Dept.	Dept. of Motor Vehicles
Wisconsin	Dept. of Revenue	Dept. of Revenue	Dept. of Revenue	Dept. of Transportation
Wyoming	...	Dept. of Revenue & Tax.	Dept. of Revenue & Tax.	Dept. of Revenue & Tax.
Dist. of Columbia	Dept. of Fin. & Revenue	Dept. of Fin. & Revenue	Dept. of Fin. & Revenue	Dept. of Fin. & Revenue

Source: The Federation of Tax Administrators.
Key:
... — Not applicable

TAXES

AGENCIES ADMINISTERING MAJOR STATE TAXES—Continued

State or jurisdiction	Tobacco	Death	Alcoholic beverage	Number of agencies administering taxes
Alabama	Dept. of Revenue	Dept. of Revenue	Alcoh. Bev. Control Bd.	2
Alaska	Dept. of Revenue	Dept. of Revenue	Dept. of Revenue	2
Arizona	Dept. of Revenue	Dept. of Revenue	Dept. of Revenue	2
Arkansas	Dept. of Fin. & Admin.	Dept. of Fin. & Admin.	Dept. of Fin. & Admin.	1
California	Bd. of Equalization	Controller	Bd. of Equalization	4
Colorado	Dept. of Revenue	Dept. of Revenue	Dept. of Revenue	1
Connecticut	Dept. of Revenue Serv.	Dept. of Revenue Serv.	Dept. of Revenue Serv.	2
Delaware	Div. of Revenue	Div. of Revenue	Div. of Revenue	2
Florida	Dept. of Business Reg.	Dept. of Revenue	Dept. of Business Reg.	3
Georgia	Dept. of Revenue	Dept. of Revenue	Dept. of Revenue	1
Hawaii	Dept. of Taxation	Dept. of Taxation	Dept. of Taxation	2
Idaho	Dept. of Revenue & Tax.	Dept. of Revenue & Tax.	Dept. of Revenue & Tax.	2
Illinois	Dept. of Revenue	Attorney General	Dept. of Revenue	3
Indiana	Dept. of Revenue	Dept. of Revenue	Dept. of Revenue	2
Iowa	Dept. of Revenue & Finance	Dept. of Revenue & Finance	Dept. of Revenue & Finance	2
Kansas	Dept. of Revenue	Dept. of Revenue	Dept. of Revenue	2
Kentucky	Revenue Cabinet	Revenue Cabinet	Revenue Cabinet	2
Louisiana	Dept. of Revenue & Tax.	Dept. of Revenue & Tax.	Dept. of Revenue & Tax.	2
Maine	Bur. of Taxation	Bur. of Taxation	Liquor Comm.	3
Maryland	Comptroller	Local	Comptroller	3
Massachusetts	Dept. of Revenue	Dept. of Revenue	Dept. of Revenue	2
Michigan	Dept. of Treasury	Dept. of Treasury	Liquor Control Comm.	3
Minnesota	Dept. of Revenue	Dept. of Revenue	Dept. of Revenue	2
Mississippi	Tax Comm.	Tax Comm.	Tax Comm.	1
Missouri	Dept. of Revenue	Dept. of Revenue	Dept. of Revenue	1
Montana	Dept. of Revenue	Dept. of Revenue	Dept. of Revenue	2
Nebraska	Dept. of Revenue	Dept. of Revenue	Liquor Control Comm.	3
Nevada	Dept. of Taxation	. . .	Dept. of Taxation	2
New Hampshire	Dept. of Revenue Admin.	Dept. of Revenue Admin.	Liquor Comm.	3
New Jersey	Dept. of Treasury	Dept. of Treasury	Dept. of Treasury	2
New Mexico	Tax & Revenue Dept.	Tax & Revenue Dept.	Tax & Revenue Dept.	1
New York	Dept. of Tax. & Finance	Dept. of Tax. & Finance	Dept. of Tax. & Finance	2
North Carolina	Dept. of Revenue	Dept. of Revenue	Dept. of Revenue	2
North Dakota	Tax Cmsr.	Tax Cmsr.	Treasurer	3
Ohio	Dept. of Taxation	Dept. of Taxation	Dept. of Taxation	2
Oklahoma	Tax Comm.	Tax Comm.	Tax Comm.	1
Oregon	Dept. of Revenue	Dept. of Revenue	Liquor Control Comm.	3
Pennsylvania	Dept. of Revenue	Dept. of Revenue	Dept. of Revenue	2
Rhode Island	Dept. of Administration	Dept. of Administration	Dept. of Administration	2
South Carolina	Tax Comm.	Tax Comm.	Tax Comm.	2
South Dakota	Dept. of Revenue	Dept. of Revenue	Dept. of Revenue	2
Tennessee	Dept. of Revenue	Dept. of Revenue	Dept. of Revenue	1
Texas	Comptroller	Comptroller	Alcoh. Bev. Comm.	3
Utah	Tax Comm.	Tax Comm.	Tax Comm.	1
Vermont	Cmsr. of Taxes	Cmsr. of Taxes	Cmsr. of Taxes	2
Virginia	Dept. of Taxation	Dept. of Taxation	Dept. of Taxation	2
Washington	Dept. of Revenue	Dept. of Revenue	Liquor Control Bd.	3
West Virginia	Tax Dept.	Tax Dept.	Alcoh. Bev. Control Cmsr.	3
Wisconsin	Dept. of Revenue	Dept. of Revenue	Dept. of Revenue	2
Wyoming	Dept. of Revenue & Tax.	Dept. of Revenue & Tax.	Liquor Comm.	2
Dist. of Columbia	Dept. of Fin. & Revenue	Dept. of Fin. & Revenue	Dept. of Fin. & Revenue	1

TAXES

Table 6.16
STATE TAX AMNESTY PROGRAMS
November 22, 1982 - Present

State or jurisdiction	Amnesty Period	legislative authorization	Major taxes covered	Accounts receivable included	Collections ($ Millions) (a)	Installment arrangements permitted (b)
Alabama	01/20/84 - 04/01/84	No (c)	All	No	3.2	No
Arizona	11/22/82 - 01/20/83	No (c)	All	No	6.0	Yes
Arkansas	09/01/87 - 11/30/87	Yes	All	No	1.2 (e)	Yes
California	12/10/84 - 03/15/85	Yes	Individual Income	Yes	154.0	Yes
		Yes	Sales	No	43.0	Yes
Colorado	09/16/85 - 11/15/85	Yes	All	No	6.4	Yes
Florida	01/01/87 - 06/30/87	Yes	Intangibles	No	13.0	No
	01/01/88 - 06/30/88	Yes (d)	All	No	8.4 (d)	No
Idaho	05/20/83 - 08/30/83	No (c)	Individual Income	No	.3	No
Illinois	10/01/84 - 11/30/84	Yes	All	Yes	152.4	No
Iowa	09/02/86 - 10/31/86	Yes	All	Yes	35.1	No
Kansas	07/01/84 - 09/30/84	Yes	All	No	.6	No
Kentucky	09/15/88 - 09/30/88	Yes (c)	All	No	60.1 (d)	No
Louisiana	10/01/85 - 12/31/85	Yes	All	No	1.2	Yes (f)
	10/01/87 - 12/15/87	Yes	All	No	.24 (e)	Yes (f)
Maryland	09/01/87 - 11/02/87	Yes	All	Yes	34.6 (g)	No
Massachusetts	10/17/83 - 01/17/84	Yes	All	Yes	85.2	Yes (h)
Michigan	05/12/86 - 06/30/86	Yes	All	Yes	109.8	No
Minnesota	08/01/84 - 10/31/84	Yes	All	Yes	12.1	No
Mississippi	09/01/86 - 11/30/86	Yes	All	No	1.0	No
Missouri	09/01/83 - 10/31/83	No (c)	All	No	.85	No
New Jersey	09/10/87 - 12/08/87	Yes	All	Yes	182.0 (e)	Yes
New Mexico	08/15/85 - 11/13/85	Yes	All (i)	No	13.6	Yes
New York	11/01/85 - 01/31/86	Yes	All (j)	Yes	401.3	Yes
North Carolina	09/01/89 - 12/01/89	Yes	All (k)	Yes	37.6	No
North Dakota	09/01/83 - 11/30/83	No (c)	All	No	.15	Yes
Oklahoma	07/01/84 - 12/31/84	Yes	Income Sales	Yes	13.9	No (l)
Rhode Island	10/15/86 - 01/12/87	Yes	All	No	1.9	Yes
South Carolina	09/01/85 - 11/30/85	Yes	All	Yes	7.1	Yes
Texas	02/01/84 - 02/29/84	No (c)	All (m)	No	.5	No
Virginia	02/01/90 - 03/31/90	Yes	All	Yes	N.A.	Yes
West Virginia	10/01/86 - 12/31/86	Yes	All	Yes	10.1 (e)	Yes
Wisconsin	09/15/85 - 11/22/85	Yes	All	Yes (n)	27.3	Yes
Dist. of Columbia	07/01/87 - 09/30/87	Yes	All	Yes	12.2	Yes

Source: The Federation of Tax Administrators.

(a) Where applicable, figure includes local portions of certain taxes collected under the state tax amnesty program.
(b) "No" indicates requirement of full payment by the expiration of the amnesty period. "Yes" indicates allowance of full payment after the expiration of the amnesty period.
(c) Authority for amnesty derived from pre-existing statutory powers permitting the waiver of tax penalties.
(d) Does not include intangibles tax and drug taxes. Gross collections totaled $22.1 million, with $13.7 million in penalties withdrawn.
(e) Preliminary figure.
(f) Amnesty taxpayers were billed for the interest owed, with payment to be made within 30 days of notification.
(g) Figure includes $1.1 million for the separate program conducted by the Department of Natural Resources for the boat excise tax.
(h) The amnesty statute was construed to extend the amnesty to those who applied to the department before the end of the amnesty period, and permitted them to file overdue returns and pay back taxes and interest at a later date.
(i) The severance taxes, including the six oil and gas severance taxes, the resources excise tax, the corporate franchise tax, and the special fuels tax were not subject to amnesty.
(j) Availability of amnesty for the corporation tax, the oil company taxes, the transportation and transmissions companies tax, the gross receipts oil tax, and the unincorporated business tax restricted to entities with 500 or fewer employees in the United States on the date of application. In addition, a taxpayer principally engaged in aviation, or a utility subject to the supervision of the State Department of Public Service was also ineligible for amnesty.
(k) Local taxes and real property taxes were not included.
(l) Full payment of tax liability required before the end of the amnesty period to avoid civil penalties.
(m) Texas does not impose a corporate or individual income tax. In practical effect, the amnesty was limited to the sales tax and other excises.
(n) Waiver terms varied depending upon the date that tax liability was assessed.

Table 6.17
STATE EXCISE RATES
(As of January 1, 1990)

State or jurisdiction	General sales and gross receipts tax (percent)	Cigarettes (cents per pack of 20)	Distilled spirits (a) ($ per gallon)	Motor fuel (b) (cents per gallon)	
				Gasoline	Diesel
Alabama	4	16.5	...	11	12
Alaska	...	29	5.60	8	8
Arizona	5	15	3.00	17	17
Arkansas	4	21	2.50 (c)	13.5	12.5
California	5 (d)	35	2.00	9	9
Colorado	3	20	2.28	20	18.5
Connecticut	8	40	4.50	20	20
Delaware	...	14	2.25	16	16
Florida	6	24	6.50	4 (e)	4 (e)
Georgia	4	12	3.79	7.5	7.5
Hawaii	4	40% (f)	5.75	11	11
Idaho	5	18	...	18	18
Illinois	6.25 (g)	30	2.00	19	21.5
Indiana	5	15.5	2.68	15	16
Iowa	4	31	...	20	22.5
Kansas	4.25	24	2.50 (h)	15	17
Kentucky	5	3 (i)	1.92 (j)	15	12
Louisiana	4	16	2.50	20	20
Maine	5	31	...	17	20
Maryland	5	13	1.50	18.5	18.5
Massachusetts	5	26	4.05	11	11
Michigan	4	25	...	15	15
Minnesota	6	38	5.03 (k)	20	20
Mississippi	6	18	...	18	18
Missouri	4.425 (u)	13	2.00	11	11
Montana	...	18	...	20	20
Nebraska	4	27	3.00	22	22
Nevada	5.75 (l)	35	2.05	16.25	22
New Hampshire	...	21	...	14	14
New Jersey	6	27 (m)	2.80 (n)	10.5	13.5
New Mexico	4.75	15	3.94	16.2	16.2
New York	4	33	5.30	8	10
North Carolina	3	2	...	21.7	21.7
North Dakota	5	30	2.50	17	17
Ohio	5	18	...	18	18
Oklahoma	4	23	5.56 (o)	16	13
Oregon	...	28	...	18	18
Pennsylvania	6	18	...	12	12
Rhode Island	6	37	3.75	20	20
South Carolina	5	7	2.72 (p)	16	16
South Dakota	4	23	3.93 (q)	18	18
Tennessee	5.5	13 (r)	4.00 (s)	21	17
Texas	6	26	2.40 (t)	15	15
Utah	5	23	...	19	19
Vermont	4	17	...	16	17
Virginia	3.5	2.5	...	17.7	16.2
Washington	6.5	34	...	18	18
West Virginia	6	17	...	15.5	15.5
Wisconsin	5	30	3.25	20.8	20.8
Wyoming	3	12	...	9	9
Dist. of Columbia	6	17	1.50	18	18

TAXES

STATE EXCISE RATES—Continued

Source: The Federation of Tax Administrators (based on legislation enacted at the 1989 sessions).

Note: . . . Indicates the tax is not applicable.

(a) Eighteen states have liquor monopoly systems. In Alabama, Idaho, Iowa, Maine, Michigan, Mississippi, Montana, New Hampshire, Ohio, Oregon, Pennsylvania, Utah, Vermont, Virginia, Washington, West Virginia and Wyoming, the state operates retail/wholesale liquor outlets. In North Carolina, liquor stores are operated by county boards. Tax rates in these states cannot be compared to others, since revenue is generated from various taxes, fees and net liquor profits. Only gallonage taxes imposed by states with a license system are reported in the table.

(b) In some states, different tax rates apply to liquefied petroleum gas, compressed natural gas and gasohol. Several states have variable-rate motor fuel taxes, under which the motor fuel tax rate is changed periodically by administrative action according to a statutory formula. Connecticut, New York and Pennsylvania have gross receipts or franchise taxes on oil companies, which are not covered in this table.

(c) Additional 20 cents per case and 3 percent off-premise or 14 percent on-premise sales taxes are imposed.

(d) Includes a temporary 0.25 percent tax increase earmarked to earthquake relief (expires December 31, 1990).

(e) The amount of the 6 percent sales tax is determined by the Department of Revenue based on average retail price, and is in addition to the gallonage rate reported in the table.

(f) Tax is based on wholesale price, approximately 36 cents per pack in November 1989.

(g) The state receives revenue from the first 5 percent, with the remainder being distributed to various local governments.

(h) Plus two additional taxes: an 8 percent enforcement tax on all sales and a 10 percent gross receipts tax.

(i) Dealers pay an additional enforcement and administrative fee of 0.1 cent per pack.

(j) Additional 5 cents per case and 9 percent wholesale taxes are imposed.

(k) An additional 1 cent per bottle tax imposed on all liquor except miniatures.

(l) Includes mandatory, statewide, state-collected 3.75 percent county and school sales tax.

(m) Includes a surtax in lieu of the state's sales tax, which is determined semi-annually by the Department of Taxation (8 cents per pack in 1990).

(n) A 7.3 percent wholesale tax is imposed in lieu of the state's sales tax.

(o) Additional $1.00 per bottle and 12 percent gross receipts taxes are imposed on all on-premise sales.

(p) An additional $5.36 per case tax and a 9 percent surtax are imposed on all liquor sales.

(q) An additional 2 percent wholesale tax is imposed.

(r) Dealers pay an additional enforcement and administrative fee of 0.05 cent per pack.

(s) Additional 15 cents per case and 15 percent (on-premise sales) taxes are imposed.

(t) Additional 12 percent (on-premise sales) and 5 cents per drink (airline sales) taxes are also imposed.

(u) Includes a temporary 0.2 percent tax increase effective October 1, 1989 through June 30, 1990.

TAXES

Table 6.18
FOOD AND DRUG SALES TAX EXEMPTIONS
(As of January 1, 1990)

State or jurisdiction	Tax rate (percentage)	Exemptions Food	Exemptions Prescription drugs	State or jurisdiction	Tax rate (percentage)	Exemptions Food	Exemptions Prescription drugs
Alabama	4		★	New Jersey	6	★	★
Arizona	5	★	★	New Mexico	4.75		
Arkansas	4		★	New York	4	★	★
California	5	★	★	North Carolina	3		★
Colorado	3	★	★	North Dakota	5	★	★
Connecticut	8	★	★	Ohio	5	★	★
Florida	6	★	★	Oklahoma	4		★
Georgia	4		★	Pennsylvania	6	★	★
Hawaii	4		★	Rhode Island	6	★	★
Idaho	5		★	South Carolina	5		★
Illinois	5	1%	1%	South Dakota	4		★
Indiana	5	★	★	Tennessee	5.5		★
Iowa	4	★	★	Texas	6	★	★
Kansas	4.25		★	Utah	5		★
Kentucky	5	★	★	Vermont	4	★	★
Louisiana	4	2%	★	Virginia	3.5		★
Maine	5	★	★	Washington	6.5	★	★
Maryland	5	★	★	West Virginia	6		★
Massachusetts	5	★	★	Wisconsin	5	★	★
Michigan	4	★	★	Wyoming	3		
Minnesota	6	★	★	Dist. of Columbia	6	★	★
Mississippi	6		★				
Missouri	4.225		★				
Nebraska	4	★	★				
Nevada	5.75	★	★				

Source: The Federation of Tax Administrators (based on legislation enacted at the 1987 sessions).

Table 6.19
STATE INDIVIDUAL INCOME TAXES
(As of January 1, 1990)

State or jurisdiction	Tax rate range (in percents) Low	Tax rate range (in percents) High	Number of brackets	Income brackets Lowest	Income brackets Highest	Personal exemptions Single	Personal exemptions Married	Personal exemptions Dependents	Federal income tax deductible
Alabama	2.0	- 5.0	3	500 (b)	- 3,000 (b)	1,500	3,000	300	★
Arizona (a)	2.0	- 8.0	7	1,290 (b)	- 7,740 (b)	2,229	4,458	1,337	★ (t)
Arkansas	1.0	- 7.0	6	3,000	- 25,000	20 (c)	40 (c)	20 (c)	
California (a)	1.0	- 9.3	6	4,020 (b)	- 26,380 (b)	55 (c)	110 (c)	55 (c)	
Colorado	5.0		1	------ Flat Rate ------		------ None ------			
Delaware	0.0	- 7.7	8	2,000	- 40,000	1,250	2,500	1,250	
Georgia	1.0	- 6.0	6	750 (e)	- 7,000 (e)	1,500	3,000	1,500	
Hawaii	2.0	- 10.0	8	1,500 (b)	- 20,500 (b)	1,040	2,080	1,040	
Idaho	2.0	- 8.2	8	1,000 (f)	- 20,000 (f)	2,000 (d)	4,000 (d)	2,000 (d)	
Illinois	3.0		1	------ Flat Rate ------		1,000	2,000	1,000	
Indiana	3.4		1	------ Flat Rate ------		1,000	2,000	1,000	
Iowa (a)	0.4	- 9.98	9	1,016	- 45,720	20 (c)	40 (c)	15 (c)	★
Kansas	4.5	- 5.95	2	27,500 (g)	- 27,500 (g)	2,000	4,000	2,000	★ (g)
Kentucky	2.0	- 6.0	5	3,000	- 8,000	20 (c)	40 (c)	20 (c)	★
Louisiana	2.0	- 6.0	3	10,000 (b)	- 50,000 (b)	4,500 (h)	9,000 (h)	1,000 (h)	★
Maine (a)	2.0	- 8.5	4	4,000 (b)	- 16,000 (b)	2,000	4,000	2,000	
Maryland	2.0	- 5.0	4	1,000	- 3,000	1,200	2,000	1,000	
Massachusetts	5.375 (i)		1	------ Flat Rate ------		2,200	4,400	1,000	
Michigan	4.6		1	------ Flat Rate ------		2,000	4,000	2,000	
Minnesota	6.0	- 8.0	2	13,000 (j)	- 13,000 (j)	2,000 (d)	4,000 (d)	2,000 (d)	
Mississippi	3.0	- 5.0	3	5,000	- 10,000	6,000	9,500	1,500	
Missouri	1.5	- 6.0	10	1,000	- 9,000	1,200	2,400	400	★
Montana (a)	2.0	- 11.0	10	1,500	- 52,500	1,200	2,400	1,200	★
Nebraska	2.0	- 5.9	4	1,800 (k)	- 27,000 (k)	1,180	2,360	1,180	
New Jersey	2.0	- 3.5	3	20,000	- 50,000	1,000	2,000	1,000	
New Mexico	1.8	- 8.5	7	5,200 (l)	- 41,600 (l)	2,000	4,000	2,000	
New York	5.0	- 7.375	4	8,000 (b)	- 16,000 (b)	0	0	1,000	
North Carolina	6.0	- 7.0	2	12,750 (m)	- 12,750 (m)	2,000	4,000	2,000	
North Dakota	3.2	- 14.6 (n)	8	3,000	- 50,000	2,000 (d)	4,000 (d)	2,000 (d)	★ (n)
Ohio	0.743	- 6.9	8	5,000	- 100,000	650 (q)	1,300 (q)	650 (q)	
Oklahoma	0.5	- 6.0 (o)	7	1,000	- 7,500	1,000	2,000	1,000	★ (o)
Oregon (a)	5.0	- 9.0	3	2,000 (b)	- 5,000 (b)	94 (c)	188 (c)	94 (c)	★ (p)
Pennsylvania	2.1		1	------ Flat Rate ------		------ None ------			
Rhode Island	22.96% Federal tax liability			...	...	...	...	...	
South Carolina (a)	2.75	- 7.0 (v)	5	2,000	- 10,000	2,000 (d)	4,000 (d)	2,000 (d)	
Utah	2.55	- 7.2	6	750 (b)	- 3,750 (b)	1,500 (b)	3,000 (d)	1,500 (d)	★ (u)
Vermont	25% Federal tax liability (r)			...	...	...	...	...	
Virginia	2.0	- 5.75	4	3,000	- 17,000	800	1,600	800	
West Virginia	3.0	- 6.5	5	10,000	- 60,000	2,000	4,000	2,000	
Wisconsin	4.9	- 6.93 (s)	3	7,500	- 15,000	0	0	50 (c)	
Dist. of Columbia	6.0	- 9.5	3	10,000	- 20,000	1,160	2,320	1,160	

Source: The Federation of Tax Administrators (based on legislation enacted at the 1989 session).

Note: This table excludes the following states taxes: Connecticut taxes interest and dividends at 1 percent to 14 percent and capital gains at 7 percent. New Hampshire taxes interest and dividends at 5 percent. Tennessee taxes interest and dividends at 6 percent.

(a) Seven states have statutory provision for automatic adjustment of tax brackets, personal exemption or standard deductions to the rate of inflation. 1989 data are shown since the inflation adjustments were not available at this time.
(b) For joint returns, the tax is twice the tax imposed on half the income.
(c) Tax credits.
(d) These states allow personal exemption provided in the Internal Revenue Code. Utah allows a personal exemption equal to three-fourths the federal exemptions.
(e) The tax brackets reported are for single individuals and married households filing jointly. For married households filing separately, the same rates apply to income brackets ranging from $500 to $5,000.
(f) For joint returns, the tax is twice the tax imposed on half the income. A $10 filing fee is charged for each return and a $15 credit is allowed for each exemption.
(g) The tax brackets reported are for single individual and married households filing separately. For married households filing jointly, the rates range from 3.65 percent for income under $35,000 to 5.15 percent for income over this amount. Different rates and brackets apply to taxpayers deducting federal income tax payments.
(h) Combined personal exemption and standard deduction.
(i) A 10 percent tax rate applies to interest, dividends and capital gains. A 5 percent rate applies to annuities and savings deposit interest.
(j) The tax brackets reported are for single individuals. The end of the lower bracket for married couples is at $19,000, and for married households filing separately at $9,500. An addition 0.5 percent tax is applied to certain income levels.
(k) The tax brackets reported are for single individual. For married couples, the same rates apply to brackets from $3,000 to $45,000.
(l) The tax brackets reported are for single individuals. For married individuals, the rate ranges from 2.4 percent under $8,000 to 8.5 percent over $64,000. Married households filing separately pay twice the tax imposed on half the income.
(m) The tax brackets reported are for single individuals. For married individuals, the same rates apply with the tax bracket changing at $21,250.
(n) Taxpayers have the option of paying 17 percent of the adjusted federal income tax liability, without a deduction of federal taxes. If approved by a referendum in 1990, the tax rates will fall to 2.67 percent of the first $3,000 to 12 percent of taxable income over $50,000. The simplified optional tax rate would drop to 14 percent.
(o) The rate range reported is for single persons not deducting federal income tax. Married persons filing jointly have the same rate and brackets that are twice as wide. Separate schedules, with rates ranging from 0.5 percent to 10 percent, apply to taxpayers deducting federal income taxes.
(p) Limited to $3,000.
(q) Taxpayers have the option of taking an additional deduction of $350 per exemption, or a $20 per exemption tax credit.
(r) If Vermont tax liability for any taxable year exceeds the tax liability determinable under federal tax law in effect on January 1, 1988, the taxpayer will be entitled to a credit of 106 percent of the excess tax. A credit of 25 percent of the federal credit, maximum $227.50.
(s) The tax brackets reported are for single individuals. For married individuals, the same rates apply to brackets from $10,000 to $20,000.
(t) 65 percent of the federal income taxes are deductible.
(u) One half of the federal income taxes are deductible.
(v) The tax rate in the lowest bracket could fall to 2.5 percent if the general fund reduction offset account is fully funded.

Table 6.20
STATE PERSONAL INCOME TAXES: FEDERAL STARTING POINTS

State or jurisdiction	Relation to Internal Revenue Code	Tax Base
Alabama	...	...
Alaska	...	...
Arizona	Current	Federal adjusted gross income
Arkansas	...	...
California	1/1/87	Federal adjusted gross income
Connecticut	...	...
Colorado	Current	Federal taxable income
Delaware	Current	Federal adjusted gross income
Florida	...	...
Georgia	1/1/89	Federal adjusted gross income
Hawaii	12/31/88	Federal taxable income
Idaho	1/1/89	Federal taxable income
Illinois	Current	Federal adjusted gross income
Indiana	1/1/89	Federal adjusted gross income
Iowa	1/1/89	Federal adjusted gross income
Kansas	Current	Federal adjusted gross income
Kentucky	1/1/85	Federal adjusted gross income
Louisiana	Current	Federal adjusted gross income
Maine	Current	Federal adjusted gross income
Maryland	Current	Federal adjusted gross income
Massachusetts	1/1/85	Federal adjusted gross income
Michigan	Current (a)	Federal adjusted gross income
Minnesota	1/1/89	Federal taxable income
Mississippi	...	...
Missouri	Current	Federal adjusted gross income
Montana	Current	Federal adjusted gross income
Nebraska	Current	Federal adjusted gross income
Nevada	...	...
New Hampshire	...	...
New Jersey	...	...
New Mexico	Current	Federal adjusted gross income
New York	Current	Federal adjusted gross income
North Carolina	1/1/89	Federal taxable income
North Dakota	Current (b)	Federal liability (b)
Ohio	Current	Federal adjusted gross income
Oklahoma	Current	Federal adjusted gross income
Oregon	12/31/88	Federal taxable income
Pennsylvania	...	...
Rhode Island	Current	Federal liability
South Carolina	12/31/88	Federal taxable income
South Dakota	...	...
Tennessee	...	...
Texas	...	...
Utah	Current	Federal taxable income
Vermont	Current (c)	Federal liability
Virginia	Current	Federal adjusted gross income
Washington	...	...
West Virginia	12/31/88	Federal adjusted gross income
Wisconsin	12/31/88	Federal adjusted gross income
Wyoming	...	...
Dist. of Columbia	1/1/89	Federal adjusted gross income

Source: The Federation of Tax Administrators (based on legislation enacted at the 1989 session).

Key:
... — State does not employ a Federal starting point
Current — State has adopted Internal Revenue Code as currently in effect. Dates indicate state has adopted Internal Revenue Code as ammended to that date.

(a) Or 1/1/87, taxpayer's option.
(b) Or federal taxable income based on current Internal Revenue Code.
(c) Not to exceed tax computed using Internal Revenue Code as of 1/1/89.

TAXES

Table 6.21
RANGE OF STATE CORPORATE INCOME TAX RATES
(As of January 1, 1990)

State or jurisdiction	Tax rate (percent)	Tax brackets Lowest	Tax brackets Highest	Number of brackets	Tax rate (a) (percent) financial institution	Federal income tax deductible
Alabama	5.0	---------- Flat Rate ----------		1	6.0	★
Alaska	1.0 - 9.4	10,000	90,000	10	1.0 - 9.4	
Arizona	2.5 - 10.5 (b)	1,000	6,000	7	2.5 - 10.5 (b)	★
Arkansas	1.0 - 6.0	3,000	25,000	5	1.0 - 6.0	
California	9.3 (c)	---------- Flat Rate ----------		1	10.644 (c)	
Colorado	5.0 - 5.4	50,000	50,000	2	5.0 - 5.4	
Connecticut	13.8 (d)	---------- Flat Rate ----------		1	13.8 (d)	
Delaware	8.7	---------- Flat Rate ----------		1	8.7 - 2.7 (e)	
Florida	5.5 (f)	---------- Flat Rate ----------		1	5.5 (f)	
Georgia	6.0	---------- Flat Rate ----------		1	6.0	
Hawaii	4.4 - 6.4 (g)	25,000	100,000	3	11.7	
Idaho	8.0 (h)	---------- Flat Rate ----------		1	8.0 (h)	
Illinois	7.3 (i)	---------- Flat Rate ----------		1	7.3 (i)	
Indiana	7.9 (j)	---------- Flat Rate ----------		1	7.9 (j)	
Iowa	6.0 - 12.0	25,000	250,000	4	5.0	★ (k)
Kansas	4.5 (l)	---------- Flat Rate ----------		1	4.25 (l)	
Kentucky	3.0 - 7.25	25,000	250,000	5	... (a)	
Louisiana	4.0 - 8.0	25,000	200,000	5	... (a)	★
Maine	3.5 - 8.93	25,000	250,000	4	1.0	
Maryland	7.0	---------- Flat Rate ----------		1	7.0	
Massachusetts	9.5 (m)	---------- Flat Rate ----------		1	12.54 (m)	
Minnesota	9.5	---------- Flat Rate ----------		1	9.5	
Mississippi	3.0 - 5.0	5,000	10,000	3	... (a)	
Missouri	5.0 - 6.5	100,000	335,000	3	7.0	★
Montana	6.75 (n)	---------- Flat Rate ----------		1	6.75 (n)	
Nebraska	4.75 - 6.65	50,000		2	... (a)	
New Hampshire	8 (o)	---------- Flat Rate ----------		1	8 (o)	
New Jersey	9 (p)	---------- Flat Rate ----------		1	3 (p)	
New Mexico	4.8 - 7.6	500,000	1,000,000	3	4.8 - 7.6	
New York	9.0 (q)	---------- Flat Rate ----------		1	9.0 (q)	
North Carolina	7.0	---------- Flat Rate ----------		1	4.5 (r)	
North Dakota	3.0 - 10.5	3,000	50,000	6	7.0 (s)	★
Ohio	5.1 - 8.9 (t)	50,000		2	... (t)	
Oklahoma	5.0	---------- Flat Rate ----------		1	5.0	
Oregon	6.6 (u)	---------- Flat Rate ----------		1	6.6 (u)	
Pennsylvania	8.5	---------- Flat Rate ----------		1	... (a)	
Rhode Island	9.0 (v)	---------- Flat Rate ----------		1	8.0 (v)	
South Carolina	5.0	---------- Flat Rate ----------		1	4.5 (w)	
South Dakota	...				6.0 (x)	
Tennessee	6.0	---------- Flat Rate ----------		1	6.0	
Utah	5.0 (y)	---------- Flat Rate ----------			5.0 (y)	
Vermont	5.5 - 8.25 (z)	10,000	250,000	4	5.5 - 8.25 (z)	
Virginia	6.0	---------- Flat Rate ----------		1	6.0 (aa)	
West Virginia	9.45	---------- Flat Rate ----------		1	9.45	
Wisconsin	7.9	---------- Flat Rate ----------		1	7.9	
Dist. of Columbia	10.0 (bb)	---------- Flat Rate ----------			10.0 (bb)	

TAXES

RANGE OF STATE CORPORATE INCOME TAX RATES—Continued

Source: The Federation of Tax Administrators (based on legislation enacted at 1987 sessions).

Note: Michigan imposes a single business tax (sometimes described as a business activities tax or value added tax) of 2.35 percent on the sum of federal taxable income of the business, compensation paid to employees, dividends, interest, royalties paid and other items.

(a) Rates listed include the corporate tax rate applied to financial institution or excise taxes based on income. Some states have other taxes based upon the value of deposits or shares.

(b) Minimum tax is $50.

(c) Minimum tax is $800. Banks and corporations electing a water's edge method of apportioning income must pay a tax of 0.3 percent of the sum of property, payroll and sales in California.

(d) Includes a 20 percent surcharge. Or 3.1 mills per dollar of capital stock and surplus (maximum tax $500,000) or $100.

(e) The marginal rate decreases over 4 brackets ranging from $20,000 to $30,000 million in taxable income. Building and loan associations are taxed at a flat 8.7 percent.

(f) An exemption of $5,000 is allowed.

(g) Capital gains are taxed at 4 percent.

(h) Minimum tax is $20. An additional tax of $10 is imposed on each return.

(i) Includes a 2.5 percent personal property replacement tax and a 20 percent surcharge.

(j) Consists of 3.4 percent on income from sources within the state plus a 4.5 percent supplemental income tax.

(k) Fifty percent of the federal income tax is deductible.

(l) Plus a surtax of 2.25 percent (2.125 percent for banks) taxable income in excess of $25,000.

(m) Rate includes a 14 percent surtax, as does the following: an additional tax of $2.60 per $1,000 on taxable tangible property (or net worth allocable to state, for intangible property corporations); minimum tax of $456.

(n) A 7 percent tax on taxpayers using water's edge combination. A 5 percent surtax is imposed on all taxes. Minimum tax is $50; for small business corporations, $10.

(o) Business profits tax imposed on both corporations and unincorporated associations.

(p) Plus a 0.375 percent surcharge. The rate reported in the table is the business franchise tax rate; there is also a net worth tax at rates ranging from 0.2 to 2 mills. The minimum tax is $25 for domestic corporations, $50 for foreign corporations. Corporations not subject to the franchise tax are subject to a 7.25 percent income tax. Banks other than savings institutions are subject to the franchise tax.

(q) Or 1.78 (0.1 for banks) mills per dollar of capital up to $350,000; or 5 percent (3 percent for banks) of the minimum taxable income; or a minimum of $1,500 to $325 depending on payroll size ($250 plus 2.5 percent surtax for banks); if any of these is greater than the tax computed on net income. An addition tax of 0.9 mills per dollar of subsidiary capital is imposed on corporations.

(r) Savings and loans are subject to the corporate income tax. The minimum bank tax is $10.

(s) Includes a 2 percent privilege tax. Minimum tax is $50.

(t) Or 5.82 mills times the value of the taxpayer's issued and outstanding share of stock; minimum tax $50. An additional litter tax is imposed equal to 0.11 percent on the first $25,000 of taxable income, 0.22 percent on income over $25,000; or 0.14 mills on net worth. Corporations manufacturing or selling litter stream products are subject to an additional 0.22 percent tax on income over $25,000 or 0.14 mills on net worth.

(u) Minimum tax is $10.

(v) Or for business corporations the tax is 40 cents per $100 of net worth, if greater than the tax computed on net income. For banks, the alternative tax is $2.50 per $10,000 of capital stock (minimum tax is $100).

(w) Savings and loans are taxed at a 6 percent rate.

(x) Minimum tax is $200 per authorized location.

(y) Minimum tax is $100.

(z) Minimum tax is $75.

(aa) State and national banks subject to the state's franchise tax on net capital is exempt from the income tax.

(bb) A 5 percent surtax is also imposed. Minimum tax is $100.

TAXES

Table 6.22
STATE SEVERANCE TAXES: 1989

State	Title and application of tax (a)	Rate
Alabama	Iron Ore Mining Tax	$.03/ton
	Forest Products Severance Tax	Varies by species and ultimate use
	Oil and Gas Conservation & Regulation of Production Tax	2% of gross value at point of production
	Oil and Gas Production Tax	8% of gross value at point of production; 4% if wells produce 25 bbl. or less oil per day or 200,000 cu. ft. or less gas per day; 6% of gross value at point of production for certain on-shore and off-shore wells; 2% of gross value of occluded natural gas from coal seams at point of production for well's first five years
	Coal Severance Tax (b)	$.135/ton
	Coal and Lignite Severance Tax	$.20/ton in addition to Coal Severance Tax
Alaska	Fisheries Business Tax	3% to 5% of fish value based on type of fish
	Oil and Gas Production Tax	The greater of $.60/bbl. for old crude oil ($.80 for all other) or 15% of gross value at production point (multiplied by economic limit factor); the greater of $.064/1,000 cu. ft. of gas or 10% of gross value at production point (multiplied by economic limit factor). Additional $.00125/bbl. of oil and $.00125/50,000 cu. ft. of gas (oil and gas conservation tax)
Arizona	Severance Tax (c)	2.5% of net severance base for mining; 1.5% of value for timbering
Arkansas	Natural Resources Severance Tax	Separate rate for each substance
	Oil and Gas Conservation Tax	Maximum 25 mills/bbl. of oil and 5 mills/1,000 cu. ft. of gas
California	Oil and Gas Production Tax	Rate determined annually by Department of Conservation (d)
Colorado	Severance Tax (e)	Separate rate for each substance
	Oil and Gas Conservation Tax	Maximum 1.5 mills/$1 of market value at wellhead (f)
Florida	Oil, Gas and Sulfur Production Tax	8% (oil); additional 12.5% for escaped oil and 5% (gas) of gross value at point of production. $2.40/long-ton produced or recovered sulfur. Wells producing less than 100 bbls./day or oil produced by tertiary methods are taxed at 5% of gross value at point of production
	Solid Minerals Tax (g)	5% of market value at point of severance, except $1.32/ton phosphate rock and $1.37/ton heavy minerals
Georgia	Tax on Phosphates	$1/ton
Idaho	Ore Severance Tax	2% of net value
	Oil and Gas Production Tax	Maximum of 5 mills/bbl. of oil and 5 mills/50,000 cu. ft. of gas (h)
	Additional Oil and Gas Production Tax	2% of market value at site of production
Illinois	Timber Fee	4% of purchase price (i)
Indiana	Petroleum Production Tax (j)	1% of value
Kansas	Severance Tax (k)	8% of gross value of oil and gas; $1/ton of coal
	Oil and Gas Assessments	13.5 mills/bbl. crude oil or petroleum marketed or used; 4 mills/1,000 cu. ft. of gas produced, sold, marketed or used
	Mined-Land Conservation & Reclamation Tax	$50, plus per ton fee of between $.03 and $.10
Kentucky	Oil Production Tax	4.5% of market value
	Coal Severance Tax	4.5% of gross value
	Natural Resource Severance Tax (l)	4.5% of gross value, less transportation expenses
Louisiana	Natural Resources Severance Tax	Rate varies according to substance
Maine	Mining Excise Tax	The greater of a tax on facilities and equipment or a tax on gross proceeds
Maryland	Mine Reclamation Surcharge	$.09/ton (as per state authority) and $.06/ton (as per county authority) of coal removed by open-pit or strip method
	Coal and Gas Severance Taxes (m)	$.30/ton of surface-mined coal
Michigan	Gas and Oil Severance Tax	5% (gas), 6.6% (oil) and 4% (oil from stripper wells and marginal properties) of gross cash market value of the total production. Maximum additional fee of 1% of gross cash market value on all oil and gas produced in state in previous year
Minnesota	Iron Severance Tax (n)	14% of value (minus credits)
	Ore Royalty Tax	14% of royalty received (minus credits)
	Taconite, Iron Sulphides and Agglomerate Taxes	$1.90/ton ($.05/ton for agglomerates)
	Semi-Taconite Tax	$.10/ton ($.05/ton if agglomerated or sintered in state), plus $.001/ton depending on percentage of iron content
	(o)	
Mississippi	Oil and Gas Severance Tax	6% of value at point of production; also, maximum 20 mills/bbl. oil or 2 mills/1,000 cu ft. gas (Oil and Gas Board maintenance tax).
	Timber Severance Tax	Varies depending on type of wood and ultimate use
	Salt Severance Tax	3% of value of entire production in state
Missouri	Surface Coal Mining Permittee Assessment	$.45/ton for first 50,000 tons sold (shipped, or otherwise disposed of) in calendar year, and $.30/ton for next 50,000 tons. One-time assessment fee based on projected production for permittees filing full-cost bonds between 9/1/88 and 9/1/93. Maximum $125,000.

TAXES

STATE SEVERANCE TAXES—Continued

State	Title and application of tax (a)	Rate
Montana	Coal Severance Tax	Varies by quality of coal and type of mine
	Metalliferous Mines License Tax (p)	Progressive rate, taxed on amounts in excess of $250,000. For concentrate shipped to smelter, mill or reduction work, 1.81%. Gold, silver or any platinum group metal shipped to refinery, 1.61%
	Oil or Gas Producers' Severance Tax	5% of total gross value of petroleum and other mineral or crude oil (q), 3% of total gross value of petroleum and other mineral or crude oil, and 2.65% of total gross value of natural gas (license tax); maximum 0.2% of market value/bbl. of oil and of each 10,000 cu. ft. of gas (conservation tax) (h)
	Micaceous Minerals License Tax	$.05/ton
	Cement License Tax (r)	$.22/ton of cement, $.05/ton of cement, plaster, gypsum or gypsum products
	Mineral Mining Tax	$25 plus 0.5% of gross value over $5,000 $25 plus 0.4% of gross value for talc
Nebraska	Oil and Gas Severance Tax	3% of value of nonstripper oil and natural gas; 2% of value of stripper oil
	Oil and Gas Conservation Tax	Maximum 4 mills/$1 of value at wellhead
	Uranium Tax	2% of gross value over $5 million
Nevada	Net Proceeds of Mine Tax	Minimum 2%, maximum 5%. Based on ratio of net proceeds to gross proceeds of whole operation.
	Oil and Gas Conservation Tax	50 mills/bbl. of oil and 50 mills/50,000 cu. ft. of gas $50 for drilling each well
New Hampshire	Refined Petroleum Products Tax	0.1% of fair market value
New Mexico	Resources Excise Tax (s)	Varies according to substance
	Severance Tax (s)	Varies according to substance
	Oil and Gas Severance Tax	3.75% of value of oil, other liquid hydrocarbons and carbon dioxide; greater of 3.75% of value or $.163/mcf at 60°F and pressure base 15.025 lbs./square inch absolute (new wells at 3.75%)
	Oil and Gas Privilege Tax	3.15% of value
	Natural Gas Processor's Tax	0.45% of value of products
	Oil and Gas Ad Valorem Production Tax	Varies
	Oil and Gas Conservation Tax (t)	Percentage varies (u)
North Carolina	Oil and Gas Conservation Tax	Maximum 5 mills/bbl. of oil and 0.5 mill/1,000 cu. ft. of gas (h)
	Primary Forest Product Assessment Tax	$.40 or $.50/1,000 board ft. and $.12 or $.20/cord depending on type of wood and use
North Dakota	Oil and Gas Gross Production Tax	5% of gross value at well
	Coal Severance Tax	$.75/ton plus $.02/ton (v)
	Oil Extraction Tax	6.5% of gross value at well (with exceptions due to price and date of well completion)
Ohio	Resource Severance Tax (w)	$.10/bbl. of oil; $.025/1,000 cu. ft. of gas; $.04/ton of salt; $.02/ton of sand, gravel, limestone and dolomite; $.07/ton of coal
Oklahoma	Oil, Gas and Mineral Gross Production Tax (x)	Separate rate for each substance
	Natural Gas and Casinghead Gas Conservation Excise Tax	$.07/1,000 cu. ft., less 7% of gross value of each 1,000 cu. ft. of gas
Oregon	Forest Products Harvest Tax	$.05/1,000 board ft. (privilege tax); $.30/1,000 board ft. (harvest tax) (y)
	Oil and Gas Production Tax	6% of gross value at well
	Severance Tax on Eastern Oregon Timber	5% of immediate harvest value and additional severance tax on reforestation land
	Severance Tax on Western Oregon Timber	6.5% of value and additional severance tax on reforestation land
South Dakota	Precious Metals Severance Tax	2% of gross yield from sale of metals plus 8% on net profits or royalties from sale of precious metals
	Energy Minerals Severance Tax	4.5% of taxable value of any energy minerals
	Conservation Tax	2.4 mills of taxable value of any energy minerals
Tennessee	Oil and Gas Severance Tax	3% of sales price
	Coal Severance Tax (z)	$.20/ton
Texas	Natural Gas Production Tax	7.5% of market value
	Oil Production Tax	The greater of 4.6% of market value or $.046/bbl.
	Sulphur Production Tax	$1.03/long ton or fraction thereof
	Cement Production Tax	$.0275/100 lbs. or fraction thereof
Utah	Mining Occupation Tax (aa)	1% of gross value for metals; 4% of value for oil, gas and other hydrocarbons at wellhead
	Oil and Gas Conservation Tax	2 mills/$1 of market value at wellhead
Virginia	Forest Products Tax	Varies by species and ultimate use
	Coal Surface Mining Reclamation Tax	Varies depending on balance of Coal Surface Mining Reclamation Fund
	Oil Severance Tax (bb)	0.5% of gross receipts from sale
Washington	Uranium and Thorium Milling Tax	$.05/lb.
	Enhanced Food Fish Tax	0.07% to 5% of value (depending on species) at point of landing
West Virginia	Natural Resource Severence Tax	Coal, 5% plus 0.35% for counties and municipalities. timber, 3.22% (cc)

TAXES

STATE SEVERANCE TAXES—Continued

State	Title and application of tax (a)	Rate
Wisconsin	Metalliferous Minerals Occupation Tax	Progressive net proceeds tax from 3% to 15%
Wyoming	Oil and Gas Production Tax	Maximum 0.8 mill/$1 of value at wellhead (h,dd)
	Mining Excise and Severance Taxes	Varies by substance from 1.5% to 3.34% of value; some additional excise taxes of 2% to 3%

Source: Commerce Clearing House, *State Tax Guide.*

(a) Application of tax is same as that of title unless otherwise indicated by a footnote.
(b) Tax scheduled to terminate upon the redemption of, and payment of all accrued interest on, bonds issued by the Alabama State Docks Department.
(c) Timber, metalliferous minerals.
(d) For 1986, $.01673/bbl. of oil or per 10,000 cu. ft. of gas.
(e) Metallic minerals, coal, oil shale, oil and gas.
(f) Currently set at 1 mill.
(g) Clay, gravel, phosphate rock, lime, shells, stone, sand, heavy minerals and rare earths.
(h) Actual rate set by administrative actions.
(i) Buyer deducts amount from payment to grower; amount forwarded to Department of Conservation.
(j) Petroleum, oil, gas and other hydrocarbons.
(k) Coal, salt, oil and gas.
(l) Coal and oil excepted.
(m) Limited to certain counties. Coal tax expires June 30, 1989.
(n) All ores; tax repealed after December 31, 1989.
(o) State also has two related taxes; Mining Occupation Tax and Proceeds Tax.
(p) Metals, precious and semi-precious stones and gems.
(q) Except 2.5 percent of gross value of incremental petroleum and other mineral or crude oil produced in tertiary recovery projects. Over $250,000 gross value to over $1 million.
(r) Cement and gypsum or allied products.
(s) Natural resources except oil, natural gas, liquid hydrocarbons or carbon dioxide.
(t) Oil, coal, gas, liquid hydrocarbons, geothermal energy, carbon dioxide and uranium.
(u) Currently, rate is .18 percent.
(v) Rate reduced by 50 percent if burned in cogeneration facility using renewable resources as fuel to generate at least 10 percent of its energy output.
(w) Oil, gas, coal, salt, limestone, dolomite, sand and gravel.
(x) Asphalt, oil, gas, uranium and metals.
(y) Additional $.26/1,000 board ft. ($.16 is part of privilege and $.10 is for administering State Forest Practices Act) on forest products harvested until July 1, 1989.
(z) Counties and municipalities also authorized to levy severance taxes on sand, gravel, sandstone, chert, and limestone and a privilege tax on nuclear materials.
(aa) Metals, oil, gas, other hydrocarbons and uranium.
(bb) May be levied by counties and cities, until July 1, 1992.
(cc) Tax rates for other natural resources will vary each year until 1994, when they will be taxed at 5 percent of gross value.
(dd) Currently, rate is .2 mill/$1.

STATE TAX COLLECTIONS IN 1988

By Gerard T. Keffer

State tax collections totaled $264 billion in fiscal 1988, up 6.9 percent from the $247 billion collected in fiscal 1987. Of their fiscal 1988 total revenue of $542 billion, the states received 48.7 percent from taxes. Major nontax revenue sources included intergovernmental payments from the federal government of $100 billion, and $90 billion from insurance trust sources (mainly employee retirement contributions). This article presents data on revenue from state government taxes only. In fiscal 1988, as in previous years, these state tax collections exceeded locally imposed collections ($264 billion versus $172 billion).

The distribution of state tax collections by major tax category has remained fairly constant over the past decade. However, in the 20 years (1958-1978) prior to that, a major realignment of tax revenue sources occurred. The primary reason was the increase in the number of states collecting individual and corporate income taxes. In 1958, 31 states collected individual income taxes, and 33 states collected corporation net income taxes; by 1973, these numbers rose to 44 and 46, respectively. These same states continue to collect individual and corporate income taxes today. And, with the additional states with income taxes, the percentage of these taxes of total taxes more than doubled from 1958 (17.2 percent) to 1978 (35.2 percent). As Table A reflects, this caused a relative decrease over the same period in sales and gross receipts taxes, license taxes, and other taxes.

General sales and gross receipts taxes were the largest source of state tax revenue at $87 billion, up 9.3 percent from 1987. Individual income taxes accounted for $80 billion, up 5.5 percent, while corporate net income taxes rose 4.6 percent to $22 billion. Selective sales taxes totaled $43 billion, an increase of 7.3 percent since 1987. Motor fuel taxes climbed 9.5 percent, to $17 billion, the largest share of selective sales taxes. Increased motor fuel tax rates in 13 states during fiscal year 1988 contributed significantly to the overall rate of the selective sales tax increase.

Tobacco product taxes showed a 4.3 percent increase to $5 billion, alcoholic beverage taxes registered a 3.2 percent growth and stood at $3 billion. Eleven states increased the cigarette tax rate in fiscal year 1988. These increases offset any decline in consumption.

Severance taxes, after declining for three straight years (down 33.9 percent in 1987, 16.1 percent in 1986, and .5 percent in 1985), rose 6.9 percent, to $4 billion. During the 1985-1987 period, the decline in severance tax revenues (mostly related to oil and gas) was so drastic in several states that it resulted in an overall decrease in total state tax revenues. The states thus affected were: Alaska, Louisiana, Oklahoma and Texas. While still not the picture of fiscal health, these state economies have benefited greatly from a reversal of the slide in severance tax revenues.

Individual State Tax Collections

State government per capita taxes reached a record high of $1,077 in 1988. Nine states collected $9 billion or more in taxes in 1988. Table B ranks these states by dollars and per capita amounts.

Taxes for the nine states listed were $140 billion or 53 percent of the total. Their collective populations were 127 million or 52 percent of the U.S. total. Their per capita tax burden was $1,108, which exceeded by 3 percent

---

Gerard T. Keffer is Chief, Taxation Branch, Governments Division, U.S. Bureau of the Census.

TAXES

Table A
Percent Distribution of State Tax Collections by Major Tax Category

Year	Sales & Gross Receipts Taxes	Income Taxes	License Taxes	Other Taxes
1958	58.6	17.2	14.7	9.5
1963	58.2	20.2	12.8	8.8
1968	57.6	24.1	10.6	7.7
1973	54.4	31.0	8.4	6.2
1978	51.5	35.2	6.8	6.5
1983	48.9	36.7	6.2	8.2
1984	48.7	37.8	6.1	7.4
1985	48.8	37.8	6.4	7.0
1986	49.3	37.7	6.5	6.5
1987	48.5	39.2	6.5	5.8
1988	49.3	38.5	6.5	5.7

the national average of $1,077. Of this group, only New York ($1,461), California ($1,274), New Jersey ($1,264) and Michigan ($1,138) exceeded the national per capita tax average.

Eight states reported state tax collections in 1988 which exceeded a 15 percent increase from the previous year: Hawaii (20.1 percent), Oklahoma (18.0 percent), Texas (19.6 percent), Alaska (17.8 percent), Kansas (17.3 percent), Maine (16.8 percent) and Florida (16.4 percent) (see Table 6.24). Only five states had increases of this magnitude between 1986 and 1987.

Table B
Selected States' Tax Collections: 1988

Name	Amount of Taxes ($ Millions)	Per Capita Amount (Hundreds)	Rank
California	36,075	1,274	9
New York	26,171	1,461	4
Texas	13,426	797	46
Pennsylvania	11,825	985	25
Florida	11,460	929	34
Illinois	11,079	954	30
Michigan	10,515	1,138	16
Ohio	9,991	920	35
New Jersey	9,762	1,264	10

Over one-quarter of Hawaii's increase was due to the collection of nearly $100 million in alcoholic beverage taxes previously paid under protest and held in escrow until 1988. Montana benefited from a surtax on its individual income tax, a rate increase on its motor fuel taxes, and newly imposed taxes on payrolls and accommodations.

Oklahoma raised its general sales and gross receipts tax to 4.0 percent from 3.25 percent, increased its motor fuels tax, and obtained significant additional income taxes as a result of an overall improvement in its economy. Most of Texas' increased tax revenues resulted from a sales and use tax base broadening and rate increase from 5.25 percent to 6.0 percent. Texas also added a 20 percent surtax on insurance sales, increased its motor vehicle sales and use tax from 5 percent to 6 percent, and raised its motor fuels tax from 10 cents to 15 cents per gallon.

Higher oil and gas production tax revenues were the principle source of Alaska's higher tax receipts. Rate, bracket, and other individual income tax revisions in Kansas produced over two-thirds of the $360 million increase in 1988 over 1987.

Reforms in Maine's personal income tax netted over one-half of the $217 million increase in total taxes. A sales and use tax rate increase to 6 percent from 5 percent resulted in nearly $1.2 billion of the $1.6 billion additional tax revenues in Florida in 1988.

At the other end of the spectrum, three states experienced a decrease in 1988 tax collections. This compares with six states that had tax revenue declines the previous year, and ten states that suffered losses in 1986. Only Wyoming had year-to-year tax revenue decreases in each of these three years. The three states affected in 1988 and their percentage changes are as follows:

Wyoming . . . . -9.3%
Oregon . . . . -5.6%
West Virginia . . . . -4.7%

In Wyoming, where heavy reliance is placed on severance taxes, oil and gas production tax revenues have halted their slide but coal taxes continued a downward spiral. West Virginia's tax revenue decline in 1988 was associated with a general downturn in its overall economy due in large measure to the depressed market for mineral resources. The decrease in Oregon's tax revenues related to larger rebates of individual income taxes.

Tax Burden

While all states rely on various types of selective sales taxes, Alaska, Delaware, Montana, New Hampshire and Oregon do not levy a general sales tax. Seven states — Alaska, Florida, Nevada, South Dakota, Texas, Washington and Wyoming — do not impose individual income taxes. Four states — Nevada, Texas, Washington and Wyoming — exclude corporation net income from taxation. Therefore, the burden of state taxation varies from state to state. Identifying the actual taxpayer is even more complicated in states with a high degree of tourism or "exported" severance taxes. For these and reasons of state versus local tax authority and distribution of responsibility for services, caution should be exercised in comparing per capita tax revenue and rankings of states.

Compared to a national state per capita average of $1,077, Alaska still leads with $2,387 in 1988. Hawaii was second ($1,857) and Delaware third ($1,543). However, New York had the highest per capita personal income tax, $758 compared to an average of $327; Tennessee had the lowest with $16. (Alaska's rate of $0.86 is not included as this reflects residual amounts collected for an income tax law now repealed.) It is important to note that while New York ranked high in per capita income tax the state ranked 31st in per capita general sales tax revenues.

Because states utilize a variety of revenue sources to support their programs, no comparison should be made or inferences drawn without a thorough background analysis of their general economy.

TAXES

Table 6.23
NATIONAL SUMMARY OF STATE GOVERNMENT TAX REVENUE, BY TYPE OF TAX: 1986 TO 1988

Tax source	Amount (in thousands of dollars)			Percent change year-to-year		Percent distribution, 1988	Per capita, 1988 (in dollars)
	1988	1987	1986	1987 to 1988	1986 to 1987		
Total collections	$264,080,470	$246,933,216	$228,081,788	6.9	8.3	100.0	$1,077.04
Sales and gross receipts	130,135,502	119,837,528	112,376,718	8.6	6.6	49.3	530.75
General sales	87,009,688	79,637,645	74,805,816	9.3	6.5	32.9	354.87
Selective sales	43,125,814	40,199,883	37,570,902	7.3	7.0	16.3	175.89
Motor fuels	17,196,209	15,705,469	14,126,153	9.5	11.2	6.5	70.13
Public utilities	6,179,474	5,987,313	6,001,473	3.2	(0.2)	2.3	25.20
Insurance premiums	6,896,341	6,382,557	5,489,842	8.0	16.3	2.6	28.13
Tobacco products	4,801,425	4,605,416	4,449,756	4.3	3.5	1.8	19.58
Alcoholic beverages	3,188,193	3,090,589	3,072,009	3.2	0.6	1.2	13.00
Parimutuels	666,922	642,522	646,264	3.8	(0.6)	0.3	2.72
Other...................	4,197,250	3,786,017	3,785,405	10.9	0.0	1.6	17.12
License	17,043,316	15,999,845	14,907,388	6.5	7.3	6.5	69.51
Motor vehicles............	8,879,338	8,308,708	7,673,270	6.9	8.3	3.4	36.21
Corporations in general.....	3,171,087	3,170,897	3,062,623	0.0	3.5	1.2	12.93
Motor vehicle operations ...	764,895	728,329	695,583	5.0	4.7	0.3	3.12
Hunting and fishing	724,138	667,984	612,364	8.4	9.1	0.3	2.95
Alcoholic beverages	244,247	251,931	239,912	(3.1)	5.0	0.1	1.00
Other.....................	3,259,611	2,871,996	2,623,636	13.5	9.5	1.2	13.29
Individual income	80,133,133	75,964,843	67,416,629	5.5	12.7	30.3	326.82
Corporation net income	21,684,670	20,724,145	18,405,994	4.6	12.6	8.2	88.44
Severance	4,328,530	4,047,878	6,125,394	6.9	(33.9)	1.6	17.65
Property	5,049,111	4,609,288	4,352,932	9.5	5.9	1.9	20.59
Death and gift...............	3,240,929	3,035,326	2,535,464	6.8	19.7	1.2	13.22
Other taxes	2,465,279	2,714,363	1,961,269	(9.2)	38.4	0.9	10.05

Source: U.S. Bureau of the Census, *State Government Tax Collections in 1988*, and unpublished data.
Note: Because of rounding, detail may not add to totals. Population figures as of July 1, 1988 were used to calculate per capita amounts; see Table 6.28.

TAXES

Table 6.24
SUMMARY OF STATE GOVERNMENT TAX REVENUE, BY STATE: 1986 TO 1988

State	Amount (in thousands of dollars)			Percent change year-to-year		Per capita, 1988 (in dollars)
	1988	1987	1986	1987 to 1988	1986 to 1987	
United States	$264,080,470	$246,933,216	$228,081,788	6.9	8.3	$1,077.04
Alabama	3,374,056	3,222,201	2,997,093	4.7	7.5	822.54
Alaska	1,251,021	1,062,391	1,856,488	17.8	−42.8	2,387.44
Arizona	3,722,112	3,469,477	3,195,720	7.3	8.6	1,066.81
Arkansas	2,020,721	1,889,066	1,826,701	7.0	3.4	843.72
California	36,075,033	35,790,750	30,878,427	0.8	15.9	1,274.11
Colorado	2,725,767	2,561,477	2,344,375	6.4	9.3	825.74
Connecticut	4,376,395	4,359,175	3,836,804	0.4	13.6	1,353.66
Delaware	1,018,367	941,932	850,254	8.1	10.8	1,542.98
Florida	11,460,299	9,846,189	9,120,166	16.4	8.0	929.09
Georgia	5,782,247	5,323,689	4,917,070	8.6	8.3	911.74
Hawaii	2,039,375	1,697,424	1,490,665	20.1	13.9	1,857.35
Idaho	893,658	829,698	744,739	7.7	11.4	890.99
Illinois	11,078,693	10,429,524	9,800,757	6.2	6.4	953.91
Indiana	5,311,824	4,774,190	4,458,168	11.3	7.1	956.05
Iowa	2,841,657	2,662,110	2,459,172	6.7	8.3	1,002.70
Kansas	2,445,284	2,085,490	1,911,548	17.3	9.1	980.07
Kentucky	3,663,591	3,520,409	3,216,343	4.1	9.5	982.99
Louisiana	3,776,254	3,448,641	3,629,513	9.5	−5.0	856.68
Maine	1,505,523	1,288,480	1,101,381	16.8	17.0	1,249.40
Maryland	5,830,888	5,204,499	4,669,561	12.0	11.5	1,261.55
Massachusetts	8,521,404	8,463,874	7,696,879	0.7	10.0	1,447.00
Michigan	10,515,368	9,857,122	9,314,194	6.7	5.8	1,138.03
Minnesota	6,143,956	5,546,422	4,898,456	10.8	13.2	1,426.50
Mississippi	2,126,254	1,943,388	1,917,330	9.4	1.4	811.55
Missouri	4,405,501	3,942,295	3,608,083	11.7	9.3	856.93
Montana	715,083	591,001	617,108	21.0	−4.2	888.30
Nebraska	1,342,868	1,203,344	1,119,382	11.6	7.5	838.24
Nevada	1,186,445	1,131,312	1,048,301	4.9	7.9	1,125.66
New Hampshire	583,168	562,712	484,478	3.6	16.1	537.48
New Jersey	9,762,360	9,491,417	8,360,193	2.9	13.5	1,264.39
New Mexico	1,793,387	1,574,692	1,462,123	13.9	7.7	1,190.04
New York	26,171,362	24,676,346	22,747,419	6.1	8.5	1,461.35
North Carolina	6,922,990	6,235,163	5,579,710	11.0	11.7	1,066.88
North Dakota	633,339	573,465	616,076	10.4	−6.9	949.53
Ohio	9,990,514	9,717,146	9,062,151	2.8	7.2	920.36
Oklahoma	3,150,072	2,669,188	2,959,632	18.0	−9.8	971.64
Oregon	2,110,963	2,235,073	1,931,346	−5.6	15.7	762.91
Pennsylvania	11,825,044	11,378,764	10,683,238	3.9	6.5	985.34
Rhode Island	1,120,534	1,050,144	885,557	6.7	18.6	1,128.43
South Carolina	3,438,186	3,158,453	2,918,975	8.9	8.2	990.83
South Dakota	475,701	416,386	403,741	14.2	3.1	667.18
Tennessee	3,855,027	3,603,331	3,271,963	7.0	10.1	787.54
Texas	13,425,516	11,227,796	11,124,708	19.6	0.9	797.19
Utah	1,602,093	1,438,325	1,364,835	11.4	5.4	947.98
Vermont	616,553	537,905	499,519	14.6	7.7	1,106.92
Virginia	6,136,607	5,526,557	4,846,627	11.0	14.0	1,020.22
Washington	5,994,964	5,639,369	5,219,292	6.3	8.0	1,289.79
West Virginia	1,743,871	1,830,168	1,848,552	−4.7	−1.0	929.57
Wisconsin	6,005,545	5,673,577	5,491,530	5.9	3.3	1,236.98
Wyoming	573,030	631,669	795,445	−9.3	−20.6	1,196.30

Source: U.S. Bureau of the Census, *State Government Tax Collections in 1988*, and unpublished data.

Note: Because of rounding, detail may not add to totals. Population figures as of July 1, 1988, were used to calculate per capita amounts; see Table 6.28.

TAXES

Table 6.25
STATE GOVERNMENT TAX REVENUE, BY TYPE OF TAX: 1988
(In thousands of dollars)

State	Total	Sales and gross receipts	Licenses	Individual income	Corporation net income	Severance	Property	Death and gift	Documentary and stock transfer	Other
Number of states using tax	50	50	50	44	46	33	41	50	29	14
United States	$264,080,470	$130,135,502	$17,043,316	$80,133,133	$21,684,670	$4,328,530	$5,049,111	$3,240,929	$2,355,178	$110,101
Alabama	3,374,056	1,825,240	280,666	929,459	177,657	60,603	72,965	15,393	12,073	...
Alaska	1,251,021	81,710	72,234	449	181,387	818,655	96,225	361	...	...
Arizona	3,722,112	2,290,007	257,043	857,710	148,134	...	138,240	30,978	...	...
Arkansas	2,020,721	1,147,721	125,078	596,899	116,202	16,302	4,784	5,745	7,283	707
California	36,075,033	14,543,985	1,670,571	12,864,291	4,781,873	26,145	1,880,708	307,460	...	...
Colorado	2,725,767	1,214,576	159,078	1,159,923	146,776	15,330	6,083	13,175	76,708	10,826
Connecticut	4,376,395	2,908,988	260,592	352,031	601,212	...	12	176,852	36,166	1,294
Delaware	1,018,367	144,793	327,530	377,782	119,323	...	...	11,479	553,382	...
Florida	11,460,299	9,122,497	685,279	...	624,032	75,023	222,918	177,168	16,642	12,518
Georgia	5,782,247	2,628,575	179,259	2,391,771	478,969	...	20,309	54,204	...	...
Hawaii	2,039,375	1,294,497	29,709	625,594	78,053	...	...	7,314	4,208	...
Idaho	893,658	478,290	70,344	280,991	61,352	675	80	1,926	...	...
Illinois	11,078,693	5,802,525	814,621	3,161,110	973,704	...	231,191	82,502	13,040	...
Indiana	5,311,824	3,018,823	178,452	1,764,498	261,125	675	23,707	64,544	...	...
Iowa	2,841,657	1,302,013	254,887	1,064,816	158,040	...	...	58,932	2,969	...
Kansas	2,445,284	1,131,923	135,926	826,318	195,520	81,812	29,280	44,505	...	...
Kentucky	3,663,591	1,684,790	183,927	1,006,992	255,760	210,046	269,912	49,056	3,108	...
Louisiana	3,776,254	2,068,833	368,558	575,693	219,894	474,899	26,827	41,550	...	...
Maine	1,505,523	737,112	96,188	555,212	84,704	...	6,237	11,913	14,157	...
Maryland	5,830,888	2,552,272	228,658	2,432,698	313,070	...	147,621	58,012	79,726	18,831
Massachusetts	8,521,404	2,913,743	248,379	3,984,746	1,068,341	...	932	254,701	50,562	...
Michigan	10,515,368	4,064,211	579,931	3,587,860	1,856,105	43,581	278,656	93,799	1	11,225
Minnesota	6,143,956	2,702,528	375,120	2,625,405	411,960	7,796	7,536	13,610	...	...
Mississippi	2,126,254	1,402,715	185,431	353,227	96,170	53,224	19,774	15,713	...	...
Missouri	4,405,501	2,286,839	337,566	1,515,970	224,228	33	10,876	28,590	...	1,399
Montana	715,083	182,094	74,058	243,768	46,200	112,779	34,958	8,745	...	12,481
Nebraska	1,342,868	726,593	98,465	432,035	73,783	2,571	3,884	3,343	2,194	...
Nevada	1,186,445	982,050	149,346	...	...	10,655	39,115	5,279	...	...
New Hampshire	583,168	256,878	82,680	29,844	145,680	...	9,894	21,933	36,259	...
New Jersey	9,762,360	5,152,735	593,844	2,557,694	1,181,849	...	27,073	163,117	86,048	...
New Mexico	1,793,387	1,013,390	127,565	303,733	49,576	291,880	3,148	4,095	...	...
New York	26,171,362	8,379,003	778,339	13,569,288	2,172,245	...	...	459,827	812,640	...
North Carolina	6,922,990	2,821,701	456,240	2,784,385	712,975	1,579	80,370	65,740	...	...
North Dakota	633,339	326,187	59,495	114,020	39,094	90,897	2,148	1,498	...	...
Ohio	9,990,514	5,169,277	806,389	3,364,689	582,026	9,353	13,562	45,218	...	...
Oklahoma	3,150,072	1,457,067	336,752	832,779	83,725	386,680	...	39,846	5,040	8,183
Oregon	2,110,963	314,949	298,191	1,283,647	167,047	31,972	...	13,647	1,508	...
Pennsylvania	11,825,044	6,015,886	1,201,892	2,805,432	1,046,443	...	140,865	401,404	213,122	...
Rhode Island	1,120,534	574,630	42,919	388,461	79,194	...	8,021	21,821	5,441	47
South Carolina	3,438,186	1,865,982	171,023	1,141,076	203,959	...	8,029	35,991	12,126	...

The Council of State Governments 331

STATE GOVERNMENT TAX REVENUE, BY TYPE OF TAX: 1988—Continued

State	Total	Sales and gross receipts	Licenses	Individual income	Corporation net income	Severance	Property	Death and gift	Documentary and stock transfer	Other
South Dakota	475,701	392,944	37,589	...	26,357	8,449	...	10,362	...	...
Tennessee	3,855,027	2,946,730	381,598	79,650	352,120	1,820	...	33,484	44,628	14,997
Texas	13,425,516	10,276,793	1,981,504	...	...	1,058,809	...	108,410	...	...
Utah	1,602,093	786,820	73,204	637,511	71,663	29,156	296	3,443	9,941	...
Vermont	616,553	303,322	48,338	201,660	44,688	...	389	6,161	...	2,054
Virginia	6,136,607	2,527,280	342,380	2,757,868	334,382	1,668	26,104	43,205	94,903	8,817
Washington	5,994,964	4,511,633	329,349	...	...	45,790	948,787	18,846	140,559	...
West Virginia	1,743,871	924,408	108,372	394,181	176,704	128,486	1,651	6,489	3,580	...
Wisconsin	6,005,545	2,674,857	297,811	2,319,967	461,369	915	128,654	98,086	17,164	6,722
Wyoming	573,030	203,087	60,926	...	...	230,272	77,288	1,457	...	...

Source: U.S. Bureau of the Census, *State Government Tax Collections in 1988*, and unpublished data.

Key:
... — Not applicable

Table 6.26
STATE GOVERNMENT SALES AND GROSS RECEIPTS TAX REVENUE: 1988
(In thousands of dollars)

State	Total	General sales or gross receipts	Selective sales and gross receipts								
			Total	Motor fuels	Public utilities	Tobacco products	Insurance	Alcoholic beverages	Parimutuels	Amusements	Other
Number of states using tax	50	45	50	50	41	50	50	50	32	26	37
All states	130,135,502	87,009,688	43,125,814	17,196,209	6,179,474	4,801,425	6,896,341	3,188,193	666,922	527,775	3,669,475
Alabama	1,825,240	927,750	897,490	275,750	251,884	71,575	138,497	97,869	...	59	61,856
Alaska	81,710	...	81,710	33,676	2,024	8,879	23,661	12,111	...	...	1,359
Arizona	2,290,007	1,706,342	583,665	314,928	91,999	52,407	72,433	40,954	10,145	799	...
Arkansas	1,147,721	777,073	370,648	216,965	...	64,483	44,416	24,229	20,555	...	...
California	14,543,985	11,515,266	3,028,719	1,292,300	48,662	252,995	1,152,508	128,720	129,544	...	23,990
Colorado	1,214,576	724,300	490,276	300,032	6,317	63,835	82,224	21,965	8,517	592	6,794
Connecticut	2,908,988	1,983,977	925,011	292,515	254,826	87,198	150,968	31,526	62,505	16,245	29,228
Delaware	144,793	...	144,793	81,402	16,726	12,465	25,188	5,023	81	...	3,908
Florida	9,122,497	6,862,627	2,259,870	764,040	217,846	340,100	316,325	453,229	119,719	2,593	46,018
Georgia	2,628,575	1,856,625	771,950	411,706	...	91,020	150,312	118,912	...	...	...
Hawaii	1,294,497	919,796	374,701	49,806	63,587	21,318	38,876	133,824	...	...	67,290
Idaho	478,290	328,453	149,837	95,204	1,323	16,253	23,532	9,160	2,296	...	2,069
Illinois	5,802,525	3,677,354	2,125,171	701,971	757,202	249,988	187,001	67,843	49,975	8,495	102,696
Indiana	3,018,823	2,361,910	656,913	401,452	...	116,253	103,489	35,705	...	14	...
Iowa	1,302,013	859,033	442,980	266,094	...	83,208	81,033	12,645	...	...	...
Kansas	1,131,923	775,633	356,290	170,035	704	59,659	72,269	47,304	6,525	767	5,552
Kentucky	1,684,790	951,756	733,034	322,736	...	14,842	147,922	49,285	21,320	304	191,420
Louisiana	2,068,833	1,300,885	767,948	366,798	35,155	74,714	184,822	49,848	1,853	196	35,095
Maine	737,112	491,936	245,176	105,779	29,400	40,672	33,464	34,008	2,726	...	...
Maryland	2,552,272	1,423,585	1,128,687	441,618	95,721	65,494	128,103	28,023	1,592	...	365,410
Massachusetts	2,913,743	2,021,093	892,650	305,517	...	168,479	248,060	78,436	32,036	9,900	50,222
Michigan	4,064,211	2,919,055	1,145,156	687,308	...	264,541	43,882	120,085	20,173	...	9,167
Minnesota	2,702,528	1,676,632	1,025,896	391,657	99,953	115,848	126,765	55,746	...	332	235,927
Mississippi	1,402,715	1,007,276	395,439	229,060	...	53,342	76,448	36,257	...	...	...
Missouri	2,286,839	1,683,481	603,358	339,738	1,113	83,214	155,402	23,891	...	...	...
Montana	182,094	...	182,094	102,404	10,494	12,052	39,510	13,208	144	...	4,282
Nebraska	726,593	447,790	278,803	165,798	1,599	38,998	34,502	15,824	673	6,507	14,902
Nevada	982,050	546,409	435,641	99,238	4,419	14,089	46,446	11,070	12	256,284	4,083
New Hampshire	256,878	...	256,878	83,016	7,074	31,695	35,299	11,383	11,489	...	76,922
New Jersey	5,152,735	3,136,801	2,015,934	330,866	1,002,496	221,826	168,138	55,092	8,233	209,201	20,082
New Mexico	1,013,390	739,904	273,486	138,703	6,004	18,814	43,483	17,471	2,330	81	46,600
New York	8,379,003	5,510,790	2,868,213	500,180	1,007,926	400,932	489,490	149,069	92,349	986	227,281
North Carolina	2,821,701	1,627,672	1,194,029	596,573	225,244	16,219	186,833	141,794	...	...	27,366
North Dakota	326,187	204,793	121,394	63,668	10,994	16,644	14,662	5,630	...	...	9,796
Ohio	5,169,277	3,218,959	1,950,318	811,365	588,233	229,124	240,836	67,399	13,361	...	...
Oklahoma	1,457,067	756,916	700,151	311,367	13,156	84,457	137,207	17,471	1,624	...	96,936
Oregon	314,949	...	314,949	166,072	5,145	70,306	58,730	10,510	4,186	249	...
Pennsylvania	6,015,886	3,846,585	2,169,301	672,262	486,312	228,881	336,488	138,368	9,652	...	297,089
Rhode Island	574,630	383,209	191,421	54,763	54,113	33,318	30,362	7,755	10,791	147	172
South Carolina	1,865,982	1,249,430	616,552	305,989	35,570	30,610	83,185	107,132	...	11,085	42,981

The Council of State Governments 333

STATE GOVERNMENT SALES AND GROSS RECEIPTS TAX REVENUE: 1988—Continued

State	Total	General sales or gross receipts	Selective sales and gross receipts								
			Total	Motor fuels	Pubic utilities	Tobacco products	Insurance	Alcoholic beverages	Parimutuels	Amusements	Other
South Dakota	392,944	262,348	130,596	61,844	760	14,282	23,480	9,013	1,000	...	20,217
Tennessee	2,946,730	2,142,276	804,454	503,496	22,270	83,142	122,438	63,125	...	...	9,983
Texas	10,276,793	6,271,018	4,005,775	1,473,821	207,836	416,997	545,808	315,536	...	133	1,045,644
Utah	786,820	589,480	197,340	129,370	4,728	21,656	25,286	16,300	...	...	...
Vermont	303,322	123,490	179,832	42,435	21,066	12,256	17,175	14,700	188	...	72,012
Virginia	2,527,280	1,188,856	1,338,424	593,677	151,045	17,075	180,460	95,379	...	111	300,677
Washington	4,511,633	3,553,516	958,117	435,456	170,965	129,724	93,619	102,010	8,882	82	17,379
West Virginia	924,408	537,499	386,909	167,658	18,013	34,216	47,155	8,645	13,780	372	97,070
Wisconsin	2,674,857	1,769,062	905,795	491,323	149,570	147,284	78,414	38,555	258	649	...
Wyoming	203,087	151,047	52,040	36,778	...	4,046	9,735	1,223	...	...	...

Source: U.S. Bureau of the Census, State Government Tax Collections in 1988, and unpublished data.

Key:
... — Not applicable

Table 6.27
STATE GOVERNMENT LICENSE TAX REVENUE: 1988
(In thousands of dollars)

State	Total	Motor vehicle	Motor vehicle operators	Corporations in general	Occupations and businesses, n.e.c.	Hunting and fishing	Alcoholic beverages	Public utilities	Amusements	Other
Number of states using tax	50	50	46	49	50	50	48	32	37	47
All states	$17,043,316	$8,879,338	$764,895	$3,171,087	$2,668,701	$724,138	$244,247	$246,743	$162,038	$182,129
Alabama	280,666	107,933	10,021	82,311	65,250	11,632	2,278	1,241	...	...
Alaska	72,234	18,358	600	892	37,772	12,678	1,632	...	302	...
Arizona	257,043	190,519	6,899	3,801	23,686	13,293	1,624	...	31	17,190
Arkansas	125,078	68,718	4,498	7,722	20,736	16,039	568	6,094	326	377
California	1,670,571	1,062,730	73,458	8,124	370,620	53,998	31,412	64,783	217	5,229
Colorado	159,078	82,358	6,259	3,428	27,826	31,060	2,463	...	49	5,635
Connecticut	260,592	185,170	21,857	9,384	31,059	2,738	5,894	...	84	4,406
Delaware	327,530	44,892	1,617	180,583	95,025	849	628	3,323	131	482
Florida	685,259	377,858	71,308	22,086	142,621	12,176	22,987	14,428	8,111	13,704
Georgia	179,259	75,107	17,631	20,335	31,199	15,988	1,720	...	...	17,279
Hawaii	29,709	18,411	...	881	7,823	212	1,002	2,312	...	70
Idaho	70,344	31,659	3,104	457	15,728	15,359	1,985	2,435	...	600
Illinois	814,621	619,767	34,015	75,261	66,053	14,278	9,958	...	1,023	2,239
Indiana	178,452	129,288	...	5,043	19,762	12,036	7,666	96	291	1,978
Iowa	254,887	184,489	9,380	12,090	11,965	11,696	7,666	4,784	11,093	1,724
Kansas	135,926	78,339	6,043	11,505	24,345	9,561	1,727	3,471	18	917
Kentucky	183,927	76,672	6,367	61,618	19,045	10,790	1,930	4,000	505	3,000
Louisiana	368,558	76,445	10,335	234,616	30,707	11,438	2,164	2,438	105	310
Maine	96,188	55,052	6,294	957	21,093	9,715	1,881	...	311	885
Maryland	228,658	133,141	8,226	4,775	73,082	7,445	360	...	18	1,611
Massachusetts	248,379	145,000	38,000	15,308	40,750	5,194	1,276	15,007	785	2,066
Michigan	579,931	413,715	26,542	9,979	48,862	41,416	11,541	...	234	12,635
Minnesota	375,120	272,876	13,690	2,917	53,982	25,535	523	...	...	5,597
Mississippi	185,431	74,507	6,827	58,384	35,831	7,739	1,169	817	...	157
Missouri	337,566	195,344	11,866	51,722	48,649	14,551	2,392	7,781	1,011	4,250
Montana	74,058	29,796	2,004	750	10,428	19,213	1,558	1,220	9,052	37
Nebraska	98,465	50,464	3,104	4,520	20,538	7,862	248	...	...	11,729
Nevada	149,346	57,233	3,775	5,058	24,738	4,500	25	...	51,632	2,385
New Hampshire	82,680	45,857	4,670	4,748	14,794	5,252	1,664	2,774	522	2,399
New Jersey	593,844	322,421	8,226	137,789	38,631	7,515	4,364	1,989	52,897	2,472
New Mexico	127,565	98,473	3,782	2,112	12,110	10,926	2	40	120	3,587
New York	778,359	417,660	66,441	24,172	165,077	23,791	29,196	44,433	4,002	1,343
North Carolina	456,240	215,513	37,654	121,156	61,999	12,424	2,650	...	3,501	4
North Dakota	59,495	33,118	2,375	610	18,616	3,240	261	10	1,261	...
Ohio	806,389	350,133	13,756	273,225	130,088	15,169	20,363	473	...	3,182
Oklahoma	336,752	244,761	9,489	30,402	30,726	11,289	3,155	4	1,717	5,209
Oregon	298,170	191,569	14,016	3,693	57,663	21,804	1,518	5,309	716	1,903
Pennsylvania	1,201,892	419,812	43,222	498,201	156,952	37,988	11,405	29,171	19	5,122
Rhode Island	42,916	31,457	...	3,048	6,527	959	235	113	92	488
South Carolina	171,023	68,256	8,338	20,491	37,393	10,021	7,497	...	7,819	11,208

STATE GOVERNMENT LICENSE TAX REVENUE: 1988—Continued

State	Total	Motor vehicle	Motor vehicle operators	Corporations in general	Occupations and businesses, n.e.c.	Hunting and fishing	Alcoholic beverages	Public utilities	Amusements	Other
South Dakota	37,589	20,869	1,300	800	8,000	5,490	186	...	144	800
Tennessee	381,598	144,464	15,102	166,504	36,195	11,799	1,440	3,580	...	2,514
Texas	1,981,504	693,988	53,542	953,201	207,660	32,723	21,499	5,561	3,457	9,873
Utah	73,204	40,349	5,340	...	12,201	14,361	420	...	...	533
Vermont	48,338	33,094	1,954	622	6,955	3,760	388	...	195	1,370
Virginia	342,380	232,882	22,518	19,263	46,471	12,761	6,042	...	37	2,406
Washington	329,349	155,977	16,228	6,434	103,515	26,100	7,354	11,850	210	1,681
West Virginia	108,372	67,868	...	3,122	15,813	8,553	5,758	5,770	...	1,488
Wisconsin	297,811	154,275	14,846	4,738	80,840	35,033	239	12	...	7,828
Wyoming	60,926	40,701	836	2,249	1,300	14,189	...	1,424	...	227

Source: U.S. Bureau of the Census, *State Government Tax Collections in 1988*, and unpublished data.
Key:
. . . — Not applicable

TAXES

Table 6.28
FISCAL YEAR, POPULATION AND PERSONAL INCOME, BY STATE

State	Date of close of fiscal year in 1988	Total population (excluding armed forces overseas) (a) (in thousands) July 1, 1988	Total population (excluding armed forces overseas) (a) (in thousands) July 1, 1987	Personal income, calendar year 1987 (b) Amount (in millions)	Personal income, calendar year 1987 (b) Per capita (in dollars)	State government portion of state-local tax revenue in fiscal 1985-86 (c) (percent)
United States		245,190	242,798	3,753,938	15,461	60.6
Alabama	September 30	4,102	4,084	49,165	12,038	72.1
Alaska	June 30	524	524	9,680	18,473	66.2
Arizona	June 30	3,489	3,400	48,699	14,323	63.1
Arkansas	June 30	2,395	2,388	27,275	11,422	75.8
California	June 30	28,314	27,653	491,393	17,770	65.4
Colorado	June 30	3,301	3,293	51,638	15,681	49.0
Connecticut	June 30	3,233	3,212	68,275	21,256	59.4
Delaware	June 30	660	648	10,564	16,302	83.2
Florida	June 30	12,335	12,022	187,476	15,594	61.0
Georgia	June 30	6,342	6,227	89,595	14,388	61.1
Hawaii	June 30	1,098	1,082	16,845	15,568	82.2
Idaho	June 30	1,003	1,000	11,793	11,793	70.7
Illinois	June 30	11,614	11,584	189,914	16,395	53.5
Indiana	June 30	5,556	5,530	77,344	13,986	66.3
Iowa	June 30	2,834	2,823	39,600	14,028	60.5
Kansas	June 30	2,495	2,475	37,341	15,087	58.5
Kentucky	June 30	3,727	3,723	44,663	11,997	77.3
Louisiana	June 30	4,408	4,448	51,176	11,505	64.5
Maine	June 30	1,205	1,186	16,595	13,992	68.2
Maryland	June 30	4,622	4,536	82,632	18,217	60.3
Massachusetts	June 30	5,889	5,856	112,027	19,130	67.0
Michigan	September 30	9,240	9,205	143,202	15,557	60.4
Minnesota	June 30	4,307	4,244	67,013	15,790	68.7
Mississippi	June 30	2,620	2,624	27,032	10,302	74.6
Missouri	June 30	5,141	5,107	74,720	14,631	62.5
Montana	June 30	805	809	9,956	12,307	57.7
Nebraska	June 30	1,602	1,594	22,475	14,100	53.8
Nevada	June 30	1,054	1,006	16,460	16,362	68.0
New Hampshire	June 30	1,085	1,056	19,100	18,087	36.5
New Jersey	June 30	7,721	7,674	155,610	20,278	57.0
New Mexico	June 30	1,507	1,496	17,781	11,886	80.8
New York	March 31	17,909	17,835	320,013	17,943	49.8
North Carolina	June 30	6,489	6,409	85,582	13,353	71.4
North Dakota	June 30	667	671	8,611	12,833	68.4
Ohio	June 30	10,855	10,816	157,638	14,575	58.7
Oklahoma	June 30	3,242	3,259	41,087	12,607	69.3
Oregon	June 30	2,767	2,723	37,869	13,907	47.6
Pennsylvania	June 30	12,001	11,942	181,487	15,197	60.5
Rhode Island	June 30	993	986	15,468	15,688	61.4
South Carolina	June 30	3,470	3,426	41,372	12,076	74.1
South Dakota	June 30	713	709	8,806	12,420	50.5
Tennessee	June 30	4,895	4,855	63,003	12,977	63.4
Texas	August 31	16,841	16,781	232,255	13,840	53.3
Utah	June 30	1,690	1,680	19,366	11,527	64.9
Vermont	June 30	557	547	7,806	14,271	59.4
Virginia	June 30	6,015	5,914	97,807	16,538	60.5
Washington	June 30	4,648	4,542	71,004	15,633	72.4
West Virginia	June 30	1,876	1,898	20,898	11,011	76.7
Wisconsin	June 30	4,855	4,807	70,541	14,675	65.5
Wyoming	June 30	479	490	6,286	12,829	58.5

Source: U.S. Bureau of the Census, *State Government Tax Collections in 1988*.
Note: Because of rounding, detail may not add to totals.
(a) Bureau of the Census, *Current Population Reports*, Series P-25, January 1989.
(b) U.S. Department of Commerce, *Survey of Current Business*, August 1988.
(c) Bureau of the Census, *Government Finances in 1986-87*, November 1988.

CHAPTER SEVEN

STATE MANAGEMENT AND ADMINISTRATION

DEVELOPMENTS IN STATE ADMINISTRATION AND MANAGEMENT

By Wayne W. Hall, Jr.

State services such as personnel, purchasing, printing, facilities, telecommunications and fleet management are generally directed by departments of administration or general services. These departments are headed by a central administrative officer charged with addressing the needs of an increasingly complex state bureaucracy. Sometimes grouped administratively with general services, state financial managers provide services that are vital to state government.

State management and administrative services may be grouped into four areas: personnel, material, information and financial management. Intelligent communications technologies and public funds investment are at the heart of challenges facing state managers. New environmental and federal challenges are also being met by state administrative officers.

In addition, states have taken steps to work together on important issues, lending their experience to each other through consulting, and banding together in cooperative purchasing efforts.

Information Management

State Librarians and Archivists

Traditional methods of information management include the use of libraries as a public information resource and archives for government records. Chief state librarians and state archivists collect and preserve the public record. As members of the information community, these executives are affected by the revolution in communication technology.

Optical transmission and electronic computing capabilities present new challenges for these managers. Storing public information using electronic media calls for new technical as well as organizational solutions. State archivists and librarians are concerned with the transfer of the public record from paper to electronic media. To be effective, electronic storage requires the active participation of those creating the record. Abandoning traditional organizational methods that deal with paper records after-the-fact, archivists are becoming more involved with the strategic planning of information systems so that critical documents such as health, social service and court records are cataloged systematically for future research.

Telecommunications

State telecommunications managers procure and manage telecommunications networks that connect state government agencies with each other and their constituents. These networks are taking advantage of advances in technology to increase the volume, speed and sophistication of information transfer. They are increasingly able to use this technology to integrate data, voice and video transmission. For instance, fiber optic lines dramatically increase the amount of information that can be sent. Sophisticated switching technologies can take information and modify it, thereby making it possible to carve personal information networks out of existing public networks.

This ability to route information has grown beyond simple telephone management. Power-

---

Wayne W. Hall, Jr. is a research assistant at The Council of State Governments. He was assisted by Sharon Hirsch, research associate, The Council of State Governments.

ful, modern networks that combine data and voice transmission serve state government in a variety of ways. For example, telecommunications technology is being used for distance learning over vast expanses in the West. States such as California, Montana and South Dakota use networks to provide statewide educational links. Videoconferencing will bring government agencies together and save travel dollars in Hawaii. Intelligent state networks connected to universities provide an attractive foundation for economic development, especially in rural areas. Land mobile radio and satellite communications warn of impending natural disasters and other emergencies.

Decisions by the Federal Communications Commission and state public service commissions play a big role in the effectiveness of state communications networks. Prohibitions against certain manufacturing and information products from Bell operating companies (agreed to by the Bell companies and AT&T at the time of divestiture) are being strenuously challenged in the Congress and before federal courts. The outcome will affect the level of competition in an increasingly competitive marketplace for telecommunications goods and services.

Information Resources

Information resource management is becoming more and more important to state government as communications functions for telecommunications, data communications and policy planning come together to form distinct information agencies. Information resource management is developing as a new centralized management function in several states. Current examples include the Inter-Technologies Group in Minnesota, the Office of Telecommunications and Information Systems in New Jersey and the Division of Information Resource Management in South Carolina.

State information resource managers are vitally interested in information technologies such as data processing and telecommunications and their applications in libraries and records management. As information resource management grows as a discipline, the states are putting new technologies together with program applications to deliver services like automated purchasing and central payroll systems. Information resource management is growing as separate information functions are connected.

Personnel Management

Personnel

State personnel directors manage human resources for the states. Their responsibilities include payroll benefits administration, recruitment and selection, performance evaluation, counseling, training and development, affirmative action, labor relations, grievance and appeals and retirement.

The state personnel managers are addressing changes in the work force of the next decade. Statistics show that Hispanics, Asians and Blacks are growing at a much faster rate as a percentage of the U.S. population. In the next century, those ethnic groups will outnumber whites for the first time. Hence, efforts to manage an increasingly diverse work force are being made. In addition, child care is an important new benefit being offered to state employees as the number of women in the work force grows. According to research conducted by the Wisconsin School of Family Resources and Consumer Sciences, 31 states have on- or near-site child care centers for state employees.

Despite tight budgets, many state training and development offices are initiating new programs to address the needs of the work force of the future including literacy training, cultural diversity awareness and customer service training. In addition, programs are being developed that address the special needs of the state government work force including a growing emphasis on ethics training. Seventeen states also belong to the National Certified Public Manager Consortium, an organization that provides training and education towards certification for public managers.

The integration of handicapped workers into the work force is growing after the passage of the Americans With Disabilities Act by Congress. HR. 2273 and SR. 933 ensure civil rights protection for the physically and mentally impaired. Wellness promotion programs are thriving in Colorado, Kansas and Washington while those states save money on their health insurance premiums. Employee assistance programs are also growing to meet the demand for counseling, especially in response to congressional passage of the Drug-Free Workplace Act. Decreased employee skill levels due to technological changes are motivating the states to offer more comprehensive skill training courses.

Material Management

Purchasing

State purchasing offices are responsible for acquiring goods and services, overseeing inventory management and coordinating the transfers of excess and surplus property for the states. In most states this is a central function with the purchasing office having responsibility to contract for most goods and services for all state agencies.

State purchasing officials continue to be concerned with unbiased competitive bidding, economy, value and public information.

Advances in computer technology are quickly changing the nature of state purchasing offices. Automation is a valuable asset for purchasers because it aids inventory management, order processing and data collection. Arizona, New Jersey and Tennessee are among the states moving toward paperless procurement systems, where user agencies can get state contract information on a network and place orders without sending paper work to the central procurement office.

Growing environmental concerns have prompted state purchasing officers to acquire environmentally safe products. This is especially true for recycled products such as paper, oil and plastic. As a group, purchasing officers are developing uniform national specifications for recycled paper in an attempt to create a greater market for such products. For example, Minnesota recently mandated that state agencies use recycled paper for stationery. Other states, for example, Virginia, require that preference be given to recycled paper.

On January 23, 1989, the U.S. Supreme Court decided a case that has a substantial impact on state set-aside quotas for minority contractors. In *City of Richmond v. J.A. Croson Co.* the Court ruled that the city's plan guaranteeing minority businesses at least 30 percent of city construction contracts was unconstitutional.

In writing the opinion for the majority, Justice Sandra Day O'Conner said that the U.S. Constitution's guarantee of "the equal protection of the laws" forbids government discrimination against whites as well as minorities, and warned that "rigid numerical quotas" would always be suspect.

Some have argued that this means states will have to disband their minority set-aside programs altogether, while others believe the court has merely insisted that these affirmative action programs be more carefully designed. The total impact of the decision has yet to be determined, but it is clear that it will have an effect on state procurement.

Printing

Slightly more than half of the states have centralized printing facilities and most states have a centralized printing authority. The central printing operation performs basic services such as typesetting, forms printing and press work. In addition, many states have legislative print shops.

State printers have recently begun to examine printing related hazardous waste because ink and other printing chemicals present disposal problems. Printing managers have agreed to work with procurement officials in studying the potential use of recycled paper products in state print shops. Minnesota recently dedicated a soybean based ink press while Missouri and Iowa are seriously considering legislation to require the use of soybean based ink in their operations. Such inks have several advantages; they offer superior printability and support a major agricultural crop while potentially cutting dependence on foreign oil.

MANAGEMENT AND ADMINISTRATION

Fleet

State fleet managers assess state fleet needs, write specifications, purchase vehicles, determine lease or rental rates to state government and arrange for vehicle maintenance and disposal. Many states agencies operate efficient fleets without centralization. However, with fleets that average between six and seven thousand vehicles, it is essential that these vehicles operate efficiently.

Congress is considering stringent rules for automobile emissions instead of expanding power plant and stationary source regulation in amendments to the 1973 Clean Air Act. Nearly half of all Americans live in cities with pollution levels that the Environmental Protection Agency considers unsafe. Such legislation would affect approximately 55 percent of the nation's vehicles, and would have significant consequences for state fleet managers. Replacement of leaking underground storage tanks also presents fleet managers with major expenditure problems. Many states require testing for leaking contaminants.

Facilities

Facilities managers maintain, construct, renovate, design and allocate or lease state office space.

Privatization affects state facilities managers more than other administrative services. The practice has many positive features, the most important of which is cost savings to the state. According to one survey by the firm Touche Ross, 31 states use some form of privatization to deliver public services. Facilities construction, contracting and operation lead the list of state services where privatization is utilized.

Asbestos abatement continues to be in the news, with conflicting information about the safest way to handle this carcinogen. Every state faces a problem to one degree or another with asbestos in state facilities. Decisions to remove the substance are often made arbitrarily because there is no universal standard defining when asbestos materials in a non-industrial setting pose a public health hazard. Many facilities managers are convinced, on the basis of significant data, that the safest course is to leave buildings containing non-damaged asbestos alone. Studies have shown that indoor levels of airborne asbestos rarely exceed outdoor levels, where asbestos occurs naturally. This controversial issue will remain a problem for many facilities managers.

Financial Management

Treasurers

State treasurers manage state financial resources through a combination of sound investments and savings.

During 1989 and 1990, developments in state financial management included an increased awareness of the social dimensions of state public funds investment. Many states are using their treasuries to invest in rural and small businesses and to assist families with the escalating cost of a college education.

States as diverse as Alabama, Florida, Michigan and Wyoming have developed programs to help middle income families with the cost of college through pre-paid tuition plans. By contracting with the state, parents can pay for their child's college education in installments. In return, the state guarantees the cost of an education at a state college or university and invests in its youth. Many states also use general obligation bond issues to help finance the cost of college.

State treasurers have been instrumental in securing low-interest loans for small businesses and farmers around the nation through linked deposit programs. Iowa, Kansas, Oklahoma and Ohio, among other states, use these programs as a convenient way of leveraging low-interest loans. In linked deposit programs, state treasurers lend money to a participating bank at low interest rates in return for the bank's guarantee that it will lend the funds to target groups at a nominal interest markup. Using this technique, the states are able to promote lending to groups in need of working capital while assuming no risk since deposits are insured by the federal government. Returns to the state in the form of an expanded tax base are reported to more than offset the initial capital outlay.

Local government investment pools have also become popular in Arizona, California, Connecticut, Georgia and Louisiana. By pooling capital with state government investments, local government is able to achieve higher rates of return on its investments.

The states are currently working to protect state and local public purpose bonds from potential federal taxation as a result of a recent U.S. Supreme Court ruling. In *South Carolina v. Baker*, the court reaffirmed earlier rulings that federal taxation of state bonds was permissible. It is estimated that taxation of state public bonds would add many billions of dollars to state government borrowing.

States Working Together

As the century draws to a close, interstate consulting projects and cooperative purchasing efforts have emerged as effective problem-solving tools. Increased information sharing amont the states is developing as an important tool in efficient state government management.

By using state government officials as consultants, the states are helping themselves with a variety of problems. Issues that have been addressed in the last two years through interstate consulting include an analysis of California's space management needs, Tennessee's telecommunications infrastructure, Minnesota's printing requirements, Delaware's purchasing procedures and Oklahoma's investigation of alternate state health insurance models. Typically, state government officials familiar with the special problems executive branch managers face donate their time and expertise to visit the host state for an intensive examination of its needs. In most cases specific recommendations are made in writing. Through this program, state management and administration needs have been assessed at nominal expense to the host state.

The states have also begun to look at cooperative purchasing as a way to enhance their bargaining positions. In one example, the states were able to bargain collectively for higher commissions for pay phones located on state property. By banding together, state telecommunications officials were able to secure a contract from a major long distance carrier with significantly higher commissions than otherwise would have been obtainable.

State purchasing officials and telecommunications directors have joined to sponsor a study of cooperative purchasing. Collectively, state governments represent a market that cannot be ignored. As specific impediments from state purchasing codes are removed, collective purchasing promises to provide state administrative officials with an effective bargaining tool.

References

State Personnel Office: Roles and Functions, The Council of State Governments/Center for Management and Administration, 1987, 44 pp.

State and Local Government Purchasing: 3rd Edition, The Council of State Governments and the National Association of State Purchasing Officials, 1988, 260 pp.

Purchasing Preference Practices: A 50-State Overview, The Council of State Governments, 1989, 27 pp.

Alternative Service Delivery and Management Improvement in State Government: A Bibliography, The Council of State Governments, 1987, 22 pp.

Preservation Needs in State Archives, The Council of State Governments/National Association of Government Archivists and Records Administrators, 1987, 66 pp.

Telecommunications — A Key to Knowledge, 1990, 68 pp. #553251-CSG001J-0390.

State Treasury Profiles, The Council of State Governments, 1989, 112 pp.

State Treasury & Finance Personnel Directory, The Council of State Governments, 1989, 132 pp.

Link Deposit Programs for Small Business and Agriculture, The Council of State Governments, 1989, 8 pp.

College Savings and Pre-payment Plans, The Council of State Governments, 1989, 10 pp.

State Treasury Activities and Functions, The Council of State Governments, 1988, 104 pp.

PERSONNEL

Table 7.1
THE OFFICE OF STATE PERSONNEL ADMINISTRATOR

				Primary responsibilities:				
State or other jurisdiction	Method of selection	Reports to governor	Reports to personnel board	Directs departmental employees	Administers policies of personnel board	Administers merit tests, establishes qualifications for classified state employees	Maintains roster of state employees, classification and compensation plans	Makes budget recommendations to legislature	Other (a)
Alabama	B		★	★	★	★	★	★	★
Alaska	G	★		★		★★	★★★	★★★	★★
Arizona	D			★		★★	★★★	★★★	
Arkansas	D	★		★		★★	★★	★★	
California State Personnel Bd.	B		★		★	★	★	★	★
Dept. of Personnel Admin.	G	★					★	★	★
Colorado	G	★	★	★	★	★★	★★★	★	
Connecticut	G			★★	★★	★★★	★★★		★★★★
Delaware	G	★★		★★★	★	★★★	★★★★	★★★	★★
Florida	G	★★		★★★	★	★★★ (n)	★★★★	★★★	★★
Georgia	G	★★		★	★	★★★	★★★		
Hawaii	G		★	★★★		★★★	★★★★		★
Idaho	B		★	★★★	★★	★★★	★★★★	★	★★
Illinois	D	★★	★★	★★		★★★	★★★★	★★★	
Indiana	G	★★		★★★		★★★	★★★★	★★	★
Iowa	G	★★		★	★★	★★★	★★★★	★★	★★
Kansas	G	★★★		★★★	★	★★★	★★★★	★★★	
Kentucky	G	★★★		★★★	★	★★★	★★★★	★★	★
Louisiana	(c)	★★★	★★	★★★		★★★	★★★★	★★★	★★★★
Maine	G	★★		★	★★	★★★	★★★★	★★	
Maryland	G	★★		★★★	★★	★★★	★★★★	★★	★★
Massachusetts	(d)	★	★	★★	★	★★★	★★★★	★★	
Michigan	B			★★★		★★★	★★★★	★★★	★★★★
Minnesota	G	★★		★★★	★	★★★	★★★★	★★★	★★★
Mississippi	B	★★★	★	★	★	★★★	★★★★	★	
Missouri	G (e)	★			★★	★★★	★★★★	★	
Montana	(f)			★★		★★★	★★★★	★★★	★★★
Nebraska	G	★★		★★★	★	★★★	★★★★	★★	★★★★
Nevada	G	★★★		★★★	★	★★★	★★★★	★	
New Hampshire	D	★★		★		★★★	★★★★	★	
New Jersey	G	★★		★	★	★★★	★★★★	★	
New Mexico	B (b)	★★★	★	★★	★	★★★	★★★★	★★★	★
New York	G	★★★		★★★	★★★★	★★★	★★★★	★★★	★★★
North Carolina	G	★★★	★★	★★		★★★	★★★★	★★★	
North Dakota	D (g)	★★		★★★★	★★	★★★	★★★★	★★	★★
Ohio	G	★		★	★	★★	★★	★★	★★
Oklahoma	G	★		★★		★★★	★★★★	★★	★
Oregon	D			★★	★	★★	★★★		★★
Pennsylvania Civil Service Comm.	(h)		★	★★	★★	★★★	★★★★		★★
Bur. of Personnel	G	★		★★★		★★★	★★★★	★★	★
Rhode Island	(h)			★★	★	★★★	★★★★		
South Carolina	(i)	★		★★★	★	★★★	★★★★	★	★★★★

The Council of State Governments 345

THE OFFICE OF STATE PERSONNEL ADMINISTRATOR—Continued

State or other jurisdiction	Method of selection	Reports to governor	Reports to personnel board	Directs departmental employees	Administers policies of personnel board	Administers merit tests, establishes qualifications for classified state employees	Maintains roster of state employees, classification and compensation plans	Makes budget recommendations to legislature	Other (a)
South Dakota	G	★	...	...	★	★	★	★	...
Tennessee	G	★	...	...	★	★	★	★	★
Texas	...	...	...	...	...	...	...	...	...
Utah	G	★	...	★	(j)	...	★	★	★
Vermont	G	★	...	★	...	...	★	★	★
Virginia	G	★	★	★	...	★	★	★	...
Washington	G (k)	...	★	★	★	★	★	★	...
West Virginia	G (l)	★	★	★	★	★	★	...	...
Wisconsin	G	★	★	★	...	★	...	★	...
Wyoming	G	★	...	★	...	★	...	...	...
Guam	G	★	...	★	...	...	★	...	...
Puerto Rico	G	...	...	...	————(m)————			...	...

Source: Information derived from survey of state personnel offices conducted by The Council of State Governments (March 1986) for the National Association of State Personnel Executives.

Key:
B — Appointment by personnel board
D — Appointment by department head
G — Appointment by governor

(a) Other responsibilities specified:
Alabama—appoints employees of Personnel Board; serves as secretary to Board.
Arizona—administers personnel rules and policies.
California—(State Personnel Board)—oversees all aspects of merit employment. (Department of Personnel Administration)—represents governor in bargaining with employee representatives; administers training, performance evaluation, benefit, labor relations, and staff reduction programs.
Connecticut—supervises affirmative action activities; conducts collective bargaining negotiations and labor management programs; administers management relations and personnel development programs, job analysis and evaluation, workers' compensation.
Delaware—administers affirmative action programs; development and training; directs labor relations for the executive branch; coordinates affirmative action; administers statewide staff development/training program, employee incentive, performance evaluation; publishes employee newsletter; coordinates state labor-management cooperate programs.
Florida—represents governor in collective bargaining negotiations; supports state agency employee training programs; administers group insurance, retirement benefit programs.
Georgia—administers health insurance plan; coordinates training programs, deferred compensation plan; serves as secretary to Personnel Board; central payroll.
Hawaii—conducts recruitment and examinations, training and safety programs, classification and compensation review, employee services, labor relations.
Illinois—negotiates collective bargaining agreements.
Indiana—administers affirmative action, rules, medical-dental plans for employees, training and continuing education; publishes newsletter; processes applications; performance appraisals; approves payroll; establishes new personnel programs and policies.
Maine—administers all aspects of employee relations and collective bargaining, workers' compensation program, and training and development programs.
Maryland—administers equal opportunity employment program; adjudicates employee grievances and appeal of disciplinary actions; administers state employee training and development program, and health benefits.
Michigan—administers employee benefits, rules of employment conditions, employee development and assistance, grievance and unfair labor practices charges, technical appeals (including selection and classification issues); regulates collective bargaining system; conducts representation elections for exclusive collective bargaining agents.
Minnesota—negotiates contracts with 16 bargaining units; represents state in labor disputes.
Missouri—recommends pay plan revisions for approval by the Board and governor; directs central training function for all state agencies; participates in central labor relations; develops standard performance appraisal system for the state.
Montana—collective bargaining supervisor; administers health benefits, deferred compensation, training and award programs, affirmative action.
Nebraska—promulgates system rules and regulations; administers health and life insurance benefits; coordinates labor relations programs.
New York—oversees agency affirmative action programs under governor's order; administers health insurance programs.
North Dakota—administers statewide appeal mechanism.
Oregon—maintains personnel system statewide.
Pennsylvania—(Civil Service Commission)—appoints staff; attends Commission meetings; recommends rules and amendments; investigates impact of Civil Service Act; appoints deputy; makes biennial report. (Bureau of Personnel)—develops personnel policy for all agencies under governor's jurisdiction; reviews and evaluates personnel programs; develops and administers senior management executive programs; administers training programs; negotiates collective bargaining.
Tennessee—administers provisions of Civil Service Act, rules of the Department of Personnel, including employment practices, classification, compensation, job performance planning and evaluation, attendance and leave, affirmative action, appeals and grievance procedures; acts as secretary of Civil Service Commission.
Utah—establishes rules and regulations.
Vermont—negotiates collective bargaining agreements; administers employee benefits; handles employee grievances.

(b) With approval by Governor.
(c) Appointed by the Louisiana Civil Service Commission following a competitive examination.
(d) Massachusetts' Civil Service Commission submits three names to the secretary of administration and finance who appoints the personnel administrator with the governor's consent. The personnel administrator serves a four-year term.
(e) From candidates certified by the Personnel Advisory Board.
(f) Selected through procedures specified in the Montana recruitment and selection rules.
(g) Director of Office of Management and Budget makes final choice from among the candidates presented by the State Personnel Board.
(h) Appointed by director of administration following a competitive examination.
(i) Selected by State Budget and Control Board, a five-member board chaired by the governor.
(j) Decentralized personnel system.
(k) From three candidates recommended by the Personnel Board.
(l) From list of eligible candidates following competitive examination.
(m) Information not available.
(n) Personnel office in Florida no longer administers merit tests.

PERSONNEL

Table 7.2
STATE PERSONNEL ADMINISTRATION: STRUCTURE AND FUNCTIONS

State or other jurisdiction	Legal basis for personnel department	Organizational status — Separate agency	Organizational status — Part of a larger agency	Human resource planning	Classification	Recruitment	Selection	Performance evaluation	Promotion	Employee assistance and counseling	Human resource development and training	Affirmative action	Labor and employee relations	Grievance and appeals	Compensation	Retirement
Alabama	C,S	★			●	★			★	★		★	★	★	★	★	
Alaska	C,S		★		●	●	●		●	★		●	★			●	
Arizona	S		★		●	★	★	★	●	●		●		●		●	
Arkansas	S		★			★						●				●	
California State Personnel Bd.	C,S,E	★			★	★	●	●		★			●	●	★		●
Dept. of Personnel Admin.	S	★															
Colorado	C,S,E	★		★	●	★	★	★	★		★		★		★	●	
Connecticut	S		★		●	●	●	●	★	●	★	★	★	●	★	●	●
Delaware	S	★			●	●	●	●	●	●	●	★	★		★	●	
Florida	S	★			★	●	●	●	●	●	●	★	●		★	●	
Georgia	C,S	★				●	●	●	●	●	●	●	●	●	●	●	●
Hawaii	C,S	★		★ ★	●	●	★			★	●	★				★	
Idaho	S	★		●	●	●	★	★		●		●	★	●	●	●	
Illinois	S		★	●	★	●	★	★	★	●	●	●			●	★	★
Indiana	S		★	★	●	●	★	●	★	●	●	★	●		●	●	★
Iowa	S		★	★	●	●	●	●	●	●	★	●	★	●	●	●	
Kansas	S	★		★	●	●	●	★	●	★	●	●		●	●	★	
Kentucky	S	★			●	●	●	●	●		●	●	★	●	★	●	
Louisiana	C	★			●	●	●	●	●	●	●	★	●		●	●	
Maine	S	★			●	★	●	●	●		★	★	★	●	★	●	
Maryland	S	★		●	●	●	●				●		●		●		
Massachusetts	S	★			●	●	●	●	●		★	★		★	★	★	
Michigan	C	★			●	★	●	●	●	★	●	★	★		●	●	
Minnesota	S	★			●	●	●	●	●	●	★	★		●	★	●	
Mississippi	S	★			●	★	●	●	●	●	●	●		★	●	●	
Missouri	C,S	★		●	●	●	●	(c)	(c)★	(c)		★				★	
Montana	S	★		●	●	●	●	●	●	●	●	★	●	★	●	●	
Nebraska	S		★ ★	★	●	●		★	●	★	●	★	★			●	
Nevada	S	★			●	●	●	★									
New Hampshire	S	★		★	●				★			★			●		
New Jersey	C,S			★	●	●			●			★					
New Mexico	S	★			●	●						★					
New York	C,S,E (b)	★		★	●	●		●	★	★	●	★		★	★	★	
North Carolina	S		★	★	●	●	●					★	★		●	★	
North Dakota	S		★		●	●	●	●		★	●	★		★	●	●	
Ohio	C		★		●	●	●	●	★	★		★	★	★	★	★	★

STATE PERSONNEL ADMINISTRATION: STRUCTURE AND FUNCTIONS—Continued

State or other jurisdiction	Legal basis for personnel department	Organizational status		Functions (a):												
		Separate agency	Part of a larger agency	Human resource planning	Classification	Recruitment	Selection	Performance evaluation	Promotion	Employee assistance and counseling	Human resource development and training	Affirmative action	Labor and employee relations	Grievance and appeals	Compensation	Retirement
Oklahoma	S	★	:	★ ●	★ ★	● ★	★ ★	★ ★	★ :	★ ●	★ ★	★ :	★ ★	: ★	● ★	: :
Oregon	S	:	★	● ●	★ ★	● ★	★ ★	★ ★	: :	● ●	: :	: :	★ ★	★ ★	● ★	: :
Pennsylvania:																
Civil Service Comm.	S	★	:	★ ★	: ●	★ ★	★ ★	: ●	★ :	★ ★	: ●	★ ●	: ●	● ●	: ★	: :
Bur. of Personnel	E	:	★	★ ★	★ ●	★ ★	★ ★	: ●	● ★	★ ●	★ ●	● ●	: ●	● ★	★ ★	: :
Rhode Island	S	:	★	★ ★	● ●	★ ★	★ ★	: ●	● ★	: ●	★ ●	: ●	: ●	★ ●	★ ●	: :
South Carolina	S	:	★	★ ★	● ●	★ ★	★ ★	: ●	● ★	: :	★ ●	: ●	: ●	★ ●	★ ●	: :
South Dakota	S	★	:	● ●	● ●	● ●	(c)	● ●	● ●	● ●	★ ●	★ ●	● ●	● ●	★ ●	: :
Tennessee	S	★	:	● ●	● ●	● ★	★	● ●	(c)	: :	: :	: :	: :	★ ★	: :	: :
Texas	S	★	:	: :	: :	: :	: :	: :	: :	: :	: :	: :	: :	: :	: :	: :
Utah	S	★	:	★ ★	● ●	★ ●	★ ●	★ ●	: ●	★ ★	★ ●	: ★	★ ★	: ●	★ ★	: :
Vermont	S	:	★	: :	: :	: :	: :	: :	: :	: :	: :	: :	: :	: :	: :	: :
Virginia	S	★	:	: :	: :	● ●	: ●	● ●	: :	: :	● ●	: ★	: :	: ★	● ●	: :
Washington	S	★ ★	:	: :	● ●	● ●	● ●	● ★	: ★	★ ★	★ ★	● ●	★ ★	★ :	● ●	: :
West Virginia	S	★	:	: :	● ●	● ●	● ●	: :	★ ●	: :	★ ●	● ●	★ ★	: :	● ●	: :
Wisconsin	S	:	★	: :	: :	● ●	● ●	: :	● ●	: :	● ●	★ ●	★ ●	: ●	● ●	: :
Wyoming	S	:	:	: :	: :	● ●	: ●	: :	: :	: :	● ●	: ●	: :	: ●	● ●	: :
Guam	S	★	:	★ ★	★ ●	★ ●	★ ●	★ ●	★ ●	★ ●	● ●	★ ●	★ ●	★ ●	★ ●	: :
Puerto Rico	S	★	:	: :	: :	: :	: :	: :	: :	★ :	: :	★ :	★ :	★ :	★ :	: :

Source: Information derived from survey of state personnel offices conducted by The Council of State Governments (March 1986) for the National Association of State Personnel Executives.

Key:
C — Constitution
S — Statute
E — Executive order

In these columns: ★—function performed in personnel department; ●—function centralized in personnel department.
(b) Also, Civil Service Commission regulations.
(c) Decentralized system.

PERSONNEL

Table 7.3
CLASSIFICATION AND COMPENSATION PLANS

State or other jurisdiction	Legal basis for plan	Current number of classifications	Classification plan: Requirement for periodic comprehensive review of plan (a)	Date of most recent comprehensive review	Legal basis for compensation plan
Alabama	(b)	1,340	★/5	1982	S,R
Alaska	S	1,000	...	1985	S
Arizona	S,R	1,450	...	1987 (c)	S,R
Arkansas	S	2,100	...	1980	S
California	C,S	4,400	★/2	...	S
Colorado	C,S	1,600	...	1975 (d)	C,S
Connecticut	S	2,500	...	1986 (c)	S,CB
Delaware	S	1,100	...	1986	S
Florida	S	1,651	...	1985	S
Georgia	S	1,500	...	1978	S
Hawaii	S,R	1,605	...	1987	S,R
Idaho	S	1,100	★/2	...	S
Illinois	S	1,620	...	1987 (c)	S
Indiana	S	1,525	...	1986 (c)	S
Iowa	S	1,116	...	1985	S,CB
Kansas	S,R	1,200	...	1986 (c)	S,R
Kentucky	S,R	1,442	...	1982	S,R
Louisiana	C	3,764	...	1987	C
Maine	S	1,497	★/10	1982	CB
Maryland	S	3,000	...	1982	S
Massachusetts	S	1,000	...	1987	S,CB
Michigan	C	1,766	...	1980	C
Minnesota	S	1,600	...	1986 (c)	S,CB
Mississippi	S	1,700	...	1987 (c)	S
Missouri	S,R	1,080 (e)	...	(f)	S
Montana	S,R	1,500	...	1985	S,R
Nebraska	S	1,300	...	1969	S
Nevada	S	1,200	★/5	1986 (c)	S
New Hampshire	S	1,470	...	1987	S
New Jersey	S,R	6,500	...	1986 (c)	S,R
New Mexico	S	800	...	...	S
New York	S	7,300	...	1954	S
North Carolina	S	3,012	...	1949	S
North Dakota	S	960	...	1986 (c)	S
Ohio	S	1,832	...	1987-88	S
Oklahoma	S	1,136	...	1981	S
Oregon	S	1,185	...	(c)	S
Pennsylvania	S,R,E	2,700	...	1970	S,R,E
Rhode Island	S	1,500	...	1957	S
South Carolina	S	2,400	...	1979	S
South Dakota	S,R	579	...	1986	S,R
Tennessee	S	1,451	...	1984	S
Texas	S	1,288 (e)	★/1	(g)	S
Utah	S	2,100	★/ (c)	1986 (c)	S
Vermont	S	1,063	...	1986 (c)	S
Virginia	S	2,100	...	1980	S
Washington	S	2,400	...	1986 (c)	S
West Virginia	S	950	...	1986	S
Wisconsin	S	2,011	...	1947	S
Wyoming	S	1,375	...	1976	S
Guam	S	900	★/2	1984	S,R
Puerto Rico	S	1,131	...	1986 (c)	S

Source: Information derived from survey of state personnel offices conducted by The Council of State Governments (March 1986) for the National Association of State Personnel Executives.

Key:
C — Constitution
S — Statute
R — Regulation
E — Executive order
CB — Collective bargaining
(a) In this column, number after slash represents frequency (in years) of required review.
(b) Authorization from state personnel board rules.
(c) Ongoing review. In Illinois, ongoing since 1969.
(d) Incremental reviews have been conducted, based on 1975 comprehensive review.
(e) Legal limit on number of classifications. Missouri—1,100; Texas—1,288.
(f) No comprehensive reviews; only reviews of sections of plan.
(g) In Texas, budget reviewed biennially by classification compensation salary administration.

PERSONNEL

Table 7.4
SELECTED EMPLOYEE LEAVE POLICIES

State or other jurisdiction	Annual leave accrual (in days/year)		Sick leave accrual (in days/year)	Average sick days used (in days/year)	Parental leave*	Other provisions	Leave sharing	Child care	
	1st year	5th year						On-site	Subsidized
Alabama	13	16.25	13	N.A.	★	...	...	...	...
Alaska	15	24	15	...	...	...	...	...	...
Arizona	12	15	12	N.A.	★	...	★	★ (a)	...
Arkansas	12	18	12	...	★ (b)	...	...	...	...
California	16.5	21	12	8.6	★	...	...	...	★
Colorado	12	15	10	7.9	...	★	★	...	...
Connecticut	12	15	15	9.31	★ (c)	★	★	★	...
Delaware	15	15	15	...	★	...	...	...	...
Florida	13	16.25	13	5.50	★	...	...	...	★
Georgia	15	18	15	...	...	...	...	...	...
Hawaii	21	21	21	...	...	★	...	...	...
Idaho	12	15	12	52 hours	...	...	...	★ (nn)	...
Illinois	10	10	12	8.7	...	★	...	★	★
Indiana	12	15	6 (d)	9.0	...	...	...	...	...
Iowa	10	15	18	7.8	...	★ (e)	...	...	...
Kansas	12	15	12	N.A.	★	...	...	★ (f)	...
Kentucky	12	(oo)	12	50 hours	...	...	★	...	...
Louisiana (g)									
Maine	12	15	12	63.2 hours	...	★	...	★	★
Maryland	10	10 (h)	15	N.A.	★ (i)	★ (j)	...	★ (k)	...
Massachusetts	10	15	15	8.6 (l)	★	...	...	★ (f)	...
Michigan	13	15	13	9.0	...	★ (m)	...	...	...
Minnesota	13 (n)	13 (n)	13	8.4	★	...	...	★	...
Mississippi	18	21	12	...	...	...	...	...	...
Missouri	15	15	15	N.A.	...	...	...	...	...
Montana	15	15	12	7-8	★ (b)	...	★ (o)	...	...
Nebraska	12	15	12 (p)	8.0	★	...	...	...	...
Nevada	15	15	15	10.3	★	...	★ (q)	★ (r)	...
New Hampshire	12	15	15	8.2	...	...	...	...	...
New Jersey	12	15	15	8.3	★	...	...	...	...
New Mexico	10	12	12	N.A.	★	...	...	...	...
New York	13 (s)	18	8-13 (t)	9.4	★ (u)	...	...	★ (v)	...
North Carolina	11.75	16.75	12	...	★	...	★	...	...
North Dakota	12	15	12	55.11 hours	★ (w)	★ (x)	...	...	...
Ohio	10	10	7	49.4 hours	★	...	...	...	...
Oklahoma	15	18	15	75.9 hours (qq)	★	...	...	...	...
Oregon	12	15	12	...	★	★ (pp)	...	...	...
Pennsylvania	5.2 (y)	15.6 (y)	13	9.7	★	...	...	★	...
Rhode Island	10	15	15	10 days	★	...	...	...	★
South Carolina	15	15	15	...	★ (z)	...	★	...	...
South Dakota	15	15	14	54.6 hours	★ (aa)	...	...	...	...
Tennessee	12	18	12	7.5 hrs./mo.	...	...	...	...	...
Texas	10.5	13.5	12	68.05 hours	★ (bb)	...	...	★ (cc)	★ (dd)
Utah	13	16.25	13	...	★	...	...	...	...
Vermont	12	15	12	9.2	...	★ (ee)	★	★	★
Virginia	12	15	15	N.A.	★	...	★	...	...
Washington	12	15	12	7.9	★	...	★	...	★
West Virginia	15	18	18	...	...	★ (ff)	...	...	...
Wisconsin	10	15	13	7.8	★	★	...	...	★ (gg)
Wyoming	12	15	12	Unknown	★	...	★ (hh)	★ (f)	...
Dist. of Columbia	13	20	13	N.A.	★ (kk)	...	(ll)	...	★ (mm)
Guam	13	19.5	13	...	★	...	...	...	...
No. Mariana Islands	13	(ii)	13	...	★ (jj)	...	...	...	...
Puerto Rico	30	30	18	...	...	...	...	...	...

PERSONNEL

SELECTED EMPLOYEE LEAVE POLICIES—Continued

Source: National Association of State Personnel Executives; based on preliminary survey data.
* Parental leave is treated as sick leave and/or annual leave without pay.
Key:
N.A. — Not available
. . . — No provision

(a) The management of the program is awarded based on a competitive bid with the Department of Administration providing the building, maintenance of the building, utilities, certain equipment and coverage under the state's risk management program at no cost to the individuals managing the day-care program.
(b) Maternity leave only.
(c) Permits employees to take up to 24 weeks of unpaid leave within any two-year period for the birth or adoption of a child, for the serious illness of a member of the immediate family or for the employee's own illness.
(d) Full-time employees with over one year of service, as of July 1, 1989, who have used all annual and sick leave, may apply for special sick leave at the rate of one week for each year of service.
(e) Sick leave may be used for maternity leave.
(f) The majority of state office facilities are not equipped to provide on-site day-care, but some facilities do provide such programs.
(g) Louisiana could not participate because less than half of their employees are covered in the present automated payroll system. There is no reason to believe that these do not represent a cross-section of state employees, so they did not feel comfortable reporting this data.
(h) 15 days at start of the sixth year.
(i) May use sick leave for illness in immediate family.
(j) 12 weeks of unpaid family leave is available.
(k) One agency has an on-site day care facility.
(l) Does not include long term disability or pregnancy leave.
(m) Provides employees with the right to an unpaid leave of absence of six months on the birth or adoption of a child. This is in addition to any other leave rights (sick or annual).
(n) Managerial personnel receive 19 1/2 days.
(o) Sick leave funds and direct grants from employee to co-worker.
(p) Increases with length of service to a top of 30 days earned per year in the 19th year.
(q) For catastrophic injury and illness only.
(r) University has on-site child care facility.
(s) Or 14 days depending on the bargaining unit and the date of hire.
(t) Depending on the bargaining unit and the date of hire.
(u) New York grants seven months of mandatory unpaid parental leave which may be extended at the discretion of the appointing agency. If both parents are state employees, they may elect to split the mandatory leave into two separate blocks with each parent entitled to one continuous period of leave. The mother may use sick leave during periods of disability while both parents may use other accrued leave to offset the amount of unpaid leave. Child care leave is also avilable in the same manner in the event of an adoption, starting any time from the date the child is placed with the family to the effective date of the adoption.

(v) At certain locations around the state.
(w) Up to 40 hours per year of family sick leave for illness or medical needs of immediate family.
(x) Up to four months unpaid family leave.
(y) As part of the collective bargaining agreement, new state employees (those hired since July 1, 1985) receive only 5.2 annual leave days in their first year of employment and 10.4 in their 5th year.
(z) Employees may use up to 5 days of accrued sick leave in a calendar year to care for illness in the immediate family including parents.
(aa) Maternity leave only, six weeks maximum.
(bb) Pregnancies are treated as any other temporary disability for sick leave with pay eligibility. If not eligible for sick leave, employees may request annual leave with pay or leave without pay, as applicable.
(cc) The Texas School for the Blind and Visually Impaired has an on-site child care facility.
(dd) The state provides an incentive to the State Purchasing and General Services Commission to allocate leasable state office building space for the provision of child care by private vendors.
(ee) 4-6 months mandatory parental leave policy.
(ff) Permanent employees are entitled to a total of 12 weeks of unpaid/family leave during any 12 month period, once all annual leave and compensatory leave has been exhausted for the birth or adoption of a child, or to care for a family member or dependent with a serious health condition.
(gg) Wisconsin has subsidized start-up costs only.
(hh) Wyoming has a sick leave donation program where individuals with over 80 hours accumulated sick leave can donate up to 16 hours to someone who has run out of leave for health purposes (16 hours per year).
(ii) After the third year, employees get 19.5 days and after six years, 26 days.
(jj) Maternity leave is 15 days; paternity leave is 2 days.
(kk) Maternity leave is offered as a combination of sick leave, annual leave, or leave without pay. A male employee may request only annual leave or leave without pay for purposes of assisting or caring for his minor children or the mother of his newborn child while she is incapacitated for maternity reasons. Any employee adopting a child may use annual leave or leave without pay in order to make family adjustments and to make arrangements for child care.
(ll) Available only to uniformed police personnel. Uniformed personnel are permitted to donate their annual leave under a catastrophic illness plan adopted in 1987 as part of the collective bargaining agreement. Legislation is currently before the Council of the District of Columbia for the enactment of a leave bank.
(mm) Available at some District government sites, although the child care is not sponsored or subsidized by the District government.
(nn) One on-site child care agency, parents must pay for services.
(oo) Between 6th and 11th year—15 days; 12th and 15th year—18 days; after 16th year—21 days.
(pp) Family care leave. Up to 12 weeks per couple allowed. May use annual leave, sick leave or leave without pay.
(qq) Includes funeral leave.

Table 7.5
STATE EMPLOYEES: PAID HOLIDAYS*

State or other jurisdiction	Major holiday (a)	Martin Luther King's Birthday (b)	Lincoln's Birthday	President's Day (c)	Washington's Birthday (c)	Good Friday	Memorial Day (d)	Columbus Day (e)	Veteran's Day	Day after Thanksgiving	Day before or after Christmas	Day before or after New Year's	Election Day (f)	Other (g)
Alabama	★★★★★	★ (h)			★		★★★★	★	★★★★★					★★
Alaska	★★★★★	(i)	(i)	★	★★★		★★★★★		★★★★★	★★	Before			★★
Arizona	★★★★★	(i) (h)	★		★		★★★★★		★★★★★					
Arkansas	★★★★★	★★	★		★★		★★★★★	★	★★★★★	★★				★★
California	★★★★★	★★	★		★		★★★★★	★	★★★★★	★★			★	
Colorado	★★★★★	★★★★★			★		★★★★★	★★★	★★★★★					
Connecticut	★★★★★	★		★ (k)	★	★★	★★★★★	★	★★★★★	★ (k)			★	
Delaware	★★★★★	★			★	★★	★★★★★		★★★★★	★	(l)			★
Florida	★★★★★	★★★★★			★		★★★★★	★★★	★★★★★	★ (l)			★★	★★
Georgia	★★★★★	★			★		★★★★★	★	★★★★★	★				★★★
Hawaii	★★★★★	★		★			★★★★★		★★★★★				★★	★
Idaho	★★★★★	★★★			★		★★★★★	★★★	★★★★★					★★★★
Illinois	★★★★★	★★	★★		★★		★★★★★	★★	★★★★★	★★	★	★	★★★ (m)	★★
Indiana	★★★★★		(i)		(i)		★★★★★		★★★★★					
Iowa	★★★★★	★★					★★★★★		★★★★★					
Kansas	★★★★★		★		★		★★★★★		★★★★★				★	★★★
Kentucky	★★★★★					★★	★★★★★		★★★★★	★★ (k)			★★★ (o)	★★★★
Louisiana	★★★★★	★★★★				★★ (n)	★★ ★★	★★	★★★★★	★ (l)			★★ (o)	★★★★
Maine	★★★★★	★★		★★	★★		★★★★★	★★	★★★★★	★★				
Maryland	★★★★★	★★			★		★★★★★	★	★★★★★	★	★	★	★	★★
Massachusetts	★★★★★	★★		★	★		★★★★★ (p)	★★	★★★★★					★★★★
Michigan	★★★★★	★★★		★★	★★		★★ ★★		★★★★★	★★		★		★★
Minnesota	★★★★★	★ (h)			★		★★★★★	★	★★★★★		Before	Before		★★
Mississippi	★★★★★	★★★			★★		★★★★★		★★★★★					★★★★
Missouri	★★★★★		★		★		★★★★★	★★	★★★★★					★★★★
Montana	★★★★★	★★			★★		★★★★★	★★	★★★★★	★★★ (q)				
Nebraska	★★★★★	★★			★		★★★★★	★★	★★★★★					
Nevada	★★★★★	★			★	★	★★★★★	★	★★★★★	★			★	★★
New Hampshire	★★★★★	★			★		★★★★★	★	★★★★★					★★
New Jersey	★★★★★	★★			★	★★	★★★★★	★	★★★★★				★	
New Mexico	★★★★★	★★★		★			★★★★★		★★★★★	★				★
New York (r)	★★★★★	★		★			★★★★★	★	★★★★★				★	
North Carolina	★★★★★	★★★	★		★	★★	★★★★★		★★★★★		Before			
North Dakota (s)	★★★★★				★		★★★★★		★★★★★					★
Ohio	★★★★★	★		★			★★★★★	★	★★★★★					
Oklahoma	★★★★★	★★	★		★		★★★★★		★★★★★		★			★
Oregon	★★★★★	★★		★			★★★★★		★★★★★					
Pennsylvania	★★★★★				★		★★★★★	★	★★★★★	★			★	★
Rhode Island	★★★★★	★★			★		★★★★★	★★	★★★★★		After			
South Carolina	★★★★★				★		★★★★★		★★★★★	★			★★	★★

STATE EMPLOYEES: PAID HOLIDAYS—Continued

State or other jurisdiction	Major holiday (a)	Martin Luther King's Birthday (b)	Lincoln's Birthday	President's Day (c)	Washington's Birthday (c)	Good Friday	Memorial Day (d)	Columbus Day (e)	Veteran's Day	Day after Thanksgiving	Day before or after Christmas	Day before or after New Year's	Election Day (f)	Other (g)
South Dakota	★	★		★	★		★	★	★					★
Tennessee	★	★(v)			★	★(v)	★	★	★	★	★(w)			
Texas (u)	★	★(x)		★			★	★	★					★
Utah	★	★(v)	★(v)				★	★(t)	★					★
Vermont (s)	★	★		★			★	★	★	★				★
Virginia	★	★(y)					★	★	★					
Washington	★	★	★	★			★	★	★	★				★
West Virginia	★	★		★	★	★(n)	★	★	★	★(q)	★(z) Before	★(z) Before	★(m)	★
Wisconsin	★	★					★							
Wyoming	★	★		★	★		★	★	★					
Dist. of Columbia	★	★					★	★	★					★
U.S. Virgin Islands	★	★		★	★	★	★	★(aa)	★		★(bb)	★(cc)		★

STATE EMPLOYEES: PAID HOLIDAYS—Continued

* Holidays in addition to any other authorized paid personal leave granted state employees.

Note: In some states, the governor may proclaim additional holidays or select from a number of holidays for observance by state employees. In some states, the list of paid holidays is determined by the personnel department at the beginning of each year; as a result, the number of holidays may change from year to year. Number of paid holidays may also vary across some employee classifications. Dates are given for 1990 and may change slightly for 1991. If holiday falls on a weekend, generally employees get the day preceding or following.

Key:
. . .—Paid holiday not granted.
(a) New Year's Day, Independence Day, Labor Day, Thanksgiving Day, and Christmas Day.
(b) Third Monday in January.
(c) Generally, third Monday in February; Washington's Birthday or Presidents' Day. In some states, the holiday is called Presidents' Day or Washington-Lincoln Day. Most frequently, this day recognized Washington and Lincoln.
(d) Last Monday in May in all states indicated, except New Hampshire where holiday is observed on May 30. Generally, states follow the Federal Government's observance (last Monday in May) rather than the traditional Memorial Day (May 30).
(e) Second Monday in October.
(f) General election day only, unless otherwise indicated.
(g) Additional holidays:
Alabama — Mardi Gras Day (varies, February 27), Thomas Jefferson's Birthday (April 13), Confederate Memorial Day (fourth Monday in April), Jefferson Davis' Birthday (first Monday in June).
Alaska — Seward's Day (last Monday in March), Alaska Day (October 18).
Arkansas — Employee's birthday.
California — Confederate Memorial Day (April 26).
Georgia — Confederate Memorial Day (April 26).
Hawaii — Prince Jonah Kuhio Kalanianaole Day (March 26), King Kamehameha Day (June 11), Admission Day (third Friday in August).
Kansas — Discretionary day (taken whenever employee chooses with supervisor's approval).
Louisiana — Mardi Gras Day (day before Ash Wednesday), Inauguration Day (every four years, in Baton Rouge only).
Maine — Patriot's Day (April 16).
Maryland — Maryland Day (March 26), Defender's Day (September 12).
Massachusetts — Evacuation Day (March 17), Patriot's Day (third Monday in April), Bunker Hill Day (June 17 normally, but observed June 18 in 1990); all three in Suffolk County only.
Michigan — One personal day.
Mississippi — Confederate's Memorial Day (last Monday in April).
Missouri — Harry Truman's Birthday (May 8).
Montana — Heritage Day (varies, set annually by Governor, November 23 in 1990).
Nebraska — Arbor Day (last Friday in April).
Nevada — Nevada Day (October 31).
New Hampshire — Floating holidays (July 1, March 1, November 1); state offices remain open.
North Dakota — Half day on Christmas Eve if Christmas Eve falls on a weekday.
Rhode Island — Victory Day (second Monday in August).
South Carolina — Discretionary day (taken whenever employee chooses with supervisor's approval).
South Dakota — Pioneer Day (second Monday in October).
Texas — Confederate Heroes Day (January 19), Texas Independence Day (March 2), Lyndon Johnson's Birthday (August 27), Sanjacinto Day (April 21), Emancipation Day (June 19), Rosh Hashanah (September 20-21), Yom Kippur (September 29). For Jewish holidays, offices open, employee may take another day.
Utah — Pioneer Day (July 24).
Vermont — Town Meeting Day (first Tuesday in March), Battle of Bennington Day (August 16).
Washington — One personal day.
West Virginia — West Virginia Day (June 20).
District of Columbia — Inauguration Day (every four years).
U.S. Virgin Islands — St. Croix Festival Day (varies, January 5 in 1990), Three Kings' Day (January 6), Transfer Day (March 31), Holy Thursday, Easter Monday, Organic Act Day (third Monday in June), Emancipation Day (July 3), Supplication Day (fourth Monday in July), Local Thanksgiving Day (third Monday in October), Liberty Day (November 1), Carnival Fair Day (halfday, varies, April 26 in 1990), and Children's Carnival Day (varies, April 27 in 1990).
(h) Also for Robert E. Lee's Birthday.
(i) In Alaska, Lincoln's Birthday is designated a floating holiday; state offices remain open, so employee must receive prior permission before taking it on February 12. In Maryland, Lincoln's Birthday, Maryland Day, and Defender's Day are floating holidays; offices remain open, so employee must receive prior approval to take it on actual holiday.
(j) Legislature is still deciding on whether employees will receive Columbus Day or Martin Luther King's Birthday.
(k) Two days given for President's Day with the second day observed on the day after Thanksgiving.
(l) In Georgia, Robert E. Lee's Birthday is observed the day after Thanksgiving and Washington's Birthday is observed the day after Thanksgiving. In Indiana, Lincoln's Birthday is observed the day after Thanksgiving and Washington's Birthday is observed the day before Christmas.
(m) Also, primary election day.
(n) Half days.
(o) In Kentucky, presidential election day only. In Louisiana, every two years.
(p) Also for Jefferson Davis' Birthday.
(q) Day after Thanksgiving at discretion of Governor.
(r) Holidays for eligible employees only, subject to the Attendance Rules for employees in New York state departments and institutions. If a holiday falls on a Sunday, it is observed on the following Monday.
(s) If a holiday falls on a Saturday, observed Friday before. If on a Sunday, observed following Monday.
(t) May observe on day after Thanksgiving.
(u) Holidays are not observed another day if one falls on the weekend.
(v) Offices open; employee may take another day.
(w) Day before and after.
(x) Called Human Rights Day; celebrates Martin Luther King and others who worked for human rights.
(y) Called King/Lee/Jackson Day.
(z) Half day on Christmas Eve and New Year's Eve if Christmas Day or New Year's Day falls on Tuesday - Friday.
(aa) And Puerto Rico Friendship Day.
(bb) Half day before and full day after.
(cc) Half day before (called Old Year's Day).

PUBLIC EMPLOYMENT

Table 7.6
SUMMARY OF STATE GOVERNMENT EMPLOYMENT: 1952-1988

Year (October)	Employment (in thousands)						Monthly payrolls (in millions of dollars)			Average monthly earnings of full-time employees		
	Total, full-time and part-time			Full-time equivalent								
	All	Education	Other	All	Education	Other	All	Education	Other	All	Education	Other
1952	1,060	293	767	958	213	745	$ 260.3	$ 65.1	$ 195.2	$ 271	$ 298	$ 262
1953	1,082	294	788	966	211	755	278.6	73.5	205.1	289	320	278
1954	1,149	310	839	1,024	222	802	300.7	78.9	221.8	294	325	283
1955	1,199	333	866	1,081	244	837	325.9	88.5	237.4	302	334	290
1956	1,268	353	915	1,136	250	886	366.5	108.8	257.7	321	358	309
1957 (April)	1,300	375	925	1,153	257	896	372.5	106.1	266.4	320	355	309
1958	1,408	406	1,002	1,259	284	975	446.5	123.4	323.1	355	416	333
1959	1,454	443	1,011	1,302	318	984	485.4	136.0	349.4	373	427	352
1960	1,527	474	1,053	1,353	332	1,021	524.1	167.7	356.4	386	439	365
1961	1,625	518	1,107	1,435	367	1,068	586.2	192.4	393.8	409	482	383
1962	1,680	555	1,126	1,478	389	1,088	634.6	201.8	432.8	429	518	397
1963	1,775	602	1,173	1,558	422	1,136	696.4	230.1	466.3	447	545	410
1964	1,873	656	1,217	1,639	460	1,179	761.1	257.5	503.6	464	560	427
1965	2,028	739	1,289	1,751	508	1,243	849.2	290.1	559.1	484	571	450
1966	2,211	866	1,344	1,864	575	1,289	975.2	353.0	622.2	522	614	483
1967	2,335	940	1,395	1,946	620	1,326	1,105.5	406.3	699.3	567	666	526
1968	2,495	1,037	1,458	2,085	694	1,391	1,256.7	477.1	779.6	602	687	544
1969	2,614	1,112	1,501	2,179	746	1,433	1,430.5	554.5	876.1	655	743	597
1970	2,755	1,182	1,573	2,302	803	1,499	1,612.2	630.3	981.9	700	797	605
1971	2,832	1,223	1,609	2,384	841	1,544	1,741.7	681.5	1,060.2	731	826	686
1972	2,957	1,267	1,690	2,487	867	1,619	1,936.6	746.9	1,189.7	778	871	734
1973	3,013	1,280	1,733	2,547	887	1,660	2,158.2	822.2	1,336.0	843	952	805
1974	3,155	1,357	1,798	2,653	929	1,725	2,409.5	932.7	1,476.9	906	1,023	855
1975	3,271	1,400	1,870	2,744	952	1,792	2,652.7	1,021.7	1,631.1	964	1,080	909
1976	3,343	1,434	1,910	2,799	973	1,827	2,893.7	1,111.5	1,782.1	1,031	1,163	975
1977	3,491	1,484	2,007	2,903	1,005	1,898	3,194.6	1,234.4	1,960.1	1,096	1,237	1,031
1978	3,539	1,508	2,032	2,966	1,016	1,950	3,483.0	1,332.9	2,150.2	1,167	1,311	1,102
1979	3,699	1,577	2,122	3,072	1,046	2,026	3,869.3	1,451.4	2,417.9	1,257	1,399	1,193
1980	3,753	1,599	2,154	3,106	1,063	2,044	4,284.7	1,608.0	2,676.6	1,373	1,523	1,305
1981	3,726	1,603	2,123	3,087	1,063	2,024	4,667.5	1,768.0	2,899.5	1,507	1,671	1,432
1982	3,747	1,616	2,131	3,083	1,051	2,032	5,027.7	1,874.0	3,153.7	1,625	1,789	1,551
1983	3,816	1,666	2,150	3,116	1,072	2,044	5,345.5	1,989.0	3,357.0	1,711	1,850	1,640
1984	3,898	1,708	2,190	3,177	1,091	2,086	5,814.9	2,178.0	3,637.0	1,825	1,991	1,740
1985	3,984	1,764	2,220	2,990	945	2,046	6,328.6	2,443.7	3,884.9	1,935	2,155	1,834
1986	4,068	1,800	2,267	3,437	1,256	2,181	6,801.4	2,583.4	4,226.9	2,052	2,263	1,956
1987	4,115	1,804	2,310	3,491	1,264	2,227	7,297.8	2,758.3	4,539.5	2,161	2,396	2,056
1988	4,236	1,854	2,381	3,606	1,309	2,297	7,842.3	2,928.6	4,913.7	2,260	2,490	2,158

Source: U.S. Bureau of the Census, annual *Public Employment* reports.
Note: Because of rounding, detail may not add to totals.

PUBLIC EMPLOYMENT

Table 7.7
EMPLOYMENT AND PAYROLLS OF STATE AND LOCAL GOVERNMENTS, BY FUNCTION: OCTOBER 1987

Functions	All employees, full-time and part-time (in thousands)			October payrolls (in millions of dollars)			Average October earnings of full-time employees
	Total	State governments	Local governments	Total	State governments	Local governments	
All functions	14,190	4,115	10,076	$24,458	$7,298	$17,160	$2,089
Education:							
Higher Education	2,056	1,681	375	2,995	2,509	487	2,414
Institutional personnel only ...	720	537	183	1,528	1,245	283	3,346
Elementary/secondary schools ...	5,234	25	5,210	9,110	40	9,070	2,096
Institutional personnel only ...	3,433	16	3,416	7,146	31	7,115	2,343
Local libraries	123	1	122	125	1	124	1,576
Other education	99	99	0	210	210	0	2,266
Selected functions:							
Highways	553	251	302	1,003	505	498	1,883
Public welfare	433	194	239	712	353	359	1,749
Hospitals	1,100	554	546	1,857	980	878	1,811
Health.......................	299	137	162	535	272	263	1,970
Police protection..............	718	82	636	1,517	195	1,322	2,343
Police officers only	525	54	471	1,264	144	1,120	2,529
Fire protection	335	0	335	629	0	629	2,585
Firefighters only	307	0	307	590	0	590	2,617
Natural resources	196	158	38	333	283	50	1,992
Correction	412	264	148	832	537	295	2,072
Social insurance administration ..	103	103	0	204	204	0	2,052
Financial administration	333	133	200	554	258	296	1,863
Judical & legal administration ...	273	99	174	563	255	308	2,235
Other government administration	360	46	314	417	91	326	1,949
Local utilities.................	433	28	406	993	82	911	2,387

Source: U.S. Bureau of the Census, *Public Employment in 1987.*
Note: Statistics for local governments are estimates subject to sampling variation. Because of rounding, detail may not add.

PUBLIC EMPLOYMENT

Table 7.8
EMPLOYMENT AND PAYROLLS OF STATE AND LOCAL GOVERNMENTS, BY FUNCTION: OCTOBER 1988

Functions	All employees, full-time and part-time (in thousands)			October payrolls (in millions of dollars)			Average October earnings of full-time employees
	Total	State governments	Local governments	Total	State governments	Local governments	
All functions	14,476	4,236	10,240	26,227	7,842	18,385	2,187
Education:							
Higher education	2,122	1,728	395	3,213	2,678	536	2,525
Instructional personnel only	749	553	196	1,624	1,313	310	3,489
Elementary/secondary schools	5,287	26	5,261	9,705	45	9,660	2,188
Instructional personnel only	3,500	17	3,483	7,617	34	7,583	2,450
Local libraries	123	1	122	140	1	139	1,690
Other education	101	101	0	206	206	0	2,202
Selected functions:							
Highways	555	253	302	1,045	527	518	1,950
Public welfare	450	202	248	761	376	385	1,804
Hospitals	1,118	562	556	2,020	1,070	950	1,936
Health	313	143	171	591	301	290	2,068
Police protection	725	85	640	1,609	214	1,396	2,450
Police officers only	530	55	475	1,341	157	1,184	2,646
Fire protection	340	0	340	664	0	664	2,690
Firefighters only	313	0	313	622	0	622	2,722
Natural resources	196	159	37	347	294	53	2,082
Correction	445	286	159	930	592	337	2,141
Social insurance administration	104	104	0	222	222	0	2,193
Financial administration	340	138	203	602	283	319	1,968
Judical and legal administration	281	103	178	618	281	337	2,371
Other government administration	372	49	323	460	101	360	2,047
Local utilities	440	28	412	1,076	83	993	2,561

Source: U.S. Bureau of the Census, *Public Employment in 1988.*
Note: Statistics for local governments are estimates subject to sampling variation. Because of rounding, detail may not add.

PUBLIC EMPLOYMENT

Table 7.9
STATE AND LOCAL GOVERNMENT EMPLOYMENT, BY STATE: OCTOBER 1987

State or jurisdiction	All employees (full-time and part-time)		Full-time equivalent employment					
			Number			Number per 10,000 population		
	State	Local	Total	State	Local	Total	State	Local
United States	4,114,545	10,075,601	12,086,379	3,491,498	8,594,881	497	143	353
Alabama	81,571	149,842	203,679	70,196	133,483	499	172	327
Alaska	22,640	24,544	39,392	20,074	19,318	750	382	368
Arizona	51,947	141,910	162,576	38,689	123,887	480	114	366
Arkansas	44,832	84,846	110,559	38,721	71,838	463	162	301
California	348,258	1,188,418	1,281,052	289,354	991,698	463	105	358
Colorado	63,207	146,850	176,783	51,566	125,217	536	156	380
Connecticut	64,234	108,411	153,661	58,219	95,442	479	181	297
Delaware	22,085	17,899	34,589	18,504	16,085	537	287	250
Florida	142,365	455,437	546,097	125,983	420,114	454	105	349
Georgia	106,400	273,198	343,417	95,460	247,957	552	153	399
Hawaii	49,945	13,157	54,506	42,185	12,321	503	390	114
Idaho	20,043	41,880	51,379	18,137	33,242	515	182	333
Illinois	158,872	479,369	517,431	130,077	387,354	447	112	334
Indiana	96,365	222,501	259,739	76,082	183,657	470	138	332
Iowa	58,677	128,391	152,693	51,585	101,108	539	182	357
Kansas	54,093	118,356	137,222	42,857	94,365	554	173	381
Kentucky	73,219	117,935	169,122	64,471	104,651	454	173	281
Louisiana	98,346	163,942	236,292	84,990	151,302	530	191	339
Maine	25,304	47,335	58,085	21,085	37,000	489	178	312
Maryland	91,958	166,744	225,764	79,754	146,010	498	176	322
Massachusetts	104,744	222,286	288,318	92,668	195,650	492	158	334
Michigan	158,706	401,109	446,266	128,892	317,374	485	140	345
Minnesota	77,822	177,123	204,049	63,806	140,243	481	150	330
Mississippi	50,527	112,054	141,997	44,382	97,615	541	169	372
Missouri	77,792	189,658	227,410	66,473	160,937	446	130	315
Montana	20,326	36,646	43,516	16,053	27,463	538	198	339
Nebraska	34,750	85,831	96,537	29,696	66,841	606	186	419
Nevada	16,857	38,275	50,039	15,275	34,764	497	152	345
New Hampshire	19,464	39,342	45,920	15,727	30,193	434	149	286
New Jersey	113,307	321,571	383,187	99,033	284,154	499	129	370
New Mexico	45,179	57,773	88,742	35,265	53,477	592	235	357
New York	298,007	953,767	1,119,537	274,956	844,581	628	154	474
North Carolina	112,899	265,654	323,088	99,778	223,310	504	156	348
North Dakota	20,217	35,323	36,742	15,229	21,513	547	227	320
Ohio	159,161	441,014	495,294	125,439	369,855	459	116	343
Oklahoma	74,842	122,882	171,607	64,364	107,243	524	197	328
Oregon	58,530	117,828	141,527	48,955	92,572	520	180	340
Pennsylvania	141,972	399,334	471,707	125,105	346,602	395	105	290
Rhode Island	25,076	27,026	44,175	19,823	24,352	448	201	247
South Carolina	78,701	168,047	180,308	69,837	110,471	526	204	323
South Dakota	16,517	35,454	36,491	13,159	23,332	515	186	329
Tennessee	81,986	180,668	232,520	70,892	161,628	479	146	333
Texas	232,159	701,362	838,871	198,769	640,102	500	118	381
Utah	37,181	63,492	80,670	32,166	48,504	480	191	289
Vermont	12,794	19,721	26,786	11,775	15,011	489	215	274
Virginia	126,420	223,077	304,222	103,849	200,373	515	176	339
Washington	105,034	170,110	233,249	84,452	148,797	514	186	328
West Virginia	39,408	67,141	94,666	33,657	61,009	499	177	322
Wisconsin	87,510	223,397	234,305	63,580	170,725	487	132	355
Wyoming	12,296	30,546	35,007	10,454	24,553	714	213	501
Dist. of Columbia	0	57,125	55,588	0	55,588	888	0	888

Source: U.S. Bureau of the Census, *Public Employment in 1987*.
Note: Statistics for local governments are estimates subject to sampling variation. Because of rounding, detail may not add to totals.

PUBLIC EMPLOYMENT

Table 7.10
STATE AND LOCAL GOVERNMENT EMPLOYMENT, BY STATE: OCTOBER 1988

State or jurisdiction	All employees (full-time and part-time)		Full-time equivalent employment					
			Number			Number per 10,000 population		
	State	Local	Total	State	Local	Total	State	Local
United States	4,235,500	10,240,175	12,404,019	3,606,475	8,797,544	505	147	358
Alabama	85,379	153,762	208,996	72,109	136,887	509	176	334
Alaska	23,849	24,725	41,359	21,018	20,341	789	401	388
Arizona	53,228	147,193	170,541	43,110	127,431	489	124	365
Arkansas	46,846	87,780	114,474	40,585	73,889	478	169	309
California	366,056	1,230,451	1,342,448	303,353	1,039,095	474	107	367
Colorado	66,534	146,856	174,856	51,539	123,317	530	156	374
Connecticut	65,790	110,017	156,521	59,145	97,376	484	183	301
Delaware	23,093	18,168	36,010	19,434	16,576	546	294	251
Florida	156,883	479,970	580,447	140,200	440,247	471	114	357
Georgia	109,930	282,831	356,187	99,702	256,485	562	157	404
Hawaii	52,506	13,536	56,725	44,032	12,693	517	401	116
Idaho	20,653	42,607	50,823	17,051	33,772	507	170	337
Illinois	159,839	481,493	520,863	130,752	390,111	448	113	336
Indiana	102,363	224,633	271,224	83,680	187,544	488	151	338
Iowa	59,723	130,710	158,751	55,820	102,931	560	197	363
Kansas	55,556	121,620	145,229	47,544	97,685	582	191	392
Kentucky	74,344	120,953	172,911	65,001	107,910	464	174	290
Louisiana	95,000	163,425	231,684	80,570	151,114	526	183	343
Maine	26,454	49,806	60,471	21,921	38,550	502	182	320
Maryland	96,191	172,630	234,901	83,908	150,993	508	182	327
Massachusetts	104,930	225,205	295,151	96,313	198,838	501	164	338
Michigan	158,249	398,672	448,226	128,012	320,214	485	139	347
Minnesota	79,597	189,814	207,911	61,786	146,125	483	143	339
Mississippi	50,256	115,488	144,405	44,393	100,012	551	169	382
Missouri	83,228	189,638	231,828	70,922	160,906	451	138	313
Montana	20,818	35,050	43,430	16,036	27,394	540	199	340
Nebraska	34,724	85,292	95,068	28,711	66,357	593	179	414
Nevada	17,786	40,685	52,437	16,231	36,206	498	154	344
New Hampshire	20,040	40,968	47,836	16,021	31,815	441	148	293
New Jersey	115,987	330,343	398,236	104,460	293,776	516	135	380
New Mexico	47,842	58,863	91,908	37,432	54,476	610	248	361
New York	304,628	956,746	1,135,976	282,241	853,735	634	158	477
North Carolina	117,192	272,383	332,554	102,975	229,579	512	159	354
North Dakota	20,348	35,443	35,958	14,964	20,994	539	224	315
Ohio	161,022	444,389	501,831	129,877	371,954	462	120	343
Oklahoma	74,510	126,234	172,682	63,261	109,421	533	195	338
Oregon	59,650	119,747	144,362	50,265	94,097	522	182	340
Pennsylvania	144,108	400,784	474,159	125,343	348,816	395	104	291
Rhode Island	24,750	28,654	46,190	20,103	26,087	465	202	263
South Carolina	83,040	125,088	185,141	73,242	111,899	534	211	322
South Dakota	15,995	35,292	35,912	12,473	23,439	504	175	329
Tennessee	83,672	188,924	241,801	71,902	169,899	494	147	347
Texas	241,879	721,520	869,485	209,570	659,915	516	124	392
Utah	38,308	64,202	81,915	33,059	48,856	485	196	289
Vermont	13,651	21,726	29,598	12,201	17,397	531	219	312
Virginia	131,666	227,198	313,058	108,668	204,390	520	181	340
Washington	107,682	175,771	238,057	85,815	152,242	512	185	328
West Virginia	39,368	69,070	94,573	33,700	60,873	504	180	324
Wisconsin	88,208	225,670	238,565	65,158	173,407	491	134	357
Wyoming	12,149	31,555	35,478	10,867	24,611	741	227	514
Dist. of Columbia	0	56,595	54,867	0	54,867	876	0	876

Source: U.S. Bureau of the Census, *Public Employment in 1988.*
Note: Statistics for local governments are estimates subject to sampling variation. Because of rounding, detail may not add to totals.

PUBLIC EMPLOYMENT

Table 7.11
STATE AND LOCAL GOVERNMENT PAYROLLS AND AVERAGE EARNINGS OF FULL-TIME EMPLOYEES, BY STATE: OCTOBER 1987

State or jurisdiction	Amount of payroll (in thousands of dollars)			Percentage of October payroll		Average earnings of full-time state and local government employees (dollars)		
	Total	State government	Local governments	State government	Local governments	All	Education employees	Other
United States	$24,457,916	$7,297,764	$17,160,152	29.8	70.2	$2,089	$2,161	$2,024
Alabama	334,571	132,235	202,335	39.5	60.5	1,667	1,733	1,602
Alaska	126,271	64,103	62,169	50.8	49.2	3,306	3,272	3,329
Arizona	368,027	106,955	261,072	29.1	70.9	2,337	2,551	2,106
Arkansas	162,521	64,652	97,869	39.8	60.2	1,505	1,564	1,442
California	3,331,492	807,608	2,523,885	24.2	75.8	2,725	2,783	2,683
Colorado	364,281	121,223	243,058	33.3	66.7	2,134	2,135	2,132
Connecticut	342,186	134,353	207,832	39.3	60.7	2,309	2,332	2,287
Delaware	67,391	34,096	33,294	50.6	49.4	2,011	2,203	1,827
Florida	1,052,042	233,335	818,706	22.2	77.8	1,968	2,071	1,885
Georgia	571,415	179,014	392,401	31.3	68.7	1,700	1,792	1,626
Hawaii	103,886	77,939	25,947	75.0	25.0	1,955	1,977	1,939
Idaho	80,712	29,876	50,836	37.0	63.0	1,659	1,648	1,672
Illinois	1,104,912	273,912	831,000	24.8	75.2	2,208	2,296	2,129
Indiana	460,705	152,583	308,122	33.1	66.9	1,849	2,083	1,574
Iowa	276,657	107,311	169,347	38.8	61.2	1,922	1,972	1,863
Kansas	229,440	69,301	160,139	30.2	69.8	1,738	1,827	1,641
Kentucky	270,139	106,925	163,214	39.6	60.4	1,641	1,701	1,567
Louisiana	364,266	142,331	221,934	39.1	60.9	1,564	1,607	1,525
Maine	97,141	37,988	59,152	39.1	60.9	1,727	1,751	1,699
Maryland	503,222	172,542	330,680	34.3	65.7	2,295	2,557	2,075
Massachusetts	610,121	202,866	407,255	33.3	66.7	2,173	2,194	2,156
Michigan	1,012,351	306,508	705,844	30.3	69.7	2,404	2,540	2,256
Minnesota	466,085	145,365	320,720	31.2	68.8	2,445	2,741	2,167
Mississippi	193,705	66,082	127,623	34.1	65.9	1,388	1,448	1,326
Missouri	389,481	107,771	281,709	27.7	72.3	1,775	1,884	1,674
Montana	75,843	30,741	45,102	40.5	59.5	1,799	1,924	1,674
Nebraska	159,512	44,935	114,577	28.2	71.8	1,716	1,689	1,741
Nevada	105,033	31,224	73,808	29.7	70.3	2,184	2,032	2,295
New Hampshire	80,165	28,534	51,631	35.6	64.4	1,803	1,807	1,798
New Jersey	857,013	238,224	618,790	27.8	72.2	2,279	2,491	2,088
New Mexico	147,477	61,836	85,641	41.9	58.1	1,720	1,752	1,687
New York	2,645,857	683,392	1,962,466	25.8	74.2	2,430	2,572	2,349
North Carolina	580,654	197,058	383,596	33.9	66.1	1,845	1,997	1,680
North Dakota	63,342	26,744	36,598	42.2	57.8	1,838	2,152	1,519
Ohio	975,955	258,745	717,210	26.5	73.5	2,043	2,248	1,848
Oklahoma	274,785	108,170	166,615	39.4	60.6	1,646	1,705	1,589
Oregon	275,052	90,845	184,207	33.0	67.0	2,042	2,095	1,993
Pennsylvania	916,932	243,066	673,866	26.5	73.5	2,011	2,121	1,908
Rhode Island	96,315	41,960	54,355	43.6	56.4	2,253	2,469	2,071
South Carolina	290,629	119,628	171,002	41.2	58.8	1,646	1,781	1,510
South Dakota	57,319	23,672	33,647	41.3	58.7	1,569	1,624	1,506
Tennessee	383,154	125,355	257,799	32.7	67.3	1,682	1,780	1,599
Texas	1,501,527	396,661	1,104,866	26.4	73.6	1,827	1,824	1,830
Utah	141,936	55,473	86,463	39.1	60.9	1,826	1,782	1,889
Vermont	46,698	22,625	24,073	48.4	51.6	1,814	1,812	1,816
Virginia	569,051	201,103	367,948	35.3	64.7	1,931	2,026	1,832
Washington	490,982	178,456	312,526	36.3	63.7	2,218	2,171	2,257
West Virginia	151,054	54,182	96,873	35.9	64.1	1,614	1,753	1,423
Wisconsin	475,627	139,147	336,480	29.3	70.7	2,135	2,281	1,979
Wyoming	64,698	19,116	45,582	29.5	70.5	1,939	2,106	1,773
Dist. of Columbia	148,284	0	148,284	0.0	100.0	2,706	2,851	2,665

Source: U.S. Bureau of the Census, *Public Employment in 1987*.
Note: Statistics for local governments are estimates subject to sampling variation. Because of rounding, detail may not add to totals.

PUBLIC EMPLOYMENT

Table 7.12
STATE AND LOCAL GOVERNMENT PAYROLLS AND AVERAGE EARNINGS OF FULL-TIME EMPLOYEES, BY STATE: OCTOBER 1988

State or jurisdiction	Amount of payroll (in thousands of dollars)			Percentage of October payroll		Average earnings of full-time state and local government employees (dollars)		
	Total	State government	Local governments	State government	Local governments	All	Education employees	Other
United States	$26,226,936	$7,842,349	$18,384,587	29.9	70.1	$2,187	$2,254	$2,126
Alabama	364,288	144,511	219,778	39.7	60.3	1,764	1,835	1,693
Alaska	130,295	65,893	64,402	50.6	49.4	3,261	3,281	3,248
Arizona	368,997	91,382	277,616	24.8	75.2	2,273	2,368	2,175
Arkansas	172,756	67,658	105,098	39.2	60.8	1,547	1,621	1,461
California	3,543,786	849,585	2,694,201	24.0	76.0	2,778	2,793	2,767
Colorado	384,422	128,021	256,401	33.3	66.7	2,265	2,264	2,266
Connecticut	389,005	159,503	229,502	41.0	59.0	2,575	2,600	2,551
Delaware	73,576	37,461	36,115	50.9	49.1	2,119	2,300	1,951
Florida	1,163,827	266,234	897,593	22.9	77.1	2,046	2,146	1,969
Georgia	615,817	191,229	424,588	31.1	68.9	1,747	1,815	1,690
Hawaii	116,264	88,028	28,236	75.7	24.3	2,086	2,136	2,051
Idaho	86,814	33,148	53,666	38.2	61.8	1,807	1,750	1,876
Illinois	1,162,170	293,443	868,727	25.2	74.8	2,315	2,424	2,219
Indiana	502,173	168,485	333,688	33.6	66.4	1,946	2,227	1,623
Iowa	298,798	116,231	182,567	38.9	61.1	2,038	2,108	1,954
Kansas	260,148	85,420	174,728	32.8	67.2	1,850	1,898	1,796
Kentucky	288,977	116,027	172,950	40.2	59.8	1,714	1,760	1,655
Louisiana	380,092	148,714	231,378	39.1	60.9	1,668	1,694	1,643
Maine	107,388	41,877	65,511	39.0	61.0	1,834	1,865	1,797
Maryland	555,624	189,204	366,420	34.1	65.9	2,435	2,728	2,197
Massachusetts	664,839	222,746	442,093	33.5	66.5	2,344	2,366	2,327
Michigan	1,061,552	316,191	745,361	29.8	70.2	2,525	2,698	2,335
Minnesota	484,826	151,655	333,171	31.3	68.7	2,459	2,638	2,287
Mississippi	211,323	73,475	137,849	34.8	65.2	1,487	1,521	1,452
Missouri	425,043	127,021	298,022	29.9	70.1	1,900	2,029	1,777
Montana	75,893	28,993	46,900	38.2	61.8	1,839	1,979	1,695
Nebraska	174,862	54,203	120,659	31.0	69.0	1,913	1,939	1,890
Nevada	114,729	33,324	81,405	29.0	71.0	2,246	2,078	2,363
New Hampshire	90,824	31,145	59,680	34.3	65.7	1,963	1,992	1,932
New Jersey	951,868	265,430	686,438	27.9	72.1	2,432	2,665	2,221
New Mexico	155,699	67,560	88,139	43.4	56.6	1,747	1,754	1,740
New York	2,882,817	770,040	2,112,777	26.7	73.3	2,614	2,744	2,542
North Carolina	617,732	209,382	408,349	33.9	66.1	1,917	2,076	1,746
North Dakota	67,681	26,891	40,790	39.7	60.3	1,988	2,245	1,682
Ohio	1,014,724	271,685	743,039	26.8	73.2	2,119	2,300	1,947
Oklahoma	281,931	108,763	173,168	38.6	61.4	1,679	1,708	1,649
Oregon	292,523	96,062	196,460	32.8	67.2	2,136	2,205	2,071
Pennsylvania	983,920	257,867	726,053	26.2	73.8	2,144	2,299	2,001
Rhode Island	105,788	45,769	60,019	43.3	56.7	2,366	2,644	2,136
South Carolina	317,714	133,164	184,550	41.9	58.1	1,758	1,924	1,598
South Dakota	56,427	21,522	34,904	38.1	61.9	1,610	1,675	1,534
Tennessee	410,844	123,186	287,659	30.0	70.0	1,732	1,869	1,616
Texas	1,600,012	417,470	1,182,542	26.1	73.9	1,876	1,898	1,850
Utah	146,862	57,844	89,017	39.4	60.6	1,859	1,801	1,941
Vermont	55,378	24,707	30,671	44.6	55.4	1,940	1,941	1,937
Virginia	620,738	221,706	399,032	35.7	64.3	2,053	2,146	1,957
Washington	519,330	185,393	333,937	35.7	64.3	2,288	2,215	2,348
West Virginia	154,213	54,932	99,281	35.6	64.4	1,651	1,806	1,441
Wisconsin	504,281	142,682	361,598	28.3	71.7	2,240	2,420	2,050
Wyoming	65,910	19,486	46,424	29.6	70.4	1,972	2,175	1,778
Dist. of Columbia	151,433	0	151,433	0.0	100.0	2,782	2,901	2,749

Source: U.S. Bureau of the Census, *Public Employment in 1988.*
Note: Statistics for local governments are estimates subject to sampling variation. Because of rounding, detail may not add due to totals.

PUBLIC EMPLOYMENT

Table 7.13
STATE GOVERNMENT EMPLOYMENT (FULL-TIME EQUIVALENT), FOR SELECTED FUNCTIONS, BY STATE: OCTOBER 1987

State	All functions	Education Higher education (a)	Education Other education (b)	Highways	Public welfare	Hospitals	Correction	Police protection	Natural resources	Financial and other governmental administration	Judicial and legal administration
United States	3,491,498	1,149,070	115,107	248,045	190,158	529,139	261,047	81,583	142,556	169,877	96,370
Alabama	70,196	25,689	4,403	3,968	3,980	11,816	3,531	1,067	3,093	2,935	1,946
Alaska	20,074	3,644	3,311	2,843	1,381	414	999	406	1,904	1,300	1,034
Arizona	38,689	15,985	2,412	1,111	2,859	5,054	1,161	1,662	1,897	673	
Arkansas	38,721	11,869	1,815	3,929	2,687	5,232	1,827	760	2,464	1,926	256
California	289,354	100,192	4,200	15,335	3,023	32,199	27,720	10,287	12,697	14,846	2,228
Colorado	51,566	25,834	1,016	3,032	1,312	6,909	2,324	877	1,706	2,434	2,322
Connecticut	58,219	13,807	3,437	4,204	3,984	12,601	4,036	1,713	952	3,578	2,516
Delaware	18,504	6,126	265	1,310	1,717	1,688	1,440	672	442	881	913
Florida	125,983	30,697	2,401	8,553	6,373	14,446	15,876	3,189	6,900	6,619	7,259
Georgia	95,460	28,273	3,218	6,347	6,212	14,041	8,320	1,956	4,784	2,674	882
Hawaii	42,185	6,420	18,121	770	943	2,675	1,357	0	1,337	1,083	1,789
Idaho	18,137	7,859	505	1,648	1,074	1,083	656	361	1,393	980	288
Illinois	130,077	47,203	2,807	8,724	12,214	15,015	10,234	3,700	3,691	9,414	2,820
Indiana	76,082	36,066	4,737	5,613	1,933	10,139	4,586	1,727	2,355	2,684	596
Iowa	51,585	22,100	1,108	2,953	3,463	9,282	1,986	798	2,724	1,867	1,876
Kansas	42,857	16,125	1,071	3,470	2,812	6,403	2,201	757	2,321	2,304	1,790
Kentucky	64,471	18,922	4,204	6,552	5,468	6,504	2,965	1,708	3,383	3,364	3,359
Louisiana	84,990	24,185	3,822	5,524	5,404	20,202	6,217	1,047	4,791	3,303	1,235
Maine	21,085	5,409	1,305	2,720	1,877	2,011	1,014	575	1,484	1,454	402
Maryland	79,754	20,421	2,182	5,234	6,745	8,801	7,849	2,212	2,264	4,920	3,431
Massachusetts	92,668	22,501	1,320	5,081	8,635	19,277	5,690	1,896	2,525	6,207	5,740
Michigan	128,892	53,613	2,090	4,087	13,287	17,812	11,757	3,176	4,058	3,891	2,468
Minnesota	63,806	32,390	1,517	4,973	1,550	7,968	1,896	870	3,090	2,595	809
Mississippi	44,382	13,888	1,367	3,075	2,700	7,323	2,352	979	3,934	1,352	367
Missouri	66,473	15,901	2,121	6,137	5,985	13,973	5,026	1,866	2,777	3,223	2,801
Montana	16,053	5,968	360	1,739	1,083	1,282	726	310	1,327	1,247	136
Nebraska	29,696	11,823	701	2,248	2,653	3,927	1,262	627	1,847	865	846
Nevada	15,275	5,383	221	1,380	672	735	1,356	343	797	1,061	249
New Hampshire	15,727	5,324	296	2,006	1,034	1,365	708	328	554	629	698
New Jersey	99,033	22,089	3,222	8,997	5,607	17,650	7,984	4,059	1,464	5,258	3,570
New Mexico	35,265	13,392	727	2,708	1,814	4,959	2,388	611	1,480	2,126	1,247
New York	274,956	45,353	5,543	14,348	8,006	72,827	27,073	5,616	3,761	17,495	15,850
North Carolina	99,778	35,518	3,288	11,204	1,050	15,092	8,935	2,755	4,774	3,441	4,162
North Dakota	15,229	6,273	326	1,106	413	2,367	297	224	1,216	435	291
Ohio	125,439	54,635	2,412	8,556	1,753	20,185	8,683	2,093	4,231	5,380	1,628
Oklahoma	64,364	22,081	1,804	3,654	6,308	7,737	3,947	1,591	6,291	2,593	1,280
Oregon	48,955	17,023	898	3,956	3,539	5,569	2,082	1,070	3,010	2,817	2,028
Pennsylvania	125,105	29,254	1,960	14,116	10,678	24,091	5,943	5,182	5,491	9,185	2,267
Rhode Island	19,823	5,357	1,101	1,048	1,720	2,707	1,138	246	659	1,267	810
South Carolina	69,837	22,904	2,949	4,613	4,497	11,982	6,027	1,481	2,040	2,949	544
South Dakota	13,159	3,873	505	1,252	1,053	1,476	621	317	785	584	451
Tennessee	70,892	26,188	1,896	5,021	5,204	9,453	5,975	1,145	2,551	3,108	1,118
Texas	198,769	74,809	3,837	15,067	13,113	34,051	17,866	2,954	7,167	7,432	2,446
Utah	32,166	16,008	765	1,597	1,762	4,034	1,126	647	1,124	1,419	724
Vermont	11,775	3,748	265	1,072	776	782	610	464	472	791	419
Virginia	103,849	36,163	2,654	10,665	1,656	19,056	8,987	2,144	3,568	4,194	2,348
Washington	84,452	35,531	1,576	5,470	3,564	7,523	5,215	1,773	3,903	2,779	982
West Virginia	33,657	10,118	1,519	5,681	2,539	3,250	801	849	1,726	1,529	920
Wisconsin	63,580	32,157	1,337	1,859	1,475	7,445	3,879	765	2,712	2,788	1,216
Wyoming	10,454	2,979	190	1,489	571	945	505	229	875	774	340

Source: U.S. Bureau of the Census, *Public Employment in 1987.*
(a) Includes instructional and other personnel.
(b) Includes instructional and other personnel in elementary and secondary schools.

PUBLIC EMPLOYMENT

Table 7.14
STATE GOVERNMENT EMPLOYMENT (FULL-TIME EQUIVALENT), FOR SELECTED FUNCTIONS, BY STATE: OCTOBER 1988

State	All functions	Education Higher education (a)	Education Other education (b)	Highways	Public welfare	Hospitals	Correction	Police protection	Natural resources	Financial and other governmental administration	Judicial and legal administration
United States	3,606,475	1,192,688	116,802	250,968	198,101	536,070	282,393	84,323	143,601	176,630	100,373
Alabama	72,109	26,580	3,964	3,923	4,113	11,955	3,608	1,175	3,435	2,894	2,455
Alaska	21,018	3,490	3,471	2,983	1,490	421	1,200	408	2,061	1,351	1,085
Arizona	43,110	18,157	2,439	1,111	2,861	763	5,696	1,646	1,995	2,030	742
Arkansas	40,585	12,615	2,484	3,712	2,846	4,414	1,921	788	2,517	1,996	273
California	303,353	104,064	4,253	16,244	3,457	34,417	29,271	10,672	15,330	15,345	2,363
Colorado	51,539	25,844	1,000	2,979	1,369	6,721	2,506	918	1,715	2,447	2,398
Connecticut	59,145	13,405	3,521	4,411	3,917	12,994	4,361	1,697	966	4,067	2,593
Delaware	19,434	6,384	260	1,378	1,696	1,660	1,580	725	491	902	1,107
Florida	140,200	33,017	1,239	8,555	7,979	16,583	21,501	3,296	6,698	7,530	7,354
Georgia	99,702	29,306	3,299	6,383	6,358	14,449	9,559	1,971	4,820	2,791	1,053
Hawaii	44,032	6,407	18,989	777	923	2,779	1,556	0	1,369	1,254	1,969
Idaho	17,051	7,080	471	1,424	639	1,042	686	361	1,365	1,259	307
Illinois	130,752	46,800	2,779	8,538	12,473	15,311	10,347	3,964	3,613	9,553	2,850
Indiana	83,680	39,395	4,913	5,621	5,099	10,240	4,705	1,793	2,427	2,775	621
Iowa	55,820	25,867	1,140	2,931	3,467	9,459	2,001	811	2,825	1,772	2,000
Kansas	47,544	16,707	1,101	3,410	2,808	9,884	2,963	923	2,234	2,017	1,843
Kentucky	65,001	20,744	4,160	6,255	5,455	4,949	3,109	1,695	3,865	3,413	3,352
Louisiana	80,570	25,074	3,628	5,323	4,618	17,454	5,541	935	4,463	3,810	1,135
Maine	21,921	5,751	1,383	2,755	1,991	1,944	1,011	597	1,506	1,493	415
Maryland	83,908	21,052	2,159	5,204	6,890	8,856	8,898	2,331	2,264	5,197	4,064
Massachusetts	96,313	23,116	1,049	4,853	8,459	20,141	4,921	2,202	2,744	6,308	5,791
Michigan	128,012	54,251	2,000	4,033	12,650	17,223	12,050	3,116	3,770	3,843	2,479
Minnesota	61,786	29,651	1,635	5,016	1,750	7,927	1,948	869	3,260	2,701	848
Mississippi	44,393	13,353	1,526	3,237	2,962	7,500	2,345	927	4,064	1,411	339
Missouri	70,922	20,655	2,119	6,243	5,862	13,506	5,444	1,871	2,073	2,944	2,852
Montana	16,036	5,624	377	1,799	1,080	1,315	748	316	1,369	1,323	141
Nebraska	28,711	10,559	663	2,426	2,694	4,094	1,551	649	1,740	897	576
Nevada	16,231	5,383	255	1,375	866	908	1,503	348	841	1,067	268
New Hampshire	16,021	5,256	313	2,067	1,211	1,326	727	330	467	665	707
New Jersey	104,460	24,271	3,610	9,101	5,814	18,059	8,670	4,347	1,492	5,228	3,969
New Mexico	37,432	13,994	757	2,598	1,779	4,635	2,418	614	1,761	2,262	1,400
New York	282,241	46,131	5,602	14,581	8,028	72,625	30,837	5,799	3,650	18,410	16,490
North Carolina	102,975	37,658	3,397	11,176	1,023	15,434	9,661	2,829	4,480	2,943	4,267
North Dakota	14,964	6,369	349	1,092	483	2,035	310	218	1,181	455	293
Ohio	129,877	58,665	2,402	8,622	1,952	19,579	9,181	2,093	4,109	5,591	1,766
Oklahoma	63,261	22,958	1,818	3,745	6,664	8,189	4,120	1,619	2,722	2,925	1,375
Oregon	50,265	17,459	1,039	3,445	3,957	5,667	2,191	1,076	3,301	2,849	1,970
Pennsylvania	125,343	29,494	2,046	13,998	10,226	23,736	6,407	5,332	5,803	9,383	2,156
Rhode Island	20,103	5,487	1,058	1,103	1,722	1,854	1,196	243	560	1,280	830
South Carolina	73,242	23,460	3,025	4,968	4,611	12,215	6,743	1,596	2,776	3,137	543
South Dakota	12,473	3,733	527	1,245	1,053	1,487	519	313	906	671	458
Tennessee	71,902	26,535	1,879	4,999	5,362	9,846	5,914	1,234	2,570	3,281	1,174
Texas	209,570	77,767	4,117	15,553	14,251	37,267	19,224	2,962	7,351	7,974	2,671
Utah	33,059	16,317	785	1,732	1,792	4,107	1,355	628	1,137	1,477	642
Vermont	12,201	3,949	340	1,102	1,125	773	577	495	635	792	430
Virginia	108,668	38,984	2,569	11,827	1,896	19,300	9,394	2,227	3,634	4,573	2,350
Washington	85,815	36,680	1,780	5,667	3,899	7,389	5,324	1,544	4,070	2,826	1,088
West Virginia	33,700	10,244	1,676	5,689	2,459	3,236	757	812	1,630	1,452	916
Wisconsin	65,158	33,593	1,260	2,128	1,439	7,472	3,820	769	2,813	3,297	1,260
Wyoming	10,867	3,353	176	1,631	603	930	518	239	733	769	345

Source: U.S. Bureau of the Census, *Public Employment in 1988.*
(a) Includes instructional and other personnel.
(b) Includes instructional and other personnel in elementary and secondary schools.

PUBLIC EMPLOYMENT

Table 7.15
STATE GOVERNMENT PAYROLLS
FOR SELECTED FUNCTIONS, BY STATE: OCTOBER 1987
(In thousands of dollars)

		Education		Selected functions							
State	All functions	Higher education (a)	Other education (b)	Highways	Public welfare	Hospitals	Correction	Police protection	Natural resources	Financial and other governmental administration	Judicial and legal administration
United States	$7,297,764	$2,508,501	$249,786	$505,201	$352,598	$979,695	$536,822	$195,262	$283,317	$349,042	$255,287
Alabama	132,235	54,522	8,685	6,807	6,903	18,386	6,254	2,126	5,420	5,357	3,928
Alaska	64,103	11,321	9,934	10,122	3,499	1,070	3,137	1,669	6,550	3,966	3,408
Arizona	106,955	63,519	4,353	1,588	4,923	1,459	9,163	2,768	4,998	3,534	1,852
Arkansas	64,652	22,254	2,993	6,924	4,124	6,997	2,692	1,447	3,806	3,167	752
California	807,608	275,146	29,136	46,844	7,408	87,046	81,625	26,806	31,723	35,454	8,720
Colorado	121,223	60,452	2,149	7,674	3,067	15,052	5,785	2,264	4,469	5,562	5,706
Connecticut	134,353	29,612	7,331	8,490	9,322	29,024	10,469	5,353	2,222	8,116	6,735
Delaware	34,096	12,156	628	2,333	2,569	2,411	2,740	1,618	853	1,548	1,774
Florida	233,335	67,308	4,121	14,209	8,473	22,912	25,844	6,754	11,603	13,214	18,000
Georgia	179,014	62,673	6,117	11,337	11,072	22,441	13,078	4,189	8,556	4,555	2,674
Hawaii	77,939	14,859	31,424	1,516	1,648	4,509	2,430	0	2,693	2,153	3,601
Idaho	29,876	11,330	994	2,842	1,702	1,489	1,477	712	2,370	1,867	860
Illinois	273,912	97,316	6,144	20,220	23,675	29,305	20,172	10,230	7,607	17,456	10,156
Indiana	152,583	83,938	6,331	9,346	2,831	17,531	7,820	3,792	4,779	4,718	1,578
Iowa	107,311	45,828	2,409	5,925	7,041	17,908	4,573	2,261	5,283	3,928	4,260
Kansas	69,301	25,473	1,889	5,855	4,093	8,759	3,862	1,494	4,181	3,885	3,184
Kentucky	106,925	33,113	8,130	10,516	8,550	8,774	4,728	3,324	5,169	5,770	5,630
Louisiana	142,331	44,335	6,840	8,656	8,668	28,066	9,899	1,980	9,506	5,925	3,298
Maine	37,988	10,208	2,408	4,523	3,122	3,405	1,978	1,266	2,817	2,549	720
Maryland	172,542	51,179	4,949	10,350	12,549	16,272	16,193	5,382	4,459	10,306	7,163
Massachusetts	202,866	50,926	3,538	11,983	17,935	35,788	12,648	5,286	5,728	14,364	12,961
Michigan	306,508	120,489	5,422	11,088	31,555	42,816	28,866	8,742	9,484	9,951	7,458
Minnesota	145,365	72,028	3,808	12,123	3,367	16,334	4,530	2,228	7,295	6,235	3,054
Mississippi	66,082	23,658	2,332	4,169	3,464	8,222	2,961	1,566	5,942	2,333	1,053
Missouri	107,771	27,920	3,288	11,319	8,881	18,064	7,632	4,220	4,397	5,196	5,784
Montana	30,741	12,258	676	3,526	1,793	1,989	1,212	644	2,575	2,211	409
Nebraska	44,935	16,653	1,271	3,645	3,852	6,100	2,004	1,187	2,302	1,418	1,621
Nevada	31,224	8,974	524	3,105	1,469	1,657	3,033	813	1,706	2,233	792
New Hampshire	28,534	9,925	558	3,503	1,830	2,413	1,449	732	812	1,200	1,326
New Jersey	238,224	60,363	8,223	22,644	11,865	34,178	18,701	10,350	3,428	11,764	11,615
New Mexico	61,836	24,585	1,358	4,785	2,988	7,255	3,993	1,172	2,986	3,671	2,534
New York	683,392	113,500	13,389	31,555	20,336	162,748	66,266	15,546	8,972	38,378	53,207
North Carolina	197,058	76,355	6,905	18,829	2,131	26,339	15,570	6,458	8,862	7,164	8,824
North Dakota	26,744	11,841	590	1,915	717	3,293	496	422	1,926	822	733
Ohio	258,745	119,601	5,320	17,572	3,535	35,588	17,709	4,988	8,113	10,948	4,029
Oklahoma	108,170	37,789	3,275	5,810	10,560	11,594	6,264	2,795	9,980	4,732	3,289
Oregon	90,845	31,332	1,837	6,726	6,211	10,062	4,237	3,062	4,876	5,046	4,250
Pennsylvania	243,066	57,398	4,072	25,790	20,506	42,230	11,421	12,310	10,757	18,604	7,219
Rhode Island	41,960	11,297	1,847	1,943	3,658	5,642	2,900	838	1,212	2,677	1,986
South Carolina	119,628	43,849	5,386	5,970	6,723	17,448	8,947	2,777	3,342	5,182	1,467
South Dakota	23,672	7,271	829	2,474	1,951	1,764	1,118	586	1,724	1,193	801
Tennessee	125,355	49,878	3,570	8,241	8,502	14,986	9,374	2,355	4,157	5,461	2,856
Texas	396,661	155,237	7,294	37,797	21,887	60,636	33,774	5,982	14,640	15,688	6,443
Utah	55,473	25,875	1,473	3,283	3,216	5,785	2,156	1,319	2,102	2,687	1,640
Vermont	22,625	8,001	511	2,108	1,218	1,268	1,018	1,087	786	1,400	938
Virginia	201,103	82,281	5,358	16,837	3,096	29,457	14,556	4,714	7,112	7,960	5,663
Washington	178,456	74,886	4,214	13,919	6,775	13,903	10,422	3,922	9,262	6,779	3,088
West Virginia	54,182	19,708	2,471	8,769	3,391	3,708	1,049	1,503	2,965	2,313	1,635
Wisconsin	139,147	72,631	3,101	4,641	3,052	14,272	7,803	1,742	5,151	6,958	3,830
Wyoming	19,116	5,452	385	3,054	896	1,343	795	483	1,661	1,446	783

Source: U.S. Bureau of the Census, *Public Employment in 1987.*
(a) Includes instructional and other personnel.
(b) Includes instructional and other personnel in elementary and secondary schools.

PUBLIC EMPLOYMENT

Table 7.16
STATE GOVERNMENT PAYROLLS
FOR SELECTED FUNCTIONS, BY STATE: OCTOBER 1988
(In thousands of dollars)

State	All functions	Education Higher education (a)	Education Other education (b)	Highways	Public welfare	Hospitals	Correction	Police protection	Natural resources	Financial and other governmental administration	Judicial and legal administration
United States	$7,842,349	$2,677,805	$250,837	$526,891	$376,193	$1,069,974	$592,244	$213,610	$294,418	$383,568	$280,944
Alabama	144,511	59,344	8,825	7,391	7,674	19,708	7,381	2,311	6,014	5,688	5,335
Alaska	65,893	11,479	10,001	9,898	3,729	1,095	3,780	1,668	6,591	4,105	3,550
Arizona	91,382	41,985	4,447	1,588	4,933	1,583	10,894	4,465	4,027	3,851	2,289
Arkansas	67,658	23,587	4,039	6,360	4,324	5,907	2,825	1,460	4,038	3,268	840
California	849,585	299,438	12,449	49,298	8,111	92,798	82,070	31,067	37,612	37,778	9,363
Colorado	128,021	65,549	2,340	7,522	3,206	14,864	6,263	2,496	4,565	5,716	6,293
Connecticut	159,503	35,088	8,439	12,738	9,424	33,364	12,128	5,238	2,549	11,707	8,910
Delaware	37,461	12,862	682	2,462	2,631	2,587	3,312	1,884	894	1,681	2,255
Florida	266,234	73,793	3,037	14,220	11,524	28,075	34,953	7,084	11,276	15,202	19,007
Georgia	191,229	66,810	6,748	11,856	11,960	23,896	12,836	4,487	8,974	5,649	2,968
Hawaii	88,028	16,417	35,943	1,645	1,704	5,056	2,701	0	2,969	2,567	4,852
Idaho	33,148	11,924	1,001	3,308	1,561	2,652	1,373	712	2,516	2,133	936
Illinois	293,443	103,284	6,342	21,886	25,579	31,646	22,882	10,365	7,974	18,863	11,303
Indiana	168,485	90,300	7,442	9,403	7,623	18,581	8,504	4,273	4,960	4,933	1,928
Iowa	116,231	50,956	2,591	6,032	7,876	18,204	4,714	2,439	5,537	4,184	4,775
Kansas	85,420	27,932	2,004	6,551	4,080	18,516	5,476	1,832	4,451	3,702	3,761
Kentucky	116,027	40,094	8,190	10,337	9,026	8,348	5,141	3,609	5,714	6,011	5,917
Louisiana	148,714	47,336	6,670	8,774	7,973	30,569	8,761	1,831	8,829	6,932	2,585
Maine	41,877	11,730	2,682	4,680	3,755	3,451	2,027	1,289	2,984	2,801	770
Maryland	189,204	55,779	5,163	11,298	13,609	17,346	17,410	5,604	5,016	11,292	8,688
Massachusetts	222,746	55,888	3,056	13,270	20,238	39,836	12,920	7,617	6,273	15,063	15,139
Michigan	316,191	122,334	5,581	11,356	31,758	44,044	31,137	9,227	9,195	10,475	9,077
Minnesota	151,655	74,473	4,188	12,562	3,906	16,615	4,757	2,354	7,656	6,764	3,238
Mississippi	73,475	25,232	2,644	4,718	4,018	11,153	2,988	1,566	6,421	2,851	1,178
Missouri	127,021	41,750	3,288	11,755	8,575	20,852	8,398	4,284	3,914	4,919	5,941
Montana	28,993	10,040	711	3,650	1,784	2,009	1,263	656	2,592	2,315	423
Nebraska	54,203	21,740	1,233	4,183	4,238	7,155	2,551	1,309	2,882	1,644	2,091
Nevada	33,324	8,974	628	3,135	1,795	1,840	3,316	826	1,796	2,339	857
New Hampshire	31,145	11,059	653	3,688	2,199	2,405	1,473	734	864	1,244	1,318
New Jersey	265,430	69,821	10,333	24,420	13,127	35,223	21,689	11,693	3,786	12,563	13,195
New Mexico	67,560	25,290	1,434	4,874	3,125	7,718	4,323	1,180	3,418	4,095	2,943
New York	770,040	120,441	16,441	37,132	16,742	189,713	79,850	18,435	11,416	46,677	54,999
North Carolina	209,382	83,340	7,531	18,872	2,223	27,040	17,617	6,695	8,955	6,652	9,675
North Dakota	26,891	12,503	642	1,844	831	2,878	503	423	1,869	850	704
Ohio	271,685	122,471	5,665	18,779	4,243	37,069	19,679	4,988	8,391	12,083	4,623
Oklahoma	108,763	38,593	3,499	6,184	11,642	13,011	6,907	3,007	3,742	5,475	3,652
Oregon	96,062	33,103	1,964	6,521	6,560	10,427	4,431	3,051	5,483	5,611	4,595
Pennsylvania	257,867	64,102	4,367	27,059	20,144	43,388	12,778	13,512	11,939	19,468	7,626
Rhode Island	45,769	12,425	2,246	2,234	3,788	4,194	3,405	930	1,401	2,864	2,010
South Carolina	133,164	48,564	5,775	7,087	7,531	18,252	10,374	3,127	4,867	5,749	1,576
South Dakota	21,522	7,598	821	2,165	1,487	1,902	808	550	1,469	1,251	893
Tennessee	123,186	53,123	3,295	6,449	7,363	14,228	10,418	2,209	3,738	5,251	3,014
Texas	417,470	167,968	8,099	29,615	24,098	67,754	33,966	6,161	15,097	17,304	7,238
Utah	57,844	26,310	1,547	3,661	3,441	6,121	2,629	1,236	2,185	2,839	1,551
Vermont	24,707	8,672	672	2,190	2,043	1,262	1,123	1,178	1,313	1,467	1,013
Virginia	221,706	89,311	5,322	21,410	3,593	31,750	16,545	5,288	7,463	9,234	5,852
Washington	185,393	76,537	3,933	14,158	8,004	14,487	11,034	3,690	9,388	7,118	3,624
West Virginia	54,932	20,776	2,832	8,562	3,332	3,777	1,013	1,301	2,773	2,236	1,632
Wisconsin	142,682	73,885	3,034	4,931	3,117	14,313	8,091	1,772	5,190	7,690	4,123
Wyoming	19,486	5,799	363	3,179	945	1,310	826	496	1,456	1,412	821

Source: U.S. Bureau of the Census, *Public Employment in 1988.*
(a) Includes instructional and other personnel.
(b) Includes instructional and otehr personnel in elementary and secondary schools.

FINANCES OF STATE-ADMINISTERED PUBLIC EMPLOYEE-RETIREMENT SYSTEMS

By Henry S. Wulf

Introduction and Summary

At the end of fiscal year 1987-88 there were 203 state-administered public employee retirement systems. These 203 state government agencies serve two main social functions. First, they provide primary protection for a large segment of public employees for retirement purposes. This protection is applicable not only for state employees, but also for a large number of local government employees as well. Second, they have accumulated vast assets that are available for investment purposes, making them important participants in the financial markets.

A total of 12.2 million public employees were members of all state and local government employee retirement systems in fiscal 1987-88. The 203 state-administered systems, however, covered 10.6 million, or 87 percent, of this total. Thus, nearly 6 out of every 7 public employee retirement system members belong to state-administered systems.

The assets of the state-administered systems amounted in 1988 to approximately $438 billion. This was 80 percent of the more than $547 billion in total assets held by all public systems including local governments. The single largest portion of these state retirement system assets was invested in corporate stocks ($137 billion), followed by federal government securities ($118 billion) and corporate bonds ($96 billion). The remainder of their portfolios included a variety of other investments such as mortgages, savings deposits and real estate holdings.

Membership

State-administered systems provided retirement coverage to 10.6 million members. This included two classes of employees, active members, consisting of current employees of state and local governments and inactive members, mostly former employees who had acquired a vested right to receive retirement benefits, or employees on military or extended leave without pay who still retained retirement credits in the system. The active members are by far the largest portion with 9.2 million members, but the nearly 1.4 million inactive members still constitute about 13 percent of the total.

System coverage

Coverage describes the types of employees eligible for membership in retirement systems. These divide broadly into two categories. General-coverage systems include employees involved in a wide variety of government activities. Limited-coverage systems are those that apply to specific job categories (teachers, police officers, fire fighters) or functions (education, highways or hospitals).

About one-third of the state-administered systems are general in their coverage, but these general systems provide retirement coverage for more than 60 percent of all members. There are 36 limited-coverage systems for public safety activities, 34 in education and the remainder in a variety of other specific operations such as judges, assessors and legislatures. The number of systems, however, is not indicative of the magnitude of membership since the education systems account for about one-third of the membership, the mis-

---

Henry S. Wulf is Chief, Finance Branch, Governments Division, U.S. Bureau of the Census.

cellaneous systems about 6 percent and the public safety less than 2 percent.

System size

State-administered retirement systems tend to be sizable in almost all respects. There are 79 systems, for example, with memberships exceeding 25,000 and only 28 with fewer than 100 members. By way of contrast, although there are about 2300 locally-administered retirement systems, only 10 had memberships exceeding 25,000 and more than 1,500 had memberships of less than 100.

The 79 very large state systems with 25,000 or more members provided retirement coverage for 10.1 million members, or more than 95 percent of the total in state-administered systems. The concentration is even greater than indicated by the previous numbers, however, because just 8 state-administered systems accounted for nearly one-third of all membership and assets. These were, in order of size (membership in parentheses): the New York State Employees (660,000), California Public Employees (595,000), Florida Retirement System (492,000), Texas Teachers Retirement Fund (487,000), New Jersey Public Employees (376,000), California State Teachers (325,000), Ohio Public Employees (315,000) and the Michigan Public School Retirement (278,000).

A recent compilation of assets for the large state systems shows just how significant they are when compared with the assets of private retirement systems. Of the top 25 public and private retirement systems, for example, 14 were state-administered systems that controlled assets ranking in size with retirement systems of such important industrial giants as AT&T, General Motors, General Electric, IBM, Ford Motor and DuPont.

Receipts

There are three sources of revenues for retirement systems: contributions from employees, contributions from governments and earnings on investments. State-administered retirement system revenue was $80 billion in fiscal 1987-88. More than one-half ($43 billion), came from earnings on investments, followed by contributions from state governments of $17 billion, from local governments of $11 billion and from employees of $10 billion.

The $43 billion in investment earnings was nearly 54 percent of total revenue. This percentage is considerably above the average of 44 percent for fiscal years 1980 through 1986. The historic high of 56 percent was reached in fiscal year 1986-87. In fiscal year 1976-77, investment earnings for these state-administered retirement systems brought in just 32 percent of the total receipts.

State government contributions increased the most of the three sources over the previous year. The almost $17 billion contributed by state governments to their systems was an increase of $4.6 billion (up nearly 40 percent), raising state contributions to about 21 percent of the total. In 1986-87 this stood at 18 percent. The impetus for this significant jump is not clear, but might be related to concerns about assuring the full funding of future retirement liabilities.

Benefit payments and other outlays

Expenditures for retirement systems fall into three categories: benefits paid, withdrawals and a miscellaneous category covering direct administrative costs and related incidental payments. The total of all three categories for state-administered retirement systems was $24.8 billion in fiscal 1987-88, up from $22.7 billion the previous year.

State-administered retirement systems paid out $22.4 billion in recurring periodic benefit payments in fiscal 1987-88. This was an increase of almost 10 percent over the previous year's total of $20.5 billion. There were also withdrawals of $1.8 billion. The remainder of the payments, $650 million, went for administrative and miscellaneous expenses.

In the past six years, benefit payments have been growing at an average annual rate of 14 percent, almost doubling 1982 total payments of $11.4 billion. There are a variety of factors that influence these payments, such as inflation, the composition and number of beneficiaries and the consolidation of smaller local government retirement systems into state systems.

Benefit payments in relation to other retirement programs

State retirement system benefits can be supplemented by a variety of retirement programs. Chief among these additional programs is federal Social Security. Some states also offer deferred compensation and investment programs. The existence of these supplementary programs can influence the amount of benefits paid directly by the state.

The precise number of state retirement system members who are covered under Social Security is not known. Where information is available, however, Social Security appears to be an important element in the overall provision of retirement benefits. In Indiana, for example, about 88 percent of the state retirement system membership is covered by Social Security.

Important changes have occurred, especially in the last decade, in the eligibility for Social Security among state government employees. Before 1951, no public employees were eligible to participate. Federal legislation at that time allowed state governments the option of participating, including employees in state-administered retirement systems. A number of states chose to participate, but retained the right to withdraw. In 1984, new federal amendments required states who were still covered by Social Security to remain in the system. A further legal change that became effective in 1986 was mandatory coverage for the health insurance portion of Social Security (Medicaid) for all newly hired state employees. State governments were given the option with this last change of extending Medicaid coverage to all employees.

Beneficiaries and monthly benefit payments

In 1988, 2.9 million beneficiaries received periodic benefit payments from state retirement systems. About nine out of every 10 of these beneficiaries (2.6 million) were retired on account of age or length of service. The remainder of the beneficiaries were divided between survivors of deceased former members (187,000) and those retired on account of disabilities (151,000). The relative size of these different beneficiary groups for the state retirement systems have remained fairly constant over the years. In 1982, for example, 87 percent of the beneficiaries were retired on account of age or length of service, there were 154,000 survivors of deceased former members and 149,000 persons retired on account of disability.

The average monthly payment for all beneficiaries was $602, up from $544 twelve months earlier. In 1982 this monthly payment was $410. Persons retired for service received the highest monthly amount ($623), followed by those retired on disability ($601) and survivors ($327).

The highest ranking states in average monthly benefit payments were Alaska ($1,201), Hawaii ($839), Connecticut ($836) and Maryland ($829). There were four states that had average payments below $300: Kansas ($298), South Dakota ($295), Iowa ($262) and Nebraska ($254).

Interpreting state averages requires considerable caution because of the multiple factors that influence these payments. Among the determinants are general wage levels for the area, the number and type of employees receiving benefits from the retirement systems and the availability of supplemental retirement programs, especially Social Security. Complicating the matter further is the fact that a number of states have instituted tiered benefit programs where new employees have different service qualifications and payment schedules than older employees.

Receipts compared with payments

Receipts for state retirement systems exceeded benefit payments by $58 billion. This is necessary because of future obligations to employees and their beneficiaries. A relative measure of the ability to meet such liabilities is a calculation of this difference as a percent of all cash and security holdings at the end of the fiscal year. The difference amounted to 14.1 percent of all cash and security holdings in fiscal 1987-88. Since 1982 this percentage has averaged 13.0 percent, with a low of 12.5 and a high of 14.1 percent.

Investments and assets

State retirement systems controlled $438 billion in cash and investment holdings at the end of fiscal 1987-88. The single largest portion of the holdings remained in corporate stocks for the third year in a row, with about one-third of all the assets. Corporate bonds were the next largest category at 22 percent, followed by U.S. Treasury securities (21 percent), cash and short-term investments (7 percent), and federal agency securities (6 percent). The remainder of the assets — less than ten percent of the total — was held in a wide variety of financial vehicles. This includes investments as diverse as bank deposits, repurchase agreements, guaranteed investment accounts, mutual fund shares, international securities, partnerships, real estate holdings, venture capital, leveraged buy outs and junk bonds.

The change in the composition of the assets in fiscal 1987-88 has been toward the three major categories of corporate stocks, corporate bonds and U.S. Treasury securities. Together these accounted for nearly 4 out of every 5 dollars in retirement system investments. This is the highest concentration in the recent past. By comparison, the three categories amounted to 73 percent of the total in 1987, 74 percent in 1986, 72 percent in 1985, 67 percent in 1984, 65 percent in 1983, 71 percent in 1982 and 76 percent in 1977.

Corporate bonds, now 22 percent of the investment total, used to be the favorite investment vehicle for state retirement systems by a large margin. As recently as 1982, for example, corporate bonds accounted for 36 percent of all assets, the next closest group being corporate stocks with 23 percent. Just five years prior to that, in 1977, corporate bonds constituted almost half of all the state retirement system assets.

Current issues

There are a number of issues under discussion in the public agenda that have ramifications for state retirement systems. Some of the more salient ones are:

Economic Development. Questions have been raised again about the possibility of using state retirement assets to stimulate economic development. The Government Finance Officers Association and the National Conference of State Legislatures, for example, recently sponsored a conference on this controversial subject.

Investment Losses. Some problems in the financial markets have made retirement system managers wary. Coupled with investment losses in West Virginia, only a portion of which affected the state retirement systems, the situation has reportedly made system managers increasingly cautious.

Involvement in Corporate Management. The two largest state retirement systems — the New York State and Local and the California Public Employees — have expressed publicly their interest in the selection of the successor to the General Motors chief executive. This is a departure for public retirement funds, which traditionally have limited themselves to purchase or divestment of investments, and have not undertaken significant involvement in corporate management decisions.

Mandatory Medicaid. There have been several efforts to expand mandatory Medicaid coverage to all state and local government employees. As indicated above, it is mandatory now only for employees hired since 1986. This has implications for the mix of benefits now being offered by the state governments, an important part of which is provided by the retirement system.

State Funding. With increasing pressure on state finances in general, it has been suggested that states cut back their contributions to retirement systems. Both long term funding of retirement system liabilities and the continued availability of funds in capital markets would be affected by such actions. There are, moreover, issues that will continue to be important for state retirement systems, for example, full funding for future liabilities, the proper use of pooled investments, changes in accounting procedures and the risks and re-

RETIREMENT

wards of investments such as venture capital. The importance of the state retirement systems in providing retirement protection for public sector employees and as a source of capital ensures that all these issues will receive full public discussion.

RETIREMENT

Table 7.17
NUMBER, MEMBERSHIP AND MONTHLY BENEFIT PAYMENTS OF STATE ADMINISTERED EMPLOYEE-RETIREMENT SYSTEMS: 1984-85 THROUGH 1986-87

Item	1986-87	1985-86	1984-85
Number of systems	201	198	203
Membership, last month of fiscal year:			
Total number	10,236,352	10,378,470	10,263,598
Active members	9,214,371	9,049,425	8,817,896
Other	1,021,981	1,329,045	1,445,702
Percent distribution	100.0	100.0	100.0
Active members	90.0	87.2	85.9
Other	10.0	12.8	14.1
Beneficiaries receiving periodic benefits:			
Total number	2,952,229	2,760,304	2,661,215
Persons retired on account of age or length of service	2,667,900	2,437,191	2,355,031
Persons retired on account of disability	126,242	146,315	140,299
Survivors of deceased former members	148,087	176,798	165,885
Percent distribution	100.0	100.0	100.0
Persons retired on account of age or length of service	90.4	88.3	88.5
Persons retired on account of disability	4.3	5.3	5.3
Survivors of deceased former members	5.0	6.4	6.2
Recurrent benefit payments for last month of fiscal year:			
Total amount (in thousands)	$1,604,885	$1,392,523	$1,263,427
To persons retired on account of age or length of service	$1,495,041	$1,267,546	$1,149,860
To persons retired on account of disability	$68,657	$77,068	$69,236
To survivors of deceased former members	$41,187	$47,908	$44,331
Percent distribution	100.0	100.0	100.0
For persons retired on account of age or length of service	93.2	91.0	91.0
For persons retired on account of disability	4.3	5.5	5.5
For survivors of deceased former members	2.6	3.4	3.5
Average monthly payment for beneficiaries:			
Average for all beneficiaries (in dollars)	$544	$504	$475
For persons retired on account of age or length of service	$558	$520	$488
For persons retired on account of disability	$464	$527	$493
For survivors of deceased former members	$326	$271	$267

Source: U.S. Bureau of the Census, *Employee Retirement Systems of State and Local Governments* (Vol. 4, No. 6).
Note: Because of rounding, detail may not add to totals.

RETIREMENT

Table 7.18
NATIONAL SUMMARY OF FINANCES OF STATE-ADMINISTERED EMPLOYEE RETIREMENT SYSTEMS: SELECTED YEARS, 1976-1987

	Amounts (in millions of dollars)						Percentage distribution			
	1986-87	1985-86	1984-85	1983-84	1982-83	1981-82	1976-77	1986-87	1985-86	1984-85	1976-77
Receipts	$ 77,706	$ 68,982	$ 55,791	$ 49,152	$ 44,847	$ 37,933	$19,287	100.0	100.0	100.0	100.0
Employee Contributions	9,428	8,939	7,901	7,278	7,196	6,672	4,223	12.1	13.0	14.2	21.9
Government Contributions	23,258	21,693	20,751	18,738	17,197	15,770	8,898	29.9	31.4	37.2	46.1
From State Government	13,199	12,162	11,976	10,458	9,611	8,898	4,847	17.0	17.6	21.5	25.1
From Local Government	10,059	9,531	8,944	8,280	7,585	6,872	4,051	12.9	13.8	16.0	21.0
Earnings on Investments	45,021	38,350	27,139	22,856	20,455	15,490	6,167	57.9	55.6	48.6	32.0
Payments	22,734	20,472	18,602	16,266	15,237	13,133	7,060	100.0	100.0	100.0	100.0
Benefits	20,537	18,187	16,183	14,578	12,757	11,430	6,048	90.3	88.8	87.0	85.7
Withdrawls	1,652	1,691	2,047	1,533	1,447	1,704	882	7.3	8.3	11.0	12.5
Other	545	595	372	155	400	335	130	2.4	2.9	2.0	1.8
Amount of cash FY	407,953	346,867	296,951	258,355	229,690	193,237	95,145	100.0	100.0	100.0	100.0
Cash and Deposits	13,960	10,651	12,267	8,381	6,063	2,427	818	3.4	3.1	4.1	0.9
Cash and Demand Deposits	2,048							0.5			
Time or Savings Deposits	11,913							2.9			
Securities	377,750	325,358	278,626	241,673	213,471	187,398	94,015	92.6	93.8	93.8	98.8
Governmental	112,660	91,483	86,589	67,432	55,826	44,167	10,096	27.6	26.4	29.2	10.6
Federal Government	112,570	91,137	86,208	66,749	55,066	43,319	9,500	27.6	26.3	29.0	10.0
U.S. Treasury	88,944	68,876	61,334	45,188	33,982	24,445	4,729	21.8	19.9	20.7	5.0
Federal Agency	23,626	22,262	24,864	21,561	21,083	18,874	4,770	5.8	6.4	8.4	5.0
State and Local Governments	90	346	381	683	760	848	596	.0	0.1	0.1	0.6
Nongovernmental	265,090	233,875	192,037	174,241	157,645	143,231	83,919	65.0	67.4	64.7	88.2
Corporate Bonds	76,741	77,138	67,208	60,646	60,563	68,948	45,364	18.8	22.2	22.6	47.7
Corporate Stocks	133,288	110,721	84,331	66,201	54,296	44,025	21,753	32.7	31.9	28.4	22.9
Mortgages	27,117	29,572	23,902	22,301	23,312	17,742	10,228	6.6	8.5	8.0	10.7
Funds held in trust	7,335							1.8			
Commercial and Finance	13,001							3.2			
Other Securities	7,609							1.9			
Other Investments	16,243	16,444	16,596	25,093	9,474	12,516	6,574		4.7	5.6	6.9
Real Property	5,523	10,858	6,058	8,301	10,156	3,412	312	1.4	3.1	2.0	0.3
Miscellaneous Investments	10,720	5,858	3,400	2,658	2,106	1,311	232	2.6	1.4	1.1	0.2
			2,658	5,643	8,050	2,101	40		1.7	0.9	0.0

Source: U.S. Bureau of the the Census, *Employee Retirement Systems of State and Local Governments* (Volume 4, Number 6).
Key:
. . . — Not available

RETIREMENT

Table 7.19
MEMBERSHIP AND BENEFIT OPERATIONS OF STATE-ADMINISTERED EMPLOYEE RETIREMENT SYSTEMS: LAST MONTH OF FISCAL YEAR 1986-87

State or jurisdiction	Membership, last month of the fiscal year	Benefit Operations, last month of fiscal year							
		Beneficiaries receiving periodic benefit payments				Periodic benefit payment for the month (in thousands of dollars)			
		Total (a)	Persons retired on account of age or length of service	Persons retired on account of disability	Survivors of deceased former members (no. of payees)	Total (a)	Persons retired on account of age or length of service	Persons retired on account of disability	To survivors of deceased former members
United States	10,236,352	2,952,229	2,677,900	126,242	148,087	1,604,885	1,495,041	68,657	41,187
Alabama	178,314	42,364	36,930	2,599	2,835	18,522	17,127	868	528
Alaska	48,807	8,069	7,868	83	118	9,332	9,059	165	107
Arizona	148,933	29,884	29,220	356	308	14,785	14,321	237	227
Arkansas	79,826	20,428	16,662	1,624	2,142	8,196	7,376	535	286
California	979,678	347,311	290,303	30,639	26,369	240,719	214,723	22,743	3,253
Colorado	111,668	37,227	31,617	3,679	1,931	22,562	21,796	0	766
Connecticut	106,580	34,369	31,077	1,977	1,315	27,283	25,388	1,215	680
Delaware	31,727	9,297	6,672	1,118	1,507	3,983	2,871	473	639
Florida	453,943	99,282	83,403	6,201	9,678	47,902	42,452	2,096	3,353
Georgia	254,056	47,775	47,372	244	159	29,637	29,546	53	39
Hawaii	55,166	17,026	15,938	1,033	55	9,384	9,021	345	18
Idaho	56,505	15,561	13,847	303	1,411	5,792	5,274	188	330
Illinois	394,949	133,337	113,436	4,770	15,131	68,368	61,219	2,995	4,153
Indiana	236,355	57,936	51,827	2,481	3,628	21,983	20,567	498	919
Iowa	128,874	58,924	58,814	37	73	10,971	10,971	45	25
Kansas	104,691	34,819	34,819	0	0	9,481	9,481	0	0
Kentucky	157,603	40,634	39,034	972	628	19,601	18,774	680	147
Louisiana	206,622	62,301	50,821	4,859	6,621	42,092	36,216	2,960	2,916
Maine	69,153	21,105	19,701	599	805	11,401	10,720	509	172
Maryland	162,754	44,147	44,147	0	0	36,385	36,385	0	0
Massachusetts	180,722	58,460	58,299	50	111	40,871	40,800	36	35
Michigan	374,863	101,125	98,021	2,183	921	66,347	65,287	707	353
Minnesota	239,363	56,202	49,862	1,636	4,704	26,391	24,171	697	1,524
Mississippi	160,762	33,301	28,846	1,598	2,857	12,884	11,328	600	956
Missouri	137,194	37,907	33,234	2,227	2,446	16,603	15,198	701	704
Montana	58,637	15,879	14,077	1,192	610	7,496	6,632	579	285
Nebraska	35,648	6,139	5,858	66	215	1,228	1,150	23	55
Nevada	68,986	9,217	7,978	502	737	5,977	5,527	259	192
New Hampshire	18,403	7,963	7,962	0	1	2,669	2,666	0	4
New Jersey	397,888	104,170	104,170	0	0	66,790	66,790	0	0
New Mexico	121,708	19,434	17,502	1,211	721	10,116	9,558	376	183
New York	765,953	305,514	301,405	1,509	2,600	162,145	160,309	914	923
North Carolina	348,477	77,735	77,687	48	0	39,775	39,775	0	0
North Dakota	24,297	5,605	5,120	89	396	1,872	1,756	23	93
Ohio	664,697	217,407	178,130	16,521	22,756	120,704	101,196	12,001	7,506
Oklahoma	119,952	43,431	40,657	880	1,894	26,735	25,268	553	914
Oregon	129,815	51,418	48,378	3,040	0	20,956	19,795	1,161	0
Pennsylvania	349,362	159,157	143,134	7,351	8,672	83,003	77,272	3,153	2,577
Rhode Island	34,452	11,530	11,364	0	166	6,923	6,833	0	89
South Carolina	247,484	37,283	31,148	3,408	2,727	18,144	15,766	1,459	919

MEMBERSHIP AND BENEFIT OPERATIONS—Continued

Benefit Operations, last month of fiscal year

State or jurisdiction	Membership, last month of fiscal year	Beneficiaries receiving periodic benefit payments				Periodic benefit payment for the month (in thousands of dollars)			
		Total (a)	Persons retired on account of age or length of service	Persons retired on account of disability	Survivors of deceased former members (no. of payees)	Total (a)	Persons retired on account of age or length of service	Persons retired on account of disability	To survivors of deceased former members
South Dakota	30,704	9,017	7,793	190	1,034	2,374	2,086	69	219
Tennessee	154,298	48,169	48,169	0	0	15,482	15,482	0	0
Texas	677,556	134,331	115,030	6,543	12,758	76,086	69,738	3,083	3,265
Utah	70,518	15,408	14,643	765	0	6,408	6,068	340	0
Vermont	21,370	4,948	4,948	0	0	1,975	1,975	0	0
Virginia	222,385	50,358	43,095	6,549	714	23,139	20,122	2,807	211
Washington	194,862	69,521	69,521	0	0	42,401	42,401	0	0
West Virginia	103,968	31,771	26,363	1,721	3,687	12,229	10,760	608	861
Wisconsin	269,076	60,296	54,835	3,281	2,180	25,906	23,792	1,840	274
Wyoming	46,148	7,737	7,163	108	466	2,804	2,252	64	488
Dist. of Columbia	11,792	9,006	6,685	595	1,726	15,311	12,748	805	1,759

Source: U.S. Bureau of the Census, *Employee Retirement Systems of State and Local Governments* (Volume 4, Number 6).
(a) Detail may not add to totals because of rounding.

RETIREMENT

Table 7.20
FINANCES OF STATE-ADMINISTERED EMPLOYEE RETIREMENT SYSTEMS, BY STATE: 1986-87
(In thousands of dollars)

State or jurisdiction	Receipts during fiscal year					Payments during fiscal year			
	Total	Employee contributions	Government contributions — From states	From local governments	Earnings on investments	Total	Benefits	Withdrawls	Other
United States	77,706,305	9,427,514	13,198,606	10,058,969	45,021,216	22,734,035	20,536,924	1,651,872	545,239
Alabama	1,007,387	156,363	251,341	992	598,691	258,063	237,606	16,443	4,014
Alaska	629,799	86,038	94,584	71,185	377,992	141,776	118,526	14,763	8,487
Arizona	1,137,459	161,921	53,913	111,211	810,414	226,291	175,801	42,000	8,490
Arkansas	603,646	40,896	105,617	19,028	438,105	113,195	98,728	10,936	3,531
California	11,137,385	1,662,309	1,577,607	1,747,593	6,149,876	3,265,593	2,963,397	217,101	85,095
Colorado	1,490,893	202,798	127,048	229,999	931,048	302,496	257,827	33,166	11,503
Connecticut	991,768	110,346	533,341	17,052	331,029	338,803	327,917	10,735	151
Delaware	280,959	15,465	77,442	0	188,052	63,305	54,652	0	8,653
Florida	2,765,393	10,736	306,738	882,993	1,564,926	557,515	528,948	3,261	25,306
Georgia	1,713,306	215,888	448,107	113,560	935,751	411,652	360,949	34,568	16,135
Hawaii	578,692	53,834	145,986	47,050	331,822	182,003	170,233	5,335	6,435
Idaho	278,676	43,833	26,150	50,793	157,900	85,576	68,433	12,510	4,633
Illinois	2,862,577	511,336	456,823	156,604	1,737,814	925,035	820,972	70,248	33,815
Indiana	830,973	115,113	219,213	90,640	406,007	297,301	268,058	22,562	6,681
Iowa	576,495	77,985	122,464	2,026	374,020	165,823	131,530	24,786	9,507
Kansas	565,202	89,782	83,120	70,157	322,143	151,459	132,061	16,850	2,548
Kentucky	974,994	178,225	227,228	42,060	527,481	275,213	248,229	21,581	5,403
Louisiana	1,343,451	243,578	360,189	23,703	715,981	633,667	571,525	54,288	7,854
Maine	369,118	51,546	129,936	22,945	164,691	150,497	136,352	7,240	6,905
Maryland	1,422,227	106,023	695,411	37,258	583,535	441,588	436,616	4,972	0
Massachusetts	865,414	241,274	437,895	0	186,245	548,478	492,697	50,826	4,955
Michigan	3,009,323	117,137	560,859	223,944	2,107,383	1,018,495	998,390	6,022	14,083
Minnesota	1,542,508	200,804	195,815	98,982	1,046,907	379,862	331,019	34,729	14,114
Mississippi	639,754	111,776	67,997	102,259	357,722	205,640	164,083	33,613	7,944
Missouri	1,132,885	139,105	148,198	150,030	695,552	240,346	204,413	24,178	11,755
Montana	255,726	58,648	21,033	46,430	129,615	104,769	89,199	14,003	1,567
Nebraska	127,503	30,785	6,331	27,475	62,912	22,425	16,674	4,130	1,621
Nevada	487,314	14,032	37,899	126,875	308,508	98,039	86,126	6,288	5,625
New Hampshire	176,943	33,663	6,383	12,049	124,848	46,560	31,859	9,496	5,205
New Jersey	2,479,824	397,294	628,380	384,310	1,069,840	884,841	800,337	74,708	9,796
New Mexico	561,590	110,730	67,995	77,179	305,686	156,766	123,972	27,347	5,447
New York	7,346,954	222,259	586,025	1,492,172	5,046,498	2,120,813	1,975,691	87,111	58,011
North Carolina	2,139,459	342,658	433,595	223,470	1,139,736	535,872	476,422	55,850	3,600
North Dakota	121,576	22,938	10,293	16,106	72,239	29,177	19,118	6,631	3,428
Ohio	6,397,487	920,490	274,752	1,267,905	3,934,340	1,948,953	1,803,629	114,998	30,326
Oklahoma	845,999	121,240	281,940	28,583	414,236	339,806	313,909	20,235	5,662
Oregon	855,538	152,357	98,713	174,806	429,662	268,766	237,541	27,577	3,648
Pennsylvania	3,819,792	394,252	877,885	462,439	2,085,216	1,336,818	1,267,916	36,494	32,408
Rhode Island	290,671	57,070	66,698	40,499	126,404	107,216	101,328	4,923	965
South Carolina	928,330	172,207	111,425	128,001	516,697	254,702	221,134	29,702	3,866
South Dakota	189,077	27,861	11,235	15,940	134,041	36,100	26,918	6,350	2,832
Tennessee	1,176,872	78,700	342,341	29,168	726,663	255,016	229,301	21,751	3,964
Texas	4,030,127	811,638	912,418	86,221	2,219,850	1,160,656	965,972	174,490	20,194
Utah	387,888	80,813	23,108	65,236	218,731	102,469	76,142	22,477	3,850
Vermont	84,770	2,289	33,002	1,122	48,357	27,577	23,696	482	3,399
Virginia	1,700,924	52,758	236,524	376,248	1,035,394	326,762	277,673	28,625	20,464
Washington	1,469,768	276,241	419,631	130,076	643,820	551,994	509,003	38,278	4,713
West Virginia	289,022	81,577	35,241	17,373	154,831	166,651	151,503	13,598	1,550
Wisconsin	2,605,964	12,521	192,799	478,622	1,922,022	427,264	380,652	43,786	2,826
Wyoming	186,903	8,382	29,938	38,600	109,983	44,351	32,247	9,829	2,275
Dist. of Columbia	341,159	28,465	52,070	173,465	87,159	187,541	182,559	1,416	3,566

Source: U.S. Bureau of the Census, *Employee Retirement Systems of State and Local Governments* (Volume 4, Number 6).
Note: Detail may not add to totals because of rounding.

RETIREMENT

FINANCES OF STATE-ADMINISTERED EMPLOYEE RETIREMENT SYSTEMS, BY STATE: 1986-87—Continued
(In thousands of dollars)

			Cash and security holdings at end of fiscal year				
				Governmental securities			
				Federal securities			
State or jurisdiction	Total	Cash and deposits	Total	U.S. treasury	Federal agency	State and local	Nongovernmental securities
United States	407,953,034	13,960,445	112,569,702	88,944,096	23,625,606	90,034	265,089,946
Alabama	5,462,307	7,949	1,116,533	146,480	970,053	0	4,335,663
Alaska	3,061,367	17,985	1,105,221	1,105,221	0	0	1,867,129
Arizona	5,622,627	44,795	1,925,400	1,612,247	313,153	0	3,647,711
Arkansas	2,936,091	306,716	1,043,679	923,300	120,379	0	1,582,795
California	62,962,618	1,175,527	6,009,959	5,518,266	491,693	10,261	53,816,472
Colorado	6,734,594	778,982	1,710,808	1,002,525	708,283	25,089	3,872,628
Connecticut	4,365,381	273,319	561,707	539,046	22,661	0	3,521,798
Delaware	1,221,712	44,359	183,084	177,859	5,225	0	414,138
Florida	11,979,640	35,672	3,815,005	1,853,209	1,961,796	0	8,128,238
Georgia	8,285,755	174,965	3,773,581	3,752,465	21,116	4,800	4,307,588
Hawaii	2,672,949	37,558	915,385	148,553	766,832	0	1,720,006
Idaho	1,137,599	57,860	202,869	179,427	23,442	0	798,592
Illinois	13,542,920	358,740	2,656,582	2,029,242	627,340	7,793	9,960,361
Indiana	3,799,179	174,338	2,066,665	1,494,816	571,849	10,778	1,544,285
Iowa	3,495,967	242,131	732,925	577,107	155,818	0	2,370,761
Kansas	2,847,188	321,228	594,932	580,917	14,015	0	1,800,130
Kentucky	4,939,130	686,717	1,782,443	1,181,701	600,742	8	2,294,052
Louisiana	6,633,846	578,863	3,416,342	2,685,991	730,351	0	2,616,237
Maine	1,190,518	142,229	241,152	159,947	81,205	0	805,461
Maryland	6,139,061	274,679	1,408,418	824,860	583,558	0	2,919,104
Massachusetts	4,470,172	33,700	34,489	33,822	667	0	2,440,333
Michigan	14,966,059	35,167	2,405,665	2,405,665	0	806	12,524,404
Minnesota	8,209,810	563,586	1,723,876	1,672,300	51,576	0	5,915,192
Mississippi	3,579,241	959,300	1,563,844	1,069,551	494,293	0	1,056,097
Missouri	7,087,121	2,868	1,276,571	395,616	880,955	3,244	5,733,905
Montana	1,188,398	64,146	131,018	108,504	22,514	1,172	980,632
Nebraska	677,477	6,166	227,070	140,818	86,252	0	340,684
Nevada	2,165,136	39,634	745,182	592,464	152,718	0	921,020
New Hampshire	922,874	18,517	232,070	169,535	62,535	0	631,764
New Jersey	15,271,791	224,931	6,018,131	5,854,530	163,601	37	8,815,222
New Mexico	2,742,212	250,002	1,413,172	976,327	436,845	0	1,075,901
New York	48,044,521	1,278,014	13,225,386	11,463,708	1,761,678	0	32,440,102
North Carolina	11,503,226	281,261	4,312,947	4,312,947	0	0	6,740,571
North Dakota	564,330	27,784	266,337	36,890	229,447	0	270,209
Ohio	30,284,401	122,536	13,866,615	7,858,407	6,008,208	3,510	14,587,810
Oklahoma	3,756,344	324,890	2,045,513	1,695,229	350,284	0	1,385,753
Oregon	6,961,259	363,078	969,887	921,775	48,112	0	5,292,417
Pennsylvania	17,205,254	1,828,207	4,758,506	4,471,773	286,733	0	8,109,632
Rhode Island	1,366,931	327,407	489,107	488,507	600	886	549,231
South Carolina	7,343,858	3,345	5,576,311	4,457,586	1,118,725	1,303	1,762,899
South Dakota	972,326	1,530	236,658	121,368	115,290	0	708,971
Tennessee	5,591,057	5,170	1,495,018	1,492,185	2,833	0	3,941,826
Texas	20,406,477	274,826	6,750,393	5,596,754	1,153,639	10,000	13,323,924
Utah	2,491,786	347,407	680,046	660,471	19,575	0	1,258,455
Vermont	459,293	96,300	39,063	39,063	0	0	323,930
Virginia	6,446,739	179,400	1,695,142	1,695,142	0	984	4,374,365
Washington	10,083,574	405,263	1,669,405	1,286,339	383,066	0	6,858,338
West Virginia	1,337,899	118,497	909,061	670,773	238,288	0	310,341
Wisconsin	11,718,424	33,315	1,996,889	1,634,544	362,345	9,363	9,551,700
Wyoming	1,104,595	9,786	553,640	128,324	425,316	0	541,169
Dist. of Columbia	1,060,512	127,656	179,821	162,776	17,045	0	753,035

RETIREMENT

Table 7.21
COMPARATIVE STATISTICS FOR STATE-ADMINISTERED PUBLIC EMPLOYEE RETIREMENT SYSTEMS: 1986-87

State	Percent of receipts paid by			Annual benefit payments as a percentage of		Average benefit payments (a)	Investment earnings as a percentage of cash and security holdings	Percentage distribution of cash and security holdings			
	Employee contribution	State government	Local government	Annual receipts	Cash and security holdings			Cash and deposits	Federal	Governmental securities State and local	Nongovernmental securities
United States	12.1	17.0	12.9	26.4	5.0	$544	11.0	3.6	29.3	0.0	67.0
Alabama	15.5	24.9	0.1	23.6	4.3	437	11.0	0.1	20.4	0.0	79.4
Alaska	13.7	15.0	11.3	18.8	3.9	1,156	12.3	0.6	36.1	0.0	61.0
Arizona	14.2	4.7	9.8	15.5	3.1	495	14.4	0.8	34.2	0.0	64.9
Arkansas	6.8	17.5	3.2	16.4	3.4	401	14.9	10.4	35.5	0.0	53.9
California	14.9	14.2	15.7	26.6	4.7	693	9.8	1.9	9.5	0.0	85.5
Colorado	13.6	8.5	15.4	17.3	3.8	606	13.8	11.6	25.4	0.4	57.5
Connecticut	11.1	53.8	1.7	33.1	7.5	794	7.6	6.3	12.9	0.0	80.7
Delaware	5.5	27.6	0.0	26.2	4.5	428	15.4	3.6	15.0	0.0	33.9
Florida	0.4	11.1	31.9	19.1	4.4	482	13.1	0.3	31.8	0.0	67.9
Georgia	12.6	26.2	6.6	21.1	4.4	620	11.3	2.1	45.5	0.1	52.0
Hawaii	9.3	25.2	8.1	29.4	6.4	551	12.4	1.4	34.2	0.0	64.3
Idaho	15.7	9.4	18.2	24.6	6.0	372	13.9	5.1	17.8	0.0	70.2
Illinois	17.9	16.0	5.5	28.7	6.1	513	12.8	2.6	19.6	0.1	73.5
Indiana	13.9	26.4	10.9	32.3	7.1	379	10.7	4.6	54.4	0.3	40.6
Iowa	13.5	21.2	0.4	22.8	3.8	187	10.7	6.9	21.0	0.0	67.8
Kansas	15.9	14.7	12.4	23.4	4.6	272	11.3	11.3	20.9	0.0	63.2
Kentucky	18.3	23.3	4.3	25.5	5.0	482	10.7	13.9	36.1	0.0	46.4
Louisiana	18.1	26.8	1.8	42.5	8.6	676	10.8	8.7	51.5	0.0	39.4
Maine	14.0	35.2	6.2	36.9	11.5	540	13.8	11.9	20.3	0.0	67.7
Maryland	7.5	48.9	2.6	30.7	7.1	824	9.5	4.5	22.9	0.0	47.5
Massachusetts	27.9	50.6	0.0	56.9	11.0	699	4.2	0.8	0.8	0.0	54.6
Michigan	3.9	18.6	7.4	33.2	6.7	656	14.1	0.2	16.1	0.0	83.7
Minnesota	13.0	12.7	6.4	21.5	4.0	470	12.8	6.9	21.0	0.0	72.1
Mississippi	17.5	10.6	16.0	25.6	4.6	387	10.0	26.8	43.7	0.0	29.5
Missouri	12.3	13.1	13.2	18.0	2.9	438	9.8	0.0	18.0	0.0	80.9
Montana	22.9	8.2	18.2	34.9	7.5	472	10.9	5.4	11.0	0.1	82.5
Nebraska	24.1	5.0	21.5	13.1	2.5	200	9.3	0.9	33.5	0.0	50.3
Nevada	2.9	7.8	26.0	17.7	4.0	648	14.2	1.8	34.4	0.0	42.5
New Hampshire	19.0	3.6	6.8	18.0	3.5	335	13.5	2.0	25.1	0.0	68.5
New Jersey	16.0	25.3	15.5	32.3	5.2	641	7.0	1.5	39.4	0.0	57.7
New Mexico	19.7	12.1	13.7	22.1	4.5	521	11.1	9.1	51.5	0.0	39.2
New York	3.0	8.0	20.3	26.9	4.1	531	10.5	2.7	27.5	0.0	67.5
North Carolina	16.0	20.3	10.4	22.3	4.1	512	9.9	2.4	37.5	0.0	58.6
North Dakota	18.9	8.5	13.2	15.7	3.4	334	4.2	4.9	47.2	0.0	47.9
Ohio	14.4	4.3	19.8	28.2	6.0	555	13.0	4.8	45.8	0.0	48.2
Oklahoma	14.3	33.3	3.4	37.1	8.4	616	11.0	8.6	54.5	0.0	36.9
Oregon	17.8	11.5	20.4	26.8	3.4	408	6.2	5.2	13.9	0.0	76.0
Pennsylvania	10.3	23.0	12.1	33.2	7.4	522	12.1	10.6	27.7	0.0	47.1
Rhode Island	19.6	22.9	13.9	34.9	7.4	600	9.2	23.9	35.8	0.1	40.2
South Carolina	18.6	12.0	13.8	23.8	3.0	487	7.0	0.0	75.9	0.0	24.0

RETIREMENT

COMPARATIVE STATISTICS: 1986-87—Continued

State	Percent of receipts paid by			Annual benefit payments as a percentage of		Average benefit payments (a)	Investment earnings as a percentage of cash and security holdings	Percentage distribution of cash and security holdings			
	Employee contribution	State government	Local government	Annual receipts	Cash and security holdings			Cash and deposits	Federal	Governmental securities State and local	Nongovernmental securities
South Dakota	14.7	5.9	8.4	14.2	2.8	263	13.8	0.2	24.3	0.0	72.9
Tennessee	6.7	29.1	2.5	19.5	4.1	321	13.0	0.1	26.7	0.0	70.5
Texas	20.1	22.6	2.1	24.0	4.7	566	10.9	1.3	33.1	0.0	65.3
Utah	20.8	6.0	16.8	19.6	3.1	416	8.8	13.9	27.3	0.0	50.5
Vermont	2.7	38.9	1.3	28.0	5.2	399	10.5	21.0	8.5	0.0	70.5
Virginia	3.1	13.9	22.1	16.3	4.3	459	16.1	2.8	26.3	0.0	67.9
Washington	18.8	28.6	8.9	34.6	5.0	610	6.4	4.0	16.6	0.0	68.0
West Virginia	28.2	12.2	6.0	52.4	11.3	385	11.6	8.9	67.9	0.0	23.2
Wisconsin	0.5	7.4	18.4	14.6	3.2	430	16.4	0.3	17.0	0.1	81.5
Wyoming	4.5	16.0	20.7	17.3	2.9	362	10.0	0.9	50.1	0.0	49.0

Source: Bureau of the Census, U.S. Department of Commerce, *Government Finances: Employee Retirement Systems of State and Local Governments.*
Note: Data for *The Book of the States* 1988-89 based on total state and local administered systems.

(a) Average benefit payment for last month of fiscal year.

STATE RECORDS

Table 7.22
FUNCTIONS AND RESPONSIBILITIES OF STATE LIBRARY AGENCIES

State	Library services to state governments							Statewide library services development														
	Documents	Information and reference service	Legislative reference	Law library	Genealogy and state history	Archives	Liaison with institutional libraries	Coordination of academic libraries	Coordination of public libraries	Coordination of school libraries	Coordination of institutional libraries	Research	Coordination of library systems	Consulting services	Interlibrary loan, reference and bibliographic service	Statistical gathering and analysis	Library legislation review	Interstate library compacts and other cooperative efforts	Specialized resource centers	Direct service to the public	Annual reports	Public relations	Continuing education
Alabama	★	★	...	...	...	...	★	...	★	...	...	★	★	★	★	★	★	★	★	†	★	★	★
Alaska	★	★	†	†	★	...	★	†	★	†	★	†	★	★	★	★	†	★	★	†	★	★	★
Arizona	★	★	★	★	★	★	★	★	★	★	★	★	★	★	★	★	★	★	★	★	★	†	★
Arkansas	★	★	...	...	...	...	★	†	★	★	★	★	★	★	★	★	★	★	★	...	★	†	★
California	★	★	★	★	★	...	★	†	★	...	†	†	★	★	★	★	★	†	★	†	★	†	†
Colorado	★	...	...	...	...	...	★	†	★	★	★	★	†	★	★	★	★	★	†	...	★	†	†
Connecticut	★	★	★	★	★	†	★	...	★	...	★	★	★	★	★	★	★	★	★	★	★	★	★
Delaware	†	★	†	...	†	...	★	★	★	★	†	★	★	★	★	†	★	★	†	★	★	★	★
Florida	★	★	†	...	★	★	★	†	...	...	★	★	★	★	★	★	★	★	★	†	★	†	★
Georgia	†	★	...	...	...	...	★	...	★	...	★	†	★	★	★	★	★	★	...	★	★	★	★
Hawaii	★	★	...	...	★	...	★	...	★	†	†	†	†	★	★	†	★	†	...	...	★	†	†
Idaho	†	★	†	...	†	†	★	...	★	...	...	★	★	★	★	★	★	★	★	†	★	★	†
Illinois	★	★	†	...	...	...	★	†	★	†	†	★	★	★	★	†	★	★	★	†	★	★	★
Indiana	★	★	†	...	★	...	★	†	★	†	†	★	★	★	★	★	★	★	†	†	★	★	†
Iowa	★	★	†	★	†	...	★	...	★	†	†	★	★	★	★	★	★	★	★	...	★	★	†
Kansas	★	★	★	...	...	...	★	†	†	★	†	★	★	★	★	★	★	★	★	...	★	†	†
Kentucky	†	★	†	...	†	★	★	†	★	...	†	†	★	★	★	★	★	★	†	†	★	★	†
Louisiana	†	★	†	...	...	★	★	†	★	†	†	★	★	★	★	★	★	★	†	†	★	★	†
Maine	★	★	†	...	★	...	★	†	★	★	†	★	★	★	★	★	★	★	★	†	★	★	†
Maryland	†	†	...	...	...	...	★	†	★	★	★	†	★	★	★	★	†	★	†	★	★	★	★
Massachusetts	...	†	...	...	...	...	★	...	★	...	★	★	★	★	†	†	★	★	★	...	★	†	†
Michigan	★	★	†	★	★	★	★	...	★	★	★	★	★	★	★	★	†	†	★	†	★	†	★
Minnesota	★	†	...	...	...	...	†	†	★	†	†	†	★	★	★	★	†	★	★	★	★	†	★
Mississippi	★	†	†	...	...	...	★	...	★	†	★	†	★	★	★	★	★	★	†	★	★	†	†
Missouri	†	†	†	...	...	...	★	†	★	...	★	★	★	★	★	†	★	★	★	★	★	★	★
Montana	†	★	...	...	...	...	★	†	★	†	†	★	★	★	★	★	†	★	★	...	★	★	★
Nebraska	★	★	†	...	...	...	★	★	★	†	★	★	★	★	★	★	★	★	★	†	★	★	†
Nevada	★	★	†	...	†	★	★	...	★	...	★	★	★	★	★	★	★	★	†	†	★	★	★
New Hampshire	★	★	★	★	★	†	★	...	★	...	★	★	★	★	★	★	★	★	...	...	★	†	★
New Jersey	★	★	†	★	★	...	★	†	★	★	†	★	★	★	★	★	★	★	†	†	★	†	★
New Mexico	★	★	†	...	†	...	★	†	★	★	★	★	★	★	★	★	★	†	★	†	★	★	★
New York	★	★	†	★	★	†	★	★	★	★	★	†	★	★	★	★	★	★	★	★	★	†	★
North Carolina	★	★	†	†	†	...	★	†	★	†	†	★	★	★	★	★	★	★	†	†	★	†	★
North Dakota	★	★	†	...	†	...	★	★	★	★	★	★	★	★	★	★	★	★	†	★	★	★	★
Ohio	★	★	...	...	†	...	★	†	★	†	†	★	★	★	★	★	★	★	†	★	†	†	†
Oklahoma	★	★	★	★	†	...	★	†	★	†	★	★	★	★	★	★	★	★	†	...	★	★	★
Oregon	★	★	★	...	...	...	★	...	★	†	★	†	★	★	★	★	★	★	★	†	★	★	★
Pennsylvania	★	★	†	★	†	...	★	★	★	★	★	★	★	★	★	★	★	★	...	★	★	★	★
Rhode Island	...	†	...	...	...	...	★	★	★	★	★	★	★	★	★	★	★	★	★	★	★	†	†
South Carolina	†	★	★	...	†	...	★	...	★	†	★	†	★	★	★	★	★	★	...	★	★	†	★
South Dakota	★	★	...	...	†	...	★	†	†	★	†	★	★	★	★	★	★	★	★	★	★	★	★
Tennessee	★	†	†	...	★	★	†	...	★	...	★	†	★	★	†	†	★	†	★	...	★	†	†
Texas	★	★	...	★	★	★	★	†	★	†	★	†	★	★	★	†	★	★	★	...	★	†	★
Utah	★	★	...	...	...	...	★	★	★	†	...	★	★	★	★	†	†	★	†	★	★	†	★
Vermont	★	★	†	★	†	...	★	...	★	...	★	†	★	★	★	★	★	★	†	★	★	★	†
Virginia	★	†	†	...	★	★	★	...	★	...	★	★	★	★	★	†	★	†	†	†	†	★	†
Washington	★	★	★	...	†	★	★	†	★	...	★	★	★	★	★	★	★	★	†	★	★	★	★
West Virginia	†	★	†	...	...	...	★	★	★	†	★	★	★	★	★	★	★	★	...	★	★	†	★
Wisconsin	†	★	†	...	...	...	★	†	★	★	★	★	★	★	★	★	★	★	...	★	★	†	★
Wyoming	★	★	...	...	†	...	★	★	†	★	†	...	★	★	★	...	★	...	★	...	†	★	†

Note: For additional information, see *Standards for Library Functions at the State Level*, 3rd edition. (American Library Association, 1985).

Key:
★ — Primary
† — Shared
... — None

STATE RECORDS

FUNCTIONS AND RESPONSIBILITIES—Continued

State	Long-range planning	Determination of size and scope of collections in the state	Mobilization of resources	Subject and reference centers	Resources—books	Resources—other printed materials	Resources—multimedia	Resources—materials for the blind and handicapped	Coordination of resources	Little-used materials	Planning of information networks	Provision of centralized facilities	Exchange of information and materials	Interstate cooperation	Administration of federal aid	Administration of state aid	Financing of library systems and networks
		Statewide development of library resources									Statewide development of information networks				Financing library programs		
Alabama	★	★	★	★	★	★	★	★	★	...	★	†	★	★	★	★	★
Alaska	★	†	†	★	†	†	★	★	★	★	†	★	†	★	★	★	†
Arizona	★	★	★	★	★	★	★	★	★	...	★	★	★	★	★	★	★
Arkansas	★	★	★	★	★	★	★	★	★	★	★	★	★	★	★	★	★
California	★	†	†	†	†	†	†	★	†	†	†	†	†	★	★	★	★
Colorado	★	†	†	†	†	†	†	★	†	†	†	†	†	†	★	★	★
Connecticut	★	★	★	★	★	★	★	★	★	★	★	★	★	★	★	★	★
Delaware	★	†	★	†	★	★	†	★	†	★	★	†	★	★	★	★	★
Florida	★	†	†	★	†	†	†	†	†	★	★	★	★	★	★	★	★
Georgia	★	★	★	★	★	★	★	★	★	★	★	★	★	★	★	★	★
Hawaii	†	†	†	†	†	†	†	★	†	★	†	†	†	†	†	†	†
Idaho	★	†	★	†	★	★	★	★	†	★	†	†	★	★	★	...	†
Illinois	†	†	†	†	†	†	†	†	†	...	†	†	†	★	★	★	★
Indiana	★	...	†	†	†	†	†	†	†	†	†	†	†	†	★	★	★
Iowa	★	★	★	★	★	★	★	†	★	★	★	★	★	★	★	★	★
Kansas	★	★	†	†	†	†	†	†	★	†	★	★	★	★	★	★	★
Kentucky	★	†	†	†	†	†	†	★	★	†	★	†	★	★	★	★	★
Louisiana	†	†	†	†	†	†	†	★	†	†	★	†	★	★	★	★	★
Maine	★	★	★	★	★	★	★	★	★	†	★	★	†	★	★	★	★
Maryland	★	...	†	†	★	...	...	★	★	...	★	†	★	★	★	★	★
Massachusetts	†	...	†	...	†	†	†	†	†	†	†	†	†	★	★	★	★
Michigan	★	†	†	†	†	†	†	★	†	†	★	...	†	★	★	★	★
Minnesota	★	†	★	†	†	†	†	★	★	★	★	†	†	★	★	★	†
Mississippi	★	★	★	★	★	★	†	†	★	★	★	★	†	†	★	★	†
Missouri	★	†	★	★	★	★	†	†	★	★	★	†	†	†	★	★	†
Montana	★	★	★	★	★	★	★	†	†	★	★	†	★	★	★	★	★
Nebraska	★	...	★	★	★	★	★	★	...	★	★	...	†	★	★	★	★
Nevada	★	†	†	†	†	†	★	★	★	★	★	★	★	★	★	★	★
New Hampshire	★	★	★	★	★	★	★	★	★	★	★	★	★	★	★	★	★
New Jersey	★	†	★	†	†	†	★	†	†	†	★	★	★	★	★	★	★
New Mexico	★	†	★	...	†	†	†	★	†	★	★	★	★	★	†	★	★
New York	★	†	†	†	★	★	★	†	★	...	★	★	★	†	★	★	★
North Carolina	★	†	★	★	★	★	†	★	★	★	★	★	★	★	★	★	★
North Dakota	★	...	★	★	★	★	★	★	★	★	★	★	★	★	★	★	★
Ohio	★	†	†	†	†	†	†	†	★	†	★	...	★	★	★	★	★
Oklahoma	★	†	★	★	★	★	★	★	★	†	★	★	★	★	★	★	★
Oregon	★	★	★	...	★	★	†	★	†	★	★	...	†	★	★	★	★
Pennsylvania	★	†	★	†	★	†	★	★	†	★	★	★	★	...	★	★	★
Rhode Island	★	†	†	†	†	†	†	★	†	...	★	†	★	★	★	★	★
South Carolina	★	†	...	★	†	†	†	★	★	...	★	★	★	★	★	★	...
South Dakota	★	†	★	†	†	★	★	★	★	★	★	†	†	†	★	...	★
Tennessee	★	...	†	†	†	†	★	†	★	†	★	†	†	★	★	★	★
Texas	★	†	†	†	†	★	†	★	†	★	★	†	★	★	★	★	★
Utah	★	†	†	†	†	†	†	★	★	...	★	†	★	†	★	★	★
Vermont	★	†	†	†	†	†	†	★	★	†	†	†	★	★	†	★	†
Virginia	★	†	†	†	†	†	†	†	†	†	★	★	★	★	★	★	†
Washington	★	...	†	†	...	...	...	†	...	†	★	★	★	★	★	★	★
West Virginia	★	...	...	†	★	...	★	★	★	★	★	★	★	★	★	†	†
Wisconsin	★	†	†	†	†	†	†	★	†	★	†	★	†	★	★	★	★
Wyoming	★	†	†	†	†	†	†	★	★	†	†	†	★	★	★	...	...

Key:
★ — Primary
† — Shared
... — None

CHAPTER EIGHT

SELECTED STATE ACTIVITIES, ISSUES AND SERVICES

INNOVATORS IN STATE GOVERNMENTS: THEIR ORGANIZATIONAL AND PROFESSIONAL ENVIRONMENT

By Keon S. Chi and Dennis O. Grady

The Innovations Transfer Program of The Council of State Governments since 1975 has recognized innovative state policies and programs that have the potential to be adapted for use in other states.

The Council annually solicits information on innovative activities across the states. Programs selected by staff are reviewed by regional panels of state officials who chose the programs reported on in the Council's *Innovations* publication series.

At each stage in the *Innovations* selection process, the following questions are used to determine whether a program or policy entry is eligible:
- Is it a state policy or program?
- Does it represent a new and creative approach to a significant problem affecting the state?
- Has the program or policy been implemented? Has it been operational for at least one year?
- Is the program or policy relatively unknown across the states?
- Has the program or policy been effective in achieving its stated goals and purposes?
- Does the program or policy address an issue or problem area that is regional or national in scope? Would it be applicable to many states?
- Could the program or policy be easily transferred to other states?

Over the past 15 years, the Council has published more than 100 *Innovations* reports, copies of which have been distributed to state policy-makers and administrators. Many of the programs submitted during the annual review are highlighted in the "Targeted Innovations" section of *State Government News*, the Council's monthly news magazine, and all are entered for reference on the Council's online *Integrated State Information System*.

Since 1975, the program has received between 300 and 500 submissions each year. With the exception of a few years, when the solicitation was targeted to specific policy areas, the requests for submissions have been sent to officials in virtually every functional or policy area in state government. Yet, the submission statistics show that officials in certain policy and program areas have been more responsive than those in other areas. More submissions have come from executive branch officials than state legislators or their staff. Some states have submitted more nominations than others.

Yet, little is known about the *innovators* in state government — the individuals who originate the ideas or who learn about them from other sources and adapt them to their own states. Out of the 1989 *Innovations* semifinalist programs, according to those submitting the entries, nearly 84 percent of these programs originated within the submitting state, while the initial ideas for about 16 percent of the programs were replicated or transferred from other states. But who are the innovators and how do they originate their ideas or obtain information on innovations from other states or other sources?

For national organizations, which are dedicated to the improvement and enhancement

---

Keon S. Chi is Senior Policy Analyst with The Council of State Governments, Strategic Planning and Innovation Group, and Dennis O. Grady is Professor at Appalachian State University, Department of Political Science/Criminal Justice.

of state decision-making, and for practitioners and scholars who are interested in the diffusion or transfer of innovative programs and policies from one state to another, it is becoming increasingly important to learn more about such state innovators.

To find out more about the innovators in state government, the Council conducted two national surveys during July and August 1989. This article contains the survey findings, and profiles the innovators, describes their organizational and professional environments, and discusses the motivations for innovation in the states. The final section summarizes the surveys' major findings.

Survey Methods

The Surveys

We used two structured questionnaires to gather information from innovation managers and innovators nationwide.

Respondents to our first survey — the Innovation Managers Survey — were drawn from the contact persons named on the innovation nominations submitted to the Council in the 1989 innovations solicitation and selection process. The survey was used to help identify individuals responsible for originating what they considered to be innovative policies or programs. Respondents to our second survey — the Innovators Survey — were the innovators themselves, most of whom were identified by the innovation managers as a result of the first survey.

The response rates for the two mail surveys were relatively high. Of the 268 innovation managers who were surveyed, 190 responded, for a 70 percent response rate. The second survey was sent to a total of 284 innovators, and 160 (or 56 percent) of the innovators responded. The quality of responses was satisfactory, and a majority of the innovators who responded to the survey enclosed their resumes, which aided our analysis of the innovators' personal backgrounds.

Distribution of Samples by Region and Policy Area

The analysis that follows discusses differences among innovators based on regional and policy area variables.

As Table A indicates, the distribution of the sample across regions is tilted toward the East and Midwest. There are, however, sufficient cases in all the regions for determining significant statistical differences among and across regions. The organization of states into regions follows The Council of State Governments' regional conference designations.

The information in Table B indicates a relatively even distribution across policy areas with the social service and state management policy areas containing the largest number of respondents. Organization of the program categories by policy areas is done for the purpose of analysis since a number of program categories have too few cases for statistical assessment. Given our approach of identifying the innovators from the Managers Survey, we expected the distribution of managers across regions and policy areas would reflect the distribution for the innovators. As shown in Tables C and D, this expectation was realized. Managers in the Eastern and Midwestern regions are represented more than managers in the South and West and the social service and state management policy areas contain the largest number of manager respondents.

Profile of Innovators

The majority of the 160 innovators surveyed were well educated and half had ex-

Table A
Regional Organization and Distribution of Sample Across Regions

Regions	States	No. of Respondents
East	CT, DE, ME, MA, NH, NJ, NY, PA, RI, VT	51
South	AL, AR, FL, GA, KY, LA, MD, MS, NC, OK, SC, TN, TX, VA, WV	30
Midwest	IL, IN, IA, KS, MI, MN, MO, NE, ND, OH, SD, WI	49
West	AK, AZ, CA, CO, HI, ID, MT, NV, NM, OR, UT, WA, WY	30

Table B
Program Organization and Distribution of Sample Across Policy Areas

Policy Areas	Program Categories	No. of Respondents
Criminal Justice	Drug Prevention	3
	Courts	2
	Corrections	5
	Public Safety	3
	Crime Prevention	5
		18
Social Services	Social Services	30
	Aging	3
	Family Services	5
		38
Education	Education	13
Environmental	Natural Resources	11
	Energy	3
	Recreation	1
		15
Health	Health	15
Economic Development/ Infrastructure	Economic Development	5
	Transportation	7
	Housing	4
		16
State Management	State Government	17
	Information Services	12
	Finance	3
	Revenue	1
	Intergovernmental Relations	1
		34
Client Oriented/ Regulatory	Insurance	2
	Agriculture	1
	Labor	6
	Civil Rights	2
		11
	Total	160

Table D
Program Organization and Distribution of Innovation Managers Across Policy Areas

Policy Areas	Program Categories	No. of Respondents
Criminal Justice	Drug Prevention	4
	Courts	1
	Corrections	8
	Public Safety	2
	Crime Prevention	4
		19
Social Services	Social Services	35
	Aging	3
	Family Services	9
		47
Education	Education	16
Environmental	Natural Resources	12
	Energy	3
	Recreation	1
		16
Health	Health	19
Economic Development/ Infrastructure	Economic Development	5
	Transportation	10
	Housing	4
		19
State Management	State Government	22
	Information Services	11
	Finance	5
	Revenue	1
	Intergovernmental Relations	1
		40
Client Oriented/ Regulatory	Labor	6
	Agriculture	6
	Civil Rights	1
	Licensing/Regulatory	1
		14
	Total	190

perience working in the private sector.

Educational Background

Table E presents information regarding the innovators' educational background. *These individuals are well educated, with virtually one-half of the sample possessing advanced degrees and only 10 percent lacked a bachelors degree from a four-year institution.*

While no comparable data are available for an average group of state employees drawn randomly, the respondents are a more educated group of individuals than the population at large.

A second consideration regarding the innovators' educational background is their aca-

Table C
Innovation Managers by Region

Regions	States	No. of Respondents
East	CT, DE, ME, MA, NH, NJ, NY, PA, RI, VT	67
South	AL, AR, FL, GA, KY, LA, MD, MS, NC, OK, SC, TN, TX, VA, WV	37
Midwest	IL, IN, IA, KS, MI, MN, MO, NE, ND, OH, SD, WI	61
West	AK, AZ, CA, CO, HI, ID, MT, NV, NM, OR, UT, WA, WY	25

Table E
Educational Background of Innovators

Degrees	Percentage of Sample
High School	3%
Some College	7
Bachelor's Degree	35
Some Graduate Work	6
Master's Degree	31
Professional Degree (MD, LLD, Ph.D.)	18
(N = 160)	

Table F
Academic Majors of Innovators
(Last Degree)

Academic Major	Percentage of Sample
Social Sciences	26%
Business	15
Education	13
Public Administration/Planning	11
Medicine	9
Law	7
Engineering	7
Humanities	6
Natural Sciences	6

demic concentration. Table F presents the percentage figures for the innovators' majors in their last (or terminal) degree program. That is, while an MD may have majored in biology as an undergraduate, Table F identifies that person's academic concentration as medicine.

Table F shows an array of academic majors, with a concentration in the social sciences (political science, sociology and history as the major concentrations within that category), business (MBAs and accounting, the major concentrations within that category), education and public administration as the dominant educational backgrounds. These results are not surprising since a person preparing for a career in government service would be advised to major in a social science for an entry-level position. Individuals with degrees in business or public administration prepared themselves for managerial positions and many respondents with these degrees were mid-career employees who returned to school to advance to managerial opportunities. The relatively large group of innovators with education degrees was employed primarily in the education policy area and reflects the professionalization of that policy area since virtually every person with a terminal degree in education possessed either a masters or Ed.D. degree.

Experience

Since there was no empirical research on the backgrounds of innovative government officials, we had little guidance as to characteristics that might make someone more innovative than other individuals. Academic theory on public organizations (e.g., Anthony Downs, *Inside Bureaucracy*, 1967) says that fresh approaches are more likely to come from newer or younger employees who are not wedded to the agencies' standard operating procedures or "normal way of doing things." We suspected our sample of innovators would be primarily younger individuals with relatively short state government careers.

Another strain of public organization research (e.g., Ralph Hummel, *The Bureaucratic Experience*, 1987) indicates that the bureaucracy itself tends to diminish creativity. Following this theory, we speculated that the innovators would be individuals with substantial experience in other types of work environments. The data supported only the second hypothesis.

Regarding the innovators' experience in other types of work settings, our sample conformed to expectations. One-half of the sample for which experiential information was provided (or 76 of 153 respondents) had prior experience in the private sector. Much of this prior private sector experience was in private non-profit organizations in the social service policy area or in private consulting firms dealing with government programs. An additional 14 percent of the sample had professional experience in another state government.

Our data depart from theoretical expectations on the age and state government experience profiles of our innovators. The average age of our sample is 44 years old and the average length of service within their state governments is 13 years. Our sample, therefore, represents primarily mid-career state employees with substantial maturity and investment in their government careers. The image portrayed in the literature of the "young turks" with fresh outlooks as the primary source of program innovation simply is not borne out by our data. *Essentially, our data indicate that innovations are coming from individuals with diverse experience and substantial expertise in the policy area who are not afraid or hesitant to experiment with new ideas and approaches.*

Of the 117 respondents who indicated their gender, 39 (33 percent of the subsample) were female. While there is no theoretical reason to assume that gender would be a factor in innovative behavior, for the sake of describing our sample, we include this information. The female innovators are employed in the social service and education policy areas (63 percent of the female respondents); are concentrated in the Eastern and Midwestern regions (79.5 percent); and possess advanced degrees (59.4 percent have either masters of professional degrees). The percentage of females in our sample mirrors the ratio of females across state and local governments earning salaries above $25,000 a year (EEOC, "Job Patterns for Minorities and Women in State and Local Government," 1985). Therefore, we believe our sample is reflective of the population of professional state government employees at least on the basis of gender.

Organizational Environment of Innovators

Because of the exploratory nature of this study, we were interested in developing a baseline of information on the organizational environment of the innovator. To that end, the respondents were asked their employment status as the innovation was developed, the role they assumed in the development of the innovation, the role that internal and external actors played in the development of and the support for the innovation, and the organizational changes required to implement the innovation. This section presents the aggregate results of their responses.

Employment Status of Innovators

Do innovations emerge primarily within the state bureaucracy by permanent employees or do they come from outside the permanent executive branch structure? To address this question, we asked the innovators about their employment status while they were developing the innovation. Table G presents this information.

Table G
Employment Status of Innovators

Status	Percentage of Respondents
State Civil Service/Central Office	35.6%
State Civil Service/Regional-Area Office	10.0
Appointed Administrator	38.8
Private Sector Employee	9.4
Other	6.2
(N = 160)	

Table G indicates that the largest number of innovators in the sample are permanent civil service employees working either in the agencies' central or field offices. The appointed administrators are central office managers involved in the development of the innovation. Unfortunately, we could not determine if these individuals were appointed specifically to generate innovative approaches or whether their innovative activities resulted from their administrative experience. Almost all of the private sector employees were employed by private non-profit organizations connected programmatically and financially to a state government program. The "Other" category includes three legislators, two federal employees, three faculty members of universities, two private citizens and a governor. *In general, these data indicate that the innovations are coming from the executive branch, with permanent civil servants slightly more involved than appointed administrators.*

The Role of the Innovator in Developing the Innovation

Do innovations emerge from individuals working on a problem who sense a need to try something different? Do they emerge as a result of supervisors prompting their employees to try a new approach? Do innovations emerge primarily from a group effort of professionals who share a common concern about a problem or opportunity? Or, do innovations emerge as some combination of these?

Respondents were asked to identify their role(s) in the development of the innovation. Four specific roles were provided in the survey, and the respondents were allowed to indicate multiple roles. The identified roles were: 1) sole responsibility for the innovation; 2) supervisor of the agency from which the innovation emerged; 3) member of an informal group developing the innovation; 4) member of a formal group developing the innovation. A fifth category of "other" was provided so respondents could specify what other role they played. The responses are presented in Table H.

Table H
Role of Innovators in Developing the Innovation

Role	Percentage of Respondents
Sole Responsibility	28.8%
Supervisor of Unit	18.7
Informal Group Member	8.1
Formal Group Member	10.6
Two Different Roles During Development	19.4
Three Different Roles During Development	6.3
Other Role	8.1
(N = 160)	

As Table H shows, *the most common singular role pattern is for innovators to generate the innovation by themselves as part of their day-to-day professional responsibilities.* The next most common role pattern is for the innovators to assume multiple roles in the development of the innovation.

The most common multiple role behavior is for the innovator to supervise the unit and be involved in a group effort to develop the innovation. Since the third most common role is to supervise the unit developing the innovation, much innovative programming is coming from the managers of innovative units, either as a manager solely or as an active participant in the development process.

If we combine all the possible permutations of managerial involvement in innovation development, 39.4 percent of the sample held a supervisory position during some stage of the process. This could indicate that the broader perspective afforded a manager who deals with the multiplicity of issues arising within a policy area is associated with identifying innovative solutions to problems within the policy area. Contrarily, it might indicate that the attributes associated with rising within the state government hierarchy also are attributes that lead a person to be willing to try new approaches to problem solving. Our data do not allow us to speculate which alternative is true, but it points to a direction for future study.

The percentages associated with group development of the innovations (18.7 percent combining formal and informal groups) are deflated since much of the group involvement was associated with other role activities. If we combine all the possible permutations which include group involvement, a total of 37.5 percent of the innovators were involved in group activity during some stage of the innovation development process.

It appears that the role activities of the innovators evolved as the innovation moved from an idea to an implementable change in the agencies' way of doing things. Perhaps sparked by the innovator's expertise and experience in the policy area, the process of bringing the innovation to fruition required the support of other actors within the policy area (group activity) and gave the innovator an opportunity to supervise some part of the innovation's development. Further study using a different research design would be necessary to confirm this speculation, but the data point in that direction.

Involvement of Groups and Individuals in Innovation Development

A prevailing model in the current study of public organizations is that public agencies operate in an open environment — one that receives support and demands from various elements. The body of research based on this model has identified a series of internal and external organizational actors who are regularly involved in agency activities. Given the exploratory nature of this study, we were interested in how involved these groups and individuals were in the development of new organizational approaches. To that end, the respondents were asked to rate on a seven-point scale (7 being Very Influential and 1 being Not Influential) how influential various groups were in the planning and development of the innovation. Table I presents the groups ranked (by group mean) from highest to lowest as involved in the development of the innovation.

The results of Table I are informative. *It is evident that, for the entire sample, the primary groups involved in helping the innovator develop the innovation are those individuals working with the innovator on a day-to-day basis — coworkers and supervisors.* Next in line are the clients, interest groups and citizens affected by the innovation. Only then do the formal institutional actors (governors and legislators) become involved in innovation development. The actors at different levels of government (federal and local) do not appear to have much influence in the development of innovations at the state level. *In general, it appears that innovators first gain the support of their immediate colleagues and supervisors, then the support of the affected citizens and only later are external formal actors brought into the process.*

Table I
Ranking of Groups Involved in Innovations' Development
(All Innovations)

Groups	Mean	St. Dev.	Median
Agency Coworkers	5.178	1.940	6.00
Agency Supervisor	4.883	2.117	6.00
State Coworkers	3.621	2.176	4.00
Clients of Agency	3.354	2.308	3.00
Interest Groups	3.307	2.270	3.00
Professional Associations	3.073	2.118	3.00
Informed Citizens	2.830	2.092	2.00
Governor's Office	2.704	2.153	1.00
Informed Legislators	2.589	2.180	1.00
University Personnel	2.527	2.012	1.00
Colleagues — Out-of-State	2.483	1.919	1.00
Legislative Staff	2.417	2.064	1.00
Federal Government Staff	2.247	1.992	1.00
Local Government Staff	2.193	1.867	1.00
Local Elected Officials	1.831	1.486	1.00
National Associations of State Offficials	1.803	1.515	1.00
(N = 150)			

Not all innovations are the same, however. As Chi (1988) has pointed out, some innovations require fundamental changes in the policy environment, such as a change in or enactment of legislation; others are less profound and require only adjustments to managerial procedures or technologies surrounding the innovator. To determine if the type of innovation affected the involvement of groups, we isolated those innovations where changes in statutory authority were required to implement the innovation. Thirty-nine cases from our sample met this criterion and are used as the basis for Table J. As expected, for those innovations that require statutory change for implementation, the ranking of groups changes considerably. Although the innovator's immediate colleagues remain the most important in developing the innovation and federal and local officials remain the least important groups, the legislators and their staffs replace the interest groups and clients in these policy innovations. Interestingly, the governors' offices remain only moderately involved in innovations requiring statutory change.

Table J
Ranking of Groups Involved in Innovations' Development
(Policy Innovations Only)

Groups	Mean	St. Dev.	Median
Agency Supervisor	4.583	2.209	5.00
Agency Coworkers	4.432	2.328	5.00
Informed Legislators	4.231	2.276	5.00
State Coworkers	4.162	2.242	5.00
Legislative Staff	4.077	2.443	4.00
Interest Groups	3.694	2.291	4.00
Professional Associations	3.389	2.168	3.50
Governors' Office	3.316	2.326	3.00
Informed Citizens	3.083	1.991	3.00
Clients	2.629	2.116	1.00
Colleagues — Out-of-State	2.541	1.966	1.00
University Personnel	2.500	2.049	1.00
Local Government Staff	2.486	2.133	1.00
Local Elected Officials	2.486	1.946	1.00
National Associations of State Officials	1.803	1.515	1.00
(N = 39)			

The final way of viewing these group rankings is to assess if the rankings remain stable across policy areas. The major work examining the influence of external actors across state agencies (Brudney and Hebert, 1987) found the influence of actors varies across policy areas. If this is true, we can speculate that the rankings of these actors' involvement in helping the innovator plan and develop the innovation should also change by policy area. We can see if this is true by displaying the rankings of the groups by policy area as displayed in Table K. The trends reported in the previous tables are generally supported for the top and bottom ranked groups with the middle-ranked groups changing in importance depending upon the policy area considered. These rankings also verify the reliability of the data base since those groups expected to be influential in some areas and not in others (e.g., local staff) operate as expected.

INNOVATIONS

Table K
Rank Ordering of Group Involvement by Policy Areas
(Means)

Groups	Crim.Jus.	Soc.Ser.	Ed.	Env.	Health	Econ.Dev.	Mgt.	Regs.
Agency Coworkers	1	1	2	1	1	1	1	1
Agency Supervisor	2	2	1	2	2	2	2	2
State Coworkers	3	4	4	3	6	8	3	9
Clients	8	3	10	4	7	11	5	3
Interest Groups	5	6	4	5	3	4	6	4
Professional Associations	6	5	6	8	4	5	9	5
Citizens	4	10	8	5	14	3	12	7
Governor's Office	9	7	9	11	11	15	4	13
Legislators	13	7	6	12	7	7	8	15
University Personnel	10	12	3	7	13	12	10	10
Colleagues Out-of-State	11	11	12	10	9	6	11	6
Legislative Staff	14	12	11	13	9	9	7	14
Federal Staff	15	9	14	9	12	10	16	8
Local Staff	7	14	14	15	5	13	14	11
Local Elected	12	15	16	14	15	16	14	11
National Associations	16	16	13	16	15	13	13	13
(N = 150)								

Support of Groups for the Innovations

While the previous discussion considered to whom the innovator looked in developing and planning the innovation, an equally important issue is the support of groups in implementing the innovation. To that end, we asked the innovators to rate on the same seven-point scale (7 being Very Influential and 1 being Not Influential), how supportive various groups were during the initial stages of the innovation. Table L presents the aggregate results.

Table L
Ranking of Groups as Supportive of Innovations
(All Innovations)

Groups	Mean	St. Dev.	Median
Agency Supervisor	5.627	2.011	7.00
Agency Coworkers	5.386	1.908	6.00
Interest Groups	4.241	2.715	5.00
State Coworkers	4.109	2.469	5.00
Clients	4.000	2.787	5.00
Informed Citizens	3.933	2.778	5.00
Governor's Office	3.918	2.537	4.00
Legislators	3.797	2.688	5.00
Legislative Staff	3.127	2.722	4.00
Federal Officials	3.037	2.829	4.00
Professional Associations	2.904	2.852	3.00
Local Governments	2.741	2.707	3.00
(N = 139)			

As Table L indicates, *the innovators found their strongest support from those with whom they work, and then from those groups most dependent upon their agencies' services.* Following closely behind are informed citizens, the governor's office and the legislature. Again, the innovators did not look to officials at other levels of government as a necessary support base. *It appears then, when promoting a new idea, the innovators look first to their agency colleagues, then to those most affected by the idea (clients and interest groups) and, if accepted, formal actors (governors and legislators) as a support base.* Table M examines only those innovations requiring statutory change to see if these aggregate rankings change when a policy innovation is implemented.

Table M
Ranking of Groups As Supportive of Innovations
(Policy Innovation Only)

Groups	Mean	St. Dev.	Median
Legislators	5.711	1.487	6.00
Governor's Office	4.909	1.974	6.00
Legislative Staff	4.861	2.380	6.00
Agency Coworkers	4.667	2.568	6.00
Interest Groups	4.378	2.564	5.00
Agency Supervisor	4.359	2.842	6.00
State Coworkers	4.237	2.655	6.00
Citizens	4.176	2.552	5.00
Local Officials	3.529	2.733	4.00
Professional Associations	3.061	2.968	3.00
Clients	2.865	2.879	1.00
Federal Officials	2.303	2.604	1.00
(N = 39)			

When policy innovations are examined separately, the rankings change dramatically. The governor's office and legislature become paramount as a support group while those most affected by the change drop in the rankings. These results are instructive. They demonstrate, from the perspective of the innovators, how they go about building a support base for their new approach. *It appears that when an innovation only involves a change in an administrative procedure or technology, the most important groups involved are the innovators immediate colleagues and their clients.* When a statutory change is necessary to implement the innovation, the innovator first gains the support of the elected officials and then includes the affected group in the process.

Is group support for policy innovation consistent across policy areas or do support rankings vary across policy areas? We can assess this question by examining the rank orderings of the groups across policy areas in Table N.

With the exception of agency coworkers and supervisors who are supportive across policy areas, the rankings indicate that support for policy innovation by groups is policy area specific. For example, the innovators working in the economic development/infrastructure policy area rank citizens as their primary support base, while innovators in the health and state management areas rank citizens near the bottom of supportive groups. Legislators are extremely important for education (ED) innovations, but virtually meaningless in the regulatory, labor and agriculture (REGS) policy areas. These data are instructive because they provide a more detailed picture of the types of groups most closely involved in promoting innovations within particular policy areas.

Despite the variation across areas, two generalizations emerge: 1) the most important group of individuals surrounding the innovator consists of the innovator's close professional colleagues (coworkers and supervisors); 2) the least significant groups surrounding the innovator are policy actors at different levels of government (local and federal officials). How important other instate actors are depends upon the type of innovation (policy change vs. managerial change) and the type of policy area.

Innovations and Organizational Change

Innovations, by their nature, affect the organizations implementing them. While this seems obvious, little research has been conducted on the effects of innovations on public organizations. *Do innovations transform the organization or do organizations simply absorb the innovation with little disruption to standard operating procedures?* To address this question, the innovators were asked to identify which of the changes listed in Table O were required to implement their innovations. Since the innovators could list multiple changes, the percentages exceed 100 percent.

The innovators' responses show in more than 80 percent of the cases, the innovation affected the organization profoundly. By far, the greatest effects of innovations are in increasing the staff of the agencies, requiring alterations in their standard operating procedures and increasing funding of agencies. Despite the era of "cut back management" experienced by many states in recent years, the innovations had little discernible effect on other agencies' budgets and program levels.

Table N
Rank Ordering of Group Support by Policy Areas
(Means)

Groups	Crim.Jus.	Soc.Ser.	Ed.	Env.	Health	Econ.Dev.	Mgt.	Regs.
Agency Coworkers	1	2	2	2	2	4	2	3
Agency Supervisor	3	1	5	1	1	2	1	1
State Coworkers	2	9	8	4	6	9	3	7
Clients	12	3	6	3	5	11	4	4
Interest Groups	8	4	1	7	3	2	8	2
Citizens	6	5	7	5	9	1	9	6
Governor's Office	4	7	4	6	4	6	5	8
Legislators	5	8	3	8	8	5	7	11
Legislative Staff	11	12	10	10	7	7	6	12
Federal Officials	9	6	12	9	12	8	11	5
Professional Associations	10	11	9	12	11	12	10	9
Local Officials	7	10	11	11	10	10	12	10
(N = 139)								

Table O
Organizational Changes Resulting from Innovations
(Percent Responding 'Yes')

Change	Percentage Yes
No Change Required	19.4%
Statutory Change(s)	24.4
Modification of Existing Regulations and Procedures	44.4
Creation of New Regulations and Procedures	40.0
New Budget Authority/Higher Appropriations	43.8
Reallocation of Existing Appropriations from One Agency to Another	17.5
Reorganization of Agency	27.5
Replacement or Elimination of Existing Program	14.4
New or Reassigned Staff Positions to Implementing Agency	51.9
(N = 160)	

It appears that these innovations were either new ventures for the organization or add-ons to existing programs rather than replacements of existing programs from other organizations.

Professional Environment

Professional networks are important to the study of innovations since through them policy innovations are disseminated (Walker 1969). Our survey instrument asked a series of questions regarding the professional networks of the innovators. Specifically, we were interested in the number and type of professional organizations the innovators belong to, the number of professional conferences the innovators attended, the sources of information used by the innovators to remain professionally current, and other states the innovators looked to as being particularly innovative in their policy area.

Professional Activities of the Innovators

A commonly-used measure of professionalism is an individual's educational background and by that measure virtually all our innovators are professionals. An additional indicator of professionalism is how active individuals are within their respective professions. In the following analysis, innovators are considered professionally active who are members of professional associations and attend professional conferences on a regular basis. We measure professionalism as the number of associations and conferences an innovator is involved with on a yearly basis. That is, the greater the number of associations and conferences, the more professionally active the innovator is considered.

As Table P indicates, the innovators in our sample are active professionally. The majority belong to at least one state and national professional association. Most belong to two or more associations. National associations appear to be more important to the innovators than regional associations. Nearly all attended at least one professional conference in the most recent year. In fact, a higher percentage attended conferences than said they belonged to the professional associations hosting the conferences.

Table P
Innovators' Involvement in Professional Associations

Types of Association	Percentage of Respondents
State Associations	
Percentage Indicating Membership	66.7%
Number of Association Memberships	
1	31.6
2	22.2
3 or more	12.7
Number of Professional Conferences (Yearly)	
1 - 2	29.7
3 - 5	31.6
6 or more	28.5
Regional/Multistate Associations	
Percentage Indicating Membership	31.4
Number of Association Memberships	
1	21.0
2	7.6
3 or more	1.9
Number of Professional Conferences	
1 - 2	41.2
3 - 5	10.1
6 or more	6.3
National Associations	
Percentage Indicating Membership	68.8
Number of Association Memberships	
1	30.4
2	25.3
3 or more	12.7
Number of Professional Conferences	
1 - 2	56.3
3 - 5	17.8
6 or more	3.2

Note: Percentages do not add to subtotals due to missing values on some variables. Valid rather than total percentages are displayed.

Given the overall high level of professional activity reported by the innovators, we wondered whether this measure of professionalism varies across regions and policy areas. Each innovator's professionalism measure was determined simply by adding together the number of state, regional and national associations indicated and the number of state, regional and national professional conferences attended. The resulting professionalism variable ranges from a low of 2 to a high of 66. The average (mean) for the sample is 16.838 with a standard deviation of 11.688. Table Q indicates that the innovator respondents from the Eastern region have the highest level of professional activity, while those from the Western region have the least. However, while these differences appear rather stark, the variation within regions is also high. From a statistical perspective, these differences are not very important. If we look at professionalism by policy areas, the results are more revealing than those of the regional analysis (see Table R).

Table Q
Innovators' Professionalism by Region

Regions	Mean	St. Dev.
East	19.023	14.446
Midwest	17.366	10.406
South	16.620	10.414
West	13.069	9.445
(N = 160)		

Table R
Innovators' Professionalism by Policy Area

Regions	Mean	St. Dev.
Environmental	23.000	14.230
Education	21.923	14.997
Criminal Justice	19.412	10.845
Client Oriented/Regulatory	17.875	5.617
Social Services	16.363	13.049
Health	16.333	12.228
Economic Development/ Infrastructure	14.533	8.659
State Management	12.100	8.652
(N = 160)		

There is considerable difference among the groups, with those working in the environmental area almost twice as professionally active as those in management. Why some policy areas are more professionally active than others remains for future research.

Sources of Information

Another aspect of the innovators' professional environment is the source (or sources) of information that allow(s) them to stay abreast of developments within their professions. We asked our sample of innovators to rate (on a seven-point scale) the importance of various information sources to their ability to keep current with professional responsibilities. The aggregate results are reported in Table S.

Table S
Innovators' Ranking of Information Sources
(Means)

Sources	Mean	St. Dev.	Median
Informal Communication/Agency Coworkers	6.070	1.383	7.00
Informal Communication/State Coworkers	5.430	1.750	6.00
Professional Association/Publications & Information	5.373	1.425	6.00
Professional Conferences, Workshops & Meetings	5.203	1.509	5.00
Informal Communication/Other States	4.842	1.661	5.00
Interest Group Information	4.728	1.615	5.00
Citizens	4.660	1.925	5.00
News Media	4.606	1.749	5.00
Academic Journals/Research Reports	4.491	1.732	5.00
Federal Government Publications/Contacts	4.352	1.688	4.00

The results indicate that the innovators rely primarily on their immediate coworkers for professional information and secondarily on the professional associations. Also, we see for the first time a recognition that lateral communication across states is an important element in the innovators' professional environments. *While other states do not appear to be instrumental in the actual development or implementation of the innovation (see Tables J, K), the innovators seem to be aware of what other states are doing within their respective policy areas.* We can speculate that these communication linkages are forged at professional conferences and maintained through ongoing, informal communication over policy concerns affecting multiple states.

Given the diversity of professional activity across policy areas as shown in Table R, it is useful to determine if the importance of different information sources varies across policy areas. Table T presents the rankings of information sources by policy areas.

With the exception of agency coworkers who are critical information sources regardless of policy area and federal information that is consistently of minor importance, the role of other information sources is policy specific. While "Other State" communications are critical to professionals in the economic development/infrastructure policy area, they are virtually meaningless in agriculture, labor, insurance and civil rights (REGS) areas. Certain policy areas rely on more "specialized" knowledge than others, reflecting somewhat of a "guild" environment within that policy area. Mosher (1982) noted that, at the federal level, certain professions essentially dominate certain agencies. These professions develop particular training requirements, continuing education expectations, and licensing requirements for entry into professional status. While the data in Table T are not appropriate to determine professional capture of any policy area, there are some, such as health and education, where the linkage from the academic community to the professional association to the professionals in the agency is stronger than in others.

Other States as Sources of Information

Having identified other states as an important source of information for innovators, we examined which states are looked to as sources of information. The question of state innovativeness as a characteristic of some states has been extensively debated by students of innovation diffusion. Within this debate are two contentions: Policy innovations diffuse within regions and each region has its innovations leader (Walker 1969); and policy innovativeness is policy area specific and different states are more or less innovative depending upon the issue area and the period of investigation (Gray 1973). As Chi (1988) has pointed out, however, most of these studies only have examined statutory innovation, which ignore much of state policy innovation not requiring legislative action. Therefore, we included items in the survey concerning which states these innovators looked to as model states within their particular policy area.

Two questions were used to determine this information. One asked if the innovators had used a program from another state as a starting point or model for their innovation. Fifty-seven respondents answered affirmatively, and then listed those states and programs that served as their models (see Table U). The table shows a diversity of states possessing model programs; 33 were mentioned by the respondents.

Table U
States With Model Programs

Frequency	States (# Mentions)
5 or more mentions	MA (11), MN (6), CA, MD, WA (5)
4 - 2 mentions	FL, NJ (4), IL, IA, OR, NY (3), CO, KY, MI, MS, OK, PA, WI, OH, TN (2)
1 mention	AK, AR, GA, ME, NM, TX, WY, DE, MO, MT, NH, VA, UT
(N = 57)	

Table V presents the same information by policy area. This information is more instructive and shows the concentration of states within policy areas. For example, seven of Massachusetts' 11 mentions are in the social service, education and economic development policy areas; four of Minnesota's six mentions are in social services. It also appears that the innovators in the social service and health fields are more likely to be aware of other state programs and willing to borrow ideas from those programs.

Table T
Ranking of Information Sources by Policy Area
(Means)

Groups	Crim.Jus.	Soc.Ser.	Ed.	Env.	Health	Econ.Dev.	Mgt.	Regs.
Agency Coworkers	1	1	1	1	4	1	1	2
State Coworkers	2	2	9	4	1	7	2	6
Prof. Assoc. Information	5	3	2	2	2	3	3	4
Prof. Assoc. Conferences	3	3	3	2	5	6	6	7
Other States	4	6	4	6	8	2	5	10
Interest Group Information	7	7	6	5	7	4	7	5
Citizens	9	5	8	7	5	5	8	1
News Media	8	10	7	8	10	8	4	3
Academic Info.	10	9	5	8	2	8	10	8
Federal Info.	6	8	10	10	8	10	9	8

INNOVATIONS

Other Innovative States

The second question concerning the innovators' knowledge of other state activity asked them to identify which states (other than their own) they perceived to be "particularly innovative or effective in addressing problems associated with your area of program responsibility." One hundred and ten respondents identified at least one other state, and together, these individuals had 225 mentions of other states (see Table W).

Table W
Innovative States by Reputation

Frequency of Mentions	States (# Mentions)
20 or More	CA(23)
19 - 15	MN(19), MA(18)
14 - 10	MI(13), NJ(11), NY(11), FL(10), IA(10)
9 - 5	OH(9), MD(8), OR(8), NC(7), PA(7), WI(7), CO(6), WA(6), IL(5), TX(5), VA(5)
4 - 1	ME(4), TN(4), AR(3), GA(3), IN(3), KY(3), KS(3), MS(3), MT(3), UT(3), AK(2), ID(2), MO(2), NM(2), SC(2), AL(1), DE(1), ND(1), OK(1), SD(1), VT(1)

(N = 110)

Results are shown in Table W. First, 40 of the 50 states are considered effective or innovative in at least one policy area. While no single state or region monopolizes the reputation for innovation, some states have a wider reputation than others. California, Minnesota and Massachusetts are, by far, best known for innovativeness and received more than 25 percent of the mentions. The next tier of states are, with the exception of Iowa, more populous and wealthier states and states that previous analyses have found to be innovative by other measures. The lower-ranked states are generally less populous.

To assess whether the reputation for innovation was regionally-based (as Walker hypothesized in 1969), we arranged mentioned states by the region of the innovator mentioning the other innovative states. Only 85 of the 225 mentions were states within the same region as the innovator. *More than 60 percent of the states mentioned were in regions other than the innovators'.* These results depart from the notion that innovators look primarily to regional neighbors when contemplating a new venture for their agencies. *It appears that the innovators' referents are all of the other states, not just those in close proximity. We might further infer that since region is not necessarily a primary referent for the state officials, the role of region in explaining the differences between and among states will continue to decrease as professional associations and the national media expand the information sources and networks of state policy innovators.*

Is a state's reputation for innovation policy-area specific? To determine this, we organized the mentioned states by policy area, as shown in Table X.

Looking at innovative states by policy area, it appears that some states' reputations are policy specific. For example, while California is mentioned overall as the most innovative state, its reputation is concentrated in the education, environmental and administrative areas (17 of 23 mentions). Minnesota, on the

Table V
Model States by Policy Area
(Number of Mentions in Parentheses)

	Crim. Jus.	Soc. Ser.	Educ.	Environ.	Health	Econ.Dev.	Admin.	Regs.
	CA(1)	MN(4)	MA(3)	PA(2)	MD(2)	MA(2)	FL(1)	WA(2)
	GA(1)	MA(3)	AK(1)	CO(1)	NJ(2)	AR(1)	KY(1)	MA(1)
	KY(1)	MD(2)	CA(1)	ME(1)	NY(2)	CA(1)	MA(1)	MI(1)
	MN(1)	FL(2)	DE(1)	MT(1)	IA(2)	FL(1)	MO(1)	MN(1)
	MS(1)	CA(1)	IL(1)	NH(1)	WI(2)	MI(1)	TN(1)	OH(1)
	NJ(1)	CO(1)	MD(1)	NM(1)	CA(1)	NY(1)	WA(1)	
	OK(1)	IL(1)		OK(1)	IL(1)	OH(1)		
	OR(1)	IA(1)		UT(1)	MA(1)	OR(1)		
		NJ(1)		WA(1)	MS(1)			
		OR(1)		WY(1)	VA(1)			
		TN(1)						
		TX(1)						
		WA(1)						
N =	8	20	8	11	15	9	6	6

other hand, has mentions more evenly distributed across seven of the eight policy areas, indicating a more general reputation for innovative programming. Further, it appears that professionals in the social services policy area have a wider perception of innovation at the state level — 28 states were mentioned as innovative, while in the criminal justice area only nine states were identified as innovative.

Motivations for Innovations

What particular events, problems or circumstances lead state officials to begin thinking about innovations? As might be expected, the innovators' responses to this survey question varied widely. What follows is a sample of answers. They are grouped under 10 subheadings: management improvement; cost savings; technology; termination of federal aid; social services; education; health care and public safety; environment; emergency; and outside the state government.

Management Improvement

"The state faced federal fiscal sanctions due to high error rates when determining eligibility for assistance programs."

"There was a total inability to aggressively enforce federal and state drug laws under existing governmental law enforcement structures."

"Increasing interest and emphasis on privatization — new competition for government — was needed for better management."

"Prior to implementation of our project, issuance of occupational licenses in the state was a very cumbersome and labor intensive process. This project streamlined that process and reduced labor by two-third."

"Lack of long-range planning in programs for low income families."

"As a state development agency we operated programs of industrial recruitment and programs to promote business retention but no specific program to encourage new business formation except incubators."

"In my duties as a performance auditor I

Table X
Innovative States by Policy Area
(Number of Mentions in Parentheses)

Crim. Jus.	Soc. Ser.	Educ.	Environ.	Health	Econ.Dev.	Admin.	Regs.
NJ(2)	MA(7)	CA(5)	CA(4)	MA(3)	MN(4)	CA(8)	MN(2)
OR(2)	MD(4)	FL(2)	TX(4)	NJ(3)	OH(4)	NC(4)	NJ(2)
AK(1)	FL(3)	MA(2)	IA(3)	WI(3)	MA(3)	CO(2)	WA(2)
CA(1)	MI(3)	AK(1)	MI(3)	CO(2)	MI(3)	MN(2)	IL(1)
ID(1)	MN(3)	AR(1)	MN(3)	IN(2)	FL(2)	PA(2)	IA(1)
MN(1)	IA(3)	CN(1)	OR(2)	MD(2)	IA(2)	UT(2)	IN(1)
NY(1)	CA(2)	DE(1)	CO(1)	MI(2)	WA(2)	VA(2)	MA(1)
OH(1)	KS(2)	GA(1)	GA(1)	NY(2)	AR(1)	FL(1)	MI(1)
PA(1)	ME(2)	IL(1)	MA(1)	OH(2)	CA(1)	IL(1)	NY(1)
	MO(2)	MN(1)	MS(1)	PA(2)	ID(1)	MD(1)	OH(1)
	NY(2)	MS(1)	MD(1)	CA(1)	IL(1)	MI(1)	WI(1)
	TN(2)	NY(1)	NJ(1)	FL(1)	NV(1)	NJ(1)	
	AL(1)	NJ(1)	NM(1)	IA(1)	NY(1)	NY(1)	
	AR(1)	ND(1)	NY(1)	ME(1)	NC(1)	OK(1)	
	CO(1)	KY(1)	NC(1)	MS(1)	OR(1)	SC(1)	
	GA(1)	OR(1)	TN(1)	TX(1)	PA(1)		
	IL(1)	TN(1)	VT(1)	VA(1)	WI(1)		
	KY(1)	VT(1)	WA(1)	WA(1)			
	MT(1)	WA(1)					
	NM(1)	WI(1)					
	OH(1)						
	OR(1)						
	PA(1)						
	SC(1)						
	SD(1)						
	VT(1)						
	VA(1)						
	WA(1)						
N = 11	51	26	31	31	30	30	14

was exposed to many state agencies and institutions where supplies of commodities and/or maintenance items were maintained. I noticed duplication/inventories of slow moving items from one inventory point to another, no awareness of the concepts of inventory control including the carrying cost of inventory, no consistent identifying scheme for items inventory and handling methods of inventory record-keeping."

"Energy was a creeping drain on the people's pocket. There was clearly a need for an indisputable symbol of integrity that would move the industry and consumers to energy efficiency."

"The answer to simple questions (how many, where, what kind, etc.) were not available on a statewide basis and policy was being made on an intuitive, knee-jerk basis without benefit of facts. The solution was obvious — develop a database."

"A fair hearing system was marred by inconsistency, poor quality and a production system from the dark ages. Approximately 80,000 hearing decisions were issued each year, with each one being hand written with minimal use of standard forms and each one being typed on a typewriter."

"The 75,000 decisions issued annually in the state were hand-drafted by administrative law judges at locations throughout the state."

Cost Savings

"Cost containment by freight management is both necessary and do-able."

"It was determined that there was a great potential for cost savings/shifting which could be realized by automating routine clerical functions."

"State facilities were aging, becoming less energy efficient and budget funds were scarce. Clearly energy projects save money over time. This program was designed to pay for those projects over time as savings are realized."

"The tremendous cost of computer maintenance, numerous contracts and my belief that most maintenance was provided by the manufacturer on a monthly fee. This is usually the most costly approach."

"It was felt that if the federal agencies would agree to uniform format, requirements and time frames, that much staff time and therefore dollars would be saved."

"Initial estimates for the time and costs involved would probably have made control of asbestos in this state's environment prohibitive. I recognized the availability of corrections' resources through the division of correctional industries and directed that they begin a feasibility study to assess the reasonableness of my proposal."

Technology

"By developing a computer program for retention schedules it is very easy to make the change without retyping the entire schedule. A pilot project is being conducted in another state agency."

"The Department needed a method to manage data, systems, purchases of computer equipment and software and do system development in a coordinated department wide manner."

"Current records management process in the state was oriented toward paper documents, based on manually prepared schedules of records inventory and disposition. To accommodate electronic records, a more automated and faster process of inventory and disposition approval was needed."

"Due to the nature of this advisory council, I have a close relationship to the leaders of high tech industry in the state. In the course of my discussions with these industry leaders, their dissatisfaction with the state graduates of vocational training programs became evident."

"In recent years there has been a dramatic growth in the number of evocation hearings against licensed facilities. The ability to track the status of these cases manually was overwhelming. By computerizing all phases of a case from initial referral to the legal offer until its ultimate resolution enables all interested parties to learn the status of any case in a matter of seconds."

"Suitable gravel material was not available on the island, only sand. Barge cost to haul suitable material was extremely expensive because of the distances involved and the short barge season in the Arctic. We began searching for a substitute."

Termination of Federal Grant Programs

"Reduced funding made it difficult to continue our full service. We needed to focus on target groups and services. We also needed to define our role within our umbrella labor/welfare agency, break down turf issues and begin really cooperating and working with welfare programs and JTPA."

"Cuts in federal funding to SSI program made us realize that SSI could not be everything to everybody. We started targeting those groups which are served by other agencies within the Department of Economic Security."

Social Services

"Courts were too overcrowded for such routine issues and no authorized surrogates (for the mentally handicapped) were available in most cases."

"Statistics revealing that hunger was a growing problem in the state, that demand for emergency food assistance was rising at an alarming rate, that providers were unable to meet all the needs and were turning people away unassisted, and that federal food assistance programs were underutilized."

"I spent eight years on committees to address the problem of affordable housing for the disabled."

"I began to realize that seniors were confused as to how much health insurance was needed as well as other forms of health insurance."

"The infant mortality rate is high. Many low income women had no reimbursement for prenatal care."

"Mission to empower poor people led me to economic development, then technological application needed for them to start small business."

"There was a lack of qualified foster parents."

"We lacked uniform service definitions and a comprehensive policies and procedures manual on long term care system."

"National issues surrounding welfare reform and child care as well as state and local concerns. Long term welfare recipients are often recycled into the welfare trap due to lack of basic job training."

"As part of my clinical work, I had to provide evaluations and treatment to mentally ill individuals involved in the criminal justice system; the lack of appropriate services and service delivery models led to my innovation in developing a program of comprehensive mental health forensic services and in developing competency and insanity evaluation methods."

"I recognized a need for clients on general assistance. Simply put, a need for an advocate to assist clients in appealing SSI, Title XX denials. Looked at overview of entire process and synthesized information obtained into working model."

"The need for greater communication between agency staff and foster parents, need for methods to address problem of foster parent retention and being responsive to training needs of foster parents."

Education

"Commissioner believed that there was disjointedness between students' belief in education and its relationship to later employment."

"The drop out rate in urban areas was my main motivation."

"There was a need for better math and science teaching."

"I read to children whose parents were illiterate while in my junior and senior years at a college."

"The need for practical teacher updating in an industry setting became critical because technology was and is changing rapidly."

"There was a need for the development of an area learning center."

"As a board of education member, it was obvious that school systems needed to plan in an organized way for a student transition from school to work to further education."

INNOVATIONS

Health Care and Public Safety

"I began thinking about the need for a specialized residence for the elderly with health care programs because our homes were unable to meet these needs and we were unable to access an appropriate placement in the generic sector."

"Ambulances had no provisions for the transport of infants and children safely and securely."

"Teen parents or teens who are pregnant find themselves in a trap without knowledge of where to seek help."

"In 1986 we had a two and a half month old child who died from methemoglobinemia as the result of ingesting well water that had a high level of nitrates."

"There was a well defined need to provide health promotion opportunities for older persons."

"One of my goals upon being appointed was to lose our dubious distinction as the leading state in terms of our fire death rate . . .. Hopefully, it will be celebrated nationwide quarterly within 10 years, and maybe the President will declare it a "Fire Prevention All Year Long.""

"The inaccessibility of clinical generic services in many areas of the state and a lack of referral of many families in need of such services."

"The rapid increase in the number of commitments to the department of corrections warranted the development of some alternative approaches. Shock incarceration prepares a person for release in six months versus a much longer time with a standard sentence."

Environment

"As we traveled the state making inspections of solid waste disposal sites, local officials kept mentioning that they had a junk vehicle problem and no funds available to solve the problem. We wrote up legislation and circulated it to the cities and counties and motor vehicle facilities for comment. During the next legislative session we had members from these groups available for testimony."

"An increase in open pit gold mining created concern for the preservation of water quality through potential discharges of associated waste streams."

"I had been staff to the waterfront commission. The development of a walkaway along the river waterfront was deemed necessary."

Emergency

"Drought and a depressed farm economy had put the rural economy into a very depressed state. Many farmers did not have the resources or the knowledge of how to handle the situation and were doing things that resulted in legal and tax problems."

"In 1986, the state was in the depths of one of the most severe agricultural recessions since the depression. I wanted capital to encourage the diversification of our economy."

Outside the State Government

"As a staff to a legislative study commission looking at prison overcrowding, my research led to examination of the deinstitutionalization movement underway in several other states and to the federal JJDP Act of 1974."

"The idea that we would do better working together as a region rather than as individual states also took root."

"The institute has developed several prototype water and waste water projects in small towns in diverse states. We were looking for an opportunity to create a statewide system."

"A nationally syndicated news column that brought to my attention and the attention of the legislative leadership the critical need for state legislatures to develop a foresight capacity."

"It was coordinated by a training team from an exemplary literacy program in an neighboring state and I became highly motivated and made plans to develop a community literacy program."

"Rural America Initiatives, our nonprofit organization, had successfully established and maintained this program model on an Indian reservation through cooperation of Indian organizations. Therefore it became important to see if the same model could be established and maintained in an urban setting and in cooperation with a non-Indian organization."

"Conversations with a long-time colleague from another state helped launch the idea."

"N.T.S.B. recommended that reliable runway lighting systems would be needed to raise the level of safety."

Innovation Managers

We surveyed the contact persons for the 1989 innovations nominations to identify the individuals who actually developed the nominated innovations. Because of the nature of the solicitation process, the contact persons generally were the managers or supervisors of the innovative programs with the exception of 51 contact persons who identified themselves as the originators of the innovations. As a result, those 51 also received the Innovators Survey. The Managers Survey was sent to the remaining 268 managers, and 190 responded. Although the primary purpose of the Managers Survey was to identify the specific innovators, items were included regarding the management of innovative agencies. This section reports on the responses.

Table Y
Employment Status of Managers

Status	Number	Percentage of Sample
Civil Service Central and Regional Offices	125	66%
Appointed Administrator	52	27
Other	13	8

Employment Status of Managers

Table Y presents data on the innovation manager's employment status. While the majority are permanent civil servants, more than one in four achieved their position through political appointment. Since previous research (Brudney and Hebert, 1987) has shown that such employment status affects how they perceive their organizational environments, we will assess this hypothesis in the following analysis. The 13 individuals not fitting into either of the above categories represented a mix of private consultants, directors of private non-profit organizations and locally-elected officials.

Managerial Perception of Group Support for Innovations

Does the perception of the support of various groups vary between those who actually developed the innovation and those who manage the innovative unit? To address this question, the Managers Survey contained the same question as the Innovators Survey regarding the support of various groups. Table Z presents the rating of the groups' support by the managers. Table AA compares the managers' ratings to those of the innovators from the previous analysis.

Table Z
Managers' Rating of Group Support for Innovations

Groups	Mean	St. Dev.	Median
Interest Groups	4.863	2.369	6.00
Clients	4.799	2.457	6.00
Governor's Staff	4.788	2.244	6.00
Others	4.610	2.663	6.00
Citizens	4.542	2.446	5.00
Legislators	4.435	2.504	5.00
Legislative Staff	4.229	2.547	5.00
Professional Associations	3.608	2.769	5.00
Local Governments	3.382	2.529	4.00
Federal Officials	3.072	2.782	4.00

Table AA
Comparison of Managers' and Innovators' Ratings of Group Support for Innovations
Means

Groups	Managers' Rating	Innovators' Rating
Interest Groups	4.863 (1)	4.241 (1)
Clients	4.799 (2)	4.000 (2)
Governor's Office	4.788 (3)	3.918 (4)
Citizens	4.542 (4)	3.933 (3)
Legislators	4.435 (5)	3.797 (5)
Legislative Staff	4.229 (6)	3.127 (6)
Professional Associations	3.608 (7)	2.904 (8)
Local Officials	3.382 (8)	2.741 (9)
Federal Officials	3.072 (9)	3.037 (7)

The results indicate a strong consistency between the managers and the innovators regarding the relative support of groups. The managers rate the governor's office slightly higher than the innovators, a finding that is not completely unexpected since the manager is probably in more direct contact with the governor's office than the staff person working on the innovation. The major difference between the managers and innovators is the significantly higher rating given each group (except federal officials) by the managers. We might speculate that the managers rate the external groups higher because they are dealing more directly with those groups as part of their managerial responsibilities.

Do appointed administrators differ from career administrators in their assessment of group support? Since previous research has found significant differences between appointed and career administrators in their view of the influence of external groups over agency operations, we wanted to determine if these differences persist in support for agency innovations. Table AB presents this comparison. While the data indicate the perception of local government officials varies in a statistically significant way, other trends in Table AB are worth noting. With the exception of interest groups and citizens, appointed administrators rate external actors higher than career managers. The higher rating of interest groups and citizens by careerists suggests the existence of a long term relationship between the career administrator and the groups providing political support for the program area. This has been found at the federal level where appointees are more responsive to political leaders while career employees are more attuned to groups relying on their programs. More detailed information would be required to confirm the possibility, but the data appear to point in that direction.

In the analysis of the innovators' perceptions of group support, we found that support of groups varied across policy areas (Table N). In Table AC the same analysis is performed for the managers' perceptions of groups by policy area. However, caution is in order in comparing Table N to Table AC. The managers did not rate the support of agency colleagues, state co-workers or agency supervisors since those groups would not be comparable from a managerial perspective.

Table AB
Managers Perception of Group Support:
Career versus Appointee
(Group Means)

Groups	Civil Service	Appointed
Governor's Office	4.806	5.021
Legislators	4.381	4.681
Legislative Staff	4.286	4.311
Local Government	3.011	4.093*
Interest Groups	4.861	4.609
Federal Officials	2.806	3.405
Professional Associations	3.576	3.738
Clients	4.657	5.022
Citizens	4.562	4.471

* Difference significant at .01 level.

The trends in relative group support perceptions between the innovators and managers are interesting. The strongest consistency between the two ratings is the low involvement of local and federal officials in terms of innovation support. Additionally, the involvement of groups appears policy area specific. The major difference is managers rated interest groups, governors and legislatures relatively higher than the innovators, perhaps reflecting a clearer understanding of how these groups are involved in permitting the innovation to come to fruition.

Agency Incentives for Innovations

While we would hope that civil servants are inventive and innovative out of a sense of professional responsibility, we also realize that individuals are motivated by incentives. Since virtually no research exists regarding different procedures within the public sector to motivate creative performance, we included a question in the Managers Survey regarding

Table AC
Managers' Rating of Group Support by Policy Areas
(Means)

Groups	Crim.Jus.	Soc.Ser.	Ed.	Env.	Health	Econ.Dev.	Mgt.	Regs.
Interest Groups	7	1	6	1	1	1	5	1
Clients	4	3	1	6	2	4	2	2
Governor	3	4	5	2	4	6	1	4
Citizens	1	2	2	3	3	2	7	3
Legislators	2	5	3	4	7	6	3	6
Legislative Staff	6	6	4	7	6	3	4	7
Professional Associations	5	8	7	5	9	9	6	5
Local Governments	8	7	9	8	5	5	8	9
Federal Staff	9	9	8	9	8	8	9	8

the incentive programs they used within their agencies. Table AD presents the results.

Table AD
Agency Incentives for Innovative Behavior
(Percent Responding Yes)

Procedures	Percentage Yes
No Procedure	20.0
Financial Incentives	36.8
Formal Recognition	52.6
Professional Activity Support	70.0
Better Working Conditions	6.8
Evaluation Procedures Emphasizing Innovation	44.7

Table AD indicates that 80 percent of the manager respondents use some incentive program to encourage innovative behavior. By far, the most frequently used incentive is support for staff involvement in professional activities by paying for travel and registration fees. Perhaps this explains the high level of professional activity among the innovators. Slightly more than half report a formal recognition system for innovative behavior through newsletters, awards and the like. This strategy relies on peer recognition as an incentive. Direct financial incentives, either through awards or performance appraisal systems, are not the norm; however, they are not unusual either. Forty-five percent of the managers' employee evaluation procedures emphasize innovative behavior and over a third of the respondents encourage innovation with specific financial incentives.

Since we found differences across policy areas in virtually all of the previous analysis, we wanted to determine whether incentive programs also vary across policy areas. Table AE presents the percentage of the respondents (by policy area) indicating that they used the various incentives.

The results show that the policy area most prone to incentives is criminal justice, while the least is health. The type of incentive used also appears to vary by policy area. For example, specific financial incentives are prevalent in the environmental area, but virtually nonexistent in the health area. Performance appraisals in most agencies in the state management area reward innovation, while only about a third of the appraisal systems in the education and environmental areas and only a quarter of the systems in the health area use this criterion for evaluation. The differences across policy areas and the impact of these differences in terms of the level of innovative activity within policy areas is an area of future research, which could be useful for the manager interested in fostering innovations.

The Impact of Innovation on the Organization

The final item in the Managers Survey was an open-ended question regarding problems and opportunities experienced by the agency as it adopted the innovation. Seventy-five percent of the managers indicated the innovation had generated problems or opportunities for their agencies and listed them. Given the free form nature of the responses, we organized responses into categories.

Previous research on the organizational benefits or opportunities arising from innovation (Downs and Mohr 1979) divide the benefits into three categories — programmatic, prestige and structural. Programmatic benefits enhance the ability of the agency to meet its primary objectives, such as increasing the number of clients served and performing more regulatory inspections. Prestige benefits

Table AE
Innovation Incentives by Policy Area
(Percent Responding Yes)

	Policy Areas							
	Crim.Jus.	Soc.Ser.	Ed.	Env.	Health	Econ.Dev.	Mgt.	Regs.
No Program	5.3	19.1	18.8	18.8	36.8	21.1	17.1	30.8
Financial	47.4	29.8	37.5	56.3	10.5	31.6	46.3	38.5
Formal Recognition	68.4	40.4	37.5	62.5	36.8	63.2	65.9	46.2
Conference Support	84.2	70.2	68.8	68.8	68.4	68.4	70.7	53.8
Working Conditions	10.5	6.4	6.3	6.3	0.0	5.3	9.8	7.7
Evaluation Procedure	47.4	44.7	31.3	37.5	26.3	47.4	58.5	46.2

enhance the reputation of the organization by actors outside the organization. Structural benefits improve the internal operation of an organization and are primarily management oriented. These three categories were used in classifying the managers' responses. In the coding process (two independent coders were used to classify the responses), a fourth category emerged — relational benefits — which fit none of the other categories. Relational benefits are those which improve the communication and coordination among agencies horizontally or vertically.

We could not identify previous work which discussed the problems associated with innovative activity in public organizations. However, the managers' listings of problems were organized into five substantive problem areas — resources, internal resistance, external resistance, coordination and managerial. Resource problems were related to the unanticipated success of the innovation creating a demand for agency services, which current budgets and personnel could not handle. Internal resistance problems were those in which agency peers and superiors were less than supportive of the innovation (e.g., "Agency employees did not understand and cared little about the effort, little buy-in to the program."). External resistance problems were those associated with outside actors (e.g., "Juvenile court judges have been very opposed to concurrent review of inpatient psychiatric care for youth."). The coordination problems represented the reverse of the relational benefits in that the innovation had required the agency to develop new relationships that were difficult to manage (e.g., "Problems originally dealt with interagency coordination and turf consciousness."). Managerial problems were related to the need to develop new procedures or policies to manage the effects of the innovation (e.g., "Contract managers had to develop new contract documents which incorporated these ideas and had to sell them to agency staff."). Table AF presents the results of the content analysis of the managers' responses.

The table indicates that the managers identified more benefits than problems in adopting the innovation. The benefits are evenly spread across the programmatic, managerial and relational categories. The major problem associated with the innovation was in the resource area. However, in combining both internal and external resistance categories, it is apparent that an equally difficult aspect of innovation adoption is overcoming inertia and complacency with current operating procedures.

Table AF
Organizational Benefits and Problems Associated with Adopting Innovations

Benefits	No. of Mentions	Percentage
Programmatic	26	29.2%
Prestige	11	12.4
Managerial	26	29.2
Relational	26	29.2
Total	89	100.0

Problems	No. of Mentions	Percentage
Resources	27	34.2%
External Resistance	13	16.5
Internal Resistance	11	13.9
Coordination	13	16.5
Managerial	15	18.9
Total	79	100.0

Conclusion

The following is a summary of our findings on the state innovator respondents to our survey:

Profile of State Innovators

• Virtually one-half of the innovators possess an advanced degree and only 10 percent lack a bachelors degree from a four-year institution.

• Innovators have a diverse array of academic majors with concentrations in the social sciences, business, education and public administration as the dominant educational backgrounds.

• One-half of the sample had prior experience in the private sector, mostly in private non-profit organizations.

• The average age of our sample is 44 years old, and the average length of service within their state governments is 13 years. Our sample represents primarily mid-career state employees.

- Of the 117 respondents who indicated their gender, 39 (or 33 percent) are female. The female innovators are largely employed in the social service and education policy areas (63 percent of the female respondents), are concentrated in Eastern and Midwestern regions, and possess advanced degrees.

Organizational Environment of Innovators

- A majority of the innovators are permanent civil service employees. Almost all of the private sector employees were employed by private non-profit organizations.
- The most common singular role pattern is for innovators to generate the innovations by themselves as part of their day-to-day professional responsibilities.
- The primary groups involved in helping the innovator develop the innovations are those individuals working with the innovator on a day-to-day basis — coworkers and supervisors.
- The innovators found their strongest support from those with whom they work, and then from those groups most dependent upon their agencies' services.
- In more than 80 percent of the cases, the innovation affected the organization profoundly. By far, the greatest impacts of innovations are: increasing the staff of the agencies; requiring alterations in standard operating-procedures; and increasing agency funding.

Professional Environment

- The innovators in the sample are active professionally. The majority belong to at least one state and national professional association; as many belong to two or more associations. National associations appear to be more important to innovators than regional associations.
- The innovators from the Eastern region have the highest level of professional activity, with those from the Western region showing the least.
- The innovators rely primarily on their immediate coworkers for professional information, and secondarily on the professional associations to which they belong. Lateral communication across states also is an important element in the innovators' professional environments.
- The innovators appear to be aware of what other states are doing within their respective policy areas.

Other States as Sources of Information

- Fifty-seven respondents said they used innovations that originated in other states as a source of information, and primarily cited programs from Massachusetts, Minnesota, California, Maryland and Washington as their models.
- According to the innovators' responses, 40 of the 50 states are considered to be innovative in at least one policy area.
- More than 60 percent of the states mentioned as innovative were in regions other than the one in which the innovator respondent resides. These results depart from the notion that innovators look primarily to regional neighbors when contemplating a new venture for their agencies.
- The respondents mentioned a diversity of states (33) as possessing model programs.

The purpose of this study was to develop a baseline of information about state policy and program innovations from the perspective of innovators themselves. The results from this initial investigation are encouraging in that the innovators' responses were sufficiently variable to permit preliminary speculation on the world of state policy innovations. However, one cross-sectional study does not allow for definitive statements regarding the people and organizations developing innovative solutions to state government concerns. Follow-up investigations and cross-sectional studies over time are necessary to confirm the findings of this study. We hope that this study will spark further research on this aspect of governance. Given the greater responsibility of the states under changing federalism, it will be increasingly important to understand how states develop and acquire innovative approaches in solving policy problems.

Selected Bibliography

Brudney, Jeffrey and F. Ted Hebert. "State Agencies and Their Environment: Examining the Influence of Important External Actors," *Journal of Politics*, Vol. 49 (1987), 186-206.

Chi, Keon, S. "Innovations Transfer in State Government," paper delivered at the annual meeting of the American Political Science Association, September 1-4, 1988, Washington, D.C.

Cope, Glen Hahn. "Innovations in State and Local Government: Consideration of a Macro-diffusion Process," paper delivered at the "Diffusion of Innovations in the Public Sector" conference sponsored by L.B.J. School of Public Affairs and the Ford Foundation in cooperation with J.F.K. School of Government, September 15-16, 1989, Austin, Texas.

Downs, Anthony. *Inside Bureaucracy*, Boston: Little, Brown and Company, 1967.

Downs, George W., Jr., and Lawrence B. Mohr. "Toward a Theory of Innovation," *Administration and Society*, Vol. 10 (1979), 379-408.

Equal Employment Opportunity Commission. "Job Patterns for Minorities and Women in State and Local Government," Washington, D.C.: U.S. Government Printing Office, 1985.

Golden, Olivia and Mary Jo Bane. "Creating and Sustaining Innovation in Human Services: Lessons from the 1986 Ford Foundation Innovations Finalists," paper delivered at the annual meeting of the American Political Science Association, September 1-4, 1988, Washington, D.C.

Gray, Virginia. "Innovation in the States: A Diffusion Study," *American Political Science Review*, Vol. 67 (1973), 1174-85.

Hummel, Ralph. *The Bureaucratic Experience*, St. Martin, 3rd ed., 1987.

Mosher, Fredrick. *Democracy and the Public Service*, 2nd ed., New York: Oxford University Press, 1982.

Walker, Jack L. "The Diffusion of Innovation Among the States," *American Political Science Association Review*, Vol. 63 (1969), 880-99.

UNIFORM STATE LAWS: 1988-1989

By John M. McCabe

In 1892, the states of the United States created the National Conference of Commissioners on Uniform State Laws (NCCUSL), the institution that produces uniform state laws. The NCCUSL is the oldest state governmental organization. It is a unique institution that couples the needs of state government with the large resources of organized bar associations. The NCCUSL allows the legal profession to donate expertise and legal drafting skills to state government. No uniform law commissioner is ever paid for the work he or she does on uniform state laws.

The uniform law commissioners form a distinguished group spanning several generations. Most great American legal scholars have participated as uniform law commissioners and most have viewed their membership in the NCCUSL as an opportunity to make major improvements in American law. Many distinguished lawyers have joined the scholars, melding academic wisdom with the pragmatism of the practicing lawyer. The result has been many individual contributions, all without compensation, to the advancement of the law in the United States.

The uniform law commissioners have assumed as their special jurisdiction, private law and private remedies. The uniform laws have been largely in the areas of contract, remedies, family law, estates and trusts, real property and conflicts of law. These are the areas of law that drive the engines of the economy, govern the functions of the family, give order to private property and eliminate conflicts between the states.

The labors of the uniform law commissioners have had two general effects that in a fashion transcend the sum of individual contributions. The first has been to equip state government to retain a position in the great gray area of concurrent powers with the Congress of the United States. State government had to have an institution that would permit it to hold its constitutional position and the NCCUSL is that institution.

The second great effect has been the empowerment of the state legislatures in the legislative image propounded in the Constitution of the United States. Whatever the founding fathers felt about the role of legislatures, courts, not the legislatures, dominated from the first days of the nation as source of private law development. We retained, as a nation, the entire English common law tradition.

Empowerment of the legislatures to legislate, rather than to leave development of the law to the courts, is a rather recent phenomenon. In fact, it did not achieve much weight or reality until the Uniform Commercial Code was adopted in nearly all the states in 1967.

The Uniform Commercial Code symbolizes a very great change in the way private law developed in the United States. It was no longer possible in the mid-20th Century — if it ever had been desirable — to leave the development of commercial law to the whims of common law. The economy had grown too large, the commercial environment too complex. The common law is too erratic and unpredictable to govern complex commercial transactions or any complex transactional environment. The Uniform Commercial Code grew from such needs and the NCCUSL provided the ready vehicle for its promulgation.

John M. McCabe is Legislative Director of the National Conference of Commissioners on Uniform State Laws.

UNIFORM LAWS

The uniform law commissioners have led and driven a revolution in the private law, if anything that takes place over a 90-year period and that continues, can be regarded as a revolution. In the spirit of that revolution, however it may be characterized, the uniform law commissioners offer the following new uniform model acts for consideration in the state legislatures. Included are substantial revisions of the Uniform Commercial Code, as the NCCUSL moves to provide, once again, the right law for the conduct of complex commercial transactions in a modern world:

Revised Uniform Commercial Code, Article 6 — Bulk Sales (UCC Article 6)

Two alternatives are presented in UCC Article 6, repeal of the entire article or adoption of a revised text. Any state that chooses not to repeal has a much improved Article 6 that protects bulk seller's creditors by requiring the bulk sale buyer to give notice of the sale to the seller's creditors. A bulk sale is the sale of more than one-half of a business' inventory to a single buyer outside the ordinary course of business. Among the improvements of Article 6 are an expedited notice requirement for a bulk sale buyer when a seller has large numbers of creditors; creditors obtain damages rather than a void sale and a return of the goods, as was the case under original Article 6; and, very small sales and very large sales are excluded from the requirements of Article 6, since creditor protection is not needed in either case.

Uniform Putative and Unknown Fathers Act (UPUFA)

A man becomes a putative father when he is identified as father of a child whose mother is not his wife. An unknown father is one whose identity is not known and cannot be found. UPUFA permits putative fathers to have their paternity adjudicated and to have child custody and visitation rights adjudicated. The act also provides standards for the termination of putative or unknown fathers' rights that conform to constitutional norms. Proper termination of parental rights is essential for successful adoptions of children.

Amendments to Uniform Securities Act (USA 1985)

Five sections of USA 1985 were amended in 1988. Included are slight changes in provisions affecting out-of-state broker-dealers and exempt non-issuer transactions. No material changes were made in any section.

Uniform Status of Children of Assisted Conception (USCACA)

Assisted conception occurs when insemination takes place by any means other than sexual intercourse, or by removal and implantation of an embryo after insemination of a woman's egg by sperm from someone other than her husband. USCACA establishes who the legal parents are when there is an assisted conception. In general, the woman who carries a child and her husband are regarded as its legal parents. No donor of sperm or egg in an assisted conception can be a legal parent. USCACA includes surrogate mother contracts. A state may choose to declare them void, or it may adopt a procedure in an appropriate court to validate such contracts. If a state adopts the second alternative, the court hears evidence very like that in an adoption proceeding, but before conception. The court then decides whether the contract is enforceable.

Uniform Statutory Power of Attorney Act (USPAA)

USPAA provides a set form for creating powers of attorney. Included in the form is a check-off list of transactional categories that a principal can choose for his/her named attorney-in-fact to perform. The only excluded category is health care decisions on behalf of an incompetent principal. The statutory form power of attorney facilitates the use of pre-printed, easily obtainable, and inexpensive forms for executing powers of attorney.

Revised Uniform Commercial Code, Article 3 — Negotiable Instruments (UCC ARTICLE 3)

The law pertaining to drafts, checks, and notes, and the rules for negotiation of these instruments have been contained in UCC Article 3 since 1951. These instruments for payment of money or creation of debt are called negotiable instruments and may be transferred freely from person to person. The revisions do not change the general character of negotiable instruments, but solve problems that have arisen in the 38 years since Article 3 was promulgated. For example, under revised Article 3, negotiability is assumed for an instrument, unless there is language on the face of the instrument making it non-negotiable. This contrasts with the original formal and mechanical rules for identifying a negotiable instrument.

Uniform Commerical Code, Article 4A — Funds Transfers (UCC ARTICLE 4A)

UCC Article 4A is an entirely new article for the Uniform Commercial Code. It governs transfers of large sums of money between commercial entities, generally by electronic means through the banking system. Consumer transactions are excluded from Article 4A and are subject to federal law under the Electronic Funds Transfer Act of 1978. Article 4A establishes basic rules governing the payment of these large sums of money, and establishes which entity or bank is liable in the event something goes wrong with an ordered payment. Generally, the liability falls to the entity responsible for the error. Banks may mitigate their liability by establishing commercially reasonable security systems for the benefit of their customers.

Revised Uniform Probate Code, Article VI (UPC ARTICLE VI)
Uniform Multiple-Person Accounts Act
Uniform Non-Probate Transfers on Death Act
Uniform POD Security Registration Act

UPC Article VI provides for multiple-party deposit accounts and pay-on-death provisions that may apply to both single-party and multiple-party accounts. Pay-on-death provisions allow an account to be paid to a named beneficiary when its last owner dies, without probate. Revised Article VI updates the law on multiple-party accounts and makes them easier to use. It also adds new provisions allowing transfer-on-death provisions for investment securities. Under them, stocks, bonds, security accounts and the like may contain provisions that permit them to be transferred on the death of the owner to a named beneficiary without probate. Revised Article VI is also offered as separate free-standing uniform acts for states that have not adopted the Uniform Probate Code.

Uniform Foreign-Money Claims Act (UFMCA)

In the United States, judgments are stated and paid in dollars, notwithstanding the fact that in litigation, arbitration and other actions pertaining to the allocation of money, a foreign currency may be the better alternative for the establishment of damages or of allocating shares in a fund of money. UFMCA dissolves the old limitations on acceptance of foreign currency in obtaining compensation in American courts.

Uniform Pretrial Detention Act (UPDA)

UPDA permits a defendant charged with a violently committed felony to be confined without bail while waiting for trial. Detention requires proof of certain specific elements pertaining to the likelihood of a successful prosecution, the objective danger to others if the defendant is released, and the lack of an appropriate release program for the defendant. The defendant has a right to counsel and a full hearing.

Uniform Rights of the Terminally Ill Act (URTIA 1989)

URTIA 1989 provides alternative means for a competent adult to provide instructions to a physician regarding withdrawal of life-sustaining treatment during the last stages of a terminal illness when the individual is no longer capable of communicating with the physician. The first alternative is a declaration that treatment be withdrawn, commonly known as a "living will." The other alternative is a declaration appointing another person to make such decisions as a surrogate or attorney-in-fact.

UNIFORM LAWS

Table 8.1
RECORD OF PASSAGE OF UNIFORM ACTS
(As of September 30, 1989)

State or other jurisdiction	Alcoholism and Intoxication Treatment (1971)	Anatomical Gift (1968) (1987)	Arbitration (1956)	Attendance of Out of State Witnesses (1931) (1936)	Audio-Visual Deposition (1978)	Certification of Questions of Law (1967)	Child Custody Jurisdiction (1968)	Class Actions (1976) (1987)	Commercial Code (1951) (1957) (1962) (1966)	Commercial Code-Article 2A (1987)	Commercial Code-Article 4A (1989)	Commercial Code-Article 6 (1989)	Commercial Code-Article 8 (1977)	Commercial Code-Article 9 (1972)	Common Interest Ownership (1982)
Alabama	...	★	...	•	...	...	★	...	•	...	...	...	...	★	...
Alaska	★	★	★	•	...	...	★	...	•	...	...	...	...	★	★
Arizona	...	★	★	•	...	...	★	...	•	...	...	...	...	★	...
Arkansas	...	•	★	★	...	...	★	...	•	...	...	...	★	★	...
California	...	•	☆	...	...	...	★	...	•	★	...	...	★	★	...
Colorado	★	★	★	•	...	★	★	...	•	...	...	...	★	★	...
Connecticut	☆	•	☆	•	...	★	★	...	•	...	...	...	★	★	★
Delaware	★	★	★	•	...	...	★	...	•	...	...	...	★	★	...
Florida	☆	★	★	•	...	☆	★	...	•	...	...	...	★	★	...
Georgia	★	★	...	•	...	...	★	...	•	...	...	...	...	★	...
Hawaii	...	•	☆	•	...	...	★	...	•	...	...	...	★	★	...
Idaho	★	...	★	★	...	...	★	...	•	...	...	...	★	★	...
Illinois	★	★	★	•	...	...	★	...	•	...	...	...	★	★	...
Indiana	...	★	★	★	...	...	★	...	•	...	...	...	★	★	...
Iowa	★	★	★	☆	...	★	★	★	•	...	...	...	★	★	...
Kansas	★	★	★	•	...	★	★	...	•	...	...	...	★	★	...
Kentucky	...	★	★	•	...	...	★	...	•	...	...	...	★	★	...
Louisiana	...	☆	★	•	...	...	★	...	...	...	...	...	★	★	...
Maine	★	★	★	•	...	☆	★	...	•	...	...	...	★	★	...
Maryland	☆	★	★	•	...	★	★	...	•	...	...	...	★	★	...
Massachusetts	☆	★	★	•	...	★	☆	...	•	...	...	...	★	★	...
Michigan	☆	★	☆	☆	...	...	★	...	•	...	...	...	★	★	...
Minnesota	☆	★	★	•	...	★	★	...	•	★	...	...	★	★	...
Mississippi	...	★	...	•	...	...	★	...	•	...	...	...	...	★	...
Missouri	...	★	☆	•	...	...	★	...	•	...	...	...	...	★	...
Montana	★	•	★	•	★	...	★	...	•	...	...	...	★	★	...
Nebraska	...	•	★	•	...	...	★	...	•	...	...	...	★	★	...
Nevada	...	•	★	•	...	...	★	...	•	...	★	...	★	★	...
New Hampshire	...	★	☆	•	...	★	★	...	•	...	...	...	★	★	...
New Jersey	...	★	☆	•	...	...	★	...	•	...	...	...	★	★	...
New Mexico	...	★	★	•	...	...	★	...	•	...	...	...	★	★	...
New York	...	★	☆	•	...	...	★	...	•	...	...	...	★	★	...
North Carolina	...	★	★	•	...	...	★	...	•	...	...	...	★	★	...
North Dakota	...	•	★	★	★	★	★	★	•	...	...	...	★	★	...
Ohio	...	★	☆	•	...	...	★	...	•	...	...	...	★	★	...
Oklahoma	★	★	★	•	...	★	★	...	•	★	...	...	★	★	...
Oregon	...	★	☆	•	...	★	★	...	•	★	...	...	★	★	...
Pennsylvania	...	★	★	•	...	...	★	...	•	...	...	...	★	★	...
Rhode Island	☆	•	☆	★	...	★	★	...	•	...	...	...	★	★	...
South Carolina	...	★	★	•	...	...	★	...	•	...	...	...	...	★	...
South Dakota	★	★	★	•	...	...	★	...	•	★	...	...	★	★	...
Tennessee	...	★	★	•	...	...	★	...	•	...	...	...	★	★	...
Texas	...	★	☆	•	...	...	★	...	•	...	...	...	★	★	...
Utah	...	•	☆	•	...	...	★	...	•	...	★	...	★	★	...
Vermont	...	★	...	•	...	...	★	...	•	...	...	...	...	...	...
Virginia	...	★	★	•	★	...	★	...	•	...	★	...	★	★	...
Washington	★	★	☆	•	...	☆	★	...	•	...	...	...	★	★	...
West Virginia	...	★	...	•	...	★	★	...	•	...	...	...	★	★	★
Wisconsin	★	★	☆	•	...	★	★	...	•	...	...	...	★	★	...
Wyoming	...	★	★	★	...	...	★	...	•	...	...	...	★	★	...
Dist. of Columbia	☆	★	★	•	...	★	★	...	•	...	...	...	...	★	...
Puerto Rico	...	...	☆	★	...	...	...	...	...	...	...	...	...	...	...
U.S. Virgin Islands	...	...	☆	...	...	...	★	...	•	...	...	...	...	...	...

Source: National Conference of Commissioners on Uniform State Laws.
Key:
★ — Enacted
• — Amended version enacted
☆ — Substantially similar version enacted
... — Not enacted

UNIFORM LAWS

PASSAGE OF UNIFORM ACTS—Continued

State or other jurisdiction	Common Trust Fund (1938) (1952)	Comparative Fault (1977) (1979)	Condominium (1977) (1980)	Conflict of Laws-Limitations (1982)	Conservation Easement (1981)	Consumer Credit Code (1968) (1974)	Consumer Sales Practices (1970) (1971)	Construction Lien (1987)	Controlled Substances (1970) (1973)	Crime Victims Reparations (1973)	Crime History Records (1986)	Criminal Procedure, Rules of (1974) (1987)	Custodial Trust (1987)	Deceptive Trade Practices (1964) (1966)	Declaratory Judgments (1922)
Alabama	★	...	...	...	★	...	...	...	★	...	...	...	...	...	★
Alaska	★	...	...	...	...	...	...	...	...	...	...	...	...	...	...
Arizona	★	...	...	...	★	...	...	...	★	...	...	...	...	...	★
Arkansas	★	...	...	★	★	...	...	...	☆	...	...	...	...	...	★
California	★	...	...	...	...	...	...	...	☆	...	...	...	...	...	...
Colorado	★	...	...	★	...	★	...	...	...	...	...	...	...	•	★
Connecticut	...	...	...	...	...	...	...	...	★	...	...	...	...	...	★
Delaware	...	...	...	...	...	...	...	...	★	...	...	...	...	★	★
Florida	★	...	...	...	...	...	...	...	☆	...	...	...	...	•	★
Georgia	...	...	...	...	...	...	...	...	☆	...	...	...	...	•	★
Hawaii	★	...	...	...	...	...	...	...	☆	...	...	...	★	•	...
Idaho	★	...	...	...	★	★	...	...	★	...	...	...	★	...	★
Illinois	★	...	...	...	...	...	...	...	☆	...	☆	...	...	★	★
Indiana	...	...	...	...	★	★	...	...	★	...	...	...	...	...	★
Iowa	•	...	...	...	...	★	...	...	★	...	...	...	...	...	★
Kansas	★	...	...	...	...	★	★	...	★	☆	...	...	...	...	...
Kentucky	...	☆	...	...	★	...	...	...	☆	★	...	...	...	...	★
Louisiana	...	...	...	...	...	...	...	...	★	...	...	...	...	...	...
Maine	★	...	•	...	★	★	...	...	...	...	...	...	...	★	★
Maryland	...	...	...	...	...	...	...	...	★	...	...	...	...	...	★
Massachusetts	•	...	...	...	...	...	...	...	★	...	...	...	...	...	★
Michigan	★	...	...	...	...	...	...	...	★	...	...	...	...	...	...
Minnesota	...	...	★	...	★	...	...	...	☆	☆	...	...	...	•	★
Mississippi	★	...	...	...	★	...	...	...	★	...	...	...	...	...	...
Missouri	★	★	...	•	...	...	...	...	★	...	...	...	...	...	★
Montana	★	...	...	...	...	...	...	...	☆	★	...	...	...	...	★
Nebraska	★	...	•	...	...	...	...	☆	★	...	...	...	...	•	★
Nevada	★	...	...	...	★	...	...	...	★	...	...	...	...	...	★
New Hampshire	•	...	★	...	...	...	...	...	...	...	...	...	...	...	...
New Jersey	...	...	...	...	...	...	...	...	★	★	...	...	...	...	★
New Mexico	★	...	•	...	...	...	...	...	★	...	...	...	...	☆	★
New York	...	...	...	...	...	...	...	...	★	...	...	...	...	...	...
North Carolina	★	...	•	...	...	...	...	...	☆	...	...	...	...	...	★
North Dakota	...	...	...	★	...	...	...	...	★	★	...	...	...	...	★
Ohio	•	...	...	...	...	...	☆	...	...	...	...	...	...	•	★
Oklahoma	•	...	...	...	...	★	☆	...	★	...	...	...	...	★	★
Oregon	•	...	...	★	★	...	...	...	★	...	...	...	...	...	★
Pennsylvania	...	...	★	...	...	...	...	...	★	...	...	...	...	...	★
Rhode Island	...	...	•	...	...	...	...	...	☆	...	...	...	...	★	★
South Carolina	...	...	...	...	...	☆	...	...	★	...	...	...	...	...	★
South Dakota	★	...	...	...	★	...	...	...	★	...	...	...	...	...	★
Tennessee	•	...	...	...	...	...	...	...	★	☆	...	...	...	...	★
Texas	★	...	...	...	★	...	...	...	★	☆	...	...	...	...	★
Utah	★	...	...	...	...	★	•	...	★	...	...	...	...	...	★
Vermont	...	...	...	...	...	...	...	...	...	...	...	...	...	...	★
Virginia	...	...	☆	...	☆	...	...	...	☆	...	...	...	...	...	★
Washington	★	☆	☆	★	...	...	...	...	★	...	...	...	...	...	★
West Virginia	★	...	...	...	...	...	...	...	★	...	...	...	...	...	★
Wisconsin	•	...	...	...	★	☆	...	...	★	...	...	...	...	...	★
Wyoming	★	...	...	...	...	★	...	...	★	...	...	...	...	...	★
Dist. of Columbia	★	...	...	...	★	...	...	...	☆	...	...	...	...	...	☆
Puerto Rico	...	...	...	...	...	...	...	...	★	...	...	...	...	...	★
U.S. Virgin Islands	...	...	...	...	...	...	...	...	★	...	...	...	...	...	★

Key:
★ — Enacted
• — Amended version enacted
☆ — Substantially similar version enacted
... — Not enacted

UNIFORM LAWS

PASSAGE OF UNIFORM ACTS—Continued

State or other jurisdiction	Determination of Death (1978) (1980)	Disclaimer of Property Interests (1973) (1978)	Disclaimer of Transfers by Wills, Intestacy or Appt. (1973) (1978)	Disclaimer of Transfers under Nontestamentary Instruments (1973) (1978)	Disposition of Community Property Rights at Death (1971)	Division of Income for Tax Purposes (1957)	Dormant Mineral Interests (1986)	Drug Dependence Treatment and Rehabilitation (1973)	Durable Power of Attorney (1979) (1987)	Duties to Disabled Persons (1972)	Enforcement of Foreign Judgments (1948) (1964)	Evidence, Rules of (1953) (1974) (1986) (1988)	Exemptions (1976) (1979)	Extradition and Rendition (1980)	Facsimile Signatures of Public Officials (1958)
Alabama	...	•	...	...	...	...	...	...	★	...	•	...	...	•	...
Alaska	•	...	•	...	★	★	...	...	★	...	•	...	•	•	...
Arizona	★	...	...	...	...	...	...	...	★	...	•	...	•	...	...
Arkansas	•	•	...	...	★	★	...	...	★	...	•	...	•	...	★
California	•	...	...	...	...	★	...	...	★	...	•	...	★	...	★
Colorado	•	...	...	...	★	★	...	...	★	★	•	...	•	•	★
Connecticut	★	...	...	...	★	☆	...	★	☆	★	•	...	•	•	★
Delaware	•	...	...	...	...	...	...	...	★	...	•	...	•	•	★
Florida	...	...	...	...	☆	...	...	...	☆	...	•	...	...	...	★
Georgia	...	•	...	...	☆	...	...	...	...	...	☆	...	...	...	...
Hawaii	...	★	...	...	★	★	...	...	•	...	•	...	...	...	★
Idaho	•	...	...	...	...	★	...	...	★	...	•	...	...	...	★
Illinois	...	...	★	...	...	★	...	...	•	...	•	★	...	...	...
Indiana	•	...	...	...	...	★	...	...	•	...	•	...	•	...	...
Iowa	...	...	...	...	...	...	...	...	★	...	•	...	...	...	...
Kansas	...	...	...	...	...	★	...	...	★	...	•	...	•	★	★
Kentucky	...	...	★	...	★	★	...	...	☆	...	...	...	...	...	...
Louisiana	...	...	...	...	...	...	...	...	...	...	...	...	...	...	...
Maine	•	...	★	★	...	★	...	...	★	...	•	...	•	...	...
Maryland	☆	★	...	...	...	...	...	...	★	...	•	...	...	...	★
Massachusetts	...	...	...	...	...	★	...	...	★	...	...	...	...	...	...
Michigan	...	...	...	...	★	★	...	...	★	...	•	...	•	•	...
Minnesota	•	...	...	...	...	☆	...	...	★	...	•	★	•	•	☆
Mississippi	•	...	...	...	...	...	...	...	☆	...	•	...	...	...	...
Missouri	...	...	...	...	...	★	...	...	★	...	•	★	...	...	★
Montana	•	...	...	...	★	★	...	...	★	...	•	...	•	•	★
Nebraska	...	...	...	...	...	...	...	...	★	...	•	★	•	...	...
Nevada	•	...	...	...	...	★	...	...	★	...	•	...	...	...	★
New Hampshire	•	...	...	...	...	☆	...	...	☆	...	•	...	...	...	★
New Jersey	...	...	★	★	...	...	...	...	★	...	...	...	★	...	...
New Mexico	...	...	...	...	...	★	...	...	★	...	•	...	•	...	★
New York	☆	...	...	...	★	★	...	...	☆	...	...	...	•	...	...
North Carolina	...	...	...	...	★	★	...	...	☆	...	...	...	...	...	...
North Dakota	•	...	...	★	...	★	...	...	★	★	•	...	•	★	★
Ohio	...	...	...	...	...	☆	...	...	★	★	•	...	...	...	...
Oklahoma	•	...	...	...	...	...	...	...	•	★	•	...	•	...	★
Oregon	•	•	★	★	★	★	...	...	☆	...	•	...	•	...	...
Pennsylvania	•	...	...	...	...	★	...	...	★	☆	•	...	...	...	★
Rhode Island	•	☆	...	...	...	...	...	...	☆	...	•	...	...	...	★
South Carolina	•	...	...	...	...	☆	...	...	★	...	...	...	...	...	...
South Dakota	...	...	...	...	...	★	...	...	★	...	•	...	•	...	...
Tennessee	•	...	...	...	...	☆	...	...	★	...	•	...	★	...	...
Texas	...	...	...	...	...	★	...	...	☆	...	•	...	•	•	...
Utah	...	...	...	...	...	☆	...	...	★	...	•	...	•	...	...
Vermont	•	★	...	...	...	★	...	...	★	...	•	...	...	...	...
Virginia	...	...	...	...	★	☆	...	...	☆	...	•	...	...	...	...
Washington	•	...	...	...	...	★	☆	...	★	...	•	...	•	•	★
West Virginia	•	•	...	...	...	...	...	...	★	...	•	...	•	...	★
Wisconsin	•	...	...	...	...	☆	...	...	•	...	•	...	•	...	...
Wyoming	★	...	...	...	★	...	...	...	☆	...	•	...	...	...	★
Dist. of Columbia	•	...	...	...	...	...	...	...	★	...	...	...	...	...	...
Puerto Rico	...	...	...	...	...	...	...	...	...	...	★	•	...	...	...
U.S. Virgin Islands	...	...	...	...	...	...	...	...	...	...	...	★	...	...	...

Key:
★ — Enacted
• — Amended version enacted
☆ — Substantially similar version enacted
... — Not enacted

UNIFORM LAWS

PASSAGE OF UNIFORM ACTS—Continued

State or other jurisdiction	Federal Lien Registration (1978) (1982)	Fiduciaries (1922)	Foreign Money Claims (1989)	Foreign Money Judgments Recognition (1962)	Franchise and Business Opportunities (1987)	Fraudulent Conveyance (1918)	Fraudulent Transfer (1984)	Guardianship and Protective Proceedings (1982) (1987)	Health Care Information (1985)	Information Practices Code (1980)	International Wills (1977)	Interstate Arbitration of Death Taxes (1943)	Interstate Compromise of Death Taxes (1943)	Jury Selection and Service (1970) (1971)	Land Security Interests (1985)
Alabama	•	★	...	...	...	...	★	•	...	...	...	...	...	...	...
Alaska	•	...	...	★	...	...	...	...	...	...	...	...	...	...	...
Arizona	...	★	...	...	...	...	★	...	...	...	...	...	...	...	...
Arkansas	•	...	...	...	...	...	★	...	...	...	...	...	...	...	...
California	★	...	...	★	...	...	★	...	...	...	...	★	★	★	...
Colorado	•	★	...	★	...	...	...	•	...	...	★	★	★	★	...
Connecticut	...	...	★	★	...	...	...	...	...	...	★	★	★	...	...
Delaware	...	...	...	...	...	★	...	...	...	...	...	...	...	...	...
Florida	...	...	...	...	...	...	★	...	...	...	...	...	...	...	...
Georgia	...	...	...	...	...	★	...	...	...	...	...	...	...	...	...
Hawaii	...	★	...	...	...	...	★	...	...	☆	...	...	...	...	...
Idaho	★	★	...	...	...	...	★	...	...	...	...	...	...	★	...
Illinois	•	★	...	★	...	...	★	...	...	...	...	...	☆	...	...
Indiana	...	★	...	...	...	...	...	...	...	...	...	...	...	☆	...
Iowa	•	...	...	...	...	...	...	...	...	...	...	...	...	...	...
Kansas	•	...	...	...	...	...	...	...	...	...	...	...	...	...	...
Kentucky	...	...	...	...	...	...	...	...	...	...	...	...	...	...	...
Louisiana	•	★	...	...	...	...	...	...	...	...	...	...	...	...	...
Maine	•	...	...	...	...	...	...	...	...	...	...	★	★	★	...
Maryland	★	★	...	★	...	★	...	...	...	...	...	...	★	★	...
Massachusetts	...	...	...	★	...	★	...	...	...	...	...	★	★	★	...
Michigan	...	...	...	★	...	★	...	...	...	...	...	★	★	★	...
Minnesota	★	★	...	★	...	...	★	...	...	...	★	☆	★	...	...
Mississippi	•	...	...	...	...	...	...	...	...	...	...	...	...	☆	...
Missouri	...	★	...	★	...	...	...	...	...	...	...	...	...	...	...
Montana	•	...	...	...	...	...	★	...	•	★	...	...	...	...	...
Nebraska	•	...	...	...	...	...	★	...	...	...	...	★	★	...	...
Nevada	★	★	...	...	...	...	★	...	...	...	...	...	...	★	...
New Hampshire	•	...	...	...	...	...	★	...	...	...	...	...	...	★	...
New Jersey	...	★	...	...	...	...	★	...	...	...	...	...	...	★	...
New Mexico	☆	★	...	...	...	...	★	...	...	...	...	...	...	...	...
New York	...	☆	...	★	...	★	...	...	...	...	...	...	...	★	...
North Carolina	...	★	...	...	...	...	...	...	...	...	...	...	...	...	...
North Dakota	•	...	...	...	...	...	★	...	...	...	★	...	...	...	★
Ohio	...	★	...	...	...	★	...	...	...	...	...	...	...	...	...
Oklahoma	•	...	...	★	...	...	★	...	...	...	...	...	...	...	...
Oregon	★	...	...	★	...	...	★	...	...	...	...	...	...	...	...
Pennsylvania	...	★	...	...	...	★	...	...	...	...	★	★	★	...	...
Rhode Island	...	☆	...	...	...	...	★	...	...	...	...	...	...	...	...
South Carolina	...	...	...	...	...	...	...	...	...	...	...	...	...	...	...
South Dakota	•	★	...	...	...	...	★	...	...	...	...	...	...	...	...
Tennessee	...	★	...	...	...	★	...	...	...	...	...	☆	☆	...	...
Texas	•	...	...	★	...	...	★	...	...	...	...	...	...	...	...
Utah	...	★	★	...	...	...	★	...	...	...	...	...	...	...	...
Vermont	...	...	...	...	...	...	...	...	...	...	...	...	...	★	★
Virginia	•	...	...	...	...	...	...	...	...	...	...	...	...	★	★
Washington	•	...	...	★	...	...	★	...	...	...	...	...	...	★	★
West Virginia	•	...	...	...	...	...	★	...	...	...	...	...	...	★	★
Wisconsin	★	★	...	...	...	...	★	...	...	...	...	...	...	★	...
Wyoming	•	★	...	...	...	...	★	...	...	...	...	...	...	...	...
Dist. of Columbia	...	★	...	...	...	...	...	☆	...	...	...	...	...	...	...
Puerto Rico	...	...	...	...	...	...	...	...	...	...	...	...	...	...	...
U.S. Virgin Islands	...	★	...	...	...	★	...	...	...	...	...	...	...	...	...

Key:
★ — Enacted
• — Amended version enacted
☆ — Substantially similar version enacted
... — Not enacted

UNIFORM LAWS

PASSAGE OF UNIFORM ACTS—Continued

State or other jurisdiction	Land Transactions (1975)(1977)(1983)	Limited Partnership (1976)(1983)(1985)	Management of Institutional Funds (1972)	Mandatory Disposition of Detainers (1958)	Marital Property (1983)	Marriage and Divorce (1970)(1973)	Multiple Persons Account (1989)	Nonprobate Transfers on Death (1989)	Motor Vehicle Accident Reparations (1972)	Notarial Acts (1982)	Parentage (1973)	Partnership (1914)	Photographic Copies as Evidence (1949)	Planned Communities (1980)
Alabama	...	★	...	...	...	...	...	...	...	...	★	☆	★	...
Alaska	...	...	...	...	...	...	...	...	...	...	...	★	★	...
Arizona	...	★	...	★	...	★	...	...	...	...	...	★	★	...
Arkansas	...	★	...	...	...	...	...	...	...	...	...	★	★	...
California	...	☆	☆	...	...	...	...	...	...	...	★	★	★	...
Colorado	...	★	★	★	...	★	...	...	...	...	★	★	★	...
Connecticut	...	★	★	...	...	...	...	...	...	...	...	★	★	...
Delaware	...	•	★	...	...	...	...	...	...	★	★	★	...	...
Florida	...	•	...	...	...	...	...	...	...	...	...	★	★	...
Georgia	...	•	★	...	...	...	☆	...	...	...	...	★	★	...
Hawaii	...	•	...	...	...	...	...	...	...	...	★	★	★	...
Idaho	...	★	...	★	...	...	...	...	...	...	...	★	★	...
Illinois	...	•	★	...	...	...	☆	...	...	...	☆	★	...	...
Indiana	...	•	★	...	...	...	...	...	...	...	...	★	★	...
Iowa	...	★	...	...	...	...	...	...	...	...	...	★	★	...
Kansas	...	•	☆	★	...	...	...	...	...	★	★	★	★	...
Kentucky	...	•	★	...	...	★	...	...	...	...	...	★	★	...
Louisiana	...	...	★	...	...	...	...	...	...	...	...	...	★	...
Maine	...	...	★	...	...	...	...	...	...	...	...	★	★	...
Maryland	...	★	★	...	...	...	...	...	...	...	...	★	★	...
Massachusetts	...	•	★	☆	...	...	...	...	...	...	...	★	★	...
Michigan	...	★	★	...	...	...	...	...	...	...	...	★	★	...
Minnesota	...	•	★	★	...	☆	...	...	...	★	★	★	★	...
Mississippi	...	•	...	...	...	...	...	...	...	...	...	★	...	...
Missouri	...	★	★	★	...	...	...	...	...	...	...	★	...	...
Montana	...	★	★	...	...	•	...	...	...	...	★	★	★	...
Nebraska	...	★	...	...	...	...	...	...	...	...	...	☆	★	...
Nevada	...	•	...	...	...	...	...	...	...	...	...	★	★	...
New Hampshire	...	•	...	...	...	...	...	...	...	...	...	★	★	...
New Jersey	...	★	★	...	...	...	...	...	...	...	...	★	★	...
New Mexico	...	•	...	...	...	...	...	...	...	...	...	★	★	...
New York	...	...	☆	...	...	...	...	...	...	...	...	★	★	...
North Carolina	...	•	★	...	...	...	...	...	...	...	...	★	★	...
North Dakota	...	•	★	★	...	...	...	...	...	...	★	★	★	...
Ohio	...	★	☆	...	...	...	...	...	...	...	☆	★	...	...
Oklahoma	...	•	...	...	...	...	...	...	...	★	...	★	★	...
Oregon	...	•	★	...	...	...	...	...	...	★	...	★	★	...
Pennsylvania	...	•	...	...	...	...	...	...	...	...	...	★	★	...
Rhode Island	...	•	★	...	...	...	...	...	...	...	★	★	★	...
South Carolina	...	★	...	★	...	...	...	...	...	...	...	★	...	...
South Dakota	...	•	...	...	...	...	...	...	...	...	...	★	★	...
Tennessee	...	•	★	...	...	...	...	...	...	...	...	★	★	...
Texas	...	•	...	...	...	...	...	...	...	...	☆	★	★	...
Utah	...	•	...	★	...	...	...	...	...	...	...	★	★	...
Vermont	...	...	★	...	...	...	...	...	...	...	...	★	★	...
Virginia	...	•	...	...	...	...	...	...	...	...	...	★	★	...
Washington	...	★	★	...	...	☆	...	...	...	...	★	★	★	...
West Virginia	...	•	★	...	...	...	...	...	...	...	...	★	★	...
Wisconsin	...	•	★	...	★	...	...	...	...	★	...	★	★	...
Wyoming	...	★	...	...	...	...	...	...	...	...	★	★	★	...
Dist. of Columbia	...	•	★	...	...	...	...	...	...	...	...	★	...	...
Puerto Rico	...	...	...	...	...	...	...	...	...	...	...	...	...	...
U.S. Virgin Islands	...	...	...	...	...	...	...	...	...	...	...	★	★	...

Key:
★ — Enacted
• — Amended version enacted
☆ — Substantially similar version enacted
... — Not enacted

UNIFORM LAWS

PASSAGE OF UNIFORM ACTS—Continued

State or other jurisdiction	Post-Conviction Procedure (1980)	Premarital Agreement (1983)	Principal and Income (1931) (1962)	Probate Court (1969) (1975) (1982) (1987) (1989)	Public Assembly (1972)	Putative and Unknown Fathers (1988)	Reciprocal Enforcement of Support (1950) (1958) (1968)	Residential Landlord and Tenant (1972)	Rights to the Terminally Ill (1985) (1989)	Securities (1985) (1988)	Simplification of Fiduciary Security Transfers (1958)	Simplifications of Land Transfers (1976) (1977) (1983)	Simultaneous Death (1940)	State Antitrust (1973) (1979)
Alabama	...	...	★	...	...	...	•	...	...	...	★	...	★	...
Alaska	...	...	•	★	...	...	•	★	★	...	...	...	★	...
Arizona	...	...	•	★	...	...	•	★	...	...	★	...	•	★
Arkansas	...	★	•	...	...	...	•	...	☆	...	...	...	•	...
California	...	•	•	...	...	...	•	...	...	...	★	...	★	...
Colorado	...	...	★	•	...	...	•	...	...	...	★	...	•	...
Connecticut	...	...	•	...	...	...	•	★	...	...	★	...	★	...
Delaware	...	...	...	...	...	...	•	...	...	...	★	...	★	...
Florida	...	...	•	...	...	...	•	★	...	...	★	...	★	...
Georgia	...	...	...	...	...	...	•	...	...	...	...	...	•	...
Hawaii	...	★	•	...	...	...	•	★	...	...	★	...	★	...
Idaho	...	...	•	★	...	...	•	...	...	...	★	...	★	...
Illinois	...	...	★	...	...	...	•	...	...	...	★	...	★	...
Indiana	...	...	•	...	...	...	•	...	...	...	...	...	★	...
Iowa	...	...	...	...	...	...	★	★	...	★	...	...	★	★
Kansas	...	★	•	...	...	...	☆	...	...	...	★	...	★	...
Kentucky	...	...	...	...	...	...	★	...	...	...	...	...	•	...
Louisiana	...	...	★	...	...	...	•	...	...	...	...	...	...	...
Maine	...	★	...	•	...	...	•	...	★	★	★	...	★	...
Maryland	...	...	•	...	...	...	•	...	...	...	★	...	★	...
Massachusetts	...	...	...	...	...	...	•	...	...	...	...	...	...	...
Michigan	...	...	•	☆	...	...	•	★	...	...	★	...	★	★
Minnesota	...	...	•	★	...	...	•	...	★	...	★	...	★	...
Mississippi	...	...	...	...	...	...	•	...	...	...	★	...	★	...
Missouri	...	...	•	...	...	...	•	...	...	...	★	...	•	...
Montana	...	★	•	★	...	...	•	★	★	...	★	...	★	...
Nebraska	...	...	...	★	...	...	•	★	...	...	★	...	★	...
Nevada	...	★	•	...	...	...	•	...	...	...	•	★	★	...
New Hampshire	...	...	...	...	...	...	•	...	...	...	...	...	★	...
New Jersey	...	...	...	☆	...	...	•	...	...	...	★	...	★	...
New Mexico	...	...	•	★	...	...	•	★	...	★	...	...	•	...
New York	...	★	•	...	...	...	•	...	...	...	★	...	★	...
North Carolina	...	...	•	...	...	...	•	...	...	...	★	...	★	...
North Dakota	★	★	•	•	...	...	•	★	...	...	★	...	★	•
Ohio	...	...	...	...	...	...	•	...	...	...	...	...	...	...
Oklahoma	...	...	★	...	★	...	•	★	...	...	...	...	•	...
Oregon	...	★	...	...	...	...	•	★	...	...	...	...	★	...
Pennsylvania	...	...	★	☆	...	...	•	...	...	...	...	...	★	...
Rhode Island	...	★	...	...	...	...	•	★	...	...	★	...	★	...
South Carolina	...	...	•	★	...	...	•	★	...	...	★	...	★	...
South Dakota	...	★	•	...	...	...	•	...	...	★	★	...	★	...
Tennessee	...	...	★	...	...	...	•	★	...	...	★	...	★	...
Texas	...	★	★	...	...	...	•	...	...	...	★	...	•	...
Utah	...	...	★	★	...	...	•	...	...	...	...	...	★	...
Vermont	...	...	★	...	☆	...	•	...	...	...	...	...	★	...
Virginia	...	★	★	...	...	...	•	★	...	...	★	...	★	...
Washington	...	...	•	...	...	...	•	☆	...	...	★	...	★	...
West Virginia	...	...	★	...	...	...	•	...	...	...	★	...	★	...
Wisconsin	...	...	★	...	...	...	•	...	...	...	★	...	★	...
Wyoming	...	...	•	...	...	...	•	...	...	...	...	...	★	...
Dist. of Columbia	...	...	...	...	...	...	•	...	...	...	★	...	•	...
Puerto Rico	...	...	...	...	...	...	•	...	...	...	...	...	...	...
U.S. Virgin Islands	...	...	...	...	...	...	•	...	...	...	...	...	•	...

Key:
★ — Enacted
• — Amended version enacted
☆ — Substantially similar version enacted
... — Not enacted

UNIFORM LAWS

PASSAGE OF UNIFORM ACTS—Continued

State or other jurisdiction	Status of Children of Assisted Conception (1988)	Status of Convicted Persons (1964)	Statutory Form Power of Attorney (1988)	Statutory Rule Against Perpetuities (1986)	Statutory Will (1984)	Succession Without Administration (1983)	Supervision of Trustees for Charitable Purposes (1954)	Testamentary Additions to Trusts (1960)	TOD Security Registration (1989)	Trade Secrets (1979) (1985)	Transboundary Pollution Reciprocal Access (1982)	Transfers to Minors (1983) (1986)	Trustees' Powers (1964)	Unclaimed Property (1981)
Alabama	...	...	...	...	...	...	...	☆	...	●	...	★	...	...
Alaska	...	...	...	...	...	...	...	★	...	●	...	●	...	★
Arizona	...	...	...	...	...	...	...	★	...	●	...	●	★	★
Arkansas	...	...	...	...	...	...	...	★	...	★	...	★	...	...
California	...	...	...	...	...	...	★	★	...	★	...	★	...	...
Colorado	...	...	...	...	...	...	...	☆	...	●	★	★	...	★
Connecticut	...	...	...	★	...	...	...	★	...	★	...	●	...	...
Delaware	...	...	...	...	...	...	...	...	...	★	...	●	...	...
Florida	...	...	...	★	...	...	...	☆	...	●	...	●	★	★
Georgia	...	...	...	...	...	...	...	★	...	...	...	...	...	...
Hawaii	...	★	...	...	...	...	...	★	...	●	...	★	★	...
Idaho	...	...	...	...	...	...	...	★	...	★	...	★	★	★
Illinois	...	...	...	...	...	★	...	☆	...	★	...	★	★	★
Indiana	...	...	...	...	...	...	...	☆	...	★	...	●	...	...
Iowa	...	...	...	...	...	...	...	★	...	...	...	★	...	...
Kansas	...	...	...	...	...	...	...	★	...	●	...	★	★	...
Kentucky	...	...	...	...	...	...	...	★	...	...	...	★	★	...
Louisiana	...	...	...	...	...	...	...	...	...	★	...	●	...	★
Maine	...	...	...	...	...	...	...	★	...	●	...	●	...	...
Maryland	...	...	...	...	...	...	...	☆	...	●	...	●	...	★
Massachusetts	...	...	...	...	★	...	...	★	...	...	...	★	...	...
Michigan	...	...	...	★	...	...	★	★	...	...	★	...	...	...
Minnesota	...	...	...	★	...	...	...	★	...	●	...	●	☆	...
Mississippi	...	...	...	...	...	...	...	☆	...	...	...	...	★	...
Missouri	...	...	...	...	...	...	...	...	...	...	...	★	...	...
Montana	...	☆	...	★	...	...	...	☆	...	★	★	●	★	☆
Nebraska	...	...	...	★	...	...	...	...	...	...	...	...	...	...
Nevada	...	...	...	★	...	...	...	★	...	●	...	★	...	★
New Hampshire	...	★	...	...	...	...	...	★	...	●	...	★	★	★
New Jersey	...	...	...	...	...	...	...	☆	...	●	★	●	...	★
New Mexico	...	...	...	...	...	...	...	★	...	●	...	●	...	★
New York	...	...	...	...	...	...	...	☆	...	...	...	...	...	...
North Carolina	...	...	...	...	...	...	...	☆	...	●	...	●	...	...
North Dakota	★	...	...	...	...	...	...	★	...	●	...	★	...	★
Ohio	...	...	...	...	...	...	...	☆	...	...	...	...	...	...
Oklahoma	...	...	...	...	...	...	...	★	...	...	...	★	...	...
Oregon	...	...	...	★	...	...	★	★	...	●	...	★	★	★
Pennsylvania	...	...	...	...	...	...	...	☆	...	...	...	●	...	...
Rhode Island	...	...	...	...	...	...	...	...	...	★	...	★	...	...
South Carolina	...	...	...	★	...	...	...	★	...	...	...	...	...	★
South Dakota	...	...	...	...	...	...	...	★	...	●	...	★	...	...
Tennessee	...	...	...	...	...	...	...	★	...	...	...	...	...	...
Texas	...	...	...	...	...	...	...	☆	...	...	...	...	...	...
Utah	...	...	...	...	...	...	...	☆	...	●	...	●	★	★
Vermont	...	...	...	...	...	...	...	★	...	...	...	...	...	...
Virginia	...	...	...	...	...	...	...	...	...	●	...	●	...	★
Washington	...	...	...	...	...	...	...	☆	...	★	...	...	...	★
West Virginia	...	...	...	...	...	...	...	★	...	●	...	★	...	...
Wisconsin	...	...	...	...	...	...	...	...	...	●	★	●	...	★
Wyoming	...	...	...	...	...	...	...	☆	...	...	...	●	★	...
Dist. of Columbia	...	...	...	...	...	...	...	☆	...	●	...	★	...	...
Puerto Rico	...	...	...	...	...	...	...	...	...	...	...	...	...	...
U.S. Virgin Islands	...	...	...	...	...	...	...	...	...	...	...	...	...	★

Key:
★ — Enacted
● — Amended version enacted
☆ — Substantially similar version enacted
... — Not enacted

UNIFORM LAWS

Table 8.2
RECORD OF PASSAGE OF MODEL ACTS
(As of September 30, 1989)

State or other jurisdiction	Act to Provide for the Appointment of Commissioners (1944)	Anti-Discrimination (1966)	Class Actions (1976) (1987)	Eminent Domain Code (1974)	Insanity Defense and Post-Trial Disposition (1984)	Juvenile Court (1968)	Land Sales Practices (1966)	Minor Student Capacity to Borrow (1969)	Periodic Payment of Judgments (1980)	Post-Mortem Examinations (1954)	Public Defender (1970) (1974)	Real Estate Cooperative (1981)	Real Estate Time-Share (1980) (1982)	State Administrative Procedures (1981)	Statutory Construction (1965)	Water Use (1958)
Alabama	★	...	...	★	...	...	...	...	...	...	...	...	...	...	...	...
Alaska	...	...	...	...	...	...	★	...	...	...	...	...	...	...	...	...
Arizona	★	...	...	...	...	...	...	★	...	...	...	...	★	...	...	...
Arkansas	★	...	...	...	...	...	...	...	...	...	...	...	...	...	...	...
California	...	...	...	...	...	...	...	...	...	...	...	...	...	...	...	...
Colorado	...	...	...	...	...	...	...	...	...	...	...	...	...	...	★	...
Connecticut	...	...	...	...	...	...	★	★	...	...	...	...	...	...	...	...
Delaware	...	...	...	...	...	...	...	...	...	...	...	...	...	...	...	...
Florida	...	...	...	...	...	...	★	...	...	...	...	...	...	...	...	...
Georgia	...	...	...	...	...	☆	☆	...	...	...	...	...	...	...	...	...
Hawaii	...	★	...	...	...	...	★	...	...	...	...	...	...	...	...	☆
Idaho	...	...	...	...	...	...	...	...	...	...	...	...	...	...	...	...
Illinois	...	...	...	...	...	...	...	...	...	...	...	...	...	...	...	...
Indiana	...	...	...	...	...	...	...	...	...	...	...	...	...	...	...	...
Iowa	★	...	★	...	...	...	...	...	...	☆	...	...	...	...	★	...
Kansas	...	...	...	...	...	...	★	...	...	...	...	...	...	...	...	...
Kentucky	★	...	...	...	...	...	...	...	...	...	...	...	...	...	...	...
Louisiana	...	...	...	...	...	...	...	...	...	...	...	...	☆	...	...	...
Maine	★	...	...	...	...	...	...	...	...	...	...	...	...	...	...	...
Maryland	...	...	...	...	...	...	...	...	...	★	...	...	☆	...	...	...
Massachusetts	...	...	...	...	...	...	...	...	...	...	...	...	...	•	...	...
Michigan	...	...	...	...	...	...	...	...	...	...	...	...	...	...	...	...
Minnesota	...	...	...	...	...	...	...	...	...	...	...	...	...	...	...	...
Mississippi	★	...	...	...	...	...	...	...	...	...	...	...	...	...	...	...
Missouri	...	...	...	...	...	...	...	...	...	...	...	...	...	...	...	...
Montana	★	...	...	...	...	...	★	☆	...	...	...	...	...	...	...	...
Nebraska	★	...	...	...	...	...	...	...	...	...	...	...	...	...	...	...
Nevada	...	...	...	...	...	...	...	...	...	...	...	...	...	...	...	...
New Hampshire	★	...	...	...	...	...	...	...	...	...	...	...	...	...	...	...
New Jersey	...	...	...	...	...	...	...	...	...	...	...	...	...	...	...	...
New Mexico	...	...	...	...	...	...	...	...	...	...	...	...	...	...	...	...
New York	...	...	...	...	...	...	...	...	...	...	...	...	...	...	...	...
North Carolina	...	...	...	...	...	...	...	...	...	...	...	...	...	...	...	...
North Dakota	...	...	...	★	...	☆	★	★	...	...	...	...	...	...	...	...
Ohio	...	...	...	...	...	...	...	...	...	...	...	...	...	...	...	...
Oklahoma	...	★	...	...	...	...	★	...	★	...	...	...	...	...	...	...
Oregon	★	...	...	...	...	...	...	...	★	...	...	...	...	...	...	...
Pennsylvania	...	...	...	...	...	...	...	...	...	...	...	...	...	...	...	...
Rhode Island	...	...	...	...	...	...	...	...	...	...	...	...	...	★	...	...
South Carolina	...	...	...	...	...	...	...	...	...	...	...	...	...	...	...	...
South Dakota	...	...	...	...	...	...	...	★	...	...	...	...	...	...	...	...
Tennessee	...	...	...	...	...	...	...	...	...	...	...	...	...	...	...	...
Texas	...	...	...	...	...	...	...	...	★	...	...	...	...	...	...	...
Utah	...	...	...	...	...	...	...	...	...	...	...	...	...	...	...	...
Vermont	...	...	...	...	...	...	...	...	...	...	...	...	...	...	...	...
Virginia	...	...	...	...	...	...	...	...	...	...	...	★	...	...	...	...
Washington	...	...	...	...	...	...	★	...	...	...	...	...	...	...	...	...
West Virginia	...	...	...	...	...	...	...	...	...	☆	...	...	...	...	...	...
Wisconsin	...	...	...	...	...	...	...	...	...	...	...	...	•	...	★	...
Wyoming	...	...	...	...	...	...	...	...	...	...	...	...	...	...	...	...
Dist. of Columbia	...	...	...	...	...	...	...	...	...	...	...	...	...	...	...	...
Puerto Rico	...	...	...	...	...	...	...	...	...	...	...	...	...	...	...	...
U.S. Virgin Islands	★	...	...	...	...	...	...	...	...	...	...	...	...	...	...	...

Source: National Conference of Commissioners on Uniform State Laws.
Key:
★ — Enacted
• — Amended version enacted
☆ — Substantially similar version enacted
... — Not enacted

EDUCATION AND CHILDREN

Table 8.3
MINIMUM AGE FOR SPECIFIED ACTIVITIES

State or jurisdiction	Age of majority (a)	Minimum age for marriage with consent (b)		Minimum age for making a will	Minimum age for buying (c)		Minimum age for serving on a jury	Minimum age for leaving school (d)
		male	female		liquor	beer or wine		
Alabama	19	14 (e)	14 (e)	19	21	21	19	16
Alaska	18	16 (f)	16 (f)	18	21	21	18	16
Arizona	18	16 (f)	16 (f)	18	21	21	18	16
Arkansas	18	17 (f)	16 (f)	18	21	21	18	17
California	18	(g)	(g)	18 (h)	21	21	18	16
Colorado	18	16 (f)	16 (f)	18	21	21 (i)	18	16
Connecticut	18	16 (f)	16 (f)	18	21	21	18	16
Delaware	18	18 (f,j)	16 (f,j)	18	21	21	18	16
Florida	18	16 (f)	16 (f)	18	21	21	18	16
Georgia	18	16 (f,j)	16 (f,j)	18	21	21	18	16
Hawaii	18	16	16 (f)	18	21	21	18	18
Idaho	18	16 (f)	16 (f)	18 (h)	21	21	18	16
Illinois	18	16 (f)	16 (f)	18	21	21	18	16
Indiana	18	17 (f)	17 (f)	18	21	21	18	16
Iowa	18	16	16	18	21	21	18	16
Kansas	18	(g)	(g)	18	21	21	18	16
Kentucky	18	(g)	(g)	18	21	21	18	16 (k)
Louisiana	18	18 (f)	16 (f)	16 (h)	21	21	18	17
Maine	18	16 (f)	16 (f)	18	21	21	18	17
Maryland	18	16 (f)	16 (f)	18	21	21	18	16
Massachusetts	18	(g)	(g)	18	21	21	18	16
Michigan	18	16	16	18	21	21	18	16
Minnesota	18	16 (l)	16 (l)	18	21	21	18	16 (m)
Mississippi	18	17 (f)	15 (f)	18	21	21	21	17
Missouri	18	15 (f)	15 (f)	18	21	21	21	16
Montana	18	18 (f)	18 (f)	18	21	21	18	16 (n)
Nebraska	19	17	17	18	21	21	19	16
Nevada	18	16 (f)	16 (f)	18	21	21	18	17
New Hampshire	18	14 (l)	13 (l)	18	21	21	18	16
New Jersey	18	16 (o)	16 (o)	18	21	21	18	16
New Mexico	18	16 (f)	16 (f)	18	21	21	18	18
New York	(p)	16	14 (l)	18	21	21	18	16 (q)
North Carolina	18	16	16 (f)	18	21	21	18	16
North Dakota	18	16	16	18	21 (r)	21 (r)	18	16
Ohio	18	18 (f)	16 (f)	18	21	19	18	18
Oklahoma	18	16 (f)	16 (f)	18	21	21	18	18
Oregon	18	17	17	18	21	21	18	18
Pennsylvania	21	16 (f)	16 (f)	18	21	21	18	17
Rhode Island	18	18 (f)	16 (f)	18	21	21	18	16
South Carolina	18	18 (f)	14 (f)	18	21	21	18	17
South Dakota	18	16 (f)	16 (f)	18	21	21 (i)	18	16 (n)
Tennessee	18	16 (f)	16 (f)	18	21	21	18	17
Texas	18	14 (l)	14 (l)	18 (h)	21	21	18	17
Utah	18	(g)	(g)	18	21	21	18	18
Vermont	18	16 (f)	16 (f)	18	21	21	18	16
Virginia	18	16 (f)	16 (f)	18	21	21	18	18
Washington	18	17 (f)	17 (f)	18	21	21	18	18
West Virginia	18	(s)	(s)	18	21	21	18	16
Wisconsin	18	16	16	18	21	21	18	18
Wyoming	19	16 (f)	16 (f)	19	21	21	19	16
Dist. of Columbia	18	16	16	18	21	21	18	17

Sources: Distilled Spirits Council of the United States, Inc.; Education Commission of the States; *The Book of the States, 1988-89;* and state constitutions.

(a) Generally, the age at which an individual has legal control over own actions and business (e.g. ability to contract) except as otherwise provided by statute. In many states, age of majority is arrived at upon marriage if minimum legal marrying age is lower than prescribed age of majority.
(b) With parental consent. Minimum age for marrying without consent is 18 years in all states, except Mississippi (21 years) and Wyoming (19 years).
(c) As of early 1986. Legislation enacted; may not yet be effective.
(d) Without graduating.
(e) Bond is required if under 18.
(f) Legal procedure for younger persons to obtain license.
(g) Statute provides that any unmarried male or female under 18 may marry with consent (usually with order of court granting permission).
(h) Age may be lower for a minor who is living apart from parents or legal guardians and managing own financial affairs, or who has contracted a lawful marriage.
(i) Eighteen, if 18 on or before 7/29/87.
(j) Parental consent not required when female is pregnant or applicants are parents of a living child.
(k) Signed parental approval prior to age 18.
(l) Parental consent and judicial consent required.
(m) Age 18, year 2000.
(n) Or completion of eighth grade, whichever is earlier.
(o) Parental consent required for ages 16 to 18; judicial approval for individuals under 16.
(p) As defined in general obligations (for purposes of contracting) and civil rights codes, 18 years.
(q) Age 17 in New York City and Buffalo.
(r) Two military bases permit 18-year-olds to purchase.
(s) Under 16, must have parental consent and approval of circuit judge.

EDUCATION AND CHILDREN

Table 8.4
GENERAL REVENUE OF PUBLIC SCHOOL SYSTEMS BY SOURCE: 1986-1987
(In thousands of dollars)

State or jurisdiction	Total (a)	Total	Intergovernmental - Directly from federal government	Intergovernmental - From state - Federal aid distributed by state	Intergovernmental - From state - Other	From other local governments	Total	From own sources - Taxes	From own sources - Parent government contributions	From own sources - Current charges - School lunch	From own sources - Current charges - Other	Other
United States	$165,856,581	$87,367,388	$1,138,949	$8,684,253	$75,184,435	$2,359,751	$72,632,221	$50,071,763	$13,351,183	$3,004,426	$1,517,622	$4,687,227
Alabama	2,076,776	1,510,042	22,892	199,834	1,114,703	172,613	308,475	190,833		70,219	4,510	42,913
Alaska	918,854	653,034	66,605	17,999	568,430		265,820		230,678	7,237	7,237	20,668
Arizona	2,162,444	1,279,044	63,683	117,584	1,018,511	79,266	883,400	744,983		45,199	19,859	73,359
Arkansas	1,266,340	719,486	4,347	106,841	606,032	2,266	449,333	346,421		22,784	42,088	38,040
California	17,860,152	12,792,897	82,033	1,079,196	11,477,586	154,082	4,583,007	3,507,758	191,595	236,130	23,406	624,118
Colorado	2,418,689	978,953	9,391	88,788	878,518	2,256	1,439,736	1,165,174		40,581	46,815	187,166
Connecticut	2,586,017	906,517	1,985	67,221	738,217	99,094	1,474,776		1,432,034	28,045	8,447	6,250
Delaware	423,756	317,226	4,587	26,631	286,008		106,530	91,595		7,646	380	6,909
Florida	6,932,938	4,054,688	35,740	439,156	3,579,792		2,878,250	2,346,731		144,848	188,269	198,402
Georgia	4,199,350	2,537,539	24,037	246,419	2,228,319	38,764	1,427,469	1,166,406		79,634	11,848	169,581
Hawaii	665,620	641,916	66,465		575,451	20	23,704 (b)					2,152
Idaho	554,744	334,698	1,819	34,325	298,534		177,020	155,084		10,113	11,439	9,364
Illinois	7,204,882	3,145,475	35,760	358,882	2,747,180	3,653	3,748,550	3,272,038		12,082	490	297,031
Indiana	3,692,899	2,004,277	7,231	141,433	1,827,700	27,913	1,446,044	1,217,135		120,532	58,949	89,007
Iowa	1,874,032	986,785	549	67,777	918,459		887,247	779,240		93,145	46,757	32,797
										69,299	5,911	
Kansas	1,647,385	825,014	9,434	38,032	669,991	107,557	780,062	653,398		40,116	17,132	69,416
Kentucky	1,870,964	1,246,097	12,787	162,527	1,069,039	1,744	479,259	367,769		35,875	12,669	62,946
Louisiana	2,498,754	1,445,273	16,499	238,929	1,182,392	7,453	848,848	718,565		37,601	17,524	75,158
Maine	799,575	366,105	4,605	35,683	325,817		364,827	126,689	204,365	9,444	9,066	15,263
Maryland	3,206,252	1,044,553	17,316	144,386	881,973	878	1,798,625		1,660,817	57,331	24,373	56,104
Massachusetts	4,265,547	1,991,206	9,836	176,968	1,566,417	237,985	2,069,430		1,967,443	71,665	12,480	17,842
Michigan	7,556,513	2,504,411	44,654	327,957	1,989,237	142,563	4,499,499	3,994,915		131,867	111,416	261,301
Minnesota	3,250,707	1,963,654	13,386	123,630	1,794,721	31,917	1,287,053	1,060,230		66,951	55,849	104,023
Mississippi	1,205,297	889,132	7,028	183,781	698,227	96	316,165	216,430	1,327	26,084	28,425	43,899
Missouri	2,864,456	1,828,764	9,865	157,142	1132817	528,940	1,035,692	836,906		54,240	67,934	76,612
Montana	631,832	431,623	28,943	22,669	302,825	77,186	200,209	164,313		8,841	1,183	25,872
Nebraska	1,100,031	334,970	10,842	45,512	211,964	66,652	765,061	641,260		22,757	55,955	45,089
Nevada	596,295	405,965	6,430	19,733	378,654	1,148	190,330	162,929		9,784	1,686	15,931
New Hampshire	619,140	59,100	2,067	17,174	39,393	466	560,040	407,483	120,404	16,028	5,476	10,649
New Jersey	6,835,878	2,525,719	13,538	262,649	2,249,532		3,696,366	2,968,115	474,332	91,169		162,750
New Mexico	1,004,102	877,986	52,808	77,212	747,966		126,116	70,628		14,144	4,090	37,254
New York	16,023,736	7,504,203	21,939	738,582	6,685,316	58,366	8,519,533	4,927,641	3,038,605	165,517	141,221	246,549
North Carolina	3,672,234	2,557,073	24,672	241,197	2,291,133	71	1,115,161		861,730	116,435	5,413	131,583
North Dakota	444,977	261,144	12,441	28,278	212,027	8,398	183,833	141,102		9,938	12,967	19,826
Ohio	6,876,512	3,398,438	19,181	333,535	3,042,638	3,084	3,478,074	3,017,418		195,118	62,687	202,851
Oklahoma	1,990,586	1,177,324	36,518	105,323	994,050	41,433	688,262	563,398		34,941	6,100	83,823
Oregon	2,060,578	703,382	35,689	88,792	534,655	44,246	1,357,196	1,221,728		30,034	35,982	69,452
Pennsylvania	8,257,326	3,621,211	21,606	405,497	3,191,791	2,317	4,179,118	3,739,419		138,420	31,784	269,495
Rhode Island	625,976	264,642	4,456	21,829	229,629	8,728	331,831		328,683	9,938	574	2,574
South Carolina	2,076,541	1,145,141	10,619	152,613	917,231	64,678	721,068	562,986		43,655	58,876	55,551

418 The Book of the States 1990-91

GENERAL REVENUE OF PUBLIC SCHOOL SYSTEMS BY SOURCE: 1986-1987—Continued

State or jurisdiction	Total (a)	Intergovernmental Total	Directly from federal government	From state: Federal aid distributed by state	From state: Other	From other local governments	From own sources Total	Taxes	Parent government contributions	Current charges: School lunch	Current charges: Other	Other
South Dakota	431,569	167,087	22,162	23,989	113,405	7,531	264,482	231,334	...	7,713	2,682	22,753
Tennessee	2,272,900	1,353,732	12,326	194,523	918,660	228,223	736,820	...	618,455	53,455	18,268	46,642
Texas	12,018,433	5,595,968	62,447	678,155	4,840,952	14,414	5,753,571	5,008,380	...	286,892	91,236	367,063
Utah	1,125,753	693,522	12,572	56,192	624,758	...	432,231	358,307	...	23,808	8,125	41,991
Vermont	449,449	133,815	1,835	18,144	113,255	581	315,634	296,359	...	5,982	1,905	11,388
Virginia	3,879,551	1,923,459	38,114	179,831	1,703,551	1,963	1,956,092	...	1,832,074	80,976	20,760	22,282
Washington	3,102,928	2,423,017	49,621	138,522	2,232,715	2,159	679,911	470,320	...	45,795	91,393	72,403
West Virginia	1,308,929	845,988	2,603	90,068	753,317	...	350,172	279,647	...	21,585	3,665	45,275
Wisconsin	3,381,971	1,607,675	8,130	145,722	1,417,810	36,013	1,774,296	1,627,069	...	53,496	13,741	79,990
Wyoming	627,781	342,958	9,396	17,391	263,137	53,034	284,823	253,627	...	7,806	8,351	15,039
Dist. of Columbia	438,630	45,460	45,460	...	...	...	393,170	...	388,641	1,469	229	2,831

Source: U.S. Bureau of the Census, *Finances of Public School Systems: January 1990*.

Note: Because of rounding, detail may not add to totals. Revenue from state sources for state dependent school systems is included as intergovernmental revenue from state rather than as parent government contributions.

(a) To avoid duplication, interschool system transactions are excluded.
(b) Revenues from charges and miscellaneous sources for Hawaii's state operated school system are included as local source revenue because these types of revenue appear under this category for the school systems in the other states.

Table 8.5
SUMMARY OF STATE GOVERNMENT DIRECT EXPENDITURES FOR EDUCATION BY STATE: 1986-87
(In thousands of dollars)

State	Total (a)	Elementary and secondary					Higher education				
				Capital outlay		Other capital outlay			Capital outlay		Other capital outlay
		Total	Current operation	Total	Construction		Total	Current operation	Total	Construction	
United States	$61,647,377	$1,301,257	$1,103,175	$198,082	$132,066	$66,016	$50,710,281	$45,246,574	$5,463,707	$2,982,765	$2,480,942
Alabama	1,506,181	34,090	26,961	7,129	7,129	...	1,056,133	929,015	127,118	71,189	55,929
Alaska	456,328	170,378	157,927	12,451	7,864	4,587	226,190	209,476	16,714	12,056	4,658
Arizona	1,010,121	...	...	...	...	...	903,008	797,882	105,126	45,815	59,311
Arkansas	617,395	...	...	...	...	...	479,537	446,281	33,256	21,293	11,963
California	6,921,315	92,605	92,605	...	...	...	5,947,259	5,244,951	702,308	470,440	231,868
Colorado	983,554	...	...	...	...	...	918,018	840,446	77,572	25,574	51,998
Connecticut	663,075	...	...	...	...	...	507,807	465,478	42,329	19,264	23,065
Delaware	314,236	...	...	...	...	...	256,806	222,964	33,842	13,837	20,005
Florida	1,513,135	...	...	...	...	...	994,622	816,620	178,002	80,137	97,865
Georgia	1,341,748	...	...	...	...	...	1,171,070	1,047,533	123,537	46,251	77,286
Hawaii	820,672	514,411	444,034	70,377	57,866	12,511	291,855	259,590	32,265	14,183	18,082
Idaho	291,367	...	...	...	...	...	258,092	220,693	37,399	20,023	17,376
Illinois	2,519,900	8,328	...	8,328	8,328	...	1,929,429	1,672,620	256,809	91,085	165,724
Indiana	1,829,609	...	...	...	...	...	1,582,322	1,453,512	128,810	46,485	82,325
Iowa	957,731	...	...	...	...	...	859,890	747,893	111,997	60,400	51,597
Kansas	653,624	19,784	19,470	44	...	44	586,889	541,148	45,741	21,171	24,570
Kentucky	1,028,769	...	...	...	...	...	829,346	757,623	71,723	31,085	40,638
Louisiana	1,141,073	27,254	27,254	...	...	...	926,493	842,822	83,671	42,939	40,732
Maine	312,580	4,077	3,470	607	591	...	242,428	211,375	31,053	21,445	9,608
Maryland	1,204,160	85,237	85,237	...	...	16	934,480	815,797	118,683	68,476	50,207
Massachusetts	1,280,979	...	...	...	...	...	1,025,416	916,663	108,753	58,265	50,488
Michigan	2,758,691	...	...	...	...	...	2,473,702	2,219,731	253,971	131,249	122,722
Minnesota	1,378,884	...	...	...	...	...	1,188,248	1,081,312	106,936	54,973	51,963
Mississippi	539,376	3,543	3,543	...	...	...	442,085	411,896	30,189	13,504	16,685
Missouri	1,099,910	...	...	...	...	...	978,048	827,271	150,777	104,885	45,892
Montana	224,574	...	...	...	...	...	175,689	151,573	24,116	9,977	14,139
Nebraska	463,385	...	...	...	...	...	413,735	355,698	58,037	29,162	28,875
Nevada	223,828	...	...	...	...	...	198,765	182,152	16,613	10,982	5,631
New Hampshire	216,430	...	...	...	...	...	188,940	155,551	33,389	24,281	9,108
New Jersey	1,534,051	...	...	...	...	...	1,275,977	1,159,121	116,856	55,512	61,344
New Mexico	474,212	16,488	9,509	6,979	6,979	...	411,168	369,856	41,312	33,418	7,894
New York	4,085,256	190	190	...	...	...	3,010,614	2,593,068	417,546	387,749	29,797
North Carolina	1,720,900	66,341	30,464	35,877	1,048	34,829	1,446,750	1,276,015	170,735	81,095	89,640
North Dakota	287,464	...	...	...	...	...	262,627	243,766	18,861	8,759	10,102
Ohio	2,679,330	...	...	...	...	...	2,472,856	2,183,361	289,495	141,222	148,273
Oklahoma	871,306	29,571	29,296	275	25	250	766,204	712,088	54,116	25,136	28,980
Oregon	674,134	...	...	...	...	...	595,240	518,758	76,482	40,052	36,430
Pennsylvania	2,080,768	19,639	...	19,639	19,639	...	1,269,705	1,146,656	123,049	62,641	60,408
Rhode Island	289,456	...	...	...	...	...	201,726	196,330	5,396	745	4,651
South Carolina	1,121,379	37,137	25,554	11,583	...	11,583	915,575	823,119	89,456	45,586	43,870

STATE GOVERNMENT DIRECT EXPENDITURES FOR EDUCATION—Continued

State	Elementary and secondary					Higher education			
	Total (a)	Total	Current operation	Capital outlay		Total	Current operation	Capital outlay	
				Total	Construction	Other capital outlay			Total	Construction	Other capital outlay

State	Total (a)	Total	Current operation	Total	Construction	Other capital outlay	Total	Current operation	Total	Construction	Other capital outlay
South Dakota	188,379	...	...	...	...	...	166,676	155,389	11,287	4,758	6,529
Tennessee	1,302,563	149,587	147,391	...	...	...	1,013,949	930,265	83,684	36,809	46,875
Texas	3,867,642	...	...	2,196	...	2,196	3,456,843	3,090,655	366,188	182,355	183,833
Utah	703,799	...	...	...	...	...	636,440	556,163	80,277	28,085	52,192
Vermont	216,407	...	...	...	...	...	178,439	167,812	10,627	3,666	6,961
Virginia	1,795,280	...	...	...	...	...	1,602,176	1,461,150	141,026	79,510	61,516
Washington	1,513,992	22,597	...	22,597	22,597	...	1,348,555	1,211,211	137,344	78,476	58,868
West Virginia	437,898	...	...	...	...	...	357,011	339,735	17,276	393	16,883
Wisconsin	1,381,103	...	...	...	...	...	1,201,713	1,140,933	60,780	23,071	37,709
Wyoming	149,428	...	...	...	...	...	133,735	122,557	11,178	3,301	7,877

Source: Bureau of the Census, Finances of Public School Systems: 1987.
Note: Detail may not add to total due to rounding.
(a) To avoid duplication, interschool system transactions are excluded.

EDUCATION AND CHILDREN

Table 8.6
FEDERAL FUNDS OBLIGATED FOR CHILD NUTRITION PROGRAMS, BY STATE: FISCAL YEAR 1988
(In thousands of dollars)

State or other jurisdiction	Total	Special Milk	School lunch	School breakfast	State administrative expense	Child care	Summer food service
UNITED STATES	$4,076,752	$18,092	$2,825,942	$465,485	$54,662	$581,821	$130,750
Alabama	99,889	34	71,031	12,278	1,294	11,632	3,620
Alaska	10,672	27	6,698	685	326	2,929	7
Arizona	56,317	206	37,752	6,705	760	9,896	998
Arkansas	47,920	27	35,694	6,260	719	4,970	250
California	425,145	715	290,801	55,821	5,534	61,044	11,230
Colorado	47,719	133	28,532	2,588	1,057	14,628	781
Connecticut	28,344	494	18,462	1,616	532	6,338	902
Delaware	10,077	32	5,328	981	288	2,664	784
Florida	189,215	119	131,289	26,498	2,134	21,273	7,902
Georgia	133,705	69	94,402	16,030	1,795	17,050	4,359
Hawaii	19,712	10	14,821	2,333	349	1,847	352
Idaho	13,983	122	11,228	532	305	1,731	65
Illinois	168,868	2,524	126,071	12,923	2,068	21,260	4,022
Indiana	57,553	333	43,828	3,058	828	8,293	1,213
Iowa	39,341	242	29,612	1,717	619	6,327	824
Kansas	40,167	393	25,239	1,096	536	12,412	491
Kentucky	81,220	276	58,350	14,250	1,021	6,098	1,225
Louisiana	137,083	84	98,180	16,765	1,630	16,652	3,772
Maine	16,411	161	10,946	840	372	3,804	288
Maryland	53,192	340	35,701	5,094	814	9,615	1,628
Massachusetts	76,425	517	41,421	7,859	1,187	23,300	2,141
Michigan	110,199	1,410	78,300	4,900	1,468	20,210	3,911
Minnesota	68,931	750	37,200	1,900	1,070	26,775	1,236
Mississippi	105,927	17	69,595	15,843	1,296	14,672	4,504
Missouri	67,284	494	47,778	5,778	865	11,057	1,312
Montana	13,050	67	8,743	779	354	2,876	231
Nebraska	23,765	220	16,453	900	447	5,429	316
Nevada	8,835	32	6,133	1,335	254	997	84
New Hampshire	8,195	200	5,679	509	278	1,328	201
New Jersey	80,250	974	57,063	5,404	1,444	12,020	3,345
New Mexico	42,929	27	28,053	3,807	663	8,246	2,133
New York	323,566	1,750	207,405	37,773	2,703	40,646	33,289
North Carolina	120,732	107	84,409	19,779	1,505	11,930	3,002
North Dakota	13,821	78	7,531	445	368	5,180	219
Ohio	151,812	1,248	112,593	15,984	1,711	17,823	2,453
Oklahoma	57,758	146	41,330	7,009	816	7,946	511
Oregon	32,732	212	23,243	2,344	538	5,824	571
Pennsylvania	135,937	797	98,411	7,600	1,669	19,309	8,151
Rhode Island	10,566	105	6,936	795	421	1,500	809
South Carolina	77,920	27	57,677	8,841	1,018	6,165	4,192
South Dakota	15,859	58	11,222	1,544	341	2,146	548
Tennessee	90,317	36	64,509	15,885	1,220	7,120	1,547
Texas	369,814	106	256,782	66,791	3,811	38,907	3,417
Utah	11,032	44	20,561	556	490	7,200	181
Vermont	6,380	187	3,966	196	271	1,721	39
Virginia	74,899	265	55,775	7,408	724	9,300	1,427
Washington	60,132	241	38,266	3,610	586	16,781	648
West Virginia	40,696	32	27,311	8,708	686	3,345	614
Wisconsin	47,701	1,562	35,523	2,208	770	7,007	631
Wyoming	7,413	22	4,551	227	279	2,239	95
Dist. of Columbia	14,635	16	10,020	1,781	326	1,972	520
American Samoa	3,294	0	2,162	958	174	0	0
Guam	2,866	0	2,012	636	211	7	0
No. Mariana Islands	1,944	0	1,254	517	173	0	0
Puerto Rico	118,336	0	97,010	16,692	1,306	0	3,328
U.S. Virgin Islands	4,267	4	3,100	114	238	380	431

Source: U.S. Department of Agriculture, Food and Nutrition Service.

EDUCATION AND CHILDREN

Table 8.7
AVERAGE ANNUAL SALARY OF INSTRUCTIONAL STAFF IN PUBLIC ELEMENTARY AND SECONDARY SCHOOLS: 1939-40 to 1988-89

State or jurisdiction	Average annual salary for: (in unadjusted dollars)					
	1939-40	1949-50	1959-60	1969-70	1979-80 (a)	1988-89 (a)
Alabama	$ 744	$2,111	$4,002	$ 6,954	$13,338	$26,150
Alaska	. . .	. . .	6,859	10,993	27,697	42,818
Arizona	1,544	3,556	5,590	8,975	16,180	31,985
Arkansas	584	1,801	3,295	6,445	12,704	22,503
California	2,351	. . .	6,600	9,980	18,626	36,381
Colorado	1,393	2,821	4,997	7,900	16,840	34,918
Connecticut	1,861	3,558	6,008	9,400	17,062	38,793
Delaware	1,684	3,273	5,800	9,300	16,873	32,763
Florida	1,012	2,958	5,080	8,600	14,875	28,697
Georgia	770	1,963	3,904	7,372	14,547	29,752
Hawaii	. . .	. . .	5,390	9,829	20,436	31,945
Idaho	1,057	2,481	4,216	7,257	14,110	24,265
Illinois	1,700	3,458	5,814	9,950	18,271	32,257
Indiana	1,433	3,401	5,542	9,574	16,256	29,642
Iowa	1,017	2,420	4,030	8,200	15,600	26,704
Kansas	1,014	2,628	4,450	7,811	14,513	29,248
Kentucky	826	1,936	3,327	7,624	15,350	26,020
Louisiana	1,006	2,983	4,978	7,220	14,020	23,100
Maine	894	2,115	3,694	8,059	13,743	25,744
Maryland	1,642	3,594	5,557	9,885	18,308	35,127
Massachusetts	2,037	3,338	5,545	9,175	22,500	33,163
Michigan	1,576	3,420	5,654	10,125	19,277	35,741
Minnesota	1,276	3,013	5,275	9,957	16,654	32,444
Mississippi	559	1,416	3,314	6,012	12,274	22,664
Missouri	1,159	2,581	4,536	8,091	14,543	27,001
Montana	1,184	2,962	4,425	8,100	15,080	26,291
Nebraska	829	2,292	3,876	7,855	14,236	26,674
Nevada	1,557	3,209	5,693	9,689	17,290	30,150
New Hampshire	1,258	2,712	4,455	8,018	12,930	26,245
New Jersey	2,093	3,511	5,871	9,500	18,851	34,390
New Mexico	1,144	3,215	5,382	8,125	15,406	25,400
New York	2,604	3,706	6,537	10,200	20,400	37,400
North Carolina	946	2,688	4,178	7,744	14,445	26,761
North Dakota	745	2,324	3,695	6,900	13,839	22,994
Ohio	1,587	3,088	5,124	8,594	16,100	30,882
Oklahoma	1,014	2,736	4,659	7,139	13,500	22,600
Oregon	1,333	3,323	5,535	9,200	16,996	30,800
Pennsylvania	1,640	3,006	5,308	9,000	17,060	31,447
Rhode Island	1,809	3,294	5,499	8,900	18,425	35,564
South Carolina	743	1,891	3,450	7,000	13,670	26,200
South Dakota	807	2,064	3,725	6,700	13,010	22,005
Tennessee	862	2,302	3,929	7,290	14,193	26,512
Texas	1,079	3,122	4,708	7,503	14,729	27,565
Utah	1,394	3,103	5,096	8,049	17,403	24,128
Vermont	981	2,348	4,466	8,225	13,300	27,265
Virginia	899	2,328	4,312	8,200	14,655	29,503
Washington	1,706	3,487	5,643	9,500	19,735	30,477
West Virginia	1,170	2,425	3,952	7,850	14,395	22,889
Wisconsin	1,379	3,007	4,870	9,150	16,335	32,600
Wyoming	1,169	2,798	4,937	8,532	16,830	28,844
Dist. of Columbia	2,350	3,920	6,280	11,075	23,027	45,603

Sources: U.S. Department of Education, National Center for Education Statistics, *Statistics of State School Systems*; National Education Association, *Estimates of School Statistics 1988-89* (Copyright 1989). Reprinted with permission.

Note: Includes supervisors, principals, classroom teachers and other instructional staff.

Key:
. . . — Not available
(a) Estimated

EDUCATION AND CHILDREN

Table 8.8
MEMBERSHIP AND ATTENDANCE IN PUBLIC ELEMENTARY AND SECONDARY SCHOOLS, BY STATE: 1987-88 AND 1988-89

State or other jurisdiction	1987-88			1988-89		
	Estimated average daily membership (ADM)	Average daily attendance (ADA)	ADA as a percent of ADM	Estimated average daily membership (ADM)	Average daily attendance (ADA)	ADA as a percent of ADM
United States	...	37,032,650	UD	...	37,240,835	UD
Alabama	727,253	689,771	94.8	723,577	686,285	94.8
Alaska	101,144	93,963	92.9	106,693	99,699	93.4
Arizona	566,098	559,008	98.7	583,249	549,922	94.3
Arkansas	431,925	409,314	94.8	429,559	411,535	95.8
California	...	4,464,085	UD	...	4,564,062	UD
Colorado	534,783	514,838	96.3	534,635	514,696	96.3
Connecticut	467,300	437,800	93.7	463,700	434,500	93.7
Delaware	94,388	87,821	93.0	95,179	88,624	93.1
Florida	1,664,999	1,530,467	91.9	1,769,113	1,644,744	93.0
Georgia	1,078,730	1,034,502	95.9	1,079,135	1,034,890	95.9
Hawaii	165,856	155,240	93.6	167,173	156,472	93.6
Idaho	...	199,563	UD	...	201,500	UD
Illinois	1,701,834	1,584,053	93.1	1,676,145	1,564,402	93.3
Indiana	933,359	882,297	94.5	927,078	876,425	94.5
Iowa	473,537	450,997	95.2	472,697	449,145	95.0
Kansas	399,666	378,771	94.8	404,870	383,703	94.8
Kentucky	612,105	578,986	94.6	606,125	574,000	94.7
Louisiana	754,300	710,700	94.2	750,900	707,500	94.2
Maine	205,414	196,399	95.6	208,404	197,500	94.8
Maryland	680,095	625,326	91.9	685,605	630,392	91.9
Massachusetts	828,621	720,504	87.0	820,078	713,076	87.0
Michigan	...	1,467,600	UD	...	1,462,600	UD
Minnesota	716,120	679,598	94.9	723,919	686,999	94.9
Mississippi	502,554	479,402	95.4	511,092	490,085	95.9
Missouri	...	723,536	UD	...	727,667	UD
Montana	145,981	139,420	95.5	145,954	139,127	95.3
Nebraska	264,218	252,399	95.5	265,375	253,813	95.6
Nevada	165,218	153,060	92.6	173,000	160,000	92.5
New Hampshire	158,788	149,627	94.2	162,010	152,614	94.2
New Jersey	1,085,800	1,008,700	92.9	1,071,700	995,600	92.9
New Mexico	272,656	245,390	90.0	276,817	246,914	89.2
New York	2,518,000	2,288,000	90.9	2,504,000	2,276,000	90.9
North Carolina	1,073,763	1,013,355	94.4	1,069,800	1,009,615	94.4
North Dakota	118,376	113,433	95.8	118,078	113,147	95.8
Ohio	1,772,217	1,656,692	93.5	1,757,673	1,643,127	93.5
Oklahoma	578,100	546,600	94.6	575,300	543,300	94.4
Oregon	449,300	420,200	93.5	455,000	425,400	93.5
Pennsylvania	1,634,400	1,520,000	93.0	1,605,280	1,495,300	93.1
Rhode Island	135,365	124,559	92.0	133,500	122,500	91.8
South Carolina	591,500	566,300	95.7	594,600	575,000	96.7
South Dakota	124,893	119,591	95.8	124,976	119,671	95.8
Tennessee	816,678	766,651	93.9	818,840	767,400	93.7
Texas	...	2,990,668	UD	...	3,028,050	UD
Utah	419,827	397,240	94.6	427,877	404,852	94.6
Vermont	90,900	86,000	94.6	93,000	88,000	94.6
Virginia	971,062	914,354	94.2	974,028	917,147	94.2
Washington	771,297	723,091	93.8	786,472	737,317	93.7
West Virginia	...	319,330	UD	...	311,592	UD
Wisconsin	735,501	693,397	94.3	737,039	695,759	94.4
Wyoming	97,517	92,419	94.8	96,815	91,534	94.5
Dist. of Columbia	85,499	77,633	90.8	85,499	77,633	90.8

Source: National Education Association, *Estimates of School Statistics 1988-89* (Copyright 1989). Reprinted with permission.
Key:
. . . — Not Available
UD — Undefined

EDUCATION AND CHILDREN

Table 8.9
ENROLLMENT, AVERAGE DAILY ATTENDANCE AND CLASSROOM TEACHERS IN PUBLIC ELEMENTARY AND SECONDARY SCHOOLS, BY STATE: 1988-89

State or jurisdiction	Enrollment	Estimated average daily attendance	Classroom teachers	Pupils per teacher based on enrollment	Pupils per teacher based on average daily attendance
United States	40,292,308	37,240,835	2,308,900	17.5	16.1
Alabama	730,032	686,285	38,079	19.2	18.0
Alaska	107,738	99,699	6,288	17.1	15.9
Arizona	655,583	549,922	33,071	19.8	16.6
Arkansas	436,387	411,535	25,462	17.1	16.2
California	4,580,105	4,564,062	201,635	22.7	22.6
Colorado	560,081	514,696	31,385	17.8	16.4
Connecticut	464,719	434,500	34,983	13.3	12.4
Delaware	96,678	88,624	5,897	16.4	15.0
Florida	1,724,939	1,644,744	100,304	17.2	16.4
Georgia	1,111,365	1,034,890	60,380	18.4	17.1
Hawaii	167,227	156,472	9,079	18.4	17.2
Idaho	214,615	201,500	10,440	20.6	19.3
Illinois	1,787,888	1,564,402	102,701	17.4	15.2
Indiana	958,530	876,425	53,870	17.8	16.3
Iowa	478,200	449,145	30,046	15.9	14.9
Kansas	426,596	383,703	28,097	15.2	13.7
Kentucky	637,627	574,000	35,736	17.8	16.1
Louisiana	782,900	707,500	43,720	17.9	16.2
Maine	208,404	197,500	13,878	15.0	14.2
Maryland	689,337	630,392	40,551	17.0	15.5
Massachusetts	816,811	713,076	59,138	13.8	12.1
Michigan	1,655,400	1,462,600	77,750	21.3	18.8
Minnesota	728,015	686,999	43,007	16.9	16.0
Mississippi	503,326	490,085	27,500	18.3	17.8
Missouri	806,639	727,667	50,692	15.9	14.4
Montana	151,944	139,127	9,595	15.8	14.5
Nebraska	268,870	253,813	17,906	15.0	14.2
Nevada	176,500	160,000	8,699	20.3	18.4
New Hampshire	169,415	152,614	10,442	16.2	14.6
New Jersey	1,080,868	995,600	79,138	13.7	12.6
New Mexico	276,817	246,914	15,255	18.1	16.2
New York	2,580,000	2,276,000	177,300	14.6	12.8
North Carolina	1,081,138	1,009,615	61,790	17.5	16.3
North Dakota	118,176	113,176	7,709	15.3	14.7
Ohio	1,778,662	1,643,127	100,659	17.7	16.3
Oklahoma	581,000	543,300	34,400	16.9	15.8
Oregon	461,800	425,400	25,147	18.4	16.9
Pennsylvania	1,654,580	1,495,300	102,450	16.2	14.6
Rhode Island	133,585	122,500	8,931	15.0	13.7
South Carolina	615,500	575,000	34,900	17.6	16.5
South Dakota	126,534	119,671	8,375	15.1	14.3
Tennessee	829,898	767,400	43,330	19.2	17.7
Texas	3,284,179	3,028,050	191,737	17.1	15.8
Utah	429,551	404,852	18,456	23.3	21.9
Vermont	95,049	88,000	6,700	14.2	13.1
Virginia	982,081	917,147	61,535	16.0	14.9
Washington	790,918	737,317	38,752	20.4	19.0
West Virginia	335,912	311,592	22,051	15.2	14.1
Wisconsin	774,857	695,759	48,542	16.0	14.3
Wyoming	97,793	91,534	6,461	15.1	14.2
Dist. of Columbia	87,539	77,633	4,951	17.7	15.7

Source: National Education Association, *Estimates of School Statistics 1988-89* (Copyright 1989). Reprinted with permission.

EDUCATION AND CHILDREN

Table 8.10
STATE COURSE REQUIREMENTS FOR HIGH SCHOOL GRADUATION

State or jurisdiction	All courses	Years of instruction in . . .							First graduating class to which requirements apply
		English/ language arts	Social studies	Mathe- matics	Science	Physical education /health	Electives	Other courses	
Alabama (a,b)									
Standard diploma	22	4	3	2	2	1½	9½	. . .	1989
Advanced diploma	22	4	4	3	3	1½	4	½ home and personal management, 2 foreign language	1989
Alaska	21	4	3	2	2	1	9	. . .	. . .
Arizona (b)	20	4	2½	2	2	. . .	9	½ free enterprise	1991
Arkansas (c)	20	4	3	3	2	1	6½	½ fine arts	1988
California (b,d)									
Standard diploma	13	3	3	2	2	2	. . .	. . .	. . .
Advanced dilpoma	16	3	3	3	2	2	. . .	2 foreign language, 1 fine arts	. . .
Colorado (e)	. . .	. . .	. . .	. . .	. . .	. . .	. . .	. . .	. . .
Connecticut	20	4	3	3	2	1	6	1 arts or vocational education	1988
Delaware (b)	19	4	2	2	2	1½	6½	. . .	1987
Florida (b,f,g,h)									
Standard diploma	24	4	3	3	3	½	9	½ practical or exploratory vocational education, ½ performing arts, or speech and debate, ½ life management skills	1989
Academic scholars	24	4	2	2	2	1½	1½	2 foreign language, 1 fine arts	1989
Georgia (b)									
Standard diploma	21	4	3	2	2	1	8	1 fine arts, vocational education, computer technology, or junior ROTC	1988
Advanced diploma	21	4	3	3	3	1	4	2 foreign language, 1 fine arts, vocational education, computer technology, or ROTC	1988
Hawaii	. . .	4	4	2	2	1½	6	½ guidance	. . .
Idaho (i)	21	4	2	2	2	1½	6	½ reading, ½ speech, ½ consumer education, 1 humanities	1989
Illinois (j)	16	3	2	2	1	4½	2¼	¼ consumer education, 1 art, foreign language, music or vocational education	1988
Indiana									
Standard diploma	19½	4	2	2	2	1½	8	. . .	1989
Academic honors	24	4	3	4	4	1	4 or 5	3 or 4 in foreign language	1990
Iowa (h,k)	. . .	. . .	. . .	. . .	. . .	1	. . .	. . .	. . .
Kansas	21	4	3	2	2	1	9	. . .	1989
Kentucky									
Standard diploma	20	4	2	3	2	1	7	1 additional mathematics science, social studies, or vocational education	1987
Commonwealth diploma	22	5	2	----------6----------		1	. . .	1 foreign language in advanced placement	1986
Louisiana (b)									
Standard diploma	23	4	3	3	3	2	7½	½ computer literacy	1989
Louisiana scholar(l)	23	4	3	3	3	2	7½	½ computer literacy	1987
Regent's scholar	24	4	3½	3	3	2	4½	3 foreign language, 1 fine arts	1983
Maine (a,f)	16	4	2	2	2	1½	3½	1 fine arts	1989
Maryland (b,m)	20	4	3	3	2	1	5	1 fine arts, industrial arts/technology education, home economics, vocational education or computer studies	1989
Massachusetts (k)	. . .	. . .	1	. . .	. . .	4	. . .	. . .	. . .
Michigan (i,n)	. . .	. . .	½	. . .	. . .	. . .	. . .	. . .	. . .
Minnesota (h)	20	4	3	1	1	1½	9½	. . .	1982
Mississippi (b,f)	18	4	2	2	2	. . .	8	. . .	1989
Missouri									
Standard diploma	22	3	2	2	2	1	10	1 practical arts, 1 fine arts	1988
College preparatory studies certificate (o)	24	4	3	3	3	1	8	1 practical arts, 1 fine arts	1988

EDUCATION AND CHILDREN

STATE COURSE REQUIREMENTS—Continued

State or jurisdiction	All courses	English/ language arts	Social studies	Mathematics	Science	Physical education /health	Electives	Other courses	First graduating class to which requirements apply
Montana (p)	20	4	1½	2	1	1	9½	...	1989
Nebraska (q)	...	...	...	...	...	...	...	...	1991
Nevada (b)	22½	4	2	2	2	2½	8½	1 arts/humanities, ½ computer literacy	1992
New Hampshire (r)	19¾	4	2½	2	2	1¼	4	½ arts, ½ computer science, 3 from 2 of the following: arts, foreign language, practical arts, and vocational education	1989
New Jersey (b)	21½	4	3	3	2	4	4	1 fine, practical or performing arts, ½ career exploration	1990
New Mexico (a,i,s)	23	4	3	3	2	1	9	1 communication skills	1990
New York (b)									
Local diploma	18½	4	4	2	2	½	varies	1 art and/or music	1989
Regent's diploma	18½	4	4	2	2	½	varies	3 to 5 in a sequence of specific courses (varying on type of diploma) chosen by the student	1989
North Carolina (b,f)									
Standard diploma	20	4	2	2	2	1	9	...	1987
Scholars program	22	4	4	3	3	2	1	1 vocational education, 1 arts education	1984
North Dakota (t)	17	4	3	2	2	1	5	...	1984
Ohio (b)	18	3	2	2	1	1	9	...	1988
Oklahoma									
Standard diploma	20	4	2	2	2	...	10	...	1987
College preparatory	15	4	2	3	2	...	...	4 from: foreign language, computer science, economics, English, geography, government, math, history, sociology, science, speech, or psychology. Total hour requirement is less, but curriculum is more rigorous and restrictive.	1988
Oregon (b,u)	22	3	3½	2	2	2	8	½ career development, 1 applied arts, fine arts, or foreign language	1988
Pennsylvania (v)	21	4	3	3	3	2	5	2 arts/humanities	1989
Rhode Island									
Standard diploma	16	4	2	2	2	...	6	...	1989
College bound	18	4	2	3	2	...	4	2 foreign language, ½ arts, ½ computer literacy	...
South Carolina (b,h,n,w)									
Standard diploma	20	4	3	3	2	1	7	...	1987
Academic achievement honors	22	4	3	3	2	1	7	2 foreign language	1986
South Dakota	20	4	3	2	2	...	8	½ computer studies, ½ fine arts	1989
Tennessee (b,x)									
Standard diploma	20	4	1	2	2	1½	9	½ economics	1989
Honors	20½	4	3	3	3	1½	2	2 in same foreign language, 2 fine/visual or performing arts (general honors) or 4 in same vocational education program (vocational education honors)	1989
Texas (b,h)									
Standard diploma	21	4	2½	3	2	2	7	½ economics/free enterprise	1988
Advanced programs	22	4	2½	3	3	1½	2	½ economics/free enterprise, 2 foreign language, 1 computer science, 1 fine arts	1988
Utah	24	3	3	2	2	2	9½	1½ arts, 1 vocational education, ½ computer science	1988
Vermont (y)	14½	4	4	----------5----------		1½	...	1 arts	1989

EDUCATION AND CHILDREN

STATE COURSE REQUIREMENTS—Continued

State or jurisdiction	All courses	Years of instruction in . . .							First graduating class to which requirements apply
		English/ language arts	Social studies	Mathe- matics	Science	Physical education /health	Electives	Other courses	
Virginia (b,h)									
Standard diploma ..	21	4	3	2	2	2	6	1 additional science or mathematics, 1 fine or practical arts	1989
Advanced studies diploma	23	4	3	3	3	2	4	3 foreign language, 1 fine or practical arts	1989
Washington (z)	19	3	2½	2	2	2	5½	1 occupational education, 1 fine, visual, or performing arts	1991
West Virginia (aa) ...	21	4	3	2	2	2	8	1 applied, fine, or performing arts or foreign language	1989
Wisconsin (m,bb)	13	4	3	2	2	2	. . .	. . .	1989
Wyoming (k)	18	. . .	1	. . .	. . .	. . .	. . .	. . .	. . .
Dist. of Columbia ...									
Comprehensive	20½	4	2	2	2	1½	7	1 foreign language, 1 lifeskills	1985
Advanced Diploma .	23	4	2	2	2	1½	1½	1 foreign language, 8 specialized preparation	1985

Source: Education Commission of the States, *Clearinghouse Notes* (September, 1989).

Key:
. . . — No requirement.
(a) Must be computer literate before graduation.
(b) Minimum competency test is required for graduation. In Ohio and South Carolina, effective by 1990. In Oregon, effective by 1992. In Maryland, a writing test and passage of a quiz on citizenship is also required.
(c) Arkansas has a social studies option of 3 units or 2 units social studies and 1 practical arts.
(d) California State Board has published "Model Graduation Requirements" to be used as a guide by local districts.
(e) Colorado accreditation requires total of 30 units covering language arts, social studies, science, mathematics, foreign language, fine/vocational/ practical arts, health/safety and physical education with local boards determining requirements. State has constitutional prohibition against state requirement.
(f) One of the science units must include lab. Florida, two of the science units must be in a lab.
(g) Florida students in vocational programs may substitute certain sequences of vocational courses to satisfy up to two of the required credits in each of the areas of English, mathematics and science.
(h) Florida, Iowa, Minnesota, South Carolina, Texas and Virginia allow students in the junior and senior classes to receive dual credits for college courses.
(i) Idaho and New Mexico have available state level minimum competency tests which districts have the option to use. If students pass the test, a special proficiency endorsement is included on their diploma.
(j) Illinois school boards may excuse pupils in 11th and 12th grades from physical education for: (1) participation in interscholastic athletics; or (2) enrollment in an academic class required for admission to college or to meet graduation requirements. Pupils in Grades 9-12 may elect to take a State Board of Education developed consumer education proficiency test. If passed, pupils will be excused from this requirement.
(k) Legislative requirements in effect for many years. Local districts determine remaining requirements.
(l) Must have ACT score of 29 or above, 3.5 GPA with no semester grade lower than a "B," no unexcused absences and no high school suspensions to receive a Scholar Program Gold Seal on diploma.
(m) Maryland students must earn 4 credits after Grade 11. Students can earn statewide certificate of merit with fulfillment of additional program. Special education certificates are available for students unable to meet requirements but who complete a special education program.

(n) Michigan state board published graduation requirement guidelines which local districts are urged to incorporate. Included in the recommendations are a minimum of 15 1/2 units; 4 units language arts, 3 social studies, 3 mathematics, 2 science, 1 physical education, other options include 2 units picked from foreign language/fine or performing arts/vocational education and 1/2 computer education. Recommendations include at least 2 years foreign language for students who are college-bound.
(o) For college preparation, specific core subjects must be taken.
(p) Effective July 1992 requirements will be changed.
(q) Local boards determine specific requirements. For graduation, state requires 200 credit hours (20 units), with at least 80 percent in core curriculum courses.
(r) Use of minimum competency test as requirement for graduation is option of the local district.
(s) Languages other than English are allowed to satisfy the communication skills requirement which emphasizes the areas of writing and speaking.
(t) North Dakota students may substitute one unit of higher level foreign language for the 4th unit of English; 1 unit of mathematics may be business math. Local education agencies are urged to establish requirements at a minimum of 20 units.
(u) Oregon students who maintain at least a 3.5 GPA will have an "Honors Degree" seal on their diploma.
(v) Pennsylvania students may option computer science instead of arts and humanities. Learning objectives and curriculum guidelines for 12 goals of quality education have been prescribed.
(w) South Carolina students who earn one unit in science and six or more in a specific occupational service area will fulfill the science requirements for a standard diploma.
(x) Tennessee students may meet the economics requirement by: 1 semester in economics, out-of-school experiences through Junior Achievement or marketing education.
(y) Vermont has combined the mathematics and science requirements in an effort to allow more flexibility for both vocational education students and for smaller or more rural districts.
(z) For Washington students graduating in 1991 an additional credit will be required in fine, visual or performing arts or any of the subject areas currently required.
(aa) West Virginia has approved but has not implemented an advanced studies certificate, Certificate of Academic Excellence.
(bb) Wisconsin recommends that districts require a total of 22 units with an emphasis in vocational education, foreign language and fine arts to make up the difference.

EDUCATION AND CHILDREN

Table 8.11
NUMBER OF INSTITUTIONS OF HIGHER EDUCATION AND BRANCHES, BY TYPE, CONTROL OF INSTITUTION AND STATE: 1987-88

State or jurisdiction	All institutions			Universities		All other 4-year institutions		2-year institutions	
	Total	Public	Private	Public	Private	Public	Private	Public	Private
United States	3,587	1,591	1,996	94	62	505	1,474	992	460
Alabama	93	59	34	2	0	17	18	40	16
Alaska	16	12	4	1	0	2	3	9	1
Arizona	35	19	16	2	0	1	12	16	4
Arkansas	38	20	18	1	0	9	10	10	8
California	314	138	176	2	4	29	139	107	33
Colorado	54	28	26	2	1	11	16	15	9
Connecticut	49	24	25	1	1	6	20	17	4
Delaware	10	5	5	1	0	1	5	3	0
Florida	94	38	56	2	1	7	42	29	13
Georgia	95	49	46	1	1	18	29	30	16
Hawaii	14	9	5	1	0	2	5	6	0
Idaho	11	6	5	1	0	3	3	2	2
Illinois	166	59	107	3	4	9	87	47	16
Indiana	78	29	49	4	1	10	37	15	11
Iowa	65	23	42	2	1	1	35	20	6
Kansas	54	29	25	3	0	5	21	21	4
Kentucky	60	22	38	2	0	6	22	14	16
Louisiana	34	20	14	1	2	13	8	6	4
Maine	31	13	18	1	0	7	13	5	5
Maryland	56	32	24	1	1	12	20	19	3
Massachusetts	120	31	89	1	7	13	65	17	17
Michigan	103	46	57	3	1	12	48	31	8
Minnesota	77	33	44	1	0	9	33	23	11
Mississippi	47	29	18	2	0	7	12	20	6
Missouri	93	27	66	1	2	12	52	14	12
Montana	18	12	6	2	0	4	3	6	3
Nebraska	35	20	15	1	1	6	12	13	2
Nevada	9	6	3	1	0	1	2	4	1
New Hampshire	33	12	21	1	0	3	17	8	4
New Jersey	63	32	31	1	2	13	24	18	5
New Mexico	26	22	4	2	0	4	4	16	0
New York	333	97	236	2	12	47	171	48	53
North Carolina	127	75	52	2	2	15	34	58	16
North Dakota	18	14	4	2	0	4	3	8	1
Ohio	155	61	94	8	1	14	64	39	29
Oklahoma	46	28	18	2	1	12	12	14	5
Oregon	46	21	25	2	0	6	24	13	1
Pennsylvania	218	64	154	3	4	40	102	21	48
Rhode Island	12	3	9	1	0	1	9	1	0
South Carolina	64	33	31	2	0	10	20	21	11
South Dakota	19	7	12	2	0	5	9	0	3
Tennessee	87	24	63	1	1	9	41	14	21
Texas	171	106	65	6	4	34	53	66	8
Utah	14	9	5	2	1	2	1	5	3
Vermont	23	6	17	1	0	3	14	2	3
Virginia	79	39	40	3	0	12	32	24	8
Washington	54	33	21	2	0	4	19	27	2
West Virginia	29	16	13	1	0	11	9	4	4
Wisconsin	64	31	33	1	1	12	29	18	3
Wyoming	9	8	1	1	0	0	0	7	1
Dist. of Columbia	18	2	16	0	5	2	11	0	0
U.S. Service Schools	10	10	0	0	0	9	0	1	0

Source: U.S. Department of Education, National Center for Education Statistics.

EDUCATION AND CHILDREN

Table 8.12
ESTIMATED UNDERGRADUATE TUITION AND FEES AND ROOM AND BOARD RATES IN INSTITUTIONS OF HIGHER EDUCATION, BY CONTROL OF INSTITUTION AND BY STATE: 1986-87

State or jurisdiction	Public institutions				Private institutions			
	Total	Tuition (in state)	Room	Board	Total	Tuition	Room	Board
Alabama	$3,406	$1,275	$1,043	$1,088	$ 6,777	$4,316	$1,172	$1,289
Alaska	3,983	975	1,429	1,579	7,245	3,719	1,589	1,937
Arizona	3,832	1,136	1,361	1,335	4,530	2,462	923	1,145
Arkansas	2,793	931	784	1,078	5,287	3,310	792	1,185
California	5,189	1,031	1,986	2,172	11,782	8,073	1,689	2,020
Colorado	4,438	1,482	1,373	1,583	10,689	7,913	1,376	1,400
Connecticut	4,317	1,527	1,370	1,420	12,567	8,534	1,964	2,069
Delaware	. . .	906	1,120	. . .	5,811	2,794	1,461	1,556
Florida	3,870	1,055	1,254	1,561	. . .	1,367	. . .	. . .
Georgia	3,623	1,369	959	1,295	8,819	5,688	1,492	1,639
Hawaii	4,249	972	1,307	1,970	5,153	3,020	1,133	1,000
Idaho	3,744	1,036	846	1,862	8,539	5,774	900	1,865
Illinois	4,450	1,708	1,339	1,403	9,955	6,560	1,729	1,666
Indiana	4,822	1,627	1,890	1,305	9,530	6,762	1,349	1,419
Iowa	3,457	1,385	1,008	1,064	8,260	5,847	1,063	1,350
Kansas	3,529	1,271	1,143	1,115	6,349	4,121	985	1,243
Kentucky	3,273	1,152	889	1,232	6,380	3,868	1,077	1,435
Louisiana	3,575	1,341	1,051	1,183	10,359	6,812	1,765	1,782
Maine	4,535	1,561	1,476	1,498	12,674	9,032	1,767	1,875
Maryland	5,325	1,682	1,889	1,754	11,140	7,274	1,914	1,952
Massachusetts	4,220	1,388	1,294	1,538	13,474	8,953	2,312	2,209
Michigan	4,738	1,877	1,212	1,649	7,727	5,093	1,208	1,426
Minnesota	4,005	1,814	1,113	1,078	9,436	6,843	1,223	1,370
Mississippi	3,865	1,603	1,050	1,212	5,535	3,890	655	990
Missouri	3,406	1,277	1,162	967	8,162	5,474	1,312	1,376
Montana	4,118	1,205	1,205	1,708	6,364	3,867	924	1,573
Nebraska	3,342	1,292	870	1,180	7,536	5,090	1,171	1,275
Nevada	3,527	988	1,302	1,237	4,900	3,100	1,800	. . .
New Hampshire	4,534	2,190	1,424	920	12,337	8,401	1,995	1,941
New Jersey	4,920	1,861	1,758	1,301	11,955	8,221	1,934	1,800
New Mexico	3,618	915	1,121	1,582	6,504	3,649	1,175	1,680
New York	4,704	1,431	1,642	1,631	11,344	7,364	2,048	1,932
North Carolina	3,057	818	1,131	1,108	8,004	5,597	1,072	1,335
North Dakota	3,130	1,198	682	1,250	5,897	4,162	687	1,048
Ohio	4,835	1,982	1,408	1,445	8,950	6,176	1,316	1,458
Oklahoma	2,925	757	944	1,224	6,151	3,662	1,120	1,369
Oregon	3,938	1,296	1,052	1,590	10,270	7,122	1,330	1,818
Pennsylvania	5,147	2,496	1,408	1,243	10,607	7,140	1,828	1,639
Rhode Island	5,398	1,845	1,803	1,750	11,941	8,187	1,952	1,802
South Carolina	4,224	1,733	1,105	1,386	7,023	4,534	1,279	1,210
South Dakota	3,408	1,409	798	1,201	7,800	5,202	1,133	1,465
Tennessee	3,375	1,133	1,029	1,213	7,696	5,075	1,391	1,230
Texas	3,853	885	1,443	1,525	8,569	5,510	1,308	1,751
Utah	3,949	1,159	1,638	1,152	. . .	1,498	. . .	. . .
Vermont	6,357	2,942	1,988	1,427	9,369	6,393	1,534	1,442
Virginia	4,983	2,070	1,482	1,431	8,875	5,724	1,672	1,479
Washington	3,940	1,339	1,268	1,333	10,109	6,837	1,611	1,661
West Virginia	4,106	1,003	1,627	1,476	8,989	6,164	1,235	1,590
Wisconsin	3,597	1,271	1,126	1,200	8,968	6,055	1,303	1,610
Wyoming	. . .	778	1,088	. . .	. . .	. . .	. . .	. . .
Dist. of Columbia	. . .	634	. . .	. . .	11,466	7,128	2,370	1,968

Source: U.S. Department of Education; National Center for Education Statistics.
Note: Data are for the entire academic year and are average charges. Tuition and fees were weighted by the number of full-time-equivalent undergraduates but are not adjusted to reflect student residency. Room and board are based on full-time students.
Key:
. . . — Not available

HIGHWAYS

Table 8.13
TOTAL ROAD AND STREET MILEAGE: 1988
(Classified by jurisdiction)

State or other jurisdiction	Rural mileage				Urban mileage			Total rural and urban mileage
	Under state control	Under local control (a)	Under federal control (b)	Total rural roads	Under state control	Under local control (a)	Total urban mileage	
United States	704,151	2,244,155	183,363	3,131,669	96,008	642,493	739,474	3,871,143
Alabama	9,392	63,244	938	73,574	1,611	15,233	16,844	90,418
Alaska (c)	10,429	...	...	10,429	1,591	169	1,760	12,189
Arizona (d)	5,812	25,882	27,073	58,767	564	10,951	11,515	70,282
Arkansas	14,955	52,991	1,494	69,440	1,216	6,438	7,654	77,094
California	14,970	59,348	17,058	91,376	3,405	67,772	71,186	162,562
Colorado	8,482	50,225	7,315	66,022	850	10,277	11,127	77,149
Connecticut	2,199	6,785	4	8,988	1,687	9,123	10,810	19,798
Delaware	3,587	228	3	3,818	1,204	365	1,569	5,387
Florida	7,669	48,989	...	56,658	4,162	43,769	47,931	104,589
Georgia	15,469	70,618	963	87,050	2,319	18,007	20,338	107,388
Hawaii	848	1,764	64	2,676	211	1,157	1,405	4,081
Idaho	4,861	27,204	26,202	58,267	251	2,135	2,396	60,663
Illinois (e)	13,057	90,572	300	103,929	4,381	27,181	31,577	135,506
Indiana	9,713	64,135	...	73,848	1,565	16,175	17,740	91,588
Iowa	9,254	94,412	114	103,780	898	7,806	8,708	112,488
Kansas	10,093	113,975	...	124,068	584	8,313	8,897	132,965
Kentucky	23,302	38,641	308	62,251	1,895	5,516	7,597	69,848
Louisiana	14,873	30,696	586	46,155	1,658	10,609	12,267	58,422
Maine	7,768	11,618	167	19,553	771	1,632	2,413	21,966
Maryland	3,946	11,966	302	16,214	1,430	10,462	12,019	28,233
Massachusetts	1,761	11,352	87	13,200	1,875	18,705	20,609	33,809
Michigan	7,692	83,207	...	90,899	1,839	25,157	26,996	117,895
Minnesota	12,214	101,833	1,647	115,694	1,186	12,764	13,950	129,644
Mississippi	9,690	54,904	318	64,912	733	6,505	7,257	72,169
Missouri	30,815	72,978	709	104,502	1,539	13,847	15,386	119,888
Montana	7,730	53,845	7,636	69,211	175	2,084	2,260	71,471
Nebraska	9,974	77,445	133	87,552	326	4,617	4,943	92,495
Nevada	4,918	23,190	13,672	41,780	288	2,763	3,053	44,833
New Hampshire	3,719	8,454	136	12,309	328	2,074	2,402	14,711
New Jersey	1,592	10,151	21	11,764	1,607	20,808	22,433	34,197
New Mexico	11,216	38,115	...	49,331	797	3,810	4,607	53,938
New York	12,270	60,801	...	73,071	4,042	33,500	37,542	110,613
North Carolina	69,937	3,538	1,767	75,242	7,429	10,922	18,571	93,813
North Dakota	7,146	76,697	690	84,533	205	1,573	1,778	86,311
Ohio	16,544	65,539	29	82,112	3,897	27,331	31,228	113,340
Oklahoma	11,951	87,256	91	99,298	995	11,108	12,105	111,403
Oregon	10,107	33,946	40,847	84,900	776	7,882	8,695	93,595
Pennsylvania	37,808	49,582	992	88,382	7,187	20,515	27,702	116,084
Rhode Island	355	1,113	...	1,468	769	3,609	4,378	5,846
South Carolina	34,964	18,813	598	54,375	5,939	3,388	9,327	63,702
South Dakota	7,754	61,944	1,963	71,661	182	1,577	1,759	73,420
Tennessee	12,440	55,548	558	68,546	2,047	13,045	15,092	83,638
Texas	68,632	146,882	963	216,477	7,804	76,163	83,967	300,444
Utah	5,087	22,174	10,293	37,554	660	4,720	5,381	42,935
Vermont (c)	2,697	10,343	71	13,111	107	862	978	14,089
Virginia	49,419	814	1,814	52,047	6,046	8,588	14,845	66,892
Washington	17,265	37,953	10,081	65,299	1,057	15,178	16,247	81,546
West Virginia (c)	30,204	645	750	31,599	1,204	1,770	2,974	34,573
Wisconsin	11,176	83,317	872	95,365	1,336	12,928	14,264	109,629
Wyoming	6,395	28,483	3,734	38,612	278	1,610	1,890	40,502
Dist. of Columbia	...	...	...	...	1,102	...	1,102	1,102

Source: Federal Highway Administration, U.S. Department of Transportation. Compiled for calendar year ending December 31, 1988 from reports of state authorities.
Note: This table does not include mileage of non-public roads.
(a) Includes mileage not identified by administrative authority.
(b) Mileage in federal parks, forests, and reservations that are not a part of the state and local highway systems.
(c) 1987 base data factored to 1988 levels (1988 base data not available).
(d) Estimated by FHWA.
(e) Municipal mileage (included in the other local roads columns) estimated from 1987 base data and factored to 1988 levels.

HIGHWAYS

Table 8.14
STATE RECEIPTS FOR HIGHWAYS: 1988
(In thousands of dollars)

State or jurisdiction	State highway user tax revenues	Roads and crossing tolls (a)	Other state imposts, general fund revenues	Miscellaneous income	Federal funds — Federal highway administration	Federal funds — Other agencies	Transfers from local governments	Bond proceeds (b)	Total receipts
United States	$24,602,218	$2,343,549	$2,272,080	$1,663,236	$13,053,529	$368,803	$510,639	$1,989,768	$46,801,822
Alabama	396,769	...	96,708	18,592	311,934	2,479	...	...	825,472
Alaska	36,766	14,448	212,038	19,989	123,727	890	...	...	407,656
Arizona	616,025	...	92,449	64,569	206,792	5,104	83,525	126,757	1,093,221
Arkansas	310,343	...	17,926	10,714	124,519	3,205	1,559	...	468,266
California	2,090,404	73,645	...	155,475	915,715	43,922	74,430	363	3,353,954
Colorado	358,322	...	49,796	19,413	231,370	3,470	7,154	...	669,525
Connecticut	418,822	13,664	...	36,658	246,053	8,317	...	341,367	1,064,881
Delaware	104,790	53,708	78,424	41,796	59,702	513	...	66,505	405,518
Florida	822,044	233,714	31,604	94,572	552,709	3,363	14,711	...	1,752,777
Georgia	377,756	1,377	89,245	63,953	478,073	3,839	...	67,017	1,071,860
Hawaii	82,249	...	28,842	3,094	65,586	549	1,109	24,551	205,980
Idaho	138,814	...	...	61	116,051	6,626	2,550	...	264,102
Illinois	1,214,990	208,213	211,484	66,799	588,147	8,274	20,528	109,034	2,427,469
Indiana	646,532	53,601	33,548	34,194	296,499	3,913	14,773	127,889	1,210,949
Iowa	443,913	11	111,043	39,831	181,527	1,719	3,263	...	781,307
Kansas	237,344	35,142	47,269	13,130	153,985	3,702	14,549	...	505,121
Kentucky	625,050	17,575	32,000	64,836	216,854	2,321	893	29,732	989,261
Louisiana	455,895	...	62,387	10,008	273,042	3,002	...	...	804,334
Maine	163,427	32,289	219	4,975	64,396	1,879	...	20,000	287,185
Maryland	877,892	57,382	...	22,050	389,373	1,951	...	7,223	1,355,871
Massachusetts (c)	...	...	...	...	...	...	...	...	...
Michigan	945,393	10,719	84,557	18,366	312,141	5,193	19,826	...	1,396,195
Minnesota	882,937	...	42,137	50,630	282,509	11,510	33,671	4,023	1,107,417
Mississippi	304,432	...	65,840	20,572	158,304	4,059	1,657	...	552,870
Missouri	614,173	...	119,269	5,642	266,134	3,075	3,987	...	912,180
Montana	127,730	...	9,851	3,830	116,467	5,328	614	...	263,820
Nebraska	212,376	...	68,699	5,714	119,211	2,266	12,004	...	420,269
Nevada	178,488	...	...	9,961	71,854	1,199	1,263	17,503	280,268
New Hampshire	119,101	29,691	...	10,173	67,000	692	3,549	15,000	245,206
New Jersey	398,571	347,429	...	234,585	290,761	1,291	...	206,078	1,478,715
New Mexico	277,626	...	58,502	8,969	113,726	1,959	1,590	...	462,371
New York	800,369	553,716	5,545	151,252	664,221	6,911	...	228,887	2,410,901
North Carolina	808,077	1,242	...	49,703	309,987	3,100	11,886	...	1,183,995
North Dakota	103,397	...	3,348	752	84,491	1,012	6,952	...	199,952
Ohio	1,153,620	81,605	...	41,650	463,523	4,859	24,118	100,152	1,869,427
Oklahoma	381,286	48,867	28,320	6,028	255,571	1,983	2,689	...	724,744
Oregon	349,441	2,012	12,913	12,650	165,191	74,178	12,588	...	628,953
Pennsylvania	1,511,187	257,455	7,233	56,771	766,046	7,624	10,108	196,997	2,813,421
Rhode Island	73,780	8,681	13,942	1,124	88,541	1,164	...	22,795	210,027
South Carolina	352,560	...	...	2,701	169,762	2,367	378	...	527,768
South Dakota	99,372	...	24,567	6,844	96,038	1,162	2,398	...	230,381
Tennessee	606,067	37	70,927	10,356	253,803	1,158	7,679	...	950,027
Texas	1,474,862	31,898	26,395	54,072	900,801	9,868	61,549	...	2,559,445
Utah	186,883	...	3,582	2,821	151,100	17,499	3,300	...	365,185
Vermont	94,626	...	1,125	2,898	45,471	626	...	...	144,746
Virginia	934,779	80,123	264,309	29,760	354,093	3,908	22,468	138,640	1,828,080
Washington	583,637	59,659	...	33,338	373,161	21,536	...	62,987	1,134,218
West Virginia	262,445	35,588	81,067	22,165	146,944	8,781	549	...	557,519
Wisconsin	603,810	...	...	27,374	226,008	1,888	25,416	51,385	935,881
Wyoming	72,687	...	34,648	7,909	63,749	51,387	1,356	...	231,736
Dist. of Columbia	72,570	...	50,316	37	82,208	382	...	25,883	231,396

Source: Federal Highway Administration, U.S. Department of Transportation. Compiled for calendar year 1988 from reports of state authorities.
Note: Totals may not add due to rounding.
Key:
... — Not applicable
(a) Toll receipts allocated for non-highway purposes are excluded.
(b) Par value of bonds issued and redeemed by refunding are excluded.
(c) 1988 State Highway Finance Data not reported for Massachusetts.

HIGHWAYS

Table 8.15
STATE DISBURSEMENTS FOR HIGHWAYS: 1988
(In thousands of dollars)

State or jurisdiction	Capital outlay — Federal aid systems — Interstate	Other federal aid systems	Other roads & streets	Total	Maintenance & traffic services	Administration & highway police	Bond interest	Grants-in-aid to local governments	Bond retirement (a)	Total disbursements
United States	$8,996,020	$13,072,494	$2,564,796	$23,909,054	$7,556,204	$5,964,597	$1,583,890	$6,811,987	$1,328,139	$47,163,871
Alabama	171,303	209,950	40,667	421,920	127,049	79,568	18,758	169,411	59,843	876,549
Alaska	53,276	96,270	7,131	156,677	108,685	36,964	9,313	65,205	30,812	407,656
Arizona	...	...	...	680,193	51,420	91,830	55,610	265,775	21,015	1,165,843
Arkansas	57,625	148,925	31,567	238,117	95,604	41,300	...	84,385	...	459,406
California	351,278	992,101	14,022	1,357,401	491,276	759,849	5,987	849,290	10,677	3,474,480
Colorado	134,882	159,873	43,663	338,418	109,186	66,176	...	140,464	...	654,244
Connecticut	212,180	283,556	18,599	514,335	70,395	72,438	72,196	29,917	59,201	818,482
Delaware	38,495	90,279	23,576	152,360	43,152	95,380	29,636	2,500	32,184	355,202
Florida	363,917	794,679	247,049	1,405,645	223,619	164,438	75,644	178,923	46,154	2,094,423
Georgia	221,790	407,417	6,194	635,401	218,596	142,202	45,284	9,710	58,154	1,109,347
Hawaii	39,401	54,051	3,396	97,148	17,506	21,264	10,441	35,772	13,821	195,952
Idaho	60,400	52,028	29,463	141,891	42,594	29,079	...	49,286	...	262,850
Illinois	358,371	613,984	298,903	1,271,258	271,296	273,693	100,265	341,978	73,091	2,331,581
Indiana	185,928	245,533	17,003	448,464	217,340	97,309	24,018	276,988	420	1,064,539
Iowa	54,163	223,485	5,224	282,872	108,383	79,777	642	291,312	3,235	766,221
Kansas	117,986	128,043	23,211	269,240	77,371	71,620	20,258	79,453	11,005	528,947
Kentucky	110,015	358,085	106,897	574,997	142,267	75,868	96,328	104,783	60,200	1,054,443
Louisiana	...	...	...	443,505	45,406	131,680	95,594	44,011	47,565	807,761
Maine	13,989	71,442	10,071	95,502	85,347	31,293	7,327	15,837	9,820	245,126
Maryland	327,841	271,538	116,978	716,357	145,060	182,721	29,315	324,533	11,693	1,409,679
Massachusetts (a)	...	...	...	...	...	...	...	...	...	...
Michigan	302,554	155,829	13,765	472,148	123,859	193,849	14,910	545,901	9,540	1,360,207
Minnesota	295,817	178,136	53,638	527,591	121,614	92,524	9,617	249,172	11,119	1,011,637
Mississippi	51,719	210,813	51,851	314,383	46,763	54,597	17,535	55,557	14,657	503,492
Missouri	90,327	317,827	5,614	413,768	208,623	164,107	...	161,630	...	948,128
Montana	38,941	84,413	51,232	174,586	11,198	24,758	10,041	18,307	...	238,890
Nebraska	51,869	139,690	2,492	194,051	42,218	32,946	111	138,354	1,000	408,680
Nevada	41,694	109,142	4,274	155,110	44,299	39,336	3,390	32,585	12,260	286,980
New Hampshire	25,665	43,823	21,586	91,074	89,997	52,418	12,152	434	10,238	256,313
New Jersey	249,575	280,349	93,821	623,745	237,656	330,311	287,730	...	73,982	1,553,424
New Mexico	79,781	148,151	5,992	233,924	67,209	72,785	5,251	32,959	50,244	462,372
New York	260,929	714,624	185,241	1,160,794	484,921	287,684	60,443	215,000	151,079	2,359,921
North Carolina	148,546	315,198	83,109	546,853	373,682	182,265	14,008	66,660	24,020	1,207,488
North Dakota	20,350	77,676	4,474	102,500	35,305	18,634	...	42,160	...	198,599
Ohio	274,774	449,129	33,943	757,846	205,841	298,855	26,834	378,554	77,250	1,745,180
Oklahoma	93,062	216,107	32,463	341,632	122,079	108,746	8,741	135,109	6,115	722,422
Oregon	69,774	198,004	...	267,778	99,316	53,605	6,899	194,374	3,300	625,272
Pennsylvania	551,659	701,319	85,722	1,338,700	625,927	279,453	164,902	242,293	134,943	2,786,218
Rhode Island	...	...	...	152,046	13,265	19,191	8,622	390	10,094	203,608
South Carolina	63,926	171,743	68,279	303,948	156,307	82,634	326	17,906	8,110	569,231
South Dakota	9,006	102,822	24,684	136,512	33,487	34,361	...	19,636	...	223,996
Tennessee	135,392	322,887	177,324	635,603	169,838	85,885	2,487	196,503	9,920	1,100,236
Texas	501,520	1,389,002	231,154	2,121,676	545,633	309,543	22,147	69,968	2,365	3,071,332
Utah	105,424	119,769	...	225,193	52,603	39,444	440	43,099	4,000	364,779
Vermont	15,396	48,007	3,614	67,017	37,096	25,103	1,749	18,567	6,305	155,837
Virginia	241,775	513,126	228,802	983,703	422,202	188,774	17,118	136,174	14,441	1,762,412
Washington	232,386	193,908	11,727	438,021	148,155	153,946	61,938	225,784	33,675	1,061,519
West Virginia	43,226	188,452	11,288	242,966	145,972	49,814	39,755	...	80,067	558,574
Wisconsin	45,373	327,441	18,041	390,855	128,154	92,767	21,321	205,020	26,139	864,256
Wyoming	48,740	90,970	8,711	148,421	50,934	29,027	...	10,358	...	238,740
Dist. of Columbia	33,980	62,598	8,341	104,919	30,499	22,786	68,807	...	4,386	231,397

Source: Federal Highway Administration, U.S. Department of Transportation. Compiled for calendar year ending December 31, 1988 from reports of state authorities.
Note: Totals may not add due to rounding.
Key:
... — Not available
(a) 1988 state highway finance data not reported for Massachusetts.

HIGHWAYS

Table 8.16
APPORTIONMENT OF FEDERAL-AID HIGHWAY FUNDS: FISCAL 1989
(In thousands of dollars)

State or other jurisdiction	Highway systems funds					Total highway systems funds (d)	Highway safety programs (d)	Bridge replacement & rehabilitation funds	Total (e)
	Consolidated primary (a)	Rural secondary (a)	Urban system (a)	Interstate (b)	Interstate resurfacing (c)				
United States	$2,301,831 (f)	$584,657	$730,438	$2,421,526	$2,543,599	$8,582,051	$128,403	$1,372,400	$12,213,203
Alabama	41,041	11,999	9,465	108,637	48,127	219,269	2,305	29,534	257,922
Alaska	74,896	32,293	3,657	13,858	21,153	145,857	647	3,431	153,453
Arizona	31,343	9,819	9,446	13,858	55,799	120,265	1,738	3,431	129,911
Arkansas	28,361	10,557	4,464	13,858	26,925	84,165	1,556	18,023	137,041
California	167,447	24,597	92,603	310,568	245,346	840,561	10,986	37,743	1,006,336
Colorado	34,512	11,058	9,801	58,611	48,872	162,854	1,363	15,404	186,442
Connecticut	25,294	3,937	10,494	39,611	32,724	112,060	1,433	64,976	265,065
Delaware	11,335	2,925	3,657	13,858	12,724	44,499	647	3,626	50,339
Florida	75,405	14,401	34,887	162,492	90,693	377,878	4,804	22,742	509,518
Georgia	55,570	15,797	13,914	65,806	90,016	241,103	3,097	32,630	383,070
Hawaii	11,335	2,925	3,657	108,246	12,724	138,887	647	3,845	144,843
Idaho	18,245	7,190	3,657	20,805	23,003	72,900	962	3,456	80,232
Illinois	89,936	17,104	40,130	13,858	90,955	251,983	5,774	40,119	368,465
Indiana	52,646	13,797	14,534	13,858	56,610	151,445	2,987	24,196	298,913
Iowa	34,887	12,511	6,652	13,858	36,470	104,378	2,097	26,893	162,251
Kansas	32,777	11,768	6,218	13,858	37,027	101,648	2,036	28,752	140,167
Kentucky	39,580	12,177	7,437	20,781	44,385	124,360	2,060	30,056	165,356
Louisiana	38,890	9,747	11,859	119,978	44,394	224,868	2,193	35,372	269,151
Maine	14,458	5,068	3,657	13,858	12,724	49,765	647	6,502	60,876
Maryland	34,031	5,794	14,387	108,466	38,981	201,659	1,955	19,874	269,324
Massachusetts	44,674	5,993	20,391	170,085	32,229	273,372	2,625	58,833	349,003
Michigan	82,743	17,483	27,574	41,172	84,148	253,120	4,745	26,248	332,717
Minnesota	43,525	14,320	11,058	39,196	47,673	155,772	2,697	17,433	185,463
Mississippi	31,796	10,727	4,663	13,858	31,680	92,724	1,612	22,150	146,891
Missouri	51,720	15,586	13,687	13,858	71,650	166,501	2,977	55,864	287,375
Montana	26,564	10,947	3,657	13,858	41,372	96,398	898	7,203	107,545
Nebraska	25,015	9,276	4,025	13,858	21,525	73,699	1,385	17,284	97,148
Nevada	18,943	7,110	3,657	13,858	22,495	66,063	687	3,431	72,104
New Hampshire	11,335	2,925	3,657	13,858	12,724	44,499	647	7,429	54,253
New Jersey	53,551	5,380	28,088	77,514	32,123	196,656	3,295	63,713	300,557
New Mexico	25,916	9,743	3,846	13,858	42,358	95,721	966	5,137	104,516
New York	134,974	17,629	63,285	13,858	88,868	318,614	8,089	137,240	658,618
North Carolina	64,824	18,495	11,330	45,708	46,439	186,796	3,161	30,840	346,034
North Dakota	17,338	7,029	3,657	13,858	20,302	62,184	959	5,339	72,768
Ohio	93,973	18,713	33,398	31,684	101,951	279,719	5,338	44,853	463,065
Oklahoma	34,508	11,738	8,137	13,858	35,658	103,899	2,132	35,627	202,053
Oregon	29,463	9,889	7,272	18,220	38,221	103,065	1,833	9,161	133,654
Pennsylvania	107,977	22,130	34,318	130,174	65,669	360,268	5,798	99,098	466,423
Rhode Island	11,335	2,925	3,657	13,858	12,724	44,499	647	3,431	107,692
South Carolina	33,008	9,198	6,717	20,757	41,389	111,069	1,790	11,414	129,566
South Dakota	18,670	7,666	3,657	13,858	25,162	69,013	872	7,602	80,480
Tennessee	47,331	13,627	11,431	13,858	63,729	149,976	2,555	44,716	277,036
Texas	132,584	36,558	47,234	133,662	203,781	553,819	8,191	55,173	943,678
Utah	19,752	6,520	5,141	16,683	39,799	87,895	999	3,431	95,130
Vermont	11,335	2,925	3,657	13,858	12,856	44,631	647	7,389	54,350
Virginia	49,955	12,881	14,816	35,708	70,638	183,998	2,724	25,547	219,482
Washington	39,531	10,103	12,669	120,515	56,493	239,311	2,333	30,353	278,705
West Virginia	23,747	7,479	3,657	13,858	18,967	67,708	1,082	39,891	112,037
Wisconsin	47,952	13,506	12,314	13,858	34,208	121,838	2,804	29,529	225,758
Wyoming	17,453	7,135	3,657	13,858	32,937	75,040	647	3,431	81,102
Dist. of Columbia	11,335	...	3,657	56,148	12,724	83,864	647	9,536	108,490
American Samoa	...	...	...	...	...	...	324	...	741
Guam	...	...	...	...	...	...	324	...	741
No. Mariana Islands	...	...	...	...	...	...	324	...	741
Puerto Rico	27,016	3,556	7,903	...	11,452	49,927	1,390	3,467	57,888
U.S. Virgin Islands	...	...	...	...	...	...	324	...	741

Source: Federal Highway Administration, U.S. Department of Transportation, *Highway Statistics 1988*.
Note: This table does not include funds from the mass transit account of the Highway Trust Fund. Totals may not add due to rounding.
Key:
 ... — Not applicable
(a) Apportioned pursuant to the surface transportation and uniform relocation assistance act of 1987.
(b) Resurfacing, rehabilitation, restoration and reconstruction.
(c) In 1985, interstate highway substitute and 85 percent minimum allocation funds were included in this category. They are not reported separately by Federal Highway Administration.
(d) Includes $9.8 million administered by the Federal Highway Administration and $118.6 million administered by National Highway Traffic Safety Administration. Does not include $2 million set-aside for commercial vehicle driver licensing programs.
(e) Does not include funds from the following programs: Emergency Relief, Forest Highways, Public Lands Highways, Parkways and Park Highways, Indian Reservation Roads, Interstate and Interstate 4-R Discretionary, Bridge Discretionary, Truck and Bus Safety Grants, Allocated Interstate Highway Substitute or Section 149 Demonstration Funds. These funds are allocated from the Highway Trust Fund.
(f) Does not include $11.3 million apportioned to the Territories as one state.

HIGHWAYS

Table 8.17
STATE MOTOR VEHICLE REGISTRATIONS: 1988

State or jurisdiction	Automobiles (a)	Motorcycles (a)	Buses (b)	Trucks (a)	1987	1988	Percentage change
United States	141,251,695	4,584,284	615,669	42,529,368	178,954,599	184,396,732	3.0
Alabama	2,919,814	50,667	8,443	952,724	3,546,583	3,880,981	9.4
Alaska	229,279	8,614	2,034	130,570	357,401	361,883	1.3
Arizona	1,927,503	83,750	4,236	773,133	2,643,437 (c)	2,704,872	2.3
Arkansas	844,810	16,608	5,258	576,982	1,444,991	1,427,050	−1.2
California	16,496,522	664,864	37,533	4,802,909	20,293,984	21,336,964	5.1
Colorado	2,121,998	105,945	5,519	795,954	3,033,354	2,923,471	−3.6
Connecticut	2,490,237	56,440	8,660	153,030 (d)	2,612,049	2,651,927	1.5
Delaware	397,286	8,843	1,796	112,858	490,494	511,940	4.4
Florida	8,713,198	199,460	35,543	2,234,913	10,683,590	10,983,654	2.8
Georgia	3,690,981	77,908	17,832	1,487,407	5,026,220	5,196,220	3.4
Hawaii	613,750	18,367	4,184	86,777	689,745	704,711	2.2
Idaho	594,228	44,554	3,464	342,466	947,254	940,178	−0.7
Illinois	6,403,462	243,735	18,030	1,443,443	7,662,322	7,864,935	2.6
Indiana	3,069,935	104,532	20,750	1,078,561	3,707,851	4,169,246	12.4
Iowa	1,817,383	193,700	8,395	741,968	2,699,427	2,567,746	−4.9
Kansas	1,523,226	78,474	3,764	682,923	2,188,039	2,209,913	1.0
Kentucky	1,861,754	35,366	9,717	923,606	2,720,197	2,795,077	2.8
Louisiana	1,970,360	38,532	19,605	947,584	2,891,234	2,937,549	1.6
Maine	709,075	40,930	5,789	226,409	927,815	941,273	1.5
Maryland	2,857,979	58,248	10,872	599,396	3,308,621	3,468,247	4.8
Massachusetts	3,322,044	61,631	10,934	485,334	3,886,852	3,818,312	−1.8
Michigan	5,556,109	212,355	22,517	1,562,865	6,944,666	7,141,491	2.8
Minnesota	2,503,362	123,271	13,078	693,917	3,171,781	3,210,357	1.2
Mississippi	1,362,686	24,812	8,340	415,833	1,760,866	1,786,859	1.5
Missouri	2,707,929	35,969	11,581	1,074,932	3,712,428	3,794,442	2.2
Montana	430,072	26,126	1,939	290,543	694,588 (c)	722,554	4.0
Nebraska	877,894	28,662	4,125	446,213	1,304,946	1,328,232	1.8
Nevada	574,212	22,378	1,753	232,338	811,970	808,303	−0.5
New Hampshire	733,529	37,857	1,640	192,945 (d)	874,011	928,114	6.2
New Jersey	5,222,761	89,073	17,427	497,664 (d)	5,519,757	5,737,852	4.0
New Mexico	788,415	37,494	3,416	474,729	1,284,706	1,266,560	−1.4
New York	8,558,985	218,508	27,345	1,251,278 (d)	9,592,732	9,837,608	2.6
North Carolina	3,597,092	58,305	33,580	1,391,956	4,870,224	5,022,628	3.1
North Dakota	385,028	24,038	2,104	267,952	650,458	655,084	0.7
Ohio	7,003,826	259,451	33,614	1,574,578	8,521,397	8,612,018	1.1
Oklahoma	1,666,947	65,585	12,724	874,347	2,526,422 (c)	2,554,018	1.1
Oregon	1,749,239	73,976	9,905	556,547	2,242,656	2,315,691	3.3
Pennsylvania	6,253,550	187,510	30,355	1,482,124 (d)	7,642,206	7,766,029	1.6
Rhode Island	555,313	24,006	1,536	113,964 (d)	653,824	670,813	2.6
South Carolina	1,799,425	31,653	13,689	600,798	2,366,144	2,413,912	2.0
South Dakota	413,668	31,490	2,003	276,961	673,796	692,832	2.8
Tennessee	3,373,276	69,879	12,814	839,400	4,026,565	4,225,490	4.9
Texas	8,455,744	211,668	60,075	3,890,394	12,298,362	12,406,213	0.9
Utah	786,942	30,181	1,155	371,338	1,113,955	1,159,435	4.1
Vermont	334,428	19,227	1,422	116,996	442,477	452,846	2.3
Virginia	3,625,109	66,679	16,245	1,028,983	4,527,987	4,670,337	0.9
Washington	2,753,299	131,110	7,640	1,126,375	3,828,067	3,887,314	1.5
West Virginia	906,488	19,520	3,772	376,374	1,193,993	1,286,634	7.8
Wisconsin	3,169,217	193,823	12,326	719,563	3,096,219	3,901,106	26.0
Wyoming	285,190	20,107	2,366	194,432	478,085	481,988	0.8
Dist. of Columbia	247,136	2,643	2,805	14,082	267,851	264,023	−1.4

Source: Federal Highway Administration, U.S. Department of Transportation, *Highway Statistics 1988.* Compiled for the calendar year ending December 31, 1988 from reports of state authorities.
Note: Where the registration year is not more than one month removed from the calendar year, registration-year data are given. Where the registration year is more than one month removed, registrations are given for the calendar year.
(a) Includes federal, state, county and municipal vehicles. Vehicles owned by the military service are not included.
(b) The numbers of private and commercial buses given here are estimates by the Federal Highway Administration of the numbers in operation, rather than the registration counts of the states.
(c) The 1987 data were revised due to additional information.
(d) The following farm trucks, registered at a nominal fee and restricted to use in the vicinity of the owner's farm, are not included in this table: Connecticut, 7,504; New Hampshire, 3,247; New Jersey 5,769; New York 24,540; Pennsylvania, 22,089; and Rhode Island, 971.

HIGHWAYS

Table 8.18
MOTOR VEHICLE LAWS
(As of 1989)

State or other jurisdiction	Minimum Age for driver's license (a)			Liability laws (b)	Vehicle inspection (c)	Transfer of plates to new owner	Child restraints mandatory for passengers under ___ years (d)	Mandatory seat belt law (e)
	Regular	Learner's	Restrictive					
Alabama	16	15 (f)	14 (g)	S	(h)	★	4	...
Alaska	16	14 (i)	14 (i)	S	spot	★	7	...
Arizona	18	15 + 7mo. (f,i)	16 (i)	C	(j)	★	5	...
Arkansas	16	(f)	14 (i,k)	S,NF	★	...	6	...
California	18	15 (k,l)	16 (l)	(m)	(j)	★	5 (n)	★ (o)
Colorado	21	15 + 6mo. (f,p)	16 (i)	S,NF	(j)	...	4 (n)	★
Connecticut	18	(q)	16 (l)	S,NF	★	...	4	★
Delaware	18	15 + 10mo. (f,k,l)	16 (l)	S,NF	★	★	5	...
Florida	16	(f)	15 (i)	(r)	...	...	6	★
Georgia	21	15	16 (i)	C,NF	(j)	★	4	★
Hawaii	18	(f)	15 (i)	S,NF	★	★	4	★
Idaho	16	(f)	14 (l)	S,C	...	...	4	★
Illinois	18	(f)	16 (i,l)	S	(s)	...	6	★
Indiana	18	15 (l,p)	16 + 1mo. (i,l)	S,C	...	...	5	★
Iowa	16	14	16 (l)	S	spot	...	6	★
Kansas	16		14 (k)	NF	spot	...	4	★
Kentucky	18	(f)	16 (i)	C,NF	...	★	(n)	...
Louisiana	17		15 (t)	C	★	★	5	★
Maine	17	(f,k)	15 (l)	S	★	...	5	(o)
Maryland	18	15 + 9mo. (f,k)	16 (i,l,t)	NF	(u)	...	5	★
Massachusetts	18	16 (f)	16 + 6mo. (i,l,t)	C,NF	★	...	5	(o)
Michigan	18	(f)	16 (i,l,v)	C,NF	spot	...	4	★
Minnesota	19	(f)	16 (l)	NF	spot (h)	★	4	★ (o)
Mississippi	15	(f)		S,F	★	...	2	...
Missouri	16		15 (p)	S	★	...	4	★
Montana	18	(f)	15 (i,l)	C	...	...	4 (n)	...
Nebraska	16	15 (f,k)	(v)	F	...	...	4	...
Nevada	18	15 + 6mo.	16 (i)	F,C	(u)	...	5	★ (o)
New Hampshire	18	(q)	16(l)	S,F	★	...	5	...
New Jersey	17	(k)	(v)	S,NF,UJ	★	...	5	★ (o)
New Mexico	16	15 (k)	15 (i,l)	S,UM	...	...	11	★
New York	18	(f,k)	16 (i,t)	S,C,NF	★	...	4	★ (o)
North Carolina	18	15 (k,l)		S,C	★	...	7	★
North Dakota	16	(f)	14 (l)	S,NF,UM,UJ	spot	★	6	★
Ohio	18 (w)	(k)	(v)	S,C	(j)	...	4 (n)	★
Oklahoma	16	(p)	15 + 6mo. (l)	S,C	★	★	5	★
Oregon	16	15 (f)	(v)	F,C,NF	spot (j)	★	16	★
Pennsylvania	18	(f)	16 (i,t)	(x)	★	...	4	★
Rhode Island	18	(f)	16 (l)	S	★	...	13	...
South Carolina	16	15 (k)	15	C,NF,UM	★	...	4	...
South Dakota	16	14 (k)	14 (t)	F,UM	...	★	5	...
Tennessee	16	15		S,F	(h)	...	4	★
Texas	18	15 (k,p)	16 (l,v)	S,F,C,UM	★	★	4	★
Utah	16 (l)	(f)		S,NF	★	...	5	★
Vermont	18	15 (k)	16 (k)	S	★	...	5	...
Virginia	18	15 + 8mo. (f,i,k)	16 (i,l)	S,NF	★	...	5	★
Washington	18	15 (f,p)	16 (l)	S,F	(j)	★	5	★ (o)
West Virginia	18	(f)	16 (i)	S,C	★	...	9	...
Wisconsin	18	(f)	16 (l)	S	spot	...	4	★
Wyoming	18	15 (k)	16 (i)	S,C	...	...	3	...
Dist. of Columbia	18	(f)	16 (i)	NF	★	...	7	★ (o)
American Samoa	18	(f,k)	16 (i,l)	C	★	★	...	...
Guam	18	15 (i,k)	16 (i)	S	★	...	...	...
Puerto Rico	18	(f)	16 (i)	(x)	★	★	...	★
U.S. Virgin Islands	18		16 (l)	C	★	★	...	...

HIGHWAYS

MOTOR VEHICLE LAWS—Continued

Source: American Automobile Association, *Digest of Motor Laws*, (1989).

Note: All jurisdictions except Guam have chemical test laws for intoxication. All except the District of Columbia have an implied consent provision. (Colorado has expressed consent law).

Key:

★ —Provision.

. . . — No provision.

(a) See Table 8.20, "Motor Vehicle Operators and Chauffeurs Licenses 1988" for additional information on driver licenses.

(b) All jurisdictions except Colorado, Hawaii, District of Columbia, American Samoa, Guam, Puerto Rico and the U.S. Virgin Islands have a non-resident service of process law. Alabama, Arkansas, California, Georgia, Illinois (applicable to hitchhikers only), New Mexico, Oregon, Texas, Utah, Virginia, Wyoming and the U.S. Virgin Islands each have a guest suit law. In this column only: S—"Security-type" financial responsibility law (following accident report, each driver/owner of the vehicles involved must show ability to pay damages which may be charged in subsequent legal actions arising from accident); F—"Future-proof type" financial responsibility law (persons who have been convicted of certain serious traffic offenses or who have failed to pay a judgment against them for damages arising from an accident must make a similar showing of financial responsibility); C—"Compulsory insurance" law (motorists must show proof of financial responsibility—liability insurance—usually as a condition of vehicle registration); NF—"No-fault insurance" law (vehicle owner looks to own insurance company for reimbursement for accident damages, rather than having to prove in court that the other party was responsible); UJ—"Unsatisfied judgment funds" law (financed with fees from motorists unable to provide evidence of insurance or from assessments levied on auto insurance companies to cover pedestrians and others who do not have no-fault insurance); UM—"Uninsured motorist" law (insurance companies must offer coverage against potential damage by uninsured motorists).

(c) "Spot" indicates spot check, usually for reasonable cause, or random roadside inspection for defective or missing equipment.

(d) The type of child restraint (safety seat or seat belt) required may differ depending upon the age of the child.

(e) These states have enacted mandatory seat belt legislation. Unless otherwise specified, legislation covers driver and front-seat passengers.

(f) Permit required. In Arkansas, for 30 days prior to taking driving test. In Delaware, for up to two months prior to 16th birthday. In Maryland, for 30 days prior to application for first license. In Minnesota, not required if driver can pass road test. In Oregon, not required if applicant can already drive.

(g) Restricted to mopeds.

(h) Cities have authority to maintain inspection stations. In Alabama, state troopers also authorized to inspect at their discretion.

(i) Guardian or parental consent required.

(j) Emission inspections. In Arizona, Colorado, Georgia, Ohio and Washington, mandatory annual emission inspections in certain counties. In California, biennial inspections are required in portions of counties which do not meet federal clean air standards. In Oregon, biennial inspections in Portland metro area and Jackson County. In Washington, also other checks (e.g., out of state purchases, salvaged).

(k) Driver must be accompanied by licensed operator. In California and Vermont (learner's permit), a licensed operator 25 years or older. In Kansas, may drive to school or work without licensed operator. In Maine, New York, Texas, Vermont (restrictive license), Virginia and Wyoming, a licensed operator 18 years or older. In Maryland, individual, 21 years or older, licensed to drive vehicle of that class, and licensed for 3 or more years. In Nebraska, a licensed operator 19 years or older. In New Jersey, an individual licensed for same classification as the learner's permit. In South Carolina, a licensed operator 21 years or older. In American Samoa, must be accompanied by parent, legal guardian, or safety instructor. In Guam, must be accompanied by parent or legal guardian.

(l) Must have successfully completed approved driver education course.

(m) Financial responsibility required of every driver/owner of motor vehicle at all times.

(n) Other restrictions. In California, Colorado, Montana and Ohio, age restriction or child under 40 pounds. In Kentucky, 40 inches in height or under.

(o) Covers other passengers in vehicle. California, Nevada, Washington and District of Columbia, all passengers. Maine, passengers between 4-12 years. Massachusetts, passengers between 5-12 years. In Minnesota, driver, front seat passengers, and anyone under 11. New Jersey, all passengers between 5 and 18 years, as well as driver and all front-seat passengers over 18 years. New York, all back seat occupants under 10 years and over 3 years, as well as all front-seat occupants.

(p) Must be enrolled in driver education course. In Colorado, if not in such course, wait until 15 + 9 mo.; in Washington, 15 + 6 mo.

(q) Required for motorcyclists only. In New Hampshire, otherwise, unlicensed persons who are being taught to drive must be accompanied by licensed operator 21 years or older.

(r) Proof of personal injury protection is required. In event of an accident in which operator is charged with a moving violation, the operator must prove liability insurance in force on date of accident.

(s) Trucks, buses and trailers only. Required for vehicle owners in certain counties.

(t) Driving hours restricted. In Louisiana, drivers under 17 not permitted to operate vehicles between hours of 11 p.m. and 5 a.m. Monday through Thursday; between midnight and 5 a.m. Friday through Sunday. In Maryland, drivers prohibited from driving between midnight and 5 a.m. unless accompanied by licensed driver 21 years or older. In Massachusetts, drivers prohibited from driving between 1 a.m. and 4 a.m., unless accompanied by parent or legal guardian. In New York, drivers 16-17 years old are restricted from driving between 8 p.m. and 5 a.m. (may not drive in New York City at any time). In Pennsylvania, drivers prohibited from driving between midnight and 5 a.m., unless accompanied by parent or spouse 18 years or older or in possession of employer's affidavit. In South Dakota, driver not permitted to operate vehicle between 8 p.m. and 6 a.m., unless accompanied by licensed driver in front seat.

(u) Mandatory inspection only under certain circumstances. In Maryland, all used cars upon resale or transfer. In Nevada, used cars registered to new owner and emissions test for first-time registration in Clark and Washoe counties.

(v) License will be granted at lower age under special conditions. In Michigan (extenuating circumstances), 14. In Nebraska (school permit), 14. In New Jersey (agriculture pursuit), 16. In Ohio (proof of hardship), 14. In Oregon, (special conditions), 14. In Texas (proof of hardship), 15.

(w) Probationary license issued to persons 16-18 upon completion of approved driver education course.

(x) Has financial responsibility law; details not available.

HIGHWAYS

Table 8.19
STATE NO-FAULT MOTOR VEHICLE INSURANCE LAWS

State or jurisdiction	Purchase of first-party benefits	Minimum tort liability threshold (a)	Maximum first-party (no-fault) benefits			
			Medical	Income loss	Replacement services	Survivors/funeral benefits
Arkansas	O	None	$5,000 if incurred within 2 yrs. of accident	70% of lost income up to $140/wk. beginning 8 days after accident, for for up to 52 wks.	Up to $70/wk. beginning 8 days after accident, for up to 52 wks.	$5,000
Colorado	M	$2,500	$50,000 if incurred within 5 yrs. (additional $50,000 for rehabilitation expenses incurred within 5 yrs. of accident)	100% of first $125/wk., 70% of next $125/wk., 60% of remainder up to $400, for up to 52 wks.	Up to $25/day for up to 52 wks.	$1,000
Connecticut	M	$400	Limited only by total benefits limit	------------ $5,000 overall max. on first-party benefits ------------ 85% of lost income up to $200/wk.	85% of replacement services up to $200/wk.	85% of actual loss for income and replacement services up to $200/wk. Funeral benefit: $2,000
Delaware	M	None, but amt. of no-fault benefits received cannot be used as evidence in suits for general damage	------ $15,000 per person, $30,000 per accident overall max. on first-party benefits ------ Limited only by total benefits limit, but must be incurred within 2 yrs. of accident	Limited only by total benefits limit, but must be incurred within 2 yrs. of accident	Limited only by total benefits limit, but must be incurred within 2 yrs. of accident	Funeral benefit: $3,000 (must be incurred within 2 yrs. of accident)
Florida	M	No dollar threshold (b)	------------ $10,000 overall max. on first-party benefits ------------ 80% of all costs	60% of lost income	Limited only by total benefits limit	Funeral benefit: $1,750
Georgia	M	$500	------------ $5,000 overall max. on first-party benefits ------------ $2,500	85% of lost income up to $200/wk.	$20/day	Max. wage loss and replacement services amounts. Funeral benefit: $1,500
Hawaii	M	$5,000 modified annually by percentage change in CPI for Honolulu metro area	------------ $15,000 overall max. on first-party benefits ------------ Limited only by total benefits limit	Up to $900/mo. for income loss and replacement services		Up to $900/mo. Funeral benefit: $1,500
Kansas	M	$2000 (b)	$4,500 (additional $4,500 for rehabilitation)	85% of lost income up to $900/mo. for mo. for 1 yr.	$25/day for 365 days	Up to $900/mo. for lost income and $25/day for replacement services for up to 1 yr., less disability payments received before death. Funeral benefit: $2,000
Kentucky	(c)	$1,000	------------ $10,000 overall max. on first-party benefits ------------ Limited only by total benefits limit	85% of lost in- come (more if tax advantage is less than 15%) up to $200/wk.	Up to $200/wk.	Up to $200/wk. each for survivors' economic loss and survivors' replacement services loss. Funeral benefit: $1,000
Maryland	M	None	------------ $2,500 overall max. on first-party benefits ------------ ------------ for expenses incurred within 3 yrs. of accident ------------ Limited only by total benefits limit	Limited only by total benefits limit	Limited only by total benefits limit; payable only to non-wage earners	Funeral benefit: limited only by total benefits limit
Massachusetts	M	$500	------------ $2,000 overall max. on first-party benefits ------------ Limited only by total benefits limit, if incurred within 2 yrs.	Up to 75% of lost income	Limited only by total benefits limit; payments made to nonfamily members for services that would have been performed by victim	Funeral benefit: limited only by total benefits limit

HIGHWAYS

STATE NO-FAULT MOTOR VEHICLE INSURANCE LAWS—Continued

State or jurisdiction	Purchase of first-party benefits	Minimum tort liability threshold (a)	Maximum first-party (no-fault) benefits			
			Medical	Income loss	Replacement services	Survivors/funeral benefits
Michigan (d)	M	No dollar threshold (e)	Unlimited	85% of lost income up to $1,475/30-day period for up to 3 yrs.; max. amt. adjusted annually for cost of living	$20/day for up to 3 yrs.	Up to $1,475/30-day period for lost income for up to 3 yrs. and $20/day for replacement services. Funeral benefits: $1,000
Minnesota	M	$4,000	$20,000	---------- $20,000 max. for first-party benefits other than medical ---------- 85% of lost income up to $250/wk.	$200/wk., beginning 8 days after accident	Up to $200/wk. ea. for survivors' economic loss and survivors' replacement services loss. Funeral benefit: $2,000
New Jersey	M	$200 or $1,500 (f)	Unlimited	Up to $100/wk. for one yr.	Up to $12/day for a max. of $4,380/person	Max. amount of benefits victim would have received. Funeral benefit: $1,000
New York	M	No dollar threshold (g)	Limited only by total benefits limit	---------- $50,000 overall max. on first-party benefits ---------- 80% of lost income up to $1,000/mo. for 3 yrs.	$25/day for 1 yr.	$2,000 in addition to other benefits
North Dakota	M	$2,500	Limited only by total benefits limit	---------- $30,000 overall max. on first-party benefits ---------- 85% of lost income up to $150/wk.	Up to $15/day	Up to $150/wk. for survivors income loss and $15/day for replacement services. Funeral benefit: $1,000
Oregon	M	None	$5,000 if incurred within 1 yr. of accident	If victim is disabled at least 14 days, 70% of lost income up to $750/mo. for up to 52 wks.	If victim is disabled at least 14 days up to $18/day for up to 52 wks.	Funeral benefit: $1,000
Pennsylvania(h)	M	None	$10,000	After 5 workdays, up to $5,000, limited to $1,000/mo. and 80% of actual lost income (i)	None	Funeral benefit: $1,500
South Carolina	O	None	Limited only by total benefits limit if incurred within 3 yrs. of accident	---------- $1,000 overall max. on first-party benefits ---------- Limited only by total benefits limit	Limited only by total benefits limit	Funeral benefit: limited only by total benefits limit
South Dakota	O	None	$2,000 if incurred within 2 yrs. of accident	$60/wk. for up to 52 wks. for disability extending beyond 14 days of date of accident	None	$10,000 if death incurs within 90 days of accident
Texas	O	None	Limited only by total benefits limit if incurred within 3 yrs. of accident	---------- $2,500 overall max. on first-party benefits ---------- Limited only by total benefits limit if incurred within 3 yrs. of accident	Limited only by total benefits limit if incurred within 3 yrs. of accident. Payable only to non-wage earners	Limited only by total benefits limit if incurred within 3 yrs. of accident
Utah	M	$3,000	$3,000	85% of lost income up to $250/wk. for up to 52 wks. subject to 3-day waiting period which does not apply if disability lasts longer than 2 wks.	$20/day for up to 365 days subject to 3-day waiting period which does not apply if disability lasts longer than 2 wks.	$3,000 survivors benefit. Funeral benefit: $1,500

STATE NO-FAULT MOTOR VEHICLE INSURANCE LAWS—Continued

State or jurisdiction	Purchase of first-party benefits	Minimum tort liability threshold (a)	Maximum first-party (no-fault) benefits			
			Medical	Income loss	Replacement services	Survivors/funeral benefits
Virginia............	O	None	$2,000 if incurred within 1 yr. of accident	100% of lost income up to $100/wk. for up to 52 wks.	None	Funeral benefit: included in medical benefit
Dist. of Columbia.....	O	(j)	$50,000 or $100,000 (medical and rehabilitation)	$12,000 or $24,000	Max. of $24,000	Funeral benefit: $4,000

Source: *No Fault Press Reference Manual*, State Farm Insurance Companies.

Key:
O — Optional
M — Mandatory

(a) Refers to minimum amount of medical expenses necessary before victim can sue for general damages ("pain and suffering"). Lawsuits allowed in all states for injuries resulting in death and permanent disability. Some states allow lawsuits for one or more of the following: serious and permanent disfigurement, certain temporary disabilities, loss of body member, loss of certain bodily functions, certain fractures, or economic losses (other than medical) which exceed stated limits.

(b) Victim cannot sue for general damages unless injury results in significant and permanent loss of important body function, permanent injury, significant and permanent scarring or disfigurement, or death.

(c) Accident victim is not bound by tort restriction if (1) he has rejected the tort limitation in writing or (2) he is injured by a driver who has rejected the tort limitation in writing. Rejection bars recovery of first-party benefits.

(d) Liability for property damage for all states with no-fault insurance is under the state tort system. Michigan has no tort liability for vehicle damage.

(e) Victim cannot sue for general damages unless injuries result in death, serious impairment of bodily function, or serious permanent disfigurement.

(f) Motorist chooses one of two optional limitations.

(g) Victim cannot recover general damages unless injury results in inability to perform usual daily activities for at least 90 days during the 180 days following the accident; dismemberment; significant disfigurement; fracture; permanent loss of use of a body organ, member, function, or system; permanent consequential limitation of use of a body organ or member; significant limitation of use of a body function or system; or death.

(h) Pennsylvania repealed its no-fault act on February 12, 1984 and replaced it with a law that requires motorists to carry certain first-party coverages but places no restriction on the right to sue for general damages.

(i) May be waived by policyholder who has no expectation of actual income loss because of age, disability, or lack of employment history. Amount includes benefits for hiring substitute to perform self-employment services and hiring special help to enable victim to work.

(j) Person can choose "Personal Injury Protection" option. If person chooses this coverage, victims who are covered by no-fault benefits have 60 days after accident to decide whether to receive no-fault benefits. Victims who choose to get no-fault benefits cannot recover damages unless injury resulted in substantial permanent scarring or disfigurement; substantial and medically demonstrable permanent impairment which has significantly affected the ability of the victim to perform professional activties or usual and customary daily activities; a medically demonstrable impairment that prevents victim from performing substantially all of his usual customary daily activities for more than 180 continuous days; or medical and rehabilitation expenses or work loss exceeding the amount of no-fault benefits available.

HIGHWAYS

Table 8.20
MOTOR VEHICLE OPERATORS AND CHAUFFEURS LICENSES: 1988

State or jurisdiction	Operators licenses			Chauffeurs licenses			Estimated total licenses in force during 1988 (in thousands) (a)
	Years for which issued	Renewal date	Amount of fee	Years for which issued	Renewal date	Amount of fee	
Alabama	4	Birthday	$15.00 (b)				2,098
Alaska	5	Birthday	10.00				300
Arizona	4	Birthday	7.00	4	Birthday	$10.00	2,352
Arkansas	2 and 4	Birth month	7.00 and 13.00	2 and 4	Birth month	7.00 and 13.00	1,677
California*	4	Birthday	10.00				18,926
Colorado*	4	Birthday	6.50				2,226
Connecticut*	4	Birthday	31.00 (b)				2,370
Delaware*	4 (e)	Birthday	10.00 (e)				469
Florida	4	Birthday	15.00 (b)	4	Birthday	15.00 (b)	8,790
Georgia*	4	Birthday	4.50				4,336
Hawaii*	2 and 4 (d)	Birthday	5.50 and 8.50 (d)				635
Idaho	3	Birthday	13.50	3	Birthday	15.50	708
Illinois*	3 and 4 (e)	Birthday	8.00 and 10.00 (f)				7,263
Indiana	4	Birth month	6.00 (f)	4	Birth month	8.00	3,773
Iowa*	2 and 4 (h)	Birthday	8.00 and 16.00 (h)	2 and 4 (i)	Birthday	15.00 and 30.00 (h)	1,887
Kansas*	4	Birthday	8.00 (b)				1,706
Kentucky	4	Birth month	8.00	4	Birth month	8.00	2,368
Louisiana	5 (g)	Birthday	12.50				2,598
Maine*	4	Birthday	18.00				867
Maryland*	4	Birthday	6.00 (j)				3,137
Massachusetts*	4	Birthday	35.00 (b)				4,250
Michigan*	4 (k)	Birthday	12.00 (j)	4	Birthday	20.00	6,389
Minnesota*	4	Birthday	29.00 (l)				2,479
Mississippi	4	Birth month	13.00				1,814
Missouri	3	Issuance	7.50	3	Issuance	15.00	3,512
Montana	4	Birthday	12.00	4	Birthday	12.00	534
Nebraska	4 (m)	Birthday	10.00 (m)				1,088
Nevada*	4	Birthday	10.00 (f)				749
New Hampshire*	4	Birthday	20.00				798
New Jersey*	4	Issuance	17.50				5,452
New Mexico*	4 (n)	30 days after Birthday	10.00 (n)				1,047
New York*	4	Birthday	33.50				10,143
North Carolina*	4	Birthday	10.00				4,422
North Dakota*	4	Birthday	10.00 (b)				431
Ohio	4	Birthday	5.00 (o)	4	Birthday	5.00 (o)	7,379
Oklahoma	2 and 4	Birth month	7.00 and 14.00 (p)	2 and 4	Birth month	11.00 and 22.00 (p)	2,219
Oregon*	4	Birthday	15.00 (j)				2,170
Pennsylvania*	4	Birth month	21.50 (i)				7,732
Rhode Island*	5 (q)	Birthday	20.00				666
South Carolina*	4	Birthday	10.00				2,306
South Dakota	4	Birthday	6.00				483
Tennessee	4	Birthday	13.00 (b)	4	Birthday	21.00	3,199
Texas	4	Birthday	16.00				11,081
Utah*	4	Birthday	10.00				978
Vermont	2 and 4	Birthday	10.00 and 16.00 (b)				406
Virginia*	5 (q)	Birth month	12.00 (q)				4,130
Washington*	4	Birthday	14.00 (b)				3,198
West Virginia	4	Issuance	10.00	4	Issuance	15.00	1,308
Wisconsin	2 and 4	Birthday	4.00 and 9.00 (b)	1	Birthday	6.00 (b)	3,268
Wyoming*	4	Birthday	5.00 (r)				349
Dist. of Columbia	4	Issuance	15.00				392

HIGHWAYS

MOTOR VEHICLE LICENSES—Continued

Sources: Highway Statistics 1988, Federal Highway Administration, U.S. Department of Transportation. Compiled from reports of state authorities and other sources. Status of requirements as of December 31, 1988.

Key:

* — Classified drivers licenses are issued; permit qualified persons to operate specified vehicles on the public highways.

(a) Compiled for calendar year ending Dec. 31, 1988 from reports of state authorities and other sources. For Alabama, Arizona, Arkansas, and Michigan, data were estimated by (and for Louisiana, data were adjusted by) the Federal Highway Administration.

(b) The following examination fees are in addition to the fee shown for an original license: Connecticut-$15 for operator and $3.50 for public service licenses; Tennessee-$2; Kansas-$3; Alabama, Massachusetts, Rhode Island, and Wisconsin-$5; North Dakota-$5 each for written and road tests; Washington-$7; Vermont-written examination fee is $10 with original learner permit. No further examination fee unless driving test is failed, then $5 additional for additional test. Florida-$19. Safe drivers may renew for 6 years at $19.

(c) An indefinite term license ($25 fee) is issued for drivers meeting specified requirements, but a reexamination (with a $1 photo fee) is required every four years.

(d) Licenses issued for two years to persons 15-24 years and 65 years and over. Cost varies depending on place of issuance; fees shown are for Honolulu.

(e) Licenses are issued for both three- and four-year terms to phase-in use of four-year term.

(f) Illinois—$5 for persons 69 years and over for four years; Indiana—$3 for three-year renewal license for persons 75 years and over; Nevada—$5 for original or renewal license for persons over 70 years.

(g) Persons 65 and over must obtain a two-year license.

(h) Two years at $8 for operator license and $15 for chauffeur license issued to persons under 18 and over 70 years old. Others may choose 2 or 4 year term.

(i) Two-year license for persons 65 years and over at $11.50.

(j) Maryland—$20 for original operators license; Oregon—$32 for original operators.

(k) Persons with unsatisfactory driving records renew for two-year term. Persons 65 and over must obtain a two-year license.

(l) Service charge of $1 if issued by Dept. of Public Safety.

(m) Original license expires on licensee's birthday in the first year after issuance that licensee's age is divisible by four. Fees are: $3.50 for one year; $5.50 for two years; $8 for three years.

(n) Persons 75 years or over renew annually at no charge.

(o) A $1.50 deputy issuance fee and $1.00 eye exam fee are charged for licenses and permits.

(p) There is an additional $4 fee for the license application before obtaining the original license. Both 2 and 4-year licenses are being issued to phase in a 4-year term.

(q) In Rhode Island, effective January 1, 1985, licenses are being issued for terms varying from 1 to 5 years at $4 per year to phase in a 5 year term. In Virginia, effective January 1, 1985, licenses are issued for terms varying from 3 to 7 years at $2.40 per year for the basic license and $1 per year for each endorsement. This will phase in a new 5-year term with licenses expiring in a year when the licensee's age is divisible by 5.

(r) Original license is $10.

COMMISSIONS

Table 8.21
STATE PUBLIC UTILITY COMMISSIONS

State or other jurisdiction	Regulatory authority	Members Number	Members Selection	Selection of chair	Length of commissioners' terms (in years)	Number of full-time employees
Alabama	Public Service Commission	3	E	E	4	137
Alaska	Public Utilities Commission	5	GS	G (a)	6	43
Arizona	Corporation Commission	3	E	C	6	217
Arkansas	Public Service Commission	3	GS	G	6	114
California	Public Utilities Commission	5	GS	G	6	1,000
Colorado	Public Utilities Commission	3	GS	G	4 (b)	98.5
Connecticut	Department of Public Utilities Control	5	GL	C	4	151
Delaware	Public Service Commission	5	GS	G	5	20
Florida	Public Service Commission	5	GS	C	4	363
Georgia	Public Service Commission	5	E	C	6	159
Hawaii	Public Utilities Commission	3	GS	G	6	22
Idaho	Public Utilities Commission	3	GS	G	6	56
Illinois	Commerce Commission	6	GS	G	5	424
Indiana	Utility Regulatory Commission	5	GS	G	4	101
Iowa	State Utilities Board	3	GS	G	6	97
Kansas	State Corporation Commission	3	GS	C	4	238.5
Kentucky	Public Service Commission	3	GS	G	4	110
Louisiana	Public Service Commission	5	E	C	6	81
Maine	Public Utilities Commission	3	GL	G	6	67
Maryland	Public Service Commission	5	GS	G	5	141
Massachusetts	Department of Public Utilities	3	G	G	4 (b)	111
Michigan	Public Service Commission	3	GS	G	6	243
Minnesota	Public Utilities Commission	5	GS	G	6	30
Mississippi	Public Service Commission	3	E	C	4	122
Missouri	Public Service Commission	5	GS	G	6	191
Montana	Public Service Commission	5	E	C	4	46
Nebraska	Public Service Commission	5	E	C	6	64
Nevada	Public Service Commission	5	G	G	4	106
New Hampshire	Public Utilities Commission	3	GC	G (c)	6	62 (d)
New Jersey	Board of Public Utilities	3	GS	G	6	382
New Mexico	Public Service Commission	3	GS	G	6	44
New York	Public Service Commission	7	GS	G	6	656
North Carolina	Utilities Commission	7	GL	G	8	135
North Dakota	Public Service Commission	3	E	C	6	57
Ohio	Public Utilities Commission	5	GS	G	5	487 (h)
Oklahoma	Corporation Commission	3	E	C	6	413
Oregon	Public Utility Commissioner	3	GS	C	4	426
Pennsylvania	Public Utility Commission	5	GS	G	5	604
Rhode Island	Public Utilities Commission	3	GS	G	6	34
South Carolina	Public Service Commission	7	L (f)	C (i)	4 (j)	141
South Dakota	Public Utilities Commission	3	E	C	6	22
Tennessee	Public Service Commission	3	E	C	6	280
Texas	Public Utility Commission	3	GS	C	6	214
Utah	Public Service Commission	3	GS	G	6	79
Vermont	Public Service Board	3	GS	G	6	17
Virginia	State Corporation Commission	3	L	C	6	581
Washington	Utilities & Transportation Commission	3	GS	G	6	234
West Virginia	Public Service Commission	3	GS	G	6	171
Wisconsin	Public Service Commission	3	GS	G (e)	6	179
Wyoming	Public Service Commission	3	GS	C	6	35
Dist. of Columbia	Public Service Commission	3	MC	MC	4	61
Puerto Rico	Public Service Commission	5	GS	GS	4	454
Virgin Islands	Public Service Commission	9 (g)	GS (g)	C	3	2

Source: National Association of Regulatory Utility Commissioners, *Annual Report on Utility and Carrier Regulation*, 1988. (Washington, D.C.: 1989 and updates).
Key:
G — Appointed by Governor.
GC — Appointed by Governor, with consent of the Governor's Council.
C — Elected by the Commission.
GS — Elected by Governor, with consent of Senate.
L — Appointed by the Legislature.
GL — Appointed by Governor, with consent of entire Legislature.
MC — Appointed by the Mayor, with consent of City Council.
E — Elected by the public.

(a) Chairman serves in that position for four years.
(b) Co-terminous with Governor's. In Colorado, two terms are co-terminous and one is staggered.
(c) With Council approval.
(d) Includes five consumer advocate positions.
(e) Chairman serves in that position for two years.
(f) Upon recommendation of State Merit Selection Panel.
(g) 7 voting, 2 non-voting. Voting members appointed by Governor and confirmed by Senate, nonvoting appointed by President of Senate.
(h) Including Board members—510.
(i) Chairmanship rotates every two years.
(j) Concurrent terms.

COMMISSIONS

Table 8.22
SELECTED REGULATORY FUNCTIONS OF STATE PUBLIC UTILITIES COMMISSIONS*

State or other jurisdiction	Controls rates of privately owned utilities on sales to ultimate consumers of				Agency has authority to:											
					Prescribe temporary rates, pending investigation			Require prior authorization of rate changes			Suspend proposed rate changes			Initiate rate investigation on its own motion		
	Electric	Gas	Telephone	CATV	Electric	Gas	Telephone	Electric	Gas	Telephone	Electric	Gas	Telephone	Electric	Gas	Telephone
Alabama	★	★	★	...	★	★	...	★	★	...	★	★	★	★	★	★
Alaska	★	★	★	...	★	★	★	★	★	★	★	★	★	★	★	★
Arizona	★	★	★	...	★	★	★	★	★	★	(a)	(a)	(a)	★	★	★
Arkansas	★	★	★	...	★	★	★	★	★	★	★	★	★	★	★	★
California	★	★	★	...	★	★(b)	★(b)	★	★	★	★	★	★	★	★	★
Colorado	★	★	★	...	★(c)	★(c)	★(c)	★	★	★	★	★	★	★	★	★
Connecticut	★	★	★	...	★	★	★	★	★	★	★	★	★	★	★	★
Delaware	★	★	★	...	★	★	★	★	★	★	★	★	★	★	★	★
Florida	★	★	★	...	★	★	★	★	★	★	★	★	★	★	★	★
Georgia	★	★	★	...	★	★	★	★	★	★	★	★	★	★	★	★
Hawaii	★	★	★	(d)	★	★	★	★	★	★	...	...	...	★	★	★
Idaho	★	★	★	...	★	★	★	★(e)	★(e)	★(e)	★	★	★	★	★	★
Illinois	★	★	★	...	★	★	★	★	★	★	★	★	★	★	★	★
Indiana	★	★	★	(s)	...	...	...	★	★	★	★	★	★	★	★	★
Iowa (r)	★	★	★	(f)	★(g)	★(g)	★(g,r)	★	★	★(g)	★	★	★(g)	★	★	★(g)
Kansas	★	★	★	...	★	★	★	★	★	★	★	★	★	★	★	★
Kentucky	★	★	★	...	★	★	★	★	★	★	★	★	★	★	★	★
Louisiana	★	★(i)	★	...	★	★	★	★	★	★	★	★	★	★	★	★
Maine	★	★	★	...	★	★	★	★	★	★	★	★	★	★	★	★
Maryland	★	★	★	...	★	★	★	★	★	★	★	★	★	★	★	★
Massachusetts	★	★	★	★(m)	★	★	★	★	★	★	★	★	★	★	★	★
Michigan	★	★	★	...	★(j)	★(j)	★(j)	★	★	★	(a)	(a)	(a)	★	★	★
Minnesota	★	★(k)	★(l)	(n)	★	★	★	★	★	★(l)	★	★	★(l)	★	★	★(l)
Mississippi	★	★	★	...	★	★	★	★	★	★	★	★	★	★	★	★
Missouri	★	★	★	...	★	★	★	★	★	★	★	★	★	★	★	★
Montana	★	★	★	...	★	★	★	★	★	★	★	★	★	★	★	★
Nebraska (o)	...	...	★	...	...	...	★	...	...	★	...	...	★	...	...	★
Nevada	★	★	★	...	★	★	★	★	★	★	★	★	★	★	★	★
New Hampshire	★	★	★	★	★	★	★	★	★	★	★	★	★	★	★	★
New Jersey	★	★	★	★	★	★	★	...	★	★	★	★	★	★	★	★
New Mexico Public Service Comm.	★	★	...	...	★	★	...	★	★	...	★	★	...	★	★	...
State Corp. Comm.	...	...	★	(p)	...	...	★	...	...	★	...	...	★	...	...	★
New York	★	★	★	(q)	★	★	★	★	★	★	★	★	★	★	★	★
North Carolina	★	★	★	...	★	★	★	★	★	★	★	★	★	★	★	★
North Dakota	★	★	★(r)	...	★	★	★	★	★	★	★	★	★	★	★	★
Ohio	★	★	★	...	★	★	★	★	★	★	★	★	★	★	★	★
Oklahoma	★	★	★	...	★	★	★	★	★	★	★	★	★	★	★	★
Oregon	★	★	★	...	★	★	★	★	★	★	★	★	★	★	★	★
Pennsylvania	★	★	★	...	★	★	★	★	★	★	★	★	★	★	★	★
Rhode Island (s)	★	★	★	...	★	★	★	★	★	★	★	★	★	★	★	★
South Carolina	★	★	★	...	★	★	...	★	★	★	...	★	★	★	★	★
South Dakota	★	★	★(t)	...	★	★	★	★	★	★	★	★	★	★	★	★
Tennessee	★	★	★	★	★(u)	★(u)	★	★	★	★	★	★	★	★	★	★
Texas Pub. Utilities Comm.	★	...	★	...	★	...	★	★	...	★	★	...	★	★	...	★
Railroad Comm.	...	★	...	...	...	★	...	...	★	...	...	★	...	...	★	...
Utah	★	★	★	★	★	★	★	★	★	★	★	★	★	★	★	★
Vermont	★	★	★	★	★	★	★	★	★	★	★	★	★	★	★	★
Virginia	★	★	★(v)	...	★	★	★	★	★	★	★	★	★	★	★	★
Washington	★	★	★	...	★	★	★	★	★	★	★	★	★	★	★	★
West Virginia	★	★	★	...	★	★	★	★	★	★	★	★	★	★	★	★
Wisconsin	★	★	★(w)	(x)	★	★	★	★	★	★	(a,s)	(a,s)	(a,s)	★	★	★
Wyoming	★	★	★	...	★	★	★	★	★	★	★	★	★	★	★	★
Dist. of Columbia (s)	★	★	★	★	...	...	...	★	★	★	★	★	...	★	★	★
Puerto Rico (s)	(q)	★	(y)	★	...	...	(y)	...	...	(y)	...	...	(y)	...	★	(y)
U.S. Virgin Islands (s)	(q)	...	★	★	★	★	★	★	★	★	(r)	★	...	...	...	★

COMMISSIONS

SELECTED REGULATORY FUNCTIONS—Continued

* Full names of commissions are shown on Table 8.21.
Source: National Association of Regulatory Utility Commissioners, *Annual Report on Utility and Carrier Regulation*, 1988 (Washington, D.C.: 1989).
Key:
★ — Yes
... — No

(a) Rates cannot be increased without hearings and a subsequent order of the Commission; consequently no suspension is required.
(b) May fix temporary rates, but practice is not followed.
(c) No specific statutory authority.
(d) Regulated by the Cable Television Division of the Department of Regulatory Agencies.
(e) Rates become effective after seven months if Commission does not take action.
(f) Under jurisdiction of Department of Administration, City of Indianapolis, Office of Telecommunications.
(g) Not for companies with less than 15,000 customers and less than 15,000 access lines.
(h) Interim rates must be approved and are collected under bond, subject to refund.
(i) Except no authority over rates charged to industrial customers by any gas company.
(j) Commission has authority to grant partial and immediate rate relief during pendency of final order, after statutory requirements are met.
(k) Rates not regulated for gas utilities serving fewer than 650 customers.
(l) Has authority only at the election of the cooperative.
(m) Massachusetts CATV Commission has jurisdiction over CATV.
(n) Minnesota Cable Commission Board.
(o) Telephone is the only regulated utility.
(p) Two-way telecommunications, data, etc.
(q) New York Commission of Cable Television has jurisdiction over CATV companies. NYPS has authority over attachments by CATV companies to utility poles and leasing of utility conduits by CATV companies.
(r) Electric public utilities with fewer than 10,000 not subject to rate regulation; gas public utilities with fewer than 2,000 customers are subject to rate regulation only upon petition by customers.
(s) Commission did not respond to request for updated information.
(t) PUC does not regulate rates of rural telephone cooperatives.
(u) Emergency only.
(v) SCC has authority to regulate rates for interchange carriers but allows them to set competitively.
(w) Of the 99 LECs operating in the state, only 12 are fully integrated.
(x) No regulation of television services.
(y) The Puerto Rico Telephone Authority, a state public corporation, purchased the Puerto Rico Telephone Company.

LABOR LEGISLATION: 1988-89

By Richard R. Nelson

The 1988-89 biennium saw continued enactment of a heavy volume of labor standards legislation covering a wide variety of subjects. Several significant measures were enacted in traditional fields, including minimum wage protection, regulation of child labor and bans on employment discrimination. Also receiving considerable attention were newer areas, including family issues such as parental leave and child care, limitations on door-to-door sales by children, restrictions on workplace smoking and regulation of employee testing for drug or alcohol abuse or for AIDS.

Wages and Hours

Minimum wages

The Federal Fair Labor Standards Amendments of 1989 (Public Law 101-157) were signed into law by the president on November 17, 1989. Among other provisions, these amendments to the Fair Labor Standards Act (FLSA) increase the federal minimum wage from $3.35 to $3.80 an hour on April 1, 1990, and to $4.25 on April 1, 1991, permit a temporary training wage for workers under 20 years of age under specified conditions, and change certain provisions relating to coverage, exemptions and enforcement. The maximum allowable tip credit will increase from 40 percent of the applicable minimum wage rate to 45 percent on April 1, 1990 and to 50 percent after March 31, 1991.

While federal legislation was being debated in 1988 and 1989, states moved ahead with their own legislation to such an extent that minimum wage was a major subject of legislative activity. A first-time law was enacted in Iowa, and new amendments, wage orders, or administrative action led to increases in Arkansas, Kansas, Maine, New Hampshire, North Dakota, Oregon, Pennsylvania, Rhode Island, South Dakota, Vermont, Wisconsin, the District of Columbia (for employees in hotel and restaurant occupations), Guam, Puerto Rico (for employees in the construction; hotel; restaurant; bar and soda fountain; recreational; sporting and amusement services industry) and the Virgin Islands. Minimum wage levels also increased during the biennium as the result of prior action in six other states (California, Connecticut, Hawaii, Massachusetts, Minnesota and Washington [1988 ballot initiative]).

A bill to enact a first-time law was vetoed in Missouri.

Measures linking state rates to any future federal rate increases were adopted in Delaware, Illinois, Maine (up to $5 per hour), Montana (up to $4 per hour) and Nevada.

The highest rates in effect on January 1, 1990 were $4.25 an hour in California, Con-

---

Richard R. Nelson is a State Standards Adviser in the Division of State Standards Programs, Wage and Hour Division, Employment Standards Administration, U.S. Department of Labor. The portion of the Occupational Safety and Health section reporting on Federal developments was prepared by Arlene Perkins, Project Officer, Directorate of Federal-State Operations, Office of State Programs, Occupational Safety and Health Administration, U.S. Department of Labor. The Workers' Compensation section was prepared by Mark Grobman, State Standards Adviser, Division of Planning, Policy and Standards, Office of Workers' Compensation Programs, Employment Standards Administration, U.S. Department of Labor.

necticut, Oregon, Rhode Island and Washington (see table 8.27). The District of Columbia and the Virgin Islands exceed $4.25 for some or all workers, and future increases in Oregon for January 1, 1991 and in Iowa by January 1, 1992 will raise these state rates to $4.75 and $4.65 respectively.

Other minimum wage and overtime changes included extension of coverage of the Oregon law to persons regulated under the Federal Fair Labor Standards Act (FLSA), most agricultural workers and others. Coverage was also extended in North Carolina and Arkansas by eliminating or changing numerical exemptions. Short-term training wages were adopted for minors under age 18 in Delaware, and for newly hired workers of any age in Iowa, Montana and Wisconsin, and retained in a revised wage order in North Dakota. Vermont eliminated a provision which had permitted payment at a lower rate for employees working for an employer less than 90 days.

In Minnesota, the phased elimination of the tip credit allowance against the minimum wage, begun in 1985, was completed as of January 1, 1989.

Wage payment and collection

Among the more important wage payment and collection developments was the enactment of a revised private sector payday law in Texas. This law specifies employer pay obligations, restricts permissible wage deductions, establishes wage claim filing, hearing, and collection procedures and establishes an administrative penalty for violation.

Labor commissioners in Idaho and Virginia were given authority to assess civil penalties for failure to pay wages. In Louisiana, employees were authorized to bring civil action to enforce payment of the undisputed portion of any wages due and in Oklahoma, employee civil court actions will no longer be limited to $1,000 per claim. The Utah Industrial Commission may now impose a penalty on employers of 5 percent of unpaid wages, assessed daily, for up to 20 days.

In other actions, the Oregon Wage Security Fund, used to pay claims of employees whose employers have gone out of business without sufficient assets to pay wage claims, was extended for 3 years.

Prevailing wage

The Louisiana prevailing wage law was repealed in 1988, continuing a trend which has seen the repeal of nine such laws since 1979. Thirty-two states currently have these laws, which specify that wage rates paid on publicly funded construction projects be not less than those prevailing in the area.[1] Efforts to repeal prevailing wage laws failed in eight states, and efforts to enact such laws failed in three.[2] In November, 1988 Massachusetts voters defeated a ballot initiative which sought repeal of the state's prevailing wage law. Among other state actions, the commissioner of labor in New York was directed to assess a civil penalty against any person demanding or receiving kickbacks of employee wages. California amendments included the addition of debarment as a penalty for violation, and authorization for local public agencies to establish labor compliance programs for public works projects and to retain fines and penalties assessed for violations.

In court action, the Illinois State Supreme Court reversed lower court decisions by holding that: it is outside the grant of home-rule power for home-rule units to exclude themselves from coverage of the state prevailing wage law.

Pay equity

The issue of equal pay for jobs of comparable value received little legislative attention during 1988 and 1989. One notable piece of legislation was adopted in North Dakota creating a pay equity implementation fund for the purpose of establishing equitable nondiscriminatory compensation among all positions and classes within the state's classification plan. Also, a measure adopted in Oregon directs the legislative assembly to provide oversight to ensure that state service compensation and classification meet legal requirements.

Employee testing

Testing of employees for drug or alcohol

abuse continued to be a headline-producing issue involving privacy rights, workplace safety and efforts to achieve "drug-free workplaces." Legislation was proposed in several jurisdictions and comprehensive new drug-testing legislation was enacted in Maine and Nebraska for all private and public employers, and in Florida for state government agencies. The Maine and Florida laws permit drug testing of job applicants offered employment and of current employees for probable cause or while undergoing substance abuse treatment. Maine also permits random testing if provided for in collective bargaining agreements and for employees in safety-sensitive positions. Florida permits testing as part of a routinely scheduled medical examination. Testing procedures, employee protections and required notifications are specified in both laws. The Nebraska measure, which applies to employers of six or more, permits drug and alcohol testing with few restrictions. A positive test may subject an employee to termination or other adverse actions. Testing and retesting procedures were specified.

Drug testing laws of limited occupational application were enacted in Illinois, Iowa, Kansas, and Tennessee.[3] A prior Rhode Island law prohibiting testing of private and public sector employees except for probable cause was amended to permit testing in the public utility mass transportation industry if required by federal law or regulation as a condition of receiving federal funds.

Testing of employees for the presence of AIDS virus (HIV) antibodies was also a controversial issue, raising questions of privacy, workplace safety and employment discrimination.

Laws prohibiting employers from requiring a test for AIDS as a condition of employment and from discriminating on the basis of a positive test were enacted in Florida, Iowa, Rhode Island, and Vermont (similar laws were enacted previously in Wisconsin and Massachusetts). In North Carolina, employers may not require or use an AIDS test to determine suitability for continued employment or discriminate against an employee with AIDS or HIV infection. They may, however, require an AIDS test for job applicants and take adverse actions, under certain conditions, against employees with AIDS. In New Mexico, disclosure of the results of an AIDS-related test may not be required as a condition of employment or continued employment unless absence of the virus infection is a bona fide occupational qualification.

Ohio employers of persons with AIDS were granted immunity from liability for damages resulting from transmission of the HIV virus to another person or for any stress-related illness or injury caused by an employee being required to work with a person with AIDS or the HIV virus.

Family issues

Changing work force demographics, especially the growing numbers of families where both parents work outside the home and of single working mothers who must reconcile the demands of work and family is increasingly being reflected in new legislation enacted to help meet the needs of these workers.

Parental leave for the birth, adoption, or serious illness of a child was the subject of active interest in 1988 and 1989, with a number of bills introduced and with legislation enacted in a few states. Maine now requires private sector employers and local governments with 25 or more employees as well as the state to grant up to eight weeks of unpaid family medical leave in any two years. In Wisconsin, private employers of 50 or more workers and the state government must provide unpaid family or medical leave of up to six weeks for the birth or adoption of a child, two weeks to care for a child, spouse, or parent with a serious health condition and two weeks personal medical leave within any 12-month period. A new law in Washington requires private and local government employers of 100 or more and state agencies to grant up to 12 weeks of unpaid leave in any 24-month period. Under this law, an employer may limit or deny family leave to those designated as key personnel, but that group may not exceed ten percent of the work force. In Connecticut, which had previously adopted a law for state employees, a private sector law was enacted initially requiring employers of 250 or more to grant up to 12 weeks of leave in any two-year period (coverage will be extended gradually in steps to include employers of 75 or more and required leave will be extended to 16 weeks).

Laws providing for parental leave in the public sector only were adopted in 1989 by North Dakota, Oklahoma and West Virginia.

Typically, parental leave laws entitle employees returning from such leave to reinstatement in the same or equivalent position without loss of benefits and several states also allow use of the leave to care for a seriously ill spouse or parent.

Among related provisions, health and insurance benefits must be continued for state employees in Massachusetts, who are granted parental leave to care for a child under three years of age. In Washington, public and private employers must allow an employee to use accrued sick leave to care for a minor child with a health condition requiring treatment or supervision. Also, a new maternity leave law in Vermont requires employers of ten or more to grant up to 12 weeks of unpaid leave to pregnant employees.

States are beginning to facilitate the provision of child care by employers. A few examples include an Oklahoma law providing for a pilot program to establish child-care centers for children of state employees, an Arizona measure providing that employers who subsidize child care through a licensed day-care center or other specified facilities will not be held liable for damages if certain conditions are met and a law in Mississippi providing income-tax credits for employers who provide child care for the children of employees during working hours.

Child labor

Child labor legislation is increasingly reflecting a growing concern for the academic performance of minors who are employed during the school year. An example is the New Hampshire Youth Employment Law which was amended to require a satisfactory level of school achievement as a prerequisite for issuing a work certificate, with revocation if this level is not maintained. As part of a literacy and school dropout prevention program, New Hampshire also limited allowable school-week work hours of 16- and 17-year-olds and created a committee to examine issues including the relationship between academic achievement and the number of weekly hours spent working or participating in sports. The Maine compulsory school attendance law was amended to prohibit the employment, without a release, of any student who is habitually truant. A study of New York child labor laws was conducted and legislation introduced (pending as of February 1, 1990) to further restrict school-term work hours by children under age 18, and resolutions were adopted in Nebraska and Tennessee asking for studies of the effect of job-holding on students and their educational progress.

The employment of minors in door-to-door sales (an area where child labor laws are frequently abused) continued to be an immerging issue during the biennium. An Alaska regulation adopted in 1989 determined such sales to be dangerous and prohibited the activity for children under age 18. Children under age 16 in Missouri may no longer be employed in door-to-door selling or similar activity unless the employer has received written permission from the director of the Division of Labor Standards. In Washington such work for children under age 16 is now prohibited unless the labor department grants a variance. Wisconsin street trades provisions have a 12-year minimum age for employment. An amendment to these provisions requires that employers of minors in door-to-door sales be certified annually by the labor department, submit specified identifying information, demonstrate financial responsibility and give minors written information on terms of employment. California now prohibits the employment of minors under age 16 in door-to-door sales more than 50 miles from their homes. These new measures join earlier restrictions adopted in Arizona, Oklahoma and Oregon.

Among other significant developments, monetary penalties were substantially increased for child labor violations in Wisconsin, the labor commissioner in New Hampshire was authorized to assess civil money penalties for violation and in South Carolina criminal penalties for violation were eliminated and replaced with a warning for a first offense and a fine determined by the commissioner of labor for each subsequent offense.

Equal employment opportunity

Prohibition of one or more of the various forms of employment discrimination continued as a major area of legislative activity during the biennium. Laws of this kind were enacted in a majority of the states, with laws concerning discrimination based on age, sex, or handicap being the most common. The age-70 upper limit for protection from age discrimination or mandatory retirement provisions was eliminated for both private and public sector employees by amendments to laws in Idaho, Kansas, South Carolina, Tennessee and Texas, and for various public sector employees by amendments in Arizona, Arkansas, Connecticut, the District of Columbia and Maryland. Some of this state activity likely was in response to Federal Age Discrimination in Employment Act amendments, effective January 1, 1987, which included removal of the age-70 upper limit on coverage.

New Massachusetts civil rights provisions ban all discrimination based on sex, race, color, creed, or national origin. A new Louisiana human rights law bars discrimination by private and public employers and apprenticeship and training programs on the basis of race, creed, color, religion, sex, age, or national origin.

Discrimination against physically or mentally handicapped persons by public and private employers was prohibited by new enactments in Delaware and Idaho. In both instances employers are required to make reasonable accommodation in the workplace for a worker's disability. North Dakota employers are also required to make reasonable accommodations for an otherwise qualified person with a physical or mental disability and for a person's religion.

Disability issues were also the subject of new laws in Texas, where the ban on discrimination on the basis of disability was amended to exclude persons with a currently communicable disease or infection, including AIDS, under certain conditions; and in Nebraska, where disability was redefined under the Fair Employment Practices Act to exclude addiction to alcohol, controlled substances, or gambling.

The Utah Anti-Discrimination Act was amended to ban employment discrimination on the basis of pregnancy, childbirth or related condition, and in Oregon it was made unlawful to refuse to transfer a pregnant employee temporarily to less strenuous or hazardous work whenever reasonable.

Massachusetts enacted a law banning discrimination in employment and other areas on the basis of sexual orientation.

Occupational safety and health

One or more laws dealing with various aspects of worker safety and health were enacted in 42 states and Guam. Many involved measures enacted to fulfill state obligations under the Federal Emergency Planning and Community Right-to-Know Act of 1986; regulation of asbestos abatement work; and restrictions on workplace smoking.

New, comprehensive, public sector right-to-know laws were enacted in Guam and Georgia. Both laws provide for safety training and notification to employees of hazardous substances in the workplace. Also, new sections were added to the Washington Worker and Community Right-to-Know Act regulating the storage and use of agricultural pesticides.

Many of the asbestos abatement enactments involved changes to meet state contractor certification responsibilities under the Federal Asbestos Hazard Emergency Response Act of 1986. Other laws provided for regulation of various aspects of this work, including the certification or licensing of contractors, safety training of workers and notification to employees of the presence of asbestos.

Maine enacted two laws of special interest. One makes a person having direct control of any employment, place of employment, or employee guilty of manslaughter if he or she intentionally or knowingly violates any federal or state occupational safety or health standard and such violation results in an employee's death. The other requires employers with 25 or more video display terminals at one location within the state to establish education and training programs for the terminal operators (a first of its kind law in Suffolk County, New York providing employee protection against possible dangers of video display terminal use was adopted in 1988, but was struck down in 1989 by the State Supreme Court which stated that the state and federal governments, not the county, should regulate workplace safety). In Connecticut, public works contracts are not to be awarded to bidders cited for specified violations of any occupational safety and health act.

Other developments included new laws or amendments pertaining to safety standards in mines, boiler and pressure vessels, and amusement ride and elevator operation. A new Texas law regulates trench excavation safety in public works construction.

Of the 25 state plan jurisdictions with occupational safety and health programs (see table 8.25), 23 operate programs covering both private and public sector employees. Two states, Connecticut and New York, cover public employees only. Of these 25 states, Virginia was granted "final approval" status during the biennium, bringing to 14 the number of state plans which have been granted final approval by OSHA.

In February 1987, California Governor Deukmejian deleted funding from the state budget for private sector activities of California's occupational safety and health program (Cal/OSHA). This controversial action engendered legislative and judicial challenges, as well as public opposition. It necessitated federal OSHA to assume concurrent jurisdiction over private sector activities in the state.

On November 8, 1988, California voters passed Proposition 97, which added a section to the state labor code mandating implementation of a full state plan. At that time, the governor and the California Department of Industrial Relations announced the restoration of a full state plan as it formerly existed, to be completed in July, 1989. In October, 1989, OSHA determined that the state occupational safety and health program approved under section 18 of the Occupational Safety and Health Act had once again been developed sufficiently to justify suspension of most concurrent federal enforcement activity. At that time, OSHA entered into a new Operational Status Agreement with the state whereby concurrent federal enforcement authority will not be initiated with regard to most federal occupational safety and health standards in the issues covered by the state's plan.

Plant closings

Federal legislation enacted in 1988 requires employers of 100 or more employees to provide 60 days' advance notice of plant closings and layoffs to affected workers or their representatives, to the state dislocated worker unit and to the appropriate unit of local government. Recourse for violation is through civil suits filed by affected workers, their representatives and/or units of local government. At the state level, Tennessee adopted a law requiring employers of 50 or more to provide notification of a major layoff, plant closure, or relocation under certain circumstances, and Wisconsin extended coverage of its law requiring advance notice to employers of 50 or more instead of 100 or more as before. Other state efforts to lessen the impact of a plant closing or substantial layoff included adoption of a Worker Adjustment Act in New York designed to provide dislocated workers with occupational training, job training and other assistance; extension of coverage, to dislocated workers, of a Rhode Island law entitling involuntarily laid-off employees to continue health insurance coverage by payment of premiums at the group rate; and funding for a business and job retention program in Washington.

Laws to encourage the formation of employee-owned enterprises were enacted in California, Montana and Pennsylvania.

Workers' compensation

Major changes in state workers' compensation laws during the biennium focused on coverage, benefit levels, funding, penalties and assessments. Other changes dealt with medical care, occupational diseases, insurance, rehabilitation, re-employment, safety and administration.

Weekly benefit levels were increased for total disability in almost every jursdiction (see Table 8.23). Colorado, Oregon and Washington raised the percentage of their average weekly wage upon which benefit levels are based. North Dakota revised the formula used to compute compensation for permanent partial disability to 33⅓ percent of the state average weekly wage (previously no percentage was established). Legislation in Alabama and Mississippi eliminated the statutory weekly benefit amounts and mandated that benefit levels now be based on a percentage of the state average weekly wage.

Coverage requirements were revised in 22 jurisdictions. Seventeen of those jurisdictions broadened coverage to new groups of workers,[4] many of which included volunteer peace officers, civil defense workers, civil air patrol members, ambulance personnel, fire company members and those who come into contact with hazardous substances. Coverage is also continuing to be extended to construction workers, employees of subcontractors, prisoners, auxiliary peace officers and participants in sheltered workshops. Five jurisdictions[5] took action to limit or exclude the coverage of out-of-state workers, inmates in training programs, seasonal workers, volunteer ski patrol members, volunteer firefighters and employees of subcontractors.

Many jurisdictions focused their attention on the costs of their workers' compensation programs. Several enactments increased penalties, assessments and fines on employers and insurers who violate the law. Also, as a cost savings measure, some jurisdictions now authorize the inclusion of medical deductibles in workers' compensation insurance policies.

Legislation was approved in Mississippi authorizing self-insurance status for the state and group self-insurance status was authorized for two or more political subdivisions.

Two states made major organizational changes. The Georgia State Board of Workers' Compensation was transferred out of the Department of Labor to function as a separate entity under the executive branch of government. The Hawaii State Workers' Compensation Fund was reorganized as the State Compensation Mutual Insurance Fund, and will operate as a nonprofit mutual insurance corporation. Insurers in Alaska are now required to establish and maintain workplace safety rate reduction programs.

Private employment agencies

California will no longer license private employment agencies and related businesses. Among other developments, Connecticut and New York laws were amended to exempt employer fee-paid agencies from regulation requirements, and the North Carolina law was amended to exempt certain employer-fee-paid consulting services or temporary help services. Coverage of the Oklahoma law was limited to agencies charging a fee to job applicants only. Illinois adopted a Job Referral and Job Listing Services Consumer Protection Act providing for the regulation of these businesses.

Other legislation

Twelve states[6] enacted or modified "whistleblower" laws designed to protect employees from employer retaliation for reporting violations to a public body, or for participating in an investigation, hearing, or court action.

Several states passed laws designed to carry out duties and responsibilities under the Federal Job Training Partnership Act. Legislation requiring background clearance checks of prospective employees in occupations involving supervision of children was also enacted in many states.

A law was enacted in New Jersey requiring apparel industry manufacturers and contractors to register annually with the Department of Labor as a condition of doing business in the state, and the New York apparel registration law was amended to cover manufacturers and contractors of men's apparel as well as the women's, children's, and infant's apparel industries as before.

Other significant enactments included a universal health-care law in Massachusetts designed to provide basic health insurance for every resident by 1992, a construction contractor registration law in Iowa under which only registered contractors will be eligible to be awarded state contracts, an amendment to the Pennsylvania Public Employee Relations Act authorizing the negotiation of fair share fee agreements and a law in Oregon making it unlawful to subject an employee or applicant to a genetic screening or brain-wave test.

New meal period requirements were enacted in Connecticut and Minnesota, and coverage of existing meal and rest period requirements were extended in Oregon.

In Texas, the Department of Labor and Standards became the Department of Licensing and Regulation, with most labor functions transferred to the Texas Employment Commission. A new consolidated Department of Employment was created in Wyoming, combining several formerly separate agencies and labor programs including the Department of Labor and Statistics. In West Virginia, under a reorganization of the executive branch of state government, the Department of Labor and several related boards and agencies were among those transferred and incorporated into a new Department of Commerce, Labor and Environmental Resources.

The federally enacted Employee Polygraph Protection Act of 1988 went into effect December 27, 1988. The act prohibits most private employers engaged in interstate commerce from using any lie detector tests, with certain exceptions, either for pre-employment screening or during the course of employment. The federal law does not preempt any state or local law or collective bargaining agreement that prohibits lie detector tests or is more restrictive than the Act, except for exemptions from the federal prohibitions for all federal, state, and local governments, for federal national defense and security functions, and for FBI contractors.

Footnotes

1. States with prevailing wage laws are Alaska, Arkansas, California, Connecticut, Delaware, Hawaii, Illinois, Indiana, Kentucky, Maine, Maryland, Massachusetts, Michigan, Minnesota, Missouri, Montana, Nebraska, Nevada, New Jersey, New Mexico, New York, Ohio, Oklahoma, Oregon, Pennsylvania, Rhode Island, Tennessee, Texas, Washington, West Virginia, Wisconsin and Wyoming. Guam and the Virgin Islands also have such laws. Laws repealed since 1979 were Florida (1979), Alabama (1980), Utah (1981), Arizona (1984), Colorado, Idaho and New Hampshire (1985), Kansas (1987) and Louisiana (1988).

2. Prevailing wage repeal efforts failed in Illinois, Indiana, Maryland, Massachusetts, New Mexico, Oklahoma, Texas, and Wisconsin. Efforts to enact laws failed in Florida, Iowa and Kansas.

3. Drug testing laws of limited application were enacted in Illinois applying to school bus drivers and to the Regional Transportation Authority; in Iowa, applicable to operators of excursion gambling boats; in Kansas for persons taking office as governor, lieutenant governor, or attorney general and for those applying for safety sensitive positions in State government; and in Tennessee applicable to Department of Correction security personnel. Prior drug testing legislation has been enacted in Connecticut, Iowa, Louisiana, Minnesota, Montana, Rhode Island, Utah and Vermont.

4. Alaska, Connecticut, Florida, Georgia, Idaho, Kansas, Louisiana, Maryland, Minnesota, New Hampshire, New York, Oklahoma, Tennessee, Utah, Virginia, Washington and Wyoming.

5. Colorado, Maine, Missouri, North Carolina and Oregon.

6. Alaska, Arizona, California, Illinois, Iowa, Maine, North Carolina, Ohio, Oregon, Rhode Island, Utah and West Virginia.

LABOR

Table 8.23
MAXIMUM BENEFITS FOR TEMPORARY TOTAL DISABILITY PROVIDED BY WORKERS' COMPENSATION STATUTES
(As of July 1989)

State or other jurisdiction	Maximum percentage of wages	Maximum payment per week Amount	Maximum payment per week Based on*	Maximum period Duration of disability	Maximum period Number of weeks	Total maximum stated in law
United States (FECA) (a)	66-2/3 (b)	$1,071.68	75% of the pay of specific grade level in federal civil service (b)	★	...	...
(LS/HWCA) (a)	66-2/3	636.24	200% of NAWW	★	...	...
Alabama	66-2/3	357.98	100% of SAWW	★	...	...
Alaska	80 of worker's spendable earnings	700.00	...	★ (c)	...	...
Arizona	66-2/3	276.15 (d)	...	★	...	...
Arkansas	66-2/3	209.08	66-2/3% of SAWW	...	450	...
California	66-2/3	224.00	...	★	...	...
Colorado	66-2/3	371.21 (e)	91% of SAWW	★	...	...
Connecticut	66-2/3	671.00 (f)	150% of SAWW	★	...	...
Delaware	66-2/3	280.64	66-2/3% of SAWW	★	...	...
Florida	66-2/3	362.00 (g)	100% of SAWW	...	350	...
Georgia	66-2/3	175.00	...	★	...	...
Hawaii	66-2/3	358.00	100% of SAWW	★	...	...
Idaho	60-90	290.70 - 403.75 (h)	90% of SAWW	...	52 (i)	...
Illinois	66-2/3	604.73	133-1/3% of SAWW	★	...	...
Indiana	66-2/3	274.00	...	...	500	$137,000
Iowa	80 of worker's spendable earnings	684.00	200% of SAWW	...	...	...
Kansas	66-2/3	271.00	75% of SAWW	★	...	100,000
Kentucky	66-2/3	343.02	100% of SAWW	★	...	...
Louisiana	66-2/3	267.00 (j)	75% of SAWW	★	...	...
Maine	66-2/3	471.83 (j)	166-2/3% of SAWW	★	...	...
Maryland	66-2/3	407.00	100% of SAWW	★	...	...
Massachusetts	66-2/3	444.21 (k)	100% of SAWW	...	260	(l)
Michigan	80 of worker's spendable earnings	409.00 (m)	90% of SAWW	★	...	...
Minnesota	66-2/3	391.00	100% of SAWW	★ (n)	...	...
Mississippi	66-2/3	206.00	66-2/3% of SAWW	...	450	92,970
Missouri	66-2/3	289.75	75% of SAWW	...	400	...
Montana	66-2/3	318.00 (o)	100% of SAWW	★	...	...
Nebraska	66-2/3	245.00	...	★	...	...
Nevada	66-2/3	368.82	100% of SAWW	★	...	...
New Hampshire	66-2/3	600.00	150% of SAWW	★	...	...
New Jersey	70	342.00	75% of SAWW	...	400	...
New Mexico	66-2/3	283.70	85% of SAWW	...	700	(p)
New York	66-2/3	300.00	...	★	...	...
North Carolina	66-2/3	376.00	110% of SAWW	★	...	...
North Dakota	66-2/3	313.00 (q)	100% of SAWW	★	...	...
Ohio	72 for first 12 weeks; 66-2/3 thereafter	400.00 (r)	100% of SAWW	★	...	...
Oklahoma	66-2/3	231.00 (s)	66-2/3% of SAWW	...	300	...
Oregon	66-2/3	388.99	100% of SAWW	★	...	...
Pennsylvania	66-2/3	399.00	100% of SAWW	★	...	...
Rhode Island	66-2/3	360.00 (t)	100% of SAWW	★	...	...
South Carolina	66-2/3	334.87	100% of SAWW	...	500	...
South Dakota	66-2/3	289.00	100% of SAWW	★	...	...
Tennessee	66-2/3	252.00	...	★	...	92,400
Texas	66-2/3	238.00 (u)	...	...	401	...
Utah	66-2/3	347.00 (v)	100% of SAWW	...	312	...
Vermont	66-2/3	544.00 (w)	150% of SAWW	★	...	...
Virginia	66-2/3	393.00	100% of SAWW	...	500	...
Washington	60-75	389.32 (x)	100% of SAMW	★	...	...
West Virginia	70	367.89	100% of SAWW	...	208	...
Wisconsin	66-2/3	363.00 (x)	100% of SAWW	★	...	...
Wyoming	66-2/3 of actual monthly earnings	354.00	100% of monthly wage	★	...	...

LABOR

MAXIMUM BENEFITS—Continued

| State or other jurisdiction | Maximum percentage of wages | Maximum payment per week | | Maximum period | | Total maximum stated in law |
		Amount	Based on*	Duration of disability	Number of weeks	
Dist. of Columbia ...	66-2/3 or 80 of worker's spendable earnings; whichever is less	513.00	100% of SAWW	★	...	...
Puerto Rico	66-2/3	65.00	...	...	312	...
U.S. Virgin Islands	66-2/3	214.00	66-2/3 of SAWW	★	...	...

Source: Branch of Workers' Compensation Studies, Division of Planning, Policy and Standards, Office of Workers' Compensation Programs, Employment Standards Administration, U.S. Department of Labor.

Key:
*SAWW — State's average weekly wage
SAMW — State's average monthly wage
NAWW — National average weekly wage.

(a) Federal Employees' Compensation Act (FECA) and the Longshoremen's and Harbor Workers' Compensation Act (LS/HWCA). LS/HWCA benefits are for private-sector maritime employees (not seamen) who work on navigable waters of the U.S., including dry docks.
(b) Benefits under FECA are computed at a maximum of 75 percent of the pay of a specific grade level in the federal civil service.
(c) Payments payable for duration of disability until date of medical stability is reached.
(d) Additional $10 monthly added to benefits of dependents residing in the U.S.
(e) Payments are subject to Social Security benefit offsets and by benefits from an employer pension or disability plan.
(f) Additional $10 weekly for each dependent child under 18 years of age, up to 50 percent of basic benefit, not to exceed 75 percent of worker's wage.
(g) Payments subject to Social Security and Unemployment Insurance benefit offsets.
(h) Additional 7 percent ($22.61) is payable for each dependent child up to five children.
(i) After 52 weeks, payments are 60 percent of SAWW for duration of disability.
(j) Payments subject to Unemployment Insurance benefit offset.
(k) Additional $6 will be added per dependent if weekly benefits are below $150.
(l) Total maximum payable not to exceed 250 times the SAWW in effect at time of injury.
(m) Payments subject to reduction by Unemployment Insurance and Social Security benefits, and those under an employer disability, retirement, or pension plan.
(n) Payments made for duration of disability until 90 days after maximum medical improvement or end of retraining.
(o) Payments subject to Social Security benefit offsets.
(p) Total maximum payable equals the sum of 700 multiplied by the maximum weekly benefit payable at the time of injury.
(q) Additional $10 per week payable for each dependent child, not to exceed worker's net wage. Benefits are reduced by 50 percent of Social Security benefits.
(r) Payments are subject to offset if concurrent and/or duplicate with those under employer non-occupational benefits plan.
(s) Payments are frozen at $231 per week from 11/1/87 until 11/1/90.
(t) Effective 9/1/89, the maximum weekly benefit will increase to $386. An additional $9 for each dependent; including a non-working spouse, aggregate not to exceed 80 percent of the worker's average weekly wage.
(u) Each cumulative $10 increase in the average weekly wage for manufacturing production workers will increase the maximum weekly benefit by $7 per week.
(v) Additional $5 for dependent spouse and each dependent child up to 4, but not to exceed 100 percent of the State average weekly wage.
(w) Additional $10 is paid for each dependent under 21 years of age.
(x) Payments subject to Social Security benefit offsets.

Table 8.24
ESTIMATES OF WORKERS' COMPENSATION PAYMENTS, BY STATE AND TYPE OF INSURANCE: 1985-86
(In thousands of dollars)

State or jurisdiction	1985				1986				Percentage change in total payment from 1985 to 1986
	Total	Insurance losses paid by private insurance (a)	State and federal fund disbursements (b)	Self insurance payments (c)	Total	Insurance losses paid by private insurance (a)	State and federal fund disbursements (b)	Self insurance payments (c)	
United States	$22,471,741	$12,340,933	$5,873,584	$4,257,224	$25,019,168	$13,840,096	$6,407,802	$4,771,270	11.3
Alabama	202,577	144,577	...	58,000	243,933	174,233	...	69,700	20.4
Alaska	109,013	91,113	...	17,900	129,417	105,917	...	23,500	18.7
Arizona	197,571	108,643	70,967	17,961	205,818	105,569	81,549	18,700	4.2
Arkansas	142,170	99,270	...	42,900	154,441	107,841	...	46,600	8.6
California	3,243,307	1,866,429	402,878	974,000	3,744,658	2,096,742	523,916	1,124,000	15.5
Colorado	284,046	130,008	114,838	39,200	354,825	146,188	155,037	53,600	24.9
Connecticut	304,811	249,880	...	54,931	347,334	285,954	...	61,380	14.0
Delaware	41,357	30,757	...	10,600	45,656	34,156	...	11,500	10.4
Florida	814,546	560,982	...	253,564	927,819	638,819	...	289,000	13.9
Georgia	360,028	310,328	...	49,700	427,056	368,056	...	59,000	18.6
Hawaii	132,757	96,807	...	35,950	135,218	99,718	...	35,500	1.9
Idaho	66,031	45,935	13,146	6,950	66,521	44,629	14,892	7,000	0.7
Illinois	911,839	665,576	...	246,263	992,646	724,646	...	268,000	8.9
Indiana	152,301	132,801	...	19,500	174,151	151,851	...	22,300	14.3
Iowa	120,688	112,488	...	8,200	131,165	124,965	...	6,200	8.7
Kansas	141,700	120,800	...	20,900	156,686	133,586	...	23,100	10.6
Kentucky	225,279	168,779	...	56,500	244,661	183,661	...	61,000	8.6
Louisiana	465,971	372,771	...	93,200	503,547	403,547	...	100,000	8.1
Maine	210,969	158,969	...	52,000	253,008	191,008	...	62,000	19.9
Maryland	305,775	210,080	38,095	57,600	327,768	224,791	46,477	56,500	7.2
Massachusetts	509,661	468,361	...	41,300	638,420	586,920	...	51,500	25.3
Michigan	782,054	435,605	38,449	308,000	829,206	450,206	52,000	327,000	6.0
Minnesota	431,420	360,349	2,171	68,900	438,473	364,822	4,651	69,000	1.6
Mississippi	97,589	89,243	...	8,346	121,998	112,798	...	9,200	25.0
Missouri	236,948	189,748	...	47,200	270,434	223,134	...	47,300	14.1
Montana	102,356	40,142	52,835	9,379	122,977	47,897	65,394	9,686	20.1
Nebraska	67,643	57,143	...	10,500	76,199	65,099	...	11,100	12.6
Nevada	123,434	920	105,950	16,564	148,675	1,014	125,724	21,937	20.4
New Hampshire	90,964	80,599	...	10,365	107,761	95,461	...	12,300	18.5
New Jersey	501,382	422,482	...	78,900	547,035	461,035	...	86,000	9.1
New Mexico	139,522	131,622	...	7,900	147,880	139,380	...	8,500	6.0
New York	985,156	533,024	271,842	180,290	1,097,946	585,877	310,069	202,000	11.4
North Carolina	241,699	180,699	...	61,000	263,005	196,505	...	66,500	8.8
North Dakota	32,731	480	32,251	...	37,536	180	37,356	...	14.7
Ohio	1,440,672	4,921	931,751	504,000	1,637,117	8,013	1,054,104	575,000	13.6
Oklahoma	291,039	201,822	43,817	45,400	268,868	188,243	39,625	41,000	–7.6
Oregon	396,111	156,380	182,631	57,100	451,637	185,637	196,000	70,000	14.0
Pennsylvania	998,343	716,951	52,392	229,000	1,133,376	807,376	66,000	260,000	13.5
Rhode Island	97,132	89,632	...	7,500	112,769	104,169	...	8,600	16.1
South Carolina	155,853	129,153	...	26,700	170,563	141,563	...	29,000	9.4

ESTIMATES OF WORKERS' COMPENSATION PAYMENTS—Continued

State or jurisdiction	1985				1986				Percentage change in total payment from 1985 to 1986
	Total	Insurance losses paid by private insurance (a)	State and federal fund disbursements (b)	Self insurance payments (c)	Total	Insurance losses paid by private insurance (a)	State and federal fund disbursements (b)	Self insurance payments (c)	
South Dakota	26,063	22,663	...	3,400	28,392	24,692	...	3,700	8.9
Tennessee	204,255	185,655	...	18,600	234,314	213,014	...	21,300	14.7
Texas	1,563,778	1,563,778	...	...	1,833,114	1,833,114	...	...	17.2
Utah	80,296	30,738	37,058	12,500	92,275	26,390	51,585	14,300	14.9
Vermont	30,328	27,828	...	2,500	35,468	32,568	...	2,900	16.9
Virginia	268,971	229,890	...	39,081	305,461	256,661	...	48,800	13.6
Washington	784,518	23,513	586,005	175,000	819,058	19,058	615,000	185,000	4.4
West Virginia	285,156	1,887	185,047	98,222	322,114	1,489	211,658	108,967	13.0
Wisconsin	287,303	228,381	...	58,922	327,002	260,002	...	67,000	13.8
Wyoming	47,043	988	46,055	...	51,003	1,484	49,519	...	8.4
Dist. of Columbia	74,179	59,343	...	14,836	75,518	60,418	...	15,100	1.8

Source: Social Security Administration, *Social Security Bulletin,* March 1989.
Note: Data for 1986 preliminary data for 1985 are revised figures. Calendar-year figures, except the data for Montana, Nevada, and West Virginia, for Federal civilian employees and "other" federal workers' compensation, and for state fund disbursements in Maryland, North Dakota, and Wyoming, represent fiscal years ended in 1985 and 1986. Includes benefit payments under the Longshoremen's and Harbor Workers' Compensation Act and extensions for the states in which such payments are made.
(a) Net cash and medical payments paid during calendar year by private insurance carriers under standard workers' compensation policies. Data primarily from A.M. Best Company, a national data-collecting agency for private insurance.
(b) Net cash and medical benefits paid by state funds compiled from state reports (published and unpublished); estimated for some states.
(c) Cash and medical benefits paid by self-insurers, plus the value of medical benefits paid by employers carrying workers' compensation policies that do not include standard medical coverage. Estimated from available state data.

LABOR

Table 8.25
STATUS OF APPROVED STATE PLANS DEVELOPED IN ACCORDANCE WITH THE FEDERAL OCCUPATIONAL SAFETY AND HEALTH ACT
(As of February 1990)

State or other jurisdiction	Operational status agreement (a)	Different standards (b)	7 (c) (l) On-site consultation agreements (c)	On-shore maritime coverage	Date of initial approval	Date certified (d)	Date of 18 (e) final approval (e)
Alaska	...	★	★	...	7/31/73	9/09/77	9/28/84
Arizona	...	...	...	...	10/29/74	9/18/81	6/20/85
California	★	★	★	★	4/24/73	8/12/77	
Connecticut (f)	...	...	★	...	10/02/73	8/19/86	
Hawaii	...	★	★	...	12/28/73	4/26/78	4/30/84
Indiana	...	...	...	...	2/25/74	9/24/81	9/26/86
Iowa	...	...	★	...	7/12/73	9/14/76	7/02/85
Kentucky	...	...	...	...	7/23/73	2/08/80	6/13/85
Maryland	...	...	★	...	6/28/73	2/15/80	7/18/85
Michigan	★	★	★	...	9/24/73	1/16/81	
Minnesota	...	...	★	★	5/29/73	9/28/76	7/30/85
Nevada	★	...	...	...	12/04/73	8/13/81	
New Mexico	★	...	...	...	12/04/75	12/04/84	
New York(f)	...	...	★	...	6/01/84		
North Carolina	★	...	★	...	1/26/73	9/29/76	
Oregon	★	★	★	★	12/22/72	9/15/82	
South Carolina	...	...	★	...	11/30/72	7/28/76	12/15/87
Tennessee	...	...	★	...	6/28/73	5/03/78	7/22/85
Utah	...	...	★	...	1/04/73	11/11/76	7/16/85
Vermont	★	...	★	★	10/01/73	3/04/77	
Virginia	...	...	★	...	9/23/76	8/15/84	11/30/88
Washington	★	★	...	★	1/19/73	1/26/82	
Wyoming	...	...	★	...	4/25/74	12/18/80	6/27/85
Puerto Rico	★	...	...	...	8/15/77	9/07/82	
U.S. Virgin Islands	...	...	...	...	8/31/73	9/22/81	4/17/84

Source: Directorate of Federal-State Operations, Office of State Programs, Occupational Safety and Health Administration, U.S. Department of Labor.

Key:
★—Yes
...—No
(a) Concurrent federal jurisdiction suspended.
(b) Standards frequently not identical to the federal.
(c) On-site consultation is available in all states either through a 7(c)(l) Agreement or under a State Plan.
(d) Developmental steps satisfactorily completed.
(e) Concurrent federal jurisdiction relinquished (supersedes Operational Status Agreement).
(f) Plan covers only state and local government employees.

Table 8.26
SELECTED STATE CHILD LABOR STANDARDS AFFECTING MINORS UNDER 18
(As of January 1990)
(Occupational coverage, exemptions and deviations usually omitted)

State or other jurisdiction	Documentary proof of age required up to age indicated (a)	Maximum daily and weekly hours and days per week for minors under 16 unless other age indicated (b)	Nightwork prohibited for minors under 16 unless other age indicated (b)
Federal (FLSA)	(c)	8-40, non-school period. Schoolday/week: 3-18 (d)	7 p.m. (9 p.m. June 1 through Labor Day) to 7 a.m.
Alabama	17; 19 in mines and quarries.	8-40-6. Schoolday/week: 3-18.	7 p.m. (9 p.m. during summer vacation) to 7 a.m. 10 p.m. before schoolday to 5 a.m., 16 and 17 if enrolled in school.
Alaska	18	6-day week, under 18. Schoolday/week: 9 (e)-23.	9 p.m. to 5 a.m.
Arizona	(f)	8-40. Schoolday/week: 3-18.	9:30 p.m. (11 p.m. before non-schoolday; 7 p.m. in door-to-door sales or deliveries) to 6 a.m.
Arkansas	16	8-48-6. 10-54-6, 16 and 17.	7 p.m. (9 p.m.) before non-schoolday) to 6 a.m. 11 p.m. before schoolday to 6 a.m., 16 and 17.
California	18	8-48-6, under 18. Schoolday/week: 4-28 (g) under 18, except 8 before non-schoolday, 16 and 17.	10 p.m. (12:30 a.m. before non-schoolday) to 5 a.m., under 18.
Colorado	16	8-40, under 18. Schoolday: 6.	9:30 p.m. to 5 a.m., before schoolday.
Connecticut	18	9-48, under 18. 8-48-6, under 18 in stores, and under 16 in agriculture. (Overtime permitted in certain industries.)	10 p.m. (midnight before non-schoolday in supermarkets) to 6 a.m., under 18. 11 p.m. (midnight before non-schoolday or if not attending school) to 6 a.m., 16 and 17 in restaurants or as usher in non-profit theater.
Delaware	18	8-48-6.	7 p.m. (10 p.m.) on Friday, Saturday and before non-schoolday) to 6 a.m.
Florida	18	10-30-6, during school year, under 18. Schoolday: 4 when followed by schoolday, except if enrolled in vocational program.	9 p.m. to 6:30 a.m. before schoolday. Midnight to 5 a.m., before schoolday, 16 and 17.
Georgia	18	8-40. Schoolday: 4.	9 p.m. to 6 a.m.
Hawaii	18	8-40-6. Schoolday: 10 (e).	7 p.m. to 7 a.m. (9 p.m. to 6 a.m. June 1 through day before Labor Day).
Idaho	(f)	9-54.	9 p.m. to 6 a.m.
Illinois	16	8-48-6. Schoolday/week: 3 [8 (e)]-23 (g).	7 p.m. (9 p.m. June 1 through Labor Day) to 7 a.m.
Indiana	17	8-40-6, under 17, except minors of 16 not enrolled in school. 9-48 during summer vacation, minors of 16 enrolled in school. Schoolday/week: 3-23.	7 p.m. (9 p.m. before non-schoolday) to 6 a.m. 10 p.m. (midnight before non-schoolday) to 6 a.m., minors of 16 enrolled in school.
Iowa	18	8-40. Schoolday/week: 4-28.	7 p.m. (9 p.m. June 1 through Labor Day) to 7 a.m.
Kansas	16 (f)	8-40.	10 p.m. before schoolday to 7 a.m.

SELECTED STATE CHILD LABOR STANDARDS—Continued

State or other jurisdiction	Documentary proof of age required up to age indicated (a)	Maximum daily and weekly hours and days per week for minors under 16 unless other age indicated (b)	Nightwork prohibited for minors under 16 unless other age indicated (b)
Kentucky	18	8-40. Schoolday/week: 3-18, under 16. 6 (8 Saturday and Sunday)-40, 16 and 17 if attending school.	7 p.m. (9 p.m. June 1 through Labor Day) to 7 a.m. 11:30 p.m. (1 a.m. Friday and Saturday) to 6 a.m. when school in session, 16 and 17.
Louisiana	18	8-40-6. Schoolday: 3.	10 p.m. to 7 a.m.
Maine	16	8-48-6. Schoolday/week: 4-28.	9 p.m. to 7 a.m., under 15. 10 p.m. to 7 a.m., 15.
Maryland	18	8-40. Schoolday/week:4-23 (g), under 16. 12 (e), under 18.	8 p.m. (9 p.m. Memorial Day through Labor Day) to 7 a.m. 8 hours of non-work, non-school time required in each 24-hour day, 16 and 17.
Massachusetts	18	8-48-6. 4-24 in farmwork, under 14. 9-48-6, 16 and 17.	7 p.m. (9 p.m. July 1 through Labor Day) to 6:30 a.m. 10 p.m. (midnight in restaurants on Friday, Saturday and vacation) to 6 a.m., 16 and 17.
Michigan	18	10-48-6, under 18. Schoolweek: 48 (e), under 18.	9 p.m. to 7 a.m. 10:30 p.m. to 6 a.m., 16 and 17 if attending school. 11:30 p.m. to 6 a.m., 16 and 17 if not attending school.
Minnesota	18	8-40.	9 p.m. to 7 a.m.
Mississippi	(f)	8-44 in factory, mill, cannery or workshop.	7 p.m. to 6 a.m. in factory, mill, cannery or workshop.
Missouri	16	8-40-6.	7 p.m. (10 p.m. before non-schoolday and for minors not enrolled in school) to 7 a.m.
Montana	18	...	...
Nebraska	16	8-48.	8 p.m. to 6 a.m. under 14. 10 p.m. (beyond 10 p.m. before non-schoolday with special permit) to 6 a.m., 14 and 15.
Nevada	17 (f)	8-48.	...
New Hampshire	18	8 on non-schoolday, 48-hour week during vacation, if enrolled in school. 48-hour week, 6-day week, during vacation, 16 and 17 if enrolled in school. Schoolday/week: 3-23 if enrolled in school. 30-hour week, 6-day week, 16 and 17 if enrolled in school.	9 p.m. to 7 a.m.
New Jersey	18	8-40-6, under 18. 10-hour day, 6-day week in agriculture. Schoolday/week: 3-18.	7 p.m. (9 p.m. during summer vacation with parental permission) to 7 a.m. 11 p.m. to 6 a.m., 16 and 17 during school term, with specified variations.
New Mexico	16	8-44 (48 in special cases), under 14.	9 p.m. to 7 a.m., under 14.
New York	18	8-48-6, 16 and 17. Schoolday/week: 3-23, under 16. 4-28, 16 if attending school.	7 p.m. to 7 a.m. Midnight to 6 a.m., 16 and 17.
North Carolina	18	8-40. Schoolday/week: 3-18 (g).	7 p.m. (9 p.m. before non-schoolday) to 7 a.m.

SELECTED STATE CHILD LABOR STANDARDS—Continued

State or other jurisdiction	Documentary proof of age required up to age indicated (a)	Maximum daily and weekly hours and days per week for minors under 16 unless other age indicated (b)	Nightwork prohibited for minors under 16 unless other age indicated (b)
North Dakota	16	8-48-6, under 18. Schoolday/week: 3-24 if not exempted from school attendance.	7 p.m. (9 p.m. June 1 through Labor Day) to 7 a.m.
Ohio	18	8-40. Schoolday/week: 3-18.	7 p.m. (9 p.m. June 1 through September 1 or during school holidays of 5 days or more) to 7 a.m.
Oklahoma	16	8-48.	6 p.m. to 7 a.m. in factories, factory workshops, pool halls or steam laundries.
Oregon	18	10-44 (emergency overtime with permit)-6. 44-hour week (emergency overtime with permit), 16 and 17.	6 p.m. to 7 a.m., except with special permit.
Pennsylvania	18	8-44-6, under 18. Schoolday/week: 4-26(g), under 16. 28 in schoolweek, 16 and 17 if enrolled in regular day school.	7 p.m. (10 p.m. during vacation from June to Labor Day) to 7 a.m. 11 p.m. (midnight before non-schoolday) to 6 a.m., 16 and 17 if enrolled in regular day school.
Rhode Island	18	8-40, 9-48, 16 and 17 during school year.	7 p.m. (9 p.m. during school vacation) to 6 a.m. 11:30 p.m. (1:30 a.m. before non-schoolday) to 6 a.m., 16 and 17 if regularly attending school.
South Carolina	(f)	8-40. Schoolday/week: 3-18.	7 p.m. (9 p.m. June 1 through Labor Day) to 7 a.m.
South Dakota	16	8-40.	After 7 p.m. in mercantile establishments, under 14.
Tennessee	18	8-40. Schoolday/week: 3-18.	7 p.m. to 7 a.m. (9 p.m. to 6 a.m. before non-schooldays).
Texas	(f)	8-48.	10 p.m. (midnight before non-schoolday or in summer if not enrolled in summer school) to 5 a.m.
Utah	(f)	8-40. Schoolday: 4.	9:30 p.m. to 5 a.m. before schoolday.
Vermont	16 (f)	8-48-6, 9-50, 16 and 17.	7 p.m. to 6 a.m.
Virginia	16	8-40-6.	7 p.m. (9 p.m. before non-schoolday and June 1 to Labor Day or with special permit) to 7 a.m.
Washington	18	8-hour day, 5-day week, under 18. Schoolday/week: 3-18.	7 p.m. (9 p.m. during summer vacation) to 7 a.m. After 9 p.m. on consecutive nights preceding schoolday, and after 9 p.m. in door-to-door sales, 16 and 17.
West Virginia	18	8-40-6.	8 p.m. to 5 a.m.
Wisconsin	18	8-24-6 when school in session and 8-40-6 in non-schoolweek. 8-40-6 when school in session and 8-48-6 in non-schoolweek (voluntary overtime per day and week permitted in non-schoolweek up to 50-hour week), 16 and 17 if required to attend school.	8 p.m. (9:30 p.m. before non-schoolday) to 7 a.m. 12:30 a.m. to 6 a.m., except where under direct adult supervision, and with 8 hours rest between end of work and schoolday, 16 and 17 if required to attend school.

SELECTED STATE CHILD LABOR STANDARDS—Continued

State or other jurisdiction	Documentary proof of age required up to age indicated (a)	Maximum daily and weekly hours and days per week for minors under 16 unless other age indicated (b)	Nightwork prohibited for minors under 16 unless other age indicated (b)
Wyoming	16	8-56.	10 p.m. (midnight before non-schoolday and for minors not enrolled in school) to 5 a.m. Midnight to 5 a.m., females 16 and 17.
Dist. of Columbia	18	8-48-6, under 18.	7 p.m. (9 p.m. June 1 through Labor Day) to 7 a.m. 10 p.m. to 6 a.m., 16 and 17.
Guam	16	8-40-6, under 18. Schoolday: 9 (e), under 18.	After 10 p.m. on schoolday, under 18.
Puerto Rico	18	8-40-6, under 18. Schoolday: 8 (e).	6 p.m. to 8 a.m. 10 p.m. to 6 a.m., 16 and 17.

Source: Division of State Standards Programs, Wage and Hour Division, Employment Standards Administration, U.S. Department of Labor.

(a) Many states require an employment certificate for minors under 16 and an age certificate for 16 and 17 year olds; in a few states other types of evidence are acceptable as proof of age. In most states the law provides that age certificates may be issued upon request for persons above the age indicated, or although not specified in the law, such certificates are issued in practice.

(b) State hours limitations on a schoolday and in a schoolweek usually apply only to those enrolled in school. Several states exempt high school graduates from the hours and/or nightwork or other provisions, or have less restrictive provisions for minors participating in various school-work programs. Separate nightwork standards in messenger service and street trades are common, but are not displayed in table.

(c) Not required. State age or employment certificates which show that the minor has attained the minimum age for the job are accepted under the Fair Labor Standards Act.

(d) Students of 14 and 15 enrolled in approved Work Experience and Career Exploration programs may work during school hours up to three hours on a schoolday and 23 hours in a schoolweek.

(e) Combined hours of work and school.

(f) Proof of age is not mandatory under state law in Arizona, Idaho, Mississippi, South Carolina, Texas and Utah; or in Kansas for minors enrolled in secondary schools, and in Nevada and Vermont for employment outside school hours. For purposes of the Fair Labor Standards Act (FLSA), federal age certificates are issued upon request by the State Department of Labor in South Carolina and by Federal Wage and Hour Offices in Mississippi and Texas. In Utah, state law directs schools to issue age certificates upon request.

Wage and Hour Offices will also issue federal age certificates upon request in Florida, Georgia, Kentucky, and Tennessee, where the states' required proof-of-age documents do not conform to those of Federal Child Labor Regulation No. 1. Also, for FLSA purposes, birth or baptismal certificates are accepted in lieu of age certificates in Alaska and Guam.

(g) More hours are permitted when school is in session less than five days.

LABOR

Table 8.27
CHANGES IN BASIC MINIMUM WAGES IN NON-FARM EMPLOYMENT UNDER STATE LAW: SELECTED YEARS 1968 TO 1990

State or other jurisdiction	1968 (a)	1970 (a)	1972	1976 (a)	1979	1980	1981	1984	1986	1988	1989	1990
Federal (FLSA)	$1.15 & $1.60	$1.30 & $1.60	$1.60	$2.20 & $2.30	$2.90	$3.10	$3.35	$3.35	$3.35	$3.35	$3.35	$3.35 (c)
Alabama	...	...	...	...	...	...	...	...	...	...	...	...
Alaska	2.10	2.10	2.10	2.80	3.40	3.60	3.85	3.85	3.85	3.85	3.85	3.85 (c)
Arizona	18.72-26.40/wk. (b)	18.72-26.40/wk. (b)	18.72-26.40/wk. (b)	...	...	...	...	...	...	...	...	...
Arkansas	1.25/day (b)	1.10	1.20	1.90	2.30	2.55	2.70	3.05	3.15	3.25	3.30	3.35
California	1.65 (b)	1.65 (b)	1.65 (b)	2.00	2.90	2.90	3.35	3.35	3.35	3.35	4.25	4.25
Colorado	1.00-1.25 (b)	1.00-1.25 (b)	1.00-1.25 (b)	1.00-1.25 (b)	1.90	1.90	1.90	2.50	3.00	3.00	3.00	3.00
Connecticut	1.40	1.60	1.85	2.21 & 2.31	2.91	3.12	3.37	3.37	3.37	3.75	4.25	4.25 (c)
Delaware	1.25	1.25	1.60	2.00	2.00	2.00	2.00	3.00	3.00	3.35	3.35	3.35 (c)
Florida	...	...	...	...	...	...	...	...	...	...	...	...
Georgia	...	...	1.25	1.25	1.25	1.25	1.25	1.25	1.25	3.25	3.25	3.25
Hawaii	1.25	1.60	1.60	2.40	2.65	2.90	3.10	3.35	3.35	3.85	3.85	3.85
Idaho	1.15	1.25	1.40	1.60	2.30	2.30	2.30	2.30	2.30	2.30	2.30	2.30
Illinois	...	...	1.40	2.10	2.30	2.30	2.30	2.65	3.35	3.35	3.35	3.35 (c)
Indiana	1.15	1.25	1.25	1.25	2.00	2.00	2.00	2.00	2.00	2.00	2.00	2.00
Iowa	...	...	...	...	...	...	...	...	...	...	...	3.85 (c)
Kansas	.65-.75 (b)	.65-.75 (b)	.65-.75 (b)	...	1.60	1.60	1.60	1.60	1.60	1.60	2.65	2.65
Kentucky	1.40	1.60	1.60	1.60	2.00	2.15	2.15	2.60	2.60	3.35	3.35	3.35
Louisiana	...	...	...	...	...	...	...	...	...	...	...	...
Maine	1.00 & 1.15	1.30	1.40-1.80	2.30	2.90	3.10	3.35	3.35	3.55	3.65	3.75	3.85 (c)
Maryland	...	...	1.60	2.20 & 2.30	2.90	3.10	3.35	3.35	3.35	3.35	3.35	3.35 (c)
Massachusetts	1.60	1.60	1.75	2.10	2.90	3.10	3.35	3.35	3.35	3.65	3.75	3.75
Michigan	1.25	1.25	1.60	2.20	2.90	3.10	3.35	3.35	3.35	3.35	3.35	3.35
Minnesota	.70-1.15 (b)	.70-1.15 (b)	.75-1.60	1.80	2.30	2.90	3.10	3.35	3.35	3.55 & 3.50	3.85 & 3.65	3.95 & 3.80 (d)
Mississippi	...	...	...	...	...	...	...	...	...	...	...	...
Missouri	...	...	...	...	...	...	...	...	...	...	...	...
Montana	1.00	1.00	1.60	1.80	2.00	2.00	2.00	2.75	3.05	3.35	3.35	3.35 (c)
Nebraska	1.25	1.30	1.00	1.60	1.60	1.60	1.60	1.60	1.60	3.35	3.35	3.35
Nevada	1.40	1.45-1.60	1.60	2.20 & 2.30	2.75	2.75	2.75	2.75	2.75	3.35	3.35	3.35 (c)
New Hampshire	1.40	1.50	1.50	2.20-2.30	2.90	3.10	3.35	3.35	3.35	3.55	3.65	3.75 (c)
New Jersey	...	...	...	2.20	2.50	3.10	3.35	3.35	3.35	3.35	3.35	3.35
New Mexico	1.15-1.40	1.30-1.60	1.30-1.60	2.00	2.30	2.65	2.90	3.35	3.35	3.35	3.35	3.35
New York	1.60	1.60	1.85	2.30	2.90	3.10	3.35	3.35	3.35	3.35	3.35	3.35
North Carolina	1.00	1.25	1.45	2.00	2.50	2.75	2.90	3.35	3.35	3.35	3.35	3.35
North Dakota	1.00-1.25	1.00-1.45	1.00-1.45	2.00-2.20	2.10-2.30	2.60-3.10	2.80-3.10	2.80-3.10	2.80-3.10	2.80-3.10	2.80-3.10	3.40
Ohio	.75-1.25 (b)	.75-1.25 (b)	.75-1.25 (b)	1.60	2.30	2.30	2.30	2.30	2.30	2.30	2.30	2.30
Oklahoma	1.00	1.00	1.40	1.80	2.00	2.00	3.10	3.35	3.35	3.35	3.35	3.35 (c)
Oregon	1.25	1.25	1.25	2.30	2.30	2.90	3.10	3.10	3.35	3.35	3.35	4.25 (c)
Pennsylvania	1.15	1.30	1.60	2.20	2.90	3.10	3.35	3.35	3.35	3.35	3.35	3.70 (c)
Rhode Island	1.40	1.60	1.60	2.30	2.30	2.65	2.90	3.35	3.35	3.65	4.00	4.25
South Carolina	...	...	...	...	...	...	...	...	...	...	...	...

CHANGES IN BASIC MINIMUM WAGE—Continued

State or other jurisdiction	1968 (a)	1970 (a)	1972	1976 (a)	1979	1980	1981	1984	1986	1988	1989	1990
South Dakota	17.00–20.00/wk.	1.00	1.00	2.00	2.30	2.30	2.30	2.80	2.80	2.80	3.35	3.35
Tennessee	...	...	...	...	...	...	...	...	...	...	...	...
Texas	...	...	1.40	1.40	1.40	1.40	1.40	1.40	1.40	3.35	3.35	3.35
Utah	1.00–1.15 (b)	1.00–1.15 (b)	1.20–1.35 (b)	1.55–1.70 (b)	2.20–2.45 (b)	2.35–2.60 (b)	2.50–2.75 (b)	2.50–2.75 (b)	2.50–2.75 (b)	2.50–2.75 (b)	2.50–2.75 (b)	2.50–2.75 (b)
Vermont	1.40	1.60	1.60	2.30	2.90	3.10	3.35	3.35	3.35	3.55	3.65	3.75 (c)
Virginia	1.60	1.60	1.60	2.00	2.35	2.35	2.65	2.65	2.65	2.65	2.65	...
Washington	1.00	1.00	1.20	2.20–2.30	2.30	2.30	2.30	3.05	2.30	2.30	3.85	4.25
West Virginia	1.25 (b)	1.30 (b)	1.45 (b)	2.00	2.20	2.20	2.75	3.05	3.05	3.35	3.35	3.35
Wisconsin	1.20	1.30	1.50	2.10	2.80	3.00	3.25	3.25	3.25	3.35	3.35	3.65
Wyoming	1.20	1.30	1.50	1.60	1.60	1.60	1.60	1.60	1.60	1.60	1.60	1.60
Dist. of Columbia	1.25–1.40	1.60–2.00	1.60–2.25	2.25–2.75	2.46–3.00	2.50–3.50	2.50–3.75	3.50–3.90	3.50–3.95	3.50–4.85	3.50–4.85	3.50–4.85 (c)
Guam	1.25	1.60	1.90	2.30	2.90	3.10	3.35	3.35	3.35	3.35	3.75	3.75 (c)
Puerto Rico	.43–1.60	.43–1.60	.65–1.60	.76–2.50	1.20–2.50	1.20–2.50	1.20–3.10	1.20–3.35	1.20–3.35	1.20–3.35	1.20–3.35	1.20–4.25
U.S. Virgin Islands	NA	NA	NA	NA	2.90	3.10	3.35	3.35	3.35	3.35	...	4.65 (c)

Source: Prepared by the Division of State Standards Programs, Wage and Hour Division, Employment Standards Administration, U.S. Department of Labor.

Note: Rates are for January 1 of each year, except in 1968 and 1972 which show rates as of February. The rates are per hour unless otherwise indicated. A range of rates, as in the District of Columbia and Puerto Rico, reflects rates which differ by industry, occupation, or other factor, as established under a wage-board type law.

Key:
... — Not applicable
NA — Not available

(a) Under the federal Fair Labor Standards Act (FLSA), the two rates shown in 1968, 1970 and 1976 reflect the former multiple-track minimum wage system in effect from 1961 to 1978. The lower rate applied to newly-covered persons brought under the act by amendments, whose rates were gradually phased in. A similar dual-track system was also in effect in certain years under the laws in Connecticut, Maryland and Nevada.

(b) The law applies only to women and minors. A 1990 enactment, effective February 14, 1990, replaced this limited law with a new act applicable to both men and women. A $3.35 per hour minimum rate was established for private and public employees, increasing to $3.80 on April 1, 1990. Subsequent to July 1, 1990, the Industrial Commission of Utah may by rule establish the minimum rate but not higher than the Federal FLSA rate.

(c) Future Federal (FLSA) increases to $3.80 and $4.25 are scheduled on April 1, 1990 and April 1, 1991 respectively (Federal rates in Puerto Rico will increase in steps to $4.25, effective on dates ranging from April 1, 1991 to April 1, 1996, depending on occupational category and industry average hourly wage). Scheduled future increases under state law will take effect as follows: Alaska to $4.30 on April 1, 1990 and to $4.75 on April 1, 1991; Connecticut to $4.27 on April 1, 1991; Delaware to $3.80 on April 1, 1990 and to $4.25 on April 1, 1991; Illinois to $3.80 on April 1, 1990 and to $4.25 on April 1, 1991; Iowa to $4.25 on January 1, 1991 and to $4.65 on January 1, 1992; Maine to $4.25 on April 1, 1991; Maryland to $3.80 on April 1, 1990 and to $4.25 on April 1, 1991; Montana to $3.80 on April 1, 1990 and to $4.00 on April 1, 1991; Nevada to $3.80 on April 1, 1990 and to $4.25 on April 1, 1991; New Hampshire to $3.85 on January 1, 1991 and to $3.95 on January 1, 1992; Oklahoma to $3.80 on April 1, 1990 and to $4.25 on April 1, 1991; Oregon to $4.75 on January 1, 1991; Pennsylvania to $3.80 on April 1, 1990 and to $4.25 on April 1, 1991; Vermont to $3.80 on April 1, 1990 and to $3.85 on July 2, 1990; retail trade occupations in the District of Columbia from $3.50 to $4.50 on April 1, 1990; Guam to $3.80 on April 1, 1990 and to $4.25 on April 1, 1991; and in the U.S. Virgin Islands to an indexed rate equal to 50 percent of the average U.S. Virgin Islands nonagricultural hourly wage beginning January 1, 1991 and each January 1 thereafter.

(d) Minnesota adopted a two-tier wage schedule effective in 1988: the higher rate applies to employers covered by the FLSA; the lower rate to employers not covered by the FLSA.

STATE REGULATION OF OCCUPATIONS AND PROFESSIONS

By Frances Stokes Berry and Pamela L. Brinegar

Occupational licensure has traditionally been an exercise of the state's inherent power to protect the health, safety and welfare of its citizens. Virginia enacted the first licensing law in 1639 to regulate fees charged by physicians and, since that time, states have maintained authority over professional regulation.[1] Today, approximately 600 occupations and professions are licensed among states, although fewer than 60 of these professions are regulated by half the states or more.[2] Issues surrounding the licensure of occupations and professions continue to crowd the agendas of state legislatures. While the federal government continues to insist that occupational and professional regulation remains an activity that rightfully belongs to the states, it has passed several laws concerning occupations and professions that mandate states to respond in particular ways and that raise the question of whether regulatory responsibilities will continue to be shifted to the federal level.

The most far-reaching federal legislation involves the establishment of a data bank for disciplinary actions (see Enforcement and Disciplinary Procedures below). In addition, the Omnibus Budget Reconciliation Act of 1987 requires states to have training and competency evaluation programs for nurse aides who are employed by nursing facilities that receive funds from Medicare and Medicaid and to establish and maintain a registry of nurse aides. The registry must be staffed to handle written and telephone inquiries from the public and health providers regarding registrants.

The Financial Institutions Reform, Recovery and Enforcement Act of 1989 (popularly known as the Savings and Loan Bailout Bill) contains a mandate that states license or certify appraisers according to federal standards established by representatives from eight major appraiser associations.

Why License Professions?

Occupational and professional groups seek licensure for many reasons: It offers practitioners an opportunity for increased status; it can lead to increased economic benefits (for example, it is sometimes a prerequisite for third-party reimbursement); and it offers mechanisms for keeping unqualified or unscrupulous practitioners from engaging in the occupations or professions.

The benefits of protecting the public from incompetent practitioners are not without negative side effects, however. There are even those who would go so far as to argue that almost all licensing laws exist primarily to provide benefits to the members of occupational groups and only incidentally to protect the public.[3] By restricting the number of people entering a profession, licensure may result in increased costs to consumers of some professional services. This restriction also can result in a shortage of licensed professional services in certain geographic areas. In many fields, auxiliaries have been under used or their abil-

---

Frances Stokes Berry is Manager of the State Leadership/Management Group and Pamela L. Brinegar is a Research Associate in the Center for Health and Regulation at The Council of State Governments. Special appreciation goes to Kara L. Schmitt, Director of Testing Services, Michigan Department of Licensing and Regulation, for her contribution to the Examinations section of this article.

ity to work independently has been hampered. Licensure often focuses on testing applicants for the initial license and is less concerned about the competence and performance of practitioners after the license is granted, although mandatory continuing education is required by many professions. State laws frequently place restrictions on advertising and on various business structures and practices. In recent years, the Federal Trade Commission has conducted numerous investigations into state licensing board rules dealing with such restrictions.[4]

State officials concerned with occupational and professional licensing today face at least four major issues: 1) setting appropriate criteria for determining which of the growing number of groups requesting licensure should receive it; 2) evaluating the organization, structure, composition and performance of licensure boards; 3) assessing the continuing competence of licensed practitioners; and 4) creating mechanisms for exchanging information.

Organization of Licensure Boards

Historically, a majority of state licensure boards were autonomous. More than 35 states have established a central agency for some or all licensure boards. Central agencies differ widely in their statutory responsibilities and the extent of the authority exercised over board decisions.[5] In a majority of states, the central agency is responsible for administrative functions such as processing applications, issuing licenses, record keeping, fee collection and routine correspondence, while the boards continue to exercise primary policy-making powers such as conducting examinations, exercising disciplinary authority and drafting administrative regulations. In other states, the central agency's powers extend to authority over board personnel, budgets, investigations and examinations. Opponents of the trend toward centralization of licensure contend that it adds to bureaucracy and red tape and reduces the responsiveness of the licensure authority to licensee needs and citizen complaints. Further, they argue that individual licensure boards with professional members best understand the issues of examinations, professional practice and discipline.

The composition of licensure boards has changed in recent years as well. Traditionally, boards were comprised exclusively of members of the regulated profession. Most states now place one or more public members on licensure boards. A related trend adds to board membership practitioners who are specialists or auxiliaries to the profession regulated by the board, such as adding a dental hygienist to a board of dentistry.

While states continue to add public members to licensure boards, the debate continues about whether public members are effective. To help train public members as effective consumer advocates, the American Association of Retired Persons has established a Citizen Participation Program.

Which Professions to License?

In the United States, five generally accepted criteria indicate when licensure is appropriate: (1) unregulated practice of the occupation poses a serious risk to a consumer's life, health, safety or economic well being, and the potential for harm is recognizable and likely to occur; (2) the practice of the occupation requires a high degree of skill, knowledge and training; (3) the functions and responsibilities of the practitioner require independent judgment and the members of the occupational group practice independently; (4) the scope-of-practice of the occupation is distinguishable from other licensed and unlicensed occupations; and (5) the economic impact on the public of regulating this occupational group is justified. Failure to meet these criteria, in general, indicate that licensure is not justified, or that some less restrictive type of regulation such as registration or certification may be appropriate.[6]

A different proposal for licensure has been developed by Ontario's Ministry of Health. This plan, which has succeeded in gaining support from the professions involved, is based on the concept that, among the health professions, it is the performance of certain acts that pose a threat to the public and it is those acts that should be licensed.[7] This approach has a likely chance of adoption in Canada.

Sunrise

State legislatures each year are approached by numerous occupations requesting state regulation. To help legislators establish licensure criteria, at least 14 states have instituted formal "sunrise" processes. Under sunrise programs, professional groups usually draft legislation providing for regulation of the profession and then attempt to convince legislators of its necessity. A legislative or legislatively-enacted body reviews applications for requests for state regulation from representatives of the unregulated occupation. Generally, the process includes a series of questions designed to measure the costs and benefits of, and need for, regulation. The reviewing body then recommends to the legislature whether regulation and what type of regulation is appropriate.[8]

Sunset

Sunset, first proposed by Colorado in 1976, was later passed by 36 states. Sunset is the automatic termination of regulatory boards and agencies unless legislative action is taken to reinstate them. The process has not resulted in the predicted wholesale deregulation of licensed professions. The most common outcomes of sunset performance reviews have been administrative and structural changes. Six states (Arkansas, Mississippi, Nebraska, New Hampshire, North Carolina and Wyoming) have repealed their sunset laws, while another six (Connecticut, Illinois, Montana, Nevada, Rhode Island and South Dakota) have inactivated the review process while leaving the laws on the books.[9] (See Table 3.25 for a summary of sunset legislation in the states.)

Enforcement and Disciplinary Procedures

Taking disciplinary action against incompetent practitioners remains a number one priority for state legislators and regulators. Legislatures have increased funding for enforcement functions and amended practice acts to expand disciplinary sanctions beyond suspension and revocation. The most frequent additional sanctions include administrative fines, reprimand and probation. State licensing boards are increasingly developing policies on dealing with practitioners who abuse drugs or alcohol, referring abusers to treatment programs for rehabilitation when possible, and tracking practitioners' successes and failures after treatment.

Despite these state initiatives, Congress authorized the federal Department of Health and Human Services to construct a national data bank on disciplinary actions taken against licensees in almost 30 professions.[10] The National Practitioner Data Bank will contain information on all clinical privilege losses, licensure disciplinary actions, malpractice payments and professional society membership losses on licensed health practitioners. The federal government plans to recover the annual operating costs of the data bank through the assessment of user fees.

Examinations

Examinations play a critical role in determining whether an individual is licensed, but often resources are not provided to ensure their validity, reliability and defensibility. Quality licensure examination is a time-consuming and complex process. Examinations must be job-related and based on well-designed and competently conducted job analyses; they must, through the use of well written individual test items and unbiased measures of competency, accurately measure the knowledge, skills and abilities required of someone entering the profession; and they must have passing points which are objectively determined and reflective of the level of minimum competence necessary to protect the public. Finally, the examinations must be administered in a secure, fair and impartial manner.

Only California, Colorado, Florida, Georgia, Indiana, Michigan, Texas, Washington and Wisconsin have established testing offices staffed by trained examination specialists who assist board members. These states' testing personnel serve boards in ways ranging from providing consultation upon request, to initiating suggestions for examination improvements, to assuming total responsibility for examination development and administration for the boards housed within the agency. Many boards that do not have access to in-house testing personnel, periodically seek assistance from independent testing experts.

Licensing examinations have successfully withstood numerous court cases in which plaintiffs have argued either that the examination was discriminatory and thus a violation of Title VII of the Civil Rights Act or that the use of an examination was anti-competitive and thus a violation of the antitrust laws. Particularly in relation to the bar examinations, but not limited to them, challenges have been made based on the 14th Amendment. Although the board's authority to establish standards has been upheld in a majority of these cases, the courts have emphasized that there must be a rational relationship between an examination and the purpose for its use.

Even though the courts have tended to support the actions of professional licensing boards, it is important that state regulators are familiar with and adhere to general testing standards and standards specific to licensure examinations.[11]

Mobility

For many licensed professions, varying state requirements pose barriers to professionals who seek to change states. If states do not coordinate standards for some professions, the professions themselves might look to the federal government to develop standards. For example, multistate accounting firms have suggested they might consider asking the federal government to look into federal licensure for accountants if more uniformity is not reached among state accountancy boards.[12] The National Association of State Boards of Accountancy and The American Institute of Certified Public Accountants are working to address these concerns.

A new licensure model that eliminates many of these barriers has been developed for the 12 European countries comprising the European Economic Community. By the end of 1991, EEC licensed professionals who provide client or patient services will be able to freely practice in any of the member countries. A striking feature of the plan is that language competency cannot be required as a condition for reciprocity. The member countries have agreed that meeting the requirements for professional licensure in a member country is sufficient for practicing in any of the others.[13]

Exchanging Information

Responding to the need for a forum to share information and discuss common problems, state licensing officials formed the National Clearinghouse on Licensure, Enforcement and Regulation (CLEAR) in 1980.

CLEAR, with staff support from The Council of State Governments, maintains an information library on state licensing practices and procedures. Sixteen publications provide comparative state information on model investigative practices, licensing structures, sunset audits, public membership and financing patterns. CLEAR also offers an annual national conference, regional meetings, training programs for investigators, and two newsletters, one providing information exchange on licensing in general, the other on specifically examination issues.

To assist states in exchanging enforcement information, CLEAR has established the National Disciplinary Information System, which provides information to states on disciplinary actions taken by states against licensed practitioners.

The Future

With the dramatic increase in federal interest in occupational and professional licensure, coupled with problems such as manpower shortages that states are trying to solve, states could be faced with taking a stronger, more unified approach to licensure or continuing to relinquish regulatory control to the federal government. At the same time that consumers are calling for strictly regulated quality of care, some professions are suggesting that relaxing the standards for entry into a profession might help ease shortages. Another suggestion to ease health manpower shortages is to create new categories of health workers that would require short training times. Actions states can take to address the shortages in professions include: 1) re-examine standards for credentialing and practice; 2) review existing scopes of practice; 3) re-examine the credentialing categories and titles in use; 4) provide for shortage situations if appropriate; 5) review barriers to mobility;[14] and 6) cross-train practitioners to perform in more than one profession.

Footnotes

1. Kara Schmitt, *Licensing and Regulation: States vs. the Federal Government in Restoring Balance in the Federal System*, 1989, The Council of State Governments, (Lexington, KY: 1989).

2. *Occupations and Professions Regulated in the States: A Comprehensive Compilation*, The National Clearinghouse on Licensure, Enforcement and Regulation (Lexington, Ky: 1990).

3. Benjamin Shimberg, "Regulation in the Public Interest: Myth or Reality?", Keynote Address delivered at the annual conference of the National Clearinghouse on Licensure, Enforcement and Regulation, Indianapolis, Sept. 8, 1989.

4. The kinds of state board rules that the Federal Trade Commission has looked into include restrictions on promotional activity, rules against referral fees, rules against the use of non-licensees to sell professional services, restrictions on payment mechanisms, restrictions on the form in which licensees can practice, restrictions on branch offices, and restrictions on the use of computers to share prescription information among pharmacies. The professions examined include architects, engineers, the funeral industry, lawyers, physicians and other health care specialists, including optometry, and surveyors. Michael McNeely, "An Overview of Recent Federal Trade Commission Investigations and Decisions," the annual conference of the National Clearinghouse on Licensure, Enforcement and Regulation, Indianapolis, Ind., Sept. 8, 1989.

5. See *Centralizing State Licensing Functions*, The Council of State Governments (Lexington, Ky: 1980).

6. "Licensure" is the most restrictive form of state regulation. Under licensure laws, it is illegal for a person to practice a profession without first meeting the standards imposed by the state. Under "certification," the state grants title protection to persons meeting predetermined standards. Those without the title may perform the services of the occupation but may not use the title. "Registration" is the least restrictive form of regulation which usually takes the form of requiring individuals to file their name, address and qualifications with a government agency before practicing the occupation. See *Occupational Licensing: Questions A Legislator Should Ask*, The Council of State Governments (Lexington, Ky: 1978) for further information on the types of regulation and the questions to answer in deciding among them.

7. *Striking a New Balance: A Blueprint for the Regulation of Ontario's Health Professions*, Ontario Ministry of Health (Ontario, Cn: 1988).

8. For detailed information on state sunrise programs, see *State Sunrise Programs: Deciding When to Regulate Occupations*, The Council of State Governments (Lexington, Ky: 1986).

9. Richard C. Kearney, "Sunset: A Survey and Analysis of the State Experience," *Public Administration Review* (January/February 1990).

10. Under Title IV of the Health Care Quality Improvement Act of 1986 and Section 5 of the Medicare-Medicaid Patient and Program Protection Act of 1987.

11. Nationally accepted guidelines are contained in *The Standards for Educational and Psychological Testing, American Psychological Association* (Washington, DC: 1985).

12. "Federal Licensing: on the Horizon?" *Professional Licensing Report*, Vol. 2, No. 7, Jan. 1990, p. 7.

13. Louis H. Orzack, "E.C. Progresses on Mutual Acceptance of Diplomas," *Europe*, March 1989.

14. David A. Montgomery, "Regulatory Responses to Manpower Shortages", CLEAR '89 Conference Proceedings, 1990, The National Clearinghouse on Licensure, Enforcement and Regulation, Lexington, Ky.

LABOR

TABLE 8.28
STATE REGULATION OF SELECTED
NON-HEALTH OCCUPATIONS AND PROFESSIONS: 1990

State or jurisdiction	Accountant, Certified Public	Architect	Auctioneer	Barber	Cosmetologist	Embalmer	Engineer, Professional	Funeral Director	Insurance Agent	Insurance Broker	Landscape Architect	Polygraph Examiner	Real Estate Agent	Real Estate Broker	Surveyor, Land
Alabama	L	L	L	L	L	L	L	L	L	L	L	L	L	L	L
Alaska	L	L	...	L	L	L	L	L	L	L	...	...	L	L	L
Arizona	L	L	L	L	L	L	L	L	L	L	L	L	L	L	L
Arkansas	L	L	...	L	L	L	L	L	L	L	L	L	L	L	L
California	L	L	L	L	L	L	L	L	L	L	L	...	L	L	L
Colorado	L	L	...	L	L	L	L	L	L	L	L	...	L	L	L
Connecticut	L	L	...	L	L	L	L	L	L	L	L	...	L	L	L
Delaware	L	L	...	L	L	L	L	L	L	L	L	...	L	L	L
Florida	L	L	L	L	L	L	L	L	L	L	L	L	L	L	L
Georgia	L	L	L	L	L	L	L	L	L	L	L	L	L	L	L
Hawaii	L	L	L	L	L	L	L	L	L	L	L	...	L	L	L
Idaho	L	L	...	L	L	L	L	L	L	L	L	L	L	L	L
Illinois	L	L	...	L	L	L	L	L	L	L	...	L	L	L	L
Indiana	L	L	L	L	L	L	L	L	L	L	L	L	L	L	L
Iowa	L	L	...	L	L	L	L	L	L	L	L	C	L	L	L
Kansas	L	L	...	L	L	L	L	L	L	L	L	L	L	L	L
Kentucky	L	L	L	L	L	L	L	L	L	L	L	L	L	L	L
Louisiana	L	L	L	L	L	L	L	L	L	L	L	L	L	L	L
Maine	L	L	L	L	L	L	L	L	L	L	L	L	L	L	L
Maryland	L	L	...	L	L	L	L	L	L	L	L	...	L	L	L
Massachusetts	L	L	L	L	L	L	L	L	L	L	L	L	L	L	L
Michigan	L	L	...	L	L	L	L	L	L	L	R	L	L	L	L
Minnesota	L	L	L	L	L	L	L	L	L	L	L	...	L	L	L
Mississippi	L	L	...	L	L	L	L	L	L	L	...	L	L	L	L
Missouri	L	L	L	L	L	L	L	L	L	L	L	L	L	L	L
Montana	L	L	...	L	L	L	L	L	L	L	L	L	L	L	L
Nebraska	L	L	L	L	L	L	L	L	L	L	L	L	L	L	L
Nevada	L	L	...	L	L	L	L	L	L	L	L	L	L	L	L
New Hampshire	L	L	...	L	L	L	L	L	L	L	...	...	L	L	L
New Jersey	L	L	...	L	L	L	L	L	L	L	L	...	L	L	L
New Mexico	L	L	...	L	L	L	L	L	L	L	L	L	L	L	L
New York	L	L	...	L	L	L	L	L	L	L	L	L	L	L	L
North Carolina	L	L	L	L	L	L	L	L	L	L	L	L	L	L	L
North Dakota	L	L	L	L	L	L	L	L	L	L	...	L	L	L	L
Ohio	L	L	L	L	L	L	L	L	L	L	L	...	L	L	L
Oklahoma	L	L	...	L	L	L	L	L	L	L	...	L	L	L	L
Oregon	L	L	...	L	L	L	L	L	L	L	L	L	L	L	L
Pennsylvania	L	L	L	L	L	L	L	L	L	L	L	...	L	L	L
Rhode Island	L	L	L	L	L	L	L	L	L	L	L	...	L	L	L
South Carolina	L	L	L	L	L	L	L	L	L	L	L	L	L	L	L
South Dakota	L	L	L	L	L	L	L	L	L	L	L	L	L	L	L
Tennessee	L	L	L	L	L	L	L	L	L	L	L	L	L	L	L
Texas	L	L	L	L	L	L	L	L	L	L	L	L	L	L	L
Utah	L	L	...	L	L	L	L	L	L	L	L	L	L	L	L
Vermont	L	L	...	L	L	L	L	L	L	L	...	...	L	L	L
Virginia	L	L	...	L	L	...	L	L	L	L	C	L	L	L	L
Washington	L	L	...	L	L	L	L	L	L	L	L	...	L	L	L
West Virginia	L	L	...	L	L	L	L	L	L	L	L	L	L	L	L
Wisconsin	L	L	...	L	L	L	L	L	L	L	...	...	L	L	L
Wyoming	L	L	...	L	L	L	L	L	L	L	...	...	L	L	L
Dist. of Columbia	L	L	L	L	L	L	L	L	L	L	L	...	L	L	...

Source: The National Clearinghouse on Licensure, Enforcement and Regulation, *Occupations and Professions Regulated in the States, 1990.*

Key:
C — Certification
L — Licensure
R — Registration

LABOR

Table 8.29
STATE REGULATION OF HEALTH OCCUPATIONS AND PROFESSIONS: 1990

State or jurisdiction	Acupuncturist	Chiropractor	Counselor, Professional	Counselor, Alcoholism	Counselor, Drug	Counselor, Pastoral	Counselor, Substance Abuse	Dentist	Dental Assistant	Dental Hygienist	Denturist	Dietitian	Emergency Medical Technologist	Hearing Aid Dealer & Fitter	Homeopath	Massage Therapist
Alabama	...	L	L	...	...	...	...	L	...	L	...	L	L	R	...	...
Alaska	L	L	...	...	...	...	...	L	O	L	L	...	L	L	...	L
Arizona	L	L	...	...	...	...	...	L	O	L	...	...	L	L	...	...
Arkansas	L	L	L	...	...	...	...	L	L	L	...	L	L	L	...	L
California	L	L	...	...	...	...	...	L	O	L	...	...	L	L	...	...
Colorado	L	L	...	...	...	...	...	L	...	L	...	...	L	L	...	...
Connecticut	...	L	L	...	...	L	...	L	...	L	...	...	L	L	...	...
Delaware	...	L	L	...	...	...	...	L	O	L	...	...	L	L	L	L
Florida	L	L	L	O	...	...	...	L	O	L	...	L	L	L	...	...
Georgia	...	L	...	...	...	...	...	L	...	L	...	R	L	L	...	...
Hawaii	L	L	...	...	...	...	...	L	L	L	...	L	L	L	...	...
Idaho	...	L	L	...	...	...	...	L	...	L	...	...	L	L	...	...
Illinois	L	L	L	...	...	...	...	L	O	L	L	...	L	L	...	...
Indiana	...	L	...	...	...	...	...	L	O	L	L	...	L	L	...	...
Iowa	...	L	...	...	...	...	R	L	...	L	...	...	L	L	...	...
Kansas	L	L	L	...	...	...	...	L	L	L	...	O	L	L	...	...
Kentucky	L	L	L	...	...	...	...	L	O	L	...	L	L	L	...	...
Louisiana	L	L	...	...	...	...	...	L	O	L	...	L	L	L	...	...
Maine	L	L	L	...	...	...	...	L	...	L	...	L	L	L	...	...
Maryland	R	L	L	...	...	...	...	L	O	L	...	L	O	...	L	...
Massachusetts	L	L	...	...	...	...	...	L	O	L	L	...	L	L	...	...
Michigan	...	L	...	...	...	...	...	L	L	L	...	...	L	L	...	L
Minnesota	L	L	L	...	...	...	...	L	O	L	...	L	L	L	...	...
Mississippi	...	L	L	...	...	...	...	L	O	L	...	...	L	L	...	...
Missouri	L	L	...	...	...	...	...	L	...	L	...	L	L	L	...	...
Montana	L	L	L	...	...	...	...	L	O	L	L	...	L	L	...	L
Nebraska	...	L	L	...	...	...	...	L	...	L	...	...	L	L	...	L
Nevada	L	L	...	...	...	...	...	L	O	L	...	...	L	L	...	...
New Hampshire	...	L	...	...	...	C	...	L	...	L	...	...	L	L	L	...
New Jersey	...	L	...	...	...	...	...	L	...	L	...	...	L	L	...	...
New Mexico	L	L	R	...	...	...	...	L	O	L	...	L	L	L	...	...
New York	R	L	L	...	...	...	...	L	L	L	...	O	L	L	...	L
North Carolina	L	L	L	...	...	...	...	L	O	L	...	L	L	L	L	L
North Dakota	...	L	...	...	...	...	...	L	...	L	...	...	L	L	...	...
Ohio	...	L	L	...	...	...	...	L	...	L	...	...	L	L	...	...
Oklahoma	L	L	L	...	...	...	...	L	L	L	...	L	L	L	...	...
Oregon	R	L	...	...	...	...	...	L	O	L	C	O	L	L	...	L
Pennsylvania	L	L	...	...	...	...	...	L	O	L	...	...	L	L	...	...
Rhode Island	L	L	L	...	...	...	...	L	...	L	...	L	L	L	...	...
South Carolina	...	...	...	...	...	...	...	L	...	L	...	...	L	L	...	...

472 The Book of the States 1990-91

STATE REGULATION OF HEALTH OCCUPATIONS AND PROFESSIONS: 1990—Continued

State or jurisdiction	Acupuncturist	Chiropractor	Counselor, Professional	Counselor, Alcoholism	Counselor, Drug	Counselor, Pastoral	Counselor, Substance Abuse	Dentist	Dental Assistant	Dental Hygienist	Denturist	Dietitian	Emergency Medical Technologist	Hearing Aid Dealer & Fitter	Homeopath	Massage Therapist
South Dakota	...	L	...	...	...	...	...	L	...	L	...	...	L	L	...	...
Tennessee	L	L	L	...	...	...	...	L	...	L	...	L	L	L	...	...
Texas	L	L	L	...	...	...	...	L	...	L	...	C	L	L	...	...
Utah	L	L	L	...	...	...	...	L	C	L	...	L	C	L	...	...
Vermont	L	L	...	...	...	...	...	L	L	L	...	...	L	...	...	...
Virginia	L	L	...	...	...	...	...	L	...	L	...	...	L	L	...	...
Washington	C	L	L	C	C	C	...	L	L	L	...	...	L	L	...	...
West Virginia	R	L	L	...	...	...	...	L	...	L	...	...	L	L	...	...
Wisconsin	...	L	...	...	...	...	...	L	...	L	...	...	L	L	...	...
Wyoming	...	...	L	...	...	...	...	...	...	...	...	...	...	...	...	...
Dist. of Columbia	L	L	L	...	...	...	...	L	L	L	...	L	L	L	...	L

Source: *Occupations and Professions Regulated in the States*, The National Clearinghouse on Licensure, Enforcement and Regulation, 1990.

Key:
C — Certification
L — Licensure
R — Registration

STATE REGULATION OF HEALTH OCCUPATIONS AND PROFESSIONS: 1990—Continued

State or jurisdiction	Masseur/Masseuse	Medical Technologist	Nuclear Medicine Technologist	Nurse, Licensed Practical	Nurse Midwife	Nurse Practitioner	Nurse, Registered	Nursing Home Administrator	Occupational Therapist	Occupational Therapy Assistant	Optician	Optometrist	Osteopath	Pharmacist	Pharmacist Assistant
Alabama	...	...	...	L	L	O	L	L	L	L	L	L	L	L	L
Alaska	...	...	...	L	O	O	L	L	L	L	...	L	L	L	L
Arizona	L	L	...	L	L	O	L	L	...	...	...	L	L	L	R
Arkansas	...	...	...	L	O	O	L	L	L	L	L	L	L	L	...
California	...	...	...	L	O	O	L	L	...	...	L	L	L	L	...
Colorado	...	...	...	L	O	O	L	L	L	L	...	L	L	L	...
Connecticut	L	L	...	L	O	O	L	L	L	L	L	L	L	L	...
Delaware	...	L	L	L	O	O	L	L	L	L	...	L	L	L	L
Florida	...	...	...	L	O	O	L	L	L	L	L	L	L	L	...
Georgia	...	...	...	L	O	O	L	L	L	L	L	L	L	L	...
Hawaii	L	L	...	L	O	...	L	L	C	C	...	L	L	L	...
Idaho	...	...	...	L	O	O	L	L	L	L	L	L	L	L	L
Illinois	...	C	...	L	O	...	L	L	L	L	...	L	L	L	...
Indiana	...	...	...	L	O	O	L	L	L	L	L	L	L	L	...
Iowa	...	...	...	L	O	O	L	L	L	L	...	L	L	L	...
Kansas	...	L	...	L	O	O	L	L	L	R	...	L	L	L	R
Kentucky	...	...	...	L	O	O	L	L	L	L	L	L	L	L	...
Louisiana	...	C	...	L	O	O	L	L	L	L	...	L	L	L	...
Maine	...	...	...	L	O	O	L	L	L	L	...	L	L	L	...
Maryland	...	...	L	L	O	O	L	L	L	L	L	L	L	L	...
Massachusetts	...	L	...	L	O	O	L	L	L	L	L	L	L	L	...
Michigan	L	L	...	L	O	O	L	L	L	L	...	L	L	L	...
Minnesota	...	...	L	L	O	...	L	L	...	...	L	L	L	L	...
Mississippi	...	...	...	L	O	O	L	L	L	L	...	L	L	L	...
Missouri	...	...	...	L	O	L	L	L	L	L	...	L	L	L	...
Montana	...	L	...	L	L	L	L	L	L	L	...	L	L	L	...
Nebraska	...	...	...	L	L	O	L	L	L	L	L	L	L	L	...
Nevada	L	...	...	L	O	L	L	L	L	L	L	L	L	L	...
New Hampshire	...	...	...	L	O	O	L	L	L	L	...	L	L	L	...
New Jersey	...	...	...	L	O	O	L	L	L	L	L	L	L	L	...
New Mexico	...	...	...	L	O	...	L	L	L	L	...	L	L	L	...
New York	...	...	...	L	O	O	L	L	L	L	L	L	L	L	...
North Carolina	...	...	...	L	O	O	L	L	L	L	L	L	L	L	...
North Dakota	...	...	...	L	O	...	L	L	L	L	...	L	L	L	...
Ohio	...	...	...	L	O	...	L	L	L	L	L	L	L	L	...
Oklahoma	...	...	...	L	O	...	L	L	...	...	...	L	L	L	L
Oregon	L	...	...	L	O	O	L	L	L	L	L	L	L	L	L
Pennsylvania	...	...	...	L	L	...	L	L	L	L	L	L	L	L	...
Rhode Island	...	...	...	L	O	O	L	L	L	L	L	L	L	L	...
South Carolina	R	...	...	L	O	O	L	L	L	L	...	L	L	L	...

STATE REGULATION OF HEALTH OCCUPATIONS AND PROFESSIONS: 1990—Continued

State or jurisdiction	Masseur/Masseuse	Medical Technologist	Nuclear Medicine Technologist	Nurse, Licensed Practical	Nurse Midwife	Nurse Practitioner	Nurse, Registered	Nursing Home Administrator	Occupational Therapist	Occupational Therapy Assistant	Optician	Optometrist	Osteopath	Pharmacist	Pharmacist Assistant
South Dakota	...	...	...	L	L	L	L	L	L	L	...	L	L	L	...
Tennessee	R	L	...	L	C	C	L	L	L	L	L	L	L	L	...
Texas	L	...	...	L	C	C	L	L	L	L	L	L	L	L	...
Utah	...	...	L	L	L	C	L	L	...	...	L	L	L	L	L
Vermont	...	...	...	L	L	C	L	L	...	...	L	L	L	L	L
Virginia	...	...	...	L	L	L	L	L	L	L	...	L	L	L	...
Washington	...	...	...	L	C	C	L	L	L	L	L	L	L	L	L
West Virginia	...	...	...	L	L	...	L	L	L	L	R	L	L	L	...
Wisconsin	...	...	L	L	L	L	L	L	L	L	...	L	L	L	...
Wyoming	...	...	...	L	L	...	L	L	...	...	...	L	L	L	...
Dist. of Columbia	...	...	...	L	C	C	L	L	L	L	L	L	L	L	R

Key:
C — Certification
L — Licensure
R — Registration

STATE REGULATION OF HEALTH OCCUPATIONS AND PROFESSIONS: 1990—Continued

State or jurisdiction	Physical Therapist	Physical Therapy Assistant	Physician	Physician Assistant	Podiatrist	Psychologist	Radiologic Technologist	Radiation Therapy Technologist	Respiratory Therapist	Sanitarian	Social Worker	Speech-Language Pathologist & Aud.	Therapist, Marriage & Family	Veterinarian	Veterinary Technician
Alabama	L	L	L	L	L	L	...	...	...	L	L	L	...	L	R
Alaska	L	L	L	L	L	L	...	...	...	...	...	L	...	L	R
Arizona	L	L	L	L	L	L	...	...	R	L	L	L	L	L	O
Arkansas	O	O	L	O	L	L	...	...	L	L	L	L	O	L	O
California	L	L	L	L	L	L	...	...	L	L	L	L	L	L	L
Colorado	L	...	L	O	L	L	...	...	...	...	...	...	...	L	O
Connecticut	L	L	L	...	L	L	L	L	O	L	L	L	O	L	L
Delaware	L	L	L	O	L	L	L	L	O	O	L	L	L	L	R
Florida	L	L	L	O	L	L	L	L	...	L	L	L	L	L	...
Georgia	O	L	L	O	L	L	L	L	O	L	R	L	L	L	R
Hawaii	L	...	L	L	L	L	L	...	...	...	...	...	...	L	R
Idaho	L	R	L	L	L	L	...	L	...	L	L	L	R	L	R
Illinois	L	...	L	L	L	O	L	L	O	O	R	L	...	L	R
Indiana	L	O	L	R	L	O	L	L	...	L	...	...	...	L	R
Iowa	L	L	L	C	L	L	L	L	...	...	L	L	...	L	R
Kansas	L	...	L	R	L	L	...	...	R	L	L	L	...	L	O
Kentucky	L	R	L	L	L	L	L	L	L	L	R	L	R	L	R
Louisiana	L	O	L	O	L	L	L	L	L	L	L	L	...	L	R
Maine	L	L	L	...	L	L	L	L	...	L	L	L	...	L	O
Maryland	L	...	L	...	L	L	L	L	L	L	L	L	...	L	...
Massachusetts	L	...	L	R	L	L	L	...	L	L	L	L	...	L	C
Michigan	L	L	L	L	L	L	...	...	...	...	L	L	...	L	R
Minnesota	L	O	L	O	L	O	L	...	L	L	L	...	L	L	R
Mississippi	L	R	L	...	L	O	L	L	...	L	O	L	...	L	O
Missouri	L	L	L	...	L	L	...	...	L	O	L	L	...	L	...
Montana	L	O	L	O	L	L	L	L	...	L	L	L	...	L	O
Nebraska	L	L	L	L	L	L	L	L	L	L	R	L	...	L	R
Nevada	L	L	L	R	L	O	L	L	...	L	R	L	O	L	R
New Hampshire	L	L	L	R	L	O	L	...	...	L	L	L	...	L	C
New Jersey	L	L	L	O	L	L	L	L	...	L	...	L	...	L	...
New Mexico	L	O	L	L	L	L	L	L	L	L	L	L	O	L	O
New York	L	L	L	R	L	L	...	...	...	L	L	L	L	L	L
North Carolina	L	L	L	R	L	O	L	...	...	L	...	L	...	L	R
North Dakota	L	L	L	O	L	O	L	L	...	L	L	L	...	L	...
Ohio	L	L	L	L	L	L	...	...	L	L	O	L	...	L	...
Oklahoma	L	L	L	C	L	L	L	L	...	L	L	L	...	L	O
Oregon	L	L	L	O	L	L	L	L	...	L	L	L	...	L	O
Pennsylvania	L	R	L	L	L	L	L	L	L	L	R	L	...	L	O
Rhode Island	L	...	L	L	L	L	L	L	L	L	L	L	...	L	...
South Carolina	L	L	L	R	L	L	L	L	...	L	R	L	...	L	R

476 The Book of the States 1990-91

STATE REGULATION OF HEALTH OCCUPATIONS AND PROFESSIONS: 1990—Continued

State or jurisdiction	Physical Therapist	Physical Therapy Assistant	Physician	Physician Assistant	Podiatrist	Psychologist	Radiologic Technologist	Radiation Therapy Technologist	Respiratory Therapist	Sanitarian	Social Worker	Speech-Language Pathologist & Aud.	Therapist, Marriage & Family	Veterinarian	Veterinary Technician
South Dakota	L	R	L	L	L	L				L	L	L		L	R
Tennessee	L	L	L	L	L	L	L	L	C	L	L	L	C	L	L
Texas	L	L	L	R	L	L	L	L	L	L	L	L	L	L	R
Utah	L		L	L	L	L	L	L		L	L	L	L	L	
Vermont	L	L	L	R	L	L				L	L	L		L	
Virginia	L	L	L	L	L	L			C	L	L	L	C	L	C
Washington	L		L	L	L	L	L			L	L		C	L	R
West Virginia	L		L	L	L	L	L	L		L	L	L		L	R
Wisconsin	L		L	L	L	L	L	L				L	C	L	C
Wyoming	L	R	L	L	L	L	L	L				L		L	R
Dist. of Columbia	L		L	L	L	L			R		L			L	L

Key:
C — Certification
L — Licensure
R — Registration

TABLE 8.30
STATUS OF MANDATORY CONTINUING EDUCATION FOR SELECTED PROFESSIONS: 1989

State or jurisdiction	Architects	Certified Public Accountants	Dentists	Engineer, Professional	Lawyers	Nurses	Nursing Home Administrator	Optometry	Psychology	Pharmacy	Physical Therapist	Physicians	Real Estate	Social Work	Licensed Practical Nurses	Veterinary Medicine
Alabama	...	★	...	...	★	E	★	★	★	★	...	★	E	...	★	★
Alaska	...	★	...	...	...	S	★	★	★	★	★	★	★	★	★	★
Arizona	E	★	...	...	...	...	★	★	E	★	★	...	E	★	★	★
Arkansas	...	★	...	...	★	...	★	★	...	★	...	...	★	★	...	★
California	...	★	★	...	...	★	★	★	...	★	...	★	★	...	★	...
Colorado	...	★	...	...	★	★	...	...	...	...	...	...	...	...	★	★
Connecticut	...	★	...	...	...	...	★	★	...	★	...	★	...	...	...	...
Delaware	...	★	...	...	★	...	★	★	★	★	★	★	★	★	★	...
Florida	E	★	★	...	★	★	★	★	★	★	...	★	★	★	★	...
Georgia	...	★	...	...	★	...	★	★	★	★	...	...	★	★	...	★
Hawaii	...	★	...	...	...	...	★	...	...	...	...	...	★	E	—	...
Idaho	...	★	...	...	★	...	★	★	★	...	...	...	★	...	★	...
Illinois	...	★	...	...	...	...	★	★	...	★	...	★	...	...	...	...
Indiana	...	★	...	...	★	...	★	★	...	★	...	...	★	...	—	E
Iowa	★	★	★	★	★	★	★	★	★	★	★	★	★	★	★	★
Kansas	...	★	★	...	★	★	★	★	★	★	★	...	E	★	★	★
Kentucky	...	★	★	...	★	★	★	★	...	★	...	...	E	E	★	★
Louisiana	...	★	...	...	★	...	★	★	E	★	...	...	S	★	...	...
Maine	...	★	...	...	...	...	★	★	★	★	...	...	★	★	★	...
Maryland	...	★	...	...	...	...	★	★	★	★	...	...	★	★	...	★
Massachusetts	...	★	★	...	...	★	★	★	E	★	...	★	★	★	★	...
Michigan	...	★	...	...	...	E	★	★	E	★	...	...	★	★	...	...
Minnesota	E	★	★	E	★	★	★	★	★	E	★	E	★	★	...	...
Mississippi	...	★	...	...	★	S	★	★	...	★	...	...	★	★	...	★
Missouri	...	★	...	...	★	...	★	★	...	★	...	...	★	—	...	...
Montana	...	★	...	...	★	...	...	★	...	...	...	★	E	★	★	★
Nebraska	...	★	...	...	...	★	★	★	★	★	...	...	E	★	★	★
Nevada	...	★	★	...	★	★	★	★	★	★	★	★	★	★	★	★
New Hampshire	E	★	E	...	...	S	★	★	★	★	...	S	★	★	...	★
New Jersey	E	★	...	...	...	...	★	★	...	★	...	...	★	...	—	...
New Mexico	E	★	...	...	★	★	★	★	...	★	...	★	★	...	★	★
New York	...	★	...	...	...	...	★	...	...	...	...	...	★	...	...	...
North Carolina	...	★	...	...	★	...	★	★	E	★	...	...	★	...	★	★
North Dakota	...	★	★	...	★	...	★	★	...	★	...	★	★	★	★	★
Ohio	...	★	...	...	★	E	★	★	★	★	...	...	★	★	...	★
Oklahoma	...	★	...	...	★	...	★	★	E	★	...	...	★	S	S	★
Oregon	...	★	...	...	★	S	★	★	★	★	...	...	★	S	S	★
Pennsylvania	...	★	...	...	...	...	★	★	...	★	...	...	S	...	E	★
Rhode Island	...	★	...	...	...	...	...	★	★	★	...	★	★	...	...	...
South Carolina	...	★	...	...	★	...	★	★	...	★	...	...	★	...	S	★
South Dakota	...	★	★	...	...	...	★	...	...	★	...	...	★	★	...	★
Tennessee	...	★	...	...	★	...	★	★	...	★	...	...	★	S	...	★
Texas	...	★	...	...	★	...	★	★	E	E	★	...	★	S	★	...
Utah	...	★	...	...	★	...	★	★	★	★	...	...	★	...	...	...
Vermont	...	★	...	...	★	...	...	★	★	E	...	...	★	...	...	...
Virginia	...	...	...	...	★	...	★	★	...	...	...	...	E	★	...	...
Washington	...	★	...	...	...	S	★	★	★	★	...	★	★	E	★	★
West Virginia	...	...	E	...	★	...	★	★	★	★	...	...	★	★	...	...
Wisconsin	...	...	...	...	★	...	★	...	...	...	★	...	★	...	—	...
Wyoming	...	★	...	...	★	S	★	★	E	★	...	...	★	★	...	...
Dist. of Columbia	...	★	...	...	...	★	E	★	...	E	★	E	★	E	★	...

Source: Louis Phillips & Associates, Athens, Georgia.

Key:
★ — Required
E — Enabling legislation
S — Under certain circumstances
— — not licensed

HEALTH

Table 8.31
STATE HEALTH AGENCIES: ORGANIZATIONAL CHARACTERISTICS AND SELECTED PUBLIC HEALTH RESPONSIBILITIES—FISCAL 1988

State or other jurisdiction	Organizational structure		Responsibilities:				
	Freestanding independent agency	Component of superagency	State crippled children's agency (Title V, SSA)	Mental health authority (PL 94-63)	Medicaid single state agency (Title XIX, SSA)	Lead environmental agency	Operates institutions
Total	35	20	42	16	8	10	16
Alabama	★	...	...	...	...	...	...
Alaska	...	★	★	...	...	...	...
Arizona	★	...	★	★	...	...	★
Arkansas	★	...	...	...	...	...	...
California	...	★	★	...	★	...	...
Colorado	★	...	★	★	...	★	...
Connecticut	★	...	★	...	...	...	...
Delaware	...	★	★	...	...	...	★
Florida	...	★	...	...	...	...	★
Georgia	...	★	★	...	...	...	...
Hawaii	★	...	★	★	...	★	★
Idaho	...	★	★	...	...	...	...
Illinois	★	...	...	...	...	...	...
Indiana	★	...	...	...	...	...	★
Iowa	★	...	...	★	...	...	...
Kansas	★	...	★	...	...	★	...
Kentucky	...	★	...	...	...	...	...
Louisiana	...	★	★	...	...	...	...
Maine	...	★	★	...	...	...	...
Maryland	★	...	★	★	...	...	★
Massachusetts	...	★	★	...	...	...	★
Michigan	★	...	★	★	...	...	★
Minnesota	★	...	★	...	...	...	...
Mississippi	★	...	★	...	...	...	...
Missouri	★	...	★	...	...	...	★
Montana	★	...	★	...	...	★	...
Nebraska	★	...	...	★	...	...	...
Nevada	...	★	★	...	...	...	...
New Hampshire	...	★	★	...	...	...	...
New Jersey	★	...	★	★	...	...	...
New Mexico	★	...	★	★	...	★	...
New York	★	...	★	...	...	...	★
North Carolina	...	★	★	...	...	...	★
North Dakota	★	...	...	...	...	★	...
Ohio	★	...	★	...	...	...	...
Oklahoma	★	...	...	...	...	★	...
Oregon	...	★	...	...	...	...	...
Pennsylvania	★	...	★	★	...	...	...
Rhode Island	★	...	★	...	...	...	...
South Carolina	★	...	★	...	...	★	...
South Dakota	★	...	★	★	...	...	...
Tennessee	★	...	★	...	★	★	...
Texas	★	...	★	...	...	...	★
Utah	★	...	★	...	★	★	...
Vermont	...	★	★	...	...	...	...
Virginia	★	...	★	...	...	...	...
Washington	...	★	★	...	...	...	...
West Virginia	★	...	...	★	...	...	★
Wisconsin	...	★	...	...	★	...	...
Wyoming	...	★	...	...	★	...	...
Dist. of Columbia	...	★	★	★	...	...	...
American Samoa	★	...	★	★	★	...	★
Guam	...	★	★	...	...	...	...
Puerto Rico	★	...	★	★	★	...	★
U.S. Virgin Islands	★	...	★	★	★	...	★

Source: Public Health Foundation, Washington, D.C.
Key:
★ — Yes
... — No

HEALTH

Table 8.32
PUBLIC HEALTH PROGRAM EXPENDITURES OF STATE HEALTH AGENCIES, BY PROGRAM: FISCAL 1988
(In thousands of dollars)

State or other jurisdiction	Total	Personal health	Environmental health	Health resources	Laboratory	General administration	Funds to LHDS not allocated to program areas
United States	$8,312,928 (a)	$6,258,244 (a)	$463,867 (a)	$720,411 (a)	$278,596 (a)	$471,487 (a)	$120,323
Alabama	90,564	61,330	1,955	3,974	5,859	9,347	8,101
Alaska	29,403	19,629	110	7,072	1,957	635	...
Arizona	145,419	126,024	735	8,003	2,594	8,062	...
Arkansas	67,265	48,829	6,859	2,115	2,283	7,178	...
California	792,670	471,914	35,432	201,609	29,275	54,440	...
Colorado	109,099	76,102	14,717	4,077	3,709	6,234	4,260
Connecticut	72,983	43,691	3,295	11,603	7,500	4,794	2,049
Delaware	52,806	44,923	2,295	1,324	1,444	2,821	...
Florida	366,796	265,915	52,325	16,481	11,410	9,103	11,564
Georgia	198,845	133,115	987	5,381	7,294	1,775	50,293
Hawaii	218,116	183,353	9,804	18,064	2,312	4,584	...
Idaho	21,005	14,562	88	2,982	2,283	1,091	...
Illinois	189,333	132,006	8,961	16,517	4,105	18,333	9,409
Indiana	106,237	78,082	8,529	4,805	3,535	11,286	...
Iowa	58,273	52,498	1,043	3,695	...	1,038	...
Kansas	46,945	26,797	9,148	3,729	2,251	5,020	...
Kentucky	110,232	68,128	4,656	23,543	2,526	2,115	9,263
Louisiana	116,726	99,961	11,651	3,976	545	594	...
Maine	25,736	19,832	1,708	1,709	2,234	253	...
Maryland	732,553	661,699	...	14,383	14,747	41,724	...
Massachusetts	281,759	244,670	6,545	10,885	13,995	5,664	...
Michigan	306,640	245,944	19,907	14,221	11,646	14,921	...
Minnesota	87,454	56,068	6,290	14,513	4,188	6,395	...
Mississippi	105,899	88,610	4,239	6,009	1,774	5,267	...
Missouri	108,825	91,497	4,749	6,082	2,733	3,763	...
Montana (a)	...	...	...	...	...	...	...
Nebraska	27,675	17,119	1,494	6,409	1,388	1,265	...
Nevada	20,050	15,083	1,390	1,832	1,360	386	...
New Hampshire	23,024	15,811	1,468	3,297	1,294	1,154	...
New Jersey	196,235	125,472	11,659	38,935	8,483	11,685	...
New Mexico	58,221	33,498	11,438	4,165	3,097	6,022	...
New York	695,766	475,682	28,297	109,935	43,698	38,153	...
North Carolina	178,872	151,227	11,036	3,166	8,245	5,198	...
North Dakota	17,487	9,006	3,050	1,587	2,269	1,049	525
Ohio	182,966	143,281	4,789	14,936	4,101	12,308	3,551
Oklahoma	88,335	61,718	14,322	4,363	2,508	5,424	...
Oregon	40,181	28,049	2,639	2,407	2,857	2,846	1,383
Pennsylvania	265,948	230,386	6,680	19,824	3,246	5,812	...
Rhode Island	35,615	18,029	4,006	6,839	4,527	2,214	...
South Carolina	181,959	127,949	25,730	5,998	7,244	15,037	...
South Dakota	20,688	16,166	52	1,920	1,629	921	...
Tennessee	178,597	118,735	35,597	11,100	6,271	6,894	...
Texas	362,715	293,710	19,376	20,950	6,569	15,055	7,055
Utah	58,012	31,066	16,541	3,252	3,121	4,032	...
Vermont	21,665	15,521	1,561	2,619	1,560	404	...
Virginia	206,196	138,210	24,254	9,818	2,169	26,275	5,469
Washington	25,987	11,714	4,301	4,755	3,659	1,559	...
West Virginia	159,720	138,828	1,845	4,868	2,470	5,182	6,528
Wisconsin	75,585	52,870	4,224	10,444	1,612	5,562	872
Wyoming	13,895	11,292	576	1,120	579	328	...
Dist. of Columbia	116,534	107,443	...	480	3,848	4,763	...
American Samoa (a)	...	...	...	...	...	...	...
Guam	7,608	4,968	1,497	205	437	502	...
Puerto Rico (a)	...	...	...	...	...	...	...
U.S. Virgin Islands (a)	...	...	...	...	...	...	...

Source: Public Health Foundation, Washington, D.C.

Note: The data in this table relate only to expenditures of official state health agencies. The public health expenditures of other agencies such as separate mental health authorities, environmental agencies, and hospital authorities are not reflected in the public health foundation's database.

(a) Data have been estimated for the state health agencies in Montana, American Samoa, Puerto Rico and the U.S. Virgin Islands, which did not report to the public health foundation for fiscal year 1988. Estimated data have been included in the United States total.

HEALTH

Table 8.33
PUBLIC HEALTH EXPENDITURES OF STATE HEALTH AGENCIES, BY SOURCE OF FUNDS: FISCAL YEAR 1988
(In millions of dollars)

Source of funds	Total	Personal health Noninstitutional	Personal health SHA-operated institutions	Environmental health	Health resources	Laboratory	General administration	Funds to LHDS not allocated to program areas
Total public health expenditures	8,312.9	5,025.1	1,233.1	463.9	720.4	278.6	471.5	120.3
Subtotal, excluding federal grant and contract funds	5,297.0	2,366.4	1,172.4	360.9	599.6	255.3	431.9	110.6
State	4,599.7	2,049.5	1,019.7	290.7	525.1	224.9	382.3	107.6
Local	140.6	99.7	—	19.8	1.9	0.9	16.3	2.1
Fees	387.9	152.6	110.7	40.5	41.9	22.1	19.1	1.0
Patient fees & reimbursements from medicaid	87.2	55.2	30.9	0.3	0.7	—	—	—
Patient fees & reimbursements from other sources	154.1	64.4	79.1	4.0	0.2	1.3	4.2	—
Other fees	146.6	32.9	0.6	—	—	—	15.0	1.0
Subtotal, federal grant and contract funds	168.8	64.7	42.0	36.2	41.0	20.9	14.2	—
Department of Health and Human Services	3,015.9	2,658.8	60.7	9.9	30.6	7.4	39.6	9.7
Public Health Service	1,128.7	902.3	55.5	103.0	120.8	23.3	17.2	9.7
Alcohol, Drug Abuse & Mental Health Administration (ADAMHA)	907.3	813.3	16.3	10.5	116.1	17.4	13.3	9.0
ADAMHA Block Grant (PL 97-35)	112.6	110.8	—	10.3	29.0	16.2	0.6	—
Other ADAMHA	84.8	83.3	—	—	1.0	—	0.6	—
Centers for Disease Control	27.7	27.5	—	—	1.0	—	0.1	—
Prev. Health & Health Services Block Grant (PL 97-35)	253.2	213.4	0.2	8.7	0.1	7.2	4.0	5.1
Immunization (PHSA, Sec. 317)	86.5	54.8	—	7.0	14.7	3.6	2.7	5.1
Refugee Assistance Act of 1980 (Sec. 412c3)	25.3	25.0	—	—	13.5	0.1	0.2	—
Venereal Disease (PHSA, Sec. 318)	10.8	10.6	—	—	—	0.1	0.1	—
Diabetes Control (PHSA, Sec. 301)	27.8	27.2	—	—	—	0.1	0.2	—
Tuberculosis (PHSA, Sec. 317)	4.3	4.1	—	—	0.1	0.4	0.1	—
Other CDC	3.7	3.7	—	—	—	—	—	—
Food and Drug Administration	94.9	88.1	0.2	1.7	1.1	3.1	0.8	—
Health Resources and Services Administration	1.9	0.3	—	1.1	0.2	—	0.3	—
Maternal and Child Health Block Grant (PL 97-35)	502.9	481.5	—	0.5	5.2	4.6	7.2	3.9
Community Health Centers (PHSA, Sec. 330)	399.9	383.2	—	0.5	1.3	4.3	6.7	3.9
Family Planning (PHSA, Title X)	4.0	4.0	—	—	—	—	—	—
Migrant Health (PHSA, Sec. 319)	78.7	78.2	—	—	—	0.2	0.3	—
National Health Planning & Res. Dev. Act (PL 93-641)	4.3	4.1	—	—	—	—	0.1	—
Other HRSA	3.0	0.4	—	—	2.6	—	—	—
National Institutes of Health	13.0	11.7	—	—	1.3	—	0.8	—
National Center for Health Statistics	31.3	7.0	16.1	—	2.9	4.4	0.3	—
Health Care Financing Administration	5.5	0.2	—	—	5.0	—	7.2	—
Medicaid Grants and Contracts (SSA, Title XIX)	178.1	64.7	38.9	0.1	69.1	1.1	3.5	0.7
Medicare Grants and Contracts (SSA, Title XVIII)	112.5	62.1	14.4	—	33.3	0.5	1.4	0.7
Other HCFA	62.5	1.8	24.5	—	34.8	0.6	0.8	—
Social Security Administration	3.1	0.8	—	—	1.0	—	1.3	—
Office of Human Development Services	16.5	—	—	—	16.5	—	—	—
Developmental Disabilities (PL 91-517, PL 94-103)	19.3	18.0	—	—	1.1	—	0.1	—
Grants for services (SSA, Title XX)	3.8	3.5	—	—	0.3	—	0.0	—
Other OHDS	11.8	11.0	—	—	0.7	—	0.1	—
Other DHHS	3.6	3.5	—	—	0.1	—	—	—
	7.5	6.2	0.3	—	0.5	0.1	0.4	—

PUBLIC HEALTH EXPENDITURES—Continued

Source of funds	Total	Personal health		Environmental health	Health resources	Laboratory	General administration	Funds to LHDS not allocated to program areas
		Noninstitutional	SHA-operated institutions					
Other federal agencies	1,860.7	1,747.9	5.2	88.4	3.0	5.6	10.5	...
Dept. of Agriculture	1,748.7	1,734.9	...	4.4	1.3	0.1	8.0	...
WIC	1,715.1	1,706.5	...	...	1.3	...	7.3	...
Other	33.6	28.4	...	4.4	...	0.1	0.7	...
Dept. of Labor	7.1	...	...	5.8	...	1.2	0.1	...
Dept. of Transportation	2.6	0.7	...	0.7	1.3	0.1	0.4	...
Consumer Product Safety Commission	0.9	—	...	...	—	0.1	0.1	...
Environmental Protection Agency	69.9	—	...	64.1	—	4.1	1.7	...
Nuclear Regulatory Commission	0.7	...	...	0.5	0.2	—	—	...
Regional Commissions	—	...	...	—	...	...	...	...
Other	30.8	12.2	5.2	12.9	0.1	—	0.2	...
Unidentified Federal	26.5	8.6	—	4.1	1.7	0.2	11.9	—

Source: Public Health Foundation, Washington, D.C.

Key:
— Dollar amounts less than $50,000.

CORRECTIONS IN THE 1990s: STATES LOOK TO INTERMEDIATE SANCTIONS AND SUBSTANCE ABUSE PROGRAMMING

By Timothy H. Matthews and Kimberly D. Roberts

Nearly all state governments today face complex issues in the management of correctional systems. Corrections budgets are absorbing more state dollars than many other government functions, yet these resources still do not meet the rising need for more prisons, jails and community corrections options. Between 1960 and 1985, state spending for corrections grew by 218 percent, more than education, public welfare, hospitals and health care, highways or law enforcement (*State Legislatures and Correctional Policies: An Overview*, 1989). The majority of this spending may be attributed to the continued increase in correctional populations due to the emphasis on public safety and crime prevention. State governments are faced with the challenge of finding creative solutions to overcrowding, while at the same time satisfying the public's demand for more accountability for offenders under correctional supervision.

Correctional Populations

At year end 1988, there were 627,402 prisoners under federal or state jurisdiction, 7.4 percent more than in 1987 and 90.2 percent more than in 1980. The incarceration rate reached an all-time high of 244 per 100,000 in 1988. State prisons were so overcrowded that 14,314 state prisoners had to be held in local jails, an increase of 18.5 percent over 1987. Although prison capacities increased by 28,000 to 31,000 beds, state prisons were still operating at 23 percent of their lowest reported capacities ("Prisoners in 1988").

As significant as the prison overcrowding crisis is the dilemma faced by probation and parole administrators. The probation population increased by 4.9 percent in 1987, bringing the total number under probation supervision to 2,356,483. Probation remains the sentence of choice for judges as there were 1.4 million admissions to probation in 1988. The parole population grew by 12.5 percent in 1988, bringing the total number of offenders on parole to 407,977. Three out of every four of the 3.7 million offenders under correctional supervision are in the community.

The Bureau of Justice Statistics reported the following facts on correctional populations for 1988:

- 1 out of every 49 adults in the U.S. is under some form of correctional supervision.
- 1 in every 27 men and 1 in every 194 women are being supervised.
- Correctional populations have increased by 7.3 percent since 1987 and 38.3 percent since 1984 (Probation and Parole 1988).

As in recent years, correctional administrators must continue to work with state legislators to identify and implement solutions to the problems posed by these increasing populations. They must engage in dialogue aimed

---

Timothy H. Matthews is a research associate/project director and Kimberly D. Roberts is a research associate in the Center for Law and Justice at The Council of State Governments' headquarters office.

Table A
Offenders Under Correctional Supervision - 1988

Supervised in the community	74.5%
Probation	63.5
Parole	11.0
Incarcerated	25.5
Jail	9.2
Prison	16.3
Total under correctional supervision	100.0

at developing policies that will effectuate positive change in the way states currently respond to convicted offenders. Many states must follow the lead of other states and enact fundamental and sweeping changes aimed at curtailing burgeoning correctional populations. One thing remains certain: Past efforts have not succeeded in reforming criminals or directing them from a criminal lifestyle. A Bureau of Justice Statistics study on prisoners released in 1983 found the following:

- Of the 108,580 persons released from 11 states in 1983, 62.5 percent were re-arrested for a felony or serious misdemeanor within 3 years, 46.8 percent were re-committed and 41.4 percent were re-incarcerated.
- An estimated 68,000 of the released prisoners were re-arrested and charged with more than 326,000 new felonies and serious misdemeanors including 50,000 violent offenses, 141,000 property offenses and 46,000 drug offenses.
- 26 percent of those released had been charged with at least 20 offenses ("Recidivism of Prisoners Released in 1985").

Correctional Policies

It is not clear that increasing incarceration rates and the movement towards massive prison construction has stymied crime rates. However, it is clear that offenders incarcerated in state prisons and local jails do not commit crimes in the public arena during their period of confinement. On the surface at least, it seems that the public's desire to lock up more offenders for longer periods of time represents sound correctional policy, particularly from a public safety point of view. The inherent problem with this call to "get tough on crime" is that, while the public supports harsher punishments for convicted offenders, it does not support increased taxes to pay for these punishments. Two things must occur if successful solutions are to be found for the current corrections dilemmas: 1) a balanced approach must be taken that incorporates a full range of sanctions from fines to long term incarceration, and 2) appropriate "programmatic" measures must be built in at every level of the supervision continuum.

Balanced Approach

Essential to the development of a balanced approach is the implementation of national sentencing policies, which include comprehensive community-based and intermediate sanctions. The most important element in state correctional systems is a state's sentencing process. Much debate has focused on whether a state should have determinate or indeterminate sentencing. Determinate sentencing enables administrators to "determine" the length of an offender's sentence and, therefore, be able to predict the release date (assuming the offender does not lose good time credits). Under an indeterminate sentencing system, the length of the sentence and release date is determined by a paroling authority. In recent years, several states have shifted toward determinate sentencing to eliminate some of the inequities in sentencing, to ensure more proportionality in the length of sentences for similar crimes and to ensure that those sentenced for violent crimes do, in fact, remain in prison for longer periods of time.

Regardless of the type of sentencing system a state employs, the impact of the system on correctional populations should not be overlooked. Particularly in a system of determinate sentencing, policy makers should be careful to project what the impact on the various correctional components will be. This will enable officials to plan for any future resources (e.g., more prisons) that may be required as a result of sentencing policies.

Intermediate Sanctions

Many of the states shifting to determinate sentencing have created guidelines for sentencing that have transferred authority for the length of sentencing from executive level agencies to judicial agencies (i.e., judges). The guidelines typically provide specific sanctions, which are tied to the severity of the offenses committed. In the past, guidelines have focused more on prison terms than community-based sanctions. With the need to circumvent overcrowding, however, more states will be looking to incorporate intermediate sanctions into the guidelines. Additionally, intermediate sanctions allow for community linkages and family ties to remain intact.

In many state systems, a vacuum exists between regular probation and incarceration, limiting judicial sentencing options. Several states (e.g., Georgia) have implemented progressive and intermediate sanctions to fill that void. Intermediate sanctions provide additional sentencing options for judges and enable them to match offender profiles and appropriate sanctions more closely. Some of the more common intermediate sanctions today include intensive supervision probation/parole, house arrest, electronic monitoring, shock probation and boot camps. Also, drug testing can be used with any of the above sanctions to monitor an offender's compliance with the conditions of supervision.

Intensive Supervision

One of the most frequently used intermediate sanctions is intensive supervision probation/parole (ISP). Used as an alternative to more costly incarceration, it is imposed on high risk offenders as a means of keeping them in the community. These programs are more restrictive than regular supervision in that they involve increased surveillance and central activities, such as home visits three times per week or nightly curfew checks. Offenders under intensive supervision are also typically required to pay restitution, participate in community service programs, maintain active employment and submit to drug testing. They may also be required to participate in community-based treatment programs.

At least 12 states have implemented system wide intensive supervision programs. These include Texas, Arizona, Georgia, Florida, Wisconsin, North Carolina, New York, New Jersey, California, Connecticut, Washington and Illinois. Several other states have ISP programs in at least one jurisdiction. Objectives of intensive supervision generally include the following:

• To increase contacts with probation/parole officers and other responsible members of the community,
• To hold offenders more accountable for their crimes through such conditions as victim restitution and community service,
• To hold offenders financially responsible for their supervision,
• To reduce recidivism by providing closer surveillance, and
• To re-integrate offenders into the community through treatment and employment opportunities ("Expanding Options for Criminal Sentencing").

House Arrest

House arrest refers to a sentence imposed by the court in which offenders are required to stay in their homes at all times, except for periods of time permitted by the court to perform special functions such as community service, to go to their jobs, to attend treatment programs or to receive other medical treatment. Several states including Utah, Michigan, Illinois and California have begun to use this form of sentencing as an alternative. The more restrictive programs were modeled after Florida's "Community Control Program" where as many as 5,000 criminals may be confined to their homes on a given day.

Florida reported significant savings, reducing the cost of supervision from $28 a day for imprisonment to $3 a day for home confinement ("House Arrest," 1987).

Electronic Monitoring

Often used as a component of intensive supervision, electronic monitoring is another method of verifying the presence of an offender at a specified location. It can be used

as a supervision tool to satisfy punishment, public safety and treatment goals by:
- Providing a cost-effective community supervision tool for offenders selected according to specific program criteria,
- Administering sanctions appropriate to the seriousness of the offense,
- Promoting public safety by providing surveillance and risk control strategies indicated by the risk and needs of the offender.
- Increasing the confidence of legislative, judicial and releasing authorities in ISP designs as a viable sentencing option ("Electronic Monitoring in Intensive Probation and Parole Programs").

The extent of control offered by electronic monitoring is generally defined as follows:
- Curfew. A curfew program includes home confinement during limited and specified hours, usually at night. Curfew is a characteristic component of intensive supervision and jail work-release programs.
- Home Detention. A detention program is more restrictive than curfew. It requires the offender to remain at home at all times except for employment, education, treatment or other specifically pre-approved and defined purposes.
- Home Incarceration. In this type of program, offenders are restricted to the home at all times except for very limited activities, such as religious worship or medical treatment.

States that have implemented electronic monitoring include New Mexico, Kentucky, Florida, Idaho, Michigan, North Carolina, South Carolina, Oregon, Utah, New Jersey and Indiana.

Shock Incarceration ("Boot Camps")

Shock incarceration is a relatively new intermediate sanction which provides an option between traditional prison incarceration and release. Typically, it is designed for the young, non-violent, first offender, age 18-25, who has a short sentence. It differs from shock probation, which was designed to show offenders how terrible imprisonment could be through a brief exposure to prison life followed by a supervised release. Ohio first instituted a form of shock probation in the 1960s, followed by Texas, Kentucky and Illinois.

More recently, states have experimented with shock incarceration (or prison "boot camps"). By 1989, eleven states had adopted forms of shock incarceration in their correctional systems. The specific components of these programs include various activities such as work, community service, education and counseling. Some programs require intensive supervision upon release. However, one similarity among the programs is a highly structured, military-type environment where offenders are required to participate in drills and physical training, all of which is directed by staff in a military, or boot camp, atmosphere. The sentence lengths are usually shorter than traditional detention. Among the benefits cited by proponents of these programs are the following:
- Alternative sentencing options. Boot camps should be considered as intermediate sanctions for offenders who pose risks too high for supervised release alone. This option reinforces "user accountability" and promotes effective drug testing programs for those on release.
- Enhanced public safety through incapacitation. Offenders in boot camps are, in fact, incapacitated for a period of time, preventing an immediate threat or opportunity for continued drug abuse or other criminal activity.
- Deterrence and punishment. The rigors of boot camp discipline, the appearance of punishment, and the threat of more serious sanctions provide a potential deterrent and the perception of punishment for some offenders.
- Rehabilitation and treatment. The system of discipline and structured rewards demonstrates the relationships of wrongful behavior and undesired consequences. The curriculum typically includes structured physical drills, life skills improvement, self-esteem enhancement, education and vocational training, confidence building, personal hygiene improvement, and substance abuse treatment.
- Reduced costs and implementation advantages. Boot camps may utilize surplus property and have shortened start-up time re-

quirements. While costs are dependent upon design features, boot camps offer potential cost-savings over prisons and experience less community resistance because they pose significantly reduced threats to the communities ("Probation and Parole in Practice").

Substance Abuse and Correctional Populations

Enhanced drug testing practices in the context of a balanced systems approach is becoming more and more critical to the functions of a criminal justice system overwhelmed by drug using offenders. There can be no doubt that test results enable officers to make better case management decisions, including taking effective restraining action before serious crimes occur.

The relationship between drug use and crime has been well documented in a number of studies. Although the exact nature of the relationship is still uncertain, much of the research establishes a definite statistical link between drug use and crime. That link points to the necessity of controlling crime through prevention, identification and treatment of drug abuse. In 1986, The Bureau of Justice Statistics sponsored a survey of inmates of state correctional facilities to examine the relationship between drug use and criminal behavior. They found:
- 35 percent of inmates in state prisons reported that they were under the influence of drugs at the time of their offense.
- Almost 80 percent of the inmates had used drugs at some time in their lives.
- Approximately half of the state prison inmates who had used drugs began by age 15.
- Half of the state prisoners sentenced for drug offenses, larceny, robbery or burglary were daily drug users.
- The more serious an offender's drug use, the more prior convictions the inmate reported ("Drug Use and Crime," 1986). The Drug Use Forecasting program, sponsored by the National Institute of Justice, compiles information from various cities to determine, by urinalysis and interviews, estimates for drug use in arrestees.

Table B reports the percent of drug use by arrestees from April through June 1987.

Table B
Percent Positive For Any Drug

City	Male	Female
Philadelphia, PA	84%	79%
San Diego, CA	80%	74%
Chicago, IL	77%	NA
New York, NY	76%	81%
New Orleans, LA	76%	65%
Miami, FL	70%	NA
Washington, D.C.	70%	88%
Birmingham, AL	70%	77%
St. Louis, MO	69%	75%
Cleveland, OH	67%	NA
Dallas, TX	67%	58%
Portland, OR	67%	75%
Kansas City, MO	64%	73%
Houston, TX	64%	64%
Detroit, MI	62%	NA
Phoenix, AZ	56%	65%

Source: National Institute of Justice

Between 56 and 84 percent of male arrestees, and 58 and 88 percent of female arrestees tested positive for one or more drugs. Also, female arrestees in Washington, D.C. (88 percent) and male arrestees in Philadelphia, PA (84 percent), were most likely to have tested positive for drugs. The increasing data confirming a correlation between drug use and crime has caused the nation to focus attention on the need for drug treatment for offenders.

State Responses to Drug Abuse Treatment

One of the major objectives of the National Drug Control Strategy, issued by the federal government in January 1990, is to encourage all states to develop state-wide treatment action plans that would ensure the coordination and provision of the necessary services, as well as, improve treatment outcomes.

In the National Drug Control Strategy, the Administration listed, "increased availability and quality in drug treatment services and development of innovative approaches to drug treatment," as funding priorities for 1991-1993. Currently, approximately 15 percent of the formula grant funds are being used for detention, rehabilitation and treatment by the states. Most states report that drug treatment services for offenders while in institutions or under correctional supervision in the community are inadequate. Almost all of the formula grants allocated in this area have been used to enhance drug treatment services available in the community and in institutions rather than to expand prisons or jails. Table C shows the formula grant allocations by state from 1987 to 1989.

Table D shows the 1989 allocation of Anti-Drug Abuse Act funds to the states for treatment, education and law enforcement.

Drug Treatment in Correctional Facilities

A comprehensive strategy for drug treatment in correctional facilities would require that all prisoners go through testing, assessment and assignment to a treatment option. The treatment options range from very structured, expensive programs (e.g, therapeutic communities) to easily implemented, inexpensive programs (e.g., self-help groups). The available options include:
- Self-help groups.
- Drug education and information.
- Individual and group counseling.
- Comprehensive drug treatment (i.e., milieu therapy).
- Intensive therapeutic communities ("Promising Approaches to Drug Treatment in Correctional Settings," 1989).

Many states have responded to the growing need for treatment services for offenders by developing innovative approaches. Table E summarizes the components of statewide drug treatment programs for corrections in six states:

Hawaii, New Jersey and Washington are in the planning phase of the program ("FY 1988 Report on Drug Control").

Programs for states interested in implementing an innovative pilot project have been funded in Iowa, Montana, New Mexico, North Carolina, Ohio and Wisconsin. The six programs target different populations and utilize different treatment approaches.

The Iowa program consists of a therapeutic community within a 30-person living unit. This community provides for a smooth transition of care and treatment throughout the release process, as well as promoting a drug-free lifestyle. Services include individual and group counseling, assignments to jobs and transition counseling ("FY 1988 Report on Drug Control").

North Carolina has developed a project called Substance Abuse Recovery Group Experience (SARGE). This program is designed to meet the needs of inmates between the ages of 14-20, who have a serious drug problem. Reducing recidivism by altering substance abuse tendencies is the goal of the program. The services include a 28-day residential treatment component at the time of admission and provides individual and group counseling, drug education, interpersonal skills, cognitive therapy techniques and assertiveness training. The treatment is then continued throughout the stay in the institution and after release, aftercare services are provided ("FY 1988 Report on Drug Control").

New York's "Stay 'n Out" therapeutic community for men at the Arthur Kill Correctional Facility and at the Bayview Correctional Facility for women operates three treatment units for men and one treatment unit for women. The counselor to prisoner ratio is approximately 1:8. Inmates are selected from the state correctional facilities and must be at least 18 years old, have a history of substance abuse, evidence of positive participation in the institution, and no history of mental illness or sex crimes. The program components include:
- An isolated unit, separated from the general prison population.
- The use of ex-addicts and ex-offenders as role models.
- A structural hierarchy where offenders are given increasing positions and status.
- Confrontation and support groups.
- Individual counseling.
- Community and relationship training.
- Program rules and penalties.
- Development of pro-social values.
- Continuity of care through networking.

State legislators need to consider a number of policy issues regarding prison drug treatment programs:
- Special treatment of prisoners in programs and opportunities to earn social status not available to the general prison population.

- Costs and benefits.
- Prison security
- Program effectiveness.
- Selection of inmates ("Promising Approaches to Drug Treatment in Correctional Settings").

Other model programs for a jail setting have been established in Arizona, Illinois and Florida to demonstrate effective methods of drug screening and drug treatment services for substance abusing offenders in a jail setting.

Drug Treatment in Community Corrections

Almost half of the states have instituted drug treatment programs for offenders under correctional supervision in the community, most of which include drug testing and/or intensive supervision, as well as referral to drug treatment programs ("FY 1988 Report on Drug Control"). Other options used by states include intermittent sentencing and TASC (Treatment Alternatives to Street Crime). Intermittent sentencing allows offenders to spend part of their time in prison and part in the community. Offenders can be released more quickly by remaining drug-free, attending treatment sessions, paying restitution and exhibiting positive behavior. The TASC program provides a bridge between treatment and corrections through a comprehensive case management system that works in coordination with courts, corrections and law enforcement to identify and assess offenders entering the criminal justice system ("Promising Approaches to Drug Treatment in Correctional Settings").

Bibliography

Dillingham, S.D., Montgomery, R.H. and Tabor, R.W. *Probation and Parole in Practice*, Anderson Publishing Co., Cincinnati, OH, 1990.

"Drug Use and Crime," U.S. Department of Justice, Bureau of Justice Statistics, 1988.

"FY 1988 Report on Drug Control," U.S. Department of Justice, Bureau of Justice Assistance, 1988.

National Drug Control Strategy, Executive Office of the President, Office of National Drug Control Policy, 1990.

NIJ Reports, U.S. Department of Justice, National Institute of Justice, 1989.

"Prisoners in 1988," U.S. Department of Justice, Bureau of Justice Statistics, 1989.

"Probation and Parole 1988," U.S. Department of Justice, Bureau of Justice Statistics, 1989.

"Recidivism of Prisoners Released in 1983," U.S. Department of Justice, Bureau of Justice Statistics, 1989.

State Legislatures and Corrections Policies: An Overview, National Conference of State Legislatures, 1989.

CORRECTIONS

Table C
Formula Grant Allocations by State

State or other jurisdiction	FY 1987	FY 1988	FY 1989	Percentage to be passed through to local jurisdiction
Total	$178,400,000	$55,600,000	$118,800,000	
Alabama	2,996,000	957,000	2,018,000	48.72%
Alaska	823,000	560,000	695,000	14.54%
Arizona	2,478,000	874,000	1,759,000	64.04%
Arkansas	1,964,000	768,000	1,388,000	53.47%
California	16,866,000	3,544,000	10,782,000	66.87%
Colorado	2,506,000	869,000	1,725,000	64.83%
Connecticut	2,470,000	860,000	1,693,000	45.13%
Delaware	886,000	571,000	739,000	25.66%
Florida	7,555,000	1,817,000	4,969,000	62.85%
Georgia	4,210,000	1,189,000	2,813,000	56.92%
Hawaii	1,154,000	620,000	903,000	48.50%
Idaho	1,124,000	613,000	871,000	61.59%
Illinois	7,660,000	1,803,000	4,805,000	65.32%
Indiana	3,913,000	1,121,000	2,556,000	58.48%
Iowa	2,290,000	822,000	1,553,000	54.77%
Kansas	2,021,000	778,000	1,420,000	54.73%
Kentucky	2,813,000	921,000	1,885,000	31.84%
Louisiana	3,282,000	1,008,000	2,158,000	53.52%
Maine	1,222,000	632,000	941,000	45.77%
Maryland	3,226,000	1,004,000	2,186,000	41.20%
Massachusetts	4,114,000	1,158,000	2,676,000	43.37%
Michigan	6,141,000	1,532,000	3,919,000	60.67%
Minnesota	3,103,000	975,000	2,078,000	67.32%
Mississippi	2,122,000	796,000	1,476,000	50.92%
Missouri	3,622,000	1,072,000	2,397,000	64.00%
Montana	1,013,000	592,000	801,000	55.39%
Nebraska	1,497,000	680,000	1,092,000	58.75%
Nevada	1,081,000	609,000	874,000	72.43%
New Hampshire	1,119,000	616,000	893,000	51.05%
New Jersey	5,194,000	1,360,000	3,352,000	60.74%
New Mexico	1,400,000	667,000	1,058,000	41.33%
New York	11,539,000	2,505,000	7,125,000	61.73%
North Carolina	4,383,000	1,214,000	2,884,000	42.50%
North Dakota	925,000	577,000	750,000	64.81%
Ohio	7,169,000	1,713,000	4,508,000	70.25%
Oklahoma	2,549,000	873,000	1,716,000	46.88%
Oregon	2,168,000	804,000	1,512,000	50.86%
Pennsylvania	7,858,000	1,841,000	4,936,000	69.41%
Rhode Island	1,101,000	610,000	866,000	44.95%
South Carolina	2,578,000	881,000	1,773,000	41.91%
South Dakota	939,000	580,000	764,000	50.62%
Tennessee	3,456,000	1,042,000	2,304,000	59.39%
Texas	10,662,000	2,382,000	6,740,000	67.87%
Utah	1,521,000	688,000	1,124,000	50.05%
Vermont	832,000	561,000	704,000	23.14%
Virginia	4,042,000	1,153,000	2,694,000	31.96%
Washington	3,237,000	1,003,000	2,187,000	56.37%
West Virginia	1,702,000	716,000	1,205,000	49.21%
Wisconsin	3,464,000	1,040,000	2,287,000	64.90%
Wyoming	816,000	557,000	682,000	57.68%
Dist. of Columbia	889,000	571,000	731,000	100.0%
American Samoa	522,000	504,000	188,100	N.A.
Guam	574,000	514,000	285,000	N.A.
No. Mariana Islands	512,000	502,000	96,900	N.A.
Puerto Rico	2,530,000	869,000	1,724,000	N.A.
U.S. Virgin Islands	567,000	512,000	539,000	

Source: Bureau of Justice Assistance, Report on Drug Control, 1989.

CORRECTIONS

Table D
Allocation of Anti-Drug Abuse Act Funds to the States for Treatment, Education and Law Enforcement: Fiscal Year 1989

State or other jurisdiction	Treatment	Education	Law Enforcement
Total	$518,497,984	$287,730,000	$118,800,000
Alabama	6,420,538	4,932,000	2,018,000
Alaska	2,449,737	1,393,000	695,000
Arizona	8,174,274	3,792,000	1,759,000
Arkansas	3,406,310	2,850,000	1,388,000
California	67,828,215	30,544,000	10,782,000
Colorado	7,658,872	3,631,000	1,725,000
Connecticut	8,204,250	3,258,000	1,693,000
Delaware	2,059,648	1,393,000	739,000
Florida	24,648,619	11,352,000	4,969,000
Georgia	8,764,514	7,554,000	2,813,000
Hawaii	2,580,291	1,393,000	903,000
Idaho	1,819,456	1,393,000	871,000
Illinois	22,288,702	13,044,000	4,805,000
Indiana	7,101,347	6,480,000	2,556,000
Iowa	4,763,097	3,216,000	1,553,000
Kansas	3,541,798	2,474,000	1,420,000
Kentucky	6,019,236	4,428,000	1,885,000
Louisiana	9,342,486	5,581,000	2,158,000
Maine	2,860,288	1,393,000	941,000
Maryland	11,583,951	4,572,000	2,186,000
Massachusetts	14,844,330	5,682,000	2,676,000
Michigan	22,180,169	10,771,000	3,919,000
Minnesota	7,878,137	4,728,000	2,078,000
Mississippi	3,428,685	3,480,000	1,476,000
Missouri	8,638,943	5,640,000	2,397,000
Montana	1,940,861	1,393,000	801,000
Nebraska	2,843,417	1,812,000	1,092,000
Nevada	2,567,746	1,393,000	874,000
New Hampshire	1,980,718	1,393,000	893,000
New Jersey	19,445,855	7,908,000	3,352,000
New Mexico	4,016,630	1,871,000	1,058,000
New York	55,734,141	18,679,000	7,125,000
North Carolina	8,463,790	7,135,000	2,884,000
North Dakota	1,366,052	1,393,000	750,000
Ohio	18,436,281	12,378,000	4,508,000
Oklahoma	4,205,249	3,810,000	1,716,000
Oregon	5,882,743	2,976,000	1,512,000
Pennsylvania	24,920,832	12,408,000	4,936,000
Rhode Island	3,135,400	1,393,000	866,000
South Carolina	4,995,522	4,111,000	1,773,000
South Dakota	1,893,438	1,393,000	764,000
Tennessee	6,563,321	5,538,000	2,304,000
Texas	30,281,932	20,893,000	6,740,000
Utah	3,972,113	2,670,000	1,124,000
Vermont	1,907,337	1,393,000	704,000
Virginia	10,971,705	6,228,000	2,694,000
Washington	9,331,013	4,961,000	2,187,000
West Virginia	3,130,048	2,238,000	1,205,000
Wisconsin	10,037,321	5,478,000	2,287,000
Wyoming	972,901	1,393,000	682,000
Dist. of Columbia	3,336,757	1,393,000	731,000
American Samoa	100,000	456,666	188,100
Guam	318,292	1,291,937	285,000
No. Mariana Islands	100,000	229,000	96,900
Puerto Rico	6,695,351	5,742,000	1,724,000
U.S. Virgin Islands	465,324	1,312,245	539,000

Source: Bureau of Justice Assistance, Report on Drug Control, 1989.

Table E
Components of Comprehensive State Departments of Corrections Treatment Strategy for Drug Abuse in Six States

ALABAMA

Operational
- Inmate drug screening, addiction assessment and treatment referral
- Database for tracking inmate treatment
- Inmate drug education
- Interim treatment prior to intensive treatment (12 step structured self-help program)
- Intensive 8-week residential treatment
- Therapeutic community 6-12 mnonths
- Prerelease transitional services
- Urinalysis in prison, probation and parole
- Evaluation research

CONNECTICUT

Operational
- Pretrial diversion of substance abusers
- Institutional treatment: drug screening, addiction assessment, treatment referral, NA/AA, AIDS intervention
- Community-based treatment: individual and group counseling, urinalysis, job referrals, vocational and educational counseling, financial referrals, NA/AA
- Community half-way houses and residential drug-free programs
- Supervision, referral, monitoring for addicted probationers

Planned
- Therapeutic community
- Information system
- Training for corrections staff

DELAWARE

Operational
- Inmate drug screening, addiction assessment and treatment referral
- Substance abuse training for corrections staff
- Interim treatment prior to intensive treatment: prison work program, counseling, substance abuse treatment
- Therapeutic community: 9-15 months

Planned
- Community residential drug-free programs: work release, progressing to supervised custody and parole supervision

FLORIDA

Operational
- Inmate drug screening, addiction assessment and treatment referral
- Training of corrections staff to improve treatment programs and unify treatment efforts
- Tier I: Inmate drug education: 35-40 hours of literature distribution, short-term counseling, group discussion, education program
- Tier II: Intensive 8-week residential treatment: individual and group counseling
- Tier III: Therapeutic community: 6-12 months
- Tier IV: Community-based treatment: 10-week program consisting of counseling, NA/AA, education groups
- Evaulation research

NEW MEXICO

Operational
- Substance abuse training for corrections staff
- Drug information resource center and satellite center
- Inmate drug eduction: graded training modules for inmates and peer counselors
- Therapeutic community: 6-12 months
- Modified therapeutic community: less intensive treatment/counseling program
- Evaluation research

NEW YORK

Operational
- Substance abuse training for corrections staff
- Therapeutic communities training
- Interim treatment prior to intensive treatment
- Therapeutic community: 9-12 months

Planned
- Expanded drug screening, assessment, treatment referral
- Treatment database
- Drug information resource center
- Expanded transitional services: employment, housing, family counseling, substance abuse services, education
- Community-based treatment programs
- Evaluation research

Source: Bureau of Justice Assistance, Report on Drug Control, 1989.

CRIMINAL JUSTICE

Table 8.34
TRENDS IN STATE PRISON POPULATION

State or jurisdiction	Total population			Population by maximum length of sentence						Incarceration rate 1988 (a)
				More than a year			Year or less and unsentenced			
	1988	1987	Percentage change	1988	1987	Percentage change	1988	1987	Percentage change	
United States	627,402	584,435	7.4	603,928	560,459	7.8	23,474	23,976	−2.1	244
Alabama	12,610	12,827	−1.7	12,357	12,602	−1.9	253	225	12.4	300
Alaska	2,588	2,528	2.4	1,862	1,767	5.4	726	761	−4.6	355
Arizona	12,158	10,948	11.1	11,639	10,558	10.2	519	390	33.1	329
Arkansas	5,519	5,441	1.4	5,519	5,441	1.4	0	0	ND	230
California	76,171	66,975	13.7	73,780	64,812	13.8	2,391	2,163	10.5	257
Colorado	5,997	4,808	24.7	5,997	4,808	24.7	0	0	ND	181
Connecticut	8,005	7,511	6.6	4,723	4,637	1.9	3,282	2,874	14.2	146
Delaware	3,166	2,939	7.7	2,359	2,116	11.5	807	823	−1.9	354
Florida	34,732	32,445	7.0	34,681	32,360	7.2	51	85	−40.0	278
Georgia	18,787	18,575	1.1	18,018	17,724	1.7	769	851	−9.6	281
Hawaii	2,367	2,268	4.4	1,510	1,536	−1.7	857	732	17.1	136
Idaho	1,548	1,435	7.9	1,548	1,435	7.9	0	0	ND	154
Illinois	21,081	19,850	6.2	21,081	19,850	6.2	0	0	ND	181
Indiana	11,406	10,827	5.3	11,271	10,634	6.0	135	193	−30.1	202
Iowa	3,034	2,851	6.4	3,034	2,851	6.4	0	0	ND	107
Kansas	5,936	5,781	2.7	5,936	5,781	2.7	0	0	ND	237
Kentucky (b)	7,119	6,436	10.6	7,119	6,436	10.6	0	0	ND	191
Louisiana	16,149	15,375	5	16,149	15,375	5.0	0	0	ND	368
Maine	1,297	1,328	−2.3	1,214	1,267	−4.2	83	61	36.1	100
Maryland	14,276	13,467	6.0	13,572	12,912	5.1	704	555	26.8	291
Massachusetts	6,733	6,265	7.5	6,733	6,265	7.5	0	0	ND	114
Michigan	27,714	23,879	16.1	27,714	23,879	16.1	0	0	ND	299
Minnesota	2,799	2,546	9.9	2,799	2,546	9.9	0	0	ND	64
Mississippi	7,438	6,880	8.1	7,304	6,719	8.7	134	161	−16.8	279
Missouri	12,354	11,146	10.8	12,354	11,146	10.8	0	0	ND	239
Montana	1,272	1,187	7.2	1,272	1,187	7.2	0	0	ND	158
Nebraska	2,205	2,086	5.7	2,111	1,963	7.5	94	123	−23.6	131
Nevada	4,881	4,434	10.1	4,881	4,434	10.1	0	0	ND	452
New Hampshire	1,019	867	17.5	1,019	867	17.5	0	0	ND	93
New Jersey (b)	16,936	15,548	8.9	16,936	15,548	8.9	0	0	ND	219
New Mexico	2,825	2,710	4.2	2,723	2,626	3.7	102	84	21.4	180
New York	44,560	40,842	9.1	44,560	40,842	9.1	0	0	ND	248
North Carolina	17,069	17,218	−0.9	16,326	16,118	1.3	743	1,100	−32.5	250
North Dakota	466	430	8.4	414	380	8.9	52	50	4.0	62
Ohio	26,113	24,220	7.8	26,113	24,220	7.8	0	0	ND	240
Oklahoma	10,448	9,639	8.4	10,448	9,639	8.4	0	0	ND	323
Oregon	5,991	5,482	9.3	5,991	5,482	9.3	0	0	ND	215
Pennsylvania	17,879	16,267	9.9	17,862	16,246	9.9	17	21	−19.0	148
Rhode Island	1,906	1,428	33.5	1,179	991	19	727	437	66.4	118
South Carolina	13,745	12,664	8.5	12,938	11,862	9.1	807	802	0.6	370
South Dakota	1,020	1,133	−10	1,020	1,133	−10	0	0	ND	143
Tennessee	7,491	7,624	−1.7	7,491	7,624	−1.7	0	0	ND	152
Texas	40,437	38,821	4.2	40,437	38,821	4.2	0	0	ND	240
Utah	2,004	1,874	6.9	1,987	1,858	6.9	17	16	6.3	117
Vermont	811	759	6.9	544	505	7.7	267	254	5.1	97
Virginia	14,184	13,321	6.5	13,928	12,931	7.7	256	390	−34.4	230
Washington	5,816	6,131	−5.1	5,816	6,131	−5.1	0	0	ND	124
West Virginia	1,458	1,461	−0.2	1,458	1,461	−0.2	0	0	ND	78
Wisconsin	6,287	6,097	3.1	6,161	6,080	1.3	126	17	641.2	126
Wyoming	962	916	5.0	962	916	5.0	0	0	ND	203
Dist. of Columbia (b)	8,705	7,645	13.9	6,340	5,614	12.9	2,365	2,031	16.4	1,031

Source: U.S. Department of Justice, Bureau of Justice Statistics, Prisoners in 1988.
Key:
ND — Not definable.

(a) The number of prisoners sentenced to more than one year per 100,000 resident population on December 31, 1988.
(b) Figures for 1987 and 1988 are not comparable to those for previous years because of the inclusion of additional jail inmates.

CRIMINAL JUSTICE

Table 8.35
ADULTS ADMITTED TO STATE PRISONS, 1980 AND 1987

State or other jurisdiction	Admissions per 1,000 selected offenses		Admissions per 100,000 adults	
	1980	1987	1980	1987
United States	25	48	80	125
Alabama	49	53	138	129
Alaska	42	116	115	245
Arizona	24	57	97	174
Arkansas	50	66	104	136
California	15	41	66	134
Colorado	16	36	55	98
Connecticut	37	52	105	112
Delaware	30	79	88	153
Florida	24	64	109	273
Georgia	49	77	156	227
Hawaii	9	28	28	54
Idaho	34	56	78	97
Illinois	32	36	78	95
Indiana	37	65	88	112
Iowa	28	45	50	70
Kansas	26	43	69	87
Kentucky	47	50 (a)	86	80
Louisiana	31	55	100	168
Maine	28	53	54	66
Maryland	30	50	107	128
Massachusetts	8	22	26	47
Michigan	20	31	67	96
Minnesota	12	24	25	45
Mississippi	43	60	97	127
Missouri	24	52	74	117
Montana	34	63	55	84
Nebraska	35	39	56	58
Nevada	26	71	136	219
New Hampshire	14	34	30	39
New Jersey	14	43	49	87
New Mexico	17	33	53	114
New York	13	39	56	116
North Carolina	61	80	158	197
North Dakota	47	79	36	56
Ohio	45	63	97	127
Oklahoma	38	71	111	214
Oregon	27	40	83	125
Pennsylvania	17	29	33	42
Rhode Island	12	15	35	34
South Carolina	47	62	153	172
South Dakota	61	119	71	107
Tennessee	33	21	89	53
Texas	38	49	129	191
Utah	15	26	39	50
Vermont	32	57	77	96
Virginia	36	84	75	123
Washington	14	20	46	63
West Virginia	30	49	38	48
Wisconsin	26	41	46	62
Wyoming	38	63	71	90
Dist. of Columbia	36	93	213	407

Sources: National Prisoner Statistics (NPS) *Crime In the United States*, 1980 and 1987; Bureau of Census estimates of population.

Note: Prison admissions refer to the number of prisoners received from courts with sentences of more than one year. Selected offenses are murder, nonnegligent manslaughter, rape, robbery, aggravated assault and burglary. Adults are the resident population age 18 and over.

(a) Admissions to custody only.

CRIMINAL JUSTICE

Table 8.36
STATE PRISON CAPACITIES, 1988

State or other jurisdiction	Rated capacity	Operational capacity	Design capacity	Population as a percent of: (a) Highest capacity	Lowest capacity
Alabama	11,162	11,162	11,162	109	109
Alaska	...	2,793	...	93	93
Arizona	...	12,240	12,240	99	99
Arkansas	...	5,530	...	100	100
California	46,279	70,706	46,279	108	165
Colorado	4,985	5,058	3,538	112	160
Connecticut	7,731	7,153	...	104	112
Delaware	2,090	2,880	2,090	110	151
Florida	38,894	35,618	27,418	89	127
Georgia	...	17,296	...	109	109
Hawaii	...	2,130	1,691	111	140
Idaho	1,163	1,406	1,163	110	133
Illinois	20,100	20,100	16,492	105	128
Indiana	10,412	...	...	110	110
Iowa	2,918	2,858	2,918	104	106
Kansas	...	4,293	...	138	138
Kentucky	6,602	6,469	...	94	96
Louisiana	12,330	12,330	12,330	100	100
Maine	934	934	934	137	137
Maryland	...	14,561	11,352	98	126
Massachusetts	...	...	3,891	173	173
Michigan	21,454	...	...	129	129
Minnesota	2,964	2,964	2,976	94	94
Mississippi	6,651	6,318	6,511	96	101
Missouri	...	12,800	...	97	97
Montana	784	1,073	784	119	162
Nebraska	...	...	1,651	134	134
Nevada	...	4,637	3,731	105	131
New Hampshire (b)	774	998	572	100	174
New Jersey	12,172	13,324	11,441	110	128
New Mexico	2,671	2,751	2,671	103	106
New York	...	45,141	40,095	99	111
North Carolina	18,668	14,767	...	91	116
North Dakota	...	516	516	90	90
Ohio	...	...	18,482	141	141
Oklahoma	...	7,378	...	142	142
Oregon	4,077	4,722	2,746	127	218
Pennsylvania	...	...	12,972	138	138
Rhode Island	1,546	1,579	1,449	121	132
South Carolina	11,793	11,793	9,443	113	141
South Dakota	1,170	1,090	1,189	86	94
Tennessee	...	7,754	...	97	97
Texas (c)	41,319	39,244	41,319	95	100
Utah	...	2,464	2,210	79	88
Vermont	597	597	597	130	130
Virginia	11,460	11,460	11,460	115	115
Washington	5,914	6,523	5,914	89	98
West Virginia (b)	1,547	1,640	1,547	85	90
Wisconsin	4,683	...	4,683	134	134
Wyoming	...	950	...	101	101
Dist. of Columbia	7,417	...	...	113	113

Source: U.S. Department of Justice, Bureau of Justice Statistics, *Prisoners in 1988*.
Key:
... - Data not available
(a) Excludes state-sentenced inmates held in local jails due to crowding where they have been included in the total prisoner count.
(b) Capacity figures available for males only. West Virginia reports an additional capacity to house 82 female prisoners.
(c) Capacity figures exclude 912 beds in halfway houses and 286 beds in psychiatric facilities.

CRIMINAL JUSTICE

Table 8.37
ADULTS ON PROBATION, 1988

State or other jurisdiction	Probation population 1/1/88	1988 Entries	1988 Exits	Probation population 12/31/88	Percent change in probation population during 1988	1988 probationers per 100,000 adult residents
Alabama (a)	23,406	10,955	9,183	25,178	7.6	843
Alaska	2,941	1,295	1,242	2,994	1.8	839
Arizona	23,158	10,648	8,338	25,468	10.0	1,004
Arkansas (a)	14,609	4,389	3,067	15,931	9.0	913
California	239,985	151,428	128,617	262,796	9.5	1,262
Colorado	22,981	21,004	20,046	23,939	4.2	984
Connecticut	43,659	30,893	28,669	45,883	5.1	1,855
Delaware	9,398	3,934	3,756	9,576	1.9	1,939
Florida	155,194	204,013	197,218	161,989	4.4	1,698
Georgia	110,484	64,800	60,016	115,268	4.3	2,525
Hawaii	8,882	7,086	6,250	9,718	9.4	1,197
Idaho (a)	4,146	2,317	2,106	4,357	5.1	623
Illinois	82,332	50,523	42,119	90,736	10.2	1,054
Indiana (a)	56,978	55,281	56,328	55,931	−1.8	1,366
Iowa	12,745	11,272	10,918	13,099	2.8	618
Kansas	18,059	10,146	8,743	19,462	7.8	1,057
Kentucky	7,181	4,075	3,858	7,398	3.0	269
Louisiana (a)	30,313	13,067	12,162	31,218	3.0	1,004
Maine (a)	4,605	4,754	3,300	6,059	31.6	672
Maryland	72,816	44,123	38,320	78,619	8.0	2,262
Massachusetts	97,571	52,852	58,076	92,347	−5.4	2,027
Michigan (a)	109,398	91,906	87,024	114,280	4.5	1,684
Minnesota	44,363	46,246	40,425	50,184	13.1	1,575
Mississippi	7,595	3,623	3,370	7,848	3.3	427
Missouri (a)	40,766	27,509	25,777	42,498	4.2	1,110
Montana	3,168	1,362	1,255	3,275	3.4	561
Nebraska (a)	11,511	15,472	15,572	11,411	−.9	968
Nevada (a)	5,338	3,223	2,636	5,925	11.0	752
New Hampshire	2,827	2,060	1,939	2,948	4.3	364
New Jersey	53,827	28,191	22,294	59,724	11.0	1,014
New Mexico	5,310	5,538	5,157	5,691	7.2	538
New York	112,461	45,903	37,555	120,809	7.4	891
North Carolina	62,940	35,136	30,912	67,164	6.7	1,384
North Dakota (a)	1,616	850	725	1,741	7.7	360
Ohio	68,769	47,641	46,204	70,206	2.1	874
Oklahoma	23,477	...	...	23,404	−.3	992
Oregon (a)	24,079	11,069	10,970	24,178	.4	1,162
Pennsylvania	85,084	49,372	42,160	92,296	8.5	1,008
Rhode Island	8,181	6,073	4,430	9,824	20.1	1,288
South Carolina	24,959	15,555	11,291	29,223	17.1	1,159
South Dakota (a)	2,594	4,500	4,590	2,504	−3.5	485
Tennessee (a)	26,403	21,805	19,447	28,761	8.9	790
Texas	289,690	139,398	140,182	288,906	−.3	2,437
Utah	5,833	3,664	3,902	5,595	−4.1	528
Vermont	5,593	3,290	2,917	5,966	6.7	1,434
Virginia	16,450	9,966	8,783	17,633	7.2	388
Washington	57,825	35,887	33,468	60,244	4.2	1,742
West Virginia	4,421	2,533	2,163	4,791	8.4	343
Wisconsin	25,188	12,036	10,477	26,747	6.2	747
Wyoming	1,917	787	890	1,814	−5.4	537
Dist. of Columbia	13,750	10,178	11,535	12,393	−9.9	2,587

Source: U.S. Department of Justice, Bureau of Justice Statistics, *Probation and Parole, 1988.*
Note: For additional information refer to source.
Key:
. . . — Not reported.

(a) Alabama, Arkansas, Louisiana, Maine, Michigan, Missouri, North Dakota, Oregon, South Dakota and Tennessee estimated entries and exits. Arkansas estimated December 1988 parole population. Idaho estimated exits. Indiana, Nebraska and Nevada estimated all data.

CRIMINAL JUSTICE

Table 8.38
ADULTS ON PAROLE, 1988

State or other jurisdiction	Parole population 1/1/88	1988 Entries	1988 Exits	Parole population 12/31/88	Percent change in parole population during 1988	1988 parolees per 100,000 adult residents
Alabama	3,456	2,361	1,116	4,701	36.0	157
Alaska	435	593	539	489	12.4	137
Arizona	2,224	3,425	3,239	2,410	8.4	95
Arkansas	3,932	1,757	1,849	3,840	−2.3	220
California	41,333	62,773	54,742	49,364	19.4	237
Colorado (b)	1,680	1,643	1,580	1,743	3.8	72
Connecticut	466	130	225	371	−20.4	15
Delaware	1,100	456	463	1,093	−.6	221
Florida	2,873	2,214	2,525	2,562	−10.8	27
Georgia	10,917	6,970	6,579	11,308	3.6	248
Hawaii	1,012	716	620	1,108	9.5	137
Idaho	865	273	345	793	−8.3	113
Illinois (b)	13,744	10,153	9,528	14,369	4.5	167
Indiana	3,071	3,792	3,452	3,411	11.1	83
Iowa	1,966	1,479	1,500	1,945	−1.1	92
Kansas	2,676	2,405	1,584	3,497	30.7	190
Kentucky	3,338	2,614	2,509	3,443	3.1	125
Louisiana	7,243	...	...	8,097	11.8	260
Maine (a)	0	0	0	0	0	0
Maryland	8,063	5,256	4,094	9,225	14.4	265
Massachusetts (b)	4,018	4,300	3,985	4,333	7.8	95
Michigan	6,342	5,886	4,551	7,677	21.1	113
Minnesota	1,444	1,799	1,604	1,639	13.5	51
Mississippi	3,456	1,315	1,594	3,177	−8.1	173
Missouri (b)	6,423	4,225	3,422	7,226	12.5	189
Montana (b)	624	269	222	671	7.5	115
Nebraska	459	676	688	447	−2.6	38
Nevada (b)	1,598	1,556	1,438	1,716	7.4	218
New Hampshire	421	213	173	461	9.5	57
New Jersey	15,709	9,943	7,189	18,463	17.5	314
New Mexico	1,194	1,281	1,395	1,080	−9.5	102
New York	31,244	17,130	14,412	33,962	8.7	251
North Carolina	4,646	8,009	6,464	6,191	33.3	128
North Dakota	133	139	109	163	22.6	34
Ohio	5,988	4,494	4,491	5,991	.1	75
Oklahoma	1,762	...	...	1,455	−17.4	62
Oregon	1,988	2,248	1,626	2,610	31.3	125
Pennsylvania	38,398	23,157	15,089	46,466	21.0	508
Rhode Island	423	403	384	442	4.5	58
South Carolina	3,469	1,247	1,044	3,672	5.9	146
South Dakota	492	776	651	617	25.4	120
Tennessee (b)	9,263	4,374	4,108	9,529	2.9	262
Texas	67,308	32,901	22,382	77,827	15.6	657
Utah	1,137	832	751	1,218	7.1	115
Vermont	200	108	126	182	−9.0	44
Virginia	6,283	6,811	6,484	6,610	5.2	145
Washington (b)	10,211	1,585	1,051	10,745	5.2	311
West Virginia (b)	841	495	529	807	−4.0	58
Wisconsin	4,009	2,413	2,316	4,106	2.4	115
Wyoming	366	114	191	289	−21.0	86
Dist. of Columbia	3,659	2,801	2,511	3,949	7.9	824

Source: U.S. Department of Justice, Bureau of Justice Statistics, Probation and Parole, 1988.
Note: For additional information refer to source.
(a) Maine abolished parole in 1976, so the number of persons remaining on parole is negligible.
(b) Illinois and Massachusetts estimated entries and exits. Colorado, Montana and West Virginia estimated exits. Tennessee estimated entries. Missouri and Washington estimated the January 1988 parole population. Nevada estimated all data.

CRIMINAL JUSTICE

Table 8.39
STATE DEATH PENALTY
(As of December 1988)

State or jurisdiction	Capital offenses	Minimum age	Persons on death row	Method of execution
Alabama	Murder during kidnaping, robbery, rape, sodomy, burglary, sexual assault, or arson; murder of peace officer, correctional officer, or public official; murder while under a life sentence; murder for pecuniary gain or contract murder; multiple murders; aircraft piracy; murder by a defendant with a previous murder conviction; murder of a witness to a crime	None	97	Electrocution
Alaska	...			
Arizona	First-degree murder	None	82	Lethal gas
Arkansas	Felony murder; arson causing death; intentional murder of a law enforcement officer, murder of a prison, jail, court or correctional personnel, or military personnel acting in line of duty; multiple murders; intentional murder of public officeholder or candidate; intentional murder while under life sentence; contract murder	15	27	Lethal injection
California	Treason; aggravated assault by a prisoner serving a life term; first-degree murder with special circumstances; train wrecking; perjury causing execution	18	229	Lethal gas
Colorado	First-degree murder; first-degree kidnaping with death of victim; felony murder	18	3	Lethal injection
Connecticut	Murder of a public safety or correctional officer; murder for pecuniary gain; murder in the course of a felony; murder by a defendant with a previous conviction for intentional murder; murder while under a life sentence; murder during a kidnaping; illegal sale of cocaine; methadone, or heroin to a person who dies from using these drugs; murder during first-degree sexual assault; multiple murders	18	1	Electrocution
Delaware	First-degree murder with aggravating circumstances	None	7	Lethal injection
Florida	First-degree murder	None	295	Electrocution
Georgia	Murder; kidnaping with bodily injury when the victim dies; aircraft hijacking; treason; kidnapping for ransom when the victim dies	17	91	Electrocution
Hawaii	...			
Idaho	First-degree murder; aggravated kidnaping	None	15	Lethal injection or firing squad
Illinois	Murder accompanied by at least one of eight aggravating factors	18	118	Lethal injection
Indiana	Murder, with aggravating circumstances	16	51	Electrocution
Iowa	...			
Kansas	...			
Kentucky	Aggravated murder; kidnaping when victim is killed	16	32	Electrocution
Louisiana	First-degree murder; treason	15	40	Electrocution
Maine	...			
Maryland	First-degree murder, either premeditated or during the commission of a felony	18	14	Lethal gas
Massachusetts	...			
Michigan	...			
Minnesota	...			
Mississippi	Capital murder includes murder of a peace officer or correctional officer, murder while under a life sentence, murder by bomb or explosive, contract murder, murder committed during specific felonies (rape, burglary, kidnaping, arson, robbery, sexual battery, unnatural intercourse with a child, nonconsensual unnatural intercourse), and murder of an elected official; capital rape is the forcible rape of a child under 14 years by a person 18 years or older; aircraft piracy	13	48	Lethal injection or lethal gas (a)

CRIMINAL JUSTICE

STATE DEATH PENALTY—Continued

State or jurisdiction	Capital offenses	Minimum age	Persons on death row	Method of execution
Missouri	First-degree murder	14	68	Lethal injection or lethal gas
Montana	Deliberate homicide; aggravated kidnaping when victim or rescuer dies; attempted deliberate homicide, aggravated assault, or aggravated kidnaping by a state prison inmate with a prior conviction for deliberate homicide or who has been previously declared a persistent felony offender	None (b)	7	Lethal injection or hanging
Nebraska	First-degree murder	18	13	Electrocution
Nevada	First-degree murder	16	44	Lethal injection
New Hampshire	Contract murder; murder of a law enforcement officer; murder of a kidnap victim; killing another after being sentenced to life imprisonment without parole	17	0	Lethal injections
New Jersey	Purposeful or knowing murder; contract murder	18	21	Lethal injection
New Mexico	First-degree murder; felony murder	None	2	Lethal injection
New York	...			
North Carolina	First-degree murder	(c)	80	Lethal injection or lethal gas
North Dakota	...			
Ohio	Assassination; contract murder; murder during escape; murder while in a correctional facility; murder after conviction of a prior purposeful killing or prior attempted murder; murder of a peace officer; murder arising from specified felonies (rape, kidnaping, arson, robbery, burglary); murder of a witness to prevent testimony in a criminal proceeding or in retaliation	18	88	Electrocution
Oklahoma	Murder with malice aforethought; murder arising from specified felonies (forcible rape, robbery with a dangerous weapon, kidnaping, escape from lawful custody, first-degree burglary, arson); murder when the victim is a child who has been injured, tortured or maimed	None (d)	92	Lethal injection
Oregon	Aggravated murder	18	15	Lethal injection
Pennsylvania	First-degree murder	None	98	Electrocution
Rhode Island	...			
South Carolina	Murder with statutory aggravating circumstances	None	36	Electrocution
South Dakota	First-degree murder; kidnaping with gross permanent physical injury inflicted on the victim; felony murder	None (e)	0	Lethal injection
Tennessee	First-degree murder	18	70	Electrocution
Texas	Murder of a public safety officer, fireman, or correctional employee; murder during the commission of specified felonies (kidnaping, burglary, robbery, aggravated rape, arson); murder for remuneration; multiple murders; murder during prison escape; murder by a state prison inmate	17	284	Lethal injection
Utah	First-degree murder; aggravated assault by prisoners involving serious bodily injury	14	8	Lethal injection or firing squad
Vermont	Murder of a police officer or correctional officer; kidnaping for ransom	None	0	Electrocution
Virginia	Murder during the commission of specified felonies (abduction, armed robbery, rape); contract murder; murder by a prisoner while in custody; murder of a law enforcement officer; multiple murders; murder of a child under 12 years old during an abduction	15	39	Electrocution
Washington	Aggravated first-degree premeditated murder	None	7	Lethal injection or hanging
West Virginia	...			
Wisconsin	...			
Wyoming	First-degree murder including felony murder	None	2	Lethal injection
Dist. of Columbia	...			

CRIMINAL JUSTICE

STATE DEATH PENALTY—Continued

Source: U.S. Department of Justice, Bureau of Justice Statistics, *Capital Punishment, 1988.*

Key:
. . . - State has no capital punishment statute.

(a) Mississippi authorizes lethal injection for those convicted after 7/1/84; executions of those convicted prior to that date are to be carried out with lethal gas.

(b) Youth as young as 12 may be tried as adults.

(c) Must be 17 unless the murderer was incarcerated for murder when a subsequent murder occurred; then may be 14.

(d) Statute partially struck by the U.S. Supreme Court on 6/29/88 held that the application of the death penalty statute to a 15-year-old defendant violated the 8th Amendment prohibition against cruel and unusual punishment.

(e) 10 years old, only after transfer hearing as an adult.

FOUR STATE ENVIRONMENTAL PROTECTION INITIATIVES FOR THE 1990s

By R. Steven Brown and John M. Johnson

During the 1980s, the states were called upon to undertake a greater role in environmental management.[1] States have always initiated new environmental programs without federal mandates, and during the 1980s state leadership not only continued, but expanded.

There are many examples in environmental management that illustrate this leadership. However, this essay will focus on four: toxic chemical use reduction, environmental management of biotechnology, state public-private partnerships and the use of ballot initiatives for environmental legislation. These four examples are by no means an exhaustive compilation of state initiatives (for example, states have also been in the forefront in addressing solid waste and medical waste management). They will serve, however, to illustrate the maturation of the new role of the states during the 1980s. This essay will attempt to review the origins of state efforts, what actions the states have already taken, and what actions might be expected during the next few years on these subjects.

Toxic Chemical Use Reduction.

During 1986, Congress' Office of Technology Assessment promoted a policy advocating the reduction of wastes as a major platform of environmental management.[2] Basically, the idea is based on "management avoidance" techniques, that is, if a waste is not produced in the first place, it will not have to be managed. However, the policy is waste-oriented. It says little about the reduction of toxic chemicals in chemical processes that lead to toxic waste by-products. When reduction of toxic chemicals in manufacturing processes is advocated by this federal policy, it is usually because that chemical results in a waste, not because the process chemical itself is inherently toxic.[3]

There is an interest, as will be described below, in using less chemicals in the first place, and not merely because this will result in less waste. Using less toxic chemicals will also reduce public and worker exposure to these chemicals and presumably the risk of contamination. It is important that this difference between waste reduction and chemical reduction be clearly understood.

During 1989, at least three states decided to tackle the problem of toxic chemical usage legislatively, and at least six others investigated the problem. These efforts originated from several sources, but seem to be centered in the work of environmental advocacy groups such as the Public Interest Research Group (PIRG), and in the concern of the public and state government over the Toxic Release Inventory (chemical emissions data) that EPA released pursuant to the federal Community Right-to-Know Act.[4]

The PIRGs in at least two states, Massachusetts and Oregon, mobilized to seek reduction of toxic chemical use by legislative means (Illinois also addressed the issues). Many states were seeking to reduce wastes during the 1989 sessions, but only a few states sought the type of reductions of process chemicals described here.

The Massachusetts effort led to the passage of a bill supported by the PIRG, the state

---

R. Steven Brown and John M. Johnson work in the Strategic Planning and Innovations Group at The Council of State Governments.

agency and industry. This bill was the more stringent of the two passed, with industries required to submit chemical use reduction plans, and civil penalties for failure to do so.[5]

The Oregon effort also led to the passage of a toxics reduction bill. This bill, too, contained provisions for industries to submit a mandatory toxic chemical use reduction plan. There are, however, no penalties for failure to submit the plan. Instead, the department can call for a public hearing on the subject.[6]

Other state-led efforts took place in California and Illinois (developing air toxics release regulations), Vermont, New Jersey, Kentucky, New York (evaluation of toxic release data), and North Carolina (establishing an advisory panel on toxicity).

More activity is expected in the years to come, based on the increase in bills being considered in 1990 as compared to 1989. As of this writing, additional bills were pending during the 1990 legislative sessions in Maine, New York, California, Tennessee, and New Jersey. A bill is also expected in Connecticut.[7]

Biotechnology

Biotechnology is, for the purposes of this article, the alteration of the genetic material of organisms (plants, animals and bacteria) through the direct manipulation of their DNA. The federal government has regulated the release of genetically engineered organisms into the environment, and products made from such organisms, for years under the auspices of several federal acts.[8]

The state role in regulation has, from the federal point of view, been relegated to commenting on proposed federal actions. These comments may be acted upon or rejected by the federal reviewing agency, but the states have little opportunity under the current federal system for the kinds of permitting or enforcement that they typically undertake in conjunction with other federal environmental programs.

During the past few years, a number of impending releases of these organisms have prompted some states to take a proactive role in the regulation of biotechnological products.[9] In the first seminal report on state regulation of biotechnology compiled by Wisconsin in 1987, five states were cited as having controls of some sort.[10] In 1989, two significant bills were passed on this subject, one in Minnesota and one in North Carolina. Both have been touted as landmark legislation.[11] This activity has attracted the attention of industry analysts, who identified state regulation as one of the ten most important issues facing biotechnology in the next decade and said "State-initiated legislation . . . will increasingly become a driving force in the industry's future."[12]

The North Carolina bill creates a permit process for review of applications for the deliberate release of modified organisms. Public notices are required and local governments are preempted from regulation. Although a comprehensive bill, it does not address the thornier question of liability in the event of environmental or health problems caused by releases.[13]

The Minnesota bill follows previous recommendations of the state's Environmental Quality Board by creating rules and a permit process for proposed releases of genetically modified organisms. Liability was not addressed in this bill, either.[14]

The number of bills of this type introduced in the various state legislatures during the 1989 session was greater than in previous sessions. It is anticipated that legislative concern about the release of engineered organisms will grow during the next decade as more releases occur, even if these releases cause no adverse effects. In the event of documentable adverse effects of a release (an unlikely event according to most scientists who have stated an opinion), an avalanche of bills to regulate further releases of engineered organisms could be expected.

Public-Private Partnerships in Environmental Development

While the need and expectations for environmental protection have continued to grow, both in terms of public perception[15] and because of federal mandates found in RCRA, CWA, SDWA and SARA, resource commitments, especially at the federal level, have declined sharply.[16] The shift in environmental responsibility away from the federal government has been especially felt at the state level, where the U.S. EPA Office of Water estimates that there will be a funding shortfall of approximately $309 million in 1995.[17] The convergence of these two trends, increased public demand and decreased federal support, will have far-reaching implications for state efforts to finance and facilitate environmental development.

One of the most promising alternatives state governments are considering is the creation and/or expansion of public-private partnerships for environmental development. Broadly defined, a public-private partnership is a contractual relationship between a public and private party that commits both to providing an environmental service.[18] Although closely related to and even drawing on some aspects of the privatization movement of the 1970s, today's public-private partnerships go far beyond traditional notions of public provision of services through private means of production.

The contemporary approach to public-private partnerships has been expanded to include not only privatization, an arrangement in which a private party owns, builds and operates a facility financed partially or totally by the private party (and usually providing services to multiple municipalities), but also environmental development applications that entail the following:

> Contract Services — an arrangement in which a private partner is contracted to deliver a specific municipal service, usually through a publicly owned facility, for example, garbage collection or operation of a waste water treatment facility;
>
> Turnkey Projects — a venture in which the private partner designs, constructs and operates an environmental facility owned by the public sector;
>
> Developer Financing — a voluntary arrangement in which a private developer finances the construction or expansion of an environmental facility in return for the right to build houses, retail stores or industrial facilities, OR an involuntary arrangement in which developers are charged an impact fee for the public construction of water, sewer or solid waste facilities to serve the developer; and
>
> Merchant Facilities — situations in which a private company makes a business decision to provide an environmental service to a community with the expectation that they will make a profit from the services provided.[19]

Although specific arrangements like those described above are usually executed without direct participation on the part of the state, there are a number of mechanisms through which state governments can act to facilitate the process. One method, used in states such as Vermont, Maine, Alaska and North Dakota, is the establishment of bond banks to provide access to capital markets for municipalities.[20] Bond banks pool multiple local debt issues into a larger bond issue, re-lending the proceeds to local government.

A similar bond option, developed in both New Jersey and Massachusetts, is the Taxable Composite Bond Program. These variable interest rate bonds are designed to provide small- and medium-sized businesses the opportunity to acquire long-term, fixed asset and working capital loans by grouping individual financing into a larger composite bond issue.[21]

Another form of public financial assistance to aid fledgling environmental partnerships is the use of tax incentives, particularly targeted investment tax credits. States including New Jersey, Oregon, Illinois and North Carolina recruit the private sector into environmental service through the use of recycling investment tax credits to manufacturers. These programs offer tax credits to manufacturers for the purchase of recycling equipment.[22] California's 1989 SB 432/AB 1308 and Maine's LD 1431 also created similar tax incentives with credits for recycling equipment up to 40 percent and 30 percent, respectively. On the other side of the public-private equation, Maine has also made available $5 million in capital grants to local and regional governments for recycling equipment and facilities.[23] Pennsylvania, on the other hand, will administer $5 million in low-interest loans to assist companies involved in recycling.[24]

In some states, enabling legislation has been required before localities could even begin to negotiate with private partners. For example, it took a 1986 law in New Jersey to enable municipalities to contract with private companies for the finance, design, construction and operation of waste water treatment plants. With the enactment of the 1986 law, and the subsequent passage of the 1987 New Jersey Statewide Mandatory Source Separation and Recycling Act, the Garden State became the nation's leader in facilitating environmental development ventures. New Jersey's comprehensive program offers an array of options for public-private partners including business recycling loans and loan guarantees, a 50 percent investment tax credit on eligible recycling equipment, a sales tax exemption on eligible recycling equipment and access to state-sponsored market development studies.[25]

Despite the progress states have made in facilitating public-private partnerships, many institutional barriers to the effective implementation of these programs remain. At the federal level, environmental regulations impose restrictions on the use and disposal of publicly owned property funded with federal grant dollars. For example, a project must reimburse the U.S. Treasury for amounts equal to the grant received if the publicly owned facility takes on a private partner. Other federal prerequisites, such as the directive in OMB's Circular A-102, require that federally funded projects remain "separate and identifiable". Furthermore, provisions in the Clean Water Act expressly prohibit loans to privately owned treatment facilities. Perhaps the greatest single impediment to the development of public-private partnerships came with the Tax Reform Act of 1986. The Act reduced the write-offs for accelerated depreciation, making it less profitable to invest in capital improvement projects, many of which involved environmental development projects that were just beginning to get off the ground. Combined with other restrictions contained in the federal tax code, the result was a substantial limitation on the benefits that might accrue to a private party working with or for a private enterprise.[26]

In 1989, however, steps were taken to alleviate some of the problems caused by the Tax Reform Act of 1986. Senate Bill 700, "The Environmental Infrastructure Act of 1989" created a new category of tax exempt bonds. Under this category, state or local governments would issue an obligation to finance any of five types of public investment including waste water treatment, hazardous waste disposal, solid waste disposal, water supply for public use and facilities needed to meet U.S. EPA regulations.[27]

Federal programs notwithstanding, states are likely to continue their efforts to develop mechanisms for facilitating public-private partnerships in the environmental service area. The growing crisis in solid waste disposal capacity will necessitate a renewed commitment to public-private cooperation.

Environmental Referenda

The 1988 election saw more voter initiatives[28] to address environmental and conservation issues than any other election in the past. Across all issues, 230 propositions were voted on in 41 states.[29] For environmental/conservation issues, 14 states considered at least 24 initiatives. Of the 24 environmental measures considered, 17 were approved. The remaining seven issues were soundly rejected. The following examples highlight some of the environmental and/or conservation issues states placed on their ballots in the 1988 election.

In the West, California considered the most propositions (four) aimed at environmental improvement. Of these, the California Safe Drinking Water Bond Law of 1988 (Prop. 81), the Water Conservation Bond Law of 1988 (Prop. 82), and the Clean Water and Water Reclamation Bond Law of 1988 (Prop. 83), were measures seeking voter approval for bond issues totaling $200M. All three measures passed.

ENVIRONMENT

One of the most controversial initiatives on the California ballot was Prop. 105, formally titled "Disclosures to Consumers, Voters, Investors — Initiative Statute." Essentially a right-to-know initiative, Prop. 105 addressed environmental concerns by forcing "advertisers [to include] warnings regarding disposal of toxic household products with exceptions."[30] Despite the complexity of the multipart initiative the measure passed with 64 to 46 percent of the vote.

Oregon voters were asked to consider two environmental initiatives, Measure #6, an extension of the Oregon Indoor Clean Air Act, and Measure #7, the Oregon Rivers Initiative. The former would have expanded the Indoor Clean Air Act to eliminate most designated smoking areas, banning smoking from all public building and even private buildings open to the public (with exceptions), and the latter will add 500 miles of natural waterways to the approximately 1,100 miles already protected by the state Scenic Rivers System.[31] Oregon Measure #6 was soundly defeated by 60 to 40 percent of the votes while Oregon Measure #7 passed by a 63 to 36 percent margin.

In Washington State, voters faced a unique decision on the Fall '88 ballot. They were asked to choose among three options: Initiative Measure 97, which stated, "Shall a hazardous waste cleanup program, partially funded by a 7/10 of 1 percent tax on hazardous substances, be enacted?"; Alternative Measure 97B, which stated, "Shall the legislature's cleanup program, with 0.8 percent hazardous substance tax raising less money, with less coverage of petroleum, be retained?"; or neither alternative. Concerned that the original initiative would result in overly stringent fines against polluters, the oil industry was successful in getting Alternative Measure 97B on the ballot. But despite the financial and political backing of the opposing industry, Initiative Measure 97 prevailed by nearly 185,000 votes over Alternative Measure 97B.

South Dakota voters were asked to decide on two initiated measures concerning environmental and conservation issues. Initiated Measure #1, the "Large-Scale Metallic Mineral Mining Reclamation Act of 1988", would have required operators of any large-scale metallic mineral surface mines to restore affected land to its approximate original contours insofar as is possible without causing rock slides, severe erosion or unstable land. Cast as a trade-off between economic development and environmental protection, the voters of South Dakota chose the former, defeating the initiative by nearly a 20 percent margin (40.5 percent for and 59.5 percent against.) Initiated Measure #2, entitled "Large-Scale Metallic Mineral Mining Tax Act", was also soundly defeated, with 65 percent voting against and 35 percent voting for the measure.

During the 1988 legislative session, Minnesota enacted a law that placed an environment and natural resources trust fund proposal on the ballot (Constitutional Amendment #1). The purpose of the trust fund is to provide a stable source of funding for long-term environmental and natural resources activities that do not receive traditional general fund appropriations.[32] Minnesota voters passed the amendment, with 77 percent of those voting indicating their approval.

The only state in the South to consider an environmentally related initiative (Constitutional Amendment #2) in the 1988 general election was Kentucky. Essentially, the amendment precludes mineral rights owners from strip-mining coal on property in cases where the Broad Form Deed was executed during years when coal was primarily deep-mined. Despite the complexity of the issue and heavy opposition by the coal industry, the measure was approved by one of the widest winning margins, nationwide, in the 1988 election — 83 percent of those voting voted for the amendment, with only 17 percent voting against.

Initiative and referenda outcomes across the nation suggest that citizens are willing to take a stand on protecting the environment at the polls. In 1988 approximately one fourth of all the states utilized some form of popular approval to decide environmental issues. Of the approximately 230 issues decided by voters across the nation, ten percent were directly related to environmental and conservation matters. While historically voters have rejected the majority of citizen initiatives, with roughly two out of three ballot questions losing,[33] there is evidence to suggest that this pattern is changing. According to Charles Price of the California State University at Chico, voters are approving approximately half of all measures securing ballot status.[34] Compare that to the over 70 percent success rate for environmental initiatives considered in the 1988 election.

Notes:

1. James P. Lester, editor, *Environmental Politics and Policy: Theories and Evidence* (Durham, NC: Duke University Press, 1989).

2. *Serious Reduction of Hazardous Wastes* (Washington, DC: U.S. Government Printing Office): 052-003-01048-8.

3. R. Steven Brown, "State Actions for Reducing Hazardous Wastes," (Lexington, KY: The Council of State Governments, 1989).

4. U.S. EPA Memorandum from Michael Strahl to Charles Elkins, October 10, 1989.

5. "Massachusetts Toxic Use Reduction Act," House Bill 6161 (1989 Session).

6. Oregon "Toxics Use Reduction and Hazardous Waste Reduction Act," (Sections 2-16), House Bill 3515 (1989 Session).

7. Tom Jacobs, DuPont de Nemours and Company, personal communication, February 16, 1990.

8. R. Steven Brown, "The State Role in Regulating Biotechnology," Policy Studies Journal 17 (Fall, 1988).

9. R. Steven Brown, "States Regulate Biotechnology," Backgrounder 088802. Lexington, Kentucky: The Council of State Governments.

10. Jule A. Stroik, "State Agency Biotechnology Report and Survey Results: Legislative and Regulatory Activities." Wisconsin Department of Natural Resources, unpublished manuscript, 1987.

11. Hope Shand, "From the States," The Gene Exchange 1 (February 1990). National Wildlife Federation newsletter.

12. Richard D. Godown, "Ten Crucial Biotech Issues in the Next Decade" Genetic Engineering News, Vol. 10, No. 1, January, 1990.

13. North Carolina "Genetically Engineered Organisms Act," (1989 Session).

14. Minnesota "Regulate the Release of Genetically Engineered Organisms," House Bill 1201 (1989 Session).

15. _____, "Roper Reports 89-1," (The Roper Organization, Inc., New York: January 1989.) A 1988 national public opinion poll found that 62% of those polled thought that the country was spending "too little" on "improving the environment," while in 1973 only 45% of those Americans polled thought that the nation was spending too little to improve the environment.

16. U.S. EPA, General Proceedings and Action Agendas from the U.S. Environmental Protection Agency's National Leadership Conference on Building Public-Private Partnerships (Washington, DC: October 26, 1988).

17. U.S. EPA, Public-Private Partnerships (P3) Strategy, PM-225, (Washington, DC: U.S. EPA July, 1989).

18. U.S. EPA, Public-Private Partnership Case Studies: Profiles of Success in Providing Environmental Services, PM-225, (Washington, DC: U.S. EPA, September 1989).

19. Ibid, 4-5.

20. U.S. EPA, Public Private Partnerships Bulletin, (Washington, DC: U.S. EPA, February 1989), 6.

21. Thomas A. Hempill, "Micro Incentives for Business," Waste Age, (February 1989), 136.

22. Ibid, 22.

23. Pete Grogan, "Nine Legislatures Choose Weapons," Waste Age, (February 1989), 53-54.

24. Ibid, 55.

25. New Jersey Department of Environmental Protection, "State Incentives for the New Jersey Recycling Industry: A Guide for the Business Community," (Trenton: New Jersey DEP, 1988).

26. U.S. EPA, Public-Private Partnerships Bulletin, (Washington, DC: U.S. EPA, June 1989), 4.

27. Hemphill, 140-141.

28. NOTE: For the purpose of this article, "voter initiative" refers to any of a number of forms of direct democracy mechanisms in-

cluding referenda; ballot questions, measures or proposals; constitutional amendments; propositions; or any other issue decision based on electorate vote. Thirteen states provide for direct initiative, five states for indirect and three states provide both options. Thirty-seven states have provisions for referenda, while the remaining states rely on some form of constitutional amendment to affect electorate decision-making.

29. Austin Ranney, "Elections '88 — Referendums." Public Opinion, (January/February 1989), 15.

30. R.H. Bork, "10 Environmental Initiatives on State Ballots for November," Initiative and Referendum Report, (September 1988), 8.

31. Ibid, 10.

32. John Helland, "A Recent History of Environmental Ballot Questions in Minnesota and Other States." House Research — Information Brief, (Minnesota House of Representatives, July 1988).

33. Patrick B. McGuigan, "Voters Look Critically at Their Legislators." Initiative and Referendum Report, (December 1988), 18.

Table 8.40
INTERSTATE WATER AGENCIES

State or other jurisdiction	Delaware River Basin Comm. (1961)	Great Lakes Comm. (1955)	Interstate Comm. on the Potomac River Basin (1940)	Interstate Sanitation Comm. (1936)	Klamath River Compact Comm. (1957)	Missouri Basin States Assn. (1981)	New England Governors' Conf., Inc. (1936)	New England Interstate Water Pollution Control Comm. (1947)	Ohio River Basin Comm. (1981)	Ohio River Valley Water Sanitation Comm. (1948)	Susquehanna River Basin Comm. (1971)	Tahoe Regional Planning Agency (1969)	Upper Colorado River Comm. (1948)	Upper Mississippi River Basin Assn. (1981)	Western States Water Council (1965)
Alabama															
Alaska															★
Arizona															★
Arkansas															
California					★							★			★
Colorado						★							★		★
Connecticut	★			★			★	★							
Delaware	★														
Florida															
Georgia															
Hawaii															
Idaho															★
Illinois		★							★	★				★	
Indiana		★							★	★					
Iowa						★								★	
Kansas						★									
Kentucky									★	★					
Louisiana															
Maine							★	★							
Maryland			★								★				
Massachusetts				★			★	★							
Michigan		★													
Minnesota		★				★								★	
Mississippi															
Missouri						★									
Montana						★									★
Nebraska						★									
Nevada											★			★	
New Hampshire							★	★							
New Jersey	★			★											
New Mexico													★		★
New York		★		★				(a)			★				
North Carolina															
North Dakota						★									
Ohio		★							★	★					
Oklahoma															
Oregon					★							★			★
Pennsylvania	★								★	★	★				
Rhode Island							★	★							
South Carolina															

INTERSTATE WATER AGENCIES—Continued

State or other jurisdiction	Delaware River Basin Comm. (1961)	Great Lakes Comm. (1955)	Interstate Comm. on the Potomac River Basin (1940)	Interstate Sanitation Comm. (1936)	Klamath River Compact Comm. (1957)	Missouri Basin States Assn. (1981)	New England Governors' Conf., Inc. (1936)	New England Interstate Water Pollution Control Comm. (1947)	Ohio River Basin Comm. (1981)	Ohio River Valley Water Sanitation Comm. (1948)	Susquehanna River Basin Comm. (1971)	Tahoe Regional Planning Agency (1969)	Upper Colorado River Comm. (1948)	Upper Mississippi River Basin Assn. (1981)	Western States Water Council (1965)
South Dakota	.	.	.	.	.	★	.	.	.	.	.	.	.	.	★
Tennessee	.	.	.	.	.	.	.	.	.	.	.	.	.	.	.
Texas	.	.	.	.	.	.	.	.	.	.	.	.	.	.	★
Utah	.	.	.	.	.	.	.	.	.	.	.	.	★	.	★
Vermont	.	.	.	.	.	.	★	★	.	.	.	.	.	.	.
Virginia	.	.	★	.	.	.	.	.	★	★	.	.	.	.	.
Washington	.	.	.	.	.	.	.	.	.	.	.	.	.	.	★
West Virginia	.	.	.	.	.	★	.	.	★	★	.	.	.	.	.
Wisconsin	.	★	.	.	.	.	.	.	.	.	.	.	.	★	.
Wyoming	.	.	.	.	.	★	.	.	.	.	.	.	★	.	★
Dist. of Columbia	.	.	★	.	.	.	.	.	.	.	.	.	.	.	.
Other information about agency:															
Federal membership	●	.	.	.	.	.	.	.	.	.	.	.	.	.	.
Advisory only	●	●	.	.	●	●	●	.	●	●	●	●	●	.	.
Enforcement powers	.	.	.	●	.	.	.	●(c)	.	.	.	.	●●(d)	.	.
Funding state	●	●	.	●	●	●	●	●	●	●	●	.	.	.	.
Funding federal/state	●	.	●	●	.	.	.	●	●	●	●	●	.	.	.

Key:
★ — Membership in agency
. . . — Not applicable
● — Yes

(a) Not a formal member; cooperates on water issues through the New England/New York Water Council which is part of this conference.
(b) Associate member.
(c) Primarily advisory; has the power to enforce water quality regulations on interstate rivers.
(d) Allocates water from Colorado River.

The Council of State Governments   509

ENVIRONMENT

Table 8.41
LOW-LEVEL RADIOACTIVE WASTE COMPACTS

State	Appalachian States Compact	Central Compact	Central Midwest Compact	Midwest Compact	Northeast Compact	Northwest Compact	Rocky Mountain Compact	Southeast Compact	Southwestern Compact
Alabama	...	...	...	...	...	...	...	★	...
Alaska	...	...	...	...	...	★	...	...	...
Arizona	...	...	...	...	...	...	...	...	★
Arkansas	...	★	...	...	...	...	...	...	...
California	...	...	...	...	...	...	...	...	★
Colorado	...	...	...	...	...	...	★	...	...
Connecticut	...	...	...	...	★	...	...	...	...
Delaware	★	...	...	...	...	...	...	...	...
Florida	...	...	...	...	...	...	...	★	...
Georgia	...	...	...	...	...	...	...	★	...
Hawaii	...	...	...	...	...	★	...	...	...
Idaho	...	...	...	...	...	★	...	...	...
Illinois	...	...	★	...	...	...	...	...	...
Indiana	...	...	...	★	...	...	...	...	...
Iowa	...	...	...	★	...	...	...	...	...
Kansas	...	★	...	...	...	...	...	...	...
Kentucky	...	...	★	...	...	...	...	...	...
Louisiana	...	★	...	...	...	...	...	...	...
Maine	---(a)---								
Maryland	★	...	...	...	...	...	...	...	...
Massachusetts	---(a)---								
Michigan	...	...	...	★	...	...	...	...	...
Minnesota	...	...	...	★	...	...	...	...	...
Mississippi	...	...	...	...	...	...	...	★	...
Missouri	...	...	...	★	...	...	...	...	...
Montana	...	...	...	...	...	★	...	...	...
Nebraska	...	★	...	...	...	...	...	...	...
Nevada	...	...	...	...	...	...	★	...	...
New Hampshire	---(a)---								
New Jersey	...	...	...	...	★	...	...	...	...
New Mexico	...	...	...	...	...	...	★	...	...
New York	---(a)---								
North Carolina	...	...	...	...	...	...	...	★	...
North Dakota	...	...	...	...	...	...	...	...	★
Ohio	...	...	...	★	...	...	...	...	...
Oklahoma	...	★	...	...	...	...	...	...	...
Oregon	...	...	...	...	...	★	...	...	...
Pennsylvania	★	...	...	...	...	...	...	...	...
Rhode Island	---(a)---								
South Carolina	...	...	...	...	...	...	...	★	...
South Dakota	...	...	...	...	(a)	...	...	...	★
Tennessee	...	...	...	...	...	...	...	★	...
Texas	---(b)---								
Utah	...	...	...	...	...	...	★	...	...
Vermont	---(a)---								
Virginia	...	...	...	...	...	...	...	★	...
Washington	...	...	...	...	...	★	...	...	...
West Virginia	★	...	...	...	...	...	...	...	...
Wisconsin	...	...	...	★	...	...	...	...	...
Wyoming	...	...	...	...	...	...	★	...	...

Source: U.S. Department of Energy.
Key:
★ — Party state
(a) Undeclared.
(b) Independent.

HOMELESSNESS IN THE STATES

By Lee Walker

Problem and Predicament

Homelessness has spread throughout America during the 1980s. From 1983 to 1989, elected officials, government agencies, advocacy groups, non-profit organizations and the media have observed the homeless, with the hope of finding the causes and cures for their predicament. But each year, the number of homeless and the complexities of homelessness appear to be greater than before.

Many observers are beginning to recognize homelessness as a widespread problem in urban and rural America. The causes and characteristics of homelessness are endemic to combinations of overlapping factors including unemployment, underemployment, mental illness, the unavailability of affordable housing, domestic violence, parentless children and other less visible personal crises.

While there is a general understanding as to who is homeless and how they became so, there is disagreement regarding the scope of the problem — how many Americans are homeless? Although state officials recognize that homelessness is a growing problem, it is a problem that is exceedingly difficult to measure at the state level and almost impossible to measure at the national level. As state officials grapple with the problem of how to measure their homeless populations, national non-profit organizations and federal agencies argue over the estimated number of homeless Americans.

The federal government's response to homelessness generally has taken the form of sporadic reactions to pressure from advocacy groups for the homeless. But neither advocates for the homeless nor state officials concerned with their state's increasing homeless populations have been more than mildly successful in their attempts to move the federal government toward addressing homelessness as a national problem. The 1987 Stewart B. McKinney Homeless Assistance Act (P.L. 100-77), for example, has been praised as a Congressional initiative. But as legislation, it has been labeled a Band-Aid and criticized for its lack of funds.[1]

Many private and non-profit groups and organizations, however, have responded overwhelmingly to homelessness. Charitable and religious groups and organizations are the foundation of support to the nation's homeless. But their resources are not abundant enough to keep pace with nationwide increases.

States' Response to Homelessness

States are becoming the pivotal level of government for dealing with homelessness and its related problems, including unemployment and underemployment; lack of affordable housing and mental health facilities; and a shortage of health and welfare services. Unable to rely as heavily on traditional federal programs and faced with limited resources, states now are willing to collaborate with local governments and the private and non-profit sectors.

States have addressed homelessness in a number of ways with varying degrees of success based on the perspectives of policymakers. The Council of State Governments gathered information on homelessness in the states in late 1988 by surveying six different state government sources: (1) governors' offices; (2) selected legislative committee chair-

---

Lee Walker is a policy analyst at The Council of State Governments' headquarters office.

men; (3) legislative service and research agencies; (4) community affairs agencies; (5) health and social service agencies; and (6) state budget offices.[2]

Governors' initiatives have taken several forms: advisory councils, task forces and interagency groups. New programs for, and policy directives to, executive branch agencies whose programs affect homeless persons are other means by which governors have addressed the problem in their states. And most significantly, they are budgeting state and federal funds to support state programs for the homeless.

Governors' offices in at least 24 states have taken policy actions or initiatives in the area of homelessness. In another eight states, initiatives were being planned. Only six of the governors' offices that responded indicated they had no specific initiatives directed toward homelessness.

Each governor who responded to The Council of State Governments' survey indicated that homelessness is a problem in his/her state — 34 percent of the governors characterized it as a serious problem, while 66 percent said it is a moderate one. In addition, 89 percent of the governors said federal programs for the homeless are inadequate in their state and 81 percent also said they have inadequate state programs for the homeless.

An overriding belief that state government should assume some of the responsibility for addressing homelessness may be another reason for the governors' initiatives. Seventeen or 46 percent respondents said the states should have the primary responsibility. It is significant to note, however, that 10 of those 17 governors further indicated that all levels of government — federal, state and local — should share responsibility. Only eight of the governors' offices that responded said the federal government should assume primary responsibility for addressing homelessness, while 10 indicated that local governments should bear the responsibility.

But homelessness in the states is not solely an executive concern. A group of legislative committee chairmen, selected from committees whose functions include programs that impact the homeless, such as housing, health, welfare and human resources, also agreed that homelessness is a problem in states. Of 30 respondents from a total of 23 states, half said that it is a serious problem, and the other half characterized it as a moderate one. In addition, 79 percent of the respondents felt that homelessness in their state is increasing, while 16 percent said it is unchanging. Only one respondent said it is decreasing.

The legislators' views regarding the scope and seriousness of homelessness in their states may account for the amount of legislative studies and legislation that have focused specifically on homelessness. The survey of legislative service and research agencies across the states revealed that along with the many task force, executive branch agency, local government and private organization reports, many state legislatures also have produced their own reports on homelessness. At least 27 states in 1988 already had enacted legislation specifically targeted toward the homeless (see Figure 1). Typically, that legislation concerns housing, health and human services for the homeless and those who are "at risk."

Estimates of the states' homeless populations

Many of the legislative service and research agencies reported problems measuring homelessness in their states by traditional quantitative methods. Eleven of the responding states could not provide estimates of the size of the homeless population in their jurisdictions. And 13 of the states said their legislatures employed no method or sources to determine the number of homeless. Of the 37 states that have tried to estimate the number of homeless, 54 percent have used a process that is of limited use for policy-making and program development.

The methods and sources identified by these legislative service and research agencies in most states are questionable. Many agencies said the only numbers available for their use are based on "guesstimates" or informal surveys. Other agencies indicated that the number was based on extrapolations from the U.S. Department of Housing and Urban Development (HUD) estimates of the national

HOUSING

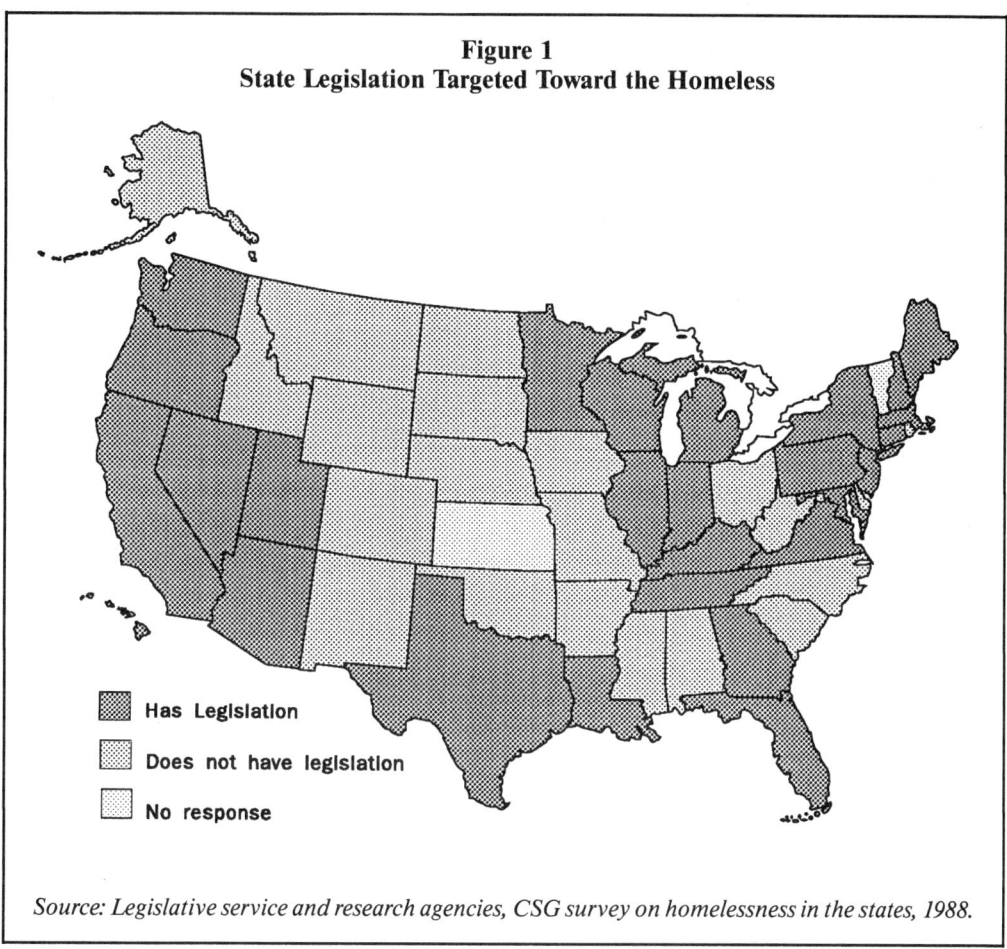

Figure 1
State Legislation Targeted Toward the Homeless

Source: Legislative service and research agencies, CSG survey on homelessness in the states, 1988.

homeless population; from case studies of homelessness in urban areas of their state; from service provider estimates of homeless served; from the number of beds or persons in shelters; or from street surveys of persons appearing to be homeless. Many legislatures also have been relying on homeless population estimates prepared by executive branch agencies that provide services to the homeless.

These approaches present problems in getting accurate and reliable estimates of a state's homeless population. The U.S. General Accounting Office (GAO), for example, found HUD's methodology and its homeless population surveys unreliable. What was unacceptable was HUD's and other organization's approach determining national estimates using urban case studies, service provider estimates and shelter or street counts (GAO said these techniques might be reliable if they were applied locally).

Urban case studies fail to count the numbers of rural homeless, while charitable groups' estimates tend to inflate the probable number of homeless or miss portions of the population altogether. Shelter and street counts miss many of the urban homeless who avoid shelters, incorrectly presume that a significant representation of homeless people are on the streets and fail to consider rural areas in which there are few shelters and little likelihood of street camping. Generally, state executive branch agencies that estimate their state's homeless population based on these numbers can only guess at the number of other homeless persons who do not come into contact with their particular agency. Although collaboration between state agencies might provide a more accurate estimate of each state's homeless population, there is little evidence that is being done.

The perspectives of executive branch service agencies

State community affairs agencies and health and social service agencies are two government agencies that might effectively collaborate services to their states' homeless population and collect and evaluate data on the recipients of their services. Each deals with direct service providers and is responsible for providing services or developing resources, including federal programs that are critical to the homeless and essential to their states' efforts in preventing homelessness.

As the primary state government connection to HUD, many community affairs agencies can provide important views on the success and appropriateness of federal programs, primarily the McKinney Act. To varying degrees, their efficiency and effectiveness in administering the housing and community development programs that constitute the core of their activities depend on the clarity of guidelines and the administrative cooperation they receive from HUD.

It is significant that community affairs agencies in at least 20 states claimed that HUD administrative support for the McKinney Act is not adequate for their individual states. Sixteen of the respondents to the survey said it is adequate. The responding agencies that gave views on administrative guideline support for the McKinney Act indicated that HUD's regulations and guidance are inconsistent and that program requirements are too inflexible and restrictive to be effective.

Sixty-two percent of the respondents, however, said McKinney Act programs are appropriate for the needs of the homeless in their state. Predictably, 95 percent of the respondents indicated McKinney Act funds are not adequate to meet the needs of their states' homeless population. It is difficult to determine whether there is a correlation between the allocation of those funds — equally distributed between state government, local government and non-profit organizations — and the agencies' perceptions that McKinney Act funds are inadequate for meeting their service needs. A distinction is necessary, for example, as to whether the amount of federal funds is inadequate, or whether funds are inadequate and the preferred remedy would be an increase in federal funds.

It is equally difficult to determine whether the states' program efforts are adequate. Of the 22 community affairs agency respondents, 59 percent said their individual state's efforts are not adequate, while 41 percent felt they are. However, many of these agencies qualified their responses by noting that in addition to increased funding support, more intergovernmental and intersectoral cooperation and collaboration is necessary. While many respondents said their states are progressing toward more collaborative approaches and sophisticated programs for the homeless, they also expressed concern that lack of funding would prevent or hamper implementation and ongoing support for those programs.

Lack of funding, in fact, is the key issue in the states' efforts to address homelessness, according to the health and social services agency respondents. Those agencies indicated that the federal and state governments are most useful as program funding sources. Perhaps more than any others in state government, these agencies are in touch with homeless individuals, citizen groups, churches and synagogues, charities and non-profit organizations. From that vantage point, they can see which providers and programs are most helpful to the needs of the homeless. It also is important that 80 percent of the respondents indicated that non-profits offer the most effective programs for helping the homeless and that in 46 percent of those states, the programs are operated with federal, state and/or local programs or support. Since the demand for non-profits' services has increased beyond existing resources, many respondents were concerned that those groups would not be able to continue providing effective assistance without an increase in state or federal funding.

That perspective is significant when coupled with the agencies' assessments of the scope of homelessness in their states. All of these agencies said that homelessness is a problem, and 38 percent characterized it as a serious one (see Figure 2). More significantly, however, 89 percent of the agencies believed that homelessness is increasing; only one respondent said it is decreasing (see Figure 3). The factors that cause and characterize homelessness — such as unemployment and underemployment, lack of mental health services and facilities, lack of affordable housing, alcoholism, drug abuse and domestic violence — are not likely to be resolved in the immediate future.

These agencies' efforts to count the homeless have been as unsuccessful as other attempts to estimate the national and state homeless populations. For example, as many as 69 percent of the respondents felt that methods to count the homeless in their state are not reasonably accurate (see Figure 4). Many legislative service and research agencies also have been unable to make accurate estimates, and many that have what they believe to be accurate estimates received the numbers from their health and social service agencies. Because the homeless constitute a mobile, dif-

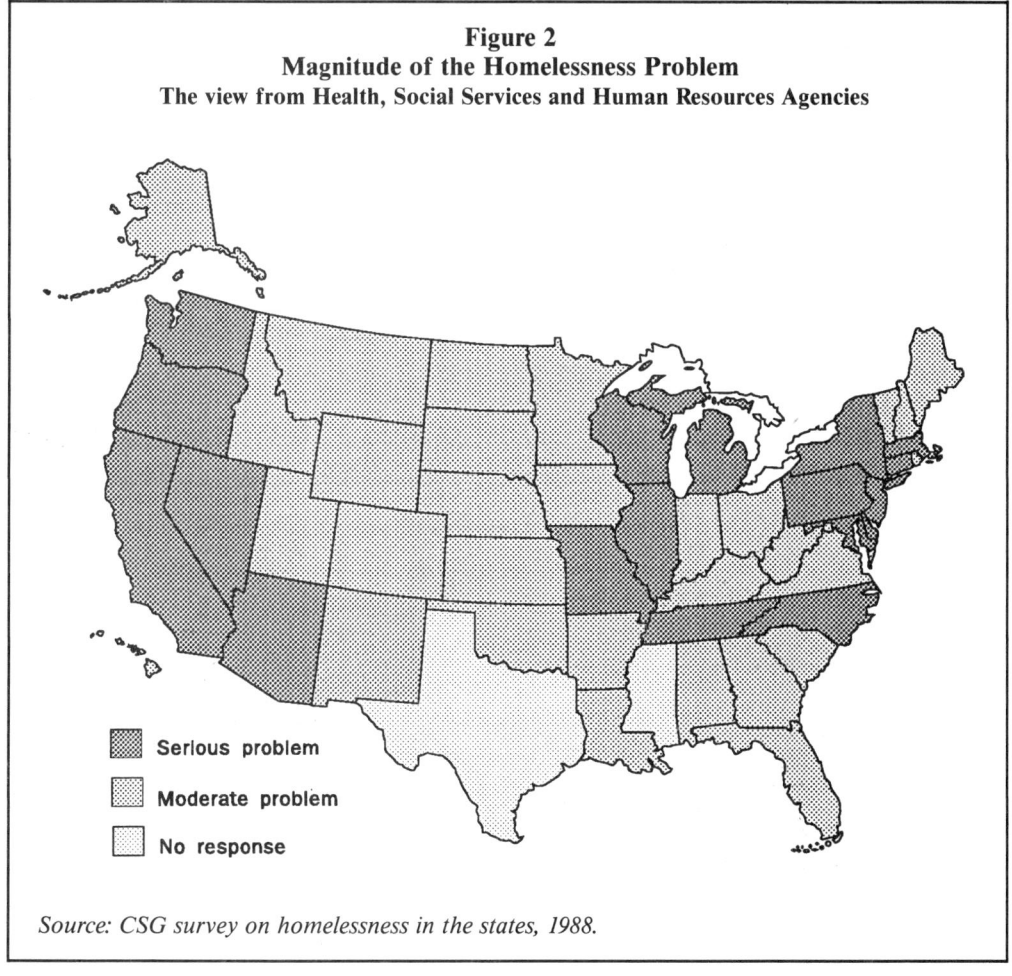

Figure 2
Magnitude of the Homelessness Problem
The view from Health, Social Services and Human Resources Agencies

- Serious problem
- Moderate problem
- No response

Source: CSG survey on homelessness in the states, 1988.

HOUSING

ficult to identify and changing population, agencies say the usual empirical methods of measurement are not effective. As a result, most state homeless population estimates are inaccurate.

Expenditures for the homeless

State budget offices have similar problems in quantifying the amount of state and federal funds budgeted and expended on each state's homeless population, unless those funds are specifically earmarked or programs are specifically entitled for the homeless. Many state and federal programs that ultimately serve the homeless, such as affordable housing, mental health, welfare and other social service programs that deal with substance abuse, domestic violence or runaway children, are not always identified as such. State budget office respondents to The Council of State Governments survey advised that state and federal funds earmarked for homeless programs were relatively easy to track. But the overlap of state and federal fiscal years, carryforward of federal funds in program areas and the allocation of funds for programs that serve the homeless as part of a larger clientele, such as the mentally ill, make tracking expenditures on each state's homeless programs an almost impossible task, given current data.

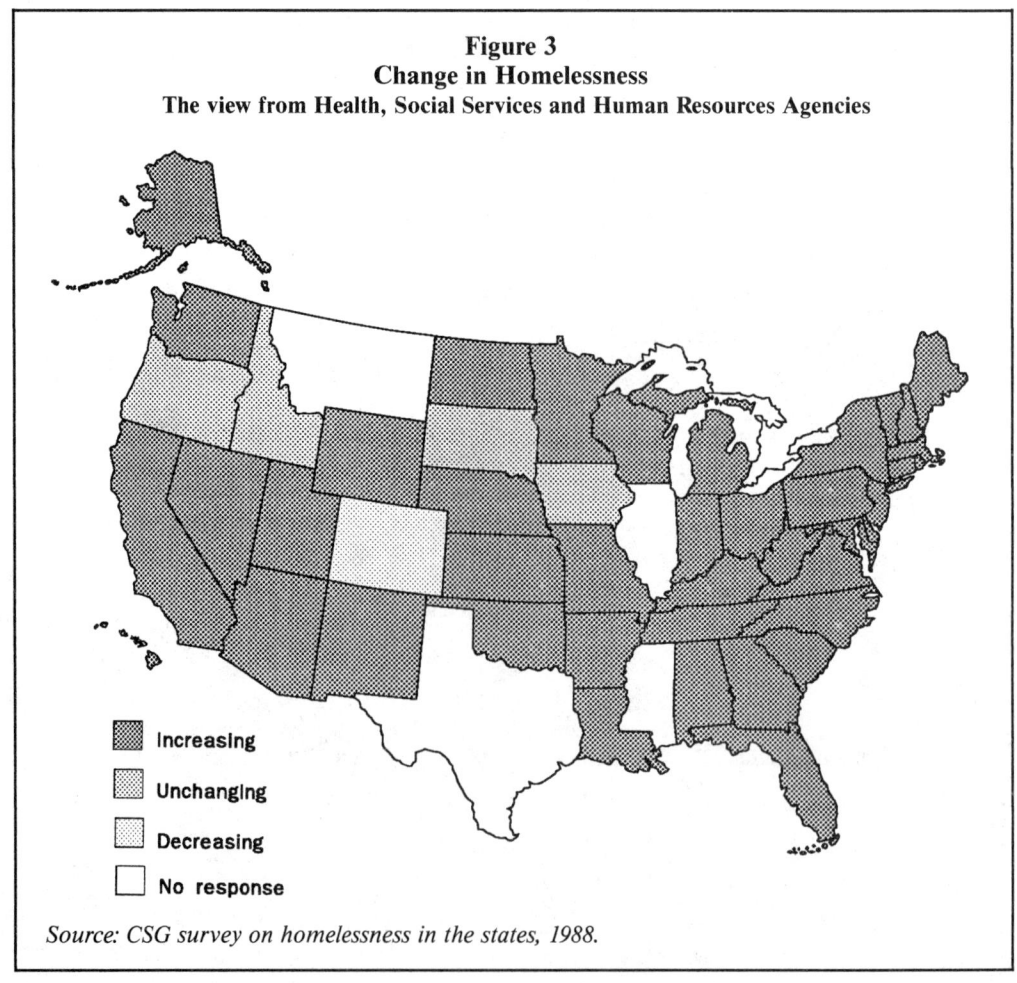

**Figure 3
Change in Homelessness
The view from Health, Social Services and Human Resources Agencies**

Source: *CSG survey on homelessness in the states, 1988.*

516 The Book of the States 1990-91

HOUSING

Consequently, it may not be significant that 13 states reported no state funds were appropriated for programs specifically entitled or targeted for the homeless in fiscal 1988; funds may have been allocated to other programs that address the cause. Comparing California's expenditure of $68.5 million for homeless programs to a state that reports no expenditures is invalid without knowing how much was spent on programs that indirectly address homelessness. In at least 19 states during 1988 state expenditures for the homeless, programs were not a significant budgetary issue, according to the budget officials who responded. As a significant budgetary issue — one that has a substantial aggregate impact on a state's expenditures or revenues — homelessness would likely capture the attention of state budget officials regardless of how dispersed or concentrated its budgetary impact.

Since homelessness is a crisis of diverse causes, a key question is whether to appropriate funds for the homeless as a target population, or instead appropriate funds to remedy the causes of homelessness. From a policy and budgetary standpoint, these are dissimilar approaches. In each case, there are questions that need to be addressed concerning program and administrative overlap, interagency cooperation, service provider capacity, the diversity of the causes of homeless-

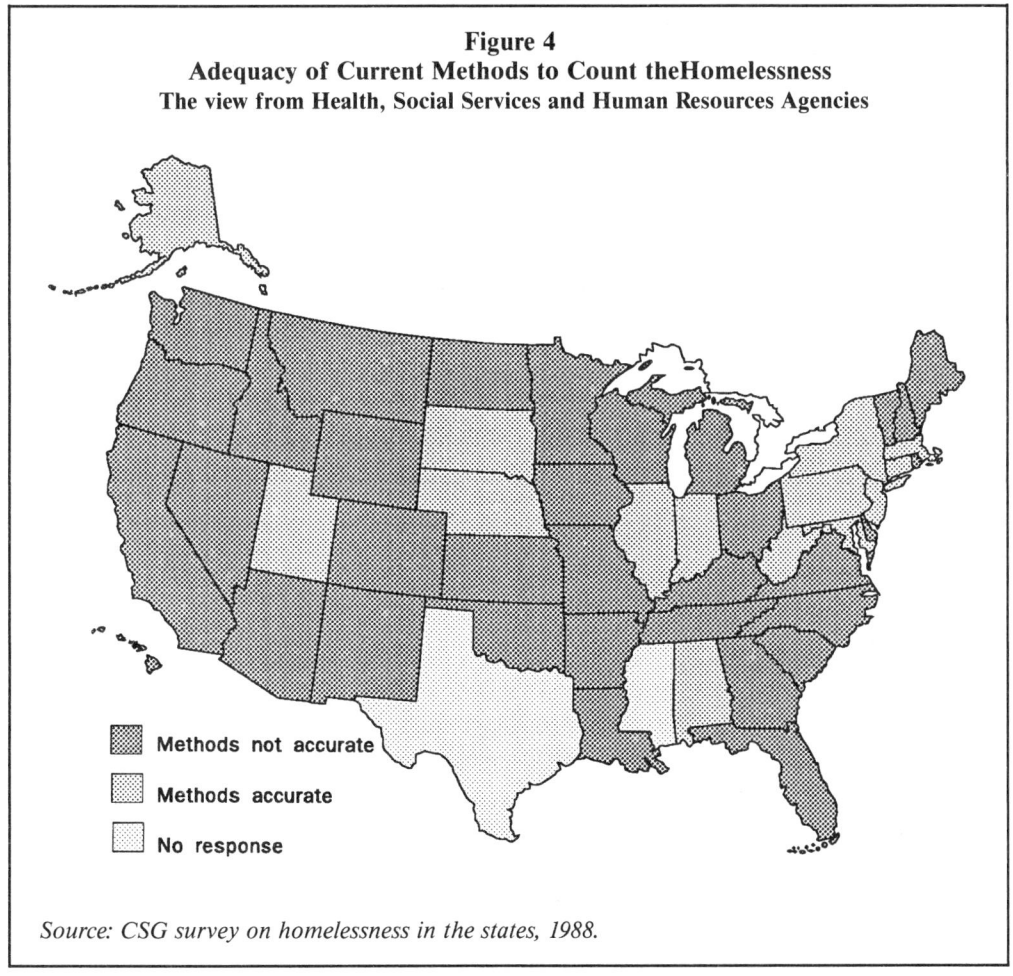

Figure 4
Adequacy of Current Methods to Count theHomelessness
The view from Health, Social Services and Human Resources Agencies

- Methods not accurate
- Methods accurate
- No response

Source: CSG survey on homelessness in the states, 1988.

ness and the size of the homeless population. For example, while a smaller, somewhat homogeneous homeless population might be easier to target, a homeless population that is large and diverse might be better served by increasing funds to a variety of existing program areas. Each state is compelled to consider these issues as they devise the strategies for developing policies and funding programs that address the homelessness problem.

Outlook

In 1990, homelessness will continue to be a complex and increasing problem in most states. All of The Council of State Governments survey respondents from governors' offices, health and social service agencies and legislative committees said their state has a homelessness problem. Eighty-five percent of the health and social service agencies claimed that homelessness in their state is increasing and 58 percent predicted that the problem will be worse in 1990. The predominant causes of homelessness are rooted deeply enough that an immediate remedy is unlikely. Personal crises that may lead to homelessness — such as mental illness, drug addiction, alcoholism, unemployment, underemployment and domestic violence — will continue to be as prevalent as they have been for the past decade. There is no indication that these social and economic trends will be altered in 1990.

Counting the states' and the nation's homeless will continue to be problematic. National counts now are based on false premises, and state estimates — when attempted — are based on unreliable methods. There is reason to believe, however, that states may reexamine their methods of counting the homeless and devise more accurate approaches for determining the size of their homeless populations. In the event that occurs, the national estimate could be calculated as the aggregate of state homeless populations. Even with variances, such a calculation would provide a more realistic number of the nation's homeless than the wide ranges that are used.

The federal response to homelessness will continue to be sporadic and incremental — spurred by homeless advocacy groups, slowed by national policy concerns and budget limitations and complicated by diverse political interests. The impact of federal domestic policies developed during the 1980s makes it improbable that any significant federal legislative or budgetary response to the nation's homelessness problem can be effected in the immediate future. In 1990, in spite of the McKinney Act's limited impact, the most that can realistically be expected in the way of a helpful federal response is cooperation, collaboration and better communication — of which, as many states complain, only a minimal amount has occurred since the emergence of homelessness as a national problem.

Regardless of the federal response, the states, local governments and third sector non-profit groups will need to form support and information-sharing networks to address the causes and characteristics of homelessness and administer the programs funded by the McKinney Act. Such initiatives and policy action may prompt Congress and the administration to develop more cooperative policies.

Third sector non-profits, religious groups and various other advocates not only have generated considerable interest and concern, but also have provided direct services to the nation's homeless. But the resources of many of these organizations, such as churches and charities, are being depleted as homelessness continues to increase. Without support and cooperation from all levels of government, their efforts will begin to erode.

In the long term, the third sector could greatly influence domestic policies and programs at all levels of government. Many national non-profit organizations advocate intergovernmental and intersectoral collaboration, with an emphasis on a more positive federal response. In the short term, the third sector supports and assists the immediate needs of the homeless. But to bring about effective government action at any level, these organizations must distinguish between the immediate needs of the homeless and the policies and programs that will be necessary to remedy and prevent homelessness in the long term.

The development of those policy and programmatic responses requires information that assesses the nature and gauges the extent of each state's homeless problem. Current policies, in the absence of such information, have overlooked crucial aspects of the homelessness problem, such as rural homelessness and the urban homeless who do not make use of shelters.

Although homelessness is a national crisis, the homeless in each state are a unique population. Each state must examine its homeless population, identify the causes and characteristics of their plight, and act accordingly. Non-profit organizations and policy-makers will then know whether emergency services — food, clothing, shelter and medical — can help the homeless out of their predicament. But more importantly, they will know whether affordable housing, employment opportunities, mental health care, education, social services, or some combination thereof, will reduce or prevent the personal crises that cause homelessness in each state.

To accomplish these tasks, states will be in the best position of all levels of government to initiate and coordinate the necessary collaboration and communication among third sector groups, local governments and the federal government. The shrinking federal domestic role will compel states to take a more active role regarding state and national policies that create domestic programs. Unable to wait for federal relief, states will be forced to take the initiative. As a result, it is reasonable to assume an intensified state advocacy effort and an evolving era in state-federal relations.

States will need to rethink their approaches to domestic problems, formulate new and more comprehensive strategies for dealing with domestic issues, devise specific methods appropriate for their circumstances and become more active in state and national domestic policy-making.

Homelessness is one of the many critical domestic policy challenges that states will continue to face. To meet the challenge, states will have to determine the causes and characteristics of their homelessness problem; develop reliable methods of counting their homeless; and serve as intergovernmental and intersectoral leaders in constructing and executing domestic policies.

Notes

1. The Stewart B. McKinney Homeless Assistance Act (P.L. 100-77) became law in July 1987. The McKinney Act includes nearly 20 different provisions to address the needs of the homeless by providing for emergency shelter, food, health care, mental health care, housing, educational programs, job training and other community services. The Act's authorization for fiscal 1987 was $442.7 million, and the final appropriation was $355 million. For fiscal 1988, it was authorized at $616 million, and $357 was appropriated. McKinney Act programs in fiscal 1988 received 43 percent less funding than in fiscal 1987.

On November 7, 1988, President Ronald Reagan signed the Omnibus McKinney Homeless Assistance Act of 1988 (P.L. 100-628), which reauthorized the McKinney Act for another two years — $634 million in fiscal 1989 and $676 million in fiscal 1990 for McKinney programs. Congress appropriated $388 million for the McKinney Act programs in fiscal 1989. President George Bush's 1990 budget proposes funding McKinney Act programs at $676 million for fiscal 1990.

2. The Council of State Governments conducted a national survey on homelessness in the states during the latter part of 1988 to gather existing data and information from officials in the best position to develop valid and useful perspectives on homelessness in their individual states. Six groups of public officials in each of the 50 states were queried: governors' offices; legislative committee chairmen; community affairs agencies; health, social services and human resources agencies; and state budget offices. The survey's purpose was to take a "point-in-time" approach to a problem that is evolving in the states, and evaluate the results within the context of the current literature and findings on homelessness.

For further details and responses from The Council of State Governments' 1988 survey refer to *Homelessness in the States* (Lexington, Ky.: The Council of State Governments, 1989).

CHAPTER NINE

INTER-GOVERNMENTAL AFFAIRS

DEVELOPMENTS IN FEDERAL-STATE RELATIONS

By Norman Beckman

Introduction

As the new decade begins, the major actors seem willing to support cooperative federalism with a focus on the states as the hinge in the intergovernmental process. States have been placed in a position of policy leadership with the federal government cheering on the one side and local governments delivering services on the other. The federal system continues adapting to incremental changes and "muddles through." Strategies being adopted for drug control, reduced air pollution, and increased educational achievement vary with the particular issues involved, focusing on bottom line feasibility rather than logical consistent division of labor. Even the prospective and elusive "peace dividend" seems unlikely to bring about sweeping changes in the way these governments do business together.

President Bush during his first year in office began a number of initiatives that marked him as a consensus builder in state capitals. The president has explicitly sought out state views in devising domestic initiatives for the war on drugs, clean air, home ownership and health care. The president also has explicitly addressed the subject of intergovernmental cooperation. In a July 1989 speech to the National Governors' Association, Bush reaffirmed his support requiring federal agencies to consider how new proposals affect state and local governments. "To cure our nation of illiteracy, drug abuse and crime, we must act in tandem, president with governor, and governor with mayor, up and down the line," he said.

Bush also revised the previous administration's 1990 budget proposal to increase aid for drought relief, the "Head Start" preschool program and math and science programs; restore $1.7 billion in Medicaid cuts and expand Medicaid to cover more poor pregnant women and infants. Bush's fiscal 1991 budget also recognized many state concerns. There is no attempt to cap Medicaid spending and, tying in with governors' concerns, funding is preserved for other entitlement programs such as foods stamps and aid to families with dependent children (AFDC), and increases for many education, environmental and anti-drug programs.

This conciliatory approach to intergovernmental cooperation is especially welcomed as several new trends complicate the intergovernmental process. One such trend is the decline in constant dollars from the federal level with an increased use of non-fiscal approaches, which include regulatory mandates and pre-emptions. These are new constraints on states at a time when the states are being encouraged to use innovative approaches in delivering services. In addition, there is an increased focusing on broad policy issues and target populations, such as the control of drug abuse, the homeless, children and the elderly. Recognition of the need to relate to the "whole person", however, is not reflected in the continuing pattern of federal categorical grants-in-aid and service delivery systems.

To measure the public's perception of the state of federalism, each year the U.S. Advisory Commission on Intergovernmental Relations polls changing public attitudes on government and taxes. The latest poll taken in June 1989 indicated that the federal role in

---

Dr. Norman Beckman is professor of political science at Howard University and was formerly director of The Council of State Governments' Washington Office.

our federal system is now being looked at more favorably than in recent years:

- For the past 18 years, the commission's poll has asked, "Which do you think is the worst tax, that is the least fair?" In 1989, local property taxes were rated as the least fair by 32 percent of the respondents. Twenty-seven percent of the public rated the federal income tax as the least fair. The result is a clear change from the 1979-1988 trend in which the federal income tax was consistently rated as the worst.
- One-third of the respondents to the 1989 poll chose the federal government as giving them the most for their money. Local government was chosen by 29 percent. These current results mark the first time since 1982 that the federal government clearly rated higher than state and local governments in this area.
- The federal government was perceived to have too much power, compared to state and local governments. Sixty-one percent of the respondents said the federal government has too much power; 9 percent said state government; and 4 percent said local government.
- The poll also asked, "Which level of government do you think needs more power today?" Twenty-two percent said state governments need more power; 34 percent said local governments and 5 percent, the federal government.

Looming over Congress and the presidency will be the November 1990 elections, including 36 gubernatorial contests. Those races will determine the two biggest issues of the early 1990s: the struggle over abortion rights and the fight to redraw the boundaries of congressional districts after the April 1990 Census. State legislatures convening in 1991 will have the responsibility for congressional redistricting, a state activity not likely to be ignored as the U.S. House of Representatives acts on legislation affecting the states. In 1990 and 1991, all politics may be state politics.

Program Initiatives

Education

The most dramatic example of federal/state cooperation was the president's September 1989 education summit with 49 of the nation's governors. During their summit at the University of Virginia, unprecedented since the time of FDR, the president and governors agreed upon six goals, which include having every preschooler ready to learn; increasing the high school graduation rate from 72 percent to at least 90 percent; making American students first in the world in mathematics and science achievement, reducing adult illiteracy from 12.5 percent to zero; making every school free of drugs and violence; and having students in grades four, eight and 12 demonstrate competency over challenging subject matter in English, math, science, geography and history.

The governors, at their February 1990 annual meeting in Washington, announced 21 objectives for reaching national education goals by the year 2000. The plan was developed by counterpart White House and National Governors' Association staff following the education summit. The specific objectives added by the governors "include preschool, nutrition and health care for all disadvantaged children, a 50 percent increase in students competent in a second language and a kindergarten through grade 12 drug prevention program in every school district." Legislation has been introduced in both houses of Congress to provide additional impetus to the goal setting and follow through.

The president's education proposals included a $250 million program for merit schools, cash awards to recognize superior teachers, a national science scholars program, a $100 million curriculum innovation addition to the magnet schools program, and help for states to develop alternative certification for teachers and principals.

Tax Exempt Financing

State officials also have a stake in congressional and presidential reaction to recommendations by the Anthony Commission on Public Finance. The commission's November 1989 report, Preserving the Federal-State-Local Partnership: The Role of Tax-Exempt Financing, urged federal tax law changes to ease financing of state and local projects. The commission called for revisions in the U.S. tax code and public policy that would:

- recognize the right of state and local governments to use tax-exempt debt to finance basic government facilities and services;
- give Congress responsibility to prevent abuses in tax-exempt financing for non-governmental projects;
- set arbitrage restrictions by limiting state and local governments' use of bond proceeds to exploit interest rate differentials created solely by the tax law;
- promote federal, state and local cooperation to encourage tax-exempt financing for public facilities and services.

Congress extended through September 30, 1990 existing tax-exempt bond provisions and tax credits of particular interest to the states. These include mortgage revenue bonds and credit certificates, low-income housing tax credits, small issue manufacturing bonds, more flexible arbitrage rebate rules, targeted jobs tax credits, employee education credits and research and development credits.

In addition, if the state and local public interest groups can reconcile their differences, there is a good chance that Congress will reverse the Bellas-Hess Supreme Court decision permitting state collection of $2.5 billion per year in sales taxes on interstate mail order sales.

Drug Control

In his anti-drug initiatives, the president called for increased federal aid to state and local criminal justice systems. In what many states see as more federal mandates without adequate funding, the plan called for states to enact minimum mandatory sentences for serious drug crimes, alternative sentencing statutes, asset forfeiture laws, school yard laws, user accountability and drug-free workplace statutes, increasing the burden on prosecutors and correctional facilities. Congress has acted by adding more money to the war on drugs. A recently released report of the Federal Courts Study Committee would shift drug case load to state courts.

Clean Air

After years of impasse, reauthorization of the Clean Air Act is expected in 1990. The Clean Air bill extends by up to 20 years deadlines for polluted areas to meet standards for ozone, carbon monoxide and particulates and prescribes new control requirements for polluted areas. The bill requires all cars sold in the United States to meet substantial reductions in tailpipe emissions standards, beginning in 1994. It also mandates reductions in utility emissions of sulfur dioxide and nitrogen oxides, which cause acid rain; and requires emissions standards to be established for major sources of nearly 200 toxic pollutants. Likely to be included in the act is an alternative fuels program for the nine most polluted cities. A majority of cities are required to set higher ozone standards by the year 2000.

Proposals to reduce acid rain include reducing 10 million tons of sulfur dioxide from emissions by the year 2000. All states will be required to develop a permit system for such emissions. States failing to do so would be subject to sanctions including a ban on construction of major new sources of air pollution, the withholding of highway funds, except for projects that enhance air quality or meet safety conditions, and the withholding of state air grants.

Civil Rights

Proposed bills would expand civil rights protections by reversing four recent U.S. Supreme Court decisions limiting the legal remedies available to women and minorities claiming job discrimination. The decisions had made job discrimination more difficult to prove, voided a city minority contract set-aside program and expanded non-minorities' right to raise claims of reverse discrimination.

The proposed Americans with Disabilities Act bars discrimination on the basis of the handicap in private-sector employment, public services and public accommodations. It mandates new or renovated public accommodations and public transportation be made accessible to the disabled. Only 17 states have laws that require public and private buildings to be accessible to disabled persons in employment, public accommodations and services, and transportation.

A committee that studied habeas corpus reform as required by the 1988 Anti-Drug Abuse Act has proposed bills to ensure fair process for defendants while speeding the appeals process. A Senate version establishes national standards for effective assistance of counsel. States adopting the higher standards would be permitted to have expedited appeals processes. Finally, proposed whistle-blower protection legislation would protect workers who call the public's attention to unsafe work conditions.

Social Concerns

A proposed National Community Services Act provides $100 million for U.S. Department of Education programs to increase school and college-based community services for youth. States would receive funds to create school-based and school-community partnership service programs. The act also provides $100 million for a full-time Youth Services Corps and $100 million for a National Service Demonstration program to make grants to states for full- or part-time national service programs.

Congress is considering increasing funding and improving the coordination of federal, state and local efforts to improve adult literacy and employability. The Stewart B. McKinney Homeless Assistance Act is due to be reauthorized. The bill's 20 programs for the homeless include housing, health and mental health care, education and job training. Proposals for substantive changes in housing programs are anticipated by consolidating funding into a block grant for emergency shelter grants, transitional and permanent housing and supplemental assistance for facilities assisting the homeless.

Hearings have been held on bills authorizing a new corporation to support state and local strategies for achieving more affordable housing for low/moderate income families and to increase home ownership. Also held were hearings on bills to provide funding to state health agencies to help achieve the national health objectives for the year 2000 to be established by the Secretary of Health and Human Services in September 1990.

National Transportation Policy

In March 1990, the secretary of Transportation announced a new transportation policy, which the National Governors' Association commended for its comprehensive multimodal approach that should help focus public and private transportation efforts. Concern was expressed over the national policy recommendations to increase the state and local share of federal transportation assistance projects, including lowering the federal matching ratios on highway assistance to get greater leverage on state, local and private funds. Federal operating assistance and share of financing for mass transit projects also would be reduced and federal hazardous material regulations would be extended to intrastate shipments.

Other Federal-State Legislation

Congress has done more than wrestle over a pay raise for itself and judge its members' ethical behavior. Among the 154 public laws enacted in 1989, Congress reauthorized programs to curb child abuse and extended for five years major nutrition programs, including the Women, Infants and Children (WIC) Supplemental Food, School Lunch and Summer Food Service. The reauthorization of the Vocational Education Act granted states more flexibility to design programs and earmarked funds to serve special populations.

Congress approved spending $166 billion over 10 years to bail out and reform saving and loan institutions. The minimum wage was raised from $3.35 to $4.55 an hour over three years. Emergency natural disaster assistance was approved for Hurricane Hugo, California's earthquake and farm drought. The Medicare Catastrophic Coverage Act, passed in 1988, was repealed. Desecration of the U.S. flag was forbidden, at least by law, if not by the Constitution.

Final action is expected on a comprehensive child care package administered through the states. Congress also considered legislation on campaign finance reform, uniform poll closing and liberalized voter registration.

Intergovernmental Fiscal Relations

Impact of the 1991 Budget on the States

The administration's budget calls for increased funding for education — including Head Start — drug abuse, space and science, air safety, and nuclear waste cleanup and other environmental programs. Some 24 program terminations are recommended. There, however, is only one example of proposed tax policy changes directly impacting on state and local governments: the budget calls for mandatory extension of the Medicare payroll tax and Social Security coverage to all public employees.

The following analysis of the budget's impact on the states is based on the February 1990 assessment by the National Governors' Association and the National Conference of State Legislatures.

The budget proposal cuts deepest in programs primarily for local government, including mass transit, economic development programs and sewage treatment grants. The proposals favor education programs such as compensatory education and Head Start and social services for children.

The administration's budget continues the federal shift in grant priorities away from physical capital investment, such as highways, bridges, and wastewater treatment facilities, and towards payments for individuals, primarily in the Medicaid program.

From 1990 to 1991, the increase in Medicaid outlays represents 48 percent of the increase in all grants and 78 percent of the increase in the category of payments for individuals. Program expansions, mandates and higher health care inflation have contributed to a rapidly growing Medicaid program.

In terms of total grant outlays, the administration's proposal returns state and local purchasing power to the position it held 10 years ago. But when Medicaid spending is removed from the totals, grants are more than $12 billion below their 1981 purchasing power.

The Fiscal Year 1991 House Budget Resolution reporting out of committee on April 23, 1990 calls for reallocating approximately half of the defense savings to increase funding beyond inflation for a series of high-priority domestic and international affairs programs with the remainder to be used for deficit reduction. Domestic programs that are to receive increases include: a package of education programs that include math and science education, and vocational education; expanded housing assistance, anti-drug abuse programs, highways, aviation, AIDS research, Head-Start and economic adjustment assistance.

Overall, the budget also affects the states in several indirect ways. Some of the aid reductions that are targeted at local government would cause states to consider replacing at least a portion of the lost aid. The proposed extension of Medicare and social security coverage to state and local government employees is significant in some states. Administration proposals to increase personal savings may affect state and local borrowing costs. Finally, the higher interest rates that result from the large budget deficit and accumulated debt increases state and local borrowing costs, and the potential for economic instability caused by the deficit threatens the fiscal health of state and local government.

Intergovernmental Legislative Priorities

The 1990 congressional lobbying targets of the National Conference of State Legislatures represent the major program and budgetary priorities that will make up the forthcoming state-federal partnership. The following are current or emerging concerns that will receive consideration:

- Agriculture and Rural Development: 1) monitoring reauthorization of the farm bill, 2) supporting responsible rural development legislation, and 3) ensuring that states are not preempted within federal pesticide regulation efforts.
- Budget and Taxation: 1) encouraging removal of numerous trust funds, such as Highway, Aviation and Employment Security from the federal budget, 2) opposing additional spending mandates on states through the Alcohol, Drug Abuse and Mental Health Block Grant.
- Commerce, Justice, and Labor: 1) encouraging new federal housing legislation, 2) opposing unfunded drug control strategy mandates, 3) monitoring possible legislation to overturn recent U.S. Supreme Court decisions dealing with affirmative action, and 4) supporting enterprise zone legislation.
- Education and Job Training: 1) encouraging reauthorization of the Vocational-Technical Education Act, 2) reviewing reauthorization of discretionary programs under the Education of the Handicapped Act, and 3) continuing involvement in proposed changes to the adult-youth training provisions of the Job Training Partnership Act (JTPA).
- Energy and Environment: 1) preserving state flexibility during reauthorization of the Clean Air Act, 2) supporting legislation that would permit states to hold the Federal facilities, and 3) ensuring that state liability and compensation fund statutes are fully protected in oil spill legislation.
- Government Operations and Pensions: 1) opposing taxation of short-term profits of public pension programs, 2) opposing mandatory Medicare coverage for public employees, 3) opposing taxation of public employees benefits, and 4) supporting reform of the federal government's cash management system.
- Health and Human Services: 1) supporting responsible child care legislation that does not impose mandates on states, 2) opposing broad mandatory Medicaid expansions, 3) monitoring legislation concerning health care access and affordability, and 4) supporting adequate funding for the JOBS program, and foster care administration costs.
- Transportation and Communications: 1) opposing any increase in the federal gas tax, 2) supporting legislation that preserves state regulatory authority regarding transportation of hazardous materials, and 3) involvement in reauthorization of highway aid programs.

Federal Aid — the Longer Perspective

To our regret, the president's 1991 budget has dropped all of the Special Analyses including Special Analysis H on Federal Aid to State and Local Governments. Its absence will be missed by those trying to understand the longer term comparative intergovernmental fiscal trends and perspectives. Perhaps meant as a substitute, the president's budget message includes a new 12-page section on "Advancing States as Laboratories." The section praises state and local governments for their innovation, some aided by federal assistance or waivers, others strictly at state and local initiative. "It is a picture of creative experimentation — not social engineering but the natural flowering of variety inherent in a healthy federal system. It is a picture that merits highlighting — and federal government support." The budget, however, does not contain new funding in support of state demonstrations and experimentation.

Aid to state and local governments in the president's 1991 budget increases to nearly $143 billion. A long-term perspective comparing federal assistance to state and local governments, between 1980 and 1991, tells a different story. Grants to state and local governments are expected to decline by 5 percent over this time period. The rest of the federal budget grew by some 29 percent in cost dollars over this period.

The House Budget Committee's analysis of the 1991 budget provides additional longer term perspectives:

One measure of federal-funding shifts is federal assistance as a percentage of state-local outlays. Since 1980, the percentage that federal assistance represents has declined from 25.8 percent to 18.2 percent in 1989, and is projected to decline to about 17 percent in 1990. The projected 1990 level would be about equal to the level that existed before 1970.

A recent report by the Census Bureau also shows that the distribution of federal grants-in-aid between state and local governments has changed significantly. The proportion of grants paid initially to local governments accounted for 25 percent of total grants in 1980 and only 15 percent in 1988, the latest year for which the data is available. Conversely, the proportion going to states was 75 percent in 1980 and 85 percent in 1988.

It is important to note that the real decrease in federal spending on grants is not expected to be uniform for all types of grants. The Office of Management and Budget (OMB) divides grants into two types: grants to individuals, administered through state and local agencies, such as Medicaid; and grants for the use of state and local governments. While grants for individuals are expected to increase by 53 percent in real terms from 1980 to 1991, real grants for state and local programs are expected to decline by 37 percent.

Restoring the Balance

Preemptions

By the beginning of 1990, concern for restoring balance in the federal system had escalated as a major concern of state and local officials' organizations. Recent years have seen an increase in federal preemption of state and local authority. Frequent use of cross-cutting and crossover grant-in-aid sanctions also add intrusions in state and local revenue raising and ability to administer their programs. The period also has seen a rise in federal mandating of programs for which state and local governments must raise the revenue. At the same time, state and local governments have been continuing to modernize their fiscal, administrative and governmental systems to respond to public needs. While the domestic spotlight shifts from the federal government to state governments, the headlines have been replete with examples of where the federal government faced problems in managing its own responsibilities.

A CSG review of current and federal pending legislation showed at least 10 examples of intrusive preemptions, including the savings and loan bailout, national wetlands law, Resource Conservation and Recovery Act reauthorization — disposal of waste, professional licensure, court-ordered taxation, welfare reform, new voter registration procedures, tax deductibility for bonds, pesticides regulation and corporate governance rules. Congress, which has caused most of the mandate and preemption frictions, has shown little interest in correcting the imbalance developing in the federal system.

A 1989 U.S. Advisory Commission on Intergovernment Relations' study began to document the extent of federal intrusion. Their survey revealed that more than 50 percent of all federal statutes preempting state and local authority enacted in the nation's history have been enacted during the last 18 years. The study also showed that few state officials are aware of the scope and variety of federal preemption and its actual effects on state government. Mandates were not particularly a problem when federal regulations requiring state and local action were financed with federal funds. The report concluded that it is the unfunded and underfunded federal mandates, especially in such areas as health and the environment, that have brought about complaints and resistance from state officials.

Constitutional Reform

Concern for intergovernmental reform was heightened by Supreme Court decisions and opinions that left the state and local governments fending for themselves in the national political process. Court decisions, preemptions and mandates led in late 1988 to the creation of an Intergovernmental Partnership Task Force made up of The Council of State

Governments, the National Conference of State Legislatures, the U.S. Conference of Mayors, the National League of Cities, the National Association of Counties and the Advisory Commission on Intergovernmental Relations. Three major joint CSG/ACIR regional hearings seeking consensus on constitutional and other reforms were held in 1989. In addition, resolutions supporting constitutional reform were adopted by the National Governors' Association, the four Council of State Governments' regional legislative conferences, the National Association of Secretaries of State, the National Association of State Treasurers, the Southern Municipal Conference and a number of individual states.

The constitutional reform proposals developed by the Intergovernmental Partnership Task Force and approved by CSG are as follows:

1. In order to make U.S. Supreme Court jurisdiction over federalism questions explicit, the following words would be added to the 10th Amendment: "Whether a power is one reserved to the states, or to the people, shall be a matter to be decided by the courts."

2. In order to open the door for state-initiated amendment proposals, the following provision would be added to Article V:

"Whenever three-fourths of the legislatures of the several states deem it necessary, they shall propose amendments to this Constitution that, after two years, shall be valid to all intents and purposes as part of this Constitution, unless disapproved by two-thirds of both Houses of Congress within two years of the date the amendments are submitted to Congress."

The most recent Court decision, *Missouri v. Jenkins*, decided on April 18, 1990, pitted federal preemption powers against a civil rights issue with a concluding that federal judges have the authority to require local governments to increase taxes to finance school desegregation, even when the tax hikes would violate state law. The state argued that the court-directed tax increase was an unconstitutional exercise of judicial power and violated the Tenth Amendment and principles of federal/state comity. Consistent with the earlier Garcia and Baker decisions, the majority in a 5-4 decision reiterated their view that the ". . . reservation of nondelegated powers to the states is not implicated by a federal-court judgement enforcing the express prohibitions of unlawful state conduct enacted by the Fourteenth Amendment [and the supremacy clause]." (*Cf. Milliken v. Bradley, supra at 291*)

The dissenting opinion in this civil rights v. federalism contest was especially vigorous, arguing that "Today's casual embrace of taxation imposed by the unelected, life-tenured federal judiciary disregards fundamental precepts for the democratic control of public institutions." The majority focused only on the question of the legality of the tax increase which overrode state and local restrictions, rather than the specific remedies in the desegregation order. The dissenting opinion, however, could not resist commenting on one of the remedies, creating a Classical Greek theme program emphasizing forensics and self-government to provide training in participatory democracy. It dryly noted that "if today's dicta become law, such lessons will be of little use to students who grow up to become taxpayers in the [Kansas City School District]."

Federalism Executive Order

One of the more promising initiatives to improve the intergovernmental process, given new life by President Bush, was the issuance of Executive Order 12612 on federalism by President Reagan on October 26, 1987. In an effort to reduce the constraints on state and local governments in administering federal programs, the Executive Order call for federal action to permit state discretion in developing policies and administering federal programs within the scope of clear constitutional authority; refraining from establishing uniform national standards for programs; preempting state law only when provided or implied in federal statute; and directing executive departments and agencies to refrain from submitting legislation that would interfere with the independence of the states, or to attach conditions to grants that are not directly related to the purpose of the grant. Each federal department and agency also was directed to designate an official to be responsible for ensuring the implementation of the Order.

Among their responsibilities are to prepare a "federalism assessment" for policy recommendations and proposals submitted to the Office of Management and Budget, including an estimate of the additional costs on the states. This assessment includes the likely source of funding for the states and their ability to fulfill the purposes of the policy. The extent to which the Executive Order has been implemented, including the designation of responsible officials has not been determined. On the positive side, President Bush has reaffirmed the Federalism Executive Order in a February 1990 memorandum to federal department and agency heads. Bush commented, "I want to stress that the principles of this order are central to my administration."

What Lies Ahead

What changes in federalism can we expect? The Heritage Foundation prescription for what needs to be done is philosophically blunt and to the point. The states should stop looking to Washington for assistance and should set a national example of restraint. The role of the federal government is not to bail out wasteful state governments, but to provide a sound national fiscal policy framework that will stimulate economic growth at the state and local level. The federal government can best help states by reducing the federal budget deficit, curbing interest rates, eliminating costly mandates and regulation and replacing the federal grants-in-aid system with a new grant program to channel aid only to those states truly in need.

The General Accounting Office's strategic plan and research themes for intergovernmental relations over the next three years seeks practical answers to valid questions. The plan lays out three major lines of inquiry for more specific research projects. The first is, "How can federal programs that rely on state and local governments be designed so that service delivery is more effective and national objectives are achieved? Research objectives will include trying to appraise the relative advantage of grants vs. loans vs. tax policy for implementing programs, assuring the use of effective and equitable grant formulas, and the proper division of labor among the three levels of government in any given federal program."

In March of 1990, the General Accounting Office issued an informational report to Congress on key intergovernmental changes over the last decade. In doing so, GAO identified three broad issues that Congress should be aware of. The first is that the fiscal gap between wealthier and poorer jurisdictions has become larger during the past decade. Second, that federal regulation of state and local governments has added tensions when coupled with decreasing federal aid. State and local governments may increasingly in the future have to choose between meeting their service responsibilities and fulfilling national regulatory objectives. Third, though the states have emerged as principal domestic partners and program innovators in their own right, these trends in state prominence could be endangered during periods when national or regional economies are weak.

A second General Accounting Office question is, "How, and to what extent, do budget and program changes affect services delivered and people served through intergovernmental programs? A more specific objective will be appraising how state and local governments are replacing federal cuts with their own resources, how program beneficiaries are affected, and the manner in which states are adapting to restrictions.

A final inquiry in improving the intergovernmental process is, "How, and to what extent, are federal regulatory and tax policy changes influencing state and local managerial and fiscal capacities?" Subjects to be addressed include agency implementation of the Regulatory Flexibility Act, federal executive branch organization for intergovernmental relations, and the effects of bond caps, income tax deductions and tax policy generally on state fiscal capacity.

Looking ahead even further, perhaps through the end of the century, what might a federalism agenda look like? Sandra Osbourn of the Congressional Research Service has identified a number of possible issues for such an agenda.

Federal-State-Relations — Should the constitutional protections of states be restored to their former strength and status? Should the Constitution be amended to guarantee this protection?

Fiscal Federalism — State and local governments have pretty much cushioned the effects of the relative decrease in domestic expenditures. Latest estimates indicate that the states are especially vulnerable. An economic down-turn would have a devastating impact on state government and state assistance to their local governments. Are strategic plans in place to deal with this eventuality?

Public Accountability — State, in addition to federal policy, has contributed directly or indirectly to a range of new actors in the governing process: although not always recorded in the Census of Governments, there is an increase in community-based organizations, special districts, public-private partnerships, private contractors, nonprofit organizations, venture capital corporations and pension fund managers. Are lines of public accountability and responsibility becoming too blurred?

Functional vs. political boundaries — What adjustments might be necessary to match political jurisdictions to new demographic, geographic, and economic realties? What role, if any, should the federal government play in any adjustment process?

State Involvement in Foreign Affairs and Defense — International economic developments are creating bonds that tie states' economies and politics closely to other countries and regional blocs throughout the world. The increased globalization of business raises each state's stake in overseas markets; draws more foreign corporations to the states; and has led to new state trade financing, venture capital programs and targeted incentives to attract foreign investment designed to benefit local economies. Individual states are involved in establishing nuclear-free zones and programs to reduce global warming. They also are involved in the resistance to sending National Guard units for exercises abroad. Will such globalization strain federal/state relations?

What will happen? Tim Conlan sees two alternative directions. One road, hopefully not to be travelled, is the aggravation of relationships by Supreme Court decisions that discount the 10th Amendment, federal preemption fueled by industry demands, unfunded mandates in drug control, environmental protection, education and health care and further constraints on state and local tax and borrowing powers. The better alternative is a resurgence of cooperative federalism based on relative equality of strength among the three levels, creativity and restraint by federal departments and agencies.

INTERGOVERNMENTAL AFFAIRS

Table 9.1
TOTAL FEDERAL AID TO STATES: FISCAL 1983-1988
(In thousands of dollars)

State or other jurisdiction	1988	1987	1986	1985	1984	1983
Total	$114,610,326	$107,962,463	$112,596,374	$105,478,200	$97,208,644	$92,692,639
Alabama	1,721,415	1,559,202	1,758,540	1,719,040	1,532,194	1,469,439
Alaska	592,779	623,914	664,264	639,871	615,698	540,720
Arizona	1,176,665	1,188,406	1,206,279	1,121,528	989,925	844,994
Arkansas	1,011,046	1,008,653	1,123,249	1,013,635	946,183	901,417
California	11,676,158	11,005,940	11,291,464	10,558,790	9,798,986	9,206,982
Colorado	1,240,940	1,151,955	1,220,384	1,165,999	1,176,127	1,057,269
Connecticut	1,542,093	1,489,038	1,501,275	1,377,388	1,221,429	1,189,471
Delaware	318,505	301,429	313,591	318,028	298,517	306,816
Florida	3,418,506	3,154,741	3,244,213	3,121,681	2,783,803	2,817,394
Georgia	2,964,083	2,511,883	2,731,619	2,371,486	2,213,733	2,109,875
Hawaii	477,207	459,687	473,368	435,570	458,783	456,678
Idaho	477,016	391,598	434,913	444,926	413,181	380,421
Illinois	4,670,274	4,467,816	5,009,911	4,688,411	4,303,812	4,189,166
Indiana	1,960,024	1,981,871	2,000,307	1,825,318	1,759,904	1,610,771
Iowa	1,199,499	1,089,827	1,158,209	1,163,730	1,091,051	980,568
Kansas	880,474	847,860	883,894	855,971	804,770	762,936
Kentucky	1,766,251	1,701,541	1,784,168	1,763,550	1,589,665	1,487,891
Louisiana	2,135,166	1,918,583	2,038,882	1,785,154	1,776,119	1,709,614
Maine	664,772	688,915	672,328	659,419	590,372	575,000
Maryland	2,004,233	2,002,057	1,959,278	1,811,665	1,697,453	1,790,362
Massachusetts	3,327,712	2,983,388	3,081,662	2,842,210	2,634,160	2,897,635
Michigan	4,242,888	4,199,194	4,353,181	3,961,474	3,775,972	3,612,150
Minnesota	2,119,637	2,037,109	2,109,814	1,982,655	1,864,551	1,764,831
Mississippi	1,324,442	1,273,712	1,344,494	1,188,296	1,175,894	1,100,151
Missouri	1,941,546	1,926,050	1,982,447	1,935,316	1,774,670	1,674,905
Montana	546,279	539,599	591,747	583,689	531,604	476,667
Nebraska	712,122	606,860	660,741	675,346	636,981	574,797
Nevada	335,985	383,980	418,308	387,267	340,350	356,360
New Hampshire	397,954	388,811	404,309	419,964	367,567	351,751
New Jersey	3,327,501	3,326,973	3,353,546	2,945,210	2,871,056	2,811,323
New Mexico	830,912	779,226	856,588	891,071	862,668	675,756
New York	12,494,241	11,932,082	12,380,416	11,092,526	10,268,490	10,031,955
North Carolina	2,298,940	2,171,329	2,281,011	2,133,677	1,929,252	1,877,549
North Dakota	461,980	418,611	433,148	452,291	453,685	371,668
Ohio	4,693,458	4,381,699	4,763,920	4,158,358	4,044,258	3,641,717
Oklahoma	1,405,840	1,317,079	1,399,610	1,235,997	1,166,536	1,075,391
Oregon	1,322,446	1,243,443	1,339,996	1,449,139	1,246,130	1,160,916
Pennsylvania	5,792,860	5,270,904	5,717,963	4,963,560	4,667,346	4,817,082
Rhode Island	643,534	549,931	570,166	573,163	547,622	486,062
South Carolina	1,353,889	1,280,001	1,322,214	1,323,560	1,168,961	1,112,715
South Dakota	443,239	439,946	457,384	480,179	435,909	360,902
Tennessee	2,225,396	2,018,033	2,128,234	2,049,340	1,885,172	1,686,750
Texas	5,167,843	4,853,015	5,224,805	4,476,730	4,136,482	3,804,616
Utah	725,196	783,799	807,257	759,414	708,143	621,539
Vermont	323,815	313,919	334,006	336,386	331,008	312,181
Virginia	1,960,899	1,905,191	1,994,506	1,816,529	1,628,438	1,664,881
Washington	2,170,381	1,978,389	1,904,876	1,826,295	1,697,921	1,536,779
West Virginia	1,056,215	1,028,299	1,062,941	904,024	819,209	840,398
Wisconsin	2,227,796	2,155,409	2,309,880	2,111,744	2,063,878	1,903,748
Wyoming	447,642	449,026	471,237	503,437	556,326	425,533
Dist. of Columbia	1,615,095	1,514,779	1,423,040	1,498,202	1,381,886	1,354,941
Puerto Rico	2,389,811	2,306,545	2,296,490	2,347,583	2,231,139	2,110,626
U.S. Virgin Islands	120,799	119,090	141,158	131,661	136,803	90,907
Other	206,633 (a)	200,780 (a)	346,486 (b)	314,330 (b)	341,672 (b)	313,147 (b)
Adjustments or undistributed to states	2,058,282	1,331,377	858,675	1,856,417	465,200	406,556

Source: U.S. Bureau of the Census, *Federal Expenditures by State for Fiscal Year 1983; 1984; 1985; 1986; 1987; and 1988.*
(a) Includes American Samoa, Guam, Northern Mariana Islands and Trust Territory.
(b) Includes American Samoa, Guam, Northern Mariana Islands, Tokelau Islands, Trust Territory of the Pacific and Saipan.

DEVELOPING STATE-LOCAL RELATIONS: 1987-1989

By Joseph F. Zimmerman

Changes in the legal, financial, and other relationships between states and their general purpose local governments continued to evolve during 1988 and 1989 with new statutory enactments, judicial decisions and advisory opinions of attorneys general. In addition, a number of study groups reported their findings and other study groups were created or had their study period extended.

The major irritant in state-local relations remains the state mandate — a constitutional, legislative, or administrative requirement that local governments undertake a specified activity or provide a service meeting minimum state standards. State restraints removing or restricting the authority of local governments also are major irritants.

Study Groups

In 1988, The Washington State Local Governance Study Commission issued a two volume report tracing the state's local governance tradition over the years and offering recommendations. The first set of recommendations is designed to improve multilateral and/or bilateral agreements between local governments on current and future service responsibilities.

The second set of recommendations deals with the citizen review process and provides for the organization of the review body, additional ways of invoking the procedure for proposed governmental structural changes and prevention of the elimination of local governments without voter approval.

The third set of recommendations contains short-term and long-term revenue proposals. Supplementary recommendations compose a fourth set dealing with special purpose districts, home rule charters, county boundary changes and vacancies in local governing bodies.

In 1989, the Virginia secretary of administration issued a report on whether a state advisory commission on intergovernmental relations was needed. The secretary recommended that "the Local Government Advisory Council be restructured so as to provide representation for all the primary parties in intergovernmental relations — local governments, the legislature, and the executive branch — and that the Council have a rotating chairmanship and a regular meeting schedule." The secretary also recommended that the staff of the Commission on Local Government should continue to support the council and the commission should be renamed the Office of State and Local Affairs. Implementing legislation was enacted by the 1989 General Assembly and the newly constituted commission became effective on January 1, 1990.

A consolidation commission, appointed by the Minnesota Municipal Board, released a report in 1988 recommending that the cities of International Falls and South International Falls be consolidated into a new city of International Falls. The merger is designed to solve problems involving water treatment, economic development, competition, maintenance of common boundary roads, cost sharing and delivery of certain services as well as differences in tax base, operating costs and level of services provided in each city.

The Ohio State and Local Government Commission issued a report, *Cooperative*

Joseph F. Zimmerman is professor of Political Science, Graduate School of Public Affairs, State University of New York at Albany.

Ventures: Strategies for the Future, in December, 1988 describing the reasons for entering into a cooperative venture, obstacles to entering a venture, and case studies of such ventures. The commission recommended that the state use financial and other incentives to encourage cooperative ventures.

Michigan Public Act 100 of 1988 created a Commission on Intergovernmental Relations to study relations between governments and to analyze any action requiring an increase in the level of service in an existing program if the action substantially increases local government costs or reduces local government revenues. Commission findings are to be reported to the governor and the Legislature.

Rhode Island Public Law 133 of 1988 established a seventeen member State-Local Relations Commission, composed of state and local officials, to study and report on issues, including relationships between and among local governments, powers and functions of local governments, impact of federal and state court decisions upon cities and towns and special problems facing local governments in interstate areas.

Virginia HB 1642 of 1989 established an eighteen member Local Government Advisory Council, and Chapter 45 of the Washington Laws of 1988 directs a state committee to conduct a comprehensive study of water use efficiency.

The Alaska Department of Community and Regional Affairs conducted ten studies in 1988 and 1989 of the feasibility of creating new boroughs (regional governments). The reports were positive in five instances, conditional in three cases, and "doubtful" in two cases.

The New York State Conference of Mayors and Other Municipal Officials in 1989 released a report, *Local Tax Burden Increasing*, revealing that state aid to general purpose local governments increased 2.4 percent since 1982 compared to an average increase of 12 percent in state aid for school districts during a period when inflation averaged 3.5 percent per year.

A special commission of business and local government leaders, appointed by Massachusetts Governor Michael Dukakis, released a report on December 15, 1989, recommending that property taxes be allowed to increase annually at the inflation rate instead of the 2.5 percent rate established by initiative proposition 2 1/2 of 1980, and that interest on funds borrowed for capital improvements be excluded from the limit.

The 1989 New Hampshire General Court (legislature) enacted Chapter 14, extending the life of a study committee created in 1988 to recommend guidelines or legislation to assist municipalities seeking to adopt a charter or revise a charter, and Chapter 199 creating a committee to study the state's revenue structure, including the relationship between the structure and local property taxes.

Chapter 886 of the Tennessee laws of 1988 created the Greater Nashville Regional Council as a replacement for the Mid-Cumberland Development District and the Mid-Cumberland Council of Governments.

The 1989 West Virginia Legislature adopted a resolution requesting the Joint Committee on Government and Finance to create an Intergovernmental Study Commission "to review, examine, and study the present structure of county and municipal government..." and make recommendations for improvements.

Local Discretionary Authority

State legislatures in 1988 and 1989 continued to broaden the discretionary authority of certain types of general purpose local governments in specific areas on a piecemeal basis.

Section 36-35-3 of the Official Code of Georgia Annotated was amended by the 1989 Legislature to place additional requirements on sponsors of petitions seeking to amend a municipal charter by the referendum method. Each sponsor must provide his or her name, address, and telephone number and swear that he or she is a resident of the municipality and all signatures on the petition were collected within the municipality.

The 1989 Georgia Legislature also amended section 21-3-64 of the code which had required four-year terms for members of municipal councils and stipulated that all elections must be held in November of odd numbered years commencing in 1993. The new law allowed municipal charters to be amended to provide for two-year terms for council members and for annual elections in November.

The 1989 New Hampshire Legislature enacted two laws broadening the authority of towns. Chapter 164 permitted a town to reduce the speed limit by ten miles per hour in a school zone forty-five minutes before and after the school day and does not require a flashing yellow light. Chapter 287 expanded the types of town meeting procedural defects which a town can "cure" by adding to existing law "any procedural act not contrary to the spirit or intent of the law."

Michigan Public Act 502 of 1988 permitted a city or village to reorganize its hospital into a public nonprofit corporation to provide greater financial flexibility and to enable the hospital to compete on a more equal basis with private hospitals. The incorporation is subject to voter approval.

In Colorado, Senate Bill 45 of 1987 stipulated that state and federal lands may be ignored for purposes of contiguity in annexation proceedings and imposes a three mile limit on the amount of annexation in a given year with specified exceptions.

With regard to noise abatement, Colorado Senate Bill 54 of 1987 authorized counties to regulate noise on public and private property under specified conditions. And Chapter 155 of the Minnesota Laws of 1987 allowed municipalities within aircraft noise zones to adopt ordinances regulating construction methods and materials for the purpose of reducing aircraft noise.

The Connecticut Legislature enacted four laws broadening the authority of cities and towns. Public Act 88-213 allowed them to regulate on-street parking in residential neighborhoods by creating neighborhood parking areas and restricting on-street parking in these areas to neighborhood residents. Public Act 87-91 permitted municipalities to extend elderly homeowner tax relief benefits to permanently and totally disabled persons regardless of age. Public Act 87-116 authorized cities and towns to defer property taxes owed by qualified senior citizens and permanently and totally disabled persons up to one hundred percent of the taxes due. And Public Act 88-234 allowed cities and towns to extend the time period over which property owners may pay their sewer assessments by allowing the last installment to be paid ten years after the maturity date of the bonds rather than one year prior to the maturity date.

In Florida, Chapter 373 of the laws of 1988 authorized water management districts to delegate to local governments storm water permitting or surface water management programs if the districts conclude such delegation is necessary or desirable.

Rhode Island Public Law 633 of 1988 established a pavement management program and declared that "roads serving longer-distance travel, connecting city and town centers, and major traffic generators shall be the state's responsibility. Roads serving local travel shall be under city or town jurisdiction." The State Planning Council designates roads as state roads or municipal roads.

Pennsylvania Act 170 of 1988, effective on February 21, 1989, made numerous changes in the Commonwealth's Municipalities Planning Code and necessitated that each municipality review and amend its land use ordinance to conform with the act.

Chapter 911 of the Tennessee Acts of 1988 authorized any municipality that lies in two or more counties to consolidate with the county in which the majority of its territory lies, and stipulated that following a consolidation the urban services tax may be levied in the part of the municipality outside the county.

States continued to enact laws authorizing local governments to enter into cooperative agreements or to form regional bodies for special purposes. Chapter 70 of the New Hampshire Laws of 1988 authorized cities and towns to enter into agreements with local governments in other states extending the authority of police in the concerned jurisdictions.

Colorado HB 1342 of 1989 clarified the authority of local governments to sign mutually binding intergovernmental agreements for joint land use planning and allowed for the adoption of comprehensive development plans incorporating various land use standards in lieu of existing zoning, subdivision, or other land use regulations.

The same statute authorized a county sheriff to contract with other law enforcement bodies or municipalities for provision of law enforcement services within the unincorporated areas of the county. Similarly, Virginia SB 512 of 1989 authorized a sheriff to provide law enforcement services for towns.

Tennessee Chapter 188 of 1989 authorized counties to enter into inter-local agreement with more than one municipality within the county. And Chapter 176 authorized the merger of contiguous municipalities in the same county subject to voter approval.

Michigan Public Act 57 of 1988 allowed two or more municipalities to incorporate a public authority to provide fire, police, emergency medical, or related services. Chapter 105 of the New Hampshire Laws of 1989 permitted municipalities to sign agreements with other cities and towns to develop and implement regional water plans and ordinances in areas where water protection needs extend beyond municipal boundaries. Chapter 324 of the New Hampshire Laws of 1989 authorized cities and towns to provide joint regional facilities for collecting, separating, or recycling solid wastes. Washington Substitute Senate Bill 5400 of 1989 goes beyond authorizing action and provides financial assistance to encourage counties "to enter into joint operating agreements with other counties to form regional" mental health support networks.

Enacted pursuant to a 1988 constitutional amendment, South Carolina Act Number 6 of 1989 allows any political subdivision (1) to enter into an agreement with another subdivision or the state for the joint administration of any function, exercise of powers, and sharing of costs, (2) provides that prohibitions against dual office-holding do not apply to any elected or appointed official or employee serving on a regional council of governments, and (3) allows counties jointly to develop an industrial or business park with other counties.

Georgia in 1989, however, took a different approach by directing the Department of Natural Resources (Official Code of Georgia Annotated, chapter 12-5) to construct and maintain regional water supply reservoirs. And Michigan Public Act 481 of 1988 directed Macomb, Oakland, and Wayne Counties and the City of Detroit to incorporate the Regional Transit Coordinating Council to replace the Southeastern Michigan Transportation Authority.

In September 1989, the California Legislature enacted a law subjecting the Oakland school district, the state's fifth largest, to a state trustee with authority to oversee the finances of the district. Eight current or former employees of the district have been indicted for embezzlement of district funds, theft of district property, and other crimes.

On October 4, 1989, the New Jersey State Board of Education employed a 1988 state law to assume control of the Jersey City school district, the second largest, on the grounds that the system was a "total educational failure." This action is the first instance of a state assuming control of the administrative and educational affairs of a *solvent* school district. On December 4, 1989, the state education commissioner appointed thirteen Jersey City residents to a fifteen member advisory board of education.

Boston University on September 6, 1989, assumed control of the Chelsea, Massachusetts, school system for a period of ten years under a 1989 state law. The system had a 50 percent drop-out rate, a high pregnancy rate, and wide-spread drug use among the approximately 3,500 students.

Environment and Land Use

Environmental issues continued to be prominent features of legislative agendas with laws often providing for a state leadership role.

Recognizing that pollution liability insurance is almost impossible to obtain, the 1989 New Hampshire General Court enacted chapter 311 establishing an Environmental Risk Insurance Pool to provide coverage for pollution claims. The law appropriated $95,000 in seed money to meet the expenses of establishing a self-insurance fund for governmental units and business firms.

Chapter 226 of the Alabama Laws of 1987 created a State Water Pollution Control Authority with broad powers "to aid in the prevention and control of water pollution, to provide state financial aid to public bodies for the prevention and control of water pollution," and to issue water pollution control bonds.

Chapter 405 of the New Hampshire Laws of 1989 required the Water Supply and Pollution Control Commission to notify by first class mail the selectmen or conservation commissions of all municipalities located within 25 air miles down stream of any point of discharge or potential discharge when an effluent permit is renewed or an application is made for a new permit. The notice requirement also must be provided by any person or firm responsible for a violation of effluent limitations.

Connecticut Public Act 87-544 directed the Commissioner of Environmental Protection to revise the state solid waste plan to include a requirement that not less than 25 percent of the solid waste generated in the state must be recycled. Each municipal solid waste plan must include a declaration of intent to process recyclable items on a regional and local basis.

Georgia Senate Bill 70 of 1989 amended the solid waste management code by requiring state certification of solid waste landfill operations, prohibiting landfills within two miles of a "significant ground-water recharge area," and requiring private landfill operators to prove financial responsibility to ensure proper closure and post closure care of landfills. Senate Bill 83 of 1989 authorized the Georgia Environmental Facilities Authority to provide low interest loans to local governments for solid waste management improvements.

The New Mexico Environmental Improvement Board issued new solid waste disposal regulations and estimated the implementation cost conservatively at fifteen million dollars. The state constitution forbids promulgation of state regulations mandating new local services or service level increases without a funding source. The Board has not identified such a source.

The 1988 Michigan Legislature enacted five laws relating to recycling. Act 414 mandated that all plastic products sold in the state be labeled with a code to make it easier to separate them for recycling. Act 415 established the Plastics Recycling Development Fund to provide grants and loans to stimulate the plastics recycling industry. Act 416 created the Recycling Target Enterprise Development Council in the Department of Natural Resources with responsibility for establishing a plan to improve recycling in the State.

Michigan Act 428 of 1988 amended the Solid Waste Management Act by specifying it is to be construed and administered to encourage source and site separation of materials from the waste stream, and required the Department of Natural Resources to encourage other environmental sound measures to prevent materials from entering the waste stream.

Michigan Act 430 of 1988 directed the Department of Natural Resources to implement a plan for recycling used motor oil and to install holding tanks at facilities where state-owned vehicles are serviced to collect and recycle oil from state vehicles and from vehicles owned by private citizens.

Michigan Act 478 of 1988 required the owner/operator of an underground petroleum storage tank to report all leaks to the Department of Natural Resources and Act 479 required the state fire marshal to administer a registration program for such tanks.

Virginia House Bill 1743 of 1989 required all local governments to adopt a local or regional solid waste management plan, subject to approval by the State Board of Waste Management, prior to siting a solid waste management facility after July 1, 1992. The plan must include a strategy to achieve a twenty-five percent recycling rate by 1995.

West Virginia Senate Bill 301 of 1989 created the West Virginia Solid Waste Management Board as a replacement for the Resource Recovery-Solid Waste Disposal Authority.

The Board is responsible for approving sites for facilities proposed by a county or regional solid waste authority. The act also created a Commercial Hazardous Waste Management Facility Siting Board.

Chapter 552 of the Tennessee Laws of 1989 repealed the authority of local governments to veto hazardous waste disposal, treatment, or storage sites within their respective jurisdictions (or within one mile for a municipality), and authorized the Commissioner of Health and Environment to make final decisions on sites.

The 1988 Virginia Legislature enacted the Chesapeake Bay Preservation Act (chapters 608 and 891) providing for the Commonwealth to join with Maryland, Pennsylvania, Washington, D.C., and the United States Environmental Agency in the clean-up and protection of the bay. The Act created the Chesapeake Bay Local Assistance Board and charged it with responsibility for developing criteria which local governments in tidal areas must employ in designating bay preservation areas. Within such areas, local governments must develop planning and zoning standards which comply with criteria promulgated by the board to protect bay water quality.

In 1989, the Virginia Legislature enacted chapters 410 and 721 authorizing the Commonwealth to regulate the use of surface water by localities. The 1989 Georgia General Assembly enacted a law (Official Code of Georgia Annotated, chapter 12-5) authorizing the Department of Natural Resources to acquire, construct, and maintain regional water supply reservoirs.

Chapter 99 of the New Hampshire Laws of 1989 empowered the State Wetlands Board to issue an emergency order requiring the immediate cessation of dredging, filling, or any other activity putting wetlands at immediate risk. Chapter 225 redefined land bordering on tidal waters under the jurisdiction of the board to include areas within 100 feet of the highest observable tide line and upland areas. A permit is required to excavate, remove fill, dredge, or construct any structure adjacent to any waters of the state.

Michigan Public Act 449 of 1988 required that pesticide applicators must register with the Department of Agriculture and complete successfully a special training program. The Georgia Legislature in 1989 enacted a law (Official Code of Georgia Annotated, chapter 12-8) requiring the Department of Natural Resources to notify any affected local government and the general public within fifteen days of the receipt of an application for a hazardous waste permit.

Chapter 285 of the New Hampshire Laws of 1988 clarified state-local powers by stipulating "the State shall have the power to regulate the extraction of minerals including the removal of dimension stone" and municipalities have authority "to regulate the removal of earth to be used as construction aggregate." The 1989 General Court enacted chapter 373 revising the excavations law by establishing a series of new minimum operational and reclamation standards applicable to all excavations, including those that were "grandfathered" (pre-1979 pits). All post-1979 pits and new excavations remain subject to local permitting procedures and locally enacted regulations, including zoning.

Rhode Island Public Law 601 of 1988 required all cities and towns to complete a comprehensive land use plan by the end of 1990. State agencies also must develop plans, and state and local goals must be coordinated.

Chapter 216 of the New Hampshire Laws of 1988 made the county responsible for planning and zoning, subdivision, and related regulations in unincorporated areas.

State Aid and Finance

The Colorado Municipal League in 1987 issued a policy statement, *Fiscal Fair Play: The Need for a State-Municipal Partnership*, describing the financial condition of municipalities, state shared revenues, property and sales tax exemptions, 104 state mandates, funding levels for municipal programs, and home rule.

In 1989, the Virginia Commission on Local Government issued a *Report on the Impact of Annexation and Immunity Actions on Affected Localities with Regard to State Aid, Mandates, and Regulations.*

With regard to state aid, an omnibus Minnesota tax law, Chapter 719 of 1988, increased local government financial aid by over 25 percent, but imposed tight levy limits on cities and required local governments to adhere to "Truth in Taxation" provisions mandating the governments to notify each property owner of proposed tax increases and to conduct a public hearing on proposed budgets. The law also provided that the state will assume responsibility for all county welfare costs.

On October 2, 1989, the Texas Supreme Court in *Edgewood Independent School District v. Kirby* overruled the decision of the Court of Appeals and held that the system of financing the education of public schools violated the state constitution. The Supreme Court pointed out "the wealthiest district has over $14,000,000 of property wealth per student, while the poorest has approximately $20,000; this disparity reflects a 700 to 1 ratio."

In his 1989 budget message to the Legislature, New Jersey Governor Thomas H. Kean proposed that the state assume from counties the costs of the welfare and state court systems, thereby saving property taxpayers more than $320 million annually.

Virginia House Bill 113 of 1989 increased by 50 percent state reimbursement for local jails to a maximum of $1.2 million annually and also increased reimbursement for regional jails to a maximum of 50 percent. And Virginia House Bill 116 of 1989 authorized local governments to join a state administered health insurance pool.

Michigan Public Act 101 of 1988, the Local Government Fiscal Responsibility Act, directed the governor to appoint a fiscal review team upon the request of a local government or following a preliminary fiscal review by the state treasurer. The act allowed the state to initiate remedial action and place a local unit in receivership.

Colorado Senate Bill 184 of 1988 reduced the assessment rate for residential property from 18 to 16 percent of actual value, and imposed additional limits on property tax increases for statutory cities and towns, counties, and special districts by reducing annual increases from six percent to five and one-half percent.

Recognizing the burden placed on certain cities and towns by tax-exempt institutions of higher education and nonprofit hospitals, the Rhode Island Legislature enacted Chapter 383 in 1987 providing that the General Assembly will appropriate to each city and town an amount equal to one-fourth of all tax revenue that would have been collected had the property been taxable.

With respect to taxation, the 1989 New York Legislature rejected Governor Mario M. Cuomo's proposals to allow New York City to extend a mortgage tax to cooperative apartments to raise approximately $47 million and the state to levy a real estate transfer tax that would have raised in excess of $125 million for local governments outside of New York City. The governor's proposals were designed to assist local governments to maintain services in view of his proposed large cuts in state aid to local governments. In general, the Legislature maintained the previous level of state aid with the exception of a reduction from $79 million to $26 million in revenue sharing funds for counties.

Chapter 565 of the New York Laws of 1989 established a state water pollution control revolving fund to maximize the amount of federal aid available to the state for municipal water pollution control projects.

In Georgia, the 1989 Legislature repealed the code section authorizing municipalities and counties levying the joint municipal sales and use tax to increase the tax rate from one to two percent for a one year period. On the other hand, the 1989 Legislature added section 48-13-51 to the Code allowing a municipality to levy a hotel/motel tax of six percent until June 30, 1990, provided 60 percent of the revenue is dedicated to tourism purposes or specified tourism facilities. The maximum municipal occupation tax upon marriage and family therapists that can be levied is restricted to $200 annually by Georgia House Bill 194 of 1989.

Colorado House Bill 1210 of 1987 allowed counties with a population exceeding 100,000 to fund various street and road improvements through the imposition of a sales tax not exceeding one-half percent. In Minnesota, the 1988 Legislature enacted Chapter 414 authorizing a town to impose a tax of up to three percent of gross receipts on a lodging establishment.

The 1987 Washington Legislature enacted Chapter 355 permitting a local government to contract with the county treasurer for the collection of special assessments, charges, excise taxes, or rates. The following year, the Legislature enacted Chapter 281 granting permission to local governments to invest in mutual funds consisting solely of bonds issued by the United States Government and money market funds consisting solely of bonds issued by the United States Government and money market funds with portfolios of bonds issued only by state and local governments in addition to traditional authorized investments.

Chapter 19 of the Washington Laws of 1987 modified the existing debt limit statute by excluding from computation of the statutory debt limit loans from the state or the federal government, and authorizing a local government to evidence a loan agreement with the state or the federal government without issuance of a formal bond instrument.

On November 8, 1988, Michigan voters approved proposition "C" authorizing the issuance of $660 million in bonds to finance environmental protection programs, including solid waste clean-up, water quality programs, and management of toxic wastes. And the 1988 Legislature enacted Public Act 498 extending from 13 to 36 months the maximum maturity for consolidated tax anticipation notes.

Chapter 279 of the New Hampshire Laws of 1989 permitted a city or town to vote to deposit receipts from a specific revenue source into a special non-lapsing fund. Previously, such a fund could be created exclusively as a capital reserve fund to which only specific dollar amounts could be appropriated. In an administrative action, the New Hampshire Board of Tax and Land Appeals, acting in response to a petition signed by more than 50 residents, reviewed the system of property assessment in the Town of Westmoreland and ordered that all properties be reassessed.

Chapter 376 of the New York Laws of 1988 required municipal officials, upon receiving a report of an external audit by an independent public accountant, to file within ten days of its receipt a copy of the report with the municipal clerk and the state comptroller. The law also authorized the municipality to provide the state comptroller with a written response to the audits and to file a copy with the municipal clerk.

Connecticut Public Act 88-346 authorized a municipality with a population exceeding 100,000 to participate in a program to facilitate the collection of parking violation fines administered by the State Department of Motor Vehicles. The department will not issue or renew a registration on a vehicle owned by a person who has more than five unpaid parking violations in that municipality except for owners engaged in the leasing or renting of motor vehicles. Connecticut Public Act 88-305 created a local housing partnership of public and private officials to develop affordable housing. The law provided a process for a municipality to receive priority consideration for certain state housing, environmental, and transportation funds, such as town aid road bonus payments.

A major development is the levying of impact fees on real estate developers to pay for road improvements and facilities. The bulk of the fees are used to finance roads, sewer lines, and schools. Orange County, California, levies an average impact fee of $185 per new housing unit to finance and equip additional fire stations, $69 a unit for sheriff's stations, and $20 a unit for child care services. Tennessee Chapter 1022 of 1988 authorized the Metropolitan Government of Nashville and Davidson county to levy impact fees.

The constitutionality of impact fees has been the subject of several court decisions since the United States Supreme Court's 1987 decision in *Nollan v. California Coastal Commission* (483 U.S. 825). Prospective purchasers of a beachfront lot situated between two public beaches sought a permit to remove an old building and replace it with a new one. The commission called for an easement across a section of the property as a condition for the permit. The court concluded that the condition violated constitutional guarantees against the taking of private property for public use without just compensation.

The Town of Guilderland, New York, enacted Local Law Number 2 of 1987, entitled "The Transportation Fee Law," requiring applicants for a building permit that will generate additional traffic to pay an impact fee with the proceeds dedicated to a fund for improvement and expansion of the road system in the town. In November 1988, the Appellate Division of the New York State Supreme Court for the Third Department in *Albany Area Builders Association v. Guilderland* (141 A.D. 2d 293) held the local law to be unconstitutional because it will inhibit new construction in the town and will shift new development to neighboring municipalities. The court specifically noted that development is a "state concern" and impact fees do not relate solely to the constitutional grant of powers to municipalities to control their own "property, affairs, or government." The decision was affirmed on October 26, 1989 by the Court of Appeals, the state's highest court.

Massachusetts cities and towns continue to experience fiscal strain attributable in part to Proposition 2½ of 1980 limiting the general property tax. A survey conducted by the Massachusetts Municipal Association revealed that 157 cities and towns placed the question of overriding Proposition 2 1/2 on the ballot during the first five months of 1989 in order to raise an additional $72 million. Only 40 percent of the proposals were approved compared to 63 percent in 1988.

Legal Decisions and Advisory Opinions

Narrow and broad interpretations of the powers of general purpose local governments continue to characterize court decisions and advisory opinions, and courts were called upon to settle disputes between local governments.

The Florida District Court of Appeal for the fifth district in *City of New Smyrna Beach v. County of Volusia* (518 So.2d 1379) in 1988 dismissed a city action challenging the validity of an amendment of the county charter establishing a Beach Trust Commission and authorizing the County Council to adopt a uniform beach code.

In 1988, the Georgia Court of Appeals in *Self v. City of Atlanta* (372 S.E.2d 283) ruled that the Georgia General Assembly did not expressly waive municipal tort immunity in the performance of governmental functions by adopting a municipal charter authorizing the municipality "to sue and be sued, and plead and be impleaded in all courts of law and equity and in all actions whatsoever."

On July 13, 1989, the Georgia Supreme Court, in *Barkley v. City of Rome*, upheld section 36-60-13 of the Official Code of Georgia Annotated which authorizes counties to use a lease-purchase agreement or a multi-year lease, or purchase facilities. A lease specifically is not deemed to create a debt for a county. To take advantage of the law, county commissioners have created the non-profit Association of County Commissioners of Georgia Leasing Corporation to sell tax-exempt bonds to cover the cost of specific county projects and to pass on to participating county governments lower debt service through the use of a lease pool. Each participating county receives its own lease and is not responsible for the payments or obligations of other participating counties. The lease pool is particularly appealing to counties with small projects because the cost of issuing bonds is high. In addition, no referendum requirement applies to a lease-purchase transaction.

The New York Court of Appeals, the state's highest court, in 1988 upheld a state law requiring New York City uniformed officers to live in the city or in Nassau, Suffolk, Westchester, Rockland, Orange, or Putnam Counties. State law does not allow such officers to live in Connecticut, New Jersey, Pennsylvania, or upstate New York.

The same court in *Matter of Frew Run Gravel Products Incorporated v. Town of Carroll* unanimously ruled that the State Mined Land Reclamation Law does not preempt provisions of a municipal zoning law which regulates land in general. The New York Court of Appeals on September 21,

1988, overturned an appellate division ruling and upheld the validity of the Town of Knox sanitary code containing standards higher than state required standards. The code specifically prohibits owners of a trailer park from dumping sewage on the surface of the ground.

The New York Court of Appeals in *Sutka v. Connors* determined in 1989 that the line-of-duty presumption for firefighters' heart-related retirement disability benefits should not be read into section 207a of the General Municipal Law which governs firefighters' sick leave benefits.

In *City of East Point v. Smith* (365 S.E. 2d 432), the Georgia Supreme Court in 1988 upheld the requirement of a municipality that all employees possessing the police power are subject to urinalysis.

The New Hampshire Supreme Court in *State v. Thibeault* upheld in 1987 the authority of a town to enact earth excavation regulations under any or all of three separate enabling statutes.

As noted in the previous section, a Guilderland, New York, local law imposing impact fees on developers was ruled to be unconstitutional. In *City of Miami Beach v. Amoco Oil Company* (510 So.2d 609), the Florida District Court of Appeal for the third district held in 1987 that the city's zoning ordinance prohibiting the sale of beer by gasoline filling stations was preempted by the state beer licensing statute.

In 1988, the Florida District Court of Appeal for the fifth district in *City of Ormond Beach v. County of Volusia* ruled that city ordinances "opting out" of the county impact fee for county roads were invalid because the ordinances did not involve the police power or a municipal governmental function.

The Connecticut Supreme Court in *Builders Service Corporation et al. v. Town of East Hampton et al.* (208 Conn. 267) ruled in 1988 that, in the absence of evidence demonstrating a rational relationship between minimum floor area requirements and any legitimate objective of zoning, the town's floor area requirements (1,400 square feet minimum) were invalid.

In *State v. Yee*, the New Hampshire Supreme Court overturned a conviction under Manchester's noise ordinance by ruling that part of the ordinance exceeded the city's authority under state law.

In *Mitchell v. Wilkerson* (372 S.E. 2d 432,), the Georgia Supreme Court in 1988 struck down the state's 1979 recall statute for failure to meet the express constitutional requirement that a recall statute state grounds for recall. In 1989, the Georgia General Assembly added sections 21-4-1 *et seq.* to the Official Code of Georgia Annotated specifying grounds for recall. The 1979 recall statute had been employed frequently to recall local government officials.

On November 20, 1989, the Pennsylvania Commonwealth Court upheld a decision of the Court of Common Pleas for Chester County invalidating a business tax enacted by the Borough of West Chester on December 1, 1988. The Commonwealth Court ruled that section 533 of Act 145, the local tax reform act, prohibits municipalities from enacting a new mercantile or business privilege tax after November 30, 1988, the date of passage of the Act. The court's decision was unexpected since most provisions in the act were contingent upon voter approval of a proposed constitutional amendment. Rejection of the proposed amendment led observers to assume Act 145 was invalid.

In 1989, the United States Court of Appeals for the Second Circuit ruled in *RRI v. Village of Southampton* in favor of the village in a section 1983 action commenced by a developer. The action was initiated in the United States District Court for the Eastern District of New York and resulted in a finding in favor of the developer and an award of $2.7 million in attorney's fees and damages. The Court of Appeals reversed the verdict and ruled that "the record was insufficient to support a finding of such a clear entitlement to the permit as to establish a property interest protected by the Fourteenth Amendment."

In 1989, a New Jersey administrative law judge approved the state Department of Education's plan to take over the Jersey City's public schools for a period of at least five years because of "deep-rooted and endemic" problems. The takeover is authorized by a 1988 urban school intervention law enacted by the Legislature.

Municipal officials continued to seek advisory opinions from state officials. In 1988, Delaware State Solicitor Michael F. Foster and Deputy Attorney General Frederick H. Schranck advised members of the Legislature that the proposed annexation of land by the City of Milford "does not meet the contiguity requirements of the Milford City Charter and would therefore be illegal if carried out."

In 1989, Delaware State Solicitor Foster and Deputy Attorney General J. Patrick Hurley advised the Secretary of Public Safety that officers of the Frederica Police Department may conduct routine traffic enforcement within one mile of the limits of the town and the revenue produced by such activity should be paid to the state.

In Informal Opinion Number 88-73, the New York Attorney General informed a town counsel that the state Agriculture and Markets Law preempts the field of prevention of cruelty to animals and local governments lack authority to regulate in the area. In Informal Opinion Number 88-22, the attorney general advised that a village may establish a penalty for violation of a local law. And, in Informal Opinion number 88-24, he advised that a village may appoint school crossing guards with authority to regulate traffic on a state highway to protect children going to and from school.

In 1989, the New York attorney general in Informal Opinion Number 89-34 informed the City of Yonkers corporation counsel that the city lacks authority to limit the number of charter commissions that may be created. Under state law, a city council, voters by petition and the mayor each may establish a charter commission.

The Corning city attorney was advised by the New York attorney general in 1989 that section 20 (32) of the General City Law does not supersede the locally established Police Commission since the section delegates authority to cities and does not mandate that action be initiated.

On August 7, 1989, the Town of Newburgh was advised by the New York attorney general that it possessed authority under the general municipal law to enact a local law containing regulations more expansive in their application than the state Public Health Law relative to the supply of water. On the same day, the attorney general advised that a director of a county laboratory may serve also as county coroner.

Mandate Relief

The growing financial burden placed upon municipalities by state mandates led to a movement in the 1970s to amend state constitutions either to restrict the authority of the state government to issue mandates or to require reimbursement by the state of mandated costs. By 1987, twelve state constitutions contained such provision.

In 1988, Alabama became the thirteenth state to amend its constitution to address the mandate issue. A voter approved amendment stipulates that no general, special, or local law mandating increased municipal expenditures becomes effective unless the law is approved by the governing body of the concerned municipalities or the law provides the "municipal governing bodies with new or additional revenues sufficient to fund such new or increased expenditures."

New Hampshire voters in 1984 ratified a proposed constitutional amendment forbidding the imposition of mandates on cities and towns unless mandated cost are reimbursed. Although the amendment persuaded the General Court (Legislature) not to adopt new mandates, the amendment has been interpreted by the state as allowing departments and agencies to issue new and expensive mandates provided the agencies possessed authority to adopt such rules and regulations prior to November 1984. To cite one example, state officials estimate that the cost of complying with new standards for elementary schools, chiefly for staff additions and larger buildings, will be $19 million.

On November 15, 1989, the executive departments and administration committee of the New Hampshire House of Representatives rejected a bill requiring the state to fund fully costs to cities and towns resulting from state rules and regulations. Agencies with authority to issue rules and regulations prior to adoption of the 1984 constitutional amendment may continue to do so without necessitating state reimbursement costs imposed upon local governments.

Chapter 213 of the Rhode Island Public Laws of 1987, (1) requires fiscal notes for all administrative rules to be prepared by a department or agency "in consultation and cooperation with the Department of Administration and the Rhode Island League of Cities and Towns," (2) defines a state mandate as "any state initiated statutory or executive action that requires a local government to establish, expand, or modify its activities in such a way as to necessitate additional expenditures from local revenue sources," (3) directs the Department of Administration, in consultation with towns and cities, to maintain "an identification of state mandates created by statute since January 1, 1970 and identify all mandates established "since July 1, 1979, which are subject to reimbursement in accordance with section 45-13-9 and the cost of each of these mandates to each city and town . . .," and, (4) requires the Department of Administration to submit to the state budget office a report of the cost of state mandates to be reimbursed.

The Rhode Island League of Cities and Towns in 1989 identified nine mandates subject to reimbursement and one mandate exempt from reimbursement. The league added ". . . the number has on the average decreased over the years . . ." and "shows that the mandate reimbursement legislation has served its intended purpose." The league also noted that several recent mandates include a funding source.

In October 1989, the Rhode Island Department of Administration issued a *Report on State Mandates* covering 22 statutes from 1988 allegedly imposing mandates on cities and towns. The department ruled that seven acts were not mandates as defined by the statutes since the requirements do not expand or modify the activities of municipalities. Five acts were determined to be nonreimburseable state mandates because a funding source was provided. Four acts were determined to be state mandates ineligible for reimbursement because they are exempt under the general laws, and six acts were held to be reimburseable mandates.

The Tennessee County Services Association reported that the lack of clarity relative to the constitutional requirement that the state share in new mandated costs imposed on local governments makes the requirement "almost meaningless." Although the state shares revenue with local governments, the state share of mandates costs often is taken from unearmarked state shared revenues.

In 1989, Alaska reimbursed boroughs and cities an average of 33.75 percent of the loss in revenue resulting from state mandates exempting the personal residence of all senior citizens and disabled veterans from local property taxes.

Chapter 377 of the New York Laws of 1989 eliminated the requirement that cities must publish annually a parcel-by-parcel list of tax-exempt property in a local newspapers. And Chapter 78 of 1989 established a grants program to assist local records management. Chapter 737 of 1987 imposed records keeping and records management mandates upon general purpose local governments.

On November 21, 1989, Judge Joseph H. Hart of the 126th Judicial District Court (Travis County) ruled that Texas law does not grant discretionary authority to the Texas Department of Corrections to delay accepting inmates from county jails and issued a writ of mandamus requiring the department to reimburse counties for costs incurred in housing inmates who belong in state prisons.

New or Expanded Mandates

The New York Local Governments Records Law (chapter 737 of 1987) mandated that each municipality, with the exception of New York City, must designate a Records Management Officer and created the State and Local Government Records Advisory Council.

Chapter 781 of the New York Laws of 1989 established a comprehensive bridge inspection and management program. Each publicly owned bridge must be inspected by a licensed professional engineer or under the supervision of such an engineer biennially and reports must be filed with the state Department of Transportation.

The 1989 New York Legislature established the Combined Local and State Parole Program directing each county to establish a three-member "local conditional release commission" to assume responsibility for part of the functions of the State Parole Board. The purpose of the program is to grant counties greater discretion in determining who should be paroled from their jails.

Connecticut Public Act 88-13 of 1988 required the review of each municipal development plan at least once a decade and mandated that consideration must be given to the need for affordable housing when preparing or updating a plan.

Georgia HB 215 of 1989 implemented recommendations of the governor's Growth Strategic Commission and directed each local government to prepare a comprehensive plan relating to economic development, the environment, human services, infrastructure and land use.

Chapter 88-130 of the 1988 Florida Laws calls for each county to achieve a 30 percent reduction in the amount of solid waste that would have been disposed of in 1994 in the absence of solid waste reduction efforts, and to initiate a recycling program for newspapers, glass, plastic bottles and aluminum cans.

Chapter 168 of the Washington Laws reversed in part a 1985 law requiring the full-text or section-by-section summary publication of all adopted municipal ordinances. The new law allows a city to publish a summary of adopted ordinances and stipulates that an inadvertent omission or error does not invalidate the ordinance.

West Virginia House Bill 2414 of 1989 required municipalities to contribute to the policemen's and firemen's pension fund an annual amount not less than the normal cost as determined by an actuarial report.

The Virginia General Assembly has not enacted new major mandates upon its political subdivisions in the period 1987-1989, but has expanded certain mandates. For example, additional emphasis has been placed on remedial programs in the area of education. The commonwealth has funded its share of all new requirements.

In 1988, the Massachusetts Department of Personnel Administration published rules implementing the Pension Reform Act of 1988 forbidding new police officers and firefighters from smoking. The law applies to all public safety officers hired after January 1, 1988. A public safety officer found, after a hearing, to have violated the prohibition is fired.

Mandate Studies

The Florida Advisory Council on Intergovernmental Relations in 1987 released a *Report on Mandates and Measures Affecting Local Government Fiscal Capacity* reporting that 49 mandates were enacted compared to 44 in the 1986 legislative session. Thirty-five mandates from 1987 required a municipality or county to perform an activity or provide a service, and 14 restricted a municipality's or county's revenues or revenue generating capacity.

The Ohio State and Local Government Commission in December 1988 released a report, *An Overview of the Mandate Problem and Recommendations for Ohio*, recommending that a catalogue of state mandates be compiled and that the State and Local Government Commission, in conjunction with the Legislative Budget Office, and local government associations, establish a mandate review committee. In addition, the Commission recommended that the state fund the cost of each mandate or provide a means of funding for the affected local governments, that no bill be voted on by the General Assembly unless there is a complete and accurate fiscal note attached to it, and that fiscal notes be attached to all administrative rules, regulations and executive orders.

The Rhode Island Department of Administration in 1988 released a report on state laws determined to be mandates. The Department in 1988 also issued a report entitled *Pro-*

cedures for Reimbursement to Cities and Towns for Costs of State Mandates Which Were Established or Became Effective Between January 1, 1979 and September 24, 1987.

In 1989, the Texas Advisory Commission on Intergovernmental Relations released a report, *Mandates to Texas Counties: A Selective Review*, containing a summary of mandate literature, a typology of mandates, fiscal note/cost estimating, reimbursement, and alternative approaches.

Local governments upset by state mandates often complain about the failure of the state government to comply with the mandates imposed upon political subdivisions. The New York Department of Environmental Conservation released in 1989 an environmental audit report revealing that 267 state facilities — armories, prisons, transportation facilities, psychiatric hospitals and fish hatcheries — were "significantly out of compliance" with at least one state environmental law.

State Restraints

Chapter 358 of the Minnesota Laws of 1987 established a program of state regulation of pesticides and preempted local regulation of pesticides except for pesticide application warning ordinances.

Chapter 88-130 of the Florida Laws of 1988 forbids the disposal of lead-acid batteries at landfills or waste-to-energy facilities.

Virginia Senate Bill 601 of 1989 forbids local governments from enacting ordinances regulating smoking in private business establishments after July 1, 1989, but the restraint sunsets on June 30, 1990. The new law also forbids local governments from restricting the use of tobacco products by their employees during off-duty hours with the exception of employees covered by the heart and lung laws.

Chapter 223 of the New Hampshire Laws of 1988 amended the Home Rule Law by placing additional substantive and procedural restrictions on home rule for cities and towns. The chapter stipulates that charter provisions may not be contrary to current state law, reduces the time period between the election of a charter commission and the date it must release a preliminary report by 30 days and a final report by 60 days, prohibits voting on petitioned charter amendments at other than regular or annual municipal elections, and restricts the authority of cities and towns to adopt ordinances or by-laws or exercise a power of function only to those granted to a municipality by the state constitution or general law.

Rhode Island Public Law 601 of 1988 established a new comprehensive planning and land use program under which cities and towns must develop plans for future land use containing specified required elements. Plans must be submitted to the Director of Administration for review to determine whether "all local comprehensive plans . . . are consistent with state goals . . ." And, Georgia House Bill 154 of 1989 preempted local building codes by substituting a statewide standard code.

In 1989, the California Legislature enacted a law making the Oakland School District the first to be controlled by a trustee. The law was precipitated by the threatened bankruptcy of the district and the trustee's authority is limited to the district's finances.

In an administrative action restricting local discretionary authority, the Massachusetts Department of Environmental Quality Engineering in 1989 imposed a moratorium on new sewer hookups in Nantucket because the town approved too many building permits and the proposed sewage treatment plants will be overloaded when they open. Furthermore, the town violated state law by allowing developers to hook onto sewers without required permits. The moratorium is similar to one imposed earlier in Burlington and Woburn.

Similarly, the New York Emergency Finance Control Board of the City of Yonkers imposed in August 1988 a citywide hiring freeze because the city faced the threat of bankruptcy resulting from large daily fines imposed by the United States District Court for the city's failure to comply with a court-ordered housing desegregation plan. In December 1988, the board lifted the freeze since the fines had been suspended pending an appeal by the city. The board was established by the 1984 Legislature when Yonkers was verging on bankruptcy.

Summary

State legislatures in the period 1987 to 1989 continued to broaden incrementally the discretionary authority of their political subdivisions, but also mandated the units to initiate specified actions and removed and restricted the authority of units in several functional areas. Similarly, court decisions and advisory opinions were mixed relative to the discretionary authority of local governments.

With respect to mandate relief, Alabama became the 13th state to adopt a constitutional provision restricting the authority of the Legislature to mandate local expenditures. Although New Hampshire voters had approved a similar constitutional amendment in 1984, the prohibition has been evaded in part because the state has interpreted the amendment as allowing agencies to issue new mandates provided they had authority to do so prior to 1984.

Recent trends suggest that most states will continue to make gradual changes in state-local relations in the form of additional grants of discretionary authority, mandates and restraints.

References

Local Discretionary Authority

David R. Berman, et al., "County Home Rule: Does Where You Stand Depend on Where You Sit?", *State and Local Government Review*, Spring 1985, pp. 232-34.

Gordon L. Clark, *Judges and Cities: Interpreting Local Autonomy* (Chicago: University of Chicago Press, 1985).

Jefferson B. Fordham, *Model Constitutional Provisions for Municipal Home Rule* (Chicago: American Municipal Association, 1953).

Michael E. Libonati, "Local Governments in State Courts: A New Chapter in Constitutional Law?" *Intergovernmental Perspective*, Summer/Fall 1987, pp. 15-17.

Model City Charter, 7th ed. (Denver: National Civic League, 1989).

Rodney L. Mott, *Home Rule for America's Cities* (Chicago: American Municipal Association, 1949).

State-Local Relations (Chicago: The Council of State Governments, 1946).

Joseph F. Zimmerman, *Measuring Local Discretionary Authority* (Washington, D.C.: United States Advisory Commission on Intergovernmental Relations, 1981).

Joseph F. Zimmerman, *State-Local Relations: A Partnership Approach* (New York: Praeger Publishers, 1983).

State-Local Relations Bodies

State-Local Relations Bodies, State ACIRS, and Other Approaches (Washington, D.C.: United States Advisory Commission on Intergovernmental Relations, 1981).

Intergovernmental Fiscal Relations

J. Richard Aronson and John Hilley, *Financing State and Local Governments*, 4th ed. (Washington, D.C.: The Brookings Institution, 1986).

Terry N. Clark, *et al.*, *Financial Handbook for Mayors and City Managers* (Florence, Kentucky: Van Nostrand Reinhold, 1986).

Proposition 2½: The Fiscal Facts (Boston: Massachusetts Department of Revenue, 1985).

Proposition 13 — How California Governments Coped with a $6 Billion Revenue Loss (Washington, D.C.: United States Government Printing Office, 1979).

United States Department of the Treasury, *Federal-State-Local Fiscal Relations: Report to the Congress* (Washington, D.C.: United States Government Printing Office, 1985).

State Mandates

Fiscal Effects of State School Mandates (Albany: New York State Legislative Commission on Expenditure Review, 1978).

State Mandates to Counties (Albany: New York State Legislative Commission on Expenditure Review, 1981).

Joseph F. Zimmerman, *State Mandating of Local Expenditures* (Washington, D.C.: United States Advisory Commission on Intergovernmental Relations, 1978).

Joseph F. Zimmerman, "The State Mandate Problem," *State and Local Government Review*, Spring 1987, pp. 78-84.

STATE AID TO LOCAL GOVERNMENTS

By David Kellerman and Henry Wulf

State intergovernmental expenditures totaled $151.7 billion during 1988, of which $149.0 billion was state aid to local governments. States' fiscal support of their local governments has kept pace with other state government spending in recent years, remaining at about 35 percent of total state general expenditures since 1983. From 1983 to 1988, state aid to local governments grew over 50 percent, from $99.1 billion to $149.0 billion. During the same period, federal government grants-in-aid to state and local governments grew only 24 percent, from $92.7 billion to $114.6 billion.

This article focuses on state aid to local governments in the form of intergovernmental expenditures. As needs for particular public services change, or as new needs come into existence, states often choose to lend financial support to their localities and allow them to provide the services. Fiscal assistance is the device that enables states to encourage localities to provide a particular service, and to control the level of services being provided.

Only the types of state aid to local governments that involve a direct transfer of funds are discussed in this article. Actually, direct provision of services by a state is the most common form of aid to localities. There is also a substantial amount of indirect aid that exists in such forms as joint investment pools, financial guidance, so-called bond banks, payments on behalf of local government employees in state-administered employee retirement systems, the administration of local public employee retirement funds and other activities.

Functional Distribution of State Aid

State aid for education continues to be the largest functional category of state payments to local governments. Local education aid makes up nearly two-thirds of all state aid. Public welfare is the next largest function, followed by general local government support and highways, as shown in Table A below.

David Kellerman is Chief, Federal Financial Staff and Henry Wulf is Chief, Finance Branch, both at the Governments Division, U.S. Bureau of the Census.

Table A
Percent Distribution of State Aid, Selected Years 1976-1988

		% Distributed by Level of Government		% Distributed by Function				
Fiscal Year	Total	To Local Governments	To Federal Government	General Local Govt. Support	Education	Public Welfare	Highways	Other
1976	100.0	98.0	2.0	9.8	58.9	16.4	5.6	9.3
1978	100.0	97.8	2.2	10.1	59.6	14.9	5.7	9.6
1980	100.0	97.9	2.1	10.2	62.3	13.0	5.2	9.2
1982	100.0	98.2	1.8	10.2	61.5	13.9	5.1	9.4
1984	100.0	98.4	1.6	9.9	62.3	12.6	5.2	10.0
1986	100.0	98.4	1.6	10.1	62.1	12.4	4.9	10.5
1988	100.0	98.3	1.7	9.8	62.9	11.6	4.6	11.1

Source: U.S Bureau of the Census

During 1988, state aid for education increased to $95.4 billion. Thirty states distributed over $1 billion each in education aid, with California outpacing all others by providing over $16 billion to local school systems.

In some states, aid for education is characterized by efforts to "equalize" the financial resources devoted to education among all areas of the state. Such decisions are based upon differences in local area fiscal capacity, and subsequently tax effort, that can result in wide differences in per pupil spending or teacher salaries within a state. Intergovernmental expenditures (state aid) can be one method of helping local governments meet statewide standards and objectives for educational spending.

The goal of equalizing local educational spending can require some differentiation in the amount of state aid being provided to local school systems. This effect cannot be tracked in the summarized data from Census Bureau surveys.

State aid for public welfare was $15.0 billion in 1988. Not all states have aid programs in public welfare. Some administer public welfare programs directly, rather than allowing their county or city governments to administer the programs. Aid for public welfare excludes state-to-federal intergovernmental expenditures, however, which was an additional $2.7 billion in 1988. Most of this is for Supplemental Security Income (SSI), which is classified as a public welfare program.

The next largest amount of state aid is for general local government support. At $14.9 billion, this area represents about 10 percent of all state aid. Much of this aid is from shared taxes, usually some portion of a state-imposed general sales tax.

State aid for highways continues to decline as a percentage of total state aid to localities. For 1988, highway aid totaled $6.9 billion, or 4.6 percent of all state intergovernmental expenditures. In absolute dollars, highway aid has risen an average of only 5.7 percent annually from 1983 to 1988 compared with annual growth of 8.5 percent annually for state intergovernmental aid overall.

This situation parallels federal aid to states for highways, which has been characterized by slower growth since 1985. Some of the federal highway aid to states is shared with local governments. Federal aid for highways was $13.5 billion in 1988. However, states have extensive direct highway expenditures of their own, and impose a variety of taxes and fees to raise highway revenue in amounts over and above the intergovernmental aid they receive from the federal government. The level of state aid to local governments for highways is affected by the extent to which a state decides to administer its own highway programs directly, as opposed to allowing its localities to do so.

The "other purposes" category of state aid is just under 10 percent of the total. The $16.7 billion in such aid for 1988 included the following: health ($5.4 billion), transit subsidies ($2.4 billion), corrections ($1 billion), housing ($1 billion) and miscellaneous ($6.9 billion).

Variations Among the States in Aid Programs

The level of state aid for local governments varies considerably among the states. Several factors influence this, including the structure and organization of the local governments, the extent to which states have relinquished control to local governments for such programs as education, welfare and highways, and even the financing (tax and revenue) choices made by state governments to fund the aid. These decisions are in turn affected by such factors as demographics, urbanization, geography and political tradition.

Nationally, state aid to local governments averaged about $608 per capita during 1988. Per capita state aid ranged from lows of $42 in Hawaii and $186 in New Hampshire, to $1,516 in Alaska and $1,151 in Wyoming. Table B displays the distribution of states for selected ranges of per capita aid to local governments. Thirty-four states have aid payments in the range of $400 to $750 per capita. Hawaii's low per capita figure reflects the fact that the state administers directly the elementary and secondary educational programs. Thus Hawaii has no state-to-local aid

Table B
State Per Capita Expenditure Distribution, 1988

Per Capita Amount	Number of States
Over $1,000	3
$750-1,000	4
$500-750	13
$400-500	21
$300-400	7
$200-300	0
Less than $200	2

for education, which is the single largest category of aid in all other states.

Other states have common factors that characterize their aid programs and the level of aid they provide. For example, the two states with the largest per capita aid to local governments — Alaska and Wyoming — channel "shared revenues" to their localities. Both get considerable revenues from natural resources that they use to support local governments.

One frequent vehicle for state aid is for property tax relief. Many states mandate tax relief programs for targeted groups, such as senior citizens. Such a program can be administered in several ways. The two most common are (1) state direct reimbursement to taxpayers (often via income tax credits or deductions) and (2) state reimbursement to local governments for tax reductions granted to the targeted groups.

Another increasingly common type of state aid derives from lottery revenue. Twenty-six states had lotteries operating in 1988 (with five more scheduled to start up). Often, lotteries have been approved by voters on the condition that profits be targeted for particular purposes such as education as is the case in California, Iowa, Michigan, New Hampshire and New Jersey.

State Aid for Different Types of Governments

Tables 9.8 and 9.9 contain a breakdown of state aid payments by type of receiving government, on a state-by-state basis. At the national level, independent school district governments are targeted for most state aid — about 52 percent during fiscal year 1988. However, school systems in general receive an even larger share of total state aid, since in many states the school systems are administered by city or county governments. In these cases, such as in Maryland, North Carolina and Virginia, the state intergovernmental expenditure to counties, municipalities, or townships contains a large amount of money for education. This can be seen more clearly in table 9.7, which shows $95.4 billion in state intergovernmental expenditures for education that includes $1.2 billion in Maryland, $3.0 in North Carolina and $2.1 in Virginia.

The counties, municipalities and townships comprise general purpose local governments. States channel about 41 percent of their aid to this group, for a variety of functions ranging from education to highways, pollution control and mass transit.

For about five percent of state aid nationally, the Census Bureau classification cannot identify the final recipient local governments. These governments are included in the "combined" category.

A small share of state intergovernmental expenditure flows to the federal government. During 1988, 32 states made such payments, which totaled $2.7 billion. This represented about 1.7 percent of all state intergovernmental expenditures. State-to-federal payments are made primarily to support the Supplemental Security Income (SSI) program. Many states have chosen to supplement the SSI payments by combining their benefit payments with the federal basic benefits. This is primarily an administrative convenience and not a true intergovernmental aid program.

Administering State Aid Programs

States face a variety of choices in administering aid programs for local governments. Once a need is identified and agreed upon, the basic decisions of how to finance an aid program and how to allocate the funds must be determined. Such decisions are not limited to aid programs created to fill a particular public need. The emergence of windfall revenues, such as those from sudden changes in severance-related revenues, sometimes prompts state officials to use these moneys to benefit citizens or their localities.

The method of financial support for state aid programs is sometimes decided based upon the type of aid program. Aid programs for a single purpose are often financed by a related revenue source — gas taxes fund highway aid or mass transit, for example. Aid programs designed to meet multiple (or general) needs are more frequently financed by general revenue — sales taxes or other general fund sources.

For aid programs targeted for a specific function, allocation decisions are usually based upon need. Equalization, previously discussed, can also be an important factor for educational programs. General local support programs, on the other hand, are more often allocated based upon an external factor, such as population or personal income. This results in a more extensive and even distribution.

Decisions about financing and allocating state aid are often related. For example, a highway aid program might be financed via a user related tax (gas tax) that is allocated according to the local county of origin (where the tax was paid). Similarly, sales taxes are usually returned to the county or city of origin when they are used to finance aid for general local government support.

Additional Data Sources

A recent report of the National Association of State Budget Officers, *State Aid to Local Governments, 1989*, furnished information on this subject similar to the Bureau of the Census' annual reports. The categorizations, explanations and tabular presentations provide a useful perspective for analytical purposes.

For historical data on this subject, consult a report done every five years since 1957 as part of the Census of Governments entitled *State Payments to Local Governments*. These publications describe the programs for financial grants and reimbursements to local governments in each state and the amounts paid under each program.

INTERGOVERNMENTAL AFFAIRS

Table 9.2
SUMMARY OF STATE INTERGOVERNMENTAL PAYMENTS: 1942 to 1988
(In millions, except per capita)

Fiscal year	Total Amount	Total Per capita	To federal governments (a)	To local governments - For general local government support	To local governments - For specified purposes Total	Education	Public welfare	Highways	All other
1942	$ 1,780	$ 13.38	...	$ 224	$ 1,556	$ 790	$ 390	$ 344	$ 32
1944	1,842	13.95	...	274	1,568	861	368	298	41
1946	2,092	15.03	...	357	1,735	953	376	339	67
1948	3,283	22.60	...	428	2,855	1,554	648	507	146
1950	4,217	28.13	...	482	3,735	2,054	792	610	279
1951	4,678	30.78	...	513	4,165	2,248	974	667	276
1952	5,044	32.57	...	549	4,495	2,523	976	728	268
1953	5,384	34.20	...	592	4,792	2,737	981	803	271
1954	5,679	35.41	...	600	5,079	2,930	1,004	871	274
1955	5,986	36.61	...	591	5,395	3,150	1,046	911	288
1956	6,538	39.26	...	631	5,907	3,541	1,069	984	313
1957	7,440	43.87	...	668	6,772	4,212	1,136	1,082	342
1958	8,089	46.65	...	687	7,402	4,598	1,247	1,167	390
1959	8,689	49.26	...	725	7,964	4,957	1,409	1,207	391
1960	9,443	52.88	...	806	8,637	5,461	1,483	1,247	446
1961	10,114	55.51	...	821	9,293	5,963	1,602	1,266	462
1962	10,906	58.97	...	839	10,067	6,474	1,777	1,327	489
1963	11,885	63.34	...	1,012	10,873	6,993	1,919	1,416	545
1964	12,968	68.15	...	1,053	11,915	7,664	2,108	1,524	619
1965	14,174	73.57	...	1,102	13,072	8,351	2,436	1,630	655
1966	16,928	86.94	...	1,361	15,567	10,177	2,882	1,725	783
1967	19,056	96.94	...	1,585	17,471	11,845	2,897	1,861	868
1968	21,950	110.56	...	1,993	19,957	13,321	3,527	2,029	1,080
1969	24,779	123.56	...	2,135	22,644	14,858	4,402	2,109	1,275
1970	28,892	142.64	...	2,958	25,934	17,085	5,003	2,439	1,407
1971	32,640	158.39	...	3,258	29,382	19,292	5,760	2,507	1,823
1972	36,759	176.27	...	3,752	33,007	21,195	6,944	2,633	2,235
1973	40,822	193.81	...	4,280	36,542	23,316	7,532	2,953	2,741
1974	45,941	216.07	$ 341	4,804	40,796	27,107	7,029	3,211	3,449
1975	51,978	242.03	975	5,129	45,874	31,110	7,137	3,225	4,402
1976	57,858	266.79	1,180	5,674	51,004	34,084	8,307	3,241	5,372
1977	62,460	285.10	1,386	6,373	54,701	36,964	8,756	3,631	5,350
1978	67,287	303.87	1,472	6,819	58,996	40,125	8,586	3,821	6,464
1979	75,963	339.25	1,493	8,224	66,246	46,196	8,675	4,149	7,226
1980	84,504	374.06	1,746	8,644	74,114	52,688	9,242	4,383	7,801
1981	93,180	406.89	1,873	9,570	81,737	57,257	11,025	4,751	8,704
1982	98,743	426.78	1,793	10,044	86,906	60,684	11,965	5,028	9,229
1983	100,887	431.77	1,765	10,364	88,758	63,118	10,920	5,277	9,443
1984	108,373	459.46	1,722	10,745	95,906	67,485	11,923	5,687	10,811
1985	121,571	510.55	1,963	12,320	107,288	74,937	12,673	6,019	13,659
1986	131,966	548.78	2,106	13,384	116,476	81,929	14,215	6,470	13,862
1987	141,426	582.48	2,455	14,245	127,180	88,253	17,331	6,785	14,811
1988	151,662	618.55	2,653	14,897	136,765	95,391	17,665	6,949	16.760

Sources: U.S. Bureau of the Census, *State Payments to Local Governments (Census of Governments: 1982,* vol. 6, no. 3) and *State Government Finances.*
(a) Represents primarily state reimbursements for the supplemental security income program. This column also duplicates some funds listed under Public welfare and All other.

INTERGOVERNMENTAL AFFAIRS

Table 9.3
STATE INTERGOVERNMENTAL EXPENDITURE, BY STATE: 1982 to 1988

State	Amount (in thousands)				Per capita amounts				Percentage change in per capita amounts		
	1988	1986	1984	1982	1988	1986	1984	1982	1986 to 1988	1984 to 1986	1982 to 1984
United States	$151,661,866	$131,966,258	$108,373,188	$98,742,976	$618.55	$548.83	$460.11	$435.86	12.7	19.3	5.6
Alabama	1,772,140	1,563,108	1,310,399	1,136,158	432.02	385.67	328.42	291.77	12.0	17.4	12.6
Alaska	794,294	863,981	1,183,094	992,519	1,515.83	1,617.94	2,366.19	2,468.95	-6.3	-31.6	-4.2
Arizona	2,014,460	1,913,685	1,547,438	1,192,237	577.37	576.93	506.86	438.64	0.1	13.8	15.6
Arkansas	1,053,029	988,755	789,131	667,184	439.68	416.84	335.94	291.86	5.5	24.1	15.1
California	29,754,786	24,929,013	19,125,775	17,625,121	1,050.89	923.95	746.46	744.68	13.7	23.8	0.2
Colorado	1,601,393	1,459,018	1,522,105	1,200,839	485.12	446.59	478.95	415.52	8.6	-6.8	15.3
Connecticut	1,477,198	1,147,052	967,483	760,415	456.91	359.69	306.75	244.66	27.0	17.3	25.4
Delaware	317,800	254,127	218,833	214,619	481.52	401.46	356.99	361.31	19.9	12.5	-1.2
Florida	6,500,752	5,198,824	3,561,701	3,512,218	527.02	445.30	324.50	360.38	18.4	37.2	-10.0
Georgia	2,928,597	2,604,968	1,947,978	1,781,763	461.78	426.76	333.73	326.15	8.2	27.9	2.3
Hawaii	49,776	30,034	25,231	27,875	45.33	28.28	24.28	28.89	60.3	16.5	-16.1
Idaho	489,765	399,356	408,686	353,787	488.30	398.16	408.28	374.77	22.6	-2.5	8.9
Illinois	5,274,272	4,797,568	3,910,634	3,725,170	454.13	415.27	339.73	326.00	9.4	22.2	4.2
Indiana	2,995,457	2,591,875	2,321,187	2,045,228	539.14	470.91	422.19	372.54	14.5	11.5	13.3
Iowa	1,802,094	1,457,094	1,321,682	1,262,391	635.88	511.08	454.19	433.22	24.4	12.5	4.8
Kansas	1,073,214	994,956	846,726	711,548	430.15	404.29	347.30	300.99	6.4	16.4	15.4
Kentucky	1,741,531	1,415,742	1,288,688	1,107,357	467.27	379.76	346.14	302.56	23.0	9.7	14.4
Louisiana	1,865,441	1,867,466	1,746,045	1,599,993	423.19	414.90	391.31	380.41	2.0	6.0	2.9
Maine	544,712	427,857	349,880	297,274	452.04	364.44	302.66	264.24	24.0	20.4	14.5
Maryland	2,233,494	1,854,629	1,635,537	1,708,142	483.23	415.56	376.07	405.06	16.3	10.5	-7.2
Massachusetts	4,127,655	3,325,747	2,617,378	2,315,564	700.91	570.26	451.43	403.62	22.9	26.3	11.8
Michigan	5,813,874	4,842,870	4,037,673	3,824,824	629.21	529.56	444.92	412.96	18.8	19.0	7.7
Minnesota	3,621,482	3,124,133	2,880,437	3,016,693	840.84	741.37	692.08	740.11	13.4	7.1	-6.5
Mississippi	1,391,664	1,237,181	1,065,912	948,128	531.17	471.31	410.28	376.09	12.7	14.9	9.1
Missouri	2,303,781	1,915,955	1,589,484	1,167,399	448.12	378.20	317.39	237.42	18.5	19.2	33.7
Montana	308,044	319,790	293,193	243,384	382.66	390.46	355.82	309.26	-2.0	9.7	15.1
Nebraska	552,488	537,476	511,721	482,635	344.87	336.34	318.63	307.41	2.5	5.6	3.6
Nevada	725,283	590,225	487,427	456,728	688.12	612.90	535.05	570.91	12.3	14.6	-6.3
New Hampshire	204,898	174,711	157,680	139,824	188.85	170.12	161.39	151.82	11.0	5.4	6.3
New Jersey	5,462,250	4,803,345	4,133,531	4,030,065	707.45	630.36	550.04	547.19	12.2	14.6	0.5
New Mexico	1,244,887	1,119,486	967,744	829,899	826.07	756.92	679.60	636.91	9.1	11.4	6.7
New York	16,767,678	15,182,153	12,262,857	11,849,950	936.27	854.27	691.45	674.90	9.6	23.5	2.5
North Carolina	4,066,203	3,402,507	2,722,596	2,440,069	626.63	537.44	441.62	414.84	16.6	21.7	6.5
North Dakota	365,329	399,754	412,386	355,610	547.72	588.15	601.15	544.58	-6.9	-2.2	10.4
Ohio	6,315,346	5,536,665	4,779,871	3,561,699	581.79	514.94	444.56	329.85	13.0	15.8	34.8
Oklahoma	1,447,844	1,478,351	1,284,809	1,160,761	446.59	447.31	389.57	383.72	-0.2	14.8	1.5
Oregon	1,201,765	1,105,928	993,012	1,014,603	434.32	409.91	371.36	385.34	6.0	10.4	-3.6
Pennsylvania	6,119,723	5,364,037	4,703,507	4,014,697	509.93	451.18	395.22	338.39	13.0	14.2	16.8
Rhode Island	374,269	347,862	275,000	235,816	376.91	356.78	285.86	249.01	5.6	24.8	14.8
South Carolina	1,574,229	1,429,440	1,095,298	1,024,500	453.67	423.16	331.91	328.16	7.2	27.5	1.1
South Dakota	221,219	194,507	165,296	160,201	310.27	274.73	234.13	231.84	12.9	17.3	0.9
Tennessee	1,685,450	1,430,475	1,105,881	1,067,709	344.32	297.83	234.45	232.57	15.6	27.0	0.8
Texas	6,625,955	6,147,106	4,965,245	4,252,176	393.44	368.49	310.54	298.84	6.8	18.7	3.9
Utah	842,039	782,272	610,987	525,165	498.25	469.83	369.85	359.46	6.0	27.0	3.8
Vermont	213,223	158,962	135,974	110,722	382.81	293.83	256.55	216.68	30.3	14.5	18.4
Virginia	3,038,790	2,513,086	1,928,473	1,658,077	505.20	434.26	342.17	310.09	16.3	26.9	10.3
Washington	3,485,095	3,011,346	2,290,339	2,128,066	749.81	674.74	526.64	515.02	11.1	28.1	2.3
West Virginia	870,197	855,734	702,912	674,956	463.86	445.93	360.10	346.13	4.0	23.8	4.0
Wisconsin	3,855,521	3,286,305	2,638,645	2,761,315	794.13	686.79	553.64	586.76	15.6	24.1	-5.2
Wyoming	551,480	590,143	529,687	369,903	1,151.32	1,163.99	1,036.57	787.03	-1.1	12.3	31.7

Source: U.S. Bureau of the Census, *State Government Finances in 1988*; and previous annual reports.

Note: Includes payments to the federal government, primarily state reimbursements for the supplemental security income program.

INTERGOVERNMENTAL AFFAIRS

Table 9.4
PER CAPITA STATE INTERGOVERNMENTAL EXPENDITURE, BY FUNCTION AND BY STATE: 1987

State	Total	General local government support	Specified functions			Miscellaneous and combined
			Education	Public welfare	Highways	
United States	$ 582.48	$ 58.67	$363.48	$ 71.38	$27.94	$ 61.00
Alabama	398.85	20.91	303.71	2.60	32.70	38.93
Alaska	1,788.33	375.65	982.38	0.00	117.15	313.15
Arizona	582.68	133.10	340.88	0.37	84.41	23.92
Arkansas	414.91	20.08	305.41	0.67	41.63	47.11
California	999.01	74.27	553.44	256.98	32.58	81.74
Colorado	463.89	7.40	299.60	83.47	48.46	24.96
Connecticut	404.59	53.64	272.73	15.17	9.31	53.74
Delaware	434.18	0.00	381.46	1.08	8.87	42.77
Florida	48.26	74.84	351.95	0.00	16.84	46.32
Georgia	448.30	2.59	369.91	23.62	6.25	45.92
Hawaii	40.52	29.00	0.00	3.43	0.00	8.10
Idaho	433.38	39.77	327.08	0.00	46.94	19.60
Illinois	444.74	46.18	302.80	11.33	30.70	53.72
Indiana	502.58	98.70	307.48	34.52	47.44	14.45
Iowa	551.65	54.13	373.62	5.21	71.56	47.13
Kansas	396.50	23.41	324.80	0.00	31.02	17.26
Kentucky	420.49	0.00	346.39	0.00	20.70	53.40
Louisana	407.15	36.22	325.85	7.45	4.51	33.11
Maine	391.89	42.50	304.58	12.77	13.39	18.65
Maryland	451.67	36.33	242.10	0.02	69.01	104.20
Massachusetts	664.50	162.89	315.80	21.17	19.32	145.33
Michigan	558.82	96.44	274.64	19.95	64.68	103.12
Minnesota	810.28	147.85	425.67	117.89	56.16	62.71
Mississippi	513.03	74.56	365.17	1.01	28.72	43.58
Missouri	409.44	1.20	341.06	1.33	23.82	42.03
Montana	393.31	24.71	298.77	10.34	17.60	41.89
Nebraska	343.60	46.21	183.05	1.14	59.08	54.12
Nevada	646.58	227.83	388.53	4.73	15.97	9.52
New Hampshire	172.37	35.42	71.94	27.46	13.14	24.41
New Jersey	646.23	134.87	368.05	90.22	1.65	51.43
New Mexico	779.59	183.76	550.67	0.00	9.36	35.80
New York	911.05	64.23	408.83	308.77	13.40	115.83
North Carolina	569.72	35.27	429.43	31.35	10.43	63.24
North Dakota	538.28	50.56	380.54	18.87	59.39	28.92
Ohio	557.30	68.95	346.07	60.72	39.71	41.85
Oklahoma	417.56	3.36	337.51	3.77	45.22	27.70
Oregon	437.24	51.14	266.36	0.90	74.50	44.34
Pennsylvania	479.02	7.65	292.30	61.37	18.39	99.32
Rhode Island	372.30	35.20	271.00	29.12	0.37	36.60
South Carolina	427.86	44.90	360.15	1.36	4.33	17.11
South Dakota	288.57	65.17	183.18	0.95	0.73	38.54
Tennessee	326.62	38.19	216.48	5.50	44.50	21.94
Texas	370.98	2.63	352.79	0.19	0.77	14.60
Utah	469.02	0.00	404.00	2.29	18.45	44.28
Vermont	328.11	7.63	253.95	13.92	37.27	15.35
Virginia	466.91	17.29	318.28	46.32	22.50	62.52
Washington	640.29	14.03	505.80	20.61	42.91	56.95
West Virginia	471.29	7.89	447.31	0.00	0.00	16.09
Wisconsin	709.18	225.62	288.25	47.72	42.02	105.58
Wyoming	1,121.93	182.41	703.06	0.68	33.35	202.44

Source: U.S. Bureau of the Census, *State Government Finances in 1987.*
Note: Includes payments to the federal governments, primarily state reimbursements for the supplemental security income program (under public welfare).

INTERGOVERNMENTAL AFFAIRS

Table 9.5
PER CAPITA STATE INTERGOVERNMENTAL EXPENDITURE, BY FUNCTION AND BY STATE: 1988

State	Total	General local government support	Specified functions			
			Education	Public welfare	Highways	Miscellaneous and unallocable
United States	$ 618.55	$ 60.76	$389.05	$ 72.04	$28.34	$ 68.36
Alabama	432.02	23.46	330.72	2.28	33.64	41.92
Alaska	1,515.83	208.61	961.85	0.00	66.35	279.00
Arizona	577.37	136.68	323.67	0.34	91.68	25.00
Arkansas	439.68	18.62	336.06	0.09	40.56	44.35
California	1,050.89	79.68	583.58	268.84	29.12	89.65
Colorado	485.12	6.68	318.46	83.05	46.52	30.41
Connecticut	456.91	62.75	320.58	14.64	9.25	49.69
Delaware	481.52	10.62	398.28	1.11	7.69	63.82
Florida	527.02	84.12	386.13	0.00	14.42	42.35
Georgia	461.78	2.54	403.51	0.00	6.87	48.85
Hawaii	45.33	29.93	0.00	3.66	0.00	11.74
Idaho	488.30	46.12	371.14	0.00	48.51	22.53
Illinois	454.13	54.29	303.16	11.92	30.73	54.03
Indiana	539.14	101.69	323.06	44.28	49.89	20.21
Iowa	635.88	54.79	448.70	9.42	75.12	47.85
Kansas	430.15	29.45	343.12	0.00	32.56	25.01
Kentucky	467.27	0.00	389.26	0.00	22.15	55.86
Louisiana	423.19	35.24	345.65	5.66	3.36	33.28
Maine	452.04	48.06	358.88	13.73	13.29	18.10
Maryland	483.23	39.91	256.34	0.01	73.11	113.86
Massachusetts	700.91	179.67	321.40	21.03	13.00	165.81
Michigan	629.21	101.63	323.71	20.49	66.05	117.32
Minnesota	840.84	151.71	446.80	112.63	65.16	64.53
Mississippi	531.17	78.78	391.30	1.30	30.56	29.24
Missouri	448.12	3.09	372.52	1.30	29.36	41.85
Montana	382.66	4.94	314.39	10.87	17.68	34.78
Nebraska	344.87	43.33	182.20	1.13	61.61	56.61
Nevada	688.12	243.40	401.81	5.25	24.14	13.53
New Hampshire	188.85	29.36	91.55	29.39	14.65	23.90
New Jersey	707.45	134.05	410.87	95.05	1.54	65.94
New Mexico	826.07	196.19	586.41	0.02	17.59	25.87
New York	936.27	61.13	450.96	287.87	8.93	127.37
North Carolina	626.63	36.16	469.95	34.20	13.13	73.19
North Dakota	547.72	68.64	369.66	21.65	63.57	24.20
Ohio	581.79	71.18	354.32	62.50	43.86	49.94
Oklahoma	446.59	4.02	347.09	1.32	51.08	43.08
Oregon	434.32	32.75	273.78	0.00	76.10	51.69
Pennsylvania	509.93	7.96	306.27	64.60	18.40	112.71
Rhode Island	376.91	36.64	298.12	28.54	0.29	13.31
South Carolina	453.67	53.62	374.31	1.63	4.22	19.89
South Dakota	310.27	64.45	206.46	0.92	0.79	37.65
Tennessee	344.32	40.85	226.57	5.16	41.19	30.56
Texas	393.44	2.52	362.68	0.00	0.69	27.54
Utah	498.25	0.00	435.46	1.44	23.90	37.45
Vermont	382.81	11.61	302.55	14.51	35.50	18.64
Virginia	505.20	5.72	341.77	53.58	23.77	80.37
Washington	749.81	13.84	543.78	40.03	45.77	106.39
West Virginia	463.86	5.89	443.35	0.00	0.00	14.61
Wisconsin	794.13	226.53	356.21	49.54	57.69	104.16
Wyoming	1,151.32	183.24	699.81	7.05	41.92	219.30

Source: U.S. Bureau of the Census, *State Government Finances in 1988*.
Note: Includes payment to the federal government, primarily state reimbursements for the supplemental security income program (under public welfare).

INTERGOVERNMENTAL AFFAIRS

Table 9.6
STATE INTERGOVERNMENTAL EXPENDITURE, BY FUNCTION AND BY STATE: 1987
(In thousands of dollars)

State	Total	General local government support	Functions – Education	Public welfare	Highways	Miscellaneous and combined
UNITED STATES	$141,425,744	$14,245,089	$88,253,298	$17,331,210	$6,784,699	$14,811,448
Alabama	1,628,921	85,400	1,240,371	10,636	133,544	158,970
Alaska	937,086	196,839	514,769	0	61,389	164,089
Arizona	1,981,109	452,544	1,158,988	1,256	286,998	81,323
Arkansas	990,802	47,950	729,328	1,608	99,420	112,496
California	27,625,639	2,053,781 (a)	15,304,352 (b)	7,106,186 (c)	900,850	2,260,470
Colorado	1,527,581	24,354	986,578	274,877	159,564	82,208
Connecticut	1,299,536	172,278	876,007	48,734	29,893	172,624
Delaware	281,350	0	247,187	700	5,750	27,713
Florida	5,890,208	899,761	4,231,178	0	202,416	556,853
Georgia	2,791,541	16,117	2,303,435	147,072	38,945	285,972
Hawaii	43,842	31,373	0	3,710	0	8,759
Idaho	433,384	39,773	327,076	0	46,938	19,597
Illinois	5,151,843	534,952	3,507,693	131,295	355,638	622,265
Indiana	2,779,292	545,801	1,700,339	190,910	262,321	79,921
Iowa	1,557,314	152,802	1,054,733	14,713	202,014	133,052
Kansas	981,336	57,942	803,890	0	76,777	42,727
Kentucky	1,565,480	0	1,289,596	0	77,081	198,803
Louisiana	1,811,000	161,116	1,449,399	33,118	20,075	147,292
Maine	464,779	50,404	361,234	15,140	15,879	22,122
Maryland	2,048,764	164,811	1,098,176	100	313,007	472,670
Massachusetts	3,891,302	953,858	1,849,301	123,959	113,117	851,067
Michigan	5,143,979	887,691	2,528,022	183,637	595,365	949,264
Minnesota	3,438,831	627,467	1,806,525	500,329	238,361	266,149
Mississippi	1,346,201	195,634	958,194	2,657	75,358	114,358
Missouri	2,091,007	6,123	1,741,806	6,801	121,652	214,625
Montana	318,184	19,992	241,702	8,365	14,240	33,885
Nebraska	547,691	73,664	291,779	1,810	94,175	86,263
Nevada	650,462	229,198	390,859	4,759	16,064	9,582
New Hampshire	182,019	37,399	75,972	29,003	13,873	25,772
New Jersey	4,959,157	1,035,030	2,824,409	692,358	12,681	394,679
New Mexico	1,166,268	274,902	823,809	0	14,006	53,551
New York	16,248,656	1,145,524	7,291,524 (d)	5,506,850 (e)	238,916	2,065,842
North Carolina	3,651,320	226,019	2,752,237	200,908	66,830	405,326
North Dakota	361,184	33,928	255,341	12,661	39,851	19,403
Ohio	6,027,790	745,742	3,743,116	656,708	429,537	452,687
Oklahoma	1,360,835	10,945	1,099,940	12,295	147,373	90,282
Oregon	1,190,596	139,246	725,285	2,443	202,871	120,751
Pennsylvania	5,720,515	91,322	3,490,650	732,837	219,668	1,186,038
Rhode Island	367,086	34,712	267,210	28,717	360	36,087
South Carolina	1,465,863	153,833	1,233,888	4,674	14,849	58,619
South Dakota	204,596	46,204	129,877	672	521	27,322
Tennessee	1,585,739	185,433	1,051,021	26,723	216,028	106,534
Texas	6,225,435	44,204	5,920,125 (f)	3,227	12,855	245,024
Utah	787,955	0	678,722	3,849	30,991	74,393
Vermont	179,476	4,174	138,908	7,616	20,384	8,394
Virginia	2,761,290	102,243	1,882,307	273,948	133,069	369,723
Washington	2,908,212	63,713	2,297,334	93,622	194,882	258,661
West Virginia	894,505	14,972	849,002	0	0	30,531
Wisconsin	3,409,036	1,084,540	1,385,605	229,395	201,981	507,515
Wyoming	549,747	89,379	344,499	332	16,342	99,195

Source: U.S. Bureau of the Census, *State Government Finances in 1987.*
Note: Totals may not add due to rounding.
(a) Includes $1,132,782,000 shared motor vehicle license taxes.
(b) Includes $12,666,555,000 redistribution of Federal funds to school districts and $1,894,852,000 community college grants.
(c) Includes $2,506,183,000 aid to local governments for families with dependent children and $1,354,877,000 reimbursement reimbursement to Federal government for supplemental security income program.
(d) Includes $6,875,384,000 general school support and $291,413,000 community college support.
(e) Includes $1,685,267,000 aid to local governments for families with dependent children, $888,531,000 vendor payment to New York City Hospital Corporation, and $451,743,000 welfare medical assistance.
(f) Includes $5,501,943,000 in support to school districts and $416,169,000 for Junior College support.

INTERGOVERNMENTAL AFFAIRS

Table 9.7
STATE INTERGOVERNMENTAL EXPENDITURE, BY FUNCTION AND BY STATE: 1988
(In thousands of dollars)

State	Total	General local government support	Functions - Education	Functions - Public welfare	Functions - Highways	Miscellaneous and combined
UNITED STATES	$151,661,866	$14,896,991	$95,390,536	$17,664,585	$6,949,190	$16,760,564
Alabama	1,772,140	96,253	1,356,615	9,344	137,992	171,936
Alaska	794,294	109,314	504,012	0	34,770	146,198
Arizona	2,014,460	476,861	1,129,298	1,200	319,866	87,235
Arkansas	1,053,029	44,591	804,872	211	97,145	106,210
California	29,754,786	2,256,180 (a)	16,523,562 (b)	7,612,029 (c)	824,568	2,538,447
Colorado	1,601,393	22,046	1,051,252	274,146	153,560	100,389
Connecticut	1,477,198	202,886	1,036,446	47,325	29,892	160,649
Delaware	317,800	7,006	262,867	730	5,078	42,119
Florida	6,500,752	1,037,564	4,762,897	0	177,903	522,388
Georgia	2,928,597	16,117	2,559,085	0	43,557	309,838
Hawaii	49,776	32,867	0	4,015	0	12,894
Idaho	489,765	46,256	372,256	0	48,656	22,597
Illinois	5,274,272	630,569	3,520,878	138,482	356,891	627,452
Indiana	2,995,457	564,966	1,794,932	246,045	277,205	112,309
Iowa	1,802,094	155,287	1,271,607	26,693	212,902	135,605
Kansas	1,073,214	73,484	856,083	0	81,239	62,408
Kentucky	1,741,531	0	1,450,761	0	82,567	208,203
Louisiana	1,865,441	155,324	1,523,643	24,951	14,825	146,698
Maine	544,712	57,907	432,448	16,540	16,010	21,807
Maryland	2,233,494	184,472	1,184,805	63	337,895	526,259
Massachusetts	4,127,655	1,058,064	1,892,744	123,870	76,546	976,431
Michigan	5,813,874	939,099	2,991,088	189,334	610,275	1,084,078
Minnesota	3,621,482	653,433	1,924,377	485,108	280,646	277,918
Mississippi	1,391,664	206,399	1,025,210	3,394	80,065	76,596
Missouri	2,303,781	15,904	1,915,102	6,680	150,926	215,169
Montana	308,044	3,978	253,084	8,747	14,236	27,999
Nebraska	552,488	69,409	291,887	1,804	98,697	90,691
Nevada	725,283	256,546	423,503	5,533	25,442	14,259
New Hampshire	204,898	31,859	99,331	31,886	15,892	25,930
New Jersey	5,462,250	1,035,036	3,172,362	733,870	11,880	509,102
New Mexico	1,244,887	295,656	883,713	24	26,504	38,990
New York	16,767,678	1,094,808	8,076,324 (d)	5,155,444 (e)	160,005	2,281,097
North Carolina	4,066,203	234,660	3,049,478	221,939	85,197	474,929
North Dakota	365,329	45,782	246,561	14,442	42,401	16,143
Ohio	6,315,346	772,619	3,846,118	678,450	476,093	542,066
Oklahoma	1,447,844	13,035	1,125,273	4,275	165,604	139,657
Oregon	1,201,765	90,633	757,537	5	210,572	143,018
Pennsylvania	6,119,723	95,494	3,675,504	775,312	220,784	1,352,629
Rhode Island	374,269	36,386	296,034	28,340	290	13,219
South Carolina	1,574,229	186,046	1,298,849	5,654	14,652	69,028
South Dakota	221,219	45,950	147,203	657	564	26,845
Tennessee	1,685,450	199,948	1,109,038	25,254	201,642	149,568
Texas	6,625,955	42,468	6,107,905 (f)	45	11,704	463,833
Utah	842,039	0	735,920	2,437	40,395	63,287
Vermont	213,223	6,465	168,521	8,080	19,776	10,381
Virginia	3,038,790	34,419	2,055,725	322,266	142,966	483,414
Washington	3,485,095	64,307	2,527,484	186,075	212,736	494,493
West Virginia	870,197	11,059	831,729	0	0	27,409
Wisconsin	3,855,521	1,099,807	1,729,405	240,510	280,099	505,700
Wyoming	551,480	87,772	335,208	3,376	20,080	105,044

Source: U.S. Bureau of the Census, *State Government Finances in 1988.*
Note: Totals may not add due to rounding.
(a) Includes $1,754,121,000 shared motor vehicle license tax.
(b) Includes $13,349,017,000 distribution of State and Federal funds to school districts and $2,158,506,000 community college grants.
(c) Includes $3,770,554,000 aid to local governments for families with dependent children and $1,846,496,000 reimbursement to Federal Government for supplemental security income program.
(d) Includes $7,627,493,000 general school support and $283,813,000 community college support.
(e) Includes $1,528,655,000 aid to local governments for families with dependent children and $992,950,000 vendor payment to New York City Hospital Corporation.
(f) Includes $5,677,244,000 in support to school districts and $430,626,000 for junior college support.

INTERGOVERNMENTAL AFFAIRS

Table 9.8
STATE INTERGOVERNMENTAL EXPENDITURE,
BY TYPE OF RECEIVING GOVERNMENT AND BY STATE: 1987
(In thousands of dollars)

State	Total intergovernmental expenditure	Type of receiving government						
		Federal	School districts	Counties	Municipalities	Townships and New England "towns"	Special districts	Combined and unallocable
United States	$141,425,744	$2,455,362	$72,862,919	$30,971,425	$22,245,511	$1,661,300	$1,431,741	$9,797,486
Alabama	1,628,921	0	1,240,371	276,642	110,269	0	0	1,639
Alaska	937,086	9,394	0	389,855	500,739	0	0	37,098
Arizona	1,981,109	1,256	1,158,988	377,912	436,129	0	0	6,824
Arkansas	990,802	134	727,953	124,317	81,472	0	8,308	48,618
California	27,625,639	1,667,314	14,562,399	9,164,361	1,870,499	0	138,683	222,383
Colorado	1,527,581	166	986,552	342,649	171,585	0	14,060	12,569
Connecticut	1,299,536	0	15,678	0	617,347	532,675	1,242	132,594
Delaware	281,350	700	247,187	11,256	8,177	0	0	14,030
Florida	5,890,208	0	4,229,840	801,793	514,931	0	20,084	323,560
Georgia	2,791,541	0	2,303,435	406,820	32,713	0	17,246	31,327
Hawaii	43,842	3,710	0	18,473	14,879	0	0	6,780
Idaho	433,384	837	325,956	74,606	23,785	0	7,063	1,137
Illinois	5,151,843	700	3,507,693	446,459	697,444	67,498	262,281	169,768
Indiana	2,779,292	15,062	1,700,339	324,362	200,059	0	3,655	535,815 (a)
Iowa	1,557,314	9,318	1,054,733	211,645	159,868	0	1,829	119,921
Kansas	981,336	186	803,890	78,538	57,739	1,886	2,622	36,475
Kentucky	1,565,480	0	1,287,870	202,050	33,282	0	20,316	21,962
Louisiana	1,811,000	16	1,449,399	162,159	34,710	0	686	164,030
Maine	464,779	8,949	0	2,787	696	6,243	0	446,104 (b)
Maryland	2,048,764	100	0	1,262,856	586,023	0	0	199,785
Massachusetts	3,891,302	112,750	78,215	0	7,585	0	351,093	3,341,659 (c)
Michigan	5,143,979	68,605	2,528,022	1,425,189	684,217	151,590	71,556	214,800
Minnesota	3,438,831	0	1,806,525	952,548	540,502	30,581	6,897	101,778
Mississippi	1,346,201	199	957,051	189,927	199,024	0	0	0
Missouri	2,091,007	9,219	1,741,806	80,123	106,540	0	1,654	151,665
Montana	318,184	872	240,568	45,285	29,630	0	0	1,829
Nebraska	547,691	1,333	286,551	70,300	74,394	0	12,463	102,650
Nevada	650,462	2,577	390,859	232,586	19,052	0	0	5,388
New Hampshire	182,019	0	14,663	30,928	34,485	32,727	614	68,602
New Jersey	4,959,157	32,254	2,036,421	1,009,429	656,581	28,048	34,751	1,161,673 (d)
New Mexico	1,166,268	0	823,809	25,701	316,366	0	0	392
New York	16,248,656	312,067	4,123,882	2,265,616	9,319,574	208,916	7,132	11,469
North Carolina	3,651,320	0	0	3,336,954	277,034	0	22,119	15,213
North Dakota	361,184	0	255,339	62,843	32,574	9,642	618	168
Ohio	6,027,790	0	3,684,739	1,293,917	159,250	29,566	7,054	853,264 (e)
Oklahoma	1,360,835	763	1,099,940	167,237	22,525	0	3,434	66,936
Oregon	1,190,596	0	725,285	322,329	88,171	0	7,255	47,556
Pennsylvania	5,720,515	72,813	3,489,924	1,192,498	436,386	109,092	290,498	129,304
Rhode Island	367,628	9,771	23,241	0	167,560	139,359	0	27,155
South Carolina	1,465,863	0	1,232,592	186,125	43,621	0	1,020	2,505
South Dakota	204,596	31	129,877	53,667	12,080	33	787	8,121
Tennessee	1,585,739	0	5,096	978,714	594,076	0	0	7,853
Texas	6,225,435	0	5,920,098	89,357	152,761	0	3,554	59,665
Utah	787,955	475	678,722	73,649	24,888	0	2,589	7,632
Vermont	179,476	7,616	138,908	0	2,584	23,255	252	6,861
Virginia	2,761,290	0	0	1,426,735	988,650	0	9,591	336,314
Washington	2,908,212	21,111	2,287,014	316,808	161,867	0	89,420	31,992
West Virginia	894,505	0	847,603	18,733	36	0	0	28,133
Wisconsin	3,409,036	84,785	1,385,605	393,844	843,617	290,189	0	410,996 (f)
Wyoming	549,747	279	328,281	50,843	97,535	0	9,315	63,494

Source: U.S. Bureau of the Census, State Government Finances in 1987.
Note: Totals may not add due to rounding.
(a) Includes $506,300,000 property tax replacement distribution to local governments.
(b) Includes $359,242,000 for local schools.
(c) Includes $1,746,382,000 education subsidies, $714,693,000 assistance to cities and towns, and $195,000,000 lottery distribution.
(d) Includes $1,034,221,000 property tax relief and shared revenues.
(e) Includes $199,346,000 tax relief payments.
(f) Includes $245,080,000 in Community Mental Health Assistance.

INTERGOVERNMENTAL AFFAIRS

Table 9.9
STATE INTERGOVERNMENTAL EXPENDITURE, BY TYPE OF RECEIVING GOVERNMENT AND BY STATE: 1988
(In thousands of dollars)

State	Total intergovernmental expenditure	Type of receiving government				
		Federal	School districts	Counties, municipalities, and townships (a)	Special districts	Combined and unallocable
United States	151,661,866	2,652,981	78,547,159	62,158,287	1,488,172	6,815,267
Alabama	1,772,140	0	1,356,615	413,503	0	2,022
Alaska	794,294	0	0	757,499	0	36,795
Arizona	2,014,460	1,200	1,129,298	874,270	0	9,692
Arkansas	1,053,029	44	804,872	199,723	5,620	42,770
California	29,754,786	1,852,530	15,474,965	12,056,870	156,933	213,488
Colorado	1,601,393	336	1,051,240	526,419	20,287	3,111
Connecticut	1,477,198	0	19,881	1,292,416	843	164,058
Delaware	317,800	725	262,170	54,905	0	0
Florida	6,500,752	0	4,761,449	1,219,121	44,349	475,833
Georgia	2,928,597	0	2,559,085	320,355	15,723	33,434
Hawaii	49,776	4,015	0	35,016	0	10,745
Idaho	489,765	591	372,206	110,365	6,551	52
Illinois	5,274,272	96	3,520,878	1,291,430	273,912	187,956
Indiana	2,995,457	17,276	1,794,932	656,360	3,944	522,945 (b)
Iowa	1,802,094	12,051	1,271,607	423,996	0	94,440
Kansas	1,073,214	114	856,083	181,365	3,005	32,647
Kentucky	1,741,531	0	1,449,609	253,146	14,740	24,036
Louisiana	1,865,441	1	1,522,394	203,742	3,759	135,545
Maine	544,712	10,782	0	9,988	0	523,942 (c)
Maryland	2,233,494	63	0	2,215,319	0	18,112
Massachusetts	4,127,655	112,206	280,563	2,886,353 (d)	410,269	438,264
Michigan	5,813,874	69,994	2,991,088	2,575,006	10,275	167,511
Minnesota	3,621,482	0	1,924,377	1,606,551	4,306	86,248
Mississippi	1,391,664	145	1,023,391	368,128	0	0
Missouri	2,303,781	12,039	1,915,102	225,194	7,117	144,329
Montana	308,044	838	251,937	53,481	0	1,788
Nebraska	552,488	1,804	286,587	142,632	11,548	109,917
Nevada	725,283	2,810	423,503	290,658	1,967	6,345
New Hampshire	204,898	0	20,151	98,553	618	85,576
New Jersey	5,462,250	37,505	2,287,201	1,973,847	9,217	1,154,480 (e)
New Mexico	1,244,887	0	883,713	356,152	0	5,022
New York	16,767,678	314,500	4,583,467	11,849,000	8,151	12,560
North Carolina	4,066,203	0	0	4,005,693	25,273	35,237
North Dakota	365,329	0	246,523	118,175	631	0
Ohio	6,315,346	0	3,766,990	1,622,605	7,867	917,884 (f)
Oklahoma	1,447,844	71	1,125,273	197,702	3,659	121,139
Oregon	1,201,765	0	757,537	435,508	6,025	2,695
Pennsylvania	6,119,723	74,430	3,674,273	1,984,046	314,319	72,655
Rhode Island	374,269	10,247	24,248	334,022	0	5,752
South Carolina	1,574,229	0	1,298,595	271,918	661	3,055
South Dakota	221,219	24	147,203	62,083	892	11,017
Tennessee	1,685,450	0	6,532	1,670,694	0	8,224
Texas	6,625,955	0	6,107,870	120,025	2,714	395,346
Utah	842,039	498	735,920	97,670	2,186	5,765
Vermont	213,223	8,080	168,521	36,288	334	0
Virginia	3,038,790	0	0	3,027,421	11,369	0
Washington	3,485,005	18,236	2,514,100	823,855	95,147	33,757
West Virginia	870,197	0	831,069	18,237	0	20,891
Wisconsin	3,855,521	89,631	1,729,405	1,656,347	50	380,088 (g)
Wyoming	551,480	99	334,736	154,635	3,911	58,099

Source: U.S. Bureau of the Census, *State Government Finances in 1988*.
Note: Totals may not add due to rounding.
(a) Counties, municipalities, and townships no longer collected as separate entities.
(b) Includes $522,894,000 property tax replacement distribution to local governments.
(c) Includes $428,271,000 for local schools.
(d) Includes $1,589,858,000 education subsidies, $817,490,000 assistance to cities and towns, and $215,000,000 lottery distribution.
(e) Includes $1,034,227,000 property tax relief and shared revenues.
(f) Includes $212,662,000 tax relief payments.
(g) Includes $234,258,000 in Community Mental Health Assistance.

Table 9.10
STATE INTERGOVERNMENTAL REVENUE FROM FEDERAL AND LOCAL GOVERNMENTS: 1987
(In thousands of dollars)

State	Total intergovernmental revenue	From federal government					From local government				
		Total (a)	Education	Public welfare	Health & hospitals	Highways	Total (a)	Education	Public welfare	Health & hospitals	Highways
United States	$102,380,659	$95,462,932	$16,883,475	$44,969,384	$3,764,484	$12,962,911	$6,917,727	$452,061	$2,116,488	$831,946	$580,478
Alabama	1,514,717	1,481,298	417,860	475,130	60,717	218,538	33,419	7,074	44	8,752	9,072
Alaska	488,932	485,378	109,301	127,530	7,451	116,854	3,554	1,969	0	152	837
Arizona	1,000,081	912,915	256,436	221,174	39,399	263,730	87,166	8,625	0	4,879	7,579
Arkansas	912,977	908,755	151,708	440,658	42,417	147,376	4,222	1,145	60,921	0	1,857
California	12,693,621	12,423,013	2,157,240	5,942,136	271,346	956,606	270,608	40,589	150	30,300	128,295
Colorado	1,245,627	1,219,900	269,652	516,704	71,722	221,621	25,727	4,662	0	0	19,900
Connecticut	1,229,293	1,208,791	167,204	532,488	95,725	240,738	20,502	112	0	0	0
Delaware	280,538	278,076	63,444	74,106	10,094	51,118	2,462	2,279	0	0	0
Florida	2,902,105	2,799,133	707,876	1,029,312	198,345	449,201	102,972	1,147	919	69,381	4,629
Georgia	2,342,370	2,287,425	461,239	1,002,526	130,472	340,809	54,945	9,642	314	0	41,860
Hawaii	429,661	425,590	109,494	180,961	20,816	38,176	4,071	153	0	0	0
Idaho	391,961	376,353	60,811	115,843	18,224	84,967	15,608	827	4,109	7,724	1,423
Illinois	4,109,404	4,027,138	855,200	1,762,712	128,575	570,590	82,266	14,795	5,756	0	54,052
Indiana	1,921,558	1,875,291	337,547	890,357	95,834	292,435	46,267	1,998	19,299	309	15,123
Iowa	1,121,355	1,044,395	219,411	426,295	69,432	170,319	76,960	0	10,057	38,756	2,767
Kansas	816,083	804,678	171,853	272,641	44,467	194,367	11,405	2,046	0	0	9,359
Kentucky	1,424,620	1,411,147	207,180	673,246	65,691	226,402	13,473	5,051	0	0	440
Louisiana	2,476,047	2,450,735	368,687	829,089	80,749	263,444	25,312	2,161	0	7,397	0
Maine	611,499	608,374	87,580	323,145	26,499	60,430	3,125	428	0	0	1,202
Maryland	1,767,093	1,721,215	321,082	693,352	53,241	388,243	45,878	430	4,928	2,381	16,112
Massachusetts	2,517,022	2,325,629	351,016	1,320,069	67,234	131,088	191,393	1,702	0	1,763	0
Michigan	4,518,404	4,019,233	707,564	2,237,040	166,103	402,047	499,171	6,921	70,080	358,644	33,691
Minnesota	1,993,472	1,903,763	314,706	927,966	58,571	294,547	89,709	1,920	58,048	13,250	12,333
Mississippi	1,165,851	1,149,563	253,124	438,932	55,983	175,857	16,288	3,485	0	0	0
Missouri	1,571,389	1,560,617	242,017	707,334	65,716	302,051	10,772	21	7	123	5,492
Montana	499,359	486,278	48,163	170,131	16,587	118,610	13,081	530	11,925	0	481
Nebraska	585,625	561,528	99,860	223,458	24,338	125,265	24,097	8,357	4,773	2,264	8,028
Nevada	308,570	299,051	56,419	71,498	14,976	82,322	9,519	2,120	1,969	596	1,599
New Hampshire	360,518	326,877	52,895	122,589	10,091	66,656	33,641	1,196	28,312	74	1,613
New Jersey	3,004,775	2,876,447	351,495	1,365,433	105,865	404,749	128,328	15,434	20,209	73,871	8,776
New Mexico	601,433	565,543	140,213	222,690	32,642	111,763	35,890	19,728	428	2,767	5,108
New York	14,669,952	10,758,412	1,042,712	7,527,983	253,635	650,012	3,911,540	69,250	1,648,575	3,525	0
North Carolina	2,194,137	2,029,557	459,707	858,151	88,860	333,770	164,580	5,721	133,805	898	11,082
North Dakota	381,967	365,738	62,538	121,221	11,999	88,775	16,229	1,137	7,972	115	4,780
Ohio	3,882,584	3,734,583	611,118	1,994,158	165,855	390,533	148,001	17,199	0	21,830	34,955
Oklahoma	1,134,466	1,107,083	206,260	499,580	44,287	174,469	27,383	11,341	0	1,224	6,587
Oregon	1,208,602	1,173,745	246,924	374,345	33,022	192,832	34,857	4,759	13,817	0	12,434
Pennsylvania	4,724,798	4,645,140	639,251	2,507,610	150,283	694,742	79,658	69,154	0	0	8,351
Rhode Island	519,509	490,013	69,570	254,812	18,166	76,417	29,496	526	0	0	0
South Carolina	1,232,507	1,197,157	267,013	560,190	75,065	134,689	35,350	11,694	4,723	6,402	444

STATE INTERGOVERNMENTAL REVENUE FROM FEDERAL AND LOCAL GOVERNMENTS: 1987—Continued

State	Total intergovernmental revenue	From federal government					From local government				
		Total (a)	Education	Public welfare	Health & hospitals	Highways	Total (a)	Education	Public welfare	Health & hospitals	Highways
South Dakota	349,374	342,645	44,691	123,031	16,265	78,365	6,729	196	2,405	1,749	1,985
Tennessee	1,883,423	1,852,262	323,953	835,821	82,331	277,766	31,161	5,966	895	10,678	10,758
Texas	4,525,129	4,508,135	1,106,045	1,667,744	199,301	902,752	16,994	14,137	0	2,247	533
Utah	804,265	778,896	187,627	258,611	55,339	153,881	25,369	13,246	2,048	694	0
Vermont	338,247	333,272	55,621	130,035	22,647	64,570	4,975	4,889	0	86	0
Virginia	2,085,530	1,948,921	445,637	669,770	93,284	370,767	136,609	2,780	0	40,457	65,846
Washington	2,089,117	1,915,402	404,041	656,565	164,652	398,637	173,715	30,638	0	114,239	2,961
West Virginia	927,727	914,581	146,720	356,265	34,103	197,672	13,146	1,076	0	0	0
Wisconsin	2,176,634	2,123,707	421,256	1,173,326	64,719	182,683	52,927	2,355	0	30	25,281
Wyoming	446,731	419,554	24,514	63,621	41,349	88,660	27,177	19,450	0	4,389	2,853

Source: U.S. Bureau of the Census, State Government Finances in 1987.
Note: Totals may not add due to rounding.
(a) Total includes revenue for other activities not shown separately in this table.

Table 9.11
STATE INTERGOVERNMENTAL REVENUE FROM FEDERAL AND LOCAL GOVERNMENTS: 1988
(In thousands of dollars)

State	Total intergovernmental revenue	From federal government					From local government			
		Total (a)	Education	Public welfare	Health & hospitals	Highways	Total (a)	Education	Public welfare	Health & hospitals	Highways
United States	$107,224,621	$100,461,496	$17,969,526	$47,908,120	$4,153,216	$13,467,477	$6,763,125	$455,397	$2,447,808	$886,975	$468,865
Alabama	1,745,442	1,711,228	493,675	534,360	63,436	319,722	34,214	6,991	85	9,654	8,586
Alaska	746,769	741,283	113,243	134,104	8,521	166,830	5,486	4,198	0	156	747
Arizona	1,021,965	943,029	282,724	280,028	43,618	202,990	78,936	3,421	60,292	10,335	73
Arkansas	946,061	940,046	153,373	485,692	35,661	129,855	6,015	1,333	0	672	2,435
California	13,036,411	12,794,593	2,208,319	6,015,249	301,958	1,075,855	241,818	40,577	555	25,697	97,240
Colorado	1,190,227	1,173,083	247,546	417,543	68,302	219,093	17,144	4,578	12	62	9,400
Connecticut	1,342,864	1,310,681	182,686	606,812	99,895	257,008	32,183	909	0	0	0
Delaware	292,391	289,980	60,404	78,792	15,901	59,090	2,411	2,318	0	0	0
Florida	3,235,790	3,109,415	750,125	1,213,923	219,231	529,145	126,375	1,722	961	89,124	7,910
Georgia	2,488,806	2,449,805	508,233	1,124,293	132,413	357,381	39,001	9,787	213	0	14,787
Hawaii	497,462	492,673	125,959	214,742	22,902	48,179	4,789	141	0	0	0
Idaho	435,392	416,516	64,108	133,430	22,361	98,403	18,876	750	3,597	10,434	2,054
Illinois	4,011,942	3,908,730	837,385	1,739,543	145,328	511,574	103,212	21,615	25,635	63	51,015
Indiana	1,991,780	1,907,967	370,966	891,044	106,095	268,773	83,813	1,340	57,561	263	14,238
Iowa	1,136,948	1,083,781	216,834	451,340	97,506	185,434	53,167	32	12,877	33,255	3,753
Kansas	852,546	838,225	186,145	263,747	47,172	186,681	14,321	2,740	0	0	11,581
Kentucky	1,638,016	1,626,658	310,385	762,972	56,384	213,841	11,358	5,231	0	0	280
Louisiana	1,920,062	1,894,325	386,048	892,589	90,747	278,425	25,737	2,440	0	6,920	0
Maine	634,050	630,575	86,265	323,987	29,160	69,247	3,475	352	0	0	1,584
Maryland	1,950,585	1,863,948	342,813	755,588	64,008	445,264	86,637	108	56,498	1,296	12,606
Massachusetts	2,912,621	2,712,009	349,808	1,571,164	82,417	246,148	200,612	1,553	0	1,834	0
Michigan	4,653,115	4,115,643	728,227	2,331,649	177,445	385,164	537,472	6,978	75,548	371,673	36,113
Minnesota	2,201,768	2,111,630	338,009	1,136,265	69,358	264,997	90,138	1,452	58,571	14,089	11,252
Mississippi	1,255,910	1,233,829	286,157	509,064	64,878	156,414	22,081	3,487	815	0	0
Missouri	1,577,569	1,566,644	259,834	749,095	65,625	259,031	10,925	107	8	95	5,345
Montana	528,283	514,080	64,619	179,528	22,378	108,878	14,203	851	11,712	0	1,124
Nebraska	595,477	577,706	110,192	245,945	24,082	111,962	17,771	2,241	2,691	2,238	9,899
Nevada	309,520	299,059	65,600	84,988	17,112	45,653	10,461	1,819	2,069	655	1,967
New Hampshire	370,130	328,700	59,655	116,420	9,363	64,319	41,430	1,593	32,412	40	4,610
New Jersey	3,586,372	3,452,853	463,825	1,539,837	169,053	582,405	133,519	18,292	22,427	68,091	20,780
New Mexico	646,969	622,170	141,058	254,268	33,866	109,328	24,799	19,576	421	2,838	1,964
New York	14,583,898	11,007,781	1,069,060	7,704,292	263,703	647,811	3,576,117	67,071	1,840,554	566	0
North Carolina	2,319,443	2,136,966	463,942	947,076	98,503	304,395	182,477	5,462	147,678	952	13,694
North Dakota	393,715	393,715	63,599	152,979	11,245	90,668	20,015	947	7,596	0	8,978
Ohio	4,213,160	4,036,110	587,352	2,254,839	181,945	415,749	177,050	17,716	0	50,654	31,829
Oklahoma	1,188,269	1,165,464	222,332	559,457	45,449	146,719	22,805	11,939	0	634	2,605
Oregon	1,350,992	1,316,615	262,862	431,209	104,680	128,283	34,377	5,115	14,731	0	10,667
Pennsylvania	4,742,001	4,680,293	686,206	2,481,451	162,454	703,888	61,708	55,885	0	0	3,649
Rhode Island	593,364	534,402	73,274	259,855	82,553	82,403	58,962	401	1,048	0	2,055
South Carolina	1,384,779	1,326,981	279,670	591,633	82,132	188,583	57,798	13,372	5,915	6,765	486

STATE INTERGOVERNMENTAL REVENUE: 1988—Continued

State	Total intergovernmental revenue	From federal government					From local government				
		Total (a)	Education	Public welfare	Health & hospitals	Highways	Total (a)	Education	Public welfare	Health & hospitals	Highways
South Dakota	392,114	385,695	55,843	136,347	20,151	80,137	6,419	128	1,904	2,791	916
Tennessee	2,092,266	2,075,922	372,980	1,031,458	81,867	231,425	16,344	6,909	854	7,597	0
Texas	5,136,774	5,112,582	1,298,949	1,829,021	233,811	1,055,902	24,192	18,025	0	4,140	214
Utah	790,014	767,657	200,050	263,080	42,658	137,628	22,357	10,934	2,568	32	0
Vermont	334,345	329,530	59,829	144,807	19,040	59,212	4,815	4,738	0	77	0
Virginia	2,151,078	2,018,713	420,599	741,915	107,379	400,620	132,365	12,741	0	41,083	40,123
Washington	2,141,081	1,953,957	440,597	735,093	165,900	347,611	187,124	34,930	0	120,627	2,732
West Virginia	982,398	965,774	160,861	360,303	31,223	235,480	16,624	823	0	0	0
Wisconsin	2,225,054	2,171,221	415,581	1,182,155	63,661	180,125	53,833	8,261	0	174	17,815
Wyoming	436,618	421,254	41,720	63,149	8,686	73,749	15,364	11,468	0	1,399	1,759

Source: U.S. Bureau of the Census, State Government Finances in 1988.
Note: Totals may not add due to rounding.
(a) Total includes revenue for other activities not shown separately in this table.

INTERSTATE COMPACTS AND AGREEMENTS

By Benjamin J. Jones and Deborah Reuter

Interstate compacts are unique and valuable tools that states jointly use to deal with common problems. They are provided for by the United States Constitution under Article 1, Section 10 which states "No State Shall, Without the Consent of Congress, . . . enter into any Agreement or Compact with another State, or with a Foreign Power." Although that phrase would seem to mean that only those agreements between states which have congressional consent are legal, the United States Supreme Court held in 1893 in *Virginia v. Tennessee*, 148 U.S. 503, that only agreements that affect the political balance within the federal system or that affect a power delegated to the national government must receive congressional consent.

A compact has both the effect of a statute in each state and the features of a binding, legal contract. Therefore, when a state adopts a compact, the state may not renounce or leave the compact except as may be provided for by compact provisions providing for withdrawal. As contracts, interstate compacts take precedence over laws that conflict with their provisions. When these characteristics are taken into consideration, it is apparent that interstate compacts are the most binding legal instruments establishing formal cooperation among states.

Until this century, such agreements were few in number and usually related to boundary issues between two states. Only 35 compacts were entered into between 1783 and 1920. However, as society has become more complex, the range of uses for compacts has expanded to include a variety of problems and concerns. This explains the growth of interstate compacts since 1920, during which time over 140 compacts have been created.

The increased use of compacts also demonstrates that these agreements have been accepted as appropriate devices for dealing with interstate problems. The increasing complexity of both government and the problems it must address have made the unique solution of interstate compacts of increasing value and importance.

Recent Developments

Among the most recent of compact developments is the proposed Midwestern Higher Education Compact. This compact would permit universities in member states to share equipment, expertise and funding. For example, the compact would allow university students in a state with no optometry school to attend a neighboring state's optometry school at in-state tuition costs.

A Midwestern Legislative Conference steering committee proposed the compact. Kansas, Michigan, Minnesota and Missouri have introduced ratification legislation or will soon do so with no state expressing resistance to the compact. However, five of the 12 Midwestern states must ratify the compact by 1995 in order for it to become effective.

Although the Midwestern states have been leaders in ensuring the quality of higher education, such factors as budget restrictions have made such assurances increasingly difficult. Twice before the Midwestern states have considered a higher education compact. The first was proposed in the mid-1960s and received little support. In 1976, the Education

---

Benjamin J. Jones is director of the Washington Office of The Council of State Governments. Deborah Reuter is an intern at the Washington Office of The Council of State Governments.

Committee of the Midwestern Conference of CSG began preparing yet another compact. The compact was endorsed by the Executive Committee of the Midwestern Conference in 1977. The compact stated that six states must join by 1981 in order for it to be activated. By the deadline, only four states had ratified the compact.

The two previous attempts to establish a higher education compact failed at least in part because Midwestern states saw it limiting the control individual states have over their universities. However, cutbacks in federal aid, economic problems in agriculture and manufacturing as well as other factors have forced states to reduce support for higher education. Few, if any, states today can provide all the educational opportunities and resources reasonably desirable. In addition, regional cooperation in higher education has proved beneficial in the southern, New England and western states. The compact is an attempt to ensure, through interstate cooperation, both high quality and low cost higher education to their citizens.

During the 1980s, the states have become increasingly concerned with issues of environmental management and natural resource protection. Enforcement responsibilities have in many cases moved from federal to state government agencies. As states lead the fight to preserve the environment, officials in Minnesota and other states have begun to consider an environmental compact as a useful tool to improve state coordination and cooperation in the environmental area.

The proposed Environmental Compact of the States would offer a forum where governors, legislators, business and environmental leaders, educators and researchers can focus on crucial environmental and natural resource issues. It would also provide a way for the public and private sectors to develop partnerships to address environmental problems that transcend individual state boundaries. It would also provide a national clearinghouse for environmental and natural resource information as well as promote education and research. In addition, the compact would offer independent analysis of environmental issues from a state perspective.

State leaders generally support coordinated drug education, treatment, prevention and law enforcement strategies. This became evident in July of 1989 when the governors of seven states signed a compact to combat drugs. Participants in the compact include Delaware, Maryland, New Jersey, New York, Pennsylvania, Virginia and West Virginia.

The Middle Atlantic Governors' Compact on Alcohol and Drug Abuse commits the states to a coordinated approach to drug and alcohol laws. The compact also provides for states to share information and training resources. In addition, it provides for prevention programs, stiff penalties and other options to incarceration for drug users. The compact is intended to serve as a coordinated strategy which attacks the drug problem on all fronts.

Residents in the central United States are unprepared for a major earthquake. Yet, outside of California, seven central states are located along the New Madrid Fault where the greatest risk for a major U.S. earthquake now exists.

The New Madrid Fault runs through southern Illinois, northeast Missouri, southern Indiana, northeast Arkansas, northwestern Mississippi, western Kentucky and western Tennessee.

On a scale of 0 to 100 for preparedness, San Francisco ranks 90 while the central United States ranks between 0 and 20. To become better prepared for an earthquake, the states threatened by the fault formed the Central U.S. Earthquake Consortium. The states' disaster officials meet quarterly to discuss methods to reduce deaths, injuries, as well as property and economic loss resulting from possible earthquakes. Although not technically a compact, this interstate coordinating and planning forum is a positive step toward coordinating earthquake planning.

The mail order business is booming as catalogues offer a variety of items ranging from clothes to major appliances. Consumers are saving close to $2 billion by buying from out-of-state firms and not paying sales tax on their purchases. As a result, a number of compacts have been created, reflecting increasing concern over revenue losses resulting from the inability of states to tax interstate mail order sales effectively.

New York and New Jersey entered into an interstate compact to exchange information gathered from in-state vendors pertaining to purchases made by residents of the other state. The effort has proven successful; millions of dollars in additional revenue have been collected.

The first multi-state effort to improve the enforcement of sales and use tax laws was undertaken by the Midwest. Illinois, Indiana, Michigan, Ohio and Wisconsin created the Great Lakes Interstate Sales Compact which requires the states to begin a number of projects designed to encourage interstate vendors to collect use taxes. Licensed vendors in each state have been asked to register for use tax collection with any of the other compact states in which they made taxable sales. The states also have attempted to register traditional retail businesses in border areas to collect use taxes for adjacent states.

Iowa, Kansas, Minnesota, Nebraska and South Dakota also have signed an interstate compact designed to collect this lost revenue. The states hope to duplicate the success of the Great Lakes Interstate Sales Compact. The plains states compact encourages in-state vendors to register with other compact states to collect use taxes on interstate purchases. The agreement will make it easier for participating states to monitor purchases made by in-state consumers from out-of-state vendors.

Minnesota has estimated the state could gain as much as $30 million a year. Nebraska could recover an additional $2 to $3 million per year while Iowa, Kansas and South Dakota figure to recover at least $1 million a year.

The use of compacts is likely to continue as states today face a wide variety of complex problems. A compact has been drafted by the states of Alaska, California and Washington with the Province of British Columbia becoming an associate, non-voting party to the compact. However, upon request of the Province of British Columbia and approval of Congress, the province may become a full party to the compact.

The purpose of the proposed compact is to 1) promote the use and protection of renewable resources while protecting fisheries, marine mammals and birds; 2) promote the better management of ocean resources that are of mutual concern; 3) address issues of mutual concern to the parties arising from the shipment of oil and hazardous materials within the region; and 4) develop a regional plan for the protection of the areas of the Pacific Ocean and adjacent waters over which the compact parties now control or may acquire. The compact also creates the Pacific Marine Resources Commission to oversee that the goals of the compact are being effectively met. The foregoing clearly indicates that compacts, far from being an archaic solution to boundary disputes, in fact continue to reflect the diverse problem-solving approaches of state governments to the broad range of issues which they face.

THE COUNCIL OF STATE GOVERNMENTS

The Council of State Governments (CSG) is the pioneer state leadership association with over half a century of experience in showcasing innovative programs, building new partnerships across the three branches of government and state agencies, promoting interstate compacts and regional action, establishing strong links with the private sector and identifying trends inside and outside state government.

The Council is a service organization whose goal is to foster excellence in all facets of state government. Founded on the premise that the states themselves are the best sources of insight, ideas and innovations, CSG provides a network for exploring new ideas, establishing useful partnerships and disseminating timely information to state policymakers. Through leadership development programs, the Council strengthens the institution of state government, giving present and future leaders the skills needed for effective governance. CSG also provides vital professional support to numerous associations of state officials, bringing these groups together under a single umbrella to ensure cross-germination of programs and ideas.

CSG is unique in its emphasis on regional and multi-state efforts. The Council is organized around four regions and serves the legislative, executive and judicial branches of government in the 50 states and six U.S. territories. CSG is a non-profit organization and its activites are non-partisan.

Through its national headquarters in Lexington, Kentucky, and regional offices in Atlanta, Chicago, New York and San Francisco, CSG works to synthesize the complex political, cultural, geographic and philosophical differences inherent in our federal system into cohesive and constructive regional and national approaches. With the approach of the 21st century, the responsibilities and challenges confronting the nation will dictate the role CSG will play in helping to improve decisionmaking at the state level.

Governing Structure

Each state has an equal voice in directing CSG activities through representation on the governing board. The governing board includes all the nation's governors and two legislators from each state and the non-state jurisdictions. Also represented on the governing board are the national organizations of lieutenant governors, attorneys general, chief justices, secretaries of state, and state auditors, comptrollers and treasurers. The governing board meets annually to provide an opportunity for the diverse members of the CSG family to interact in sessions on current and emerging state issues.

An executive committee is selected to manage the day-to-day activities of the Council. Its members also serve with approximately 150 colleagues on the Council's governing board. State officials also serve on several standing committees that advise the executive committee.

CSG is funded in part through direct contributions by the states, U.S. territories and other non-state jurisdictions. In addition CSG administers federal and private foundation grants which support research and information-gathering projects on topics of interest to state officials. CSG also generates revenue from the sale of publications and by conducting workshops and conferences.

The national headquarters office in Lexington is organized around four groups, Strategic Planning and Innovations, State Leadership and Management, Communications and Development, and Finance and Administration. These groups are responsible for an array of national programs including strategic planning, trends analysis, secretariat services, publications, state information inquiry services, data processing services and interstate consulting.

Also reporting to the executive director is the Intergovernmental Affairs Office in Washington, D.C., which monitors developments at the federal level and evaluates their impact on state legislation and policies. The office helps facilitate contact and cooperation among officials at the federal, state and local levels.

Regional Offices

CSG's regional structure distinguishes it among state service agencies. Offices in Atlanta, Chicago, New York and San Francisco serve regional conferences of state officials (Southern Legislative Conference, Midwestern Legislative Conference, Eastern Regional Conference and Western Legislative Conference, respectively, as well as the Southern Governors' Association and the Midwestern Governors Association). Regions are the backbone of CSG, providing elected and appointed state officials the opportunity to address issues pertinent to specific areas of the country. Regional task forces and committees actively address their states' needs in agriculture and rural development, energy, environment and natural resources, fiscal affairs and other priority areas.

The issues and activities of each regional office are selected by a regional executive committee of state officials. Regional offices of CSG produce newsletters and substantive issue reports for officials in their region. In addition, annual conferences of regional organizations of state officials are staffed by CSG's regional offices.

Publications

CSG publishes a variety of materials about state government, including policy reports, reference works, directories, periodicals, information briefs and newsletters. Major CSG publications are:

- *The Book of the States*, a biennial reference guide to all major aspects of state government. This volume contains quantitative and comparative data as well as essays written by experts in state operations.
- *State Elective Officials and the Legislatures, State Legislative Leadership, Committees and Staff*, and *State Administrative Officials Classified by Function*, supplemental directories that include names, addresses and telephone numbers of state officials.
- *Suggested State Legislation*, an annual volume of draft legislation and legislative ideas selected by a committee of state officials.
- *State Government News*, CSG's monthly magazine on state developments, issues and innovations. It is distributed to over 17,000 subscribers, including all elected state officials, and features the Conference Calendar, a monthly listing of meetings involving CSG and its associated organizations.
- *The Journal of State Government*, a quarterly publication that provides a forum for the discussion of state issues from political, academic and practitioner viewpoints.
- *State Government Research Checklist*, a bimonthly inventory of state government reports and current information sources.
- *Backgrounders*, a series of brief, special issue reports covering current state actions and trends.

Affiliated, Cooperating and Adjunct Organizations

CSG is an umbrella organization that allows officials from the different branches of state government to come together on a regular basis and consider issues and challenges of mutual concern. CSG has a relationship with a wide range of state officials and their national associations. The more than 55 associated and cooperating organizations of CSG encompass nearly all constitutional offices and many functional areas. Among the groups with which the Council enjoys formal ties are lieutenant governors, state treasurers, secretaries of state, general services officers, purchasing officials, surplus property administrators, personnel executives, archivists and records administrators, telecommunications directors, emergency medical services directors and controlled substances administrators.

A list of CSG affiliated, cooperating and adjunct groups begins on page 571.

THE COUNCIL OF STATE GOVERNMENTS
OFFICES AND DIRECTORS

Headquarters Office

Daniel Sprague, Executive Director
Iron Works Pike
P.O. Box 11910
Lexington, Kentucky 40578-1910
(606) 231-1939

Eastern Office
Alan V. Sokolow, Director
270 Broadway, Suite 513
New York, New York 10007
(212) 693-0400

Southern Office
Colleen Cousineau, Director
3384 Peachtree Road, N.E., Suite 830
Atlanta, Georgia 30326
(404) 266-1271

Midwestern Office
Virginia Thrall, Director
641 East Butterfield Road, Suite 401
Lombard, Illinois 60148
(708) 810-0210

Western Office
Andrew Grose, Director
121 Second Street, 4th Floor
San Francisco, California 94105
(415) 974-6422

Washington Office
Benjamin Jones, Director
Hall of the States
444 North Capitol Street
Washington, D.C. 20001
(202) 624-5460

THE COUNCIL OF STATE GOVERNMENTS

AFFILIATED ORGANIZATIONS

Conference of Chief Justices
Conference of State Court Administrators
National Association of Attorneys General
National Association of Secretaries of State
National Association of State Auditors, Comptrollers and Treasurers
National Association of State Directors of Administration and General Services
National Association of State Personnel Executives
National Association of State Purchasing Officials
National Association of State Treasurers
National Clearinghouse on Licensure, Enforcement and Regulation
National Conference of Lieutenant Governors
National Conference of State Legislatures

COOPERATING ORGANIZATIONS

Adjutants General Association of the United States
American Probation and Parole Associations
Association of State Correctional Administrators
Association of State Dam Safety Officials
Association of State Floodplain Managers
Association of State and Interstate Water Pollution Control Administrators
Chief Officers of State Library Agencies
Coastal States Organization
Council on Governmental Ethics Laws
Federation of Tax Administrators
Interstate Conference on Water Policy
National Association of Government Archives and Records Administrators
National Association of Regulatory Utility Commissioners
National Association of State Agencies for Surplus Property
National Association of State Boating Law Administrators
National Association of State Controlled Substances Authorities
National Association of State Departments of Agriculture
National Association of State Emergency Medical Services Directors
National Association of State Facility Administrators
National Association of State Foresters
National Association of State Information Resource Executives
National Association of State Juvenile Correctional Agencies
National Association of State Land Reclamationists
National Association of State Mental Health Program Directors
National Association of State Telecommunications Directors
National Association of State Training and Development Directors
National Association of State Units on Aging
National Association of State Unclaimed Property Administrators
National Conference of Commissioners on Uniform State Laws
National Conference of State Fleet Administrators
National Conference of States on Building Codes and Standards
National Criminal Justice Association
National Emergency Management Association
National Reciprocal and Family Support Association
National State Printing Association
Ohio River Basin Commission
Parole and Probation Compact Administrators' Association

THE COUNCIL OF STATE GOVERNMENTS

ADJUNCT ORGANIZATIONS

Association of Paroling Authorities International
International Association of Corporation Administrators
National Association of Governmental Labor Officials
Organization of State Broadcasting Executives
Correctional Industries Association

THE COUNCIL OF STATE GOVERNMENTS
THE REGIONAL CONFERENCES 1989-90

EAST
Eastern Regional Conference
Representative Christopher Boyle, Rhode Island

Eastern Association of Attorneys General
Attorney General Jeffrey Amestoy, Vermont

MIDWEST
Midwestern Governors' Conference
Governor Tommy G. Thompson, Wisconsin

Midwestern Legislative Conference
Representative Jane M. Barnes, Illinois

SOUTH
Southern Governors' Association
Governor Ray Mabus, Mississippi

Southern Legislative Conference
Delegate Tyras Athey, Maryland

WEST
Western Legislative Conference
Representative H. L. Jensen, Wyoming

THE COUNCIL OF STATE GOVERNMENTS
OFFICERS AND EXECUTIVE COMMITTEE
1989-1990

Chairman
House Speaker Thomas B. Murphy, Georgia
President
Governor Michael N. Castle, Delaware
Chairman Elect
Senator W. Paul White, Massachusetts
President-Elect
Governor Terry Branstad, Iowa
Vice Chairman
Speaker Pro Tem John H. Connors, Iowa
Vice President
Governor Rose Mofford, Arizona

Senate President Stanley J. Aronoff, Ohio
Governor John Ashcroft, Missouri
Delegate Tyras S. Athey, Maryland
Representative Jane Barnes, Illinois
Representative Christopher Boyle, Rhode Island
Senator Bill Bradbury, Oregon
Lieutenant Governor Bobby L. Brantley, Florida
Senator Paul Burke, Kansas
Representative Charles W. Capps, Jr., Mississippi
Chief Justice Harry L. Carrico, Virginia
Senate President Arnold Christensen, Utah
Representative Lee A. Daniels, Illinois
Director Bruce Douglas, Department of Regulatory Agencies, Colorado
Senator Ross O. Doyen, Kansas
Senator Hugh T. Farley, New York
Senator Bettye Fahrenkamp, Alaska
Treasurer Jimmie Lou Fisher, Arkansas
Lieutenant Governor Jim Folsom, Jr., Alabama
Governor Booth Gardner, Washington
Speaker Bob F. Griffin, Missouri
Senator Kemp Hammon, New York
Representative Roy Hausauer, North Dakota
Senator Douglas Henry, Jr., Tennessee
Representative Robert C. Hunter, North Carolina
Representative H. L. Jensen, Wyoming
Attorney General Jim Jones, Idaho
Attorney General Frank J. Kelley, Michigan
Senator John J. Marchi, New York
Representative Jane Maroney, Delaware
Governor James G. Martin, North Carolina
Speaker John L. Martin, Maine
Director Phyllis Mayes, Human Resources Management, South Carolina
Comptroller Edward Mazur, Virginia
Chief Justice Vincent L. McKusick, Maine

THE COUNCIL OF STATE GOVERNMENTS

Representative Elizabeth Millard, New Hampshire
Representative John E. Miller, Arkansas
Senator Roger D. Moe, Minnesota
Secretary of State Ralph Munro, Washington
Senate President Pro Tem Samuel B. Nunez, Jr., Louisiana
Governor William A. O'Neill, Connecticut
State Auditor Edward Renfrow, North Carolina
Senator Mark Ricks, Idaho
Senate President Pro Tem David A. Roberti, California
Senate Deputy President Pro Tem Kenneth C. Royall, Jr., North Carolina
Treasurer Janet C. Rzewnicki, Delaware
Representative Ronald A. Silver, Florida
Representative Donna Sytek, New Hampshire
Secretary of State Julia H. Tashjian, Connecticut
Representative John J. Thomas, Indiana
Governor James R. Thompson, Illinois
Governor Tommy G. Thompson, Wisconsin
Assemblyman Robert C. Wertz, New York
Representative Charlie Williams, Mississippi
Treasurer Mary Ellen Withrow, Ohio
Chief Deputy Director Elizabeth Yost, Department of General Services, California

CHAPTER TEN

STATE PAGES

STATE PAGES

Table 10.1
OFFICIAL NAMES OF STATES AND JURISDICTIONS, CAPITALS, ZIP CODES AND CENTRAL SWITCHBOARDS

State or other jurisdiction	Name of state capitol(a)	Capital	Zip code	Area code	Central switchboard
Alabama, State of	State Capitol	Montgomery	36130	205	261-2500
Alaska, State of	State Capitol	Juneau	99811	907	465-2111
Arizona, State of	State Capitol	Phoenix	85007	602	542-4900
Arkansas, State of	State Capitol	Little Rock	72201	501	682-2345
California, State of	State Capitol	Sacramento	95814	916	322-9900
Colorado, State of	State Capitol	Denver	80203	303	866-5000
Connecticut, State of	State Capitol	Hartford	06106	203	566-2211
Delaware, State of	Legislative Hall	Dover	19901	302	736-4000
Florida, State of	The Capitol	Tallahassee	32399	904	488-1234
Georgia, State of	State Capitol	Atlanta	30334	404	656-2000
Hawaii, State of	State Capitol	Honolulu	96813	808	548-2211
Idaho, State of	State Capitol	Boise	83720	208	334-2411
Illinois, State of	State House	Springfield	62706	217	782-2000
Indiana, State of	State House	Indianapolis	46204	317	232-3140
Iowa, State of	State Capitol	Des Moines	50319	515	281-5011
Kansas, State of	State House	Topeka	66612	913	296-0111
Kentucky, Commonwealth of	State Capitol	Frankfort	40601	502	564-2500
Louisiana, State of	State Capitol	Baton Rouge	70804	504	342-6600
Maine, State of	State House	Augusta	04333	207	289-1110
Maryland, State of	State House	Annapolis	21401	301	858-3000
Massachusetts, Commonwealth of	State House	Boston	02133	617	727-2121
Michigan, State of	State Capitol	Lansing	48909	517	373-1837
Minnesota, State of	State Capitol	St. Paul	55515	612	296-6013
Mississippi, State of	New Capitol	Jackson	39201	601	359-1000
Missouri, State of	State Capitol	Jefferson City	65101	314	751-2000
Montana, State of	State Capitol	Helena	59620	406	444-2511
Nebraska, State of	State Capitol	Lincoln	68509	402	471-2311
Nevada, State of	Legislative Hall	Carson City	89710	702	885-5000
New Hampshire, State of	State House	Concord	03301	603	271-1110
New Jersey, State of	State House	Trenton	08625	609	292-2121
New Mexico, State of	State Capitol	Santa Fe	87503	505	827-4011
New York, State of	State Capitol	Albany	12224	518	474-2121
North Carolina, State of	State Legislative Building	Raleigh	27611	919	733-1110
North Dakota, State of	State Capitol	Bismarck	58505	701	224-2000
Ohio, State of	State House	Columbus	43215	614	466-2000
Oklahoma, State of	State Capitol	Oklahoma City	73105	405	521-2011
Oregon, State of	State Capitol	Salem	97310	503	378-3131
Pennsylvania, Commonwealth of	Main Capitol Building	Harrisburg	17120	717	787-2121
Rhode Island and Providence Plantations, State of	State House	Providence	02903	401	277-2000
South Carolina, State of	State House	Columbia	29211	803	734-1000
South Dakota, State of	State Capitol	Pierre	57501	605	773-3011
Tennessee, State of	State Capitol	Nashville	37219	615	741-3011
Texas, State of	State Capitol	Austin	78711	512	463-4630
Utah, State of	State Capitol	Salt Lake City	84114	801	538-3000
Vermont, State of	State House	Montpelier	05602	802	828-1110
Virginia, Commonwealth of	State Capitol	Richmond	23219	804	786-0000
Washington, State of	Legislative Building	Olympia	98504	206	753-5000
West Virginia, State of	State Capitol	Charleston	25305	304	348-3456
Wisconsin, State of	State Capitol	Madison	53702	608	266-2211
Wyoming, State of	State Capitol	Cheyenne	82002	307	777-7011
District of Columbia	District Building	Washington	20004	202	727-1000
American Samoa, Territory of	Maota Fono	Pago Pago	96799	684	633-4116
Federated States of Micronesia	. . .	Kolonia	96941	. . .	NCS
Guam, Territory of	Congress Building	Agana	96910	671	472-8931
Marshall Islands	. . .	Majuro	96960	. . .	NCS
No. Mariana Is., Commonwealth of	Civic Center	Saipan	96950	. . .	NCS
Puerto Rico, Commonwealth of	The Capitol	San Juan	00904	809	721-6040
Republic of Belau	. . .	Koror	96940	. . .	NCS
U.S. Virgin Islands, Territory of	Capitol Building	Charlotte Amalie	00802	809	774-0880

NCS—No central switchboard.

(a) In some instances the name is not official.

STATE PAGES

Table 10.2
HISTORICAL DATA ON THE STATES

State or other jurisdiction	Source of state lands	Date organized as territory	Date admitted to Union	Chronological order of admission to Union
Alabama	Mississippi Territory, 1798(a)	March 3, 1817	Dec. 14, 1819	22
Alaska	Purchased from Russia, 1867	Aug. 24, 1912	Jan. 3, 1959	49
Arizona	Ceded by Mexico, 1848(b)	Feb. 24, 1863	Feb. 14, 1912	48
Arkansas	Louisiana Purchase, 1803	March 2, 1819	June 15, 1836	25
California	Ceded by Mexico, 1848	(c)	Sept. 9, 1850	31
Colorado	Louisiana Purchase, 1803(d)	Feb. 28, 1861	Aug. 1, 1876	38
Connecticut	Fundamental Orders, Jan. 14, 1638; Royal charter, April 23, 1662(e)	...	Jan. 9, 1788(f)	5
Delaware	Swedish charter, 1638; English charter, 1683(e)	...	Dec. 7, 1787(f)	1
Florida	Ceded by Spain, 1819	March 30, 1822	March 3, 1845	27
Georgia	Charter, 1732, from George II to Trustees for Establishing the Colony of Georgia(e)	...	Jan. 2, 1788(f)	4
Hawaii	Annexed, 1898	June 14, 1900	Aug. 21, 1959	50
Idaho	Treaty with Britain, 1846	March 4, 1863	July 3, 1890	43
Illinois	Northwest Territory, 1787	Feb. 3, 1809	Dec. 3, 1818	21
Indiana	Northwest Territory, 1787	May 7, 1800	Dec. 11, 1816	19
Iowa	Louisiana Purchase, 1803	June 12, 1838	Dec. 28, 1846	29
Kansas	Louisiana Purchase, 1803(d)	May 30, 1854	Jan. 29, 1861	34
Kentucky	Part of Virginia until admitted as state	(c)	June 1, 1792	15
Louisiana	Louisiana Purchase, 1803(g)	March 26, 1804	April 30, 1812	18
Maine	Part of Massachusetts until admitted as state	(c)	March 15, 1820	23
Maryland	Charter, 1632, from Charles I to Calvert(e)	...	April 28, 1788(f)	7
Massachusetts	Charter to Massachusetts Bay Company, 1629(e)	...	Feb. 6, 1788(f)	6
Michigan	Northwest Territory, 1787	Jan. 11, 1805	Jan. 26, 1837	26
Minnesota	Northwest Territory, 1787(h)	March 3, 1849	May 11, 1858	32
Mississippi	Mississippi Territory(i)	April 7, 1798	Dec. 10, 1817	20
Missouri	Louisiana Purchase, 1803	June 4, 1812	Aug. 10, 1821	24
Montana	Louisiana Purchase, 1803(j)	May 26, 1864	Nov. 8, 1889	41
Nebraska	Louisiana Purchase, 1803	May 30, 1854	March 1, 1867	37
Nevada	Ceded by Mexico, 1848	March 2, 1861	Oct. 31, 1864	36
New Hampshire	Grants from Council for New England, 1622 and 1629; made Royal province, 1679(e)	...	June 21, 1788(f)	9
New Jersey	Dutch settlement, 1618; English charter, 1664(e)	...	Dec. 18, 1787(f)	3
New Mexico	Ceded by Mexico, 1848(b)	Sept. 9, 1850	Jan. 6, 1912	47
New York	Dutch settlement, 1623; English control, 1664(e)	...	July 26, 1788(f)	11
North Carolina	Charter, 1663, from Charles II(e)	...	Nov. 21, 1789(f)	12
North Dakota	Louisiana Purchase, 1803(k)	March 2, 1861	Nov. 2, 1889	39
Ohio	Northwest Territory, 1787	May 7, 1800	March 1, 1803	17
Oklahoma	Louisiana Purchase, 1803	May 2, 1890	Nov. 16, 1907	46
Oregon	Settlement and treaty with Britain, 1846	Aug. 14, 1848	Feb. 14, 1859	33
Pennsylvania	Grant from Charles II to William Penn, 1681(e)	...	Dec. 12, 1787(f)	2
Rhode Island	Charter, 1663, from Charles II(e)	...	May 29, 1790(f)	13
South Carolina	Charter, 1663, from Charles II(e)	...	May 23, 1788(f)	8
South Dakota	Louisiana Purchase, 1803	March 2, 1861	Nov. 2, 1889	40
Tennessee	Part of North Carolina until land ceded to U.S. in 1789	June 8, 1790(l)	June 1, 1796	16
Texas	Republic of Texas, 1845	(c)	Dec. 29, 1845	28
Utah	Ceded by Mexico, 1848	Sept. 9, 1850	Jan. 4, 1896	45
Vermont	From lands of New Hampshire and New York	(c)	March 4, 1791	14
Virginia	Charter, 1609, from James I to London Company(e)	...	June 25, 1788(f)	10
Washington	Oregon Territory, 1848	March 2, 1853	Nov. 11, 1889	42
West Virginia	Part of Virginia until admitted as state	(c)	June 20, 1863	35
Wisconsin	Northwest Territory, 1787	April 20, 1836	May 29, 1848	30
Wyoming	Louisiana Purchase, 1803(d,j)	July 25, 1868	July 10, 1890	44
Dist. of Columbia	Maryland(m)	...	...	...
American Samoa	------Became a territory, 1900------			
Federated States of Micronesia	...	May 10, 1979	...	...
Guam	Ceded by Spain, 1898	Aug. 1, 1950	...	...
Marshall Islands	...	May 1, 1979	...	...
No. Mariana Is.	...	March 24, 1976	...	...
Puerto Rico	Ceded by Spain, 1898	...	July 25, 1952(n)	...
Republic of Belau	...	Jan. 1, 1981	...	...
U.S. Virgin Islands	------Purchased from Denmark, March 31, 1917------			

The Council of State Governments

STATE PAGES

HISTORICAL DATA—Continued

(a) By the Treaty of Paris, 1783, England gave up claim to the 13 original Colonies, and to all land within an area extending along the present Canadian border to the Lake of the Woods, down the Mississippi River to the 31st parallel, east to the Chattahoochie, down that river to the mouth of the Flint, east to the source of the St. Mary's, down that river to the ocean. The major part of Alabama was acquired by the Treaty of Paris, and the lower portion from Spain in 1813.
(b) Portion of land obtained by Gadsden Purchase, 1853.
(c) No territorial status before admission to Union.
(d) Portion of land ceded by Mexico, 1848.
(e) One of the original 13 Colonies.
(f) Date of ratification of U.S. Constitution.
(g) West Feliciana District (Baton Rouge) acquired from Spain, 1810; added to Louisiana, 1812.
(h) Portion of land obtained by Louisiana Purchase, 1803.
(i) See footnote (a). The lower portion of Mississippi also was acquired from Spain in 1813.
(j) Portion of land obtained from Oregon Territory, 1848.
(k) The northern portion of the Red River Valley was acquired by treaty with Great Britain in 1818.
(l) Date Southwest Territory (identical boundary as Tennessee's) was created.
(m) Area was originally 100 square miles, taken from Virginia and Maryland. Virginia's portion south of the Potomac was given back to that state in 1846. Site chosen in 1790, city incorporated 1802.
(n) On this date, Puerto Rico became a self-governing commonwealth by compact approved by the U.S. Congress and the voters of Puerto Rico as provided in U.S. Public Law 600 of 1950.

STATE PAGES

Table 10.3
STATE STATISTICS

State or other jurisdiction	Land area		Population			Percentage change 1970 to 1980	Density per square mile	No. of Representatives in Congress	Capital	Population	Rank in state	Largest city	Population
	In square miles	Rank in nation	Size	Rank in nation									
Alabama	50,767	28	3,893,888	22	13.1	76.7	7	Montgomery	177,857	3	Birmingham	284,413
Alaska	570,833	1	401,851	50	32.8	0.7	1	Juneau	19,528	3	Anchorage	174,431
Arizona	113,508	6	2,718,215	29	53.1	23.9	5	Phoenix	789,704	1	Phoenix	789,704
Arkansas	52,078	27	2,286,435	33	18.9	43.9	4	Little Rock	158,461	1	Little Rock	158,461
California	156,299	3	23,667,902	1	18.5	151.4	45	Sacramento	275,741	7	Los Angeles	2,966,850
Colorado	103,595	8	2,889,964	28	30.8	27.9	6	Denver	492,365	1	Denver	492,365
Connecticut	4,872	48	3,107,576	25	2.5	637.8	6	Hartford	136,392	2	Bridgeport	142,546
Delaware	1,932	49	594,338	47	8.4	307.6	1	Dover	23,512	3	Wilmington	70,195
Florida	54,153	26	9,746,324	7	43.5	180.0	19	Tallahassee	81,548	11	Jacksonville	540,920
Georgia	58,056	21	5,463,105	13	19.1	94.1	10	Atlanta	425,022	1	Atlanta	425,022
Hawaii	6,425	47	964,691	39	25.3	150.1	2	Honolulu (a)	762,874	1	Honolulu (a)	762,874
Idaho	82,412	11	943,935	41	32.4	11.5	2	Boise	102,451	2	Boise	102,451
Illinois	55,645	24	11,426,518	5	2.8	205.3	22	Springfield	99,637	4	Chicago	3,005,072
Indiana	35,932	38	5,490,224	12	5.7	152.8	10	Indianapolis	700,807	1	Indianapolis	700,807
Iowa	55,965	23	2,913,808	27	3.1	52.1	6	Des Moines	191,003	1	Des Moines	191,003
Kansas	81,778	13	2,363,679	32	5.1	28.9	5	Topeka	115,266	3	Wichita	279,272
Kentucky	39,669	37	3,660,777	23	13.7	92.3	7	Frankfort	25,973	9	Louisville	298,451
Louisiana	44,521	33	4,205,900	19	15.4	94.5	8	Baton Rouge	219,419	2	New Orleans	557,515
Maine	30,995	39	1,124,660	38	13.2	36.3	2	Augusta	21,819	6	Portland	61,572
Maryland	9,837	42	4,216,975	18	7.5	428.7	8	Annapolis	31,740	5	Baltimore	786,775
Massachusetts	7,824	45	5,737,037	11	0.8	733.6	11	Boston	562,994	1	Boston	562,994
Michigan	56,954	22	9,262,078	8	4.3	162.6	18	Lansing	130,414	5	Detroit	1,203,339
Minnesota	79,548	14	4,075,970	21	7.1	51.2	8	St. Paul	270,230	2	Minneapolis	370,951
Mississippi	47,233	31	2,520,638	31	13.7	53.4	5	Jackson	202,895	1	Jackson	202,895
Missouri	68,945	18	4,916,686	15	5.1	71.3	9	Jefferson City	33,619	12	St. Louis	453,085
Montana	145,388	4	786,690	44	13.3	5.4	2	Helena	23,938	5	Billings	66,798
Nebraska	76,644	15	1,569,825	35	5.7	20.5	3	Lincoln	171,932	2	Omaha	314,255
Nevada	109,894	7	800,493	43	63.8	7.3	2	Carson City	32,022	5	Las Vegas	164,674
New Hampshire	8,993	44	920,610	42	24.8	102.4	2	Concord	30,400	3	Manchester	90,936
New Jersey	7,468	46	7,364,823	9	2.7	986.2	14	Trenton	92,124	5	Newark	329,248
New Mexico	121,335	5	1,302,894	37	28.1	10.7	3	Santa Fe	48,953	2	Albuquerque	331,767
New York	47,377	30	17,558,072	2	-3.7	370.6	34	Albany	101,727	6	New York	7,071,639
North Carolina	48,843	29	5,881,766	10	15.7	120.4	11	Raleigh	150,255	3	Charlotte	314,447
North Dakota	69,300	17	652,717	46	5.7	9.4	1	Bismarck	44,485	2	Fargo	61,383
Ohio	41,004	35	10,797,630	6	1.3	263.3	21	Columbus	564,871	2	Cleveland	573,822
Oklahoma	68,655	19	3,025,290	26	18.2	44.1	6	Oklahoma City	403,213	1	Oklahoma City	403,213
Oregon	96,184	10	2,632,105	30	25.9	27.4	5	Salem	89,233	3	Portland	366,383
Pennsylvania	44,888	32	11,863,895	4	0.5	264.3	23	Harrisburg	53,264	10	Philadelphia	1,688,210
Rhode Island	1,055	50	947,154	40	-0.3	987.8	2	Providence	156,804	1	Providence	156,804
South Carolina	30,203	40	3,121,820	24	20.5	103.4	6	Columbia	101,208	1	Columbia	101,208
South Dakota	75,952	16	690,768	45	3.7	9.1	1	Pierre	11,973	9	Sioux Falls	81,343
Tennessee	41,155	34	4,591,120	17	16.9	111.6	9	Nashville	455,651	2	Memphis	646,356
Texas	262,017	2	14,229,191	3	27.1	54.3	27	Austin	345,496	6	Houston	1,595,138
Utah	82,073	12	1,461,037	37	37.9	17.8	3	Salt Lake City	163,033	1	Salt Lake City	163,033
Vermont	9,273	43	511,456	48	15.0	55.2	1	Montpelier	8,241	5	Burlington	37,712

The Council of State Governments

STATE STATISTICS—Continued

State or other jurisdiction	Land area In square miles	Land area Rank in nation	Population Size	Population Rank in nation	Percentage change 1970 to 1980	Density per square mile	No. of Representatives in Congress	Capital	Population	Rank in state	Largest city	Population
Virginia	39,704	36	5,346,818	14	14.9	134.7	10	Richmond	219,214	3	Norfolk	266,979
Washington	66,511	20	4,132,156	20	21.1	62.1	8	Olympia	27,447	15	Seattle	493,846
West Virginia	24,119	41	1,949,644	34	11.8	80.8	4	Charleston	63,968	1	Charleston	63,968
Wisconsin	54,426	25	4,705,767	16	6.5	86.5	9	Madison	170,616	2	Milwaukee	636,212
Wyoming	96,989	9	469,557	49	41.3	4.8	1	Cheyenne	47,283	2	Casper	51,016
Dist. of Columbia	63		638,333		-15.6	10,132.3	1 (b)					
American Samoa	76		32,395		18.9	419.0		Pago Pago	3,075		Pago Pago	3,075
Federated States of Micronesia	271		73,160					Kolonia, Ponape				
Guam	209		105,816		24.7	506.3	1 (b)	Agana	5,549		Moen, Truk	10,351
Marshall Islands	70		31,042		34.9	443.5		Majuro	896		Tamuning	8,862
No. Mariana Is.	184		16,780		74.1	91.1		Saipan	8,667		Majuro	8,667
Puerto Rico	3,421		3,187,570		17.9	931.8	1 (b)	San Juan	424,600		Saipan	14,549
Republic of Belau	192		12,177		8.1	63.4		Koror	6,222		San Juan	424,600
U.S. Virgin Islands	132		95,591		54.6	724.2	1 (b)	Charlotte Amalie, St. Thomas	11,842		Charlotte Amalie, St. Thomas	11,842

Key:
(a) Honolulu County.
(b) Delegate with committee voting privileges only.

STATE PAGES

Alabama

Nickname	The Heart of Dixie
Motto	*We Dare Maintain Our Rights*
Animal	*Racking Horse*
Flower	Camellia
Bird	Yellowhammer
Tree	Southern (Longleaf) Pine
Song	*Alabama*
Insect	Monarch butterfly
Stone	Marble
Entered the Union	December 14, 1819
Capital	Montgomery

ELECTED EXECUTIVE BRANCH OFFICIALS

Governor	Guy Hunt
Lieutenant Governor	Jim Folsom Jr.
Secretary of State	Perry Hand
Attorney General	Don Siegelman
Treasurer	George C. Wallace Jr.
Auditor	Jan Cook
Commr. of Agriculture & Industries	Albert McDonald

SUPREME COURT

E. C. Hornsby, Chief Justice
Reneau P. Almon
Hugh Maddox
Richard L. Jones
Janie L. Shores
Henry B. Steagall II
Oscar W. Adams Jr.
Gorman Houston
Mark Kennedy

LEGISLATURE

President of the Senate	Lt. Gov. Jim Folsom Jr.
President Pro Tem of the Senate	Ryan deGraffenried Jr.
Secretary of the Senate	McDowell Lee
Speaker of the House	James Clark
Speaker Pro Tem of the House	James M. Campbell
Clerk of the House	John W. Pemberton

STATISTICS

Land Area (square miles)	50,767
Rank in Nation	28th
Population	3,893,888
Rank in Nation	22nd
Density per square mile	76.7
Number of Representatives in Congress	7
Capital City	Montgomery
Population	177,857
Rank in State	3rd
Largest City	Birmingham
Population	284,413
Number of Cities over 10,000 Population	40

Alaska

Motto	*North to the Future*
Flower	Forget-me-not
Marine Mammal	Bowhead Whale
Bird	Willow Ptarmigan
Tree	Sitka Spruce
Song	*Alaska's Flag*
Fish	King Salmon
Fossil	Woolly Mammoth
Sport	Dog Mushing
Gem	Jade
Mineral	Gold
Purchased from Russia by the United States	March 30, 1867
Entered the Union	January 3, 1959
Capital	Juneau

ELECTED EXECUTIVE BRANCH OFFICIALS

Governor	Steve Cowper
Lieutenant Governor	Stephen McAlpine

SUPREME COURT

Warren W. Matthews, Chief Justice
Edmond W. Burke
Allen Compton
Daniel Moore
Jay A. Rabinowitz

LEGISLATURE

President of the Senate	Tim Kelly
Secretary of the Senate	Nancy Quinto
Speaker of the House	Sam Cotten
Chief Clerk of the House	Irene Cashen

STATISTICS

Land Area (square miles)	570,833
Rank in Nation	1st
Population	401,851
Rank in Nation	50th
Density per square mile	0.7
Number of Representatives in Congress	1
Capital City	Juneau
Population	19,528
Rank in State	3rd
Largest City	Anchorage
Population	174,431
Number of Cities over 10,000 Population	3

STATE PAGES

Arizona

Nickname .... The Grand Canyon State
Motto .... *Ditat Deus* (God Enriches)
Flower .... Blossom of the Saguaro Cactus
Bird .... Cactus Wren
Tree .... Palo Verde
Song .... *Arizona March Song* and *Arizona*
Gemstone .... Turquoise
Official Neckwear .... Bola Tie
Entered the Union .... February 14, 1912
Capital .... Phoenix

ELECTED EXECUTIVE BRANCH OFFICIALS

Governor .... Rose Mofford
Secretary of State .... Jim Shumway
Attorney General .... Robert K. Corbin
Treasurer .... Ray Rottas
Auditor General .... Douglas R. Norton
Supt. of Public Instruction .... C. Diane Bishop
Mine Inspector .... Douglas K. Martin

SUPREME COURT

Frank X. Gordon Jr., Chief Justice
Stanley G. Feldman, Vice Chief Justice
James Duke Cameron
Robert J. Corcoran
James Moeller

LEGISLATURE

President of the Senate .... Robert B. Usdane
President Pro Tem of the Senate .... Leo Corbet
Secretary of the Senate .... Shirley L. Wheaton

Speaker of the House .... Jane Dee Hull
Speaker Pro Tem
   of the House .... Bill English
Chief Clerk of the House .... Jane Richards

STATISTICS

Land Area (square miles) 113,508
   Rank in Nation 6th
Population 2,718,215
   Rank in Nation 29th
   Density per square mile 23.9
Number of Representatives in Congress 5
Capital City .... Phoenix
   Population 789,704
   Rank in State 1st
Largest City .... Phoenix
Number of Places over 10,000 Population 17

Arkansas

Nickname .... The Land of Opportunity
Motto .... *Regnat Populus* (The People Rule)
Flower .... Apple Blossom
Bird .... Mockingbird
Tree .... Pine
Song .... *Arkansas*
Gem .... Diamond
Entered the Union .... June 15, 1836
Capital .... Little Rock

ELECTED EXECUTIVE BRANCH OFFICIALS

Governor .... Bill Clinton
Lieutenant Governor .... Winston Bryant
Secretary of State .... W.J. "Bill" McCuen
Attorney General .... Steve Clark
Treasurer .... Jimmie Lou Fisher
Auditor .... Julia Hughs Jones
Land Commr. .... Charlie Daniels

SUPREME COURT

Jack Holt, Jr., Chief Justice
Robert H. Dudley
Tom Glaze
Steele Hays
Darrell Hickman
David Newbern
John I. Purtle

GENERAL ASSEMBLY

President
   of the Senate .... Lt. Gov. Winston Bryant
President Pro Tem
   of the Senate .... Nick Wilson
Secretary of the Senate .... Hal Moody

Speaker of the House .... Ernest Cunningham
Speaker Pro Tem
   of the House .... L. L. Bryan
Chief Clerk of the House .... Jo Kenshaw

STATISTICS

Land Area (square miles) 52.078
   Rank in Nation 27th
Population 2,286,435
   Rank in Nation 33rd
   Density per square mile 43.9
Number of Representatives in Congress 4
Capital City .... Little Rock
   Population 158,461
   Rank in State 1st
Largest City .... Little Rock
Number of Places over 10,000 Population 29

California

Nickname	The Golden State
Motto	*Eureka* (I Have Found It)
Animal	California Grizzly Bear
Flower	Golden Poppy
Bird	California Valley Quail
Tree	California Redwood
Song	*I Love You, California*
Fossil	Saber-Toothed Cat
Marine Mammal	California Gray Whale
Entered the Union	September 9, 1850
Capital	Sacramento

ELECTED EXECUTIVE BRANCH OFFICIALS

Governor	George Deukmejian
Lieutenant Governor	Leo T. McCarthy
Secretary of State	March Fong Eu
Attorney General	John Van de Kamp
Treasurer	Thomas Hayes
Controller	Gray Davis
Supt. of Public Instruction	Bill Honig

SUPREME COURT

Malcolm M. Lucas, Chief Justice
Stanley Mosk
Allen E. Broussard
Edward Panelli
Joyce Luther Kennard
David N. Eagleson
Marcus M. Kaufman

LEGISLATURE

President of the Senate	Lt. Gov. Leo T. McCarthy
President Pro Tem of the Senate	David A. Roberti
Secretary of the Senate	Darryl R. White
Speaker of the Assembly	Willie Lewis Brown Jr.
Speaker Pro Tem of the Assembly	Mike Roos
Acting Chief Clerk of the Assembly	R. Brian Kidney

STATISTICS

Land Area (square miles)	156,299
Rank in Nation	3rd
Population	23,667,902
Rank in Nation	1st
Density per square mile	151.4
Number of Representatives in Congress	45
Capital City	Sacramento
Population	275,741
Rank in State	7th
Largest City	Los Angeles
Population	2,966,850
Number of Places over 10,000 Population	256

Colorado

Nickname	The Centennial State
Motto	*Nil Sine Numine* (Nothing Without Providence)
Flower	Columbine
Bird	Lark Bunting
Tree	Blue Spruce
Song	*Where the Columbines Grow*
Fossil	Stegosaurus
Gemstone	Aquamarine
Animal	Bighorn Sheep
Entered the Union	August 1, 1876
Capital	Denver

ELECTED EXECUTIVE BRANCH OFFICIALS

Governor	Roy Romer
Lieutenant Governor	C. Michael Callihan
Secretary of State	Natalie Meyer
Attorney General	Duane Woodard
Treasurer	Gail S. Schoettler

SUPREME COURT

Joseph R. Quinn, Chief Justice
Luis D. Rovira
Mary J. Mullakey
George E. Lohr
William E. Erickson
Anthony Vollack
Howard M. Kirshbaum

GENERAL ASSEMBLY

President of the Senate	Ted L. Strickland
President Pro Tem of the Senate	Harold L. McCormick
Secretary of the Senate	Joan M. Albi
Speaker of the House	Carl "Bev" Bledsoe
Speaker Pro Tem of the House	Paul D. Schauer
Chief Clerk of the House	Lee C. Bahrych

STATISTICS

Land Area (square miles)	103,595
Rank in Nation	8th
Population	2,889,964
Rank in Nation	28th
Density per square mile	27.9
Number of Representatives in Congress	6
Capital City	Denver
Population	492,365
Rank in State	1st
Largest City	Denver
Number of Places over 10,000 Population	25

STATE PAGES

Connecticut

Nickname	The Constitution State
Motto	*Qui Transtulit Sustinet*
	(He Who Transplanted Still Sustains)
Animal	Sperm Whale
Flower	Mountain Laurel
Bird	American Robin
Tree	White Oak
Song	*Yankee Doodle*
Mineral	Garnet
Insect	Praying Mantis
Entered the Union	January 9, 1788
Capital	Hartford

ELECTED EXECUTIVE BRANCH OFFICIALS

Governor	William A. O'Neill
Lieutenant Governor	Joseph J. Fauliso
Secretary of State	Julia H. Tashjian
Attorney General	Clarine Nardi Riddle
Treasurer	Francisco Borges
Comptroller	J. Edward Caldwell

SUPREME COURT

Ellen Ash Peters, Chief Justice
Robert J. Callahan
Arthur H. Healey
David M. Shea
Robert D. Glass
Alfred V. Covello
T. Clark Hull

GENERAL ASSEMBLY

President of the Senate	Lt. Gov. Joseph J. Fauliso
President Pro Tem of the Senate	John B. Larson
Clerk of the Senate	Thomas P. Sheridan
Speaker of the House	Richard J. Balducci
Deputy Speaker of the House	Ronald Smoko
Clerk of the House	Penn J. Ritter

STATISTICS

Land Area (square miles)	4,872
Rank in Nation	48th
Population	3,107,576
Rank in Nation	25th
Density per square mile	637.8
Number of Representatives in Congress	6
Capital City	Hartford
Population	136,392
Rank in State	2nd
Largest City	Bridgeport
Population	142,546
Number of Places over 10,000 Population	22

Delaware

Nickname	The First State
Motto	Liberty and Independence
Flower	Peach Blossom
Bird	Blue Hen Chicken
Tree	American Holly
Song	*Our Delaware*
Mineral	Sillimanite
Beverage	Milk
Entered the Union	December 7, 1787
Capital	Dover

ELECTED EXECUTIVE BRANCH OFFICIALS

Governor	Michael N. Castle
Lieutenant Governor	Dale E. Wolf
Secretary of State	Michael E. Harkins
Attorney General	Charles M. Oberly III
Treasurer	Janet C. Rzewnicki
Auditor	R. Thomas Wagner Jr.
Insurance Commr.	David N. Levinson

SUPREME COURT

Andrew D. Christie, Chief Justice
Henry R. Horsey
Andrew G. T. Moore II
Joseph T. Walsh
Randy J. Holland

GENERAL ASSEMBLY

President of the Senate	Lt. Gov. Dale E. Wolf
President Pro Tem of the Senate	Richard S. Cordrey
Secretary of the Senate	Bernard J. Brady
Speaker of the House	Terry R. Spence
Chief Clerk of the House	JoAnn Hedrick

STATISTICS

Land Area (square miles)	1,932
Rank in Nation	49th
Population	594,338
Rank in Nation	47th
Density per square mile	307.6
Number of Representatives in Congress	1
Capital City	Dover
Population	23,512
Rank in State	3rd
Largest City	Wilmington
Population	70,195
Number of Places over 10,000 Population	3

STATE PAGES

Florida

Nickname	The Sunshine State
Motto	*In God We Trust*
Animal	Florida Panther
Flower	Orange Blossom
Bird	Mockingbird
Tree	Sabal Palmetto Palm
Song	*The Swanee River (Old Folks at Home)*
Marine Mammal	Manatee
Saltwater Mammal	Porpoise
Gem	Moonstone
Shell	Horse Conch
Entered the Union	March 3, 1845
Capital	Tallahassee

ELECTED EXECUTIVE BRANCH OFFICIALS

Governor	Bob Martinez
Lieutenant Governor	Bobby Brantley
Secretary of State	Jim Smith
Attorney General	Bob Butterworth
Treasurer/Insurance Commr.	Tom Gallagher
Comptroller	Gerald A. Lewis
Commr. of Education	Betty Castor
Commr. of Agriculture	Doyle Conner

SUPREME COURT

Raymond Ehrlich, Chief Justice
Ben F. Overton
Parker Lee McDonald
Leander J. Shaw Jr.
Rosemary Barkett
Stephen Grimes
Gerald Kogan

LEGISLATURE

President of the Senate	Robert B. Crawford
President Pro Tem of the Senate	Arnett E. Girardeau
Secretary of the Senate	Joe Brown
Speaker of the House	Tom Gustafson
Speaker Pro Tem of the House	Sam Mitchell
Clerk of the House	John B. Phelps

STATISTICS

Land Area (square miles)	54,153
Rank in Nation	26th
Population	9,746,324
Rank in Nation	7th
Density per square mile	180
Number of Representatives in Congress	19
Capital City	Tallahassee
Population	81,548
Rank in State	11th
Largest City	Jacksonville
Population	540,920
Number of Places over 10,000 Population	96

Georgia

Nickname	The Empire State of the South*
Motto	*Wisdom, Justice and Moderation*
Flower	Cherokee Rose
Bird	Brown Thrasher
Tree	Live Oak
Song	*Georgia on My Mind*
Butterfly	Tiger Swallowtail
Insect	Honeybee
Fish	Largemouth Bass
Entered the Union	January 2, 1788
Capital	Atlanta

*Unofficial

ELECTED EXECUTIVE BRANCH OFFICIALS

Governor	Joe Frank Harris
Lieutenant Governor	Zell B. Miller
Secretary of State	Max Cleland
Attorney General	Michael J. Bowers
Auditor	G. W. Hogan
Commr. of Insurance	Warren Evans
Superintendent of Schools	Werner Rogers
Commr. of Agriculture	Thomas T. Irvin
Commr. of Labor	Joe Tanner

SUPREME COURT

Harold G. Clarke, Chief Justice
George T. Smith
Charles L. Weltner
Richard Bell
Willis B. Hunt
Robert Benham
Norman Fletcher

GENERAL ASSEMBLY

President of the Senate	Lt. Gov. Zell B. Miller
President Pro Tem of the Senate	Joseph F. Kennedy
Secretary of the Senate	Hamilton McWhorter Jr.
Speaker of the House	Thomas B. Murphy
Speaker Pro Tem of the House	Jack Connell
Clerk of the House	Glenn W. Ellard

STATISTICS

Land Area (square miles)	58,056
Rank in Nation	21st
Population	5,463,105
Rank in Nation	13th
Density per square mile	94.1
Number of Representatives in Congress	10
Capital City	Atlanta
Population	425,022
Rank in State	1st
Largest City	Atlanta
Number of Places over 10,000 Population	39

STATE PAGES

Hawaii

Nickname . . . . The Aloha State
Motto . . . . *Ua Mau Ke Ea O Ka Aina I Ka Pono*
(The Life of the Land Is Perpetuated in Righteousness)
Flower . . . . Hibiscus
Bird . . . . Hawaiian Goose
Tree . . . . Kukui Tree (Candlenut)
Song . . . . *Hawaii Ponoi*
Gem . . . . Black Coral
Marine Mammal . . . . Humpback Whale
Entered the Union . . . . August 21, 1959
Capital . . . . Honolulu

ELECTED EXECUTIVE BRANCH OFFICIALS
Governor . . . . John D. Waihee III
Lieutenant Governor . . . . Benjamin J. Cayetano
Attorney General . . . . Warren Price III
Comptroller . . . . Russel S. Nagata

SUPREME COURT
Herman T. F. Lum, Chief Justice
Yoshimi Hayashi
Frank D. Padgett
James H. Wakatsuki
(1 Vacancy)

LEGISLATURE
President of the Senate . . . . Richard S. H. Wong
Vice President
  of the Senate . . . . James Aki
Clerk of the Senate . . . . T. David Woo Jr.

Speaker of the House . . . . Daniel J. Kihano
Vice Speaker of the House . . . . Emilio S. Alcon
Clerk of the House . . . . Gerald I. Miyoshi

STATISTICS
Land Area (square miles) 6,425
  Rank in Nation 47th
Population 964,691
  Rank in Nation 39th
  Density per square mile 150.1
Number of Representatives in Congress 2
Capital City . . . . Honolulu
  Population (county & city) 762,874
  Rank in State 1st
Largest City . . . . Honolulu
Number of Places over 10,000 Population 12

Idaho

Nickname . . . . The Gem State
Motto . . . . *Esto Perpetua* (Let It Be Perpetual)
Flower . . . . Syringa
Bird . . . . Mountain Bluebird
Tree . . . . Western White Pine
Song . . . . *Here We Have Idaho*
Horse . . . . Appaloosa
Fossil . . . . Hagerman Horse
Gemstone . . . . Idaho Star Garnet
Entered the Union . . . . July 3, 1890
Capital . . . . Boise

ELECTED EXECUTIVE BRANCH OFFICIALS
Governor . . . . Cecil D. Andrus
Lieutenant Governor . . . . C. L. Otter
Secretary of State . . . . Pete T. Cenarrusa
Attorney General . . . . Jim Jones
Treasurer . . . . Lydia J. Edwards
Auditor . . . . J. D. Williams
Supt. of Public Instruction . . . . Jerry L. Evans

SUPREME COURT
Robert E. Bakes, Chief Justice
Stephen Bistline
Byron Johnson
Larry M. Boyle
Charles F. McDevitt

LEGISLATURE
President
  of the Senate . . . . Lt. Gov. C. L. Otter
President Pro Tem
  of the Senate . . . . Michael Crapo
Secretary of the Senate . . . . Dorothea Baxter

Speaker of the House . . . . Tom Boyd
Chief Clerk of the House . . . . Phyllis Watson

STATISTICS
Land Area (square miles) 82,412
  Rank in Nation 11th
Population 943,935
  Rank in Nation 41st
  Density per square mile 11.5
Number of Representatives in Congress 2
Capital City . . . . Boise
  Population 102,451
  Rank in State 1st
Largest City . . . . Boise
Number of Places over 10,000 Population 11

STATE PAGES

Illinois

Nickname	The Prairie State
Great Seal	*State Sovereignty-National Union*
Animal	White-tailed Deer
Flower	Native Violet
Bird	Cardinal
Tree	White Oak
Song	*Illinois*
Mineral	Fluorite
Fish	Blue Gill
Entered the Union	December 3, 1818
Capital	Springfield

ELECTED EXECUTIVE BRANCH OFFICIALS

Governor	James R. Thompson
Lieutenant Governor	George H. Ryan Sr.
Secretary of State	James Edgar
Attorney General	Neil F. Hartigan
Treasurer	Jerry Cosentino
Comptroller	Roland W. Burris

SUPREME COURT

Thomas J. Moran, Chief Justice
Horace L. Calvo
William G. Clark
Ben Miller
Howard C. Ryan
John J. Stamos
Daniel P. Ward

GENERAL ASSEMBLY

President of the Senate	Philip J. Rock
Minority Leader of the Senate	James Philip
Secretary of the Senate	Linda Hawker
Speaker of the House	Michael J. Madigan
Minority Leader of the House	Lee A. Daniels
Chief Clerk of the House	John F. O'Brien

STATISTICS

Land Area (square miles)	55,645
Rank in Nation	24th
Population	11,426,518
Rank in Nation	5th
Density per square mile	205.3
Number of Representatives in Congress	22
Capital City	Springfield
Population	99,637
Rank in State	4th
Largest City	Chicago
Population	3,005,072
Number of Places over 10,000 Population	177

Indiana

Nickname	The Hoosier State
Motto	*Crossroads of America*
Flower	Peony
Bird	Cardinal
Tree	Tulip Poplar
Song	*On the Banks of the Wabash, Far Away*
Poem	*Indiana* by Franklin Mapes
Stone	Limestone
Entered the Union	December 11, 1816
Capital	Indianapolis

ELECTED EXECUTIVE BRANCH OFFICIALS

Governor	Evan Bayh
Lieutenant Governor	Frank L. O'Bannon
Secretary of State	Joseph H. Hogsett
Attorney General	Linley E. Pearson
Treasurer	Marjorie H. O'Laughlin
Auditor	Ann G. DeVore
Supt. of Public Instruction	H. Dean Evans

SUPREME COURT

Randall T. Shepard, Chief Justice
Roger O. DeBruler
Richard M. Givan
Alfred J. Pivarnik
Brent E. Dickson

GENERAL ASSEMBLY

President of the Senate	Lt. Gov. Frank L. O'Bannon
President Pro Tem of the Senate	Robert D. Garton
Principal Secretary of the Senate	Carolyn J. Tinkle
Democrat Speaker of the House	Michael K, Phillips
Republican Speaker of the House	Paul S. Mannweiler
Democrat Speaker Pro Tem of the House	Chester F. Dobis
Republican Speaker Pro Tem of the House	Jeffrey K. Espich
Democrat Principal Clerk	Betty Masariu
Republican Principal Clerk	Sharon Thuma

STATISTICS

Land Area (square miles)	35,932
Rank in Nation	38th
Population	5,490,224
Rank in Nation	12th
Density per square mile	152.8
Number of Representatives in Congress	10
Capital City	Indianapolis
Population	700,807
Rank in State	1st
Largest City	Indianapolis
Number of Places over 10,000 Population	61

The Council of State Governments

STATE PAGES

Iowa

Nickname . . . . The Hawkeye State
Motto . . . . *Our Liberties We Prize and
Our Rights We Will Maintain*
Flower . . . . Wild Rose
Bird . . . . Eastern Goldfinch
Tree . . . . Oak
Song . . . . *The Song of Iowa*
Stone . . . . Geode
Entered the Union . . . . December 28, 1846
Capital . . . . Des Moines

ELECTED EXECUTIVE BRANCH OFFICIALS

Governor . . . . Terry E. Branstad
Lieutenant Governor . . . . Jo Ann Zimmerman
Secretary of State . . . . Elaine Baxter
Attorney General . . . . Thomas J. Miller
Treasurer . . . . Michael L. Fitzgerald
Auditor . . . . Richard D. Johnson
Secy. of Agriculture . . . . Dale Cochran

SUPREME COURT

Arthur A. McGiverin, Chief Justice
James H. Carter
David K. Harris
Jerry L. Larson
Louis A. Lavorato
Linda K. Newman
Louis W. Schultz
Bruce M. Snell, Jr.

GENERAL ASSEMBLY

President
 of the Senate . . . . Lt. Gov. Jo Ann Zimmerman
President Pro Tem
 of the Senate . . . . Tom Mann Jr.
Secretary of the Senate . . . . John F. Dwyer

Speaker of the House . . . . Don Avenson
Speaker Pro Tem of the House . . . . John H. Connors
Chief Clerk of the House . . . . Joseph J. O'Hern

STATISTICS

Land Area (square miles) 55,965
 Rank in Nation 23rd
Population 2,913,808
 Rank in Nation 27th
 Density per square mile 52.1
Number of Representatives in Congress 6
Capital City . . . . Des Moines
 Population 191,003
 Rank in State 1st
Largest City . . . . Des Moines
Number of Places over 10,000 Population 29

Kansas

Nickname . . . . The Sunflower State
Motto . . . . *Ad Astra per Aspera*
(To the Stars through Difficulties)
Animal . . . . American Buffalo
Flower . . . . Wild Native Sunflower
Bird . . . . Western Meadowlark
Tree . . . . Cottonwood
Song . . . . *Home on the Range*
Reptile . . . . Ornate Box Turtle
Insect . . . . Honeybee
Entered the Union . . . . January 29, 1861
Capital . . . . Topeka

ELECTED EXECUTIVE BRANCH OFFICIALS

Governor . . . . Mike Hayden
Lieutenant Governor . . . . Jack D. Walker
Secretary of State . . . . Bill Graves
Attorney General . . . . Robert T. Stephan
Treasurer . . . . Joan Finney
Commr. of Insurance . . . . Fletcher Bell

SUPREME COURT

Robert H. Miller, Chief Justice
Richard W. Holmes
Kay McFarland
Harold S. Herd
Tyler C. Lockett
Donald L. Allegrucci
Frederick N. Six

LEGISLATURE

President
 of the Senate . . . . Paul Burke
Vice President
 of the Senate . . . . Eric Yost
Secretary of the Senate . . . . Lu Kenney

Speaker of the House . . . . James D. Braden
Speaker Pro Tem
 of the House . . . . Dale Sprague
Chief Clerk of the House . . . . Janet E. Jones

STATISTICS

Land Area (square miles) 81,778
 Rank in Nation 13th
Population 2,363,679
 Rank in Nation 32nd
 Density per square mile 28.9
Number of Representatives in Congress 5
Capital City . . . . Topeka
 Population 115,266
 Rank in State 3rd
Largest City . . . . Wichita
 Population 279,272
Number of Places over 10,000 Population 34

STATE PAGES

Kentucky

Nickname . . . . The Bluegrass State
Motto . . . . *United We Stand, Divided We Fall*
Animal . . . . Gray Squirrel
Flower . . . . Goldenrod
Bird . . . . Cardinal
Tree . . . . Kentucky Coffee Tree
Song . . . . *My Old Kentucky Home*
Fossil . . . . Brachiopod
Fish . . . . Kentucky Bass
Entered the Union . . . . June 1, 1792
Capital . . . . Frankfort

ELECTED EXECUTIVE BRANCH OFFICIALS

Governor . . . . Wallace G. Wilkinson
Lieutenant Governor . . . . Brereton C. Jones
Secretary of State . . . . Bremer Ehrler
Attorney General . . . . Fredric J. Cowan
Treasurer . . . . Robert Mead CPA
Auditor of Public Accounts . . . . Bob Babbage
Supt. of Public Instruction . . . . John H. Brock
Commr. of Agriculture . . . . Ward Burnette

SUPREME COURT

Robert F. Stephens, Chief Justice
Dan Jack Combs
William M. Gant
Joseph E. Lambert
Charles M. Leibson
Roy N. Vance
Donald C. Wintersheimer

GENERAL ASSEMBLY

President
  of the Senate . . . . Lt. Gov. Brereton Jones
President Pro Tem
  of the Senate . . . . John A. Rose
Chief Clerk of the Senate . . . . Julie Haviland

Speaker of the Assembly . . . . Donald J. Blandford
Speaker Pro Tem
  of the Assembly . . . . Pete Worthington
Chief Clerk of the House . . . . Evelyn Marston

STATISTICS

Land Area (square miles) 39,669
  Rank in Nation 37th
Population 3,660,777
  Rank in Nation 23rd
  Density per square mile 92.3
Number of Representatives in Congress 7
Capital City . . . . Frankfort
  Population 25,973
  Rank in State 9th
Largest City . . . . Louisville
  Population 298,451
Number of Places over 10,000 Population 30

Louisiana

Nickname . . . . The Pelican State
Motto . . . . *Union, Justice and Confidence*
Flower . . . . Magnolia
Bird . . . . Eastern Brown Pelican
Tree . . . . Bald Cypress
Song . . . . *Give Me Louisiana*
Crustacean . . . . Crawfish
Dog . . . . Catahoula Leopard
Entered the Union . . . . April 30, 1812
Capital . . . . Baton Rouge

ELECTED EXECUTIVE BRANCH OFFICIALS

Governor . . . . Charles E. "Buddy" Roemer
Lieutenant Governor . . . . Paul Hardy
Secretary of State . . . . W. Fox McKeithen
Attorney General . . . . William J. Guste Jr.
Treasurer . . . . Mary L. Landrieu
Supt. of Education . . . . Thomas G. Clausen
Commr. of Agriculture . . . . Bob Odom
Commr. of Insurance . . . . Douglas D. Green
Commr. of Elections . . . . Jerry M. Fowler

SUPREME COURT

John A. Dixon Jr., Chief Justice
Pascal F. Calogero Jr.
Luther F. Cole
James L. Dennis
Harry T. Lemmon
Walter F. Marcus Jr.
Jack Crozier Watson

LEGISLATURE

President of the Senate . . . . Allen R. Bares
President Pro Tem
  of the Senate . . . . Samuel B. Nunez
Secretary of the Senate . . . . Michael S. Baer III

Speaker of the House . . . . Jimmy N. Dimos
Speaker Pro Tem
  of the House . . . . Huntington B. Downer
Clerk of the House . . . . Alfred W. Speer

STATISTICS

Land Area (square miles) 44,521
  Rank in Nation 33rd
Population 4,205,900
  Rank in Nation 19th
  Density per square mile 94.5
Number of Representatives in Congress 8
Capital City . . . . Baton Rouge
  Population 219,419
  Rank in State 2nd
Largest City . . . . New Orleans
  Population 557,515
Number of Places over 10,000 Population 34

The Council of State Governments

STATE PAGES

Maine

Nickname	The Pine Tree State
Motto	*Dirigo* (I Direct)
Animal	Moose
Flower	White Pine Cone and Tassel
Bird	Chickadee
Tree	White Pine
Song	*State of Maine Song*
Fish	Landlocked Salmon
Mineral	Tourmaline
Entered the Union	March 15, 1820
Capital	Augusta

ELECTED EXECUTIVE BRANCH OFFICIALS

Governor .... John R. McKernan Jr.

SUPREME JUDICIAL COURT

Vincent L. McKusick, Chief Justice
Robert W. Clifford
Samuel W. Collins
Caroline D. Glassman
D. Brock Hornby
David G. Roberts
Daniel E. Wathen

LEGISLATURE

President of the Senate .... Charles P. Pray
Secretary of the Senate .... Joy J. O'Brien

Speaker of the House .... John L. Martin
Clerk of the House .... Edwin H. Pert

STATISTICS

Land Area (square miles)	30,995
Rank in Nation	39th
Population	1,124,660
Rank in Nation	38th
Density per square mile	36.3
Number of Representatives in Congress	2
Capital City	Augusta
Population	21,819
Rank in State	6th
Largest City	Portland
Population	61,572
Number of Places over 10,000 Population	12

Maryland

Nicknames	The Old Line State and Free State
Motto	*Fatti Maschii, Parole Femine* (Manly Deeds, Womanly Words)
Flower	Black-eyed Susan
Bird	Baltimore Oriole
Tree	White Oak
Song	*Maryland, My Maryland*
Dog	Chesapeake Bay Retriever
Boat	The Skipjack
Fish	Striped Bass
Entered the Union	April 28, 1788
Capital	Annapolis

ELECTED EXECUTIVE BRANCH OFFICIALS

Governor	William Donald Schaefer
Lieutenant Governor	Melvin A. Steinberg
Secretary of State	Winfield M. Kelly Jr.
Attorney General	J. Joseph Curran Jr.
Comptroller of Treasury	Louis L. Goldstein
Treasurer	Lucille Maurer

COURT OF APPEALS

Robert C. Murphy, Chief Judge
William H. Adkins II
John F. McAuliffe
Albert T. Blackwell Jr.
John C. Eldridge
Harry A. Cole
Lawrence F. Rodowsky

GENERAL ASSEMBLY

President of the Senate .... Thomas V. Mike Miller Jr.
President Pro Tem of the Senate .... Frederick C. Malkus Jr.
Secretary of the Senate .... Oden Bowie

Speaker of the House .... R. Clayton Mitchell Jr.
Speaker Pro Tem of the House .... Dennis C. Donaldson
Chief Clerk of the House .... Jacqueline M. Spell

STATISTICS

Land Area (square miles)	9,837
Rank in Nation	42nd
Population	4,216,975
Rank in Nation	18th
Density per square mile	428.7
Number of Representatives in Congress	8
Capital City	Annapolis
Population	31,740
Rank in State	5th
Largest City	Baltimore
Population	786,775
Number of Places over 10,000 Population	17

STATE PAGES

Massachusetts

Nickname	The Bay State
Motto	*Ense Petit Placidam Sub Libertate Quietem* (By the Sword We Seek Peace, but Peace Only under Liberty)
Animal	Morgan Horse
Flower	Mayflower
Bird	Chickadee
Tree	American Elm
Song	*All Hail to Massachusetts*
Fish	Cod
Insect	Ladybug
Dog	Boston Terrier
Beverage	Cranberry Juice
Gem	Rhodenite
Mineral	Babingtonite
Entered the Union	February 6, 1788
Capital City	Boston

ELECTED EXECUTIVE BRANCH OFFICIALS

Governor	Michael S. Dukakis
Lieutenant Governor	Evelyn F. Murphy
Secretary of the Commonwealth	Michael J. Connolly
Attorney General	James M. Shannon
Treasurer	Robert Q. Crane
Auditor of the Commonwealth	A. Joseph DeNucci

SUPREME JUDICIAL COURT

Paul J. Liacos, Chief Justice
Ruth I. Abrams
John M. Greaney
Neil L. Lynch
Joseph R. Nolan
Francis P. O'Connor
Herbert P. Wilkins

GENERAL COURT

President of the Senate	William M. Bulger
Clerk of the Senate	Edward B. O'Neill
Speaker of the House	George Keverian
Clerk of the House	Robert E. MacQueen

STATISTICS

Land Area (square miles)	7,824
Rank in Nation	45th
Population	5,737,037
Rank in Nation	11th
Density per square mile	733.3
Number of Representatives in Congress	11
Capital City	Boston
Population	562,994
Rank in State	1st
Largest City	Boston
Number of Places over 10,000 Population	149

Michigan

Nicknames	The Wolverine State and Great Lake State
Motto	*Si Quaeris Peninsulam Amoenam Circumspice* (If You Seek a Pleasant Peninsula, Look About You)
Flower	Apple Blossom
Bird	Robin
Tree	White Pine
Insect	Dragonfly
Song	*Michigan, My Michigan*
Stone	Petoskey Stone
Gem	Chlorastrolite
Fish	Trout
Entered the Union	January 26, 1837
Capital	Lansing

ELECTED EXECUTIVE BRANCH OFFICIALS

Governor	James Blanchard
Lieutenant Governor	Martha Griffiths
Secretary of State	Richard H. Austin
Attorney General	Frank J. Kelley
Treasurer	Robert A. Bowman

SUPREME COURT

Dorothy Comstock Riley, Chief Justice
Dennis Wayne Archer
Patricia J. Boyle
James H. Brickley
Michael F. Cavanagh
Robert Griffin
Charles L. Levin

LEGISLATURE

President of the Senate	Lt. Gov. Martha Griffiths
President Pro Tem of the Senate	Nick Smith
Secretary of the Senate	Willis H. Snow
Speaker of the House	Lewis N. Dodak
Speaker Pro Tem of the House	Teola P. Hunter
Clerk of the House	David H. Evans

STATISTICS

Land Area (square miles)	56,954
Rank in Nation	22rd
Population	9,262,078
Rank in Nation	8th
Density per square mile	162.2
Number of Representatives in Congress	18
Capital City	Lansing
Population	130,414
Rank in State	5th
Largest City	Detroit
Population	1,203,339
Number of Places over 10,000 Population	88

STATE PAGES

Minnesota

Nickname	The North Star State
Motto	*L'Etoile du Nord* (The Star of the North)
Flower	Pink and White Lady's-Slipper
Bird	Common Loon
Tree	Red Pine
Song	*Hail! Minnesota*
Fish	Walleye
Grain	Wild Rice
Mushroom	Morel
Entered the Union	May 11, 1858
Capital	St. Paul

ELECTED EXECUTIVE BRANCH OFFICIALS

Governor	Rudy Perpich
Lieutenant Governor	Marlene Johnson
Secretary of State	Joan Anderson Growe
Attorney General	Hubert H. Humphrey III
Treasurer	Michael A. McGrath
Auditor	Arne H. Carlson

SUPREME COURT
Peter S. Popovich, Chief Justice
Glenn E. Kelley
M. Jeanne Coyne
Lawrence R. Yetka
Rosalie E. Wahl
John E. Simonett
A. M. Keith

LEGISLATURE

President of the Senate	Jerome M. Hughes
Secretary of the Senate	Patrick E. Flahaven
Speaker of the House	Robert Vanasek
Chief Clerk of the House	Edward A. Burdick

STATISTICS

Land Area (square miles)	79,548
Rank in Nation	14th
Population	4,075,970
Rank in Nation	21st
Density per square mile	51.2
Number of Representatives in Congress	8
Capital City	St. Paul
Population	270,230
Rank in State	2nd
Largest City	Minneapolis
Population	370,951
Number of Places over 10,000 Population	65

Mississippi

Nickname	The Magnolia State
Motto	*Virtute et Armis* (By Valor and Arms)
Animal	White-tailed deer
Flower	Magnolia
Bird	Mockingbird
Water Mammal	Bottlenosed Dolphin
Tree	Magnolia
Song	*Go, Mississippi*
Fish	Black Bass
Beverage	Milk
Entered the Union	December 10, 1817
Capital	Jackson

ELECTED EXECUTIVE BRANCH OFFICIALS

Governor	Ray Mabus
Lieutenant Governor	Brad Dye
Secretary of State	Dick Molpus
Attorney General	Mike Moore
Treasurer	Marshall Bennett
Auditor of Public Accounts	Pete Johnson
Commr. of Agriculture and Commerce	Jim Buck Ross
Commr. of Insurance	George Dale

SUPREME COURT
Roy Noble Lee, Chief Justice
Reuben V. Anderson
Armis E. Hawkins
Joel Blass
Dan M. Lee
Lenore L. Prather
James Robertson
Michael Sullivan
Ed Pittman

LEGISLATURE

President of the Senate	Lt. Gov. Brad Dye
President Pro Tem of the Senate	Glen DeWeese
Secretary of the Senate	Frank Barber
Speaker of the House	Tim Ford
Clerk of the House	Charles J. Jackson Jr.

STATISTICS

Land Area (square miles)	47,233
Rank in Nation	31st
Population	2,520,638
Rank in Nation	31st
Density per square mile	53.4
Number of Representatives in Congress	5
Capital City	Jackson
Population	202,895
Rank in State	1st
Largest City	Jackson
Number of Places over 10,000 Population	27

STATE PAGES

Missouri

Nickname .... The Show Me State
Motto .... *Salus Populi Suprema Lex Esto*
(The Welfare of the People Shall Be the Supreme Law)
Flower .... White Hawthorn
Bird .... Bluebird
Insect .... Honeybee (Apis Melliferr)
Tree .... Flowering Dogwood
Song .... *Missouri Waltz*
Stone .... Mozarkite
Mineral .... Galena
Fossil .... Crinoid
Entered the Union .... August 10, 1821
Capital .... Jefferson City

ELECTED EXECUTIVE BRANCH OFFICIALS

Governor .... John Ashcroft
Lieutenant Governor .... Mel Carnahan
Secretary of State .... Roy D. Blunt
Attorney General .... William L. Webster
Treasurer .... Wendell Bailey
Auditor .... Margaret B. Kelly

SUPREME COURT

Charles B. Blackmar, Chief Justice
William H. Billings
Ann K. Covington
Andrew J. Higgins
Albert L. Rendlen
Edward D. Robertson Jr.
Warren D. Welliver

GENERAL ASSEMBLY

President
  of the Senate .... Lt. Gov. Mel Carnahan
President Pro Tem
  of the Senate .... James L. Mathewson
Secretary of the Senate .... Terry L. Spieler

Speaker of the House .... Robert F. Griffin
Speaker Pro Tem
  of the House .... Patrick J. Hickey
Chief Clerk of the House .... Douglas W. Burnett

STATISTICS

Land Area (square miles) 68,945
  Rank in Nation 18th
Population 4,916,686
  Rank in Nation 15th
  Density per square mile 71.3
Number of Representatives in Congress 9
Capital City .... Jefferson City
  Population 33,619
  Rank in State 12th
Largest City .... St. Louis
  Population 453,085
Number of Places over 10,000 Population 51

Montana

Nickname .... The Treasure State
Motto .... *Oro y Plata* (Gold and Silver)
Animal .... Grizzly Bear
Flower .... Bitterroot
Bird .... Western Meadowlark
Tree .... Ponderosa Pine
Song .... *Montana*
State Ballad .... *Montana Melody*
Gem stones .... Yogo Sapphire and Agate
State Fossil .... Duck-billed Dinosaur
Entered the Union .... November 8, 1889
Capital .... Helena

ELECTED EXECUTIVE BRANCH OFFICIALS

Governor .... Stan Stephens
Lieutenant Governor .... Allen Kolstad
Secretary of State .... Mike Cooney
Attorney General .... Marc Racicot
Treasurer .... Dave Ashley
Auditor .... Andrea Bennett
Supt. of Public Instruction .... Nancy Keenan

SUPREME COURT

Jean Turnage, Chief Justice
Diane Barz
John C. Harrison
William E. Hunt
John C. Sheehy
R. C. McDonough
Fred J. Weber

LEGISLATURE

President of the Senate .... Jack Galt
President Pro Tem
  of the Senate .... Matt Himsl
Secretary of the Senate .... Myrna Omholt

Speaker of the House .... John Vincent
Speaker Pro Tem of the House .... Kelly Addy
Chief Clerk of the House .... Larry Fasbender

STATISTICS

Land Area (square miles) 145,388
  Rank in Nation 4th
Population 786,690
  Rank in Nation 44th
  Density per square mile 5.4
Number of Representatives in Congress 2
Capital City .... Helena
  Population 23,938
  Rank in State 5th
Largest City .... Billings
  Population 66,798
Number of Places over 10,000 Population 9

The Council of State Governments 593

STATE PAGES

Nebraska

Nickname .... The Cornhusker State
Motto .... *Equality Before the Law*
Mammal .... White-tailed Deer
Flower .... Goldenrod
Bird .... Western Meadowlark
Tree .... Western Cottonwood
Song .... *Beautiful Nebraska*
Insect .... Honeybee
Gemstone .... Blue Agate
Entered the Union .... March 1, 1867
Capital .... Lincoln

ELECTED EXECUTIVE BRANCH OFFICIALS

Governor .... Kay A. Orr
Lieutenant Governor .... William E. Nichol
Secretary of State .... Allen J. Beermann
Attorney General .... Robert M. Spire
Treasurer .... Frank Marsh
Auditor of Public Accounts ...... Ray A. C. Johnson

SUPREME COURT

William C. Hastings, Chief Justice
Dale E. Fahrenbruch
D. Nick Caporale
C. Thomas White
John T. Grant
Leslie Boslaugh
Thomas M. Shanahan

UNICAMERAL LEGISLATURE

President of the
  Legislature .... Lt. Gov. William E. Nichol
Speaker of the Legislature .... William E. Barrett
Chairman of Executive Board,
  Legislative Council .... Bernice Labedz
Vice Chairman of Executive Board,
  Legislative Council .... Richard Peterson
Clerk of the Legislature .... Patrick J. O'Donnell

STATISTICS

Land Area (square miles) 76,644
  Rank in Nation 15th
Population 1,569,825
  Rank in Nation 35th
  Density per square mile 20.5
Number of Representatives in Congress 3
Capital City .... Lincoln
  Population 171,932
  Rank in State 2nd
Largest City .... Omaha
  Population 314,255
Number of Places over 10,000 Population 12

Nevada

Nickname .... The Silver State
Motto .... *All for Our Country*
Animal .... Desert Bighorn Sheep
Flower .... Sagebrush
Bird .... Mountain Bluebird
Tree .... Bristlecone Pine and Single-leaf Pinon
Song .... *Home Means Nevada*
Fish .... Lahontan Cutthroat Trout
Fossil .... Ichthyosaur
Entered the Union .... October 31, 1864
Capital .... Carson City

ELECTED EXECUTIVE BRANCH OFFICIALS

Acting Governor and
  Lieutenant Governor .... Robert J. Miller
  (Governor was elected to U.S. Senate in 1988)
Secretary of State .... Frankie Sue Del Papa
Attorney General .... Brian McKay
Treasurer .... Ken Santor
Controller .... Darrel R. Daines

SUPREME COURT

Clifton C. Young, Chief Justice
Thomas L. Steffen
John C. Mowbray
Charles E. Springer
Robert E. Rose

LEGISLATURE

President
  of the Senate .... Acting Gov. Robert J. Miller
President Pro Tem
  of the Senate .... Lawrence E. Jacobsen
Secretary of the Senate .... Janice L. Thomas
Speaker of the Assembly .... Joseph E. Dini Jr.
Speaker Pro Tem
  of the Assembly .... Myrna T. Williams
Chief Clerk
  of the Assembly .... Mouryne B. Landing

STATISTICS

Land Area (square miles) 109,894
  Rank in Nation 7th
Population 800,493
  Rank in Nation 43rd
  Density per square mile 7.3
Number of Representatives in Congress 2
Capital City .... Carson City
  Population 32,022
  Rank in State 5th
Largest City .... Las Vegas
  Population 164,674
Number of Places over 10,000 Population 6

STATE PAGES

New Hampshire

Nickname	The Granite State
Motto	*Live Free or Die*
Animal	White-tailed Deer
Flower	Purple Lilac
Bird	Purple Finch
Tree	White Birch
Song	*Old New Hampshire*
Insect	Ladybug
Gem	Smoky Quartz
Entered the Union	June 21, 1788
Capital	Concord

ELECTED EXECUTIVE BRANCH OFFICIALS

Governor .... Judd Greg

SUPREME COURT

David A. Brock, Chief Justice
William F. Batchelder
David H. Souter
William R. Johnson
W. Stephen Thayer III

GENERAL COURT

President of the Senate .... William S. Bartlett Jr.
President Pro Tem
  of the Senate .... Eleanor P. Podles
Clerk of the Senate .... Wilmont S. White

Speaker
  of the House .... W. Douglas Scamman Jr.
Deputy Speaker of the House ...... Harold W. Burns
Chief Clerk of the House .... James A. Chandler

STATISTICS

Land Area (square miles)	8,993
Rank in Nation	44th
Population	920,610
Rank in Nation	42nd
Density per square mile	102.4
Number of Representatives in Congress	2
Capital City	Concord
Population	30,400
Rank in State	3rd
Largest City	Manchester
Population	90,936
Number of Places over 10,000 Population	12

New Jersey

Nickname	The Garden State
Motto	*Liberty and Prosperity*
Animal	Horse
Flower	Purple Violet
Bird	Eastern Goldfinch
Tree	Red Oak
Insect	Honeybee
Entered the Union	December 18, 1787
Capital	Trenton

ELECTED EXECUTIVE BRANCH OFFICIALS

Governor	James F. Florio
Secretary of State	Joan Haberle
Attorney General	Robert DelTufo
Treasurer	Douglas Berman

SUPREME COURT

Robert N. Wilentz, Chief Justice
Robert L. Clifford
Marie L. Garibaldi
Alan B. Handler
Daniel J. O'Hern
Stewart G. Pollock
Gary S. Stein

LEGISLATURE

President of the Senate .... John A. Lynch
President Pro Tem
  of the Senate .... John F. Russo
Secretary of the Senate .... John McCarthy

Speaker of the Assembly .... Joseph V. Doria Jr.
Speaker Pro Tem
  of the Assembly .... Chuck Hardwick
Clerk of the Assembly .... Virginia E. Haines

STATISTICS

Land Area (square miles)	7,468
Rank in Nation	46th
Population	7,364,823
Rank in Nation	9th
Density per square mile	986.2
Number of Representatives in Congress	14
Capital City	Trenton
Population	92,124
Rank in State	5th
Largest City	Newark
Population	329,248
Number of Places over 10,000 Population	110

STATE PAGES

New Mexico

Nickname .... The Land of Enchantment
Motto .... *Crescit Eundo* (It Grows As It Goes)
Flower .... Yucca (Our Lord's Candles)
Bird .... Chaparral Bird
Tree .... Pinon
Songs .... *Asi es Nuevo Mexico* and
O, Fair New Mexico
Gem .... Turquoise
Fossil .... Ceolophysis Dinosaur
Animal .... Black Bear
Entered the Union .... January 6, 1912
Capital .... Santa Fe

ELECTED EXECUTIVE BRANCH OFFICIALS

Governor .... Garrey Carruthers
Lieutenant Governor .... Jack L. Stahl
Secretary of State .... Rebecca D. Vigil-Giron
Attorney General .... Hal Stratton
Treasurer .... James L. Lewis
Auditor .... Harold H. Adams

SUPREME COURT
Tony Scarborough, Chief Justice
Dan Sosa Jr.
Harry E. Stowers Jr.
Richard E. Ransom
Mary Walters

LEGISLATURE
President
  of the Senate .... Lt. Gov. Jack L. Stahl
President Pro Tem
  of the Senate .... Manny M. Aragon
Chief Clerk of the Senate .... Juanita M. Pino

Speaker of the House .... Raymond G. Sanchez
Chief Clerk of the House .... Stephen R. Arias

STATISTICS
Land Area (square miles) 121,335
  Rank in Nation 5th
Population 1,302,894
  Rank in Nation 37th
  Density per square mile 10.7
Number of Representatives in Congress 3
Capital City .... Santa Fe
  Population 48,953
  Rank in State 2nd
Largest City .... Albuquerque
  Population 331,767
Number of Places over 10,000 Population 13

New York

Nickname .... The Empire State
Motto .... *Excelsior* (Ever Upward)
Animal .... American Beaver (Castor Canadensis)
Flower .... Rose
Bird .... Bluebird
Tree .... Sugar Maple
Song .... *I Love New York*
Gem .... Garnet
Fossil .... Sea Scorpion
Entered the Union .... July 26, 1788
Capital .... Albany

ELECTED EXECUTIVE BRANCH OFFICIALS

Governor .... Mario M. Cuomo
Lieutenant Governor .... Stan Lundine
Attorney General .... Robert Abrams
Comptroller .... Edward V. Regan

COURT OF APPEALS
Sol Wachtler, Chief Judge
Richard D. Simons
Judith S. Kaye
Fritz W. Alexander II
Vito J. Titone
Stewart F. Hancock Jr.
Joseph W. Bellacosa

LEGISLATURE
President of the Senate .... Lt. Gov. Stan Lundine
President Pro Tem
  of the Senate .... Ralph J. Marino
Secretary of the Senate .... Stephen Sloan

Speaker of the Assembly .... Melvin H. Miller
Speaker Pro Tem
  of the Assembly .... William F. Passannante
Clerk of the Assembly .... Francine M. Misasi

STATISTICS
Land Area (square miles) 47,377
  Rank in Nation 30th
Population 17,558,072
  Rank in Nation 2nd
  Density per square mile 370.6
Number of Representatives in Congress 34
Capital City .... Albany
  Population 101,727
  Rank in State 6th
Largest City .... New York
  Population 7,071,639
Number of Places over 10,000 Population 86

STATE PAGES

North Carolina

Nicknames .... The Tar Heel State and Old North State
Motto .... *Esse Quam Videri* (To Be Rather Than to Seem)
Flower .... Dogwood
Bird .... Cardinal
Tree .... Pine
Song .... *The Old North State*
Mammal .... Grey Squirrel
Dog .... Plott Hound
Beverage .... Milk
Entered the Union .... November 21, 1789
Capital .... Raleigh

ELECTED EXECUTIVE BRANCH OFFICIALS

Governor .... James G. Martin
Lieutenant Governor .... James C. Gardner
Secretary of State .... Rufus L. Edmisten
Attorney General .... Lacy H. Thornburg
Treasurer .... Harlan E. Boyles
Auditor .... Edward Renfrow
Supt. of Public Instruction .... Bob Etheridge
Commr. of Agriculture .... James A. Graham
Commr. of Labor .... John C. Brooks
Commr. of Insurance .... James E. Long

SUPREME COURT

James G. Exum, Chief Justice
Louis B. Meyer   Henry E. Frye
Burley B. Mitchell Jr. John Webb
Harry C. Martin   Willis P. Whichard

GENERAL ASSEMBLY

President
 of the Senate .... Lt. Gov. James C. Gardner
President Pro Tem
 of the Senate .... Henson P. Barnes
Secretary of the Senate .... Sylvia M. Finks

Speaker of the House .... J. L. Mavretic
Speaker Pro Tem
 of the House .... R. Don Beard
Clerk of the House .... Grace Collins

STATISTICS

Land Area (square miles) 48,843
 Rank in Nation 29th
Population 5,881,766
 Rank in Nation 10th
 Density per square mile 120.4
Number of Representatives in Congress 11
Capital City .... Raleigh
 Population 150,255
 Rank in State 3rd
Largest City .... Charlotte
 Population 314,447
Number of Places over 10,000 Population 43

North Dakota

Nickname .... Peace Garden State
Motto .... *Liberty and Union, Now and Forever, One and Inseparable*
Animal .... Flickertail Gopher
Flower .... Prairie Rose
Bird .... Western Meadowlark
Tree .... American Elm
Song .... *North Dakota Hymn*
March .... *Spirit of the Land*
Stone .... Teredo Petrified Wood
Fish .... Northern Pike
Entered the Union .... November 2, 1889
Capital .... Bismarck

ELECTED EXECUTIVE BRANCH OFFICIALS

Governor .... George A. Sinner
Lieutenant Governor .... Lloyd B. Omdahl
Secretary of State .... James Kusler
Attorney General .... Nicholas Spaeth
Treasurer .... Robert Hanson
Auditor .... Robert Peterson
Supt. of Public Instruction .... Wayne Sanstead
Commr. of Agriculture .... Sarah Vogel
Commr. of Labor .... Bryon Kneetson
Commr. of Insurance .... Earl Pomeroy
Tax Commissioner .... Hedi Heitcamp

SUPREME COURT

Ralph J. Erickstad, Chief Justice
Gerald W. VanderWalle
H. F. Gierke
Herbert L. Meschke
Beryl J. Levine

LEGISLATIVE ASSEMBLY

President of the Senate .... William Heigaard
President Pro Tem
 of the Senate .... Herschel Lashkowitz
Secretary of the Senate .... Patricia Conrad

Speaker of the House .... William Kretschmar
Chief Clerk of the House .... Roy Gilbreath

STATISTICS

Land Area (square miles) 69,300
 Rank in Nation 17th
Population 652,717
 Rank in Nation 46th
 Density per square mile 9.4
Number of Representatives in Congress 1
Capital City .... Bismarck
 Population 44,485
 Rank in State 2nd
Largest City .... Fargo
 Population 61,383
Number of Places over 10,000 Population 9

The Council of State Governments 597

STATE PAGES

Ohio

Nickname	The Buckeye State
Motto	*With God, All Things Are Possible*
Animal	White-tailed Deer
Flower	Scarlet Carnation
Bird	Cardinal
Tree	Buckeye
Song	*Beautiful Ohio*
Stone	Ohio Flint
Insect	Ladybug
Entered the Union	March 1, 1803
Capital	Columbus

ELECTED EXECUTIVE BRANCH OFFICIALS

Governor	Richard F. Celeste
Lieutenant Governor	Paul R. Leonard
Secretary of State	Sherrod Brown
Attorney General	Anthony J. Celebrezze Jr.
Treasurer	Mary Ellen Withrow
Auditor	Thomas E. Ferguson

SUPREME COURT

Thomas J. Moyer, Chief Justice
Andrew Douglas
Craig Wright
Robert E. Holmes
Herbert R. Brown
A. William Sweeney
Alice Robie Resnick

GENERAL ASSEMBLY

President of the Senate	Stanley J. Aronoff
President Pro Tem of the Senate	David L. Hobson
Clerk of the Senate	Martha L. Butler
Chief Executive Officer of the Senate	James R. Tilling
Speaker of the House	Vernal G. Riffe
Speaker Pro Tem of the House	Barney Quilter
Executive Secretary of the House	Aristotle L. Hutras

STATISTICS

Land Area (square miles)	41,004
Rank in Nation	35th
Population	10,797,630
Rank in Nation	6th
Density per square mile	263.3
Number of Representatives in Congress	21
Capital City	Columbus
Population	564,871
Rank in State	2nd
Largest City	Cleveland
Population	573,822
Number of Places over 10,000 Population	150

Oklahoma

Nickname	The Sooner State
Motto	*Labor Omnia Vincit* (Labor Conquers All Things)
Animal	American Buffalo
Flower	Mistletoe
Bird	Scissor-tailed Flycatcher
Tree	Redbud
Song	*Oklahoma*
Rock	Barite Rose (Rose Rock)
Grass	Indian Grass
Entered the Union	November 16, 1907
Capital	Oklahoma City

ELECTED EXECUTIVE BRANCH OFFICIALS

Governor	Henry Bellmon
Lieutenant Governor	Robert S. Kerr III
Attorney General	Robert H. Henry
Treasurer	Ellis Edwards
Auditor and Inspector	Clifton H. Scott
Supt. of Public Instruction	Gerald E. Hoeltzel
Insurance Commr.	Gerald Grimes
Corporation Commrs.	Bob Anthony
	Bob Hopkins
	James B. Townsend

SUPREME COURT

Rudolph Hargrave, Chief Justice
Marian Opala, Vice Chief Justice

Robert E. Lavendar	Robert D. Simms
Ralph B. Hodges	Hardy Summers
Marian P. Opala	Rudolph Hargrave
Yvonne Kauger	John B. Doolin
Alma Wilson	

LEGISLATURE

President of the Senate	Lt. Gov. Robert S. Kerr III
President Pro Tem of the Senate	Robert V. Cullison
Secretary of the Senate	Lance Ward
Speaker of the House	Stephen C. Lewis
Speaker Pro Tem of the House	Jim Glover
Chief Clerk of the House/ Administrator	Larry Warden

STATISTICS

Land Area (square miles)	68,655
Rank in Nation	19th
Population	3,025,290
Rank in Nation	26th
Density per square mile	44.1
Number of Representatives in Congress	6
Capital City	Oklahoma City
Population	403,213
Rank in State	1st
Largest City	Oklahoma City
Number of Places over 10,000 Population	33

STATE PAGES

Oregon

Nickname...................... The Beaver State
Motto.............. *She Flies with Her Own Wings*
Animal........................ American Beaver
Flower........................... Oregon Grape
Bird........................ Western Meadowlark
Tree............................... Douglas Fir
Song....................... *Oregon, My Oregon*
Gemstone............................. Sunstone
Insect...................... Swallowtail Butterfly
Entered the Union............... February 14, 1859
Capital................................. Salem

ELECTED EXECUTIVE BRANCH OFFICIALS

Governor...................... Neil Goldschmidt
Secretary of State................. Barbara Roberts
Attorney General................. Dave Frohnmayer
Treasurer............................ Tony Meeker
Supt. of Public Instruction .... John W. Erickson
Labor Commr................... Mary W. Roberts

SUPREME COURT

Edwin J. Peterson, Chief Justice
Wallace P. Carlson Jr.
Edward N. Fadeley
W. Michael Gillette
Robert E. Jones
Hans A. Linde
George A. VanHoomissen

LEGISLATIVE ASSEMBLY

President of the Senate............. John Kitzhaber
President Pro Tem
 of the Senate .... Frank Roberts
Secretary of the Senate.............. Donna Merrill

Speaker of the House .... Vera Katz
Speaker Pro Tem of the House .... Mike Burton
Chief Clerk of the House.......... Ramona Kenady

STATISTICS

Land Area (square miles).................... 96,184
 Rank in Nation........................... 10th
Population............................ 2,632,105
 Rank in Nation........................... 30th
 Density per square mile.................... 27.4
Number of Representatives in Congress 5
Capital City............................... Salem
 Population............................. 89,233
 Rank in State............................ 3rd
Largest City............................. Portland
 Population............................ 366,383
Number of Places over 10,000 Population 29

Pennsylvania

Nickname..................... The Keystone State
Motto........... *Virtue, Liberty and Independence*
Animal....................... White-tailed Deer
Flower........................ Mountain Laurel
Game Bird......................... Ruffed Grouse
Tree................................. Hemlock
Insect................................. Firefly
Fossil............................ Phacopsrana
Entered the Union............. December 12, 1787
Capital............................. Harrisburg

ELECTED EXECUTIVE BRANCH OFFICIALS

Governor........................ Robert P. Casey
Lieutenant Governor .... Mark S. Singel
Attorney General .... Ernest D. Preate Jr.
Treasurer.................. Catherine Baker Knoll
Auditor........................ Barbara Hafer
Acting Secretary of State ...... Christopher A. Lewis

SUPREME COURT

Robert N. C. Nix Jr., Chief Justice
Rolf Larsen
John P. Flaherty Jr.
James T. McDermott
Stephen A. Zappala
Nicholas P. Papadakos
(1 vacancy)

GENERAL ASSEMBLY

President of the
 Senate.................. Lt. Gov. Mark S. Singel
President Pro Tem
 of the Senate................ Robert C. Jubelirer
Secretary of the Senate .... Mark R. Corrigan

Speaker of the House.......... James J. Manderino
Chief Clerk of the House........... John J. Zubeck

STATISTICS

Land Area (square miles).................. 44,888
 Rank in Nation........................... 32nd
Population........................... 11,863,895
 Rank in Nation............................. 4th
 Density per square mile................... 264.3
Number of Representatives in Congress 23
Capital City.......................... Harrisburg
 Population............................. 53,264
 Rank in State............................ 10th
Largest City.......................... Philadelphia
 Population.......................... 1,688,210
Number of Places over 10,000 Population 83

STATE PAGES

Rhode Island

Nicknames	Little Rhody and Ocean State
Motto	*Hope*
Animal	Quahaug
Flower	Violet
Bird	Rhode Island Red
Tree	Red Maple
Song	*Rhode Island*
Rock	Cumberlandite
Mineral	Bowenite
Entered the Union	May 29, 1790
Capital	Providence

ELECTED EXECUTIVE BRANCH OFFICIALS

Governor	Edward D. DiPrete
Lieutenant Governor	Roger N. Begin
Secretary of State	Kathleen S. Connell
Attorney General	James E. O'Neil
Treasurer	Anthony J. Solomon

SUPREME COURT

Thomas F. Fay, Chief Justice
Thomas F. Kelleher
Joseph R. Weisberger
Florence K. Murray
Donald F. Shea

GENERAL ASSEMBLY

President of the Senate	Lt. Gov. Roger N. Begin
President Pro Tem of the Senate	John F. Correia
Secretary of the Senate	Kathleen S. Connell
Speaker of the House	Joseph DeAngelis
Speaker Pro Tem of the House	Alfred W. Cardente
Clerk of the House	Eugene J. McMahon

STATISTICS

Land Area (square miles)	1,055
Rank in Nation	50th
Population	947,154
Rank in Nation	40th
Density per square mile	987.8
Number of Representatives in Congress	2
Capital City	Providence
Population	156,804
Rank in State	1st
Largest City	Providence
Number of Places over 10,000 Population	27

South Carolina

Nickname	The Palmetto State
Mottos	*Animis Opibusque Parati* (Prepared in Mind and Resources) and *Dum Spiro Spero* (While I Breathe, I Hope)
Animal	White-tailed Deer
Flower	Yellow Jessamine
Bird	Carolina Wren
Tree	Palmetto
Song	*Carolina and South Carolina on My Mind*
Stone	Blue Granite
Fish	Striped Bass
Entered the Union	May 23, 1788
Capital	Columbia

ELECTED EXECUTIVE BRANCH OFFICIALS

Governor	Carroll A. Campbell Jr.
Lieutenant Governor	Nick A. Theodore
Secretary of State	John T. Campbell
Attorney General	T. Travis Medlock
Treasurer	Grady L. Patterson Jr.
Comptroller General	Earle E. Morris Jr.
Supt. of Education	Charlie G. Williams
Commr. of Agriculture	D. Leslie Tindal
Adjutant General	T. Eston Marchant

SUPREME COURT

George Tillman Gregory Jr., Chief Justice
David W. Harwell
A. Lee Chandler
Ernest A. Finney Jr.
Jean Hoeter Toal

GENERAL ASSEMBLY

President of the Senate	Lt. Gov. Nick A. Theodore
President Pro Tem of the Senate	Marshall Burns Williams
Clerk of the Senate	Frank B. Caggiano
Speaker of the House	Robert J. Sheheen
Speaker Pro Tem of the House	John I. Rogers III
Clerk of the House	Sandra K. McKinney

STATISTICS

Land Area (square miles)	30,203
Rank in Nation	40th
Population	3,121,820
Rank in Nation	24th
Density per square mile	103.4
Number of Representatives in Congress	6
Capital City	Columbia
Population	101,208
Rank in State	1st
Largest City	Columbia
Number of Places over 10,000 Population	26

South Dakota

Nicknames .... The Coyote State
                                The Sunshine State
Motto .... *Under God the People Rule*
Animal .... Coyote
Flower .... American Pasque
Bird .... Ringnecked Pheasant
Tree .... Black Hills Spruce
Song .... *Hail, South Dakota*
Mineral .... Rose Quartz
Fish .... Walleye
Insect .... Honeybee
Grass .... Western Wheat Grass
Entered the Union .... November 2, 1889
Capital City .... Pierre

ELECTED EXECUTIVE BRANCH OFFICIALS

Governor .... George S. Mickelson
Lieutenant Governor .... Walter D. Miller
Secretary of State .... Joyce Hazeltine
Attorney General .... Roger Tellinghuisen
Treasurer .... David L. Volk
Auditor .... Vernon L. Larson
Commr. of School
  and Public Lands .... Timothy H. Amdahl
Commrs. of Public Utilities ..... Kenneth Stofferahn
                                  Laska Schoenfelder
                                  James Burg

SUPREME COURT

George Wuest, Chief Justice
Robert E. Morgan
Frank E. Henderson
Richard Sabers
Robert A. Miller

LEGISLATURE

President of the
  Senate .... Lt. Gov. Walter D. Miller
President Pro Tem
  of the Senate .... Harold W. Halverson
Secretary of the Senate .... Fee Jacobsen

Speaker of the House .... Royal J. Wood
Speaker Pro Tem
  of the House .... Jim Hood
Chief Clerk of the House .... Paul Inman

STATISTICS

Land Area (square miles) 75,952
  Rank in Nation 16th
Population 690,768
  Rank in Nation 45th
  Density per square mile 9.1
Number of Representatives in Congress 1
Capital City .... Pierre
  Population 11,973
  Rank in State 9th
Largest City .... Sioux Falls
  Population 81,343
Number of Places over 10,000 Population 10

Tennessee

Nickname .... The Volunteer State
Motto .... *Agriculture and Commerce*
Animal .... Raccoon
Flower .... Iris
Bird .... Mockingbird
Tree .... Tulip Poplar
Wildflower .... Passion Flower
Songs .... *When It's Iris Time in Tennessee;*
  The Tennessee Waltz; My Homeland, Tennessee;
                My Tennessee; and *Rocky Top*
Insects .... Lady beetle and Firefly
Gem .... Freshwater Pearl
Rocks .... Limestone and Agate
Slogan .... Tennessee—America at Its Best
Entered the Union .... June 1, 1796
Capital City .... Nashville

ELECTED EXECUTIVE BRANCH OFFICIALS

Governor .... Ned McWherter
*Lt. Governor .... John Sheldon Wilder
*elected by the Senate

CONSTITUTIONAL OFFICIALS

Interim Secretary of State .... Milton Rice
Attorney General .... Charles W. Burson
Treasurer .... Steve Adams
Comptroller of the Treasury ... William R. Snodgrass

SUPREME COURT

Frank F. Drowota III, Chief Justice
Robert E. Cooper
William H. D. Fones
Charles H. O'Brien
William J. Harbison

GENERAL ASSEMBLY

Speaker
  of the Senate .... Lt. Gov. John S. Wilder
Speaker Pro Tem
  of the Senate .... Robert Rochelle
Chief Clerk
  of the Senate .... Clyde W. McCullough Jr.

Speaker of the House .... Ed Murray
Speaker Pro Tem
  of the House .... Lois M. DeBerry
Chief Clerk of the House .... Bryant Millsaps

STATISTICS

Land Area (square miles) 41,155
  Rank in Nation 34th
Population 4,591,120
  Rank in Nation 17th
  Density per square mile 111.6
Number of Representatives in Congress 9
Capital City .... Nashville
  Population 455,651
  Rank in State 2nd
Largest City .... Memphis
  Population 646,356
Number of Places over 10,000 Population 37

STATE PAGES

Texas

Nickname	The Lone Star State
Motto	*Friendship*
Flower	Bluebonnet, Buffalo Clover, Wolf Flower
Bird	Mockingbird
Tree	Pecan
Song	*Texas, Our Texas*
Stone	Palmwood
Gem	Topaz
Grass	Side Oats Grama
Dish	Chili
Seashell	Lightning Whelk
Fish	Guadalape Bass
Entered the Union	December 29, 1845
Capital	Austin

ELECTED EXECUTIVE BRANCH OFFICIALS

Governor	William P. Clements
Lieutenant Governor	William P. Hobby Jr.
Secretary of State	George Bayoud Jr.
Attorney General	Jim Mattox
Treasurer	Ann W. Richards
Auditor	Lawrence F. Alvin
Comptroller of Public Accounts	Bob Bullock
Commr. of Agriculture	Jim Hightower
Commr. of General Land Office	Garry Mauro

SUPREME COURT
Thomas R. Phillips, Chief Justice

Franklin E. Spears	Paul A. Gonzalez
C. L. Ray	Oscar H. Mauzy
Eugene H. Cook	Lloyd Doggett
Jack Hightower	Nathan L. Hecht

COURT OF CRIMINAL APPEALS
John F. Onion Jr., Presiding Judge

Charles F. Campbell Jr.	Michael J. McCormick
Sam Houston Clinton	Charles Miller
Thomas G. Davis	Marvin O. Teague
Wilbur C. Davis	Bill White

LEGISLATURE

President of the Senate	Lt. Gov. William P. Hobby Jr.
President Pro Tem of the Senate	John Leedom
Secretary of the Senate	Betty King
Speaker of the House	Gibson D. Lewis
Speaker Pro Tem of the House	Hugo Berlanger
Chief Clerk of the House	Betty Murray

STATISTICS

Land Area (square miles)	262,017
Rank in Nation	2nd
Population	14,229,191
Rank in Nation	3rd
Density per square mile	54.3
Number of Representatives in Congress	27
Capital City	Austin
Population	345,496
Rank in State	6th
Largest City	Houston
Population	1,595,138
Number of Places over 10,000 Population	151

Utah

Nickname	The Beehive State
Motto	*Industry*
Flower	Sego Lily
Animal	Elk
Bird	Seagull
Tree	Blue Spruce
Fish	Rainbow Trout
Song	*Utah, We Love Thee*
Gem	Topaz
Insect	Honeybee
Entered the Union	January 4, 1896
Capital	Salt Lake City

ELECTED EXECUTIVE BRANCH OFFICIALS

Governor	Norman Bangerter
Lieutenant Governor	W. Val Oveson
Attorney General	R. Paul VanDam
Treasurer	Edward T. Alter
Auditor	Tom L. Allen

SUPREME COURT
Gordon R. Hall, Chief Justice
Christine M. Durham
Richard C. Howe
I. Daniel Stewart
Michael D. Zimmerman

LEGISLATURE

President of the Senate	Arnold Christensen
Secretary of the Senate	Sophia C. Buckmiller
Speaker of the House	Nolan E. Karras
Chief Clerk of the House	Carole E. Peterson

STATISTICS

Land Area (square miles)	82,073
Rank in Nation	12th
Population	1,461,037
Rank in Nation	37th
Density per square mile	17.8
Number of Representatives in Congress	3
Capital City	Salt Lake City
Population	163,033
Rank in State	1st
Largest City	Salt Lake City
Number of Places over 10,000 Population	22

STATE PAGES

Vermont

Nickname .... The Green Mountain State
Motto .... *Freedom and Unity*
Animal .... Morgan Horse
Flower .... Red Clover
Bird .... Hermit Thrush
Tree .... Sugar Maple
Song .... *Hail, Vermont!*
Insect .... Honeybee
Beverage .... Milk
Entered the Union .... March 4, 1791
Capital .... Montpelier

ELECTED EXECUTIVE BRANCH OFFICIALS

Governor .... Madeleine M. Kunin
Lieutenant Governor .... Howard B. Dean
Secretary of State .... James H. Douglas
Attorney General .... Jeffrey L. Amestoy
Treasurer .... Paul W. Ruse Jr.
Auditor of Accounts .... Alexander V. Acebo

SUPREME COURT

Frederic W. Allen, Chief Justice
Louis P. Peck
Ernest W. Gibson III
John A. Dooley
James L. Morse

GENERAL ASSEMBLY

President of the Senate .... Lt. Gov. Howard B. Dean
President Pro Tem
 of the Senate .... Douglas A. Racine
Secretary of the Senate .... Robert H. Gibson

Speaker of the House .... Ralph G. Wright
Clerk of the House .... Robert L. Picher

STATISTICS

Land Area (square miles) 9,273
 Rank in Nation 43rd
Population 511,456
 Rank in Nation 48th
 Density per square mile 55.2
Number of Representatives in Congress 1
Capital City .... Montpelier
 Population 8,241
 Rank in State 5th
Largest City .... Burlington
 Population 37,712
Number of Places over 10,000 Population 3

Virginia

Nickname .... The Old Dominion
Motto .... *Sic Semper Tyrannis*
 (Thus Always to Tyrants)
Animal .... Foxhound
Flower .... Dogwood
Bird .... Cardinal
Tree .... Dogwood
Song .... *Carry Me Back to Old Virginia*
Shell .... Oyster
Boat .... Chesapeake Bay
Entered the Union .... June 25, 1788
Capital .... Richmond

ELECTED EXECUTIVE BRANCH OFFICIALS

Governor .... L. Douglas Wilder
Lieutenant Governor ...... Donald Sternoff Beyer Jr.
Attorney General .... Mary Sue Terry

SUPREME COURT

Harry Lee Carrico, Chief Justice
Henry H. Whiting
A. Christian Compton
Elizabeth B. Lacy
Charles S. Russell
Roscoe B. Stephenson Jr.
Leroy R. Hassell

GENERAL ASSEMBLY

President
 of the Senate .... Lt. Gov. Donald S. Beyer Jr.
President Pro Tem
 of the Senate .... Stanley C. Walker
Clerk of the Senate .... Jay T. Shropshire

Speaker of the House .... A.L. Philpott
Clerk of the House .... Joseph H. Holleman Jr.

STATISTICS

Land Area (square miles) 39,704
 Rank in Nation 36th
Population 5,346,818
 Rank in Nation 14th
 Density per square mile 134.7
Number of Representatives in Congress 10
Capital City .... Richmond
 Population 219,214
 Rank in State 3rd
Largest City .... Norfolk
 Population 266,979
Number of Places over 10,000 Population 33

STATE PAGES

Washington

Nickname .... The Evergreen State
Motto .... *Alki* (Chinook Indian word meaning By and By)
Flower .... Coast Rhododendron
Bird .... Willow Goldfinch
Tree .... Western Hemlock
Song .... *Washington, My Home*
Dance .... Square Dance
Gem .... Petrified Wood
Entered the Union .... November 11, 1889
Capital .... Olympia

ELECTED EXECUTIVE BRANCH OFFICIALS

Governor .... Booth Gardner
Lieutenant Governor .... Joel Pritchard
Secretary of State .... Ralph Munro
Attorney General .... Kenneth O. Eikenberry
Treasurer .... Dan Grimm
Auditor .... Robert V. Graham
Supt. of Public Instruction .... Judith Billings
Insurance Commr. .... Richard G. Marquardt
Commr. of Public Lands .... Brian J. Boyle

SUPREME COURT
Keith Callow, Chief Justice
Robert F. Utter   Richard Guy
Robert F. Brachtenbach   James A. Anderson
James M. Dolliver   Barbara Durham
Fred H. Dore   Charles Smith

LEGISLATURE

President
  of the Senate .... Lt. Gov. Joel Pritchard
President Pro Tem
  of the Senate .... A. L. Rasmussen
Secretary of the Senate .... Sid Snyder

Speaker of the House .... Joseph E. King
Speaker Pro Tem
  of the House .... John O'Brien
Chief Clerk of the House .... Alan Thompson

STATISTICS

Land Area (square miles) 66,511
  Rank in Nation 20th
Population 4,132,156
  Rank in Nation 20th
  Density per square mile 62.1
Number of Representatives in Congress 8
Capital City .... Olympia
  Population 27,447
  Rank in State 15th
Largest City .... Seattle
  Population 493,846
Number of Places over 10,000 Population 36

West Virginia

Nickname .... The Mountain State
Motto .... *Montani Semper Liberi* (Mountaineers Are Always Free)
Animal .... Black Bear
Flower .... Big Rhododendron
Bird .... Cardinal
Tree .... Sugar Maple
Songs .... *West Virginia, My Home Sweet Home; The West Virginia Hills;* and *This Is My West Virginia*
Fruit .... Apple
Fish .... Brook Trout
Entered the Union .... June 20, 1863
Capital .... Charleston

ELECTED EXECUTIVE BRANCH OFFICIALS

Governor .... W. Gaston Caperton III
Secretary of State .... Ken Hechler
Attorney General .... Roger Tompkins
Treasurer .... Thomas E. Loehr
Auditor .... Glen B. Gainer Jr.
Commr. of Agriculture .... Cleve Benedict

SUPREME COURT OF APPEALS
Richard Neely, Chief Justice (01-90/12-90)
Thomas E. McHugh
Thomas B. Miller
W. T. Brotherton Jr.
Margaret Workman

LEGISLATURE

President of the Senate .... Keith Burdette
Clerk of the Senate .... Darrell E. Holmes

Speaker of the House .... Robert Chambers
Clerk of the House .... Donald L. Kopp

STATISTICS

Land Area (square miles) 24,119
  Rank in Nation 41st
Population 1,949,644
  Rank in Nation 34th
  Density per square mile 80.8
Number of Representatives in Congress 4
Capital City .... Charleston
  Population 63,968
  Rank in State 1st
Largest City .... Charleston
Number of Places over 10,000 Population 15

Wisconsin

Nickname	The Badger State
Motto	*Forward*
Animal	Badger
Flower	Wood Violet
Bird	Robin
Tree	Sugar Maple
Song	*On, Wisconsin!*
Fish	Muskellunge
Mineral	Galena
Entered the Union	May 29, 1848
Capital	Madison

ELECTED EXECUTIVE BRANCH OFFICIALS

Governor	Tommy G. Thompson
Lieutenant Governor	Scott McCallum
Secretary of State	Douglas J. La Follette
Attorney General	Donald J. Hanaway
Treasurer	Charles P. Smith
Supt. of Public Instruction	Herbert J. Grover

SUPREME COURT

Nathan S. Heffernan, Chief Justice
Shirley S. Abrahamson
William A. Bablitch
William G. Callow
Louis J. Ceci
Roland B. Day
Donald W. Steinmetz

LEGISLATURE

President of the Senate	Fred A. Risser
Chief Clerk of the Senate	Donald J. Schneider
Speaker of the Assembly	Thomas A. Loftus
Pro Temp of the Assembly	David E. Clarenbach
Chief Clerk of the Assembly	Thomas Melvin

STATISTICS

Land Area (square miles)	54,426
Rank in Nation	25th
Population	4,705,767
Rank in Nation	16th
Density per square mile	86.5
Number of Representatives in Congress	9
Capital City	Madison
Population	170,616
Rank in State	2nd
Largest City	Milwaukee
Population	636,212
Number of Places over 10,000 Population	55

Wyoming

Nicknames	The Equality State and The Cowboy State
Motto	*Equal Rights*
Animal	Bison
Flower	Indian Paintbrush
Bird	Western Meadowlark
Tree	Cottonwood
Song	*Wyoming*
Gem	Jade
Entered the Union	July 10, 1890
Capital	Cheyenne

ELECTED EXECUTIVE BRANCH OFFICIALS

Governor	Mike Sullivan
Secretary of State	Kathy Karpan
Treasurer	Stan Smith
Auditor	Jack Sidi
Supt. of Public Instruction	Lynn Simons

SUPREME COURT

G. Joseph Cardine, Chief Justice
Michael Golden
Richard J. Macy
Richard V. Thomas
Walter C. Urbigkit Jr.

LEGISLATURE

President of the Senate	Russell W. Zimmer
Vice President of the Senate	Jerry B. Dixon
Chief Clerk of the Senate	Liv Hanes
Speaker of the House	Bill McIlvain
Speaker Pro Tem of the House	William A. Cross
Chief Clerk of the House	Paul Galeotos

STATISTICS

Land Area (square miles)	96,989
Rank in Nation	9th
Population	469,557
Rank in Nation	49th
Density per square mile	4.8
Number of Representatives in Congress	1
Capital City	Cheyenne
Population	47,283
Rank in State	2nd
Largest City	Casper
Population	51,016
Number of Places over 10,000 Population	8

STATE PAGES

District of Columbia

Motto .... *Justitia Omnibus* (Justice for All)
Flower .... American Beauty Rose
Bird .... Wood Thrush
Tree .... Scarlet Oak
Became U.S. Capital .... December 1, 1800

ELECTED EXECUTIVE BRANCH OFFICIALS
Mayor .... Marion S. Barry Jr.

U.S. COURT OF APPEALS FOR THE DISTRICT OF COLUMBIA
Chief Judge .... Patricia M. Wald

DISTRICT OF COLUMBIA COURT OF APPEALS
Chief Judge .... Judith W. Rogers

U.S. DISTRICT COURT FOR THE DISTRICT OF COLUMBIA
Chief Judge .... Aubrey E. Robinson Jr.
U.S. Attorney .... Jay B. Stephens

THE SUPERIOR COURT OF THE DISTRICT OF COLUMBIA
Chief Judge .... Fred B. Ugast

COUNCIL OF THE DISTRICT OF COLUMBIA
Chairman .... David A. Clarke
Chairman Pro Tem .... Nadine P. Winter

STATISTICS
Land Area (square miles) 67
Population 626,000
   Density per square mile 9343.3
   Delegate to Congress* 1

*Committee voting privileges only.

American Samoa

Motto .... *Samoa-Muamua le Atua*
   (Samoa, God Is First)
Flower .... Paogo (Ula-fala)
Plant .... Ava
Song .... *Amerika Samoa*
Became a Territory of the United States 1900
Capital .... Pago Pago

ELECTED EXECUTIVE BRANCH OFFICIALS
Governor .... Peter T. Coleman
Lieutenant Governor .... Galeai P. Poumele

HIGH COURT
F. Michael Kruse, Chief Justice
Grover J. Rees, III, Associate Chief Justice
Malaetasi Togafa, District Court Judge
Faisiota Tauanu'u, Chief Associate Judge
Olo Letuli, Associate Judge
Kalasa Afuola
Vaivao M. Fruean
Matautia Tuiafono

LEGISLATURE
President of the Senate .... Letuli Toloa
Vice-President
   of the Senate .... A.P. Lutali
Secretary of the Senate .... Fialupe Fiaui

Speaker of the House .... Tuana'itau F. Tuia
Vice Speaker
   of the House .... Moananu A. Va
Clerk of the House .... Wally Utu

STATISTICS
Land Area (square miles) 77
Population 34,500
   Density per square mile 448.0
Capital City .... Pago Pago
   Population 3,075
Largest City .... Pago Pago
Number of Villages 76

Guam

Nickname .... Hub of the Pacific
Flower .... *Puti Tai Nobio* (Bougainvillea)
Bird .... *Toto* (Fruit Dove)
Tree .... *Ifit* (Intsiabijuga)
Song .... *Stand Ye Guamanians*
Stone .... Latte
Animal .... Iguana
Ceded to the United States
   by Spain .... December 10, 1898
Became a Territory .... August 1, 1950
Request to become a
   Commonwealth Plebiscite .... November 1987
Capital .... Agana

ELECTED EXECUTIVE BRANCH OFFICIALS
Governor .... Joseph Ada
Lieutenant Governor .... Frank F. Blas

SUPERIOR COURT
Paul J. Abbate, Presiding Judge
Benjamin J.F. Cruz
Ramon V. Diaz
Joaquin V.E. Manibusan
Peter C. Siguenza Jr.
Janet Healy Weeks

LEGISLATURE
Speaker .... Joe T. San Agustin
Vice Speaker .... Ted S. Nelson
Legislative Secretary .... Pilar C. Lujan

STATISTICS
Land Area (square miles) 209
Population 102,977
   Density per square mile 572.0
Delegate to Congress* 1
Capital City .... Agana
   Population 896
Largest City .... Tamuning
   Population 13,580

*Committee voting privileges only.

Northern Mariana Islands

Tree .... Flame Tree
Flower .... Plumeria
Administered by the United States as a trusteeship for
the United Nations .... July 18, 1947
Voters approved a
   proposed constitution .... June 1975
U.S. President signed covenant agreeing to
Commonwealth status for the
islands .... March 24, 1976
Became a self-governing Commonwealth
.... January 9, 1978
Capital .... Saipan

ELECTED EXECUTIVE BRANCH OFFICIALS
Governor .... Lorenzo I. DeLeon Guerrero
Lieutenant Governor .... Benjamin T. Manglona

COMMONWEALTH TRIAL COURT
Robert A. Hefner, Chief Judge
Jose S. Dela Cruz
Ramon G. Villagomez

LEGISLATURE
President
   of the Senate .... Joseph S. Inos
Vice President
   of the Senate .... Henry DLG. San Nicolas
Speaker
   of the House .... Pedro R. Guerrero
Vice Speaker
   of the House .... Luis C. Benavente

STATISTICS
Land Area (square miles) 183.5
Population 20,000
   Density per square mile 91.1
Capital City .... Saipan
   Population 16,532
Largest City .... Saipan

STATE PAGES

Puerto Rico

Nickname . . . . Island of Enchantment
Motto . . . . *Joannes Est Nomen Ejus*
(John Is Thy Name)
Flower . . . . Maga
Bird . . . . The Pitirre
Tree . . . . The Flamboyan
Song . . . . *La Borinquena*
Animal . . . . Coqui
Became a territory of the United States
. . . . December 10, 1898
Became a self-governing Commonwealth
. . . . July 25, 1952
Capital . . . . San Juan

ELECTED EXECUTIVE BRANCH OFFICIALS

Governor . . . . Rafael Hernandez-Colon
Secretary of State . . . . Antonio J. Colorado
Secretary of Justice . . . . Hector Rivera-Cruz
Attorney General . . . . Hector Rivera-Cruz
Treasurer . . . . Ramon Garcia-Santiago
Auditor . . . . Ilena Colon-Carlo
Education . . . . Jose Lema-Moya
Health . . . . Jose Ediberto Soler-Zapata

SUPREME COURT

Victor M. Pons Nunez, Chief Justice
Rafael Alonso-Alonso
Federico Hernandez-Denton
Antonio Negron-Garcia
Peter Ortiz-Gustafson
Francisco Rebollo-Lopez
Miriam Naveira de Rodon

LEGISLATIVE ASSEMBLY

President
of the Senate . . . . Miguel Hernandez-Agosto
Vice President
of the Senate . . . . Sergio Pena Clos
Secretary
of the Senate . . . . Celeste Benitez-Rivera

Speaker of the House . . . . . . Jose R. Jarabo-Alvarez
Vice President
of the House . . . . Samuel Ramirez
Chief Clerk
of the House . . . . Fredinand Marcade-Ramos

STATISTICS

Land Area (square miles) 3,421
Population 3,187,570
   Density per square mile 931.8
Delegate to Congress* 1
Capital City . . . . San Juan
   Population 424,600
Largest City . . . . San Juan
Number of Places over 10,000 Population 31

---

*Committee voting privileges only.

U.S. Virgin Islands

Nicknames . . . . St. John, St. Croix, and
St. Thomas
Flower . . . . Yellow Elder or Ginger Thomas
Bird . . . . Yellow Breast or Banana Quit
Song . . . . *Virgin Islands March*
Purchased from Denmark . . . . March 31, 1917
Capital . . . . Charlotte Amalie, St. Thomas

ELECTED EXECUTIVE BRANCH OFFICIALS

Governor . . . . Alexander Farreley
Lieutenant Governor . . . . Derek M. Hodge

FEDERAL DISTRICT COURT

Almeric L. Christian, Chief Judge
David V. O'Brien

LEGISLATURE

President . . . . Ruby M. Rouss
Vice President . . . . Bingley G. Richardson
Legislative
Secretary . . . . Alicia Hansen

STATISTICS

Land Area (square miles) 132
   St. Croix (square miles) 80
   St. John (square miles) 20
   St. Thomas (square miles) 32
Population 95,591
   St. Croix 49,725
   St. John 2,472
   St. Thomas 44,372
   Density per square mile 724.2
Delegate to Congress* 1
Capital City . . . . Charlotte Amalie, St. Thomas
   Population 11,842

---

*Committee voting privileges only.

SUBJECT INDEX

(Page numbers in **boldface** indicate tables; a complete list of tables in on page vi)

A

Acid rain
   Reduction proposals, 524
Adjutants general
   Salaries, **90**
   Selection, methods of, **85**
Administration and management
   Developments in, 340-344
   Facilities management, 343
   Fleet management, 343
   Organization, administrative
      Cabinet systems, **71**
      Executive branch, 75-76
   Personnel, 341-342
      Administrative officials
         Salaries, **90**
         Selection, methods of, **85**
         Office of administrator: primary responsibilities, **345**
         Structure and functions, **347**
   Printing, 343
   Purchasing, 342
   State librarians and Archivists, 340
   Telecommunications, 340-341
Administrative officials
   Salaries, **90**
   Selection, methods of, **85**
   Terms, length and number of, **83**
   See also titles of individuals officials
Age Discrimination in Employment Act, 200
Age, minimum
   For holding office
      Attorneys general, **102**
      Governors, **64**
      Legislators, **125**
      Lieutenant governors, **96**
      Secretaries of state, **99**
   For specified activities
      Buying liquor, **417**
      Employment, selected, **459**
      Leaving school, **417**
      Making a will, **417**
      Marriage, **417**
      Obtaining age of majority, **417**
      Serving on a jury, **417**
Agriculture,
   Administrative officials
      Salaries, **90**

      Selection, methods of, **85**
   Elected officials, terms, length and number of, **83**
   Federal-state cooperation, 527
Aid to local governments 549-552
   Distribution of state aid, 1976-1988, **549**
   Per capita expenditure, 1988, **551**
   See also Intergovernmental affairs
AIDS
   Guidelines for courts regarding, 199-200
   Testing of applicants or employees, 448
Air pollution *See* Environmental and natural resource problems
Alcoholic beverages *See* Taxation and tax revenue
Alt, Ronald, 310-312
Americans with Disabilities Act, 525
Amusements, *See* Tax revenue
Anti-Drug Abuse Act, 488, 491, **525**
Asbestos abatement, 343, 450
Asbestos Hazard Emergency Response Act of 1986, 450
Assistance and subsidies *See* Finances, state
Attorneys general
   Duties
      Advisory, **103**
      Antitrust, **104**
      Consumer protection, **104**
      Counsel for state, **105**
      Prosecutorial, **103**
      To administrative agencies, **105**
   Minimum age for office, **102**
   Qualifications for office, **102**
   Relationships with governors, 57
   Salaries, **90**
   Selection, methods of, **85, 102**
   Separately elected offical, 57
   Subpoena powers, **104**
   Terms, length and number of, **83**
   To be elected: 1990-91, **232**
Auditors
   Terms, length and number of, **83**
   To be elected: 1990-91, **232**

B

Baker v. Carr, 108
Banking
   Administrative officials
      Salaries, **90**
      Selection, methods of, **85**
   See also Finances, state

SUBJECT INDEX

Beckman, Norman, 522-531
Berry, Frances Stokes, 465-470
Beyle, Thad L., 50-61, 75-82
Brinegar, Pamela L., 465-470
Brown, R. Steven, 501-507
Budgets
  Administrative officials
    Salaries, **90**
    Selection, methods of, **85**
  Balanced budgets and deficit limitations: constitutional and statutory provisions, **309**
  Budgetary calendars, by state, **286**
  Gubernatorial powers, **67, 290**
  Legislative
    Appropriations process: budget documents and bills, **171**
    Authority, **290**
  Preparation, review and controls, officials or agencies responsible for, **287** See also Finance, state
Burrell v. Mississippi Tax Commission, 23

C

Cabinet systems, **71**
Campaign finance laws See Elections
Candidates for state offices
  Methods of nominating, **234**
Capital outlay See Finances, state, expenditure
Capital punishment, **498**
Capitals, **576**
Chavez v. Virgil-Giron, 29
Chi, Keon S., 382-404
Chief justice See Judiciary, judges
Child
  Labor standards, 449, **459**
  Nutrition programs, federal aid to: fiscal 1986, **422**
  Restraint laws, **436**
Cigarettes See Taxation, tobacco products; Tax revenue, tobacco products
Civil Rights
  Administrative officials
    Salaries, **91**
    Selection, methods of, **86**
  Federal initatives, 524, 525
Clean Air Act, 343, 524-525
Commerce
  Administrative officials
    Salaries, **91**
    Selection, methods of, **86**
Community affairs
  Administrative officials
    Salaries, **91**
    Selection, methods of, **86**
Compacts and agreements, interstate, 565-567
  Low-level radioactive wastes, **510**
  See also Intergovernmental affairs
Compensation
  Classification and compensation plans, **349**
  Governors, **65**
  Holidays, paid, state employees, **352**

Judges of appellate and general trial courts, **221**
Legislative
  Compensation commissions, **132**
  House leaders, additional for, **141**
  Interim payments and other direct payments, **135**
  Method of setting, **131**
  Regular and special sessions, **133**
  Senate leaders, additional for, **139**
  Tied or related to state employees' salaries, **131**
Wages and hours legislation, 446-447
See also, Employment, state; Salaries
Comptrollers
  Salaries, **91**
  Selection, methods of, **86**
  Terms, length and number of, **83**
Computers
  Computer services, administrative officials
    Salaries, **91**
    Selection, methods of, **86**
  Information resources, 341
  Legislative activities performed with, **187**
    Fiscal, budget, economic applications, **187**
    Legislative management, **187**
    Statutory, bill systems, legal applications, **187**
  Telecommunications in administration and management, 340-341
Constitutional reform, 528-529
Constitutions and constitutional revision, 20-39
  Amendment procedures, constitutional provisions for
    By initiative, **44**
    By the legislature, **42**
    Constitutional conventions, **45**
  Amendments
    Number adopted, **40**
    Number submitted, **40**
  Changes by method of initiation, **21**
    Constitutional commissions, **21,** 23-25
      Operative: 1987-90, **47**
    Constitutional conventions, **21,** 22-23
      Burrell v. Mississippi State Tax Commission, 23
      In session: 1988-90, **47**
    Constitutional initiative, 21, **21**
    Legislative proposal, 21-23, **21**
  Dates of adoption, **40**
  Effective date of present constitution, **40**
  Estimated length, **40**
  Extraordinary votes by legislatures, **175, 177**
  General information, **40**
  Number by state, **40**
  Sources and resources, 35-39
  Substantive changes, **22,** 25-35
    Amendments, 33-35
      County Organization Reform Amendment, 29-30
    Bills of rights, 25-27
    Constitutional revisions, 33-35
    Elections, 25-27
    Government, three branches of, 27-29
      Chavez v. Virgil-Giron, 29

SUBJECT INDEX

Local government finance, 29-33
State functions, 33-35
Suffrage, 25-27
Construction *See* Finances, state
Consumer affairs
 Administrative officials
  Salaries, **91**
  Selection, methods of, 86
Continuing education, *See* Education
Contracting, *See* Privatization
Corrections
 Administrative officials
  Salaries, **91**
  Selection, methods of, **86**
 Balanced approach, 484
 Boot camps, 486
 Correctional policies, 484
 Death penalty, **498**
 Drug abuse treatment, 487-489
  Correctional facilities, 488
  Community corrections, 489
  Comprehensive corrections treatment strategy, **492**
  Substance Abuse Recovery Group Experience, 488
 Employment and payrolls
  State
   October 1987, **362, 364**
   October 1988, **363, 365**
  State and local
   October 1987, **356**
   October 1988, **357**
 In the 1990's, 483-492
  Funding
   Anti-Drug Abuse Act, **491**
   Education, **491**
   Law enforcement, **491**
   Treatment, **491**
   Grant allocations, formula, **490**
   Percent local jurisdiction, **490**
 Intermediate sanctions, 484-485
  Electronic monitoring, 485-486
  House arrest, 485
  Intensive supervision probation/parole (ISP), 485
 Offenders under correctional supervision: 1986, 484
 Parole
  Adults on, **497**
 Populations, correctional, 483-484, **484**
 Prisons
  Adults admitted: 1980 and 1987, **494**
  Capacities: 1988, **495**
  Population trends, **493**
 Probation, adults on, **496**
 Shock treatment, 486
 Substance abuse, 487
  Offenders under correctional supervision (1988), **484**
  Percent positive for any drug, **487**
Council of State Governments, 568-574
 Affiliated and cooperating organizations, 571-572

 Governing structure, 568-569
 Offices and directors, 570
 Officers and executive committee, 573-574
 Publications, 569
 Regional conferences 1989-90, 572
 Regional offices, 569, 570
Courts, *See* Judiciary
Criminal justice, *See* Corrections
Current operation, *See* Finances, state

D

Davis v. Michigan Department of the Treasury, 310
Death penalty, 498
Debt redemption, *See* Finances, state
Delado v. Smith, 26
Direct expenditures, *See* Finances, state
Direct legislation
 Initiative provisions for state legislation
  Circulating petition, **268**
  Preparing to place on ballot, **270**
  Requesting permission to circulate petition, **267**
  Signatures required, **267**
  Voting, **272**
 Referendum provisions for state legislation
  Circulating petition, **274**
  Preparing to place on ballot, **275**
  Requesting permission to circulate petition, **273**
  Signatures required, **273**
  Voting, **276**
Drug control, 524-525
Drugs and Drug testing
 Employee, 279, 448
 Middle Atlantic Governors' Compact on Alcohol and Drug Abuse, 566
 See also Corrections; Employment, state; Judiciary
Drug Treatment, *See* Corrections

E

Economic development
 Administrative officials
  Salaries, **91**
  Selection, methods of, **86**
Education
 Administrative officials
  Salaries, **91**
  Selection, methods of, **86**
 Board members to be elected: 1990-91, **232**
 Continuing, mandatory for professions, **478**
 Elected state officials, provisions for terms of, **83**
 Employees, average earnings
  October 1987, **360**
  October 1988, **361**
 Employment and payrolls, state and local
  October 1987, **356**
  October 1988, **357**
 Employment, by state
  October 1987, **362**
  October 1988, **363**
 Employment, summary of: 1952-1986, **355**
 Federal initiatives, 523, 525, 527

SUBJECT INDEX

Payrolls, state
  October 1987, **364**
  October 1988, **365**
Revenue, intergovernmental
  Per capita by state: 1987, **555**; 1988, **556**
  Summary of state payments: 1942 to 1988, **553**
  Totals by state: 1987, **557**; 1988, **558**
Superintendents of public instruction
  To be elected: 1990-91, **232**

Education, elementary and secondary
Average daily attendance
  1987-88 and 1988-89, **424, 425**
  1987-88 and 1988-89, **424**
Capital outlay: 1986-87, **420**
Classroom teachers: 1988-89, **425**
Course requirements for high school graduation, **426**
Employment and payrolls, state and local
  October 1987, **356**
  October 1988, **357**
Employment, by state
  October 1987, **362**
  October 1988, **363**
Enrollment: 1988-89, **425**
Finance
  Expenditure: 1986-87, **420**
  Revenue, by source: 1986-87, **418**
Membership by state: 1987-88, 1988-89, **424**
Payrolls
  October 1987, **364**
  October 1988, **365**
Pupils per teacher: 1988-89, **425**
Salaries and wages: 1986-87, **420**
Salary, average annual, of instructional staff: 1939-40 to 1988-89, **423**
School lunches, federal funds for: fiscal 1988, **422**

Education, higher
Administrative officials
  Salaries, **92**
  Selection, methods of, **87**
Capital outlay: 1986-87, **420**
Employment and payrolls, state and local
  October 1987, **356**
  October 1988, **357**
Expenditures: 1985-86, **420**
Institutions of
  Estimated undergraduate tuition fees: 1986-87, **430**
  Number by type and control: 1986-87, **429**
Midwestern Higher Education Compact, **565**
Payrolls, state
  October 1987, **364**
  October 1988, **365**
Salaries and wages: 1985-86, **420**

Elected state officials
Terms, provisions for length and number of, **83**

Elections
Administrative officials
  Salaries, **91**
  Selection, methods of, **86**
Campaign finance laws
  Filing requirements, **237**
  Limitations on contributions
    By individuals, **247**
    By organizations, **242**
  Limitations on expenditures, **253**
  Regulation, 229-230
  Funding of: tax provisions and public financing, **259**
Gubernatorial, 50-51
  Campaign costs: 1977-89, **53**
  Campaign costs: 1986-89, **52**
  Voting statistics for, **264**
Legislation, 226-231
  Absentee ballot procedures, 228-29
  Election technology, 227-228
  Electronic voter registration, 230
  Finance regulations, 229-230
  Handicapped access to the polls, 227
  Legislative districting, 108-109
  Voter registration, 226-227, 230
Legislative, use of surplus campaign funds, **149**
Nominating candidates for state offices, methods of, **234**
Polling hours, **262**
Primaries, election information, **236**
State officials to be elected: 1990-91, **232**
Voting
  Gubernatorial elections, statistics for, **264**
  Voter registration information, **261**
  Voter turnout
    For presidential elections: 1980, 1984, 1988, **266**
    In non-presidential election years: 1978, 1982, 1986, **265**
  See also Direct legislation, recall of state officials

Emergency management
Administrative officials
  Salaries, **92**
  Selection, methods of, **87**

Employee retirement systems, finances of, 366-370
Benefit payments and other outlays, 367
Comparative statistics for: 1986-87, **377**
Current issues, 369
Economic development, 369
Legislative benefits, **143**
Holdings at end of fiscal year, by state: 1986-87, **375**
Investment losses, 369
Investments and assets, 369
Involvement in corporate management, 369
Mandatory medicaid, 369
Membership and benefit operations of: last month of fiscal 1986-87, **373**
Membership, number and monthly benefit payments of 1984-85 through 1986-87, **371**
Receipts and payments, 367-369
  By state: 1986-87, **375**
  National summary: 1976-1987, **372**
State funding, 369-370
System coverage and size, 366-367

SUBJECT INDEX

Employment security administration, *See* Finances, state
Employment, state
  Average monthly earnings, summary: 1952-1986, **355**
  Classification and compensation plans, **349**
  Drug Free Workplace Act, 341
  For selected functions
    October 1987, **362**
    October 1988, **363**
  Holidays, paid, **352**
  Leave policies, selected, **350**
  Payrolls
    For selected functions
      October 1987, **364**
      October 1988, **365**
    Monthly summary of: 1952-1988, **355**
  Personnel administration
    Office of administrator: primary responsibilities, **345**
    Structure and function, **347**
  Services
    Administrative officials
      Salaries, **92**
      Selection, methods of, **87**
  Summary of: 1952-1988, **355**
  Wages and hours legislation, 446-447
  See also Compensation; Labor; Salaries
Employment, state and local
  Average earnings
    October 1987, **356, 360**
    October 1988, **357, 361**
  By function
    October 1987, **356**
    October 1988, **357**
  By individual states
    October 1987, **358**
    October 1988, **359**
  Payrolls
    October 1987, **356, 360**
    October 1988, **357, 361**
Energy resources
  Administrative officials
    Salaries, **92**
    Selection, methods of, **87**
  Low-level radioactive waste compacts, **510**
Environmental and natural resource problems
  Air quality
    Acid rain, 524
    Asbestos in buildings, state actions on, 343, 450
    Clean Air Act, 343, 524, 527
  Central U.S. Earthquake Consortium, 566
  Environmental Compact of the States, proposed, 566
  Environmental referenda, 504-506
  Hazardous waste, 501-502
    Biotechnology, 502
    Low-level radioactive waste compacts, **510**
    Toxic chemicals, 501-502
  Initiatives, addressing, 501-507
  Legislation, federal

    Clean Air Act, 343
  Pacific Marine Resources Commission, 567
  Publicprivate involvement, 502-504
  Solid waste
    Water and wastewater
      Interstate agencies, **508**
  See also Intergovernmental relations, state-local relations
Environmental protection agencies
  Administrative officials
    Salaries, **92**
    Selection, methods of, **87**
Equal Employment Opportunity Act, 200
Equipment, *See* Finances, state
Executive branch
  Organization and issues: 1988-89, 75-82
    Ethics, 79-80
    Management techniques, 78
    Planning, 79
    Productivity, 78-79
    Reorganization, 75-78
      Corrections, 77-78
      Economic development, 76-77
      Environment, 78
      Higher Education, 78
      State agency heads, 79
    Sunset, 78
  See also Governors
Expenditure, *See* Finances, state

F

Fair Labor Standards Act (FLSA), 446
Farming, *See* Agriculture and rural development
Federal aid,
  Decline in, 522, 527
  To child nutrition programs: Fiscal 1988, **422**
  To education
    1987, **561**
    1988, **563**
  To health agencies: fiscal 1988, **481**
  To health and hospitals
    1987, **561**
    1988, **563**
  To highways
    1987, **561**
    1988, **563**
    Fiscal 1989, **434**
  To mass transit: fiscal 1989, **434**
  To public school systems: 1986-87, **418**
  To public welfare, **522**
    1987, **561**
    1988, **563**
  To states, 522, 526-530
    1987, **561**
    1988, **563**
    Fiscal 1981-1986, **532**
Federal-state relations, *See* Intergovernmental relationships

SUBJECT INDEX

Finances, state, 282-285
  Administrative officials
    Employment
      October 1987, **362**
      October 1988, **363**
    Payrolls
      October 1987, **364**
      October 1988, **365**
    Salaries, **92**
    Selection, methods of, **87**
  Agencies, administering
    Major state taxes, **313**
  Borrowing, extraordinary legislative vote, **177**
  Campaign finance regulation, 229-230
  Cash and security holdings, 285
    At end of fiscal 1987, **292**
    At end of fiscal 1988, **293**
    National totals, selected years: 1974-88, **294**
  Current issues, 285
  Debt, 284-285
    National totals, selected years: 1974-88, **294**
    Outstanding: end of fiscal 1985, **292, 308**
    Outstanding: end of fiscal 1986, **293, 309**
  Expenditure, 283-284, **284**
    Assistance and subsidies
      By state: 1987, **300**; 1988, **302**
      National totals: 1974-88, **294**
    By character and object
      By state: 1987, **300**; 1988 **302**
      National totals: 1974-88, **294**
    Capital outlay
      By state: 1987, **300**; 1988 **302**
      National totals: 1974-88, **294**
    Construction
      By state: 1987, **300**; 1988, **302**
      National totals: 1974-88, **294**
    Corrections
      By state: 1987, **304**; 1988 **306**
      National totals: 1974-88, **294**
    Current operation
      By state: 1987, **300**; 1988, **302**
      National totals: 1974-88, **294**
    Debt redemption
      National totals: 1974-88, **294**
    Direct expenditure
      By state: 1987, **300**; 1988 **302**
      National totals: 1974-88, **294**
    Education
      By state: 1987, **304**; 1988, **306**
      Intergovernmental, by state: 1987, **557**; 1988, **558**
      National totals: 1974-88, **294**
      Per capita, by state: 1987, **555**; 1988, **556**
      To local government for: 1942 to 1988, **553**
    Employment security administration
      By state: 1987, **304**; 1988, **306**
      National totals: 1974-88, **294**
    Equipment
      By state: 1987, **300**; 1988, **302**
      National totals: 1974-88, **294**

    Financial administration
      By state: 1987, **304**; 1988, **306**
      National totals: 1974-88, **294**
    General
      By function: 1987, **304**; 1988, **306**
      By state: 1985, **292**; 1986, **293**
      National totals: 1974-88, **294**
    Health and hospitals
      By state: 1987, **304**; 1988, **306**
      National totals: 1974-88, **294**
    Highways
      By state: 1987, **304**; 1988, **306**
      Intergovernmental, by state: 1987, **557**; 1988, **558**
      National totals: 1974-88, **294**
      Per capita, by state: 1987, **555**; 1988, **556**
      To local governments for: 1942 to 1988, **553**
    Insurance benefits and repayments
      By state: 1987, **300**; 1988, **302**
      National totals: 1974-88, **294**
    Insurance trust
      By state: 1985, **292**; 1986, **293**
      National totals: 1974-88, **294**
    Interest on debt
      By state: 1987, **300**; 1988, **302**
      National totals: 1974-88, **294**
    Intergovernmental, 285
      By function: 1987, **557**; 1988, **558**
      By state: 1982-88, **554**; 1987, **300**; 1988, **302**
      By type of receiving government: 1987, **559**; 1988, **560**
      National totals: 1974-88, **294**
      Per capita by function: 1987, **555**; 1988, **556**
      Per capita distribution: 1988, **551**
      Percent distribution: 1976-88, 549
      Summary of payments: 1942-88, **553**
    Investments, 285
    Land and existing structures
      By state: 1987, **300**; 1988, **302**
      National totals: 1974-88, **294**
    Local government support
      By state: 1987, **557**; 1988, **558**
      Per capita by state: 1987, **555**; 1988, **556**
      Summary of payments: 1942-88, **553**
    Liquor stores
      By state: 1987, **292**; 1988, **293**
      National totals: 1974-88, **294**
    Natural resources
      By state: 1987, **304**; 1988, **306**
      National totals: 1974-88, **294**
    Police
      By state: 1987, **304**; 1988, **306**
      National totals: 1974-88, **294**
    Public welfare
      By state: 1987, **557**; 1988, **558**
      National totals: 1974-88, **294**
      Per capita by state: 1987, **555**; 1988, **556**
      To local government for: 1942-88, **553**
    Salaries and wages
      By state: 1987, **300**; 1988, **302**

SUBJECT INDEX

Securities
  National totals: 1974-88, **294**
  Totals
    By state: 1985, **292**; 1986, **293**
    National totals: 1974-88, **294**
  Utilities
    By state: 1987, **292**; 1988, **293**
    National totals: 1974-88, **294**
Financial Institutions Reform, Recovery and Enforcement Act of 1989, 465
Federal-state tax relations, 523, 524
  Fiscal year, population and personal income, **337**
  Louisiana Tax Reform Amendment, 30
  National totals for selected years: 1974-88, **294**
  Revenue, 282-283, **284**
    Administrative officials
      Salaries, **94**
      Selection, methods of, **89**
    Borrowing
      By state: 1987, **292**; 1988, **293**
      National totals: 1974-88, **294**
    General
      By source and state: 1987, **296**; 1988, **298**
      By state: 1985, **292**; 1986, **293**
      National totals: 1974-88, **294**
    Insurance trust
      By state: 1987, **292**; 1988, **293**
      National totals: 1974-88, **294**
    Intergovernmental
      By state: 1987, **296, 561**; 1988, **298, 563**
      National totals: 1974-88, **294**
      Total federal aid to states: fiscal 1983-88, **532**
    Liquor Stores
      By state: 1987, **292**; 1988, **293**
      National totals: 1974-88, **294**
    Sources of state revenue, **283**
    Summary financial aggregates
      By state: 1987, **292**; 1988, **293**
    Taxes
      By state: 1987, **296**; 1988, **298**
      National totals: 1974-88, **294**
    Totals
      By state: 1987, **292**; 1988, **293**
      National totals: 1974-88, **294**
    Utilities
      By state: 1987, **292**; 1988, **293**
      National totals: 1974-88, **294**
    See also Budgets; Federal aid; Taxation; Tax revenue
Finances, state and local, 538-541
  Administration
    Employment and payrolls
      October 1987, **356**
      October 1988, **357**
    See also Intergovernmental affairs
Financial administration, *See* Finances, state
Fire protection
  Employment and payrolls, state and local
    October 1987, **356**
    October 1988, **357**

Fiscal notes
  Content and distribution, **173**
Fiscal year
  Date of close of: 1988, **337**
  Population and personal income, **337**
Fish and wildlife
  Administrative officials
    Salaries, **92**
    Selection, methods of, **87**

G

General services
  Administrative officials
    Salaries, **92**
    Selection, methods of, **87**
  See also Finances, state
Gona, Deborah, 1-17
Governors, 50-61, **62**
  Access to state transportation, **65**
  Birthdates, **62**
  Birth places, **62**
  Budgetary powers, **67**
  Campaign costs, 51-53, **52**
  Compensation, **65**
  Consecutive terms allowed, numbers of, **62**
  Date of first service, **62**
  Date present term ends, **62**
  Elections, 50-53
    Campaign costs: 1977-89, **53**
    Voting statistics for, **264**
  Executive orders: authorization, provisions, procedures, **69**
    Impeachments
      Provisions for, **73**
  Lieutenant governors
    Joint election with, **62**
    Relationships with, 56-57
  Names of, **62**
  National Governors Association, 53, 58
  Number of previous terms, **62**
  Office, 55
  Party affiliation of, **62**
  Powers, 53-55, **67**
    Appointment, 55
    Veto, 54, **67**
  Qualifications for office, **64**
  Residence, official, **65**
  "Rules of the Game", 55-56
  Salaries, **90**
  Selection, methods of, **85**
  Separately elected officials, 56-58
  Succession to governorship, **62**
  Terms, length and number of, 50-51, **62, 83**
  To be elected: 1990-91, **232**
  Transition, provisions and procedures for, **72**
  Travel allowance, **65**
  See also Executive branch
Grady, Dennis O., 382-404

The Council of State Governments 615

SUBJECT INDEX

H

Handicapped persons
  Access to the polls, 227
  Americans With Disabilities Act, 525
Hall, Wayne W., Jr., 340-344
Health agency programs
  Administrative officials
    Salaries, **92**
    Selection, methods of, **87**
  Employment and payrolls, state and local
    October 1987, **356**
    October 1988, **357**
  Expenditures
    By program: fiscal 1988, **480**
    By source of funds: fiscal 1988, **481**
  Funding: fiscal 1988, **481**
  Medicaid, 522, 526, 527
  Medicare, 526
  Occupations and professions, state regulation of: 1990, **472**
  Organization and responsibilities: fiscal 1988, **479**
  See also Finances, state
Highways
  Administrative officials
    Salaries, **92**
    Selection, methods of, **87**
  Aid to local governments for: 1942 to 1988, **553**
  Disbursements for: 1988, **433**
  Employment and payrolls, state and local
    October 1987, **356**
    October 1988, **357**
  Employment, by state
    October 1987, **362**
    October 1988, **363**
  Expenditures for
    Intergovernmental by state: 1987, **557**; 1988, **558**
    Per capita by state: 1987, **555**; 1988, **556**
    Summary of state payments: 1942 to 1988, **553**
  Federal funds
    Apportionment of: fiscal 1989, **434**
    By state: 1988, **432**
  Mileage, road and street: 1988, **431**
  Payrolls, state
    October 1987, **364**
    October 1988, **365**
  Receipts
    By state: 1988, **432**
  Revenue, intergovernmental: 1987, **561**; 1988, **563**
  Tolls, receipts from: 1988, **432**
  See also Finances, state
Historic preservation
  Administrative officials
    Salaries, **93**
    Selection, methods of, **88**
Holidays, paid
  State employees, **352**
Homelessness, 511-519
  Changes in, **516**
  Expenditures, 516-518
  Government action
    Federal, 511-512, 518-519
    Legislation targeted toward, 513
    Local, 511-512, 518
  McKinney Act, 511, 514, 518
  Methods to count, 515-517
  Population, 512-514, 518-519, 515, 517
  Private party action, 518-519
  Outlook, 518-519
  State perspective, 514-516
  State response, 511-518
Hospitals
  Employment and payrolls, state and local
    October 1987, **356**
    October 1988, **357**
  Employment, state
    October 1987, **362**
    October 1988, **363**
  Payrolls, state
    October 1987, **364**
    October 1988, **365**
  See also Finances, state
House of Representatives, *See* Legislatures
Housing, *see* Homelessness

I

Impeachment
  Provisions for, **73**
Income
  Personal, per capita: 1987, **337**
Income taxes, *See* Taxation; Tax revenue
Information resources, 340, 341, 342
Infrastructure, *See* Intergovernmental affairs
Initiative, *See* Direct legislation
Innovators, Innovations, 382-404
  Managers, 399-402
    Agency incentives, 400-401, **401**
    Employment status, 399, **399**
    Impact on organization, 401-402, **402**
    Managerial perception of group support, 399-400, **399, 400**
  Motivations, 395-399
    Cost savings, 396
    Education, 397
    Emergency, 398
    Environment, 398
    Health care and public safety, 398
    Management improvement, 395-396
    Outside the state government, 398-399
    Social services, 397
    Technology, 396-397
    Termination of federal grant programs, 397
  Organizational environment, 386-391, 403
    Employment status, 386
    Innovations and organizational change, 390-391, **391**
    Involvement groups and individuals, 387-388, **388**
    Role of the innovator, 386-387, **387**
    Support of groups for, 389-390, **389, 390**
  Professional environment, 391-395, 403
    Activities of, 391-392, **391, 392**

SUBJECT INDEX

Other states, 394-395, **394, 395**
Other states as source, 393, 403, **393**
Sources of information, 392-393, **392, 393**
Profile of innovators, 383-386, 403
   Educational background, 384-385, **384, 385**
   Experience, 385-386
Survey Methods, 383
   Distribution of samples, 383-384, **383, 384**

Insurance
Administrative officials
   Salaries, **93**
   Selection, methods of, **88**
Elected officials, terms, length and number of, **83**
No-fault motor vehicle laws, **438**
See also Finances, state; Labor, workers' compensation; Tax revenue

Intergovernmental affairs
Council of State Governments, 568-574
Federal-state relations, 522-531
   Agriculture and rural development, 527
   Anti-Drug Abuse Act, 525
   Civil Rights, 524, 525
   Commerce, justice and labor, 527
   Drug control, 524
   Education, 523, 525, 527
   Environment
     Acid Rain, 524
     Clean Air, 524, 527
     Oil Spills, 527
   Federalism
     Constitutional reform, 528,529
     Executive order on federalism, 529, 530
     Intergovernmental Partnership Task Force, 528, 529
     Milliken v. Bradley, 529
     Missouri v. Jenkins, 529
     Preemptions, 528
   Finance
     Anthony Commission on Public Finance, 524
     Bellas-Hess Supreme Court decision, 524
     Federal funding, 522, 526-530
     Taxation, 523, 524, 529
   Foreign Affairs, 531
   General Accounting Office research, 530
   Government operations and pensions, 527
   Health and human services, 525, 527
     Americans with Disabilities Act, 525
     Homeless Assistance Act, 525
     Medicaid, 522, 526, 527
     Medicare, 526
     National Community Services Act, 525
   Job Training, 527
   Transportation policy, 525, 527
Finances, 222, 223
   Expenditure
     Aid to local governments, 549-551
     By state: 1980 to 1986, **454**; 1985, **238**; 1986, **240**
     By function and state: 1985, **457**; 1986, **458**
     By type of receiving government: 1985, **459**; 1986, **460**
     For local public works, by state: fiscal 1986
     Bonds and loans, **423**
     Grants, taxes, user fees, **422**
     Per capita by function and state: 1985, **455**; 1986, **456**
     Per capita distribution: 1986, **452**
     Percent distribution, selected years, 1976-86, **451**
     Summary of payments: 1942 to 1986, **453**
   Revenue
     By source and state: 1987, **296**; 1988, **298**
     From federal and local governments: 1985, **461**; 1986, **463**
     Total federal aid to states: fiscal 1981-86, **444**
   Great Lakes Interstate Sales Compact, 567
State-local relationships, 533-548
   Barkley v. City of Rome, 541
   Builders Service Corporation et. at. v. Town of East Hampton et. al., 542
   City of East Point v. Smith, 542
   City of Miami Beach v. Amoco Oil Company
   City of New Smyrna Beach v. County of Volusia, 541
   City of Ormond Beach v. County of Volusia, 542
   Finance, 538-541
   Legal decisions and advisory opinions, 541-543
   Local discretionary authority, 534-536
   Matter of Frew Run Gravel Products Incorporated v. Town of Carroll, 541
   Mitchell v. Wilkerson, 542
   Nolan v. California Coastal Commission, 540
   RRI v. Village of Southampton, 542
   Self v. City of Atlanta, 541
   State mandates, 543-546
   State v. Thiebeault, 542
   State v. Yee, 542
   Sutka v. Connors, 542
Interstate compacts and agreements, 565-567

J

Johnson, John M., 501-507
Jones, Benjamin J., 565-567
Jones, Rich, 108-117
Judges, *See* Judiciary
Judiciary, 194-203
   Access, Public perception of, 198-199
   Administrative offices of the courts, **223**
   AIDS guidelines for courts, 199-200
   Case Management, 196
   "Courts of the Future", 195-196
   Dispute resolution, alternate, 197-198
   Drug courts, 197
     Bureau of Justice Assistance, 197
     Comprehensive Adjudication of Drug Arrestees Program, 197
     Differentiated case management, 197
   Fairness in the courts, 199-200

SUBJECT INDEX

Judges
  Chief justice
    Selection, methods of, **204**
    Terms in years, **204**
    Compensation, 200-201, **221**
  Courts of last resort
    Qualifications, **208**
    Selected, methods of, **204**
    Terms in years, **204**
    To be elected: 1990-91, **232**
  General trial courts
    Number and terms, **206**
    Qualifications, **208**
  Intermediate appellate courts
    Number and terms, **206**
    Qualifications, **208**
    To be elected: 1990-91, **232**
  Removal of, methods for, **213**
    Extraordinary votes by legislature, **175, 177**
    Selection and retention of, 200-201, **210**
    Vacancies, methods for filling, **213**
  Technology and the courts, 194-195
    Facsimile Machines, 195
    Videotape, 195

K

Keffer, Gerard T., 326-328
Kellerman, David, 549-552
Knoebel, Dixie, 194-202

L

Labor
  Administrative officials
    Salaries, **93**
    Selection, methods of, **88**
  Child labor standards, 449, **459**
  Elected state officials, terms, length and number, **83**
  Employee drug testing, 447-448
  Equal employment opportunity, 450
  Family issues, 448-449
  Legislation, 446-453
  Occupational safety and health, 450-451
  Occupations, regulation **463, 471**
  Plant closings, 451
  Private employment agencies, 452
  Wages and hours, 446-447
    Minimum wage, 446-447
      Fair Labor Standards Act, 446
      Non-farm employment: 1968 to 1990, **463**
    Pay equity, 447
    Prevailing wage, 447
    Wage payment and collection, 447
  Workers' compensation, 451-452
    Estimates of payments: 1985-86, **456**
    Maximum benefits for temporary total disability, **454**
Land and existing structures, *See* Finances, state

Land area
  By state, **581**
Land use, *See* Agriculture and rural development
Laws, *See* Legislation
Legislation
  Asbestos abatement, 450
  Child restraint, **436**
  Elections, 226-229
    Absentee ballot procedures, 228-229
    Election technology, 227-228
    Federal write-in ballot, 180
    Handicapped access to the polls, 179, 180
    Voter registration, 179
  Environment and land use, 536-538
  Finance, state-local, 538-541
  Introductions and enactments
    Regular sessions: 1988 and 1989, **160**
    Special sessions: 1988 and 1989, **163**
  Hazardous substance information, 369
  Labor, 446-453
    Child labor, 449
    Employee drug testing, 342, 447-448
    Equal employment opportunity, 450
    Family issues, 448-449
    Occupational safety and health, 450-451
    Plant closings, 451
    Wages and hours, 446-447
      Minimum wage, 446-447
      Pay equity, 447
      Prevailing wage, 447
      Wage payment and collection, 447
    "Whistleblower" laws, 452
    Workers' compensation, 451-452
  Local discretionary authority, 534-536
  Model acts, record of passage of, **416**
  Motor vehicles, **436**
  No-fault motor vehicle insurance, **438**
  Seat belt, mandatory, **436**
  Sunrise programs, 467
  Sunset laws, **183**, 467
  Uniform acts, record of passage of, **409**
  Uniform state laws: 1988-89, 405-408
    Commercial Code, Revised, Article 3-Negotiable Instruments, 407, **409**
    Commercial Code, Article 4A-Funds Transfers, 407, **409**
    Commercial Code, Article 6-Bulk Sales, 406, **409**
    Foreign-Money Claims Act, 407, **409**
    Pretrial Detention Act, 407, **409**
    Probate Code, Revised, Article VI, 407, **409**
    Multiple-Person Accounts Act, 407, **409**
      Non-Probate Transfers on Death Act, 407, **409**
      POD Decurity Registration Act, 407, **409**
    Putative and Unknown Fathers Act, 406, **409**
    Rights of the Terminally Ill Act, 407-408, **409**
    Securities Act, Amendments, 406, **409**
    Status of Children of Assisted Conception, 406, **409**
    Statutory Power of Attorney Act, 406, **409**
  Vetoed by governors
    Regular session: 1988 and 1989, **160**

SUBJECT INDEX

Special session: 1988 and 1989, **163**
Legislators, *See* Legislatures and Legislative procedures
Legislatures and legislative procedures, 108-117
  Activities performed with computers, **187**
  Appropriations process: budget documents and bills, **171**
  Bill and resolution introductions and enactments
    Regular sessions, 1988 and 1989, **160**
    Special sessions, 1988 and 1989, **163**
  Bill introduction, time limits on, 111, **151**
  Bill pre-filing, reference and carryover, **154**
  Budget documents and bills, **171**
  Campaign funds, use of surplus, **149**
  Convening places, **118**
  Decentralization of management control, 115
  Effective date of enacted legislation, **157**
  Explusion, extraordinary vote required, **175, 177**
  Extraordinary votes, **175, 177**
  Evolving legislature, 115-116
    Competition, increase in, 115-116
    Growth in, 115
    Time, increased demands, 115
    Public awareness, increase in, 115
  Facilities, 113
  Fiscal notes, content and distribution, **173**
  Frequency of legislative cycles, **286**
  Information systems, 113
  Initiative provisions for state legislation, **267, 268, 270, 272**
  Leadership positions
    Decline in authority of, 115
    Selection, methods of
      House, **129**
      Senate, **127**
    Legal provisions for, **119**
  Legislative districting, 108-109
    Baker v. Carr, 108
    Reynolds v. Sims, 108
  Legislators
    "Full-time," 110-111, 115
    Minimum age, **125**
    Number, terms, and party affiliations, **123**
    Qualifications for election, **125**
    Salaries and other compensation, 111-112, 131
      Additional compensation
        For House leaders, **141**
        For Senate leaders, **139**
      Compensation commission **132**
      Method of setting **131**
      Retirement benefits **143**
      Tied or related to employees' salaries **131**
      Interim and other direct payments, **135**
      Per diem, **133, 135**
      Regular and special sessions, **133**
      Travel allowance, **133, 135**
    To be elected:; 1990-91, **232**
  Lobbyists
    As defined in state statutes, **189**
    Registration and reporting **191**
  Membership turnover: 1986, **90**

Names of, **118**
Party control, 114-115
Powers
  Budgetary, **171**
  Impeachment, **73**
  Veto override, **157**
Referendum provisions for state legislation, **273, 274, 275, 276**
Review of administrative regulations
  Powers, **181**
  Structures and procedures, **179**
Scheduling, 111
Sessions
  Regular
    Legal provisions for, **119**
    Length and duration of: 1988, 1989, 109-110, **160**
  Special
    Legal provisions for, **119**
    Length and duration of: 1988, 1989, **163**
Staff services, 112-113, 115-116
  For individual legislators, **165**
  For standing committees, **166**
Standing committees
  Appointment and number, **167**
  Procedure, **169**
Trends, 115-116
See also Direct legislation
Library agencies
  Administrative officials
    Salaries, **94**
    Selection, methods of, **89**
  Employment and payrolls, state and local
    October 1987, **356**
    October 1988, **357**
  Functions and responsibilities, 340, **379**
Licensing
  Administrative officials
    Salaries, **93**
    Selection, methods of, **88**
  Licenses, tax revenue from
    By state: 1987, **296**; 1988, **298**; 1988, **331, 335**
    National summary **319**
    Percent of collections, selected years, **265**
Lieutenant governors
  Consecutive terms allowed, **96**
  Governors, joint election with, **62**
  Powers and duties, **97**
  Qualifications and terms, **96**
  Role in the executive and legislative branches, 28, 29
  Salaries, **90**
  Selection, methods of, **85**
  Separately elected official, 56-57
  Terms, length and number of, **83**
  To be elected: 1990-91, **232**
Liquor stores, *See* Finances, state; Taxation, alcoholic beverages;
Tax revenue, alcoholic beverages
Lobbyists
  As defined in state statutes, **189**

SUBJECT INDEX

Registration and reporting, **191**
Louisiana Tax Reform Amendment, 30

M

McCabe, John M., 405-408
McKinney Act, 511, 514, 518, 525
Management, *See* Administration and management
Mass transit, local
  Federal funding for, **434**
Matthews, Timothy H., 483-492
May, Janice, 20-39
Mental health and retardation
  Administrative officials
    Salaries, **93**
    Selection, methods of, **88**
  See also Health agency programs
Meyer v. Grant, 27
Minimum wage
  Non-farm employment: 1968-90, **463**
Model acts
  Record of passage of, **416**
Montero v. Meyer, 26
Motor vehicles
  Insurance, no-fault, **438**
  Laws, **436**
  Operators and chauffeurs licenses: 1988, **441**
  Registrations: 1988, **435**
  See also Tax revenue

N

National Conference of Commissioners on Uniform State Laws, 405
National Governors' Association, 53, 525, 526, 552
Natural resources
  Administrative officials
    Salaries, **93**
    Selection, methods of, **88**
  Employment and payrolls, state and local
    October 1987, **356**
    October 1988, **357**
  Employment, state
    October 1987, **362**
    October 1988, **363**
  Payrolls, state
    October 1987, **364**
    October 1988, **365**
  See also Environmental and natural resource problems; Finances, state
Nelson, Richard R., 446-453
Nominating candidates for state offices
  Methods of, **234**

O

Omnibus Budget Reconciliation Act, 465
Occupational safety and health
  Legislation, 450-451
Occupational Safety and Health Act, 451
  Status of approved state plans in accordance with, **458**
Occupational Safety and Health Administration (OSHA), 451
Occupations and professions, state regulation of, 465-470, **471**
  Continuing education, **478**
  Enforcement and disciplinary procedures, 467
  Examinations, 467
  Financial Institutions Reform, Recovery and Enforcement Act of 1989, 465
  Licensure, 466
  Mobility, 468
  Omnibus Budget Reconciliation Act, 465
  Organization of licensure boards, 385
  Regulation, **471**
  Sunrise programs, 467
  Sunset laws, 467

P

Pay equity
  Legislation, 366
Parental leave, 350
Parimutuels, *See* Tax revenue
Parks and recreation
  Administrative officials
    Salaries, **93**
    Selection, methods of, **88**
Parole
  Adults on, **497**
  Release programs, 485-486
  See also Corrections
Personnel management, *See* Administration and management
Planning
  Administrative officials
    Salaries, **93**
    Selection, methods of, **88**
Police protection
  Employment and payrolls, state and local
    October 1987, **356**
    October 1988, **357**
  Employment, state
    October 1987, **362**
    October 1988, **363**
  Payrolls, state
    October 1987, **364**
    October 1988, **365**
  State police administrators
    Salaries, **94**
    Selection, methods of, **89**
  See also Finances, state
Pollution, *See* Environmental and natural resource problems
Population
  Capitals, by state, **579**
  Largest cities, by state, **579**
  Totals, by state, **337, 579**

SUBJECT INDEX

Post audit
  Administrative officials
    Salaries, **93**
    Selection, methods of, **88**
Pre-audit
  Administrative officials
    Salaries, **94**
    Selection, methods of, **89**
Primaries, *See* Elections
Prisons, 483-492
  Adults admitted: 1980-1987, **494**
  Capacities: 1988, **495**
  Population trends, **493**
  See also Corrections
Probation
  Adults on, **496**
  See also Corrections
Property taxes, *See* Tax revenue
Public assistance, *See* Public welfare
Public health, *See* Health agency programs
Public instruction
  Superintendents of
    To be elected: 1990-91, **232**
  See also Education; Education, elementary and secondary
Public library, *See* Library agencies
Public school systems, *See* Education, elementary and secondary
Public utilities
  Commissions, **443**
    Administrative officials
      Salaries, **94**
      Selection, methods of, **89**
    Commissioners
      Length of terms, **443**
      To be elected: 1990-91, **232**
    Number of members and employees, **443**
    Regulatory authority, **443**
    Regulatory functions of, selected, **444**
    Selection of members, **443**
  Employment and payrolls, state and local
    October 1987, **356**
    October 1988, **357**
Public welfare
  Administrative officials
    Salaries, **94**
    Selection, methods of, **89**
  Aid to local governments for: 1942-88, **553**
  Employment and payrolls, state and local
    October 1987, **356**
    October 1988, **357**
  Employment, state
    October 1987, **362**
    October 1988, **363**
  Expenditure for
    Intergovernmental by state: 1987, **557**; 1988, **558**
    Per capita by state: 1987, **555**; 1988, **556**
    Summary of state payments: 1942-88, **553**
  Homeless Assistance Act, 525
  Medicaid, 522, 526, 527
  Medicare, 526
  National Community Services Act, 525
  Payrolls, state
    October 1987, **364**
    October 1988, **365**
  Revenue, intergovernmental; 1987, **561**; 1988, **563**
  See also Finances, state
Public works, local
  Federal-state assistance for, 438-440
    Decline in federal grants, 414, 415
Purchasing
  Administrative officials
    Salaries, **94**
    Selection, methods of, **89**

R

Recall of state officials
  Applicability to state officials, **277**
  Petitions, **277**
  Review, appeal and election, **279**
Referendum, *See* Direct legislation
Retirement systems, *See* Employee retirement systems
Reuter, Deborah, 565-567
Revenue, *See* Finances, state
Reynolds v. Simms (1965), 108
Roads, *See* Highways
Roberts, Kimberly D., 483-492

S

Safety and health, *See* Occupational safety and health
Salaries
  Administrative officials, **90**
  Court administrative officials, **223**
  Education
    Elementary and secondary
      Average annual instructional staff: 1939-40 to 1988-89, **423**
      by state: 1986-87, **420**
    Higher, by state: 1986-87, **420**
  Governors, **65**
  Judges of appellate and general trial courts, 200-201, **221**
  Legislators, **33, 35, 139, 141**
  See also Compensation; Finances, state; and titles of individual officials
Secretaries of state
  Duties
    Custodial, **101**
    Election, **100**
    Legislative, **101**
    Publication, **101**
    Registration, **100**
  Qualifications for office, **99**
  Salaries, **90**
  Selection, methods of, **85, 99**
  Separately elected official, 58

SUBJECT INDEX

Terms, length and number of, **83**
To be elected: 1990-91, **232**
Senate, *See* Legislatures and legislative procedures
Smolka, Richard G., 226-231
Social insurance administration
  Employment and payrolls, state and local
    October 1987, **356**
    October 1988, **357**
Social services
  Administrative officials
    Salaries, **94**
    Selection, methods of, **89**
  See also Public welfare
State-local relationships, *See* Intergovernmental relationships
State pages
  Historical data, **577**
  Official names, capitals, zip codes and central switchboards, **576**
  Selected officials and statistics, by state, 581-608
  Statistics, **579**
State police, *See* Police protection
Substance abuse
  Testing employees for, 447-448
  See also Corrections; Drugs and Drug Testing
Sunrise programs, 467
Sunset legislation, 78, 467, **183**
Supreme Court (U.S.) decisions
  Legislative districting
    Baker v. Carr, 77
    Reynolds v. Sims, 77

T

Tax amnesty programs, 312
  November 22, 1982 - Present **315**
Taxation
  Agencies administering, **313**
  Alcoholic beverages, 312
    Agencies administering, **313**
    Excise rates, **316**
  Cigarettes, *See* Taxation, tobacco products
  Death
    Agencies administering, **313**
    Distilled spirits
      Excise rates, **316**
    Excise rates, **316**
  Federal-state tax relations, 523, 524, 529
  Gasoline
    Agencies administering, **313**
  Income
    Corporate, 311
      Agencies administering, **313**
      Rates, **321**
    IndividualPersonal, 310-311
      Agencies administering, **313**
      By income brackets, **319**
      Federal starting points, **320**
  Motor fuel, 311-312
    Excise rates. **316**

  Motor vehicle
    Agencies administering, **313**
  Pension
    Davis v. Michigan Department of the Treasury, 310
  Sales, 311
    Agencies administering, **313**
    Exemptions for food and drugs, **318**
  Severance: 1989, **323**
  Tobacco products, 312
    Agencies administering, **313**
    Cigarette excise rate, **316**
  Trends, 1988-89, 310-312
  See also Finances, state, revenue; Tax revenue
Tax provisions and public financing
  Funding state elections, **259**
Tax Reform Act of 1986, 310
Tax revenue
  Alcoholic beverages
    License: 1988, **335**
    National summary: 1986 to 1988, **329**
    Sales and gross receipts: 1988, **333**
  Amusements
    License: 1988, **271**
    Sales and gross receipts: 1988, **333**
  By source and state: 1987, **296**; 1988, **298**
  By state, summary of: 1986 to 1988, **329**
  By type of tax
    By state: 1988, **331**
    National summary: 1986 to 1988, **329**
  Collections
    By major tax category, percent distribution of, **327**
    In state: 1988, 326-328
    For selected states: 1988, **327**
  Corporations in general, licenses
    By state: 1988, **335**
    National summary: 1986 to 1988, **329**
  Death and gift
    By state: 1988: **331**
    National summary: 1986 to 1988, **329**
  Documentary and stock transfer: 1988, **331**
  Hunting and fishing license
    By state: 1988, **335**
    National summary: 1986 to 1988, **329**
  Income, corporate and individual
    By state: 1987, **296**; 1988, **298**; 1988, **331**
    National summary: 1986 to 1988, **329**
    Percent distribution of tax collections, **327**
  Insurance
    National summary: 1986 to 1988, **329**
    Sales and gross receipts: 1988, **333**
  Licenses
    By state: 1987, **296**; 1988, **298**; 1988, **331**, **335**
    National summary: 1986 to 1988, **329**
    Percent distribution of tax collections, **327**
  Motor fuels
    National summary: 1986 to 1988, **329**
    Sales and gross receipts: 1987, **296**; 1988, **298**; 1988, **333**

SUBJECT INDEX

Motor vehicle license
  By state: 1987, **296**; 1988, **298**; 1988, **333**
  National summary: 1986 to 1988, **329**
Motor vehicle operators license
  By state: 1988, **335**
  National summary: 1986 to 1988, **329**
Occupations and businesses, license
  By state: 1988, **335**
Parimutuels
  Sales and gross receipts: 1988, **333**
Property taxes
  By state: 1988, **333**
  National summary: 1986 to 1988, **329**
Public utilities
  License: 1988, **335**
  National summary: 1986 to 1988, **329**
  Sales and gross receipts: 1986 to 1988, **329**
Sales and gross receipts
  By source and state: 1988, **333**
  By state: 1987, **296**; 1988, **331**
  Percent distribution of tax collections, **327**
  Selective: by state: 1988, **333**
Severance taxes
  By state: 1988, **331**
  National summary: 1986 to 1988, **329**
Tobacco products
  National summary: 1986 to 1988, **329**
  Sales and gross receipts: 1988, **333**
  See also Finances, state
Telecommunications, 340-341
  See also Computers; Judiciary
Tobacco products, *See* Taxation; Tax revenue
Tourism
  Administrative officials
    Salaries, **94**
    Selection, methods of, **89**
Toxic chemicals 501-502
  See also Environmental and natural resource problems
Transportation
  Administrative officials
    Salaries, **94**
    Selection, methods of, **89**
  Fleet management,
  See also Highways, Mass transit
Travel allowance
  Governors, **65**
  Legislators, **131**, **133**
Treasurers
  Management responsibilities, 343-344
  Salaries, **90**
  Selection, methods of, **85**
  Separately elected official, 58
  Terms, length and number of, **83**
  To be elected: 1990-91, **232**

U

Uniform state laws: 1988-89, 405-408
  Record of passage of, **409**
  Titles of
    Commercial Code, Revised, Article 3-Negotiable Instruments, 407
    Commercial Code, Article 4A-Funds Transfers, 407
    Commercial Code, Article 6-Bulk Sales, 406
    Foreign-Money Claims Act, 407
    Pretrial Detention Act, 407
    Probate Code, Revised, Article VI, 407
      Multiple-Person Accounts Act, 407
      Non-Probate Transfers on Death Act, 407
      POD Decurity Registration Act, 407
    Putative and Unknown Fathers Act, 406
    Rights of the Terminally Ill Act, 407-408
    Securities Act, Amendments, 406
    Status of Children of Assisted Conception, 406
    Statutory Power of Attorney Act, 406
Utilities, *See* Public utilities

V

Veto
  Gubernatorial power, 54, **67**, **157**
  Measures vetoed by governor
    Regular sessions: 1988 and 1989, **160**
    Special sessions: 1988 and 1989, **163**
  Override powers of legislatures, **67**, **157**, **175**, **179**
Virginia v. Tennessee, 565
Voter registration, 226-227, 230
Voting, *See* Elections, voting
Voting Rights,
  Delgado v. Smith, 26
  Montero v. Meyer, 26

Y

Yniguez v. Mofford, 26

W

Wages and hours
  Legislation, 446-447
    Minimum wage, 446-447
      Non-farm employment: 1968 to 1988, **463**
    Pay equity, 447
    Prevailing wage, 447
    Wage payment and collection, 447
  See also Compensation; Salaries
Walker, Lee, 511-519
Wastewater, *See* Environmental and natural resource problems; Public works, local
Water, *See* Environmental and natural resource problems; Public works, local
"Whistleblower" laws, 452, 525
Workers' compensation, *See* Labor, workers' compensation
Wulf, Henry S., 282-285, 366-370, 549-552

Z

Zip codes
  Of state capitals, **576**
Zimmerman, Joseph F., 533-548

CURRENT
CONVENIENT
WELL-ORGANIZED

Looking for Someone?

Three directories that put you in touch with important state leaders:

State Elective Officials and the Legislatures 1989-90 lists the names, addresses, parties and districts of state legislators as of January, 1989. Geographically arranged, this directory also includes listings of key executive branch officials and supreme court justices. 150 pages. Soft cover, ISBN 0-87292-085-2. $30. ($21 for state officials.)

State Legislative Leadership, Committees and Staff 1989-90 is your one-stop source for names, addresses and telephone numbers of state legislative leaders, committees and chairpersons, officers and principal legislative staff. Arranged in easy to use format of geographic, title, and function headings. 297 pages. Soft cover. ISBN 0-87292-087-9. $30. ($21 for state officials.)

State Administrative Officials Classified by Function 1989-90 puts at your fingertips the names, addresses and telephone numbers of thousands of key administrators in more than 130 areas of state government, including definitions of administrative functions. 289 pages. Soft cover. ISBN0-87292-088-7. $30. ($21 for state officials.)

To order, write or call: Order Department, The Council of State Governments, Iron Works Pike, P.O. Box 11910, Lexington, KY 40578-1910, (606) 231-1850. Or FAX your order, (606) 231-1858.

WHO's WHO IN STATE GOVERNMENT

STAFFORD LIBRARY
COLUMBIA COLLEGE
COLUMBIA, MO 65216